PHILIP'S

iniAtlas
ondon

Contents

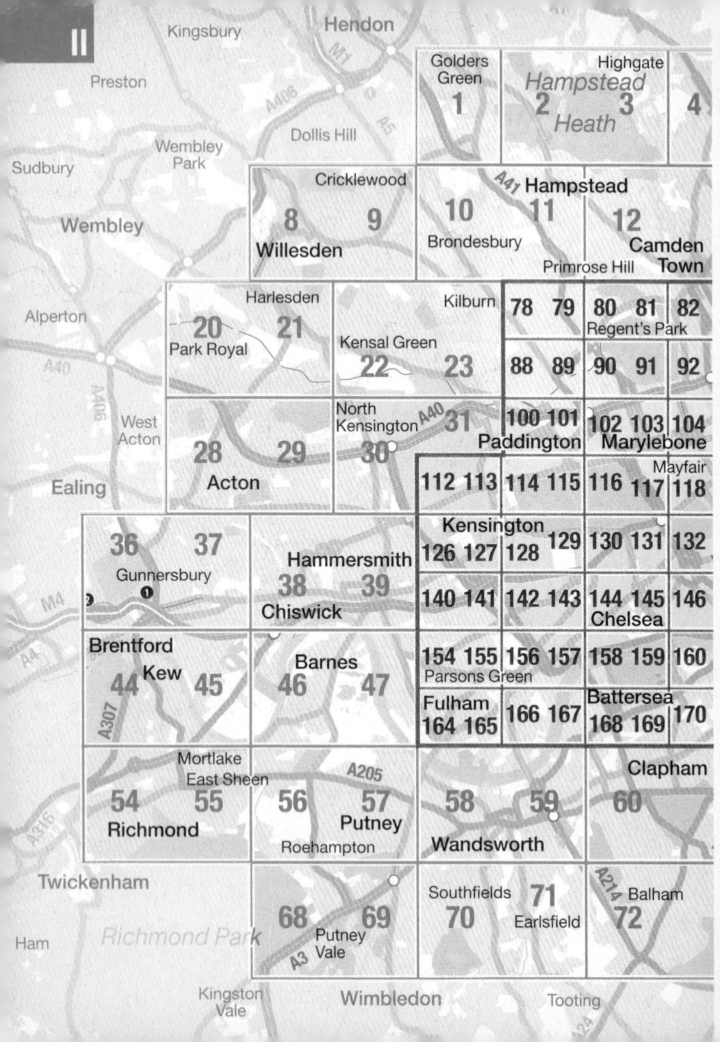

Kingsbury
Hendon
M1
Preston
A406
A5
Dollis Hill
Golders Green
1
Highgate
Hampstead Heath
2
3
4
Sudbury
Wembley Park
Cricklewood
8
9
Willesden
Wembley
A41
Hampstead
10
11
12
Brondesbury
Camden Town
Primrose Hill
Harlesden
Kilburn
78
79
80
81
82
Regent's Park
Alperton
20
21
Park Royal
Kensal Green
22
23
88
89
90
91
92
A40
A406
West Acton
North Kensington
A40
31
100
101
102
103
104
Paddington
Marylebone
28
29
30
Acton
Ealing
Mayfair
112
113
114
115
116
117
118
Kensington
126
127
128
129
130
131
132
36
37
Gunnersbury
Hammersmith
38
39
Chiswick
M4
140
141
142
143
144
145
146
Chelsea
A4
Brentford
Kew
44
45
A307
Barnes
46
47
154
155
156
157
158
159
160
Parsons Green
Fulham
164
165
166
167
Battersea
168
169
170
Mortlake
East Sheen
A205
54
55
56
57
58
59
60
Richmond
Putney
Roehampton
Wandsworth
Clapham
A316
Twickenham
Southfields
70
71
Earlsfield
A214
Balham
72
68
69
Putney Vale
A3
Ham
Richmond Park
Kingston Vale
Wimbledon
Tooting
A24

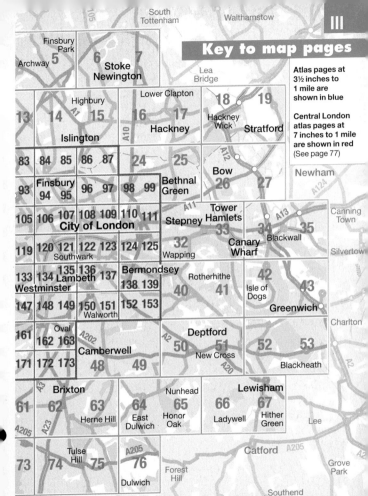

Key to map pages

Atlas pages at
3½ inches to
1 mile are
shown in blue

Central London
atlas pages at
7 inches to 1 mile
are shown in red
(See page 77)

South Tottenham

Walthamstow

Finsbury Park

Archway **5**

6 Stoke Newington **7**

Lea Bridge

Highbury

13 **14** **15**
Islington

Lower Clapton

16 **17**
Hackney

18 **19**

Hackney Wick

Stratford

Newham

83 **84** **85** **86** **87** **24** **25**

Bow

26 **27**

93 **94** **95** **96** **97** **98** **99**
Finsbury
Bethnal Green

105 **106** **107** **108** **109** **110** **111**
City of London

Tower Hamlets
Stepney **33**

34 **35**
Blackwall

Canning Town

Silvertown

119 **120** **121** **122** **123** **124** **125**
Southwark

Wapping

32

Canary Wharf

133 **134** **135** **136** **137** **138** **139**
Lambeth
Westminster
Bermondsey

Rotherhithe

40 **41**

42 **43**
Isle of Dogs

Greenwich

Charlton

147 **148** **149** **150** **151** **152** **153**
Walworth

161 **162** **163**
Oval

171 **172** **173**

Camberwell

48 **49**

Deptford

50 **51**
New Cross

52 **53**

Blackheath

61 **62** **63**
Brixton

Herne Hill

64
East Dulwich

Nunhead

65
Honor Oak

Lewisham

66 **67**
Ladywell   Hither Green

Lee

73 **74** **75**
Tulse Hill

76
Dulwich

Forest Hill

Catford

Grove Park

Streatham

Crystal Palace

Southend

Downham

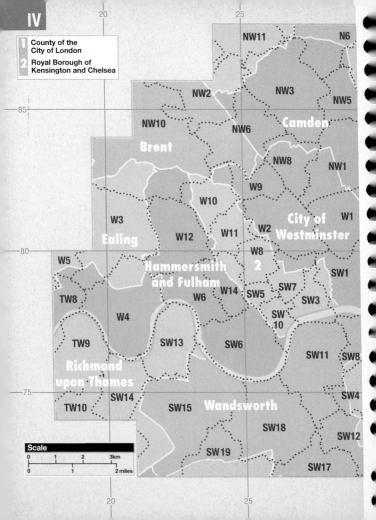

IV

1 County of the City of London
2 Royal Borough of Kensington and Chelsea

NW11　N6

NW2　NW3　NW5

NW10　Camden

Brent　NW6

NW8　NW1

W9

W10

W3　W11　W2　City of

Ealing　W12　Westminster　W1

W8

W5　SW1

Hammersmith and Fulham　2

TW8　SW5　SW7

W14　SW3

W6　SW10

W4　SW13　SW6

TW9

SW11　SW8

Richmond upon Thames

TW10　SW14　SW4

SW15　Wandsworth

SW18　SW12

SW19　SW17

Scale
0　1　2　3km
0　1　2 miles

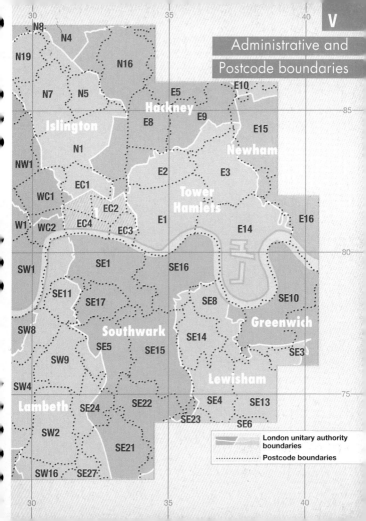

Key to map symbols

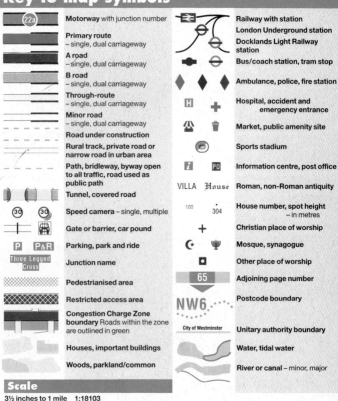

Motorway with junction number

Primary route
– single, dual carriageway

A road
– single, dual carriageway

B road
– single, dual carriageway

Through-route
– single, dual carriageway

Minor road
– single, dual carriageway

Road under construction

Rural track, private road or
narrow road in urban area

Path, bridleway, byway open
to all traffic, road used as
public path

Tunnel, covered road

Speed camera – single, multiple

Gate or barrier, car pound

Parking, park and ride

Junction name

Pedestrianised area

Restricted access area

Congestion Charge Zone
boundary Roads within the zone
are outlined in green

Houses, important buildings

Woods, parkland/common

Railway with station

London Underground station

Docklands Light Railway
station

Bus/coach station, tram stop

Ambulance, police, fire station

Hospital, accident and
emergency entrance

Market, public amenity site

Sports stadium

Information centre, post office

VILLA House   Roman, non-Roman antiquity

House number, spot height
– in metres

Christian place of worship

Mosque, synagogue

Other place of worship

Adjoining page number

Postcode boundary

Unitary authority boundary

Water, tidal water

River or canal – minor, major

Scale

3½ inches to 1 mile   1:18103

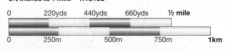

| 0 | 220yds | 440yds | 660yds | ½ mile |

| 0 | 250m | 500m | 750m | 1km |

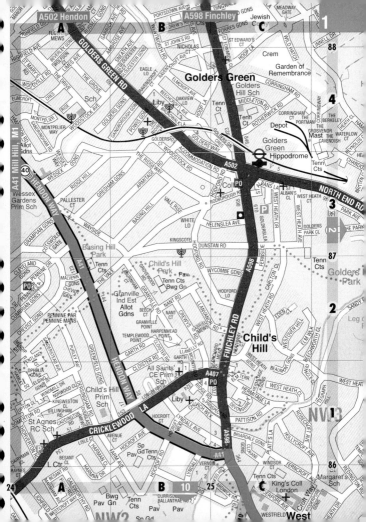

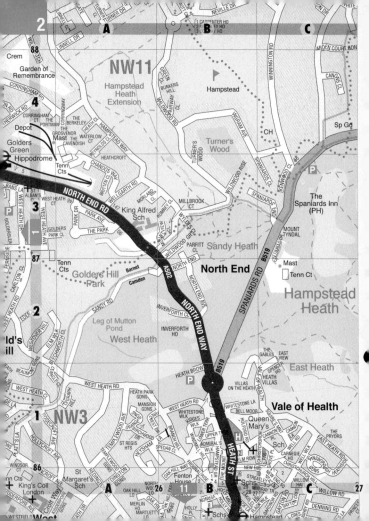

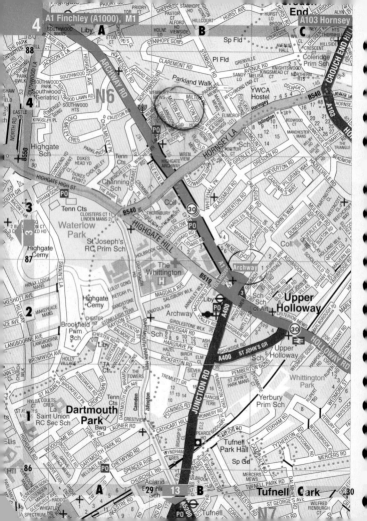

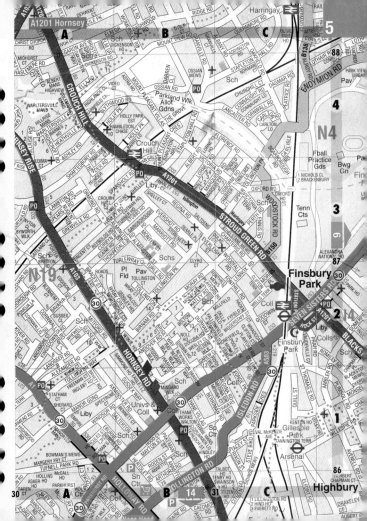

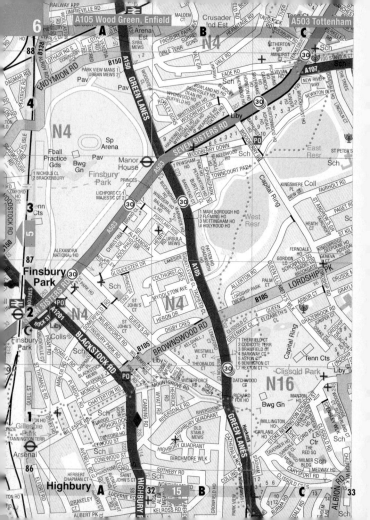

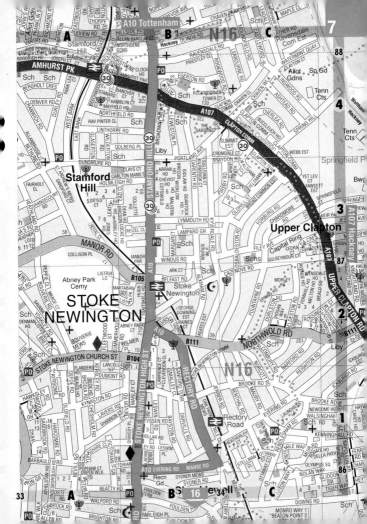

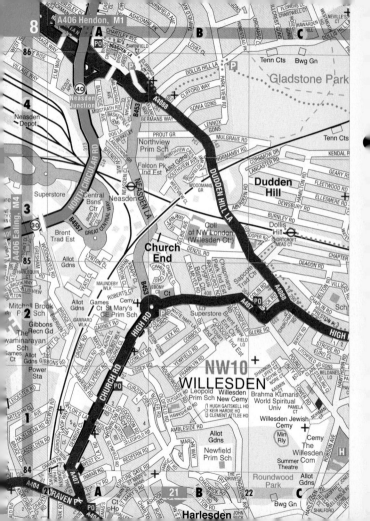

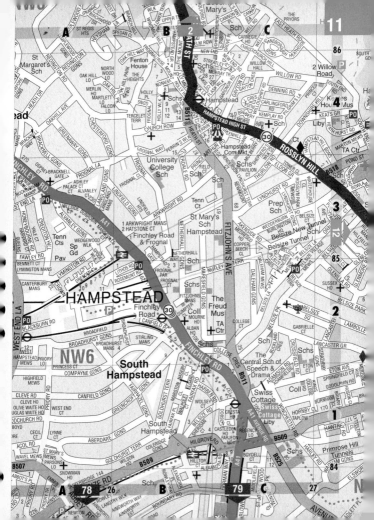

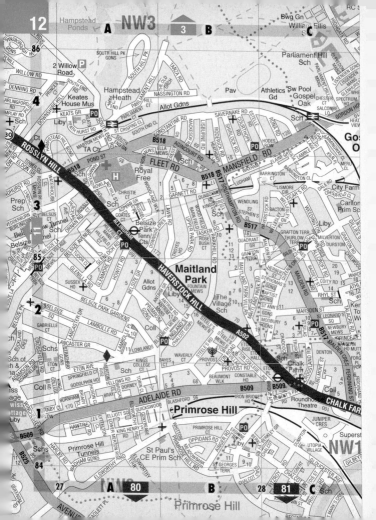

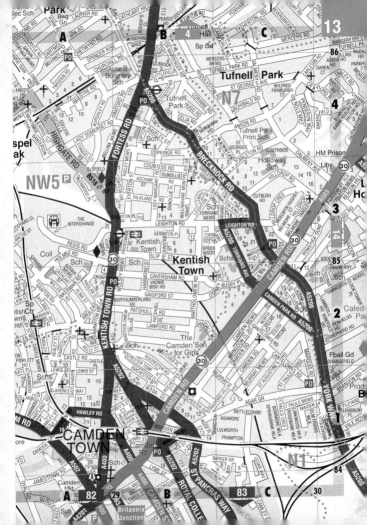

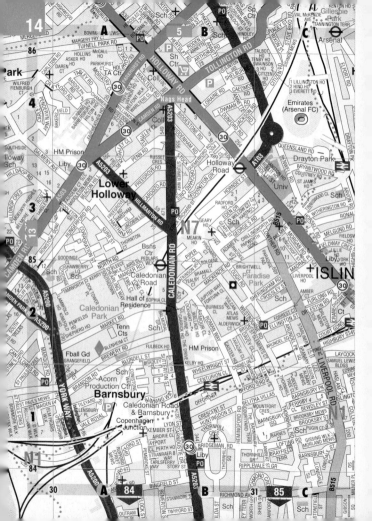

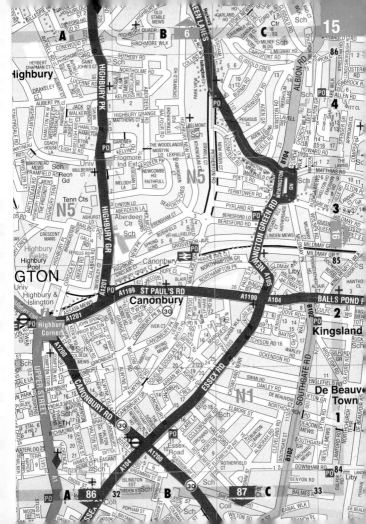

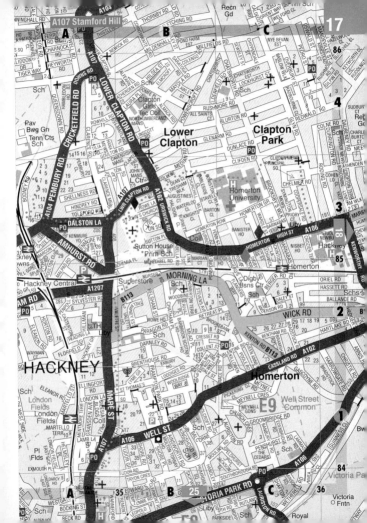

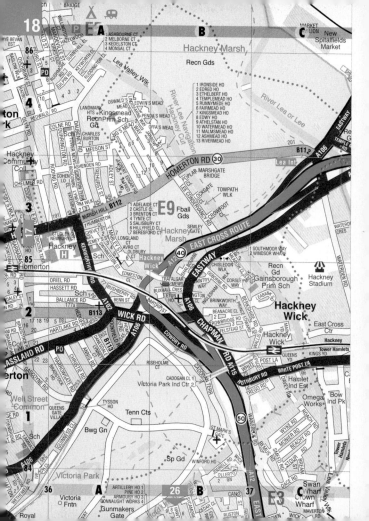

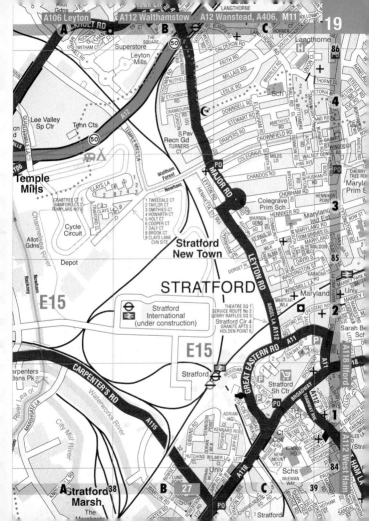

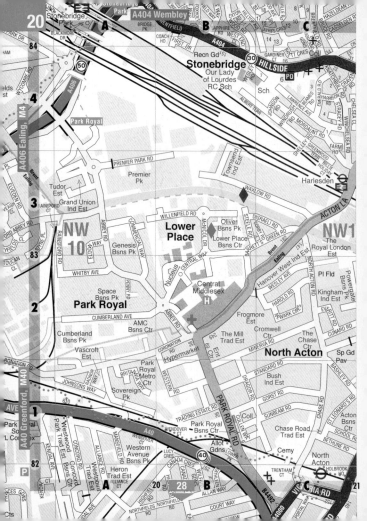

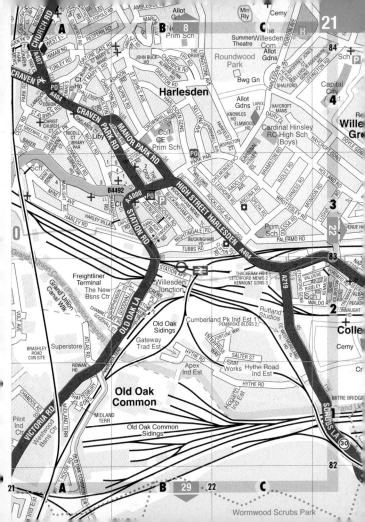

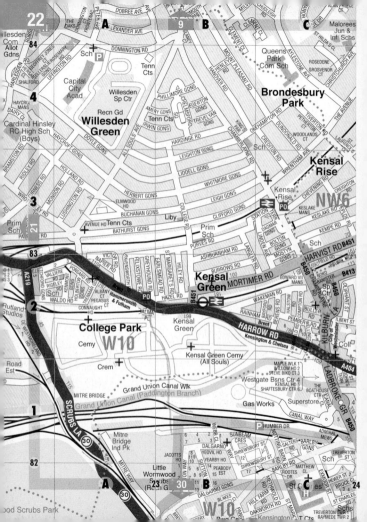

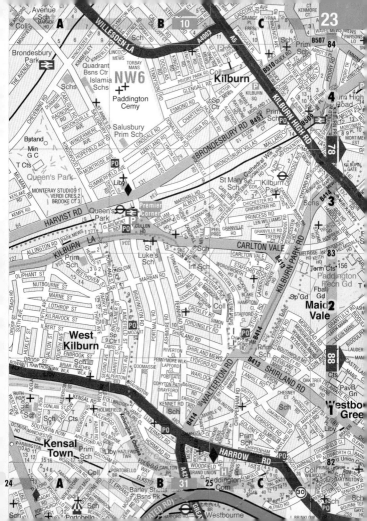

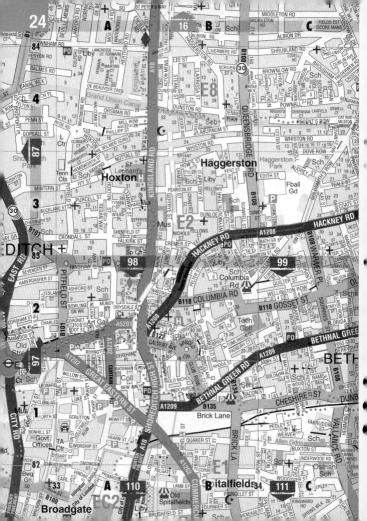

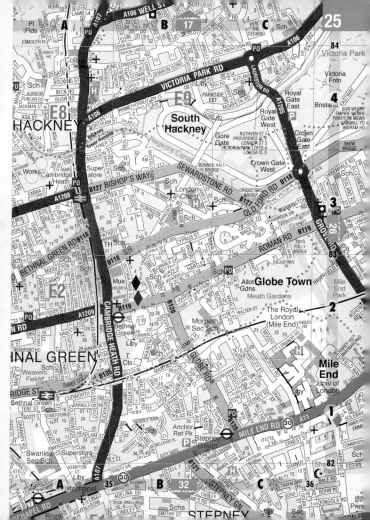

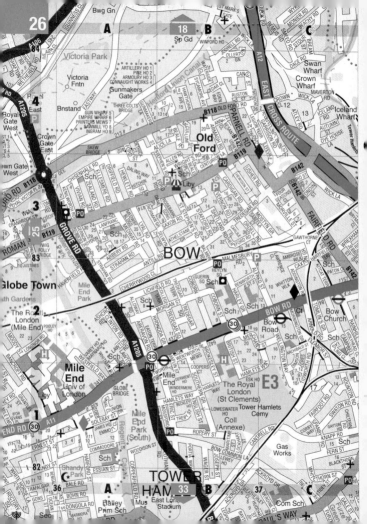

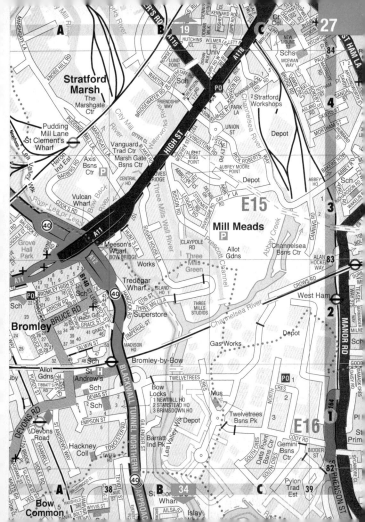

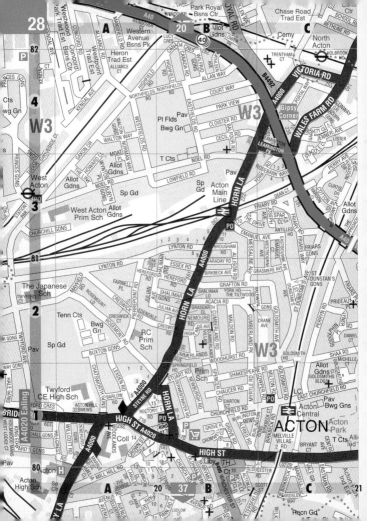

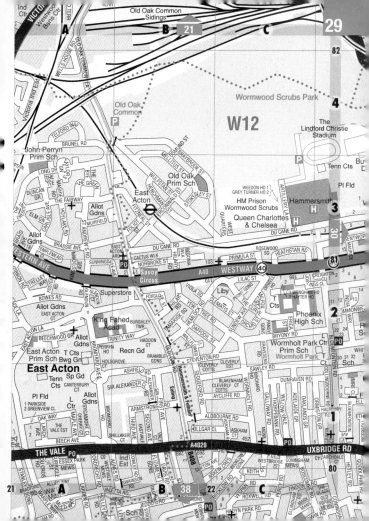

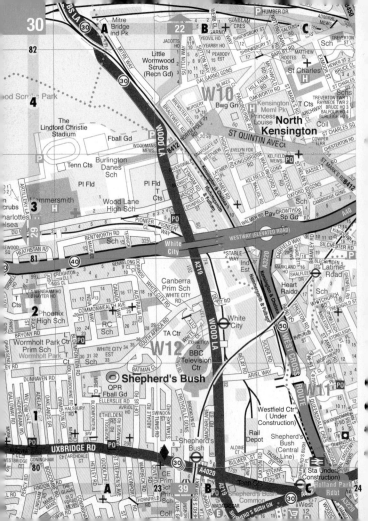

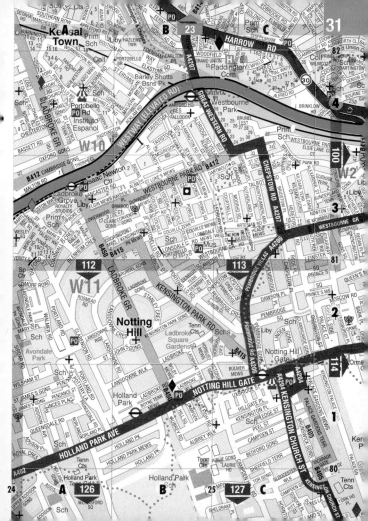

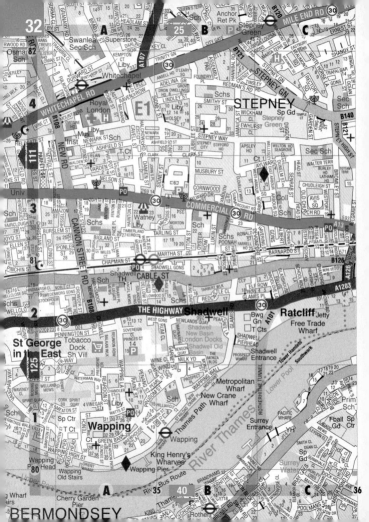

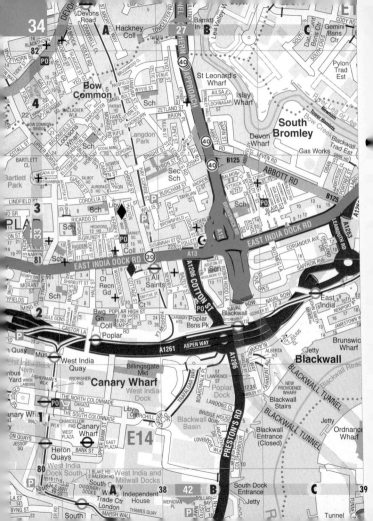

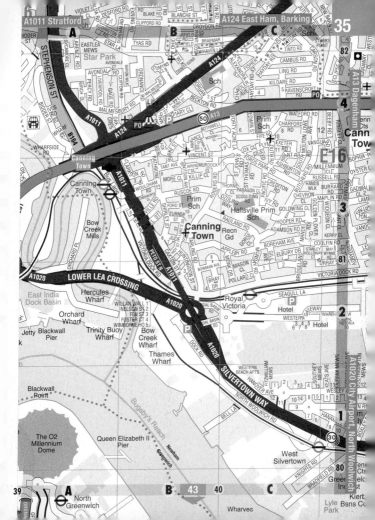

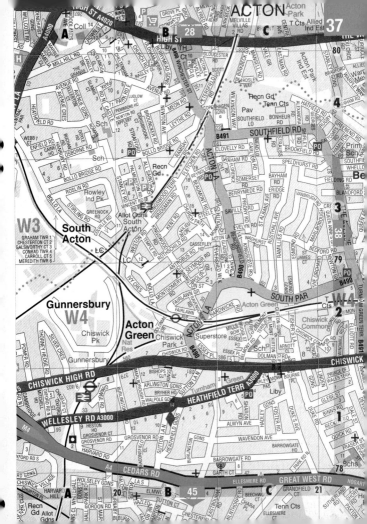

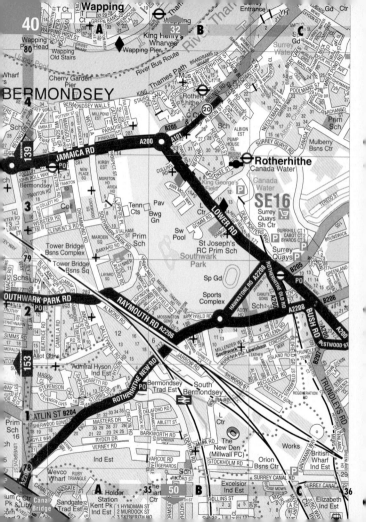

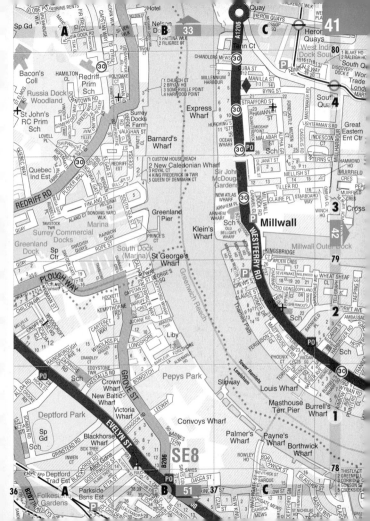

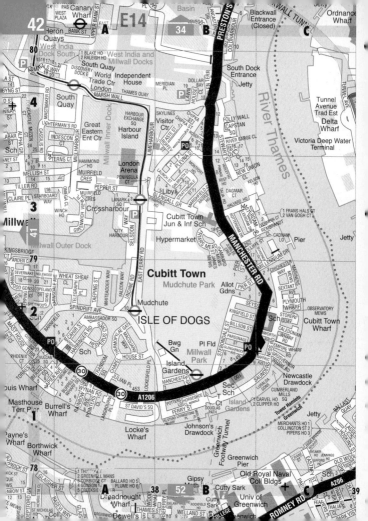

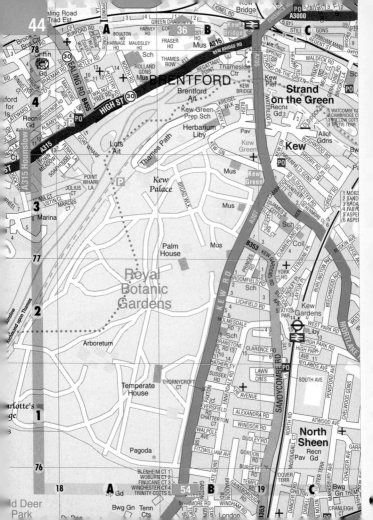

ealing Road
Trad Est

BURFORD RD
BOULTON HO
HARVEY
COF
GREEN DRAGON LA
36
STILE GDNS
C
LIONEL RD
Kew Bridge
A3000
PO
KINGSLEY
HARNAGE
MAUDSLEY HO
Sch
A
FRASER HO
HO
B
Mus A315
KEW BRIDGE RD
Kew Bridge
PINKHAM MANS
REGENT ST
WALDECK RD

78
Griffin
Gd
30
GRAEMAR RD
BROOK RD
NETLEY RD
NORTH RD
POTTERY RD
HOLLAND GDNS
THAMES ROW
Mus
REGATTA RD
Thameside
Ctr
Kew
Pier
STRAND-ON-THE-GREEN
Strand on the Green

4
KINGSLEY RD
EALING RD B455
MAFEKING RD
WALNUT TREE RD
+
HIGH ST 30
BRENTFORD
Brentford Ait
Kew Green Prep Sch
Kew
Bridge
BUSH
Kew
Pav
Green
Kew
Kew
WATCOMBE
CAMBRIDGE
WILLOW COTT

ford
for
A315 Hounslow
ALBANY RD
PO
GOAT WHARF
FERRY LA
Lots
Ait
Thames Path
Herbarium
Liby
Kew
Green
Allot
Gdns
BUSHWOOD RD
PO
PRIORY RD
MORTI
SAND
BROA
FABY
ASPE

3
Marina
POINT WHARF LA
JULIUS CT
MARCUS CT
P
SOAP HOUSE LA
Kew
Palace
BROAD WLK
Mus
Mus
Sch
JAMES'S
COTT'S
Coll

77
Richmond upon Thames
Palm
House
Mus
B353
KEW GARDENS RD
CUMBERLAND RD
YORK RD
BURLINGTON AVE
BEECHWOOD AVE

2
Royal Botanic Gardens
KEW RD
A307
BROOMFIELD RD
Sch
LICHFIELD RD
STATION PAR
Kew
Gardens
Liby
WEST PARK RD
HIGH PARK RD
MORTLAKE
Arboretum
HOLMESDALE RD
Sch
BRANSTONE RD
CLARENCE RD
HATHERLEY
RD
SUSSEX HO
HIGH PARK
AVE
NYLANDS AVE

1
arlotte's
ge
Temperate
House
THORNYCROFT CT
PAXTON CL
EVERSFIELD RD
CHATTERTON RD
WALPOLE AVE
FITZWILLIAM AVE
ENNERDALE RD
LAWN CRES
THE AVENUE
ALEXANDRA RD
WINDSOR RD
DUDLEY RD
GORDON RD
BURDETT RD
SANDYCOMBE RD
SOUTH AVE
NORTH AVE
ATWOOD RD
North Sheen
Recn
Pav
Gd
CHELWOOD GDNS
PENSFORD RD

76
Pagoda
18
A
BLENHEIM CT 1
WOBURN CT 2
FINUCANE CT 3
WINCHESTER CT 4
TRINITY COTTS 5
Gd
54
B
GAINSBOROUGH RD
BRAOUNDON RD
19
C
Bwg
Gn
DOVER TERR
CHILTON RD
DARELL RD
MARYSBURY AVE
CHAUCER AVE
GARR
CRANLEIGH
d Deer
Park
Bwg Gn
Tenn
Cts
WINDHAM RD
London
B353

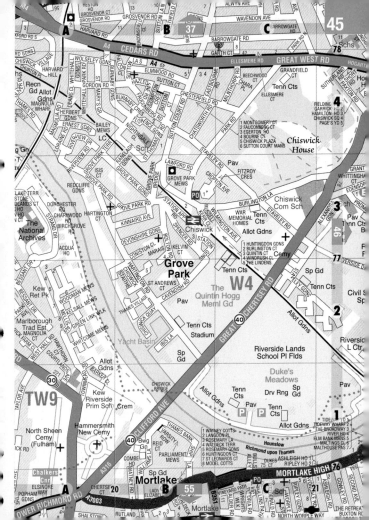

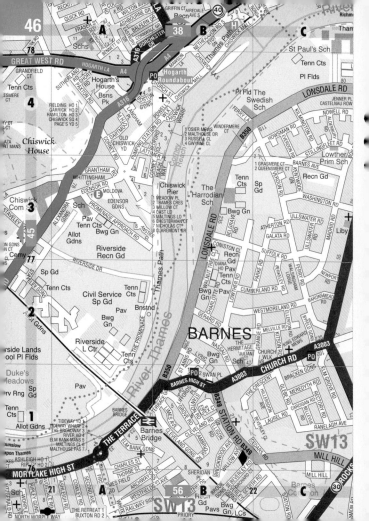

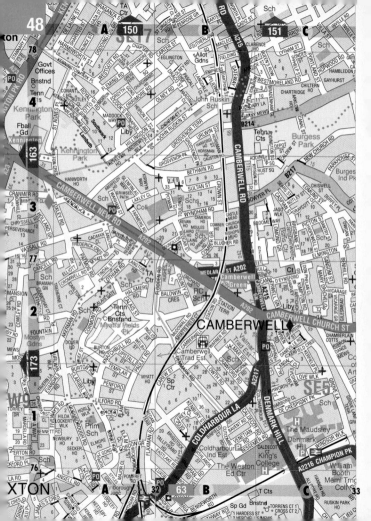

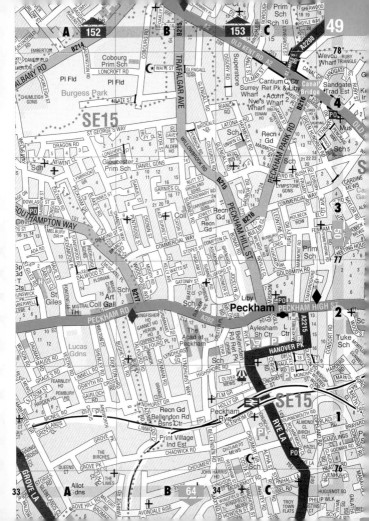

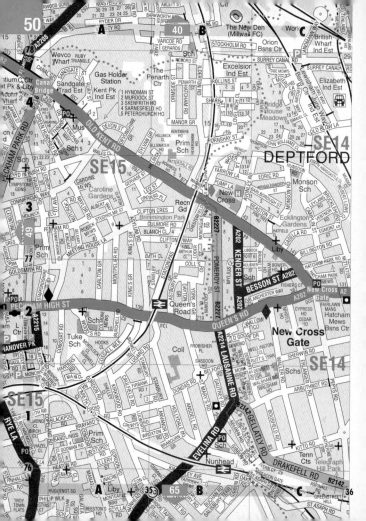

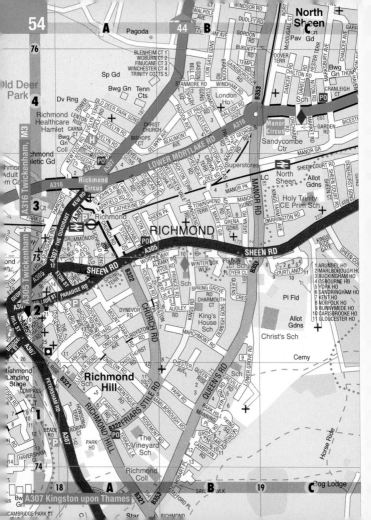

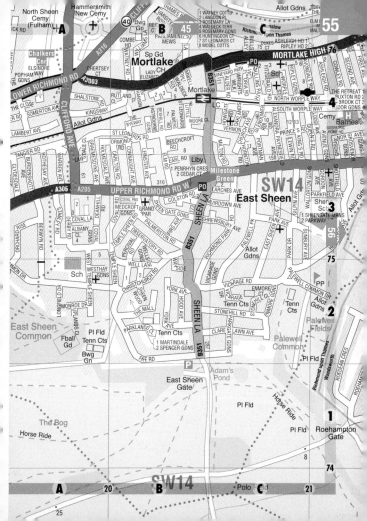

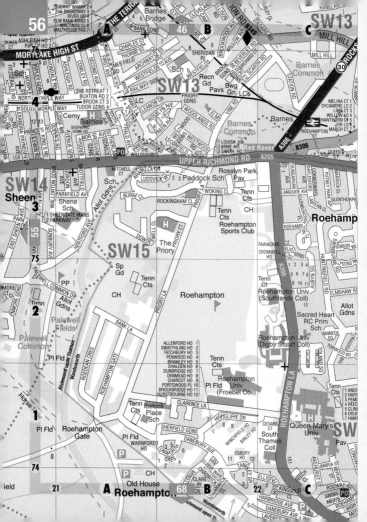

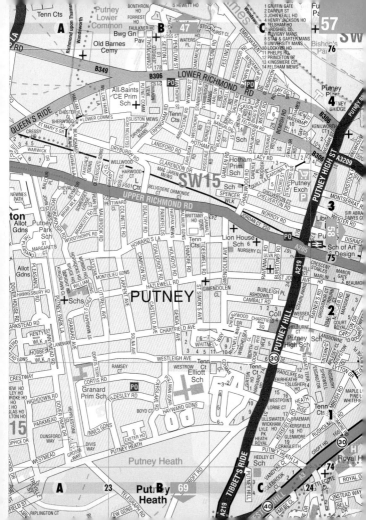

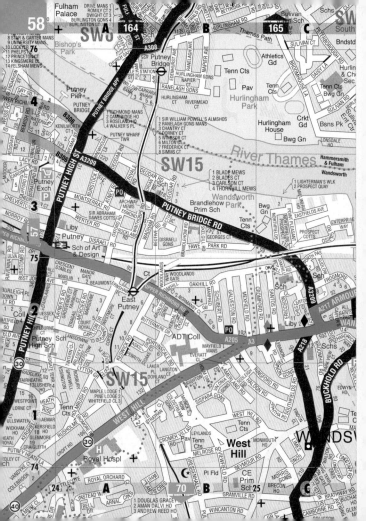

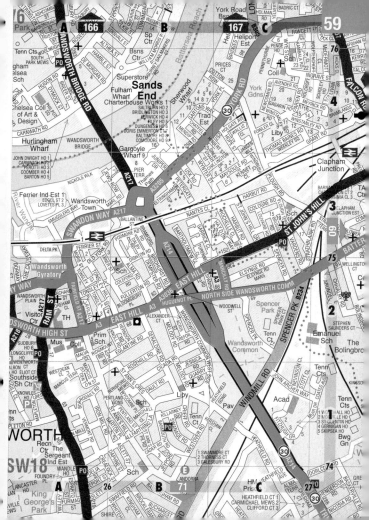

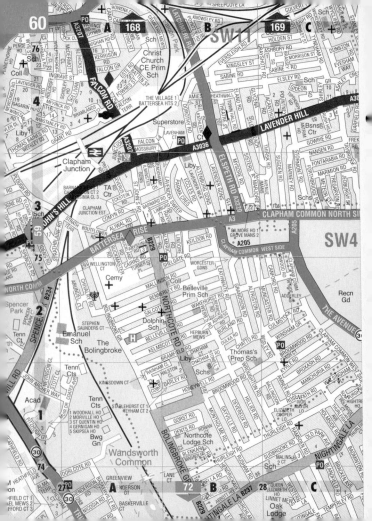

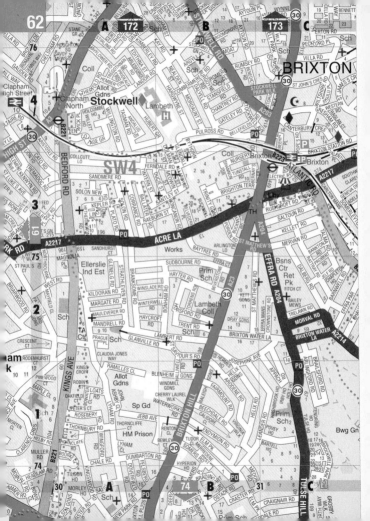

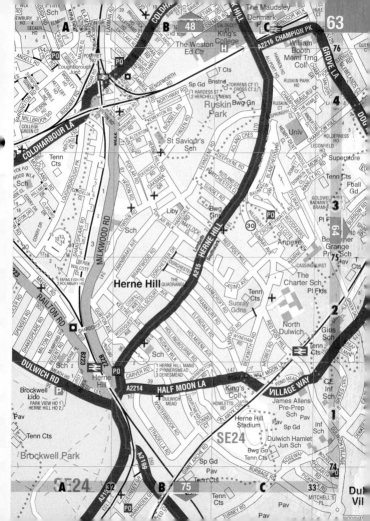

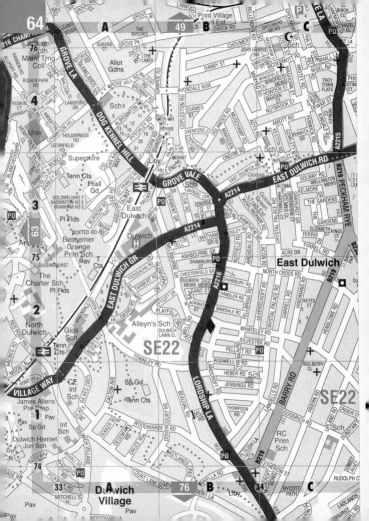

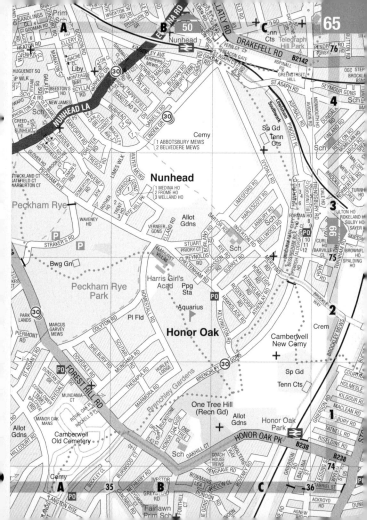

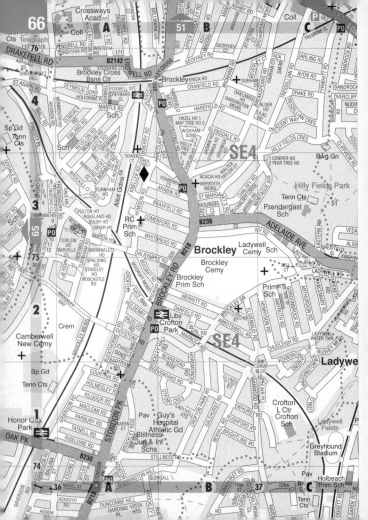

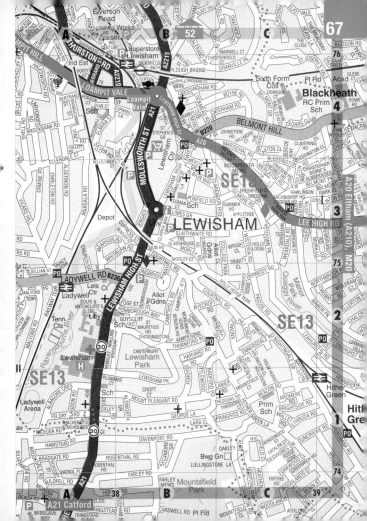

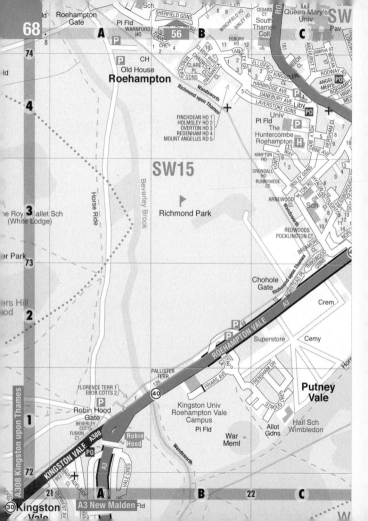

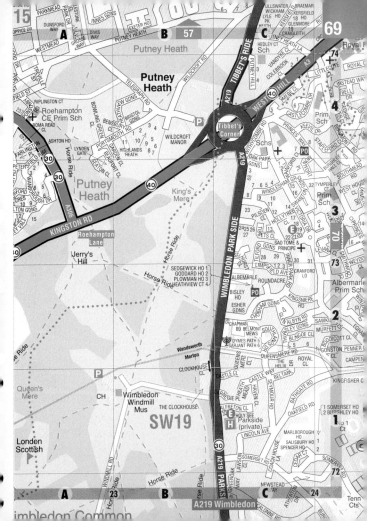

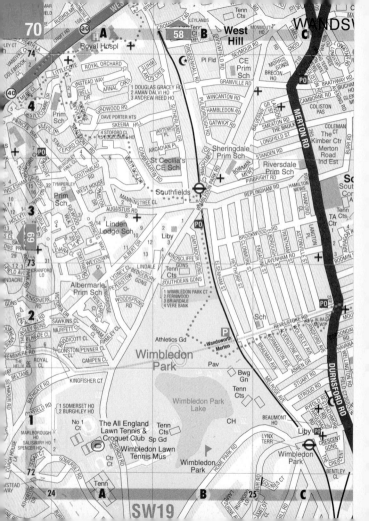

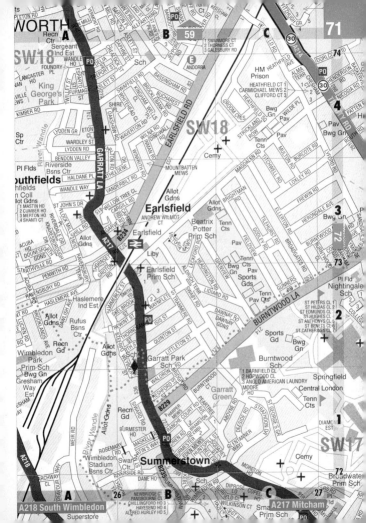

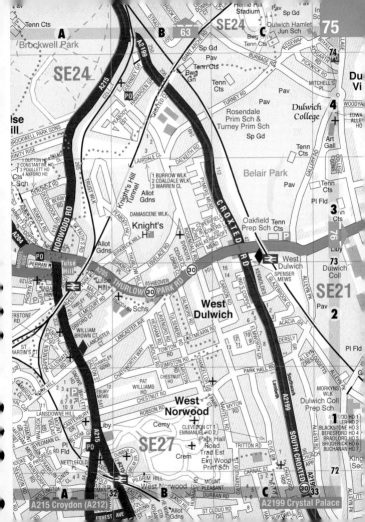

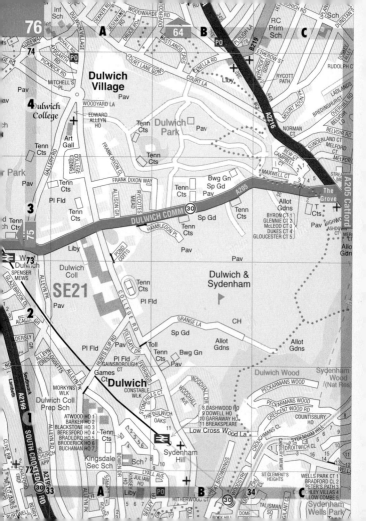

Key to enlarged map pages

78 79 St John's Wood	Primrose Hill **80 81** Regent's	**82 83** Somers Town	Islington **84 85** King's Cross	**86 87**	
Maida Vale **88 89** Westbourne Green	Park **90 91** Lisson Grove	**92 93** Bloomsbury	St Pancras **94 95**	**Finsbury** **96 97**	Shoreditch Bethnal **98 99** Green Spitalfields
Paddington **100 101**	**Marylebone** **102 103**	Fitzrovia **104 105**	Holborn **106 107** St Giles	**City** **108 109**	**110 111** Whitechapel
Notting Hill **112 113** Kensington	Bayswater **114 115** Hyde Park	Mayfair **116 117**	**118 119** St James	Strand **120 121** South Bank	**122 123** **Southwark**	St George in **124 125** the East
Kensington Holland Pk **126 127** West	Gardens Knightsbridge **128 129** Brompton	**130 131**	Green Park **132 133**	Waterloo **134 135**	The Borough **136 137**	**138 139** **Bermondsey**
Kensington **140 141** Earl's Ct	South Kensington **142 143**	**Westminster** **144 145** Belgravia	Victoria **146 147** Pimlico	**Lambeth** **148 149** Vauxhall	Newington **150 151** Kennington	**152 153** Walworth
West Brompton **154 155** Parsons Green	Walham **156 157** Green	**Chelsea** **158 159** Battersea Park	**160 161** Nine Elms	**162 163**		
Fulham **164 165**	**166 167**	**Battersea** **168 169**	**170 171**	South Lambeth **172 173** Stockwell	Congestion Charge Zone	

Additional symbols on enlarged maps

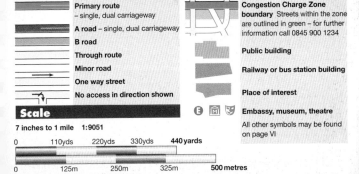

	Primary route – single, dual carriageway
	A road – single, dual carriageway
	B road
	Through route
	Minor road
→	**One way street**
	No access in direction shown

Congestion Charge Zone boundary Streets within the zone are outlined in green – for further information call 0845 900 1234

Public building

Railway or bus station building

Place of interest

E ⋔ ♨ Embassy, museum, theatre

All other symbols may be found on page VI

Scale

7 inches to 1 mile **1:9051**

0	110yds	220yds	330yds	**440 yards**

0	125m	250m	325m	**500 metres**

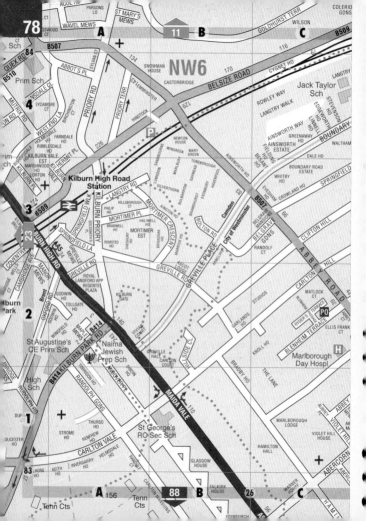

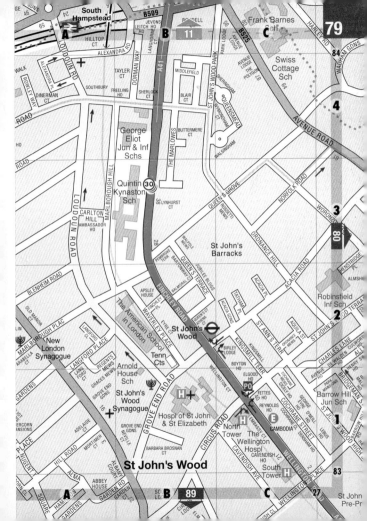

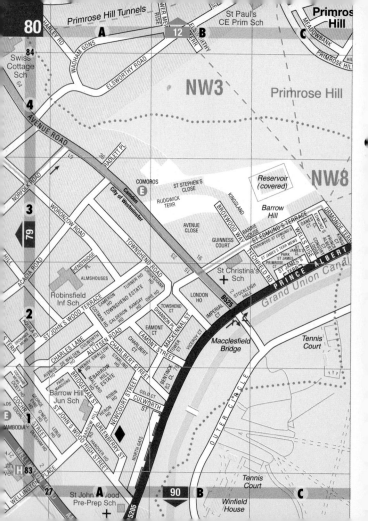

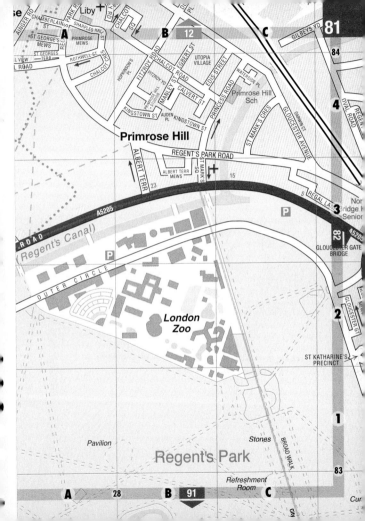

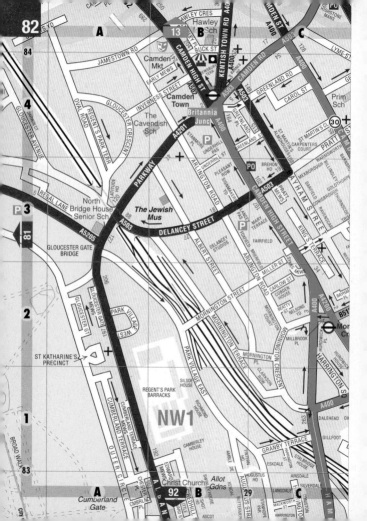

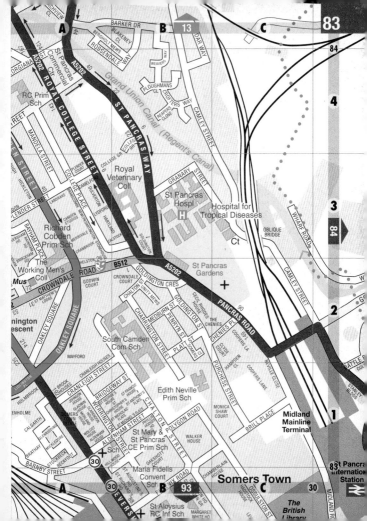

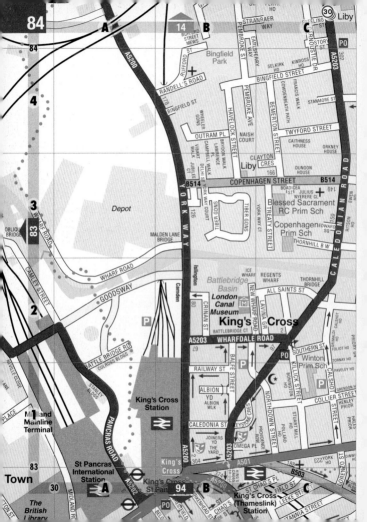

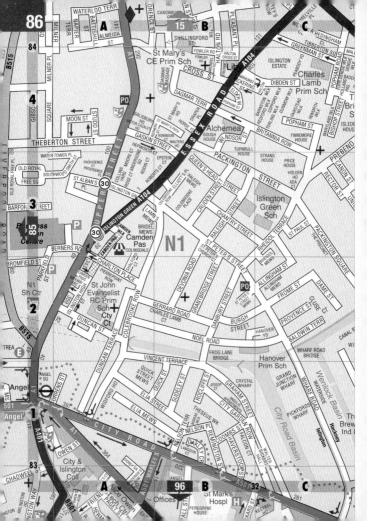

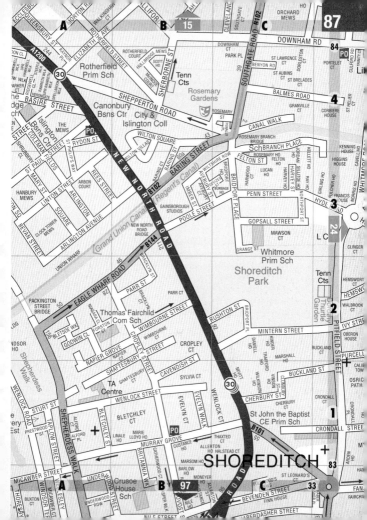

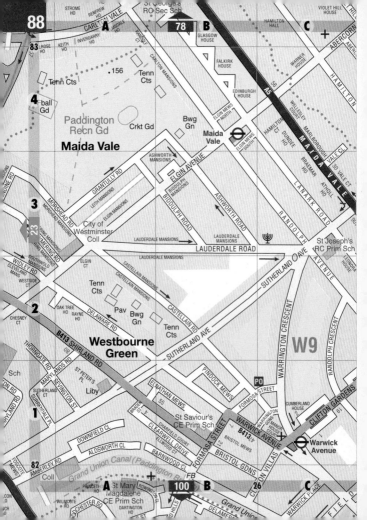

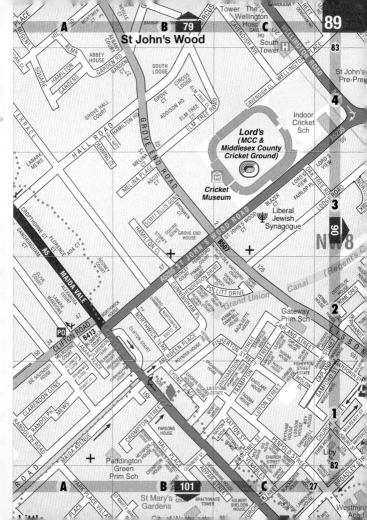

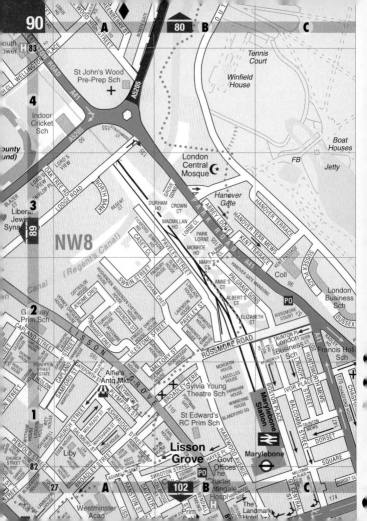

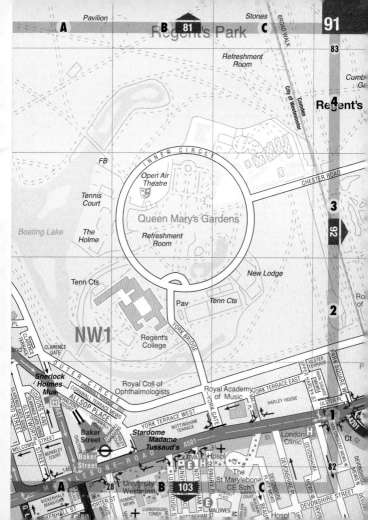

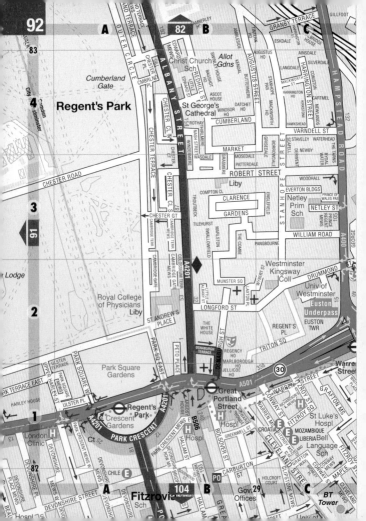

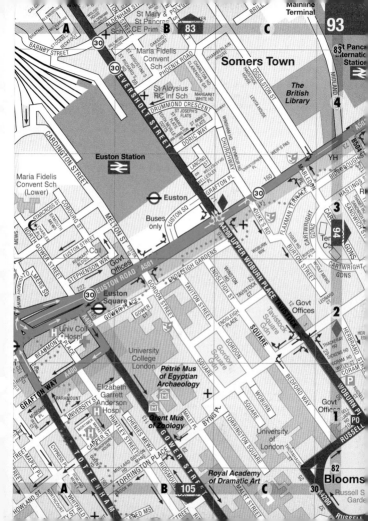

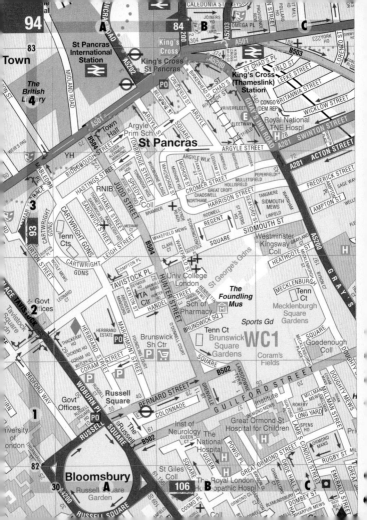

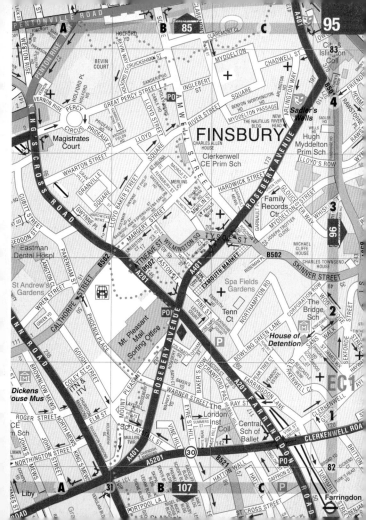

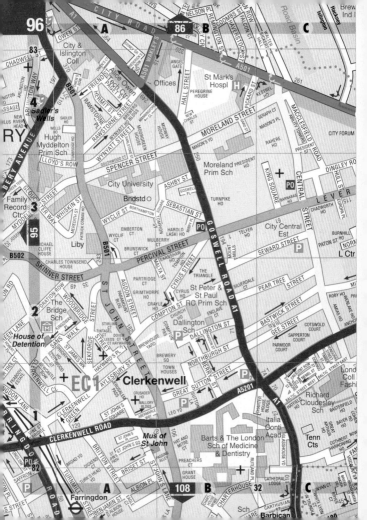

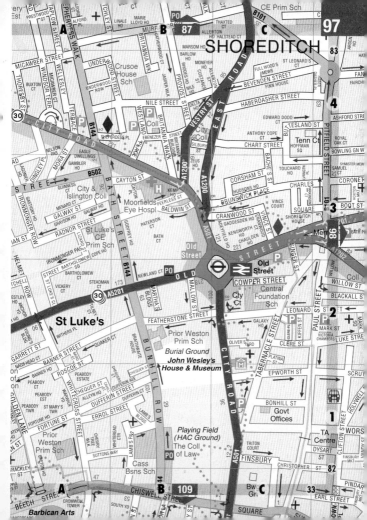

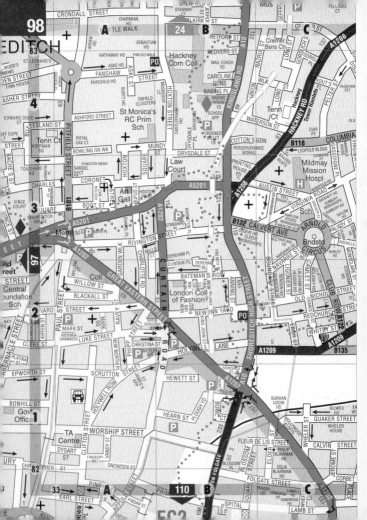

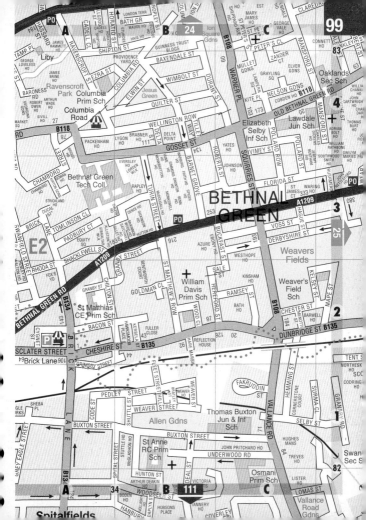

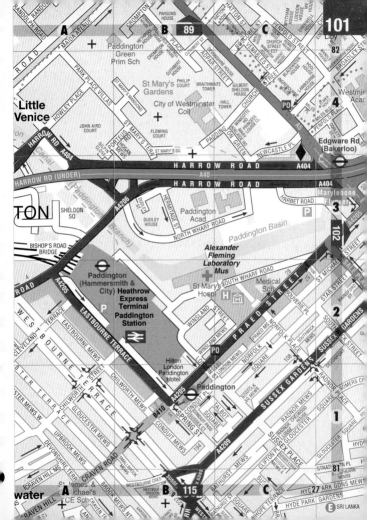

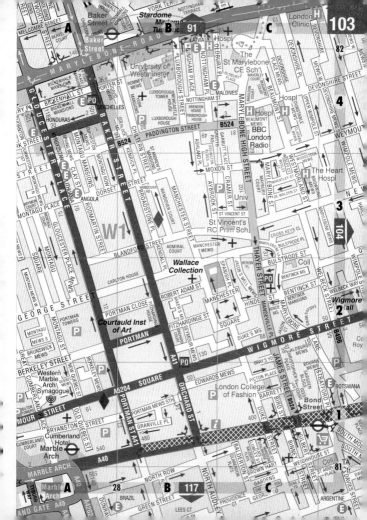

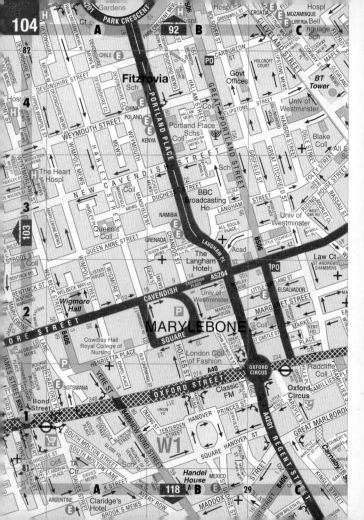

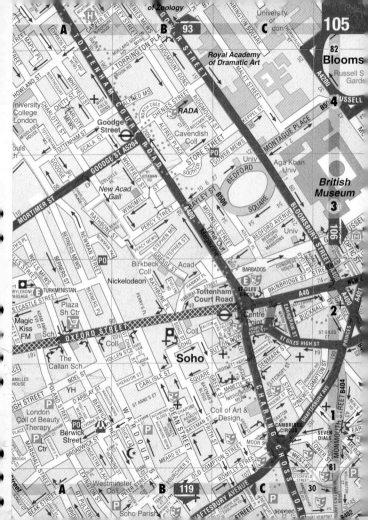

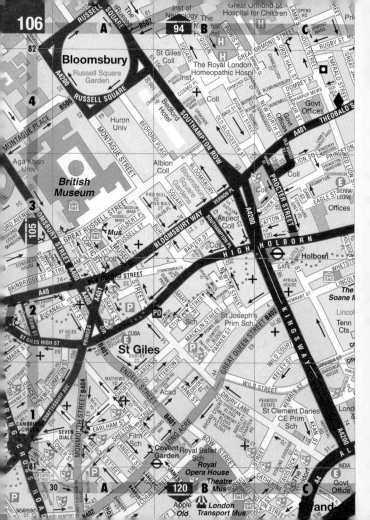

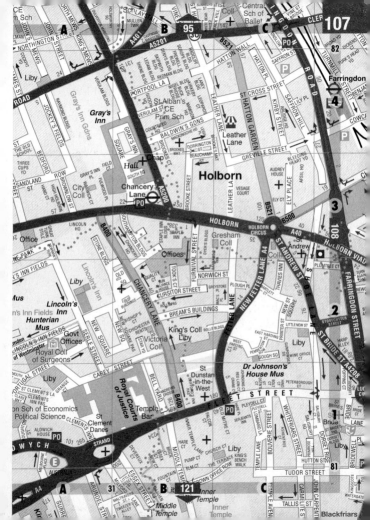

Central Sch of Ballet

Holborn

Gray's Inn

Gray's Inn Gdns

St Alban's CE Prim Sch

Leather Lane

Hatton Garden

Farringdon

Chancery Lane

Gresham Coll

Holborn Circus

St Andrew Coll

Lincoln's Inn Fields

Lincoln's Inn Hunterian Mus

Royal Coll of Surgeons

Govt Offices

King's Coll Liby

Dr Johnson's House Mus

Royal Courts of Justice

St Clement Danes

Temple Bar

St Dunstan-in-the-West

FLEET STREET

Bride

London Sch of Economics & Political Science

STRAND

ALDWYCH

Middle Temple

Inner Temple

Blackfriars

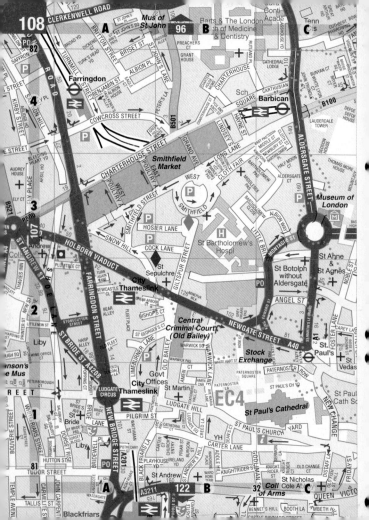

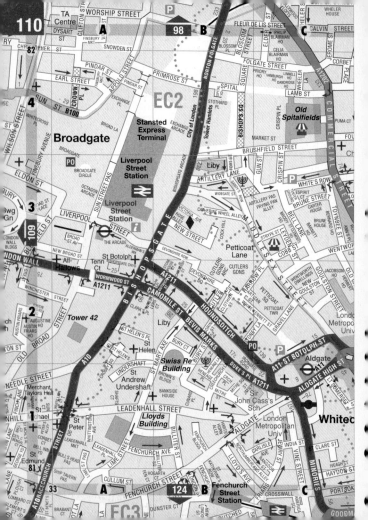

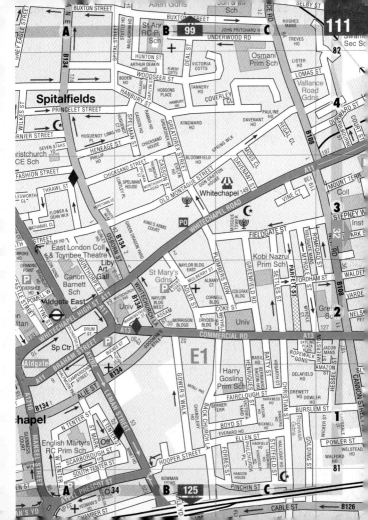

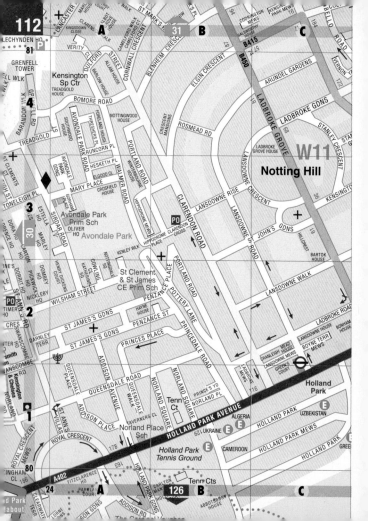

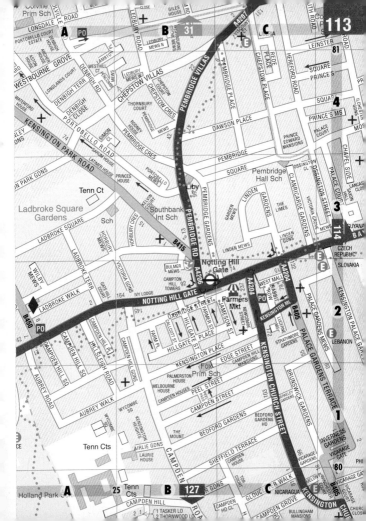

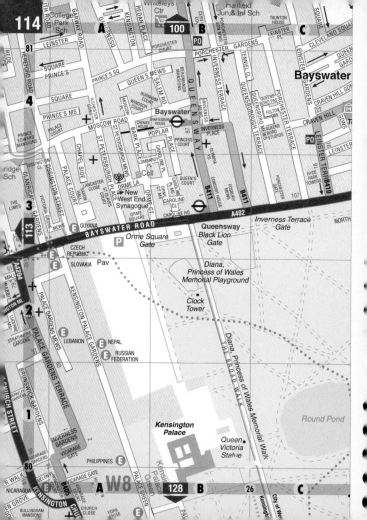

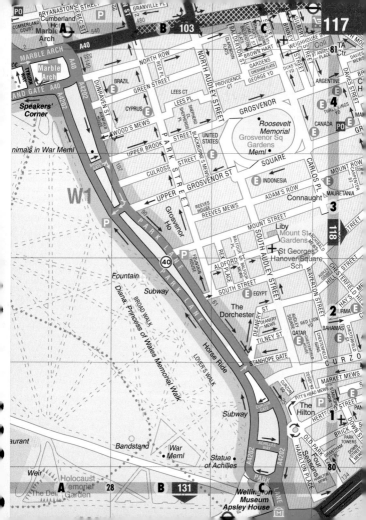

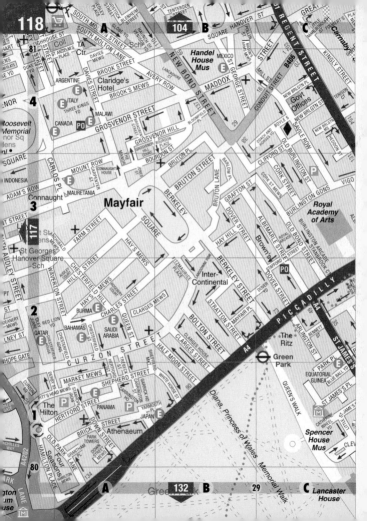

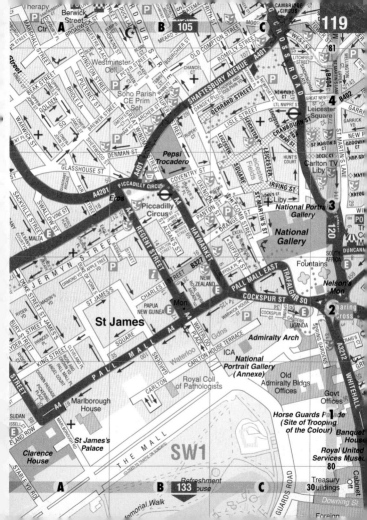

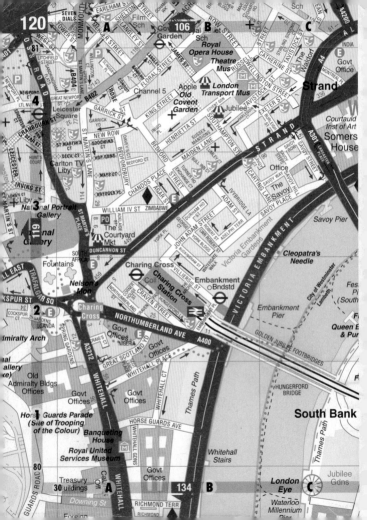

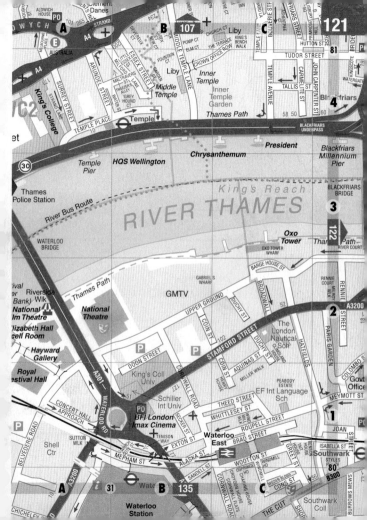

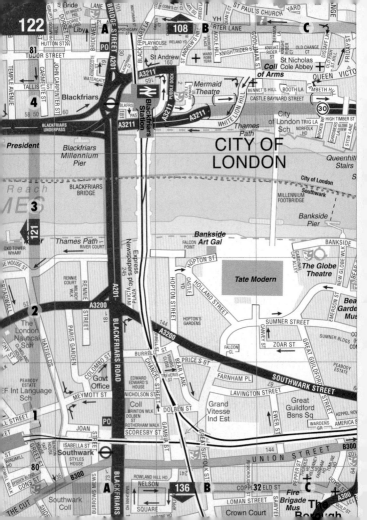

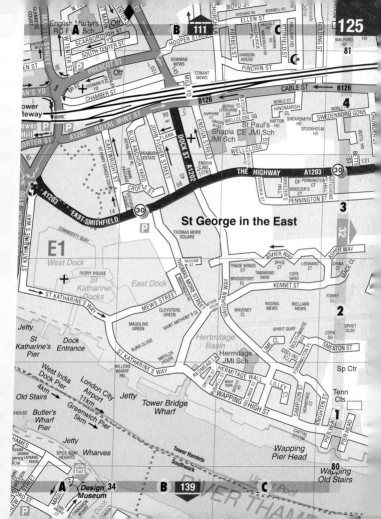

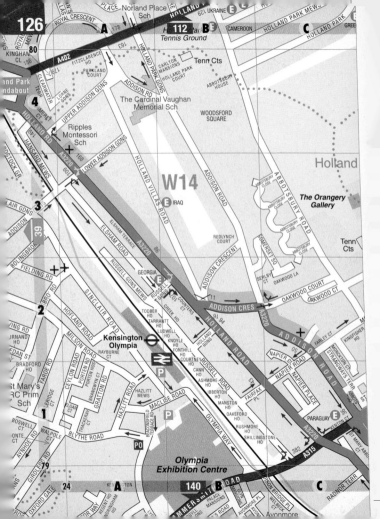

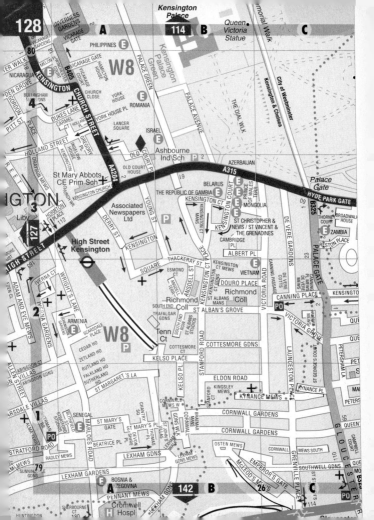

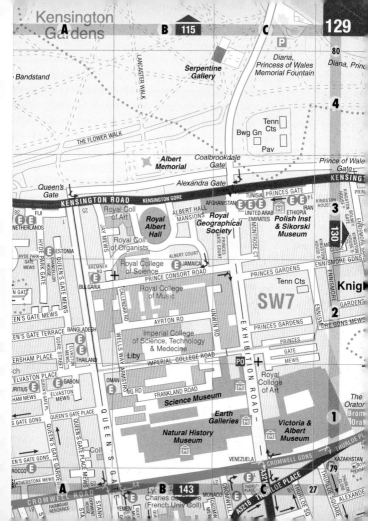

Kensington Gardens

A

B 115

C

80

Diana, Princess of Wales Memorial Fountain

Diana, Princ

P

4

Serpentine Gallery

Bandstand

LANCASTER WALK

THE FLOWER WALK

Tenn Cts

Bwg Gn

Pav

Albert Memorial

Coalbrookdale Gate

Prince of Wale Gate

Queen's Gate

Alexandra Gate

KENSING

KENSINGTON ROAD

KENSINGTON GORE

TUNISIA PRINCES GATE PL

AFGHANISTAN

KINGSTON HOUSE S

KINGSTON HOUSE N

PRIN

38

FIJI

E

NETHERLANDS

Royal Coll of Art

25

ALBERT HALL MANSIONS

Royal Albert Hall

Royal Geographical Society

UNITED ARAB EMIRATES

E E E ETHIOPIA

IRAN

Polish Inst & Sikorski Museum

KINGSTON HOUSE S CLOSE

BOLNEY GATE

KING'S CT

3

JAY MEWS

Royal Coll of Organists

MONTROSE CT

PRINCE'S GATE MEWS

130

ENNISMORE GDNS

ESTONIA

E

HYDE PARK GATE MEWS

CHANCELLOR HOUSE

QUEEN'S GATE

BREMNER RD

Royal College of Science

ALBERT COURT

E JAMAICA

PRINCE'S GATE COURT

PRINCES GARDENS

ENNISMORE

Knig

GATE

E

BULGARIA

PRINCE CONSORT ROAD

Tenn Cts

GARDENS

2

N GATE

Royal College of Music

SW7

CALLENDAR RD

EN'S GATE MEWS

BANGLADESH

E E ELVASTON MEWS

AYRTON RD

UNWIN RD

PRINCES GARDENS

ENNISM

DRE GDNS MEWS

GORE STREET

WELLS WAY

PRINCES

ERSHAM PLACE

E THAILAND

Imperial College of Science, Technology & Medecine

GATE MEWS

EN'S GATE TERRACE

ARMSTRONG RD

Liby

IMPERIAL COLLEGE ROAD

ELVASTON PLACE

E GABON

OMAN

PO

rich

URITIUS

E QUEEN'S GATE PL

ELVASTON MEWS

NG RD

FRANKLAND ROAD

EXHIBITION ROAD

Royal College of Art

The Orator

Brom

HAM MEWS

GORROCCO

E

QUEEN'S GATE GARDE

QUEEN'S GATE PLACE

Science Museum

Ora

1

S GATE GDNS

QUEEN'S GATE

Earth Galleries

Victoria & Albert Museum

Natural History Museum

M

M

M

M

COLI

VENEZUELA

CROMWELL GDNS

KAZAKHSTAN

79

NORTH TERRA

N'S GATE GDNS

ATHERSTONE MEWS

FAIRBRIAR RESIDENCE

THURLOE PL

ALEXANDE

CROMWELL ROAD

A4

B 143

A3218

THURLOE PLACE

THURLOE SQ

27

Charles de Gaulle (French Univ Coll)

MONACO

E

A

E

B

C

STANH

E

E YEMEN

FAIRBRIAR RESIDENCE

QUEEN'S

LZ

STA

GROVEN

ROCCO

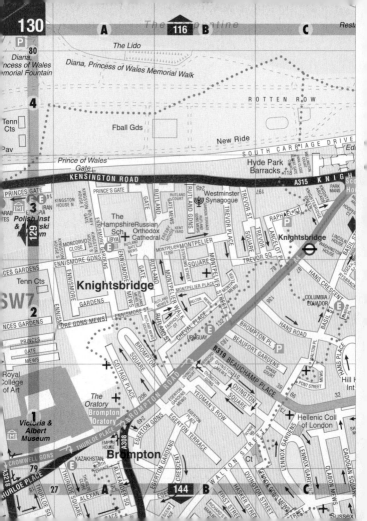

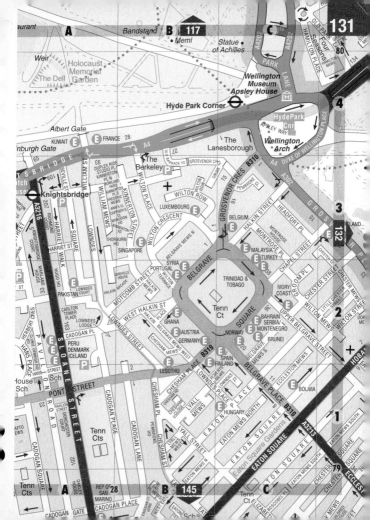

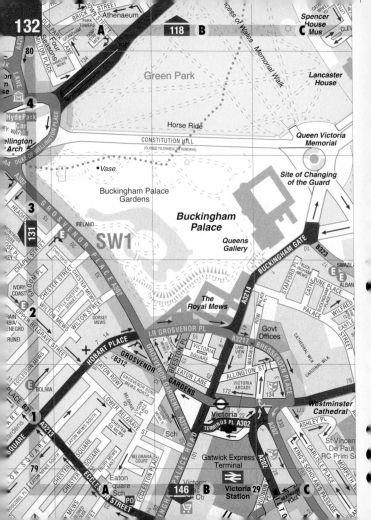

BRICK STREET
Athenaeum
OLD PARK LANE
Four Seasons
PARK TOWERS
GRANTHAM
HAMILTON PLACE
HAMILTON MEWS

ncess of Wales Memorial Walk

Spencer House Mus
CLEV

80

Green Park

Lancaster House

HydePark Cnr
MAY FAIR
WAY
Wellington Arch
4

Horse Ride

Queen Victoria Memorial

A4
DUKE OF WELLINGTON PLACE
A4

CONSTITUTION HILL
(CLOSED TO TRAFFIC ON SUNDAYS)

A302

Vase

Site of Changing of the Guard

HEADCO
3

GROSVENOR PLACE

Buckingham Palace Gardens

131

CHAPEL STREET
MONTROSE
SE PL
KEY
IRELAND
SW1

Buckingham Palace

Queens Gallery

A302

IVORY COAST
E

GROOM PL

CHESTER CL
CHESTER STREET
CHESTER MEWS
LITTLE CHESTER STREET

BUCKINGHAM GATE
B323
SWAZIL

E E
ALBAN

RAIN
RBIA/
ENEGRO
RUNEI

2
UPPER BELGRAVE STREET

WILTON MEWS
WILTON STREET

DORSET MEWS

CATHERINE PLACE
STAFFORD PL
BUCK INGHAM PLACE
WILFRED

A3214

The Royal Mews

PALACE
CATHEDRAL
CASTLE
STREET

LR GROSVENOR PL
A3217
DRESSEDREN PLACE

Govt Offices

BOLIVIA
E

ECCLESTON MEWS

HOBART PLACE
B312
GROSVENOR ROW
EATON ROW

GROSVENOR PL
BEESTON LANE
VICTORIA SQUARE

LAKE VIEW CT
WARW
CARDINAL WLK

CARDINAL WLK

1
A3213
B3

EATON MEWS SOUTH
LOWER BELGRAVE ST
BELGRAVE MEWS
GROSVENOR GDNS MEWS NORTH

EATON LANE
ALLINGTON ST
VICTORIA ARCADE
134

Westminster Cathedral

ASHLEY PL

79

BUCKINGHAM PALACE ROAD
GROSVENOR GARDENS
A3215

EATON MEWS SOUTH
CHESTER SQ MEWS
Sch

Victoria
TERMINUS PL
A302
22

St Vincent De Paul RC Prim Sc

KING'S SCHOLAR'S PASSAGE
MORPETH

N S O U A R E
ardens
CHESTER SQUARE
CHESTER SQUARE
BELGRAVIA COURT

Sch
BURY EATON GAS

Eaton Square Sch

Victoria Ctr

Gatwick Express Terminal

CARLISLE PLACE

MOSCBEL PL
ECCLESTON STREET
EATON MEWS SOUTH
MEWS
PO

Victoria 29 Station

HUDSON
NEATHOUSE PLACE

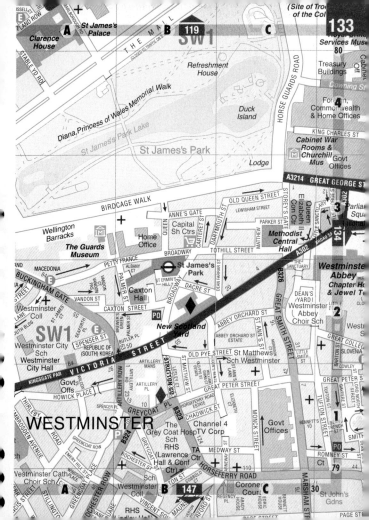

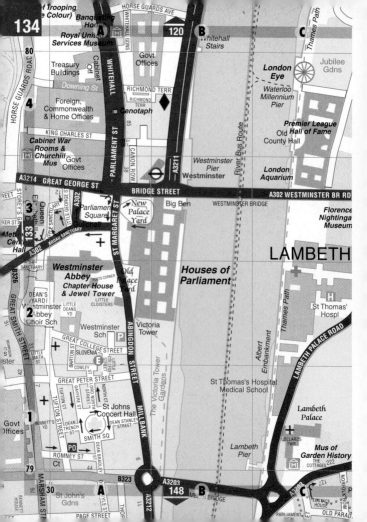

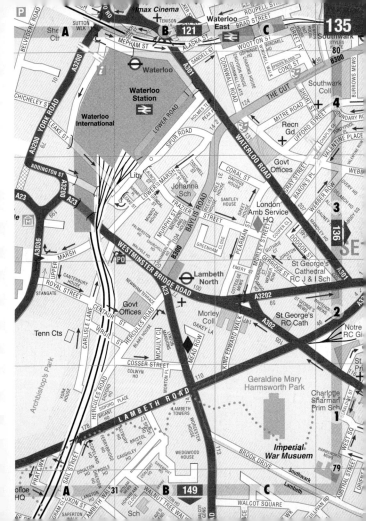

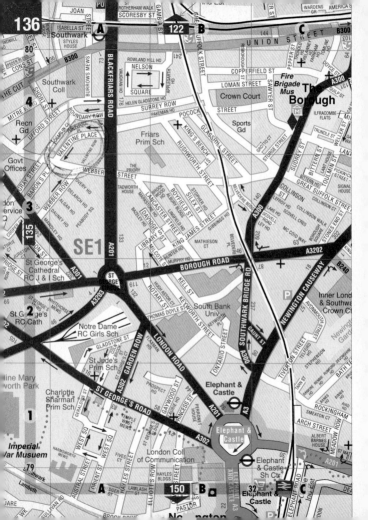

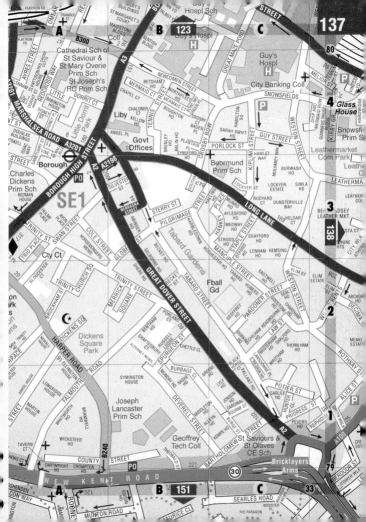

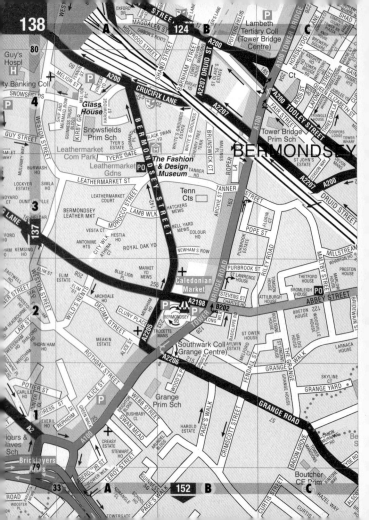

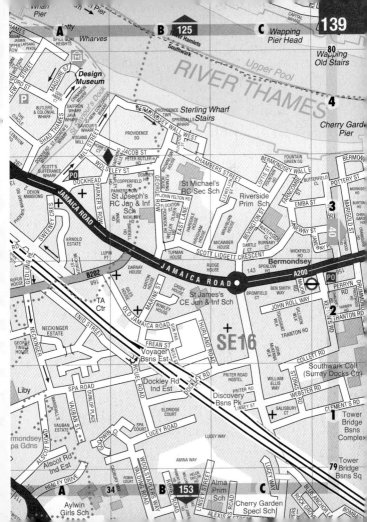

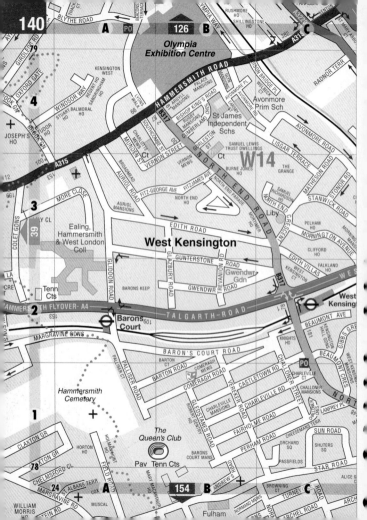

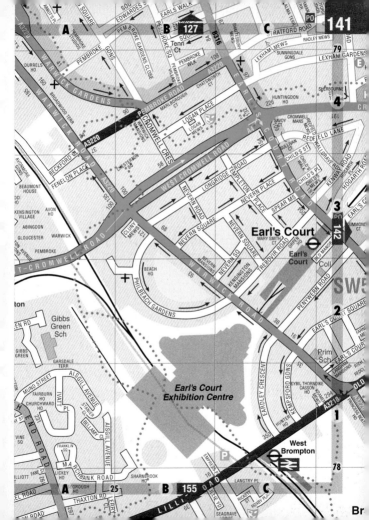

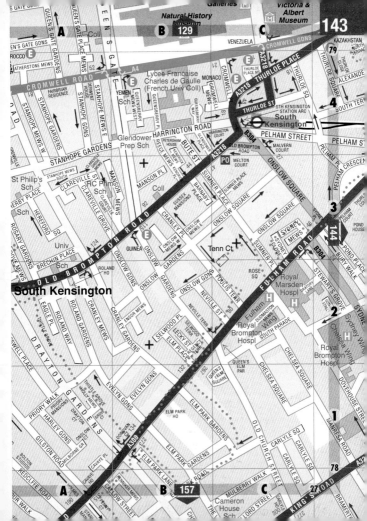

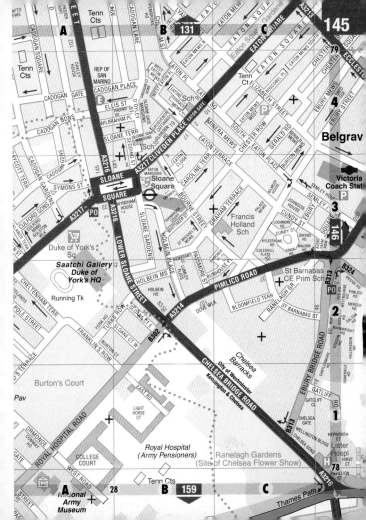

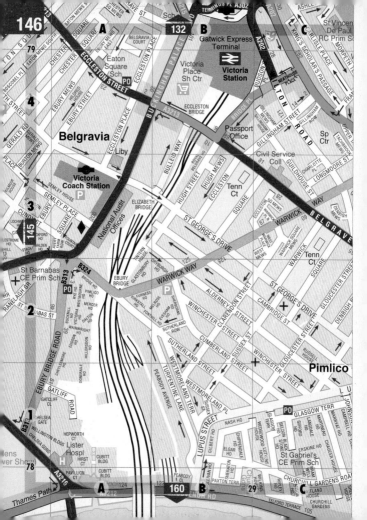

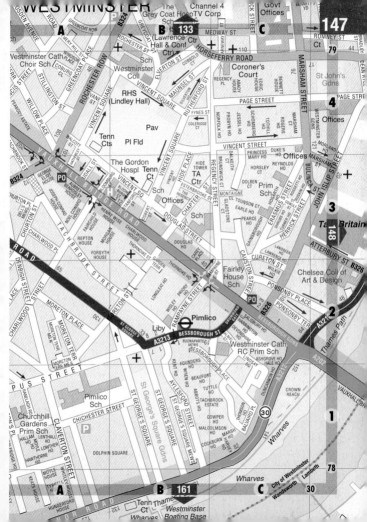

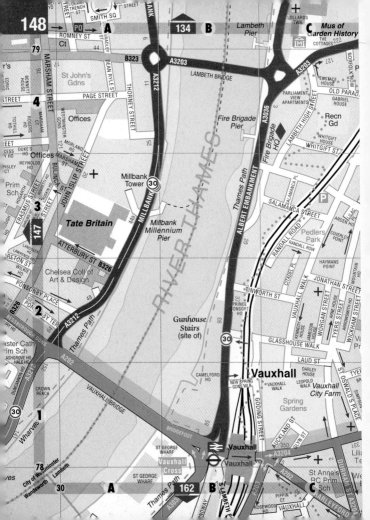

SMITH SQ

A

Lambeth Pier

LOLLARDS TWR

Mus of arden History

THE COTTAGES 222

ROMNEY ST Ct

PO

B323

A3203

79

St John's Gdns

A3212

LAMBETH BRIDGE

EUSTACE HOUSE

A3203

PAGE STREET

DEAN RYLE ST

THORNEY STREET

PARLIAMENT VIEW APARTMENTS

OLD PARAD

GABRIEL HOUSE

4

MARSHAM STREET

Offices

WESTMINSTER GDNS

MORLAND HO

A3036

Fire Brigade Pier

LAMBETH HIGH STREET

Recn Gd

WHITGIFT HOUSE

WHITGIFT ST

STREET

Prim Sch

ERASMUS STREET

JOHN ISLIP STREET

MARSHAM STREET

Millbank Tower

30

Fire Brigade HQ

SALAMANCA STREET

ALBERT EMBANKMENT

P

3

147

Tate Britain

MILLBANK

Millbank Millennium Pier

Thames Path

RANDALL ROAD

PEDLEY PARK

COVERLEY POINT

RANDALL ROW

ATTERBURY ST

B326

CITADEL PL

HAYMANS POINT

Chelsea Coll of Art & Design

JONATHAN STREET

WORGAN STREET

MOUNTAIN

WICKHAM STREET

PONSONBY PLACE

TINWORTH ST

VAUXHALL WALK

TYERS STREET

2

B326

PONSONBY TER

A3212

PRINCE CONSORT RD

GLASSHOUSE WALK

ster Cath rim Sch

Thames Path

A202

Gunhouse Stairs (site of)

30

LAUD ST

Spring

VAUXHALL BRIDGE

CAMELFORD HO

NEW SPRING GDNS WALK

Vauxhall

DARLEY HOUSE

LEOPOLD WALK

Vauxhall City Farm

30

1

CROWN REACH

BRIDGEFOOT

NEW SPRING GDNS WLK

VAUXHALL WALK

GODING STREET

Spring Gardens

St O'SWALDS PLACE

Wharves

ST GEORGE WHARF

Vauxhall

AUCKLAND ST

FLYIN ST

A3204

A202

St Anne's RC Prim Sch

78

City of Westminster Lambeth

Vauxhall Cross

ST GEORGE WHARF

Vauxhall

Vauxhall

PIPPIN CT

Lilia Te

30

A

Wandsworth

Thames Path

162 B

ROSEWOOD

VAUXHALL

HARLEYFORD

C

RIVER THAMES

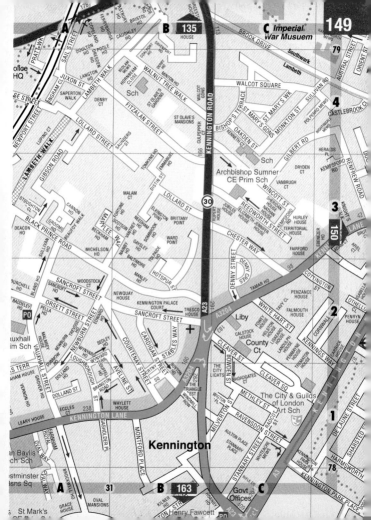

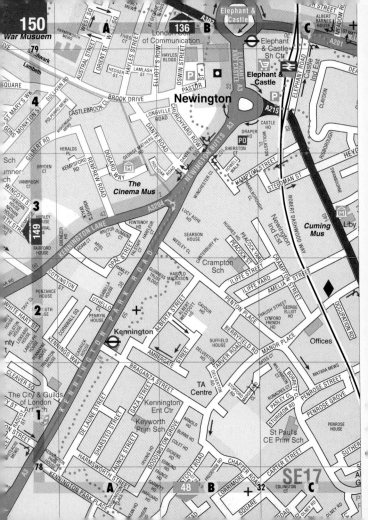

79 Southwark

Lambeth

SQUARE

4 ST MARY'S WK

GDNS, MONKTON S

Sch mmner ch

3

149

2

1

WEST SQ

London Museum of Communication

136

A302

Elephant & Castle

C

ALBERT BARNES MEADOW RD

A201

Elephant & Castle Sh Ctr

Elephant & Castle Ind Est

Newington

CASTLE HO

PO

CLANDON

HEYG

The Cinema Mus

Newington Ind Est

Cuming Mus

Liby

Kennington

Crampton Sch

Searson House

Offices

78

Kennington

TA Centre

Kennington Ent Ctr

Keyworth Prim Sch

The City & Guilds of London Art Sch

St Paul's CE Prim Sch

Penrose House

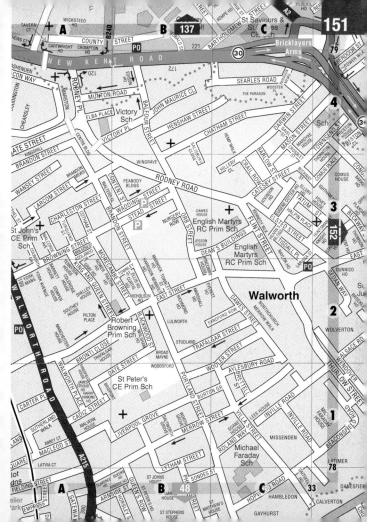

TAVERN CT

WICKSTEED HO

A

CARTWRIGHT

COUNTY

CROMPTON

B240

STREET

B

137

CHENEY ST

St Saviours & St Olaves CE Sch

C

Bricklayers Arms

79

BERDOUR ST

PO

221

BARTHOLOMEW

30

NEW KENT ROAD

172

SEARLES ROAD

THE PARAGON

4

DARWIN STREET

MASON STREET

Sch

PRESTON ST

PRESTON CL

CONG

120

MUNTON ROAD

RODNEY PL

MARSTON

CHEARSLEY

ELBA PLACE

Victory Sch

JOHN MAURICE CL

HENSHAW STREET

CHATHAM STREET

WOOSTER

MARDYKE

THORNTON STREET

COMUS PLACE

COMUS HOUSE

DATE STREET

KINGSHILL

BRANDON STREET

CENTRE BLDG

VICTORY PL

BALFOUR STREET

HEMP WALK

HILLERY CL

CRAIL ROW

CATESBY STREET

BARLOW STREET

WINGRAVE

RODNEY ROAD

3

BECKWAY

POVEY HO

TATUM

BECKWAY

KNIGHT HO

152

EAST

WANSEY STREET

LARCOM STREET

BRANDON MEWS

PEABODY BLDGS

STEAD STREET

WADDING STREET

NURSERY ROW

ORB STREET

DAWES HOUSE

English Martyrs RC Prim Sch

JESSON HOUSE

HALPIN PLACE

ELSTED STREET

TISDALL PL

MAYOR HO

CHARLESTON STREET

COTHAM ST

BROWNING STREET

MORECAMBE STREET

KING AND QUEEN STREET

English Martyrs RC Prim Sch

DEAN'S BUILDINGS

PO

2

St John's CE Prim Sch

YORK MANS

BARRETT HOUSE

SHELLEY HO

PILTON PLACE

NICHOLSON ST

EAST STREET

MARSHALL

MERROW WALK

Walworth

DUNNICO HO

MEDLAR WAY

WOLVERTON

BRONTI CLOSE

Robert Browning Prim Sch

BLACKWOOD ST

LULWORTH

SANDFORD ROW

STUDLAND

TRAFALGAR STREET

DATE STREET

BROAD MAYNE

WOODSFORD

St Peter's CE Prim Sch

LIVERPOOL GROVE

PORTLAND STREET

BURTON GR

WOOLER STREET

AYLESBURY ROAD

INVILLE ROAD

1

CARTER PLACE

MALVERN HOUSE

CADIZ STREET

MERROW STREET

ROLAND WAY

LEES ROAD

VILLA ST

MISSENDEN

BEACONSFIELD

SUTHERLAND WALK

ABBEY CT

MACLEOD ST

A215

LATVIA CT

LYTHAM STREET

SONDES ST

PH

Michael Faraday Sch

78

LATIMER

33

SQUARE

FIELDING STREET

EMPRESS

A

GATEWAY

ARNSIDE ST

QUEEN'S ROW

B

48

ST JOHNS HOUSE

HOPLEY

ROAD

C

ROAD

HAMBLEDON

DANESFIE

ST MATTHEW'S HOUSE

GAYHURST

CALVERTON

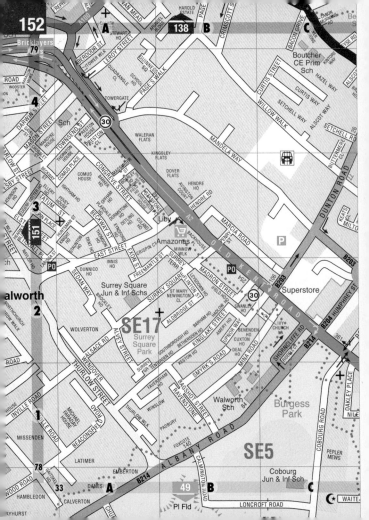

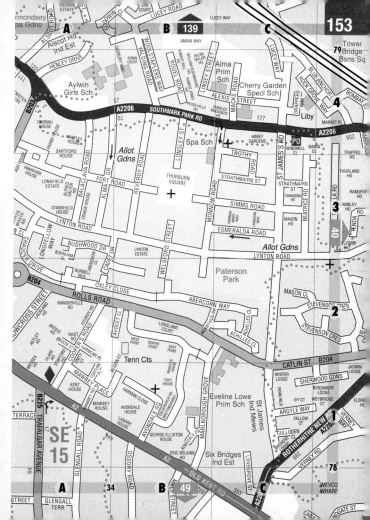

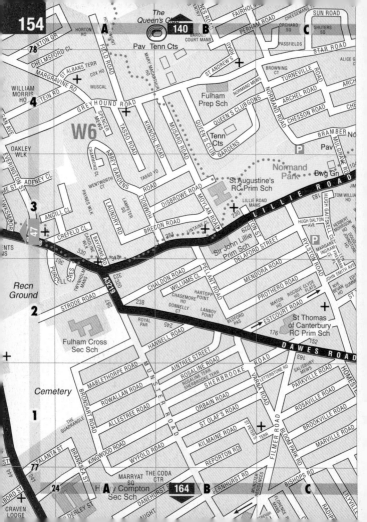

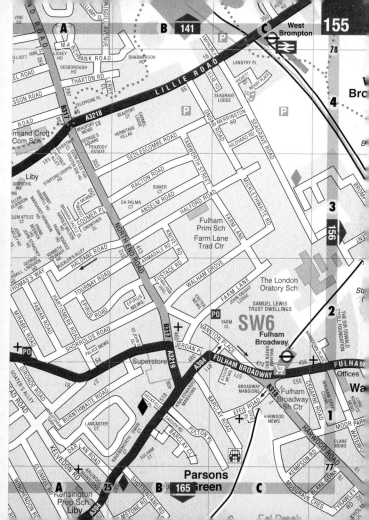

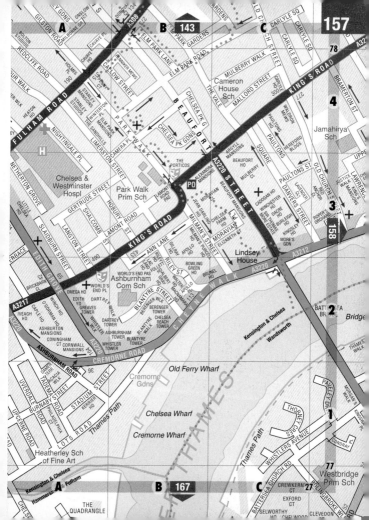

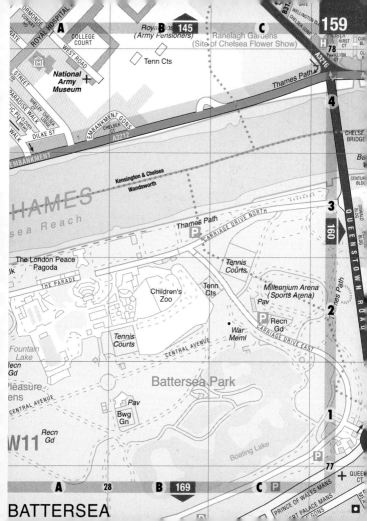

ORMONDE
GATE
CONWAY
 RD
ROYAL HOSPITAL
A
COLLEGE
COURT
WEST ROAD
STREET
SHELEY CHELSEA
PARADISE WALK
CLOVER
CT

M
**National
Army
Museum**

DILKE ST

EMBANKMENT GDNS
CHELSEA
CT
A3212

EMBANKMENT

Royal Hos
(Army Pensioners)
B
Tenn Cts

145

Ranelagh Gardens
(Site of Chelsea Flower Show)
C

B3
GATE
WELLINGTON PLA
CHELSEA GORSE

A3216

159

H

HOSP
HIRST CT

CUI
BL

CLB

Thames Path
A

4

CHELSE
BRIDGE

Ba

CENTUR
BLDG

Kensington & Chelsea
Wandsworth

HAMES
sea Reach

Thames Path
P

CARRIAGE DRIVE NORTH

3

160

OSWALD
BLDG

QUEENSTOWN ROAD

The London Peace
Pagoda

THE PARADE

Children's
Zoo

Tenn
Cts

Tennis
Courts

Millennium Arena
(Sports Arena)
Pav

Thames Path

2

Tennis
Courts

P Recn
Gd

CARRIAGE DRIVE EAST

War
Meml

CENTRAL AVENUE

Battersea Park

Fountain
Lake

ecn
Gd

**Pleasure
ens**

CENTRAL AVENUE

W11 Recn
Gd

Pav

Bwg
Gn

Boating Lake

1

P

77

QUEE
CT

A   28   **B** **169**   **C** P

PRINCE OF WALES MANS

BATTERSEA

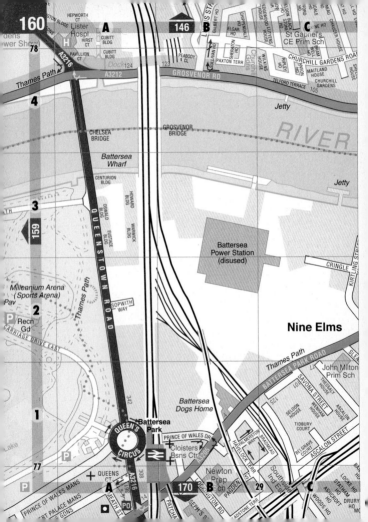

A

B

C

HEPWORTH CT
Lister Hospl
CUBITT BLDG
HIRST CT
PAVILLION CT
CUBITT BLDG
Dock 124
123
H
78
A3216
A3212

St Gabriel's
CE Prim Sch
EDGWORTH HOUSE
GILBERT ST
ELGAR
HO
CHIPPENHALL
WILKIE HO
PAXTON TERR
PEABODY
CL
Churchill
Gdns
RIPLEY
HO
MAITLAND
HOUSE
CHURCHILL GARDENS ROAD
TELFORD TERRACE
CHURCHILL
GARDENS
105

GROSVENOR RD

Thames Path

CHELSEA
BRIDGE

GROSVENOR
BRIDGE

Jetty

RIVER

4

Battersea
Wharf

CENTURION
BLDG

HOWARD
BLDG

Jetty

3

CHELSEA

159

OSWALD
BLDG

EUSTACE
BLDG

WARWICK
BLDG

QUEENSTOWN ROAD

Battersea
Power Station
(disused)

CRINGLE

KIRTLING STREET

Millennium Arena
(Sports Arena)
Pav

P

2

Recn
Gd

CARRIAGE DRIVE EAST

SOPWITH
WAY

Thames Path

Nine Elms

Thames Path

BATTERSEA PARK ROAD

SLEA

John Milton
Prim Sch

SAVONA STREET

1

342

Battersea
Dogs Home

SELDON
HOUSE

WIMMERA
HOUSE

TIDBURY
COURT

BELGRAVE
COURT

ASCALON STREET

ASCALON
HOUSE

Lake

P

77

Battersea
Park

QUEEN'S
CIRCUS

PRINCE OF WALES DR

Cloisters
Bsns Ctr

HAVELOCK TERR

LORD PALMERSTON

BRANDAD

South
Ind Est

P

PRINCE OF WALES MANS

ALBERT PALACE MANS

LEAS GDNS

QUEENS
CT

308

A3216

HEATH ST

PO

Newton
Prep Sch

KENNINGTON RD

PARDEN

AUSTONE TERR

WOODS HO

SEPH'S S

PATCHA

14

198

B

29

C

A

Prim Sch
Hallam Ho
Moyle Lowry Ho
Kents Ho
Hawthorne Ho
Moyle House
Tyrrell House
Hungerford House

DOLPHIN SQUARE

MALCOLMSON HO
MARSH HO
Cockburn St

City of Westminster
Lambeth
Wandsworth

Wharves

Wharves

78

GROSVENOR ROAD
129

132
137

Tenn Ct   Thames Path
Wharves
Westminster Boating Base
Grosvenor Pier

Wharf

RIVERSIDE COURT
30

4

A3205

THAMES

Wharves

Thames Path   ELM QUAY

South Bank Bsns Ctr

New Covent Garden
Flower Market

3

162

56
A3205
NINE ELMS LANE

Tideway Ind Est

POST OFFICE WAY   PONTON ROAD

SW8

62

2

PASCAL STREET
BRAMLEY CRES

DARMAN RD
LOCKYER D
DAVIDSON G
ALDI

BROOKS COURT

WANDSWORTH ROAD

BASI HO
ADRIAN HO
WIL

HEMANS STREET

DARLINGTON HOUSE
HUNTER HOUSE
HEMANS ESTATE

CONFI HO
FOXBRIDGE WD

THORNCROF

STREET
STREET

Sleaford Ind Est

P

CRIMSWORTH ROAD

MILL POND CL

WEBB HOUSE
JOHNSON HOUSE
EVANS HOUSE

FOUNT ST

1

SHELDON CT
DEAN C

BUR

283

St George's CE Prim Sch

New Covent Garden
Fruit & Vegetable Market
PO

GOLDSBORO RD

THORPARCH ROAD

ANDREW PL

TILLMAN

KEMP CT

STAFFO CT
SUMNER CT
LEY DR

77

CORUNNA RD

M HO
HO
BRADY HO

ORGAN HO
MARSH HO

HORP

TAIT CT

LEN EDWARDS DR
WALLIS
BANCROFT
BENSON CT

Lambeth Coll

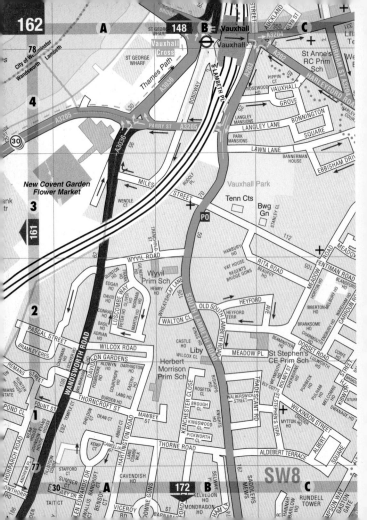

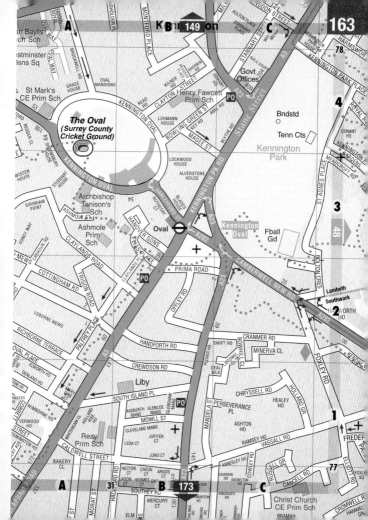

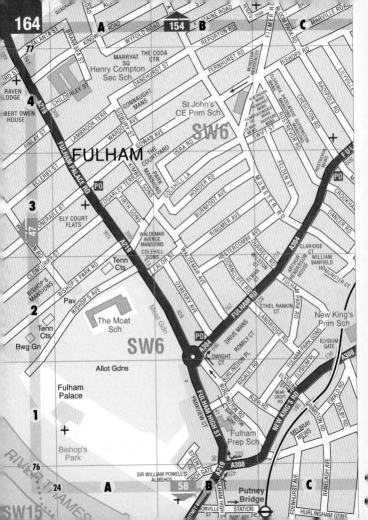

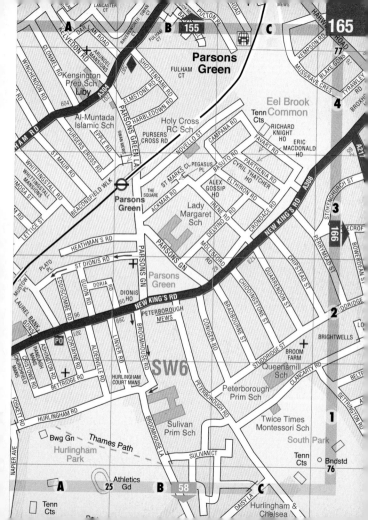

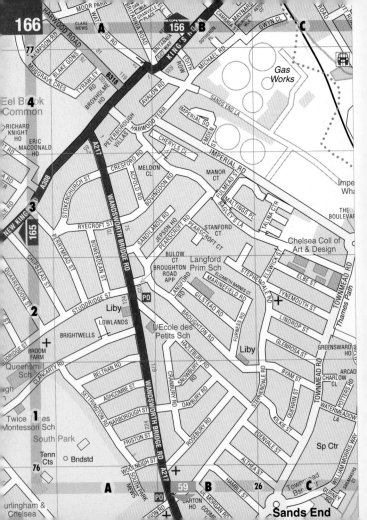

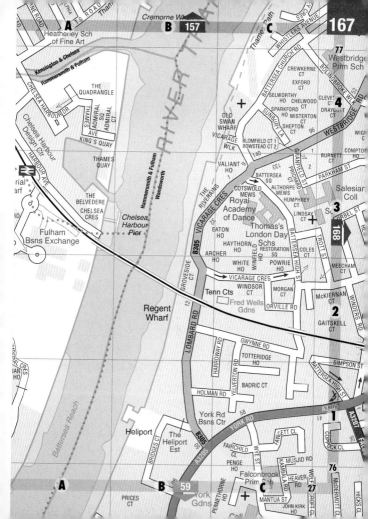

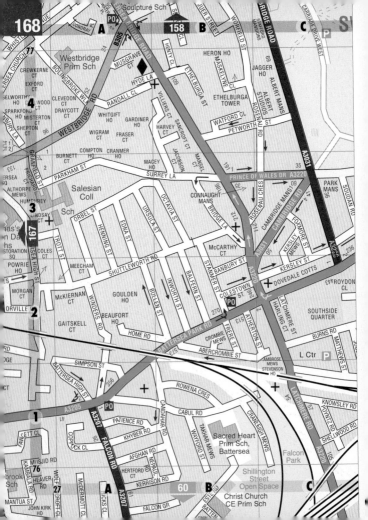

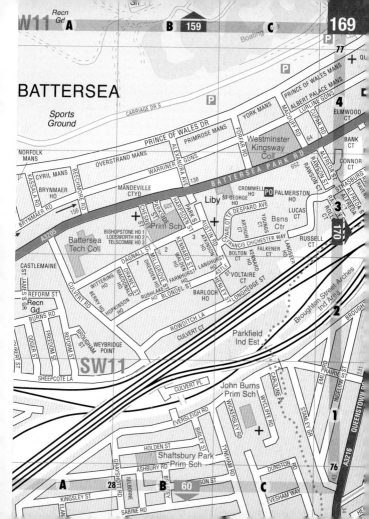

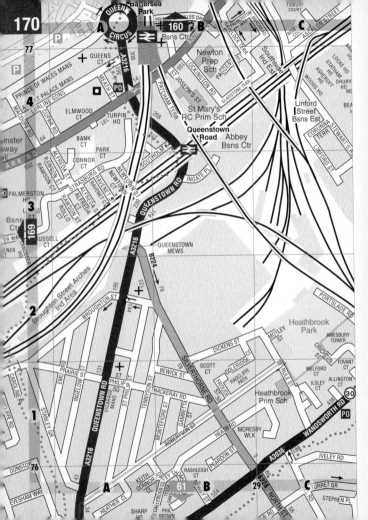

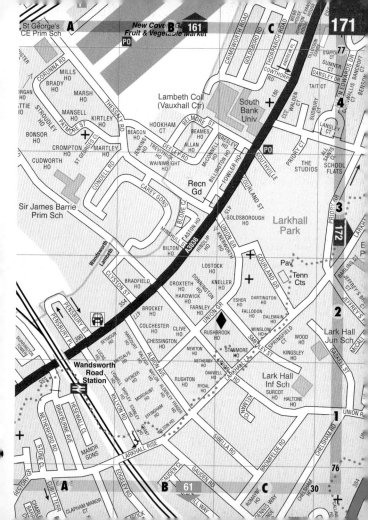

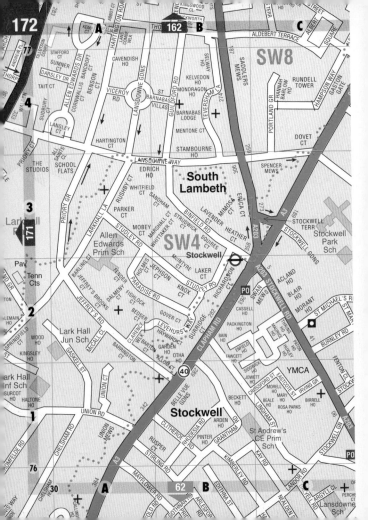

Index

Church Rd **6** Beckenham BR2..........**53** C6 **228** C6

Place name	**Location number**	**Locality, town or village**	**Postcode district**	**Standard scale reference**	**Enlarged scale reference**
May be abbreviated on the map	Present when a number indicates the place's position in a crowded area of mapping	Shown when more than one place (outside London postal districts) has the same name	District for the indexed place	Page number and grid reference for the standard mapping	Page number and grid reference for the central London enlarged mapping, underlined in red

Public and commercial buildings are highlighted in magenta
Places of interest are highlighted in blue with a star✶
Cities, towns and villages are listed in CAPITAL LETTERS

Abbreviations used in the index

Acad	Academy	Ct	Court	Int	International	Prom	Promenade
App	Approach	Ctr	Centre	Intc	Interchange	RC	Roman Catholic
Arc	Arcade	Crkt	Cricket	Jun	Junior	Rd	Road
Art Gall	Art Gallery	Ctry Pk	Country Park	Junc	Junction	Rdbt	Roundabout
Ave	Avenue	Cty	County	La	Lane	Ret Pk	Retail Park
Bglws	Bungalows	Ctyd	Courtyard	L Ctr	Leisure Centre	Sch	School
Bldgs	Buildings	Dr	Drive	Liby	Library	Sec	Secondary
Bsns Ctr	Business Centre	Ent Ctr	Enterprise Centre	Mans	Mansions	Sh Ctr	Shopping Centre
Bsns Pk	Business Park	Ent Pk	Enterprise Park	Mdw/s	Meadow/s	Sp	Sports
Bvd	Boulevard	Est	Estate	Meml	Memorial	Specl	Special
Cath	Cathedral, Catholic	Ex Ctr	Exhibition Centre	Mid	Middle	Sports Ctr	Sports Centre
CE	Church of England	Ex Hall	Exhibition Hall	Mix	Mixed	Sq	Square
Cemy	Cemetery	Fst	First	Mkt	Market	St	Street, Saint
Cir	Circus	Gdn	Garden	Mon	Monument	Sta	Station
Circ	Circle	Gdns	Gardens	Mus	Museum	Stad	Stadium
Cl	Close	Gn	Green	Obsy	Observatory	Tech	Technical
Cnr	Corner	Gr	Grove	Orch	Orchard		Technology
Coll	College	Gram	Grammar	Par	Parade	Terr	Terrace
Com	Community	Her Ctr	Heritage Centre	Pas	Passage	Trad Est	Trading Estate
Comm	Common	Ho	House	Pav	Pavilion	Twr/s	Tower/s
Comp	Comprehensive	Hospl	Hospital	Pk	Park	Univ	University
Con Ctr	Conference Centre	Hts	Heights	Pl	Place	Wlk	Walk
Cotts	Cottages	Ind Est	Industrial Estate	Prec	Precinct	Yd	Yard
Cres	Crescent	Inf	Infant	Prep	Preparatory		
Cswy	Causeway	Inst	Institute	Prim	Primary		

Abady Ho SW1 . . . . **147** C4
Abberley Mews 9
SW8 . . . . 61 A4
Abbess Cl SW2 . . . . 75 A3
Abbeville Mews 3
SW4 . . . . 61 C3
Abbeville Rd SW4 . 61 B2
Abbey Bsns Ctr 7
SW8 . . . . **170** B4
Abbey Ct
6 Bedford Pk
W12 . . . . 38 A3
Camberwell SE17 . . **151** A1
St John's Wood
NW8 . . . . 78 C2
Abbeyfield Rd
SE16 . . . . 40 B2
Abbey Gdns
Bermondsey SE1 6 . **153** C4
St John's Wood
NW8 . . . . 79 A1
West Kensington
W6 . . . . **154** A3
Abbey Ho NW8 . . . 89 A4
Abbey La E15 . . . . . 27 C3
Abbey Lo NW8 . . . . 90 B3
Abbey Orchard St
SW1 . . . . **133** C2
Abbey Orchard Street
Est SW1 . . . . **133** C2
Abbey Rd
St John's Wood
NW8 . . . . 78 C2
Wembley NW10 . . . . 20 A4
Abbey Rd Motorist Ctr
NW6 . . . . 78 A4
Abbey St SE1 . . . . **138** C2
Abbot Ct SW8 . . . . **162** A1
Abbot Ho 14 E14 . . 34 A2
Abbotsbury Cl
Kensington W14 . . **126** C3
Mill Meads E15 . . . . 27 B3
Abbotsbury Ho
W14 . . . . **126** B4
Abbotsbury Mews
SE15 . . . . 65 B4
Abbotsbury Rd
W14 . . . . **126** C3
Abbotshade Rd 15
SE16 . . . . 32 C1
Abbots Ho
Kensington W14 . . **126** C1
Pimlico SW1 . . . . . **147** B1
Abbots La SE1 . . . **124** B1
Abbots Pk SW2 . . . 74 C3
Abbot's Pl NW6 . . . 78 A4
Abbot St E8 . . . . . . 16 B2
Abbotstone Ho 4
E5 . . . . 7 C2
Abbotstone Rd
SW15 . . . . 57 B4
Abbotswell Rd
SE4 . . . . 66 B2
Abbotswood Rd
London SE22 . . . . . 64 A3
Streatham SW16 . . 73 C1
Abbott Ho SW12 . . 72 B4
Abbott Rd E14 . . . . 34 C3
Abbotts Cl N1 . . . . 15 B2
Abbotts Wharf 4
E14 . . . . 33 C3
Abchurch La EC4,
EC4 . . . . **123** C4
Abchurch Yd EC4. **123** B4

Abdale Rd W12 . . . . 30 A2
Abel Ho SE11 . . . . **163** B4
Aberavon Rd E3 . . . 26 A2
Abercorn Cl NW8 . . **88** C4
Abercorn Mans
NW8 . . . . 79 A1
Abercorn Mews 10
TW10 . . . . 54 B3
Abercorn Pl NW8 . . 78 C1
Abercorn Way
SE1 . . . . **153** B2
Abercrombie Ho 11
W12 . . . . 30 A2
Abercrombie St
SW11 . . . . **168** B2
Aberdale Ct 22
SE16 . . . . 40 C4
Aberdare Gdns
NW6 . . . . 11 A1
Aberdeen Ct
Canonbury N5 . . . . 15 B3
Paddington W9 . . . . **89** B1
Aberdeen La N5 . . . 15 B3
Aberdeen Mans
WC1 . . . . **94** A2
Aberdeen Pk N5 . . . 15 B3
Aberdeen Pl NW8 . . **89** B2
Aberdeen Rd
Canonbury N5 . . . . 15 B4
Dudden Hill NW10 . . 8 B3
Aberdeen Terr
SE3 . . . . 52 C1
Aberdour St SE1 . **152** A4
Aberfeldy Ho SE5 . . 48 A3
Aberfeldy St E14 . . 34 B3
Abersham Rd E8 . . 16 B3
Ability Plaza 8
E8 . . . . 16 B1
Ability Twrs EC1 . . **96** A4
Abingdon W14 . . . **141** A3
Abingdon Cl
Kentish Town NW1 . 13 C2
Abingdon Cts 8
W8 . . . . **127** C1
Abingdon Ho
E2 . . . . 24 B1 **98** C2
Abingdon Mans
W8 . . . . **127** B2
Abingdon Rd W8 . **127** C1
Abingdon St SW1 **134** A2
Abingdon Villas
W8 . . . . **127** C1
Abinger Gr SE8 . . . 51 B4
Abinger Ho SE1 . . **137** B3
Abinger Mews
W9 . . . . 23 C1
Abinger Rd W4 . . . 38 A3
Ablett St SE16 . . . . 40 B1
Abney Gdns 5 N16 . 7 B2
Abney Park
Cemetery*
N16 . . . . 7 A2
Abney Park Ct N16 . 7 B2
Aboyne Rd SW17 . . 71 C1
Abyssinia Cl SW11 . 60 A3
Abyssinia Rd
SW11 . . . . 60 A3
Acacia Cl SE8 . . . . . 41 A2
Acacia Gdns NW8 . **79** C2
Acacia Gr SE21 . . . 75 C2
Acacia Ho
Brockley SE4 . . . . . 66 B3
Stoke Newington N16 . 6 C2

Acacia Pl NW8 . . . . **79** C2
Acacia Rd
Acton W3 . . . . 28 B2
St John's Wood
NW8 . . . . **79** C2
Acacia Wlk SW10 . **157** A1
Acad at Peckham The
SE15 . . . . 49 B2
Academy Ct 6 E2 . . 25 B2
Academy Gdns
W8 . . . . **127** B4
Academy Sch The
NW3 . . . . 11 C4
Academy The 2
N19 . . . . 4 B3
Acad of Live &
Recorded Arts The
SW18 . . . . 59 C1
Acanthus Dr SE1 . **153** B2
Acanthus Rd
SW11 . . . . 60 C4
Accommodation Rd
NW11 . . . . 1 B3
Acer Ct 2 NW2 . . . . 9 C4
Acfold Rd SW6 . . . **166** A3
Achilles Cl SE1 . . . **153** C2
Achilles Ho 6 E2 . . 25 A3
Achilles Rd NW6 . . 10 C3
Achilles St SE14 . . 51 A3
Achilles Way W1 . . **117** C1
Acklam Rd W10 . . . 31 B4
Ackmar Rd SW6 . . **165** B3
Ackroyd Dr E3 . . . . 33 C4
Acland Burghley Sch
NW5 . . . . 13 A4
Acland Cres SE5 . . 63 C4
Acland Ho SW9 . . . **172** C2
Acland Rd NW2 . . . . 9 A2
Acol Ct 11 NW6 . . . 10 C1
Acol Rd NW6 . . . . . 11 A1
Acorn Ct 5 E3 . . . . 26 C3
Acorn Gdns W3 . . . 28 C4
Acorn Par 7 SE15 . 50 A3
Acorn Production Ctr
N7 . . . . 14 A1
Acorns The 21
E1 . . . . 32 A1
Acorn Wharf SE15 . 49 C4
Acorn Wlk SE16 . . . 33 A1
Acqua Ho TW9 . . . . 45 A3
Acre Dr SE22 . . . . . 64 C3
Acre La SW2 . . . . . 62 B3
Acris St SW18 . . . . 59 B2
ACTON 28 C1
Acton Bsns Ctr
NW10 . . . . 20 C1
Acton Central Ind Est
4 W3 . . . . 28 B1
Acton Central Sta
3 W3 . . . . 28 C1
ACTON GREEN . . . 37 B2
Acton High Sch
W3 . . . . 36 C4
Acton Hill Mews
W3 . . . . 28 A1
Acton Ho
8 Acton W3 . . . . . . 28 B3
10 Haggerston E8 . . 24 B4
Acton Hospl W3 . . . 36 C4
Acton La
Acton Green W4 . . . 37 B2
Harlesden NW10 . . 20 C3
Acton Main Line Sta
W3 . . . . 28 A3
Acton Mews E8 . . . 24 B4

Acton Park Ind Est
W3 . . . . 37 C4
Acton St WC1 . . . . . **94** C3
Acton Town Sta
W3 . . . . 36 C4
Acton Vale Ind Pk
W3 . . . . 29 B1
Acuba Ho SW18 . . . 71 A3
Acuba Rd SW18 . . . 71 A2
Ada Ct Islington N1 . **86** C3
St John's Wood W9 . **89** A3
Ada Gdns E14 . . . . 34 C3
Ada Ho 23 E2 . . . . . 24 C4
Adair Ho SW3 . . . . **158** B4
Adair Rd W10 . . . . 23 A1
Adair Twr 7 W10 . . 23 A1
Ada Kennedy Ct 6
SE10 . . . . 52 B3
Adam Ct SE11 . . . . **150** A3
Adam & Eve Ct
W1 . . . . **105** A2
Adam & Eve Mews
W8 . . . . **127** C2
Adamfields SW11 . . 11 C1
Adams Gardens Est 5
SE16 . . . . 40 B4
Adams Ho 3 E14 . . 34 C3
Adams Mews
SW17 . . . . 72 B2
Adamson Rd
Hampstead NW3 . . 11 C1
Newham E16 . . . . . 35 C3
Adams Pl N7 . . . . . 14 B3
Adam's Row W1 . . **117** C3
Adam St WC2 . . . . **120** B3
Adam Wlk SW6 . . . 47 B3
Ada Pl E2 . . . . 24 C4
Ada Rd SE5 . . . . . . 49 A3
Adare The
SW16 . . . . 74 A1
Adare Wlk SW16,
SW2 . . . . 74 B2
Ada St E8 . . . . 25 A4
Adderley Gr SW11 . 60 C2
Adderley St E14 . . . 34 B3
Addey Ho SE8 . . . . 51 B3
Addey & Stanhope
Sch SE14 . . . . 51 C2
Addington Ct 7
SW14 . . . . 55 C4
Addington Ho
SW9 . . . . **173** A1
Addington Rd E3 . . 26 C2
Addington Sq SE5 . 48 C3
Addington St SE1 . **135** A3
Addis Ho 50 E1 . . . 32 B4
Addison Ave
W11 . . . . . . 31 A1 **112** A4
Addison Bridge Pl
W14 . . . . **140** C4
Addison Cres
W14 . . . . **126** B2
Addison Gdns
W14 . . . . 39 C3
Addison Gr W4 . . . 38 A3
Addison Ho NW8 . . **89** B4
Addison Park Mans 12
W14 . . . . 39 C4
Addison Pl
W11 . . . . . . 31 A1 **112** A4
Addison Prim Sch
W14 . . . . 39 B3
Addison Rd W14 . **126** C2
Addle Hill EC4 . . . . **108** B1
Addle St EC2 . . . . **109** A3
Addlestone Ho 4
W10 . . . . 30 B4

Addy Ho SE16 . . . . 40 B2
Adela Ho 9 W6 . . . 39 B1
Adelaide Ave SE4 . . 66 C3
Adelaide Gr W12 . . 29 C2
Adelaide Ct
Hackney E5 . . . . . . 18 A3
St John's Wood
NW8 . . . . **79** A1
Adelaide Gr W12 . . 29 C1
Adelaide Rd
Primrose Hill NW3 . 12 A1
Richmond TW9 . . . . 54 B3
2 Wandsworth
SW18 . . . . 58 C2
Adelaide St WC2 . **120** A3
Adela St W10 . . . . 23 A1
Adelina Gr E1 . . . . 32 B4
Adelina Mews
SW12 . . . . 73 C3
Adeline Pl WC1 . . . **105** C3
Adelphi Ct 20
SE16 . . . . 40 C4
Adelphi Terr WC2 . **120** B3
Adeney Rd W6 . . . . 47 C4
Aden Gr N16 . . . . . 15 C4
Aden Ho 12 E1 . . . . 32 C4
Aden Lo N16 . . . . . 15 C4
Adeyfield Ho EC1 . . **97** C3
Adie Rd W6 . . . . . . 39 B3
Adisham Ho 4 E5 . . 17 A3
Adler St E1 . . . . **111** B2
Adley St E5 . . . . . . 18 A3
Admiral Ct
Chelsea SW10 . . . **167** A4
Marylebone W1 . . . **103** B3
Admiral Hyson Ind Est
SE16 . . . . 40 A1
Admiral Mews
W10 . . . . 22 C1
Admiral Pl SE16 . . . 33 A1
Admirals Ct
Bermondsey SE1 . . **124** C1
32 Putney SW19 . . 69 C3
Admirals Gate
SE10 . . . . 52 A2
Admiral Sq SW10 . **167** A4
Admiral St SE8 . . . . 51 C2
Admirals Way E14 . 41 C4
Admiral's Wlk NW3 . 2 B1
Admiralty Arch*
SW1 . . . . **119** C2
Admiralty Cl 1
SE8 . . . . 51 C2
Admiral Wlk W9 . . 31 C4
Adolphus Rd N4 . . . 6 A2
Adolphus St SE8 . . 51 B3
Adpar St W2 . . . . . **101** B4
Adrian Bolt Ho 2
E2 . . . . 25 A2
Adrian Ho
Islington N1 . . . . . **85** A3
South Lambeth
SW8 . . . . **162** A2
Stratford E15 . . . . . 19 C1
Adrian Mews
SW10 . . . . **156** B4
Adriatic Bldg 18
E14 . . . . 33 A2
Adriatic Ho 10 E1 . 25 C1
Adron Ho 13 SE16 . 40 B2
Adstock Ho 5 N1 . . 15 A1
ADT Coll SW15 . . . 58 B2
Adventurers Ct 17
E14 . . . . 34 C2
Adys Lawn NW2 . . . 9 A2

Adys Rd SE15 . . . . 64 B4

Aegean Apts [7]
E16 . . . . 35 C2

Aegon Ho [3] E14 . . 42 A3
Affleck St N1 . . . . . 85 A1
Afghan Rd SW11 . . 168 A1
Africa Ho WC2 . . . . 106 C2
Afsil Ho EC1 . . . . . . 107 C3

Aga Khan Univ
WC1 . . . . 105 C3

Agamemnon Rd
NW6 . . . . 10 B3
Agar Gr NW1 . . . . . . 13 C1
Agar Pl NW1 . . . . . . 13 C1
Agar St WC2 . . . . . 120 B3
Agate Rd W6 . . . . . . 39 B3
Agatha Cl E1 . . . . . . 32 B1
Agave Rd NW2 . . . . . 9 B4
Agdon St EC1 . . . . . 96 A2

Agincourt Rd
NW3 . . . . 12 B4
Agnes Ct [11] SW18 . 59 C3
Agnes Ho [13] W11 . 30 C2
Agnes Rd W3 . . . . . . 38 B4
Agnes St E14 . . . . . . 33 B3

Aigburth Mans
SW9 . . . . 163 B1
Ailsa St E14 . . . . 34 B4
Ainger Rd NW3 . . . . 12 B1
Ainsdale NW1 . . . . . 92 C4
Ainsdale Dr SE1 . . 153 B1
Ainsley St E2 . . . . . . 25 A2
Ainslie Wlk [6]
SW12 . . . . 73 A4
Ainsty St [20] SE16 . 40 B4
Ainsworth Cl SE5 . . 49 A1
Ainsworth Est
NW8 . . . . 78 C4
Ainsworth Ho
NW8 . . . . 78 B3
Ainsworth Rd E9 . . . 17 B1
Ainsworth Way
NW8 . . . . 78 B4
Aintree St SW6 . . . 154 B2
Aird Ho SE1 . . . . . . 136 C1
Airdrie Cl N1 . . . . . . 14 B1
Airedale Ave W4 . . . 38 B1
Airedale Ave S
W4 . . . . 38 B1
Airedale Rd SW12 . . 72 B4
Airlie Gdns
W8 . . . . . . 31 C1 113 B1
Air St W1 . . . . 119 A3
Aisgill Ave SW5 . . . 141 A1
Aiten Pl W6 . . . . 38 C2
Aithan Ho [13] E14 . 33 B3
Aitken Cl E8 . . . . 24 C4
Ajax Ho [3] E2 . . . . . 25 A3
Ajax Rd NW6 . . . . . . 10 C3
Akbar Ho [7] E14 . . . 42 A2
Akehurst St SW15 . . 68 C4
Akenside Ct [3]
NW3 . . . . 11 C3
Akenside Rd NW3 . . 11 C3
Akerman Rd SW9 . . . 48 A2
Akintaro Ho [7]
SE8 . . . . 51 B4
Alamaro Lo [5]
SE10 . . . . 43 B3
Aland Ct SE16 . . . . . 41 A3
Alan Preece Ct
NW6 . . . . 9 C1
Alaska Bldg [12]
SE13 . . . . 52 A2
Alaska St SE1 . . . . 121 B1

Alastor Ho [10] E14 . 42 B3
Albacore Cres
SE13 . . . . 67 A1
Alba Mews SW18,
SW19 . . . . 70 C2
Alban Ho
Hampstead NW3 . . . . 11 B2
New Cross SE14 . . . . 51 B2
Albans Cl SW16 . . . . 74 A1
Albany W1 . . . . 118 C3
Albany Cl SW14 . . . . 55 A3
Albany Ct
College Pk NW10 . . . . 22 A2
NW8 . . . . 79 B1
Westminster SW1 . . 133 B2
Whitechapel E1 . . . . 111 B2
Albany Ctyd SW1 . . 119 A3
Albany Ho [6] TW8 . . 44 A4
Albany Mans
SW11 . . . . 158 B1
Albany Mews
Camberwell SE5 . . . . 48 B4
Islington N1 . . . . 14 C1
Albany Par [4]
TW8 . . . . 44 A4
Albany Pas [12]
TW10 . . . . 54 A2
Albany Rd
Camberwell SE5 . . . . 49 A4
Richmond TW10 . . . . 54 A2
Albany St NW1 . . . . 92 B4
Albany Terr [6]
TW10 . . . . 54 B2
Albemarle SW19 . . . 69 C2
Albemarle Ho
[2] Brixton SW2 . . . . 62 C4
Rotherhithe SE8 . . . . 41 B2
Albemarle Mans
NW3 . . . . 11 A4
Albemarle Prim Sch
SW19 . . . . 70 A2
Albemarle St W1 . . 118 C3
Albemarle Way
EC1 . . . . 96 A1
Alberta Ct [1]
TW10 . . . . 54 B2
Alberta Ho E14 . . . . 34 B1
Alberta St SE17 . . . 150 B2
Albert Ave SW8 . . . 162 C1
Albert Barnes Ho
SE1 . . . . 136 C1
Albert Bigg Point
E15 . . . . 27 B4
Albert Bridge Rd
SW11 . . . . 158 C1
Albert Cl [1] E9 . . . . 25 A4
Albert Cotts E1 . . . 111 B4
Albert Ct
Knightsbridge
SW7 . . . . 129 B3
[6] Putney SW19 . . . . 70 A3
Albert Dr SW19 . . . . 70 A3
Albert Emb SE1 . . . 148 B3
Albert Gate Ct
SW1 . . . . 130 C3
Albert Gdns E1 . . . . 32 C3
Albert Gray Ho
SW10 . . . . 157 B2
Albert Hall Mans
SW7 . . . . 129 B3
Albert Mans
Battersea SW11 . . . 168 C4
Hornsey N8 . . . . 5 A4
Albert Meml 129 B3
Albert Mews W8 . . . 128 C2

Albert Palace Mans
SW11 . . . . 169 C4
Albert Pl W8 . . . . . . 128 B3
Albert Rd
Finsbury Pk N4 . . . . . . 5 B4
Kilburn NW6 . . . . 23 B3
Richmond TW10 . . . . 54 B2
Albert's Ct NW1 . . . . 90 B2
Albert Sq SW8 . . . . 162 C1
Albert St NW1 . . . . . 82 B3
Albert Starr Ho [7]
SE8 . . . . 40 C2
Albert Studios
SW11 . . . . 168 C4
Albert Terr
Camden Town
NW1 . . . . 81 B3
Stonebridge NW10 . . . 20 B4
Albert Terr Mews
NW1 . . . . 81 B3
Albert Way SE15 . . . 50 A3
Albion Ave SW8 . . . 171 B1
Albion Cl W2 . . . . . 116 B4
Albion Coll WC1 . . . 106 B3
Albion Ct [7] W6 . . . 39 A2
Albion Dr E8 . . . . . . 16 C1
Albion Est SE16 . . . . 40 B4
Albion Gate W2 . . . 116 B4
Albion Gdns [1]
W6 . . . . 39 A2
Albion Gr N16 . . . . . 16 A4
Albion Ho
[17] Deptford SE8 . . . 51 C3
EC1 . . . . 108 A4
Albion Mews
Bayswater W2 . . . . . 116 B4
[6] Hammersmith
W6 . . . . 39 A2
Islington N1 . . . . 85 B4
Albion Pl
Broadgate EC2 . . . . 109 C3
Clerkenwell EC1 . . . 108 A4
Hammersmith W6 . . . 39 A2
Albion Prim Sch
SE16 . . . . 40 B4
Albion Rd N16 . . . . . 15 C4
Albion Riverside
SW11 . . . . 158 A2
Albion Sq E8 . . . . . . 16 B1
Albion St
Bayswater W2 . . . . . 116 B4
Rotherhithe SE16 . . . 40 B4
Albion Terr E8 . . . . . 16 B1
Albion Way
Barbican EC1 . . . . . 108 C3
Lewisham SE13 . . . . 67 B3
Albion Wlk N1 . . . . . 84 B1
Albion Works Studios
E8 . . . . 16 C3
Albon Yd N1 . . . . 87 A3
Albon Ho SW18 . . . . 59 A1
Albrighton Rd SE5,
SE22 . . . . 64 A4
Albury Bldgs SE1 . . 136 B3
Albury Ct SE8 . . . . . 51 C4
Albury Lo [2] SW2 . . 74 B4
Albury St SE8 . . . . . 51 C4
Albyn Rd SE8 . . . . . 51 C2
**Alchemea Coll of
Audio Engineering**
N1 . . . . 86 B4
Alconbury Rd E5 . . . . 7 C2
Aldbourne Rd
W12 . . . . 29 C1

Aldbridge St
SE17 . . . . 152 B2
Aldburgh Mews
W1 . . . . 103 C2
Aldbury Ho SW3 . . 144 A3
Aldebert Terr
SW8 . . . . 162 C1
Aldeburgh Pl
SE10 . . . . 43 C2
Aldeburgh St
SE10 . . . . 43 C1
Aldenham Ho
NW1 . . . . 83 A1
Aldenham St NW1 . . 83 B1
Alden Ho E8 . . . . 25 A4
Aldensley Rd W6 . . . 39 A3
Alderbrook Prim Sch
SW12 . . . . 73 A4
Alderbrook Rd
SW12 . . . . 61 A1
Aldebury Rd
SW13 . . . . 46 C4
Aldergrove Ho [3]
E5 . . . . 7 C2
Alder Ho
Camberwell SE15 . . . 49 B4
[1] Maitland Pk
NW3 . . . . 12 B2
St Johns SE4 . . . . . . 66 C4
Alderley Ho SW8 . . 171 B1
Alder Lo SW6 . . . . . 47 C2
Aldermanbury
EC2 . . . . 109 A2
Aldermanbury Sq
EC2 . . . . 109 A3
Alderman's Wlk
EC2 . . . . 110 A3
Alderney Ho [21]
N1 . . . . 15 B2
Alderney Mews
SE1 . . . . 137 B2
Alderney Rd E1 . . . . 25 C1
Alderney St SW1 . . 146 B2
Alder Rd SW14 . . . . 55 C4
Aldersford Cl SE4 . . 65 C3
Aldersgate Ct
EC1 . . . . 108 C3
Aldersgate St
EC1 . . . . 108 C3
Aldershot Rd NW6 . . 23 B4
Alderson St W10 . . . 23 A1
Alderton Rd SE24 . . 63 B4
Alderville Rd
SW6 . . . . 165 A2
Alderwick Ct N7 . . . 14 B2
Aldford St W1 . . . . . 117 C2
Aldgate EC3 . . . . . . 110 B1
Aldgate East Sta
E1 . . . . 111 A2
Aldgate High St
EC3 . . . . 110 C1
Aldgate Sta EC3 . . 110 C1
Aldham Ho SE4 . . . . 51 B2
Aldine Ct W12 . . . . . 30 B1
Aldine St W12 . . . . . 39 B4
Aldington Ct [8]
E8 . . . . 16 C1
Aldred Rd NW6 . . . . 10 C3
Aldren Rd SW17 . . . 71 B1
Aldrich Terr SW18 . . 71 B2
Aldrick Ho N1 . . . . . 85 A2
Aldridge Ct W11 . . . 31 B4
Aldridge Rd Villas
W11 . . . . 31 B4
Aldsworth Cl W9 . . . 88 A1
Aldwich Ho WC2 . . 107 A1

Aldworth Gr SE13 . . 67 B1
Aldwych WC2 . . . . . 107 A1
Aldwych Bldgs
WC2 . . . . 106 B2
Aldwyn Ho SW8 . . . 162 A1
Alexander Ave
NW10 . . . . 9 A1
Alexander Ct
SW18 . . . . 59 B2
*Alexander Fleming
Laboratory Mus* ★
W2 . . . . 101 C2
Alexander Ho [15]
E14 . . . . 41 C3
Alexander Mews
W2 . . . . 100 A2
Alexander Pl
SW7 . . . . 144 A4
Alexander Rd N19 . . 5 A2
Alexander Sq
SW3 . . . . 144 A4
Alexander St W2 . . . 31 C3
Alexandra Ave
SW11 . . . . 169 B3
Alexandra Cl SE8 . . 51 B4
Alexandra Cotts
SE14 . . . . 51 B2
Alexandra Ct
Paddington W9 . . . . . 89 A2
[5] Shacklewell N16 . 16 B4
[1] Shepherd's Bush
W12 . . . . 30 B3
Alexandra Gdns
W4 . . . . 46 A3
Alexandra Gr N4 . . . 6 A3
Alexandra Ho [1]
W6 . . . . 39 B1
Alexandra Mans
Chelsea SW3 . . . . . . 157 B3
Cricklewood NW2 . . . . 9 C3
[6] Hampstead
NW6 . . . . 10 C3
[9] Shepherd's Bush
W12 . . . . 30 B1
**Alexandra National
Ho** N4 . . . . 6 A2
Alexandra Pl NW8 . . 79 A4
Alexandra Rd
Acton W4 . . . . 37 C4
Hampstead NW8 . . . 11 C1
Mortlake SW14 . . . . . 55 C4
Richmond TW9 . . . . . 44 B1
Alexandra St
[5] Deptford SE14 . . . 51 A3
Newham E16 . . . . . . 35 C4
Alex Gossip Ho
SW6 . . . . 165 B3
Alexis St SE16 . . . . 153 C4
Alfearn Rd E5 . . . . . 17 B4
Alford Ct N1 . . . . . . 87 A1
Alford Pl N1 . . . . 87 A1
Alfreda Ct SW11 . . 170 A3
Alfreda St SW11 . . 170 A3
Alfred Butt Ho
SW17 . . . . 72 B1
Alfred Cl W4 . . . . . . 37 C2
Alfred Ho E9 . . . . . . 18 A3
Alfred Mews W1,
WC1 . . . . 105 A4
Alfred Nunn Ho
NW10 . . . . 21 B4
Alfred Pl WC1 . . . . 105 B4
Alfred Rd
Acton W3 . . . . 28 B1
Paddington W2 . . . . . 31 C4
Alfred Salter Ho
SE1 . . . . 153 A3

Alfred Salter Prim
Sch SE16. . . . . .40 C4
Alfred St E3. . . . . .26 B2
Alfreton Cl SW19. . . . . .69 C1
Alfriston Rd SW11. . .60 B2
Algar Rd SE1. . . . . .136 A3
Algarve Rd SW18. . .71 A3
Algernon Rd
Kilburn NW6. . . . . .23 C4
Lewisham SE13. . . . . . . .67 A3
Algiers Rd SE13. . . . . .66 C3
Alice Gilliott Ct
W14. . . . . .155 A4
Alice La E3. . . . . .26 B4
Alice Owen Tech Ctr
EC1. . . . . .96 A4
Alice Shepherd Ho 12
E14. . . . . .42 B4
Alice St SE1. . . . . .138 A1
Alice Walker Cl 2
SE24. . . . . .63 A3
Alie St E1. . . . . .111 A1
Aliwal Rd SW11. . . . . .60 A3
Alkerden Rd W4. . . . . .38 A1
Alkham Rd N16. . . . . . . .7 B2
Allam Ho
W11. . . . . .31 A2 112 A4
Allanbridge N16. . . . . . . .7 A4
Allan Ho SW8. . . . . . .171 B4
Allan Way W3. . . . . . . .28 B4
Allard Gdns SW4. . . .61 C2
Allardyce St SW4,
SW9. . . . . .62 B3
Allbrook Ho 4
SW15. . . . . .68 C4
Allcroft Rd NW5. . . . .12 C2
Allendale Cl SE5. . . . .48 C2
Allen Edwards Dr
SW8. . . . . .172 A4
Allen Edwards Prim
Sch SW4. . . . . .172 A3
Allenford Ho
SW15. . . . . .56 B1
All England Lawn
Tennis & Croquet
Club The SW19. . . . .70 A1
Allen Ho W8. . . . . . . .127 C2
Allen Mans W8. . . . . .127 C2
Allen Rd
Old Ford E3. . . . . .26 B3
Stoke Newington
N16. . . . . .16 A4
Allensbury Pl
7 Camden Town
NW1. . . . . .13 C1
Camden Town NW1. .14 A1
Allen St W8. . . . . .127 C1
Allenswood 12
SW19. . . . . .70 A3
Allerdale Ho 7 N4. . . .6 C4
Allerton Ho N1. . . . . .87 C1
Allerton St N1. . . . . . .97 C4
Allerton Wlk 17 N7. . .5 B2
Allestree Rd SW6. . .154 A1
Alleyn Cres SE21. . . .75 C2
Alleyn Ho
Bermondsey SE1. . . .137 B1
St Luke's EC1. . . . . . . .97 A1
Alleyn Pk SE21. . . . . .76 A1
Alleyn Rd SE21. . . . . .76 A1
Alleyn's Sch SE22. . .64 A2
Allfarthing La
SW18. . . . . .59 B1
Allfarthing Prim Sch
SW18. . . . . .59 B1
Allgood St 10 E2. . . .24 B3

Allhallows La EC4. .123 B3
Alliance Ct W3. . . . . . .28 A4
Alliance Rd W3. . . . . . .20 A1
Allied Ind Est W3. . . .29 A1
Allied Way W3. . . . . . .38 A4
Allingham Ct NW3. . .12 A3
Allingham Mews
N1. . . . . .86 C2
Allingham St N1. . . . . .86 C2
Allington Cl SW8. . . .170 C1
Allington Rd W10. . . .23 A3
Allington St SW1. . . .132 B1
Allison Cl SE10. . . . . . .52 B2
Allison Gr SE21. . . . . . .76 A3
Allison Rd W3. . . . . . . .28 B2
Allison Ho
E2. . . . . .24 B2 99 A3
Allitsen Rd NW8. . . . .80 A2
Allnatt Way SW4. . . .61 C2
Allom Ct SW4. . . . . . .172 B1
Allonby Ho E14. . . . . .33 A4
Alloway Rd E3. . . . . . . .26 A2
Allport Ho SE5. . . . . . .63 C4
Allport Mews 44
E1. . . . . .25 B1
All Saints CE Prim
Sch
SW15. . . . . .57 B4
All Saints' CE Prim
Sch
Blackheath Vale
SE3. . . . . .53 A1
Child's Hill NW2. . . .1 B1
All Saints Church 1
N19. . . . . .4 C1
All Saints Ct
Lower Clapton E5. . . .17 B4
10 Shadwell E1. . . . . .32 B2
All Saints Dr SE3. . . .53 B1
All Saints Ho 2
W11. . . . . .31 B4
All Saints Pas
SW18. . . . . .58 C2
All Saints Rd W11. . .31 B3
All Saints Rd W3. . . . .37 B3
All Saints St N1. . . . . .84 C2
Allsop Pl NW1. . . . . . .91 A1
All Souls' Ave
NW10. . . . . .22 A4
All Souls CE Prim Sch
W1. . . . . .104 C3
All Souls' Pl 1 W1. . .104 B3
Alma Birk Ho 1
NW6. . . . . .10 B1
Almack Rd E5. . . . . . . .17 B4
Alma Gr SE1. . . . . . . .153 A3
Alma Ho 7 TW8. . . . . .44 A4
Alma PL NW10. . . . . . .22 A2
Alma Prim Sch
SE16. . . . . .153 C4
Alma Rd SW18. . . . . . .59 B2
Alma Sq NW8. . . . . . . .89 A4
Alma St
Camden Town
NW5. . . . . .13 A2
Stratford New Town
E15. . . . . .19 C2
Alma Terr
Earl's Ct W8. . . . . . . .127 C1
Wandsworth SW18. . .71 C4
Almeida St 10 N1. . . .15 A1
Almeric Rd SW11. . . .60 B3
Almington St N4. . . . . .5 B3
Almond Ave W5. . . . . .36 A3

Almond Cl SE15. . . . . .49 C1
Almond Ho SE4. . . . . .51 B1
Almond Rd SE16. . . . .40 A2
Almorah Rd N1. . . . . .15 C1
Al-Muntada Islamic
Sch SW6. . . . . .165 A4
Alperton St W10. . . . .23 B1
Alphabet Sq E3. . . . . .33 C4
Alpha Cl NW8. . . . . . . .90 B3
Alpha Gr E14. . . . . .41 C4
Alpha Ho
16 Brixton SW4. . . . .62 B3
Kilburn NW6. . . . . .23 C3
Lisson Gr NW8. . . . . . .90 B1
Alpha Pl
Chelsea SW3. . . . . . .158 B4
Kilburn NW6. . . . . .23 C3
Alpha Rd SE14. . . . . . .51 B2
Alpha St SE15. . . . . . . .49 C1
Alpine Gr 37 E9. . . . . .17 B1
Alpine Rd SE16. . . . . . .40 C1
Al Rd N4. . . . . .5 C4
Alsace Rd SE17. . . . .152 A2
Al Sadiq & Al Zahra
Schs NW6. . . . . .23 A4
Alscot Road Ind Est
SE1. . . . . .139 A1
Alscot Way SE1. . . . .152 B4
Altair Ct N1. . . . . .15 C2
Altenburg Gdns
SW11. . . . . .60 B3
Althea St SW6. . . . . . . .59 A4
Althorpe Mews
SW11. . . . . .167 C3
Althorp Rd SW17. . . .72 B3
Altima Ct SE22. . . . . . .64 C3
Alton Ho 3 E3. . . . . . .27 A2
Alton Rd
Richmond TW10,
TW9. . . . . .54 A3
Roehampton SW15. . .68 C3
Alton St E14. . . . . .34 A4
Alumni Ct SE1. . . . . .139 A4
Alvaney Ct NW3. . . . .11 A3
Alvanley Gdns
NW6. . . . . .11 A3
Alvanley Ho SW9. . .173 B4
Alverstone Ho SW18,
SW19. . . . . .70 C2
Alverstone Ho
SE11. . . . . .163 B3
Alverstone Rd NW2. .9 B1
Alverton St SE8. . . . . .51 B4
Alvey St SE17. . . . . . .152 A2
Alvington Cres E8. . . .16 B3
Alwyn Ave W4. . . . . . . .37 C1
Alwyne La N1. . . . . . . .15 A1
Alwyne Pl N1. . . . . . . .15 B2
Alwyne Rd N1. . . . . . . .15 B1
Alwyne Sq N1. . . . . . . .15 B2
Alwyne Villas N1. . . . .15 A1
Alwyn Gdns W3. . . . . .28 A3
Alzette Ho 11 E2. . . .25 C3
Aman Dalvi Ho
SW18. . . . . .70 A4
Amazonas SE1. . . . . .152 B3
Amazon St E1. . . . . . . .32 A3
Ambassador Ct 9
NW6. . . . . .10 C3
Ambassador Ho
NW8. . . . . .79 A3
Ambassador Sq
E14. . . . . .42 A2
Amber Ct N7. . . . . .14 C2

Ambergate St
SE17. . . . . .150 B2
Amberley Ct 2
SW9. . . . . .63 A4
Amberley Rd W9. . . . .31 C4
Amber Wharf 28
E2. . . . . .24 B4
Ambler Prim Sch
N4. . . . . .6 A2
Amber Rd N4. . . . . .6 A1
Ambleside
13 Putney SW19. . . . .70 A3
Regent's Pk NW1. . . .82 B1
Ambleside Cl 11
E9. . . . . .17 B3
Ambleside Point 1
SE15. . . . . .50 B3
Ambleside Rd
NW10. . . . . .8 B1
Ambrose Ave
SW1. . . . . .133 A1
Ambrose Ho 9
E14. . . . . .33 C4
Ambrose Mews
SW11. . . . . .168 C2
Ambrose St SE16. . . .40 A2
Ambrose Wlk 3 E3. .26 C3
AMC Bsns Ctr
SW9. . . . . .63 A3
Amelia Cl W3. . . . . .37 A4
Amelia Ho 3 W6. . . . .39 B1
Amelia St SE17. . . . . .150 C2
Amen Cnr EC4. . . . . . .108 B1
Amen Ct EC4. . . . . . . .108 B1
American
Intercontinental Univ
W1. . . . . .103 C3
American Sch in
London The W8. . . .79 B2
American Univ in
London The N7. . . . . . .5 B1
America Sq EC3. . . . .124 C4
America St SE1. . . . . .122 C1
Ameriand Rd
SW18. . . . . .58 B1
Amersham Gr
SE14. . . . . .51 B3
Amersham Rd
SE14. . . . . .51 B3
Amersham Vale SE14,
SE8. . . . . .51 B3
Amery Gdns
NW10. . . . . .22 A4
Amery Ho SE17. . . . .152 B2
Amesbury Ave
SW2. . . . . .74 B2
Amesbury Twr
SW8. . . . . .170 C2
Ames Cotts 3 E3. . . .33 A4
Ames Ho 10 E2. . . . . .25 C3
Amethyst Rd E15. . . .19 C4
Amhurst Ct N4. . . . . . . .6 C4
Amhurst Par N16. . . . .7 B4
Amhurst Pk N4, N16. .7 A4
Amhurst Rd E8,
N16. . . . . .16 C3
Amhurst Terr E8. . . . .16 C4
Amias Ho EC1. . . . . . . .96 C2
Amiel St 18 E1. . . . . . .25 B1
Amies St SW11. . . . . . .60 B4
Amigo Ho SE1. . . . . . .135 C2
Amina Way SE16. . . .139 B1
Amner Rd SW11. . . . . .60 C1
Amor Rd W6. . . . . .39 B3
Amory Ho N1. . . . . . . .85 A2
Amott Rd SE15. . . . . . .64 C4
Amoy Pl E14. . . . . .33 C2
Ampton Pl WC1. . . . . .94 C3

Alf–Ang 177

Ampton St WC1. . . . . .94 C3
Amstel Ct 12 SE15. . .49 B3
Amsterdam Rd
E14. . . . . .42 B3
Amundsen Ct 7
E14. . . . . .41 C1
Amwell St EC1. . . . . . .95 B4
Amyruth Rd SE4. . . . . .66 C2
Anatola Rd N19. . . . . . .4 B2
Anchorage Point 1
E14. . . . . .41 C4
Anchor Ho EC1. . . . . . .96 C2
Anchor Mews
SW12. . . . . .61 A1
Anchor Ret Pk E1. . . .25 B1
Anchor St SE16. . . . . . .40 A2
Anchor Terr SE1. . . . .123 A2
Anchor Yd EC1. . . . . . .97 A2
Ancill Cl W6. . . . . .154 A3
Ancona Rd NW10. . . .21 C3
Andalus Rd SW9. . . . .62 A4
Andaman Ho 3
E1. . . . . .33 A4
Andersens Wharf 7
E14. . . . . .33 B3
Anderson Ho N19. . . . .5 A2
Anderson Cl W3. . . . . .28 C3
Anderson Ho
E14. . . . . .34 B2
Anderson Rd E9. . . . . .17 C1
Andersons Sq N1. . . .86 A3
Anderson St SW3. . .144 C2
Anderton Ct SE5. . . . .63 C4
Andover Ho 5 N7. . . . .5 B2
Andover Pl NW6. . . . . .78 A1
Andover Rd N7. . . . . . . .5 B2
Andoversford Ct 2
SE15. . . . . .49 A4
Andre St E8. . . . . .16 C3
Andrew Borde St
WC2. . . . . .105 C2
Andrewes Ho
EC2. . . . . .109 A3
Andrew Ho
New Cross SE4. . . . . . .51 B1
Putney SW15. . . . . . . .56 C2
Andrew Logan's Glass
House SE1. . . . . .138 A4
Andrew Marvell Ho
N16. . . . . .16 A4
Andrew PI SW8. . . . .171 C4
Andrew Reed Ho
SW18. . . . . .70 A4
Andrews Crosse
WC2. . . . . .107 B1
Andrew's Rd E8. . . . . .25 A4
Andrew St E14. . . . . . .34 B3
Andrews Wharf 14
E8. . . . . .25 A4
Andrews Wlk
SE17. . . . . .48 A4
Andrew Wilmot Ct
SW18. . . . . .71 B3
Anfield Cl SW12. . . . .73 B4
Angel EC1. . . . . .86 B1
Angela Davis Ind Est
20 SW9. . . . . .63 A3
Angel Ct
Broadgate EC2. . . . . .109 C2
St James SW1. . . . . . .119 A1
5 Willesden NW2. . . .8 C2
Angel Gate EC1. . . . . .96 B4
Angel Ho N1. . . . . .85 C1
Angelina Ho 2
SE15. . . . . .49 C2

Angelis Apartments
N1 . . . . **86 B1**
Angel La E15 . . . . **19** C2
Angell Park Gdns 🖪
SW9 . . . . .62 C4
Angell Rd SW9 . . . .63 A4
Angel Mews
Finsbury N1 . . . . . . **85** C1
Putney SW15 . . . . . .68 C4
Stepney E1 . . . . .32 A2
Angel Pas EC4 . . **123 B3**
Angel Pl SE1 . . . **137 B4**
Angel Sq N1 . . . . . . **85** C1
Angel St EC1 . . . **108** C2
Angel Sta EC1 . . . . **85** C1
Angel Wlk W6 . . . .39 B2
Angerstein Bsns Pk
SE10 . . . . .43 C2
Angerstein La SE3 . **53** B2
Anglebury 🖪 W2 . . .31 C3
Anglers La NW5 . . .13 A2
Anglesey Ho 🔟
E14 . . . . .33 C3
Anglia Ho 🔟 E14 . . .33 A3
Anglo American
Laundry SW12 . . . . .71 B1
Anglo Rd 🔟 E3 . . .26 B3
Angrave Ct 🖪 E8 . .24 B4
Angrave Pas 🖪
E8 . . . . .24 B4
Angus Ho 🔟
SW12 . . . . .73 C4
Angus St SE14 . . . .51 A3
Anhalt Rd SW11 . . **158** B2
Animals in War
Meml ⚹ W1 . . . . . . **117** A4
Anley Rd W14 . . . . .39 C4
Annabel Cl E14 . . . .34 A3
Anna Cl E8 . . . . .24 B4
Annandale Rd
Chiswick W4 . . . . . . .38 A1
Greenwich SE10 . . . .43 B1
E1 . . . . .32 B3
Anne Goodman Ho 🖪
E1 . . . . .32 B3
Anne Kerr Ct 🔟
SW15 . . . . .57 C1
Anne's Ct NW8 . . . .90 B2
Annesley Ho SW9 **173 B4**
Annesley Wlk N19 . .4 B2
Annette Cres 🔟
N1 . . . . .15 B1
Annette Ct N7 . . . . . .5 B1
Annette Rd N7 . . . .14 B4
Annie Besant Cl
E3 . . . . .26 B4
Anning St
E2 . . . . .24 A1 **98** B2
Annis Rd E9 . . . . . . .18 A2
Ann La SW10 . . . . **157** B3
Ann Moss Way
SE16 . . . . .40 B3
Ann's Cl SW1 . . . **131** B3
Ann's Pl E1 . . . . . . **110** C3
Ansdell Rd SE15 . . .50 B1
Ansdell St W8 . . . **128** B2
Ansdell Terr W8 . **128** B2
Ansell Ho E1 . . . . . .32 B4
Ansell Rd SW17 . . .72 B1
Anselm Rd SW6 . . **155** B3
Ansleigh Pl W11 . . .30 C2
Anson Ho
Pimlico SW1 . . . . . **160** C4
🔳 Tower Hamlets
E1 . . . . .26 A1

Anson Prim Sch
NW2 . . . . .9 C3
Anson Rd
Cricklewood NW2 . . . .9 B3
Tufnell Pk N7 . . . . . . .13 C4
Anstey Ct 🖪 W3 . . .37 A4
Anstey Ho 🖪 E9 . .25 B4
Anstey Rd SE15 . . . .64 C4
Anstice Cl W4 . . . . .46 A3
Antenor Ho 🔟 E2 . .25 A3
Anthony Cope Ct 🖪
N1 . . . . .97 C4
Anthony Ho NW8 . . **90** A1
Anthony St E1 . . . . .32 A3
Antill Rd E3 . . . . . . .26 A2
Antill Terr E1 . . . . . .32 C3
Antonine Hts SE1 **138** A3
Anton St E8 . . . . . . .16 C3
Antony Ho
🗗 Deptford SE14 . . .50 C3
🔳 Rotherhithe
SE16 . . . . .40 B2
Antrim Gr NW3 . . . .12 B2
Antrim Ho SW11 . . .60 C4
Antrim Mans NW3 .12 B2
Antrim Rd NW3 . . . .12 B2
Antrobus Rd W4 . . .37 B3
Apex Ind Est
N10 . . . . .21 B1
Aphrodite Ct 🔟
E14 . . . . .41 C2
Apollo Bldg 🖪
E14 . . . . .41 C2
Apollo Ho
Chelsea SW10 . . . **157** B3
🔳 Hackney E2 . . . . .25 A3
Highgate N6 . . . . .3 B4
Apollo Ind Bsns Ctr 🔟
SE8 . . . . .50 C4
Apollo Pl SW10 . . **157** B2
Apollo Studios 🔟
NW5 . . . . .13 C3
Apothecary St
EC4 . . . . **108** A1
Appach Rd SW2 . . .62 C1
Appleby St 🖪 E2 . .37 B4
Appleby Rd
Hackney E8 . . . . .16 C1
Newham E16 . . . . . . .35 C3
Appleby St E2 . . . . .24 B3
Appledore Cl SW12,
SW17 . . . . .72 B2
Appleford 🔟 NW5 . .13 B3
Appleford Ho 🖪
W10 . . . . .23 A1
Appleford Rd W10 .23 A1
Applegarth Ho
Borough The SE1 . **136** B4
🖪 Camberwell
SE15 . . . . .49 C3
Applegarth Rd
W14 . . . . .39 C3
Apple Mkt WC2 . . **120** B4
Appleshaw Ho 🗗
SE5 . . . . .64 A4
Appleton Ct 🗵 E8 .17 A3
Appletree Ct SE13 .67 C3
Apple Tree Yd
SW1 . . . . **119** A2
Appold St EC2 . . . **110** A4
Appollo Cl SW9 . . **173 B4**
Apprentice Way 🖪
E5 . . . . .17 A4
Approach Cl N16 . .16 A4

Approach Rd E2 . . .25 B3
Approach The W3 . .28 C3
April Ct 🗵 E2 . . . . .24 C3
April St E8 . . . . .16 B4
Apsley Ho
Stepney E1 . . . . .32 B4
St John's Wood
NW8 . . . . .79 B2
Apsley Way W1 . . **131** C4
Aquila St NW8 . . . . **79** C2
Aquinas St SE1 . . **121** C1
Arabella Ct NW8 . . **79** A2
Arabella Dr SW15 . .56 A3
Arabian Ho 🗵 E1 . .26 A1
Arabin Rd SE4 . . . . .66 B3
Aragon Twr SE8 . . .41 B2
Arakan Ho 🔼 N16 . .15 C4
Arapiles Ho 🖪
E14 . . . . .34 C3
Arbery Rd E3 . . . . . .26 A3
Arbon Ct N1 . . . . . . .87 A3
Arbor Ct N16 . . . . . . .6 C2
Arborfield Cl SW2 . .74 B3
Arborfield Ho 🗗
E14 . . . . .33 C2
Arbour Ho 🖪 E1 . . .32 C3
Arbour Sq E1 . . . . . .32 C3
Arbuthnot Rd
SE14 . . . . .50 C1
Arbutus St E8 . . . . .24 B4
Arcade The
Broadgate EC2 . . . **110** A3
🔼 Tufnell Pk N7 . . . .14 A4
Arcadian Ho 🖪 E14 .34 A4
Arcadian Pl SW18 . .70 B4
Arcadia St E14 . . . . .33 C3
Archangel St SE16 .40 C4
Archbishop Coggan
Ho SE13 . . . . .67 C3
Archbishop Michael
Ramsey Tech Coll
SE5 . . . . .48 A3
Archbishop's Pl 🔼
SW2 . . . . .74 B4
Archbishop Sumner
CE Prim Sch
SE11 . . . . **149** C3
Archbishop Tenison's
Sch SE11 . . . . **163** A3
Archdale Ct W12 . . .30 A1
Archdale Ho SE1 . **138** A2
Archdale Rd SE22 . .64 B3
Archel Rd W14 . . . **154** C4
Archer Ho
Battersea SW11 . . **167** C2
🔼 Hoxton N1 . . . . . . .24 A4
🔳 New Cross SE14 . .51 A2
Notting Hill
W11 . . . . . . .31 B2 **113** A4
Archer Sq SE14 . . . .51 A4
Archer St W1 . . . . **119** B4
Archery Cl W2 . . . **102** B1
Archery Fields Ho
WC1 . . . . .95 B4
Archery Stps W2 . **116** B4
Arches The WC2 . . **120** B2
Archibald Mews
W1 . . . . **118** A3
Archibald Rd N7 . . . .13 C4
Archibald St E3 . . . .26 C2
Archie St SE1 . . . . **138** B3
Arch St SE1 . . . . . . **136** C1
Archway N19 . . . . . . .4 B2
Archway Bsns Ctr 🖪
N19 . . . . .4 C1

Archway Cl
North Kensington
W10 . . . . .30 C4
🔼 Upper Holloway
N19 . . . . .4 B2
Archway Hts 🖪
N19 . . . . .4 B3
Archway Mews
SW15 . . . . .58 A3
Archway Rd N6 . . . . .4 A4
Archway St SW13,
SW14 . . . . .56 A4
Archway Sta N19 . . .4 B2
Arcola St E8 . . . . . . .16 B3
Arctic St NW5 . . . . . .13 A3
Ardbeg Rd SE24 . . . .63 C2
Arden 🔟 SW19 . . . . .69 C3
Arden Cres E14 . . . .41 C2
Arden Ho
🗾 Hoxton N1 . . . . . .24 A3
Stockwell SW9 . . . **172 B1**
Vauxhall SE11 . . . **148** C3
Ardent Ho 🖪 E3 . . .26 A3
Ardilaun Rd N5 . . . . .15 B4
Ardleigh Rd N1 . . . .16 A2
Ardlui Rd SE27 . . . . .75 B2
Ardmere Rd SE13 . .67 C1
Ardshiel Cl SW15 . .57 C4
Ardwell Rd SW2 . . .74 A2
Ardwick Rd NW2 . . .10 C4
Ares Ct 🔞 E14 . . . . .41 C2
Arethusa Ho 🗎
E14 . . . . .42 A2
Argo Bsns Ctr 🗾
NW6 . . . . .23 C2
Argon Mews SW6 **155** C1
Argos Ct SW9 . . . **173 B4**
Argos Ho 🖪 E2 . . . .25 A3
Argosy Ho
Fitzrovia W1 . . . . . . **92** B1
🔼 Rotherhithe SE8 . .41 A2
Argyle Ho E14 . . . . .42 B3
Argyle Mans 🗛
NW2 . . . . .9 C4
Argyle Pl W6 . . . . . . .39 A2
Argyle Prim Sch
WC1 . . . . .94 A4
Argyle Rd E1 . . . . . .25 C1
Argyle Sq WC1 . . . . .94 B4
Argyle St WC1 . . . . . .94 B4
Argyle Way SE16 . **153** C1
Argyle Wlk WC1 . . .94 B3
Argyll Cl SW9 . . . . . .62 B4
Argyll Ct 🔞 SW2 . . .74 A4
Argyll Mans
Chelsea SW3 . . . . . **157** C4
West Kensington
W14 . . . . **140** B4
Argyll Rd W8 . . . . **127** C3
Argyll St W1 . . . . . **104** C1
Arica Ho SE16 . . . . . .40 A3
Arica Rd SE4 . . . . . . .66 A4
Ariel Ct
🗾 Hammersmith
W12 . . . . .39 C3
Newington SE11 . . . **150** A3
Ariel Rd NW6 . . . . . .10 C2
Ariel Way W12 . . . . .30 B1
Aristotle Rd SW4 . . .61 C4
Arizona Bldg 🔟
SE13 . . . . .52 A2
Arkansas Ho 🗃
N19 . . . . .4 C4
Ark Ct N16 . . . . .7 B2
Arklow Ho SE17 . . . .48 C4
Arklow Rd SE14 . . . .51 B4

Arklow Road Trad Est
SE14 . . . . .51 B4
Arkwright Ho 🗱
SW2 . . . . .74 A4
Arkwright Mans
NW3 . . . . .11 B3
Arkwright Rd
NW3 . . . . .11 B3
Arlesey Cl SW15 . . **58** A2
Arlesford Rd SW9 . .62 A4
Arlidge Ho EC1 . . . **107** C4
Arlingford Rd
SW2 . . . . .62 C1
Arlington Ave N1 . . .87 A3
Arlington Cl SE13 . . .67 C2
Arlington Ct 🖪
W3 . . . . .28 A1
Arlington Gdns
W4 . . . . .37 B1
Arlington Ho
🖪 Deptford SE8 . . . .51 B4
Finsbury EC1 . . . . . . **95** C4
🗎 Shepherd's Bush
W12 . . . . .30 A1
Arlington Lo SW2 . .62 B3
Arlington Park Mans
🗎 W4 . . . . .37 B1
Arlington Pl 🔞
SE10 . . . . .52 B3
Arlington Rd NW1 . **82** B3
Arlington Sq N1 . . . .87 A3
Arlington St SW1 **118** C2
Arlington Way EC1 . **95** C4
Armada Ct 🔟 SE8 . .51 C4
Armadale Rd
SW6 . . . . **155** B3
Armada St 🔟 SE8 . .51 C4
Armagh Rd E3 . . . . .26 B4
Arminger Rd W12 . .30 A1
Armitage Ho
NW1 . . . . **102** B4
Armitage Rd
Golders Green
NW11 . . . . .1 B3
Greenwich SE10 . . . .43 B1
Armour Cl N7 . . . . . .14 B2
Armoury Ho E3 . . . .26 A4
Armoury Rd SE8 . . .52 A1
Armoury Way
SW18 . . . . .58 C2
Armsby Ho 🔟 E1 . . .32 B4
Armstrong Ho 🖪
SW15 . . . . .57 C1
Armstrong Rd
Eaton Green W3 . . . .29 B1
Knightsbridge SW7 **129** B1
Arnal Cres SW18 . . .70 A4
Arncliffe NW6 . . . . . .78 B3
Arndale Wlk 🖪
SW18 . . . . .59 A2
Arne Ho SE11 . . . . **148** C2
Arne St WC2 . . . . . **106** B1
Arneway St SW1 . . **133** C1
Arnewood Cl
SW15 . . . . .68 C3
Arnhem Pl E14 . . . . .41 C3
Arnhem Way 🖪
SE22 . . . . .64 A2
Arnhem Wharf
E14 . . . . .41 C3
Arnhem Wharf Prim
Sch E14 . . . . .41 C3
Arnold Cir
E2 . . . . .24 B2 **98** C3
Arnold Est SE1 . . . **139** A3
Arnold Ho
Newington SE17 . . . **150 B1**

Arnold Ho *continued*
- 9 Stoke Newington
  N16 . . . . 7 A1
Arnold House Sch
  NW8 . . . . 79 B1
Arnold Rd E3 . . . . 26 C2
Arnot Ho 22 SE5 . . . . . . 48 B3
Arnott Cl W4 . . . . 37 C2
Arnould Ave SE5 . . . . . 63 C3
Arnside Ho 2
  SE17 . . . . 48 C4
Arnside St SE17 . . . . . 48 C4
Arodene Rd SW2 . . . . . 62 B1
Arragon Rd SW18 . . . . 70 C3
Arran Ho
  5 Canary Wharf
  E14 . . . . 34 B1
  Stoke Newington N16 . 7 B3
Arran Wlk N1 . . . . 15 B1
Arrol Ho SE1 . . . . 137 A1
Arrowe Ct 6 E5 . . . . . . 17 A4
Arrow Ho 28 N1 . . . . . . 24 A4
Arrow Rd E3 . . . . 27 A2
Arrowsmith Ho
  SE11 . . . . 148 C2
Arsenal Sta N5 . . . . 5 C1
Arta Ho 23 E1 . . . . 32 B3
Artemis Ct 14 E14 . . . . 41 C2
Artemis Pl SW18 . . . . . 70 B4
Artesian Rd W2 . . . . . . 31 C3

Arthur Ct
  Battersea SW11 . . . . . 169 C3
  10 North Kensington
  W10 . . . . 30 C3
  Paddington W2 . . . . . 100 A2
Arthur Deakin Ho
  E1 . . . . 111 C4
Arthurdon Rd SE4 . . . . 66 C2
Arthur Henderson Ho
  7 Crouch End N19 . . . . 4 C4
  Fulham SW6 . . . . 164 C2
Arthur Newton Ho 20
  SW11 . . . . 59 C4
Arthur Rd N7 . . . . 14 B4
Arthur St EC4 . . . . 123 C4
Arthur Wade Ho
  E2 . . . . 24 B2 99 A4
Artichoke Hill 8
  E1 . . . . 32 A2
Artichoke Mews 6
  SE5 . . . . 48 C2
Artichoke Pl SE5 . . . . . 48 C2
Artillery Ho
  Bow E3 . . . . 26 A4
  Westminster SW1 . . . 133 B1
Artillery La
  Broadgate E1 . . . . . . 110 B3
  North Kensington
  W12 . . . . 29 C3
Artillery Pas E1 . . . . . 110 B3
Artillery Pl SW1 . . . . . 133 B1
Artillery Row
  SW1 . . . . 133 B1
Artisan Ct E8 . . . . 16 C2
Artisan Mews 9
  NW10 . . . . 22 C2
Artisan Quarter 10
  NW10 . . . . 22 C2
Artizan St E1 . . . . 110 B2
Arton Wilson Ho 12
  SW15 . . . . 56 C2
Arts Educational Sch
  The W4 . . . . 38 A2
Arundel Bldgs
  SE1 . . . . 138 B1
Arundel Cl SW11 . . . . . 60 A2

Arundel Ct
  Barnes SW13 . . . . 47 A4
  Chelsea SW3 . . . . . . 144 B2
  Putney SW15 . . . . 57 C2
Arundel Gdns
  W11 . . . . 31 B2 112 C4
Arundel Gr N16 . . . . . . 16 A3
Arundel Ho
  Islington N1 . . . . 86 B4
  Richmond TW10 . . . . . 54 C2
  3 South Acton W3 . . . 37 A4
Arundel Lo 10 N19 . . . . 5 A2
Arundel Mans
  Barnes SW13 . . . . 47 A4
  Fulham SW6 . . . . 165 A4
Arundel Pl N1 . . . . 14 C2
Arundel Sq N7 . . . . 14 C2
Arundel St WC2 . . . . . 121 A4
Arundel Terr
  SW13 . . . . 47 A4
Arvon Rd N5 . . . . 14 C3
Asaph Ho SE14 . . . . . . 51 B2
Ascalon Ct 18
  SW2 . . . . 74 B4
Ascalon Ho SW8 . . . . 160 C1
Ascalon St SW8 . . . . . 160 C1
Ascham St NW5 . . . . . 13 B3
Ascot Ct
  8 Brixton SW4 . . . . . . 62 A3
  St John's Wood
  NW8 . . . . 89 B3
Ascot Ho
  6 Acton Green
  W4 . . . . 37 B1
  1 Paddington W9 . . . . 31 C4
  Regent's Pk NW1 . . . . 92 B4
Ascot Lo NW6 . . . . 78 B2
Ascot Par 5 SW4 . . . . . 62 A3
Ascott Ave W5 . . . . 36 A4
Ashbourne Gr
  Chiswick W4 . . . . 38 A1
  East Dulwich SE22 . . . 64 B3
Ashbourne Ind Sch
  W8 . . . . 128 A3
Ashbridge Ct 3
  W6 . . . . 39 A3
Ashbridge St NW8 . . . . 90 A1
Ashbrook Rd N19 . . . . . 4 C2
Ashburn Gdns
  SW7 . . . . 142 C4
Ashburnham Com Sch
  SW10 . . . . 157 B2
Ashburnham Gr
  SE10 . . . . 52 A3
Ashburnham Pl
  SE10 . . . . 52 A3
Ashburnham Rd
  Chelsea SW10 . . . . . 157 A1
  Kensal Rise NW10 . . . 22 B2
Ashburnham Retreat 4
  SE10 . . . . 52 A3
Ashburnham Twr
  SW10 . . . . 157 B2
Ashburn Pl SW7 . . . . . 142 C3
Ashburton Mans
  SW10 . . . . 157 A2
Ashburton Rd E16 . . . . 35 C3
Ashbury Rd SW11 . . . . 60 C4
Ashby Ct NW8 . . . . 89 C2
Ashby Gr N1 . . . . 15 B1
Ashby Ho
  6 Brixton SW9 . . . . . . 48 A1
  7 Islington N1 . . . . . . 15 B1
Ashby Mews
  10 Clapham Pk
  SW2 . . . . 62 A2

Ashby Mews *continued*
  New Cross SE4 . . . . . 51 B1
Ashby Rd SE4 . . . . 51 B1
Ashby St EC1 . . . . 96 B3

Ashchurch Ct 2
  W12 . . . . 38 C3
Ashchurch Gr
  W12 . . . . 38 C3
Ashchurch Park Villas
  W12 . . . . 38 C3
Ashchurch Terr
  W12 . . . . 38 C3
Ashcombe Ct 4
  SW15 . . . . 58 A2
Ashcombe Ho 30
  E3 . . . . 27 A2
Ashcombe St
  SW6 . . . . 166 A1
Ashcroft Ho SW8 . . . . 170 C4
Ashcroft Rd E3 . . . . . . 26 A2
Ashcroft Sq 8
  W6 . . . . 39 B2
Ash Ct
  Clapham SW11 . . . . . . 60 C2
  Marylebone W1 . . . . . 102 C2
  6 Rotherhithe
  SE16 . . . . 33 A4
  Upper Holloway N19 . . . 4 B2
Ashdale Ho N4 . . . . 6 C4
Ashdene 5 SE15 . . . . . 50 A3
Ashdon Rd NW10 . . . . . 21 B4
Ashdown Cres
  NW5 . . . . 12 C3
Ashdown Ct SE22 . . . . 76 C3
Ashdown Ho 7 E5 . . . . 7 C2
Ashdown Way
  SW17 . . . . 72 C2
Ashdown Wlk 20
  E14 . . . . 41 C2
Ashenden SE17 . . . . . . 151 A4
Ashenden Rd E5 . . . . . 18 A3
Ashen Gr SW19 . . . . . . 70 C2
Ashentree Ct EC4 . . . . 107 C1
Asher Way E1 . . . . 125 C3
Ashfield Ho 5 N5 . . . . 15 B3
Ashfield Rd W3 . . . . . . 29 B1
Ashfield St E1 . . . . 32 B4
Ashfield Yd 22 E1 . . . . 32 B4
Ashford Ct NW2 . . . . . . 9 C4
Ashford Ho
  10 Brixton SW9 . . . . . 63 A3
  2 Deptford SE8 . . . . . 51 B4
Ashford Rd NW2 . . . . . . 9 C4
Ashford St
  N1 . . . . 24 A2 98 A4
Ash Gr
  Cricklewood NW2 . . . . 10 A4
  Ealing W5 . . . . 36 A3
  Hackney E8 . . . . 25 A4
Ashgrove Ct 2
  W9 . . . . 31 C4
Ashgrove Ho
  SW1 . . . . 147 C2
Ash Ho
  4 Canary Wharf
  E14 . . . . 42 B4
  Fulham SE1 . . . . 153 A3
Ashington 1 NW5 . . . . 12 C2
Ashington Ho 18
  E1 . . . . 25 A1
Ashington Rd
  SW6 . . . . 165 A1
Ashland Pl W1 . . . . . . 103 B4
Ashleigh Ho SW14 . . . . 56 A4
Ashleigh Rd SW14 . . . . 56 A4
Ashley Cres SW11 . . . . 60 C4

Ashley Ct
  Hampstead NW3 . . . . . 11 A3
  10 Kingsland N16 . . . . 16 A3
Ashley Pl SW1 . . . . . . 132 C1
Ashley Rd
  Hornsey N19 . . . . 5 A4
  Richmond TW9 . . . . . . 54 A4
Ashlin Rd E15 . . . . 19 C4
Ashlone Rd SW15 . . . . 57 C4
Ashlone Rd SW15 . . . . 57 C4
Ashmead Bsns Ctr 8
  E16 . . . . 27 C1
Ashmead Ho E9 . . . . . 18 A3
Ashmead Mews 1
  SE8 . . . . 51 C1
Ashmead Rd SE8 . . . . 51 C1
Ashmere Gr 11 SW2 . . 62 A3
Ashmere Ho 11
  SW2 . . . . 62 A3
Ashmill St NW8 . . . . . 102 A4
Ashmole Prim Sch
  SW8 . . . . 163 A3
Ashmole St SW8 . . . . 163 A3
Ashmore NW1 . . . . 83 B3
Ashmore Cl SE15 . . . . 49 B3
Ashmore Ho W14 . . . . 126 B1
Ashmore Rd W9 . . . . . 23 B2
Ashmount Prim Sch
  N19 . . . . 4 B4
Ashmount Rd N19 . . . . 4 C4
Ashness Rd SW11 . . . . 60 B2
Ashpark Ho 4
  E14 . . . . 33 B3
Ashtead Ct 18
  SW19 . . . . 69 C3
Ashtead Rd E5 . . . . 7 C4
Ashton Ho
  Kennington SW9 . . . . 163 C1
  Roehampton SW15 . . . 69 A4
Ashton Rd E15 . . . . 19 C3
Ashton St E14 . . . . 34 B2
Ashurst Lo 4 N5 . . . . . 15 A3
Ashwin St E8 . . . . 16 B2
Ashworth Cl SE5 . . . . . 48 C1
Ashworth Mans
  W9 . . . . 88 B3
Ashworth Rd W9 . . . . . 88 B3
Aske Ho N1 . . . 24 A2 98 A4
Asker Ho N7 . . . . 14 A4
Aske St N1 . . . 24 A2 98 A4
Askew Cres W12 . . . . . 38 C4
Askew Mans 14
  W12 . . . . 38 C4
Askew Rd W12 . . . . 38 C4
Askham Ct W12 . . . . . . 29 C1
Askham Rd W12 . . . . . . 29 C1
Askill Dr SW15 . . . . . . 58 A2
Asland Rd E15 . . . . 27 C4
Aslett St SW18 . . . . . . 71 B4
Asmara Rd NW2 . . . . . . 10 A3
Asolando Dr SE17 . . . . 151 A3
Aspect Coll WC1 . . . . 106 B3
Aspect Ho 7 E14 . . . . . 42 B4
Aspen Cl Ealing W5 . . . 36 B4
  9 Upper Holloway
  N19 . . . . 4 B2
Aspen Ct
  18 Acton W3 . . . . 28 B3
  12 Hackney E5 . . . . . . 16 C3
  Richmond TW9 . . . . . . 44 C3
Aspen Gdns 3
  W6 . . . . 39 A1
Aspen Ho
  2 Deptford SE15 . . . . 50 B4
  4 Maitland Pk
  NW3 . . . . 12 B2

Aspen Ho *continued*
  Richmond TW9 . . . . . . 44 C3
Aspenlea Rd W6 . . . . . 47 C4
Aspen Way E14 . . . . . . 34 B2
Aspern Gr NW3 . . . . . . 12 A3
Aspinall Ho SW12 . . . . 74 A3
Aspinall Rd SE4 . . . . . 65 C4
Aspinden Rd SE16 . . . . 40 A2
Aspire Bld 2
  SW15 . . . . 58 B2
Aspley Rd SW18 . . . . . 59 A2
Assam St E1 . . . . 125 A1
Assam St E1 . . . . 111 B2
Assata Mews N1 . . . . . 15 A2
Assembly Pas E1 . . . . . 32 B4
Assisi Ct SW12 . . . . . . 72 B3
Astbury Bsns Pk 5
  SE15 . . . . 50 B2
Astbury Ho SE11 . . . . 135 B1
Astbury Rd SE15 . . . . . 50 B2
Astell St SW3 . . . . 144 B2
Aster Ho 3 SE13 . . . . . 52 B1
Aste St E14 . . . . 42 B4
Astey's Row 1 N1 . . . . 15 B1
Astle St SW11 . . . . . . 169 C2
Astley Ho
  Fulham SE1 . . . . 153 A2
  9 Paddington W2 . . . . 31 C4
Aston Ho
  Notting Hill
  W11 . . . . 31 B2 113 A4
  South Lambeth
  SW8 . . . . 171 B3
Aston St E14 . . . . 33 A4
Astonville St
  SW18 . . . . 70 C3
Astor Ct SW6 . . . . 156 C1
Astoria Mans 10
  SW16 . . . . 74 A1
Astoria Par SW16 . . . . 74 A1
Astoria Wlk SW9 . . . . . 62 C4
Astra Ho
  4 Bow E3 . . . . 26 B2
  Hornsey N4 . . . . 5 B4
Astrop Mews W6 . . . . . 39 B3
Astrop Terr W6 . . . . . . 39 B4
Astwood Mews
  SW7 . . . . 142 C4
Asylum Rd SE15 . . . . . 50 A3
Atalanta St
  SW6 . . . . 47 C3 154 A1
Atheldene Rd
  SW18 . . . . 71 B3
Athelstane Gr E3 . . . . . 26 B3
Athelstane Mews
  N4 . . . . 5 C3
Athelstan Gdns 8
  NW6 . . . . 10 A1
Athelstan Ho
  Hackney Wick E9 . . . . 18 B3
  Stoke Newington
  N16 . . . . 16 A4
Athena Ct
  Bermondsey SE1 . . . . 138 A3
  St John's Wood
  NW8 . . . . 79 B2
Athenia Ho 7 E14 . . . . 34 C3
Athenlay Rd SE15 . . . . 65 C2
Atheneoum Ct N5 . . . . 15 B4
Athens Gdns W9 . . . . . 23 C1
Atherden Rd E5 . . . . . . 17 B4
Atherfield Ct
  SW18 . . . . 59 A1

Atherfold Rd SW9 ..62 A4
Atherstone Ct
W2 .... 100 B4
Atherstone Mews
SW7 .... 143 A4
Atherton Rd SW13 .46 C3
Atherton St SW11 168 B2
Athlone Cl 24 .65 ..17 A3
Athlone Ho
16 Camden Town
NW5 ....12 C2
9 Stepney E1 ....32 B3
Athlone House N6 ...3 B4
Athlone Rd SW2 ..74 C4
Athlone St NW5 ....12 C2
Athol Cl SW N4 ......5 B2
Athol Ho W9 .....88 C3
Athol Sq E14 ....34 B3
Atkins Ct 13 E3 .....26 B4
Atkins Lo W8 .....127 B4
Atkinson Ho
Battersea SW11.. 169 B3
15 Hackney E2....24 C3
Walworth SE17... 151 C3
Atkins Rd SW4,
SW12 ....73 C4
Atlanta Bldg 4
SE13 ....52 A2
Atlantic Ct 10 E14 .34 C2
Atlantic Ho
1 Putney SW15 ..58 B2
4 Tower Hamlets
E1 ....33 A4
Atlantic Rd SW2, SW9,
SE24 ....62 C3
Atlas Mews
Dalston E8 ......16 B2
Islington N7 .....14 B2
Atlas Rd NW10 ....21 A2
Atley Rd E3 ....26 C4
Atney Rd SW15 ....58 A3
Atterbury St SW1 148 A3
Attilburgh Ho
SE1 ....138 C2
Attlee Ho E1 .....111 A3
Attneave St WC1 ...95 B3
Atwater Cl SW2 ...74 C3
Atwell Rd 5 SE15 .49 C1
Atwood Ave TW9 ..44 C1
Atwood Ho SE21 ..76 A1
Atwood Rd W6 ....39 A2
Aubert Ct N5 .....15 A4
Aubert Pk N5 .....15 A4
Aubert Rd N5 .....15 A4
Aubrey Beardsley Ho
SW1 ....147 A3
Aubrey Mans
NW1 ....102 A4
Aubrey Moore Point
E15 ....27 B3
Aubrey Pl NW8 ....78 C1
Aubrey Rd
W14 ......31 B1 113 A1
Aubrey Wlk
W14 ......31 B1 113 A1
Auburn Cl SE14 ...51 A3
Aubyn Sq SW15 ...56 C2
Auckland Ho 11
W12 ....30 A2
Auckland Rd
SW11 ....60 A3
Auckland St SE11 148 C1
Auden Pl NW1 ....81 B4
Audley Cl 8
SW11 ....60 C4

Audley Ct W1 .....118 A2
Audley Rd TW10 ...54 B2
Audley Sq W1 ....117 C2
Audley St E2 ......24 C3
Augustine Ho
Broadgate EC2... 109 C2
Forest Gate SE4.. 51 B2
Augustine Rd
W14 ....39 C3
Augustines Ct E9 ..17 B3
Augustus Cl W12 ..39 A3
Augustus Ct
6 Putney SW19 ..70 A3
Streatham SW16 ..73 C2
Augustus Ho NW1 92 C4
Augustus Rd
SW19 ....70 A3
Augustus St NW1 ..92 B4
Aura Ho 8 TW9 ...45 A2
Auriga Mews N1 ...15 C3
Auriol Mans W14 140 A3
Auriol Rd W14 ....140 A3
Aurora Bldg 4
E14 ....34 B1
Aurora Ho E14 ....34 A3
Austen Ho 5
NW6 ....23 C2
Austin Friars EC2 109 C2
Austin Friars Ho
EC2 ....109 C2
Austin Friars Sq
EC2 ....109 C2
Austin Ho
5 Brixton SW2 ...62 B2
3 New Cross E14 .51 B3
Austin Rd SW11 .169 B3
Austins Ct SE15 ...64 C4
Austin St 2 E2 ....98 C3
Australia Rd W12 ..30 A2
Austral St SE11 ...150 A4
Autumn Rise 3
W4 ....37 C1
Autumn St E3 .....26 C4
Avalon Rd SW6 ..166 A4
Avebury Ct N1 ....87 B3
Avebury St N1 ....87 B3
Aveline St SE11 ..149 B1
Aveling Ho 12 N19.. 4 B1
Ave Maria La EC4. 108 B1
Avenell Mans N5 ..15 A4
Avenell Rd N5 ......6 A1
Avenfield Ho W1 .117 A4
Avening Terr
SW18 ....70 C4
Avenue Cl NW8 ....80 B3
Avenue Cres W3 ..37 A4
Avenue Ct
Chelsea SW3 ....144 C3
Cricklewood NW2 ..1 A1
Avenue Gdns
Mortlake SW14 ...56 A4
South Acton W3 ..37 A4
Avenue Ho
St John's Wood
NW8 ....80 A1
Upper Clapton N16.. 7 C2
Willesden Green
NW10 ....22 A3
Avenue Lo 12
NW8 ....11 C1
Avenue Mans
Clapham SW11....60 C3
Hampstead NW3 ..11 A3

Avenue Mans continued
Willesden NW2 .....9 A2
Avenue Park Rd SE21,
SE27 ....75 A2
Avenue Rd
Crouch End N6 ....4 C4
Harlesden NW10 ..21 B3
Primrose Hill NW8 80 A4
South Acton W3 ..37 A4
Avenue Sch The
NW6 ....10 C2
Avenue The
Bedford Pk W4 ...38 A3
Brondesbury Pk
NW6 ....23 A4
Clapham SW4 ....60 C2
Greenwich SE10 ..52 C3
Richmond TW9 ...44 B1
Wandsworth SW18,
SW12 ....72 A4
Wimbledon SW19 46 C1
Avery Farm Row
SW1 ....146 A3
Avery Hill Coll (Mile
End Annexe) E3 ..26 B1
Avery Row W1 ....118 B4
Aviary Ct E16 .....35 B4
Avignon Rd SE4 ..65 C4
Avingdor Ct 13
W3 ....28 B1
Avington Ct SE1 ..152 B3
Avis Sq E1 ....32 C3
Avocet Cl SE1 ....153 B2
Avon Ct
1 Acton W3 ......28 B3
7 Putney SW15 ..58 A2
Avondale Ct E16 ..35 A4
Avondale Ho
Bermondsey SE1 .153 B1
6 Mortlake SW14 .55 C4
Avondale Mans
SW6 ....164 C4
Avondale Park Gdns
W11 ....31 A2 112 A3
Avondale Park Prim
Sch W11 ..31 A2 112 A3
Avondale Rd
Mortlake SW14 ...55 C4
Newham E16 .....35 A4
Avondale Rise
SE15 ....64 B4
Avondale Sq 1 SE1 153 B1
Avon Ho
2 Islington N1 ....14 C1
14 Stoke Newington
N16 ....7 A3
West Kensington
W14 ....141 A3
Avonhurst Ho
NW6 ....10 A1
Avonley Rd SE14 ..50 B3
Avonmore Gdns
W14 ....141 A3
Avonmore Pl
W14 ....140 B4
Avonmore Prim Sch
W14 ....140 B4
Avonmore Rd
W14 ....140 C4
Avonmouth
SE1 ....136 C2
Avon Pl SE1 ......137 A3
Avriol Ho W10 ....30 A1
Avro Ct E9 ....18 A3

Axford Ho SW2 ....75 A3
Axis Bsns Ctr E15 .27 A4
Axis Ct SE10 ....53 A4
Axminster Rd N7 ...5 B1
Aybrook St W1 ...103 B3
Aycliffe Rd W12 ..29 C1
Aylesbury Ho 13
SE15 ....49 C4
Aylesbury Rd
SE17 ....151 C1
Aylesbury St EC1 ..96 A1
Aylesford Ho SE1 137 C3
Aylesford St SW1 147 B1
Aylesham Sh Ctr
SE15 ....49 C2
Aylestone Ave
NW6 ....22 C4
Aylmer Ho SE10 ..42 C1
Aylmer Rd W12 ...38 B4
Aylton Est 28 SE16 40 B4
Aylward St E1 .....32 C3
Aylwin Est SE1 ...138 B2
Aylwin Girls Sch
SE1 ....153 A4
Aynhoe Mans
W14 ....39 C2
Aynhoe Rd W14 ...39 C3
Ayres St SE1 .....137 A4
Ayrsome Rd N16 ...7 A1
Ayrton Gould Ho 8
E2 ....25 C2
Ayrton Rd SW7 ..129 B2
Aysgarth Rd SE21 .76 A4
Ayshford Ho E1 ...25 A2
Ayston Ho 19 SE8..40 C2
Aytoun Ct SW9 ..173 A1
Aytoun Pl SW9 ..173 A1
Aytoun Rd SW9 ..173 A1
Azalea Ho SE14 ...51 B3
Azania Mews
NW5 ....13 A2
Azenby Rd SE15 ..49 B1
Azof St SE10 ......43 A2
Azov Ho 10 E1 ....26 A1
Aztec Ct 8 N16 ...16 A2
Azure Ho 2 E2 ....99 B3

B

Baalbec Rd N5 ....15 A3
Babington Ct
WC1 ....106 B4
Babington Ho
SE1 ....137 A4
Bacchus Wlk 12
N1 ....24 A3
Bache's St N1 .....97 C3
Back Church La
E1 ....111 B1
Back Hill EC1 ......95 C1
Back La NW3 .....11 B4
Bacon Gr SE1 ....138 C1
Bacon's Coll SE16 .41 A4
Bacon St
E1, E2 ......24 B1 99 A2
Bacton NW5 ......12 C3
Bacton St 2 E2 ....25 B2
Baddeley Ho
SE11 ....149 A2
Baddow Wlk N1 ...86 C4
Baden Pl SE1 ....137 B4
Badminton Ct 9
N4 ....6 B4

Badminton Ho
SE22 ....64 A3
Badminton Mews 9
E16 ....35 C1
Badminton Rd
SW12 ....60 C1
Badric Ct SW11 ..167 C1
Badsworth Rd
SE5 ....48 B2
Bagley's La SW6 .166 B3
Bagnigge Ho WC1 .95 B3
Bagshot Ho NW1 ..92 B4
Bagshot St SE17 .152 B1
Baildon 27 E2 .....25 B3
Baildon St SE8 ....51 B3
Bailey Ct 9 W10 ..30 C3
Bailey Ho 11 SW10 156 B2
Bailey Mews
Brixton SW2 .....62 C2
Chiswick W4 .....45 A4
Bainbridge St
WC1 ....105 C2
Bain Ho SW9 ....172 B2
Baird Ho 29 W12 ..30 A2
Baird St EC1 ......97 A2
Baizdon Rd SE3 ..53 A1
Baker Ho E3 ......27 A2
Baker Rd NW10 ...21 A4
Bakers Field N7 ...14 A4
Bakers Hall Ct
EC3 ....124 B3
Baker's Mews W1 103 B2
Bakers Pas 22
NW3 ....11 B4
Bakers Rents
E2 ....24 B2 98 C3
Baker's Row EC1 ..95 B1
Baker St W1, W1 103 A4
Baker Street W1 ..103 A4
Baker Street Sta
NW1 ....91 A1
Baker's Yd C1 ......95 B1
Bakery Cl SW9 ...163 A1
Balaclava Rd SE1 153 A3
Balchier Rd SE22 .65 A1
Balcombe Ho
Lisson Gr NW1 ...90 C2
8 Streatham SW2 .74 B3
Balcombe St NW1 .90 C1
Balcorne St E9 ....17 B1
Balderton Flats
W1 ....103 C1
Balderton St 1 .....103 C1
Baldock St 31
SE5 ....48 B1
Baldock St 3 E3 ...27 A3
Baldwin Ho 18
SW2 ....74 C3
Baldwin Cres SE5 .48 B2
Baldwin St EC1 ...97 B3
Baldwin's Gdns
EC1 ....107 B4
Baldwin St EC1 ...97 B3
Baldwin Terr N1 ...86 C2
Baldwin Gdns W3 .28 C2
Balearic Apts 3
E16 ....35 C2
Bale Rd E1 ....33 A4
Bales Coll W10 ....22 C2
Balfern Gr W4 .....38 A1
Balfern St SW11 .168 B2
Balfe St N1 ....84 B1
Balfour Ho W10 ...30 C4
Balfour Mews
W1 ....117 C2

Balfour Pl
Mayfair W1 . . . . **117** C3
Putney SW15 . . . . **57** A3
Balfour Rd
Highbury N5 . . . . 15 B4
North Acton W3 . . . . . . 28 B4
Balfour St SE17 . . **151** B4
Balfron Twr [4]
E14 . . . . 34 B3
BALHAM 72 C4
Balham Gr SW12 . . 72 C4
Balham High Rd SW12,
SW17 . . . . 72 C3
Balham Hill SW12 . . 61 A1
Balham New Rd
SW12 . . . . 73 A4
Balham Park Mans
SW12 . . . . 72 B3
Balham Park Rd
SW12 . . . . 72 B3
Balham Sta SW12 . . 73 A3
Balham Station Rd
SW12 . . . . 73 A3
Balin Ho SE1 . . . . **137** B4
Balkan Ho [1] 32 A2
Balladier Wlk E14 . . 34 A4
Ballance Rd E9 . . . . 18 A2
Ballantine St
SW18 . . . . 59 B3
Ballantrae Ho
NW2 . . . . 10 B4
Ballard Ho SE10 . . . 52 A4
Ballast Quay SE10 . 42 C1
Ballater Rd SW2,
SW4 . . . . 62 A3
Ball Ct EC3 . . . . . . **109** C1
Ballin Ct E14 . . . . . 42 B4
Ballingdon Rd
SW11 . . . . 60 C1
Ballinger Point [8]
E3 . . . . 27 A2
Balliol Ho [1]
SW15 . . . . 57 C1
Balliol Rd W10 . . . . 30 C3
Ballogie Ave NW10 . . 8 A4
Ballow Cl [5] SE5 . . 49 A3
Ball's Pond Pl [3]
N1 . . . . 15 C2
Ball's Pond Rd N1 . 16 A2
Balman Ho [8]
SE16 . . . . 40 C2
Balmer Rd E3 . . . . . 26 B3
Balmes Rd N1 . . . . **87** C4
Balmoral Cl [1]
SW15 . . . . 57 C1
Balmoral Ct
[21] Rotherhithe
SE16 . . . . 32 C1
St John's Wood
NW8 . . . . **79** B2
Balmoral Gr N7 . . . 14 B2
Balmoral Ho
[1] Isle of Dogs
E14 . . . . 42 A3
Stoke Newington N4 . . 6 B3
West Kensington
W14 . . . . **140** A4
Balmoral Mews
W12 . . . . 38 B3
Balmoral Rd NW2 . . 9 A2
Balmore Cl E14 . . . . 34 B3
Balmore St N19 . . . . 4 A2
Balmuir Gdns
SW15 . . . . 57 B3
Balnacraig Ave
NW10 . . . . 8 A4
Balniel Gate SW1 **147** C2

Balsam Ho [6] E14 . 34 A2
Baltic Apts [5] E16 . 35 C2
Baltic Ho [7] SE5 . . 48 B1
Baltic St E EC1 . . . **96** C1
Baltic St W EC1 . . . **96** C1
Baltimore Ho
Clapham SW18 . . . . . . 59 B3
Kennington SE11 . . . **149** B2
Balvaird Pl SW1 . . **147** C1
Balvernie Gr
SW18 . . . . 70 C4
Bamber Rd [5]
SE15 . . . . 49 B2
Bamborough Gdns [12]
W12 . . . . 39 B4
Bamford Ct E15 . . . 19 A3
Banbury Ct WC2 . . **120** A4
Banbury Ho [9] E9 . 17 C1
Banbury Rd E9 . . . 17 C1
Banbury St SW11 . **168** B2
Bancroft Ct SW8 . **172** A4
Bancroft Ho [11] E1 . 25 B1
Bancroft Rd E1 . . . 25 C1
Banff Ho [1] NW3 . . 12 A2
Banfield Rd SE15 . . 65 A4
Bangabandhu Prim
Sch E2 . . . . 25 B2
Bangalore St
SW15 . . . . 57 C4
Banim St W6 . . . . . 39 A2
Banister Ho
Hackney E9 . . . . 17 C3
Nine Elms SW8 . . . . . **171** A4
[9] West Kilburn
W10 . . . . 23 A2
Banister Ho [9]
W10 . . . . 23 A2
Bank Ct SW11 . . . . **170** A4
Bank End SE1 . . . . **123** A2
Bank St E14 . . . . . . **34** A1
Bank of England *
EC2 . . . . **109** B1
Bank of England
Mus * EC2 . . . . . . **109** B1
Banks Ho SE1 . . . . **136** C1
Bankside
Borough The SE1 . . . **122** C3
Borough The SE1 . . . **123** A2
Bankside Art Gal *
SE1 . . . . **122** B3
Bankside Ave [1]
SE13 . . . . 67 B4
Bankside Ho EC3 . **110** B1
Bankside Pier
SE1 . . . . **122** C3
Bank St E14 . . . . . . 34 A1
Bank Sta EC3 . . . . **109** C1
Bankton Rd SW2 . . 62 C3
Banner Cl [3] SE16 . . 40 A1
Banner St EC1 . . . **97** A1
Bannerman Ho
SW8 . . . . **162** C3
Banner St EC1 . . . **97** A2
Banning Ho [4]
SW19 . . . . 69 C3
Banning St SE10 . . 43 A1
Bannister Cl SW2 . 74 C3
Bannister Ho [27]
SE14 . . . . 50 C4
Banquering Ho *
SW1 . . . . **120** A1
Banstead Ct N4 . . . 6 B3
Banstead St SE15 . . 65 B4
Bantock Ho [8]
W10 . . . . 23 A2
Bantry Ho [13] E1 . 25 C1
Bantry St SE5 . . . . 48 C3

Banville Ho SW8 . **163** A1
Banyan Ho [6]
NW3 . . . . 11 A2
Banyard Rd SE16 . . 40 A3
Baptist Gdns NW5 . 12 C2
Barandon Wlk [9]
W11 . . . . 30 C2
Baranel Ho [28]
E1 . . . . 25 B1
Barbara Brosnan Ct
NW8 . . . . **79** B1
Barbara Castle Cl
SW6 . . . . **155** A3
Barbara Rudolph Ct
[5] N19 . . . . 5 A4
Barbauld Rd N16 . . . 7 A1
Barber Beaumont Ho
[2] E1 . . . . 25 C2
Barbers Rd E15 . . . 27 A3
BARBICAN **109** A3
Barbican N1 . . . . **96** C1
Barbican Arts & Con
Ctr * EC2 . . . . **109** A4
Barbican Sta EC1 . **108** C4
Barb Mews W6 . . . 39 B3
Barbon Cl WC1 . . . **106** C4
Barbrook Ho [17] E9 . 17 B2
Barchard St SW18 . 59 A2
Barchester St E14 . 34 A4
Barclay Cl SW6 . . . **155** B1
Barclay Ho [21] E9 . 17 B1
Barclay Rd SW6 . . **155** C1
Barcombe Ave
SW2 . . . . 74 B2
Bardell Ho [21] SE1 . **139** B3
Bardolph Rd
Richmond TW9 . . . . . 54 B4
Tufnell Pk N7 . . . . . . 14 A4
Bard Ho N16 . . . . . . 20 C2
Bardsey Pl [8] E1 . 25 B1
Bardsey Wlk [5]
N1 . . . . 15 B2
Bardsley Ho [6]
SE10 . . . . 52 B4
Bardsley La SE10 . . 52 B4
Barents Ho [1] E1 . . 25 C1
Barfett St W10 . . . . 23 B1
Barfleur La SE8 . . . 41 B2
Barford Ho [3] E3 . 26 B3
Barford St N1 . . . . **85** C3
Barforth Rd SE15 . . 65 A4
Barge House St
SE1 . . . . **121** C2
Barge La [10] E3 . . 26 B4
Barham Ho SE17 . . **152** B2
Baring Ct N1 . . . . . **87** B3
Baring Ho [5] E14 . 33 C3
Baring St N1 . . . . . **87** B3
Barker Ct TW9 . . . . 45 A1
Barker Dr NW1 . . . . 13 C1
Barker Ho
Dulwich SE21 . . . . . . 76 A1
Walworth SE17 . . . . . **152** A3
Barker Mews SW4 . 61 A3
Barker St SW10 . . **156** C4
Barker Wlk SW16 . . 73 C1
Barkston Gdns
SW5 . . . . **142** A3
Barkway Ct N4 . . . . 6 B2
Barkwith Ho [27]
SE14 . . . . 50 C4
Barkworth Rd
SE16 . . . . 40 B1
Barlborough St
SE14 . . . . 50 C3
Barlby Gdns W10 . . 22 C1

Barlby Prim Sch
W10 . . . . 22 C1
Barlby Rd W10 . . . . 30 C4
Barleycorn Way
E14 . . . . 33 B2
Barley Mow Pas
Chiswick W4 . . . . 37 C1
Clerkenwell EC1 . . . . **108** B3
Barley Shotts Bsns Pk
W10 . . . . 23 B1
Barling [8] N1 . . . . . 13 A1
Barling Ct SW4 . . . **172** A2
Barlings Ho [2]
SE4 . . . . 65 C3
Barloch Ho SW11 . **169** B2
Barlow Ho
[14] Bermondsey
SE16 . . . . 40 A2
[15] Notting Hill
W11 . . . . 31 A2 **112** A4
Shoreditch N1 . . . . . **97** B4
Barlow Pl W1 . . . . **118** B3
Barlow Rd
Acton W3 . . . . 28 A1
Brondesbury NW6 . . . 10 B2
Barlow St SE17 . . . **151** C3
Barmouth Rd
SW18 . . . . 59 B1
Barnabas Ho EC1 . . **96** C3
Barnabas Lo SW8 . **172** B4
Barnabas Rd E9 . . . 17 C3
Barnaby Pl SW7 . . **143** B3
Barnard Ct SW16 . . 74 B1
Barnard Ho [17] E2 . 25 A2
Barnard Lo [10] W9 . 31 C4
Barnard Mews
SW11 . . . . 60 A3
Barnardo Gdns [1]
E1 . . . . 32 C2
Barnardo St E1 . . . 32 C3
Barnard Rd SW11 . 60 A3
Barnard's Inn EC4 **107** C2
Barnbrough N1 . . . **82** C4
Barnby St NW1 . . . **93** A4
Barn Cl [19] NW5 . . 13 C3
Barnersbury Ho
N7 . . . . 14 A4
BARNES 46 B2
Barnes Ave SW13 . . 46 C3
Barnes Bridge Sta
SW13 . . . . 46 A1
Barnes Common *
SW13 . . . . 56 C4
Barnes Ct N1 . . . . . 14 C1
Barnes High St
SW13 . . . . 46 B1
Barnes Ho
[14] Bethnal Green
E2 . . . . 25 B3
Camden Town NW1 . . **82** B4
[20] Deptford SE14 . . . 50 C4
Hornsey N19 . . . . 5 A4
Barnes Hospl
SW14 . . . . 56 A4
Barnes Prim Sch
SW13 . . . . 56 B4
Barnes St E14 . . . . 33 A3
Barnes Sta SW13 . . 56 C4
Barnes Terr SE8 . . . 41 B1
Barnet Gr
E2 . . . . 24 C2 **99** B3
Barnet Ho [35] SE5 . 48 B1
Barnett Ho EC1 . . **110** C3
Barnett St [11] E1 . 32 A3
Barn Field NW3 . . . 12 B3

Barnfield Cl
London N4 . . . . 5 A4
Wandsworth SW17 . . 71 B1
Barnfield Pl E14 . . . 41 C2
Barnham St SE1 . . **138** B4
BARNSBURY 14 A1
Barnsbury Gr N7 . . 14 B1
Barnsbury Ho [2]
SW4 . . . . 61 C1
Barnsbury Pk N1 . . 14 C1
Barnsbury Rd N1 . . **85** B3
Barnsbury Sq N1 . . 14 C1
Barnsbury St N1 . . 14 C1
Barnsbury Terr
N1 . . . . 14 B1
Barnsdale Ave
E14 . . . . 41 C2
Barnsdale Rd W9 . . 23 B1
Barnsley St E1 . . . . 25 A1
Barn St N16 . . . . . . 7 A2
Barnstaple La
SE13 . . . . 67 B3
Barnston Wlk N1 . . **86** C4
Barnwell Ho [5]
SE5 . . . . 49 A2
Barnwell Rd SW2 . 62 C2
Barnwood Cl W9 . . **88** B1
Baron Cl N1 . . . . . . **85** B2
Baroness Rd
E2 . . . . 24 B2 **99** A4
Barons Court Mans
W14 . . . . **140** B1
Baron's Court Rd
W14 . . . . **140** B2
Barons Court Sta
W14 . . . . **140** A2
Barons Gate [6]
W4 . . . . 37 B3
Barons Keep
W14 . . . . **140** A2
Barons Lo [9] E14 . 42 B2
Baronsmead Rd
SW13 . . . . 46 C2
Baronsmede W5 . . 36 B4
Baron's Pl SE1 . . . **135** C3
Baron St N1 . . . . . . **85** B2
Baron Wlk E16 . . . . 35 B4
Barque Mews SE8 . 51 C4
Barradell Ho [18]
W14 . . . . 39 C3
Barras Ho [15] N1 . 15 A1
Barratt Ind Pk E3 . 27 B1
Barratt Ho NW6 . . . 23 C4
Barratt's Gr N16 . . 16 A3
Barratt's Green Rd
NW10 . . . . 20 C3
Barrett St W1 . . . **103** C1
Barrhill Rd SW2 . . 74 A2
Barriedale SE14 . . . 51 A1
Barrie Ho
Acton W3 . . . . 37 B4
Bayswater W2 . . . . . **115** A3
Primrose Hill NW8 . . **80** B3
Stoke Newington
N16 . . . . 7 A1
Barrington Cl
NW5 . . . . 12 C3
Barrington Ct
[9] Acton W3 . . . . . . 37 A4
Kentish Town NW5 . . 12 C3
South Lambeth
SW9 . . . . **172** B1

Barrington Rd
SW9 . . . .**63** A4

Barrowgate Ho
W4 . . . .**37** C1

Barrowgate Rd
W4 . . . .**37** C1

Barrow Hill Est
NW8 . . . .**80** A1

Barrow Hill Jun Sch
NW8 . . . .**80** A1

Barrow Hill Rd
NW8 . . . .**80** A1

Barry Ct SW4 . . . .**61** B1
Barry Ho 4 SE16 . . . .**40** A1
Barry Lo 4 . . . .**5** B4
Barry Par SE22 . . . . . .**64** C3
Barry Rd SE22 . . . . . .**64** C2
Barset Rd SE15 . . . . . .**65** B4
Barston Rd SE27 . . . .**75** B1
Barstow Cres SW2 . . .**74** B3
Bartell Ho SW2 . . . . . .**62** C1
Barter St WC1 . . . . . .**106** B3
Bartholomew Cl
Barbican EC1 . . . .**108** C3
Wandsworth SW18 . .**59** B3

Bartholomew Ct
16 Blackwall E14 . . . .**34** C2
St Luke's EC1 . . . .**97** A2

Bartholomew Ho 22
SE5 . . . .**48** B1

Bartholomew La
EC2 . . . .**109** C1

Bartholomew Pas
EC1 . . . .**108** B3

Bartholomew Pl
EC1 . . . .**108** C3

Bartholomew Rd
NW5 . . . .**13** B2

Bartholomew Sq
18 Bethnal Green
E1 . . . .**25** A1
St Luke's EC1 . . . .**97** A2

Bartholomew St
SE1 . . . .**137** C1

Bartholomew Villas
NW5 . . . .**13** B2
Bartle Rd W11 . . . .**31** A3
Bartlett Cl E14 . . . . . .**33** C3
Bartlett Ct EC4 . . . . .**107** C2
Bartok Ho
W11 . . . . . **31** B2 **112** C3
Barton Ct
Hackney E9 . . . .**17** B3
Peckham SE15 . . . . . .**65** A4

Barton Ct
South Lambeth
SW4 . . . .**172** A2
West Kensington
W14 . . . .**140** B2

Barton Ho
6 Bromley E3 . . . . . .**27** A2
Islington N1 . . . .**15** A1
Sands End SW6 . . . . . .**59** A4
Barton Rd W14 . . . . .**140** B1
Barton St SW1 . . . . .**134** A2
Bartonway NW8 . . . . .**79** B2
Bartram Rd SE4 . . . . .**66** A1
Bartrip St E9 . . . .**18** B2
Barts & The London
Sch of Medicine &
Dentistry EC1 . . . . .**96** B1
Barville Cl SE4 . . . . . .**66** A3
Barwell Ho
E2 . . . .**24** C1 **99** C2
Barwick Ho 7 W3 . . .**37** B4

Bascome St 13
SW2 . . . .**62** C1
Base Apartments 6
N1 . . . .**15** B1
Baseline Business
Studios 10 W11 . . . . .**30** C1
Basevi Way SE8 . . . . .**52** A4
Bashley Rd NW10 . . . .**20** C1
Basildon Ct W1 . . . .**103** C4
Basil Ho
South Lambeth
SW8 . . . .**162** A2
Whitechapel E1 . . . . .**111** C2
Basil Mans SW1 . . . .**130** C3
Basil St
Knightsbridge
SW1 . . . .**130** C3
Knightsbridge SW1,
SW3 . . . .**130** C2
Basin App 20 E14 . . . .**33** A3
Basing Ct 13 SE15 . . .**49** B2
Basingdon Way
SE5 . . . .**63** C3
Basinghall Ave
EC2 . . . .**109** B2
Basinghall St EC2 . . .**109** B2
Basing Hill NW11 . . . .**1** B3
Basing House Yd
E2 . . . .**24** A2 **98** B4
Basing Pl
E2 . . . .**24** A2 **98** B4
Basing St W11 . . . . . .**31** B3
Basire St N1 . . . .**87** A4
Baskerville Ct
SW18 . . . .**72** A4
Baskerville Gdns
NW10 . . . .**8** A4
Baskerville Rd
SW18 . . . .**72** A4
Baslow Wlk 6 E5 . . . .**17** C4
Basnett Rd 9
SW11 . . . .**60** C4
Basque Ct 21 SE16 . . .**40** C4
Bassano St SE22 . . . .**64** B2
Bassein Park Rd
W12 . . . .**38** B4
Bassett Rd W10 . . . . .**30** C3
Bassett St NW5 . . . . .**12** C2
Bassingbourn Ho 3
N1 . . . .**15** A1
Bassingham Rd
SW18 . . . .**71** B4
Bassishaw Highwalk
EC2 . . . .**109** B3
Basswood Cl 8
SE15 . . . .**65** A4
Basterfield Ho EC1 . .**96** C1
Bastion Highwalk
EC2 . . . .**108** C3
Bastwick St EC1 . . . . .**96** C2
Basuto Rd SW6 . . . .**165** C3
Batavia Ho 1
SE14 . . . .**51** A3
Batavia Mews 3
SE14 . . . .**51** A3
Batavia Rd SE14 . . . . .**51** A3
Batchelor St N1 . . . . .**85** C3
Bateman Ho 8
SE17 . . . .**48** A4
Bateman's Bldgs
W1 . . . .**105** B1
Bateman's Row
EC2 . . . .**24** A1 **98** B2
Bateman St W1 . . . . .**105** B1
Bate St 10 E14 . . . . . .**33** B2
Bath Cl SE15 . . . .**50** A3

Bath Ct
Finsbury EC1 . . . .**97** B3
3 Forest Hill SE26 . .**76** C1
Holborn EC1 . . . .**95** B1
Bathgate Ho 8
SW9 . . . .**48** A1
Bathgate Rd
SW19 . . . .**69** C1
Bath Gr 22 . . . .**24** C3
Bath Ho
Bethnal Green
E2 . . . .**24** C1 **99** C2
Borough The SE1 . . .**137** A2
Bath Pl
11 Hammersmith
W6 . . . .**39** B1
Shoreditch
EC2 . . . .**24** A2 **98** A3
Bath Rd W4 . . . .**38** A2
Bath St EC1 . . . .**97** B3
Bath Terr SE1 . . . . . .**136** C2
Bathurst Gdns
NW10 . . . .**22** A3
Bathurst Ho 7
W12 . . . .**30** A2
Bathurst Mews
W2 . . . .**115** C4
Bathurst St W2 . . . . .**115** C4
Batley Pl 3 N16 . . . . .**7** B1
Batley Rd N16 . . . .**7** B1
Batman Cl W12 . . . . . .**30** A1
Batoum Gdns W6 . . . .**39** B3
Batson Ho 1 E1 . . . . .**111** C1
Batson St W12 . . . . . .**38** C4
Batten Ho
1 London SW4 . . . . .**61** B2
10 West Kilburn
W10 . . . .**23** A2
Batten St SW11 . . . . . .**60** A4
BATTERSEA **169** A4
Battersea Bridge Rd
SW11 . . . .**158** A1
Battersea Bsns Ctr
SW11 . . . .**60** C4
Battersea Church Rd
SW11 . . . .**167** C4
Battersea Dogs Home
SW8 . . . .**160** B1
Battersea High St
SW11 . . . .**167** B1
Battersea Hts
SW11 . . . .**60** B4
Battersea Park ✱
SW11 . . . .**159** B1
Battersea Park Rd
SW11, SW8 . . . .**169** A3
Battersea Park Sta
SW8 . . . .**160** A1
Battersea Rise
SW11 . . . .**60** A3
Battersea Sq
SW11 . . . .**167** C3
Battishill St 9 N1 . . .**15** A1
Battlebridge Ct
NW1 . . . .**84** B2
Battle Bridge La
SE1 . . . .**124** A1
Battle Bridge Rd
NW1 . . . .**84** A2
Battledean Rd N5 . . .**15** A3
Battle Ho 8 SE15 . . . .**49** C4
Batty St E1 . . . .**111** C2
Baty Ho SW2 . . . .**74** B3
Baulk The SW18 . . . . .**70** C4

Bavaria Rd N19 . . . . .**5** A2
Bavent Rd SE5 . . . . . .**48** B1
Bawdale Rd SE22 . . . .**64** B2
Bawtree Rd SE14 . . . .**51** A3
Baxendale
E2 . . . .**24** C2 **99** B4
Baxter Ho 10 E3 . . . . .**27** A2
Baxter Rd N1 . . . .**15** C2
Baycliffe Ho 5 E9 . . .**17** C2
Bay Ct Ealing W5 . . . .**36** A3
7 Stepney E1 . . . .**25** C1
Bayer Ho EC1 . . . .**96** C1
Bayes Ct NW3 . . . .**12** B1
Bayfield Ho 8
SE4 . . . .**65** C3
Bayford Ho E8 . . . . . .**24** C4
Bayford St Ind Ctr 6
E8 . . . .**17** A1
Bayford St 3 E8 . . . . .**17** A1
Bayham Pl NW1 . . . . .**83** A3
Bayham Rd W4 . . . . . .**37** C3
Bayham St NW1 . . . . .**82** C3
Bayhurst Ho 4 N4 . . . .**6** B4
Bayley St WC1 . . . . . .**105** B3
Baylis Rd SE1 . . . .**135** B3
Baynes Mews 2
NW3 . . . .**11** C2
Baynes St NW1 . . . . . .**13** B1
Bayon Ho 27 N19 . . . . .**4** C4
Bayonne Rd W6 . . . .**154** A3
Bayston Rd N16 . . . . . .**7** B1
BAYSWATER **114** C4
Bayswater Rd W2 . . .**115** B3
Bayswater Sta
W2 . . . .**114** B4
Bayton Ct 2 E8 . . . . . .**16** C1
Baytree Rd SW2 . . . . .**62** B3
Bazalgette Ho
NW8 . . . .**89** C2
Bazeley Ho SE1 . . . . .**136** A3
Bazely St E14 . . . .**34** B2
BBC Television Ctr
W12 . . . .**30** B1
Beach Ho SW5 . . . . .**141** B2
Beachy Rd E3 . . . .**18** C1
Beaconfield Terrace
Rd W14 . . . .**126** A1
Beacon Gate SE14 . . .**65** C4
Beacon Hill N7 . . . . . .**14** A3
Beacon Ho
11 Camberwell
SE5 . . . .**49** A3
7 Isle of Dogs E14 . .**42** A1
South Lambeth
SW8 . . . .**171** B4
Beacon Rd SE13 . . . . .**67** C1
Beaconsfield Cl
Acton Green W4 . . . . .**37** B1
Greenwich SE3 . . . . . .**53** C4
Beaconsfield Rd
Acton W4 . . . .**37** C3
Greenwich SE3 . . . . . .**53** C4
Walworth SE17 . . . . .**152** A1
Willesden NW10 . . . . .**8** B2
Beaconsfield Wlk
SW6 . . . .**165** A3
Beadon Rd W6 . . . . . .**39** B2
Beak St W1 . . . .**119** A4
Beale Ho SW9 . . . . . .**172** C1
Beale Pl E3 . . . .**26** B3
Beale Rd E3 . . . .**26** B4
Beames Ho SW8 . . . .**171** B4
Beames Rd NW10 . . . .**20** C4
Beaminster Ho
SW8 . . . .**162** C2
Beamish Ho 7
SE16 . . . .**40** B2

Beanacre Cl E9 . . . . . .**18** B2
Bear Alley EC4 . . . . .**108** A2
Bear Croft Ho
SW6 . . . .**164** C1
Beardsley Way
W3 . . . .**37** C4
Bear Gardens Mus ✱
SE1 . . . .**122** C2
Bear Gdns SE1 . . . . .**122** C2
Bear La SE1 . . . .**122** B1
Bear St WC2 . . . .**119** C4
Bearstead Rise
SE4 . . . .**66** B2
Beaton Cl SE15 . . . . . .**49** B2
Beatrice Ho
1 Brixton SW2 . . . . .**62** B2
4 Hammersmith
W6 . . . .**39** B1
2 Stepney E1 . . . . . .**32** A4
Beatrice Pl W8 . . . . .**128** A1
Beatrice Rd
Bermondsey SE1 . . . .**153** C3
Finsbury Pk N4 . . . . . .**5** C4
2 Richmond TW10 . .**54** B2
Beatrice Tate Sch
E2 . . . .**25** A2
Beatrice Webb Ho 3
E3 . . . .**26** A3
Beatrix Ho SW5 . . . .**142** B2
Beatrix Potter Prim
Sch SW18 . . . .**71** B3
Beatson Wlk 23
SE16 . . . .**32** C1
Beattie Ho SW8 . . . .**171** A4
Beatty Ho 10 E14 . . . .**41** C4
Beatty Rd N16 . . . .**16** A4
Beatty St NW1 . . . . . .**82** C2
Beauchamp Cl 7
W4 . . . .**37** B3
Beauchamp Pl
SW3 . . . .**130** B1
Beauchamp Rd
SW11 . . . .**60** B3
Beauchamp St
EC1 . . . .**107** B3
Beauchamp Terr
SW15 . . . .**57** A4
Beauclerc Rd W6 . . . .**39** A3
Beauclerk Ho 10
SW16 . . . .**74** A1
Beaufort Cl SW19 . . .**69** A4
Beaufort Ct SW6 . . .**155** B4
Beaufort Gdns
SW3 . . . .**130** B2
Beaufort Ho
Battersea SW11 . . . .**168** A2
Chelsea SW3 . . . .**157** C3
20 Millwall E14 . . . .**41** C4
Pimlico SW1 . . . .**147** B1
Beaufort Mans
SW3 . . . .**157** C3
Beaufort Mews
SW6 . . . .**155** A4
Beaufort St SW3 . . . .**157** B4
Beaufoy Ho
South Lambeth
SW8 . . . .**162** C2
3 West Norwood
SE27 . . . .**75** A1
Beaufoy Rd 11
SW8 . . . .**61** A4
Beaufoy Wlk
SE11 . . . .**149** A3
Beaulieu Cl SE5 . . . . .**63** C4
Beaulieu Pl W4 . . . . . .**37** B3
Beaumanor Mans
W2 . . . .**114** A4

Beaumaris Twr **2**
W3 . . . . 37 A4
Beaumont SW15 . . . . 58 A2
Beaumont Ave
Richmond TW9 . . . . . 54 B4
West Kensington
W14 . . . . **140 C2**
Beaumont Bldgs
WC2 . . . . **106 B1**
Beaumont Cres
W14 . . . . **140 C1**
Beaumont Ct
10 Acton Green
W4 . . . . 37 B1
Marylebone W1 . . . **103 C4**
7 Mile End E1 . . . . 26 A2
Beaumont Gdns
NW3 . . . . 1 C1
Beaumont Gr E1 . . . 25 C1
Beaumont Ho
1 Streatham
SW2 . . . . 74 A3
West Kensington
W14 . . . . **141 A3**
Wimbledon SW19 . . 70 C1
Beaumont Lo E8 . . . 16 C2
Beaumont Pl NW1,
WC1, W1. . . . . **93 A2**
Beaumont Rd
Putney SW15,
SW19 . . . . 70 A4
South Acton W4 . . . 37 B3
Beaumont Rise
N19. . . . . 4 C3
Beaumont Sq E1 . . 32 C4
Beaumont St W1 . . **103 C4**
Beaumont Wlk
NW3 . . . . 12 B1
Beauvale **6** NW1. . 12 C1
Beauval Rd SE22 . . 64 B1
Beavis Ho N7 . . . . . . 7 A1
Beavor La W6 . . . . . 38 C1
Beccles St E14 . . . . 33 B2
Beck Cl SE13 . . . . . . 52 A2
Beckers The N16 . . . 16 C4
Becket Ho SE1 . . . . **137 B3**
Becket St SE1 . . . . . **137 B2**
Beckett Cl
Streatham SW16 . . . 73 C2
Willesden NW10 . . . . 8 A2
Beckett Ho
London SW9 . . . . . **172 B1**
15 Stepney E1 . . . . 32 B4
Beckfoot NW1. . . . . **83 A1**
Beckford Cl W14 . . **141 A3**
Beckford Ho **18**
N16. . . . . 16 A3
Beckford Prim Sch
NW6 . . . . 10 B3
Beckham Ho
SE11 . . . . **149 A3**
Beck Ho N16 . . . . . . 7 A1
Beckington **18**
NW5 . . . . 12 C2
Beckley Ho E3 . . . . 26 B1
Becklow Gdns
Chiswick W12 . . . . . 38 B4
1 Shepherd's Bush
W12 . . . . 38 C4
Becklow Mews **7**
W12 . . . . 38 C4
Becklow Rd W12 . . 38 C4
Beck Rd E8 . . . . 25 A4
Beckton Rd E16 . . . 35 B4
Beckway St SE17 . . **152 A3**
Beckwith Ho **22**
E2 . . . . 25 A3

Beckwith Rd SE24 . . 63 C2
Bective Pl SW15 . . . 58 B3
Bective Rd SW15 . . 58 B3
Bedale St SE1 . . . . **123 B1**
Bedefield WC1 . . . . **94 B3**
Bede Ho
London SE14 . . . . . . 51 B2
5 Putney SW15 . . . 57 C1
Bedford Ave WC1 . **105 C3**
Bedfordbury WC2 **120 A3**
Bedford Cl W4 . . . . 46 B4
Bedford Cnr **3**
W4 . . . . 38 A2
Bedford Court Mans
WC1 . . . . **105 C3**
Bedford Ct
6 Richmond TW9 . . 54 B3
St James WC2 . . . . **120 A3**
Bedford Gardens Ho
W8 . . . . 31 C1 **113 C1**
Bedford Gdns
W8 . . . . 31 C1 **113 C1**
Bedford Hill SW12 . 73 A2
Bedford Ho
2 Acton W4 . . . . . . 38 A2
2 Stockwell SW4 . . 62 A3
Bedford Park Cnr **3**
W4 . . . . 38 A2
Bedford Park Mans **4**
W4 . . . . 37 C2
Bedford Pas SW6 . **154 B2**
Bedford Rd W4 . . . **106 A4**
Bedford Rd
Acton W4 . . . . 38 A3
Stockwell SW2,
SW4 . . . . 62 A3
Bedford Row
WC1 . . . . **107 A3**
Bedford Sq WC1 . . **105 C3**
Bedford St WC2 . . **120 B3**
Bedford Way WC1 . **93 C1**
Bedgebury Gdns
SW19 . . . . 70 A2
Bedlam Mews
SE11 . . . . **149 B4**
Bedlow Cl NW8 . . . **89 C1**
Bedser Cl SE11 . . . **163 A4**
Bedser Ct SW4 . . . **172 A2**
Bedwell Ho SW9 . . **173 B1**
Beech Ave W3 . . . . 29 A1
Beech Cl
Deptford SE8 . . . . . 51 B4
Putney SW15 . . . . . 68 C4
Beechcroft Ave
NW11 . . . . 1 B4
Beechcroft Ct
3 Golders Green
NW11 . . . . 1 C4
Greenwich SE3 . . . . 53 C2
Beech Croft Ct N5 . 15 A4
Beechcroft Rd
Mortlake SW14 . . . . 55 B4
Upper Tooting
SW17 . . . . 72 A2
Beechcroft Way
N19 . . . . 4 C3
Beech Ct
Child's Hill NW2 . . . . 1 B2
Marylebone W1 . . . **102 C2**
43 Notting Hill W2 . 31 C4
7 Rotherhithe
SE16 . . . . 33 A1
Beechdale Rd
SW2 . . . . 62 B1
Beechdene **4**
SE15 . . . . 50 A2

Beeches Rd SW17 . . 72 B1
Beeches The **1**
N19. . . . . 5 A3
Beechey Ho **30** E1 . 32 A1
Beech Gdns W5 . . . 36 A3
Beech Ho
6 Maitland Pk
NW3 . . . . 12 B2
5 Rotherhithe
SE16 . . . . 40 B4
9 Stoke Newington
N16. . . . . 6 C2
Beechmore Rd
SW11 . . . . **169 A3**
Beech St EC2 . . . . **109 A4**
Beech Tree Cl N1 . . 14 C1
Beechwood Ave
TW9 . . . . 44 C2
Beechwood Ct
Chiswick W4 . . . . . . 45 C4
Stamford Hill N16 . . . 7 A4
Beechwood Gr
W3 . . . . 29 A2
Beechwood Ho **23**
E2 . . . . 24 C3
Beechwood Rd E8 . 16 B2
Beechworth Cl
NW3 . . . . 1 C2
Beecroft Mews
SE4 . . . . 66 A2
Beecroft Rd SE4 . . . 66 A2
Beehive Cl E8 . . . . . 16 B1
Beehive Pl SW9 . . . 62 C4
Beemans Row **7**
SW18 . . . . 71 B2
Beeston Cl **5** E8 . 16 C3
Beeston Pl SW1 . . **132 B2**
Beeston's Ho SE15 . 65 A4
Beethoven St
W10 . . . . 23 A2
Begbie Ho **5** SW9 . **173 A2**
Begonia Wlk W12 . 29 B3
Beira St SW12 . . . . 73 A4
Beis Chinuch Lebonos
Girls Sch N4 . . . . . . 6 B4
Beis Rochel d'Satmar
Girls Sch N16 . . . . . . 7 A4
Bekesbourne St **17**
E14 . . . . 33 A3
Beldanes Lo NW10 . 8 C1
Belenoyd Ct SW16 . 74 B1
Belfast Rd N16 . . . . 7 B2
Belford Ho **7** E8 . 24 B4
Belfort Rd SE15 . . . 50 B1
Belfry Cl **13** SE16 . 40 A1
Belgrade Ho N16 . . 16 A4
Belgrade Rd N16 . . 16 A4
Belgrave Cl **11** W3 . 37 B4
Belgrave Ct
4 Acton Green
W4 . . . . 37 B1
22 Limehouse E14 . 33 B2
Nine Elms SW8 . . . **160 C1**
Belgrave Gdns
Kilburn NW8 . . . . . **78 C3**
St John's Wood
NW8 . . . . **78 C3**
Belgrave Mans
NW8 . . . . **78 C3**
Belgrave Mews N
SW1 . . . . **131 B3**
Belgrave Mews S
SW1 . . . . **131 C2**
Belgrave Mews W
SW1 . . . . **131 B2**

Belgrave Pl SW1 . . **131 C1**
Belgrave Rd
Barnes SW13 . . . . . . 46 B3
Westminster SW1 . . **146 C3**
Belgrave Sq SW1 . **131 B2**
Belgrave St E1 . . . . 32 C3
Belgrave Yd SW1 . **132 A1**
BELGRAVIA **146 A4**
Belgravia Ct SW1 . **132 A1**
Belgravia Ho **11**
SW4 . . . . 61 C1
Belgrove St WC1 . . **94 B4**
Belham Wlk **13**
SE5 . . . . 48 C2
Belinda Rd **8**
SW9 . . . . 63 A4
Belitha Villas N1 . . 14 C1
Bellamy Cl
12 Millwall E14 . . . 41 C4
West Kensington
SW5 . . . . **141 A1**
Bellamy's Ct **16**
SE16 . . . . 32 C1
Bellamy St SW12 . . 73 A4
Bellasis Ave SW2 . . 74 A2
Bell Ct SW13 . . . . . 56 C2
Bell Dr SW18 . . . . . 70 A4
Bellefields Rd
SW9 . . . . 62 B4
Bellenden Prim Sch
SE15 . . . . 49 C1
Bellenden Rd
SE15 . . . . 49 B1
Bellenden Rd Ret Pk
SE15 . . . . 49 C2
Bellenden Road Bsns
Ctr SE15 . . . . 49 B1
Bellerbys Coll SE8 . 51 C4
Belleville Prim Sch
SW11 . . . . 60 B2
Belleville Rd
SW11 . . . . 60 B2
Belle Vue Gdns
SW9 . . . . **172 B1**
Bellevue Pl E1 . . . . 25 B1
Bellevue Rd
Barnes SW13 . . . . . . 46 C1
Upper Tooting
SW17 . . . . 72 B3
Bellew St SW17 . . . 71 B1
Bell Flats **4** NW2 . 8 C2
Bellflower Ct
SE13 . . . . 67 A3
Bellgate Mews
NW5 . . . . 4 A1
Bellgrave Lo **9**
W4 . . . . 37 A1
Bell Ho
Greenwich SE10 . . . 52 B4
5 Streatham SW2 . 74 C4
Bellina Mews
NW5 . . . . 13 B4
Bell Ind Est **2** W4 . 37 B2
Bell Inn Yd EC3 . . **109 C1**
Bell La
Newham E16 . . . . . . 35 C1
Spitalfields E1 . . . . **110 C3**
Bell Language Sch
W1 . . . . **92 C1**
Bellmaker Ct **13**
E3 . . . . 33 C4
Bell Moor NW3 . . . . 2 B1
Belio Ct SE24, SW2 . 75 A3
Bellot Gdns **1**
SE10 . . . . 43 A1
Bellot St SE10 . . . . 43 A1

Bell Wharf La
EC4 . . . . **123 A4**
Bellwood Rd SE15 . 65 C3
Bell Yard Mews
SE1 . . . . **138 B3**
Bell Yd WC2 . . . . . **107 B1**
Belmont Cl SW4 . . 61 B4
Belmont Ct
1 Highbury N5 . . . 15 B4
6 Stamford Hill N16 . 7 A3
Belmont Gr
Chiswick W4 . . . . . 37 C2
Lewisham SE13 . . . 67 C4
Belmont Hall Ct
SE13 . . . . 67 C4
Belmont Hill SE13 . 67 C4
Belmont Mews
SW19 . . . . 69 C2
Belmont Prim Sch
W4 . . . . 37 C2
Belmont Rd
Clapham SW4 . . . . . 61 B4
London W4 . . . . 37 C2
Belmont St NW1 . . 12 C1
Belmont Terr W4 . . 37 C2
Belmore Ho N7 . . . 13 C3
Belmore La N7 . . . . 13 C3
Belmore St SW8 . . **171 B4**
Beloe Cl SW15 . . . . 56 C3
Belper Ct **11** E5 . . 17 C4
Belsham St E9 . . . . 17 B2
Belsize Ave NW3 . . 12 A3
Belsize Court Garages
1 NW3 . . . . 11 C3
Belsize Cres NW3 . 11 C3
Belsize Ct NW3 . . . 11 C3
Belsize Gr NW3 . . . 12 A2
Belsize La NW3 . . . 11 C3
Belsize Mews
NW3 . . . . 11 C3
Belsize Park Gdns
NW3 . . . . 12 A2
Belsize Park Mews **1**
NW3 . . . . 11 C3
Belsize Park Sta
NW3 . . . . 12 A3
Belsize Pk NW3 . . . 11 C3
Belsize Pl NW3 . . . 11 C3
Belsize Rd NW6 . . . **78 B4**
Belsize Sq NW3 . . . 11 C2
Belsize Terr NW3 . . 11 C2
Beltane Dr SW19 . . 69 C1
Belthorn Cres
SW12 . . . . 73 B4
Belton Rd NW2 . . . 8 C2
Belton Way E3 . . . . 33 C4
Beltran Rd SW6 . . **166 A1**
Belvedere Bldgs
SE1 . . . . **136 B3**
Belvedere Ct
Brondesbury NW2 . . 9 C2
7 Clapham Pk
SW4 . . . . 61 C1
Putney SW15 . . . . . 57 B3
53 Shoreditch N1 . 24 A4
Belvedere Hts
NW8 . . . . **90 A2**
Belvedere Mews
SE15 . . . . 65 B4
Belvedere Pl
Brixton SW2 . . . . . . 62 B3
Lambeth SE1 . . . . **136 B3**
Belvedere Rd SE1 . **121 A1**
Belvedere The
SW10 . . . . **167 A3**

Belvoir Lo SE22 ....76 C4
Belvoir Rd SE22 ....76 C4
Bembridge Cl
NW6 ....10 A1
Bembridge Ho
🟡 Deptford SE8 ....41 B2
Wandsworth SW18 ....59 A1
Bemerton St N1 ....84 C4
Bemish Rd SW15 ....57 C4
Benabo Ct 🟨 E8 ....16 C3
Benbow Ct W6 ....39 A3
Benbow Ho 🟨

SE8 ....51 C4
Benbow Rd W6 ....39 A3
Benbow St SE8 ....51 C4
Bence Ho 🟩 SE8 ....41 A2
Bendall Mews
NW1 ....102 B4
Bendemeer Rd
SW15 ....57 C4
Benden Ho SE13 ....67 B2
Bendon Valley
SW18 ....71 A4
Benedict Rd SW9 ....62 B4
Benenden Ho
SE17 ....152 B2
Ben Ezra Ct SE17 ....151 A3
Benfleet Ct 🟨 E8 ....24 B4
Bengal Ct EC3 ....109 C1
Bengal Ho E1 ....32 C4
Bengeworth Rd
SE5 ....63 B4
Benham Cl 🟨

SW11 ....59 C4
Benham Ho SW10 ....156 B2
Benham's Pl 🟨

NW3 ....11 B4
Benhill Rd SE5 ....48 C2
Benington Ct N4 ....6 B2
Benjamin Cl E8 ....24 C4
Benjamin Ho 🟨

W3 ....28 A1
Benjamin Mews
SW12 ....73 B4
Benjamin St EC1 ....108 A4
Ben Jonson Ct 🟥

N1 ....24 A3
Ben Jonson Prim Sch
E1 ....26 A1
Ben Jonson Rd E1 ....33 A4
Benledi Rd E14 ....34 C3
Bennelong Cl
W12 ....30 A3
Bennerley Rd
SW11 ....60 B2
Bennet's Hill EC4 ....122 B4
Bennett Ct
Hampstead NW6 ....11 A2
Lower Holloway N7 ....5 B1
🟥 Tufnell Pk N19 ....4 C4
Bennett Gr SE13 ....52 A2
Bennett Ho
🟨 Streatham

SW4 ....73 C4
Westminster SW1 ....147 C4
Bennett St
Chiswick W4 ....38 A1
St James SW1 ....118 C2
Bennett's Yd SW1 ....133 C1
Benn Ho E2 ....24 C2 99 B3
Benn St E9 ....18 A2
Benns Wlk 🟨

TW9 ....54 A3
Bensbury Cl SW15 ....69 B4

Ben Smith Way
SE16 ....139 C2
Benson Ct
South Lambeth
SW8 ....172 A4
🟥 Tufnell Pk N19 ....13 B4
Benson Ho
Lambeth SE1 ....121 C1
🟨 Shoreditch
E2 ....24 B1 98 C2
Benson Quay E1 ....32 B2
Benthal Ct N16 ....7 C1
Benthal Prim Sch
N16 ....7 C1
Benthal Rd N16 ....7 C1
Bentham Ct 🟥 N1 ....15 B1
Bentham Ho SE1 ....137 B2
Bentham Rd E9 ....17 C2
Bentinck Cl NW8 ....80 B1
Bentinck Ho 🟨

W12 ....30 A2
Bentinck Mans
W1 ....103 C2
Bentinck Mews
W1 ....103 C2
Bentinck St W1 ....103 C2
Bentley Cl SW19 ....70 C1
Bentley Ct SE13 ....67 B3
Bentley Ho
🟥 Bow E3 ....26 C1
🟩 Camberwell SE5 ....49 A2
Bentley Rd N1 ....16 A2
Bentworth Ct
E2 ....24 C1 99 B2
Bentworth Prim Sch
W12 ....30 A3
Bentworth Rd
W12 ....30 A3
Benwell Rd N7 ....14 C3
Benwick Cl SE16 ....40 A2
Benworth St E3 ....26 B2
Benyon Ho EC1 ....95 C4
Benyon Rd N1 ....87 C4
Benyon Wharf 🟥

E8 ....24 A4
Beormund Prim Sch
SE1 ....137 C3
Bequerel Ct SE10 ....43 B3
Berberis Ho 🟥 E3 ....33 C4
Berber Pl 🟨 E14 ....33 C2
Berber Rd SW11 ....60 B2
Berebinder Ho 🟥

E3 ....26 B3
Berenger Twr
SW10 ....157 B2
Berenger Wlk
SW10 ....157 B2
Berens Rd NW10 ....22 C2
Beresford Ct E9 ....18 A3
Beresford Ho
Dulwich SE21 ....76 A1
🟥 Stockwell SW4 ....62 A3
Beresford Lo N4 ....15 C3
Beresford Rd N5 ....15 C3
Beresford Terr 🟥

N5 ....15 B3
Bere St E1 ....32 C2
Berestede Rd 🟨

W6 ....38 B1
Bergen Ho SE5 ....48 B1
Bergen Sq SE16 ....41 A3
Berger Prim Sch
E9 ....17 C2
Berger Rd E9 ....17 C2
Berghem Mews
W14 ....39 C3
Bergholt Cres N16 ....7 A4

Bergholt Mews
NW1 ....13 C1
Berglen Ct E14 ....33 A2
Bering Sq E14 ....41 C1
Berisford Mews
SW18 ....59 B1
Berkeley Ct
🟥 Golders Green
NW11 ....1 B4
Marylebone NW1 ....91 A1
Willesden NW10 ....8 A4
Berkeley Gdns
W8 ....31 C1 113 C1
Berkeley Ho
🟥 Bow E3 ....26 C2
🟨 Deptford SE8 ....41 B1
Berkeley Mews
W1 ....103 A1
Berkeley Rd SW13 ....46 C2
Berkeley Sq W1 ....118 B3
Berkeley St W1 ....118 B3
Berkeley The NW11 ....2 A4
Berkley Gr NW1 ....12 C1
Berkley Rd NW1 ....12 B1
Berkshire Ho
WC2 ....106 A2
Berkshire Rd E9 ....18 B2
Bermans Way
NW10 ....8 B4
BERMONDSEY 40 A4
Bermondsey Leather
Mkt SE1 ....138 A3
Bermondsey Mkt* ....
SE1 ....138 B2
Bermondsey Sq
SE1 ....138 B2
Bermondsey St
SE1 ....138 A3
Bermondsey Trad Est
SE16 ....40 B1
Bermondsey Wall E
SE16 ....40 A4
Bermondsey Wall W
SE1, SE16 ....139 B4
Bernard Angell Ho 🟨

SE10 ....52 C4
Bernard Cassidy St 🟨

E16 ....35 B4
Bernard Ho E1 ....110 C3
Bernard Shaw Ct 🟥

NW1 ....13 B1
Bernard Shaw Ho 🟨

NW10 ....20 C4
Bernard St WC1 ....94 B1
Bernay's Gr SW9 ....62 B3
Berners Ho N1 ....85 B2
Berners Mews
W1 ....105 A3
Berners Pl W1 ....105 A2
Berners Rd N1 ....86 A3
Berners St W1 ....105 A2
Berner Terr 🟥 E1 ....111 C1
Bernhard Baron Ho 🟨

E1 ....111 C1
Bernhardt Cres
NW8 ....90 A2
Bernie Grant Ho 🟥

E9 ....17 B1
Berridge Mews
NW6 ....10 C3
Berriman Rd N7 ....5 B1
Berry Cotts 🟨

E14 ....33 A3

Berryfield Rd
SE17 ....150 B2
Berry Ho
Battersea SW11 ....169 A2
🟨 Bethnal Green
E1 ....25 A1
Berrymead Gdns
W3 ....37 B4
Berrymede Inf Sch
W3 ....37 B4
Berrymede Jun Sch
W3 ....37 B4
Berrymede Rd W4 ....37 C3
Berry Pl EC1 ....96 B3
Berry St EC1 ....96 B1
Berry Way W5 ....36 A3
Bertha Neubergh Ho 🟨

SE5 ....48 B2
Berthon St SE8 ....51 C4
Bertie Rd NW10 ....8 C2
Bertram St N19 ....4 A2
Bertrand Ho 🟥

SW16 ....74 A1
Bertrand St SE13 ....67 A4
Bertrum House Sch
SW17 ....72 C2
Berwick St W1 ....105 A1
Berwyn Ho 🟥 N16 ....7 B3
Berwyn Rd
Mortlake SW14,
TW10 ....55 A3
Streatham SE24 ....75 A3
Beryl Rd W6 ....39 C1
Besant Ct NW2 ....1 A1
Besant Ho NW8 ....78 C3
Besant Pl SE22 ....64 B3
Besant Rd NW2 ....10 A4
Besant Wlk N7 ....5 B2
Besford Ho 🟨 E2 ....24 C3
Bessant Dr TW9 ....45 A2
Bessborough Gdns
SW1 ....147 C2
Bessborough Pl
SW1 ....147 C2
Bessborough Rd
SW15 ....68 C3
Bessborough St
SW1 ....147 B2
Bessemer Ct 🟨

NW1 ....13 B1
Bessemer Grange
Prim Sch SE5 ....64 A3
Bessemer Park Ind
Est 🟥 SE24 ....63 A3
Bessemer Rd SE5 ....48 B1
Bessingham Wlk
SE4 ....65 C2
Besson St SE14 ....50 C2
Bessy St E2 ....25 B2
Bestwood St SE8 ....40 C2
Beswick Mews 🟥

NW6 ....11 A2
Beta Pl 🟥 SW4 ....62 B3
Betchworth Ho 🟥

N7 ....13 C3
Bethersden Ho
SE17 ....152 B2
Bethlehem Ho 🟥

E14 ....33 B2
Bethnal Green Rd
Bethnal Green
E2 ....24 C2 99 B3
Shoreditch E1,
E2 ....24 B1 99 A2

Bethnal Green Sta
Bethnal Green E1 ....25 A1
Bethnal Green E2 ....25 B2
Bethnal Green Tech
Coll E2 ....24 B2 99 A3
Bethune Rd
North Acton NW10 ....20 C1
Stamford Hill N16 ....7 A4
Bethwin Rd SE5 ....48 B3
Betsham Ho SE1 ....137 B4
Betterton Ho
WC2 ....106 B1
Betterton St WC2 ....106 B1
Bettridge Rd
SW6 ....165 A1
Betts Ho E1 ....32 A2
Betts St E1 ....32 A2
Betty Layward Prim
Sch N16 ....6 C1
Betty May Gray Ho 🟨

E14 ....42 B2
Bevan St N1 ....87 A3
Bev Callender Cl 🟨

SW8 ....61 A4
Bevenden St N1 ....97 C4
Beveridge Rd 🟥

NW10 ....8 A1
Beverley Cl
🟥 Acton Green
W4 ....37 B1
🟥 Barnes SW13 ....46 C1
🟥 Wandsworth
SW11 ....59 C3
Beverley Cotts
SW15 ....68 A3
Beverley Ct
🟥 Acton Green
W4 ....37 B1
🟥 Acton W12 ....38 A4
Brockley SE4 ....66 B4
Islington N5 ....15 A2
Beverley Gdns
Barnes SW13 ....56 B4
Hendon NW11 ....1 A4
Beverley Lo 🟨

TW10 ....54 A2
Beverley Path 🟨

SW13 ....46 B1
Beverley Rd
Barnes SW13 ....56 B4
Chiswick W4 ....38 B1
Beversbrook Rd
N19 ....4 C1
Beverstone Rd
SW2 ....62 B2
Beverston Mews
NW1 ....102 C3
Bevin Cl SE16 ....33 A1
Bevin Ct WC1 ....95 A4
Bevington Prim Sch
W10 ....31 A4
Bevington Rd
W10 ....31 A4
Bevington St
SE16 ....139 C3
Bevin Ho
🟥 Bethnal Green
E2 ....25 B2
🟥 Bow E3 ....26 C2
Bevin Sq SW17 ....72 B1
Bevin Way WC1 ....95 B4
Bevis Marks EC3 ....110 B2
Bew Ct SE21 ....76 C4
Bewdley Ho N4 ....6 B4
Bewdley St N1 ....14 C1
Bewick Mews
SE15 ....50 A3
Bewick St SW8 ....170 B1
Bewley Ct SW2 ....62 B1

Bewley Ho 7 E1 . . . . 32 A2
Bewley St E1 . . . . 32 A2
Bexhill Rd
  Catford SE4 . . . . . . 66 B1
  Mortlake SW14 . . . . 55 B4
Bexley Ho SE4 . . . . . . 66 A3
BFI London Imax
  Cinema E1 . . . . . . 121 B1
Bianca Rd SE1,
  SE15 . . . . 49 C4
Bicester Rd TW9 . . . . 55 A4
Bickenhall Mans
  W1 . . . . 103 A4
Bickenhall St W1 103 A4
Bickerton Rd N19 . . . . 4 B2
Bicknell Ho E1 . . . . . 111 C1
Bicknell Rd SE5 . . . . . 63 B4
Bicknor Ho 2 E9 . . . . 17 C2
Bidborough St N1,
  WC1 . . . . 94 A3
Biddenham Ho 10
  SE16 . . . . 40 C2
Bidder St E16 . . . . . . 35 A4
Biddesden Ho
  SW3 . . . . 144 C3
Biddestone Rd N7 . . 14 B4
Biddulph Mans
  W9 . . . . 88 B3
Biddulph Rd W9 . . . . . 88 B3
Bidwell St SE15 . . . . . 50 A2
Big Ben * SW1 . . . . 134 B3
Biggerstaff Rd
  E15 . . . . 27 B4
Biggerstaff St N4 . . . . 5 C2
Bigg's Row SW15 . . . 57 C4
Bigland Green Prim
  Sch E1 . . . . 32 A3
Bigland St E1 . . . . . . 32 A3
Bilberry Ho 18 E3 . . 33 C4
Billie Holiday Ct
  NW10 . . . . 20 C3
Billingford Cl SE4 . . 65 C3
Billing Ho 7 E1 . . . . 32 C3
Billingley N1 . . . . 82 C3
Billing Pl SW10 . . . . 156 B2
Billing Rd SW10 . . . 156 B2
Billingsgate Mkt
  E14 . . . . 34 A1
Billing St SW10 . . . . 156 B2
Billington Ho
  SW8 . . . . 171 C3
Billington Rd
  SE14 . . . . 50 C3
Billiter Sq EC3 . . . . 110 B1
Billiter St EC3 . . . . . 110 B1
Billson St E14 . . . . . . 42 B2
Bilton Ho 2 SW8 . . . 171 B3
Bilton Twrs W1 . . . . 103 A1
Bina Gdns SW5 . . . . 142 C3
Binbrook Ho 13
  W10 . . . . 22 B1
Binden Rd W12 . . . . . 38 B3
Binfield Ct SE5 . . . . . 48 B1
Binfield Rd SW4 . . . 172 B3
Bingfield St N1 . . . . . 84 C4
Bingham Pl W1 . . . . 103 B4
Bingham St N1 . . . . . 15 C2
Binley Ho SW15 . . . . 56 B1
Binney St W1 . . . . . 103 C1
Binnie Ct SE10 . . . . . 52 A3
Binnie Ho SE1 . . . . 136 C1
Binns Rd W4 . . . . 38 A1
Binns Terr 3 W4 . . . 38 A1
Binstead Ho SW18 . . 58 A3
Binyon Ho 8 N16 . . 16 A4
Birbeck Ho 4 N19 . . 4 C3
Bircham Path SE4 . . 65 C3

Birch Cl
  Newham E16 . . . . . 35 A4
  Peckham SE15 . . . . 49 C1
  Upper Holloway N19 . 4 B1
Birchdown Ho 82
  E3 . . . . 27 A2
Birches The SE5 . . . . 49 A1
Birchfield Ho 8
  E14 . . . . 33 C2
Birchfield St E14 . . . 33 C2
Birchgrove Ho
  TW9 . . . . 45 A3
Birch Ho
  New Cross Gate
  SE14 . . . . 51 B2
  5 Tulse Hill SW2 . . 62 C1
Birchington Ct
  NW6 . . . . 78 A4
Birchington Ho 1
  E5 . . . . 17 A3
Birchington Rd
  NW6 . . . . 23 C4
Birchin La EC3 . . . . 109 C1
Birchlands Ave
  SW12 . . . . 72 B4
Birchmere Lo 19
  SE16 . . . . 40 A1
Birchmere Row
  SE3 . . . . 53 B1
Birchmore Wlk N5 . . . 6 B1
Birch Vale Ct NW8 . . 89 C2
Birchwood Dr NW3 . . 2 A1
Birdcage Wlk
  SW1 . . . . 133 B3
Birdhurst Rd
  SW18 . . . . 59 B2
Bird In Bush Rd
  SE15 . . . . 49 C3
Bird In Hand Yd 22
  NW3 . . . . 11 B4
Birdsall Ho 5 SE5 . . 64 A4
Birdsfield La 12
  E3 . . . . 26 B4
Bird St W1 . . . . 103 C1
Birkbeck Ave W3 . . 28 B2
Birkbeck Coll W1 105 B2
Birkbeck Ct W3 . . . . 37 C4
Birkbeck Hill SE21 . . 75 A3
Birkbeck Mews 5
  E8 . . . . 16 B3
Birkbeck Pl SE21 . . 75 B2
Birkbeck Rd
  Acton W3 . . . . 28 C1
  Dalston E8 . . . . 16 B3
Birkbeck St E2 . . . . 25 A2
Birkdale Cl 30
  SE16 . . . . 40 A1
Birkenhead Ho 11
  N7 . . . . 14 C3
Birkenhead St
  WC1 . . . . 94 A4
Birkwood Cl SW12 . 73 C4
Birley Lo NW8 . . . . . 79 C2
Birley St SW11 . . . . 169 B1
Birnam Rd N4 . . . . 5 B2
Birrell Ho SW9 . . . . 172 C1
Birse Cres NW10 . . . 8 A4
Birtwhistle Ho 8
  E3 . . . . 26 B4
Biscay Ho 11 E1 . . . 25 C1
Biscay Rd W6 . . . . . . 39 C1
Biscoe Way SE13 . . 67 C4
Biscott Ho 3 E3 . . . 27 A1
Bisham Gdns N6 . . . 3 C3

Bishop Challoner
  Collegiate Sch
  E1 . . . . 32 B3
Bishop Ct 20 SW2 . . 62 C1
Bishop Duppa's
  Almshouses 7
  TW10 . . . . 54 A2
Bishop King's Rd
  W14 . . . . 140 B4
Bishop's Ave SW6 . 164 A2
Bishop's Ct N19 . . . . 4 B1
Bishops Ct
  Bayswater W2 . . . 100 B2
  Richmond TW9 . . . . 54 A4
Bishop's Ct
  Holborn EC4 . . . . 108 A2
  Holborn WC2 . . . . 107 B2
Bishopsdale Ho 6
  NW6 . . . . 23 C4
Bishopsgate EC2 . . 110 A2
Bishopsgate Arc
  E1 . . . . 110 B3
Bishopsgate
  Churchyard EC2 . 110 A2
Bishops Ho SW8 . . 162 B1
Bishop's Mans
  SW6 . . . . 47 C1
Bishops Mead SE5 . 48 B3
Bishop's Park Rd
  SW6 . . . . 47 C1
Bishops Rd SW6 . . 164 C4
Bishops Sq E1 . . . . 110 B4
Bishop St N1 . . . . . . 86 C4
Bishop's Terr
  SE11 . . . . 149 C4
Bishopstone Ho
  SW11 . . . . 169 B2
Bishop's Way E2 . . . 25 B3
Bishopswood Rd
  N6 . . . . 3 B4
Bishop Way NW10 . . 8 A1
Bishop Wilfred Wood
  Cl SE15 . . . . 49 C1
Bisseville Ho SE13 . 52 A1
Bisson Rd E15 . . . . . 27 B3
Bittern Ct 7 SE8 . . . 51 C4
Bittern St SE1 . . . . 136 C3
Blackall St
  EC2 . . . . 24 A1 98 A2
Blackburn Ct 21
  SW2 . . . . 62 C1
Blackburne's Mews
  W1 . . . . 117 B3
Blackburn Rd
  NW6 . . . . 11 A2
Blackdown Ho E8 . . 16 C4
Blackett St SW15 . . 57 C4
Blackfriars Bridge
  EC4 . . . . 122 A4
Blackfriars Ct
  EC4 . . . . 122 A4
Blackfriars La
  EC4 . . . . 108 A1
Blackfriars Pas
  EC4 . . . . 122 A4
Blackfriars Pier
  EC4 . . . . 122 A4
Blackfriars Rd
  SE1 . . . . 122 A1
Blackfriars Sta
  EC4 . . . . 122 A4

Blackfriars Underpass
  EC4 . . . . 121 C2
Blackheath * SE3 . . 53 A2
Blackheath Ave
  SE3 . . . . 53 A3
Blackheath Bsns Ctr
  SE10 . . . . 52 B2
Blackheath Gr
  SE3 . . . . 53 B1
Blackheath High Sch
  Blackheath SE3 . . . 53 B1
  Greenwich SE3 . . . 53 C3
Blackheath Hill
  SE10 . . . . 52 B2
Blackheath Prep Sch
  SE3 . . . . 53 C2
Blackheath Rd
  SE10 . . . . 52 A2
Blackheath Rise
  SE13 . . . . 52 B1
BLACKHEATH VALE
  SE3 . . . . 53 B1
Blackheath Vale
  SE3 . . . . 53 A1
Blackheath Village
  SE3 . . . . 53 B1
Black Horse Ct
  SE1 . . . . 137 C2
Blackhorse Rd
  SE8 . . . . 51 A4
Blacklands Terr
  SW3 . . . . 145 A3
Black Lion La W6 . . 38 C2
Black Lion Mews
  W6 . . . . 38 C2
Blackmore Ho
  Islington N1 . . . . . . 85 A3
  2 Wandsworth
  SW18 . . . . 59 A2
Blackmore Twr 1
  W3 . . . . 37 B3
Blackpool Rd
  SE15 . . . . 50 A1
Black Prince Rd SE1,
  SE11 . . . . 149 A3
Black Roof Ho 9
  SE5 . . . . 48 A2
Black's Rd W6 . . . . . 39 B2
Blackstock Ho 2
  N5 . . . . 6 A1
Blackstock Mews
  N4 . . . . 6 A1
Blackstock Rd N4,
  N5 . . . . 6 A2
Blackstone Ho
  Dulwich SE21 . . . . 76 A1
  Pimlico SW1 . . . . 146 C1
Blackstone Rd NW2 . 9 B4
Black Swan Yd
  SE1 . . . . 138 A4
Blackthorn Ct
  20 Camberwell
  SE15 . . . . 49 B3
  4 Leyton E15 . . . . 19 C4
Blackthorn St E3 . . . 26 C1
Blackwall Ho 1
  SW9 . . . . 62 C4
BLACKWALL 34 C2
Blackwall Sta E14 . . 34 B2
Blackwall Trad Est
  E14 . . . . 34 C4
Blackwall Tunnel E14,
  SE10 . . . . 34 C3
Blackwall Tunnel App
  SE10 . . . . 43 A4

Blackwall Tunnel
  Northern Approach
  E14, E3 . . . . 27 B1
Blackwall Way
  E14 . . . . 34 B2
Blackwater St
  SE22 . . . . 64 B2
Blackwell Cl 16
  E5 . . . . 17 C4
Blackwell Ho 3
  SW4 . . . . 61 C1
Blackwood Ho 11
  E1 . . . . 25 A1
Blackwood St
  SE17 . . . . 151 B2
Bladen Ho 4 E1 . . . 32 C3
Blades Ct
  4 Hammersmith
  W6 . . . . 39 A1
  Putney SW15 . . . . 58 B3
Blades Ho SE11 . . . 163 B3
Blades Lo 18 SW2 . . 62 C1
Blagdon Rd SE13 . . 67 A1
Blagrove Rd 1
  W10 . . . . 31 B4
Blair Cl N1 . . . . 15 B2
Blair Ct NW8 . . . . . . 79 B4
Blairderry Rd
  SW2 . . . . 74 A2
Blairgowrie Ct 13
  E14 . . . . 34 C3
Blair Ho SW9 . . . . . 172 C2
Blair St E14 . . . . 34 C3
Blake Coll W1 . . . . 104 C4
Blake Ct
  8 Bermondsey
  SE16 . . . . 40 A1
  Kilburn NW6 . . . . 23 C2
Blake Gdns SW6 . . 166 A4
Blake Ho
  2 Deptford SE8 . . . 51 C4
  Isle of Dogs E14 . . 42 A4
  14 Kentish Town
  N19 . . . . 13 C3
  Lambeth SE1 . . . . 135 B2
  14 Stoke Newington
  N16 . . . . 16 A4
Blake Mews
  TW9 . . . . 44 C2
Blakemore Rd
  SW16 . . . . 74 A1
Blakeney Cl
  14 Camden Town
  NW1 . . . . 13 C1
  4 Dalston E8 . . . . . 16 C3
Blakenham Ct
  W12 . . . . 29 C1
Blaker Rd E15 . . . . . 27 B4
Blakes Cl W10 . . . . . 30 B4
Blake's Rd SE15 . . . 49 A3
Blanca Ho 16 N1 . . 24 A3
Blanchard Way
  E8 . . . . 16 C2
Bland Cl SE15 . . . . . 50 B3
Blanchedowne
  SE5 . . . . 63 C3
Blandfield Rd
  SW12 . . . . 72 C4
Blandford Ct
  Brondesbury Pk
  NW6 . . . . 10 A1

Blandford Ct continued
6 De Beauvoir Town
N1 . . . . 16 A1
Blandford Ho
SW8 . . . . 162 C2
Blandford Rd W4 . . . 38 A3
Blandford Sq NW1 . 90 B1
Blandford St W1 . . . 103 B3
Bland Ho SE11 . . . . . 149 A2
Blantyre St SW10 . 157 B2
Blantyre Twr
SW10 . . . . 157 B2
Blantyre Wlk
SW10 . . . . 157 B2
Blashford NW3 . . . . 12 B1
Blasker Wlk 8
E14 . . . . 42 A1
Blaxland Ho 12
W12 . . . . 30 A2
Blazer Ct NW8 . . . . 89 C3
Blechynden Ho 17
W10 . . . . 30 C3
Blechynden St
W10 . . . . 30 C2
Bleeding Heart Yd
EC1 . . . . 107 C3
Blemundsbury
WC1 . . . . 106 C4
Blendworth Point 4
SW15 . . . . 69 A3
Blenheim 26
SW19 . . . . 69 C3
Blenheim Cres
Notting Hill W11 . . . 31 A3
Notting Hill
W11 . . . 31 A2 112 B4
Blenheim Ct
Barnsbury N7 . . . . . 14 A2
Richmond TW9 . . . . 54 B4
7 Rotherhithe
SE16 . . . . 32 C1
Upper Holloway N19 . 5 A2
Blenheim Gdns
Clapham Pk SW2 . . . 62 B1
Dollis Hill NW2 . . . . 9 B3
Blenheim Gr SE15 . 49 C1
Blenheim Pas
NW8 . . . . 78 C2
Blenheim Rd
Acton W4 . . . . 38 A3
St John's Wood
NW8 . . . . 79 A2
Blenheim St W1 . . 104 A1
Blenheim Terr
NW8 . . . . 78 C2
Blenkarne Rd
SW11 . . . . 60 B1
Blessed Sacrament
RC Prim Sch N1 . . 84 C3
Blessington Cl
SE13 . . . . 67 C4
Blessington Rd
SE13 . . . . 67 C3
Bletchley Ct N1 . . . 87 B1
Bletchley St N1 . . . 87 A1
Bletsoe Wlk N1 . . . 87 A2
Blick Ho 8 SE16 . . . 40 B3
Blincoe Cl SW19 . . 69 C2
Blissett St SE10 . . . 52 B2
Bliss Mews 14
W10 . . . . 23 A2
Blisworth Ho 12
E2 . . . . 24 C4
Blithfield St W8 . . 128 A1

Bloemfontein Ave
W12 . . . . 30 A1
Bloemfontein Rd
W12 . . . . 30 A2
Blomfield Ct
Battersea SW11 . . . 167 C4
Paddington W9 . . . . 89 A2
Blomfield Ho 2
E14 . . . . 34 A2
Blomfield Mans 8
W12 . . . . 30 B1
Blomfield Rd W9 . 100 C4
Blomfield St EC2 . 109 C3
Blomfield Villas
W9 . . . . 100 C4
Blondel St SW11 . 169 B2
Blondin St E3 . . . . . 26 C3
Bloomburg St
SW1 . . . . 147 A3
Bloomfield Ho 6 E1 111 B3
Bloomfield Pl W1 . 118 B4
Bloomfield Terr
SW1 . . . . 145 C2
Bloom Gr SE27 . . . . 75 A1
Bloom Park Rd
SW6 . . . . 154 C1
BLOOMSBURY . . 106 A4
Bloomsbury Ct
WC1 . . . . 106 B3
Bloomsbury Ho 10
SW4 . . . . 61 C1
Bloomsbury Pl
London SW18 . . . . . 59 B2
St Giles WC1 . . . . . 106 B3
Bloomsbury Sq
WC1 . . . . 106 B3
Bloomsbury St
WC1 . . . . 105 C3
Bloomsbury Way
WC1 . . . . 106 B3
Blore Cl SW8 . . . . . 171 B3
Blore Ct W1 . . . . . . 119 B4
Blore Ho SW10 . . . 156 B2
Blossom Cl W5 . . . . 36 A4
Blossom Pl
E1 . . . . 24 A1 98 B1
Blossom St
E1 . . . . 24 A1 98 B1
Blount St E14 . . . . . 33 A3
Blucher Rd SE5 . . . 48 B3
Blue Anchor Alley 4
TW9 . . . . 54 A3
Blue Anchor La
SE16 . . . . 40 A2
Blue Anchor Yd
E1 . . . . 125 B4
Blue Ball Yd SW1 . 118 C1
Bluebell Cl 10 E9 . . 25 B4
Blue Gate Fields Jun
& Inf Schs E1 . . . . 32 B2
Bluegate Mews
E1 . . . . 32 A2
Blue Lion Pl SE1 . . 138 A2
Blueprint Apartments
15 SW12 . . . . 73 A4
Blundell Cl E8 . . . . 16 C4
Blundell St N7 . . . . 14 A2
Blurton Rd E5 . . . . . 17 C4
Blyth Cl 4 E14 . . . . 42 C2
Blythe Ho SE11 . . . 163 C4
Blythe Mews 2
W14 . . . . 39 C3
Blythendale Ho 34
E9 . . . . 24 C3
Blythe Rd W14 . . . 126 A1
Blythe St E2 . . . . . . 25 A2
Blyth's Wharf E14 . 33 A2

Blythwood Rd N4 . . 5 A4
Bnois Jerusalem Sch
N16 . . . . 6 C4
Boades Mews 3
NW3 . . . . 11 C4
Boadicea St N1 . . . 84 C3
Boardwalk Pl E14 . 34 B1
Boarley Ho SE17 . . 152 A3
Boathouse Ctr The
W10 . . . . 22 C1
Boathouse Wlk 24
SE15 . . . . 49 B3
Boat Lifter Way 16
SE16 . . . . 41 A2
Bobbin Cl SW4 . . . 61 B4
Bob Marley Way 11
SE24 . . . . 62 C3
Bocking St E8 . . . . . 25 A4
Boddicott Cl
SW19 . . . . 70 A2
Boddington Gdns
W3 . . . . 36 C4
Boddington Ho 2
SE14 . . . . 50 B2
Bodeney Ho 10
SE5 . . . . 49 A2
Boden Ho 1 E1 . . . 111 B4
Bodington Ct 2
W12 . . . . 39 C4
Bodley Manor Way
SE24 . . . . 74 C4
Bodmin St SW18 . . 70 C3
Bodney Rd E5, E8 . 17 B3
Bogart Ct 13 E14 . . 33 C2
Bohemia Pl 1 E8 . . 17 A2
Bohn Rd E1 . . . . 33 A4
Boileau Rd SW13 . . 47 A4
Boilerhouse SE1 . . 124 C1
Boisseau Ho 11
E1 . . . . 32 B4
Bolden St SE8 . . . . 52 A1
Boldero Pl NW8 . . . 90 A1
Boleyn Rd N16 . . . . 16 A3
Bolina Rd SE16 . . . 40 B1
Bolingbroke Gr
SW11 . . . . 60 B1
Bolingbroke Hospl
The SW11 . . . . 60 A2
Bolingbroke Rd
W14 . . . . 39 C3
Bolingbroke Wlk
SW11 . . . . 168 A4
Bollo Bridge Rd
W3 . . . . 37 B4
Bollo Ct 2 W3 . . . . 37 B3
Bollo La W3 . . . . . . 37 A3
Bolney Gate SW7 . 130 A3
Bolney St SW8 . . . 162 C1
Bolsover St W1 . . . . 92 B1
Bolt Ct EC4 . . . . . . 107 C1
Bolton Cres SE5 . . 48 A3
Bolton Gdns
Kensal Rise NW10 . . 22 C3
South Kensington
SW5 . . . . 142 B2
Bolton Gdns Mews
SW10 . . . . 142 C2
Bolton Ho 3 SE10 . 43 A1
Bolton Pl SW5 . . . . 142 C2
Bolton Rd
Chiswick W4 . . . . . . 45 B3
Harlesden NW10 . . . 21 A4
Kilburn NW8 . . . . . . 78 B3
Boltons Ct SW5 . . . 142 B2
Bolton St W1 . . . . . 118 B2

Boltons The
SW10 . . . . 142 C2
Bolton Studios
SW10 . . . . 143 A1
Bolton Wlk N7 . . . . 5 B2
Bombay Ct 8
SE16 . . . . 40 B4
Bombay St SE16 . . 40 A2
Bomore Rd
W11 . . . . . 31 A2 112 A4
Bonar Rd SE15 . . . . 49 C3
Bonchurch Rd
W10 . . . . 31 A4
Bond Ct EC4 . . . . . 109 B1
Bond Ho 4 NW6 . . . 23 B3
Bonding Yard Wlk
SE16 . . . . 41 A3
Bond St W4 . . . . . . 37 C2
Bond Street Sta
W1 . . . . 103 C1
Bonfield Rd SW8 . . 162 B4
Bonfield Rd SE13 . . 67 B3
Bonham Ho
W11 . . . . . 31 B1 112 C2
Bonham Rd SW2 . . 62 B2
Bonheur Rd W4 . . . 37 C4
Bonhill St EC2 . . . . 97 C1
Bonington Ho N1 . . 84 C1
Bonita Mews SE15 . 65 C4
Bonner Ho 3
SW15 . . . . 56 C2
Bonner Prim Sch
E2 . . . . 25 B2
Bonner Rd E2 . . . . . 25 B3
Bonner St E2 . . . . . 25 B3
Bonneville Gdns
SW4 . . . . 61 B1
Bonneville Prim Sch
SW4 . . . . 61 B1
Bonnington Sq
SW8 . . . . 162 C4
Bonny St NW1 . . . . 13 B1
Bonsor Ho SW8 . . . 171 A4
Bonsor St SE5 . . . . 49 A3
Bonthron Ho
SW15 . . . . 47 B1
Booker Cl 11 E3 . . . 33 B4
Boord St SE10 . . . . 43 A3
Boothby Rd N19 . . . 4 C2
Booth Cl 10 E9 . . . . 25 A4
Booth Ho 2 SW2 . . 74 C4
Booth La EC4 . . . . . 122 C4
Booth's Pl W1 . . . . 105 A3
Boot St N1 . . . . 24 A2 98 A3
Bordon Wlk 5
SW15 . . . . 68 C4
Boreas Wlk N1 . . . . 86 B1
Boreham Ave E16 . 35 C3
Boreman Ho 11
SE10 . . . . 52 B4
Borland Rd SE15 . . 65 B3
Borneo St SW15 . . 57 B4
Borough High St
SE1 . . . . 123 B2
Borough Mkt* 123 B1
Borough Rd SE1 . . 136 B2
Borough Sq SE1 . . 136 C3
Borough Sta SE1 . . 137 A3
BOROUGH THE . . 136 C4
Borrett Cl SE17 . . . 150 C1
Borrodaile Rd
SW18 . . . . 59 A1
Borrowdale NW1 . . 92 C3
Borthwick St SE8 . . 41 C1
Boscastle Rd NW5 . 4 A1

Boscobel Ho 4
E8 . . . . 17 A2
Boscobel Pl SW1 . 145 C4
Boscobel St NW8 . . 89 C1
Boscombe Cl E5 . . 18 A3
Boscombe Rd
W12 . . . . 38 C4
Boss Ho SE1 . . . . . 138 C4
Boss St SE1 . . . . . . 138 C4
Boston Gdns W4 . . 46 A4
Boston Ho
24 Camberwell
SE5 . . . . 48 B1
Earl's Ct SW5 . . . . 142 B3
Lisson Gr NW1 . . . . 90 C2
Boston Pl NW1 . . . . 90 C1
Bosun Cl 22 E14 . . 41 C4
Boswell Ct
Bloomsbury WC1 . . 106 B4
9 Hammersmith
W14 . . . . 39 C3
Boswell Ho WC1 . . 106 B4
Boswell St WC1 . . 106 B4
Bosworth Ho 4
W10 . . . . 23 A1
Bosworth Rd W10 . 23 A1
Bothwell Cl E16 . . . 35 B4
Bothwell St 6
W6 . . . . 47 C4
Botolph Alley
EC3 . . . . 124 A4
Botolph La EC3 . . . 124 A4
Bott's Mews W2 . . . 31 C3
Boughton Ho SE1 . 137 B4
Boulcott St E1 . . . . 32 C3
Boulevard The
Chelsea SW6 . . . . . 167 A3
4 Upper Tooting
SW17 . . . . 72 C2
Boulogne Ho SE1 . 138 C2
Boulter Ho 4
SE14 . . . . 50 B2
Boulton Ho TW8 . . 36 A1
Boundaries Mans 3
SW12 . . . . 72 C3
Boundaries Rd
SW12 . . . . 72 C3
Boundary Ho
Balham SW12 . . . . . 73 A3
1 Camberwell SE5 . 48 B3
18 Notting Hill W11 . 30 C1
Boundary La SE17 . 48 B4
Boundary Pas
E2 . . . . 24 B1 98 C2
Boundary Rd NW8 . 79 A4
Boundary Road Est
NW8 . . . . 78 C3
Boundary Row
SE1 . . . . 136 A4
Boundary St
E2 . . . . 24 B1 98 C2
Bourchier St W1 . . 119 B4
Bourdon Pl W1 . . . 118 B4
Bourdon St W1 . . . 118 B3
Bourke Cl
London SW4 . . . . . . 62 A1
Willesden NW10 . . . . 8 A2
Bourlet Cl W1 . . . . 104 C3
Bourne Ct W4 . . . . 45 B4
Bourne Ho 5
SW4 . . . . 61 B3
Bourne Mews
W1 . . . . 103 C1
Bournemouth Cl
SE15 . . . . 49 C1
Bournemouth Rd
SE15 . . . . 49 C1

Bourne Pl W4 ....37 C1
Bourne St SW1...145 B3
Bourne Terr W2 ....100 B4
Bousfield Prim Sch
  SW10 ....142 C2
Bousfield Rd SE14 ..50 C1
Boutcher CE Prim Sch
  SE1 ....152 C4
Boutflower Rd
  SW11 ....60 A3
Bouverie Mews
  N16...................7 A2
Bouverie Pl W2 ...101 C2
Bouverie Rd N16......7 A3
Bouverie St EC4 ...107 C1
Bovingdon Cl 4
  N19....................4 B2
Bovingdon Rd
  SW6 ....166 B3
BOW 26 B3
Bowater Cl SW2 ....62 A1
Bowater Ho EC1 ....97 A1
Bow Brook The 20
  E2 ....25 C3
Bow Church Sta
  ....26 C2
E3 ....26 C2
BOW COMMON 34 A4
Bow Common La
  E3 ....26 B1
  E3 ....26 B1
Bowden Ho 22 8 ..27 A2
Bowden St SE11 ..149 C1
Bowditch SE8 ....41 B1
Bowen Ct 2 N5 ....15 A4
Bowen Dr SE21.......76 A1
Bowen St E14 ....34 A3
Bower Ave SE3 ......53 A3
Bowerdean St
  SW6 ....166 A2
Bowerman Ave
  SE14.................51 A4
Bowerman Ho 1
  N19....................4 C2
Bower St E1 ....32 C3
Bowes-Lyon Hall 13
  E16 ....35 C1
Bowes Rd W3 ....29 A2
Bowfell Rd W6 ......47 B4
Bowhill Cl SW9 ....163 C2
Bow Ho 3 E3 ....26 C2
Bowie Cl SW4 ....73 C4
Bow Ind Pk E15 ....18 C1
Bow La EC2, EC4 ..109 A1
Bowland Ho N4 ......6 B4
Bowland Rd SW4 ...61 C3
Bowland Yd SW1 ..131 A3
Bowl Ct EC2 ....24 A1 98 B1
Bowles Rd 1 SE1 ..49 C4
Bowley Ho SE16 ..139 B2
Bowling Green Cl
  SW19..................69 A4
Bowling Green Ho
  SW10 ....157 B2
Bowling Green La
  EC1 ....95 C2
Bowling Green Pl
  SE1 ....137 B4
Bowling Green St
  SE11 ....163 B4
Bowling Green Wlk
  N1 ....24 A2 98 A4
Bowman Ave E16...35 B2
Bowman Mews
  St George in East
    E1 ....125 A4
  Wandsworth SW18 ..70 B3

Bowman's Mews
  N7 ....5 A1
Bowman's Pl N7 ......5 A1
Bowmore Wlk
  NW1 ....13 C1
Bowness Cl 6 E8 ..16 B2
Bowness Ho SE15 ..50 B3
Bowood Rd SW11 ..60 C2
Bow Rd E3 ....26 C2
Bow Road Sta 26 C2
Bowry Ho 14 E14 ...33 B4
Bow Sch E3 ....26 C2
Bowsprit Point 1
  E14 ....41 C4
Bow St WC2 ....106 B1
Bowstead Ct
  SW11 ....167 C3
Bow Triangle Bsns Ctr
  17 E3 ....26 C2
Bowyer Ho
  27 Shoreditch N1......24 A4
  9 Shepherd's Bush
    W11 ....30 C1
Bowyer Pl SE5 ....48 B3
Bowyer St 15 SE5 ..48 B3
Boxall Rd SE21 ....64 A1
Boxley Ho 8 E5 ....17 A3
Boxmoor Ho
  16 Hackney E2 ...24 C4
  9 Shepherd's Bush
    W11 ....30 C1
Box Tree Ho SE8 ....41 B2
Boxworth Gr N1 ....85 A4
Boyce Ho 1 W10 ..23 A2
Boyd Ct SW15 ....57 B1
Boydell Ct NW8 ....11 C1
Boyd St E1 ....111 C1
Boyfield St SE1 ....136 B3
Boyle St W1...........118 C4
Boyne Rd SE13 ......67 C4
Boyne Terr Mews
  W11 ....31 B1 112 C2
Boyson Rd 10
  SE17.................48 C4
Boyton Cl E1 ....25 C1
Boyton Ho
  Kennington SE11 ..149 B1
  St John's Wood
    NW8 ....79 C2
Brabant Ct EC3 ....124 A4
Brabazon St E14 ...34 A3
Brabner Ho
  E2 ....24 C2 99 B4
Braburn Gr SE15 ..50 B3
Bracer Ho 1 N1 ....24 A3
Bracewell Rd W10 ..30 B4
Bracey Mews 1
  N4 ....5 A2
Bracey St N4 ....5 A2
Bracken Ave
  SW12 ....72 C4
Brackenbury N4 ......5 B3
Brackenbury Gdns
  W6 ....39 A3
Brackenbury Prim
  Sch W6 ....39 A3
Brackenbury Rd
  W6 ....39 A3
Bracken Gdns
  SW13 ....46 C1
Bracken Ho 15 E3 ..33 C4
Brackley Ave SE15 ..65 B4
Brackley Ct NW8 ...89 C2
Brackley Rd W4 .....38 A1
Brackley St EC1 ...109 A4
Brackley Terr 6
  W4 ....38 A1

Bracklyn Ct N1......87 B2
Bracklyn St N1......87 B2
Bracknell Gate
  NW3 ....11 A3
Bracknell Gdns
  NW3 ....11 A4
Bracknell Way
  NW3 ....11 A4
Bradbeer Ho 24
  E2 ....25 B2
Bradbourne St
  SW6 ....165 C2
Bradbury Ct 2
  SE3 ....53 C3
Bradbury Ho 4 E1 ..111 A2
Bradbury St 28
  N16...................16 A3
Bradby Ho NW8 ....78 B3
Braddon Rd TW9 ...54 B4
Braddyll St SE10 ...43 A1
Bradenham 1
  SE17.................48 C4
Bradenham Cl
  SE17.................48 C4
Braden St 7 W9 ....88 A1
Bradfield Ct 14
  NW1 ....13 A1
Bradfield Ho
  SW8 ....171 B2
Bradford Ho 4
  W14 ....39 C3
Bradford Rd W3 ....38 A4
Bradgate Rd SE6 ...67 A1
Brading Rd SW2....74 B4
Brading Terr W12 ..38 C3
Bradiston Rd W9 ...23 B2
Bradley Cl N7 ....14 B2
Bradley Ho
  Bermondsey SE16 ...40 A2
  1 Bromley E3 ......27 A2
Bradley Mews
  SW12 ....72 B3
Bradley's Cl N1 ......85 C2
Bradlord Ho SE21 ..76 A1
Bradmead SE8 .....160 C1
Bradmore Park Rd
  W6 ....39 A2
Brad St SE1 ....121 C1
Bradstock Ho E9 ...18 A1
Bradstock Rd E9 ...17 C2
Bradwell Ho NW6 ...78 A3
Brady Ho
  London SW4 ....61 C2
  South Lambeth
    SW8 ....171 A4
Brady St E1 ....25 A1
Braefoot Ct SW15 ..57 C2
Braemar SW15 ......57 C1
Braemar Ave SW18,
  SW19..................70 C2
Braemar Ho W9 ....88 C3
Braemar Mans
  W8 ....128 B1
Braes St N1 ....15 A1
Braganza St SE17 ..150 A1
Braham Ho SE11 ..149 A1
Braham St E1 ....111 A2
Brahma Kumaris
  World Spiritual Univ
    NW10 ....8 A3
Braid Ave W3 ....29 A3
Braid Ho SE10 ....52 B2
Braidwood St
  SE1 ....124 A1
Brailsford Rd SW2 ..62 C1
Braintree Ho 6
  E1 ....25 B1

Braintree St E2 .....25 B2
Braithwaite Ho
  EC1 ....97 B2
Braithwaite Twr
  W2 ....101 B4
Bramah Gn SW9 ..173 C4
Bramah Mus of Tea &
  Coffee* SE1 .....123 A1
Bramall Ct N7 ....14 B2
Bramber WC1 ....94 A3
Bramber Ct TW8 ...36 A2
Bramber Rd W14 ..154 C4
Brambledown 8
  SW6 ....47 A4
Bramble Gdns
  W12 ....29 B2
Bramble Ho 13 E3 ..33 C4
Brambling Ct 25
  SE8 ....51 B4
Bramcote Gr SE16 ..40 B1
Bramcote Rd
  SW15..................57 A3
Bramerton NW6 .....9 C1
Bramerton St
  SW3 ....158 A4
Bramfield Ct N4 ......6 B2
Bramfield Rd
  SW11 ....60 B2
Bramford Rd
  SW18..................59 B3
Bramham Gdns
  SW5 ....142 B3
Bramham Ho
  SE22..................64 A3
Bramlands Cl
  SW11 ....60 A4
Bramley Cres
  SW8 ....161 C2
Bramley Ct SE13 ...67 C2
Bramley Ho
  8 North Kensington
    W10................30 C3
  Roehampton SW15 ..56 B1
Bramley Rd W10 ...30 C3
Brampton WC1.....106 C3
Bramshaw Rd E9 ..17 C2
Bramshill Gdns
  NW5 ....4 A1
Bramshill Rd
  NW10 ....21 B3
Bramshurst NW8 ..78 B3
Bramston Rd
  Harlesden NW10 ...21 C3
  Wandsworth SW17 ..71 B1
Bramwell Ho
  Borough The SE1 ..137 A1
  Chelsea SW1 ......160 C4
Bramwell Mews
  N1 ....85 A4
Brancaster Ho
  22 Globe Town E1 ...25 C2
  Islington N5 ....15 A3
Brancaster Rd
  SW16 ....74 A1
Branch Hill NW3 ....2 B1
Branch Pl N1 ....87 C4
Branch Rd E14 ......33 A2
Branch St SE15......49 A3
Brand Cl N4 ....6 A3
Brandon La 10 W4 ..37 B1
Brandlehow Rd
  SW15..................58 B3
Brandon Mews
  Barbican EC2 .....109 B4
  Walworth SE17....151 A3
Brandon Rd N7 ......14 A1
Brandon St SE17 ..151 A3

Brandrams Wharf
  SE16 ....40 B4
Brandreth Rd
  SW17 ....73 A2
Brand St SE10 ......52 B3
Brangton Rd
  SE11 ....149 A1
Brangwyn Ct
  W14 ....126 A1
Branksea St SW6 ..154 A1
Branksome Ho
  SW8 ....162 C2
Branksome Rd
  SW2 ....62 A2
Bransby Ct 4 N16...16 A4
Branscombe NW1 ...83 A3
Branscombe St
  SE13 ....67 A4
Bransdale Cl NW6 ..23 C4
Branstone Ct 9
  TW9 ....44 B2
Branstone Rd
  TW9 ....44 B2
Branston Ho N7 ....14 C3
Brantwood Ho 9
  SE5 ....48 B3
Brantwood Rd
  SE24 ....63 B2
Brasenose Dr
  SW13 ....47 B4
Brashley Road Cvn
  Site NW10 ....21 A2
Brassey Ho 1 E14 ..42 A2
Brassey Rd NW6....10 B2
Brassey Sq SW11 ..60 C4
Brassie Ave W3 .....29 A3
Brass Talley Alley 31
  SE16 ....40 C4
Brathay NW1 ....83 A1
Brathway Rd
  SW18..................70 C4
Bratley St
  E1 ....24 C1 99 B1
Bravington Pl W9 ..23 B1
Bravington Rd W9 ..23 B2
Brawne Ho 12
  SE17.................48 A4
Braxfield Rd SE4 ...66 B3
Bray NW3 ....12 A1
Brayard's Rd SE15 ..50 A1
Braybrook St W12 ..29 B3
Brayburne Ave
  SW4 ....171 A1
Bray Cres SE16......40 C4
Braydon Rd N16 .....7 C3
Bray Dr E16 ....35 B2
Brayfield Terr N1 ..14 C1
Brayford Sq 17 E1 ..32 B3
Bray Pl SW3 ....144 C3
Bread St EC2, EC4 ..109 A1
Breakspeare SE21 ..76 B1
Breakspears Mews
  SE4 ....51 C1
Breakspears Rd
  SE4 ....66 C4
Breakwell Ct 18
  W10 ....23 A1
Breamore Cl
  SW15..................68 C3
Breamore Ho 21
  SE15 ....49 C3
Bream's Bldgs
  EC4 ....107 B2
Bream St E3 ....18 C1
Breasley Cl SW15...57 A3

Brechin Pl SW7 . . . **143 A3**

Brecknock Prim Sch
N7 . . . . **13** C2

Brecknock Rd
N19 . . . . **13** C4

Brecon Ho
Stamford Hill N16 . . . . . . **7** B3
Wandsworth SW18 . . . . **70** C4

Brecon Rd W6 . . . . . . **154 B3**
Bredel Ho E14 . . . . **33** C4
Bredgar SE13 . . . . **67** A2
Bredgar Rd N19 . . . . **4** B2

Bredinghurst
SE22 . . . . **76** C4

Bredinghurst Sch
SE15 . . . . **65** C3
Bredin Ho SW10 . . . **156 B2**
Breer St SW6 . . . . **59** C4
Breezer's Ct E1 . . . . . **125** C3
Breezer's Hill E1 . . . **125** C3
Brehon Ho NW1 . . . . . . **82** C3
Bremner Rd SW7 . . . **129 A2**
Brenchley Gdns SE15,
SE22, SE23 . . . . **65** C1
Brenda Rd SW17 . . . . **72** B2
Brendon Ave NW10 . . **8** A4
Brendon Ho W1 . . . . **103 B4**
Brendon St W1 . . . . . **102 B2**
Brenley Ho SE1 . . . . . **137 B4**

Brenmands Cl
N19 . . . . **4** B1

**Brent Adult Comm
Education Service**
Coll NW10 . . . . **20** C4
Brent Ct B W12 . . . . . **38** A3

Brentford Fountain L
Ctr W4 . . . . **36** C1
Brent Ho E9 . . . . **17** B2
Brenthouse Rd E9 . . . **17** B2

Brenthurst Rd
NW10 . . . . **8** B2
Brent Mus★ NW10 . . **9** A2

Brent New Ent Ctr
NW10 . . . . **8** B2
Brenton Ct E9 . . . . **18** A3
Brenton St E14 . . . . . . **33** A3
Brent Rd E16 . . . . **35** C4

Brent Trad Est
NW10 . . . . **8** A3

Brentwick Gdns
TW8 . . . . **36** A2

Brereton Ho 4
SW2 . . . . **74** C4

Bressenden Pl
SW1 . . . . **132 C2**

Breton Ho
Bermondsey SE1 . . . . **138** C2
St Luke's EC2 . . . . **97 A1**
Brett Cl N16 . . . . **7** A2
Brett Cres NW10 . . . . **20** C4
Brettell St SE17 . . . . **151** C1
Brett Ho B SW15 . . . **69** C4

Brett House Cl 2
SW15 . . . . **69** C4
Brettinghurst SE1 **153** B1
Bretton Ho N19 . . . . **5** A3
Brett Pas B8 E8 . . . . . . **17** A3
Brett Rd E8 . . . . **17** A3

Brewers Bldgs
EC1 . . . . **96 A4**
Brewers Ct W2 . . . . . **100** C2
Brewer's Gn SW1 **133 B2**

Brewers Hall Gdns
EC2 . . . . **109 A3**
Brewer St W1 . . . . . . **119 A4**

Brewery Ind Est The
N1 . . . . **87 A1**
Brewery Rd N7 . . . . . . **14** A2

Brewery Sq
Bermondsey SE1 . . . . **124** C1
Clerkenwell EC1 . . . . . . **96 B2**

Brewhouse La
Putney SW15 . . . . **58** A4
Wapping E1 . . . . **32** A1

Brewhouse St
SW16 . . . . **33** A1

Brewhouse Yd
EC1 . . . . **96 A2**

Brewster Gdns
W10 . . . . **30** B4

Brewster Ho
Bermondsey SE1 . . . . **153** A4
Poplar E14 . . . . **33** B2
Briant Ho SE1 . . . . . . **135 A1**
Briant St SE14 . . . . . . **50** C3
Briar Ct 7 Bow E3 . . **26** C3
Dalston E8 . . . . **16** B1
Briardale SW19 . . . . . . **70** B3

Briardale Gdns
NW3 . . . . **1** C1

Briardale Ho 12
N16 . . . . **7** A3
Briar Rd NW2 . . . . **9** B4
Briar Wlk
Putney SW15 . . . . **57** A3
West Kilburn W10 . . . . **23** A1

Briarwood Rd
SW4 . . . . **61** C2
Briary Cl NW3 . . . . **12** A1
Briary Ct 10 E16 . . . . **35** B3

Brickbarn Cl
SW10 . . . . **157 A2**
Brick Ct EC4 . . . . **107 B1**

Brick Farm Cl
TW9 . . . . **45** A2

Brick La
Shoreditch
E2 . . . . **24 B2 99 A4**
Spitalfields
E1 . . . . **24 B1 99 A1**

Bricklayers Arms
SE1 . . . . **137** C1
Brick St W1 . . . . **118 A1**

Brickworth Ho
SW9 . . . . **173 C4**
Brideale Cl SE15 . . . . **49** B4
Bride Ct EC4 . . . . **108 A1**
Bride La EC4 . . . . **108 A1**
Bridel Mews N1 . . . . **86** A3
Bride St N7 . . . . **14** B2

Bridewain St SE1 **138** C2

Bridewell Pl
Holborn EC4 . . . . **108 A1**
28 Wapping E1 . . . . . . **32** A1

Bridford Mews
W1 . . . . **104 A4**
Bridge App NW3 . . . . **12** C1
Bridge Ave W6 . . . . . **39** B1

Bridge Avenue Mans
1 W6 . . . . **39** B1
Bridge Cl 11 W10 . . . **30** C3
Bridge Ct
1 Blackwall E14 . . . **34** C2
9 Willesden NW10 . . **8** A1

Bridge Field Ho
W2 . . . . **100 A2**
Bridgefoot SE1 . . . . **148 B1**
Bridge Gdns N16 . . . . **15** C4
Bridge Ho
Brockley SE4 . . . . **66** B3
1 Camden Town
NW1 . . . . **12** C1

Bridge Ho continued
Homerton E9 . . . . **17** C3

Bridge House Quay
E14 . . . . **34** B1
Bridge La SW11 . . . **168 B3**
Bridgeland Rd
E16 . . . . **35** C2
Bridgeman Ho 19
E9 . . . . **17** B1
Bridgeman Rd N1 . . **14** B1
Bridgeman St
NW8 . . . . **80** A1
Bridge Meadows
SE14 . . . . **50** C4
Bridgend Rd
SW18 . . . . **59** B3
Bridgen Ho 9 E1 . . **32** A3
Bridge Pk 7
SW18 . . . . **58** C2
Bridge Pl NW1 . . . **146 B4**
Bridgeport Pl E1 . . **125** C2
Bridge Rd
Stratford Marsh
E15 . . . . **27** C4
Willesden NW10 . . . . **8** A2
Bridge Sch The
Clerkenwell EC1 . . . . . . **96 A2**
Shoreditch N1 . . . . **87 A4**
Bridges Ct SW11 . . **167 B1**
Bridges Ho 18 SE5 . . **48** C3
Bridge St
Chiswick W4 . . . . **37** C2
Westminster SW1 . . . **134 B3**
Bridge Terr E15 . . . . . **19** C1
Bridgeview 2 W6 . . **39** B1
Bridgewater Rd
E15 . . . . **27** C4
Bridgewater Sq
EC2 . . . . **108** C4
Bridgewater St
EC2 . . . . **108** C4
Bridgeway St NW1 **83 A1**
Bridge Wharf 18
E2 . . . . **25** C3
Bridge Yd SE1 . . . . . **123** C2
Bridgford St SW17,
SW18 . . . . **71** B1
Bridgman Rd W4 . . **37** B3
Bridgnorth Ho 15
SE15 . . . . **49** C4
Bridgwater Ho
W2 . . . . **100** C2
Bridle La W1 . . . . . . **119 A4**
Bridlington Ho
SW18 . . . . **59** B3
Bridport SE17 . . . . . **151 A1**
Bridport Ho N1 . . . . . **87** C3
Bridport Pl N1 . . . . . . **87** C3
Bridstow Pl W2 . . . . **31** C3
Brief St SE5 . . . . **48** A2
Brierfield NW1 . . . . . **82** C3
Brierley Rd
Leyton E11 . . . . **19** C4
Upper Tooting
SW12 . . . . **73** B2
Brierly Gdns E2 . . . . **25** B3
Brigade St SE3 . . . . . . **53** B1
Briggeford Cl 5
E5 . . . . **7** C2
Briggs Ho
E2 . . . . **24 B2 99 A4**
Brightling Rd SE4 . . **66** B1
Brightlingsea Pl 5
E14 . . . . **33** B2
Brightman Rd
SW18 . . . . **71** C3

Brighton Bldgs
SE1 . . . . **138 A1**
Brighton Ct SW15 . . **58** B1
Brighton Gr SE14 . . . **51** A2
Brighton Ho 7
SW9 . . . . **62** B3
Brighton Rd N16 . . . **16** A4
Brighton Terr
SW9 . . . . **62** B3
Brightside Rd
SE13 . . . . **67** C1
Bright St E14 . . . . **34** A4
Brightwell Ct N7 . . . **14** B3
Brightwells Rd SW6 **166 A2**
Brig Mews SE8 . . . . . **51** C4
Brigstock Ho SE5 . . . **48** B1
Brill Pl NW1 . . . . **83** C1
Brimsdown Ho E3 . . **27** B1
Brindley Ho
27 Notting Hill W2 . . **31** C4
22 Streatham
SW12 . . . . **74** A4
Brindley St SE14 . . . . **51** B2
Brine Ho 11 E3 . . . . . **26** A3
Brinklow Ho W2 . . **100** A3
Brinkworth Way
E9 . . . . **18** B2
Brinsley Ho 17 E1 . . **32** B3
Brinsley St 8 E1 . . . **32** A3
Brinton Wlk SE1 . . . **122 A1**
Brion Pl E14 . . . . **34** B4
Brisbane Ho 3
W12 . . . . **30** A2
Brisbane St SE5 . . . . **48** C3
Briset Rd SE1 . . . . **96 A1**
Briset St EC1 . . . . **96 A1**
Briset Way N7 . . . . **5** B2
Bristol Gdns
Putney SW15 . . . . **69** B4
Westbourne Green
W9 . . . . **88 B1**
Bristol Ho SE11 . . . **135 B1**
Bristol Mews W9 . . . **88** B1
Bristowe Cl 24
SW2 . . . . **62** C1

**Britain at War
Experience★**
SE1 . . . . **124 A1**

Britannia Building
N1 . . . . **97 B4**
Britannia Cl SW4 . . . **61** C3
Britannia Gate B
E16 . . . . **35** C1
Britannia Junc
NW1 . . . . **82** B4
Britannia Rd
22 Millwall E14 . . . . **41** C2
Walham Green
SW6 . . . . **156 A1**
Britannia Row N1 . . **86** C4
Britannia St WC1 . . . **94** C4
Britannia Way
NW10 . . . . **20** A1
Britannia Wlk N1 . . . **97** B4
**British Coll of
Osteopathic
Medicine** NW3 . . . . . **11** B2
British Gr W4 . . . . **38** B1
British Grove Pas 2
W4 . . . . **38** B1
British Grove S 3
W4 . . . . **38** B1
British Library The★
WC1 . . . . **93** C4
British Mus★
WC1 . . . . **106 A3**
British St E3 . . . . **26** B2

British Wharf Ind Est
SE14 . . . . **50** C4
Britley Ho 11 E14 . . **33** B3
Brittany Ho SW15 . . **57** B3
Brittany Point
SE11 . . . . **149 B3**
Britten Cl NW11 . . . . . . **2** A3
Britten Ho SW3 . . . **144 B2**
Britten St SW3 . . . . **144 A2**
Britton St EC1 . . . . . . **96 A1**
BRIXTON **62** C4
Brixton Day Coll
SW9 . . . . **62** A4
Brixton Hill SW2 . . . **62** B1
Brixton Hill Ct 5
SW2 . . . . **62** B2
Brixton Hill Pl
SW2 . . . . **74** A4
Brixton Mkt SW9 . . . **62** C3
Brixton Oval 7
SW2 . . . . **62** C3
Brixton Rd SW9 . . . **173 B2**
Brixton Sta SW9 . . . **62** C3
Brixton Station Rd
SW9 . . . . **62** C4
Brixton Water La
SW2 . . . . **62** B2
Broadbent Cl N6 . . . . **4** A3
Broadbent St W1 . . **118 A4**
Broadbridge Cl
SE3 . . . . **53** C3

Broad Common Est
N16 . . . . **7** C3
Broad Ct WC2 . . . . . **106 B1**
Broadfield NW6 . . . . **11** A2

Broadfield La
NW1 . . . . **14** A1
Broadfields Way
NW10 . . . . **8** B3
Broadford Ho 12
E1 . . . . **26** A1
BROADGATE **110 A4**
Broadgate EC2 . . . . **110 A4**
Broadgate Circ
EC2 . . . . **110 A3**
Broadgates Ct
SE11 . . . . **149 C1**
Broadgates Rd
SW18 . . . . **71** C3
Broadhinton Rd
SW4 . . . . **61** B4
Broadhurst Cl
Hampstead NW6 . . . . . **11** B2
9 Richmond TW10 . . **54** B2
Broadhurst Gdns
NW6 . . . . **11** A2
Broadhurst Mans
NW6 . . . . **11** A2
Broad La EC2 . . . . . . **110 A4**
Broadlands N6 . . . . . . **3** C4
Broadlands Ave
SW16 . . . . **74** A2
Broadlands Cl
Highgate N6 . . . . **3** C4
Streatham SW16 . . . . . **74** A2
Broadlands Lo N6 . . . **3** B4
Broadlands Mans 2
SW16 . . . . **74** A2
Broadlands Rd N6 . . . **3** B4
Broadley St NW8 . **102 A4**
Broadley Terr
NW1 . . . . **90 B1**
Broadmayne
SE17 . . . . **151 B2**
Broadmead W14 . . **140 A3**

Broadoak Ct 8
SW9 . . . . .62 C4
Broadoak Ho NW6 . . **78** B3
Broad St Ave EC2 **110** A3
Broad Sanctuary
SW1 . . . . **134** A3
Broadstone Ho
SW8 . . . . **162** C1
Broadstone Pl
W1 . . . . **103** B3
Broad Street Pl
EC2 . . . . **109** C3
Broadwalk Ho
SW7 . . . . **128** C3
Broadwalk La
NW11 . . . . .1 A4
Broadwall SE1 **121** C2
Broadway
Stratford E15 . . . . .19 C1
Westminster SW1 . . **133** B2
Broadway Arc 3
W6 . . . . .39 B2
Broadway Ctr The 8
W6 . . . . .39 B2
Broadway Ho 2
E8 . . . . .25 A4
Broadway Mans
SW6 . . . . **155** C1
Broadway Market
E8 . . . . .25 A4
Broadway Market
Mews E8 . . . . .24 C4
Broadway Mews E5 . .7 B4
Broadway Ret Pk
NW2 . . . . .9 C4
Broadway The
Barnes SW13 . . . . .46 A1
South Acton W3 . . . . . .37 A4
Broadway Wlk 4
E14 . . . . .41 C3
Broadwick St W1 **105** A1
Brnad Wlk
Mayfair W1, SW1 . . **117** B2
Regent's Pk NW1 . . **81** C1
Richmond TW9 . . . . . . .54 A4
Broad Wlk The
W8 . . . . **114** B1
Broadwood Terr
W14 . . . . **141** A4
Broad Yd EC1 . . . . . **96** A1
Brocas Cl NW3 . . . . .12 A1
Brockbridge Ho
SW15 . . . . .56 B1
Brocket Ho SW8 . .**171** B3
Brockham Dr SW2 . .74 B4
Brockham Ho
Camden Town
NW1 . . . . .83 A3
11 Streatham SW2 . .74 B4
Brockham St SE1 **137** A2
Brockhurst Ho N4 . .6 C4
Brockill Cres SE4. . .66 A3
Brocklebank Rd
SW18 . . . . .71 B4
Brocklebank Road Ind
Est SE7 . . . . .43 C2
Brocklehurst St
SE14 . . . . .50 C3
BROCKLEY 66 B3
Brockley Cross
SE4 . . . . .66 B4
Brockley Cross Bssns
Ctr SE4 . . . . .66 A4
Brockley Gdns
SE4 . . . . .51 B1
Brockley Gr SE4. . . .66 B2

Brockley Hall Rd
SE4 . . . . .66 A2
Brockley Mews
SE4 . . . . .66 A2
Brockley Prim Sch
SE4 . . . . .66 B2
Brockley Rd SE4. . . .66 B2
Brockley Way SE4 . .66 A2
Brockmer Ho 5
E1 . . . . .32 A2
Brock Pl E3 . . . . .27 A1
Brock St SE15 . . . . . .65 B4
Brockweir 22 E2 . . . .25 B3
Brockwell Ct 2
SW2 . . . . .62 C2
Brockwell Ho
SE11 . . . . **163** A4
Brockwell Park . . . . . .★
SE24 . . . . .63 A1
Brockwell Park Gdns
SE24 . . . . .75 A4
Brockwell Park Row
SW2 . . . . .62 C1
Broderick Ho
SE21 . . . . .76 A1
Brodia Rd N16 . . . . . . .7 A1
Brodick Ho 12 E3. . .26 B3
Brodie Ho SE1 . . . **153** A2
Brodie St SE1 . . . . **153** A2
Brodlove La E1 . . . . .32 C2
Brodrick Rd SW17. . .72 A2
Brody Ho E1 . . . . . **110** C3
Broken Wharf
EC4 . . . . **122** C4
Brokesley St E3 . . . .26 B2
Broke Wlk
Hackney E8 . . . . .24 B4
11 Hackney E8 . . . . . .24 C4
Bromar Rd SE5 . . . . .64 A4
Bromehead St 8
E1 . . . . .32 B3
Bromell's Rd SW4 . .61 B3
Bromfelde Rd
SW4 . . . . **171** C1
Bromfield Ct
SE16 . . . . **139** C2
Bromfield St N1. . . **85** C2
Bromleigh Ho
SE1 . . . . **138** C2
BROMLEY 27 A2
Bromley-by-Bow Sta
E3 . . . . .98 A4
Bromley Hall Rd
E14 . . . . .34 B4
Bromley High St
E3 . . . . .27 A2
Bromley Lo 2 W3. . .28 B3
Bromley Pl W1 . . . **104** C4
Bromley St E1 . . . . . .32 C3
BROMPTON **130** A1
Brompton Arc
SW1 . . . . **131** A3
Brompton Oratory
SW3 . . . . **130** A1
Brompton Park Cres
SW6 . . . . **156** A3
Brompton Pl
SW3 . . . . **130** B2
Brompton Rd
SW3 . . . . **130** B2
Brompton Sq
SW3 . . . . **130** A2
Bromstone Ho
SW9 . . . . **173** B3
Bromwich Ave N6 . .3 C2

Bromwich Ho 3
TW10 . . . . .54 A1
Bromyard Ave W3 . .29 A2
Bromyard Ho
3 Acton W3 . . . . .29 A1
3 Peckham SE15 . . . .50 A3
Bron Ct NW6 . . . . . .23 C4
BRONDESBURY . . .10 A2
Brondesbury Coll for
Boys NW6 . . . . .10 A1
Brondesbury Ct
NW2 . . . . .9 C2
Brondesbury Mews 4
NW6 . . . . .10 C1
BRONDESBURY
PARK 22 C4
Brondesbury Park Sta
NW6 . . . . .23 A4
Brondesbury Pk
NW2 . . . . .9 C1
Brondesbury Rd
NW6 . . . . .23 B3
Brondesbury Sta
NW6 . . . . .10 B1
Brondesbury Villas
NW6 . . . . .23 C3
Bronsart Rd SW6 **154** A1
Bronte Ho SW4 . .39 C3
Bronte Ho
Kilburn NW6 . . . . . . .23 C2
6 Stoke Newington
N16 . . . . .16 A3
Bronti Cl SE17 . . . **151** A2
Bronwen Ct NW8. . .89 B3
Bronze St SE8 . . . . . .51 C3
Brookbank Rd
SE13 . . . . .67 A4
Brook Cl SW17 . . . . .72 C2
Brook Com Prim Sch
E8 . . . . .16 C3
Brook Ct
Mortlake SW14 . . . . .56 A4
Stratford New Town
E15 . . . . .19 B3
Brookdale Rd SE6 . .67 A1
Brook Dr SE11 . . . **150** A4
Brooke Ct W10 . . . . .23 A3
Brooke Ho 4
SE14 . . . . .51 A2
Brooke Rd E5, N16 . . .7 C1
Brooke's Ct EC1 . **107** B4
Brooke's Mkt EC1 **107** C4
Brooke St EC1 . . . **107** B3
Brookfield
Dartmouth Pk N6 . . . . .3 C1
11 Finsbury Pk N4 . . .5 C2
Brookfield Ho 23
E2 . . . . .25 A3
Brookfield Pk NW5 . .4 A1
Brookfield Prim Sch
N19 . . . . .4 A2
Brookfield Rd
Acton W4 . . . . .37 C4
Homerton E9 . . . . .18 A2
Brookgate N16 . . . . . .6 C2
Brook Gate W1 . . . **117** A3
Brook Gdns SW13 . .56 B4
Brook Gn W6 . . . . . . .39 C2
BROOK GREEN 39 C2
Brook Green Flats 11
W14 . . . . .39 C3
Brook Ho
5 Clapham Pk
SW4 . . . . .61 B2
Ealing W3 . . . . .36 C4
4 Hammersmith
W6 . . . . .39 B2

Brook Ho continued
Marylebone WC1 . . **105** B4
Brook Hos NW1 . . **83** A1
Brooklands Ave
SW18 . . . . .71 A2
Brooklands Court
Apartments 3
NW6 . . . . .10 B1
Brooklands Ct 2
NW6 . . . . .10 B1
Brooklyn Ct W12 . . .30 A1
Brookmarsh Ind Est
SE10 . . . . .52 A3
Brook Mews N
W2 . . . . **115** A4
Brookmill Rd SE8 **51** C2
Brooksbank Ho 7
E9 . . . . .17 B2
Brooksbank St 9
E9 . . . . .17 B2
Brooksby Ho 9
N1 . . . . .14 C1
Brooksby Mews
N1 . . . . .14 C1
Brooksby St N1 . . . .14 C1
Brooksby's Wlk
E9 . . . . .17 C3
Brooks Ct
London SW1 . . . . . **172** A2
Nine Elms SW8 . . . **161** A2
Brooks Ho 6
SW2 . . . . .74 C3
Brookside Rd N19 . . .4 B2
Brooks La W4 . . . . . .44 C4
Brook's Mews
W1 . . . . **118** A4
Brooks Rd W4 . . . . . .36 C1
Brook St
Bayswater W2 . . . . **115** C4
Mayfair W1 . . . . **118** A4
Brookstone Ct
SE15 . . . . .65 A3
Brooksville Ave
NW6 . . . . .23 A4
Brookville Rd
SW6 . . . . **154** C1
Brookwood Ave
SW13 . . . . .46 B1
Brookwood Ho
SE1 . . . . **136** B3
Brookwood Rd
SW18 . . . . .70 C3
Broome Ct 3
TW9 . . . . .44 C2
Broome Ho 7 E5 . . .17 A3
Broome Way SE5 . . .48 C3
Broom Farm SW6 **165** C2
Broomfield 7
NW1 . . . . .12 C1
Broomfield Ho
SE17 . . . . **152** B2
Broomfield House
Sch TW9 . . . . .44 B2
Broomfield St E14 . .34 A4
Broomgrove Rd
SW9 . . . . **173** A1
Broomhill Rd
SW18 . . . . .58 C2
Broomhouse La
SW6 . . . . **165** B2
Broomhouse Rd
SW6 . . . . **165** B2
Broomsleigh St
NW6 . . . . .10 B3

Broomwood Hall Sch
SW12 . . . . .72 C4
Broomwood Rd
SW11 . . . . .60 C2
Brougham Rd
Acton W3 . . . . .28 B3
Hackney E8 . . . . .24 C4
Brougham St
SW11 . . . . **169** A2
Brough Cl SW8 . . **162** B1
Broughton Dr 10
SW9 . . . . .63 A3
Broughton Rd
SW6 . . . . **166** B2
Broughton Road App
SW6 . . . . **166** B2
Broughton St
SW8 . . . . **170** A2
Brouncker Rd W3 . .37 B4
Browne Ho 12 SE8 . .51 C3
Brownfield St E14. . .34 B3
Brownfield Ho
SE4 . . . . .66 A3
Brown Hart Gdns
W1 . . . . **117** C4
Browning Cl W9. . . . **89** A1
Browning Ct W14 **154** C4
Browning Ho
2 London SE14. . . . . .51 A2
7 Shepherd's Bush
W12 . . . . .30 B3
10 Stoke Newington
N16 . . . . .16 A4
Browning Mews
W1 . . . . **103** C3
Browning St SE17 **151** A3
Brownlow Ho
SE16 . . . . **139** B3
Brownlow Mews
WC1 . . . . **95** A1
Brownlow Rd
Hackney E8 . . . . .24 C4
Willesden NW10 . . . . .8 A1
Brownlow St
WC1 . . . . **107** A3
Brown's Bldgs
EC3 . . . . **110** B1
Brown St W1 . . . . **102** C2
Brownswood Rd
N4 . . . . .6 B2
Broxash Rd SW11 . .60 C1
Broxbourne Ho 11
E3 . . . . .27 A1
Broxholme Ho
SW6 . . . . **166** A4
Broxholm Rd SE27,
SW16 . . . . .74 C1
Broxwood Way
NW8 . . . . **80** B3
Bruce Cl W10 . . . . . .30 C4
Bruce Glasier Ho 12
N19 . . . . .4 C4
Bruce Ho
4 Clapham Pk
SW4 . . . . .61 C1
North Kensington
W10 . . . . .30 C4
Putney SW15 . . . . . . .57 A2
Bruce Rd E3 . . . . . . .27 A2
Bruckner St W10 . . .23 B2
Bruges Pl 13 NW1 . .13 B1
Brune Ho E1 . . . . **110** C3
Brunel Ct 5 SW13 .46 B1

Brunel Engine House
Rotherhithe★
SE16.....................40 B4
Brunel St W2 ....31 C4
Brunel Ho
Chelsea SW10 .....**157** C2
4 Gospel Oak
NW5 ....13 A4
Millwall E14 ....42 A1
New Cross SE8.....51 B3
22 Streatham SW2 .74 A4
Brunel Mews
NW10 ....22 C2
Brunel Rd
Acton W3 ....29 A4
Wapping SE16 ....32 B1
Brunel St E16 ......35 B3
Brune St E1 ....**110** C3
Brunlees Ho SE1 .**137** A1
Bruno Ct 5 E8.......16 C2
Brunswick Ct
Bermondsey SE1 ..**138** B4
Finsbury EC1 ....**96** A3
Westminster SW1 .**147** C3
Brunswick Gdns
W8 ....31 C1 **113** C1
Brunswick Ho
4 Haggerston E2...24 B3
Lisson Gr NW1.......**90** C2
Brunswick Mews
W1 ....**103** A2
Brunswick Park Prim
Sch SE5.................48 C3
Brunswick Pk SE5 .49 A2
Brunswick Pl N1 ..**97** C3
Brunswick Quay
SE16 ....40 C3
Brunswick Rd E14 .34 B3
Brunswick Sh Ctr
WC1 ....**94** B2
Brunswick Sq
WC1 ....**94** B2
Brunswick Villas 2
SE5 ....49 A2
Brunton Pl E14.....33 A3
Brushfield St E1 ..**110** C4
Brussels Rd SW11 .59 C3
Bruton La W1 ......**118** B3
Bruton Pl W1 ......**118** B3
Bruton St W1 ......**118** B3
Brutus Ct SE11....**150** A3
Bryan Ave NW10....9 A1
Bryan Ct W1 ......**102** C2
Bryan Ho SE16 .....41 B4
Bryan Rd SE16......41 B4
Bryanston Ct W1 .**102** C2
Bryanston Ho 12
SE15 ....49 B2
Bryanston Mans
W1 ....**102** C4
Bryanston Mews E
W1 ....**102** C3
Bryanston Mews W
W1 ....**102** C2
Bryanston Pl W1 .**102** C3
Bryanston Sq W1 .**102** C2
Bryanston St W1 .**103** A1
Bryant Ct
Acton W3 ....28 C1
Haggerston E2 ....24 B3
Bryantwood Rd N5,
N7 ....14 C3
Bryce Ho 28 SE14...50 C4
Brydale Ho 2
SE16 ....40 C2

Brydges Pl WC2.....**120** A3
Brydges Rd E15......19 C3
Brydon Wlk N1 ....**84** B4
Bryer Ct EC2 ....**108** C4
Bryett Rd N7..........5 A1
Bryher Ho W4 ....37 B1
Brymay Cl E3 ....26 C3
Brymon Ct W1 ......**103** A3
Brynmaer Ho
SW11 ....**169** A3
Brynmaer Rd
SW11 ....**169** A3
Bryony Rd W12......29 C2
BT Telecom Twr★
W1 ....**104** C4
Buccleuch Ho E5......7 C4
Buchanan Ct 16
SE16 ....40 C2
Buchanan Gdns
NW10 ....22 A3
Buchanan Ho
Dulwich SE21.........76 A1
Wandsworth SW18 .70 C4
Buchan Ho W3 ....37 A4
Buchan Rd SE15.....65 B4
Bucharest Rd
SW18 ....71 B4
Buckfast St
E2 ....24 C2 **99** C3
Buck Hill Wlk W2 ..**115** C3
Buckhold Rd
SW18 ....58 C1
Buckhurst Ho 18
N7 ....13 C3
Buckhurst St E1......25 A1
Buckingham Gate
SW1 ....**133** A2
Buckingham Ho
Finsbury Pk N4 ....6 B3
Richmond TW10 .....54 C2
Buckingham Mans
NW6 ....11 A3
Buckingham Mews
Harlesden NW10 ....21 B3
7 Kingsland N1.......16 A2
Westminster SW1 .**132** C2
Buckingham Pal★
SW1 ....**132** C3
Buckingham Palace
Rd SW1 ....**146** B4
Buckingham Pl
SW1 ....**132** C2
Buckingham Rd
Harlesden NW10 ....21 B3
Kingsland N1.........16 A2
Buckingham St
WC2 ....**120** B3
Buckingham Yd
NW10 ....21 B3
Buckland Cres
NW3 ....11 C2
Buckland Ct 6
N1 ....24 A3
Buckland Ho 8
N1 ....14 C1
Buckland St N1 ......**87** C1
Buckland Wlk 2
W3 ....37 B4
Buckler's Alley
SW6 ....**155** A2
Bucklersbury EC2,
EC4 ....**109** B1
Buckle St
Whitechapel E1 ....**111** A2
Whitechapel E1 ....**111** B2
Buckley Ct 5
NW6 ....10 B1

Buckley Ho NW6 ....10 B1
Buckmaster Cl 1
SW9 ....**62** C4
Buckmaster Ho 7
N7 ....14 B4
Buckmaster Rd
SW11 ....60 A3
Bucknall St WC1 ..**106** A2
Bucknell Cl SW2.....62 B3
Buckner Rd SW2.....62 B3
Buckridge Bldg
EC1 ....**107** B4
Buckshead Ho 18
W2 ....31 C4
Buck St NW1 ....13 A1
Buckstone Cl
SE23 ....65 B1
Buckters Rents
SE16 ....33 A1
Buckthorne Rd
SE4 ....66 A2
Budge Row EC4 ...**109** B1
Budge's Wlk W2 ..**115** A2
Budleigh Ho 16
SE15 ....49 C3
Buer Rd SW6 ....**164** B1
Bugsby's Way
SE10 ....43 B2
Buick Ho 4 E3 ....26 C1
Bulbarrow Wlk 8
NW1 ....78 B3
Bulinca St SW1 ....**147** C3
Bullace Row SE5.....48 C2
Bullards Pl 2 E2 ...25 C2
Bulleid Way SW1 ..**146** B3
Bullen Ho 8 E1 .....25 A1
Bullen St SW11 .....**168** B2
Buller Cl SE15........49 C3
Buller Rd NW10 .....22 C2
Bullfinch Ct 7
SE21 ....75 C2
Bullingham Mans
SW5 ....31 C1 **113** B2
Bull Inn Ct WC2 ...**120** B3
Bullivant St 9
E14 ....34 B2
Bulls Alley SW14 ...44 C1
Bull's Gdns SW3 .**144** B4
Bulls Head Pas
EC3 ....**110** A1
Bull Yd SE15 ....49 C2
Bulmer Mews
W11 ....31 C1 **113** B2
Bulow Ct SW6.......**166** B2
Bulstrode Pl W1 ..**103** C3
Bulstrode St W1 ..**103** C2
Bulwer St W12.......30 B1
Bunbury Ho SE15...49 C3
Bunhill Row EC1 ...**97** B1
Bunhouse Pl SW1 .**145** C2
Bunkers Hill NW11 ...2 B4
Bunning Ho 7 N7 ...14 A4
Bunning Way N7 ...14 B1
Bunsen Ho 2 E3.....26 A3
Bunsen St 3 E3......26 A3
Bunyan Ct EC2 ....**108** C4
Buonaparte Mews
SW1 ....**147** B2
Burbage Cl SE1 ...**137** B1
Burbage Ho
16 Deptford SE14 ...50 C4
Shoreditch N1 ....87 C3
Burbage Rd SE21,
SE24 ....75 C4
Burbage Sch N1 ....24 A3
Burcham St E14.....34 B3
Burchell Ho SE11 .**149** A2
Burchell Rd SE15...50 A2

Burcher Gale Gr 6
SE15 ....49 B3
Burcote Rd SW18...71 C4
Burden Ho SW8 ...**162** A1
Burdenshott Ave
TW10 ....55 A3
Burder Cl N1...........16 A2
Burder Rd N1 ....16 A2
Burdett Coutts &
Townshend CE Prim
Sch SW1 ....**147** C3
Burdett Mews
W2 ....**100** A2
Burdett Rd
Richmond TW9 ......54 B4
Tower Hamlets E3 ...33 B4
Burdett St SE1 ....**135** C2
Burford Ct SE8 .....51 C4
Burford Ho
1 Brentford TW8 ....36 A1
South Lambeth
SW9 ....**173** A1
Burford Rd
Brentford TW8 ....36 A1
6 Stratford Marsh
E15 ....27 C4
Burford Wlk SW6 .**156** B1
Burgate Ct 9
SW9 ....**62** C4
Burges Gr SW13....47 A3
Burgess Hill NW2 ..10 C4
Burgess Ho 3
SE5 ....48 B3
Burgess Ind Pk
SE5 ....48 C3
Burgess Park Mans
NW6 ....11 A4
Burgess St E14 ......33 C4
Burge St SE1 ....**137** C1
Burghley Hall Cl
SW19 ....70 A3
Burghley Ho
SW19 ....70 A1
Burghley Rd NW5 ..13 A4
Burghley Twr W3 ...29 B2
Burgh St N1 ....86 B2
Burgon St EC4 ....**108** B1
Burgos Gr SE10 .....52 A2
Burgoyne Rd SW9 ..62 B4
Burhan Uddin Ho
E1 ....24 B1 **98** C1
Buriton Ho 9
SW15 ....69 A3
Burke Cl SW15 ......56 A3
Burke Ho 1 SW11...59 C3
Burke St E16 ....35 B4
Burland Rd SW11...60 B2
Burleigh Ho
Chelsea SW3 ......**157** C3
North Kensington
W10 ....30 C4
Burleigh Pl SW15...57 C2
Burleigh St WC2 ..**120** C4
Burley Ho E1 ....32 C3
Burlington Arc
W1 ....**118** C3
Burlington Ave
TW9 ....44 C2
Burlington Cl W9 ...23 C1
Burlington Ct
Chiswick W4 ....45 B3
Highgate N6 ....3 C3
Burlington Danes Sch
W12 ....30 A3
Burlington Gdns
Acton Green W4.....37 B1
Acton W3 ....28 B1

Burlington Gdns
continued
Fulham SW6 ....**164** B1
Marylebone W1 ....**118** C3
Burlington Ho
NW3 ....11 C3
Burlington La W4 ..45 C3
Burlington Mews
Acton W3 ....28 B1
2 Putney SW15 .....58 B2
Burlington Pl
SW6 ....**164** B1
Burlington Rd
Acton Green W4.....37 B1
Fulham SW6 ....**164** B1
Burma Rd N16 ......15 C4
Burmarsh 6 NW5 ..12 C2
Burmester Ho
SW17 ....71 B1
Burmester Rd
SW17 ....71 B1
Burnaby Cres W4 ..45 B4
Burnaby Ct SE16 .**139** C3
Burnaby Gdns W4 ..45 A4
Burnaby St SW10 **157** A1
Burnand Ho 3
W14 ....39 C3
Burnbury Rd
SW12 ....73 B3
Burne Jones Ho
W14 ....**140** B3
Burnell Ho 18
SW9 ....74 C3
Burnell Wlk SE1...**153** A2
Burness Cl N7........14 B2
Burne St NW1 .....**102** A4
Burnett Cl E9 ....17 B3
Burnett Ct SW11 .**168** A3
Burnett Ho 6
SE13 ....52 B1
Burney St SE10.....52 B3
Burnfoot Ave
SW6 ....**164** B3
Burnham NW3 ......12 A1
Burnham Cl SE1 ..**153** A3
Burnham Ct W2 ..**114** B4
Burnham Est 5
E2 ....25 B2
Burnham St E2.....25 B2
Burnhill Ho EC1 ...**96** C3
Burnley Rd
London SW9 ....**172** C2
Willesden NW10 .....8 C3
Burnsall St SW3 .**144** B2
Burns Ho
18 Bethnal Green
E2 ....25 B2
1 Islington N7 ......14 B2
Kennington SE17 ...**150** B1
11 Stoke Newington
N16 ....16 A4
Burns Rd SW11 ...**168** C2
Burnside Cl SE16...32 C1
Burns Rd SW11 ...**168** C2
Burn's Rd NW10...21 B4
Burnthwaite Ho
SW6 ....**155** A1
Burntwood Cl
SW18 ....72 A3
Burntwood Ct
SW17 ....71 B1
Burntwood Grange Rd
SW18 ....72 A3
Burntwood La
SW17 ....71 C2
Burntwood Sch
SW17 ....71 C2

Buross St E1 . . . . .32 A3
Burrage Ct 17
  SE16 . . . . .40 C2
Burrard Ho 11 E2 . . . . . .25 B3
Burrard Rd NW6 . . . . . . .10 C4
Burr Cl E1 . . . . .125 B2
Burrell St SE1 . . . . .122 A2
Burrell's Wharf Sq
  E14 . . . . .42 A1
Burrhill Ct SE16 . . . . .40 C3
Burrow Ho SW9 . . . . . . .173 A1
Burrow Rd SE22 . . . . .64 A3
Burrows Mews
  SE1 . . . . .136 A4
Burrows Rd NW10 . . . . . .22 B2
Burrow Wlk SE21 . . . . . . .75 B4
Burr Rd SW18 . . . . .70 C4
Bursar St SE1 . . . . .124 A1
Burslem St E1 . . . . .111 C1
Burstock Rd SW15 . . . . . .58 A3
Burston Rd SW15 . . . . . . .57 C2
Burtley Cl N4 . . . . .6 B3
Burton Bank N1 . . . . .15 C1
Burton Ct SW3 . . . . .145 A2
Burton Gr SE17 . . . . .151 B1
Burton Ho
  8 Bermondsey
  SE16 . . . . .40 A4
  Brixton SE5 . . . . .48 A2
Burton Lo 6
  SW15 . . . . .58 B2
Burton Mews
  SW1 . . . . .145 C3
Burton PI WC1 . . . . .93 C3
Burton Rd
  Brixton SW9 . . . . .48 A1
  Brixton SW9 . . . . .173 B2
  Brondesbury NW6 . . . . .10 B1
Burtons Ct E15 . . . . .19 C1
Burton St WC1 . . . . .93 C2
Burtonwood Ho N4 . . . . . .6 C4
Burt Ho N1 . . .24 A2 98 A4
Burwash Ho SE1 . . . . . .137 C3
Burwell Cl 22 E1 . . . . .32 A3
Burwell Wlk 48 E3 . . . . . .26 C1
Burwood Ho 11
  SW9 . . . . .63 A3
Burwood PI W2 . . . . .102 B2
Bury Cl SE16 . . . . .32 C1
Bury Ct EC3 . . . . .110 B2
Buryfield Ct 9
  SE8 . . . . .40 C2
Bury PI WC1 . . . . .106 B3
Bury St
  St James SW1 . . . . .119 A2
  Whitechapel EC3 . . . . . .110 B2
Bury Wlk SW3 . . . . .144 A2
Busbridge Ho 24
  E14 . . . . .33 C4
Busby Mews 5
  NW1 . . . . .13 C2
Busby PI NW5 . . . . .13 C2
Bushbaby Cl SE1 . . . . . .138 A1
Bushberry Rd E9 . . . . . . .18 A2
Bush Cotts 12
  SW18 . . . . .58 C2
Bush Ct 7 W12 . . . . .39 C4
Bushell St E1 . . . . .125 C2
Bushey Down
  SW12 . . . . .73 A2
Bushey Hall SE5 . . . . .48 B2
Bushey Hill Rd
  SE5 . . . . .49 B2
Bushfield Ho N5 . . . . .15 B3
Bush Ind Est
  NW10 . . . . .20 C1
Bush La EC4 . . . . .123 B4

Bushnell Rd SW17 . .73 A1
Bush Rd
  Bermondsey SE8 . . . . . .40 C2
  Hackney E8 . . . . .25 A4
  Richmond TW9 . . . . . . .44 B4
Bushwood Dr
  SE1 . . . . .153 A3
Bushwood Rd
  TW9 . . . . .44 C4
Business Design Ctr*
  N1 . . . . .85 C3
Buspace Studios 2
  W10 . . . . .23 A1
Butcher Row E1 . . . . .32 C3
Butchers Rd E16 . . . . .35 C3
Bute Gdns W6 . . . . .39 C2
Bute House Prep Sch
  W6 . . . . .39 C2
Bute St SW7 . . . . .143 B4
Bute Wlk 18 N1 . . . . .15 C2
Butfield Ho 6 E9 . . . . . . .17 B2
Butler Ho
  2 Bethnal Green
  E2 . . . . .25 B2
  3 Brixton SW9 . . . . . . .48 A2
  11 Poplar E14 . . . . .33 B3
Butler PI SW1 . . . . .133 B2
Butler Rd NW10 . . . . .8 B1
Butlers & Colonial
  Wharf SE1 . . . . .139 A4
Butler St 3 E2 . . . . .25 B2
Butler's Wharf W
  SE1 . . . . .124 C1
Butley Ct 3 E3 . . . . .26 A3
Butterfield Cl 1
  SE16 . . . . .40 A4
Butterfly Wlk 2
  SE5 . . . . .48 C2
Buttermere NW1 . . . . . . .92 B4
Buttermere Cl
  Bermondsey SE1 . . . . . .152 C3
  Leyton E11 . . . . .19 C4
Buttermere Ct
  NW8 . . . . .79 B4
Buttermere Dr
  SW15 . . . . .58 A2
Buttermere Ho 13
  E3 . . . . .26 B2
Buttermere Wlk 9
  E8 . . . . .16 B2
Butterwick W6 . . . . .39 B2
Butterworth Ct
  SW16 . . . . .74 A1
Buttesland St N1 . . . . . . .97 C4
Buxhall Cres E9 . . . . .18 B2
Buxted Rd
  Camberwell SE22 . . . . . .64 A3
  Dalston E8 . . . . .16 B1
Buxton Ct N1 . . . . .97 A4
Buxton Gdns W3 . . . . . . .28 A2
Buxton Ho 3
  SW11 . . . . .59 C3
Buxton Rd
  Mortlake SW14 . . . . .56 A4
  Upper Holloway N19 . . .4 C3
  Willesden NW2 . . . . .9 A2
Buxton St
  E1 . . . . .24 B1 99 A1
Byam Shaw Sch of Art
  N19 . . . . .4 C2
Byam St SW6 . . . . .166 C1
Byards Ct SE16 . . . . .40 C3
Byas Ho 6 E3 . . . . .26 B2
Byefield Cl SE16 . . . . .41 A4
Byelands Cl 12
  SE16 . . . . .32 C1
Bye The W3 . . . . .29 A3

Byeway The SW14 . . . . . .55 B4
Byfeld Gdns SW13 . . . . . .46 C2
Bygrove Prim Sch
  E14 . . . . .34 A3
Bygrove St E14 . . . . .34 A3
Byng PI WC1 . . . . .93 B1
Byng St E14 . . . . .41 C4
Byrne Ho 11
  SW2 . . . . .62 B2
Byrne Rd SW12 . . . . .73 A2
Byron Cl E8 . . . . .24 C4
Byron Ct
  Chelsea SW3 . . . . .144 B3
  Dulwich SE21 . . . . .76 C3
  8 Hampstead NW6 . . . .11 B1
  Paddington W9 . . . . . . .23 C1
  St Pancras WC1 . . . . . . .94 C2
Byron Mews
  Hampstead NW3 . . . . . .12 B4
  2 Maida Vale W9 . . . . . .23 C1
Byron St E14 . . . . .34 B3
Bythorn St SW9 . . . . .62 B3
Byward St EC3 . . . . .124 B3
Bywater PI SE16 . . . . .33 A1
Bywater St SW3 . . . . . . .144 C2
Bywell PI W1 . . . . .104 C3
Byworth Wlk N19 . . . . . . .5 A3

C

Cabbell St NW1 . . . . .102 A3
Cabinet Off SW1 . . . . .76 C3
Cabinet War Rooms &
  Churchill Mus*
  SW1 . . . . .133 C4
Cable Ho WC1 . . . . .95 B4
Cable PI SE10 . . . . .52 B2
Cable St E1 . . . . .32 A2
Cabot Ct SE16 . . . . .40 C3
Cabot Sq E14 . . . . .33 C1
Cabul Rd SW11 . . . . .168 B1
Cactus Cl SE5 . . . . .49 A1
Cactus Wlk W12 . . . . .29 B3
Cadbury Way
  SE1 . . . . .153 A4
Caddington Rd
  NW2 . . . . .1 A1
Cadell Ct E2 . . . . .24 B3
Cadell Ho 12 E2 . . . . .24 B3
Cade Rd SE10 . . . . .52 C2
Cader Rd SW18 . . . . .59 B1
Cadet Dr SE1 . . . . .153 A2
Cade Tyler Ho 10
  SE10 . . . . .52 B2
Cadiz St SE17 . . . . .151 A1
Cadman Cl SW9 . . . . .48 A3
Cadmore Ho 4
  N1 . . . . .15 A1
Cadmus Cl 9
  SW4 . . . . .61 C4
Cadmus Ct SW9 . . . . . . .173 B4
Cadnam Lo E14 . . . . .42 C3
Cadnam Point 15
  SW15 . . . . .69 A3
Cadogan Ct 8 E9 . . . . . . .18 B1
Cadogan Ct SW3 . . . . . .144 C3
Cadogan Ct Gdns
  SW1 . . . . .145 B4
Cadogan Gate
  SW1 . . . . .145 A4
Cadogan Gdns
  SW3 . . . . .145 A3
Cadogan Ho SW3 157 C3
Cadogan La SW1 . . . . . . .131 B1
Cadogan PI SW1 . . . . . . .131 A1
Cadogan Sq SW1 . . . . . . .131 A1
Cadogan St SW3 . . . . . . .144 C3

Cadogan Terr E9 . . . . . . .18 B1
Caedmon Rd N7 . . . . . . .14 B4
Caernarvon Ho
  W2 . . . . .100 C2
Caesar Ct 26 E2 . . . . .25 C3
Cahill St EC1 . . . . .97 A1
Cahir St E14 . . . . .42 A2
Caine Ho W3 . . . . .37 A4
Caird St W10 . . . . .23 B2
Cairns Ho 3 N7 . . . . .14 B4
Cairns Rd SW11 . . . . .60 A2
Caister Ho N1 . . . . .14 B2
Caister Ho 10
  SW12 . . . . .73 A4
Caister Mews
  SW12 . . . . .73 A4
Caister Rd SW12 . . . . . . .73 A4
Caithness Ho N1 . . . . . . .84 C4
Caithness Rd W14 . . . . . .39 C3
Calabria Rd N5 . . . . .15 A3
Calais Gate SE5 . . . . .48 A2
Calais St SE5 . . . . .48 A2
Calbourne Rd
  SW12 . . . . .72 C4
Calcraft Ho 10 E2 . . . . . . .25 B3
Caldecot Ct SE5 . . . . .48 B1
Caldecot Rd SE5 . . . . . . .48 B1
Calder Ct SE16 . . . . .33 B1
Calderon Ho NW8 . . . . . .80 A2
Calderon PI 27
  W10 . . . . .30 B4
Caldervale Rd
  SW4 . . . . .61 C2
Caldew St SE5 . . . . .48 C3
Caldwell St SW9 . . . . . . .163 A1
Caldy Wlk 18 N1 . . . . .15 B2
Caleb St SE1 . . . . .137 A4
Caledonia Ho 15
  E14 . . . . .33 A3
Caledonian Market
  SE1 . . . . .138 B2
Caledonian Rd
  Islington N1 . . . . .84 C3
  Lower Holloway N7 . . . .14 B2
Caledonian Road &
  Barnsbury Sta
  N7 . . . . .14 B1
Caledonian Road Sta
  N7 . . . . .14 B1
Caledonian Sq 6
  NW1 . . . . .13 C2
Caledonian Wharf Rd
  E14 . . . . .42 C2
Caledonia St N1 . . . . .84 B1
Cale St SW3 . . . . .144 A2
Caletock Way
  SE10 . . . . .43 B1
Calgarth NW1 . . . . .83 A1
Calgary Ct 30
  SE16 . . . . .40 B4
Caliban Twr 9
  N1 . . . . .24 A3
Calico Ho 4
  SW11 . . . . .59 B4
Calico Row 5
  SW11 . . . . .59 B4
Calidore Cl SW2 . . . . .62 B1
Callaby Terr 11
  N1 . . . . .15 C2
Callahan Cotts 3
  E1 . . . . .32 B4
Callan Sch The
  W1 . . . . .105 A2
Callcott Ct NW6 . . . . .10 B1
Callcott Rd NW6 . . . . . . .10 B1

Callcott St
  W8 . . . . .31 C1 113 B1
Callendar Rd
  SW7 . . . . .129 B2
Callingham Cl 15
  E14 . . . . .33 B3
Callingham Ho 4
  SW4 . . . . .62 A4
Callow St SW3 . . . . .157 B3
Calmington Rd
  SE5 . . . . .49 A4
Calshot Ho N1 . . . . .84 C2
Calshot St N1 . . . . .84 C1
Calstock NW1 . . . . .83 B3
Calstock Ho SE11 . . . . . .149 C2
Calthorpe St WC1 . . . . . . .95 A2
Calton Ave SE21 . . . . . . .64 A1
Calver 13 NW5 . . . . .13 A4
Calverley Gr N19 . . . . .4 C3
Calvert Ave
  E2 . . . . .24 B2 98 C3
Calvert Ct
  1 London N19 . . . . .4 B3
  5 Richmond TW9 . . . . . .54 B3
Calvert Ho 8
  W12 . . . . .30 A2
Calverton SE5 . . . . .49 A4
Calvert Rd SE10 . . . . .43 B1
Calvert's Bldgs
  SE1 . . . . .123 B1
Calvin St E1 . . . .24 B1 98 C1
Calypso Cres 6
  SE15 . . . . .49 B3
Calypso Way SE8,
  SE16 . . . . .41 B2
Cambalt Ho 3
  SW15 . . . . .57 C2
Cambalt Rd SW15 . . . . . .57 C2
Cambay Ho 7 E1 . . . . .26 A1
Camber Ho 4
  SE15 . . . . .50 B4
Camberley Ho
  NW1 . . . . .82 B1
CAMBERWELL 48 B2
Camberwell Bsns Ctr
  SE5 . . . . .48 C3
Camberwell Church
  St SE5 . . . . .48 C2
Camberwell Coll of
  Arts
  Camberwell SE5 . . . . . . .49 A2
  Camberwell SE15 . . . . . .49 B3
Camberwell Glebe
  SE5 . . . . .49 A2
Camberwell Gn
  SE5 . . . . .48 C2
Camberwell Gr
  SE5 . . . . .49 A1
Camberwell Green
  SE5 . . . . .48 B2
Camberwell New Rd
  SW9 . . . . .48 A3
Camberwell Rd
  SE5 . . . . .48 B3
Camberwell Station
  Rd SE5 . . . . .48 B2
Camberwell Trad Est
  SE5 . . . . .48 B2
Camborne Rd
  SW18 . . . . .70 C4
Cambourne Mews 6
  W11 . . . . .31 A3
Cambray Rd SW12 . .73 B3

Cambria Ho **14**
E14 . . . . .33 A3
Cambria Lo **8**
SW15 . . . . .58 B2
Cambrian Cl SE27 . .75 A1
Cambrian Rd
TW10 . . . . .54 B1
Cambria Rd SE5 . . . .63 B4
Cambria St SW6 . .156 B1
Cambridge Ave
NW6 . . . . .23 C3
Cambridge Cir
WC2 . . . . .105 C1
Cambridge Cotts
TW9 . . . . .44 C4
Cambridge Cres **20**
E2 . . . . .25 A3
Cambridge Ct
20 Bethnal Green
E2 . . . . .25 A3
7 Hammersmith
W6 . . . . .39 B2
2 Kilburn NW6 . . . .23 C3
Marylebone W2 . . .102 A3
Stamford Hill N16 . . .7 A4
Cambridge Gate
NW1 . . . . .92 A2
Cambridge Gate
Mews NW1 . . . . . . .92 B2
Cambridge Gdns
Kilburn NW6 . . . . . .23 C3
North Kensington
W10 . . . . .31 A3
Cambridge Gr W6 . .39 A2
Cambridge Grove Rd
E1, E2 . . . . .25 B2
Cambridge Heath Rd
E1, E2 . . . . .25 A3
Cambridge Heath Sta
E2 . . . . .25 A3
Cambridge Ho
SW6 . . . . .58 A4
Cambridge Mans
SW11 . . . . .168 C3
Cambridge Pas **9**
E9 . . . . .17 B1
Cambridge Pl W8 . .128 B3
Cambridge Rd N
Barnes SW13 . . . . . .46 B1
Battersea SW11 . . .168 C3
Kilburn NW6 . . . . . .23 C2
Kilburn NW6 . . . . . .23 C3
Richmond TW9 . . . . .44 C2
Cambridge Rd N
W4 . . . . .37 A1
Cambridge Rd S **5**
W4 . . . . .37 A1
Cambridge Sch
W6 . . . . .39 A2
Cambridge Sq
W2 . . . . .102 A2
Cambridge St
SW1 . . . . .146 C2
Cambridge Terr
NW1 . . . . .92 B3
Cambridge Terr Mews
NW1 . . . . .92 B3
Cambus Rd E16 . . . .35 C4
Cam Ct **2** SE15 . . .49 B4
Camden Coll of
English NW1 . . . . . .12 C1
Camden Gdns
NW1 . . . . .13 A1
Camden High St
NW1 . . . . .82 C3
Camden Ho **6**
SE8 . . . . .41 B1

Camdenhurst St
E14 . . . . .33 A3
Camden Lock Pl
NW1 . . . . .13 A1
Camden Mews
NW1 . . . . .13 C2
Camden Mkt* . . . . .
NW1 . . . . .13 C2
Camden Park Rd
NW1 . . . . .13 C2
Camden Pas N1 . . . .86 A3
Camden Rd NW1 . . .82 B4
Camden Road Sta
NW1 . . . . .13 B1
Camden Row SE3 . .53 A1
Camden Sch for Girls
The NW5 . . . . .13 B2
Camden Sq NW1 . . .13 C2
Camden St NW1 . . . .83 A3
Camden Studios
NW1 . . . . .83 A3
Camden Terr **17**
NW1 . . . . .13 C2
CAMDEN TOWN . .13 A1
Camden Town Sta
NW1 . . . . .82 B4
Camden Wlk N1 . . . .86 A3
Cameford Ct **20**
SW12 . . . . .74 A4
Camelford NW1 . . . .83 A3
Camelford Ct **19**
W11 . . . . .31 A3
Camelford Ho
SE1 . . . . .148 B1
Camelford Wlk **13**
W11 . . . . .31 A3
Camellia Ho SE8 . . .51 B3
Camellia St SW8 . .162 A1
Camelot Ho **13**
NW1 . . . . .13 C2
Camelot Prim Sch
SE15 . . . . .50 A4
Camera Pl SW10 . .157 B4
Cameret Ct **3**
W11 . . . . .39 C4
Cameron Ct **3**
SW19 . . . . .70 A3
Cameron Ho
Camberwell SE5 . . . .48 B3
St John's Wood
NW8 . . . . .80 A2
Cameron House Sch
SW10 . . . . .157 C4
Cameron Pl SW16 . .74 C2
Camerton Ct **8**
E8 . . . . .16 B1
Camilla Rd SE16 . . .40 A2
Camlet St
E2 . . . . .24 B1 **98** C2
Camley St NW1 . . . .83 C2
Camomile St EC3 . .110 B2
Campaign Ct W9 . . .23 B1
Campana Rd SW6 . .165 C4
Campbell Ct
Dulwich SE21 . . . . . .76 C3
South Kensington
SW7 . . . . .128 C1
Campbell Gordon
Way NW2 . . . . .9 A4
Campbell Ho
Paddington W2 . . . . .89 B1
Pimlico SW1 . . . . .146 C1
30 Shepherd's Bush
W12 . . . . .30 A2
Campbell Rd E3 . . . .26 C2
Campbell Wlk N1 . . .84 B4
Campdale Rd N7 . . . .4 C1

Campden Gr W8 . .127 C4
Campden Hill W8 . .127 B4
Campden Hill Ct
W8 . . . . .127 C4
Campden Hill Gate
W8 . . . . .127 B4
Campden Hill Gdns
W8 . . . . .31 C1 113 B2
Campden Hill Mans
W8 . . . . .31 C1 113 C2
Campden Hill Pl
W14 . . . . . . .31 B1 113 A2
Campden Hill Rd
W8 . . . . .127 B4
Campden Hill Sq
W14 . . . . . . .31 B1 113 A2
Campden Ho **4**
NW6 . . . . .11 C1
Campden Hos
W8 . . . . .31 C1 113 B1
Campden House Cl
W8 . . . . .127 C4
Campden St
W8 . . . . .31 C1 113 B1
Campen Cl SW19 . . .70 A2
Camperdown St
E1 . . . . .111 A1
Campion Ho **13**
N16 . . . . .16 A3
Campion Rd SW15 . .57 B2
Camplin St SE14 . . .50 C3
Campshill Pl SE13 . .67 B2
Campshill Rd
SE13 . . . . .67 B2
Campton Hill Twrs
W8 . . . . .31 C1 113 B2
Cam Rd E15 . . . . . . .27 C4
Camsey Ho **8**
SW2 . . . . .62 B2
Canada Cres W3 . . .20 B1
Canada Gdns SE13 . .67 B2
Canada Sq E14 . . . . .34 A1
Canada St SE16 . . . .40 C4
Canada Water Sta
SE16 . . . . .40 C3
Canada Way W12 . . .30 A2
Canal App SE8 . . . . .51 A4
Canal Bldg N1 . . . . .86 C2
Canal Bridge SE15 . .49 C4
Canal Cl
Mile End E1 . . . . . . .26 A1
North Kensington
W10 . . . . .22 C1
Canal Gr SE15 . . . . .50 A4
Canal Head Public Sq
1 SE15 . . . . .49 C2
Canal Path **2** E2 . . .24 C4
Canalside Studios **20**
N1 . . . . .24 A4
Canal St SE5 . . . . . .48 C4
Canal Way W10 . . . .22 C1
Canal Wlk N1 . . . . . .87 C4
CANARY WHARF . . .34 A1
Canary Wharf* . . . .
E14 . . . . .34 A1
Canary Wharf Pier
(River Bus) E14 . . . .33 B1
Canary Wharf Sta
E14 . . . . .34 A1
Canary Wharf Sta
(DLR) E14 . . . . .33 C1
Canberra Prim Sch
W12 . . . . .30 A2
Canbury Mews
SE26 . . . . .76 C1

Cancell Rd SW9 . . .173 C4
Candahar Rd
SW11 . . . . .168 B1
Candida Ct **9**
NW1 . . . . .13 A1
Candishe Ho SE1 . .138 C4
Candle Gr SE15 . . . .65 A4
Candlemakers **25**
SW11 . . . . .59 C3
Candover St W1 . . .104 C3
Candy St E3 . . . . . . .26 B4
Canfield Gdns
NW6 . . . . .11 A1
Canfield Pl NW6 . . . .11 B2
Canford Rd SW11 . . .60 C2
Canham Rd W3 . . . . .38 A4
Cann Ho W14 . . . . .126 B1
Canning Cross
SE5 . . . . .49 A1
Canning Ho **23**
W12 . . . . .30 A2
Canning Pas W8 . . .128 C2
Canning Pl W8 . . . .128 C2
Canning Pl Mews
W8 . . . . .128 C2
Canning Rd N5 . . . . . .6 A1
Cannington **14**
NW5 . . . . .12 C2
CANNING TOWN . .35 B3
Canning Town
E16 . . . . .35 A3
Canning Town Sta
E16 . . . . .35 A3
Cannock Ho N4 . . . . .6 C4
Cannon Dr **21** E14 . .33 C2
Cannon Hill NW6 . . .10 C3
Cannon Ho SE11 . .149 A3
Cannon La NW3 . . . . .2 C1
Cannon Pl NW3 . . . . .2 C1
Cannon St EC4 . . . .123 A4
Cannon Street Rd
E1 . . . . .32 A3
Cannon Street Sta
EC4 . . . . .123 B4
Cannon Wharf Bsns
Ctr **12** SE8 . . . . . . .41 A2
Canon Barnett Prim
Sch E1 . . . . .111 A2
Canon Beck Rd
SE16 . . . . .40 B4
CANONBURY 15 B2
Canonbury Bsns Ctr
N1 . . . . .87 A4
Canonbury Cres
N1 . . . . .15 B1
Canonbury Ct **1**
N1 . . . . .15 A1
Canonbury Gr N1 . . .15 B1
Canonbury Hts **8**
N1 . . . . .15 C2
Canonbury La N1 . . .15 A1
Canonbury Pk N
N1 . . . . .15 B2
Canonbury Pk S
N1 . . . . .15 B2
Canonbury Pl N1 . . .15 A2
Canonbury Prim Sch
N1 . . . . .15 A2
Canonbury Rd N1 . . .15 A1
Canonbury Sq N1 . . .15 A1
Canonbury St N1 . . .15 B1
Canonbury Sta N1,
N5 . . . . .15 B3
Canonbury Villas
N1 . . . . .15 A1
Canon Murnane Rd
SE1 . . . . .138 C1

Canon Row SW1 . .134 A3
Canons Cl N2 . . . . . . .2 C4
Canon St N1 . . . . . . .86 C3
Canrobert St E2 . . . .25 A2
Cantelowes Rd
NW1 . . . . .13 C2
Canterbury Cl **16**
SE5 . . . . .48 B1
Canterbury Cres
SW9 . . . . .62 C4
Canterbury Ct
Acton W3 . . . . .29 A1
Kilburn NW6 . . . . . .23 C3
Canterbury Gr SE27,
SW16 . . . . .74 C1
Canterbury Ho
6 Bromley E3 . . . . .27 A2
Lambeth SE1 . . . . .135 A2
Canterbury Ind Pk **18**
SE15 . . . . .50 B4
Canterbury Mans
NW6 . . . . .11 A2
Canterbury Pl
SE17 . . . . .150 B3
Canterbury Rd
NW6 . . . . .23 C3
Canterbury Terr
NW6 . . . . .23 C3
Cantium Ret Pk
SE1 . . . . .49 C4
Canton St E14 . . . . .33 C3
Cantrell Rd E3 . . . . .26 C1
Canute Ct SW16 . . .74 C1
Canute Gdns SE16 . .40 C2
Canvey St SE1 . . . .122 C2
Cape Henry Ct **13**
E14 . . . . .34 C2
Capel Ho **17** E9 . . .17 B1
Capel Lo
6 Richmond TW9 . .44 B2
2 Streatham SW2 . .74 B4
Capern Rd SW18 . . .71 B3
Capio Nightingale
Hospl SW3 . . . . . . .144 B1
Capital City Acad
NW10 . . . . .22 A4
Capital East Apts **9**
E16 . . . . .35 C2
Capital Interchange
Way TW8 . . . . .36 C1
Capital Sh Ctrs
SW1 . . . . .133 B3
Capital Wharf E1 . .125 C1
Capland Ho NW8 . . .89 C2
Capland St NW8 . . . .89 C2
Caple Ho SW10 . . .157 A2
Caple Rd NW10 . . . .21 B3
Capper St WC1 . . . . .93 A1
Capstan Ho **8**
E14 . . . . .42 B2
Capstan Rd SE8 . . . .41 B2
Capstan Sq E14 . . . .42 B4
Capstan Way E14 . . .34 A1
Capulet Mews **1**
E16 . . . . .35 C1
Caradoc Cl W2 . . . . .31 C3
Caradoc St SE10 . . .43 A1
Caradon Cl N11 . . . .14 C1
Caraway Villas **5**
W11 . . . . .30 C1
Caravel Cl E14 . . . . .41 C3
Caravel Mews **14**
SE8 . . . . .51 C4
Caraway Hts E14 . . .34 B2
Carbery Ave W3 . . . .36 B4

Carbis Rd E14 . . . . .33 B3
Carbroke Ho 9
　E9 . . . . .25 B4
Carburton St W1 . . . . . .92 B1
Cardale St 11 E14 . . . . . .42 B3
Carden Rd SE15 . . . . . . .65 A4
Cardiff Ho 9
　SE15 . . . . .49 C4
Cardigan Rd
　Barnes SW13 . . . . .46 C1
　Bow E3 . . . . .26 B3
　Richmond TW10 . . . . . .54 A1
Cardigan St SE11 . 149 B2
Cardigan Wlk 10
　. . . . . .15 B1
Cardinal Bourne St
　SE1 . . . . 137 C1
Cardinal Cap Alley
　SE1 . . . . 122 C3
Cardinal Hinsey Cl
　. . . . . .21 C3
Cardinal Hinsley RC
　High Sch (Boys)
　NW10 . . . . .21 C4
Cardinal Pl SW15 . .57 C3

London E9 . . . . .17 C1
London E8 . . . . .18 A3
Cardinals Way N19 . .4 C3
Cardinal Vaughan
　Meml Sch The
　W14 . . . . 126 A4
Cardinal Wlk
　SW1 . . . . 132 C1
Cardine Mews
　SE15 . . . . .50 A3
Cardington St
　NW1 . . . . .93 A3
Cardozo Rd N7 . . . . . .14 A3
Cardross St W6 . . . . . .39 A3
Cardwell Rd 3
　N7 . . . . .14 A4
Career Ct 11 SE16 . . .40 C4
Carew Cl N7 . . . . .5 B2
Carew Ct 15 SE14 . . . .50 C4
Carew Ho SW16 . . . . .74 C1
Carew St SE5 . . . . .48 B1
Carey Ct 8 SE5 . . . . .48 B3
Carey Gdns SW8 . 171 B3
Carey La EC2 . . . . . 108 C2
Carey Pl SW1 . . . . . 147 B3
Carfax Pl SW4* 61 C3
Carfree Cl 5 N1 . . . . .14 C1
Cargill Rd SW18 . . . . .71 B3
Carinthia Ct 3
　SE8 . . . . .41 A2
Carisbrooke Ct
　Acton W3 . . . . .37 B4
　1 Streatham SW16 . .74 B1
Carisbrooke Gdns
　SE15 . . . . .49 B3
Carisbrooke Ho
　TW10 . . . . .54 C2
Carleton Gdns
　N19 . . . . .4 C3
Carleton Rd N7 . . . . .13 C4
Carlile Cl E3 . . . . .26 B3
Carlile Ho SE1 . . . . 137 C1
Carlingford Rd
　NW3 . . . . .11 C4
Carlisle Ave
　Acton W3 . . . . .29 A3
　Whitechapel EC3 . . 110 C1
Carlisle Ho 6 NW5 . .4 B1
Carlisle La SE1 . . . . 135 A2

Carlisle Pl SW1 . . . 132 C1
Carlisle Rd
　Finsbury Pk N4 . . . . . .5 C4
　Kilburn NW6 . . . . .23 A4
Carlisle St W1 . . . . 105 B1
Carlisle Wlk 6 E8 . .16 B2
Carlos Pl W1 . . . . . 118 A3
Carlow St NW1 . . . . . .82 C2
Carlson Ct SW13 . . . .58 B3
Carlton Ct
　Brixton SW9 . . . . . . .48 A2
　Kilburn NW6 . . . . .78 B2
　9 Willesden NW2 . . . .9 B2
Carlton Dr SW15 . . . .58 B2
Carlton Gdns
　SW1 . . . . 119 B1
Carlton Gr SE15 . . . . .50 A2
Carlton Hill NW8 . . . .78 C2
Carlton Ho
　2 Kilburn NW6 . . . . .23 B3
　Kilburn NW6 . . . . .23 C3
　Marylebone W1* . 103 A2
Carlton House Terr
　SW1 . . . . 119 C2
Carlton Lo N4 . . . . .5 C4
Carlton Mans
　Brixton SW9 . . . . . . .62 C3
　Cricklewood NW2 . . . .9 C3
　Kensington W14 . . . 126 A4
　4 Maida Vale W9 . . .88 B4
　5 North Hampstead
　. . . . . .10 C1
　Stamford Hill N16 . . .7 B3
Carlton Prim Sch
　NW5 . . . . .12 C3
Carlton Rd
　Acton W4 . . . . .37 C4
　Finsbury Pk N4 . . . . . .5 C4
　Mortlake SW14 . . . . .55 B3
Carlton Sq E1 . . . . . . .25 C1
Carlton St SW1 . . . 119 B3
Carltons The 5
　SW15 . . . . .58 A2
Carlton Tower Pl
　SW1 . . . . 131 A2
Carlton Vale NW6 . . .23 C3
Carlton Vale Inf Sch
　NW6 . . . . .23 B2
Carlyle Ho
　4 Camberwell
　SE5 . . . . .48 B3
　Chelsea SW3 . . . . . 157 C4
　12 Stoke Newington
　N16 . . . . .7 A1
Carlyle Mans
　SW3 . . . . 158 A3
Carlyle Mews 24
　E1 . . . . .25 C1
Carlyle Pl SW15 . . . .57 C3
Carlyle Rd 1
　NW10 . . . . .20 C4
Carlyle's Ho*
　SW3 . . . . 158 A3
Carlyle Sq SW3 . . . 143 C1
Carmalt Gdns
　SW15 . . . . .57 B3
Carmarthen Ho 8
　SW15 . . . . .69 B4
Carmarthen Pl
　SE1 . . . . 138 A4
Carmel Ct W8 . . . . . 128 A4
Carmelite St EC4 . . 121 C4
Carmel Lo SW6 . . . 155 B4
Carmen St E14 . . . . . .34 A3
Carmichael Cl 9
　. . . . . .59 C4

Carmichael Ct 5
　SW13 . . . . .46 B1
Carmichael Ho 6
　E14 . . . . .34 B2
Carmichael Mews
　SW18 . . . . .71 C4
Carminia Rd
　SW17 . . . . .73 A2
Carnaby St* W1 . . 104 C1
Carnac St SE21,
　SE27 . . . . .75 C1
Carna Ct TW9 . . . . . . .54 A4
Carnegie Ho NW3 . . .2 C1
Carnegie Pl SW19 . .69 C1
Carnegie St N1 . . . . . .85 A3
Carnicot Ho 2
　SE15 . . . . .50 A2
Carnoustie Dr N1 . . .14 B1
Carnwath Ho SW6 . .59 A4
Carnwath Rd SW6 . .59 A4
Caroline Cl
　Bayswater W2 . . . . 114 B3
　Streatham SW16 . . .74 B1
Caroline Gdns
　E2 . . . . .24 A2 98 B4
Caroline Ho
　Bayswater W2 . . . . 114 B3
　20 Hammersmith
　W6 . . . . .39 B1
Caroline Martyn Ho
　8 N19 . . . . .4 C4
Caroline Pl
　Bayswater W2 . . . . 114 B3
　Clapham SW11 . . . 169 C1
Caroline Pl Mews
　W2 . . . . 114 B3
Caroline St E1 . . . . . .32 C3
Caroline Terr
　SW1 . . . . 145 B3
Caroline Wlk W6 154 A3
Carol St NW1 . . . . . . .82 C4
Caroline Ct 4
　SE16 . . . . .41 A2
Carpenter Ho
　11 Tower Hamlets
　E14 . . . . .33 C4
　5 Tufnell Pk N19 . . .13 C4
Carpenters Bsns Pk
　E15 . . . . .19 A1
Carpenters Ct
　NW1 . . . . .82 C4
Carpenter's Pl
　SW4 . . . . .61 C3
Carpenters Prim Sch
　E15 . . . . .27 B4
Carpenter's Rd
　E15 . . . . .19 A1
Carpenter St W1 . . 118 A3
Carradale Ho 2
　E14 . . . . .34 B3
Carrara Cl 11 SW9 . .63 A3
Carrara Wharf
　SW6 . . . . .58 A4
Carriage Dr E 3
　SW11 . . . . 159 C3
Carriage Drive E
　SW11 . . . . 159 C3
Carriage Drive N SW11,
　SW8 . . . . 159 C3
Carriage Dr N
　SW11 . . . . 158 C2
　Battersea SW11,
　SW11 . . . . 159 C3
Carriage Dr S
　SW11 . . . . 169 B4

Carriage Dr W
　SW11 . . . . 158 C1
Carrick Ho
　Islington N7 . . . . . . .14 B2
　Kennington SE11 . . 150 A2
Carrick Mews SE8 .51 C4
Carrington Ct
　SW11 . . . . .60 A3
Carrington Ho
　W1 . . . . 118 A1
Carrington Lo 3
　TW10 . . . . .54 A2
Carrington Rd
　TW10 . . . . .54 C3
Carrington St W1 . 118 A1
Carrol Cl NW5 . . . . . .13 A4
Carroll Ct
　Acton W3 . . . . .37 A3
　4 Shacklewell E5 . . .7 C3
Carroll Ho W2 . . . . 115 B4
Carron Cl E14 . . . . . . .34 A3
Carroun Rd SW8 . 162 C2
Carr St 8 E14 . . . . . . .33 A3
Carslake Rd SW15 . .57 B1
Carson Rd
　Dulwich SE21 . . . . . .75 C2
　Newham E16 . . . . . . .35 C4
Carter Ct EC4 . . . . . 108 B1
Carteret Ho 8
　W12 . . . . .30 A2
Carteret St SW1 . . 133 B3
Carteret Way SE8 . .41 A2
Carter Ho
　11 London Bridge
　SW1 . . . . .62 C2
　Spitalfields E1 . . . . 110 C3
Carter La EC4 . . . . 108 B1
Carter Pl SE17 . . . 151 A1
Carters Cl 10 NW5 .13 C2
Carter's Yd SW18 . .58 C2
Carthew Rd W6 . . . . .39 A3
Carthew Villas
　W6 . . . . .39 A3
Carthusian St
　EC1 . . . . 108 C4
Cartier Circ E14 . . . .34 B1
Carting La WC2 . . . 120 B3
Cartmel NW1 . . . . . . .92 C4
Carton Ho
　Bermondsey SE16 . 139 B2
　12 Shepherd's Bush
　W11 . . . . .30 C2
Cartoon Mus The*
　WC1 . . . . 106 A3
Cartwright Gdns
　WC1 . . . . .94 A3
Cartwright Ho
　SE1 . . . . 137 A1
Cartwright St E1 . . 125 A3
Cartwright Way
　SW13 . . . . .47 A3
Carvel Ho E14 . . . . . .42 B1
Carver Cl 18 W4 . . . .37 B3
Carver Rd SE24 . . . . .63 B1
Carville Cres SW8 . .62 C1
Caryl Ho 6 SW19 . . .69 C3
Carysfort Rd N16 . . .15 C4
Casella Rd SE14 . . . .50 C3
Casey Cl NW8 . . . . . . .90 B3
Casino Ave SE24 . . . .63 C2
Caspian Ho 10 E1 . .32 C4
Caspian St SE5 . . . . .48 C3
Cassandra Ct 7
　NW2 . . . . .9 B2
Cass Bsns Sch EC1 .97 B1
Cassell Ho SW9 . . 172 B2

Casserley Ho W4 . . .37 C3
Cass Ho 22 E9 . . . . . .17 C2
Cassidy Rd SW6 . . 155 B1
Cassilis Rd E14 . . . . . .41 C4
Cassinghurst SE24 . .63 C2
Cassland Rd E9 . . . . .17 C2
Casson Ho 1 . . . . . . 111 B4
Casson St E1 . . . . . . 111 B3
Castalia Sq 6 E14 . .42 B4
Castellain Mans
　W9 . . . . .88 A2
Castellain Rd W9 . . .88 B2
Castell Ho 11 SE8 . .51 C3
Castello Ave SW15 . .57 B2
Castelnau SW13 . . . .47 A3
Castelnau Gdns
　SW13 . . . . .47 A4
Castelnau Mans
　SW13 . . . . .47 A4
Castelnau Row
　SW13 . . . . .47 A4
Casterbridge
　Kilburn NW6 . . . . .78 B4
　1 Notting Hill W11 .31 C3
Casterton St E8 . . . .17 A2
Castleacre W2 . . . . 102 A1
Castle Baynard St
　EC4 . . . . 122 C4
Castlebrook Cl
　SE11 . . . . 150 A4
Castle Cl
　2 Acton W3 . . . . . . .37 B4
　Homerton E9 . . . . . . .18 A3
　South Acton W3 . . . .37 A4
　Wimbledon SW19 . .69 C1
Castlecombe Dr
　SW19 . . . . .69 C4
Castle Ct EC3 . . . . . 109 C1
Castleden Ho
　. . . . . .11 C1
Castleford Ct NW8 .89 C2
Castlefrank Ho
　N1 . . . . .24 A2 98 B4
Castlegate TW9 . . . . .54 B4
Castlehaven Rd
　. . . . . .13 A1
Castle Ho
　Newington SE1 . . . 150 C4
　South Lambeth
　SW8 . . . . 162 B2
Castle Ind Est
　SE17 . . . . 150 C4
Castle La SW1 . . . . 132 C2
Castlemaine
　SW11 . . . . 169 A2
Castlemaine St 2
　E1 . . . . .32 A4
Castle Mead SE5 . . .48 B3
Castle Mews NW1 . .13 A2
Castle Pl
　8 Acton W4 . . . . . . .38 A2
　Camden Town W4 . .13 A2
Castle Rd NW1 . . . . . .13 A2
Castlereagh St
　W1 . . . . 102 C2
Castleton Ho 6
　E14 . . . . .42 B2
Castletown Rd
　W14 . . . . 140 B1
Castleview Cl N4 . . . .6 B2
Castle Way SW19 . . .69 C1
Castlewood Ho
　WC1 . . . . 105 C2
Castle Yd
　Highgate N6 . . . . .3 C4

Castle Yd continued
Lambeth SE1 . . . . . . **122** B2
Castor La E14 . . . . **34** A2
Catalpa Ct SE13 . . . . . **67** C1
Caterham Rd
SE13 . . . . **67** C4
Catesby Ho 25 E9 . . . **17** B1
Catesby St SE17 . . . **151** C3
Cathay Ho SE16 . . . . **40** A4
Cathay St 1 SE16 . . . **40** A4
Cathcart Hill N19 . . . . **4** B1
Cathcart Rd
SW10 . . . . **156** C4
Cathcart St NW5 . . . **13** A2
Cathedral Ct EC4 . . . **108** B1
Cathedral Lo EC1 . . . **108** C4
Cathedral Sch of St
Saviour & St Mary
Overie Prim Sch
SE1 . . . . **137** A4
Cathedral St SE1 . . . **123** B2
Cathedral Wlk
SW1 . . . . **132** C2
Catherall Rd N5,
N16 . . . . **6** B1
Catherine Baird Ct 12
SW12 . . . . **73** A4
Catherine Dr SW4 . . . **54** A3
Catherine Gr SE10 . . **52** A2
Catherine Griffiths Ct
EC1 . . . . **95** C2
Catherine Ho 16
N1 . . . . **24** A4
Catherine Pl SW1 **132** C2
Catherine St WC2 **120** C4
Catherine Wheel Alley
E1 . . . . **110** B3
Catherine Wheel Yd
SW1 . . . . **118** C1
Catherwood Ct N1 **87** B1
Cathles Rd SW12 . . . **73** A4
Cathnor Rd W12 . . . . **39** A4
Catlin St SE16 . . . . . . **40** A1
Catman Ho N4 . . . . **5** B3
Cato Rd SW4 . . . . **61** C3
Cator St
Camberwell SE15 . . . **49** B3
Camberwell SE15 . . . **49** B4
Cato St W1 . . . . **102** B2
Catton St WC1 . . . . . **106** C3
Caughley Ho
SE11 . . . . **135** B1
Caulfield Ct 13
NW1 . . . . **13** B1
Caulfield Rd SE15 . . . **50** A1
Causeway The
SW18 . . . . **59** A2
Causton Cotts 3
E14 . . . . **33** A3
Causton Ho 5 . . . . . **48** B3
Causton Rd N6 . . . . . . **4** A4
Causton St SW1 . . . **147** C2
Cautley Ave SW4 . . . **61** B2
Cavalry Gdns
SW15 . . . . **58** B2
Cavaye Ho SW10 . . . **157** A4
Cavaye Pl SW10 . . . **143** A1
Cavell Ct 3 N19 . . . . **4** B2
Cavell Ho 6 N1 . . . . . **24** A4
Cavell St E1 . . . . **32** A4
Cavendish Ave
NW8 . . . . **79** C1
Cavendish Cl
Brondesbury NW6 . . **10** B2
 3 Putney SW15 . . . . **58** A2

Cavendish Cl continued
St John's Wood
NW8 . . . . **89** C4
Cavendish Coll
WC1 . . . . **105** B4
Cavendish Ct EC2 **110** B2
Cavendish Gdns
SW4 . . . . **61** B1
Cavendish Ho
South Lambeth
SW8 . . . . **172** A4
St John's Wood
NW8 . . . . **79** C1
Cavendish Mans
 2 Clapham Pk
SW12 . . . . **61** B1
Hackney E5 . . . . **17** B3
Holborn EC1 . . . . . . **95** B1
 8 West Hampstead
NW6 . . . . **10** C3
Cavendish Mews N
W1 . . . . **104** B4
Cavendish Mews S
W1 . . . . **104** B3
Cavendish Par
SW12 . . . . **61** A1
Cavendish Pl
Balham SW4 . . . . **61** A1
Brondesbury NW2 . . . **9** C2
Marylebone W1 . . . . **104** B2
Cavendish Prim Sch
W4 . . . . **46** A3
Cavendish Rd
Brondesbury NW6 . . **10** B1
Chiswick W4 . . . . . . **45** B2
Clapham Pk SW12 . . **61** B1
Cavendish Sch W1 **104** B2
Cavendish Sch The
NW1 . . . . **82** B4
Cavendish Sq W1 **104** B2
Cavendish St N1 . . . **87** B1
Cavendish Terr 11
E3 . . . . **26** B2
Cavendish The
NW11 . . . . **2** A4
Caversham Ho 7
SE15 . . . . **49** C4
Caversham Rd
NW5 . . . . **13** B2
Caversham St
SW3 . . . . **158** C4
Caverswall St
W12 . . . . **30** B3
Cavour Ho SE17 . . . **150** B2
Caxton Gr 5 E3 . . . . **26** C2
Caxton Hall *
SW1 . . . . **133** B2
Caxton Rd W12 . . . . **39** C4
Caxton St N E16 . . . **35** B3
Caxton St SW1 . . . . **133** B2
Caxton Wlk WC2 . . . **105** C1
Cayford Ho 3
NW3 . . . . **12** B3
Cayley Prim Sch
E14 . . . . **33** A3
Cayton Pl EC1 . . . . . **97** B3
Cayton St EC1 . . . . . **97** B3
Cazenove Mans 1
N16 . . . . **7** C2
Cazenove Rd N16 . . . **7** C2
Cecil Ct
Chelsea SW10 . . . . **156** C4
South Hampstead
NW6 . . . . **11** A1
 3 St James WC2 . . **120** A3
Cecilia Rd E8 . . . . . . **16** C3
Cecil Mans 2
SW17 . . . . **72** C2

Cecil Rd Acton W3 . . **28** B4
Harlesden NW10 . . . . **21** A4
Cecil Rhodes Ho
NW1 . . . . **83** B2
Cedar Ct
Old Ford E3 . . . . **26** B4
West Norwood
SE21 . . . . **75** B2
Cedar Ct
Islington N1 . . . . **15** B1
Marylebone W1 . . . . **102** B2
Mortlake SW14 . . . . . **55** B3
Wimbledon SW19 . . . **69** C1
Cedar Gr W5 . . . . **36** A3
Cedar Ho
 5 Cubitt Town
E14 . . . . **42** B4
Kensington W8 . . . . **128** A2
New Cross Gate
SE14 . . . . **50** C2
 5 Richmond TW9 . . **45** A2
 16 Rotherhithe
SE16 . . . . **40** C4
Cedar Lo
Brondesbury NW2 . . **10** B2
Fulham SW6 . . . . **47** C2
Cedarne Rd SW6 . **156** A1
Cedar Rd NW2 . . . . . . **9** B4
Cedars Cl SE13 . . . . . **67** C4
Cedars Ct SW15 . . . . **56** C1
Cedars Ho 1 SW2 . . **62** B3
Cedars Mews
SW4 . . . . **61** A3
Cedars Rd
Barnes SW13 . . . . . . **46** C1
Clapham SW4 . . . . . . **61** A3
Cedars The E9 . . . . . **17** C1
Cedar Terr TW9 . . . . **54** A3
Cedar Way 7 NW1 . . **83** B4
Cedar Way Ind Est
NW1 . . . . **83** B4
Cedra Ct N16 . . . . **7** C3
Cedric Chambers
NW8 . . . . **89** B2
Celandine Cl E3,
E14 . . . . **33** C4
Celandine Dr E8 . . . **16** B1
Celbridge Mews
W2 . . . . **100** B2
Celestial Gdns
SE13 . . . . **67** C3
Celia Blairman Ho
E1 . . . . **110** C4
Celia Ct 7 TW9 . . . . **44** B2
Celia Ho 10 N1 . . . . **24** A3
Celia Rd N19 . . . . . . **13** B4
Celtic St E14 . . . . . . **34** A4
Cenacle Cl NW3 . . . . . **1** C1
Centaur Ct 3
TW8 . . . . **36** A1
Centaur St SE1 . . . . **135** A2
Central Ave SW11 **159** A1
Central Bsns Ctr
NW10 . . . . **8** A3
Central Criminal
Court (Old Bailey) *
EC4 . . . . **108** B2
Central Foundation
Boys' Sch EC2 . . . . **97** C2
Central Foundation
Lower Girls Sch The
E3 . . . . **26** A2
Central Foundation
Upper Girls Sch The
E3 . . . . **26** B2
Central Ho E15 . . . . . **27** B3
Central Middlesex
Hospl NW10 . . . . . . **20** B2

Central Par W3 . . . . . **37** A4
Central St Martins
Coll EC1 . . . . **95** C1
Central St Martin's
Coll of Art & Design
W1 . . . . **105** C1
Central St Martins
Coll of Art & Design
(The London Inst)
WC1 . . . . **106** C3
Central Sch of Ballet
EC1 . . . . **95** C1
Central Sch of Speech
& Drama The
NW3 . . . . **11** C1
Central St EC1 . . . . . **96** C3
Central Way
NW10 . . . . **20** B2
Centre Ave W3 . . . . . **28** C1
Centre Bldg SE17 **151** A4
Centre Hts 3
NW3 . . . . **11** C1
Centre Point SE1 **153** B2
Centre Point Ho
WC2 . . . . **105** C2
Centre St E2 . . . . **25** A3
Centurion Bldg
SW8 . . . . **160** A3
Centurion Cl N7 . . . . **14** B1
Centurion La E3 . . . . **26** B3
Centurion Ho SE13 . . **52** A1
Cephas Ave E1 . . . . . **25** B1
Cephas Ho 9 E1 . . . . **25** B1
Cephas St E1 . . . . **25** B1
Cerise Rd SE15 . . . . . **49** C2
Cerney Mews W2 **115** B4
Cervantes Ct W2 **100** B1
Cester St E2 . . . . **24** C4
Ceylon Rd
 8 Hammersmith
W14 . . . . **39** C3
Kensington W14 . . . **126** A1
Chabot Dr SE15 . . . . **65** A4
Chadacre Ho 10
SW9 . . . . **63** A3
Chadbourn St E14 . . **34** A4
Chadston Ho 17
N1 . . . . **15** A1
Chadswell WC1 . . . . **94** B3
Chadwell St EC1 . . . **95** C4
Chadwick Cl
SW15 . . . . **68** B4
Chadwick Rd
Harlesden NW10 . . . . **21** B4
Peckham SE15 . . . . . **49** B1
Chadwick St SW1 **133** B1
Chadworth Ho
Finsbury EC1 . . . . . . **96** C3
Finsbury Pk N4 . . . . . . **6** B3
Chagford Ho
 30 Bromley E3 . . . . . **27** A2
Marylebone NW1 . . . **90** C1
Chagford St NW1 . . . **91** A1
Chalbury Ho 3
SW9 . . . . **62** B3
Chalbury Wlk N1 . . **85** B2
Chalcot Cres NW1 **81** A4
Chalcot Gdns
NW3 . . . . **12** B2
Chalcot Mews
SW16 . . . . **74** A1
Chalcot Rd NW1 . . . . **81** B4
Chalcot Sq NW1 . . . . **12** C1
Chaldon Rd SW6 . . **154** B2
Chale Rd SW2 . . . . . . **62** A1
Chalfont Ct NW1 . . . . **91** A1

Chalfont Ho 2
SE16 . . . . **40** A3
Chalford 7 NW3 . . . **11** B2
Chalford Ct 13
SW15 . . . . **57** C1
Chalkers Cnr TW9 . . **55** A4
Chalk Farm Sta
NW3 . . . . **12** C1
Chalk Hill Rd W6 . . . **39** C2
Chalkwell Ho 10
E1 . . . . **32** C3
Challenge Cl
NW10 . . . . **21** A4
Challenger Ho 7
E14 . . . . **33** A2
Challice Way SW2 . . **74** B3
Challoner Cres
W14 . . . . **140** C1
Challoner Mans
W14 . . . . **140** C1
Challoner St W14 **140** C1
Chalmers Ho 6
SW11 . . . . **59** B4
Chalmer's Wlk 14
SE17 . . . . **48** A4
Chalner Ho SW2 . . . **74** C3
Chaloner Ct SE1 . . . **137** B4
Chalsey Lodge
SE4 . . . . **66** B3
Chalsey Rd SE4 . . . . **66** B3
Chalton St NW1 . . . . **83** B1
Chamberlain Cotts
SE5 . . . . **48** C2
Chamberlain Ho 6
E1 . . . . **32** B2
Chamberlain St 1
NW1 . . . . **12** B1
Chamberlayne Mans
 3 NW10 . . . . **22** C2
Chamberlayne Rd
NW10 . . . . **22** B1
Chambers La NW10 . . **9** B1
Chambers Rd N7 . . . **14** A4
Chambers St
SE16 . . . . **139** C3
 9 Chamber St E1 . . **125** B4
Chambon Pl 7
W6 . . . . **38** C2
Chambord Ho
E2 . . . . **24** B2 **99** A3
Chambord St
E2 . . . . **24** B2 **99** A3
Champion Gr SE5 . . **63** C4
Champion Hill
SE5 . . . . **63** C4
Champion Pk SE5 . . **48** C1
Champlain Ho 26
W12 . . . . **30** A2
Chancel Ct W1 . . . . **119** B4
Chancellor Gr
SE21 . . . . **75** B1
Chancellor Ho
South Kensington
SW7 . . . . **129** A2
 29 Wapping E1 . . . **32** A1
Chancellor Pas
E14 . . . . **33** C1
Chancellors' Ct
WC1 . . . . **106** C4
Chancellor's Rd
W6 . . . . **39** B1
Chancellors St
W6 . . . . **39** B1
Chancellors Wharf 21
W6 . . . . **39** B1
Chancel St SE1 . . . . **122** A1

Chancery Bldgs 🏠
E1 . . . . 32 B2
Chancery Ho
WC2 . . . . 107 B3
Chancery La EC4 . 107 B2
Chancery Lane Sta
WC1 . . . . 107 B3
Chancery Mews
SW17 . . . . 72 A2
Chance St
E2 . . . . 24 B1 98 C2
Chandler Ave E16 . 35 C4
Chandlers Mews
E14 . . . . 41 C4
Chandler St E1 . . . . 32 A1
Chandlers Way 🏠
SE24 . . . . 74 C4
Chandler Way
SE15 . . . . 49 B3
Chandlery Ho E1 . 111 B1
Chandos Pl WC2 . 120 A3
Chandos Rd
Cricklewood NW2 . . . 9 B3
Old Oak Comm
NW10 . . . . 21 A1
Stratford New Town
E15 . . . . 19 C3
Chandos St W1 . . 104 B3
Chandos Way
NW11 . . . . 2 A3
Change Alley EC3 109 C1
Channel Gate Rd
NW10 . . . . 21 A2
Channel Ho E14 . . . 33 A4
Channelsea Bsns Ctr
E15 . . . . 27 C3
Channelsea Rd
E15 . . . . 27 C4
Channing Sch N6 . . 4 A3
Chantrey Rd SW9 . . 62 B4
Chantry Cl W9 . . . . 23 B1
Chantry Cres NW10 . 8 B2
Chantry Ct SW6 . . . 58 A4
Chantry Sq W8 . . . 128 A1
Chantry St N1 . . . . . 86 B3
Chant Sq E15 . . . . . 19 C1
Chant St E15 . . . . . 19 C1
Chapel Cl NW10 . . . 8 B2
Chapel Ct SE1 . . . 137 B4
Chapel House St
E14 . . . . 42 A2
Chapel Market N1. 85 B2
Chapel Pl
Islington N1 . . . . . . 85 C2
Marylebone W1. . . 104 A1
Shoreditch
EC2 . . . . . . 24 A2 98 A3
Chapel Side W2 . . 114 A3
Chapel St
Paddington NW1 . 102 A3
Westminster SW1 . 131 C3
Chapleton Ho
SW2 . . . . 62 C2
Chaplin Cl SE1 . . . 136 A4
Chaplin Ho 🏠
SW9 . . . . 62 C4
Chaplin Rd NW2. . . . 8 C2
Chaplow Cl SW6 . . 166 C1
Chapman Ho
🏠 Stepney E1 . . . . 32 A3
🏠 West Norwood
SE27 . . . . 75 A1
Chapman Rd E9 . . . 18 B2
Chapmans Park Ind
Est NW10 . . . . 8 B2
Chapman Sq
SW19 . . . . 69 C2

Chapman St E1 . . . . 32 A2
Chapone Pl W1 . . . 105 B1
Chapter Cl 🏠 W4 . 37 B3
Chapter House &
Jewel Twr★
SW1 . . . . 134 A2
Chapter Rd
Kennington SE17 . 150 B1
Willesden NW2 . . . . . 8 C3
Chapter St SW1 . . 147 B3
Chara Pl W4 . . . . . 45 C4
Charcot Ho SW11 . 56 B1
Charcroft Ct 🏠
W14 . . . . 39 C4
Chard Ho 🏠 N7 . . . 5 B2
Chardin Ho SW9 . 173 C4
Chardin Rd 🏠 W4. 38 A2
Chardmore Rd N16 . 7 C3
Charecroft Way
W12 . . . . 39 C4
Charfield Ct W9 . . . 88 B1
Charford Rd E16 . . 35 C4
Chargrove Cl 🏠
SE16 . . . . 40 C4
Charing Cross
SW1 . . . . 120 A2
Charing Cross Hospl
W6 . . . . 39 C1
Charing Cross Rd
WC2 . . . . 105 C1
Charing Cross Sta
WC2 . . . . 120 B2
Chariot Cl 🏠 E3 . . 26 C4
Charlbert Ct NW8 . 80 A2
Charlbert St NW8 . 80 A2
Charles Allen Ho
EC1 . . . . 95 B4
Charles Auffray Ho 🏠
E1 . . . . 32 B4
Charles Barry Cl
SW4 . . . . 61 B4
Charles Burton Ct
E5 . . . . 18 A4
Charles Coveney Rd
🏠 SE15 . . . . 49 B2
Charles Darwin Ho 🏠
E2 . . . . 25 A2
Charles Dickens Ho
🏠 E2 . . . . 25 A2
Charles Dickens Prim
Sch SE1 . . . . 136 C3
Charles Edward
Brooke Sch SW9 . 48 A2
Charles Edward
Brooke Sch (Dennen
Site) SE5 . . . . 48 A2
Charles Flemwell
Mews 🏠 E16 . . . . 35 C1
Charles Haller St 🏠
SW2 . . . . 74 C4
Charles Harrod Ct
SW13 . . . . 47 B4
Charles Hobson Ho 🏠
NW10 . . . . 21 A4
Charles Hocking Ho
🏠 W3 . . . . 37 B4
Charles II Pl SW3 144 C1
Charles II St SW1 . 119 B2
Charles La NW8 . . . 80 A2
Charles Lamb Ct
N1 . . . . 86 B3
Charles Lamb Prim
Sch N1 . . . . 86 C4
Charles Mackenzie Ho
🏠 SE16 . . . . 153 C4
Charles Pl NW1 . . . 93 A3

Charles Rowan Ho
WC1 . . . . 95 B3
Charles Sq N1 . . . 97 C3
Charles St
Barnes SW13 . . . . 46 A1
Mayfair W1 . . . . . 118 A2
Charleston St
SE17 . . . . 151 A3
Charlesworth Ho 🏠
E14 . . . . 96 A2
Charles Utton Ct
E8 . . . . 16 C4
Charlesworth Ho 🏠
E14 . . . . 96 A2
Charleville Ct
W14 . . . . 140 C1
Charleville Mans
W14 . . . . 140 B1
Charleville Rd
W14 . . . . 140 C1
Charlotte Ct 🏠
W6 . . . . 38 C2
Charlotte Despard
Ave SW11 . . . . . . 169 C3
Charlotte Ho 🏠
W6 . . . . 39 B1
Charlotte Mews
Marylebone W1 . . 105 A4
North Kensington
W10 . . . . 30 C3
West Kensington
W14 . . . . 140 A4
Charlotte Pl
Marylebone W1 . . 105 A3
Westminster SW1 . 146 C3
Charlotte Rd
Barnes SW13 . . . . 46 B2
Shoreditch
EC2 . . . . . . 24 A1 98 A2
Charlotte Row
SW4 . . . . 61 B4
Charlotte Sharman
Prim Sch SE1 . . . 136 A1
Charlotte Sq 🏠
TW10 . . . . 54 B1
Charlotte St W1 . . 105 A4
Charlotte Terr N1 . 85 A3
Charlton Ct
🏠 Hackney E2 . . 24 B4
🏠 Kentish Town
N7 . . . . 13 C3
Charlton Ho
🏠 Brentford TW8 . 44 A4
Somers Town NW1 . 93 B4
Charlton King's Rd
NW5 . . . . 13 C3
Charlton Pl N1 . . . . 86 A2
Charlton Rd NW10 . 21 A4
Charlton Way SE10,
SE3 . . . . 53 A2
Charlwood Ho
Richmond TW9 . . . . 45 A3
🏠 Streatham SW2 . 74 B3
Westminster SW1 . 147 B3
Charlwood Pl
SW1 . . . . 147 A3
Charlwood Rd
SW15 . . . . 57 C3
Charlwood St
SW1 . . . . 147 A2
Charlwood Terr 🏠
SW15 . . . . 57 C3
Charman Ho
🏠 London SW2 . . 62 C1
South Lambeth
SW8 . . . . 162 A2

Charmian Ho 🏠
N1 . . . . 24 A3
Charmouth Ct
TW10 . . . . 54 B2
Charmouth Ho
SW8 . . . . 162 C2
Charnock Ho 🏠
W12 . . . . 30 A2
Charnwood Gdns
E14 . . . . 41 C2
Charrington Ho 🏠
E1 . . . . 25 B1
Charrington St
NW1 . . . . 83 B2
Charter Bldgs 🏠
SE10 . . . . 52 A2
Charter Ct
Finsbury Pk N4 . . . . . 5 C3
Marylebone W1 . . 102 B3
Charter Ho WC2 . 106 B1
Charterhouse Bldgs
EC1 . . . . 96 C1
Charterhouse Mews
EC1 . . . . 108 B4
Charterhouse Rd
E8 . . . . 16 C3
Charterhouse Sq
EC1 . . . . 108 B4
Charterhouse Square
Sch EC1 . . . . 108 B4
Charterhouse St
EC1 . . . . 108 A3
Charterhouse Works
SW18 . . . . 59 B3
Charteris Rd
Finsbury Pk N4 . . . . . 5 C3
Kilburn NW6 . . . . . 23 B4
Charter Nightingale
Hospl The NW1 . . 102 B4
Charter Sch The
SE24 . . . . 63 C2
Chartes Ho SE1 . . 138 B2
Chartfield Ave
SW15 . . . . 57 B2
Chartfield Sch
SW15 . . . . 57 A2
Chartfield Sq
SW15 . . . . 57 C2
Chartham Ct 🏠
SW9 . . . . 62 C4
Chartham Gr SE27 . 75 A1
Chartham Ho SE1 137 C2
Chart House The 🏠
E14 . . . . 42 A1
Chartridge Ct 🏠
SW9 . . . . 48 C4
Chart St N1 . . . . . . 97 C4
Chartwell 🏠
SW19 . . . . 69 C3
Chase Ct SW3 . . . 130 C1
Chase Ctr The
NW10 . . . . 20 C2
Chaseley Ct W4 . . . 37 A1
Chaseley St E14 . . 33 A3
Chasemore Ho 🏠
SW6 . . . . 154 B2
Chase Rd NW10 . . 20 C1
Chase Road Trad Est
NW10 . . . . 20 C1
Chase The SW4 . . . 61 A4
Chater Ho 🏠 E2 . . 25 C2
Chatfield Rd
SW11 . . . . 59 B4
Chatham Ct SW11 . 60 B2
Chatham Ho 🏠
SE5 . . . . 49 A1
Chatham Pl E9 . . . . 17 B2
Chatham Rd SW11 . 60 B2

Chatham St SE17 . 151 C4
Chatsworth Ct
Brondesbury NW2 . . 9 C2
Clapton Pk E5 . . . . 17 C4
Earl's Ct W8 . . . . 141 B4
Chatsworth Est
E5 . . . . 17 C4
Chatsworth Gdns
W3 . . . . 28 A1
Chatsworth Lo 🏠
W4 . . . . 37 C1
Chatsworth Rd
Brondesbury NW2 . . 9 C2
Chiswick W4 . . . . . 45 B4
Clapton Pk E5 . . . . 17 C4
Chatsworth Way
SE27 . . . . 75 B1
Chattenden Ho 🏠
N4 . . . . 6 C4
Chatterton Ct
TW9 . . . . 44 B1
Chatterton Rd N4 . . 6 A1
Chatto Rd SW11 . . 60 B2
Chaucer Ave TW9 . 44 C1
Chaucer Ct 🏠
N16 . . . . 16 A4
Chaucer Dr SE1 . . 153 A3
Chaucer Ho SW1 . 146 C1
Chaucer Rd
Acton W3 . . . . 28 B1
Herne Hill SE24 . . . 63 A2
Chaulden Ho EC1 . 97 C3
Cheadle Ct NW8 . . 89 C2
Cheadle Ho 🏠
E14 . . . . 33 B3
Cheam St 🏠 SE15 . 65 A4
Cheapside EC2 . . . 109 A1
Chearsley SE17 . . . 151 A4
Cheddington Ho 🏠
E2 . . . . 24 C4
Chedworth Cl E16 . 35 B3
Chedworth Ho 🏠
E5 . . . . 7 C2
Cheesemans Terr
W14 . . . . 140 C1
Chelmer Rd E9 . . . 17 C3
Chelmsford Cl W6 . 47 C4
Chelmsford Ho 🏠
N7 . . . . 14 B4
Chelmsford Sq
NW10 . . . . 22 B4
CHELSEA 144 B1
Chelsea Barracks★
SW1 . . . . 145 C1
Chelsea Bridge
SW1 . . . . 160 A4
Chelsea Bridge Rd
SW1 . . . . 145 C1
Chelsea Cl NW10 . 20 C4
Chelsea Cloisters
SW3 . . . . 144 B3
Chelsea Coll of Art &
Design
Chelsea SW3 . . . 144 A1
Pimlico SW1 . . . . 148 A2
Chelsea Cres
Brondesbury NW2 . 10 B2
Chelsea SW10 . . . 167 A3
Chelsea Ct SW3 . . 159 B4
Chelsea Emb
SW3 . . . . 158 C4
Chelsea Est SW3 . 158 A3
Chelsea Farm Ho
SW10 . . . . 157 C3

Chelsea Gate
SW1 . . . . **145** C1
Chelsea Gdns
SW1 . . . . **145** C1
Chelsea Harbour
Design Ctr SW10 **167** A4
Chelsea Harbour Dr
SW10 . . . . **167** A4
Chelsea Harbour Pier
SW10 . . . . **167** B3
Chelsea Lo SW3 . **159** A4
Chelsea Manor Ct
SW3 . . . . **158** B2
Chelsea Manor Gdns
SW3 . . . . **144** B1
Chelsea Manor St
SW3 . . . . **144** B1
Chelsea Manor
Studios SW3 . . **144** B1
Chelsea Park Gdns
SW3 . . . . **157** B4
Chelsea Physic Gdn ★
SW1 . . . . **158** C4
Chelsea Reach Twr
SW10 . . . . **157** B2
Chelsea Sq SW3 . . **143** C1
Chelsea Twrs
SW3 . . . . **158** B3
Chelsea &
Westminster Hospl
SW10 . . . . **157** A3
Chelsfield Ho
SE17 . . . . **152** A3
Chelsfield Point **3**
E9 . . . . **17** C1
Chelsham Ho **1**
SW4 . . . . **61** C4
Chelsham Rd SW4 . **61** C4
Cheltenham Pl
10 Acton W3 . . . . . **28** A1
Acton W3 . . . . **37** A4
1 South Acton W3 . **37** A4
Cheltenham Rd
SE15 . . . . **65** B2
Cheltenham Terr
SW3 . . . . **145** A2
Chelverton Ct
SW15 . . . . **57** C3
Chelverton Rd
SW15 . . . . **57** C3
Chelwood Ct
SW11 . . . . **167** C4
Chelwood Gdns
TW9 . . . . **44** C1
Chelwood Ho W2 . **101** C1
Chenies Ho W2 . . **114** A4
Chenies Mews
WC1 . . . . **93** B1
Chenies Pl NW1 . . **83** C2
Chenies St WC1 . . **105** B4
Chenies The NW1 . **83** C2
Cheniston Gdns
W8 . . . . **128** A2
Chepstow Cl
SW15 . . . . **58** A2
Chepstow Cres
W11 . . . **31** C2 **113** B4
Chepstow Ct
W11 . . . . **31** C2 **113** B4
Chepstow Pl
W2 . . . . **31** C2 **113** C4
Chepstow Rd W2 . . **31** C3
Chepstow Villas
W11 . . . **31** C2 **113** B4

Chequers Ct EC1 . . **97** B1
Chequers Ho NW8 . **90** A2
Chequer St EC1 . . . **97** A1
Cherbury Ct N1 . . . **87** C1
Cherbury St N1 . . . **87** C1
Cheriton Ho **3** E5 . **17** A3
Cheriton Sq SW17 . **72** C2
Cherry Cl **12** SW2 . . **74** C4
Cherry Ct
Acton W3 . . . . **29** A1
1 Rotherhithe
SE16 . . . . **33** A1
Cherry Garden Ho **7**
SE16 . . . . **40** A4
Cherry Garden Sch
SE16 . . . . **153** C4
Cherry Garden St
SE16 . . . . **40** A4
Cherry Laurel Wlk
SW2 . . . . **62** B1
Cherry Tree Cl **11**
E9 . . . . **25** B4
Cherry Tree Ct
1 Camden Town
NW1 . . . . **13** B1
11 Peckham SE15 . . **50** A2
Cherry Tree Dr
SW16 . . . . **74** A1
Cherrytree Ho **8**
W10 . . . . **22** C2
Cherry Tree Ho
SE14 . . . . **51** B1
Cherry Trees Sch The
E3 . . . . **26** C2
Cherry Tree Terr
E1 . . . . **138** B4
Cherry Tree Wlk
EC1 . . . . **97** A1
Cherrywood Cl E3 . **26** A2
Cherrywood Dr
SW15 . . . . **57** C2
Chertsey Ct SW14 . **55** A4
Chertsey Ho
E2 . . . . **24** B2 **98** C3
Cherwell Ho NW8 . **89** C1
Cheryls Cl SW6 . . **166** B4
Chesham Cl SW1 . **131** B1
Chesham Ct SW18 . **71** C4
Chesham Flats
W1 . . . . **117** C4
Chesham Ho
SW1 . . . . **131** B1
Chesham Mews
SW1 . . . . **131** B2
Chesham Pl SW1 . **131** B1
Chesham St SW1 . **131** B1
Cheshire St
E2 . . . . **24** B1 **99** A2
Chesholm Rd N16 . . **7** A1
Cheshunt Ho NW6 . **78** A3
Chesil Ct
17 Bethnal Green
E2 . . . . **25** B3
Chelsea SW3 . . . . **158** B4
Chesilton Rd
SW6 . . . . **164** C4
Chesney Ct W9 . . . **23** C1
Chesney Ho SE13 . . **67** C3
Chesney St SW11 . **169** B3
Chessington Ho
SW8 . . . . **171** B2
Chesson Rd W14 . **155** A4
Chessum Ho E8 . . . **16** C2
Chester Ave TW10 . **54** B1
Chester Cl
Barnes SW13 . . . . . **57** A4
Knightsbridge SW1 . **132** A3

Chester Cl *continued*
1 Richmond TW10 . . **54** B1
Chester Close N
NW1 . . . . **92** B4
Chester Close S
NW1 . . . . **92** B3
Chester Cres E8 . . . **16** B3
Chester Ct
Bermondsey SE8 . . . **40** C1
4 Camberwell SE5 . **48** C3
Gospel Oak NW5 . . . **12** C4
Regent's Pk NW1 . . . **92** B3
Chesterfield Ct
SE13 . . . . **67** B4
Chesterfield Gdns
Greenwich SE10 . . . **52** C3
Mayfair W1 . . . . . **118** A2
Chesterfield Gr
SE22 . . . . **64** B2
Chesterfield Hill
W1 . . . . **118** A3
Chesterfield Ho
Highgate N6 . . . . **3** C3
Mayfair W1 . . . . . **117** C2
Chesterfield Rd
W4 . . . . **45** B4
Chesterfield St
W1 . . . . **118** A2
Chesterfield Way
SE15 . . . . **50** B3
Chesterford Gdns
NW3 . . . . **11** A4
Chester Gate NW1 . **92** B3
Chester Ho
Dartmouth Pk N19 . . **4** A2
2 Deptford SE8 . . . **51** B4
Chesterman Ct
W4 . . . . **46** A3
Chester Mews
SW1 . . . . **132** A2
Chester Pl NW1 . . . **92** A4
Chester Rd
Dartmouth Pk N19 . . **4** A3
Regent's Pk NW1 . . . **92** A4
Chester Row
SW1 . . . . **145** C1
Chester Sq SW1 . . **146** A4
Chester Sq Mews
SW1 . . . . **132** A1
Chester St
Bethnal Green
E2 . . . . . . **24** C1 **99** C2
Westminster SW1 . **131** C2
Chester Terr NW1 . **92** A4
Chester Way
SE11 . . . . **149** C3
Chestnut Alley
SW6 . . . . **155** A3
Chestnut Ave **11**
SW14 . . . . **55** C4
Chestnut Cl
New Cross Gate
SE14 . . . . **51** B2

Chestnut Cl *continued*
1 Stoke Newington
N16 . . . . **6** C2
Chestnut Ct SW6 . **155** A4
Chestnut Gr SW12 . **72** C3
Chestnut Grove Sch
SW12 . . . . **72** C3
Chestnut Ho
11 Acton W4 . . . . . **38** A2
Brockley SE4 . . . . . . **66** B4
7 Maitland Pk
NW3 . . . . **12** B2
West Norwood
SE27 . . . . **75** B1
Chestnut Rd SE21,
SE27 . . . . **75** B1
Chestnuts The **1**
N5 . . . . **15** A4
Chettle Cl SE1 . . . **137** B2
Chetwode Ho
NW8 . . . . **90** A2
Chetwode Rd
SW17 . . . . **72** B1
Chetwynd Rd NW5 . **4** A1
Cheval Ct SW15 . . . **57** A3
Cheval Pl SW7 . . . **130** B2
Cheval St E14 . . . . . **41** C3
Chevening Rd
Cubitt Town SE10 . . **43** B1
Kilburn NW6 . . . . . . **23** A4
Cheverell Ho **2**
E2 . . . . **24** C3
Cheverton Rd N19 . . **4** C3
Chevet St E9 . . . . . . **18** A3
Chevington NW2 . . **10** B2
Cheviot Ct **18**
SE14 . . . . **50** B3
Cheviot Gate NW2 . **1** A2
Cheviot Gdns NW2 . **1** A2
Cheviot Ho N16 . . . . **7** B3
Chevron Cl E16 . . . **35** C3
Cheylesmore Ho
SW1 . . . . **146** A2
Cheyne Ct SW3 . . **158** C4
Cheyne Gdns
SW3 . . . . **158** B3
Cheyne Mews
SW3 . . . . **158** B3
Cheyne Pl SW3 . . . **158** C4
Cheyne Row SW3 . **158** A3
Cheyne Wlk
SW10 . . . . **157** B2
Cheyney Ho **2** E9 . **17** C2
Chichele Mans
NW2 . . . . **9** C3
Chichele Rd NW2 . . . **9** C3
Chicheley St SE1 . **135** A4
Chichester Ct **2**
NW1 . . . . **13** B1
Chichester Ho
NW6 . . . . **23** C3
Chichester Rd
Bayswater W2 . . . . **100** B4
Kilburn NW6 . . . . . . **23** C3
Chichester Rents
WC2 . . . . **107** B2
Chichester St
SW1 . . . . **147** A1
Chichester Way
E14 . . . . **42** C2
Chicksand Ho E1 . **111** B4
Chicksand St E1 . . **111** A3
Chicksand Street
E1 . . . . **111** B3
Chiddingstone
SE13 . . . . **67** B2

Chiddingstone St
SW6 . . . . **165** C2
Chigwell Ct **1** E9 . . **18** A2
Chigwell Hill E1 . . . **32** A2
Chiham Ho **5**
SE15 . . . . **50** B4
Chilcombe Ho **6**
SW15 . . . . **68** C4
Chilcot Cl **13** E14 . . **34** A3
Childebert Rd
SW17 . . . . **73** A2
Childeric Prim Sch
SE14 . . . . **51** A3
Childeric Rd SE14 . . **51** A3
Childerley St
SW6 . . . . **164** A4
Childers St SE8 . . . **51** B1
Child La SE10 . . . . . **43** B3
CHILD'S HILL **1** C2
Child's Hill Prim Sch
NW2 . . . . **1** A1
Child's Mews
SW5 . . . . **141** C3
Child's Pl SW5 . . . **141** C3
Child's St SW5 . . . **141** C3
Child's Wlk SW5 . . **141** C3
Chilham Ct **13**
SW9 . . . . **62** C4
Chilham Ho SE1 . . **137** C2
Chillington Dr
SW11 . . . . **59** C3
Chillingworth Rd
N7 . . . . **14** C3
Chiltern Ct
22 Deptford SE14 . . **50** B3
Marylebone NW1 . . . **91** A1
Chiltern Ho
Camberwell SE17 . . **48** C4
2 Kensal Town
W10 . . . . **31** A4
9 Stamford Hill N16 . **7** B3
Chiltern Rd E3 . . . . **26** C1
Chiltern St W1 . . . **103** B4
Chilton Gr SE8 . . . . **41** A2
Chilton Rd TW9 . . . **54** C4
Chilton St
E2 . . . . **24** B1 **99** A2
Chilver St SE10 . . . . **43** B1
Chilworth Ct **8**
SW19 . . . . **69** C3
Chilworth Mews
W2 . . . . **101** B1
Chilworth St W2 . . **101** A1
Chimney Ct **22** E1 . **32** A1
China Cl **1** E14 . . . **32** A4
China Hall Mews **8**
SE16 . . . . **40** B3
China Mews **17**
SW2 . . . . **74** B4
Chindit Ho **11** N16 . **15** C4
Ching Ct WC2 . . . **106** A1
Chinnocks Wharf
E14 . . . . **33** A2
Chipka St E14 . . . . . **42** B4
Chipley St SE14 . . . **51** A4
Chippendale Ho
SW1 . . . . **146** B1
Chippenham Gdns
NW6 . . . . **23** C2
Chippenham Mews
W9 . . . . **23** C1
Chippenham Rd
W9 . . . . **23** C1
Chip St SW4 . . . . . . **61** C3
Chipstead Ho **4**
SW2 . . . . **74** A3

Chipstead St
SW6 ....165 C2
Chirk Ct SE4 ......51 B1
Chisenhale Prim Sch
E3 ....26 A3
Chisenhale Rd E3 ..26 A3
Chisholm Ct 11
W6 ....38 C1
Chisholm Rd 13
TW10 ....54 B1
Chisledon Wlk E9 .18 B2
Chislehurst Rd
TW10 ....54 A2
Chislet 5 NW5 ....12 C2
Chiswell St
Barbican EC1 .....109 B4
Camberwell SE5 ...48 C3
CHISWICK 38 B1
Chiswick & Bedford
Park Prep Sch
W4 ....38 A2
Chiswick Ave
W4 ....37 C2
Chiswick Com Sch
W4 ....45 C3
Chiswick Green
Studios 11 W4 ...37 B2
Chiswick High Rd
W4 ....38 A2
Chiswick High Road
(North Circular Rd)
W4 ....36 C1
Chiswick Ho* W4 ..45 C4
Chiswick La W4 ....38 A1
Chiswick La S W4 ..46 B4
Chiswick Mall W4 ..38 B1
Chiswick Maternity
Hospl W4 ....38 B1
Chiswick Park Sta
W4 ....37 B2
Chiswick Pier W4 ..46 B3
Chiswick Pk W4 ....37 C2
Chiswick Plaza
W4 ....45 B4
Chiswick Quay
W4 ....45 B2
Chiswick Rd W4 ....37 B2
Chiswick Rdbt W4 ..36 C1
Chiswick Sq W4 ....46 A4
Chiswick Sta W4 ...45 B3
Chiswick Staithe
W4 ....45 B2
Chiswick Terr 6
W4 ....37 B2
Chiswick Village
W4 ....45 A4
Chiswick Wharf
W4 ....46 B4
Chitty St W1 .....105 A4
Chivalry Rd SW11 ..60 A2
Chiveston 27
SW19 ....69 C3
Chobham Gdns
SW19 ....69 C2
Chobham Rd E15 ...19 C3
Cholmeley Cres N6 ..4 A4
Cholmeley Lo N6 .....4 A3
Cholmeley Pk N6 .....4 A4
Cholmley Gdns
NW6 ....10 C3
Cholmondeley Ave
NW10 ....21 C3
Chopin's St SE8 ...51 B4
Chopwell Cl E15 ...19 C1
Choumert Gr SE15 .49 C1
Choumert Mews
SE15 ....49 C1

Choumert Rd
SE15 ....49 B1
Choumert Sq 4
SE15 ....49 C1
Chow Sq 8 E8 .....16 B3
Chrisp Ho SE10 ....53 A4
Chrisp St E14 .....34 A3
Christ Church
TW9 ....54 A4
Christchurch Ave
NW6 ....10 A1
Christchurch
Bentinck CE Prim
Sch NW1 ....102 B3
Christchurch CE Prim
Sch SW3 ....158 C4
Christ Church CE
Prim Sch
Battersea SW11 ...60 A4
Brondesbury NW6 ..10 B1
Cubitt Town SW19 ..42 B4
Christchurch CE Sch
E1 ....111 A3
Christ Church Ct
11 Brondesbury Pk
NW6 ....10 A1
Harlesden NW10 ...21 A4
Christchurch Hill
NW3 ....11 C4
Christchurch Ho 2
SW2 ....74 A3
Christchurch Pas
NW3 ....2 B1
Christ Church Prim
Sch, Hampstead
NW3 ....2 B1
Christchurch Rd
Mortlake SW14 ....55 B2
Streatham SW2 ....74 C3
Christ Church Sch
NW1 ....92 B4
Christchurch Sq 2
E9 ....25 B4
Christ Church St
SW3 ....158 C4
Christ Church
Streatham CE Prim
Sch SW2 ....74 B3
Christchurch Terr
SW3 ....158 C4
Christchurch Way
SE10 ....43 A1
Christian Ct SE16 .33 B1
Christian St E1 ...111 C1
Christie Ct
Maitland Pk NW3 ..12 A3
2 Upper Holloway
N19 ....5 A2
Christie Ho 2
SE10 ....43 B1
Christie Rd E9 ....18 A2
Christina Sq N4 ....6 A3
Christina St
EC2 ......24 A1 98 A2
Christopher Boone's
Almshouses SE13 .67 C3
Christopher Cl
SE16 ....40 C4
Christopher France
Ho 6 E1 ....26 A2
Christopher Hatton
Prim Sch EC1 .....95 B1
Christopher Lo 2
N6 ....4 C4

Christopher Pl
NW1 ....93 C3
Christopher St
EC2 ....97 C1
Christ's Sch TW10 .54 C2
Christ the King RC
Prim Sch N4 ....5 B2
Christ the King Sixth
Form Coll SE13 ...67 C4
Chryssell Rd SW9 .163 C1
Chubworthy St 5
SE14 ....51 A4
Church Ave
Camden Town
NW1 ....13 A2
Mortlake SW14 ....55 C4
Church Cl W8 .....128 A4
Church Cres E9 ....17 C1
Churchcroft Cl
SW12 ....72 C4
Church Ct
Holborn EC4 .....107 B1
Rotherhithe SE16 ..41 B4
Churchdale Ct 1
W4 ....37 A1
CHURCH END 8 A4
Church Entry EC4 .108 B1
Church Estate
Almshouses 8
TW9 ....54 B3
Church Gdns
W3 ....28 B1
Churchfield Ho
W2 ....89 B1
Churchfield Mans
SW6 ....165 A1
Churchfields SE10 .52 B4
Church Garth 4
N19 ....4 C2
Church Gate SW6 ..58 A4
Church Gn SW9 ...173 C2
Church Gr SE13 ...66 C2
Churchill Gardens
Prim Sch SW1 ....147 A1
Church Ho EC1 ....96 B2
Churchill Ct
Finsbury Pk N4 .....5 C4
Peckham SE5 ......49 C1
Willesden NW2 .....9 A3
Churchill Gdns
SW1 ....160 C4
Churchill Gdns Rd
SW1 ....160 C4
Churchill Pl E14 ...34 A1
Churchill Rd
Gospel Oak NW5 ..13 A4
Willesden NW2 .....9 B2
Churchill Wlk E9 ..17 B3
Church Mead SE5 .48 B3
Churchmead Rd
NW10 ....8 C2
Church Path W4 ...37 B3
Church Rd
Acton W3 ....37 B3
Barnes SW13 .....46 C2
2 Canonbury N1 ...15 B2
Richmond TW10,
TW9 ....54 A2

Church Rd continued
Willesden NW10 ....8 A1
Church Row NW3 ..11 B4
Church St
Chiswick W4 ......46 B4
Lisson Gr NW8 ....90 A1
Church Street Est
NW8 ....89 C1
Church Studios 16
NW1 ....13 C2
Churchward Ho
Camberwell SE17 ..48 A4
West Kensington
SW5 ....141 A1
Churchway NW1 ...93 C4
Church Wlk
Barnes SW13 .....46 C2
Canonbury N16 ...15 C4
Child's Hill NW2 ....1 B1
Dartmouth Pk N6 ...3 C1
Churchyard Row
SE11 ....150 B4
Churnfield 2 N4 ....5 C2
Churston Cl 16
SW2 ....74 C3
Churston Mans
WC1 ....95 A1
Churton Pl
Brentford W4 .....45 A4
Pimlico SW1 .....147 A3
Churton St SW1 ..147 A3
Chute Ho SW9 ...173 B1
Chuter Ede Ho
SW6 ....155 A3
Cicada Rd SW18 ...59 B2
Cicely Ho NW8 ....79 C1
Cicely Rd SE15 ....49 C2
Cinema Mus The*
SE11 ....150 A3
Cinnabar Wharf
Central E1 ....125 C2
Cinnabar Wharf East
E1 ....125 C2
Cinnabar Wharf West
E1 ....125 C2
Cinnamon Cl 2
SE15 ....49 B3
Cinnamon Row 3
SW11 ....59 B4
Cinnamon St E1 ...32 A1
Cinnamon Wharf
SE1 ....139 A4
Circle Ho 14 E14 ..34 C3
Circle The SE1 ...139 A4
Circus Lo NW8 ....89 B4
Circus Mews W1 ..102 C4
Circus Pl EC2 ....109 C3
Circus Rd NW8 ....79 B1
Circus St SE10 ....52 B3
Cirencester St
W2 ....100 A4
Citadel Pl SE11 ..148 C2
Citizen Ho N7 .....14 C4
Citizen Rd N7 .....14 C4
Citron Terr 4
SE15 ....65 A4
Citrus Ho 14 SE8 .41 B1
City Banking Coll
SE1 ....137 C4
City Bsns Ctr 33
SE16 ....40 B4
City Central Est
EC1 ....96 C3
City Coll N1 ......97 B4

City Coll of London
The WC1 ....107 A3
City Forum EC1 ....96 C4
City Garden Row
N1 ....86 B1
City Gate E1 ......25 B1
City & Guilds of
London Art Sch The
SE11 ....149 C1
City Harbour E14 ..42 A3
City & Islington 6th
Form Coll EC1 ....96 A4
City & Islington Coll
Finsbury Pk N4 .....6 A2
Lower Holloway N7 .14 A4
Lower Holloway N7 .14 B4
Shoreditch EC1 ...97 A3
Shoreditch N1 .....87 B4
City Lights The
SE11 ....149 C1
CITY OF LONDON
 ....122 A4
City of London Sch
EC4 ....122 C4
City of London Sch
for Girls EC2 ....109 A4
City of Westminster
Coll
Paddington NW1 ..102 B4
Paddington NW1 ..101 B4
City of Westminster
Coll, Maida Vale Ctr
W9 ....88 A3
City of Westminster
Coll, Queens Park
Ctr W9 ....23 C2
City Rd EC1 ....97 A4
City Thameslink Sta
EC4 ....108 A1
City University
EC1 ....96 A3
City Wlk SE1 .....138 A3
Civil Service Coll
SW1 ....146 C3
Clabon Mews
SW1 ....144 C4
Clack St SE16 .....40 B4
Claire Ct NW2 .....10 A2
Claire Pl E14 .....41 C3
Clancarty Rd
SW6 ....165 C1
Clandon Cl W3 ....37 A4
Clandon St SE8 ...51 C1
Clanfield Ho 12
SW15 ....68 C3
Clanricarde Gdns
W2 ....31 C2 113 C3
CLAPHAM 61 A4
Clapham Common*
 ....61 A3
Clapham Common
North Side SW4 ...60 C3
Clapham Common
South Side SW4 ...61 B2
Clapham Common Sta
SW4 ....61 B3
Clapham Common
West Side
Clapham SW4,
SW11 ....60 B3
Clapham SW11 ....60 C2

Clapham Computer &
Secretarial Coll
SW11 . . . . .60 B2
Clapham Court Terr
2 SW4 . . . . .62 A2
Clapham Cres
SW4 . . . . .61 C3
Clapham Ct 3
SW4 . . . . .62 A2
Clapham High St
SW4 . . . . .61 C3
Clapham High Street
Sta SW4 . . . . .61 C4
Clapham Junction Est
SW11 . . . . .60 A3
Clapham Junction Sta
SW11 . . . . .60 A4
Clapham Manor Ct 1
SW4 . . . . .61 B4
Clapham Manor Prim
Sch SW4 . . . . .61 B4
Clapham Manor St
SW4 . . . . .61 C4
Clapham Mans
SW4 . . . . .61 A1
Clapham North Bsns
Ctr 10 SW4 . . . . . . .61 C4
Clapham North Sta
SW4 . . . . .62 A4
CLAPHAM PARK . . .61 C2
Clapham Park Rd
SW4 . . . . .61 C3
Clapham Park Terr 4
SW2 . . . . .62 A2
Clapham Rd SW9 .162 A3
Clapham South Sta
SW4 . . . . .61 A1
Clapton Comm E5 . . .7 C4
Clapton Girls Tec Coll
E5 . . . . .17 B4
CLAPTON PARK 18 A2
Clapton Pas E5 . . . . .17 B3
Clapton Sq E5 . . . . . .17 B3
Clapton Terr E5 . . . . . .7 C3
Clapton Way E5 . . . .16 C4
Clara Grant Ho 10
E14 . . . . .41 C3
Clara Grant Prim Sch
The E3 . . . . .26 C1
Clare Ct WC1 . . . . . .94 B3
Claredale Ho 3
E2 . . . . .25 A3
Claredale St E2 . . . .24 C3
Clare Gdns W11 . . . .31 A3
Clare Ho
Bermondsey SE1 . .153 A2
6 Old Ford E3 . . . . .26 B4
Clare La N1 . . . . . . .15 B1
Clare Lawn Ave
SW14 . . . . .55 C2
Clare Mews SW6 . . .156 A1
Clare Mkt WC2 . . . .107 A1
Claremont 1
SW15 . . . . .58 A2
Claremont Cl
Finsbury N6 . . . . . . .85 C1
4 Streatham SW2 . .74 B3
Claremont Ct 1
W9 . . . . .23 B3
Claremont Gr W4 . . .46 A3
Claremont Rd
Highgate N6 . . . . .4 B4
West Kilburn W9 . . .23 B3
Claremont Sq N1 . . .85 B1

Claremont St
SE10 . . . . .52 A4
Clarence Ave SW4 . .61 C1
Clarence Cres
SW4 . . . . .61 C1
Clarence Ct 10
W6 . . . . .39 A2
Clarence Gate
NW1 . . . . .91 A2
Clarence Gate Gdns
NW1 . . . . .91 A1
Clarence Gdns
NW1 . . . . .92 B3
Clarence Ho SE17 . .48 B4
Clarence Ho*
SW1 . . . . .119 A1
Clarence La SW15 . .56 B1
Clarence Mews
Balham SW12 . . . . . .73 A4
Hackney E5 . . . . . . .17 A3
1 Rotherhithe
SE16 . . . . .32 C1
Clarence Pl 5 E5 . . . .17 A3
Clarence Rd
Brentford W4 . . . . . .36 C1
Brondesbury NW6 . . .10 B1
Lower Clapton E5 . . .17 A4
Richmond TW9 . . . . .44 C2
Clarence St 6
TW9 . . . . .54 A3
Clarence Terr
NW1 . . . . .91 A2
Clarence Way
NW1 . . . . .13 A1
Clarence Wlk
SW4 . . . . .172 A2
Clarendon Cl
Bayswater W2 . . . . .116 A4
30 Hackney E9 . . . . .17 B1
Clarendon Cross
W11 . . . . .31 A2 112 B3
Clarendon Ct
Paddington W9 . . . . .89 A2
1 Richmond TW9 . . .44 C2
Willesden NW2 . . . . . .9 B1
Clarendon Dr
SW15 . . . . .57 B3
Clarendon Flats
W1 . . . . .103 C1
Clarendon Gdns
W9 . . . . .89 A1
Clarendon Gr NW1 . .93 B4
Clarendon Ho
NW1 . . . . .83 A1
Clarendon Mews
W2 . . . . .116 A4
Clarendon Pl W2 . . .116 A4
Clarendon Rd
W11 . . . . .31 A2 112 B3
Clarendon Rise
SE13 . . . . .67 B3
Clarendon St
SW1 . . . . .146 B2
Clarendon Terr
W9 . . . . .89 A2
Clarendon Wlk 11
W11 . . . . .31 A3
Clare Pl SW15 . . . . .68 B4
Clare Rd
New Cross Gate
SE14 . . . . .51 B2
Willesden NW10 . . . . .8 C1
Clare St E2 . . . . .25 A3
Clareville Ct 7
SW7 . . . . .143 A3
Clareville Gr SW7 . .143 A3
Clareville Grove Mews
SW7 . . . . .143 A3

Clareville St SW7 . .143 A3
Clarewood Ct W1 . .102 C3
Clarewood Wlk
SW9 . . . . .62 C3
Clarges Ho W1 . . . .118 A2
Clarges Mews
W1 . . . . .118 A2
Clarges St W1 . . . . .118 B2
Clariat Ct W3 . . . . . .36 C4
Claribel Rd SW9 . . . .48 A1
Claridge Ct SW6 . . .164 C3
Clarissa Ho 7
E14 . . . . .34 A3
Clarissa St E8 . . . . . .24 B4
Clarke Ho 2 SW4 . . .61 B4
Clarke Path N16 . . . . .7 C3
Clarkes Mews
W1 . . . . .103 C4
Clark Ho SW10 . . . .156 C2
Clarkson Rd E16 . . . .35 B3
Clarkson Row
NW1 . . . . .82 C1
Clarkson St E2 . . . . .25 A2
Clark's Pl EC2 . . . . .110 A2
Clark St E1 . . . . .32 B4
Classic Mans 33
E9 . . . . .17 B1
Classinghall Ho 14
SW15 . . . . .57 C1
Claude Rd SE15 . . . . .50 A1
Claude St E14 . . . . . .41 C2
Claudia Jones Way
SW2 . . . . .62 A1
Claudia Pl SW19 . . . .70 A3
Clavell St 8 SE10 . . .52 B4
Claverdale Rd
SW2 . . . . .74 C4
Clavering Ave
SW13 . . . . .47 A4
Clavering Ho SE13 . .67 C3
Claverton St SW1 . .147 A1
Clave St E1 . . . . .32 B1
Claxton Gr
W6 . . . . .39 C1 140 A1
Claybank Gr SE13 . . .67 A4
Claybrook Rd W6 . . .47 C4
Claydon SE17 . . . . .150 C4
Clayhall Ct 23 E3 . . .26 B3
Claylands Pl SW8 . .163 B2
Claylands Rd
SW8 . . . . .163 A3
Claypole Rd E15 . . . .27 B3
Claypons Ave
TW8 . . . . .36 A2
Claypons Hospl &
Day Treatment Ctr
TW8 . . . . .36 A2
Claypons La TW8 . .36 A1
Clays Ct N16 . . . . .7 B3
Clays La E15 . . . . . . .19 A3
Clays Lane Cl E15 . . .19 A3
Clays Lane Cvn Site
E15 . . . . .19 B3
Clay St W1 . . . . . . .103 A3
Clayton Cres N1 . . . .84 C3
Clayton Ct N16 . . . . . .7 C4
Clayton Ho 22 E9 . . .17 B1
Clayton Mews
SE10 . . . . .52 C2
Clayton Rd SE15 . . . .49 C2
Clayton St SE11 . . .163 B4
Clearbrook Way 13
E1 . . . . .32 B3
Clear Water Ho 9
TW10 . . . . .54 A2

Clearwater Terr 4
W11 . . . . .39 C4
Clearwell Dr W9 . . . .88 B1
Cleaver Ho 6
NW3 . . . . .12 B1
Cleaver Sq SE11 . . .149 C1
Cleaver St SE11 . . . .149 C2
Cleeve Ho
E2 . . . . .24 A2 98 B3
Cleeve Way SW15 . .68 B4
Cleeve Workshops
E2 . . . . .24 A2 98 B3
Clegg St 16 E1 . . . . .32 A1
Cleland Ho 10 E2 . . .25 B3
Clematis St W12 . . . .29 C2
Clem Atlee Par
SW6 . . . . .155 A3
Clem Attlee Ct
SW6 . . . . .155 A3
Clemence St E14 . . . .33 B4
Clement Attlee Ho
NW10 . . . . .8 B1
Clement Ave SW4 . .61 C3
Clement Cl
Acton W4 . . . . .37 C2
Hampstead NW6 . . . . .9 B1
Clement Danes Ho 2
W12 . . . . .30 A3
Clement Ho
1 Deptford SE8 . . . .41 A2
17 North Kensington
W10 . . . . .30 B4
Clements Ave 1
E16 . . . . .35 C2
Clements Inn
WC2 . . . . .107 A1
Clements Inn Pas
WC2 . . . . .107 A1
Clement's La EC2,
EC4 . . . . .123 C4
Clement's Rd
SE16 . . . . .40 A3
Clemson Ho 9 E8 . . .24 B4
Clennam St SE1 . . . .137 A4
Clenston Mews
W1 . . . . .102 C2
Clent Ho 4 N16 . . . . .7 B3
Cleopatra's Needle*
WC2 . . . . .120 C3
Clephane Rd 13
N1 . . . . .15 B2
Clephane Rd N N1 . .15 B2
Clephane Rd S N1 . .15 C2
Clere Pl EC2 . . . . . . .97 C2
Clere St EC2 . . . . . . .97 C2
CLERKENWELL 96 A1
Clerkenwell Cl
EC1 . . . . .95 C1
Clerkenwell Gn
EC1 . . . . .96 A1
Clerkenwell Parochial
CE Prim Sch EC1 . .95 B3
Clerkenwell Rd
EC1 . . . . .96 A1
Clermont Rd E9 . . . . .25 B4
Clevedon Cl
Battersea SW11 . . . .168 A4
Dulwich SE21 . . . . . .75 C1
Clevedon Mans
NW5 . . . . .12 C4
Cleve Ho NW6 . . . . .11 A1
Cleveland Ave W4 . .38 B2
Cleveland Ct W1 . . . .93 A1
Cleveland Gdns
Barnes SW13 . . . . . .46 B1
Paddington W2 . . . . .100 C1

Cleveland Gr 39
E1 . . . . .25 B1
Cleveland Mans
Brixton SW9 . . . . . .163 B1
8 Brondesbury
NW6 . . . . .10 B1
Paddington W9 . . . . .23 C1
Cleveland Mews
W1 . . . . .104 C4
Cleveland Pl SW1 . .119 A2
Cleveland Rd
Barnes SW13 . . . . . .46 B1
Islington N1 . . . . . . .15 C1
5 South Acton W4 . .37 B3
Cleveland Row
SW1 . . . . .119 A1
Cleveland Sq W2 . . .100 C1
Cleveland St W1 . . . .92 C1
Cleveland Terr
W2 . . . . .101 A2
Cleveland Way E1 . .25 B1
Clevendon Cl N16 . . . .7 B1
Cleve Rd NW6 . . . . .11 A1
Cleverly Cotts
W12 . . . . .29 B1
Cleverly Est W12 . . .29 C2
Cley Ho SE4 . . . . . . .65 C3
Clichy Ho 32 E1 . . . .32 B4
Clifden Mews E5 . . .17 C3
Clifden Rd E5 . . . . . .17 C3
Cliff Ct 14 NW1 . . . .13 C2
Cliffe Ho 5 SE10 . . . .43 B1
Clifford Ave
Mortlake SW14 . . . . .45 B1
Mortlake SW14,
TW9 . . . . .55 A4
Clifford Ct
Bayswater W2 . . . . .100 A3
Wandsworth SW18 . .71 C4
Willesden NW10 . . . . .8 A4
Clifford Dr SW9 . . . . .63 A3
Clifford Gdns
NW10 . . . . .22 B3
Clifford Haigh Ho
SW6 . . . . .47 C3
Clifford Ho W14 . . . .140 C3
Clifford's Inn Pas
EC4 . . . . .107 B1
Clifford St W1 . . . . .118 C3
Clifford Way NW10 . . .8 B4
Cliff Rd NW1 . . . . . . .13 C2
Cliff Road Studios 10
NW1 . . . . .13 C2
Cliffsend Ho SW9 . .173 C3
Clifton Ct SE8 . . . . . .51 C1
Cliffview Rd SE13 . . .66 C4
Cliff Villas NW1 . . . .13 C2
Clifton Ave W12 . . . .29 B1
Clifton Cres SE15 . . .50 A3
Clifton Ct
Finsbury Pk N4 . . . . . .5 C2
Paddington NW8 . . . .89 B2
Peckham SE15 . . . . .50 A3
Putney SW15 . . . . . .57 C2
Clifton Gate
SW10 . . . . .156 C4
Clifton Gdns
Chiswick W4 . . . . . . .37 C2
Paddington W9 . . . . .88 C1
Clifton On E8 . . . . . . .16 C2
Clifton Hill NW8 . . . .78 C3
Clifton Ho
E2 . . . . .24 B1 98 C2
Clifton Mans 4
SW9 . . . . .62 C3

Clifton Pl
Paddington W2 . . . . . **101** C1
Rotherhithe SE16 . . . . **40** B4
Clifton Rd
Harlesden NW10 . . . . . **21** C3
Newham E16 . . . . . . **35** A4
Paddington W9 . . . . . . **89** A2
Clifton Rise SE14 . . **51** A3
Clifton St
EC2 . . . . . . **24** A1 **98** A1
Clifton Terr N4 . . . . . . **5** C2
Clifton Villas W9 . **100** C4
Clifton Way SE15 . . **50** B3
Climsland Ho SE1 **121** C2
Clinch Ct E16 . . . . **35** C4
Cline Ho SW15 . . . . **56** C2
Clinger Ct N1 . . . . . **24** A4
Clink St SE1 . . . . . **123** B2
Clinton Rd E3 . . . . . **26** A2
Clipper Appts 12
SE10 . . . . **52** B4
Clipper Cl 3 SE16 . **40** C4
Clipper Ho E14 . . . . **42** B1
Clipper Way SE13 . **67** B3
Clipstone Ho 10
SW15 . . . . **56** C2
Clipstone Mews
W1 . . . . **104** C4
Clipstone St W1 . . **104** C4
Clissold Cres N16 . **15** C4
Clissold Ct N4 . . . . . **6** B2
Clissold Ho 4 N16 . **6** C2
Clissold Rd N16 . . . . **6** C1
Clitheroe Rd SW9 **172** B1
Clive Ct W9 . . . . **89** A2
Cliveden Ho SW1 . **145** B4
Cliveden Pl SW1 . **145** B4
Clive Ho
Clapham SW8 . . . . **171** B2
Greenwich SE10 . . . . **52** B4
Clive Rd SE21,
SE27 . . . . **75** C1
Cloak La EC4 . . . . **123** B4
Clochar Ct NW10 . . **21** B4
Clock Ho N16 . . . . . . **7** B4
Clockhouse Cl
SW19 . . . . **69** B1
Clockhouse Pl
SW15 . . . . **58** A1
Clockhouse The
SW19 . . . . **69** B1
Clock Mus* EC2 **109** A2
Clock Tower Mews
N1 . . . . **87** A3
Clock Tower Pl
N7 . . . . **14** A2
Cloister Rd
Acton W3 . . . . **28** B4
Child's Hill NW2 . . . . **1** B2
Cloisters Ct N6 . . . . . **4** A3
Cloisters The
SW9 . . . . **173** C3
Clonbrock Rd N16 . **16** A4
Cloncurry St SW6 . **47** C1
Clone Ct 4 W12 . . . **38** A3
Clonmel Rd SW6 . **165** A4
Clonmore St
SW18 . . . . **70** B3
Clorane Gdns NW3 . . **1** C1
Close The
Lewisham SE3 . . . . . **52** C1
Mortlake TW9 . . . . . **55** A4
Cloth Ct EC1 . . . . . **108** B3
Cloth Fair EC1 . . . . **108** B3
Clothier St E1 . . . . **110** B2
Cloth St EC1 . . . . . **108** C4

Cloudesdale Rd
SW17 . . . . **73** A2
Cloudesley Mans
N1 . . . . **85** C3
Cloudesley Pl N1 . . **85** C3
Cloudesley Rd N1 . **85** C3
Cloudesley Sq N1 . **85** C3
Cloudesley St N1 . . **85** C3
Clove Cres E14 . . . . **34** C2
Clovelly Ct NW2 . . . . **9** B3
Clovelly Ho W2 . . **100** C2
Clovelly Rd W4 . . . . **37** C4
Clovelly Way E1 . . . **32** B3
Clover Mews
SW3 . . . . **159** A4
Clowes Ho 3
E2 . . . . **24** B1 **98** C3
Clunbury St N1 . . . . **87** C1
Clunie Ho SW1 . . **131** A2
Cluny Mews SW5 . **141** B3
Cluny Pl SE1 . . . . . **138** A2
Cluse Ct N1 . . . . **86** C2
Clutton St E14 . . . . **34** A4
Clyde Ct NW1 . . . . . **83** C2
Clyde Flats SW6 . **154** C2
Clydesdale Gdns
TW10 . . . . **55** A3
Clydesdale Ho 4
W11 . . . . **31** B3
Clydesdale Rd
W11 . . . . **31** B3
Clyde St SE8 . . . . . . **51** B4
Clynes Ho 3 E2 . . **25** C2
Clyro Ct N4 . . . . **5** B3
Clyston St SW8 . . . **171** A2
Coach & Horses Yd
W1 . . . . **118** C4
Coach House La
Highbury N5 . . . . . . **15** A4
Wimbledon SW19 . . **69** C1
Coach House Mews
SE23 . . . . **65** C1
Coach House Yd 3
NW3 . . . . **11** C4
Coachmaker Mews 4
SW9 . . . . **62** A4
Coalbrook Mans 3
SW12 . . . . **73** A3
Coaldale Wlk
SE21 . . . . **75** B4
Coalecroft Rd
SW15 . . . . **57** B3
Coalport Ho SE11 **149** B4
Coatbridge Ho 6
N1 . . . . **14** B1
Coates Ave SW18 . . **60** A1
Coates Ct NW3 . . . . **12** A3
Coate St E2 . . . . **24** C3
Coates Wlk TW8 . . **36** A1
Cobbett St SW8 . . **163** A1
Cobble La N1 . . . . . . **15** A1
Cobble Mews N4,
N5 . . . . **6** B1
Cobbold Ct SW1 . **147** B4
Cobbold Ind Est
NW10 . . . . **8** B2
Cobbold Mews
W12 . . . . **38** B4
Cobbold Rd
Bedford Pk W12 . . . **38** B4
Willesden NW10 . . . . **8** B3
Cobb's Hall 1
SW6 . . . . **47** C4
Cobb St E1 . . . . . . **110** C3

Cobden Bldgs
WC1 . . . . **94** C4
Cobden Ho
Bethnal Green
E2 . . . . **24** C2 **99** C4
Regent's Pk NW1 . . . **82** C2
Cobham Cl SW11 . . **60** A1
Cobham Mews 3
NW1 . . . . **13** C1
Coborn Mews 9
E3 . . . . **26** B2
Coborn Rd E3 . . . . . **26** B2
Coborn St E3 . . . . . **26** B2
Cobourg Prim Sch
SE5 . . . . **49** B4
Cobourg Rd SE5 . . . **49** B4
Cobourg St NW1 . . **93** A3
Coburg Cl SW1 . . . **147** A4
Coburg Cres SW2 . . **74** C3
Coburg Dwellings
11 E1 . . . . **32** B2
Cochrane Cl NW8 . . **79** C1
Cochrane Ho 19
E14 . . . . **41** C4
Cochrane Mews
NW8 . . . . **79** C1
Cochrane St NW8 . . **79** C1
Coci Ho W14 . . . . . **141** A3
Cockburn Ho
SW1 . . . . **147** C1
Cock Hill E1 . . . . . . **110** B3
Cock La EC1 . . . . . **108** B3
Cockpit Yd WC1 . . **107** A4
Cockspur Ct SW1 . **119** C2
Cockspur St SW1 . **119** C2
Coda Ctr The
SW6 . . . . **164** B4
Code St E1 . . **24** B1 **99** A1
Codicote Ho 22
SE8 . . . . **40** C2
Codicote Terr N4 . . . . **6** B2
Codling Cl E1 . . . . **125** C2
Codrington Ct 7
E1 . . . . **33** A1
Codrington Ho 1
E1 . . . . **25** A1
Codrington Mews
W11 . . . . **31** A3
Cody Rd E16 . . . . . . **27** C1
Coffey St SE8 . . . . . **51** C3
Cohen Lo E5 . . . . . . **18** A3
Coin St SE1 . . . . . . **121** B2
Coity Rd NW5 . . . . . **12** C2
Cokers La SE21 . . . . **75** C2
Coke St E1 . . . . **111** C2
Colas Mews 7
NW6 . . . . **23** C4
Colbeck Mews
SW5 . . . . **142** B3
Colberg Pl N16 . . . . . **7** A4
Colbert 1 SE5 . . . . **49** B2
Colborne Ho 8
E14 . . . . **33** C2
Colchester Ho 1
SW8 . . . . **171** B2
Colchester St E1 . **111** A2
Coldbath Sq EC1 . . **95** B2
Coldbath St SE13 . . **52** A1
Cold Blow La
SE14 . . . . **51** A3
Coldharbour E14 . . **34** B1
Coldharbour Ind Est
SE5 . . . . **48** B1
Coldharbour La
SW9 . . . . **63** A4
Coldharbour Pl
SE5 . . . . **48** C1

Coldstream Gdns
SW18 . . . . **58** B1
Colebeck Mews
N1 . . . . **15** A2
Colebert Ave E1 . . . **25** B1
Colebert Ho 21 E1 . **25** B1
Colebrook Cl
SW19 . . . . **69** C4
Colebrook Ct
SW3 . . . . **144** B3
Colebrooke Pl N1 . **86** B3
Colebrooke Row
Islington N1 . . . . . . **86** B3
Islington N1, N1 . . . **86** B2
Colebrook Ho 1
E14 . . . . **34** A3
Coleby Path 2
SE5 . . . . **48** C3
Colechurch Ho 1
SE1 . . . . **153** B1
Colefax Bldg 21
E1 . . . . **111** C2
Coleford Rd SW18 . **59** B2
Colegrave Prim Sch
E15 . . . . **19** C3
Colegrave Rd E15 . **19** C3
Colegrove Rd
SE15 . . . . **49** B4
Coleherne Ct
SW10 . . . . **142** B1
Coleherne Mans
SW5 . . . . **142** B2
Coleherne Mews
SW10 . . . . **142** A1
Coleherne Rd
SW10 . . . . **142** A1
Colehill Gdns
SW6 . . . . **164** A3
Colehill La SW6 . . **164** B3
Cole Ho SE1 . . . . . **135** C3
Coleman Ct SW18 . **70** C4
Coleman Fields
N1 . . . . **87** A4
Coleman Mans N19 . **5** A4
Coleman Rd SE5 . . . **49** A3
Coleman St EC2 . . **109** B2
Coleman Street Bldgs
EC2 . . . . **109** B2
Colenso Rd E5 . . . . . **17** B4
Coleraine Rd SE3 . . **53** B4
Coleridge Cl SW8 **170** B1
Coleridge Gdns
NW6 . . . . **11** B1
Coleridge Ho
Pimlico SW1 . . . . . **147** A1
Walworth SE17 . . . **151** A2
Coleridge Prim Sch
N8 . . . . **4** C4
Coleridge Rd N4,
N7 . . . . **5** C2
Coleridge Sq
SW10 . . . . **156** C2
Coles Ct SW11 . . . **167** C3
Coleshill Flats
SW1 . . . . **145** C3
Cole St SE1 . . . . . **137** A3
Colestown St
SW11 . . . . **168** B2
Colet Gdns W14 . . . **39** C2
Colet Ho SE17 . . . . **150** B1
Colette Ct 5 SE16 . **40** C4
Coley St WC1 . . . . . **95** A1
Colfe & Hatchcliffe's
Glebe SE13 . . . . . . **67** A2
Colgate Ho SE13 . . **52** A1
Colin Blanchard Ho
SE4 . . . . **51** C1

Colin Ct SW16 . . . **73** C2
Colinette Rd
SW15 . . . . **57** B3
Colin Rd NW10 . . . . . **8** C2
Colinsdale N1 . . . . . **86** A3
Colin Winter Ho 46
E1 . . . . **25** B1
Coliston Pas
SW18 . . . . **70** C4
Coliston Rd SW18 . **70** C4
Collamore Ave
SW18 . . . . **72** A3
Collard Pl NW1 . . . . **13** A1
Collcutt Lo SW4 . . **62** A3
College App SE10 . **52** B4
College Cl E5 . . . . . **17** B3
College Cres NW3 . **11** C2
College Cross N1 . **14** C1
College Ct
Chelsea SW3 . . . . . **145** A1
3 Hammersmith
W6 . . . . **39** B1
Hampstead NW3 . . . **11** C2
College Gdns
Dulwich SE21 . . . . . . **76** A3
Upper Tooting
SW17 . . . . **72** A2
College Gr NW1 . . . **83** B4
College Green Ct
SW9 . . . . **63** A4
College Hill EC4 . . **123** A4
College La NW5 . . . **13** A4
College Mews 5
SW18 . . . . **59** A2
COLLEGE PARK . . **22** A2
College Park Cl
SE13 . . . . **67** C3
College Park Sch
W2 . . . . **100** A1
College Pl
Camden Town
NW1 . . . . **83** A3
Chelsea SW10 . . . . **156** C2
College Rd
Dulwich SE19,
SE21 . . . . **76** A2
Kensal Green NW10 . **22** B3
College St EC4 . . . **123** A4
College Terr E3 . . . . **26** B2
Collent Ho 17 E9 . . **17** B2
Collent St E9 . . . . . **17** B2
Collerston Ho
SE10 . . . . **43** B1
Collette Ho N16 . . . . **7** B3
Collett Ho SE13 . . . **67** A4
Collett Rd SE16 . . **139** C2
Colley Ho 12 N7 . . . **13** C3
Collier St N1 . . . . . . **84** C1
Collingbourne Rd
W12 . . . . **30** A1
Collingham Gdns
SW5 . . . . **142** B3
Collingham Pl
SW5 . . . . **142** B4
Collingham Rd
SW5 . . . . **142** B3
Collingham Sixth
Form Coll SW5 . . **142** B3
Collington St
SE10 . . . . **42** C1
Collingwood Ho
27 Bethnal Green
E1 . . . . **25** A1
Marylebone W1 . . . **104** C4

Collingwood St
E1 . . . . .25 A1
Collins Ct E8 . . . . .16 C2
Collins Ho
6 Cubitt Town
E14 . . . . .43 B1
4 Poplar E14 . . . . . . .34 B2
Collinson Ct SE1 . .**136** C3
Collinson Ho **14**
SE15 . . . . .49 C3
Collinson St SE1 . .**136** C3
Collinson Wlk
SE1 . . . .**136** C3
Collins Rd N5, N16 ..15 B4
Collins Sq SE3 . . . . . .53 B1
Collins St SE3 . . . . . . .53 A1
Collins Yd N1 . . . . . .86 A3
Collison Pl N16 . . . . . .7 A3
Coll of Arms*
EC4 . . . .**122** C4
Coll of Central
London The
EC2 . . . . .24 A1 **98** A2
Coll of Law The
EC1 . . . .**97** B1
Coll of NW London
NW6 . . . . .23 C4
Coll of NW London
(Willesden Centre)
NW10 . . . . .8 B3
Coll of Optometrists
The SW1 . . . .**120** A2
Coll Sharp Ct
E2 . . . . .24 B2 **98** C3
Coll's Rd SE15 . . . . . .50 B2
Collyer Pl SE15 . . . . . .49 C2
Colmans Wharf **5**
E14 . . . . .34 A4
Colmar Cl **3** E1 . . . .25 C1
Colmore Mews
SE15 . . . . .50 A2
Colnbrook St SE1 .**136** A2
Colne Ho NW8 . . . . .89 C1
Colne Rd E5 . . . . .18 A4
Cologne Rd SW11 . . .59 C3
Colombo St SE1 . .**122** A1
Colomb St SE10 . . . . .43 A1
Colonades The **4**
SE5 . . . . .48 C2
Colonial Dr W4 . . . . . .37 B2
Colonnade WC1 . . . .**94** B1
Colonnade Ho
SE3 . . . . .53 B1
Colonnades The **6**
E8 . . . . .17 A2
Colonnade The **7**
SE8 . . . . .41 B2
Colorado Bldg **9**
SE13 . . . . .52 A2
Colosseum Terr
NW1 . . . .**92** B2
Colour Ho SE1 . . . .**138** B3
Colstead Ho **22** E1 . . .32 A3
Colston Rd SW14 . . .55 B3
Colthurst Cres N4 . . . .6 B2
Coltman Ho SE10 . . . .52 B4
Coltman St E14 . . . . . .33 A4
Columba Ho SE14 . . .51 B2
Columbas Dr NW3 . . .2 C3
Columbia Ho **18**
E3 . . . . .26 C2
Columbia Point **7**
SE16 . . . . .40 B3
Columbia Prim Sch
E2 . . . . .24 B2 **99** A4

Columbia Rd
9 Hackney E2 . . . . .24 C3
Shoreditch
E2 . . . . .24 B2 **98** C4
Columbia Road Mkt
E2 . . . . .24 B2 **99** A4
Colverson Ho **16**
E1 . . . . .32 B4
Colvestone Cres
E8 . . . . .16 B3
Colvestone Prim Sch
E8 . . . . .16 B3
Colville Gdns W11 ..31 B3
Colville Ho **17**
E2 . . . . .25 B3
Notting Hill W11 . . . . .31 B3
Colville Mews
W11 . . . . .31 B3
Colville Pl W1 . . . .**105** A3
Colville Prim Sch
W11 . . . . .31 B3
Colville Rd
Notting Hill W11 . . . . .31 B3
South Acton W3 . . . .37 A3
Colville Sq W11 . . . . .31 B3
Colville Terr W11 . . . .31 B3
Colwall Ho **10** SW9 .173 A1
Colwell Rd SE22 . . . .64 B2
Colwick Cl N6 . . . . . . .4 C4
Colwith Rd W6 . . . . . .47 B4
Colworth Gr SE17 .**151** A3
Colwyn Ho SE1 . . . .**135** B1
Colyton Rd SE22 . . . .65 A2
Combe Ave SE3 . . . . .53 B3
Combedale Rd
SE10 . . . . .43 C1
Combe Ho
Mortlake SW14 . . . . .45 B1
20 Paddington W2 . . .31 C4
Combemartin Rd
SW18 . . . . .70 A3
Combe Mews **2**
SE3 . . . . .53 B3
Comber Gr SE5 . . . . .48 B3
Comber Grove Prim
Sch SE5 . . . . .48 B3
Comber Ho SE5 . . . . .48 B3
Combermere Rd
SW9 . . . . .62 B4
Combe The NW1 . . . .92 B3
Com Coll Hackney
The E8 . . . . .25 A4
Comeragh Mews
W14 . . . .**140** B1
Comeragh Rd
W14 . . . .**140** B1
Comerford Rd SE4 . .66 B3
Comet Pl SE8 . . . . . .51 C3
Comet St SE8 . . . . . .51 C3
Comins Ho SW4 . . . .61 B2
Commercial Rd
Stepney E1 . . . . .32 B3
Whitechapel E1 . . . .**111** C2
Commercial St
E1 . . . .**110** C4
Commercial Way
Peckham SE15 . . . . .49 C3
Wembley NW10 . . . . .20 A3
Commerell Pl
SE10 . . . . .43 B1
Commerell St
SE10 . . . . .43 A1
Commodity Quay
E1 . . . .**125** A3
Commodore Ct
SE8 . . . . .51 C2

Commodore Ho **7**
E14 . . . . .34 B2
Commodore St E1 . .26 A1
Commondale
SW15 . . . . .57 B4
Common Rd
SW13 . . . . .56 C4
Common View
SW15 . . . . .57 B4
Commonwealth Ave **11**
Shepherd's Bush
W12 . . . . .30 A2
8 Shepherd's Bush
W12 . . . . .30 A2
Commonwealth Ho
WC1 . . . .**106** B2
Community Rd
E15 . . . . .19 C3
Comodore Ho
SW18 . . . . .59 B3
Compania Bldg **12**
E1 . . . .**32** C2
Compass Ct SE1 .**124** C1
Compass Ho
Bayswater W2 . . . .**100** A1
London SE8 . . . . .52 A1
Compass Point **10**
E14 . . . . .33 C2
Compayne Gdns
NW6 . . . . .11 A1
Compton Ave
Islington N1 . . . . . . .15 A2
London N6 . . . . .3 A4
Compton Cl
Camberwell SE15 . . .49 B3
Regent's Park NW1 ..92 B3
Compton Cres W4 . .45 B4
Compton Ho
SW11 . . . .**168** A4
Compton Pas EC1 . .96 B2
Compton Pl WC1 . . .94 A2
Compton Rd
Islington N1 . . . . . . .15 A2
Kensal Green NW10 . .22 C2
Compton St EC1 . . . .96 B2
Compton Terr N1 . . . .15 A2
Comus Ho SE17 . . .**152** A3
Comus Pl SE17 . . . .**152** A3
Comyn Rd SW11 . . . .60 A3
Comyns Cl E16 . . . . . .35 B4
Conant Ho SE11 . . . .48 A4
Conant Mews E1 . .**125** B4
Concanon Rd SW4 . .62 B3
Concert Hall App
SE1 . . . .**121** A1
Concord Bsns Ctr
W3 . . . . .28 A4
Concorde Way
SE16 . . . . .40 C2
Concordia Wharf **10**
E14 . . . . .34 B1
Concord Rd W3 . . . .20 A1
Condell Rd SW8 . . .171 A3
Conder St E14 . . . . . .33 A3
Condray Pl SW11 . .158 A1
Conduit Ct WC2 . . .120 A4
Conduit Ho SE10 . . . .52 C2
Conduit Mews
W2 . . . .**101** B1
Conduit Pas W2 . . .101 B1
Conduit Pl W2 . . . .101 B1
Conduit St W1 . . . .118 C4
Coney Acre SE21 . . . .75 B3
Coney Way SW8 . . .163 A3

Congers Ho SE8 . . . .51 C3
Congress Ho
WC1 . . . .**105** C2
Congreve Ho **10**
N16 . . . . .16 A3
Congreve St SE17 .152 A3
Conifer Ct **28**
SW19 . . . . .69 C3
Conifer Gdns
SW16 . . . . .74 B1
Conifer Ho SE4 . . . . .66 B3
Coniger Rd SW6 . .165 B2
Coningham Ct
SW10 . . . . .157 A2
Coningham Mews
W12 . . . . .29 C1
Coningham Rd
W12 . . . . .39 A4
Coningsby Rd N4 . . . .6 A4
Conington Rd
SE13 . . . . .52 B1
Conisbrough NW1 .82 C3
Coniston NW1 . . . . . .92 C4
Coniston Cl
Barnes SW13 . . . . . .46 B3
Chiswick W4 . . . . . . .45 B3
Coniston Ct
Marylebone W2 . . .102 B1
6 Rotherhithe
SE16 . . . . .40 C4
Conistone Way
N7 . . . . .14 A1
Coniston Ho
16 Bow E3 . . . . . . .26 B2
11 Camberwell SE5 .48 B3
Coniston Wlk E9 . . . .17 B3
Conlan St W10 . . . . . .23 A1
Conley Rd NW10 . . . .8 A2
Conley St SE10 . . . . .43 A1
Connaught Ave
SW14 . . . . .55 B3
Connaught Cl W2 .102 B1
Connaught Ho
College Pk NW10 . . . .22 A2
Mayfair W1 . . . . . . .118 A3
Connaught Lo N4 . . . .5 C4
Connaught Mans
Battersea SW11 . . .168 B3
1 Brixton SW9 . . . .62 C3
18 Canonbury N16 . .15 C4
Fulham SW6 . . . . . .164 A4
Connaught Pl W2 .102 C1
Connaught Rd
Finsbury Pk N4 . . . . . .5 C4
Harlesden NW10 . . . .21 A3
5 Richmond TW10 . .54 B2
Connaught Sq
W2 . . . .**102** C1
Connaught St W2 .102 B1
Connaught Works
E3 . . . . .26 A4
Connell Ct **6**
SE14 . . . . .50 C4
Connor Ct SW11 . . .170 A3
Connor St E9 . . . . . . .25 C4
Conrad Ho
3 Limehouse
SE16 . . . . .33 A2
South Lambeth
SW8 . . . .**162** A2
12 Stoke Newington
N16 . . . . .16 A3
Conrad Twr W3 . . . . .37 A3
Consort Ho W2 . . . .114 B3
Consort Lo NW8 . . .80 C3
Consort Rd SE15 . . . .50 A1
Cons St SE1 . . . . . .135 C4

Constable Ct **11**
SE16 . . . . .40 A1
Constable Ho
22 Millwall E14 . . . .41 C4
Primrose Hill NW3 . . .12 B1
Constable Wlk
SE21 . . . . .76 A1
Constant Ho **28**
E14 . . . . .34 A2
Constantine Ho
SW2 . . . . .75 A3
Constantine Rd
NW3 . . . . .12 A4
Constitution Hill SW1,
W1 . . . .**132** B4
Consul Ho **3** E3 . . .26 C1
Content St SE17 . . .151 B3
Convent Gdns
W11 . . . . .31 B3
Convent of Jesus &
Mary Language Coll
NW10 . . . . .21 B4
Convent of Jesus &
Mary RC Inf Sch
NW2 . . . . .9 B2
Conway Gr W3 . . . . .28 C4
Conway Ho
Chelsea SW3 . . . . .145 A1
5 Millwall E14 . . . .42 A2
6 Streatham SW2 . .74 A3
Conway Mews W1 . .92 C1
Conway St W1 . . . . .92 C1
Conybeare NW3 . . . .12 A1
Conyer St **23** E3 . . .26 A3
Cookham Cres
SE16 . . . . .40 C4
Cookham Ho
E2 . . . . .24 B1 **98** C2
Cook's Rd
Camberwell SE17 . . .48 A4
Stratford Marsh
E15 . . . . .27 A3
Coomassie Rd W9 . .23 B1
Coombe Ho **10** N7 . .13 C3
Coombe Rd W4 . . . . .38 A1
Coomber Ho SW6 . . .59 A4
Coombs St N1 . . . . .86 B1
Coomer Mews
SW6 . . . .**155** A3
Coomer Pl SW6 . . .155 A3
Cooperage The
SE1 . . . .**124** C1
Cooper Cl SE1 . . . .135 C3
Cooper Ct E15 . . . . . .19 B3
Cooper Ho NW8 . . . .89 B1
Cooper Rd NW10 . . . .8 C3
Coopersale Rd E9 . . .17 C3
Coopers Cl E1 . . . . . .25 B1
Coopers Ct
3 Acton W3 . . . . . .28 B1
Tower Hamlets E3 . .26 B1
Coopers La NW1 . . .83 C1
Cooper's Lo SE1 . .138 C4
Cooper's Rd SE1 . .153 A2
Cooper's Row
EC3 . . . .**124** C4
Cooper St **10** E16 . .35 B4
Coopers Yd N1 . . . . .15 A1
Cope Ho EC1 . . . . . .97 A3
Copeland Dr E14 . . .41 C2
Copeland Ho
SE11 . . . .**135** A1
Copeland Rd SE15 . .50 A1
Copenhagen Gdns
W4 . . . . .37 C4
Copenhagen Ho
N1 . . . . .85 B3

Copenhagen Pl E14....33 B3
Copenhagen Prim Sch N1....84 C3
Copenhagen St N1....84 C3
Cope Pl W8....127 B1
Cope St SE16....40 C2
Copford Wlk N1....86 C4
Copleston Rd SE15....64 B4
Copley Cl 15 SE17....48 A4
Coppedhall 2 SE21....75 C2
Copperas St SE8....52 A4
Copper Beech N6....3 C4
Copperbeech Cl NW3....11 C3
Copperfield Ho SE1....139 B3
Copperfield Rd E3....33 A4
Copperfields 1 W3....36 C4
Copperfield St SE1....136 C4
Copper Mews 4 W4....37 B3
Coppice Dr SW15....57 A1
Coppin Ho SW2....75 A3
Coppock Cl SW11....168 A1
Copse Cl SW15....58 A2
Copthall Ave EC2....109 C2
Copthall Bldgs EC2....109 C2
Copthall Cl EC2....109 B2
Copthorne Ave SW12....73 C4
Coptic St WC1....106 A3
Copton Cl E3....33 C4
Coral Apts 6 E16....35 C2
Coral Ho 5 E1....26 A1
Coral Row 14 SW11....59 B4
Coral St SE1....135 C2
Coram Ho
　Bloomsbury WC1....94 A2
　9 Chiswick W4....38 A1
Coram Mans WC1....94 C1
Coram St WC1....94 A1
Corbden Cl SE15....49 B2
Corbet Cl 5 ....109 C1
Corbet Ho SE8....41 B4
Corbet Pl E1....111 A4
Corbett Ho SW10....156 C4
Corbett's La SE16....40 B2
Corbetts Pas 8 SE16....40 B2
Corbidge Ct SE8....52 A4
Corbiere Ho 5 N1....24 A4
Corbin Ho 7 E3....27 A2
Corbridge Cres E2....25 A3
Corbyn St N4, N19....5 A3
Corby Rd NW10....20 C3
Corby Way E3....26 C1
Cordelia Cl SE24....63 A3
Cordelia Ho 57 N1....24 A3
Cordelia St E14....34 A3
Cording St E14....34 A4
Cordwainers Ct 11 E9....17 B1
Corfe Ho SW8....162 C2
Corfe Lodge 15 SE21....75 C2

Corfe Twr 6 W3....37 B4
Corfield St E2....25 A2
Coriander Ave E14....34 C3
Coriander Ct SE1 139 A4
Corinne Rd N19....13 B4
Cork St Mews W1....118 C3
Cork St W1....118 C3
Corlett St NW1....102 A3
Cormont Rd SE5....48 A2
Cormorant Ct
　38 Deptford SE8....51 B4
　5 Dulwich SE21....75 C2
Cornbury Ho 5 SE8....51 B4
Cornelia St N7....14 B2
Cornell Bldg 1 E1....111 B2
Corner Fielde SW2....74 B3
Corner Gn SE3....53 C1
Corner House St WC2....120 A2
Cornerstone Ct 1 E1....99 C1
Cornerways SW15....56 C3
Corney Rd W4....46 A4
Corney Reach Way W4....46 A3
Cornflower Terr SE22....65 A1
Cornford Gr SW12....73 A2
Cornhill EC3....109 C1
Cornick Ho 7 SE16....40 A3
Cornish Ho
　Brentford TW8....36 B1
　17 Camberwell SE17....48 A4
Cornmill La SE13....67 B4
Cornmow Dr NW10....8 C3
Cornwall Ave E2....25 B2
Cornwall Cres W11....31 A3
Cornwall Flats SE1....135 C4
Cornwall Gdns
　Kensington SW7....128 B1
　Willesden NW10....9 A1
Cornwall Gdns Wlk SW7....128 B1
Cornwall Gr W4....38 A1
Cornwall Ho
　Marylebone NW1....91 A1
　5 Putney SW15....69 B4
Cornwallis Ct SW8....172 A4
Cornwallis Ho 24 W12....30 A2
Cornwallis Rd N19....5 A2
Cornwallis Sq N19....5 A2
Cornwall Mans
　Chelsea SW10....157 A2
　Marylebone NW1....91 A1
Cornwall Mews S SW7....128 C1
Cornwall Mews W SW7....128 B1
Cornwall Rd
　Finsbury Pk N4....5 C4
　Lambeth SE1....135 C4
Cornwall Sq SE11....150 A2
Cornwall St 4 E1....32 A2
Cornwall Terr NW1....91 A1

Cornwall Terrace Mews NW1....91 A1
Cornwood Dr E1....32 B3
Coronation Ave N16....16 B4
Coronation Ct 19 W10....22 B1
Coronet St 24 A2 98 A3
Corporation Row EC1....95 C2
Corporation St N7....14 A3
Corpus Christi RC Prim Sch SW2....62 B2
Corrance Rd SW4....62 A3
Corringham Ct NW11....1 C4
Corringham Ho 1 E1....32 C3
Corringham Rd NW11....1 C4
Corringway NW11....1 C4
Corry Dr SW9....63 A3
Corry Ho 2 E14....34 A2
Corsham St N1....97 C3
Corsica St N5....15 A2
Corsley Way E9....18 B2
Cortayne Rd SW6 165 A2
Cortis Rd SW15....57 A1
Cortis Terr SW15....57 A1
Corunna Rd SW8 171 A4
Corunna Terr SW8....170 C4
Corvette Sq 5 SE10....52 C4
Coryton Path W9....23 B1
Cosbycote Ave SE24....63 B2
Cosgrove Ho 11 E2....24 C4
Cosmo Pl WC1....106 B4
Cosmur Cl W12....38 B3
Cossall Wlk SE15....50 A2
Cossar Mews 10 SW2....62 C2
Cosser St SE1....135 B2
Costa St SE15....49 C1
Coston Wlk 4 SE4....65 C3
Cosway Mans NW1....102 A3
Cosway St NW1....102 A3
Cotall St E14....33 C4
Cotes Ho NW8....90 A1
Cotham St SE17....151 A3
Cotherstone Rd SW2....74 B3
Cotleigh Rd NW6....10 C1
Cotman Cl SW15....57 C2
Cotman Ho NW8....80 A2
Cotrill Gdns E8....17 A2
Cotswold Ct EC1....96 C2
Cotswold Gate NW2....1 A3
Cotswold Ho N16....7 B3
Cotswold Mews SW11....167 C3
Cottage Gn SE5....48 C3
Cottage Gr SW9....62 A4
Cottage Pl SW3....130 A1
Cottage St E14....34 A2
Cottages The SE1....134 C1
Cottage Wlk 2 N16....7 B1
Cottenham Ho 3 N19....5 A2

Cottesbrook St SE14....51 A3
Cottesloe Ho NW8....90 A2
Cottesloe Mews SE1....135 C2
Cottesmore Ct W8....128 B2
Cottesmore Gdns W8....128 B2
Cottingham Rd SW8....163 A2
Cottington Ct SE11....150 A2
Cottington St SE11....149 A3
Cotton Ave W3....28 C3
Cotton Ho
　Bedford Pk W12....38 B4
　18 Streatham SW12....74 A4
Cotton Row SW11....59 C4
Cotton's Gdns E2....24 A2 98 A4
Cottons La SE1....123 C2
Cotton St E14....34 B2
Cottrell Ct SE10....43 B2
Couchman Ho 8 SW4....61 B1
Coulgate St SE4....66 A4
Coulson St SW3....144 C2
Coulter Rd W6....39 A3
Coults Cres N5....15 A4
Councillor St SE5....48 B3
Counters Ct W14....126 B2
Counter St SE1....124 A1
Countess Rd NW5....13 B3
Country Gr SE5....48 B2
County Ho
　22 Herne Hill SE24....63 A3
　South Lambeth SW9....173 B4
County St SE1....137 A1
Courier Ho 17 SW2....74 C4
Courland Gr SW8....171 C3
Courland St SW8....171 C3
Courtauld Ho 2 E2....24 C3
Courtauld Inst of Art*
　Marylebone W1....103 A2
　Strand WC2....120 C4
Courtauld Rd N19....5 A3
Courtenay Ave N6....3 A4
Courtenay Sq SE11....149 B1
Courtenay St SE11....149 B2
Courtfield Gdns SW5....142 B3
Courtfield Ho EC1....107 B4
Courtfield Mews SW5....142 B3
Courtfield Rd SW7....142 C3
Court Gdns N7....14 C2
Courthill Rd SE13....67 B3
Courthope Rd
　14 Rotherhithe SE16....40 B4
　South Lambeth SW8....162 A1

Courthope Rd NW3....12 B4
Court La SE21....76 B4
Courtlands TW10....54 C2
Courtlands Ave TW9....45 A1
Court Lane Gdns SE21....76 A4
Court Mans W6....38 C2
Courtmead Cl SE24....63 B1
Courtnell St W2....31 C3
Courtney Ct N7....14 C3
Courtney Ho W14....126 B2
Courtney Rd N7....14 C3
Courtrai Rd SE23....66 A1
Court Royal SW15....58 A2
Court St E1....32 A4
Courtville Ho 17 W10....23 A2
Court Way W3....28 C4
Courtyard The
　Fulham SW6....164 A1
　Islington N1....14 B1
　13 Wandsworth SW18....59 C3
Cousin La EC4....123 B3
Couzens Ho 8 E3....33 B4
Coval Gdns SW14....55 A3
Coval La SW14....55 A3
Coval Pas SW14....55 B3
Coval Rd SW14....55 B3
Covell Ct 16 SE8....51 C3
Covent Garden Sta WC2....106 B1
Covent Garden* WC2....120 B4
Coventry Cl NW6....23 C4
Coventry Rd E1....25 A1
Coventry St W1....119 B3
Coverdale Rd
　Brondesbury NW2....10 A2
　Hammersmith W12....39 A4
　Hampstead NW6....9 C1
Coverham Ho 5 SE4....65 C3
Coverley Cl E1....111 C4
Coverley Point SE11....148 C3
Cowcross St EC1....108 A4
Cowdenbeath Path N1....84 C4
Cowdray Hall Royal Coll of Nursing W1....104 A2
Cowdray Ho 22 SE22....64 A4
Cowdry Rd E9....18 B2
Cowley Rd
　Brixton SW9....173 C4
　East Acton W3....29 B1
　Mortlake SW14....56 A4
Cowley St SW1....134 A1
Cowling Cl W11....31 A1 112 A2
Cowper Ho
　Pimlico SW1....147 C1
　Walworth SE17....151 A2
Cowper Rd
　Acton W3....28 C1
　Stoke Newington N16....16 A4
Cowper's Ct EC3....109 C1

Cowper St EC1, EC2.....97 C2
Cowper Terr W10...30 C4
Cowthorpe Rd SW8.....119 C4
Cox Ho W6.....154 A4
Coxson Way SE1..138 C3
Coysh Ct **8** SW15...58 A2
Crabtree Cl E2.....24 B3
Crabtree Ct E15.....19 A3
Crabtree Hall SW6.47 B3
Crabtree La SW6.....47 C3
Craddock St NW5.....12 C2
Cragie Ho SE1.....153 A3
Craigleith SW15.....57 C1
Craignair Rd SW2.74 C4
Craig's Ct SW1.....120 A2
Craik Ct W12.....23 B3
Crail Row SE17.....151 C3
Cramer St W1.....103 C3
Crammond Cl
 W6.....154 A3
Crampton Sch
SE17.....150 B2
Crampton St
SE17.....150 C2
Cranbourn Alley
WC2.....119 C4
Cranbourne Ct
SW11.....158 B2
Cranbourne Rd
E15.....19 B4
Cranbourn Ho **6**
SE16.....40 A4
Cranbourn Pas **5**
SE16.....40 A4
Cranbourn St
WC2.....119 C4
Cranbrook NW1.....83 A3
Cranbrook Ho **5**
E5.....17 A3
Cranbrook Rd
Chiswick W4.....38 A1
St Johns SE8.....51 C2
Cranbrook St E2....25 C3
Cranbury Rd SW6 166 B1
Crandale Ho **8**
E5.....17 A3
Crandley Ct SE8...41 A2
Crane Ave W3....28 B2
Crane Ct
7 Acton W12.....38 A4
Holborn EC4.....107 C1
Crane Gr N7.....14 C2
Crane Ho
24 Bow E3.....26 A3
16 Peckham SE15...49 B2
Crane Mead SE16.40 C2
Crane St
Greenwich SE10....42 C1
6 Peckham SE15...49 B2
Cranfield Ct NW1..102 B3
Cranfield Ho
WC1.....106 B4
Cranfield Rd SE4...66 B4
Cranford Cotts **8**
E1.....32 C2
Cranford Lo SW19..69 C2
Cranford St E1.....32 C2
Cranhurst Rd NW2..9 B3
Cranleigh
W11.....31 B1 112 C2
Cranleigh Ct
Richmond TW9.....54 C4
4 Stamford Hill N16..7 A3

Cranleigh Hos
NW1.....83 A1
Cranleigh Mews
SW11.....168 C1
Cranleigh St NW1..83 A1
Cranley Gdns
SW7.....143 B2
Cranley Mews
SW7.....143 A2
Cranley Pl SW7....143 B3
Cranmer Ct SW3..144 B3
Cranmer Ho
SW11.....168 A4
Cranmer Rd SW9 163 C2
Cranswick Rd
SE16.....40 A1
Cranwell Cl E3....27 A1
Cranwich Rd N16....7 A4
Cranworth Gdns
SW9.....173 B4
Cranworth Ho **6**
N7.....14 B4
Craster Rd SW2...74 B4
Craston Ho **2**
SE5.....49 A1
Craven Cl N16.....7 C4
Craven Cottage
(Fulham FC)
SW6.....47 C2
Craven Ct NW10...21 A4
Craven Hill W2....115 A4
Craven Hill Gdns
W2.....114 C4
Craven Hill Mews
W2.....115 A4
Craven Ho **2**
SW14.....55 C4
Craven Lo
Bayswater W2....115 A4
Fulham SW6.....47 C2
Craven Mews **4**
SW11.....60 C1
Craven Park Mews
NW10.....21 A4
Craven Park Rd
NW10.....21 A4
Craven Pas SW1..120 A2
Craven Pk NW10...21 A4
Craven Rd
Paddington W2....101 A1
Stonebridge NW10..20 C4
Craven St W2.....120 A2
Craven Terr W2...115 A4
Craven Wlk E5, N16..7 C4
Crawford Bldgs
NW1.....102 B3
Crawford Mews
W1.....102 B3
Crawford Pas EC1..95 C1
Crawford Pl W1...102 B3
Crawford Place
Dwellings NW1..102 B3
Crawford Point **4**
E16.....35 B3
Crawford Prim Sch
SE5.....48 B2
Crawford Rd SE5...48 B1
Crawford St W1...102 C3
Crawshay Gr SW9 173 C4
Crawshay Ho **13**
N16.....15 C4
Crawthew Gr SE22 64 B3
Crayford Ho
Bermondsey SE1..137 C3

Crayford Ho continued
5 Lower Holloway
N7.....14 A4
Crayford Rd N7....14 A4
Crayle Ho SE11....149 B2
Crealock St SW18..59 A1
Creasy Est SE1....138 A1
Crebor St SE22....64 C1
Credenhill Ho **7**
SE15.....50 A3
Crediton Hill NW6..11 A3
Crediton Rd
Brondesbury Pk
NW10.....22 C4
Newham E16.....35 C3
Credon Rd SE16...40 A1
Creechurch La
EC3.....110 B1
Creechurch Pl
EC3.....110 B1
Creed Ct **5** EC4...108 B1
Creed Ho SE15....65 A4
Creed La EC4.....108 B1
Creek Ho W14....126 B2
Creek Rd SE10,
SE8.....52 A4
Creek Road Ind Est
SE8.....52 A4
Creekside SE8....52 A4
Creekside Foyer
SE8.....52 A4
Crefeld Cl W6....154 A3
Creighton Cl W12..30 A2
Creighton Rd
NW6.....22 C3
Cremer Bsns Ctr **8**
E2.....24 B3
Cremer Ho **9** SE8..51 C3
Cremer St E2.....24 B3
Cremorne Rd
SW10.....157 B2
Creon Ct SW9....173 B4
Crescent EC3.....124 C4
Crescent Arc **1**
SE10.....52 B4
Crescent Ct SW4...61 C2
Crescent Gdns
SW19.....70 C1
Crescent Gr SW4...61 B3
Crescent Ho SE13..52 A1
Crescent La SW4...61 C2
Crescent Mans
Islington N5.....15 A3
Notting Hill
W11.....31 A2 112 B4
Crescent Pl SW3..144 B4
Crescent Row EC1..96 C1
Crescent St N1....14 B1
Crescent Stables
SW15.....58 A2
Crescent The
Acton W3.....29 A3
Barnes SW13.....46 C1
Wimbledon SW19...70 C1
Crescent Way SE4..66 C4
Crescent Wood Rd
SE21, SE26.....76 C1
Cresford Rd SW6 166 A3
Cressage Ho **9**
TW8.....44 A4
Cressall Ho **14**
E14.....41 C3
Cresset Ho **8** E9...17 B2
Cresset Rd E9....17 B2

Cresset St SW4....61 C4
Cressfield Cl NW5..12 C3
Cressida Rd N19....4 C3
Cressingham Rd
SE13.....67 B4
Cressington Cl **4**
N16.....16 A3
Cresswell Gdns
SW5.....142 C2
Cresswell Pl
SW10.....143 A2
Cressy Ct
Hammersmith W6...39 A3
6 Stepney E1.....32 B4
Cressy Ho SW13...57 A4
Cressy Hos **7** E1...32 B4
Cressy Pl E1.....32 B4
Cressy Rd NW3....12 B4
Cresta Ho
7 Bow E3.....26 C1
Hampstead NW6...11 C1
Crestfield St N1,
WC1.....94 B4
Crestway SW15....57 A1
Creswick Ct W3....28 A2
Creswick Rd W3....28 A2
Creswick Wlk **7**
E3.....26 C2
Crewdson Rd
SW9.....163 B1
Crewe Pl NW10...21 B2
Crewkerne Ct
SW11.....167 C4
Crews St E14.....41 C2
Crewys Rd
Child's Hill NW2....1 B2
London SE15.....50 A1
Crichton St SW8..170 C2
Cricketers Mews **4**
SW4.....59 A2
Cricketfield Rd E5..17 A4
Cricklade Ave
SW2.....74 B2
CRICKLEWOOD.....9 B4
Cricklewood
Broadway NW2.....9 C4
Cricklewood La
NW2.....1 B1
Cricklewood Sta
NW2.....9 C4
Crieff Rd SW18....59 B1
Criffel Ave SW2....73 C3
Crimscott St SE1..138 B1
Crimsworth Rd
SW8.....161 C1
Crinan St N1.....84 B2
Cringle St SW8...160 C2
Cripplegate St
EC1.....109 A4
Crispe Ho N1.....85 A3
Crispian Cl NW10...8 A4
Crispin Cl SE17...152 A3
Crispin Pl E1.....110 C4
Crispin St E1.....110 C3
Crisp Rd W6.....39 B1
Cristowe Rd SW6 165 A1
Criterion Mews
N19.....4 C2
Crockerton Rd
SW17.....72 B2
Croft Ct SE13.....67 B1
Croftdown Rd NW5..4 A1
Crofters Ct **5** SE8..41 A2
Crofters Way NW1..83 B4
Croft Ho
Putney SW15.....58 A1

Croft Ho continued
11 West Kilburn
W10.....23 A2
Crofton Ave W4....45 C3
Crofton Gate Way
SE4.....66 A2
Crofton L Ctr SE4..66 C1
Crofton Park Rd
SE4.....66 B1
Crofton Park Sta
SE4.....66 A2
Crofton Rd SE5....49 A1
Crofton Sch SE4...66 C1
Crofton Terr
Homerton E5.....18 A3
Richmond TW9....54 B3
Crofts Ho **21** E2...24 C3
Crofts St E1.....125 B3
Croft St SE8.....41 A2
Croft The NW10...21 B3
Crogsland Rd
NW1.....12 C1
Cromartie Rd N19...4 C4
Cromarty Ho **3**
E1.....33 A4
Crombie Mews
SW11.....168 B2
Cromdale St N16....7 B4
Cromer Ct
Streatham SW16...74 A1
Wandsworth SW18..58 B1
Crome Rd NW10....8 A2
Cromer St WC1....94 B3
Cromer Terr E8....16 C3
Cromer Villas Rd
SW18.....58 B1
Cromford Path **1**
E5.....17 C4
Cromford Rd
SW18.....58 C2
Crompton Ct SW3 144 A4
Crompton Ho
Borough The SE1..137 A1
Paddington W2....89 B1
South Lambeth
SW8.....171 A3
Crompton St W2...89 B1
Cromwell Ave
Hammersmith W6...39 A2
Highgate N6.....4 A3
Cromwell Cl
2 Gunnersbury
W4.....37 A1
Cromwell Cres
SW5.....141 B4
Cromwell Ctr
NW10.....20 C2
Cromwell Gdns
SW7.....129 C1
Cromwell Gr W6...39 B3
Cromwell Ho
Battersea SW11...169 C3
Putney SW15.....56 C3
Cromwell Hospl
SW5.....142 A4
Cromwell Lo **40**
E1.....25 B1
Cromwell Mans
SW5.....141 C4
Cromwell Mews
SW7.....143 C4
Cromwell Pl
1 Acton W3.....28 B1
Highgate N6.....4 A3
Mortlake SW14....55 B4

Cromwell Pl continued
South Kensington
SW7 . . . . **143 C4**
Cromwell Rd
Brixton SW9 . . . . 48 A2
South Kensington
SW7 . . . . **143 A4**
Cromwell Twr
EC2 . . . . **109 A4**
Crondace Rd
SW6 . . . . **165 C3**
Crondall Ct 7 N1 . . . 24 A3
Crondall Ho SW15 . . 68 C3
Crondall Pl 18 N1 . . . 24 A3
Crondall St N1 . . . . 24 A3
Crone Ct 5 NW6 . . . 23 B3
Cronin St SE15 . . . . 49 B3
Crooked Billet Yd
E2 . . . . 24 A2 98 B4
Crooke Rd SE8 . . . . 41 A1
Crookham Rd
SW6 . . . . **164 C3**
Croom's Hill SE10 . . 52 C3
Croom's Hill Gr
SE10 . . . . 52 B3
Cropley Ct N1 . . . . **87 B2**
Cropley St N1 . . . . **87 B2**
Cropthorne Ct 9 W9 . **89 A3**
Crosby Ct 1 SE1 . . . **137 B4**
Crosby Ho 19 E14 . . 42 B3
Crosby Row 1 SE1 . . **137 B4**
Crosby Sq EC3 . . . . **110 A2**
Crosby Wlk
8 Dalston E8 . . . . 16 B2
Streatham SE24 . . . 74 C4
Crosfield Ct 9
W10 . . . . 30 C3
Crosfield Ho
W11 . . . . 31 A2 **112 A3**
Crosland Pl 5
SW11 . . . . 60 C4
Crossbow Ho 18
N1 . . . . 24 A4
Cross Cl SE15 . . . . 50 A1
Cross Ct SE5 . . . . . 63 C4
Crossfield Rd
NW3 . . . . 11 C2
Crossfield St SE8 . . 51 C3
Crossford St SW9 . . **172 C1**
Crossharbour Sta
E14 . . . . 42 A3
Cross Keys Cl N1 . . **103 C3**
Cross La EC3 . . . . . **124 A3**
Crossleigh Ct 3
SE14 . . . . 51 B3
Crosslet St SE17 . . **151 C4**
Crosslet Vale
SE10 . . . . 52 A2
Crossley St N7 . . . . 14 C2
Crossman Hos 19
SW12 . . . . 73 A4
Crossmount Ho 5
SE5 . . . . 48 B3
Cross Rd SE5 . . . . 49 A1
Cross St
Islington N1 . . . . **86 B4**
Mortlake SW13 . . . 56 A4
Crossthwaite Ave SE5,
SE24 . . . . 63 C3
Crosstrees Ho 7
E14 . . . . 41 C3
Crosswall EC3 . . . . **124 C4**
Crossway E8, N16 . . 16 A3
Crossway Ct SE4 . . 51 A1
Crossways Acad
SE4 . . . . 51 A1
Croston St E8 . . . . 24 C4

Crouch End Hill N8 . . 4 C4
Crouch Hall Ct N19 . 5 A3
Crouch Hill N4, N8,
N19 . . . . 5 A3
Crouch Hill Sta N4 . 5 B4
Crouchmans Ct SE21,
SE26 . . . . 76 C1
Crowder St E1 . . . . 32 A2
Crowfield Ho N5 . . . 15 B4
Crowfoot Cl 2 E9 . . 18 B3
Crowhurst Cl
SW9 . . . . **173 C2**
Crowhurst Ho 5
SW9 . . . . **173 A1**
Crowland Ho NW8 . . **78 C3**
Crowland Terr N1 . . 15 C1
Crowline Wlk 4
N1 . . . . 15 B2
Crown Cl
City of London
4 Bow E3 . . . . . 26 B3
Kentish Town NW5 . 13 A4
Crown Close Bsns Ctr
12 E3 . . . . 26 C4
Crown Ct
City of London
EC4 . . . . **109 A1**
4 Putney SW15 . . 57 C3
St Giles WC2 . . . . **106 B1**
St John's Wood
NW8 . . . . **90 B3**
Crowndale Ct
NW1 . . . . **83 B2**
Crowndale Rd
NW1 . . . . **83 A2**
Crowne Ho SE1 . . . **123 A1**
Crownfield Rd
E15 . . . . 19 C4
Crowngate Ho 33
E3 . . . . 26 B3
Crownhill Rd
NW10 . . . . 21 B4
Crownleigh Ct
SW2 . . . . 62 C2
Crown Lo SW3 . . . **144 B3**
Crown Mews 9
E1 . . . . 32 C4
Crown Office Row
EC4 . . . . **121 B4**
Crown Pas SW1 . . **119 A1**
Crown Pl
Broadgate EC2 . . **110 A4**
Kentish Town NW5 . 13 A2
Crown Reach
SW1 . . . . **147 C1**
Crown St
Acton W3 . . . . . . 28 A1
3 Camberwell SE5 . 48 B3
Crownstone Ct 1
SW2 . . . . 62 C2
Crownstone Rd
SW2 . . . . 62 C2
Crown Terr TW9 . . . 54 B3
Crows Rd E15 . . . . 27 C2
Crowther Ave
TW8 . . . . 36 A2
Crowther Cl 11 SW6 . **155 B3**
Crowthorne Cl
SW18 . . . . 70 B3
Crowthorne Rd
W10 . . . . 30 C3
Croxley Rd W9 . . . . 23 B2
Croxted Cl SE21 . . . 75 B4
Croxted Rd SE21,
SE24 . . . . 75 C3
Croxteth Ho SW8 . . **171 B2**
Croydon Ho SE1 . . **135 C4**
Crozier Ho SW8 . . **162 C1**
Crozier Terr E9 . . . 17 C3

Crucifix La SE1 . . . **138 A4**
Cruden Ho
5 Bow E3 . . . . . 26 B3
11 Camberwell
SE17 . . . . 48 A4
Cruden St N1 . . . . **86 B3**
Cruickshank St
WC1 . . . . **95 B4**
Cruikshank Ho
NW8 . . . . **80 B2**
Crusader Ho EC1 . . **96 A1**
Crusoe House Sch
N1 . . . . **97 B4**
Crusoe Mews N16 . . 6 C2
Crutched Friars
EC3 . . . . **124 B4**
Crystal Palace Rd
SE22 . . . . 64 C2
Crystal Wharf N1 . . **86 B1**
Cuba St E14 . . . . 41 C4
Cubitt Bldg SW1 . . **146 A1**
Cubitt St WC1 . . . . **95 A3**
Cubitt Terr SW4 . . . 61 B4
CUBITT TOWN . . . 42 C2
Cubitt Town Jun & Inf
Sch E14 . . . . 42 B3
Cuddington SE17 . . **151 A4**
Cudworth Ho
SW8 . . . . **171 A3**
Cudworth St E1 . . . 25 A1
Cuffley Ho 3 W10 . . 30 B4
Cuff Point
E2 . . . . 24 B2 **98 C4**
Culand Ho SE17 . . **152 A3**
Culford Gdns
SW3 . . . . **145 A3**
Culford Gr N1 . . . . 16 A2
Culford Mans
SW3 . . . . **145 A3**
Culford Mews N1 . . 16 A2
Culham Ho
21 Paddington W2 . 31 C4
2 Shoreditch
E2 . . . . 24 B2 **98 C3**
Cullen Ho W9 . . . . 23 B3
Cullen Way NW10 . . 20 B1
Culling Rd SE16 . . . 40 B3
Cullingworth Rd
NW10 . . . . 9 A3
Culloden Cl 16 SE16 . **153 C1**
Culloden Prim Sch
E14 . . . . 34 B3
Cullum St EC3 . . . **124 A4**
Culmore Rd SE15 . . 50 B3
Culmstock Rd
SW11 . . . . 60 C2
Culpepper Ct
SE11 . . . . **149 B4**
Culross Bldgs
NW1 . . . . **84 A2**
Culross St W1 . . . **117 B3**
Culver Ct SW18 . . . 59 A1
Culverden Rd
SW12 . . . . 73 B2
Culverhouse WC1 . . **106 C3**
Culverhouse Gdns
SW16 . . . . 74 B1
Culvert Ct 1 N7 . . 14 B3
Culvert Pl SW11 . . **169 B2**
Culvert Rd N15 . . . 7 A1
Culvert Rd SW11 . . **169 A2**
Culworth Ho NW8 . . **80 A2**
Culworth St NW8 . . **80 A1**

Cumber Ho SW18 . . 70 C2
Cumberland Ave
NW10 . . . . 20 A2
Cumberland Bsns Pk
NW10 . . . . 20 A2
Cumberland Cl E8 . 16 B2
Cumberland Cres
W14 . . . . **140 B4**
Cumberland Ct
W1 . . . . **103 A1**
Cumberland Gate
W1 . . . . **117 A4**
Cumberland Gdns
WC1 . . . . **95 B4**
Cumberland Ho
Paddington W9 . . . 88 C2
1 Putney SW15 . . 69 B4
Cumberland Mans
Marylebone W1 . . **102 C2**
7 West Hampstead
NW6 . . . . 10 C3
Cumberland Market
NW1 . . . . **92 B4**
Cumberland Mills Sq
E14 . . . . 42 C1
Cumberland Park Ind
Est NW10 . . . . . . 21 C2
Cumberland Pk
W3 . . . . 28 B2
Cumberland Pl
NW1 . . . . **92 A4**
Cumberland Rd
Acton W3 . . . . . . 28 B2
Barnes SW13 . . . . 46 C2
Richmond TW9 . . . 44 C3
Cumberland St
SW1 . . . . **146 B2**
Cumberland Terr
NW1 . . . . **82 A1**
Cumberland Terrace
Mews NW1 . . . . . **82 A1**
Cumberland Villas
Acton W3 . . . . . . 28 B2
Cumberland Wharf 12
SE16 . . . . 40 B4
Cumbrian Gdns
NW2 . . . . 1 A2
Cuming Mus* . . . .
Cumming St N1 . . . **85 A1**
Cumnor Cl SW9 . . **173 A2**
Cunard Pl EC3 . . . **110 B1**
Cunard Rd NW10 . . 20 C2
Cunard Wlk 3
SE16 . . . . 41 A2
Cundy St SW1 . . . **145 C3**
Cunningham Ct
W2 . . . . **89 B1**
Cunningham Ho 10
SE5 . . . . 48 C3
Cunningham Pl
NW8 . . . . **89 B2**
Cunnington St W4 . . 37 B2
Cupar Rd SW11 . . **169 C4**
Cureton St SW1 . . **147 C3**
Curlew Ho
7 Brockley SE4 . . . 66 A3
2 Peckham SE15 . . 49 B2
Curlew St SE1 . . . **139 A4**
Curness St SE13 . . 67 B3
Curran Ho SW3 . . **144 A3**
Curricle St W3 . . . 29 A1
Currie Ho 13
SW12 . . . . 73 C4
Cursitor St EC4 . . **107 B2**
Curtain Pl
EC2 . . . . 24 A1 **98 B2**

Curtain Rd
EC2 . . . . 24 A1 **98 B2**
Curtis Dr W3 . . . . 28 C3
Curtis Ho SE17 . . . **151 B2**
Curtis St SE1 . . . . **152 C4**
Curtis Way SE1 . . . **152 C4**
Curve Bldg The
SE4 . . . . 66 B2
Curve The W12 . . . 29 C2
Curwen & New Acad
Gall* W1 . . . . . . **105 B3**
Curwen Rd W12 . . 38 C4
Curzon Cres NW10 . 8 A1
Curzon Gate W1 . . **117 C1**
Curzon Sq W1 . . . **117 C1**
Curzon St W1 . . . **118 A2**
Custance Ho N1 . . **87 B1**
Custance St N1 . . . **97 B4**
Custom House
EC3 . . . . **124 A3**
Custom House Reach
SE16 . . . . 41 B3
Cutbush Ho N7 . . . 13 C3
Cutcombe Rd SE5 . 48 B1
Cuthbert Harrowing
Ho EC1 . . . . **96 C1**
Cuthbert Ho W2 . . **101 B4**
Cuthbert St W2 . . . **89 B1**
Cuthill Wlk 5 SE5 . 48 C2
Cutlers Gdns EC2 . **110 B2**
Cutlers Gdns Arc
EC2 . . . . **110 B2**
Cutlers Sq 4 E14 . . 41 C2
Cutler St EC2 . . . . **110 B2**
Cut The SE1 . . . . . **135 C4**
Cutty Sark* SE10 . . 52 C4
Cutty Sark Ho 10
E14 . . . . 42 A2
Cutty Sark Ret
Development
SE10 . . . . 52 B4
Cutty Sark Sta
SE10 . . . . 52 B4
Cuxton Ho SE17 . . **152 B2**
Cyclops Mews 12
E14 . . . . 41 C2
Cygnet Ho NW8 . . **78 C4**
Cygnet House N 8
E14 . . . . 34 A3
Cygnet House S 9
E14 . . . . 34 A3
Cygnet St
E1 . . . . 24 B1 **99 A2**
Cygnus Bsns Ctr
NW10 . . . . 8 B2
Cynthia St N1 . . . . **85 A1**
Cyntra Pl 8 E8 . . . 17 A1
Cypress Ct 3 E11 . . 19 C4
Cypress Ct E14 . . . 42 A4
Cypress Gdns SE4 . 66 A2
Cypress Ho SE14 . . 50 C2
Cypress Pl W1 . . . **93 A1**
Cyprus Pl 22 E2 . . 25 B3
Cyprus St E2 . . . . 25 B3
Cyrena Rd SE22 . . 64 B2
Cyril Jackson Prim
Sch (North Bldg)
E14 . . . . 33 B2
Cyril Jackson Prim
Sch (South Bldg)
E14 . . . . 33 B2
Cyril Mans SW11 . . **169 A3**
Cyril Thatcher Ho
SW6 . . . . **165 C3**
Cyrus Ho EC1 . . . . **96 B2**

Cyrus St EC1 . . . . **96** B2
Czar St SE8 . . . .**51** C4

D

Dabb's La EC1 . . . . **95** C1
Dabin Cres SE10 . . . . .52 B2
Dacca St SE8 . . . . .51 B4
Dace Rd E3 . . . . .26 C4
Dacre Ho SW3 . . . . **157** C3
Dacre St SW1 . . . . . **133** B2
Daffodil St W12 . . . . .29 B2
Dafforne Rd SW17 . .72 C1
Dagmar Ct E14 . . . . . .42 B3
Dagmar Gdns
NW10 . . . . .22 C3
Dagmar Pas N1 . . . . **86** B4
Dagmar Rd
  Camberwell SE5 . . . . .49 A2
  Finsbury Pk N4 . . . . . . .5 C4
Dagmar Terr N1 . . . . **86** B4
Dagnall St SW11 . . **169** B3
Dagnan Rd SW12 . . .73 B4
Dagobert Ho **27**
  E1 . . . . .32 B4
Daimler Ho **8** . . .26 C1
Dainton Ho **22** 31 C4
Dainty Way **5** 38 B2
Dairy Cl NW10 . . . . . .21 C4
Dairyman Cl NW2 . . . .1 A1
Daisy Dormer Ct **11**
  SW9 . . . . .62 B3
Daisy La SW6 . . . . . . .58 C4
Dakin Pl **8** E1 . . . . .33 A4
Dakota bldg **6**
  SE13 . . . . .52 A2
Dalberg Rd SW2 . . . .62 C2
Dalbury Ho **8**
  SW9 . . . . .62 B3
Dalby Rd SW18 . . . . .59 B3
Dalby St NW5 . . . . . . .13 A2
Dalebury Rd SW17 . .72 B2
Dale Croft N4 . . . . .6 B1
Dalehead NW1 . . . . **82** C1
Daleham Gdns
  NW3 . . . . .11 C2
Daleham Mews
  NW3 . . . . .11 C2
Dale Ho
  London SE4 . . . . .66 A3
  St John's Wood
  NW8 . . . . **78** C4
Dalemain Ho **8**
  SW8 . . . . **171** C2
Dalemain Mews **12**
  E16 . . . . .35 C1
Dale Rd
  Camberwell SE17 . . . .48 A4
  Gospel Oak NW5 . . . .12 C3
Dale Row W11 . . . . . .31 A3
Dale St W4 . . . . .38 A1
Daley Ho **6** W12 . .30 A3
Daley St E9 . . . . .17 C2
Daley Thompson Way
  7 SW8 . . . . .61 A4
Dalgarno Gdns
  W10 . . . . .30 B4
Dalgarno Way
  W10 . . . . .22 B1
Daling Way E3 . . . . . .26 A3
Dalkeith Ct SW1 . . **147** C3
Dalkeith Ho **6**
  SW9 . . . . .48 A2
Dalkeith Rd SE21 . . .75 B4

Dalling Rd W6 . . . . . . .39 A2
Dallington Sch
  EC1 . . . . **96** B2
Dallington St EC1 . . **96** B2
Dalmeny Ave N7 . . . .13 C4
Dalmeny Avenue Est
  3 N7 . . . . .13 C4
Dalmeny Ct SW4 . . **172** A2
Dalmeny Rd N7 . . . . .13 C4
Dalmeyer Rd NW10 . .8 B2
Dalmore Rd SE21 . . .75 B2
Dalrymple Rd SE4 . .66 A3
DALSTON 16 C2
Dalston Jct E8 . . . . . .16 C2
Dalston Kingsland Sta
  E8 . . . . .16 B3
Dalston La E8 . . . . . . .16 C3
Dalton Ho
  7 Balham SW12 . .73 A4
  10 Bow E3 . . . . . .26 A3
  14 Deptford SE14 . .50 C4
Dalton St SE27 . . . . . .75 A1
Dalwood St SE5 . . . .49 A2
Daly Ct E15 . . . . .19 B3
Dalyell Rd SW9 . . . . .62 B4
Damascene Wlk
  SE21 . . . . .75 B2
Damer Ho **9** 54 B1
  Damer Terr SW10 **157** A1
Dame St N1 . . . . **86** C2
Damien Ct **12** E1 . .32 A3
Damien St E1 . . . . . . .32 A3
Damory Ho **1**
  SE16 . . . . .40 B2
Dan Bryant Ho **5**
  SW12 . . . . .73 B4
Danby Ho
  7 Hackney E9 . . . .17 B1
  3 West Kilburn
  W10 . . . . .23 B2
Danby St SE15 . . . . . .64 B4
Dancer Rd
  Fulham SW6 . . . . . **164** C3
  Richmond TW9 . . . . .54 C4
Dandridge Cl
  SE10 . . . . .43 B1
Dandridge Ho **11**
  E1 . . . . **110** C4
Danebury W10 . . . . . .30 B4
Danebury Ave
  SW15 . . . . .56 B1
Danecroft Rd
  SE24 . . . . .63 C2
Dane Ho **16** SE5 . .48 B1
Danehurst St
  SW6 . . . . **164** A4
Danemere St
  SW15 . . . . .57 B4
Dane Pl E3 . . . . .26 B3
Danes Ct NW8 . . . . **80** C3
Danesdale Rd E9 . . .18 A2
Danesfield SE5 . . . . . .49 A4
Danes Ho **10** W10 .30 B4
Dane St WC1 . . . . . **106** C3
Daneville Rd SE5 . . .48 C2
Daniel Bolt Cl E14 . .34 A4
Daniel Ct W3 . . . . . . .29 A2
Daniel Gdns SE15 . .49 B3
Daniell Ho N1 . . . . . **87** C2
Daniel's Rd SE15 . . .65 B4
Dan Leno Wlk
  SW6 . . . . **156** A1
Dansey Pl W1 . . . . **119** B4
Dante Pl SE11 . . . . **150** B3
Dante Rd SE11 . . . **150** A4

Danube Ct **13**
  SE15 . . . . .49 B3
Danube St SW3 . . . **144** B2
Danvers Ho **1**
  E1 . . . . **111** C1
Danvers St SW3 . . **157** C3
Da Palma Ct SW6 . **155** B3
Daphne St SW18 . . .59 B1
Daplyn St E1 . . . . . . **111** B4
D'arblay St W1 . . . **105** A1
Darcy Ho E8 . . . . .25 A4
Darell Prim Sch
  TW9 . . . . .54 C4
Darell Rd TW9 . . . . . .54 C4
Daren Ct N7 . . . . .14 A4
Darent Ho **4**
  NW8 . . . . **101** C4
Darenth Rd N16 . . . . . .7 B3
Darfield NW1 . . . . . **82** C3
Darfield Way W10 . .30 C3
Darfur St SW15 . . . **57** C4
Darien Ho
  8 London SW11 . . .59 C4
  11 Stepney E1 . . . .32 C4
Darien Rd SW11 . . . .59 C4
Daring Ho **28** E3 . .26 A3
Darlan Rd SW6 . . . **155** A1
Darley Ho SE11 . . . **148** C1
Darley Rd SW11 . . . .60 B1
Darling Ho **1** 25 A1
Darling Row E1 . . . . .25 A1
Darlington Ho
  SW8 . . . . **161** C1
Darnall Ho **4**
  SE10 . . . . .52 B2
Darnay Ho SE16 . . **139** B2
Darnell Ho **9**
  SE10 . . . . .52 A3
Darnley Ho **7** E14 .33 A3
Darnley Rd E9 . . . . . .17 B2
Darnley Terr **12**
  W11 . . . . .30 C1
Darrell Rd SE22 . . . .64 C2
Darren Cl N4 . . . . .5 B4
Darsley Dr SW8 . . . **172** A4
Dartford Ho SE1 . . **153** A4
Dartford St SE17 . . .48 B4
Dartington NW1 . . . . **83** A3
Dartington Ho
  Bayswater W2 . . . . **100** A4
  London SW8 . . . . . **171** C2
Dartle Ct SE16 . . . . **139** C3
Dartmoor Wlk **10**
  E14 . . . . .41 C2
Dartmouth Cl
  W11 . . . . .31 C3
Dartmouth Gr
  SE10 . . . . .52 B2
Dartmouth Hill
  SE10 . . . . .52 B2
Dartmouth Ho
  Dartmouth Pk N19 . . .4 A2
  Lewisham SE10 . . . . .52 B1
DARTMOUTH PARK
  .4 A1
Dartmouth Park Ave
  NW5 . . . . .4 A1
Dartmouth Park Hill
  N19 . . . . .4 A2
Dartmouth Park Rd
  NW5 . . . . .4 A1
Dartmouth Pl W4 . . .46 A4
Dartmouth Rd NW2 . .9 C2
Dartmouth Row
  SE10 . . . . .52 B2

Dartmouth St
  SW1 . . . . **133** C3
Dartmouth Terr
  SE10 . . . . .52 C2
Darton Ct W3 . . . . . . .28 B1
Dartrey Twr
  SW10 . . . . **157** B2
Dartrey Wlk
  SW10 . . . . **157** A2
Dart St W10 . . . . .23 B2
Darville Rd N16 . . . . . .7 B1
Darwen Pl E2 . . . . . . .25 A4
Darwin Ho NW1 . . . **81** C4
Darwin Ho **8**
  SE13 . . . . .52 B1
Darwin St SE17 . . . **151** C4
Daryngton Ho
  SW8 . . . . **162** A1
Dashwood Ho
  SE21 . . . . .76 B1
Data Point Bsns Ctr
  E16 . . . . .27 C1
Datchelor Pl **14**
  SE5 . . . . .48 C2
Datchet Ho NW1 . . **92** B2
Datchett Ho
  E2 . . . . .24 B2 **98** C3
Datchwood Ct N4 . . . .6 B1
Datchworth Ho **3**
  N1 . . . . .15 A1
Date St SE17 . . . . . **151** B1
Daubeney Prim Sch
  E5 . . . . .18 A4
Daubeney Rd E5 . . . .18 A4
Daubeney Twr **2**
  SE8 . . . . .41 B1
Dault Rd SW18 . . . . .59 B1
Dauney Ho SE1 . . . **136** A3
Dave Adams Ho **8**
  E3 . . . . .26 B3
Davenant Ho **11**
  E1 . . . . **111** C4
Davenant Rd N19 . . . .4 C2
Davenant St E1 . . . **111** C3
Davenport Ho
  SE11 . . . . **135** B1
Davenport Mews **8**
  W12 . . . . .30 A1
Davenport Rd SE6 . .67 B1
Daventry St NW1 . . **102** A4
Dave Porter Hts
  SW19 . . . . .70 A4
Daver Ct SW3 . . . . **144** B1
Davern Cl SE10 . . . . .43 B2
Davey Cl N7 . . . . .14 B2
Davey Rd E9 . . . . .18 C1
Davey's Ct WC2 . . **120** A4
Davey St SE15 . . . . **49** B4
David Beckham Acad
  The SE10 . . . . .43 B4
David Devine Ho **7**
  E8 . . . . .16 C3
David Game Coll
  SW7 . . . . **143** B3
Davidge Ho SE1 . . **135** C3
Davidge St SE1 . . . **136** B3
David Hewitt Ho **2**
  E3 . . . . .34 A4
David Ho
  5 Putney SW15 . . .56 C2
  South Lambeth
  SW8 . . . . **162** A2
David Mews W1 . . . **103** A4
Davidson Gdns
  SW8 . . . . **162** A2
Davidson Ho **7**
  N19 . . . . .13 B4
David St E15 . . . . .19 C3

Davies Laing & Dick
  Coll W1 . . . . **103** C2
Davies Mews W1 . . **118** A4
Davies St W1 . . . . . **118** A4
Davina Ho
  Brondesbury NW2 . .10 B2
  17 Hackney E5 . . . .17 A3
Da Vinci Ct **15**
  SE16 . . . . .40 A1
Davis Ho **32** W12 . .30 A2
Davis Rd W3 . . . . .38 B4
Davisville Rd W12 . .38 C4
Dawes Ho SE17 . . . **151** B3
Dawes Rd SW6 . . . **154** C2
Dawes St SE17 . . . **151** C2
Dawlish Ave SW18 . .71 A2
Dawlish Rd NW2 . . . . .9 C2
Dawnay Gdns
  SW18 . . . . .71 C2
Dawnay Rd SW17,
  SW18 . . . . .71 C2
Dawn Cres E15 . . . . .27 C4
Dawson Ho
  22 Bethnal Green
  E2 . . . . .25 B2
  3 Camberwell SE5 .49 A2
Dawson Pl
  W2 . . . . .31 C2 **113** C4
Dawson Rd NW2 . . . .9 B4
Dawson St E2 . . . . . . .24 B3
Day Ho **2** SE5 . . . .48 B3
Daylesford Ave
  SW15 . . . . .56 C3
Daynor Ho **4**
  NW6 . . . . .23 C4
Daysbrook Rd
  SW2 . . . . .74 B3
Dayton Gr SE15 . . . .50 B2
Deacon Ho SE11 . . **149** A3
Deacon Mews N1 . .15 C1
Deacon Rd NW2 . . . . .8 C2
Deacon Way
  SE17 . . . . **151** A4
Deal Ho
  Deptford SE15 . . . . . .50 C4
  Walworth SE17 . . . **152** B2
Deal Porters Way
  SE16 . . . . .40 C3
Deal St E1 . . . . **111** B4
Dealtry Rd SW15 . . .57 B3
Deal Wlk SW9 . . . . **163** C1
Dean Bradley St
  SW1 . . . . **134** A1
Dean Cl
  Hackney E9 . . . . .17 B3
  Rotherhithe SE16 . . .32 C1
Dean Coll of London
  N7 . . . . .5 B1
Deancross St E1 . . .32 B3
Dean Ct Acton W3 . .28 C3
  South Lambeth
  SW8 . . . . **162** A1
Deanery Mews
  W1 . . . . **117** C2
Deanery St W1 . . . **117** C2
Dean Farrar St
  SW1 . . . . **133** C2
Deanhill Ct **2**
  SW14 . . . . .55 A3
Deanhill Rd SW14 . .55 A3
Dean Ho London N4 . .6 B4
  New Cross SE14 . . . .51 B3
  2 Stamford Hill N16 . .7 B3
  3 Stepney E1 . . . . .32 B3
Dean Rd NW2 . . . . . . .9 B2
Dean Ryle St
  SW1 . . . . **148** A4

Dean's Bldgs
SE17 . . . . **151** C3
Deans Cl W4 . . . . .45 A4
Dean's Ct EC4 . . . . . **108** B1
Deanshanger Ho 🔟
SE8 . . . . .41 B2
Dean's Mews W1 . . **104** B2
Dean St W1 . . . . **105** B1
Dean Stanley St
SW1 . . . . **134** A1
Dean's Yd SW1 . . . . **133** C2
Dean Trench St
SW1 . . . . **134** A1
Dearmer Ho 🔞
SW2 . . . . .74 C4
Deason St E27 . . . . . .27 B4
Deauville Ct
🔟 London SW4 . . . .61 B1
🔟 Rotherhithe
SE16 . . . . .40 C4
Deauville Mans
SW4 . . . . .61 B1
De Barowe Mews 🔟
N5 . . . . .15 A3
Debdale Ho 🔞 E2 . . . .24 C4
De Beauvoir Cres
N1 . . . . .24 A4
De Beauvoir Ct
N1 . . . . .15 C1
De Beauvoir Pl 🗓
N1 . . . . .16 A2
De Beauvoir Prim Sch
N1 . . . . .16 A1
De Beauvoir Rd
N1 . . . . .16 A1
De Beauvoir Sq
N1 . . . . .16 A1
DE BEAUVOIR TOWN
. . . . .16 A1
Debenham Ct E8 . . . .24 C4
Debnams Rd SE16 . . .40 B2
Decima St SE1 . . . . . **138** C2
Deck Cl SE16 . . . . . . .32 C1
De Crespigny Pk
SE5 . . . . .48 C1
Deeley Rd SW8 . . . . **171** B4
Deepdale N4 . . . . .6 A1
Deepdene Gdns
SW2 . . . . .74 B4
Deepdene Ho N16 . . . .6 C3
Deepdene Lo 🗓
SW2 . . . . .74 B4
Deepdene Mans
SW6 . . . . **164** C4
Deepdene Rd SE5,
SE24 . . . . .63 C3
Deerbrook Rd SE24,
SW2 . . . . .75 A3
Dee Rd TW9 . . . . .54 B3
Deerdale Rd SE24 . . .63 B3
Deerhurst Ho 🔟
SE15 . . . . .49 C4
Deerhurst Rd NW2 . . .9 C2
Deer Lo SW6 . . . . . . .58 A4
Deeside Rd SW17 . . .71 C1
Dee St E14 . . . . .34 B3
Defoe Ave TW9 . . . . .44 C3
Defoe Ho
Barbican EC2 . . . . . **108** C4
🗓 Stoke Newington
N16 . . . . .7 A1
Defoe Pl EC2 . . . . . **108** C4
Defoe Rd
Rotherhithe SE16 . . .41 B4
Stoke Newington N16 . .7 A1
De Gama Pl 🗓
E14 . . . . .41 C1

Dekker Ho 🔟 SE5 . .48 C3
Dekker Rd SE21 . . . . .64 A1
Delafield Ho E1 . . . . **111** C1
Delaford Rd SE16 . . . .40 A1
Delaford St SW6 . . . **154** B3
Delamere Ho 🔟 N4 . . .6 C4
Delamere Rd W5 . . . .36 A4
Delamere St W2 . . . **100** C3
Delamere Terr
W2 . . . . **100** B4
Delancey Pas NW1 . **82** B3
Delancey St NW1 . . **82** B3
Delancey Studios
NW1 . . . . **82** B3
Delany Ho SE10 . . . . .52 B4
Delarch Ho SE1 . . . **136** A3
De Laune St SE17 . . **150** A1
Delaware Rd W9 . . . . **88** A2
Delawyk Cres
SE24 . . . . .63 C1
Delft Way 🗓 SE22 . . .64 A2
Delhi St N1 . . . . **84** B3
Delia St SW18 . . . . . .71 A4
Delius Gr E15 . . . . . . .27 B3
Dellafield N4 . . . . .5 C2
Dell Cl E15 . . . . .27 C4
Dellow Ho 🔟 E1 . . . . .32 A2
Dellow St E1 . . . . .32 A2
Dell's Mews SW1 . . **147** A3
Deloraine Ho SE8 . . . .51 C2
Deloraine St SE8 . . . .51 C2
Delorme St W6 . . . . . .47 C4
Delta Bldg 🔟 E14 . . .34 B3
Delta Ho N1 . . . . **97** B4
Delta St E2 . . . . **99** B4
Delta Point
🔟 E2 . . . . 24 C2 **99** B4
Delta St E2 . . . . 24 C2 **99** B4
Delverton Ho
SE17 . . . . **150** B2
Delverton Rd
SE17 . . . . **150** B2
Delvino Rd SW6 . . . **165** C3
De Montfort Ct 🗓
SW16 . . . . .74 A1
De Montfort Rd
SW16 . . . . .74 A2
De Morgan Rd
SW6 . . . . .59 A4
Dempster Rd
SW18 . . . . .59 B2
Denbigh Cl
Notting Hill
W11 . . . . 31 B2 **113** A4
Willesden NW10 . . . . .8 A1
Denbigh Gdns
TW10 . . . . .54 B2
Denbigh Ho
Knightsbridge
SW1 . . . . **131** A2
🗓 Notting Hill W11 . .31 B3
Notting Hill
W11 . . . . 31 B2 **113** A4
Denbigh Mews
SW1 . . . . **146** C3
Denbigh Pl SW1 . . . **146** C2
Denbigh Rd
W11 . . . . 31 B2 **113** A4
Denbigh St SW1 . . . **147** A2
Denbigh Terr
W11 . . . . 31 B2 **113** A4
Denbury Ho 🔞 E3 . . .27 A2
Denby Ct SE11 . . . . **149** A4
Dence Ho
🔟 E2 . . . . 24 C2 **99** B3
Denchworth Ho 🗓
SW9 . . . . **173** B1

Dene Cl SE4 . . . . .66 A3
Denehurst Gdns
Acton W3 . . . . .28 A1
Richmond TW10 . . . . .54 A1
Dene Mans 🔟
NW6 . . . . .10 C2
Denesmead SE24 . . . .63 B2
Denewood Rd N6 . . . . .3 B4
Dengie Wlk N1 . . . . . **86** C4
Denham Ho
🔟 W12 . . . . .30 A2
Denham St SE10 . . . .43 C1
Denholme Rd W9 . . . .23 B2
Denland Ho SW8 . . . **163** A1
Denman Ho N16 . . . . .7 A2
Denman Rd SE15 . . . .49 B1
Denman St W1 . . . . **119** B3
Denmark Gr N1 . . . . **85** B2
Denmark Hill SE5 . . . .48 C1
Denmark Hill Sta
SE5 . . . . .48 B2
Denmark Mans 🔟
SE5 . . . . .48 B1
Denmark Pl
🔟 Bromley E3 . . . . . .26 C2
Soho WC2 . . . . **105** C2
Denmark Rd
Camberwell SE5 . . . . .48 B1
Kilburn NW6 . . . . .23 B3
Denmark St WC2 . . **105** C2
Denmead Ho
SW15 . . . . .56 B1
Denne Terr E8 . . . . . .24 B4
Dennett's Gr SE14 . . .50 C1
Dennett's Rd SE14 . . .50 C2
Denning Cl NW8 . . . . **89** A3
Denning Point E1 . . **111** A2
Denning Rd NW3 . . . .11 C4
Dennington Park
Mansions 🔢
NW6 . . . . .10 C2
Dennington Park Rd
NW6 . . . . .10 C2
Dennis Ct SE10 . . . . .52 B2
Dennis Ho 🔢 E3 . . . .26 B3
Dennison Point
E15 . . . . .19 B1
Dennis Way SW4 . . . .61 C4
Denny Cres SE11 . . **149** C2
Denny St SE11 . . . . **149** C2
Densham Ho NW8 . . **79** C1
Denstone Ho 🗓
SE15 . . . . .49 C4
Denton Ho N1 . . . . . . .15 A1
Denton NW1 . . . . **12** C2
Denton St SW18 . . . . .59 A1
Dents Rd SW11 . . . . .60 B1
Denver Rd N16 . . . . . . .7 A4
Denyer Ho 🔟
NW5 . . . . .13 A4
Denyer St SW3 . . . . **144** B4
Denys Bldg EC1 . . . **107** B4
Denzil Rd NW10 . . . . . .8 B3
Deodar Rd SW15 . . . .58 A3
Depot App NW2 . . . . . .9 C4
Depot Rd W12 . . . . . .30 B2
Depot St SE5 . . . . . . .48 C4
DEPTFORD 50 C3
Deptford Bridge
SE8 . . . . .51 C2
Deptford Bridge Sta
SE8 . . . . .51 C2
Deptford Broadway
SE8, SE14 . . . . .51 C2
Deptford Church St
SE8 . . . . .51 C3

Deptford Ferry Rd 🔢
E14 . . . . .41 C2
Deptford Gn 🗓 SE8 . .51 C4
Deptford Green Sch
SE14 . . . . .51 B3
Deptford Green Sch
(Annex) SE14 . . . . . .51 A3
Deptford High St
SE8 . . . . .51 C3
Deptford Park Prim
Sch SE8 . . . . .41 A1
Deptford Sta SE8 . . . .51 C3
Deptford Trad Est
SE8 . . . . .50 C4
Deptford Wharf
SE8 . . . . .41 B2
Dept of Transport &
Environment
SW1 . . . . **133** C1
De Quincey Mews 🗓
E16 . . . . .35 C1
Derby Ct 🔞 E5 . . . . . .17 C4
Derby Gate SW1 . . . **134** A4
Derby Ho SE11 . . . . **149** B4
Derby Rd
Mortlake SW14 . . . . .55 A3
South Hackney E9 . . .25 C4
Derbyshire St
E2 . . . . 24 C2 **99** C3
Derby St W1 . . . . . . **117** C1
Dereham Ho 🔟
SE4 . . . . .65 C3
Dereham Pl
EC2 . . . . 24 A1 **98** B2
Derek Walcott Cl
SE24 . . . . .63 A2
Dericote St E8 . . . . . .25 A4
Dering St W1 . . . . . . **104** B1
Dermody Gdns
SE13 . . . . .67 C2
Dermody Rd SE13 . . .67 C2
Deronda Rd SE24,
SW2 . . . . .75 A3
Derrick Ho 🔞
SW2 . . . . .74 C3
Derrycombe Ho 🔞
W11 . . . . .31 C4
Derry St W8 . . . . . . **128** A3
Dersingham Rd
NW2 . . . . .1 A1
Derwent NW1 . . . . . . **92** C3
Derwent Ct
🔢 Hammersmith
W6 . . . . .38 C2
🗓 Rotherhithe
SE16 . . . . .40 C4
Derwent Gr SE22 . . . .64 B3
Derwent Ho
South Kensington
SW7 . . . . **143** A4
Tower Hamlets E3 . . .26 B1
Derwent St SE10 . . . .43 A1
Derwentwater Mans
🔢 W3 . . . . .28 B1
Derwentwater Prim
Sch W3 . . . . .28 B1
Derwentwater Rd
W3 . . . . .28 B1
Desborough Cl
W2 . . . . **100** B4
Desborough Ho
W14 . . . . **155** A4
Desenfans Rd
SE21 . . . . .64 A1
Desmond St SE14 . . .51 A4
Despard Ho SW2 . . . .74 C2
Despard Rd N19 . . . . . .4 B3

Desvignes Dr
SE13 . . . . .67 C1
Dethick Ct 🗓 E3 . . . .26 A4
Detling Ho SE17 . . . **152** A3
Devas St E3 . . . . .27 A1
Deventer Cres 🔞
SE22 . . . . .64 A2
De Vere Cotts
W8 . . . . **128** C2
De Vere Gdns W8 **128** C3
Deverell St SE1 . . . **137** B1
De Vere Mews
W8 . . . . **128** C2
Devereux Ct WC2 . **107** B1
Devereux Ho 🗓
SW15 . . . . .56 C2
Devereux La
SW13 . . . . .47 A3
Devereux Rd
SW11 . . . . .60 B1
Devitt Ho 🗓 E14 . . . .34 A2
Devizes St N1 . . . . . . **87** C3
Devonhurst Pl 🔢
W4 . . . . .37 C1
Devonia Rd N1 . . . . . **86** B2
Devon Mans SE1 . . **138** B4
Devonport 🗓
W2 . . . . **102** A2
Devonport Ho
Greenwich SE10 . . . .52 B4
🔢 Paddington W2 . . .31 C4
Devonport Rd
W12 . . . . .39 A4
Devonport St E1 . . . . .32 C3
Devonshire Cl
W1 . . . . **104** A4
Devonshire Ct
🔢 Balham SW12 . . . .73 A4
🗓 Richmond TW9 . . .44 B2
Devonshire Dr
SE10 . . . . .52 A2
Devonshire Gdns
W4 . . . . .45 B3
Devonshire Gr
SE15 . . . . .50 A4
Devonshire Hall 🔢
E9 . . . . .17 B2
Devonshire Ho
Brondesbury NW6 . . .10 B2
Newington SE1 . . . . **136** C2
Paddington W2 . . . . **101** C4
🗓 Putney SW15 . . . . .69 B4
Westminster SW1 . . **147** C2
Devonshire Hospl
W1 . . . . **103** C4
Devonshire House
Prep Sch NW3 . . . . .11 C3
Devonshire House
Sch NW3 . . . . .11 B3
Devonshire Mews 🔞
W4 . . . . .38 A1
Devonshire Mews N
W1 . . . . **104** A4
Devonshire Mews S
W1 . . . . **104** A4
Devonshire Mews W
W1 . . . . **103** C4
Devonshire Pl
Child's Hill NW2 . . . . . .1 C1
Kensington W8 . . . . **128** A1
Marylebone W1 . . . **103** C4
Devonshire Place
Mews W1 . . . . **103** C4
Devonshire Rd
W4 . . . . .38 A1

Devonshire Row
EC2 . . . . 110 B3
Devonshire Row
Mews W1 . . . . 92 B1
Devonshire Sq
EC2 . . . . 110 B3
Devonshire St
Chiswick W4 . . . . A3
Marylebone W1 . . . 104 A4
Devonshire Terr
W2 . . . . 101 A1
Devons Rd E3 . . . . 27 A1
Devons Road Sta
E3 . . . . A1
Devon St SE15 . . . 50 A4
De Walden Ho
NW8 . . . . A2
De Walden St W1 103 C3
Dewar St SE15 . . . 64 C4
Dewberry St E14 . . 34 B4
Dewey Rd N1 . . . . 85 B2
Dewhurst Rd W14 . 39 C3
Dewsbury Ct ▣
W4 . . . . 37 B2
Dewsbury Rd NW10 . 8 C3
Dewsbury Terr
NW1 . . . . 82 B4
D'eynsford Rd SE5 . 48 C2
Dhonau Ho SE16 . 153 A4
Diadem Ct W1 . . . 105 B2
Dial Wlk The W8 . 128 B4
Diamond Est
SW17 . . . . 72 A1
Diamond Ho ㉒
E3 . . . . 26 A3
Diamond St SE15 . 49 A3
Diamond Terr
SE10 . . . . 52 B2
Diana ㉗ SE8 . . . 51 B4
Diana Ho
Barnes SW13 . . . . 46 B2
▣ Brixton SW2 . . . 62 B2
Diana, Princess of
Wales Mml Wlk
W2 . . . . 114 C1
Dibden Ho ▣ SE5 . 49 A3
Dibden St N1 . . . . 86 C4
Dibdin Ho W9 . . . . 78 A1
Dicey Ave NW2 . . . 9 B4
Dickens Ct EC1 . . . 96 A1
Dickens Ho
Bloomsbury WC1 . . 94 A2
Kennington SE17 . . 150 B1
Kilburn NW6 . . . . . 23 C2
Paddington NW8 . . 89 C2
Dickens House Mus*
WC1 . . . . 95 A1
Dickenson Rd N8 . . . 5 A4
Dickens Sq SE1 . . 137 A2
Dickens St SW8 . 170 B2
Dickinson Ho
E2 . . . . 24 C2 99 B3
Dicksee Ho NW8 . . 89 B1
Dick Shepherd Ct ㄇ
SW2 . . . . 62 C1
Dickson Ho ▣ E1 . . 32 A3
Didbin Ho N7 . . . . 5 B2
Digby Cres N4 . . . . 6 B2
Digby Mans W6 . . 39 B1
Digby Rd E9 . . . . . 17 C2
Digby St E2 . . . . . 25 B2
Diggon St E1 . . . . 32 C4
Dighton Ct SE17 . . 48 B4
Dighton Rd SW18 . 59 B3

Dignum St N1 . . . . 85 B2
Digswell St N7 . . . . 14 C2
Dilke St SW3 . . . . 159 A4
Dilston Gr SE16 . . 40 B2
Dilton Gdns SW15 . 69 A3
Dimes Pl ▣ W6 . . . 39 A2
Dimson Cres E3 . . 26 C2
Dinerman Ct NW8 . 79 A4
Dingle Gdns E14 . . 33 C2
Dingley La SW16 . 73 C2
Dingley Pl EC1 . . . 97 A3
Dingley Rd EC1 . . . 96 C3
Dingwall Rd SW18 . 71 B4
Dinmont Ho ㉒ E2 . 24 C3
Dinmont St ▣ E2 . 25 A3
Dinmore Ho ▣ E9 . 25 B4
Dinnington Ho ㄇ
E1 . . . . 25 A1
Dinsdale Rd SE3 . . 53 B4
Dinsmore Rd
SW12 . . . . 73 A4
Dinton Ho NW8 . . . 90 A2
Dinwiddy Ho N1 . . 84 C1
Dionis Ho SW6 . . 165 B3
Disbrowe Rd W6 . 154 B3
Discovery Bsns Pk
E14 . . . . 139 C1
Discovery Dock E
E14 . . . . 42 A4
Discovery Ho ▣
E14 . . . . 34 B2
Disney Pl SE1 . . . 137 A4
Disney St SE1 . . . 137 A4
Disraeli Cl ㄇ W4 . . 38 A2
Disraeli Gdns
SW15 . . . . 58 B3
Disraeli Rd
Acton NW10 . . . . . 20 C3
Putney SW15 . . . . 58 B3
Diss St E2 . . . 24 B2 98 C4
Distaff La EC4 . . . 122 C4
Distillery La ㄇ W6 . 39 B1
Distillery Rd W6 . . 39 B1
Distillery Wlk ㄇ
TW8 . . . . 44 A4
Distin St SE11 . . . 149 B3
Ditchburn St E14 . 34 B2
Ditton Ho ㄇ E5 . . . 17 A3
Divis Way SW15 . . 57 A1
Dixon Clark Ct N1 . 15 A2
Dixon Ho ㉕ NW10 . 30 C3
Dixon Rd SE14 . . . 51 A2
Dixon's Alley ㄇ
SE16 . . . . 40 A4
Dobree Ave NW10 . . 9 A1
Dobson Cl NW6 . . 11 C1
Dobson Ho ㄇ
SE14 . . . . 50 C4
Doby Ct EC4 . . . . 123 A4
Dockers Tanner Rd ㉖
E14 . . . . 41 C2
Dockhead SE1 . . . 139 A3
Dockhead Wharf
SE1 . . . . 139 A4
Dock Hill Ave
SE16 . . . . 40 C4
Docklands Ct ㉕
E14 . . . . 33 B3
Docklands Heritage
Mus* SE16 . . . . . . 33 B1
Dockley Rd SE16 139 B1
Dockley Road Ind Est
SE16 . . . . 139 B1
Dock Offices ㄇ
SE16 . . . . 40 B3
Dock St E1 . . . . . . 125 B4

Doctor Spurstowe
Almshouses ▣
E8 . . . . 17 A2
Docura Ho N7 . . . . 5 B2
Docwras Bldgs
N1 . . . . 16 A2
Dodbrooke Rd
SE27 . . . . 75 A1
Dodd Ho ㄅ SE16 . 40 A2
Doddington Gr
SE17 . . . . 150 B1
Doddington Pl ▣
SE17 . . . . 48 A4
Dodson St SE1 . . 135 C3
Dod St E14 . . . . . . 33 C3
Dog Kennel Hill
SE22 . . . . 64 A4
Dog Kennel Hill Sch
SE22 . . . . 64 A4
Dog La NW10 . . . . . 8 A4
Dolben Ct SW1 . . 147 C3
Dolben St SE1 . . 122 B1
Dolby Rd SW6 . . . 164 C1
Doleman Ho ㄇ
SE10 . . . . 52 A2
Dolland Ho SE11 . 149 A1
Dolland St SE11 . 149 A1
Dollar Bay E14 . . . 42 B4
DOLLIS HILL 9 A4
Dollis Hill Sta NW2 . . 8 C3
Dolman Rd W4 . . . 37 C2
Dolman St SW4 . . 62 B3
Dolphin Cl ▣
SE16 . . . . 40 C4
Dolphin Ct N7 . . . . 13 C4
Dolphin La E14 . . . 34 A2
Dolphin Sch SW11 . 60 B2
Dolphin Sq SW1 . 147 B1
Dolphin Twr ㉑
SE8 . . . . 51 B4
Dombey Ho
Bermondsey SE1 . 139 B3
▣ Shepherd's Bush
W11 . . . . 30 C1
Dombey St WC1 . . 106 C4
Domett Cl SE5 . . . 63 C3
Domfe Pl E5 . . . . . 17 B4
Domingo St EC1 . . 96 C1
Dominion St EC2 . 109 C4
Donaghue Cotts ㄇ
E14 . . . . 33 A4
Donald Ho ㄇ
NW6 . . . . 23 B4
Donegal Ho ㉒ E1 . 25 B1
Donegal St N1 . . . 85 A1
Doneraile Ho
SW1 . . . . 146 A1
Doneraile St SW6 . 47 C2
Dongola Rd E1 . . . 33 A4
Don Gratton Ho ㄇ
E1 . . . . 111 B3
Donkey Alley
SE22 . . . . 64 C1
Donkin Ho ㄅ
SE16 . . . . 40 A2
Donne Ct SE24 . . 63 B1
Donne Ho
㉖ Canonbury N16 . 15 C4
㉕ Deptford SE14 . . 50 C4
ㄇ Poplar E14 . . . . 33 C3
Donne Pl SW3 . . 144 B4
Donnington Ct
ㄇ Camden Town
NW1 . . . . 13 A1

Donnington Ct
continued
Willesden NW10 . . . 9 A1
Donnington Ho
SW8 . . . . 171 B2
Donnington Prim Sch
NW10 . . . . 22 A4
Donnington Rd
NW10 . . . . 22 A4
Donovan Ct SW7 143 B1
Donovan Ho ▣ E1 . 32 B2
Don Phelan Cl
SE5 . . . . 48 C2
Doon St SE1 . . . . 121 B2
Doradus Ct ㉒
SW19 . . . . 69 C3
Dora Ho
ㄇ Shepherd's Bush
W11 . . . . 30 C2
ㄇ Tower Hamlets
E14 . . . . 33 B3
Dorando Cl W12 . . 30 A2
Doran Wlk
Stratford E15 . . . . 19 B1
Stratford Marsh E15 . 27 A4
Dora St E14 . . . . . 33 B3
Dorcas St ▣
SW8 . . . . 59 C3
Dorchester Ct
ㄇ De Beauvoir Town
N1 . . . . 16 A1
Herne Hill SE24 . . 63 B2
Knightsbridge SW1 131 A1
ㄇ Streatham
SW16 . . . . 74 A2
Dorchester Dr
SE24 . . . . 63 B2
Dorchester Gr W4 . 38 B1
Dorchester Ho
TW9 . . . . 45 A3
Dordrecht Rd W3 . 29 A1
Doria Rd SW6 . . . 165 A2
Doric Ho ㄇ E2 . . . 25 C3
Doric Way NW1 . . 93 B4
Doris Emmerton Ct
SW18 . . . . 59 C3
Dorking Cl SE8 . . . 51 B4
Dorking Ho SE1 . 137 C2
Dorland Ct SW15 . 58 B1
Dorlcote Rd SW18 . 72 A4
Dorleston Ct N1 . . 87 C4
Dorman Way NW8 . 79 B4
Dormay St SW18 . 59 A2
Dormstone Ho
SE17 . . . . 152 A3
Dornberg Cl SE3 . . 53 C3
Dorncliffe Rd
SW6 . . . . 164 B2
Dorney NW3 . . . . . 12 A1
Dornfell St NW6 . . 10 C3
Dornoch Ho ㉖ E3 . 26 B3
Dornton Rd SW12,
SW17 . . . . 73 B2
Dorothy Charrington
Ho ㄇ SW2 . . . . . 64 C2
Dorothy Rd SW11 . 60 B4
Dorrien Wlk SW16 . 73 C2
Dorrington Point ㉖
E3 . . . . 27 A2
Dorrington St
EC1 . . . . 107 B4
Dorrit Ho ㉒ W11 . 30 C1
Dorrit St SE1 . . . . 137 A4
Dorset Bldgs EC4 108 A1
Dorset Cl NW1 . . 102 C4
Dorset Ct ㉓ N1 . . 16 A1

Dorset Mans ㉒
W6 . . . . 47 C4
Dorset Mews
SW1 . . . . 132 A2
Dorset Pl E15 . . . . 19 C2
Dorset Rd SW8 . . 162 C2
Dorset Rise EC4 . 108 A1
Dorset Sq NW1 . . 90 C1
Dorset St ㄇ W1 . . 103 A3
Dorton Cl ▣ SE15 . 49 A3
Dorville Cres W6 . . 39 A3
Doughty Ct ㄇ E1 . . 32 A1
Doughty Mews
WC1 . . . . 94 C1
Doughty St WC1 . . 94 C1
Douglas Bldgs
SE1 . . . . 137 A2
Douglas Ct ▣
NW6 . . . . 10 C1
Douglas Gracey Ho
SW18 . . . . 70 A4
Douglas Ho
Putney SW15 . . . . 56 C1
ㄇ Westminster SW1 147 B3
Douglas Johnstone
Ho SW6 . . . . 154 C3
Douglas Mews
NW2 . . . . 1 A1
Douglas Path E14 . 42 B1
Douglas Rd
Islington N1 . . . . . 15 B1
Kilburn NW6 . . . . . 23 B4
ㄇ Newham E16 . . . 35 C4
Douglas Rd N N1 . . 15 B2
Douglas Rd S N1 . . 15 B2
Douglas St SW1 . 147 B3
Douglas Waite Ho
NW6 . . . . 11 A1
Douglas Way SE8 . 51 B3
Doulton Ho SE11 149 A4
Doulton Mews ▣
NW6 . . . . 11 A2
Dounesforth Gdns
SW18 . . . . 71 A3
Douro Pl W8 . . . . 128 B2
Douro St E3 . . . . . 26 C3
Douthwaite Sq
E1 . . . . 125 C2
Dovecote Gdns ▣
SW14 . . . . 55 C4
Dovedale Cotts
SW11 . . . . 168 C2
Dovedale Ho N16 . . 6 C4
Dovedale Rd SE22 . 65 B1
Dovehouse St
SW3 . . . . 144 A1
Dove Mews SW7 . 143 A2
Dovercourt Rd
SE22 . . . . 64 B1
Dover Ct
Clerkenwell EC1 . . 96 A2
ㄇ Greenwich SE10 . 52 A2
Dove Rd N1 . . . . . 15 C2
Doverfield Rd
SW2 . . . . 74 A4
Dover Flats SE1 . 152 B3
Dover Ho
Brixton SE5 . . . . . 48 A2
ㄇ Deptford SE15 . . 50 B4
Dover House Rd
SW15 . . . . 57 A2
Dover Mans ㄇ
SW9 . . . . 62 C4
Dove Row E2 . . . . 24 C4
Dover Park Dr
SW15 . . . . 57 A1

Dover St W1..... 118 C2
Dover Terr TW9 .....44 C1
Doves Yd N1..... 85 B3
Doves St SW8 .... 172 C4
Doveton Ho 7 E1.. 25 B1
Doveton St 8 E1....25 B1
Dove Wlk SW1 ... 145 B2
Dovey Lo 4 N1.... 14 C1
Dowdeny Cl 13
SE5 ....56 A3
Dowding Ho N6.... 3 C4
Dowell Ho SE21... 76 B1
Dowes Ho 13
SW16 ....91 A4
Dowgate Hill EC4. 123 B4
Dowland St W10 .. 23 A2
Dowlas St SE5 ....49 A3
Dowlen Ct 14 E14 .41 C4
Dowler Ho 1..... 111 C1
Downbarton Ho
SW9 .... 173 B4
Downbury Mews 2
SW18 ....58 C2
Downend Ct 1
SE15 ....49 A4
Downer's Cotts
SW4 ....61 B3
Downey Ho 6 E1 .25 C1
Downfield Cl W9 . 88 A1
Downham Ct 13
N1.....................15 C1
Downham Rd N1 ..15 C1
Downing Ho
2 North Kensington
W10 ....30 C3
5 Putney SW15... 56 C2
Downing St*
SW1 .... 134 A4
Down Pl W6 ....39 A1
Down St Mews
W1 .... 118 A1
Downs Ct 18 E8 ...17 A3
Downsell Prim Sch
E15 ....19 C4
Downsell Rd E15 ..19 C4
Downshire Hill
NW3 ....11 C4
Downside 2
SW15 ....58 A2
Downside Cres
NW3 ....12 A3
Downs La 2 E5 ....17 A4
Downs Park Rd E5,
E8 ....16 C3
Downs Rd E5, N16..16 C4
Down St W1........ 118 A1
Downsview Sch
E5 ....17 A4
Downton Ave SW2..74 B2
Downtown Rd
SE16 ....41 A4
Dowrey St N1...... 85 B4
Dowson Cl SE5....63 C3
Dowson Ct SE13...67 C4
Dowson Ho 8 E1 ..32 C3
Doyce St SE1..... 136 C4
Doyle Gdns NW10 .22 A4
Doyle Ho W3 ....37 A4
D'Oyley St SW1 .. 145 B4
Doynton St N19 ....4 A2
Draco St SE17.....48 B4
Dragon Ct WC2 .. 106 B2
Dragon Rd SE15...49 A4
Dragon Yd WC1 .. 106 B2

Dragoon Rd SE8....41 B1
Dragor Rd NW10 ..20 B1
Drake Cl 30 SE16 ..40 C4
Drake Croft N16 ....6 C2
Drake Ct 8 W12 ...39 A4
Drakefell Rd
SE14 ....65 C4
Drakefield Rd
SW17 ....72 C1
Drake Ho
1 Limehouse E14. .33 A2
2 Stepney E1.......32 B4
Drakeley Ct N5.....15 A4
Drake St WC1 .... 106 C3
Drakes Ctyd NW6...10 B1
Drake St WC1 .... 106 C3
Draper Ho 1..... 150 B4
Draper Pl N1....... 86 B4
Drapers Almshouses
3 E3 ....26 C2
Drapers Gdns
EC2................. 109 C2
Drapers Rd E15 .. 19 C4
Drappers Way
SE16 .... 153 C4
Draycott Ave
SW3 .... 144 B3
Draycott Cl SE5 .. 48 C3
Draycott Cl SW11 168 A4
Draycott Pl SW3 . 144 C3
Draycott Pl N1.... 144 C3
Draycott Terr
SW3 .... 145 A3
Drayford Cl W9 ... 23 B1
Dray Gdns SW2 ... 62 B2
Draymans Ct 4
SW9 ....62 B4
Drayson Mews
W8 .... 127 C3
Drayton Gdns
SW10 .... 143 A1
Drayton Ho 14
SE5 ....49 A2
Drayton Park Mews
12 N5 ....15 A3
Drayton Park Prim
Sch N5 ....14 C3
Drayton Park Sta
N5.......................14 C3
Drayton Pk N5, N7 ..14 C4
Drayton Rd NW10 .21 B4
Dreadnought St
SE10 ....43 A3
Dresden Cl NW6...11 A2
Dresden Ho
Clapham SW11 .. 169 B2
Lambeth SE11 ... 149 A4
Dresden Rd N19 ....4 C3
Dressington Ave
SE4 ....66 C1
Drewett Ho E1 ... 111 C1
Drew Ho 2 SW16 ..74 A1
Drewstead La
SW16 ....73 C2
Drewstead Rd
SW16 ....73 C2
Driffield Rd E3 .....26 A3
Driftway Ho 19
N1.......................24 A3
Drinkwater Ho 11
SE5 ....48 C3
Drive Mews SW2. 164 B2
Drive The
Acton W3 ....28 B3
Harlesden NW10 ..21 B4
Hendon NW11 .....1 A4
Islington N7 ....14 B2

Dr Johnson Ave
SW17 ....73 A1
Dr Johnson's House
Mus* E4 .... 107 C1
Droitwich Cl SE26 .76 C1
Dromore Rd SW15..58 A1
Dron Ho E1 ....32 B4
Droop St W10 ......23 A1
Drovers Ct SE13 ...67 B4
Drovers Pl SE15 ...50 A3
Druce Rd SE21 ....64 A1
Druid St SE1 ...... 138 C3
Drummer Lo N7 .....5 B1
Drummond Cres
NW1 .... 93 B4
Drummond Gate
SW1 .... 147 C2
Drummond Ho 15
E2 ....24 C3
Drummond Rd
SE16 ....40 A3
Drummonds Pl
TW9 ....54 A3
Drummond St
NW1 .... 92 C2
Drum St E1 .... 111 A2
Drury Ho SW8.... 170 C4
Drury La WC2 .... 106 B1
Dryad St SW15 ....57 C4
Dryburgh Ho
SW1 .... 146 B2
Dryburgh Mans
SW15 ....57 B4
Dryburgh Rd
SW15 ....57 B4
Dryden Bldg 1 ... 111 B2
Dryden Cl SE11 .. 149 C3
Dryden Ho
6 Camberwell
SE5 ....49 A2
18 Stoke Newington
N16 ....7 A1
Dryden St WC2... 106 B1
Dryfield Wlk 8
SE8 ....51 C4
Drysdale Flats 3
E8 ....16 B3
Drysdale Ho 8
E2 ....24 B3
Drysdale Pl
N1.......................24 A2 98 B4
Drysdale St
N1.......................24 A2 98 B4
Dublin Ave E8 .....24 C4
Ducal St E2 .... 24 B2 99 A3
Ducane Cl 6 W12..30 B3
Du Cane Ct SW12 .72 C3
Du Cane Rd W12 ..29 C3
Ducavel Ho SW2 ..74 B3
Duchess Mews
W1 .... 104 B3
Duchess of Bedford Ho
W8 .... 127 B3
Duchess of Bedford's
Wlk W8 .... 127 B3
Duchess St W1 .. 104 B3
Duchy St SE1 .... 121 C2
Ducie Ho 2 SW15..57 B2
Ducie St SW4 .....62 B3
Duckett St E1 .....33 A4
Duck La W1 .... 105 B1
DUDDEN HILL 8 C3
Dudden Hill La
NW10 ....8 B3
Dudley Ct
Marylebone W1 .. 102 C1

Dudley Ct continued
St Giles WC2..... 106 A2
Dudley Ho
Brixton SW9..... 173 B2
Paddington W2 .. 101 B3
Dudley Mews 14
SW2 ....62 C1
Dudley Rd
Kilburn NW6.......23 B3
Richmond TW9 ....44 B1
Dudley St W2 .... 101 B3
Dudmaston Mews
SW3 .... 143 C2
Duffell Ho SE11 . 149 A1
Dufferin Ave EC1 . 97 B1
Dufferin Ct EC1 ... 97 B1
Dufferin St EC1 ... 97 A1
Duffield Ho N4 .....6 B4
Duff St E14 ....34 A3
Dufour's Pl W1 .. 105 A1
Dugard Way SE11 150 A3
Dugdale Ho 10 N7..13 C3
Duke Humphrey Rd
SE3 ....53 A1
Duke of Wellington Pl
SW1, W1......... 131 C4
Duke of York's Sq
SW3 .... 145 A3
Duke of York St
SW1 .... 119 A2
Duke Rd W4 ....37 C1
Duke St Hill SE1 . 123 C2
Duke St St James's
SW1 .... 119 A2
Duke's Ave W4....37 C1
Dukes Ct
Dulwich SE22 .... 76 C3
East Dulwich SE22 ..65 A2
Lewisham SE13 ...52 B1
Mortlake SW14 ...45 C1
Dukes Gate 4 W4..37 B2
Dukes Head Yd N6..4 A3
Duke's Ho SW1 .. 147 C4
Duke Shore Wharf
E14 ....33 B2
Dukes La W8 .... 128 A4
Duke's Mews W1 103 C2
Duke's Pl EC3 ... 110 B1
Dukes Point N6 ....4 A3
Duke's Rd WC1 ... 93 C3
Duke St W1 ...... 103 C1
Duke Street Mans
W1 .... 103 C1
Duke's Yd W1 ... 117 C4
Dulas St N4 ....5 B3
Dulford St
W11 ....31 A2 112 A4
Dulka Rd SW11 ...60 B2
Dulverton NW1 ....83 A3
Dulverton Mans
WC1 .... 95 A1
DULWICH 76 A1
Dulwich Coll SE21..76 A1
Dulwich Coll Picture
Gall* SE21 ....76 A4
Dulwich Coll Prep
Sch SE21 ....76 A1
Dulwich Comm
SE21 ....76 B2
Dulwich Hamlet Jun
Sch SE21 ....63 C1
Dulwich Hospl
SE22 ....63 A3
Dulwich Lawn Cl 5
SE22 ....64 B2
Dulwich Mead
SE24 ....63 B1

Dulwich Mews
East Dulwich SE22..64 B3
1 East Dulwich
SE22 ....64 B3
Dulwich Oaks The
SE21 ....76 B1
Dulwich Rd SE24 .63 A1
DULWICH VILLAGE
..........................76 A4
Dulwich Village
SE21 ....64 A1
Dulwich Village CE Inf
Sch SE21 .... 150 A3
Dumain Ct SE11 . 150 A3
Du Maurier Ho 2
NW3 ....12 B3
Dumbarton Ct 16
SW2 ....74 A4
Dumbarton Rd
SW2 ....62 A1
Dumont Rd N16 ....7 A1
Dumphreys Ho 5
SW4 ....73 C4
Dumpton Pl NW1 .12 C1
Dunbar St SE27 ...75 B1
Dunbar Wharf 27
E14 ....33 B2
Dunboyne Rd
NW3 ....12 B3
Dunbridge Ho
SW15 ....56 B1
Dunbridge St
Bethnal Green E2...25 A1
E2 ....25 A1 99 C2
Duncan Ct 3 E14 ..34 B4
Duncan Gr W3.....29 A3
Duncan Ho 3
NW3 ....12 B1
Duncannon Ho
SW1 .... 147 C1
Duncannon St
WC2 .... 120 A3
Duncan Rd
Hackney E8........25 A4
Richmond TW9 ...54 A3
Duncan St N1 ..... 86 A2
Duncan Terr N1 ... 86 A2
Dunch St 33 E1 ...32 A3
Duncombe Ho 7
SW19 ....69 C3
Duncombe Prim Sch
N19 ....5 A3
Duncombe Rd N19 ..4 C3
Duncrievie Rd
SE13 ....67 C1
Dundalk Ho 2 E1 .32 B3
Dundalk Rd SE4 ..66 A4
Dundas Ho 12 E2 .25 B3
Dundas Rd SE15 .50 B1
Dundee Ct 31 E1 .32 A1
Dundee Ho W9 ... 88 C4
Dundee St E1 .....32 A1
Dundee Wharf
E14 ....33 B2
Dundonald Rd
NW10 ....22 C4
Dundry Ho 8
SE26 ....76 C1
Dunelm Gr SE27 ..75 B1
Dunelm St E1 .....32 C3
Dunford Rd N7 ....14 B4
Dungarvan Ave
SW15 ....56 C3

Dungeness Ho
SW18 . . . . 59 B3
Dunhill Point 12
SW15 . . . . 69 A3
Dunkeld Ho 6
E14 . . . . 34 C3
Dunlace Rd E5 . . . . 17 C4
Dunlin Ct 12 SE1 . . 75 C2
Dunlin Ho 18 SE16 . . 40 C2
Dunloe Ct 7 E2 . . . 24 B3
Dunloe St E2 . . . . . 24 B3
Dunlop Pl SE16 . . 139 A1
Dunmore Point
E2 . . . . 24 B2 98 C3
Dunmore Rd NW6 . . 23 A4
Dunmow Ho SE11 149 A2
Dunmow Rd E15 . . . 19 C4
Dunmow Wlk N1 . . 86 C4
Dunnage Cres
SE16 . . . . 41 A2
Dunne Mews 11
NW5 . . . . 13 B3
Dunnet Ho 22 E3 . . 26 B3
Dunnico Ho SE17 152 A2
Dunnock Ct 8
SE21 . . . . 75 C2
Dunn's Pas WC1 . . 106 B2
Dunn St E8 . . . . . . 16 B3
Dunollie Pl NW5 . . 13 B3
Dunollie Rd NW5 . . 13 B3
Dunoon Ho N1 . . . . 84 C3
Dunraven Ho 14
TW9 . . . . 44 B2
Dunraven Rd W12 . . 29 C1
Dunraven Sch
SW16 . . . . 74 B1
Dunraven St W1 . . 117 A4
Dunrobin Ct NW3 . . 11 A3
Dunsany Rd W14 . . 39 C3
Dunsfold Ho 4
SW2 . . . . 74 B4
Dunsford Way
SW15 . . . . 57 A1
Dunsmure Rd N16 . . 7 A3
Dunstable Ct 3
SE3 . . . . 53 C3
Dunstable Mews
W1 . . . . 103 C4
Dunstable Rd TW10,
TW9 . . . . 54 A3
Dunstall Ho 9
SE15 . . . . 49 C2
Dunstan Ho SE4 . . 51 B1
Dunstan Ho 5
E1 . . . . 32 B4
Dunstan Rd NW11 . . 1 C3
Dunstan's Gr SE22 . 65 A1
Dunstan's Rd SE22 . 64 C1
Dunster Ct EC3 . . 124 B4
Dunster Gdns
NW6 . . . . 10 B1
Dunsterville Way
SE1 . . . . 137 C3
Dunston Rd
Clapham SW11 . . 169 C1
Hackney E8 . . . . . 24 B4
Dunston St E8 . . . . 24 B4
Dunton Ho 14
SW16 . . . . 74 A1
Dunton Rd SE1 . . . 152 C3
Dunthill Rd
SW18 . . . . 71 A3
Dunworth Mews
W11 . . . . 31 B3
Duplex Ride SW1 . 131 A3

Durand Gdns
SW9 . . . . 173 A3
Durand Prim Sch
SW9 . . . . 173 A3
Durant St
E2 . . . . 24 C2 99 B4
Durban Ho 26
W12 . . . . 30 A2
Durdans Ho 8
NW1 . . . . 13 B1
Durfey Pl SE5 . . . . 48 C3
Durford Cres
SW15 . . . . 69 A3
Durham Ct
Brockley SE4 . . . . 66 C4
4 Kilburn NW6 . . . 23 C3
Durham Ho
7 Dartmouth Pk
NW5 . . . . 4 B1
Lisson Gr NW8 . . . 90 B3
Durham House St
WC2 . . . . 120 B3
Durham Rd N4,N7 . . 5 B2
Durham Row E1 . . . 33 A4
Durham St SE11 . . 162 C4
Durham Terr W2 . . 100 A2
Durley Rd N16 . . . . 7 A4
Durlock Ho SW9 . . 173 B4
Durlston Rd E5 . . . . 7 C2
Durnford St 4
SE10 . . . . 52 B4
Durnsford Ave
SW19 . . . . 71 A1
Durnsford Rd SW18,
SW19 . . . . 70 C1
Durrell Rd SW6 . . 164 C3
Durrels Ho W14 . . 141 A4
Durrington Rd E5 . . 18 A4
Durrington Twr
SW8 . . . . 171 A2
Durrisdeer Ho
NW2 . . . . 10 B4
Durston NW5 . . . . . 12 C3
Durward St E1 . . . . 32 A4
Durweston Mews
W1 . . . . 103 A4
Durweston St W1 103 A3
Dutch Yd SW18 . . . 58 C2
Dutton Ho SW2 . . . 75 A3
Dutton St SE10 . . . 52 B2
Dwight Ct SW6 . . 164 B2
Dycer Ho 19 E9 . . . 17 C2
Dye House La E3 . . 26 C4
Dyer Ho SE3 . . . . . 53 A1
Dyer's Bldgs EC1 . 107 B3
Dyer's La SW15 . . . 57 A3
Dykes Ct 11 SW2 . . 74 B3
Dylan Rd 2 SE24 . . 63 A3
Dylways SE5 . . . . . 63 C3
Dymchurch Ho 10
E5 . . . . 17 A3
Dymes Path SW19 . 69 C2
Dymock St SW6 . . 59 A4
Dyne Rd NW6 . . . . 10 B1
Dynevor Rd
Richmond TW10 . . 54 A2
Shacklewell N16 . . . 7 B1
Dynham Rd NW6 . . 10 C1
Dyott St
Soho WC1 . . . . . . 105 C2
St Giles WC1, WC2 106 A2
Dysart St
EC2 . . . . 24 A1 98 A1
Dyson Ho 3 SE10 . 43 B1

Eade Rd N4 . . . . . . 6 B4
Eagle Cl SE16 . . . . 40 B1
Eagle Ct
10 Dulwich SE21 . . 75 C2
Holborn EC1 . . . . 108 A4
Eagle Dwellings
EC1 . . . . 97 A4
Eagle Ho
22 Bethnal Green
E1 . . . . 25 A1
Finsbury Pk N7 . . . . 5 B1
Eagle Hts 15
SW11 . . . . 60 A4
Eagle Mans N16 . . 16 B3
Eagle Mews N1 . . . 16 A2
Eagle Pl
South Kensington
SW7 . . . . 143 A2
St James SW1 . . . 119 A3
Eagle St WC1 . . . 106 C3
Eagle Wharf E15 . . 124 C1
Eagle Wharf Rd
N1 . . . . 87 A2
Eagle Works
E1 . . . . 24 B1 99 A1
Eagling Cl 25 E3 . . 26 C2
Ealing, Hammersmith
& West London Coll
W14 . . . . 140 A2
Ealing Tertiary Coll
W3 . . . . 28 A1
Eamann Casey Ho
SW9 . . . . 173 C3
Eamont Ct NW8 . . 80 B2
Eamont St NW8 . . . 80 B2
Eardley Cres SW5 141 C1
Earldom Rd SW15 . 57 B3
Earle Ho SW1 . . . 147 C3
Earlham St WC2 . . 106 A1
Earl Ho NW1 . . . . . 90 B1
Earlom Ho WC1 . . . 95 B3
Earl Rd SW14 . . . . 55 B3
Earls Court Ex Ctr★
SW5 . . . . 141 B1
Earl's Court Gdns
SW5 . . . . 142 A3
Earl's Court Rd SW5,
W8 . . . . 141 C3
Earl's Court Sq
SW5 . . . . 142 A2
Earl's Court Sta
SW5 . . . . 141 C3
Earlsferry Way N1 . 14 A1
EARLSFIELD 71 B3
Earlsfield Prim Sch
SW18 . . . . 71 B2
Earlsfield Rd
SW18 . . . . 71 B4
Earlsfield Sta
SW18 . . . . 71 B3
Earlsmead Rd
NW10 . . . . 22 B2
Earls Terr W8 . . . 127 A1
Earlsthorpe Mews 3
SW12 . . . . 60 C1
Earlston Gr E9 . . . . 25 A4
Earls Wlk W8 . . . 127 B1
Earlswood Cl 10
SE10 . . . . 43 A1

Earlswood Ho 2
SW2 . . . . 74 B3
Earlswood St
SE10 . . . . 43 A1
Early Mews NW1 . . 82 B4
Earnshaw Rd E1 . . 96 B3
Earnshaw St WC1,
WC2 . . . . 105 C2
Earsby St W14 . . . 140 B4
Earth Galleries★
SW7 . . . . 129 C1
Eashing Point 5
SW15 . . . . 69 A3
Easleys Mews
W1 . . . . 103 C2
EAST ACTON 29 A1
East Acton Arc
W3 . . . . 29 B3
East Acton Ct 3 . . 29 A2
East Acton La W3 . 29 A2
East Acton Prim Sch
W3 . . . . 29 A2
East Acton Sta
W12 . . . . 29 B3
East Arbour St E1 . 32 C3
East Bank N16 . . . . 7 A4
East Block 5 E1 . . 32 C2
Eastbourne Ave
W3 . . . . 28 C3
Eastbourne Gdns
SW14 . . . . 55 B4
Eastbourne Mews
W2 . . . . 101 A2
Eastbourne Rd
W4 . . . . 45 B4
Eastbourne Terr
W2 . . . . 101 A2
Eastbury Gr W4 . . 38 A1
Eastbury Terr E1 . . 25 C1
Eastcastle St W1 . 105 A2
Eastcheap EC3 . . 124 A4
East Churchfield Rd
W3 . . . . 28 C1
Eastcote St SW9 . 172 C1
East Cross Ctr
E15 . . . . 18 C2
East Cross Route
Bow E3 . . . . 26 C4
Hackney Wick E9 . 18 B4
Eastdown Ho E8 . . 16 C4
Eastdown Pk SE13 . 67 C3
EAST DULWICH . . 64 A2
East Dulwich Gr
SE22 . . . . 64 A2
East Dulwich Rd SE15,
SE22 . . . . 64 C2
East Dulwich Sta
SE22 . . . . 64 B3
Eastern Rd SE4 . . . 66 C3
East Ferry Rd E14 . 42 A2
Eastfields Ave
SW18 . . . . 58 C3
Eastfields Rd W3 . . 28 B4
Eastfield St E14 . . . 33 A4
East Harding St
EC4 . . . . 107 C2
East Heath Rd NW3 . 2 C1
East Hill SW18 . . . 59 B2
East India Bldgs 9
E14 . . . . 33 C2
East India Ct 7
SE16 . . . . 40 B4
East India Dock
Basin★ E14 . . . . . 35 A2
East India Dock Rd
E14 . . . . 34 A2

East India Dock Road
Tunnel 18 E14 . . . 34 C3
East India Sta E14 . 34 C2
East La 16 . . . . . . 139 B3
East London Ho NW8 . 89 C3
Eastlake Rd SE5 . . 48 B1
Eastlands Cres
SE21 . . . . 64 B1
Eastleigh Wlk 9
SW15 . . . . 68 C4
East London Coll &
Toynbee Theatre
E1 . . . . 111 A3
East London Stad
E3 . . . . 33 B4
Eastman Dental Hospl
WC1 . . . . 94 C2
Eastman Ho 7
SW4 . . . . 61 B1
Eastman Rd W3 . . . 37 C4
Eastmearn Rd SE21,
SE27 . . . . 75 B2
East Mount St E1 . 32 A4
East Parkside 11
Greenwich SE10 . . 42 C1
Eastry Ho 11
SW8 . . . . 162 A1
Easton Ho 5
SE27 . . . . 75 A1
Easton St WC1 . . . 95 B2
East Parkside
SE10 . . . . 43 B4
East Pas EC1 . . . . 108 C4
East Plaza E14 . . . 34 A1
East Point SE1 . . . 153 B2
East Poultry Ave
EC1 . . . . 108 A3
East Putney Sta
SW15 . . . . 58 A2
East Rd
Chelsea SW1 . . . 145 B1
Shoreditch N1 . . . . 97 C4
East Row W10 . . . 23 A1
Eastry Ho SW8 . . 162 A1
EAST SHEEN 55 C3
East Sheen Ave
SW14 . . . . 55 C3
East Sheen Prim Sch
SW14 . . . . 56 A3
East Smithfield
E1 . . . . 125 A3
East St SE17 . . . . 151 B2
East Surrey Gr
SE15 . . . . 49 B3
East Tenter St 3 111 A1
Eastvale W3 . . . . . 29 B1
East View NW3 . . . . 2 C2
Eastway
South Hackney E3,
E9 . . . . 26 A4
Temple Mills E9,
E10 . . . . 18 C4
Eastwell Ho SE1 . 137 C2
Eastwick Ct 2
SW19 . . . . 69 C3
Eastwood Cl 2
N7 . . . . 14 C3
Eaton Cl SW1 . . . 145 B3
Eaton Dr SW9 . . . . 63 A3
Eaton Gate SW1 . 145 B4
Eaton Ho
Battersea SW11 . . 167 C3
23 Limehouse E14 . 33 B2
Eaton House Sch
SW1 . . . . 145 B4
Eaton House The
Manor Sch SW4 . . 61 A3
Eaton La SW1 . . . 132 B1
Eaton Mans SW1 . 145 B3

Eat–Eli 209

Eaton Mews N SW1 131 C1
Eaton Mews S SW1 132 A1
Eaton Mews W SW1 145 C4
Eaton Pl SW1 131 C1
Eaton Row SW1 132 A1
Eaton Sq SW1 131 C1
Eaton Square Sch SW1 146 A4
Eaton Terr
Belgravia SW1 145 C4
Bow E3 26 A2
Eaton Terr Mews SW1 145 B4
Eatonville Rd SW17 72 B2
Eatonville Villas SW17 72 B2
Ebbisham Dr SW8 162 C3
Ebbsfleet Rd NW2 10 A4
Ebenezer Ho SE11 150 A3
Ebenezer Mussel Ho 5 E2 25 B3
Ebenezer St N1 97 B4
Ebley Cl SE15 49 B4
Ebner St SW18 59 A2
Ebony Ct NW10 8 B2
Ebony Ho
Bethnal Green E2 24 C2 99 B3
10 West Hampstead NW3 11 A2
Ebor Cotts SW15 68 A1
Ebor St E1, E2 24 B1 98 C2
Eburne Rd N7 5 A1
Ebury Bridge Rd SW1 145 C1
Ebury Mews
Belgravia SW1 146 A4
West Norwood SE27 75 A1
Ebury Mews E SW1 132 A1
Ebury Sq SW1 145 C3
Ebury St SW1 146 A4
Ecclesbourne Rd N1 15 B1
Eccles Ct SE11 149 A1
Eccles Rd SW11 60 B3
Eccleston Ho 1 SW2 62 C1
Eccleston Mews SW1 131 C1
Eccleston Pl SW1 146 A4
Eccleston Sq SW1 146 B3
Eccleston Sq Mews SW1 146 C3
Eccleston St SW1 146 A4
Eckford St N1 85 B2
Eckstein Rd SW11 60 A3
Edans Ct W12 38 B4
Edbrooke Rd W9 23 C1
Eddisbury Ho 7 SE26 76 C1
Eddiscombe Rd SW6 165 A2
Eddison Ct N19 5 A2
Eddystone Rd SE4 66 A2
Eddystone Twr SE8 41 A1
Edenbridge Cl 29 SE16 40 A1
Edenbridge Rd E9 17 C1
Eden Cl
Child's Hill NW3 1 C2
Kensington W8 127 C2
Edendale W3 28 A2
Eden Gr N7 14 B3
Edenham Way W10 31 B4
Eden Ho
15 Battersea SW11 60 A4
Lisson Gr NW8 90 A1
Edenhurst Ave SW6 58 B4
Eden Lodge NW6 9 C1
Eden Mews SW17 71 B1
Edensmuir Ct SE3 53 C3
Edensor Gdns W4 46 A3
Edensor Rd W4 46 A3
Edenvale St SW6 166 C1
Eden Way E3 26 B4
Edgar Ho
Homerton E9 18 A3
South Lambeth SW8 162 A2
Edgar Kail Way SE22 64 A3
Edgarley Terr SW6 164 A3
Edgar Rd E3 27 A2
Edgar Wallace Cl 4 SE15 49 A3
Edgcott Ho 2 W10 30 B4
Edgecombe Ho
4 London SE5 49 A1
Putney SW19 70 A4
Edgecote Cl 7 W3 28 B1
Edgehill Ho 4 SW9 48 A1
Edgeley La SW4 61 C4
Edgeley Rd SW4 61 C4
Edgel St SW18 59 A3
Edge St W8 31 C1 113 C2
Edgeworth Ho NW8 78 C4
Edgson Ho SW1 146 A2
Edgware Acad WC2 106 B1
Edgware Rd W1, W2, NW1, NW8 102 A3
Edgware Road Sta (Bakerloo) NW1 102 A3
Edgware Road Sta (Met, Distr, Circle) NW1 102 B3
Edinburgh Cl 7 E2 25 B3
Edinburgh Ct 10 SE16 32 C1
Edinburgh Ho
3 Acton W3 28 C3
Maida Vale W9 88 B4
Edington 20 NW5 12 C2
Edison Bldg 7 E14 41 C4
Edison Ct SE10 43 B3
Edison Ho SE1 151 B4
Edis St NW1 81 C4
Editha Mans SW10 156 C3
Edith Cavell Cl 2 N19 5 A4
Edith Gr SW10 157 A2
Edith Ho 6 W6 39 B1
Edithna St SW9 62 A4
Edith Neville Cotts NW1 93 B4
Edith Neville Prim Sch NW1 83 B1
Edith Ramsay Ho 2 E1 33 A4
Edith Rd
Stratford New Town E15 19 C3
West Kensington W14 140 B3
Edith Row SW6 166 B4
Edith St E2 24 C3
Edith Summerskill Ho SW6 154 C2
Edith Terr SW10 156 C2
Edith Villas W14 140 C2
Edith Yd SW10 157 A2
Edmeston Cl E9 18 A2
Edmond Ct SE14 50 B2
Edmonton Ct 5 SE16 40 B3
Edmund Halley Way SE10 43 A4
Edmund Ho
Kennington SE17 150 B1
New Cross Gate SE14 51 B2
Edmundsbury Ct Est 16 SW9 62 B3
Edmund St SE5 48 C3
Edmund Waller Prim Sch SE14 50 C1
Ednam Ho SE15 49 C4
Edna St SW11 168 A3
Edred Ho E9 18 A4
Edrich Ho SW4 172 A3
Edric Ho SW1 147 C4
Edric Rd SE14 50 C3
Edridge Ho 9 SE27 75 A1
Edward Alleyn Ho SE21 76 A4
Edward Ct 2 E16 35 C4
Edward Dodd Ct N1 97 C4
Edward Edward's Ho SE1 122 A1
Edwardes Pl W8 127 A1
Edwardes Sq W8 127 A1
Edward Friend Ho 6 N16 7 A1
Edward Ho
Paddington W2 89 B1
Vauxhall SE11 149 A2
Edward Kennedy Ho 18 W10 23 A1
Edward Mann Cl 13 E1 32 C3
Edward Mews NW1 82 B1
Edward Pl SE8 51 B4
Edward Robinson Ho 3 SE14 50 C3
Edward's Cotts 11 N1 15 A1
Edward's La N16 7 A2
Edwards Mews
Islington N1 14 C1
Marylebone W1 103 B1
Edward Sq
Islington N1 84 C3
1 Rotherhithe SE16 33 A1
Edward St SE14 51 B3
Edward VII Mans NW10 22 C2
Edward Wilson Prim Sch W2 100 A4
Edwin Ho SE15 49 C3
Edwin's Mead E9 18 A4
Edwin St
Bethnal Green E1 25 B1
Newham E16 35 C4
Edwy Ho E9 18 B4
Edwyn Ho SW18 59 A1
Effie Pl SW6 155 C1
Effie Rd SW6 155 C1
Effingham Ho SW8 171 B1
Effra Ct SW2 62 B2
Effra Mans SW2 62 C2
Effra Par SW2 62 C2
Effra Rd SW2 62 C2
Effra Road Ret Pk SW2 62 C2
EF International Language Sch SE1 121 C1
Egbert Ho E9 18 A3
Egbert St NW1 81 B4
Egbury Ho SW15 56 B1
Egerton Cres SW3 144 B4
Egerton Ct 5 TW10 54 A2
Egerton Dr SE10 52 A2
Egerton Gdns
Knightsbridge SW3 130 A1
Willesden NW10 22 B4
Egerton Gdns Mews SW3 130 B1
Egerton Ho W4 45 B4
Egerton Pl SW3 130 B1
Egerton Rd N16 7 B4
Egerton Terr SW3 130 B1
Egham Cl SW19 70 A2
Eglantine Rd SW18 59 B2
Eglington Ct SE17 48 B4
Egliston Mews SW15 57 B4
Egliston Rd SW15 57 B4
Egmont St SE14 50 C3
Egremont Ho SE13 52 A1
Egremont Rd SE27 74 C1
Egret Ho 11 SE16 40 C2
Eider Ct 38 SE8 51 B4
Elaine Ct 13 NW3 12 B2
Elaine Gr NW5 12 C3
Elaine Ho N4 5 A3
Elam Cl SE5 48 A1
Elam St SE5 48 A1
Elan Ct E1 32 A4
Eland Rd SW11 60 B4
Elba Pl SE17 151 A4
Elbe St SW6 166 C2
Elborough St SW18 70 C3
Elbury Dr E16 35 C3
Elcho St SW11 158 B1
Elcot Ave SE15 50 A3
Elderberry Rd W5 36 A4
Elderfield Ho 4 E14 33 C2
Elderfield Rd E5 17 B4
Elder St E1 24 B1 98 C1
Elder Wlk
Islington N1 86 B4
2 Lewisham SE13 67 B4
Eldon Ct NW6 23 C4
Eldon Gr NW3 11 C3
Eldon Ho SW9 63 A4
Eldon Rd W8 128 B1
Eldon St EC2 109 C3
Eldon Way NW10 20 A3
Eldridge Ct SE16 139 B1
Eleanor Cl SE16 40 C4
Eleanor Ct 13 E2 24 C4
Eleanor Gr SW13 56 A4
Eleanor Ho
18 Hammersmith W6 39 B1
1 Kentish Town NW5 13 B3
Eleanor Palmer Prim Sch NW5 13 B4
Eleanor Rathbone Ho 1 N6 4 C4
Eleanor Rd E8 17 A1
Eleanor St E3 26 C2
Electra Ct 6 NW2 9 B2
Electric Ave SW9 62 C3
Electric Ho 18 E3 26 C2
Electric La 2 SW9 62 C3
Electric Mans 1 SW9 62 C3
Elephant & Castle
Newington SE1 150 B4
Newington SE1 136 B1
Elephant & Castle Sh Ctr SE1 150 C4
Elephant & Castle Sta
Lambeth SE1 136 B1
Newington SE17 150 C4
Elephant La SE16 40 B4
Elephant Rd SE17 150 C4
Elfindale Rd SE24 63 B2
Elfort Rd N5 14 C4
Elf Row E1 32 B2
Elgar Ave W5 36 A4
Elgar Cl SE8 51 C3
Elgar Ct W14 126 A1
Elgar Ho
Pimlico SW1 146 B1
South Hampstead NW6 11 B1
Elgar St SE16 41 A3
Elgin Ave
Hammersmith W12 39 A3
Westbourne Green W9 88 B4
Elgin Cl W12 39 A4
Elgin Cres W11 31 A2 112 B4
Elgin Ct W9 88 A2
Elgin Ho 8 E14 34 A3
Elgin Mans W9 88 A3
Elgin Mews W11 31 A3
Elgin Mews N W9 88 B4
Elgin Mews S W9 88 B4
Elgood Cl W11 31 A1 112 A1
Elgood Ho NW8 79 C1
Elham Ho 13 E5 17 A3
Elia Mews N1 86 A1
Elias Pl SW8 163 B3
Elia St N1 86 A1
Elim Est SE1 138 A2

Elim St SE1 . . . . . . **138** A2
Eliot Cotts SE3 . . . . . . 53 A1
Eliot Ct SW18 . . . . . . 59 A1
Eliot Gdns SW15 . . . . 56 C3
Eliot Hill SE13 . . . . . . 52 B1
Eliot Ho **10** TW10 . . 54 A1
Eliot Mews NW8 . . . . 78 C1
Eliot Pk SE13 . . . . 52 B1
Eliot Pl SE3 . . . . 53 A1
Eliot Vale SE3 . . . . . . 52 C1
Elizabeth Ave
  Islington N1 . . . . . . 15 C1
  Shoreditch N1 . . . . . 87 A4
Elizabeth Barnes Ct
  SW6 . . . . **166** B2
Elizabeth Blount Ct **4**
  E14 . . . . 33 A3
Elizabeth Cl
  Paddington W9 . . . . . **89** A1
  12 Poplar E14 . . . . . 34 A3
Elizabeth Cooper Pl
  SW12 . . . . 60 C1
Elizabeth Cotts **5**
  TW9 . . . . 44 C2
Elizabeth Ct
  Chelsea SW10 . . . . . **157** C3
  East Dulwich SE22 . . 64 C3
  Marylebone NW8 . . . 90 B2
  Westminster SW1 . . **133** C1
Elizabeth Finn Ho **1**
  W12 . . . . 38 C4
Elizabeth Garrett
Anderson Hospl
  NW1 . . . . **93** A1
Elizabeth Garrett
Anderson Language
  Coll N1 . . . . 85 A1
Elizabeth Gdns
  W3 . . . . 29 B1
Elizabeth Ho
  15 Hammersmith
  W6 . . . . 39 B1
  Lambeth SE11 . . . . **149** C3
Elizabeth Ind Est
  SE14 . . . . 50 C4
Elizabeth Kenny Ho
  N1 . . . . 15 B2
Elizabeth Mews
  28 Hackney E2 . . . . 24 C3
  Maitland Pk NW3 . . 12 B2
Elizabeth Selby Inf
  Sch E2 . . . . 24 C2 **99** C4
Elizabeth Sq **13**
  SE16 . . . . 33 A2
Elizabeth St SW1 . . **145** C4
Elkington Point
  SE11 . . . . **149** C3
Elkstone Rd W10 . . . 31 B4
Ellacombe Ho **1**
  SW2 . . . . 74 C4
Ellaline Rd W6 . . . . . 47 C4
Elland Ho **11** E14 . . 33 B3
Elland Rd SE15 . . . . . 65 B3
Ella Rd N4, N8 . . . . . 5 C4
Ellenborough Ho **5**
  W12 . . . . 30 A2
Ellenborough Pl
  SW15 . . . . 56 C3
Ellen St E1 . . . . **111** C1
Ellen Wilkinson Ho
  7 Globe Town E2 . . 25 C2
  West Brompton
  SW6 . . . . **155** A3
Ellerby St SW6 . . . . . 47 C2

Ellerdale Cl **16**
  NW3 . . . . 11 B4
Ellerdale Rd NW3 . . . 11 B3
Ellerdale St SE13 . . . 67 A4
Ellerker Gdns
  TW10 . . . . 54 A1
Ellerslie Gdns
  NW10 . . . . 21 C4
Ellerslie Ind Est
  SW2 . . . . 62 A2
Ellerslie Rd W12 . . . 30 A1
Ellerton St W3 . . . . . 37 A4
Ellerton Rd
  Barnes SW13 . . . . . 46 C1
  Wandsworth SW17,
  SW18 . . . . 71 C3
Ellery Cl **8** NW10 . . 21 B3
Ellery Ho SE17 . . . . **151** C3
Ellery St SE15 . . . . . 50 A1
Ellesmere Ct W4 . . . 45 C4
Ellesmere Rd
  Bow E3 . . . . 26 A3
  Chiswick W4 . . . . . 45 C4
  Willesden NW10 . . . 8 C3
Ellesmere St E14 . . . 34 A3
Ellingfort Rd E8 . . . . 17 A1
Ellingham Rd
  Leyton E15 . . . . . . 19 C4
  Shepherd's Bush
  W12 . . . . 38 C4
Ellington Ho SE1 . . **137** A1
Ellington St N7 . . . . 14 C2
Elliott Rd
  Acton W4 . . . . 38 A2
  Brixton SW9 . . . . . 48 A2
  Camberwell SW9 . . 48 A2
Elliott Sch SW15 . . . 57 B1
Elliott's Pl N1 . . . . . 86 B3
Elliott Sq NW3 . . . . 12 A1
Elliott's Row SE11 . . **150** B4
Ellis Cl NW10 . . . . . 9 B2
Ellisfield Dr SW15 . . 68 C4
Ellis Franklin Ct
  NW8 . . . . 78 C2
Ellistield Rd SE17 . . **151** B2
Ellison Ho **1** SE13 . . 52 B1
Ellison Rd SW13 . . . 46 B1
Ellis St SW1 . . . . . . **145** B4
Ellsworth St E2 . . . . 25 A2
Ellwood Ct W9 . . . . 88 B1
Elmar Rd E14 . . . . . **164** B2
Elm Bank Gdns
  SW13 . . . . 46 A1
Elm Bank Mans
  SW13 . . . . 46 A1
Elmbourne Rd
  SW17 . . . . 73 A1
Elmbridge Wlk E8 . . 16 C1
Elm Cl N19 . . . . 4 B2
Elmcourt Rd SE21;
  SE27 . . . . 75 A2
Elm Court Sch
  SE27 . . . . 75 B2
Elm Cres W5 . . . . . . 36 A4
Elmcroft N6 . . . . . . 4 B4
Elmcroft Ave NW11 . 1 B4
Elmcroft Cres
  NW11 . . . . 1 A4
Elmcroft St E5 . . . . 17 B4
Elm Ct
  Brixton SW9 . . . . . **173** B4
  Lewisham SE13 . . . 67 C4
  42 Notting Hill W2 . 31 C4
  Strand EC4 . . . . . . **121** B4
Elmer Ho NW1 . . . . **102** A4
Elmfield Ho
  6 Canonbury N5 . . 15 B3

Elmfield Ho continued
  Paddington W9 . . . . **23** C1
Elmfield Mans **5**
  SW17 . . . . 72 C2
Elmfield Rd SW17 . . 73 A2
Elmfield Way W9 . . . 31 C4
Elm Friars Wlk
  NW1 . . . . 13 C1
Elm Gn W3 . . . . 29 A3
Elm Gr
  Cricklewood NW2 . . 9 C4
  Peckham SE15 . . . . 49 C1
Elm Grove Rd
  Barnes SW13 . . . . . 46 C1
  Ealing W5 . . . . 36 A4
Elm Ho **14** E14 . . . . 42 B4
Elmhurst Mans
  SW4 . . . . 61 C4
Elmhurst St SW4 . . . 61 C4
Elmhurst Villas
  SE15 . . . . 65 B3
Elmington Rd SE5 . . 48 C3
Elmira St SE13 . . . . 67 A4
Elm Lo SW6 . . . . . . 47 C2
Elmore St N1 . . . . . 15 C1
Elm Park Gdns
  SW10 . . . . **143** B1
Elm Park Ho
  SW10 . . . . **143** B1
Elm Park La SW3 . . **143** B1
Elm Park Mans
  SW10 . . . . **157** A4
Elm Pk SW2 . . . . . . 74 B4
Elm Pk Rd SW3 . . . **157** B4
Elm Quay SW8 . . . . **161** B3
Elm Rd SW14 . . . . . 55 B3
Elms Cres SW4 . . . . 61 C1
Elms Mews W2 . . . **115** B4
Elms Rd SW4 . . . . . 61 B2
Elmslie Point **2**
  E3 . . . . 33 B4
Elms The
  Barnes SW13 . . . . . 56 B4
  3 Harlesden
  NW10 . . . . 21 A3
Elmstone Rd SW6 . . **165** C3
Elm Terr NW2 . . . . . 1 C1
Elmton Ct NW8 . . . . **89** B2
Elm Tree Cl NW8 . . . **89** B4
Elm Tree Ct
  6 Camberwell
  SE5 . . . . 48 B2
  St John's Wood
  NW8 . . . . **89** B4
Elm Tree Rd NW8 . . **89** B4
Elm Way NW10 . . . . 8 A4
Elm Wlk NW3 . . . . . 1 C2
Elmwood Ct
  SW11 . . . . **170** A4
Elm Wood Prim Sch
  SE27 . . . . 75 C1
Elmwood Rd
  Chiswick W4 . . . . . 45 B4
  Herne Hill SE24 . . . 63 C2
Elmworth Gr SE21 . . **75** C2
Elnathan Mews
  W9 . . . . **88** B1
Elphinstone St N5 . . 15 A4
Elrington Rd E8 . . . . 16 C2
Elsa St E1 . . . . 33 A4
Elsdale Ho **8** E9 . . . 17 B2
Elsdale St E9 . . . . . 17 B1

Elsden Mews E2 . . . 25 B3
Elsenham St SW18,
  SW19 . . . . 70 B2
Elsfield NW5 . . . . . . 13 A3
Elsham Rd W14 . . . **126** A3
Elsham Terr W14 . . **126** A3
Elsie Lane Ct W2 . . **100** A3
Elsiemaud Rd SE4 . . **66** B2
Elsie Rd SE22 . . . . . 64 B3
Elsinore Gdns NW2 . 1 A1
Elsinore Ho
  12 Camberwell
  SE5 . . . . 48 B1
  Islington N1 . . . . . **85** B3
Elsinore Way TW9 . . 55 A4
Elsley Rd SW11 . . . . 60 C4
Elsley Sch SW11 . . . 60 C4
Elspeth Rd SW11 . . . 60 B3
Elstead Ho **9**
  SW2 . . . . 74 B4
Elsted St SE17 . . . . **151** C3
Elstow Grange
  NW6 . . . . 9 C1
Elswick Rd SE13 . . . 52 A1
Elswick St SW6 . . . **166** C2
Elsworthy Rd NW3 . . 80 A4
Elsworthy Rise
  NW3 . . . . 12 A1
Elsworthy Terr
  NW3 . . . . 12 A1
Elsynge Rd SW18 . . 59 C2
Elsynge Road Mans
  SW18 . . . . 59 C2
Elthiron Rd SW6 . . **165** C3
Elthorne Rd N19 . . . 4 C2
Elthruda Rd SE13 . . 67 C1
Elton Ho **3** E3 . . . . 26 B4
Elton Pl N16 . . . . . . 16 A3
Elton St **2** N16 . . . 16 A3
Eltringham St
  SW18 . . . . 59 B3
Elvaston Mews
  SW7 . . . . **129** A2
Elvaston Pl SW7 . . . **129** A1
Elveden Ho **20**
  SW9 . . . . 63 A3
Elver Gdns
  E2 . . . . 24 C2 **99** C4
Elverson Rd SE8 . . . 52 A1
Elverson Rd Sta
  SE8 . . . . 52 A1
Elverton St SW1 . . **147** B4
Elvin Ho **2** E9 . . . . 17 B2
Elvis Rd NW2 . . . . . 9 B2
Elwin St E2 . . . 24 C2 **99** B4
Elwood Ho N5 . . . . . 6 A1
Elworth Ho SW8 . . **163** A1
Ely Cotts SW8 . . . . **162** C1
Ely Court Flats
  SW6 . . . .
Ely Ct Holborn EC1 . **107** C3
  3 Maida Vale NW6 . 23 C3
Ely Ho **22** SE15 . . . 49 C3
Ely Pl EC1 . . . . **107** C3
Elysium Gate
  SW6 . . . . **164** C2
Elysium Pl SW6 . . . **164** C1
Elysium St SW6 . . . **164** C1
Elystan Ct SW15 . . . 57 A2
Elystan Pl SW3 . . . **144** C2
Elystan St SW3 . . . **144** B3
Elystan Wlk N1 . . . . **85** B3
Emanuel Ave W3 . . . 28 B3
Emanuel Ct W3 . . . . 28 C3
Emanuel Sch
  SW11 . . . . 60 A2

Embankment
  SW15 . . . . 47 C1
Embankment Gdns
  SW3 . . . . **159** A4
Embankment Pier
  WC2 . . . . **120** B2
Embankment Pl
  WC2 . . . . **120** B2
Embankment Sta
  WC2 . . . . **120** B2
Embassy Ct NW8 . . **79** C1
Embassy Ho **2**
  NW6 . . . . 10 C1
Emba St SE16 . . . . **139** C3
Ember Ct **2** W12 . . 38 A3
Emberton SE5 . . . . . 49 A4
Emberton Ct EC1 . . **96** A3
Embleton Rd SE13 . . 67 A3
Emden St SW6 . . . . **166** B4
Emerald Rd NW10 . . 20 C4
Emerald St WC1 . . **106** C4
Emerson Ho N16 . . . 16 A3
Emerson St SE1 . . . **122** C2
Emery Hill St
  SW1 . . . . **133** A1
Emery St SE1 . . . . **135** C2
Emily St **7** E16 . . . 35 B3
Emirates Stad
  (Arsenal FC) N7 . . . 14 C4
Emlyn Gdns **3**
  W12 . . . . 38 A3
Emlyn Rd W12 . . . . 38 B3
Emmanuel CE Prim
  Sch NW6 . . . . 10 C3
Emmanuel Ho
  Dulwich SE21 . . . . . 75 C1
  Lambeth SE11 . . . . **149** B3
Emmanuel Rd
  SW12 . . . . 73 C3
Emma St E2 . . . . . . 25 A3
Emminster NW6 . . . 78 A4
Emmott Cl E1 . . . . . 26 A1
Emperor's Gate
  SW7 . . . . **142** C4
Empingham Ho **20**
  SE8 . . . . 40 C2
Empire Mews SW16 . **74** A1
Empire Ho SW3 . . . **130** A1
Empire Sq N19 . . . . 5 A1
Empire Wharf E3 . . . 26 A4
Empire Wharf Rd
  E14 . . . . 42 C2
Empress Mews **36**
  SE5 . . . . 48 B1
Empress Pl SW6 . . **141** B1
Empress St SE17 . . **48** B4
Empson St E3 . . . . 27 A1
Emsworth St SW2 . . 74 B2
Emu Rd SW8 . . . . . **170** A1
Enard Ho **25** E3 . . . 26 B3
Enbrook St W10 . . . 23 A2
Enclave Ct EC1 . . . . **96** B2
Endell St WC2 . . . . **106** A1
Enderby St SE10 . . . 43 A1
Endlesham Ct **2**
  SW12 . . . . 72 C4
Endlesham Rd
  SW12 . . . . 72 C4
Endsleigh Gdns
  WC1 . . . . **93** B2
Endsleigh Mans **4**
  SW16 . . . . 74 A1
Endsleigh Pl WC1 . . **93** C2
Endsleigh St WC1 . . **93** C2
Endwell Rd SE4 . . . 51 A1
Endymion Rd
  Harringay N4 . . . . . 6 A4
  Tulse Hill SW2 . . . . 62 B1

Energen Cl NW10 . . . . 8 A2
Enfield Cloisters
 N1 . . . . 24 A2 98 A4
Enfield Ho SW9 . . . . . 172 B2
Enfield Rd
De Beauvoir Town E8,
 N1 . . . . 24 A1
South Acton W3 . . . . 37 A4
Enford St W1 . . . . . . 102 C4
Engadine St SW18 . .70 C3
Engate St SE13 . . . . . . 67 B3
England's La NW3 . . 12 B2
Englefield NW1 . . . . . 92 C3
Englefield Rd N1 . .16 A1
Englewood Rd
 SW12 . . . . 61 B1
English Gardening
 Sch The SW3 . . . 158 C4
English Grounds
 SE1 . . . . 124 A1
English Martyrs RC
 Prim Sch E1 . . . . 111 A1
English St E3 . . . . .26 B1
Enid St SE16 . . . . . . 139 A2
Enid Stacy Ho 11
 N19 . . . . .4 C4
Enmore Ct SW14 . . .55 C2
Enmore Gdns
 SW14 . . . . .55 C2
Enmore Rd SW15 . .57 B2
Ennerdale Ho 3
 N4 . . . . .6 C4
Ennerdale Rd
 TW9 . . . . .44 B1
Ennersdale Rd
 SE13 . . . . .67 C2
Ennis Ho 16 E14 . . .34 A3
Ennismore Ave
 W4 . . . . .38 B2
Ennismore Gdns
 SW7 . . . . 130 A2
Ennismore Gdns
 Mews SW7 . . . . . 130 A2
Ennismore Mews
 SW7 . . . . 130 A2
Ennismore St
 SW7 . . . . 130 A2
Ennis Rd N4 . . . . .5 C3
Ensbury Ho SW8 . . 162 C2
Ensign Cl E1 . . . . . . 125 C3
Ensign Ho 6 E14 . .41 C4
Ensign St E1 . . . . . . 125 B4
Ensor Mews SW7 . 143 B2
Enterprise Ho 38
 E9 . . . . .17 B1
Enterprise Way
College Pk NW10 . . . .21 C2
Wandsworth SW18 . . .58 C3
Enterprise Way
 SE23 . . . . .41 B2
Epirus Mews
 SW6 . . . . 155 B2
Epirus Rd SW6 . . . 155 A2
Epping Cl E14 . . . . . .41 C2
Epping Ho 5 E5 . . . . .7 C2
Epping Pl N1 . . . . .14 C2
Epple Rd SW6 . . . . 165 A4
Epstein Ct N1 . . . . . .86 B3
Epworth St EC2 . . . .97 C1
Equity Sq
 E2 . . . . 24 B2 99 A3
Erasmus St SW1 . 147 C3
Erconwald St W12 . .29 B3
Eresby Ho SW7 . . . 130 B3
Eresby Pl NW6 . . . .10 C1
Erica Ct SW4 . . . . . 172 B3
Erica Ho SE4 . . . . . . .66 B4

Erica St W12 . . . . .29 C2
Ericcson Cl SW18 . .58 C2
Eric Fletcher Ct 15
 N1 . . . . .15 B1
Eric Rd NW10 . . . . .8 B2
Eric Macdonald Ho
 W6 . . . . 165 C3
Eric Rd NW10 . . . . . .67 C3
Ericson Ho
London SE13 . . . . .67 C3
Stamford Hill N16 . . . . .7 B3
Eric St E3 . . . . .26 B1
Eric Wilkins Ho
 SE1 . . . . 153 B1
Eridge Ho SE22 . . . .64 B4
Eridge Rd W4 . . . . . . .37 C3
Erin Ct NW2 . . . . .9 B2
Erlanger Rd SE14 . .50 C1
Ermine Rd SE13 . . . .67 A3
Ernest Bevin Coll
 SW17 . . . . .72 A2
Ernest Gdns W4 . . . .45 A4
Ernest Simmonds Ho
 SE14 . . . . .50 B1
Ernest St E1 . . . . .25 C1
Ernshaw Pl SW15 . .58 A2
Eros (Shaftesbury
 Meml)* W1 . . . . 119 B3
Erpingham Rd
 SW15 . . . . .57 B4
Errington Rd W9 . . .23 B1
Errol St EC1 . . . . .97 A1
Erskine Ho SW1 . . 146 C1
Erskine Rd NW3 . . . .12 B1
Escuan Lo N5 . . . . . . .15 B3
Esher Gdns SW19 . .69 C2
Esher Ho SW8 . . . . 171 C2
Eskdale NW1 . . . . . . .82 C1
Esk Ho E3 . . . . .26 B1
Esme Ho SW15 . . . . .56 B3
Esmeralda Rd
 SE1 . . . . 153 C3
Esmond Ct W8 . . . 128 B2
Esmond Gdns W4 . .37 C2
Esmond Rd
Acton W4 . . . . .37 C3
Kilburn NW6 . . . . .23 B4
Esmond St SW15 . .58 A3
Esparto St SW18 . . .71 A4
Espirit Ct E1 . . . . . . 110 C3
Espirit Ho 6
 SW15 . . . . .58 A2
Essendine Mans
 W9 . . . . .23 C2
Essendine Prim Sch
 W9 . . . . .23 C2
Essendine Rd W9 . .23 C2
Essex Ct
Barnes SW13 . . . . .46 B1
Hammersmith W6 . . . .39 B3
Holborn EC4 . . . . 107 B1
Essex Ho 2 E14 . . . .34 A3
Essex Pl W4 . . . . .37 B2
Essex Place Sq 5
 W4 . . . . .37 C2
Essex Rd Acton W3 . .28 B2
Chiswick W4 . . . . .37 C2
Islington N1 . . . . .86 B4
Willesden NW10 . . . . . .8 A1
Essex Road Sta
 N1 . . . . .15 B1
Essex St WC2 . . . . 121 B4
Essex Villas W8 . . 127 B3
Essian St E1 . . . . .33 A4
Essington SW15 . . . .58 A1
Estcourt Rd SW6 . 154 C2

Estella Ho 15 W11 . .30 C2
Estelle Rd NW3 . . . .12 B4
Esterbrooke St
 SW1 . . . . 147 B3
Este Rd SW11 . . . . 168 A1
Estoria Cl 22 SW2 . .74 C4
Etal Ho N1 . . . . .15 A1
Etchingham Rd
 E15 . . . . .19 B4
Eternit Wlk SW6 . . .47 C2
Ethelbert Ho E9 . . . .18 A4
Ethelbert St SW12 . .73 A3
Ethelburga St
 SW11 . . . . 168 B4
Ethelburga Twr
 SW11 . . . . 168 B4
Ethelden Rd W12 . . .30 A1
Ethel Rankin Ct
 SW6 . . . . 164 C2
Ethel St SE17 . . . . . 151 A3
Ethelworth Ct 4
 SW2 . . . . .74 C3
Etherow St SE22 . . .64 C1
Ethnard Rd SE15 . . .50 A4
Eton Ave NW3 . . . . . .12 A1
Eton Cl SW18 . . . . . .71 A4
Eton College Rd
 NW3 . . . . .12 B2
Eton Ct NW3 . . . . . . .11 C1
Eton Garages 11
 NW3 . . . . .12 A2
Eton Hall NW3 . . . . . .12 B2
Eton Ho
Hackney E9 . . . . .18 B2
Highbury N5 . . . . .15 A4
Eton Pl NW1 . . . . . . .12 C1
Eton Rd NW3 . . . . . . .12 B2
Eton Rise NW3 . . . . .12 B2
Eton St TW10 . . . . . .54 A2
Eton Villas NW3 . . . .12 B2
Etta St SE8 . . . . .51 A4
Ettrick St E14 . . . . . .34 B3
Eugene Cotter Ho
 SE17 . . . . 151 C3
Eugenia Rd SE16 . . .40 B2
Euro Cl NW10 . . . . . . .8 C2
Eurolink Bsns Ctr
 SW2 . . . . .62 C2
Europa Pl EC1 . . . . .96 C3
Eustace Bldg
 SW8 . . . . 160 A3
Eustace Ho SE11 . 148 C4
Eustace Rd SW6 . . 155 B2
Euston Rd NW1 . . . .93 A2
Euston Sq NW1 . . . .93 B3
Euston Square Sta
 WC1 . . . . .93 A2
Euston St NW1 . . . . .93 A3
Euston Sta NW1 . . .93 A3
Euston Underpass
 NW1 . . . . .92 C2
Evandale Rd SW9 . 173 C2
Evangelist Rd
 NW5 . . . . .13 A4
Evans Cl E8 . . . . .16 B2
Evans Ho
14 Shepherd's Bush
 W12 . . . . .30 A2
South Lambeth
 SW8 . . . . 161 C1
Evelina Mans 9
 SE5 . . . . .48 C3
Evelina Rd SE15 . . .50 B1
Eveline Lowe Prim
 Sch SE1 . . . . 153 C1
Evelyn Ct
Marylebone W1 . . . . . 102 C1

Evelyn Ct continued
Shacklewell E8 . . . . . .16 C4
Shoreditch N1 . . . . . . .87 B1
Evelyn Denington Ct
 2 N1 . . . . .15 A1
Evelyn Fox Ct
 W10 . . . . .30 B4
Evelyn Gdns
Richmond TW9 . . . . . .54 A3
South Kensington
 SW7 . . . . 143 B1
Evelyn Ho
Bedford Pk W12 . . . . .38 B4
3 Brixton SW2 . . . . . .62 B2
Spitalfields E1 . . . . . 111 B3
Evelyn Rd
Acton W4 . . . . .37 C3
Richmond TW9 . . . . . .54 A4
Evelyn St SE8 . . . . . .41 A1
Evelyn Terr TW9 . . . .54 A4
Evelyn Wlk N1 . . . . . .87 B1
Evelyn Yd W1 . . . . . 105 B2
Evenwood Cl
 SW15 . . . . .58 A2
Everard Ho E1 . . . . 111 C1
Everatt Cl SW18 . . . .58 B2
Everdon Rd SW13 . .46 C4
Everest Pl E14 . . . . .34 B4
Everett Ho
Islington N7 . . . . .14 C4
Walworth SE17 . . . . 151 B2
Evergreen Sq 8
 E8 . . . . .16 B1
Everilda St N1 . . . . . .85 A3
Evering Rd E5, N16 . .7 C1
Everington St W6 . . .47 C4
Everitt Rd NW10 . . . .20 C2
Everleigh St N4 . . . . .5 B3
Eversfield Rd TW9 . .44 B1
Evershed Ho E1 . . . 111 A2
Evershed Wlk W4 . . .37 C2
Eversholt St NW1 . . .93 B4
Evershot Rd N4 . . . . .5 B3
Eversleigh Rd
 SW11 . . . . 169 B1
Eversley Ho
 E2 . . . . 24 C2 99 B3
Everthorpe Rd
 SE15 . . . . .64 B4
Everton Bldgs
 NW1 . . . . .92 C3
Evesham Ct 2
 TW10 . . . . .54 B1
Evesham Ho
1 Bethnal Green
 E2 . . . . .25 B3
Pimlico SW1 . . . . . . 146 B2
St John's Wood
 NW8 . . . . .78 C3
Evesham St W11 . . .30 C2
Evesham Way
 SW11 . . . . .60 C4
Evesham Wlk
Brixton SW9 . . . . . . 173 B2
Camberwell SE5 . . . .48 C1
Ewald Rd SW6 . . . 164 C1
Ewart Pl 17 E3 . . . . .26 B3
Ewe Cl N7 . . . . .14 A2
Ewen Henderson Ct
 10 SE14 . . . . .51 A3
Ewen Ho N1 . . . . .84 C3
Ewer St SE1 . . . . . . 122 C1
Ewhurst 19 SW15 . .57 C1
Ewhurst Cl E1 . . . . . .32 B4
Ewhurst Rd SE4 . . . .66 B1

Exbury Ho
Hackney E9 . . . . .17 B2
4 London SW9 . . . . . .62 B3
Excel Ct WC2 . . . . . 119 C3
Excelsior Gdns
 SE13 . . . . .52 B1
Excelsior Ind Est
 SE16 . . . . .50 B4
Exchange Arc
 EC2 . . . . 110 B4
Exchange Ct WC2 . 120 B3
Exchange Mans 2
 NW11 . . . . .1 B4
Exchange Pl EC2 . 110 A4
Exeter Ct NW6 . . . . .23 C3
Exeter Ho
Paddington W2 . . . . . 100 C2
11 Peckham SE15 . . .49 C4
Putney SW15 . . . . . . .57 B1
12 Exeter Mans NW2 .10 A2
Exeter Mews
Fulham SW6 . . . . . . 155 B2
12 Hampstead
 NW6 . . . . .11 A2
Exeter Rd
Brondesbury NW2 . . . .10 A2
Newham E16 . . . . .35 C4
Exeter St WC2 . . . . 120 C4
Exeter Way 2
 SE14 . . . . .51 B3
Exford Ct SW11 . . . 167 C4
Exhibition Cl W12 . .30 B2
Exhibition Rd
 SW7 . . . . 129 C2
Exmoor Ho 25 E3 . .26 A3
Exmoor St W10 . . . .30 C4
Exmouth Ho
Clerkenwell EC1 . . . . . .95 C2
6 Millwall E14 . . . . . .42 A2
Exmouth Market
 EC1 . . . . .95 C2
Exmouth Mews
 NW1 . . . . .93 A3
Exmouth Pl E8 . . . . .17 A1
Exmouth St E1 . . . . .32 B3
Exonbury NW8 . . . . .78 B3
Exton St SE1 . . . . . 121 B1
Eynella Rd SE21 . . .76 B4
Eynham Rd W12 . . . .30 B3
Eynsford Ho
Borough The SE1 . . . 137 B4
7 Deptford SE15 . . . .50 B4
Walworth SE17 . . . . 152 A3
Eyot Gdns W6 . . . . . .38 B1
Eyot Gn W4 . . . . .38 B1
Eyre Ct NW8 . . . . . . .79 B2
Eyre St Hill EC1 . . . .95 B1
Eythorne Rd SW9 . 173 C4
Ezra St E2 . . . . 24 B2 99 A4

F

Fabian Rd SW6 . . . 155 A2
Fabyc Ho TW9 . . . . . .44 C3
Fairacres SW15 . . . .56 C3
Fairbairn Gn 1
 SW9 . . . . .48 A2
Fairbriar Residence
 SW7 . . . . 143 A4

Fairbridge Rd N19... 4 C2
Fairburn Ct SW15 ... 58 A2
Fairburn Ho
6 Stamford Hill
N16................... 7 A3
West Kensington
SW5 .... 141 A1
Fairby Ho SE1... 153 A4
Faircharm Trad Est
SE8................... 52 B3
Fairchild Cl SW11 167 C1
Fairchild Ho
13 Hackney E9..... 17 B1
Pimlico SW1.......
Shoreditch
N1..........24 A2 98 A4
Fairchild Pl
EC2...........24 A1 98 B1
Fairchild St
EC2...........24 A1 98 B1
Fairclough St E1 111 C1
Faircourt 14 NW3 .12 B2
Faircroft N16...... 6 C3
Fairdale Gdns
SW15................ 57 A3
Fairdene Ct N7....14 A3
Fairfax Ho
Brixton SW9...... 173 C1
6 Putney SW15 ...56 C2
Fairfax Mews
SW15................ 57 B3
Fairfax Pl
Kensington W14.. 126 B1
South Hampstead
NW6................. 11 B1
Fairfax Rd
Acton W4 .... 38 A3
South Hampstead
NW6................. 11 B1
Fairfield
Camden Town
NW1................ 82 C3
4 Stepney E1....32 B4
Fairfield Ct
Harlesden NW10 ..21 C4
1 London SW18 ...59 A2
Fairfield Dr SW18 59 A2
Fairfield Rd E3.....26 C3
Fairfield St SW18 ..59 A2
Fairfoot Rd E3......26 C1
Fairford Ho SE11. 149 C3
Fairhazel Gdns
NW6................. 11 B1
Fairheathe SW15...57 C1
Fairholme Rd
W14................ 140 B1
Fairholt Cl N16.....7 A3
Fairholt Ho N16....6 C3
Fairholt St SW7.. 130 B2
Fairhurst 4 NW6..11 B2
Fairlawn Ave W4 ..37 B2
Fairlawn Ct 5 W4 ..37 B2
Fairlawn Gr W4 ....37 B2
Fairlawn Mans
SE14................ 50 C2
Fairlawns SW15...57 C2
Fairlead Ho 6
E14.................. 41 C3
Fairley House Sch
SW1................ 147 C2
Fairlie Ct
22 Bromley E3 ....27 A2
1 Tufnell Pk N7...13 C4
Fairlight Ave
NW10................ 21 A3

Fairlight Ct 4
NW10................ 21 A3
Fairlop Pl NW8..... 89 C3
Fairmead Ho E9....18 A4
Fairmead Rd N7,
N19.................. 5 A1
Fairmont Ave E14 .34 C1
Fairmont Ho 1
E3.................... 26 C1
Fairmount Rd
SW2.................. 62 B1
Fair St SE1...... 138 C4
Fairstead Wlk N1 ..86 C4
Fairthorn Rd SE7,
SE10................. 43 C1
Fairview Ho 14
SW2.................. 74 B4
Fairview Pl SW2...74 B4
Fairwall Ho 6
SE5.................. 49 A2
Fairway Cl NW11...2 B4
Fairway Ct 13
SE16................. 40 C4
Fairway The 3
W3.................... 29 A3
Fairweather Ho
N7.................... 14 A4
Faith Ct NW2 ...... 9 A2
Faithfull Ho N5 ...15 B3
Fakruddin St
E1.............24 C1 99 C1
Falconberg Ct
W1................. 105 C2
Falconberg Mews
W1................. 105 C2
Falconbrook Prim Sch
SW11................ 59 C4
Falcon Cl
Chiswick W4......45 B4
Lambeth SE1.... 122 B2
Falcon Ct
14 Dulwich SE21...75 C2
Holborn EC4...... 107 B1
Islington N1....... 86 B1
Falcon Gr SW11....60 A4
Falcon Ho 11 SE15..49 B2
Falcon La SW11....60 A4
Falcon Lo
11 Paddington W9..31 C4
West Hampstead
NW3................. 11 A4
Falcon Pk Ind Est
NW10................. 8 A3
Falcon Point SE1. 122 B3
Falcon Rd SW11....60 A4
Falcon Terr SW11 ..60 A4
Falcon Way E14....42 A2
Falconwood Ct
SE3.................. 53 B1
Falkener Ct SW11 169 C3
Falkirk Ct 11 SE16 .32 C1
Falkirk Ho W9 .....88 B4
Falkirk St N1.......24 A3
Falkland Ho
Kensington W8.. 128 A1
West Kensington
W14................ 140 C2
Falkland Pl 2
NW5................. 13 B3
Falkland Rd NW5...13 B3
Falkner House Sch
SW7................ 143 A2
Fallodon Ho
London SW8 ..... 171 C2
Paddington W11 ...31 B4
Fallow Ct SE16 ... 153 C1
Fallowfield N4 ......5 B2

Falmouth Ho
Bayswater W2 ... 116 A4
Kennington SE11 149 C2
Falmouth Rd SE1 137 A1
Falstaff Ct SE11 .. 150 A3
Falstaff Ho 11 N1..24 A3
Fane St W14 ...... 155 A4
Fann St EC1....... 97 A1
Fanshaw St
N1.............24 A2 98 A4
Fanthorpe St
SW15................ 57 B4
Faraday Cl N7....14 B2
Faraday Ho
2 Balham SW12 ...73 A4
6 Gospel Oak
NW5................. 13 A4
Kensal Town W10...31 A4
Poplar E14 .... 33 B2
Faraday Lo SE10 ...43 B3
Faraday Rd
Acton W3 .... 28 B2
Kensal Town W10...31 A4
Fareham Ho 13
SW15................ 68 C3
Fareham St W1 .. 105 B2
Farjeon Ho NW6 ..11 C1
Farleigh Pl N16 ...16 B4
Farleigh Rd N16...16 B4
Farley Ct
Kensington W14.. 126 C2
Marylebone NW1 . 91 B1
Farlington Pl
SW15................ 69 A4
Farlow Rd SW15...57 C4
Farlton Rd SW18 ..71 A4
Farm Ave NW2 ....1 B1
Farm Cl SW6..... 155 C2
Farmdale Rd SE10 .43 C1
Farmer Ho 4
SE16................. 40 A3
Farmers Rd SE5...48 A3
Farmer St
W8.............31 C1 113 B2
Farm La SW6..... 155 C2
Farm Lane Trad Ctr
SW6.............. 155 C3
Farmleigh Ho
SW9.................. 63 A2
Farm Pl
W8.............31 C1 113 B2
Farm Rd NW10.....20 C4
Farm St W1...... 118 A3
Farnaby Ho 2
W10.................. 23 B2
Farnborough Ho 1
SW15................ 68 C3
Farncombe St
SE16................ 139 C3
Farndale Ho NW6 .78 A4
Farnell Mews
SW5............... 142 A2
Farnell Pl W3.....28 A2
Farnfield Ho 12
SW2.................. 62 B2
Farnham Ct 2 N16..7 A3
Farnham Ho
Borough SE1 .... 122 C1
Marylebone NW1 . 90 B1
Farnham Pl SE1 .. 122 B1
Farnham Royal
SE11............... 149 A1
Farnhurst Ho
SW11............... 169 B2
Farningham Ho 9
N4.................... 6 C4

Farnley Ho SW8 .. 171 B2
Farnsworth Ct
SE10................. 43 B3
Farnworth Ho 5
E14.................. 42 C2
Faroe Rd W14......39 C3
Farquhar Rd
SW19................ 70 C1
Farrance St E14 ...33 C3
Farrant Ho 18
SW11................ 59 C4
Farrell Ho E1......32 B3
Farrer Ho SE8......51 C3
Farriers Mews
SE15................. 65 B4
Farrier St NW1.....13 B1
Farrier Wlk SW10 156 C4
Farringdon La EC1 95 C1
Farringdon Rd
EC1................ 108 A2
Farringdon St
EC4................ 108 A2
Farringdon Sta
EC1................ 108 A2
Farrins Rents
SE16................. 33 A1
Farrow La SE14 ...50 B3
Farrow Pl SE16....41 A3
Farthingale Wlk
E15.................. 19 C1
Farthing Alley
SE1................ 139 B3
Farthing Fields 8
E1.................... 32 A1
Fashion & Design Mus
The★ SE1......... 138 A4
Fashion Retail Acad
The W1............ 105 B2
Fashion St E1..... 111 A3
Fassett Rd E8......16 C2
Fassett Sq E8......16 C2
Fauconberg Ct
W4.................. 45 B4
Fauconberg Rd
W4.................. 45 B4
Faulkner Ho SW15 .47 B1
Faulkner's Alley
EC1................ 108 A4
Faulkner St SE14 ..50 B2
Faunce Ho 1
SE17................ 150 A1
Faunce St SE17 .. 150 A1
Favart Rd SW6 ... 165 C4
Faversham Ho
Camden Town
NW1................ 83 A3
Walworth SE17... 152 A1
Fawcett Cl SW11. 167 C1
Fawcett Est E5.....7 C3
Fawcett Ho SW9 . 172 B2
Fawcett Rd NW10 ..8 B1
Fawcett St SW10 . 156 C4
Fawe Park Rd
SW15................ 58 B3
Fawe St E14 ....34 A4
Fawkham Ho SE1 153 A3
Fawley Ct SE27....75 A2
Fawley Lo 2 E14 ...42 C2
Fawley Rd NW6....11 A3
Fawnbrake Ave
SE24................. 63 B2
Fayetville Ho 26
N19.................. 4 C4
Faygate Rd SW2....74 B2
Fazerley Ct 10 W2 .31 C4
Fearnley Ho SE5 ...49 A1
Fearon St SE10.....43 C1

Feathers Pl SE10 ...52 C4
Featherstone St
EC1................. 97 B2
Featley Rd SW9 ...63 A4
Felbridge Ho 21
SE22................. 64 A4
Felday Rd SE13....67 A1
Felden St SW6 ... 164 C3
Feldman Cl N16 ...7 C3
Felgate Mews 4
W6.................. 39 A2
Felix St E2 25 A3
Felixstowe Rd
NW10................ 22 A2
Fellbrigg Rd SE22 .64 B2
Fellbrigg St E1.....25 A1
Fell Ho 11 N19 ....4 B1
Fellows Ct E2......24 B3
Fellows Rd NW3...12 A1
Felltram Way SE7 .43 C1
Felmersham Cl 2
SW4................. 61 C3
Felsberg Rd SW2...74 A4
Felsham Ho SW15 .57 C4
Felsham Mews
SW15................ 57 C4
Felsham Rd SW15 .57 C4
Felstead Gr E9 ...18 C2
Felstead Wharf
E14.................. 42 B1
Felton Ho N1 ...... 87 C3
Felton St N1 ...... 87 C3
Fenchurch Ave
EC3................ 110 A1
Fenchurch Bldgs
EC3................ 110 B1
Fenchurch Pl
EC3................ 124 B4
Fenchurch St
EC3................ 124 B4
Fenchurch Street Sta
EC3................ 124 B4
Fen Ct EC3....... 124 A4
Fendall St SE1 ... 138 B1
Fender Ct SW4... 172 A2
Fendt Cl 8 E16 ....35 B3
Fenelon Pl W14 .. 141 A3
Fenham Rd SE15...50 A3
Fenner Cl SE16.....40 A2
Fenner Ho 20 E1 ..32 A1
Fenner Sq 10
SW11................ 59 C4
Fenning St SE1 .. 138 A4
Fen St E9...........17 B3
Fen St E16.......35 C2
Fenstanton 3 N4...5 B3
Fenstanton Prim Sch
SW2.................. 74 C3
Fentiman Rd
SW8................ 162 C2
Fenton Cl
Dalston E8 ....16 B2
South Lambeth
SW9................ 172 C1
Fenton Ho SE14 ...51 A3
Fenton House ★
NW3.................. 2 B1
Fentons SE3 ...... 53 B3
Fenton St E1.......32 A3
Fenwick Gr SE15 . 64 C4
Fenwick Pl SW9...62 A4
Fenwick Rd SE15 . 64 C4
Ferdinand Ho 1
NW1................ 13 A1
Ferdinand Pl NW1 .12 C1

Ferdinand St NW1 . . 12 C1
Ferguson Dr W3 . . . . 28 C3
Ferguson Ho SE10 . . 52 B2
Ferguson's Cl E14 . . 41 C2
Fergus Rd N5 . . . . . . 15 A3
Fermain Ct E N1 . . . . 24 A4
Fermain Ct N N1 . . . . 24 A4
Fermain Ct W N1 . . . 24 A4
Fermoy Rd W9 . . . . . 23 B1
Fernbank Mews
SW12 . . . . 61 B1
Fern Cl 🔳 N1 . . . . . . 24 A3
Ferncliff Rd E8 . . . . . 16 C3
Ferncroft Ave
NW3 . . . . 10 C4
Fern Ct SE14 . . . . . . 50 C1
Ferndale Ct 🔳
SE3 . . . . 53 B3
Ferndale Ho N16 . . . . 6 C3
Ferndale Rd SW4,
SW9 . . . . 62 B3
Ferndene Rd SE24 . . 63 B3
Ferndown Lo 🔳
E14 . . . . 42 B3
Fernhead Rd W9 . . . 23 B2
Fernhill Ho E5 . . . . . . 7 C2
Fernholme Rd
SE15 . . . . 65 C2
Fernhurst Rd
SW6 . . . . 164 B4
Fernie Ho SE22 . . . 64 B4
Fernlea Rd SW12 . . . 73 A3
Fernleigh Cl W9 . . . . 23 B2
Fernsbury St WC1 . . 95 B3
Fernshaw Mans
SW10 . . . . 156 C3
Fernshaw Rd
SW10 . . . . 156 C3
Fernside NW11 . . . . . 1 C3
Fernside Rd SW12 . . 72 C4
Fern St E3 . . . . 26 C1
Ferntower Rd N5 . . . 15 C3
Fern Wlk SE16 . . . . 153 C1
Fernwood SW19 . . . . 70 B3
Ferrey Mews
SW9 . . . . 173 B1
Ferriby Cl N1 . . . . . . 14 C1
Ferrier Ind Est
SW18 . . . . 59 A3
Ferrier Point 🔳
E16 . . . . 35 C4
Ferrier St SW18 . . . . 59 A3
Ferrings SE21 . . . . . 76 A1
Ferris Rd SE22 . . . . 64 C3
Ferrybridge Ho
SE11 . . . . 135 A1
Ferry La
Barnes SW13 . . . . . 46 B4
Brentford TW8 . . . . 44 A4
Richmond TW9 . . . . 44 C3
Ferry Rd SW13 . . . . 46 C2
Ferry Sq 🔳 TW8 . . . 44 A4
Ferry St E14 . . . . . . 42 B1
Festing Rd SW15 . . . 57 C4
Festival Ct 🔳 E8 . . . 16 B1
Festival Pier SE1 . . 120 C2
Festival Pleasure
Gdns SW11 . . . . . 158 C1
Fetter La EC4 . . . . . 107 C2
Fettes Ho NW8 . . . . 79 C1
Ffinch St SE8 . . . . . . 51 C3
Field Ct
Hampstead NW3 . . . 11 B3
Holborn WC1 . . . . 107 A3
Lower Holloway N7 . 14 A3
Wimbledon SW19 . . . 70 C1

Fieldgate Mans
E1 . . . . 111 C3
Fieldgate St E1 . . . . 111 C3
Field Ho NW10 . . . . 22 C2
Fieldhouse Rd
SW12 . . . . 73 B3
Fielding Ho
Chiswick W4 . . . . . 46 A4
🔳 Kilburn NW6 . . . 23 C2
St John's Wood
NW8 . . . . 78 C4
Fielding Mews
SW13 . . . . 47 A4
Fielding Rd
Acton W4 . . . . 38 A3
Hammersmith W14 . 39 C3
Fielding St SE17 . . . 48 B4
Field Lo NW10 . . . . . 8 B2
Field Rd W6 . . . . . 154 A4
Fields Est E8 . . . . . . 16 C1
Field St WC1 . . . . . . 94 C4
Fieldsway Ho N5 . . . 14 C3
Fieldview SW17,
SW18 . . . . 71 C3
Fieldview Ct 🔳
N5 . . . . 15 A3
Fieldway Cres N5,
N7 . . . . 14 C3
Fieldwick Ho 🔳
E9 . . . . 17 C2
Fife Rd
Mortlake SW14 . . . 55 B2
Newham E16 . . . . . 35 C4
Fife Terr N1 . . . . . . 85 A2
Fifth Ave W10 . . . . . 23 A2
Fig Tree Cl NW10 . . 21 A4
Filey Ave N16 . . . . . . 7 C3
Filey Ho SW18 . . . . 59 B3
Filigree Ct SE16 . . . 33 B1
Filmer Ho NW6 . . . 164 B4
Filmer Mews
SW6 . . . . 164 B4
Filmer Rd SW6 . . . 154 C1
Filton Ct 🔳 SE14 . . 50 B3
Finborough Rd
SW10 . . . . 156 B4
Finchdean Ho
SW15 . . . . 68 B4
Finch Ho 🔳 SE8 . . . 52 A3
Finch La EC2, EC3 . 109 C1
Finchley Pl NW8 . . . 79 B2
Finchley Rd
Hampstead NW3 . . 11 B2
St John's Wood
NW8 . . . . 79 B2
Finchley Road &
Frognal Sta NW3 . 11 B3
Finchley Road Sta
NW3 . . . . 11 B2
Finch Lo 🔳 W9 . . . . 31 C4
Finch Mews 🔳
SE15 . . . . 49 B2
Finch's Ct 🔳 E14 . . . 34 A2
Findhorn St 🔳
E14 . . . . 34 B3
Findon Cl SW18 . . . 58 C1
Findon Rd W12 . . . . 38 C4
Fineran Ct 🔳
SW11 . . . . 59 C3
Fingal St SE10 . . . . 43 B1
Fingest Ho NW8 . . . 90 A2
Finland Rd SE4 . . . . 66 A4
Finland St SE16 . . . 41 A3
Finlay St SW6 . . . . . 47 C2
Finley Ct 🔳 SE5 . . . 48 B3
Finmere Ho 🔳 N4 . . 6 B4
Finnemore Ho N1 . . 86 C4

Finn Ho N1 . . . . 97 C4
Finnis St E2 . . . . 25 A1
FINSBURY 95 C4
Finsbury Ave 🔳 EC2 109 C3
Finsbury Cir EC2 . . 109 C3
Finsbury Coll N4 . . . . 5 C2
Finsbury Lo 🔳
EC2 . . . . 109 B4
Finsbury Market
EC2 . . . . 98 A1
Finsbury Mkt
EC2 . . . . . 24 A1 98 A1
FINSBURY PARK . . . 5 C2
Finsbury Park N4,
N5 . . . . 5 C2
Finsbury Park Sta
N4 . . . . 5 C2
Finsbury Pavement
EC2 . . . . 109 C4
Finsbury Sq EC2 . . 109 C4
Finsbury St EC2 . . . 109 B4
Finsen Rd SE5 . . . . 63 B4
Finstock Rd W10 . . . 30 C3
Finton House Sch
SW17 . . . . 72 B2
Finucane Ct TW9 . . . 54 B4
Finwhale Ho E14 . . . 42 A3
Fiona Ct 🔳 NW6 . . . 23 B3
Firbank Rd SE15 . . . 50 A1
Fircroft N1 . . . . 86 B4
Fircroft Prim Sch
SW17 . . . . 72 B1
Fircroft Rd SW17 . . 72 B1
Fire Brigade Pier
SE1 . . . . 148 B4
Firecrest Dr NW3 . . . 2 A1
Firle Ho W10 . . . . . . 30 B4
Fir Lo SW15 . . . . . . 57 A3
Firmston Ho 🔳
SW14 . . . . 55 C4
Firs Ave SW14 . . . . 55 B3
Firsby Rd N16 . . . . . . 7 C3
First Ave
East Acton W3 . . . . 29 B1
Mortlake SW14 . . . 56 A4
West Kilburn W10 . . 23 B1
Firth Gdns SW6 . . . 164 A3
Fir Tree Ho 🔳
SE14 . . . . 50 B3
Fir Trees Cl SE16 . . 33 A1
Fisher Ho
Islington N1 . . . . . 85 B3
🔳 Shadwell E1 . . . 32 B2
🔳 Tufnell Pk N19 . . 4 B1
Fishermans Dr
SE16 . . . . 40 C4
Fishers Cl SW16 . . . 73 C1
Fishers Ct SE14 . . . 50 C2
Fisher's La W4 . . . . 37 C2
Fisher St
Holborn WC1 . . . . 106 C3
Newham E16 . . . . . 35 C4
Fisherton St NW8 . . 89 C2
Fisherton Street Est
NW8 . . . . 89 C1
Fishlock Ct SW4 . . . 172 A2
Fish St Hill EC3 . . . 123 C3
Fitch Ct SW2 . . . . . 62 C2
Fitzalan St SE11 . . . 149 B4
Fitzclarence Ho
W11 . . . . 126 A4
Fitz-George Ave
W14 . . . . 140 A3
Fitzgerald Ave
SW14 . . . . 56 A4

Fitzgerald Ho
Brixton SW9 . . . . . 173 B1
🔳 Poplar E14 . . . . 34 A3
Fitzgerald Rd
SW14 . . . . 55 C4
Fitzhardinge Ho
W1 . . . . 103 B2
Fitzhardinge St
W1 . . . . 103 B2
Fitzherbert Ho 🔳
TW10 . . . . 54 B1
Fitzhugh Gr SW18 . . 59 C1
Fitzjames Ave
W14 . . . . 140 B3
Fitzjohn's Ave
NW3 . . . . 11 C3
Fitzjohns Mans
NW3 . . . . 11 B2
Fitzjohns Prim Sch
NW3 . . . . 11 C3
Fitzmaurice Ho 🔳
SE16 . . . . 40 A2
Fitzmaurice Pl
W1 . . . . 118 B2
Fitzneal St W12 . . . 29 B3
Fitzroy Cl N6 . . . . . . 3 B3
Fitzroy Cres W4 . . . 45 C3
Fitzroy Ct W1 . . . . . 93 A1
Fitzroy Ho
Bermondsey SE1 . . 153 A2
🔳 Tower Hamlets
E14 . . . . 33 B3
Fitzroy Mews W1 . . . 92 C1
Fitzroy Pk N6 . . . . . . 3 C3
Fitzroy Rd NW1 . . . 81 B4
Fitzroy Sq W1 . . . . . 92 C1
Fitzroy St W1 . . . . . 92 C1
Fitzroy Yd NW1 . . . 81 B4
Fitzwarren Gdns
N19 . . . . 4 B3
Fitzwilliam Ave
TW9 . . . . 44 B1
Fitzwilliam Mews
E16 . . . . 35 C1
Fitzwilliam Rd
SW4 . . . . 61 B4
Fives Ct SE11 . . . . 136 A1
Fiveways Rd SW9 . . 173 C1
Flamborough Ho 🔳
SE15 . . . . 49 C2
Flamborough St
E14 . . . . 33 A3
Flamingo Ct 🔳
SE8 . . . . 51 C3
Flamsteed Ct 🔳
SE13 . . . . 52 A2
Flamsteed Ho *
SE10 . . . . 52 C4
Flanchford Rd
W12 . . . . 38 B3
Flanders Ho N16 . . . 7 A1
Flanders Mans 🔳
W4 . . . . 38 B2
Flanders Rd W4 . . . 38 A2
Flanders Way E9 . . . 17 C2
Flank St E1 . . . . . . 125 B4
Flansham Ho 🔳
E14 . . . . 33 B3
Flask Cotts 🔳
NW3 . . . . 11 C4
Flask Wlk NW3 . . . . 11 C4
Flatiron Sq SE1 . . . 123 A1
Flatiron Yd SE1 . . . 123 A1
Flavell Mews SE10 . 43 A1
Flaxman Ct W1 . . . 105 B1

Flaxman Ho
🔟 Chiswick W4 . . . 38 A1
Newington SE1 . . . 136 B2
Flaxman Rd SE5 . . . 48 A1
Flaxman Terr WC1 . . 93 C3
Flecker Ho 🔳 SE5 . . 48 C3
Fleece Wlk N7 . . . . 14 A2
Fleet Ct 🔳 W12 . . . 38 A3
Fleetfield WC1 . . . . 94 B4
Fleet Ho
🔳 Brixton SW2 . . . 62 C2
🔳 Limehouse E14 . 33 A2
Fleet Pl EC4 . . . . . 108 A2
Fleet Prim Sch
NW3 . . . . 12 B3
Fleet Rd NW3 . . . . . 12 B3
Fleet Sq WC1 . . . . . 95 A3
Fleet St EC4 . . . . . 107 C1
Fleet Street Hill
E1 . . . . 24 C1 99 A1
Fleet Wood 🔳 N16 . . 7 B2
Fleetwood Rd
NW10 . . . . 8 C3
Fleetwood St N16 . . 7 A2
Fleming Cl 🔳 W9 . . 23 C1
Fleming Ct W2 . . . 101 B4
Fleming Ho
Bermondsey SE16 . 139 B3
Finsbury Pk N4 . . . 6 B3
🔳 Newington SE17 . 48 A4
Fletcher Bldgs 🔳
WC2 . . . . 106 B1
Fletcher Ct 🔳
NW5 . . . . 13 A4
Fletcher Ho 🔳
N16 . . . . 16 A4
Fletcher Path 🔳
SE8 . . . . 51 C3
Fletcher Rd W4 . . . . 37 B3
Fletcher St 🔳 E1 . . 125 C4
Fleur De Lis St
E1 . . . . 24 B1 98 C1
Fleur Gates 🔳
SW19 . . . . 69 C4
Flinders Ho 🔳 E1 . . 32 A1
Flinton St SE17 . . . 152 B2
Flint St SE17 . . . . . 151 C3
Flitcroft St WC2 . . . 105 C1
Flitton Ho 🔳 N1 . . . 15 A1
Flock Mill Pl
SW18 . . . . 71 A3
Flodden Rd SE5 . . . 48 B2
Flood St SW3 . . . . 158 B4
Flood Wlk SW3 . . . 158 B4
Flora Cl E14 . . . . . . 34 A3
Flora Gardens Prim
Sch W6 . . . . 39 A2
Flora Gdns 🔳 W6 . . 39 A2
Floral St WC2 . . . . 120 A4
Florence Ct W9 . . . . 89 A3
Florence Gdns
W4 . . . . 45 B4
Florence Ho
🔟 Bermondsey
SE16 . . . . 40 A1
🔳 Brixton SW2 . . . 62 B2
🔳 Shepherd's Bush
W11 . . . . 30 C2
🔳 Wandsworth
SW18 . . . . 59 C3
Florence Mans
SW6 . . . . 164 C4
Florence Nightingale
Ho 🔳 N1 . . . . 15 B2

Florence Nightingale
Mus ★ SE1 . . . . . **135** A3

Florence Rd
Acton W4 . . . .**37** C3
Finsbury Pk N4. . . . . .**5** C4
New Cross Gate
SE14. . . . .**51** B2

Florence St N1 . . . . .**15** A1

Florence Terr
Kingston u T SW15. . .**68** A1
New Cross Gate
SE14. . . . .**51** B2

Florence Way
SW12 . . . .**72** B3

Flores Ho 15 E1 . . . . .**32** C4

Florfield Rd E8 . . . . .**17** A2

Florian SE5 . . . .**49** A2

Florian Rd SW15 . . . .**58** A3

Florida St
E2 . . . .**24** C2 **99** C3

Florida State Univ
WC1 . . . .**105** C3

Florin Ct SE1 . . . . . .**138** C3

Floris Pl 7 SW4. . . . .**61** B4

Florys Ct SW19 . . .**70** A3

Floss St SW15 . . . . . .**47** B1

Flower & Dean Wlk
E1 . . . .**111** A3

Flowersmead
SW17 . . . .**72** C2

Flowers Mews
N19 . . . .**4** B2

Flower Wlk The
SW7 . . . .**129** A4

Floyer Cl TW10 . . . .**54** B2

Flynn Ct 13 E14 . . .**33** C2

Foley Ho 19 E1 . . . .**32** B3

Foley St W1 . . . . . .**104** C3

Folgate St E1 . . . . .**110** C4

Foliot Ho N1 . . . .**84** C2

Foliot St W12 . . . . . .**29** B3

Follett Ho SW10 . . .**157** B2

Follett St E14 . . . . . .**34** B3

Folly Wall E14 . . . . .**42** B4

Fonda Ct 14 E14 . . . .**33** C2

Fontarabia Rd
SW11 . . . .**60** C3

Fontenelle SE5 . . . . .**49** A2

Fontenoy Ho
SE11 . . . .**150** A3

Fontenoy Rd SW12,
SW17 . . . .**73** B2

Fonthill Ho
Kensington W14 . . . .**126** B2
Pimlico SW1 . . . . . .**146** B2

Fonthill Mews N4 . . .**5** B2

Fonthill Rd N4 . . . . . .**5** C2

Fontley Way
SW15 . . . .**68** C4

Footpath The
SW15 . . . .**56** C2

Forber Ho 2 E2 . . .**25** B2

Forbes Ho 2 W4. . .**36** C1

Forbes St E1 . . . . . .**111** C1

Forburg Rd N16. . . . .**7** C3

Ford Cl 12 E3 . . . . .**26** A3

Fordcombe 13
NW5 . . . .**12** C2

Fordham Ho 11
SE14. . . . .**51** A3

Fordham St E1 . . . .**111** C2

Fordingley Rd W9 . .**23** B2

Ford Rd E3. . . . .**26** B3

Fords Park Rd
E16. . . . .**35** C3

Ford Sq E1. . . . .**32** A4

Ford St Bow E3 . . . . .**26** A3
Canning Town E16 . .**35** B3

Fordwych Ct NW2 . .**10** A2

Fordwych Rd
NW2 . . . .**10** A3

Fordyce Rd SE13 . . .**67** B2

Forecastle Ct E14 . .**41** C4

Foreign,
Commonwealth &
Home Offices
SW1 . . . .**134** A4

Foreland Ho
W11 . . . .**31** A2 **112** A4

Foreshore SE8 . . . . .**41** B2

Fore St EC2 . . . .**109** A3

Forest Cl NW6 . . . . .**10** A1

Forester Rd SE15. . . .**65** A4

Forest Gr E8 . . . .**16** B2

Forest Hill Rd
SE22. . . . .**65** A1

Forest Rd
Dalston E8 . . . .**16** B2
Richmond TW9 . . . . .**44** C3

Fore Street Ave
EC2 . . . .**109** B3

Forest Way 19 N19 . .**4** B2

Forfar Rd SW11. . . .**169** C4

Forge Pl NW1 . . . . . .**12** C2

Forman Ho SE4 . . . . .**65** C3

Forman Pl N16 . . . . .**16** B4

Formby Ct 2 N7 . . . .**14** C3

Formosa Ho E1 . . . . .**26** A1

Formosa St W9 . . . . .**88** B1

Formunt Cl E16 . . . . .**35** B4

Forrest Ct N7 . . . . . .**14** C2

Forrest Ho SW15 . . .**47** B1

Forset St W1 . . . . . .**102** B2

Forset St W1 . . . . . .**102** B2

Forster Rd SW2 . . . . .**74** A4

Forston St N1 . . . . . .**87** A2

Forsyth Gdns
SE17 . . . .**48** A4

Forsyth Ho
14 Hackney E9. . . . .**17** B1
Pimlico SW1 . . . . . .**147** A3

Forsythia Ho SE4 . . .**66** A4

Fortescue Ave 1
E8 . . . .**17** A1

Fortess Gr NW5 . . . .**13** B3

Fortess Rd NW5 . . . .**13** B4

Fortess Wlk NW5 . . .**13** A3

Forthbridge Rd
SW11 . . . .**60** C3

Forth Ho 50 E3 . . . . .**26** B3

Forties The 9
NW5 . . . .**13** B3

Fortior Ct N6. . . . .**4** B4

Fortnam Rd N19 . . . .**4** C2

Fort Rd SE1 . . . .**153** A3

Fortrose Cl E14 . . . .**34** C3

Fortrose Gdns SW2,
SW12 . . . .**74** A3

Fort St E1 . . . .**110** B3

Fortuna Cl N7 . . . . . .**14** B2

Fortune Ct 6 E8 . . . .**16** B1

Fortune Gate Rd
NW10 . . . .**21** A4

Fortune Green Rd
NW6 . . . .**10** C4

Fortune Ho
Lambeth SE11 . . . . .**149** B3
St Luke's EC1 . . . . . .**97** A1

Fortune St EC1 . . . . .**97** A1

Fortune Way
NW10 . . . .**21** C2

Forty Acre La E16 . . .**35** C4

Forum Cl 7 E3 . . . . .**26** C4

Forward Bsns Ctr The
3 E16 . . . .**27** C1

Fosbrooke Ho
SW8 . . . .**162** A1

Fosbury Ho 7
W2 . . . .**114** B3

Foscote Mews W9 .**31** C4

Foskett Rd SW6 . . .**165** A1

Fossil Rd SE13 . . . . .**66** C4

Foster Ct
8 Camden Town
NW1 . . . .**13** B1
Canning Town E16 . .**35** B2

Foster Ho SE14. . . . .**51** B2

Foster La EC2 . . . . .**108** C2

Foster Rd
Acton W3 . . . .**29** A2
Chiswick W4. . . . . . .**37** C1

Foubert's Pl W1 . . .**104** C1

Foulden Rd N16 . . . .**16** B4

Foulden Terr N16. . .**16** B4

Foulis Terr SW7 . . .**143** C2

Foundary Ho 6
E14. . . . .**34** A4

Founders Ct EC2 . . .**109** B2

Founders Ho
SW1 . . . .**147** B2

Foundling Ct WC1. . .**94** A2

Foundling Mus The ★
WC1 . . . .**94** B2

Foundry Cl SE16. . . .**33** A1

Foundry Mews
NW1 . . . .**93** A2

Foundry Pl
Stepney E1 . . . .**32** B4
Wandsworth SW18 . .**71** A4

Fountain Ct
11 Shepherd's Bush
W11 . . . .**39** C4
Strand EC4 . . . .**121** B4

Fountain Green Sq
SE16 . . . .**139** C3

Fountain Ho
Bermondsey SE16 . .**139** C3
3 Brondesbury Pk
NW6 . . . .**10** A1
Mayfair W1. . . . . . .**117** B2

Fountain Mews
5 Highbury N5 . . . . .**15** B4
Maitland Pk NW3 . . .**12** B2

Fountain Pl SW9 . .**173** C3

Fountayne Rd N16 . .**7** C2

Fount St SW8 . . . . .**161** C1

Fournier St E1 . . . .**111** A4

Fourscore Mans
E8. . . . .**16** C1

Four Seasons Cl
E3 . . . .**26** C3

Fourth Ave W10. . . .**23** A2

Fovant Ct SW8 . . . .**170** C1

Fowey Cl E1 . . . . . .**125** C1

Fowey Ho SE11 . . .**149** C2

Fowler Cl SW11 . . . .**59** C4

Fowler Ho
5 Camberwell
SE5. . . . .**49** A1
Islington N1 . . . .**86** B4
South Lambeth
SW8 . . . .**171** C3

Fowler Rd N1 . . . . . .**86** B4

Fownes St SW11 . . .**60** A4

Fox and Knot St
EC1 . . . .**108** B4

Foxberry Ct SE4 . . . .**66** B3

Foxberry Rd SE4 . . .**66** A4

Foxborough Gdns
SE4 . . . .**66** C2

Foxbourne Rd
SW17 . . . .**72** C2

Fox Cl
Bethnal Green E1 . . .**25** B1
Newham E16 . . . . . .**35** C4

Foxcombe Rd 6
SW15 . . . .**68** C3

Foxcote SE5 . . . . . .**152** B1

Foxcroft N1. . . . .**85** A1

Foxfield NW1. . . . . .**82** B3

Foxglove St W12 . . .**29** B2

Foxham Rd N19 . . . . .**4** C1

Fox Ho 2 SW11 . . . .**59** C3

Foxley Cl E8 . . . .**16** C3

Foxley Ho 4 E3 . . . .**27** A2

Foxley Rd SW9 . . . .**48** A3

Foxley Sq 3 SW9 . .**48** A2

Foxmore St SW11 . .**168** C3

Fox Prim Sch
W8 . . . .**31** C1 **113** B1

Fox Rd E16. . . . .**35** B4

Fox's Yd E2 . .**24** B1 **99** A2

Foxwell Mews
SE4 . . . .**66** A4

Foxwell St SE4 . . . . .**66** A4

Foyle Rd SE3 . . . . . .**53** B4

Fradel Lo N16 . . . .**6** C4

Framfield Rd N5 . . . .**15** A3

Frampton NW1. . . . .**13** C1

Frampton Ct 3
W3 . . . .**37** B4

Frampton Ho NW8 .**89** C1

Frampton Park Rd
E9 . . . .**17** B1

Frampton St NW8 . .**89** C1

Francemary Rd
SE4 . . . .**66** C2

Franche Court Rd
SW17 . . . .**71** B1

Francis Chichester
Way SW11 . . . .**169** C4

Francis Cl 6 E14. . . .**42** C2

Francis Ct 12 SE14 .**50** C4

Francis Ho
Harlesden NW10 . . . .**21** B4
11 Shoreditch N1 . . .**24** A4
Walham Green
SW10 . . . .**156** B2

Francis Holland Sch
Belgravia SW1 . . . .**145** C3
Marylebone NW1 . . .**90** C2

Francis Snary Lo 11
SW18 . . . .**58** C2

Francis St E1 . . . . . .**147** A4

Francis Terr N19 . . . .**4** B1

Francis Terrace Mews
13 N19 . . . .**4** B1

Francis Wlk N1 . . . . .**84** C4

Franconia Rd
SW4 . . . .**61** C2

Frank Barnes Sch
NW3 . . . .**11** C1

Frank Beswick Ho
SW6 . . . .**155** A3

Frank Dixon Cl
SE21 . . . .**76** A3

Frank Dixon Way
SE21 . . . .**76** A3

Frankfurt Rd SE24. .**63** B2

Frankham Ho 8
SE8 . . . .**51** C3

Frankham St SE8. . .**51** C3

Frank Ho SW8. . . . .**162** A2

Frankland Cl SE16. .**40** A2

Frankland Ho 4
SW12 . . . .**73** A4

Frankland Rd
SW7 . . . .**129** B1

Franklin Bldg 5
E14 . . . .**41** C4

Franklin Cl
Greenwich SE13 . . . .**52** A2
West Norwood
SE27 . . . .**75** A1

Franklin Ho
New Cross SE4. . . . .**51** A1
26 Wapping E1. . . . .**32** A1

Franklin Pl SE13. . . .**52** A2

Franklin Sq SW5 . .**141** A1

Franklin's Row
SW3 . . . .**145** A2

Franklyn Rd NW10. . .**8** B2

Frank Soskice Ho
SW6 . . . .**155** A3

Frank Whymark Ho 4
SE16 . . . .**40** B4

Frans Hals Ct E14 . .**42** C3

Fraserburgh Ho 29
E3 . . . .**26** B3

Fraser Ct SW11. . . .**168** A4

Fraser Ho
Brentford TW8 . . . . .**36** B1
Clapham SW8. . . . .**171** B1

Fraser Regnart Ct 12
NW5 . . . .**12** B3

Fraser St W4. . . . . . .**38** A1

Frazier St SE1 . . . .**135** B3

Frean St SE16 . . . .**139** B2

Frearson Ho 41 WC1 .**95** A4

Freda Corbett Cl 10
SE15 . . . .**49** C3

Frederica St 4
N7. . . . .**14** B1

Frederick Blg 1 . . .**16** A2

Frederick Charrington
Ho 4 E1. . . . .**25** B1

Frederick Cl W2 . .**116** C4

Frederick Cres
SW9 . . . .**48** A3

Frederick Ct SW6 . .**58** A4

Frederick's Pl
EC2 . . . .**109** B1

Frederick Sq 11
SE16 . . . .**33** A2

Frederick's Row
EC1 . . . .**96** A4

Frederick St WC1 . . .**94** C3

Frederick Terr E8 . . .**16** B1

Frederic Mews
SW1 . . . .**131** B3

Freedom St
SW11 . . . .**169** A2

Freegrove Rd N7. . . .**14** A3

Freeling Ho NW8 . . .**79** B4

Freeling St 2 N1 . . .**14** B1

Freeman Ho 13
SW2 . . . .**74** A4

Freemantle St
SE17 . . . .**152** A2

Freemens Hos 1
SW9 . . . .**62** B3

Freke Rd SW11. . . . .**60** C4

Fremantle Ho 14
E1. . . . .**25** A1

Fremont St E9 . . . . .**25** B4

French Pl
E1. . . . .**24** A1 **98** B2

Frendsbury Rd
SE4 . . . . 66 A3
Frensham Ct N5 . . . 15 B3
Frensham Dr
SW15 . . . . 68 C2
Frensham St SE15 . . 49 C4
Frere St SW11 . . . . . 168 B2
Freshfield Ave E8 . 16 B1
Freshfield Cl SE13 . .67 C3
Freshford St
SW18 . . . . 71 B1
Freston Rd W10,
W11 . . . . 30 C2
Freswick Ho 6 . . . .41 A2
Freud Mus The *
NW3 . . . . 11 B2
Frewell Bldg EC1 . .108 B3
Frewin Rd SW18 . . . .71 C3
Friar Mews SE27 . . . 75 A1
Friars Ave SW15 . . . 68 B1
Friars Cl SE1 . . . . . 122 B1
Friars Gdns W3 . . . .28 C3
Friars Mead E14 . . .42 B3
Friars Place La
W3 . . . . .28 C2
Friars Prim Sch
SE1 . . . . 136 B3
Friars Stile Pl 9
TW10 . . . . 54 A1
Friars Stile Rd
TW10 . . . . 54 A1
Friar St EC4 . . . . . . 108 B1
Friars Way W3 . . . . .28 C3
Friary Park Ct 12
W3 . . . . .28 B3
Friary Rd
Acton W3 . . . . .28 C3
Peckham SE15 . . . . .49 C3
Friday Grove Mews 11
SW12 . . . . .73 B4
Friday St EC4 . . . . . 122 C4
Frideswide Pl
NW5 . . . . 13 B3
Friendly Pl 16
SE13 . . . . 52 A2
Friendly St SE8 . . . .51 C2
Friendly Street Mews
SE8 . . . . .51 C1
Friendship Way
E15 . . . . .27 B4
Friend St EC1 . . . . . .96 A4
Friern Rd SE22 . . . . 64 C1
Frigate Ho 7 E14 . . .42 B2
Frigate Mews SE8 . .51 C4
Frimley Cl SW19 . . . 70 A2
Frimley Way E1 . . . .25 C1
Frinstead Ho 1
W10 . . . . 30 C2
Friston St SW6 . . . 166 A1
Frith Ho
Bethnal Green
E2 . . . . .24 C2 99 B3
Paddington NW8 . . .89 C1
Frith Rd E11 . . . . . . .19 C4
Frith St W1 . . . . 105 B1
Frithville Ct 2
W12 . . . . 30 B1
Frithville Gdns
W12 . . . . 30 B1
Frobisher Ct
6 Greenwich
SE10 . . . . 52 C4
5 Shepherd's Bush
W12 . . . . 39 B4
Frobisher Ho 27
E1 . . . . .32 A1

Frobisher Pas E14 . .33 C1
Frobisher Pl SE14 . .50 B2
Frobisher St SE10 . .53 A4
Frogley Rd SE22 . . . 64 B3
Frogmore SW18 . . . .58 C2
Frogmore Est
NW10 . . . . .20 B2
Frogmore Ind Est
N5 . . . . .15 C3
Frognal NW3 . . . . . . 11 B3
Frognal Cl NW3 . . . . 11 B3
Frognal Ct NW3 . . . . 11 B2
Frognal Gdns
NW3 . . . . 11 B3
Frognal La NW3 . . . . 11 A3
Frognal Par NW3 . . . 11 B2
Frognal Rise NW3 . . 11 B4
Frognal Way NW3 . . 11 B4
Frome Ho SE15 . . . . 65 B3
Frome St N1 . . . . . . .86 C2
Fromow's Cnr 14
W4 . . . . .37 B1
Frontenac NW10 . . . .9 A1
Frostic Wlk E1 . . . . 111 A3
Froude St SW8 . . . . 170 B1
Frye Ct 5 E3 . . . . . . 26 B2
Frying Pan Alley
E1 . . . . 110 C3
Fry Rd NW10 . . . . . . 21 B4
Fulbourne St 11
E1 . . . . .32 A4
Fulbrook Rd N19 . . . 13 B4
Fulcher Ct 13 SE8 . .51 B4
Fulcher Ho
13 Deptford SE8 . . . 41 B1
10 Shoreditch N1 . . . 24 A4
Fulcher Rd
N19 . . . . .5 A1
Fulford Mans 3
N19 . . . . .5 A1
Fulford St SE16 . . . . 40 A4
FULHAM 47 C2
Fulham Broadway
SW6 . . . . 155 C1
Fulham Broadway Sh
Ctr SW6 . . . . 155 C1
Fulham Broadway Sta
SW6 . . . . 155 C2
Fulham Bsns
Exchange SW6 . . . 167 A3
Fulham Cross Sec Sch
SW6 . . . . 154 A1
Fulham Ct SW6 . . . 165 B4
Fulham High St
SW6 . . . . 164 B1
Fulham Pal *
SW6 . . . . 164 A1
Fulham Palace Rd
SW6, W6 . . . . .47 C4
Fulham Park Gdns
SW6 . . . . 164 C2
Fulham Park Rd
SW6 . . . . 164 C2
Fulham Prep Sch
Fulham W6 . . . . . . 164 B1
Fulham W14 . . . . . 154 B4
Fulham Prim Sch
SW6 . . . . 155 B3
Fulham Rd
Chelsea SW10 . . . . 157 A4
Fulham SW6 . . . . . 165 A4
Fuller Cl E2 . . 24 C1 99 B2
Fuller's Ho 8
SW18 . . . . 58 C2
Fullerton Rd
SW18 . . . . 59 B2
Fullwood's Mews
N1 . . . . .97 C4
Fulmar Ct 6 SE21 . .75 C2

Fulmar Ho
12 Bermondsey
SE16 . . . . .40 C2
Marylebone NW8 . . .90 B1
Fulmead St SW6 . . .166 B3
Fulneck 1 E1 . . . . . 32 B4
Fulthorp Rd SE3 . . . 53 C1
Fulton Mews W2 . . 114 C4
Fulwood Pl WC1 . . 107 A3
Fulwood Wlk
SW19 . . . . 70 A3
Furber St W6 . . . . . .39 A3
Furley Ho 4 SE15 . .49 C3
Furley Rd SE15 . . . . 49 C3
Furlong Rd N7 . . . . . 14 C2
Furmage St SW18 . .71 A4
Furness Ho SW1 . . . 146 A2
Furness Lo 4
SW14 . . . . 55 A3
Furness Prim Sch The
NW10 . . . . 21 A4
Furness Rd
Harlesden NW10 . . .21 C3
Sands End SW6 . . . 166 B2
Furnival St EC4 . . . 107 B2
Furrow La E9 . . . . . . 17 B3
Fursecroft W1 . . . . 102 C2
Furze St E3 . . . . 33 C4
Fusion Ct SW15 . . . .68 A1
Futters Ct 1
NW10 . . . . 21 A3
Fyfield N4 . . . . .5 C2
Fyfield Rd 6 SW9 . .62 C4
Fynes St SW1 . . . . . 147 B4

G

Gable Ho 12 W4 . . . .38 A2
Gables Cl SE5 . . . . . 49 A2
Gables The
1 Clapham SW4 . . .61 B4
Hampstead NW3 . . . .2 C2
Gabriel Ho SE11 . . 148 C4
Gabrielle Ct NW3 . . .11 C2
Gabriel Mews NW2 . .1 B2
Gabriel's Wharf
SE1 . . . . 121 B2
Gaddesden Ho
EC1 . . . . .97 C3
Gadsden Ho
6 Homerton E9 . . . .17 C2
8 Kensal Town
W10 . . . . .23 A1
Gagarin Ho SW11 . .59 C4
Gage Rd E16 . . . . . . 35 A4
Gage St WC1 . . . . . 106 B4
Gainford Ho 5 E2 . . 25 A2
Gainford St N1 . . . . .85 B4
Gainsborough Ct
6 Bermondsey
SE16 . . . . .40 A1
8 Dulwich SE21 . . .76 A2
Shepherd's Bush
W12 . . . . .39 B4
Gainsborough Gdns
Golders Green
NW11 . . . . .1 B4
Hampstead NW3 . . . .2 C1
Gainsborough Ho
Finsbury Pk N4 . . . . .5 B3
1 Stepney E1 . . . . . 32 C4
8 Limehouse E14 . . 33 A2
Westminster SW1 . .147 C3
Gainsborough Prim
Sch E9 . . . . .18 C2

Gainsborough Rd
Bedford Pk W4 . . . . .38 B2
Richmond TW9 . . . . 54 B4
Gainsborough St 5
E9 . . . . 18 B2
Gainsborough Studios
N1 . . . . 87 B3
Gainsford St SE1 . . 139 A4
Gairloch Ho 2
NW1 . . . . 13 C1
Gairloch Rd SE5 . . . 49 A1
Gaisford St NW5 . . . 13 B2
Gaitskell Ct SW11 . 168 A2
Gaitskell Ho SE17 . .48 C4
Gaitskell Way
SE1 . . . . 136 C4
Galata Rd SW13 . . . 46 C3
Galatea Sq SE15 . . . 65 A4
Galaxy Bldg 6
E14 . . . . 41 C2
Galaxy Ho EC2 . . . . .97 C2
Galbraith St E14 . . . 42 B3
Gale Ho 10 SW2 . . .62 B2
Galena Ho 6 W6 . . .39 A2
Galena Rd W6 . . . . . 39 A2
Galen Pl WC1 . . . . . 106 B3
Galesbury Rd
SW18 . . . . 59 B1
Gales Gdns E2 . . . . .25 A2
Gale St E3 . . . . 33 C4
Galgate Cl 4
SW19 . . . . 70 A3
Galleon Cl SE16 . . . .40 C4
Galleon Ho 8 E14 . . 42 B2
Gallery Ct SW10 . . . 156 C3
Gallery Rd SE21 . . . 75 C3
Galleywall Rd
SE16 . . . . .40 A2
Galleywall Road Trad
Est 3 SE16 . . . . . . .40 A1
Galleywood Ho 1
W10 . . . . 30 B4
Gallia Rd N5 . . . . 15 A3
Galloway Rd W12 . . 29 C1
Galsworthy Ave
E14 . . . . 33 A4
Galsworthy Ct W3 . .37 A3
Galsworthy Ho 4
W11 . . . . 31 A3
Galsworthy Rd
NW2 . . . . .10 A4
Galton St W10 . . . . . 23 A2
Galveston Ho 2
E1 . . . . 26 A1
Galveston Rd
SW15 . . . . 58 B2
Galway Cl 22 SE16 . .40 A1
Galway Ho
Finsbury EC1 . . . . . .97 A3
1 Stepney E1 . . . . . 32 C4
Galway St EC1 . . . . .97 A3
Gambetta St SW8 . 170 B1
Gambia St SE1 . . . . 122 B1
Gambier Ho EC1 . . . .97 A3
Gamlen Rd SW15 . . .57 C3
Gandolfi St 5
SE5 . . . . 49 A4
Ganley Ct 19
SW11 . . . . 59 C4
Gannet Ct 5 SE21 . .75 C2
Gannet Ho SE15 . . . 49 B2
Ganton St W1 . . . . . 105 A1
Garand Ct 6 N7 . . . 14 B3
Garbett Ho 2
SE17 . . . . .48 A4
Garbutt Pl W1 . . . . 103 C3
Garden Cl SW15 . . . .69 A4

Garden Ct
4 Richmond TW9 . .44 B2
10 South Acton W4 . 37 B3
St John's Wood
NW8 . . . . 89 B4
Strand EC4 . . . . 121 B4
Garden Flats
SW16 . . . . 74 A1
Garden Ho SW9 . . . 172 B2
Garden La SW2 . . . . 74 B3
Garden Mews
W2 . . . . 31 C2 113 C3
Garden Pl 12 E2 . . . 24 B4
Garden Rd
Richmond TW9 . . . . 54 C4
St John's Wood
NW8 . . . . 89 A4
Garden Row SE1 . . 136 A2
Garden Royal 18
SW15 . . . . 57 C1
Garden St E1 . . . . . . 32 C4
Gardens The
East Dulwich SE22 . 64 C3
Stamford Hill N16 . . .7 B4
Garden Terr
Knightsbridge
SW7 . . . . 130 B3
Pimlico SW1 . . . . . 147 B2
Garden Wlk
EC2 . . . . .24 A1 98 A2
Gardiner Ave NW2 . . .9 B3
Gardiner Ct NW10 . .20 C4
Gardiner Ho
SW11 . . . . 168 A4
Gardner Ct N5 . . . . . 15 B4
Gardners La EC4 . . 122 C4
Gardnor Mans 14
NW3 . . . . 11 B4
Gardnor Rd NW3 . . . 11 C4
Gard St EC1 . . . . . . .96 B4
Gareth Gr BR1 . . . . .11 C1
Garfield Ho W2 . . . 102 C1
Garfield Mews 7
SW11 . . . . 60 C4
Garfield Rd SW11 . . 60 C4
Garford St E14 . . . . . 33 C2
Garland Ct 12 E14 . .33 C2
Garland Ho N16 . . . . .6 C1
Garlands Ho NW8 . . 78 B2
Garlick Hill EC4 . . . 123 A4
Garlinge Ho SW9 . . 173 B4
Garlinge Rd NW2 . . .10 B2
Garnault Mews
EC1 . . . . .95 C3
Garnault Pl EC1 . . . .95 C3
Garner St E2 . . . . . . 24 C3
Garnet Rd NW10 . . . .8 A2
Garnet St E1 . . . . . . 32 B2
Garnett Ho 5 . . . . . 12 B3
Garnett Rd NW3 . . . 12 B3
Garnham Cl 2 N16 . .7 B2
Garnham St 1 N16 . .7 B2
Garnies Cl SE15 . . . 49 B3
Garrad's Rd SW16 . .73 C1
Garratt Wlk NW10 . .8 A2
Garratt Ho 8 N16 . . .7 A3
Garratt La SW18 . . . 71 A3
Garratt Park Sch
SW18 . . . . 71 A2
Garraway Ct SW13 . 47 B3
Garraway Ho SE21 . .76 B1
Garrett Cl W3 . . . . . 28 C4
Garrett Ho 5
W12 . . . . 30 A3

Garrett St EC1 . . . . . **97 A2**
Garrick Cl SW18 . . . . . 59 B3
Garrick Ho
  Chiswick W4 . . . . .46 A4
  Mayfair W1 . . . . **118 A1**
Garrick Rd TW9 . . . . .44 C1
Garrick St WC2 . . . . **120 A4**
Garrick Yd WC2 . . . . **120 A4**
Garsdale Terr
  SW5 . . . . **141 A2**
Garsington Mews
  SE4 . . . . .66 B4
Garson Ho W2 . . . . . **115 B4**
Garston Ho E 6 N1 . . . 15 A1
Garter Way SE16 . . . .40 C4
Garth Ct W4 . . . . .45 C4
Garth Ho NW2 . . . . . . .1 B2
Garth Rd
  Child's Hill NW2 . . . . . .1 B2
  ■ Chiswick W4 . . . . . .37 C1
Gartmoor Gdns
  SW19 . . . . .70 B3
Garton Ho 6 N6 . . . . .4 C4
Garton PI SW18 . . . . .59 B1
Gartons Way
  SW11 . . . . .59 B4
Garway Rd W2 . . . . **100 A1**
Gascoigne PI
  E2 . . . . .24 B2 **98 C3**
Gascony Ave NW6 . . .10 C1
Gascoyne Ho 2
  E9 . . . . .17 C1
Gascoyne Rd E9 . . . . .17 C1
Gaselee St E14 . . . . .34 B2
Gasholder PI
  SE11 . . . . **149 A1**
Gaskarth Rd SW12 . . .61 A1
Gaskell St SW4 . . . . **172 A2**
Gaskin Ho N16 . . . . . .6 C1
Gaskin St N1 . . . . **86 A4**
Gaspar Ct SW7 **142 B4**
Gaspar Mews
  SW5 . . . . **142 B4**
Gasson Ho 24
  SE14 . . . . .50 C4
Gastein Rd W6 . . . . . .47 C4
Gastigny Ho EC1 . . . **97 A3**
Gaston Bell Cl
  TW9 . . . . .54 B4
Gaston Gate SW8 **172 C4**
Gataker Ho 5
  SE16 . . . . .40 A3
Gataker St 6
  SE16 . . . . .40 A3
Gatcliff Cl SE1 . . . . **145 C1**
Gatcombe Ho 20
  SE22 . . . . .64 A4
Gatcombe Rd
  ■ Newham E16 . . . . .35 C1
  Tufnell Pk N19 . . . . . . .4 C1
Gatefield Ct SE15 . . .64 C4
Gateforth St NW8 . . **90 A1**
Gate Hill Ct
  W11 . . . . . . 31 B1 **113 A2**
Gatehouse Sch E2 . .25 C3
Gatehouse Sq
  SE1 . . . . **123 A2**
Gateley Ho 6 SE4 . . .65 C3
Gateley Rd SW9 . . . . .62 B4
Gate Mews SW7 . . . **130 B3**
Gatesborough St
  EC2 . . . . . .24 A1 **98 A2**
Gates St SE17 . . . . . **150 C2**
Gatesden WC1 . . . . . **94 B3**
Gateside Rd SW17 . .72 B1

Gate St WC2 . . . . . **106 C2**
Gateway SE17 . . . . . .48 B4
Gateway Arc N1 . . . . **86 A2**
Gateway Ho SW12 . . .61 A1
Gateway Mews 2
  E8 . . . . .16 B3
Gateway Prim Sch
  NW8 . . . . **89 C2**
Gateways The
  SW3 . . . . **144 B3**
Gateway Trad Est
  NW10 . . . . .21 B2
Gathorne St E2 . . . . .25 C3
Gatliff Rd SW1 . . . . **146 A1**
Gatonby St SE15 . . . .49 B2
Gatwick Ho 3
  E14 . . . . .33 B3
Gatwick Rd SW18 . . .70 B4
Gauden Cl SW4 . . . . .61 C4
Gauden Rd SW4 . . . . .61 C4
Gaunt St SE1 . . . . . **136 B2**
Gautrey Rd SE15 . . . .50 B1
Gaverick Mews 8
  E14 . . . . .41 C2
Gaviller PI 3 E5 . . . .17 A4
Gawber St E2 . . . . . . .25 B2
Gay Cl NW2 . . . . .9 A3
Gaydon Ho W2 . . . . **100 A4**
Gayfere St SW1 . . . **134 A1**
Gayford Rd W12 . . . . .38 B4
Gay Ho N16 . . . . .16 A3
Gayhurst SE17 . . . . . .48 C4
Gayhurst Ho NW8 . . **90 B2**
Gayhurst Prim Sch
  E8 . . . . .16 C1
Gayhurst Rd E8 . . . . .16 C1
Gaymead NW8 . . . . . **78 B3**
Gay Rd E15 . . . . .27 C3
Gaysley Ho SE11 . . **149 B3**
Gayton Cres NW3 . . .11 C4
Gayton Ho E3 . . . . . . .26 C1
Gayton Rd NW3 . . . . .11 C4
Gayville Rd SW11 . . .60 B1
Gaywood Cl SW2 . . . .74 C3
Gaywood St SE1 . . . **136 B1**
Gaza St SE17 . . . . . **150 A1**
Gaze Ho 10 E14 . . . .34 C3
Gean Ct E11 . . . . .19 C4
Geary Ho N7 . . . . .14 B3
Geary Rd NW10 . . . . . .8 C3
Geary St N7 . . . . .14 B3
Gedling Ho SE22 . . . .64 B4
Gedling PI SE1 . . . . **139 A2**
Gees Ct W1 . . . . **103 C1**
Gee St EC1 . . . . **96 C2**
Geffrye Ct N1 . . . . . . .24 A3
Geffrye Mus ★ E2 . .24 B3
Geldart Rd SE15 . . . .50 A3
Geldeston Rd E5 . . . . .7 C2
Gellatly Rd SE14 . . . .50 C1
Gemini Bsns Ctr
  E16 . . . . .27 C1
Gemini Ho 11 E3 . . . .26 C4
General Wolfe Rd
  SE10 . . . . .52 C2
Genesis Bsns Pk
  NW10 . . . . .20 A3
Geneva Ct
  1 Putney SW15 . . . .57 C2
  Stoke Newington N16 . .6 C3
Geneva Dr SW9 . . . . .62 C3
Genoa Ave SW15 . . . .57 B2

Genoa Ho 19 E1 . . . .25 C1
Geoffrey Chaucer
  Tech Coll SE1 . . . . **137 C1**
Geoffrey Cl SE5 . . . . .48 B1
Geoffrey Ct SE4 . . . . .66 B4
Geoffrey Ho SE1 . . . **137 C2**
Geoffrey Jones Ct
  NW10 . . . . .21 C4
Geoffrey Rd SE4 . . . .66 B4
George Beard Rd 11
  SE8 . . . . **41 B2**
George Beare Lo 9
  SW4 . . . . **61 B2**
George Belt Ho 8
  E2 . . . . .25 C2
George Ct WC2 . . . . **120 B3**
George Downing Est
  N16 . . . . .7 B2
George Eliot Ho
  SW1 . . . . **147 A3**
George Eliot Jun & Inf
  Schs NW8 . . . . **79 B4**
George Elliot Ho
  SE17 . . . . **150 C2**
George Elliston Ho 1
  SE1 . . . . **153 B1**
George Eyre Ho
  NW8 . . . . **79 C1**
George Green's Sec
  Sch E14 . . . . .42 B1
George Inn Yd
  SE1 . . . . **123 B1**
George La SE13 . . . . **67 B1**
George Lansbury Ho
  1 Bow E3 . . . . .26 B2
  3 Willesden NW10 . . .8 A1
George Lashwood Ct
  12 SW9 . . . . .62 B3
George Leybourne Ho
  E1 . . . . **125 C4**
George Lindgren Ho
  SW6 . . . . **155 A2**
George Loveless Ho
  2 . . . . .24 B2 **99 A4**
George Mathers Rd
  SE11 . . . . **150 A4**
George Mews
  NW1 . . . . **92 C3**
George Peabody Ct
  NW1 . . . . **102 A4**
George Row SE16 . . **139 B3**
George's Rd N7 . . . . .14 B3
George's Sq SW6 . . **155 A4**
George St
  6 Canning Town
  E16 . . . . .35 B3
  Marylebone W1 . . . **103 A2**
George Tingle Ho
  SE1 . . . . **139 A2**
Georgette PI SE10 . . .52 B3
George Vale Ho 38
  E2 . . . . .24 C3
George Walter Ho 11
  SE16 . . . . .40 B2
George Wyver Cl
  SW18 . . . . .70 A4
George Yd
  City of London
  EC3 . . . . **109 C1**
  Mayfair W1 . . . . . . **117 C4**
Georgian St SW1 . . **83 A4**
Georgian Ct 12 E9 . .25 B4
Georgina Gdns 6
  E2 . . . . .24 B2 **99 A4**
Geraldine Rd
  Brentford W4 . . . . . . .44 C4
  Wandsworth SW18 . . .59 B2

Geraldine St
  SE11 . . . . **136 A1**
Gerald Mews
  SW1 . . . . **145 C4**
Gerald Rd SW1 . . . . **145 C4**
Gerard Ct NW2 . . . . . .9 C3
Gerard Ho SE14 . . . . .50 C3
Gerards Cl SE16 . . . .40 B1
Gernigan Ho
  SW18 . . . . .59 C1
Gernon Rd E3 . . . . . . .26 A3
Gerrard Ho 5
  SE14 . . . . .50 C3
Gerrard Pl W1 . . . . . **119 C4**
Gerrard Rd N1 . . . . . **86 B2**
Gerrard St W1 . . . . . **119 C4**
Gerridge Ct SE1 . . . **135 C2**
Gerridge St SE1 . . . **135 C2**
Gerry Raffles Sq
  E15 . . . . .19 C2
Gertrude St
  SW10 . . . . **157 A3**
Gervase St SE15 . . . .50 A3
Getters Talmud Torah
  N16 . . . . .6 C4
Ghent Way E8 . . . . . .16 B2
Giant Arches Rd
  SE24 . . . . .63 B1
Gibbings Ho SE1 . . **136 B3**
Gibbins Rd E15 . . . . .19 B1
Gibbon Ho NW8 . . . **89 C1**
Gibbon Rd
  Acton W3 . . . . .29 A2
  Nunhead SE15 . . . . . .50 B1
Gibbons Rd NW10 . . . .8 A2
Gibbon's Rents
  SE1 . . . . **124 A1**
Gibbs Grn W14 . . . . **141 A2**
Gibbs Green Rd
  W14 . . . . **140 C2**
Gibbs Green Sch
  W14 . . . . **141 A2**
Gibraltar Ho
  NW10 . . . . .21 A3
Gibraltar Wlk
  E2 . . . . .24 B2 **99 A3**
Gibson Cl E1 . . . . . . **25 B1**
Gibson Gdns N16 . . . .7 B2
Gibson Rd SE11 . . . **149 A3**
Gibson Sq N1 . . . . . **85 C4**
Gibson St SE10 . . . . .43 A1
Gideon Rd SW11 . . . .60 C4
Giesbach Rd N19 . . . .4 C2
Giffen Square Mkt
  SE8 . . . . .51 C3
Giffin St SE8 . . . . . . .51 C3
Gifford Ho
  5 Clapham SW4 . . . .61 C3
  Greenwich SE10 . . . . .42 C1
  Pimlico SW1 . . . . . **146 C1**
Gifford St N1 . . . . . . .14 A1
Gilbert Ho
  Barbican EC2 . . . . **109 A3**
  Deptford SE8 . . . . . . .51 C4
  5 Globe Town E2 . . .25 C2
  Pimlico SW1 . . . . . **146 B1**
  South Lambeth
  SW8 . . . . **162 A2**
Gilbert PI WC1 . . . . **106 A3**
Gilbert Rd SE11 . . . **149 C4**
Gilbert Sheldon Ho
  W2 . . . . **101 C4**
Gilbertson Ho 111
  E14 . . . . .41 C3
Gilbert St W1 . . . . . **103 C1**

Gilbeys Yd NW1 . . . .12 C1
Gilby Ho 5 E9 . . . . . .17 C2
Gilda Cres N16 . . . . . .7 C3
Gildea St W1 . . . . . **104 B3**
Gilden Cres NW5 . . . .12 C3
Giles Ho
  Bermondsey SE16 . . **139 B2**
  Notting Hill W11 . . . . .31 C3
Gilesmead SE5 . . . . .48 C2
Gilkes Cres SE21 . . . .64 A1
Gilkes Pl SE21 . . . . . .64 A1
Gillam Ho 9 SE16 . . .40 B2
Gill Ave E16 . . . . .35 C3
Gillender St E3 . . . . . .27 B1
Gillespie Prim Sch
  N5 . . . . .6 A1
Gillespie Rd N4, N5 . .6 A1
Gillett Pl 27 E8 . . . . .16 A3
Gillett St E8, N16 . . .16 A3
Gillfoot NW1 . . . . . . **82 C1**
Gillian St SE13 . . . . .67 A2
Gillies St NW5 . . . . . .12 C3
Gilling Ct 5 NW3 . . .12 A2
Gillingham Ho
  SW1 . . . . **146 C4**
Gillingham Mews
  SW1 . . . . **146 C4**
Gillingham Rd NW2 . .1 A1
Gillingham Row
  SW1 . . . . **146 C4**
Gillingham St
  SW1 . . . . **146 C4**
Gillison Wlk SE16 . **139 C2**
Gillman Ho 24 E2 . . .24 C3
Gillray Ho SW10 . . . **157 B3**
Gill St E14 . . . . .33 B2
Gilmore Ho SW4 . . . .60 B3
Gilmore Rd SE13 . . . .67 C3
Gilpin Ave SW14 . . . .55 C3
Gilpin Cl W2 . . . . . . **101 A4**
Gilpin Rd E5 . . . . . . **115 B4**
Gilstead Rd SW6 . . **166 B2**
Gilston Rd SW10 . . **143 A1**
Giltspur St EC1 . . . **108 B2**
Gilwell Ct 7 E5 . . . . .17 A4
Gipsy Cnr W3 . . . . . .28 C4
Gipsy La SW15 . . . . .57 A4
Gipsy Moth IV ★
  SE10 . . . . .52 B4
Giraud St E14 . . . . . .34 A3
Girdlers Rd W14 . . . .39 C2
Girdlestone Wlk
  N19 . . . . .4 B2
Girdwood Rd SW18,
  SW19 . . . . .70 A4
Girling Ho 9 N1 . . . .24 A4
Gironde Rd SW6 . . . **155 A1**
Girton Ho SW15 . . . .57 C1
Girton Villas 6
  W10 . . . . .30 C3
Gisburn Ho 23
  SE15 . . . . .49 C3
Gissing Wlk N1 . . . . .14 C1
Glade The W12 . . . . . **39 A4**
Glading Terr N16 . . . .7 B1
Gladsmuir Rd N19 . . .4 B3
Gladstone Ct
  Westminster SW1 . **147 C3**
  Willesden NW2 . . . . . .9 A3
Gladstone Ho 16
  E14 . . . . .33 C3
Gladstone Park Sch
  NW10 . . . . .9 A4
Gladstone Rd W4 . . . .37 C3
Gladstone St SE1 . . **136 A2**

Gladstone Terr
SW8 . . . . 170 B4
Gladwin Ho NW1 . . 83 A1
Gladwyn Rd SW15 . 57 C4
Gladys Rd NW6 . . . 10 C1
Glaisher St SE8 . . . 52 A4
Glamis Ct W3 . . . . . 37 A4
Glamis Est **3** E1 . . 32 C2
Glamis Pl E1 . . . . . . 32 B2
Glamis Rd E1 . . . . . 32 B2
Glanville Ho **4**
SW12 . . . . 73 B4
Glanville Rd SW2 . 62 A2
Glasbury Ho **5**
SW9 . . . . 62 B3
Glaserton Rd N16 . 7 A4
Glasgow Ho W9 . . . 78 B1
Glasgow Terr
SW1 . . . . 146 C1
Glasshill St SE1 . . 136 B4
Glasshouse Fields
E1 . . . . 32 C2
Glasshouse St
W1 . . . . 119 A3
Glasshouse The
SE13 . . . . 67 B3
Glasshouse Wlk
SE11 . . . . 148 C2
Glasshouse Yd
EC1 . . . . 96 C1
Glass St **4** E2 . . . . . 25 A1
Glastonbury Ct **12**
SE14 . . . . 50 B3
Glastonbury Ho
SW1 . . . . 146 A2
Glastonbury Pl **22**
E1 . . . . 32 B3
Glastonbury St
NW6 . . . . 10 B3
Glaucus St E3 . . . . 34 A4
Glazbury Rd W14 . 140 B2
Glazebrook Cl
SE21 . . . . 75 C2
Glebe Cl **1** W4 . . . . 38 A1
Glebe Ct **13** E3 . . . . 27 A2
Glebe Ho **8** SE16 . . 40 A3
Glebelands Cl SE5 . 64 A4
Glebe Pl SW3 . . . . 158 A4
Glebe Rd
Barnes SW13 . . . . . 46 C1
Dalston E8 . . . . 16 B1
Willesden NW10 . . . 8 A2
Glebe St W4 . . . . . . 38 A1
Gledhow Gdns
SW5 . . . . 142 C3
Gledstanes Rd
W14 . . . . 140 B1
Glegg Pl **3** SW15 . 57 C3
Glenaffric Ave
E14 . . . . 42 C2
Glen Albyn Rd
SW19 . . . . 69 C2
Glenalmond Ho **2**
SW15 . . . . 57 C1
Glenarm Rd E5 . . . 17 C4
Glenbrook Prim Sch
SW4 . . . . 61 C1
Glenbrook Rd
NW6 . . . . 10 C3
Glenburnie Rd
SW17 . . . . 72 B1
Glencoe Mans
SW9 . . . . 163 B1
Glendall St SW9 . . 62 B3
Glendarvon
SW15 . . . . 57 C4

Glendower Gdns **10**
E14 . . . . 55 C4
Glendower Pl
SW7 . . . . 143 B4
Glendower Prep Sch
SW7 . . . . 143 B4
Glendower Rd
SW14 . . . . 55 C4
Glendun Ho **2**
E8 . . . . 16 C3
Glendun Ct W3 . . . 29 A2
Glendun Rd W3 . . . 29 A2
Gleneagles Cl **21**
SE16 . . . . 40 A1
Glenelg Rd SW2 . . 62 A2
Glenfield Rd
SW12 . . . . 73 B3
Glenfinlas Way
SE5 . . . . 48 A3
Glenforth St SE10 . 43 B1
Glengall Gr E14 . . . 42 B3
Glengall Pass **2**
NW6 . . . . 23 C4
Glengall Rd
Camberwell SE15 . . 49 B4
Kilburn NW6 . . . . . . 23 B4
Glengall Terr
SE15 . . . . 49 B4
Glengarnock Ave
E14 . . . . 42 B2
Glengarry Rd
SE22 . . . . 64 B2
Glenhurst Ave
NW5 . . . . 12 C4
Glenilla Rd NW3 . . 12 A2
Glenister Rd SE10 . 43 B1
Glenkerry Ho **1**
E14 . . . . 34 B3
Glenloch Ct **2**
NW3 . . . . 12 A2
Glenloch Rd NW3 . 12 A3
Glenluce Rd SE3 . . 53 C4
Glenmore SW15 . . 57 C1
Glenmore Ho **6**
TW10 . . . . 54 A1
Glenmore Rd
NW3 . . . . 12 A2
Glennie Ct SE21 . . 76 C3
Glennie Ho SE10 . . 52 B2
Glennie Rd SE27,
SW16 . . . . 74 C1
Glenridding NW1 . . 83 A1
Glenrosa St SW6 . 166 C2
Glenroy St W12 . . . 30 B3
Glensdale Rd SE4 . 66 B4
Glenshaw Mans
SW9 . . . . 163 B1
Glentanner Way
SW17 . . . . 71 C1
Glen Terr E14 . . . . . 42 B4
Glentham Gdns
SW13 . . . . 47 A4
Glentham Rd
SW13 . . . . 47 A4
Glenthorne Mews
W6 . . . . 39 A2
Glenthorne Rd
W6 . . . . 39 A2
Glenthorpe SW15 . 56 C3
Glentworth St
NW1 . . . . 91 A1
Glenville Gr SE8 . . 51 B3
Glenville Mews
SW18 . . . . 70 C4
Glenworth Ave
E14 . . . . 42 C2
Gliddon Dr E5 . . . . 17 A4

Gliddon Rd W14 . . 140 A2
Globe Pond Rd
SE16 . . . . 33 A1
Globe Prim Sch
E2 . . . . 25 B2
Globe Rd E1, E2 . . . 25 B1
Globe St SE1 . . . . . 137 B3
Globe Terr **9** E2 . . . 25 B2
Globe Theatre The ★
SE1 . . . . 122 C3
GLOBE TOWN 25 C2
Globe View **4**
EC4 . . . . 122 C4
Globe Yd W1 . . . . . 104 A1
Gloucester Wlk . . . 141 A3
Gloucester Ave
NW1 . . . . 81 C4
Gloucester Cir
SE10 . . . . 52 B3
Gloucester Cres
NW1 . . . . 82 A4
Gloucester Ct
Borough The SE1 . . 137 A2
City of London EC3 . 124 B3
Dulwich SE22 . . . . . 76 C3
Richmond TW9 . . . . 44 C3
Gloucester Dr N4 . . 6 A2
Gloucester Gate
NW1 . . . . 82 A2
Gloucester Gate
Mews NW1 . . . . 82 A2
Gloucester Gdns
Golders Green
NW11 . . . . 1 B4
Paddington W2 . . . 100 C2
Gloucester Ho
Kilburn NW6 . . . . . . 23 C3
Richmond TW9 . . . . 54 C2
Gloucester Mews
W2 . . . . 101 A1
Gloucester Mews W
W2 . . . . 101 A1
Gloucester Pk
SW7 . . . . 142 C4
Gloucester Pl W1 . 103 A4
Gloucester Pl Mews
W1 . . . . 103 A3
Gloucester Prim Sch
SE15 . . . . 49 A3
Gloucester Rd
Acton W3 . . . . 37 B4
Richmond TW9 . . . . 44 C3
South Kensington
SW7 . . . . 142 C4
Gloucester Road Sta
SW7 . . . . 142 C4
Gloucester Sq
6 Hackney E2 . . . . 24 C4
Paddington W2 . . . 102 A1
Gloucester St
SW1 . . . . 146 C2
Gloucester Terr
W2 . . . . 101 A1
Gloucester Way
EC1 . . . . 95 C3
Gloucester Wlk
W8 . . . . 127 C4
Glover Ho
London SE15 . . . . . . 65 A3
2 South Hampstead
NW6 . . . . 11 B1
Glycena Rd SW11 . 60 B4
Glyn Ct SE27 . . . . . 74 C1
Glynde Mews
SW3 . . . . 130 B1
Glynde Reach
WC1 . . . . 94 B3

Glynde St SE4 . . . . 66 B1
Glynfield Rd NW10 . 8 A1
Glynn Mans W14 . 140 B4
Glyn Rd E5 . . . . 17 C4
Glyn St SE11 . . . . . 148 C1
Goater's Alley
SW6 . . . . 155 A1
Goat Wharf TW8 . . 44 A4
Godalming Rd
E14 . . . . 34 A4
Goddard Ho SW19 . 69 C2
Goddard Pl N19 . . . 4 B1
Godfrey Ho EC1 . . . 97 B3
Godfrey St
Chelsea SW3 . . . . . 144 B2
Mill Meads E15 . . . . 27 B3
Goding St SE11 . . . 148 B1
Godley Rd SW18 . . 71 C3
Godliman St EC4 . 122 C4
Godman Rd SE15 . . 50 A1
Godolphin Ho
Primrose Hill NW3 . 12 A1
7 Streatham SW2 . 74 C3
Godolphin & Latymer
Sch W6 . . . . 39 A2
Godolphin Pl W3 . . 28 C2
Godolphin Rd
W12 . . . . 39 A4
Godson St N1 . . . . . 85 B2
Godstone Ct **1**
N16 . . . . 7 A3
Godstone Ho SE1 . 137 C2
Godwin Cl N1 . . . . . 87 A2
Godwin Ct NW1 . . . 83 A2
Godwin Ho
2 Haggerston E2 . . 24 B3
Kilburn NW6 . . . . . . 78 A2
Goffers Ho SE3 . . . 53 A1
Goffers Rd SE3,
SE13 . . . . 53 A1
Goffton Ho SW9 . . 173 A1
Goldbeaters Gdns
NW11 . . . . 1 B4
Golborne Gdns
5 Kensal Town
W10 . . . . 23 A1
West Kilburn W10 . . 23 B1
Golborne Mews **5**
W10 . . . . 31 A4
Golborne Rd W10 . 31 A4
Golden Cross Mews
2 W11 . . . . 31 B3
Golden Hinde The ★
SE1 . . . . 123 B2
Golden La EC1 . . . . 97 A1
Golden Plover Cl
E16 . . . . 35 C3
Golden Sq W1 . . . . 119 A4
Golders Ct NW11 . . 1 B4
Golders Gdns
NW11 . . . . 1 B4
GOLDERS GREEN . 1 C4
Golders Green Coll
NW11 . . . . 1 C4
Golders Green Cres
NW11 . . . . 1 C4
Golders Green Rd
NW11 . . . . 1 A4
Golders Green Sta
NW11 . . . . 1 B4
Golders Hill Sch
NW11 . . . . 1 C4
Golderslea NW11 . . 1 C3
Golders Park Cl
NW11 . . . . 1 C3
Golders Way NW11 . 1 B4

Goldhawk Ind Est The
W6 . . . . 39 A3
Goldhawk Mews **2**
W12 . . . . 39 A4
Goldhawk Rd W12 . 38 C4
Goldhawk Road Sta
W12 . . . . 39 B4
Goldhurst Terr
NW6 . . . . 11 B1
Goldie Ho N19 . . . . 4 C4
Goldie St SE5 . . . . 48 A2
Golding St E1 . . . . 111 C1
Goldington Cres
NW1 . . . . 83 B2
Goldington St
NW1 . . . . 83 B2
Goldman Cl
E2 . . . . 24 C1 99 B2
Goldney Rd W9 . . . 23 C1
Goldsboro Rd
SW8 . . . . 161 C1
Goldsborough Ho
SW8 . . . . 171 C3
Goldsmith Ave
W3 . . . . 28 C2
Goldsmith Ct
WC1 . . . . 106 B2
Goldsmith Ho W3 . 28 C2
Goldsmith Rd
Acton W3 . . . . 28 C1
Peckham SE15 . . . . 49 C2
Goldsmiths Bldgs
W3 . . . . 28 C1
Goldsmiths Cl W3 . 28 C1
Goldsmiths Coll, Univ
of London SE14 . . . 51 A2
Goldsmith's Pl
NW6 . . . . 78 A3
Goldsmith's Row
E2 . . . . 24 C3
Goldsmith's Sq **17**
E2 . . . . 24 C3
Goldsmith St EC2 . 109 A2
Goldthorpe NW1 . . 82 C3
Goldwell Ho SE22 . 64 A3
Goldwin Cl SE14 . . 50 B2
Goldwing Cl E16 . . 35 C3
Gomm Rd SE16 . . . 40 B3
Gondar Gdns NW6 . 10 B3
Gondar Mans
NW6 . . . . 10 B3
Gonson St SE8 . . . 52 A4
Gonston Cl SW19 . 70 A2
Gonville Ho **6**
SW15 . . . . 57 C1
Gonville St SW6 . . 58 A4
Gooch Ho EC1 . . . 107 B4
Goodall Ho **10** SE4 . 65 C3
Goodenough Coll
WC1 . . . . 94 C2
Goodfaith Ho **18**
E14 . . . . 34 A2
Goodge Pl W1 . . . 105 A3
Goodge St W1 . . . 105 A3
Goodge Street Sta
W1 . . . . 105 B4
Goodhall St NW10 . 21 B2
Good Hart Pl E14 . . 33 A2
Goodhope Ho **17**
E14 . . . . 34 A2
Goodinge Cl N7 . . . 14 A2
Goodinge Rd N7 . . 14 A2
Goodman Cres
SW2 . . . . 73 C2

Goodman's Stile
E1 . . . . **111** B2

Goodman's Yd E1,
EC3 . . . . **124** C4

Goodrich Com Sch
SE22 . . . . .64 C1

Goodrich Ct 9
W10 . . . . .30 C3

Goodrich Ho
20 Bethnal Green
E2 . . . . .25 B3
Stamford Hill N16 . . . .7 A4

Goodrich Rd SE22 . .64 C1

**Good Shepherd RC
Prim Sch The**
W12 . . . . .38 B4

Goodson Rd NW10 . .8 A1

Goodspeed Ho 20
E14 . . . . .34 A2

Goodsway NW1 . . . .84 A2

Goodway Gdns
E14 . . . . .34 C3

Goodwill Ho 22
E14 . . . . .34 A2

Goodwin Cl SE16 **139** A1

Goodwin Ho 2
SE15 . . . . .65 A4

Goodwin Rd W12 . . .38 C4

Goodwins Ct
WC2 . . . . .120 A4

Goodwin St N4 . . . . .5 C2

Goodwood Ct W1 **104** B4

Goodwood Ho 3
W4 . . . . .37 B1

Goodwood Mans 3
SW9 . . . . .62 C4

Goodwood Rd
SE14 . . . . .51 A3

**Goose Green Prim
Sch** SE22 . . . . .64 B3

Goose Green Trad Est
SE22 . . . . .64 C3

Gophir La EC4 . . . .**123** B4

Gopsall St N1 . . . . .**87** C3

Gordon Ave SW14 . .56 A3

**Gordonbrock Prim
Sch** SE4 . . . . .66 C2

Gordonbrock Rd
SE4 . . . . .66 C2

Gordon Cl 5 W12 . .30 B3

Gordon Ct 3 W12 . .30 B3

Gordondale Rd SW18,
SW19 . . . . .70 C2

Gordon Gr SE5 . . . . .48 A1

Gordon Ho 17 E1 . . .32 B2

Gordon Hospl The
SW1 . . . .**147** B3

Gordon House Rd
NW5 . . . . .12 C4

Gordon Lo N16 . . . . .6 C3

Gordon Mans WC1 **93** B1

Gordon Pl W8 . . . .**127** C4

Gordon Rd
Chiswick W4 . . . . . . .45 A4
Leyton E15 . . . . .19 B4
Peckham SE15 . . . . . .50 A1
Richmond TW9 . . . . . .44 B1

Gordon Sq WC1 . . . .93 C2

Gordon St WC1 . . . .93 B2

Gorefield Ho NW6 . .23 C3

Gorefield Pl NW6 . . .23 C3

Gore Rd E9 . . . . . . .25 B4

Gore St SW7 . . . . .**129** A2

Gorham Ho 12
SW4 . . . . .61 B1

Gorham Pl
W11 . . . . . .31 A2 **112** A3

Goring St EC3 . . . . .**110** B2

Gorleston St W14 . .**140** B4

Gorse Cl E16 . . . . . .35 C3

Gorsefield Ho 6
E14 . . . . .33 C2

Gorst Rd
London SW11 . . . . . . .60 B1
North Acton NW10 . . .20 C1

Gorsuch Pl
E2 . . . . .24 B2 **98** C4

Gorsuch St
E2 . . . . .24 B2 **98** C4

Gosberton Rd
SW12 . . . . .72 C3

Gosfield St W1 . . . .**104** C3

Gosford Ho 25 E3 . . .26 B3

Goslett Yd WC2 . . . .**105** C2

Gosling Ho 2 E1 . . . .32 B2

Gosling Way SW9 . .**173** B4

Gospatric Home Ho
SW14 . . . . .56 A4

GOSPEL OAK 12 C4

Gospel Oak Prim Sch
NW5 . . . . .12 C4

Gospel Oak Sta
NW5 . . . . .12 C4

Gosport Ho 9
SW15 . . . . .68 C3

Gosterwood St
SE8 . . . . .51 A4

Goswell Pl EC1 . . . . .96 B3

Goswell Rd EC1 . . . . .96 B4

Gothic Ct 17 SE5 . . .48 B3

Gottfried Mews
NW5 . . . . .13 B4

Gough Ho N1 . . . . . .86 B4

Gough Sq EC4 . . . .**107** C2

Gough St WC1 . . . . .95 A1

Gough Wlk 14 E14 . .33 C3

Goulden Ho
SW11 . . . .**168** A2

Gouldman Ho 33
E1 . . . . .25 B1

Gould Terr 28 E8 . . .17 A3

Goulston St E1 . . . .**110** C2

Goulton Rd E5 . . . . .17 A4

Govan St E2 . . . . . . .24 C4

Gover Ct SW4 . . . . .**172** B2

Gowan Ave SW6 . . .**164** A4

Gowan Ho
E2 . . . . .24 B2 **98** C3

Gowan Rd NW10 . . . .9 A2

Gower Cl SW4 . . . . .61 B1

Gower Ct WC1 . . . . .93 B2

Gower Ho SE17 . . . .**151** A2

Gower Mews
WC1 . . . .**105** C4

Gower Pl NW1,
WC1 . . . . .93 B2

Gower Sch The
N7 . . . . .14 A2

Gower St WC1 . . . . .93 B1

Gower's Wlk E1 . . .**111** B1

Gowlett Rd SE15 . . .64 C4

Gowrie Rd SW11 . . .60 C4

Gracechurch St EC2,
EC4 . . . .**123** C4

Gracefield Gdns
SW16 . . . . .74 A1

Gracehill 2 E1 . . . . .32 B4

Grace Ho SE11 . . . .**163** A4

Grace Jones Cl
E8 . . . . .16 C2

Grace Pl E3 . . . . . . .27 A2

Graces Mews NW8 . .79 A1

Grace's Mews SE5 . .49 A1

Grace's Rd SE5 . . . . .49 A1

Grace St E3 . . . . . . .27 A2

Graemesdyke Ave
SW14 . . . . .55 A3

Grafton Cres NW1 . .13 A2

Grafton Ct 10 E8 . . .16 C3

Grafton Ho
10 Bow E3 . . . . .26 C2
2 Deptford SE8 . . . . .41 B1

Grafton Mans
SW4 . . . . .61 B3

Grafton Mews W1 . .92 C1

Grafton Pl NW1 . . . .93 C3

Grafton Prim Sch
N7 . . . . .5 A1

Grafton Rd
Acton W3 . . . . .28 B2
Gospel Oak NW5 . . . .12 C3

Grafton Sq SW4 . . . .61 B4

Grafton St W1 . . . .**118** B3

Grafton Terr NW5 . . .12 C3

Grafton Way W1 . . . .93 A1

Grafton Yd NW5 . . . .13 A2

Graham Ct 5
SE14 . . . . .50 C4

Graham Ho
5 Balham SW12 . . . . .73 A4
6 Tufnell Pk N19 . . . .13 C4

Graham Mans 2
E8 . . . . .17 A2

Graham Rd
Acton W4 . . . . .37 C3
Dalston E8 . . . . .16 C2

Graham St N1 . . . . .86 B1

Graham Terr
SW1 . . . .**145** C3

Graham Twr W3 . . . .37 A3

Grainger Ct 23
SE5 . . . . .48 B3

Grampian Gdns
NW2 . . . . .1 A3

Grampians The 10
W14 . . . . .39 C4

Granard Ave
SW15 . . . . .57 A2

Granard Ho 20 E9 . .17 C2

Granard Prim Sch
SW15 . . . . .57 A1

Granard Rd SW11,
SW12 . . . . .72 B4

Granary Rd E1 . . . . .25 A1

Granary Sq N1 . . . . .14 C2

Granary St NW1 . . . .83 B3

Granary The SE8 . . .51 C3

Granby St SE1 . . . .**135** B3

Granby St
Bethnal Green
E2 . . . . .24 C1 **99** B2
Shoreditch
E2 . . . . .24 B1 **99** A2

Granby Terr NW1 . .**82** C1

Grand Ave EC1 . . . .**108** B4

Grandfield Ct W4 . . .45 C4

Grandison Rd
SW11 . . . . .60 B2

Grand Junction Wharf
N1 . . . . .86 C1

Grand Par SW14 . . . .55 B3

Grand Union Cl
W9 . . . . .31 B4

Grand Union Cres
E8 . . . . .24 C4

Grand Union Ind Est
NW10 . . . . .20 A3

Grand Vitesse Ind Est
SE1 . . . .**122** B1

Granfield St
SW11 . . . .**167** C3

Grangecourt Rd
N16 . . . . .7 A3

Grange Ct
Peckham SE15 . . . . . .49 B1
Strand WC2 . . . .**107** A1

Grangefield NW1 . . .14 A1

Grange Gdns NW3 . . .2 A1

Grange Gr N1 . . . . . .15 B2

Grange Ho
Bermondsey SE1 . . . .**138** C3
Willesden NW10 . . . . .9 A1

Grange La SE21 . . . .76 B2

Grangemill 11 . . . . .13 A4

GRANGE MILLS 73 B3

Grange Mills
SW12 . . . . .73 B3

Grange Pl NW6 . . . .10 C1

Grange Prim Sch
SE1 . . . .**138** A1

Grange Rd
Barnes SW13 . . . . . .46 C2
Bermondsey SE1 . . . .**138** C1
Gunnersbury W4 . . . .37 A1
Willesden NW10 . . . . .9 A2

Grange St N1 . . . . . .87 C3

Grange The
Bermondsey SE1 . . . .**138** C1
7 Gunnersbury
W4 . . . . .37 A1
2 Hammersmith W12 .39 A3
3 Maitland Pk
NW3 . . . . .12 B2
South Acton W3 . . . . .37 A4
West Kensington
W14 . . . .**140** C3

Grangeway NW6 . . . .10 C1

Grange Wlk SE1 . . .**138** C1

Grange Yd SE1 . . . .**138** C1

Granite Apts E15 . . .19 C2

Grannary The 10 . . .16 C1

Gransden Ave E8 . . .17 A1

Gransden Ho 5
SE8 . . . . .41 B1

Gransden Rd W12 . . .38 B4

Grantbridge St N1 . .86 B2

Grantham Ct 9
SE16 . . . . .40 C4

Grantham Ho 20
SE15 . . . . .49 C4

Grantham Pl W1 . . .**118** A1

Grantham Rd
Chiswick W4 . . . . . . .46 A3
South Lambeth
SW9 . . . .**172** B1

Grant Ho
Clapham SW8 . . . . . .**171** B1
Clerkenwell EC1 . . . .**108** B4

Grantley Ho
2 Deptford SE14 . . . .50 C4
5 Putney SW19 . . . . .69 C3

Grantley St E1 . . . . .25 C1

**Grant Mus of Zoology
& Comparative
Anatomy** ★ W1 . . . .93 B1

Grant Rd SW11 . . . . .60 A4

Grant St N1 . . . . . . .85 B2

Grantully Rd W9 . . . .88 A3

Granville Ct
8 Deptford SE14 . . . .51 A3
Shoreditch N1 . . . . . .87 C4

Granville Gr SE13 . . .67 B4

Granville Ho 18 . . . . .33 C3

Granville Mans 8
W12 . . . . .39 B4

Granville Pk SE13 . . .67 C4

Granville Pl
Marylebone W1 . . . .**103** B1
Walham Green
SW6 . . . .**156** A1

Granville Point
NW2 . . . . .1 B2

Granville Rd
Child's Hill NW2 . . . . . .1 B2
Kilburn NW6 . . . . . . .23 C3
Wandsworth SW18 . . .70 B4

Granville Sq
SE15 . . . . .49 A3
Finsbury WC1 . . . . . .95 A3

Granville St WC1 . . .95 A3

Grape St WC2 . . . . .**106** A2

Grasgarth Cl W3 . . .28 B2

Grasmere NW1 . . . . .92 B3

Grasmere Ave W3 . .28 C2

Grasmere Ct
SW13 . . . . .46 C4

Grasmere Ho 20
N16 . . . . .16 C4

Grasmere Point 2
SE15 . . . . .50 B3

Grasmere Prim Sch
N16 . . . . .15 C4

Grateley Ho 10
SW15 . . . . .69 A3

Gratton Rd W14 . . .**126** A1

Graveley Ho 7
SE8 . . . . .41 A2

Gravel La E1 . . . . . .**110** C2

Gravesend Rd
W12 . . . . .29 C2

Grayfriars Pas
EC1 . . . .**108** B2

Gray Ho SE17 . . . . .**151** A2

Grayland Ct WC1 . . .94 C3

Grayling Rd N16 . . . . .6 C2

Grayling Sq
E2 . . . . .24 C2 **99** C4

Grayshott Rd
SW11 . . . . .60 C4

Gray's Inn PI WC1 **107** A4

Gray's Inn Rd WC1 . .95 A2

Gray's Inn Sq
WC1 . . . .**107** B4

Grayson Ho EC1 . . . .97 A3

Gray St SE1 . . . . . .**135** C3

Grayswood Point 14
SW15 . . . . .68 C3

Gray's Yd W1 . . . . .**103** C2

Grazebrook Prim Sch
N16 . . . . .7 A2

Grazebrook Rd N16 . .6 C2

Great Arthur Ho
EC1 . . . . .96 C1

Great Bell Alley
EC2 . . . .**109** B2

Great Castle St
W1 . . . .**104** C2

Great Central St
NW1 . . . .**102** C4

Great Chapel St
W1 . . . .**105** B2

Great Chart St
SW11 . . . . .59 B3

Great Chertsey Rd
SW14, W4 . . . . 45 C2
Great Church La
W6 . . . . 39 C1
Great College St
SW1 . . . . 134 A2
Great Croft WC1 . . . 94 B3
Great Cross Ave
SE3 . . . . 53 A3
Great Cumberland
Mews W1 . . . . 102 C1
Great Cumberland Pl
W1 . . . . 103 A1
Great Dover St
SE1 . . . . 137 B2
Great Eastern Bldgs
10 E8 . . . . 17 A2
Great Eastern Ent Ctr
E14 . . . . 42 A4
Great Eastern Pier
E14 . . . . 41 C1
Great Eastern Rd
E15 . . . . 19 C2
Great Eastern St
EC2 . . . . . . 24 A1 98 A2
Great Eastern Wharf
SW11 . . . . 158 B1
Great Field **7**
NW5 . . . . 13 B3
Greatfield Cl
London SE4 . . . . 66 C3
4 Tufnell Pk N19 . . 13 B4
Great George St
SW1 . . . . 133 C3
Great Guildford Bsns
Sq SE1 . . . . 122 C1
Great Guildford St
SE1 . . . . 122 C1
Greatham Wlk **8**
SW15 . . . . 68 C3
Great James St
WC1 . . . . 106 C4
Great Marlborough St
W1 . . . . 104 C1
Great Maze Pond
SE1 . . . . 137 C4
Great Newport St
WC2 . . . . 120 A4
Greatorex Ho E1 . . 111 B4
Greatorex St E1 . . . 111 B4
Great Ormond St
Hospl for Children
WC1 . . . . 94 C1
Great Ormond St
WC1 . . . . 94 C1
Great Percy St
WC1 . . . . 95 B4
Great Peter St
SW1 . . . . 133 C1
Great Portland St
W1 . . . . 104 B4
Great Portland Street
Sta W1 . . . . 92 B1
Great Pulteney St
W1 . . . . 119 A4
Great Queen St
WC2 . . . . 106 B2
Great Russell Mans
WC1 . . . . 106 A3
Great Russell St
WC1 . . . . 106 A3
Great St Helen's
EC3 . . . . 110 A2
Great St Thomas
Apostle EC4 . . . . . . 123 A4
Great Scotland Yd
SW1, WC2 . . . . 120 A2

Great Smith St
SW1 . . . . 133 C2
Great Spilmans
SE22 . . . . 64 A2
Great Suffolk St
SE1 . . . . 122 B1
Great Sutton St
EC1 . . . . 96 B1
Great Swan Alley
EC2 . . . . 109 B2
Great Titchfield St
W1 . . . . 104 C3
Great Tower St
EC3 . . . . 124 A4
Great Trinity La
EC4 . . . . 123 A4
Great Turnstile
WC2 . . . . 107 A3
Great Western Rd W2,
W9 . . . . 31 B4
Great West Rd W4 . . 45 C4
Great West Road
Cedars Rd W4 . . . . . 45 B4
Great West Road
Hogarth La W4 . . . . 46 A4
Great Winchester St
EC2 . . . . 109 C2
Great Windmill St
W1 . . . . 119 B4
Great Yd SE1 . . . . . 138 B4
Greaves Cotts **10**
E14 . . . . 33 A4
Greaves Twr
SW10 . . . . 157 A2
Grebe Ct **16** E14 . . . . 42 B4
Greek Ct W1 . . . . . . 105 C1
Greek St W1 . . . . . . 105 C1
Greenacre Ct E8 . . . . 16 C3
Greenacre Sq **20**
SE16 . . . . 40 C4
Green Arbour Ct
EC1 . . . . 108 A2
Greenaway Gdns
NW3 . . . . 11 A4
Greenaway Ho
Finsbury WC1 . . . . . . 95 B3
St John's Wood
NW8 . . . . 78 C4
Greenberry St
NW8 . . . . 80 A1
Green Cl NW11 . . . . . . 2 B4
Greencoat Pl
SW1 . . . . 147 A3
Greencoat Row
SW1 . . . . 133 A1
Greencourt Ho **25**
E1 . . . . 25 C1
Greencroft Gdns
NW6 . . . . 11 B1
Green Ct **2** NW10 . . . 8 A4
Green Dale SE22 . . . . 64 A2
Greendale SE22 . . . . . 64 A2
Green Dragon Ct
SE1 . . . . 123 B1
Green Dragon Ho
WC1 . . . . 106 B2
Green Dragon La
TW8 . . . . 36 B1
Green Dragon Prim
Sch TW8 . . . . 44 A4
Green Dragon Yd
E1 . . . . 111 B3
Greene Ct **20** SE14 . . 50 C4
Greene Ho SE1 . . . . 137 B1
Greenend Rd W4 . . . 38 A4

Greener Ho **3**
SW4 . . . . 61 C4
Greenfell Mans
SE8 . . . . 52 A4
Greenfield Gdns
NW2 . . . . 1 A1
Greenfield Ho **28**
SW19 . . . . 69 C3
Greenfield Rd E1 . . 111 C2
Greenham Cl SE1 . . 135 B3
Greenham Ho **5**
E9 . . . . 25 B4
Greenheath Bsns Ctr
8 E2 . . . . 25 A1
Greenhill NW3 . . . . . . 11 C4
Greenhill Pk
NW10 . . . . 21 A4
Greenhill Rd
NW10 . . . . 21 A4
Greenhill's Rents
EC1 . . . . 108 A4
Greenhills Terr **16**
N1 . . . . 15 C2
Green Ho The **5**
SW19 . . . . 70 A3
Green Hundred Rd
SE15 . . . . 49 C4
Greening Ho SE13 . . 67 C3
Greenland Ho
Bermondsey SE8 . . . . 40 C1
4 Mile End E1 . . . . 26 A1
Greenland Mews
SE8 . . . . 40 C1
Greenland Pl NW1 . . 82 B4
Greenland Quay
SE16 . . . . 40 C2
Greenland Rd
NW1 . . . . 82 C4
Greenland St NW1 . . 82 B4
Green Lanes N4, N8,
N15 . . . . 6 A4
Greenleaf Cl **8**
SW2 . . . . 74 C4
Green Link Wlk
TW9 . . . . 45 A2
Greenman St N1 . . . . 86 C4
Greenmead Sch
SW15 . . . . 57 A2
Greenock Rd **11**
W3 . . . . 37 B3
Green Park Sta
W1 . . . . 118 C2
Greenroof Way
SE10 . . . . 43 B3
Greens Ct W1 . . . . . 119 B4
Green's Ct
W11 . . . . . . 31 B1 112 C1
Greenside Prim Sch
W12 . . . . 38 C4
Greenside Rd
W12 . . . . 38 C4
Green St W1 . . . . . . 117 B4
Greenstead Gdns
SW15 . . . . 57 A2
Greenstreet Hill
SE4 . . . . 65 C4
Greensward Ho
SW6 . . . . 166 C2
Green Terr EC1 . . . . . 95 C3
Green The W3 . . . . . . 29 A1
Greenview Cl W3 . . . 29 A1
Greenview Ct
East Dulwich SE22 . . 64 C3
Wandsworth SW18 . . 72 A4

Greenwell St W1 . . . 92 B1
GREENWICH 52 C3
Greenwich Acad
SE10 . . . . 52 A2
Greenwich Bsns Ctr
SE10 . . . . 52 A3
Greenwich Bsns Pk
SE10 . . . . 52 A3
Greenwich Church St
SE10 . . . . 52 B4
Greenwich Coll
SE10 . . . . 52 B3
Greenwich Ct **11**
E1 . . . . 32 A3
Greenwich High Rd
SE10 . . . . 52 A3
Greenwich Ho
SE13 . . . . 67 C1
Greenwich Ind Est
SE10 . . . . 52 A3
Greenwich Mkt
SE10 . . . . 52 B4
Greenwich Mkt **2**
SE10 . . . . 52 B4
Greenwich Park* 53 A3
Greenwich Park St
SE10 . . . . 52 C4
Greenwich Quay
SE8 . . . . 52 A4
Greenwich South St
SE10 . . . . 52 B2
Greenwich Sta
SE10 . . . . 52 A3
Greenwich View Pl
E14 . . . . 42 A3
Green Wlk SE1 . . . . 138 A1
Greenwood **8**
SW19 . . . . 69 C3
Green Wood NW5 . . . 13 B3
Greenwood Ho
Finsbury WC1 . . . . . . 95 B3
6 Nunhead SE4 . . . 65 C3
Greenwood Pl
NW5 . . . . 13 A3
Greenwood Rd E8 . . 16 C2
Greenwood Terr
NW10 . . . . 20 C3
Green Yd WC1 . . . . . . 95 A2
Green Yd The SE1 . . 135 C3
Greet St SE1 . . . . . . 121 C1
Gregor Mews SE3 . . . 53 C3
Gregory Pl W8 . . . . 128 A4
Greig Terr SE17 . . . . . 48 A4
Grenada Ho **19**
E14 . . . . 33 B2
Grenade St E14 . . . . . 33 B2
Grena Rd TW9, ... 54 B3
Grena Rd TW10,
TW9 . . . . 54 B3
Grendon Cl SE15 . . . 49 C3
Grendon Ho
20 Hackney E9 . . . . 17 B1
Pentonville N1 . . . . . 84 C1
Grendon St NW8 . . . . 90 A2
Grenfell Ho SE5 . . . . 48 B3
Grenfell Rd W11 . . . . 30 C2
Grenfell Twr **5**
W11 . . . . 30 C2
Grenfell Wlk **4**
W11 . . . . 30 C2
Grenier Apartments
15 SE15 . . . . 50 A3
Grenville Ho
20 Bow E3 . . . . 26 A3
4 Deptford SE8 . . . . 51 C4
Grenville Lo N6 . . . . . . 4 B4

Gre–Gri **219**

Grenville Mans
WC1 . . . . 94 A2
Grenville Mews
SW7 . . . . 142 C3
Grenville Pl SW7 . . . 142 C4
Grenville Rd N19 . . . . . 5 A3
Grenville St WC1 . . . . 94 B1
Gresham Almshouses
3 SW9 . . . . 62 B3
Gresham Coll
EC1 . . . . 107 C3
Gresham Gdns
NW11 . . . . 1 A3
Gresham Pl **2** N19 . . . 4 C2
Gresham Rd SW9 . . . 62 C4
Gresham St EC2 . . . 109 A2
Gresham Way
SW19 . . . . 70 C1
Gresham Way Est
SW19 . . . . 71 A1
Gresley Ho SW8 . . . 171 C4
Gresley Rd N19 . . . . . . 4 B4
Gressenhall Rd
SW18 . . . . 70 B4
Gresse St W1 . . . . . . 105 B2
Greswell St SW6 . . . . 47 C2
Greta Ho SE3 . . . . 53 B4
Gretton Ho **2** E2 . . . 25 B2
Greville Hall NW6 . . . 78 B2
Greville Ho
Knightsbridge
SW1 . . . . 131 B2
Putney SW15 . . . . 57 C4
Greville Lo **2** W2 . . 100 A2
Greville Mews
NW6 . . . . 78 A3
Greville Pl W9 . . . . . . 78 B2
Greville Rd
Kilburn NW6 . . . . 78 B2
Richmond TW10 . . . . . 54 B1
Greville St EC1 . . . . 107 C4
Grey Coat Hospital
Sch (St Michaels)
The SW1 . . . . 147 B3
Grey Coat Hospital
Sch The SW1 . . . . . 133 B1
Greycoat Pl SW1 . . . 133 B1
Greycoat St SW1 . . . 133 B1
Grey Eagle St
E1 . . . . 24 B1 99 A1
Greyfriars **16** SE26 . . 76 C1
Greyfriars Ho SE3 . . . 53 B4
Grey Ho **2** W12 . . . . 30 A2
Greyhound Ct
WC2 . . . . 121 B4
Greyhound Rd
College Pk NW10 . . . . 22 A2
Fulham W6 . . . . 154 A4
Greyladies Gdns
SE10 . . . . 52 B1
Greystoke Ho
SE15 . . . . 49 C4
Greystoke Pl EC4 . . 107 C2
Grey Turner Ho
W12 . . . . 29 C3
Grice Ct N1 . . . . 15 B2
Grierson Rd SE23 . . . . 66 A1
Griffin Cl NW10 . . . . . . 9 A3
Griffin Ct
3 Brentford TW8 . . 44 A4
Chiswick W4 . . . . 38 B1
Shepherd's Bush
W12 . . . . 30 A1
Griffin Gate SW15 . . 57 C4

Griffon Ho 🖪
SW11 . . . . .60 A4
Grigg's PI SE1 . . . . . **138** B1
Grimaldi Ho N1 . . . . **84** C2
Grimsby St
Bethnal Green
E2 . . . . .24 C1 **99** A2
Shoreditch
E2 . . . . .24 B1 **99** A2
Grimsel Path SE5 . . . .48 A3
Grimshaw Cl N6 . . . . . .3 C4
Grimston Rd SW6 **164** C1
Grimthorpe Ho
EC1 . . . . .96 A2
Grimwade Cl SE15 . .65 B4
Grindall Ho 🖾 E1 . .25 A1
Grindal St SE1 . . . . . **135** B3
Grindley Ho 🖪 E3 . .33 B4
Grinling Gibbons Prim
Sch SE8 . . . . .51 B4
Grinling PI SE8 . . . . .51 C4
Grinstead Rd SE8 . . .41 A1
Grisedale NW1 . . . . . .92 C4
Grittleton Rd W9 . . .23 C1
Groombridge Rd
E9 . . . . .17 C1
Groom Cres SW18 . .71 C4
Groome Ho SE11 . . . **149** A3
Groom PI SW1 . . . . . **131** C2
Grosse Way SW15 . .57 A1
Grosvenor Ave
Canonbury N5 . . . . . .15 B3
Mortlake SW14 . . . . . .56 A4
Richmond TW10 . . . . .54 A2
Grosvenor Bridge
SW1 . . . . **160** B4
Grosvenor Cotts
SW1 . . . . **145** B4
Grosvenor Court
Mans W2 . . . . **102** C1
Grosvenor Cres
SW1 . . . . **131** C3
Grosvenor Cres Mews
SW1 . . . . **131** B3
Grosvenor Ct
Brondesbury Pk
NW6 . . . . .22 C4
Gunnersbury W4 . . . . .37 A1
🖾 Poplar E14 . . . . . . .33 B3
Putney SW15 . . . . . . .58 A2
Grosvenor Gdns
Cricklewood NW2 . . . . .9 B3
Mortlake SW14 . . . . . .56 A4
Westminster SW1 . . **132** B1
Grosvenor Gdns
Mews E SW1 . . . . **132** B2
Grosvenor Gdns
Mews N SW1 . . . . **132** A1
Grosvenor Gdns
Mews S SW1 . . . . **132** B1
Grosvenor Hill
W1 . . . . **118** A4
Grosvenor Hill Ct
W1 . . . . **118** A4
Grosvenor Ho E5 . . . . .7 C4
Grosvenor Park
SE5 . . . . .48 B3
Grosvenor Pier
SW1 . . . . **161** B4
Grosvenor PI SE5 . . .48 B4
Grosvenor PI
SW1 . . . . **132** A3
Grosvenor Rd
Acton Green W4 . . . . .37 B1

Grosvenor Rd continued
Pimlico SW1 . . . . . . **161** A4
Richmond TW10 . . . . .54 A2
Grosvenor Residences
🖪 W1 . . . . .39 C3
Grosvenor Sq W1 . . **117** C4
Grosvenor St W1 . . **118** A4
Grosvenor Terr
SE5 . . . . .48 B4
Grosvenor The
NW11 . . . . .2 A4
Grosvenor Wharf Rd
E14 . . . . .42 C2
Grote's Bldgs SE3 . .53 A1
Grote's PI SE3 . . . . .53 A1
Groton Rd SW18 . . . .71 A2
Grotto Ct SE1 . . . . **136** C4
Grotto Pas W1 . . . . **103** B4
Grove Crescent Rd
E15 . . . . .19 C2
Grove Ct
Camberwell SE5 . . . . .49 A1
Clapham SW4 . . . . . .61 B4
South Kensington
SW10 . . . . **143** A1
St John's Wood
NW8 . . . . **89** B4
Grovedale Rd N19 . . . .4 C2
Grove Dwellings
E1 . . . . .32 B4
Grove End NW5 . . . . .13 A4
Grove End Ho
NW8 . . . . **89** B3
Grove End Rd
NW8 . . . . **89** B3
Grove Gdns NW8 . . **90** B3
Grove Hall Ct
Bow E3 . . . . .26 C3
St John's Wood
NW8 . . . . **89** A4
Grove Hill Rd SE5 . .64 A4
Grove Ho
Blackheath SE3 . . . . .53 B1
Chelsea SW3 . . . . . **158** B4
Grove La SE5 . . . . . . .64 A4
Groveland Ct EC4 **109** A1
Grovelands Cl SE5 . .49 A1
Grove Lane Terr
SE5 . . . . .48 C1
Groveley Ho 🖾 N4 . . .6 B4
Grove Lo SW4 . . . . . .61 B3
Grove Mans
London SW4 . . . . . . .60 B3
🖾 Shepherd's Bush
W6 . . . . .39 B4
🖪 Stamford Hill N16 . .7 C3
Grove Mews W6 . . . .39 B3
GROVE PARK 45 B2
Grove Park Bridge
W4 . . . . .45 B3
Grove Park Gdns
W4 . . . . .45 B3
Grove Park Mews
W4 . . . . .45 B3
Grove Park Prim Sch
W4 . . . . .45 B4
Grove Park Rd
W4 . . . . .45 A3
Grove Park Terr
W4 . . . . .45 A3
Grove Pk SE5 . . . . . .49 A1
Grove PI Acton W3 . .28 B1
Balham SW12 . . . . . .61 A1
Hampstead NW3 . . . . .2 C1
Grover Ct SE13 . . . . .52 A1

Grove Rd Acton W3. .28 B1
Barnes SW13 . . . . . . .46 B1
Bow E3 . . . . .26 A3
Richmond TW10 . . . . .54 B1
Willesden NW2 . . . . . .9 B2
Grover Ho
🖾 London SW4 . . . . .61 B2
Vauxhall SE11 . . . . . **149** A1
Groveside Ct
SW11 . . . . **167** B2
Grove St SE8 . . . . . . .41 B1
Grove Terr NW5 . . . . .13 A4
Grove Terrace Mews
NW5 . . . . .4 A1
Grove The
Dulwich SE21 . . . . . . .76 C3
Hendon NW11 . . . . . . .1 A4
Highgate N6 . . . . .3 C3
Stroud Green N4 . . . . .5 B4
Grove Vale SE22 . . . .64 B3
Grove Way SW9 . . . **173** A3
Grovewood 🖸
TW9 . . . . .44 C2
Grummant Rd
SE15 . . . . .49 B2
Grundy St E14 . . . . . .34 A3
Guardian Angels RC
Prim Sch E3 . . . . . .26 A2
Guards Mus The★
SW1 . . . . **133** A3
Guation Ave SE24 . . .63 A2
Guerin Sq E3 . . . . . . .26 B2
Guernsey Gr SE24 . . .75 B4
Guernsey Ho 🔟
N1 . . . . .15 B2
Guernsey Rd 🖽
N1 . . . . .15 B2
Guildford Gr SE10 . .52 A2
Guildford Ho 🖾
SE5 . . . . .48 B1
Guildford Rd
SW8 . . . . **172** A4
Guild Hall★ EC2. . **109** A2
Guildhall Bldgs
EC2 . . . . **109** B2
Guildhall Ho EC2 . . **109** B2
Guildhall Sch Music &
Drama EC2 . . . . . . **109** A4
Guildhall Yd EC2 . . **109** A2
Guildhouse St
SW1 . . . . **146** C3
Guilford PI WC1 . . . . **94** C1
Guilford St WC1 . . . . **94** B1
Guillemot Ct 🖪
SE8 . . . . .51 B4
Guinness Cl E9 . . . . .18 A1
Guinness Ct
Chelsea SW3 . . . . . **144** C3
Finsbury EC1 . . . . . . **97** A3
Primrose Hill NW8 . . **80** B3
Whitechapel E1 . . . . **111** B1
Guinness Sq SE1 . . **152** A4
Guinness Trust Bldgs
Bermondsey SE1 . . **138** A4
🔼 Bethnal Green
E2 . . . . .24 C3
Chelsea SW3 . . . . . **144** C3
Hammersmith W6 . . . .39 B1
Kennington SE11 . . **150** A2
Guion Rd SW6 . . . . **165** A2
Gujarat Ho 🖪 N16 . . . .7 A1

Gulland Wlk 🟤
N1 . . . . .15 B2
Gullane Ho 🖾 E3 . . . .26 B3
Gulliver St SE16 . . . .41 B3
Gulston Wlk SW3 **145** A3
Gunmakers La E3 . . .26 A4
GUNNERSBURY 37 A2
Gunnersbury Avenue
(North Circular Rd)
W3 . . . . .36 C3
Gunnersbury Cl 🟤
W4 . . . . .37 A1
Gunnersbury Cres
W3 . . . . .36 B3
Gunnersbury Ct 🟤
W3 . . . . .37 A4
Gunnersbury Dr
W5 . . . . .36 B4
Gunnersbury Gdns
W3 . . . . .36 B4
Gunnersbury La
W3 . . . . .36 C4
Gunnersbury Mews 🟤
W4 . . . . .37 A1
Gunnersbury Park
W3 . . . . .36 C2
Gunnersbury Park
Mus★ W3 . . . . . . .36 C3
Gunnersbury Sta
W4 . . . . .37 A1
Gunners Rd SW18 . . .71 C3
Gunpowder Sq
EC4 . . . . **107** C2
Gun St E1 . . . . **110** C3
Gunstor Rd N16 . . . . .16 A4
Gunter Gr SW6 . . . **156** C2
Gunterstone Rd
W14 . . . . **140** B2
Gunthorpe St E1 . . **111** A2
Gunwhale Cl SE16 . .32 C1
Gun Wharf
Old Ford E3 . . . . .26 A4
Wapping E1 . . . . .32 B1
Gurdon Ho 🖾 E14 . . .33 B3
Gurdon Rd SE7 . . . . .43 C1
Gurney Ho
Bayswater W2 . . . . **100** A2
🔼 Bethnal Green
E2 . . . . .24 C3
Gurney Rd SW6 . . . . .59 B4
Guthrie Ct SE1 . . . **135** C3
Guthrie St SW3 . . . **144** A2
Gutter La EC2 . . . . **108** C2
Guyscliff Rd SE13 . .67 B2
Guy's Hospl SE1 . . **137** C4
Guy's Hospl Sch
SE1 . . . . **123** C1
Guy St SE1 . . . . . . **137** C4
Gwalior Rd SW15 . .57 C4
Gwendolen Ave
SW15 . . . . .57 C2
Gwendolen Cl
SW15 . . . . .57 C2
Gwendwr Rd
W14 . . . . **140** B2
Gwent Ct 🗓 SE16 . .32 C1
Gwilym Maries Ho 🖪
E2 . . . . .25 A2
Gwyn Cl SW6 . . . . . **156** C1
Gwynne Ho
Finsbury WC1 . . . . . . **95** B3
🖪 Streatham SW2 . . .74 B3
Whitechapel E1 . . . . .32 A4
Gwynne PI WC1 . . . . **95** A3
Gwynne Rd SW11 **167** C2
Gye Ho 🖪 SW4 . . . . .62 A3

Gylcote Cl SE5 . . . . . .63 C3

H

Haarlem Rd 🖽
W14 . . . . .39 C3
Haberdasher PI
N1 . . . . .24 A2 **98** A4
Haberdashers' Aske's
Hatcham Coll
SE4 . . . . .51 A1
Haberdasher St
N1 . . . . **97** C4
Hackford Rd SW9 **173** A4
Hackford Wlk
SW9 . . . . **173** B3
HACKNEY 17 A2
Hackney Central Sta
E8 . . . . .17 A2
Hackney Coll (Poplar
Ctr) E3 . . . . .27 B1
Hackney Com Coll
N1 . . . . .24 A2 **98** B4
Hackney Downs Sta
E8 . . . . .17 A3
Hackney Free &
Parochial CE Sec
Sch E9 . . . . .17 C2
Hackney Gr E8 . . . . .17 A2
Hackney Hospl E9. .18 A3
Hackney Rd E2 . . . . .24 C3
Hackney Stadium
Mkt★ E15 . . . . .18 C2
HACKNEY WICK 18 C2
Hackney Wick E9 . . .18 C2
Hackney Wick Sta
E9 . . . . .18 C2
Hackworth Point 🖾
E3 . . . . .27 A2
Hacon Sq 🖪 E8 . . . . .17 A1
Haddo Ho
Gospel Oak NW5 . . . . .13 A4
Greenwich SE10 . . . . .52 A4
Haddon Ct W3 . . . . . .29 B2
Haddo St SE10 . . . . .52 B4
Haden Ct N4 . . . . .5 C2
Hadfield Ho 🖸 E1 . **111** C1
Hadleigh Cl 🖪 E1 . . .25 B1
Hadleigh Ho 🔟
E1 . . . . .25 B1
Hadleigh St E2 . . . . .25 B2
Hadley Ct N16 . . . . . . .7 C3
Hadley Gdns W4 . . . .37 C1
Hadley St NW1 . . . . . .13 A2
Hadlow Ho SE17. . **152** B2
Hadrian Cl 🖪 E3 . . . .26 C4
Hadrian Ct SE4 . . . . .66 C4
Hadrian Est 🖪 E2 . . .24 C3
Hadrian St SE10 . . . .43 A1
Hadstock Ho NW1 . . **93** C4
Hadyn Park Ct 🖪
W12 . . . . .38 C4
Hadyn Park Rd
W12 . . . . .38 C4
Hafer Rd SW11 . . . . .60 B3
HAGGERSTON 24 B3
Haggerston Rd E8. .24 B4
Haggerston Sch
E2 . . . . .24 B3
Haggerston Studios
🖾 E8 . . . . .24 B4
Hague Prim Sch
E2 . . . . .25 A1
Hague St 🖪 E2 .24 C2 **99** C3
Haig Ho 🖪 E2 . . . . . .24 C3

Hailsham Ave
SW2 . . . . 74 B2
Hainford Cl SE4 . . . . . . 65 C3
Haining Cl 3 W4 . . . . 36 C1
Hainton Cl E1 . . . . 32 A3
Halcomb St N1 . . . . . . 24 A4
Halcrow St E1 . . . . 32 A4
Halcyon Wharf
E1 . . . . 125 C2
Haldane Pl SW18 . . . . 71 A3
Haldane Rd SW6 . . . . 155 A3
Haldon Rd SW18 . . . . 58 B1
Hale Ho SW1 . . . . 147 C2
Hales Ho 3 SW12 . . . 73 A4
Hales Prior N1 . . . . . . 84 C1
Hales St SE8 . . . . 51 C3
Hale St E14 . . . . 34 A2
Halesworth Rd
SE13 . . . . 67 A4
Half Moon Cres
N1 . . . . 85 A2
Half Moon Ct EC1 . . 108 C3
Half Moon La
SE24 . . . . 63 B1
Halfmoon Pas E1 . . . 111 A1
Half Moon St W1 . . . 118 B1
Halford Ho 3
SW15 . . . . 57 C2
Halford Rd
Richmond TW10 . . . . 54 A2
West Brompton
SW6 . . . . 155 B3
Haliday Ho 3 . . . . 15 C2
Haliday Wlk 4 N1 . . . 15 C2
Halidon Cl E9 . . . . 17 B3
Haliwell Ho 3 NW6 . . 78 A3
Halkett Ho 3 E2 . . . . 25 B4
Halkin Arc SW1 . . . . 131 A2
Halkin Mews
SW1 . . . . 131 B2
Halkin Pl SW1 . . . . . . 131 B2
Halkin St SW1 . . . . . . 131 C3
Hallam Ct W1 . . . . . . 104 B4
Hallam Ho
London SW9 . . . . . . 173 B4
Pimlico SW1 . . . . . . 147 A1
Hallam Mews W1 . . . 104 B4
Hallam St W1 . . . . . . 104 B4
Halley Gdns SE13 . . . 67 C3
Halley Ho
16 Bethnal Green
E2 . . . . 24 C3
6 Cubitt Town
SE10 . . . . 43 B1
Halley Prim Sch
E14 . . . . 33 A4
Halley St E14 . . . . 33 A4
Hallfield Jun & Inf
Schs W2 . . . . 100 B1
Hall Gate NW8 . . . . . 89 A4
Halliday Ho 6 E1 . . . 111 C1
Halliford St N1 . . . . . . 15 C1
Halling Ho SE1 . . . . . 137 C3
Hallings Wharf
Studios 2 E15 . . . . 27 C4
Halliwell Ct 4
SE22 . . . . 64 C2
Halliwell Rd SW2 . . . 62 B1
Hall Oak Wlk NW6 . . 10 B2
Hall Pl W2 . . . . 89 B1
Hall Rd Leyton E15 . . 19 C4
St John's Wood
NW8 . . . . 89 A3
Hall Sch The NW3 . . . 11 C2
Hall St SW Wimbledon
SW15 . . . . 68 C1

Hall St EC1 . . . . 96 B4
Hallsville Prim Sch
E16 . . . . 35 C3
Hallsville Rd E16 . . . . 35 B3
Hall Twr W2 . . . . 101 C4
Halpin Pl SE17 . . . . . 151 C3
Halsbury Ho 4
N7 . . . . 14 B4
Halsbury Rd W12 . . . 30 A1
Halsey St SW3 . . . . . . 144 C4
Halsmere Rd SE5 . . . 48 A2
Halstead Ct N1 . . . . . . 87 C1
Halston Cl SW11 . . . . 60 B1
Halstow 2 NW5 . . . . . 12 C2
Halstow Prim Sch
SE10 . . . . 43 C1
Halstow Rd
Greenwich SE3,
SE10 . . . . 43 C1
Kensal Green NW10 . 22 C2
Halton Cross St
N1 . . . . 86 B4
Halton Ho 22 N1 . . . . 15 A1
Halton Mans N1 . . . . 15 A1
Halton Pl N1 . . . . 86 C4
Halton Rd N1 . . . . 86 B4
Halyard Ho E14 . . . . . 42 B3
Hambalt Rd SW4 . . . . 61 B2
Hambledon SE17 . . . . 48 C4
Hambledon Chase
N4 . . . . 5 A4
Hambledon Ho E5 . . . 17 A4
Hambledon Pl
SE21 . . . . 76 B3
Hambledon Rd
SW18 . . . . 70 B4
Hamble St SW6 . . . . . 59 A4
Hambley Ho 5
SE16 . . . . 40 A2
Hamblyn Ct N16 . . . . 7 B4
Hambridge Way
SW2 . . . . 74 C4
Hambrook Ct 12
NW5 . . . . 13 A4
Hamers Ho 10
SW2 . . . . 74 C4
Hamilton Cl
Rotherhithe SE16 . . . 41 A4
St John's Wood
NW8 . . . . 89 B3
Hamilton Ct W9 . . . . 88 C4
Hamilton Gdns
NW8 . . . . 89 A4
Hamilton Hall
NW8 . . . . 78 C1
Hamilton Ho
22 Bow E3 . . . . 26 B2
Chiswick W4 . . . . 46 A4
Kensington W8 . . . . 128 A4
1 Poplar E14 . . . . . . 33 B2
Putney SW15 . . . . . . 56 C2
18 Richmond TW9 . . 44 C2
St John's Wood
NW8 . . . . 89 B4
Hamilton La N5 . . . . . 15 A4
Hamilton Lo 57 E1 . . 25 B1
Hamilton Mews
W1 . . . . 132 A4
Hamilton Pk N5 . . . . . 15 A4
Hamilton Pk W
N5 . . . . 15 A4
Hamilton Pl W1 . . . . 117 C1
Hamilton Rd
Acton W4 . . . . 38 A4
Hendon NW11 . . . . . . 1 A4
Willesden NW10 . . . . 8 C3

Hamilton Sq SE1 . . . 137 C4
Hamilton St SE8 . . . . 51 C4
Hamilton Terr
NW8 . . . . 89 A4
Hamlet Ct
18 Hammersmith
W6 . . . . 39 A2
Kennington SE11 . . . 150 A2
Hamlet Gdns W6 . . . 38 C2
Hamlet Gdns Ind Est
E9 . . . . 18 C1
Hamlet The SE5 . . . . . 63 C4
Hamlets Way E3 . . . . 26 B1
Hamlet The SE5 . . . . . 63 C4
Hamlet Way SE1 . . . 137 C4
Hammelton Rd 3 . . . . 48 A2
Hammersley Ho 3
SE14 . . . . 50 B3
HAMMERSMITH . . . 39 B2
Hammersmith Bridge
Rd W6, SW13 . . . . . . 39 B1
Hammersmith
Broadway
Hammersmith W6 . . . 39 B1
5 Hammersmith
W6 . . . . 39 B2
Hammersmith Flyover
W6 . . . . 39 B1
Hammersmith Gr
W6 . . . . 39 B3
W12 . . . . 30 A3
Hammersmith Hospl
W6 . . . . 39 B3
Hammersmith Rd
Hammersmith W6 . . . 39 C2
Kensington W14 . . . 140 B4
Hammersmith Sta
W6 . . . . 39 B2
Hammersmith Terr 8
W6 . . . . 38 C1
Hammett St EC3 . . . 124 C4
Hammond Ho
10 Deptford SE14 . . . 50 B3
Millwall E14 . . . . 42 A3
Hammond Lo 6
W9 . . . . 31 C4
Hammonds SW5 . . . . 13 B2
Hamond Sq N1 . . . . . 24 A3
Hampden Cl NW1 . . . 83 C2
Hampden Gurney CE
Prim Sch W1 . . . . . . 102 B2
Hampden Gurney St
W1 . . . . 102 C1
Hampden Rd N19 . . . 4 C2
Hampshire Ct 8
SW13 . . . . 46 B1
Hampshire Hog La
8 Hammersmith
W6 . . . . 39 A1
6 Hammersmith
W6 . . . . 39 A2
Hampshire Sch The
SW7 . . . . 130 A3
Hampshire St
NW5 . . . . 13 C2
Hampson Way
SW8 . . . . 172 C4
HAMPSTEAD 11 B2
Hampstead Coll of
Fine Arts &
Humanities NW3 . . . 12 A2
Hampstead Gate
NW3 . . . . 11 B3
Hampstead Gn
NW3 . . . . 12 A3
Hampstead Gr NW3 . 2 B1

Hampstead Heath*
NW3 . . . . 2 C3
Hampstead Heath Sta
NW3 . . . . 12 A4
Hampstead High St
NW3 . . . . 11 C4
Hampstead Hill Gdns
NW3 . . . . 12 A4
Hampstead Hill Sch
NW3 . . . . 12 A3
Hampstead La NW3 . . 3 A4
Hampstead Parochial
CE Prim Sch
NW3 . . . . 11 B4
Hampstead Rd
NW1 . . . . 92 C4
Hampstead Sch
NW2 . . . . 10 A4
Hampstead Sq 1
NW3 . . . . 2 B1
Hampstead Sta
NW3 . . . . 11 B4
Hampstead West 4
NW6 . . . . 10 C2
Hampstead Wlk 1
E3 . . . . 26 B4
Hampton Cl NW6 . . . 23 C2
Hampton Ct
1 Islington N1 . . . . . 15 A2
13 Rotherhithe
SE16 . . . . 32 C1
Hampton St SE1 . . . 150 B3
Hamstead Gates 13
NW5 . . . . 13 A2
Ham St TW10 . . . . . . 119 B4
Hana Mews E5 . . . . . . 17 A4
Hanbury Ho
Bethnal Green E1 . . 111 B4
South Lambeth
SW8 . . . . 162 B3
Hanbury Mews N1 . . 87 A3
Hanbury Rd W3 . . . . . 37 A4
Hanbury St E1 . . . . . . 111 A4
Hancock Nunn Ho 6
NW3 . . . . 12 B1
Hancock Rd E3 . . . . . 27 B2
Handa Wlk 3 N1 . . . . 15 B2
Hand Ct WC1 . . . . . . 107 A3
Handel Mans
Barnes SW13 . . . . . . 47 B3
Bloomsbury WC1 . . . 94 B2
Handel St WC1 . . . . . 94 B2
Handel Way E14 . . . . 105 B3
Handforth Rd
SW9 . . . . 163 B2
Handley Rd E9 . . . . . . 25 B4
Hands Wlk E16 . . . . . 35 C3
Hanford Cl SW18 . . . 70 C3
Hankey Pl SE1 . . . . . 137 C3
Hanley Ct N4 . . . . 5 B3
Hanley Gdns N4 . . . . 5 B3
Hanley Rd N4, N19 . . 5 A3
Hanmer Wlk N7 . . . . . 5 B2
Hannah Mary Way
SE1 . . . . 153 C3
Hannay La N8 . . . . . . 4 C4
Hannay Wlk SW16 . . 73 C2
Hannell Rd SW6 . . . . 154 B2
Hannen Ho SE5 . . . . . 63 C4
Hannen Rd SE27 . . . . 75 A1
Hannibal Rd E1 . . . . . 32 B4
Hannington Rd
SW4 . . . . 61 A4
Hanover Ave E16 . . . 35 C1
Hanover Cl TW9 . . . . 44 C3
Hanover Ct
Shepherd's Bush
W12 . . . . 29 C1

Hanover Ct continued
Stamford Hill N16 . . . 7 B3
Hanover Gate Mans
NW1 . . . . 90 B2
Hanover Gdns
SE11 . . . . 163 B3
Hanover Ho NW8 . . . 80 A1
Hanover Mans 5
SW2 . . . . 62 C2
Hanover Pk SE15 . . . 49 C2
Hanover Pl
16 Bow E3 . . . . 26 B2
St Giles WC2 . . . . . . 106 B1
Hanover Rd NW10 . . 22 B4
Hanover Sq W1 . . . . 104 B1
Hanover St W1 . . . . . 104 B1
Hanover Stps W2 . . . 102 B1
Hanover Terr NW1 . . 90 C3
Hanover Terrace
Mews NW1 . . . . 90 B3
Hanover West Ind Est
NW10 . . . . 20 C2
Hanover Yd N1 . . . . . 86 C2
Hansard Mews
W14 . . . . 39 C4
Hanscomb Mews
SW4 . . . . 61 B3
Hans Cres SW1 . . . . 130 C2
Hansler Ct 14
SW19 . . . . 70 A3
Hansler Rd SE22 . . . . 64 B2
Hanson Cl
Balham SW12 . . . . . . 73 A4
Mortlake SW14 . . . . . 55 B4
Hanson Ho E1 . . . . . 125 C4
Hanson St W1 . . . . . 104 C4
Hans Pl SW1 . . . . . . 130 C2
Hans Rd SW3 . . . . . . 130 C2
Hans St SW1 . . . . . . 131 A1
Hanway Ho SW9 . . . 173 C4
Hanway Pl W1 . . . . . 105 B2
Hanway St W1 . . . . . 105 B2
Hanworth Ho SE5 . . . 48 A3
Harben Rd NW6 . . . . 11 B1
Harberson Rd
SW12 . . . . 73 A3
Harberton Rd N19 . . 4 B3
Harbet Rd W2 . . . . . 101 C3
Harbinger Prim Sch
E14 . . . . 42 A2
Harbinger Rd E14 . . . 42 A2
Harbin Ho 5 SW2 . . 74 C3
Harbledown Ho
SE1 . . . . 137 B3
Harbledown Rd
SW6 . . . . 165 B4
Harbord Cl SE5 . . . . . 48 C1
Harbord Ho 5
SE16 . . . . 40 C2
Harbord St SW6 . . . . 47 C2
Harborough Sch
N19 . . . . 4 C2
Harbour Ave
SW10 . . . . 167 A3
Harbour Exchange Sq
E14 . . . . 42 A4
Harbour Rd SE5 . . . . 63 B4
Harbridge Ave
SW15 . . . . 68 C4
Harbut Rd SW11 . . . . 59 C3
Harcombe Rd N16 . . . 7 A1
Harcourt Ho
Clapham SW8 . . . . . 171 B2

Harcourt Ho *continued*
Marylebone W1 . . . . **104** A2
4 Willesden NW10 . . . **9** B2
Harcourt Rd SE4 . . . . **66** B4
Harcourt St W1 . . . . **102** B3
Harcourt Terr
SW10 . . . . **142** B1
Hardcastle Ho
3 New Cross Gate
SE14 . . . . **51** A2
8 Peckham SE15 . . .**49** C2
Hardel Rise SW2 . . .**75** A3
Hardel Wlk SW2,
SW2 . . . .**74** C4
Harden Ho SE5 . . . . **49** A1
Harders Rd SE15 . . **50** A1
Hardess St SE24 . . . **63** B4
Hardham Ho **5**
SW2 . . . .**62** C1
Harding Cl SE17 . . . **48** B4
Hardinge Rd
NW10 . . . . **22** B4
Hardinge St E1 . . . . **32** B3
Harding Ho SW13 . .**47** A4
Hardington **2**
NW1 . . . . **12** C1
Hardwick Ho **14**
E3 . . . . **27** A2
Hardwick Mews
WC1 . . . . **95** A3
Hardwicke Ho W4 . .**37** C2
Hardwick Ho
London SW8 . . . . . . **171** B2
Marylebone NW8 . . . . **90** B2
Hardwick St EC1 . . **95** C3
Hardwick's Way
SW18 . . . . **58** C2
Hardwidge St
SE1 . . . . **138** A4
Hardy Ave 4 E16 . .**35** C1
Hardy Cl SE16 . . . . .**40** C4
Hardy Cotts **2**
SE10 . . . .**52** C4
Hardy Ct SE3 . . . . . .**53** B4
Hardy Rd SE3 . . . . . **53** B4
Hare and Billet Rd
SE3 . . . .**52** C1
Harecourt Rd N1 . . **15** B2
Hare Ct EC4 . . . . . . **107** B1
Haredale Ho
SE16 . . . . **139** B3
Haredale Rd SE24 . .**63** B3
Harefield Mews
SE4 . . . .**66** B4
Harefield Rd SE4 . . **66** B4
Hare Marsh
E2 . . . .**24** C1 **99** B2
Hare Pl EC4 . . . . . . **107** C1
Hare Row E2 . . . . . . **25** A3
Hare Wlk N1 . . . . . . **24** A3
Harewood Ave
NW1 . . . . **90** B1
Harewood Pl W1 . . **104** B1
Harewood Row
NW1 . . . . **102** B4
Harfield Gdns **1**
SE5 . . . .**64** A4
Harfleur Ct SE11 . . **150** A3
Harford Ho
Camberwell SE5 . . . . **48** B4
Notting Hill W11 . . . . **31** B4
Harford Mews **5**
N19 . . . .**4** C1
Harford St E1 . . . . . .**26** A1

Hargrave Mans **3**
N19 . . . .**4** C2
Hargrave Park Prim
Sch N19 . . . . **4** B2
Hargrave Pk N19 . . . .**4** B2
Hargrave Pl N7 . . . .**13** C3
Hargrave Rd N19 . . . .**4** B2
Hargraves Ho **14**
W12 . . . .**30** A2
Hargwyne St SW9 . .**62** B4
Harkness Ho E1 . . .**111** C1
Harlech Twr **5**
W3 . . . .**37** B4
Harlescott Rd
SE15 . . . .**65** C3
HARLESDEN **21** B4
Harlesden Gdns
NW10 . . . .**21** B4
Harlesden Plaza **2**
NW10 . . . .**21** B3
Harlesden Prim Sch
NW10 . . . .**21** A3
Harlesden Rd
NW10 . . . .**21** C4
Harlesden Sta
NW10 . . . .**20** C3
Harleyford Ct
SW8 . . . . **162** C4
Harleyford Manor **8**
W3 . . . .**28** B1
Harleyford Rd
SE11 . . . . **162** C4
Harleyford St
SE11 . . . . **163** B3
Harley Gdns
SW10 . . . . **143** A1
Harley Gr E3 . . . .**26** B2
Harley Ho NW1 . . . . **91** C1
Harley Pl W1 . . . . . **104** A3
Harley St W1 . . . . . **104** A3
Harley Villas
NW10 . . . .**21** A3
Harling Ct SW11 . . **168** C2
Harlowe Ho **13** E8 . .**24** B4
Harlynwood **19**
SE5 . . . .**48** B3
Harman Cl
Bermondsey SE1 . . . **153** B1
Cricklewood NW2 . . . .**1** A1
Harman Dr NW2 . . . .**10** A4
Harmon Ho **7**
SE8 . . . .**41** B2
Harmood Gr NW1 . .**13** A1
Harmood Ho **7**
NW1 . . . .**13** A1
Harmood St NW1 . .**13** A1
Harmsworth St
SE17 . . . . **150** A1
Harmsworth Way
SW19 . . . .**69** B1
Harney Ct SE14 . . . .**51** A2
Harold Ct SE16 . . . . **40** C4
Harold Est SE1 . . . . **138** B1
Harold Ho **16** E2 . . **25** C3
Harold Laski Ho
EC1 . . . .**96** B3
Harold Maddison Ho
SE17 . . . . **150** B2
Harold Rd NW10 . . .**20** C2
Harold Wilson Ho
SW6 . . . . **155** A3
Harp Alley EC4 . . . **108** A2
Harpenden Rd SE27,
SW16 . . . .**75** A2

Harpenmead Point
NW2 . . . .**1** B2
Harper Ho **3** SW9 . .**63** A4
Harper Mews
SW17 . . . .**71** B1
Harper Rd SE1 . . . . **137** A2
Harp La EC3 . . . . . . **124** A3
Harpley Sq E1 . . . . . **25** C1
Harpsden St
SW11 . . . . **169** B3
Harpur Mews
WC1 . . . . **106** C4
Harpur St WC1 . . . . **106** C4
Harrier Ho **9**
SW11 . . . .**60** A4
Harriet Cl E8 . . . . . . **24** C4
Harriet Ho SW6 . . . **156** B1
Harriet St SW1 . . . . **131** A3
Harriet Tubman Cl **2**
SW2 . . . .**74** C4
Harriet Wlk SW1 . . **131** A3
Harrington Ct
South Kensington
SW7 . . . . **143** C4
3 West Kilburn W9 . **23** B2
Harrington Gdns
SW7 . . . . **142** C3
Harrington Ho
Regent's Pk NW1 . . . **92** C4
Westminster SW1 . . . **147** C2
Harrington Rd
SW7 . . . . **143** B4
Harrington Sq
NW1 . . . . **82** C1
Harrington St
NW1 . . . . **92** C4
Harriott Cl SE10 . . . **43** B2
Harriott Ho **11** E1 . .**32** B3
Harris Girl's Acad
SE15 . . . .**65** B2
Harris Ho
11 Bow E3 . . . .**26** C2
2 Brixton SW9 . . . **62** C4
Harrison Ho SE17 . . **151** B2
Harrison Rd NW10 . **20** C4
Harrisons Ct **1**
SE14 . . . .**50** C4
Harrison St WC1 . . **94** B3
Harris St SE5 . . . . . .**48** C3
Harrodian Sch The
SW13 . . . .**46** B3
Harrogate Ct **2**
SE26 . . . .**76** C1
Harrold Ho **1**
NW3 . . . .**11** B1
Harroway Rd
SW11 . . . . **167** C2
Harrowby St W1 . . **102** B2
Harrowgate Ho **22**
E9 . . . . **17** C2
Harrowgate Rd
E9 . . . . **18** A1
Harrow La E14 . . . . .**34** B2
Harrow Pl E1 . . . . . **110** B2
Harrow Rd
Little Venice W2 . . . . **101** A3
Westbourne Green W2,
W9 . . . . **23** C1
Harrow St NW1 . . . **102** A4
Harry Gosling Prim
Sch E1 . . . . **111** C1
Harry Hinkins Ho
SE17 . . . . **151** A1
Harry Lambourn Ho
10 SE15 . . . . **50** A3
Hartfield Terr E3 . . **26** C3
Hartham Cl N7 . . . . **14** A3

Hartham Rd N7 . . . . **14** A3
Hart Ho SW2 . . . . . . **74** C3
Hartington Ct
Chiswick W4 . . . .**45** A3
South Lambeth
SW8 . . . . **172** A4
Hartington Rd
Chiswick W4 . . . .**45** B2
South Lambeth
SW8 . . . . **162** A1
Hartismere Rd
SW6 . . . . **155** A2
Hartlake Rd E9 . . . . **18** A2
Hartland NW1 . . . . . **83** A3
Hartland Rd
Camden Town
NW1 . . . . **13** A1
Kilburn NW6 . . . .**23** B4
Hartley Ho
Bermondsey SE1 . . . **153** A4
Putney SW15 . . . .**56** C2
Hartley St E2 . . . . . . **25** B2
Hartnoll Ho **4** N7 . .**14** C3
Hartnoll St N7 . . . . .**14** B3
Harton Lodge **2**
SE8 . . . .**51** C2
Harton St SE8 . . . . . **51** C2
Hartopp Ct **20** N16 . .**7** A1
Hartopp Point
SW6 . . . . **154** B2
Hartshorn Alley
EC3 . . . . **110** B1
Hart's La SE14 . . . . .**51** A2
Hart St EC3 . . . . **124** B4
Hartswood Ho **10**
SW2 . . . .**74** A3
Hartswood Rd
W12 . . . .**38** B3
Hartwell Cl SE22 . . **64** C3
Hartwell St E8 . . . . .**16** B2
Harvard Ct NW6 . . . **11** A3
Harvard Hill W4 . . . .**45** A4
Harvard Ho
3 Camberwell
SE17 . . . .**48** A4
Putney SW15 . . . .**57** C1
Harvard Mans **7**
SW11 . . . .**59** C3
Harvard Rd
Acton Green
W4 . . . .**37** B1
Gunnersbury W4 . . . .**37** A1
Lewisham SE13 . . . . .**67** B2
Harvey Ct SW11 . . . **168** B4
Harvey Ho
10 Bethnal Green
E1 . . . .**25** A1
Brentford TW8 . . . . . .**36** A1
Pimlico SW1 . . . . **147** C1
Shoreditch N1 . . . . . .**87** C3
Harvey Lo **8** W9 . . . **31** C4
Harvey Point **1**
E16 . . . .**35** C4
Harvey Rd SE5 . . . . .**48** C2
Harvey St N1 . . . . . . **87** C3
Harvington Wlk
E8 . . . . **16** C1
Harvist Rd NW6 . . . **23** A3
Harwood Ct
Putney SW15 . . . .**57** B3
Shoreditch N1 . . . . . .**87** C3
Harwood Point
SE16 . . . . **41** B4
Harwood Rd SW6 . . **156** A1
Harwood Terr
SW6 . . . . **166** A4

Hascombe Ho **11**
SW15 . . . .**69** A3
Hascombe Terr **2**
SE5 . . . .**48** C1
Haselrigge Rd
SW4 . . . .**61** C3
Hasker St SW3 . . . . **144** B4
Haslam Cl N1 . . . . . **14** C1
Haslam Ho **12** N1 . . **15** B1
Haslam St SE15 . . . **49** B2
Haslemere Ave
SW18 . . . .**71** A2
Haslemere Ct **5**
N16 . . . .**7** A3
Haslemere Ind Est
SW18 . . . .**71** A2
Haslemere Rd N8 . . .**5** A4
Hassard St E2 . . . . . **24** B3
Hassett Rd E9 . . . . . **18** A2
Hassop Rd NW2 . . . . .**9** C4
Hastings Cl **17**
SE15 . . . .**49** C3
Hastings Ho **6**
W12 . . . .**30** A2
Hastings Hos WC1 . **94** A3
Hastings St WC1 . . . **94** A3
Hatcham Mews Bsns
Ctr SE14 . . . . **50** C2
Hatcham Park Mews
SE14 . . . .**50** C2
Hatcham Park Rd
SE14 . . . .**50** C2
Hatchard Rd N19 . . . .**5** A2
Hatchers Mews
SE1 . . . . **138** B3
Hatcliffe Almshouses
SE10 . . . .**43** A1
Hatcliffe St SE10 . . .**43** B1
Hatfield Cl SE3 . . . . **53** C3
Hatfield Ho EC1 . . . **96** C1
Hatfield Rd W4 . . . . **37** C4
Hatfields SE1 . . . . . **121** C2
Hathaway Ho
N1 . . . .**24** A3 **98** A4
Hatherley Ct W2 . **100** A2
Hatherley Gr W2 . **100** A2
Hatherley Rd TW9 . **44** B2
Hatherley St SW1 . **147** A3
Hathersage Ct N1 . **15** C3
Hathersley Ho **3**
SW2 . . . .**74** C4
Hathorne Cl **3**
SE15 . . . .**50** A1
Hathway Ho **3**
SE15 . . . .**50** B1
Hathway St **4**
SE15 . . . .**50** B1
Hatley Rd N4, N7 . . . .**5** B2
Hat & Mitre Ct
EC1 . . . . **96** B1
Hatstone Ct NW3 . . **11** B3
Hatteraick St **6**
SE16 . . . .**40** B4
Hatton Gdn EC1 . . **107** C4
Hatton Ho E1 . . . . . **125** C4
Hatton Pl EC1 . . . . **107** C4
Hatton Row NW8 . . **89** C1
Hatton St NW8 . . . . **89** C1
Hatton Wall EC1 . . **107** C4
Haunch of Venison Yd
W1 . . . . **104** A1
Hauteville Court Gdns
3 W6 . . . . **38** B3
Havana Rd SW18,
SW19 . . . .**70** C2

Havannah St E14 . . . . . .41 C4
Havelock Cl 13
  W12 . . . . .30 A2
Havelock Ct 8
  SE15 . . . . .50 A3
Havelock St N1 . . . . . .84 B4
Havelock Terr
  SW8 . . . . .160 B1
Haven Cl SW19 . . . . . .69 C1
Havenpool NW8 . . . . .78 B3
Haven St 18 NW1 . . . . .13 A1
Haven The TW9 . . . . . .54 C4
Havercourt 3
  NW3 . . . . .12 A2
Haverfield Gdns
  TW9 . . . . .44 C3
Haverfield Rd E3 . . . . .26 A2
Haverhill Rd SW12 . . .73 B3
Havering 8 NW1 . . . . .13 A1
Havering Ho N4 . . . . . .6 B4
Havering Pl 32 C3
Haversham Lo NW2 . . .9 C3
Haversham Pl N6 . . . . .3 B2
Haverstock Hill
  NW3 . . . . .12 B2
Haverstock Rd
  NW5 . . . . .12 C3
Haverstock Sch
  NW1 . . . . .12 C2
Haverstock St N1 . . . .86 B1
Havil St SE5 . . . . .49 A2
Havisham Ho
  SE16 . . . . .139 B3
Hawarden Gr
  SE24 . . . . .75 B4
Hawberry Lo N7 . . . . .14 A2
Hawes St N1 . . . . .15 A1
Hawgood St E3 . . . . . .33 C4
Hawke Ho 20 E1 . . . . .25 C1
Hawke Pl 22 SE16 . . . .40 C4
Hawkesbury Rd
  SW15 . . . . .57 A2
Hawkesworth Ho 3
  SW4 . . . . .61 B1
Hawke Twr 4
  SE14 . . . . .51 A4
Hawk Ho 7 SW11 . . . .60 A4
Hawkins Ho 3
  SE8 . . . . .51 C4
Hawkins Rd NW10 . . . .8 A1
Hawkley Gdns
  SE27 . . . . .75 A2
Hawkridge 12
  NW5 . . . . .12 C2
Hawkshaw Cl 28
  SW2 . . . . .74 A4
Hawkshead NW1 . . . .92 C4
Hawkshead Rd
  Acton W4 . . . . .38 A4
  Willesden NW10 . . . . .8 B1
Hawkslade Rd
  SE15 . . . . .65 C2
Hawksley Rd N16 . . . . .7 A1
Hawksmoor Mews
  E1 . . . . .32 A2
Hawksmoor Pl
  E2 . . . . .24 C1 99 B2
Hawksmoor St 8
  W6 . . . . .47 C4
Hawkstone Rd
  SE16 . . . . .40 B2
Hawkwell Wlk N1 . . . .87 A4
Hawley Cres NW1 . . . .13 A1
Hawley Inf Sch
  NW1 . . . . .13 A1

Hawley Mews 4
  NW1 . . . . .13 A1
Hawley Rd 3
  NW1 . . . . .13 A1
Hawley St NW1 . . . . . .13 A1
Haworth Ho 7
  SW2 . . . . .62 C1
Hawstead Rd SE6 . . . .67 A1
Hawthorn Ave E3 . . . .26 B4
Hawthorn Ct
  Putney SW15 . . . . . . .57 A4
  Richmond TW9 . . . . . .45 A2
Hawthorne Cl N1 . . . .16 A2
Hawthorne Ho
  SW1 . . . . .147 A1
Hawthorn Ho
  SE14 . . . . .51 B2
Hawthorn Rd NW10 . . .8 C1
Hawthorn Wlk
  W10 . . . . .23 A1
Hawtrey Rd NW3 . . . .12 A1
Haycroft Gdns
  NW10 . . . . .22 A4
Haycroft Mans
  SW2 . . . . .62 C2
Haycroft Rd SW2 . . . .62 A2
Hay Currie St E14 . . . .34 A3
Hayday Rd E16 . . . . . .35 C4
Hayden Piper Ho
  SW3 . . . . .158 C4
Hayden's Pl W11 . . . . .31 B3
Haydon St E1, EC3 . . .124 C4
Haydon Way
  SW11 . . . . .59 C3
Haydon Wlk 11 . . . . .111 A1
Hayes Ct
  23 Camberwell
  SE5 . . . . .48 B3
  Streatham SW12 . . . . .74 A3
Hayes Gr SE15 . . . . . .65 B3
Hayes Pl NW1 . . . . . . .90 B1
Hayfield Pas 1 . . . . . .25 B1
Hayfield Yd 2 . . . . . . .25 B1
Hay Hill W1 . . . . .118 B3
Hayhurst N1 . . . . .86 B4
Hayles Bldgs
  SE11 . . . . .150 A4
Hayles St SE11 . . . . . .150 A4
Hayling 20 N16 . . . . . .16 A3
Haymans Point
  SE11 . . . . .148 C2
Haymarket SW1 . . . . .119 B3
Haymerle Ho 6
  SE15 . . . . .49 C3
Haymerle Sch
  SE15 . . . . .49 C4
Hayne Ho
  W11 . . . . .31 A1 112 A2
Haynes Ho 3 E9 . . . . .17 C2
Hay's Galleria ★
  SE1 . . . . .124 A2
Hay's La SE1 . . . . . . .124 A2
Hay's Mews W1 . . . . .118 A2
Hay St E2 . . . . .24 C4
Hayter Ho
  W12 . . . . .29 C2
Hayter Rd SW2 . . . . . .62 B2
Haythorn Ho
  SW11 . . . . .167 C3
Hayton Cl 11 E8 . . . . .16 B2
Hayward Ct SW4 . . . .172 B2
Hayward Gallery ★
  SE1 . . . . .121 A2
Hayward Gdns
  SW15 . . . . .57 B1

Hayward Ho N1 . . . . . .85 B2
Haywards Pl EC1 . . . . .96 A2
Hayward's Pl EC1 . . . .96 A2
Haywood Lo 23
  N7 . . . . .13 C3
Hazelbourne Rd
  SW12 . . . . .61 A1
Hazel Cl
  Peckham SE15 . . . . . .49 C1
  Upper Holloway N19 . .4 B2
Hazel Ct SE16 . . . . . . .33 A1
Hazeldon Rd SE4 . . . .66 A2
Hazel Ho
  London SE4 . . . . .66 B4
  8 Maitland Pk
  NW3 . . . . .12 B2
Hazellville Rd N19 . . . .4 C3
Hazelmere Ct 10
  SW2 . . . . .74 B3
Hazelmere Rd
  NW6 . . . . .23 B4
Hazel Rd NW10 . . . . . .22 B2
Hazel Way SE1 . . . . .152 C4
Hazelwood Cl W5 . . . .36 A4
Hazelwood Ho 11
  SE8 . . . . .41 A2
Hazelwood Mans
  SW6 . . . . .164 C4
Hazlebury Rd
  SW6 . . . . .166 B2
Hazledene Rd W4 . . . .45 B4
Hazlewell Rd
  SW15 . . . . .57 B2
Hazlewood Cres
  W10 . . . . .23 A1
Hazlewood Twr
  W10 . . . . .23 B2
Hazlitt Mews
  W14 . . . . .126 A1
Hazlitt Rd W14 . . . . . .126 A1
Headbourne Ho
  SE1 . . . . .137 C2
Headcorn 10 NW5 . . . .12 C2
Headfort Pl SW1 . . . .131 C3
Headington Rd
  SW18 . . . . .71 B2
Headlam Rd SW4 . . . .73 C4
Headlam St E1 . . . . . .25 A1
Heads Mews W11 . . . .31 C3
Head St E1 . . . . .32 C3
Heald St SE8, SE14 . . .51 C2
Healey Ho
  24 Bow E3 . . . . .26 C2
  SW9 . . . . .163 C2
Healey St NW1 . . . . . .13 A2
Hearne Rd W4 . . . . . . .44 C4
Hearn's Bldgs
  SE17 . . . . .151 C3
Hearnshaw St 1
  E14 . . . . .33 A3
Hearn St
  EC2 . . . . .24 A1 98 B1
Heart Hosp The
  W1 . . . . .103 C3
Heart Raido W10 . . . .30 C2
Heathbrook Prim Sch
  SW4 . . . . .170 C4
Heath Brow NW3 . . . . .2 B1
Heath Cl NW11 . . . . . . .2 A4
Heathcote Point 28
  E9 . . . . .17 C2
Heathcote St WC1 . . . .94 C3
Heathcroft W5 . . . . . . .36 A3
Heath Ct
  2 Hampstead
  NW3 . . . . .11 B2

Heath Ct continued
  Stoke Newington N16 . .6 C3
Heath Dr NW3 . . . . . . .11 A3
Heather Cl SW8 . . . . . .61 A4
Heather Ct SW4 . . . .172 B3
Heather Ho 11
  E14 . . . . .34 B3
Heatherley Sch 15 . . . .7 C1
Heatherley Lo 16 . . . . .7 C2
Heather Wlk W10 . . . .23 A1
Heathfield Ave
  SW18 . . . . .71 C4
Heathfield Ct
  3 Bow E3 . . . . .26 C3
  4 Chiswick W4 . . . . . .37 B1
  Wandsworth SW18 . . .71 C4
Heathfield Gdns
  Acton Green W4 . . . . .37 B1
  Blackheath SE3 . . . . . .53 A1
  Wandsworth SW18 . . .59 C1
Heathfield Ho SE3 . . . .53 A1
Heathfield Pk NW2 . . . .9 B2
Heathfield Rd
  South Acton W3 . . . . .37 A4
  Wandsworth SW18 . . .59 C1
Heathfield Sq
  SW18 . . . . .71 C4
Heathfield Terr
  W4 . . . . .37 C1
Heathgate Pl NW3 . . .12 B4
Heath Hurst Rd
  NW3 . . . . .12 A4
Heath La SE3 . . . . .52 C1
Heathland Rd N16 . . . .7 A3
Heath Mans
  3 Hampstead
  NW3 . . . . .11 B4
  Putney SW15 . . . . . . .57 C1
Heathman's Rd
  SW6 . . . . .165 A3
Heath Mead SW19 . . .69 C1
Heathmere Prim Sch
  SW15 . . . . .68 C3
Heath Park Gdns
  NW3 . . . . .2 A1
Heathpool Ct 8
  E1 . . . . .25 A1
Heath Rd SW8 . . . . . .170 B1
Heath Rise SW15 . . . .57 C1
Heath Royal SW15 . . .57 C1
Heathshott 2
  TW10 . . . . .54 A1
Heathside NW3 . . . . . .11 C4
Heathside Prep Sch
  NW3 . . . . .11 B4
Heathstan Rd
  W12 . . . . .29 C3
Heath View NW5 . . . . .12 C4
Heathview Ct
  SW19 . . . . .69 C2
Heathview Gdns
  SW15 . . . . .69 B4
Heath Villas NW3 . . . . .2 C1
Heathville Rd N4,
  N19 . . . . .5 A4
Heathwall St
  SW11 . . . . .60 B1
Heathway SE3 . . . . . . .53 C3
Heathway Ct NW3 . . . .1 C2
Heathwood Ct
  SW12 . . . . .73 B3
Heaton Ho
  Chelsea SW10 . . . . .157 A4
  6 Peckham SE15 . . . .50 A1
Heaton Rd SE15 . . . . .50 A1

Heaven Tree Cl
  N1 . . . . .15 B3
Heaver Rd 24
  SW11 . . . . .59 C4
Hebden Ct 24 E2 . . . . .24 B4
Hebdon Rd SW17 . . . .72 A1
Heber Prim Sch
  SE22 . . . . .64 B1
Heber Rd
  Cricklewood NW2 . . . . .9 C4
  East Dulwich SE22 . . .64 B1
Hebron Rd W6 . . . . . . .39 A3
Heckfield Pl SW6 . . . .155 B1
Heckford Ho E14 . . . . .34 A3
Heckford St E1 . . . . . .32 C2
Hector Cl
  London SW9 . . . . . . .173 B4
  Putney SW15 . . . . . . .57 C2
Hector Ho 14 E2 . . . . .25 A3
Heddington Gr N7 . . . .14 B3
Heddon St W1 . . . . . .118 C4
Hedger's Gr E9 . . . . . .18 A2
Hedger St SE11 . . . . .150 A4
Hedingham Cl 9
  N1 . . . . .15 B1
Hedley Ct SW15 . . . . .57 C1
Hedley Ho E14 . . . . . .42 B3
Hedley Row N5,
  N16 . . . . .15 C3
Hedsor Ho
  E2 . . . . .24 B1 98 C2
Heidegger Cres
  SW13 . . . . .47 A3
Heights The NW3 . . . .11 B4
Heiron St SE17 . . . . . .48 A4
Helby Rd SW4 . . . . . . .61 C1
Heldar Ct SE1 . . . . . .137 C3
Helen Gladstone Ho
  SE1 . . . . .136 A4
Helen Mackay Ho 10
  E14 . . . . .34 C3
Helen Peele Cotts 10
  SE16 . . . . .40 B3
Helenslea Ave
  NW11 . . . . .1 C3
Helen St 6
  SE18 . . . . .25 A3
Helen Taylor Ho 6
  SE16 . . . . .153 B4
Heliport Est The
  SW11 . . . . .167 B1
Helix Ct 17 W11 . . . . .30 C1
Helix Gdns SW2 . . . . .62 B1
Helix Rd SW2 . . . . . . .62 B1
Helix The SW19 . . . . .69 C2
Hellenic Coll of
  London SW1 . . . . . . .130 C1
Hellings St E1 . . . . . .125 C1
Helmet Row EC1 . . . . .97 A2
Helmsdale Ho
  NW6 . . . . .78 A1
Helmsley Pl E8 . . . . . .17 A1
Helmsley St 7 E8 . . . .17 A1
Helperby Rd NW10 . . . .8 A1
Helsby Ct NW8 . . . . . .89 B2
Helsinki Sq SE16 . . . . .41 A3
Helston NW1 . . . . .82 C2
Helston Ho SE11 . . . .149 C2
Hemans Est SW8 . . . .161 C1
Hemans St SW8 . . . . .161 C1

Hemberton Rd
SW9 . . . . **62** A4

Hemingford Rd
N1 . . . . **85** A4

Hemlock Rd W12 . . **29** B2

Hemming St
E1 . . . . .24 C1 **99** C1

Hemmingway Cl
NW5 . . . . **12** C4

Hemp Wlk SE17 . . **151** C4

Hemstal Rd NW6 . . .10 C1

Hemsworth Ct N1 . .24 A3

Hemsworth St N1 . .24 A3

Hemus Pl SW3 . . . **144** B1

Henchman St W12 . .29 B3

Henderson Ct

8 Deptford SE14 . . . .50 C4

Hampstead NW3 . . . .11 C3

Wandsworth SW18 . .72 A4

Henderson Dr
NW8 . . . . **89** B2

Henderson Rd
SW18 . . . . .72 A4

Hendham Rd
SW17 . . . . .72 B2

Hendre Ho SE1 . . . **152** B3

Hendre Rd SE1 . . . **152** B3

Hendrick Ave
SW12 . . . . .72 B4

Heneage La EC3 . . **110** B1

Heneage Pl EC3 . . **110** B1

Heneage St E1 . . . **111** A4

Henfield Cl N19 . . . .4 B3

Henley Cl SE16 . . . .40 B4

Henley Ct

Brondesbury NW2 . . . .9 C2

Peckham SE15 . . . . .64 C4

Henley Dr SE1 . . . **153** A4

Henley Ho
E2 . . . . .24 B1 **99** A2

Henley Prior N1 . . **84** C1

Henley Rd NW10 . . .22 B4

Henley St SW11 . . **169** C2

Henniker Mews
SW3 . . . . **157** B4

Henniker Rd E15 . . .19 C3

Henning St SW11 **168** A3

Henrietta Cl SE8 . . .51 C4

Henrietta Ho **11**

W6 . . . . .39 B1

Henrietta Mews
WC1 . . . . **94** B2

Henrietta Pl W1 . . **104** A2

Henrietta St

Strand WC2 . . . . . **120** B4

Stratford New Town

E15 . . . . .19 B3

Henriques St E1 . . **111** C1

Henry Cavendish Prim
Sch SW12 . . . . .73 B3

Henry Compton Sec
Sch SW6 . . . . **164** A4

Henry Dent Cl SE5 . .63 C4

Henry Dickens Ct
W11 . . . . .31 A1 **112** A2

Henry Fawcett Prim
Sch SE11 . . . . **163** B4

Henry Ho

Lambeth SE1 . . . . . **121** C1

South Lambeth

SW8 . . . . **162** A2

St John's Wood

NW8 . . . . **80** A2

Henry Jackson Ho
SW15 . . . . .57 C4

Henry Jackson Rd
SW15 . . . . .57 C4

Henry Rd N4 . . . . . . .6 B3

Henryson Rd SE4 . . .66 C2

Henry Wise Ho
SW1 . . . . **147** A3

Henshall Point **10**
E3 . . . . .27 A2

Henshall St N1 . . . .15 C2

Henshaw St SE17 . **151** B4

Hensley Point **28**
E9 . . . . .17 C2

Henslowe Rd
SE22 . . . . .64 C2

Henslow Ho **12**
SE15 . . . . .49 C3

Henson Ave NW2 . . .9 B3

Henson Ct **3** N5 . . .15 B4

Henstridge Pl
NW8 . . . . **80** A3

Henty Cl SW11 . . . **168** B4

Henty Wlk SW15 . . .57 A2

Hepburn Mews
SW11 . . . . .60 B2

Hepplestone Cl
SW15 . . . . .57 A1

Hepscott Rd E9 . . . .18 C1

Hepworth Ct

Chelsea SW1 . . . . . **146** A1

Islington N1 . . . . **86** A4

Hera Cl **11** E14 . . . .41 C2

Heralds Pl SE11 . . **150** A4

Herald St **5** E2 . . . .25 A1

Herbal Hill EC1 . . . **95** C1

Herbert Chapman Ct
N5 . . . . .15 A4

Herbert Cres
SW1 . . . . **131** A2

Herbert Gdns

Chiswick W4 . . . . .45 A4

Willesden Green

NW10 . . . . .22 A3

Herbert Ho E1 . . . **110** C2

Herbert Mews **13**
SW2 . . . . .62 C1

Herbert Morrison Ho
SW6 . . . . **154** C3

Herbert Morrison
Prim Sch NW8 . . . **162** A1

Herbert St NW5 . . . .12 C2

Herbrand Est WC1 . **94** A2

Herbrand St WC1 . . **94** A2

Hercules Ct **7**
SE14 . . . . .51 A4

Hercules Rd SE1 . . **135** A1

Hercules St N7 . . . . .5 A1

Hereford Bldgs
SW3 . . . . **157** C4

Hereford Ho

1 Brixton SW2 . . . . .62 C3

25 Camberwell SE5 . .48 B1

8 Knightsbridge **130** B2

Walham Green

SW10 . . . . **156** B2

Hereford Mans **10**
W2 . . . . .31 C3

Hereford Mews **11**
W2 . . . . .31 C3

Hereford Pl SE14 . . .51 B3

Hereford Rd

Acton W3 . . . . .28 B2

Bayswater

W2 . . . . . .31 C2 **113** C4

Hereford Retreat **5**
SE15 . . . . .49 C3

Hereford Sq SW7 . **143** A3

Hereford St
E2 . . . . .24 C1 **99** B2

Hereward House Sch
NW3 . . . . .11 C2

Heritage Cl SW9 . . .63 A4

Heritage Ct SE8 . . . .40 C1

Heritage Ho **22**
SW19 . . . . .69 C3

Hermes Cl **5** W9 . .23 C1

Hermes Ct SW9 . . .173 B4

Hermes St N1 . . . . . **85** B1

Hermitage Ct

2 Child's Hill NW2 . . .1 C1

Wapping E1 . . . . . . **125** C1

Hermitage Gdns
NW2 . . . . .1 C1

Hermitage La NW2 . .1 C1

Hermitage Prim Sch
E1 . . . . **125** C2

Hermitage Row **8**
E8 . . . . .16 C3

Hermitage St W2 . . **101** B3

Hermitage The

Barnes SW13 . . . . . .46 B2

Richmond TW10 . . . . .54 A2

Hermitage Villas
SW6 . . . . **155** B4

Hermitage Wall
E1 . . . . **125** C1

Hermit Pl NW6 . . . . **78** A3

Hermit St EC1 . . . . . **96** A4

Herndon Rd SW18 . .59 B2

HERNE HILL 63 B2

Herne Hill SE24 . . . .63 B3

Herne Hill Ho
SE24 . . . . .63 A1

Herne Hill Mans
SE24 . . . . .63 B1

Herne Hill Rd
SE24 . . . . .63 B2

Herne Hill Sch
SE24 . . . . .63 B2

Herne Hill Sta
SE24 . . . . .63 A1

Herne Hill Stad
SE24 . . . . .63 C1

Herne Pl SE24 . . . . .63 A2

Heron Cl NW10 . . . . .8 A2

Heron Ct

16 Cubitt Town

E14 . . . . .42 B3

7 Dulwich SE21 . . . .75 C2

Heron Dr N4 . . . . . . .6 B2

Herongate N1 . . . . **87** A4

Heron Ho

Battersea SW11 . . . **168** B4

Peckham SE15 . . . . .49 B2

St John's Wood

NW8 . . . . **80** A1

Heron Pl

Marylebone W1 . . . **103** C2

Rotherhithe SE16 . . . .33 A1

Heron Quays E14 . . .33 C1

Heron Quays Sta
E14 . . . . .33 C1

Heron Rd SE24 . . . . .63 B3

Heron Trad Est
W3 . . . . .28 A4

Herrick Ho

16 Camberwell

SE5 . . . . .48 C3

17 Canonbury N16 . .15 C4

Herrick Rd N5 . . . . . .6 B1

Herrick St SW1 . . . **147** C3

Herries St W10 . . . . .23 A3

Hersant Cl NW10 . . .21 C4

Herschell's Mews
SE5 . . . . .63 B4

Hersham Cl SW15 . .68 C4

Hershell Ct **1**
SW14 . . . . .55 A3

Hertford Ave
SW14 . . . . .56 A3

Hertford Ct **10**
SW11 . . . . .60 A4

Hertford Lo **10**
SW19 . . . . .70 A3

Hertford Pl W1 . . . . **93** A1

Hertford Rd N1 . . . . .24 A4

Hertford St W1 . . . **118** A1

Hertmitage The **5**
SE13 . . . . .52 B1

Hertslet Rd N7 . . . . . .5 B1

Hertsmere Rd E14 . .33 C2

Hesewall Cl SW4 . . **171** A1

Hesketh Pl
W11 . . . . . .31 A2 **112** A3

Heslop Ct **1** 72 C3

Heslop Rd SW12 . . .72 B3

Hesper Mews
SW5 . . . . **142** A3

Hesperus Cres
E14 . . . . .42 A2

Hessel St E1 . . . . . . .32 A3

Hestercombe Ave
SW6 . . . . **164** B3

Hester Rd SW11 . . **158** A1

Hester Terr TW9 . . . .54 C4

Hestia Ho SE1 . . . . **138** A3

Heston Ho

Gunnersbury W4 . . . .37 A1

3 St Johns SE8 . . . . .51 C2

Heston St SE14 . . . . .51 C2

Hetherington Rd SW2,
SW4 . . . . .62 A3

Hethpool Ho W2 . . **89** B1

Hetley Rd W12 . . . . .39 A4

Hetty Rees Ct **6**
N19 . . . . .5 A4

Hevelius Cl SE10 . . .43 B1

Hever Ho SE15 . . . . .50 C4

Heversham Ho
SE15 . . . . .50 B4

Heward Ct SE13 . . . .52 B1

Hewer Ho **1** SW4 . .61 B2

Hewett Ho SW15 . . .47 B1

Hewett St
EC2 . . . . . .24 A1 **98** B1

Hewison St E3 . . . . .26 B3

Hewlett Rd E3 . . . . . .26 A3

Hewling Ho **1**
N16 . . . . .16 A3

Hexagon The N6 . . . .3 B3

Hexham Rd SE27 . . .75 B2

Hexton Ct N4 . . . . . . .6 B2

Heybridge **9**
NW1 . . . . .13 A2

Heydon Ho **3**
SE14 . . . . .50 B2

Heyford Ave SW8 . **162** B2

Heyford Terr
SW8 . . . . **162** B2

Heygate St SE17 . . **151** A4

Heylyn Sq E3 . . . . . .26 B2

Heysham La NW3 . . . .2 A1

Heythorp St SW18 . .70 B2

Heywood Ho

11 Deptford SE14 . . .50 C4

6 Tulse Hill SW2 . . . .62 C1

Heyworth Rd E5 . . . .17 A4

Hibbert Ho **13** E14 . .41 C3

Hibbert St SW11 . . . .59 C4

Hichisson Rd SE15 . .65 B2

Hickes Ho **9** NW6 . .11 C1

Hickey's Almshouses
7 TW9 . . . . .54 B3

Hickin St **2** E14 . . . .42 B3

Hickleton NW1 . . . . **83** A3

Hickling Ho **10**
SE16 . . . . .40 A3

Hickmore Wlk
SW4 . . . . .61 B4

Hicks Cl SW11 . . . . . .60 A4

Hicks St SE8 . . . . . . .41 A1

Hide Pl SW1 . . . . . . **147** B3

Hide Twr SW1 . . . . **147** B3

Hieover SE21 . . . . . . .75 B2

Higgins Ho **7** N1 . . .24 A4

Higginson Ho **2**
NW3 . . . . .12 B1

Higgs Ind Est **9**
SE24 . . . . .63 A4

Highbridge Ct **13**
SE14 . . . . .50 B3

High Bridge Wharf
SE10 . . . . .42 C1

Highbury Mans **24**
N1 . . . . .15 A1

HIGHBURY 15 A4

Highbury Cnr N5 . . . .15 A2

Highbury Corner
N5 . . . . .15 A2

Highbury Cres N5 . . .14 C3

Highbury Fields Sch
N5 . . . . .15 A3

Highbury Gr N5 . . . . .15 B3

Highbury Grange
N5 . . . . .15 B4

Highbury Grove Ct
N5 . . . . .15 A2

Highbury Grove Sch
N5 . . . . .15 B3

Highbury Hill N5 . . . .15 A3

Highbury & Islington
Sta N1 . . . . .15 A2

Highbury New Pk
N5 . . . . .15 B4

Highbury Pk N5 . . . . .15 A4

Highbury Quadrant
Prim Sch N5 . . . . . . .15 C4

Highbury Quadrant
N5 . . . . .15 B4

Highbury Station Rd
N1 . . . . .14 C2

Highbury Terr N5 . . . .15 A3

Highbury Terrace
Mews N5 . . . . .15 A3

Highcliffe Dr
SW15 . . . . .56 B1

Highcroft Rd N19 . . . .5 A4

Highcross Way **4**
SW15 . . . . .68 C3

Highdown Rd
SW15 . . . . .57 A1

Highfield Ave
NW11 . . . . .1 A4

Highfield Cl SE13 . . . .67 C1

Highfield Mews
NW6 . . . . .11 A1

Highfield Rd W3 . . . .28 B4

Highfield Sch
SW18 . . . . .72 A4

Highfields Gr N6 . . . . .3 B3

HIGHGATE 3 C4

Highgate Archway
N6 . . . . 4 B3
Highgate Ave N6 . . . . 4 A4
Highgate Cemetery★
N19 . . . . 4 A2
Highgate Cl N6 . . . . 3 C4
Highgate High St
N6 . . . . 4 A3
Highgate Hill N19 . . . 4 B3
Highgate Ho 🔢
SE26 . . . . 76 C1
Highgate Rd NW5 . . 13 A4
Highgate Sch
Highgate N6 . . . . 3 B4
Highgate N6 . . . . 3 C4
Highgate West Hill
N6 . . . . 3 C2
Highgrove Point 🔢
NW3 . . . . 11 B4
High Holborn
WC1 . . . . 106 C3
High Holborn Ho
WC1 . . . . 106 C3
Highlands Ave W3 . . 28 B2
Highlands Cl N4 . . . . . 5 A4
Highlands Heath
SW15 . . . . 69 A4
Highlever Rd W10 . . 30 B4
High London SE13 . . 67 C4
Highmore Rd SE3 . . 53 A3
High Mount N4 . . . . . . 5 A4
High Park Ave
TW9 . . . . 44 C2
High Park Rd TW9 . . 44 C2
High Par Rd
SW16 . . . . 74 A1
High Point N6 . . . . 3 C4
High Rd NW10 . . . . . 8 B2
Highshore Rd
SE15 . . . . 49 B1
Highshore Sch
SE15 . . . . 49 B2
High St Acton W3 . . 28 A1
Brentford TW8 . . . . . . 44 A4
Stratford Marsh E15 . 27 B4
High Street Harlesden
NW10 . . . . 21 B3
High Street
Kensington Sta
W8 . . . . 128 A3
High The SW16 . . . . 74 A1
High Timber St
EC4 . . . . 122 C4
High Trees SW2 . . . . 74 C3
Hightrees Ho
SW12 . . . . 60 C1
Highview N8 . . . . 5 A4
Highview Ct 🔢
SW19 . . . . 70 A3
High View Prim Sch
SW11 . . . . 59 C3
Highway Bsns Pk The
🔢 E1 . . . . 32 C2
Highway The E1 . . . . 32 C2
Highway Trad Ctr The
🔢 E1 . . . . 32 C2
Highwood Cl SE22 . . 76 C3
Highwood Rd N19 . . 5 A1
Highworth St
NW1 . . . . 102 B4
Hilary Cl SW6 . . . . . 156 A2
Hilary Rd W12 . . . . . 29 B2
Hilborough Ct 🔢
E8 . . . . 24 B4
Hilborough Rd 🔢
E8 . . . . 16 B1

Hilda Lockert Wlk
SW9 . . . . 48 A1
Hilda Terr SW9 . . . 173 C2
Hildith Ho 🔢
TW10 . . . . 54 B1
Hildred Ho SW1 . . . 146 A4
Hildreth St SW12 . . 73 A3
Hildreth Street Mews
🔢 SW12 . . . . 73 A3
Hildyard Rd SW6 . . 155 C4
Hiley Rd NW10 . . . . 22 B2
Hilgrove Rd NW6 . . 11 B1
Hillary Ct 🔢 W12 . . 39 B4
Hillbeck Cl
Deptford SE15 . . . . . . 50 B3
Deptford SE15 . . . . . . 50 B3
Hillbrow 🔢 TW10 . . 54 A1
Hillbury Rd SW17 . . 73 A1
Hillcourt Rd SE22 . . 65 A1
Hillcrest
Camberwell SE24 . . . 63 C3
Highgate N6 . . . . 3 C4
Notting Hill
W11 . . . . 31 B2 112 C3
Hillcrest Ct NW2 . . 10 A3
Hillcrest Rd W3 . . . . 28 A1
Hill Ct
Hampstead NW3 . . . 12 A4
Putney SW15 . . . . 57 C2
Hilldrop Cres N7 . . . 13 C3
Hilldrop La N7 . . . . . 13 C3
Hilldrop Rd N7 . . . . . 13 C3
Hillersdon Ave
SW13 . . . . 46 C1
Hillersdon Ho
SW1 . . . . 146 A2
Hillery Cl SE17 . . . . 151 C3
Hill Farm Rd W10 . . 30 C4
Hillfield Ct NW3 . . . 12 A3
Hillfield Ho N5 . . . . . 15 B3
Hillfield Mans
NW3 . . . . 12 A3
Hillfield Rd NW6 . . 10 C3
Hillgate Pl
Balham SW12 . . . . . . 73 A4
Kensington
W8 . . . . 31 C1 113 B2
Hillgate St
W8 . . . . 31 C1 113 B2
Hill House Sch
SW1 . . . . 131 A1
Hilliard Ho 🔢 E1 . . 32 A1
Hilliard's Ct E1 . . . . 32 B1
Hillier Ho 🔢 NW1 . . 13 C1
Hillier Rd SW11 . . . 60 B1
Hillingdon St
SE17 . . . . 48 A4
Hill Lo SW11 . . . . . . 59 C3
Hillman Dr 🔢
NW10 . . . . 22 B1
Hillman St E8 . . . . . . 17 A2
Hillmarton Rd N7 . . 14 A3
Hillmead Dr SW9 . . 63 A3
Hill Mead Prim Sch
SW9 . . . . 63 A3
Hillmore Ct SE13 . . 67 C4
Hill Rd NW8 . . . . 79 A1
Hillrise Mans N19 . . 5 A4
Hillrise Rd N19 . . . . 5 A4
Hillsboro Rd SE22 . . 64 A2
Hillsborough Ct 🔢
NW6 . . . . 78 A3
Hillside
Greenwich SE10 . . . . 52 C3
Stonebridge NW10 . . 20 C4
Hillside Cl NW8 . . . . 78 B2
Hillside Ct NW3 . . . 11 A3

Hillside Gdns SW2 . . 74 C2
Hillside Rd SW2 . . . 74 C2
Hillsleigh Rd
W14 . . . . 31 B1 113 A2
Hills Pl W1 . . . . 104 C1
Hill St W1 . . . . 118 A2
Hillstone Ct 🔢 E3 . . 27 A1
Hilltop Ct
🔢 London SW18 . . . 59 C3
South Hampstead
NW8 . . . . 11 B1
Hilltop Ho 🔢 N6 . . . 4 C4
Hilltop Rd NW6 . . . 10 C1
Hill View NW1 . . . . 81 A4
Hillway N6 . . . . 3 C2
Hill Wood Ho NW1 . 83 B1
Hillworth Rd SW2 . . 74 C4
Hillyard St SW9 . . . 173 B3
Hillyfield Cl E9 . . . . 18 A3
Hilly Fields Cres
SE4 . . . . 66 C4
Hilsea Point 🔢
SW15 . . . . 69 A3
Hilsea St E5 . . . . 17 B4
Hilton Ho
Lower Holloway
N7 . . . . 14 A4
🔢 Nunhead SE4 . . . 65 C3
Hilversum Cres 🔢
SE22 . . . . 64 A2
Hinckley Rd SE15 . . 64 C3
Hind Ct EC4 . . . . . . 107 C1
Hinde Mews W1 . . . 103 C2
Hinde St W1 . . . . . . 103 C2
Hind Gr E14 . . . . 33 C3
Hindhead Point 🔢
SW15 . . . . 69 A3
Hind Ho
🔢 Deptford SE14 . . 50 C4
Islington N7 . . . . 14 C4
Hindle Ho E8 . . . . . . 16 B3
Hindley Ho N7 . . . . . 5 B1
Hindlip Ho SW8 . . . 171 B3
Hindmans Rd
SE22 . . . . 64 C2
Hindmarsh Cl E1 . . 125 C4
Hindrey Rd E5 . . . . . 17 A3
Hinstock Ho NW6 . . 78 A4
Hinton Rd SE24 . . . . 63 A4
Hippodrome Mews
W11 . . . . 31 A2 112 A3
Hippodrome Pl
W11 . . . . 31 A2 112 B3
Hirst Ct SW1 . . . . . . 146 A1
Hitchin Sq 🔢 E3 . . . 26 A3
Hithe Gr 🔢 SE16 . . 40 B3
Hitherfield Prim Sch
SW16 . . . . 74 C2
Hitherfield Rd SW16,
SW2 . . . . 74 C1
Hither Green La
SE13 . . . . 67 C1
Hither Green Prim
Sch SE13 . . . . 67 C1
Hitherlands SW12 . . 73 A2
HM Prison
Wormwood Scrubs
W12 . . . . 29 C3
HMS Belfast★
SE1 . . . . 124 B2
Hoadly Rd SW16 . . 73 C2
Hobart Pl SW1 . . . . 132 A2
Hobbes Wlk SW15 . 57 A2
Hobb's Ct 🔢 SE1 . . 139 A4
Hobbs' Pl N1 . . . . . . 24 A4
Hobday St E14 . . . . 34 A3

Hobhouse Ct
SW1 . . . . 119 C3
Hobsons Pl E1 . . . . 111 B4
Hobury St SW10 . . 157 B3
Hocker St
E2 . . . . 24 B2 98 C3
Hockett Cl SE8 . . . . 41 B2
Hockley Ho 🔢 E9 . . 17 B2
Hockliffe Ho 🔢
W10 . . . . 30 B4
Hockney Ct 🔢
SE16 . . . . 40 A1
Hockworth Ho 🔢
N16 . . . . 7 A3
Hocroft Ave NW2 . . 1 B1
Hocroft Ct NW2 . . . 1 B1
Hocroft Rd NW2 . . . 1 B1
Hocroft Wlk NW2 . . 1 B1
Hodford Lo NW11 . . 1 C2
Hodford Rd NW11 . . 1 C3
Hodister Cl 🔢 SE5 . 48 B3
Hoffman Sq N1 . . . . 97 C4
Hofland Rd W14 . . 126 A2
Hogan Mews W2 . . 101 B4
Hogan Way 🔢 E5 . . . 7 C2
Hogarth Bsns Pk
W4 . . . . 46 A4
Hogarth Ct
🔢 Camden Town
NW1 . . . . 13 B1
City of London EC3 . 124 B4
Whitechapel E1 . . . . 111 C1
Hogarth Ho SW1 . . 147 C3
Hogarth Ind Est
NW10 . . . . 21 C1
Hogarth La W4 . . . . 46 A4
Hogarth Pl SW5 . . . 142 A3
Hogarth Rd SW5 . . 142 A3
Hogarth Roundabout
W4 . . . . 46 A4
Hogarth's House★
W4 . . . . 46 A4
Holbeach Mews 🔢
SW12 . . . . 73 A3
Holbeck Row
SE15 . . . . 49 C3
Holbein Ho SW1 . . 145 B2
Holbein Mews
SW1 . . . . 145 B2
Holbein Pl SW1 . . . 145 B3
Holberton Gdns
NW10 . . . . 22 A2
HOLBORN 107 C3
Holborn EC1 . . . . . 107 C3
Holborn Cir EC1 . . 107 C3
Holborn Ho 🔢
W12 . . . . 30 A3
Holborn Pl WC1 . . 106 C3
Holborn Sta WC1 . 106 C3
Holborn Viaduct
EC1 . . . . 108 A3
Holbrook Cl N19 . . . 4 A3
Holbrooke Ct N7 . . 14 A4
Holbrook Ho
Acton W3 . . . . 28 C4
🔢 Streatham SW2 . 74 B3
Holcombe Ho
SW9 . . . . 62 A4
Holcombe Pl SE4 . . 66 A4
Holcombe St W6 . . 39 A2
Holcroft Ct W1 . . . 104 C4
Holcroft Ho
Battersea SW11 . . . . 59 C4
🔢 Lewisham SE10 . . 52 B2
Holcroft Rd E9 . . . . 17 B1
Holdenby SE4 . . . . . 66 A2

Hig–Hol 225

Holden Ho
🔢 Deptford SE8 . . . 51 C3
Islington N1 . . . . 86 C3
Holden Point E15 . . 19 C2
Holden St SW11 . . . 169 B1
Holdernesse Rd 🔢
SW17 . . . . 72 C2
Holderness Ho
SE5 . . . . 64 A4
Holdsworth Ho 🔢
SW2 . . . . 74 C4
Holford Ho
🔢 Bermondsey
SE16 . . . . 40 A2
Finsbury WC1 . . . . . 95 A4
Holford Pl WC1 . . . 95 A4
Holford Rd NW3 . . . 2 B1
Holford St WC1 . . . 95 A4
Holford Yd WC1 . . . 85 B1
Holgate Ave SW11 . 59 C4
Holland Gdns
Brentford TW8 . . . . . 44 A4
Kensington W14 . . 126 B2
Holland Gr SW9 . . 163 C1
Holland Park
W11 . . . . 31 B1 112 C1
Holland Park Ave
W11 . . . . 31 A1 112 B1
Holland Park Ct 🔢
W14 . . . . 126 B4
Holland Park Gdns
W14 . . . . 126 A4
Holland Park Mews
W11 . . . . 31 B1 112 C1
Holland Park Rd
W14 . . . . 127 A4
Holland Park Rdbt
W12 . . . . 39 C4
Holland Park Sch
W8 . . . . 127 A4
Holland Park Sta
W11 . . . . 31 B1 112 C1
Holland Pas 🔢 N1 . . 86 C4
Holland Pl W8 . . . . 128 A4
Holland Rd
West Kensington
W14 . . . . 126 B2
Willesden Green
NW10 . . . . 22 A3
Holland Rise Ho
SW9 . . . . 163 A1
Holland St
Kensington W8 . . . . 127 C4
Lambeth SE1 . . . . . . 122 B2
Holland Villas Rd
W14 . . . . 126 A3
Holland Wlk
Kensington W14 . . 127 A3
Upper Holloway N19 . 4 C3
Hollar Rd N16 . . . . . 7 B1
Hollen St W1 . . . . . . 105 B2
Holles Ho SW9 . . . 173 B2
Holles St W1 . . . . . 104 B2
Holley Rd W3 . . . . . 38 A4
Holliday Sq 🔢
SW11 . . . . 59 C4
Hollies The SW12 . . 73 B2
Hollies Way 🔢
SW12 . . . . 72 C4
Hollingbourne Rd
SE24 . . . . 63 B2
Hollins Ho N7 . . . . . 14 A4
Hollisfield WC1 . . . . 94 B3

Holloway Rd
Lower Holloway
N7 . . . . .14 B4
Upper Holloway N19 . .4 C2
Holloway Road Sta
N7 . . . . .14 B3
Holloway Sch N7 . . .13 C3
Holly Berry La 6
NW3 . . . . .11 B4
Hollybush Gdns
E2 . . . . .25 A2
Holly Bush Hill 4
NW3 . . . . .11 B4
Hollybush Ho 28
E2 . . . . .25 A2
Hollybush Pl E2 . . . .25 A2
Holly Bush Steps 6
NW3 . . . . .11 B4
Holly Bush Vale 10
NW3 . . . . .11 B4
Hollycroft Ave NW3 . .1 C1
Hollydale Prim Sch
SE15 . . . . .50 B1
Hollydale Rd SE15 . .50 B1
Hollydene
Hither Green SE13 . . .67 C1
⊞ Peckham SE15 . . . .50 A2
Holly Gr SE15 . . . . . .49 C1
Hollyhedge Ho
SE3 . . . . .52 C1
Holly Hedge Terr
SE13 . . . . .67 C2
Holly Hill NW3 . . . . .11 B4
Holly Lo W8 . . . . . .127 B4
Holly Lodge SE13 . . .67 C1
Holly Lodge Gdns
N6 . . . . .3 C3
Holly Lodge Mans
N6 . . . . .3 C2
Holly Mews SW10 143 A1
Holly Mount NW3 . . .11 B4
Hollymount Cl 9
SE10 . . . . .52 B2
Holly Park Est N4 . . . .5 B4
Holly Pk N4 . . . . .5 B4
Holly Pl NW3 . . . . . .11 B4
Holly Rd 6 W4 . . . . .37 C2
Holly St E8 . . . . .16 B1
Holly Terr N6 . . . . .3 C3
Hollytree Cl SW19 . .69 C3
Holly Tree Ho SE4 . . .66 B4
Holly Village N6 . . . . .4 A2
Holly Wlk NW3 . . . . .11 B4
Hollywood Lofts
E1 . . . . .24 B1 98 C1
Hollywood Mews
SW10 . . . . .156 C4
Hollywood Rd
SW10 . . . . .156 C4
Holman Ho 2 E2 . .25 C2
Holm Hunt Ho
W14 . . . . .140 A1
Holman Rd SW11 167 B1
Holmbrook 1 NW1 . .83 A1
Holmbury Ct
SW17 . . . . .72 B1
Holmbury Ho SW9 . .63 A2
Holmbush Rd
SW15 . . . . .58 A1
Holmcote Gdns
N5 . . . . .15 B3
Holmdale Rd NW6 . .10 C3
Holmdene Ave
SE24 . . . . .63 B2
Holmead Rd SW6 156 B1

Holmefield Ct 4
NW3 . . . . .12 A2
Holmefield Ho
W10 . . . . .23 A1
Holmes Cl SE22 . . . .64 C3
Holmes Ct
⊞ South Acton
W4 . . . . .37 B3
South Lambeth
SW4 . . . . .172 A2
Holmesdale Ave
SW14 . . . . .55 A3
Holmesdale Ho 12
NW6 . . . . .23 C4
Holmesdale Rd
Highgate N6 . . . . .4 A4
Richmond TW9 . . . . . .44 B2
Holmesley Rd
SE23 . . . . .66 A1
Holmes Pl SW10 . .157 A4
Holmes Rd NW5 . . . .13 A3
Holmes Terr SE1 . .135 B4
Holmewood Gdns
SW2 . . . . .74 B4
Holmewood Rd
SW2 . . . . .74 B4
Holmhurst SE13 . . . .67 C1
Holmleigh Prim Sch
N16 . . . . .7 A3
Holmleigh Rd N16 . . .7 A3
Holm Oak Cl
SW15 . . . . .58 B1
Holmsbury Ho 6
N7 . . . . .13 C3
Holmsdale Ho 14
E14 . . . . .34 A2
Holmside Ct SW12 . .60 C1
Holmside Rd
SW12 . . . . .60 C1
Holmsley Ho
SW15 . . . . .68 B4
Holm Wlk SE3 . . . . . .53 C1
Holmwood Ct 3
N16 . . . . .7 B4
Holocaust Meml
Gdn* W2 . . . . .131 A4
Holroyd Rd SW15 . . .57 B2
Holsgrove Ct W3 . . .29 A1
Holst Mans SW13 . . .47 B3
Holsworthy Ho 49
E3 . . . . .27 A2
Holsworthy Sq
WC1 . . . . .95 A1
Holt Ct
Greenwich SE10 . . . . .52 B4
Stratford New Town
E15 . . . . .19 B3
Holt Ho SW2 . . . . . . .62 C1
Holton St E1 . . . . . . .25 C1
Holwood Pl 7
SW4 . . . . .61 C3
Holybourne Ave
SW15 . . . . .68 C4
Holy Cross RC Sch
SW6 . . . . .165 B4
Holy Family RC Prim
Sch E14 . . . . .33 C2
Holy Ghost RC Prim
Sch SW12 . . . . .72 C4
Holyhead Cl E3 . . . . .26 C2
Holyoake Ct SE16 . . .41 B4
Holyoak Rd SE11 . .150 B3
Holyport Rd SW6 . . .47 C3
Holyrood Ho N4 . . . . .6 B3
Holyrood Mews 10
E16 . . . . .35 C1
Holyrood St SE1 . .124 A1

Holy Trinity CE Prim
Sch
Belgravia SW1 . . . . .145 B4
Dalston E8 . . . . .16 B2
Hampstead NW3 . . . .11 B2
Richmond TW10 . . . . .54 C3
Streatham SW2 . . . . .74 B4
Holy Trinity & Saint
Silas CE Prim Sch
NW1 . . . . .13 A1
Holywell Cl
⊞ Bermondsey
SE16 . . . . .40 A1
3 Greenwich SE3 . . .53 C4
Holywell La
EC2 . . . . .24 A1 98 B2
Holywell Row
EC2 . . . . .24 A1 98 B1
Homan Ho 6
SW4 . . . . .73 C4
Homecross Ho 7
W4 . . . . .37 C2
Homefield Ave W4 . .38 B1
Homefield St 14
N1 . . . . .24 A3
Homeleigh Ct 8
SW16 . . . . .74 A1
Homeleigh Rd
SE15 . . . . .65 C2
Homemead SW12 . . .73 A2
Home Office SW1 133 B3
Home Park Rd
SW19 . . . . .70 B1
Home Rd SW11 . . . .168 A2
Homer Dr E14 . . . . . .41 C2
Homer Rd E9 . . . . . . .18 A2
Homer Row W1 . . . .102 B3
Homer St W1 . . . . . .102 B3
HOMERTON 17 C1
Homerton Coll of
Technology E9 . . .17 B3
Homerton Gr E9 . . . .17 C3
Homerton High St
E9 . . . . .17 C3
Homerton Rd E9 . . . .18 B3
Homerton Row E9 . . .17 B3
Homerton Sta E9 . . .17 C2
Homerton Terr E9 . . .17 C2
Homerton University
Hospl E9 . . . . .17 C3
Homestall Rd
SE22 . . . . .65 B2
Homestead Rd
SW6 . . . . .155 A1
Homewoods 2
SW12 . . . . .73 B4
Homildon Ho 10
SE26 . . . . .76 C1
Honduras St EC1 . . .96 C2
Honeybourne Rd
NW6 . . . . .11 A3
Honeybrook Rd SW12,
SW4 . . . . .73 B4
Honeyfield N4 . . . . . . .5 C2
Honey La EC2 . . . . .109 A1
Honey Lane Ho
SW10 . . . . .156 B4
Honeyman Cl NW6 . . .9 C1
Honeywell Jun & Inf
Schs SW11 . . . . . . .60 B1
Honeywell Rd
SW11 . . . . .60 B1
Honeywood Ho 5
SE15 . . . . .49 C2
Honeywood Rd
NW10 . . . . .21 B3

Honiton Gdns 1
SE15 . . . . .50 B1
Honiton Ho 26
SE5 . . . . .48 B1
Honiton Rd NW6 . . . .23 B3
HONOR OAK 65 B2
Honor Oak Park Sta
SE23 . . . . .65 C1
Honor Oak Pk
SE23 . . . . .65 C1
Honor Oak Rise
SE23 . . . . .65 B1
Honwell Ho 24
W2 . . . . .31 C4
Hood Ave SW14 . . . .55 B2
Hood Ct N7 . . . . .5 B1
Hood Ho 17 SE5 . . . .48 C3
Hooke Ct SE10 . . . . .52 B2
Hooke Ho 22 E3 . . . .26 A3
Hookham Ct SW8 171 B4
Hooks Cl SE15 . . . . . .50 A2
Hooper Ho 9
SW18 . . . . .58 B2
Hooper Rd E16 . . . . .35 C3
Hooper's Ct SW1 . .130 C3
Hooper's Mews 4
W3 . . . . .28 B1
Hooper St E1 . . . . . .111 B1
Hope Cl
Brentford TW8 . . . . . .36 A1
Canonbury N1 . . . . . .15 B2
Hope Ct 4
SE15 . . . . .49 C4
Hope Gdns 10 W3 . .37 A4
Hope St SW11 . . . . . .59 C4
Hopetown St E1 . . .111 A3
Hopewell St SE5 . . . .48 C3
Hopewell Yd 6 SE5 . .48 C3
Hop Gdns WC2 . . . .120 A3
Hopgood St 5
W12 . . . . .30 B1
Hopkins Ho 17
E14 . . . . .33 C3
Hopkinson Ho
SW11 . . . . .169 B2
Hopkinson's Pl
NW1 . . . . .81 B4
Hopkins St W1 . . . .105 B1
Hopping La N1 . . . . .15 A2
Hop St SE10 . . . . . . .43 B2
Hopton Ho 5
SW9 . . . . .48 A1
Hopton's Gdns
SE1 . . . . .122 B2
Hopton St SE1 . . . .122 B2
Hopwood Cl SW17 . .71 B1
Hopwood Rd SE17 . .48 C4
Hopwood Wlk E8 . . .16 C1
Horatio Ho 13 E2 . . .24 B3
Horatio Pl 8 E14 . . . .34 B1
Horatio St 11 E2 . . . .24 B3
Horbury Cres
W11 . . . . .31 C2 113 B3
Horbury Mews
W11 . . . . .31 B2 113 A3
Horder Rd SW6 . . . .164 B3
Hordle Prom E 8
SE15 . . . . .49 B3
Hordle Prom N 4
SE15 . . . . .49 B3
Hordle Prom S 3
SE15 . . . . .49 B3
Horizon Bldg 22
E14 . . . . .33 C2
Horizon Sch N16 . . . .16 A4
Horle Wlk SE5 . . . . . .48 A1
Hormead Rd W9 . . . .23 B1

Hornbeam Cl
SE11 . . . . .149 B4
Hornbeam Ho 2
NW3 . . . . .12 B2
Hornbeam Sq 6
E3 . . . . .26 B4
Hornblower Cl 2
SE16 . . . . .41 C3
Hornby Cl NW3 . . . . .11 C1
Hornby Ho SE11 . .163 C4
Horndean Cl 3
SW15 . . . . .68 C3
Horne Hos 18 N1 . . .24 A4
Horne Way SW15 . . .47 B1
Horn La Acton W3 . . .28 B3
Greenwich SE10 . . . . .43 C2
Horn Link Way
SE10 . . . . .43 C2
Hornsby House Sch
SW12 . . . . .72 C3
Hornsey La N6 . . . . . .4 B4
Hornsey Lane Gdns
N6 . . . . .4 B4
Hornsey Rd N7, N19, .5 B2
Hornsey Rise Gdns
N19 . . . . .5 A4
Hornsey St N7 . . . . .14 B3
Hornshay St SE15 . . .50 B4
Hornton Ct W8 . . . .127 C3
Hornton Pl W8 . . . .127 C3
Hornton St W8 . . . .127 C4
Horrocks Ho
SW15 . . . . .57 A2
Horse & Dolphin Yd
W1 . . . . .119 C4
Horseferry Pl
SE10 . . . . .52 B4
Horseferry Rd
Limehouse E14 . . . . . .33 A2
Westminster SW1 . . .147 C4
Horseferry Rd Est
SW1 . . . . .133 B1
Horse Guards Ave
SW1 . . . . .120 A1
Horse Guards Par★
SW1 . . . . .119 C1
Horse Guards Rd
SW1 . . . . .133 C4
Horsell Rd N5 . . . . . .14 C3
Horselydown La
SE1 . . . . .124 C1
Horselydown Mans
SE1 . . . . .138 C4
Horsemongers Mews
SE1 . . . . .137 A2
Horsendon Ho 11
N7 . . . . .13 C3
Horseshoe Cl E14 . . .42 B1
Horse Yd 1 N1 . . . . .86 B4
Horsfield Ho 8
N1 . . . . .15 B1
Horsford Rd SW2 . . .62 B2
Horsley Ct SW1 . . . .147 C3
Horsley Ho 11 SE4, .65 C3
Horsley St 3
SE17 . . . . .48 C4
Horsman Ho 5 . . . . .48 B4
Horsman St SE5 . . . .48 B4
Horsmonden Rd
SE4 . . . . .66 B1
Horston Ho N4 . . . . . .6 B4
Hortensia Ho
SW10 . . . . .156 C2
Hortensia Rd
SW10 . . . . .156 C2
Horticultural Pl 6
W4 . . . . .37 C1

Horton Ave NW2 . . .10 A4

Horton Ho
13 Deptford SE15 . . . .50 B4
South Lambeth
SW8 . . . . .162 C2
West Kensington
W14 . . . . .140 A1
Horton Rd E8 . . . . . .17 A2
Horton St SE13 . . . . .67 A4

Horwood Ho
24 Bethnal Green
E2 . . . . .25 A2
Marylebone NW8 . . .90 B2
Hosack Rd SW12 . . .
SW17 . . . . .72 C2
Hosier La EC1 . . . .108 B3
Hoskins St SE10 . . .42 C1

Hospl for Tropical
Diseases
Fitzrovia WC1 . . . . .93 A1
Somers Town NW1 . .83 C3

Hospl of St John & St
Elizabeth NW8 . . . .79 B1
Hotham Prim Sch
SW15 . . . . .57 B4
Hotham Rd SW15 . . .57 B4
Hothfield Pl SE16 . . .40 B3
Hotspur St SE11 . . .149 B2
Houblon Rd TW10 . . .54 A2
Houghton Cl **10**
E8 . . . . .16 B2
Houghton Sq SW9 . .62 A4
Houghton St
WC2 . . . . .107 A1
Houndsditch EC3 . .110 B2
Houseman Way **20**
SE5 . . . . .48 C3
House of Detention *
EC1 . . . . .95 C2
Houses of
Parliament *
SW1 . . . . .134 B2
Hoveden Rd NW2 . . .10 A3
Howard Bldg
SW8 . . . . .160 A3
Howard Cl
Acton W3 . . . . .28 A3
Cricklewood NW2 . . .10 A4
Howard Ct
Lewisham SE10 . . . .52 B2
Peckham SE15 . . . .64 C4
Howard Ho
16 Brixton SW9 . . . . .9 C4
14 Deptford SE8 . . . .51 B4
Fitzrovia W1 . . . . . .92 B1
Howard Mews N5 . . .15 A4
Howard Rd
Canonbury N16 . . . .15 C4
Cricklewood NW2 . . .9 C4
Howard's La SW15 . .57 B3
Howarth Ct E15 . . . .19 B3
Howbury Rd SE15 . .65 B4
Howcroft Ho **3**
E3 . . . . .26 B2
Howden St SE15 . . . .64 C4
Howell Ho **6** N7 . . .13 C3
Howell Wlk SE1 . . .150 B3
Howgate Rd SW14 . .55 C4
Howick Pl SW1 . . . .133 A1
Howie St SW11 . . . .158 A1
Howitt Cl
6 Maitland Pk
NW3 . . . . .12 A2
Stoke Newington
N16 . . . . .16 A4
Howitt Rd NW3 . . . .12 A2

Howland Ho **9**
SW16 . . . . .74 A1
Howland Mews E
W1 . . . . .105 A4
Howland St W1 . . . .105 A4
Howland Way
SE16 . . . . .41 A4
Howletts Rd SE24 . . .63 B1
Howley Pl W2 . . . .101 A4
Howsman Rd
SW13 . . . . .46 C4
Howson Rd SE4 . . . .66 A3
Howson Terr
TW10 . . . . .54 A1
How's St E2 . . . . . . .24 B3
HOXTON 24 A3
Hoxton Mkt
N1 . . . . .24 A2 **98** A3
Hoxton Point
EC1 . . . . .24 A2 **98** A3
Hoxton Sq
N1 . . . . .24 A2 **98** A3
Hoxton St N1 . . . . . .24 A3
Hoylake Rd W3 . . . .29 A3
Hoyland Cl **4**
SE15 . . . . .50 A3
Hoy St E16 . . . . .35 B3
Hub Buildings The **4**
SW12 . . . . .73 A3
Huberd Ho SE1 . . . .137 C2
Hubert Gr SW9 . . . .62 A4
Hubert Ho NW8 . . . .90 A1
Huddart St E3 . . . . . .33 C4
Huddleston Cl E2 . . .25 B3
Huddleston Rd
NW2 . . . . .13 C2
Huddleston Rd N7 . .13 B4
Hudson Cl **15** W12 . .30 A2
Hudson Ct **1** E14 . . .41 C1
Hudson Ho
Chelsea SW10 . . . .156 C2
5 Notting Hill W11 . .31 A3
Hudsons Ho N1 . . . .97 C3
Hudson's Pl SW1 . .146 C4
Huggin Ct EC4 . . . .123 A4
Huggin Hill EC4 . . .123 A4
Huggins Ho **9** E3 . . .26 C2
Huggins Pl SW2 . . . .74 B3
Hughan Rd E15 . . . .19 C3
Hugh Astor Ct
SE1 . . . . .136 B2
Hugh Dalton Ave
SW6 . . . . .154 C3
Hughenden Ho
NW8 . . . . .90 A2
Hughendon Terr
E15 . . . . .19 B4
Hughes Ho
28 Bethnal Green
E2 . . . . .25 B2
Camberwell SE5 . . .48 B2
18 Deptford SE8 . . . .51 C4
Newington SE17 . . .150 B3
Hughes Mans
E1 . . . . .24 C1 **99** C1
Hughes Terr **3**
E16 . . . . .35 B4
Hugh Gaitskell Cl
SW6 . . . . .154 C3
Hugh Gaitskell Ho
Stoke Newington
N16 . . . . .7 B2
Willesden NW10 . . . .8 B1
Hugh Mews SW1 . .146 B3
Hugh Morgan Ho **4**
SW4 . . . . .61 C4

Hugh Myddelton Prim
Sch EC1 . . . . .95 C3
Hugh Platt Ho **29**
E2 . . . . .25 A3
Hugh St SW1 . . . . .146 B3
Hugo Ho SW1 . . . . .131 A2
Hugon Rd SW6 . . . .59 A4
Hugo Rd N19 . . . . . .13 B4
Huguenot Ct E1 . . .111 A4
Huguenot Pl
London SW18 . . . . .59 B2
Spitalfields E1 . . . .111 A4
Huguenot Sq
SE15 . . . . .65 A4
Hullbridge Mews
N1 . . . . .87 B4
Hull Cl SE16 . . . . . .32 C1
Hull Ct SE5 . . . . . . .48 C1
Hull St EC1 . . . . . . .96 C3
Hulme Pl SE1 . . . . .137 A3
Humber Dr W10 . . . .22 C1
Humber Rd SE3 . . . .53 B4
Humberton Cl E9 . . .18 A3
Humbolt Rd W6 . . .154 A3
Hume Ct N1 . . . . . . .15 A1
Hume Ho **4** W11 . . .30 C1
Humphrey Ct
SW11 . . . . .167 C3
Humphrey St SE1 . .152 C2
Humphry Ho **10**
SW15 . . . . .57 C2
Hungerford Bridge
SE1 . . . . .120 C2
Hungerford Ho
SW1 . . . . .161 A4
Hungerford La
WC2 . . . . .120 B2
Hungerford Prim Sch
N7 . . . . .13 C2
Hungerford Rd
2 Camden Town
N7 . . . . .13 C2
Lower Holloway N7 . .14 A3
Hungerford St **21**
E1 . . . . .32 A3
Hunsdon Rd SE14 . .50 C3
Hunslett St E2 . . . . .25 B3
Hunstanton Ho
NW1 . . . . .102 B4
Hunt Cl W11 . . . . . .30 C1
Hunter Cl
Borough The SE1 . . .137 C1
Upper Tooting
SW12 . . . . .72 C3
Huntercombe
Roehampton Hospl
The SW15 . . . . . . .68 C4
Hunter Ct
8 London SE5 . . . .63 C3
12 Streatham SW2 . . .74 C4
Hunter Ho
Bloomsbury WC1 . . .94 B2
Lambeth SE1 . . . . .136 B3
South Lambeth
SW8 . . . . .161 C1
4 Tufnell Park N19 . . . .4 B1
West Brompton
SW5 . . . . .141 C1
Hunterian Mus *
WC2 . . . . .107 A2
Hunter Lo **9** W9 . . .31 C4
Hunter St WC1 . . . . .94 B2
Huntingdon Ct
SW14 . . . . .55 B4
Huntingdon Gdns
W4 . . . . .45 B3

Huntingdon Ho
SW5 . . . . .141 C4
Huntingdon St
Canning Town E16 . . .35 B3
Islington N1 . . . . . . .14 B1
Huntingfield Rd
SW15 . . . . .56 C2
Huntingford Ho
SW15 . . . . .47 B1
Huntington Ho
NW2 . . . . .9 B2
Huntley St WC1 . . . .93 B1
Hunts Cl SE3 . . . . . .53 C1
Hunt's Ct WC2 . . . .119 C3
Huntshaw Ho **37**
E3 . . . . .27 A2
Hunt's La E15 . . . . . .27 B3
Huntsman St
SE17 . . . . .152 A3
Huntspill St SW17 . .71 B1
Hunts Slip Rd
SE21 . . . . .76 A2
Huntsworth Mews
NW1 . . . . .90 C1
Hurdwick Ho NW1 . .82 C2
Hurdwick Pl NW1 . . .82 C2
Hurleston Ho **11**
SE8 . . . . .41 B1
Hurley Cres SE16 . . .40 C4
Hurley Ho
Lambeth SE11 . . . .149 C3
Shoreditch
E2 . . . . .24 B2 **98** C3
Hurley Lo SE22 . . . .65 B1
Hurlingham Bsns Pk
SW6 . . . . .58 C4
Hurlingham &
Chelsea Sec Sch
SW6 . . . . .58 C4
Hurlingham Ct
SW6 . . . . .58 B4
Hurlingham Gdns
SW6 . . . . .58 B4
Hurlingham Rd
SW6 . . . . .165 A1
Hurlingham Sch
SW15 . . . . .58 B3
Hurlingham Sq
SW6 . . . . .59 A4
Hurlock Ho **1** N5 . . .6 A1
Hurlock St N5 . . . . . .6 A1
Huron Rd SW17 . . . .72 C1
Huron Univ Vol 106 A4
Hurstbourne Ho
SW15 . . . . .56 B1
Hurstdene Gdns
N15 . . . . .7 A4
Hurst Ho N1 . . . . . . .85 A1
Hurst St SE24 . . . . .63 A1
Hurstway Wlk **2**
W11 . . . . .30 C2
Husborne Ho **8**
SE8 . . . . .41 A2
Huson Cl NW3 . . . . .12 A1
Hutching's St E14 . .41 C4
Hutching's Wharf **11**
E14 . . . . .41 C4
Hutchins Cl E15 . . . .19 B1
Hutchins Ho **3**
SW4 . . . . .73 C4
Hutchinson Ho
SE14 . . . . .50 B3
Hutton Ct N4 . . . . . .5 B3

Hor–Ica 227

Hutton Ho
E2 . . . . .24 C2 **99** B3
Hutton St EC4 . . . .107 C1
Huxbear St SE4 . . . .66 B2
Huxley Ho
London SW9 . . . . .172 C2
Paddington NW8 . . .89 C1
Huxley St W10 . . . . .23 A2
Hyacinth Rd SW15 . .68 C3
Hyde Farm Mews
SW12 . . . . .73 C3
Hyde La SW11 . . . .168 A4
Hyde Park * W2 . . .116 C1
Hyde Park Cnr
SW1 . . . . .131 C3
Hyde Park Corner Sta
SW1 . . . . .131 C4
Hyde Park Cres
W2 . . . . .102 A1
Hyde Park Gate Mews
SW7 . . . . .129 A3
Hyde Park Gdns
W2 . . . . .115 C4
Hyde Park Gdns Mews
W2 . . . . .116 A4
Hyde Park Mans
NW1 . . . . .102 A3
Hyde Park Pl W2 . .116 B4
Hyde Park Sq W2 . .102 A1
Hyde Park Square
Mews W2 . . . . . .102 A1
Hyde Park St W2 . .102 A1
Hyde Park Twrs
W2 . . . . .114 C3
Hyde Rd
Richmond TW10 . . . .54 B2
Shoreditch N1 . . . . .24 A4
Hyde's Pl **12** N1 . . .15 A1
Hyde St SE8 . . . . . .51 C4
Hydethorpe Rd
SW12 . . . . .73 B3
Hyde Vale SE10 . . . .52 B3
Hylda Ct NW5 . . . . . .3 C1
Hyndman Ho **4**
N19 . . . . .13 C4
Hyndman St SE15 . .50 A4
Hyperion Ho
27 Bow E3 . . . . . . .26 A3
Streatham SW2 . . . .74 B4
Hyson Rd SE16 . . . .40 A1
Hythe Ho **14** SE16 . .40 B4
Hythe Rd NW10 . . . .21 C1
Hythe Road Ind Est
NW10 . . . . .21 C1

Ian Hamilton Ho
NW1 . . . . .93 B4
Ian Mikardo Sch
E3 . . . . .27 A2
Ibberton Ho
Kensington W14 . . .126 B1
South Lambeth
SW8 . . . . .162 C2
Ibbotson Ave E16 . .35 B3
Ibbott St E1 . . . . . . .25 B1
Ibis Ct **16** SE8 . . . . .51 B4
Ibis La W4 . . . . .45 B2
Ibsley Gdns SW15 . .68 C3
Ibstock Place Sch
SW15 . . . . .56 A1
Icarus Ho **2** E3 . . . .26 B2

Iceland Rd E3 ....26 C4
Iceland Wharf
SE16 ....41 A2
Iceni Ct **E2** E3 ....26 B4
Ice Wharf NW1 ......84 B2
Idaho Bldg **7**
SE13 ....52 A2
Ida St E14 ....34 B3
Idmiston Rd E15,
SE27 ....75 B2
Idol La EC3 ....124 A3
Idonia St SE8 ....51 C3
Iffley Ho E2 ....24 B2 98 C3
Iffley Rd W6 ....39 A3
Ifield Ho SE17 ....152 B2
Ifield Rd SW10 ....156 B4
Ifor Evans Pl E1 ....25 C1
Ightham Ho SE17 .....152 A3
Ikon Ho **21** E1 ....32 B2
Ikra Prim Sch N16 ..16 B4
Ilbert St W10 ....23 A2
Ilchester Gdns
W2 ....114 A4
Ilchester Mans
W8 ....127 B2
Ilchester Pl W14 .....127 A2
Ildersly Gr SE21 ......75 C2
Ilderton Prim Sch
SE16 ....40 B1
Ilderton Rd SE15,
SE16 ....50 B4
Ilex Rd NW10 ....8 B2
Ilford Ho **14** N1 ....15 C2
Ilfracombe Flats
SE1 ....137 A4
Iliffe St SE17 ....150 B2
Iliffe Yd SE17 ....150 B2
Ilkeston Ct **7** E5 ....17 C4
Ilminster Gdns
SW11 ....60 A3
Ilsley Ct SW8 ....170 C1
Imber Ct N1 ....87 B3
Imperial Ave **5**
N16 ....16 A4
Imperial College Rd
SW7 ....129 B2
Imperial Cres
SW6 ....167 A1
Imperial Ct NW8 ......80 B2
Imperial Ho
1 Bow E3 ....26 A2
2 Poplar E14 ....33 B2
Strand WC2 ....106 C1
Imperial Rd SW6 ....166 B3
Imperial Sq SW6 ....166 B4
Imperial St E3 ....27 B2
Imperial Twrs **3**
NW3 ....11 B4
Imperial War Mus*
SE1, SE11 ....135 C1
Imperial Wharf Sta
SW10 ....167 A3
Imre Ct W12 ....30 A1
Independent Pl
E8 ....16 B3
Indescon Ct E14 ......42 A4
Indiana Bldg **7**
SE8 ....51 C2
India St EC3 ....110 C1
India Way W12 ....30 A2
Indigo Mews N16 ......6 C1
Indus Ct **10** SE15 ....49 B3

Ingate Pl SW8 ....**170** B3
Ingelow Ho W8 ......**128** A4
Ingersoll Rd W12 .....30 A1
Ingestre Pl W1 ....**105** A1
Ingestre Rd NW5 .....13 A4
Ingham Rd NW6 ....10 C4
Inglebert St EC1 .....**95** B4
Ingleborough St
SW9 ....**173** B2
Ingleby Rd N7 ....5 A1
Inglefield Sq **10**
E1 ....32 A1
Ingle Ho **3** SW12 ...73 C3
Inglesham Wlk E9 ...18 B2
Ingleside Gr SE3 .....53 B4
Inglethorpe Ho **6**
E5 ....17 C2
Inglethorpe St
SW6 ....47 C2
Ingleton St SW9 ....**173** B2
Inglewood Cl E14 ....41 C2
Inglewood Mans **11**
NW6 ....10 C3
Inglewood Rd
NW6 ....10 C3
Inglis Ho **1** SW15 ..57 B2
Inglis St SE5 ....48 A2
Ingram Ave NW11 .....2 B4
Ingram Cl SE11 ......**149** A4
Ingram Ho E3 ....26 A4
Ingram Lo **3** SW4 ..61 C1
Ingrave St SW11 .....60 A4
Ingrebourne Ho
NW8 ....**101** C4
Ingress St **4** W4 ...38 A1
Inigo Pl WC2 ....**120** A4
Inkerman Rd NW5 ...13 A2
Inkerman Terr
W8 ....**127** C1
Inkster Ho **9**
SW11 ....60 A4
Inman Rd
Harlesden NW10 .....21 A4
Wandsworth SW18 ..71 B4
Inner Circ NW1 ......**91** B4
Inner Park Rd
SW19 ....69 C2
Inner Temple* **7**
EC4 ....**121** B3
Inner Temple La
EC4 ....**107** B1
Innes Gdns SW15 ...57 A1
Innisfree Ho NW2 .....9 C2
Innis Ho SE17 ....**152** A2
Insley Ho **13** E3 .....27 A2
Inst for Child Health
WC1 ....94 C1
Institute PI **8** E8 ....17 A3
Instituto Espanol
Vicente Canada
Blanch W10 ....31 A4
Inst of Neurology
Bloomsbury WC1 ...**106** B4
St Pancras WC1 ....94 B1
Int Coll of
Accountancy The
WC1 ....72 B1
Interchange The
NW5 ....13 A2
International House
Language Sch
WC2 ....**106** B2
International Sch of
London W3 ....36 C2
Inver Ct
Bayswater W2 ......**100** B1

Inver Ct continued
4 Hammersmith
W6 ....38 C3
Inverclyde Gdns
IG1 ....
Inverforth Cl NW3 ....2 B2
Inverforth Ho NW3 ...2 B2
Invergarry Ho
NW6 ....**78** A1
Invermead Cl W6 ....38 C2
Inverness Mews
W8 ....**114** A4
Inverness PI W2 .....**114** A4
Inverness St NW1 ..**82** B4
Inverness Terr
W2 ....**114** A4
Inverton Rd SE15 ....65 C3
Invicta Cl **3** E3 ....33 C4
Invicta Plaza SE1 ..**122** A2
Invicta Prim Sch
SE3 ....53 C3
Invicta Rd SE3,
SE7 ....53 C4
Inville Rd SE17 ......**151** C1
Inwen Ct SE8 ....41 A1
Inwood Ct **12** NW1 .13 B1
Inwood Ho **16**
SE22 ....64 A4
Inworth St SW11 ...**168** B2
Inworth Wlk N1 ....86 C4
Ion Ct **16** E2 ....24 C3
Ionian Bldg **19**
E14 ....33 A2
Ionian Ho **22** E1 ...25 C1
Ipsden Bldgs SE1 ..**135** C4
Ipswich Ho SE4 ......65 C2
Ireland Yd EC4 ......**108** B1
Irene Rd SW6 ....**165** C3
Ireton Ho SW9 ......**173** C1
Ireton St **13** E3 .....26 C1
Iris Ct **8** SE15 ......50 A1
Iroko Ho **7** NW3 ...11 A2
Iron Bridge Cl
NW10 ....8 A3
Iron Bridge Ho
NW3 ....12 B1
Irongate Ho EC3 ...**110** B2
Iron Mill PI SW18 ...59 A1
Iron Mill Rd SW18 ..59 A1
Ironmonger La
EC2 ....**109** B1
Ironmonger Pas
EC1 ....**97** A3
Ironmonger Row
EC1 ....**97** A3
Ironmongers' PI **2**
E14 ....41 C2
Ironside Cl SE16 ....40 C4
Ironside Ho E9 ....18 A4
Ironworks **1** E3 ....26 C4
Irvine Ct W1 ....93 A1
Irvine Ho N7 ....14 B2
Irving Gr SW9 ....**172** C1
Irving Ho SE17 ......**150** A1
Irving Mews N1 .....15 B2
Irving Rd W14 ....39 C3
Irving St WC2 ....**119** C3
Irwell Est **51** SE16 .40 B4
Irwin Gdns NW10 ..22 A4
Isabella Ct **8**
TW10 ....54 B1
Isabella Ho
19 Hammersmith
W6 ....39 B1
Kennington SE11 ...**150** A2
Isabella Rd E9 ....17 B3

Isabella St SE1 ......**122** A1
Isabel St SW9 ....**173** A4
Isambard Mews
E14 ....42 B3
Isambard PI SE16 ...32 B1
Iseldon Ct N7 ....14 A4
Isel Way **4** SE22 ...64 A2
Isis Cl SW15 ....57 B3
Isis Ct W4 ....45 A3
Isis Ho NW8 ....**89** C1
Isis St SW18 ....71 B2
Islamia Girls' High
Sch NW6 ....23 A4
Islamia Prim Sch
NW6 ....23 A4
Islamic Coll for
Advanced Studies
NW10 ....9 A2
Island Gardens Sta
E14 ....42 B1
Island Ho E14 ....27 C2
Island Rd SE16 ....40 C2
Island Row E14 ......33 B3
Islay Wlk **17** N1 ...15 B2
Isleden Ho N1 ....86 C4
Isledon Rd N4, N7 ...5 C1
ISLE OF DOGS 42 B2
ISLINGTON 14 C2
Islington Arts &
Media Sch N4 ....5 B3
Islington Bsns Ctr
N1 ....**87** A4
Islington Est N1 .....86 C4
Islington Gn N1 ......86 A3
Islington Green Sch
N1 ....86 C4
Islington High St
N1 ....**86** A2
Islington Park Mews
N1 ....15 A1
Islington Park St
N1 ....15 A1
Islington Sixth Form
Ctr N7 ....14 C4
Islip St NW5 ....13 B3
Isokon Flats **3**
NW3 ....12 B3
Issac Way SE1 ......**137** A4
Italia Conti Acad of
Theatre Arts EC1 ..**96** C1

Ivanhoe Ho
11 Balham SW12 ...73 A4
21 Bow E3 ....26 A3
Ivanhoe Rd SE5 .....64 B4
Ivatt Pl W14 ....**141** A1
Iveagh Cl E9 ....25 C4
Iveagh Ct EC3 ....**110** C1
Iveagh Ho
2 Brixton SW9 ....48 A1
Chelsea SW10 ....**157** A2
Ivebury Ct **9** W10 ..30 B3
Iveley Rd SW4 ......**170** C1
Iver Ct N1 ....15 B2
Iverna Ct W8 ....**127** C2
Iverna Gdns W8 ....**127** C2
Iverson Rd NW6 .....10 C2
Ives Rd E16 ....35 A4
Ives St SW3 ....**144** B4
Ivimey St **24** E2 ....99 C4
Ivinghoe Ho **14**
N7 ....13 C3
Ivor Ct NW1 ....90 C2
Ivories The N1 ....15 B1
Ivor Mayor Lo
SW12 ....60 C1
Ivor PI NW1 ....90 C1
Ivor St NW1 ....13 B1

Ivory Ho
9 London SW11 ...59 B4
St George in t East
E1 ....**125** A2
Ivory Sq **10** SW18 ..59 B4
Ivybridge Ho **8**
SE22 ....64 A4
Ivybridge La WC2 ..**120** B3
Ivy Church La SE1,
SE17 ....**152** C2
Ivy Cres W4 ....37 B2
Ivy Ct SE16 ....**153** C1
Ivydale Prim Sch
SE15 ....65 C3
Ivydale Rd SE15 .....65 C3
Ivyday Gr SW16 ......74 B1
Ivy Lo W8 ...31 C1 **113** B2
Ivymount Rd SE27 ..74 C1
Ivy Rd Brockley SE4 ..66 C3
Cricklewood NW2 .....9 B4
Newham E16 ....35 C3
Ivy St N1 ....24 A3
Ixworth PI SW3 .....**144** A3

J

Jacaranda Gr E8 .....16 B1
Jackman Ho **24**
E1 ....32 A1
Jackman St E8 ....25 A4
Jackson Cl E9 ....17 C1
Jackson Ho **18**
SW11 ....59 C4
Jackson Rd N7 ....14 B4
Jackson's La N6 ....4 A4
Jack Taylor Sch
NW8 ....**78** C4
Jack Tizard Sch
W12 ....30 A1
Jack Walker Ct
N5 ....6 A1
Jacobin Lo N7 ....14 A3
Jacob Mans **15** E1 ..32 A3
Jacobson Ct
SW11 ....**168** B3
Jacobson Ho E1 ....**110** C2
Jacob St SE1 ....**139** B4
Jacob's Well Mews
W1 ....**103** C2
Jacotts Ho W10 ......22 B1
Jacqueline Ho **8**
E1 ....32 C4
Jaggard Way
SW12 ....72 B4
Jago Wlk **9** SE5 ...48 C3
Jamahirya Sch
SW3 ....**158** A4
Jamaica Rd
Bermondsey SE1 ..**139** A3
Bermondsey SE16 ..40 A3
Jamaica St E1 ....32 B4
James Allen's Girls'
Sch SE22 ....63 C1
James Anderson Ct **20**
E2 ....24 A3
James Ave NW2 ....9 B3
James Brine Ho
E2 ....24 B2 **99** A4
James Campbell Ho
2 E2 ....25 B3
James Collins Cl
W9 ....23 B1

James Docherty Ho
4 E2 ....25 B3
James Hammett Ho
9 E2 ....24 B3
James Ho
Mile End E1 ....26 A1
39 Rotherhithe
SE16 ....63 A3
James Joyce Wlk **7**
SE24 ....25 B3
James Leicester Hall
of Residence N7 ..14 A2
James Lind Ho **6**
SE8 ....41 B2
Jameson Ct E2 ....25 B3
Jameson Ho **8**
SE11 ....148 C2
Jameson Pl **11**
W3 ....37 B4
Jameson St
W8 ....31 C1 113 C2
James's Cotts
TW9 ....44 C3
James St
Marylebone W1 ..103 C3
Strand WC2 ....120 B4
James Stewart Ho
NW6 ....10 B1
James Stroud Ho
SE17 ....151 A1
Jamestown Rd
NW1 ....82 A4
Jamestown Way
E14 ....34 C2
James Wolfe
Sch SE10 ....52 B3
Jamuna Cl E14 ....33 A4
Jane St E1 ....32 A3
Janet St E14 ....41 C3
Janeway Pl **2**
SE16 ....40 A4
Janeway St SE16 139 C3
Jansen Ho **5**
SW15 ....56 C2
Jansen Wlk SW11 ..59 C3
Japan Cres N4 ......5 B3
Jardine Rd E1 ......32 C2
Jarman Ho
Bermondsey SE16 ..40 C2
16 Stepney E1 ......32 B4
Jarrett Ct SW2 ....75 A3
Jarrow Rd SE16 ....40 B1
Jarrow Way E19 ....18 A4
Jarvis Ho **9** SE15 ..49 C2
Jarvis Rd SE22 ....64 A3
Jasmin SE1 ....125 A1
Jasmine Sq E3 ....26 B4
Jasmin Ho SE4 ....66 B4
Jasmin Lo **17**
SE16 ....40 A1
Jason Ct
London SW9 ....173 B4
Marylebone W1 ....103 C2
Jasper Wlk N1 ......97 B4
Java Wharf SE1 ..139 A4
Jay Ho SW15 ......47 B1
Jay Mews SW7 ..129 A3
Jean Darling Ho
SW10 ....157 B3
Jean Pardies Ho **28**
E1 ....32 B4
Jebb Av SW2 ......62 A1
Jebb St E3 ....26 C3
Jedburgh St
SW11 ....60 C3

Jeddo Mews W12 ..38 B4
Jeddo Rd W12 ......38 B4
Jefferson Bldg **3**
E14 ....41 C4
Jeffrey's Ct SW4 172 A2
Jeffrey's Pl NW1 ..13 B1
Jeffrey's Rd SW4 172 A2
Jeffrey's St NW1 ..13 B1
Jeff Wooller Coll
WC1 ....106 B3
Jeger Ave E2 ......24 C4
Jeff Rd SW2 ....62 C2
Jellicoe Ho
5 Bethnal Green
E2 ....24 C3
Fitzrovia NW1 ......92 C1
11 Putney SW15 ....57 C2
Jemotts Ct **9**
SE14 ....50 C4
Jenkins Rd SW8 ..171 B4
Jenkinson Ho **12**
E2 ....25 C2
Jenner Ave W3 ....28 C4
Jenner Ho **5**
SE3 ....53 A4
Jenner Pl SW13 ....47 A4
Jenner Rd N16 ......7 B1
Jennifer Ho SE11 149 C3
Jennings Ho SE10 ..42 C1
Jennings Rd SE22 ..64 B1
Jensen Ho SE10 **4** 172 B1
Jephson Ct **3**
SW4 ....172 B1
Jephson Ho **6**
SE17 ....48 A4
Jephson St SE5 ....48 C2
Jephtha Rd SW18 ..58 C1
Jerdan Pl SW6 ....155 B2
Jeremiah St **11**
E14 ....34 A3
Jeremy Bentham Ho
E2 ....24 C2 99 C3
Jermyn St SW1 ..119 A2
Jerningham Ct
SE14 ....51 A2
Jerningham Rd
SE14 ....51 A2
Jerome Cres NW8 ..90 A2
Jerome Ho NW1 ..102 B4
Jerome St
E1 ....24 B1 98 C1
Jerome Twr **5**
W3 ....37 A4
Jerrard St SE13 ....67 A4
Jerrold Lo SW11 ..167 A4
Jerrold St N1 ....24 A3
Jersey Ho **8** N1 ....15 B2
Jersey Rd N1 ......15 B2
Jersey St E2 ....25 A2
Jerusalem Pas
EC1 ....96 A1
Jervis Bay Ho **9**
E14 ....34 C3
Jervis Ct
2 Greenwich
SE10 ....52 B3
Marylebone W1 ..104 B1
Jessel Ho
St Pancras WC1 ....94 A3
Westminster SW1 147 C4
Jessica Rd SW18 ..59 B2
Jessie Blythe La **4**
N19 ....5 A4
Jessie Duffett Ho **11**
SE5 ....48 B3
Jesson Ho SE17 ..151 B3
Jessop Ct N1 ......86 B1
Jessop Ho **9** W4 ..37 C2

Jessop Prim Sch
SE24 ....63 B3
Jessop Sq E14 ....33 C1
Jeston Ho **10** SE27..75 A1
Jethou Ho **10** N1 ..15 B2
Jevons Ho **9**
NW8 ....11 C1
Jewell Ho **8**
SW12 ....73 B4
Jewish Mus The*
NW1 ....13 B1
Jewry St EC3 ......110 C1
Jews Row SW18 ..59 B3
Jeymer Ave NW2 ....9 B3
Jeypore Rd SW18 ..59 B1
Jim Griffiths Ho
SW6 ....155 A3
Joanna Ho **4** W6 ..39 B1
Joan St SE1 ....122 A1
Jocelin Ho N1 ......85 A3
Jocelyn Rd TW9 ..54 A4
Jocelyn St SE15 ..49 C2
Jockey's Fields
WC1 ....107 A4
Jodane St SE8 ....41 B2
Jodrell Rd E3 ......18 B1
Johanna Prim Sch
SE1 ....135 B3
Johanna St SE1 ..135 B3
John Adam St
WC2 ....120 B3
John Aird Ct W2 ..101 A4
John Archer Way
SW18 ....59 C1
John Ashby Cl
SW2 ....62 A1
John Ball Prim Sch
SE3 ....53 B1
John Barker Ho
NW6 ....10 A1
John Betts' Ho
W12 ....38 C3
John Betts Prim Sch
W6 ....39 A3
John Bond Ho **2**
E3 ....26 B3
John Brent Ho **8**
SE8 ....40 C2
John Buck Ho
NW10 ....21 B4
John Burns Prim Sch
SW11 ....169 C1
John Campbell Rd **26**
N16 ....16 A3
John Carpenter St
EC4 ....122 A4
John Cartwright Ho
7 E2 ....25 A2
John Clynes Ct
SW15 ....57 A3
John Conwey Ho **23**
SW2 ....62 C1
John Dee Ho **3**
SW14 ....55 C4
John Donne Prim Sch
SE15 ....50 A2
John Dwight Ho
SW6 ....59 A4
John Fearon Wlk **5**
W10 ....23 A2
John Felton Rd
SE16 ....139 B3
John Fielden Ho **10**
E2 ....25 A2
John Fisher St
E1 ....125 B4

John F. Kennedy
Specl Sch E15....27 C1
John Harris Ho
SE15 ....64 C3
John Harrison Way
SE10 ....43 B3
John Islip St SW1 148 A3
John Keall Ho
SW15 ....57 C4
John Keble CE Prim
Sch NW10 ....21 B4
John Kennedy Ct **1**
N1 ....15 C2
John Kennedy Ho **1**
SE16 ....40 C2
John Kennedy Lo **2**
N1 ....15 C2
John King Ct **5**
N19 ....4 C2
John Kirk Ho
22 Battersea
SW11 ....59 C4
5 Streatham
SW16 ....74 A1
John Knight Lo
SW6 ....155 C2
John McDonald Ho **4**
E14 ....42 B3
John McKenna Wlk
SE16 ....139 C2
John & Mary Sch
NW5 ....13 C3
John Maurice Ct
SE17 ....151 B4
John Milton Prim Sch
SW8 ....160 C1
John Nettleford Ho
E2 ....25 A2
John Orwell Sports
Ctr E1 ....32 A1
John Parker Sq **8**
SW11 ....59 C4
John Parry Ct **28**
N1 ....24 A3
John Paul II Sch
SW19 ....69 C4
John Penn Ho
SE8 ....51 B3
John Penn St
SE13 ....52 A2
John Perryn Prim Sch
W3 ....29 A3
John Prince's St
W1 ....104 B2
John Pritchard Ho
1 E1 ....24 C1 99 C1
John Ratcliffe Ho **6**
NW6 ....23 C2
John Rennie Wlk **1**
E1 ....32 B1
John Roan Sch The
SE3 ....53 A3
John Roll Way
SE16 ....139 C2
John Ruskin Prim Sch
SE5 ....48 B4
John Ruskin St
SE5 ....48 B4
John Scurr Ho **18**
E14 ....33 A3
John Scurr Prim Sch
E1 ....25 B1
John Silkin La
SE8 ....40 C1
John's Mews WC1 ..95 A1
John Smith Ave
SW6 ....154 C2

John Smith Mews
E14 ....34 C2
Johnson Cl E8 ....24 C4
Johnson Ct **10**
SW18 ....59 C3
Johnson Ho
Belgravia SW1 ....145 C3
Bethnal Green
E2 ....24 C2 99 C3
Somers Town NW1..83 A1
South Lambeth
SW8 ....161 C1
Johnson Lo **12**
W9 ....31 C4
Johnson Rd NW10..20 C4
Johnsons Ct EC4 107 C1
Johnson's Pl SW1 146 C1
Johnson St E1 ......32 B3
Johnsons Way
NW10 ....20 A1
John Spencer Sq
N1 ....15 A2
John's Pl E1 ....32 A3
John St WC1 ....95 A1
John Stainer Com
Prim Sch SE4 ......66 A4
Johnston Ct SW9 173 A3
Johnstone Ho
SE13 ....67 C4
John Strachey Ho
SW6 ....155 A3
John Trundle Ct
EC2 ....108 C4
John Tucker Ho **8**
E14 ....41 C3
John Wesley's House
& Mus* EC1 ....97 C2
John Wheatley Ho
14 London N19......4 C1
West Brompton
SW6 ....155 A3
John Williams Cl
SE14 ....50 C4
Joiners Arms Yd **5**
SE5 ....48 C2
Joiner St SE1 ......123 C1
Joiners Yd N1 ......84 B1
Jolles Ho **9** E3 ....27 A2
Jonathan Ct **9**
W4 ....38 A2
Jonathan St SE11 148 C2
Jones Ho
4 South Bromley
E14 ....34 C3
Stamford Hill N16....7 A3
Jones St W1 ....118 A3
Jones Wlk **6**
TW10 ....54 B1
Jonson Ho
Borough The SE1....137 C1
16 Canonbury N16..15 C4
Jordan Ct SW15 ....57 C3
Jordan Ho
12 London SE4......65 C3
Shoreditch N1 ......87 C3
Jordans Ho N16 ....90 A1
Joscoyne Ho **5**
E1 ....32 A3
Joseph Ave W3 ....28 C3
Joseph Conrad Ho
SW1 ....147 A3
Joseph Ct N16 ......7 A4
Joseph Hardcastle
SE14 ....50 C3

Josephine Ave
SW2 . . . . .62 B2
Joseph Irwin Ho **11**
E14 . . . . .33 B2
Joseph Lancaster
Prim Sch SE1 . . . .137 B1
Joseph Powell Cl **1**
SW12 . . . . .61 B1
Joseph Priestley Ho
12 E2 . . . . .25 A2
Joseph St E3 . . . . .26 B1
Joseph Trotter Cl
EC1 . . . . .95 C3
Joshua St SW4 . . . . . .34 B3
Joslings Cl W12 . . . . . .29 C2
Josseline Ct **8** E3 . . .26 A3
Joubert Mans
SW3 . . . . .144 B3
Joubert St SW11 . . . .169 A2
Jowett Ho SW9 . . . . .172 B1
Jowett St SE15 . . . . . .49 B3
Jubet Ho **9** E16 . . . .15 C4
Jubilee Bldgs
NW8 . . . . .79 B2
Jubilee Cl **4**
NW10 . . . . .21 B3
Jubilee Cres E14 . . . . .42 B3
Jubilee Ct N1 . . . . .84 B4
Jubilee Ho **1** 149 C3
Jubilee Hts NW2 . . . . .10 B2
Jubilee Mans **10**
E1 . . . . .32 B3
Jubilee Mkt WC2 . . . .120 B4
Jubilee Pl SW3 . . . . .144 B2
Jubilee Prim Sch
London SW2 . . . . .62 C1
Stamford Hill N16 . . . . .7 C3
Jubilee St E1 . . . . .32 B4
Jubilee The **2**
SE10 . . . . .52 A3
Jubilee Yd SE1 . . . . . .138 C4
Judd St WC1 . . . . .94 A3
Jude St E16 . . . . .35 B3
Judges' Wlk NW3 . . . .2 B1
Juer St SW11 . . . . . . .158 B1
Julian Ave W3 . . . . . . .28 A2
Julian Ct SW13 . . . . . .46 B2
Julian Pl E14 . . . . .42 A1
Julia St NW5 . . . . .12 C3
Juliet Ho **11** N1 . . . . .24 A3
Julius Ho **8** E14 . . . .34 C3
Julius Nyerere Cl
N1 . . . . .84 C3
Junction App
Battersea SW11 . . . . .60 A4
Lewisham SE13 . . . . .67 B4
Junction Mews
W2 . . . . .102 A2
Junction Pl W2 . . . . .101 C2
Junction Rd N19 . . . . .4 B1
Juniper Cres NW1 . . .12 C1
Juniper Ct N16 . . . . . . .6 C2
Juniper Dr SW18 . . . .59 B3
Juniper Ho
6 Peckham SE14,
SE15 . . . . .50 B3
9 Richmond TW9 . . .45 A2
Juniper St **18** E1 . . . .32 B2
Juno Ct SW9 . . . . . . .163 B1
Juno Ho **2** E3 . . . . . .26 C4
Juno Way SE14 . . . . . .50 C4
Juno Way Ind Est
SE14 . . . . .50 C4
Jupiter Ct SW9 . . . . .163 B1

Jupiter Way N7 . . . . . .14 B2
Jupp Rd E15 . . . . .19 C1
Jupp Rd W E15 . . . . . .27 C4
Jura Ho SE16 . . . . . . .41 A2
Jurston Ct SE1 . . . . . .135 C3
Justines Pl E2 . . . . . . .25 C2
Jutland Cl N19 . . . . . . .5 A3
Jutland Ho **4** SE5 . . .48 B1
Juxon St SE11 . . . . . .149 A4

K

Kambala Rd SW11 . . . .59 C4
Kara Way NW2 . . . . . . .9 C4
Karen Ct
3 Camberwell
SE5 . . . . .64 A4
Forest Hill SE23 . . . . .66 A1
Karen Ho **7** N16 . . . .15 C4
Kasmin Ct NW10 . . . . .8 C1
Kassala Rd SW11 . . . .169 A3
Katherine Cl **3**
SE16 . . . . .32 C1
Katherine Ho **11**
W10 . . . . .23 A1
Katherine Sq
W11 . . . . .31 A1 112 A2
Kathleen Ave W3 . . . . .28 B4
Kathleen Rd SW11 . . .60 B4
Kay Rd SW9 . . . . .172 C1
Kay St E2 . . . . .24 C3
Kean Ho **5** SE17 . . . .48 A4
Kean St WC2 . . . . . . .106 C1
Keates Cl
Bermondsey SE1 . . . .152 C3
Hampstead NW3 . . . . .12 A4
Keats Cl
22 Bethnal Green
E2 . . . . .25 B2
30 Camberwell SE5 . .48 B3
Chelsea SW1 . . . . . . .161 A4
Keats House Mus ★
NW3 . . . . .12 A4
Keats Pl EC2 . . . . . . .109 B3
Keble Ho **4** SW15 . . .57 C1
Keble Pl SW13 . . . . . .47 A4
Kedelston Ct E15 . . . . .18 A4
Kedge Ho **18** E14 . . .41 C3
Kedleston Wlk **21**
E2 . . . . .25 A2
Keel Cl SE16 . . . . .32 C1
Keel Ct **8** E14 . . . . . .34 C2
Keeley St WC2 . . . . . .106 C1
Keeling Ho **4** E2 . . . .25 A3
Keelson Ho **9**
E14 . . . . .41 C3
Keen's Yd N1 . . . . .15 A2
Keeper Wharf E1 . . . . .32 C2
Keepier Wharf **18**
E14 . . . . .34 C2
Keep The SE3 . . . . . . .53 C1
Keeton's Rd SE16 . . . .40 A3
Keevil Dr SW19 . . . . . .70 A4
Keighley Cl N7 . . . . . .14 A4
Keildon Rd SW11 . . . . .60 B3
Keir Hardie Ho
Fulham W6 . . . . .47 C4
15 Upper Holloway
N19 . . . . .4 C4
Willesden NW10 . . . . .8 B1
Keir Hardy Prim Sch
E16 . . . . .35 C4

Keith Connor Cl **5**
SW8 . . . . .61 A4
Keith Gr W12 . . . . .29 C1
Keith Ho NW6 . . . . . . .78 A1
Kelby Ho N7 . . . . .14 B2
Kelfield Ct **1**
W10 . . . . .30 C3
Kelfield Gdns
W10 . . . . .30 C3
Kelfield Mews
W10 . . . . .30 C3
Kellett Ho N1 . . . . . . .87 C3
Kellett Rd SW2 . . . . . .62 C3
Kellow Ho SE1 . . . . . .137 B4
Kell St SE1 . . . . .136 B2
Kelly Ave SE15 . . . . . .49 B2
Kelly Ct **18** E14 . . . . .33 C2
Kelly Mews **4** W9 . . .23 B1
Kelly St NW1 . . . . .13 A2
Kelman Cl SW4 . . . . .171 C1
Kelmore Gr SE22 . . . .64 C3
Kelmscott Gdns
W12 . . . . .38 C3
Kelmscott Rd
SW11 . . . . .60 B2
Kelross Rd N5 . . . . .15 B4
Kelsall Mews TW9 . . . .45 A2
Kelsey St E2 . . . . .24 C1 99 C2
Kelshall Ct N4 . . . . .6 B2
Kelson Ho E14 . . . . . . .42 B3
Kelso Pl W8 . . . . .128 B2
Kelvedon Ho
SW8 . . . . .172 B4
Kelvedon Rd SW6 . . .155 A1
Kelvin Ct
Chiswick W4 . . . . .45 B3
Notting Hill
W11 . . . . .31 C2 113 B3
Kelvington Rd
SE15 . . . . .65 C2
Kelway Ho W14 . . . . .140 C1
Kelyway Ho **20**
SW2 . . . . .74 C4
Kember St N1 . . . . . . .14 B1
Kemble Ho SW9 . . . . .63 A4
Kemble St WC2 . . . . .106 C1
Kemerton Rd SE5 . . . .63 B4
Kemey's St E9 . . . . . . .18 A3
Kemp Ct SW8 . . . . . . .162 A1
Kemp Ho **14** E2 . . . . .25 C3
Kempe Rd NW6 . . . . . .22 C3
Kemp Ho
Finsbury EC1 . . . . .97 B3
1 Globe Town E2 . . . .25 C3
Kempis Way **5**
SE22 . . . . .64 A2
Kemplay Rd NW3 . . . .11 C4
Kemps Dr E14 . . . . . . .33 C2
Kempsford Gdns
SW5 . . . . .141 C1
Kempsford Rd
Lambeth SE11 . . . . . .149 C3
1 Newington SE11 . .150 A3
Kemps Gdns SE13 . . .67 B2
Kempson Rd SW6 . . .155 C1
Kempthorne Rd
SE8 . . . . .41 B2
Kempton Ct E1 . . . . . .32 A4
Kempton Ho **13**
N1 . . . . .24 A4
Kemsing Ho SE1 . . . .137 C3
Kemsing Rd SE10 . . . .43 C1
Kemsley SE13 . . . . . . .67 A2
Kenbrook Ho
Kensington W14 . . . .127 A1

Kenbrook Ho *continued*
5 Kentish Town
NW5 . . . . .13 B3
Kenbury Gdns **10**
SE5 . . . . .48 B1
Kenbury Mans **18**
SE5 . . . . .48 B1
Kenbury St SE5 . . . . . .48 B1
Kenchester Cl
SW8 . . . . .162 B1
Kendal NW1 . . . . .92 B4
Kendal Ave W3 . . . . . .28 A4
Kendal Cl SE5 . . . . . . .48 A3
Kendal Ct NW2 . . . . . .10 A3
Kendal Ho
29 Hackney E9 . . . . .17 B1
Islington N1 . . . . .85 A2
Kendall Ct **3**
SE22 . . . . .64 C2
Kendall Pl W1 . . . . . .103 B3
Kendal Pl SW15 . . . . .58 B2
Kendal Rd NW10 . . . . .8 C4
Kendal St W2 . . . . . . .102 B1
Kendal Stps W2 . . . . .102 B1
Kender Prim Sch
SE14 . . . . .50 B2
Kender St SE14 . . . . . .50 B2
Kendoa Rd **1**
SW4 . . . . .61 C3
Kendon Ho E15 . . . . . .19 C1
Kendrick Ct **12**
SE15 . . . . .50 A2
Kendrick Mews
SW7 . . . . .143 B3
Kendrick Pl SW7 . . . .143 B3
Kenilford Rd
SW12 . . . . .73 A4
Kenilworth Ct
SW6 . . . . .58 A4
Kenilworth Rd
Bow E3 . . . . .26 A3
Kilburn NW6 . . . . .23 B4
Kenley Wlk
W11 . . . . .31 A2 112 A3
Kenmont Gdns
NW10 . . . . .22 A2
Kenmont Prim Sch
NW10 . . . . .22 A2
Kenmure Ct TW9 . . . .44 C3
Kenmure Rd E8 . . . . . .17 A3
Kenmure Yd E8 . . . . . .17 A3
Kennacraig Cl **6**
E16 . . . . .35 C1
Kennard Ho
SW11 . . . . .169 C3
Kennard Rd E15 . . . . .19 C1
Kennard St SW11 . . . .169 B3
E16 . . . . .35 B4
Kennedy Cox Ho **9**
E16 . . . . .35 B4
Kennedy Ho SE11 . . .148 C2
Kennedy Wlk
SE17 . . . . .151 C3
Kenneth Campbell Ho
NW8 . . . . .89 C2
Kenneth Cres NW2 . . .9 A3
Kenneth Ct SE11 . . . .149 C4
Kenneth Ho NW6 . . . .89 C1
Kenneth Younger Ho
SW6 . . . . .155 A3
Kennet Ho NW8 . . . . .89 C1
Kennet Rd W9 . . . . . . .23 B1
Kennet St E1 . . . . .125 C2
Kennet Wharf La
EC4 . . . . .123 A4

Kenning Ho **6** N1 . . .24 A4

Kenning St **18**
SE16 . . . . .40 B4
Kennings Way
SE11 . . . . .149 C2
KENNINGTON 149 B1
Kennington Ent Ctr
SE17 . . . . .150 A1
Kennington La
SE11 . . . . .149 C1
Kennington Oval
SE11 . . . . .163 A3
Kennington Palace Ct
SE11 . . . . .149 B2
Kennington Park
Gdns SE17 . . . . .48 A4
Kennington Park Ho
SE11 . . . . .149 C2
Kennington Park Pl
SE11 . . . . .48 A4
Kennington Park Rd
SE11 . . . . .150 A2
Kennington Rd
SE11 . . . . .149 B3
Kennington Sta
SE17 . . . . .150 A2
Kennoldes SE21 . . . . .75 C2
Kenrick Pl W1 . . . . . .103 B3
KENSAL GREEN . . .22 B2
Kensal Green Cemy
(All Souls) ★
NW10 . . . . .22 B2
Kensal Green Sta
NW10 . . . . .22 B2
Kensal Ho W10 . . . . . .22 C1
Kensal Rd W10 . . . . . .23 A1
KENSAL RISE 22 C3
Kensal Rise Prim Sch
NW6 . . . . .22 C3
Kensal Rise Sta
NW10 . . . . .22 C3
KENSAL TOWN 23 A1
KENSINGTON 127 C3
Kensington &
Chelsea Coll
Chelsea SW10 . . . . . .156 C2
Kensal Town W10 . . . .31 A4
Kensington Church Ct
W8 . . . . .128 A3
Kensington Church St
W8 . . . . .31 C1 113 C1
Kensington Church
Wlk W8 . . . . .128 A3
Kensington Court
Mans W8 . . . . .128 B3
Kensington Court
Mews W8 . . . . .128 B3
Kensington Court Pl
W8 . . . . .128 B2
Kensington Ct Gdns
W8 . . . . .128 B2
Kensington Gardens ★
W2 . . . . .115 A1
Kensington Gate
W8 . . . . .128 C2
Kensington Gdns Sq
W2 . . . . .100 A1
Kensington Gore
SW7 . . . . .129 B3
Kensington Hall Gdns
W14 . . . . .140 C2
Kensington High St
W8 . . . . .127 C2
Kensington Ho **3**
NW5 . . . . .13 B3

Kensington Hts
W8 . . . . . . 31 C1 113 B1
Kensington Mall
W8 . . . . . . 31 C1 113 C2
Kensington Mans
SW5 . . . . 141 C2
Kensington Olympia
Sta W14 . . . . . . 126 A2
Kensington Pal*
W8 . . . . 114 B1
Kensington Palace
Gdns W8 . . . . . 114 A2
Kensington Park Gdns
W11 . . . . . 31 B2 113 A2
Kensington Park Mews
Mews W11 . . . . . . 31 B3
Kensington Park Rd
W11 . . . . . 31 B2 113 A2
Kensington Pl
W8 . . . . . 31 C1 113 B2
Kensington Prep Sch
SW6 . . . . 165 A4
Kensington Rd
SW7 . . . . . 31 A2 112 A4
Kensington Sports Ctr
W11 . . . . . 31 A2 112 A4
Kensington Sq
W8 . . . . 128 A3
Kensington Village
W14 . . . . 141 A3
Kensington W
W14 . . . . 140 A4
Kenworth Ho EC1 97 C3
Kent Ct 3 E2 . . . . . 24 B3
Kent Ho
Camberwell SE1 . 153 A1
13 Chiswick W4 . . . 38 A1
Marylebone W1 . . 104 C2
Pimlico SW1 . . . . 147 A1
Richmond TW10 . . 54 C2
Kentish Bldgs
SE1 . . . . 123 B1
KENTISH TOWN . 13 A2
Kentish Town CE Prim
Sch NW5 . . . . . . 13 A3
Kentish Town Rd
NW1 . . . . 13 A2
Kentish Town Sta
NW5 . . . . 13 B3
Kentish Town West
Sta NW5 . . . . . . 13 A2
Kent Lo 9 SW19 . . 69 C3
Kentmere Ho
SE15 . . . . 50 B4
Kenton Ct W14 . . 126 C1
Kenton Ho
20 Globe Town E1 . . 25 B1
Highbury N5 . . . . . 5 C1
Kenton Rd E9 . . . . 17 C2
Kenton St WC1 . . . 94 A2
Kent Pas NW1 . . . . 90 B3
Kent Pk Ind Est
SE15 . . . . 50 A4
Kent Rd
Richmond TW9 . . . 44 C3
South Acton W4 . . 37 B3
Kent St E2 . . . . 24 B3
Kent Terr NW1 . . . 90 B3
Kentwell Cl SE4 . . 66 A3
Kentwode Gn
SW13 . . . . 46 C3
Kent Yard SW7 . . 130 B3
Kenway Rd SW5 . 142 A3
Ken Wilson Ho 16
E2 . . . . 24 C3
Kenwood Cl NW3 . . 2 C3

Kenwood Ho 15
SW9 . . . . 63 A3
Kenwood Ho*
NW3 . . . . 3 A3
Kenworthy Rd E9 . 18 A2
Kenwrick Ho N1 . . 85 A3
Kenwyn Rd SW4 . . 61 C3
Kenyon Ho 9 SE10 . 48 B3
Kenyon St SW6 . . 47 C2
Kepler Ho 9 SE10 . 43 B1
Kepler Rd SW2,
SW4 . . . . 62 A3
Keppel Ho
Brompton SW3 . . 144 A3
5 Deptford SE8 . . . 41 B1
Keppel Row SE1 . 122 C1
Keppel St WC1 . . 105 C4
Kerbela St
E2 . . . . 24 C1 99 B2
Kerbey St E14 . . . 34 A3
Kerfield Cres SE5 . 48 C2
Kerfield Pl SE5 . . . 48 C2
Kerridge Ct N1 . . . 16 A2
Kerrier Ho SW10 . 157 A1
Kerrington Ct 7
W12 . . . . 39 B4
Kerrison Rd
Battersea SW11 . . 60 A4
Mill Meads E15 . . . 27 C4
Kerry N7 . . . . 14 A2
Kerry Ho 6 E1 . . . 32 B3
Kerry Path SE8 . . . 51 B4
Kerry Rd SE8 . . . . 51 B4
Kerscott Ho 30 E3 . 27 A2
Kersfield Ho
SW15 . . . . 57 C1
Kersfield Rd
SW15 . . . . 57 C1
Kershaw Cl SW18 . 59 C1
Kershaw Ho 7
SE27 . . . . 75 A1
Kersley Mews
SW11 . . . . 168 C3
Kersley Rd N16 . . . 7 A1
Kersley St SW11 . 168 C2
Kerwick Cl 1 N7 . 14 B1
Keslake Mans
NW10 . . . . 22 C3
Keslake Rd NW6 . . 22 C3
Keston Ho SE17 . . 152 B2
Keston Rd SE15 . . . 64 C4
Kestrel Ave SE24 . . 63 B2
Kestrel Ho
4 Battersea
SW11 . . . . 60 A4
Finsbury EC1 . . . . 96 C4
Kestrel Pl SE14 . . . 51 A4
Keswick Broadway 1
SW15 . . . . 58 B2
Keswick Ct 2
SE22 . . . . 64 C2
Keswick Ho 5
SE5 . . . . 48 B2
Keswick Hts 9
SW15 . . . . 58 A4
Keswick Ho E8 . . . . 16 C3
Keswick Rd SW15 . 58 A2
Kett Gdns SW2 . . . 62 B2
Kettleby Ho NW9 . . 63 A4
Ketton Ho 11 W10 . 22 B1
Kevan Ho SE5 . . . . 48 B3
KEW 44 C4
Kew Bridge TW8 . . 36 B1
Kew Bridge Ct 8
W4 . . . . 36 C1

Kew Bridge
Distribution Ctr
TW8 . . . . 36 B1
Kew Bridge Rd
TW8 . . . . 36 B1
Kew Bridge Sta
TW8 . . . . 36 B1
Kew Bridge Steam
Mus* TW8 . . . . . . 36 B1
Kew Coll TW9 . . . . 44 B3
Kew Foot Rd TW9 . 54 A4
Kew Gardens Rd
TW9 . . . . 44 C2
Kew Gardens (Royal
Botanic)* TW9 . . . 44 A3
Kew Gardens Sta
TW9 . . . . 44 B2
Kew Gn TW9 . . . . . 44 B4
Kew Green TW9 . . . 44 B4
Kew Green Prep Sch
TW9 . . . . 44 B4
Kew Lo 11 TW9 . . . 44 B2
Kew Montessori Sch
TW9 . . . . 44 C2
Kew Pal* TW9 . . . . 44 A3
Kew Pier TW9 . . . . 44 B4
Kew Rd TW9, W4 . . 44 B2
Kew Ret Pk TW9 . . 44 C3
Kew Riverside Prim
Sch TW9 . . . . . . 45 A1
Key Cl E1 . . . . 25 A1
Keyes Ct SE22 . . . . 64 C2
Keyes Rd NW2 . . . . 9 C3
Keyham Ho 9 W2 . . 31 C4
Key Ho SE11 . . . . 163 B4
Keymer Rd SW2 . . . 74 B2
Keynsham Ho 2
N4 . . . . 6 B4
Keyse Rd SE1 . . . 138 C1
Keystone Cres N1 . 84 B1
Keyworth Cl E5 . . . 18 A4
Keyworth Pl SE1 . 136 B2
Keyworth Prim Sch
SE17 . . . . 150 A2
Keyworth St SE1 . 136 B2
Kezia St SE8 . . . . . 41 A1
Khyber Rd SW11 . 168 A1
Kibworth St SW8 . 162 C1
Kidbrooke Gdns
SE3 . . . . 53 C2
Kidderpore Ave
NW3 . . . . 10 C4
Kidderpore Gdns
NW3 . . . . 10 C4
Kiffen St EC2 . . . . 97 C2
Kilbrennan Ho 9
E14 . . . . 34 B3
KILBURN 23 C4
Kilburn Bridge 14
NW6 . . . . 23 C4
Kilburn Gate NW6 78 A2
Kilburn High Rd
NW6 . . . . 23 C4
Kilburn High Road Sta
NW6 . . . . 23 C4
Kilburn Ho 15 W9 . 23 B2
Kilburn La W10 . . . 23 A3
Kilburn Park
Foundation Sch The
NW6 . . . . 23 B3
Kilburn Park Rd
NW6 . . . . 23 C2
Kilburn Park Sta
NW6 . . . . 23 C3
Kilburn Pl NW6 . . . 23 C4
Kilburn Priory
NW6 . . . . 78 A3

Kilburn Sq NW6 . . 23 C4
Kilburn Sta NW2 . . 10 B2
Kilburn Vale NW6 . 78 A3
Kilburn Vale Est 13
NW6 . . . . 23 C4
Kilby Ct SE10 . . . . 43 B3
Kildare Ct W2 . . . . 31 C3
Kildare Gdns W2 . . 31 C3
Kildare Rd E16 . . . 35 C4
Kildare Terr W2 . . 31 C3
Kildare Wlk E14 . . 33 C3
Kildoran Rd SW2 . . 62 A2
Kilgour Rd SE23 . . 66 A1
Kilkie St SW6 . . . 166 C1
Killarney Rd SW18 . 59 B1
Killick St N1 . . . . . 84 C1
Killieser Ave SW2 . 74 A2
Killip Cl E16 . . . . . 35 B3
Killoran Ho 2 E14 . 42 B3
Killowen Rd E9 . . . 17 C2
Killyon Rd SW8 . . 171 B1
Kilmaine Rd SW6 . 154 B1
Kilmarsh Rd W6 . . 39 B2
Kilmington Rd
SW13 . . . . 46 C4
Kilmore Ho 17
E14 . . . . 34 A3
Kilmuir Ho SW1 . 145 C3
Kiln Ct E14 . . . . . . 33 B2
Kilner Ho SE11 . . 163 B4
Kilner St E14 . . . . 33 C4
Kiln Pl NW5 . . . . . 12 C3
Kiloh Ct 1 SW11 . . 60 A4
Kilpatrick Ct N16 . . 7 B3
Kilpeck Ho 9 N4 . . 6 B4
Kilravock St W10 . 23 A2
Kilronan 5 W3 . . . 28 C3
Kimbell Gdns
SW6 . . . . 164 A3
Kimber Ctr The
SW18 . . . . 70 C4
Kimberley Ave
SE15 . . . . 65 B4
Kimberley Ct NW6 . 23 A4
Kimberley Ho 6
E14 . . . . 42 B3
Kimberley Rd
Kilburn NW6 . . . . 23 A4
Stockwell SW9 . . . 62 A4
Kimber Rd SW18 . . 71 A4
Kimble Ho
Lisson Gr NW8 . . . 90 B2
1 Lower Holloway
N7 . . . . 14 A3
Kimbolton Row
SW3 . . . . 144 A3
Kimpton Ct 12
SE5 . . . . 48 C2
Kimpton Ho SW15 . 68 C4
Kimpton Rd SE5 . . 48 C2
Kinburn St SE16 . . 40 C4
Kincaid Rd SE15 . . 50 A3
Kincardine Gdns
W9 . . . . 23 C1
Kindell Ho 4
SW14 . . . . 55 C4
Kinder Ho N1 . . . . 87 C2
Kindersley Ho E1 . 111 C1
Kinder St 15 E1 . . . 32 A3
Kinefold Ho N7 . . . 14 A2
Kinfauns Rd SW2 . . 74 C2
King Alfred Sch
NW11 . . . . 2 A3
King Arthur Cl
SE15 . . . . 50 B3
King Charles Ct 17
SE17 . . . . 48 A4

King Charles Ho
SW6 . . . . 156 B2
King Charles St
SW1 . . . . 134 A1
King Charles Terr 11
E1 . . . . 32 A2
King Charles Wlk 6
SW19 . . . . 70 A3
King David La E1 . 32 B2
Kingdon Ho 8
E14 . . . . 42 B3
Kingdon Rd NW6 . 10 C2
Kingdown Cl W10 . 30 C3
King Edward Mans 12
E8 . . . . 25 A4
King Edward Mews
SW13 . . . . 46 C2
King Edwards Mans
SW6 . . . . 155 B1
King Edward's Rd
E9 . . . . 25 B4
King Edward St
EC1 . . . . 108 C2
King Edward The
Third Mews 11
SE16 . . . . 40 A4
King Edward VII Hospl-
Sister Agnes W1 103 C4
King Edward Wlk
SE1 . . . . 135 C2
King Fahed Acad
W3 . . . . 29 B2
Kingfield St E14 . . 42 B2
Kingfisher Ct
1 Battersea
SW11 . . . . 60 A4
7 Cubitt Town E14 . 42 B4
Putney SW19 . . . . 70 A2
Kingfisher Ho
6 Battersea
SW18 . . . . 59 B4
Peckham SE15 . . . 49 B2
West Kensington
W14 . . . . 126 C2
Kingfisher Mews
SE13 . . . . 67 A2
Kingfisher Sq 16
SE8 . . . . 51 B4
King Frederick IX Twr
SE16 . . . . 41 B3
King George Sq
TW10 . . . . 54 B1
King George St
SE10 . . . . 52 B3
Kingham Cl
1 Shepherd's Bush
W11 . . . . 39 C4
Wandsworth SW18 . 71 B4
Kingham Ind Est
NW10 . . . . 20 C2
King Henry's Rd
NW3 . . . . 12 A1
King Henry's Reach
W6 . . . . 47 B4
King Henry St
N16 . . . . 16 A3
King Henry's Wlk
N1 . . . . 16 A2
King Henry's Yd 5
N16 . . . . 16 A3
King Henry Terr 10
E1 . . . . 32 A2
King Ho 5 W12 . . . 30 A3
Kinghorn St EC1 . 108 C3

King James St
SE1 . . . . **136** A3
King John Ct
EC2 . . . . 24 A1 98 B2
King John St E1 . . . . 32 C4
Kinglake St SE17 . . 152 B2
Kingly Ct W1 . . . . . . 119 A4
Kingly St W11 . . . . . 118 C4
King & Queen St
SE17 . . . . 151 A2
King's Arms Ct
E1 . . . . 111 B3
King's Arms Yd
EC2 . . . . 109 B2
Kings Ave SW4 . . . . 62 A1
Kings Avenue Sch
SW4 . . . . 62 A2
King's Bench St
SE1 . . . . 136 B4
King's Bench Wlk
EC4 . . . . 107 C1
Kingsbridge N16 . . 6 C3
Kingsbridge Ave
W3 . . . . 36 B4
Kingsbridge Ct
E14 . . . . 41 C2
Kingsbridge Rd
W10 . . . . 30 B3
Kingsbury Rd N1 . . 16 A2
Kingsbury Terr
N1 . . . . 16 A2
Kingsclere Cl
SW15 . . . . 68 C4
Kingscliffe Gdns
SW19 . . . . 70 B3
King's Coll
Dulwich Village
SE24 . . . . 63 C1
Strand WC2 . . . . 121 A4
Kings College Ct
NW3 . . . . 12 A1
King's College Hospl
SE5 . . . . 48 C2
Kings College Rd
NW3 . . . . 11 C1
King's Coll London
(Hampstead)
NW3 . . . . 10 C4
King's Coll Univ
SE1 . . . . 121 B1
Kingscote NW11 . . 1 B3
Kingscote Rd W4 . . 37 C3
Kingscote St EC4 . 122 A4
King's Court N
SW3 . . . . 144 A1
Kingscourt Rd
SW16 . . . . 74 A1
King's Court S
SW3 . . . . 144 A1
King's Cres N4, N5 . 6 B1
Kingscroft SW4 . . 62 A1
Kingscroft Rd
NW2 . . . . 10 B2
KING'S CROSS . . . 84 C2
King's Cross WC1 . 94 B4
King's Cross Bridge
WC1 . . . . 94 B4
King's Cross Rd
WC1 . . . . 95 A3
King's Cross, St
Pancras N1 . . . . 94 A4
King's Cross Sta
N1 . . . . 84 B1
King's Cross (Thames
Link) Sta WC1 . . 94 B4

Kings Ct
6 Barnsbury N7 . . . . 14 B1
Chiswick W6 . . . . . . 38 C2
East Dulwich SE22 . . 64 C3
Primrose Hill NW8 . 80 C3
11 Putney SW15 . . . . 68 C4
Kingsdale Gdns
W11 . . . . 30 C1
Kingsdale Sec Sch
SE21 . . . . 76 A1
Kingsdown Ave
W3 . . . . 29 A2
Kingsdown Cl
28 Deptford SE16 . . 40 A1
6 Notting Hill W11 . 31 A3
Kingsdown Ct
SW11 . . . . 60 A1
Kingsdown Ho 1
E8 . . . . 16 C3
Kingsdown Rd 4
N19 . . . . 5 A2
Kings Farm Ave
TW10 . . . . 54 C3
Kingsfield Ho 18
N16 . . . . 7 A1
Kingsford St NW5 . 12 B3
Kingsgate Est N1 . 16 A2
Kingsgate Ho
SW9 . . . . 173 C4
Kingsgate Par
SW1 . . . . 133 A1
Kingsgate PI NW6 . 10 C1
Kingsgate Prim Sch
NW6 . . . . 10 C1
Kingsgate Rd
NW6 . . . . 10 C1
King's Gdns 6
NW6 . . . . 10 C1
King's Gr
Peckham SE15 . . . . 50 A2
Peckham SE15 . . . . 50 A3
Kingshall Mews
SE13 . . . . 67 B4
King's Head Yd
SE1 . . . . 123 B1
Kingshill SE17 . . . 151 A4
Kings Ho
16 Limehouse E14 . . 33 B2
South Lambeth
SW8 . . . . 162 B2
Kingshold Rd E9 . . 17 B1
King's House Sch
TW10 . . . . 54 B2
King's House Sch
(Jun) TW10 . . . . . 54 B2
King's Keep 5
SW15 . . . . 57 C2
KINGSLAND 16 A2
Kingsland NW8 . . 80 B3
Kingsland Gn 1 E8,
N1 . . . . 16 A2
Kingsland High St
E8 . . . . 16 B3
Kingsland Pas 2
E8 . . . . 16 A2
Kingsland Rd E2 . . 24 A3
Kingsland Sh Ctr 12
E8 . . . . 16 B3
Kingslawn Cl
SW15 . . . . 57 A2
Kingsley Ct NW2 . . 9 A2
Kingsley Flats
SE1 . . . . 152 B3
Kingsley Ho
Chelsea SW3 . . . . 157 C3
Clapham SW4 . . . 171 C2

Kingsley Mews
Kensington W8 . . . 128 B1
15 St George in t East
E1 . . . . 32 A2
Kingsley PI N6 . . . . 3 C4
Kingsley Rd NW6 . . 23 B4
Kingsley St SW11 . 60 B4
Kings Mall Sh Ctr
W6 . . . . 39 B2
King's Mans SW3 . 158 A3
Kingsmead TW10 . . 54 B1
Kingsmead Ct N6 . . 4 C4
Kingsmead Ho E9 . 18 A4
Kingsmead Prim Sch
E9 . . . . 18 A4
Kingsmead Way E5,
E9 . . . . 18 A4
Kingsmere Cl
SW15 . . . . 57 C4
Kingsmere PI N16 . 6 C3
Kingsmere Rd
SW19 . . . . 69 C2
King's Mews
1 Clapham Pk
SW4 . . . . 62 A2
Gray's Inn WC1 . . . 95 A1
Kingsmill NW8 . . . 79 C2
Kingsmill Terr
NW8 . . . . 79 C2
Kingsnorth Ho 17
W10 . . . . 30 C3
King's Par
1 Hammersmith
W12 . . . . 38 C3
Willesden NW10 . . . 22 B4
Kings PI W4 . . . . . . 37 B2
King's PI SE1 . . . . 136 C3
King Sq EC1 . . . . . . 96 C3
King's Quay SW10 167 A4
Kings Rd
Richmond TW10,
TW9 . . . . 54 B2
Willesden NW10 . . . 9 A1
King's Rd
Chelsea SW3 . . . . 144 B1
Chelsea SW3 . . . . 157 B3
Mortlake SW14 . . . 55 C4
Kings Ride Gate
TW10 . . . . 54 C3
Kingsridge SW19 . 70 A2
King's Scholars' Pas
SW1 . . . . 146 C4
King St W Acton W3 . 28 B1
Hammersmith W6 . . 38 C2
St James SW1 . . . 119 A2
Strand WC2 . . . . . 120 A4
Whitechapel EC2 . 109 A1
King Stairs Cl
SE16 . . . . 40 A4
King's Terr NW1 . . 82 C3
Kingston Ho 6
NW6 . . . . 10 A1
Kingston Ho E
SW7 . . . . 130 A3
Kingston Ho N
SW7 . . . . 130 A3
Kingston Ho S
SW7 . . . . 130 A3
Kingston Rd SW15,
SW19 . . . . 69 A3
Kingston Univ
Roehampton Vale
Campus SW15 . . . 68 B1
Kingston Vale
SW15 . . . . 68 A1

Kingstown St NW1 . 81 B4
Kingswater PI
6 W6 . . . . 39 A2
King Street Coll
W12 . . . . 39 A4
Kingsway
Mortlake SW14,
TW9 . . . . 55 A4
St Giles WC2 . . . . 106 C2
Kingsway Coll
NW5 . . . . 13 A2
Kingsway Mans
WC1 . . . . 106 C4
Kingsway PI EC1 . . 96 A2
Kingswear Rd NW5 . 4 A1
Kings Well 28
NW3 . . . . 11 B4
Kings Wlk Sh Mall
SW3 . . . . 144 C2
Kingswood 51
E2 . . . . 25 B3
Kingswood Ave
NW6 . . . . 23 A3
Kingswood Cl
SW8 . . . . 162 B1
Kingswood Ct
Hither Green SE13 . 67 C1
7 Richmond TW10 . 54 B2
Kings Wood Ct 4
NW6 . . . . 10 C1
Kingswood Rd
South Acton W4 . . . 37 B3
Streatham SW2 . . . 74 A4
Kingswood Terr
W4 . . . . 37 B3
Kingthorpe Rd
NW10 . . . . 8 A1
Kington Ho NW6 . . 78 B3
Kingward Ho E1 . . 111 B4
Kingweston Ct
N16 . . . . 7 A1
King William La 3
SE10 . . . . 43 A1
King William St
EC4 . . . . 123 C4
King William Wlk
SE10 . . . . 52 B4
Kingwood Rd
SW6 . . . . 154 A1
Kinloch St N7 . . . . 5 B1
Kinnaird Ave W4 . . 45 B3
Kinnear Rd W12 . . 38 B4
Kinnerton PI N
SW1 . . . . 131 A3
Kinnerton PI S
SW1 . . . . 131 A3
Kinnerton St
SW1 . . . . 131 B3
Kinnerton Yd
SW1 . . . . 131 B3
Kinnoull Mans 10
E5 . . . . 17 A4
Kinnoul Rd W6 . . . 154 A4
Kinross Ho N1 . . . . 84 C4
Kinsale Rd SE15 . . 64 C4
Kinsham Ho
E2 . . . . 24 C1 99 C2
Kintore Way SE1 . 152 C4
Kintyre Ct 17 SW2 . 74 A4
Kintyre Ho 41 E14 . 34 B1
Kinver Ho N4 . . . . 6 C4
Kipling Ho 82 SE5 . 48 B3
Kipling St SE1 . . . 137 C4
Kipling Terr 8 N9 . 37 B3
Kirby Est SE16 . . . 40 A3
Kirby Gr SE1 . . . . 138 A4
Kirby St EC1 . . . . 107 C4

Kirkeby Bldg EC1. 107 B4
Kirkland Wlk 4
E8 . . . . 16 B2
Kirkley Ho N16 . . . 7 A3
Kirkman Ho W1 . . 105 B3
Kirkman PI W1 . . . 105 B3
Kirkmichael Rd
E14 . . . . 34 B3
Kirkside Rd SE3 . . 53 C4
Kirkstall Gdns
SW2 . . . . 74 A3
Kirkstall Ho SW1 . 146 A2
Kirkstall Rd SW2 . 74 A3
Kirkstead Ct E5 . . 18 A4
Kirkstone NW1 . . . 92 C4
Kirkwall PI E2 . . . 25 B2
Kirkwood Rd SE15 . 50 A1
Kirtley Ho SW8 . . 171 A4
Kirtling St SW8 . . 160 C2
Kirton Cl W4 . . . . 37 C2
Kirton Gdns
E2 . . . . 24 B2 99 A3
Kirwin Way SE5 . . 48 A3
Kitcat Terr E3 . . . 26 C2
Kite Ho 5 SW11 . . 60 A4
Kite PI E2 . . 24 C2 99 C4
Kitson Rd
Barnes SW13 . . . . . 46 C2
Camberwell SE5 . . . 48 B3
Kittiwake St SE8 20
SE8 . . . . 51 B4
Kiver Rd N19 . . . . 5 A2
Klea Ave SW4 . . . 61 B1
Kleffens Ct 2 SE3 . 53 B3
Kleine Wharf 50
N1 . . . . 24 A4
Knapp Cl NW10 . . 8 A2
Knapp Rd E3 . . . . 26 C1
Knaresborough Dr
SW18 . . . . 71 A3
Knaresborough Ho 4
N4 . . . . 6 B4
Knaresborough Pl
SW5 . . . . 142 A4
Knatchbull Rd
Brixton SE5 . . . . . . 48 A2
Stonebridge NW10 . 20 C4
Knebworth Ho
South Lambeth
SW8 . . . . 171 C3
2 Stoke Newington
N16 . . . . 16 A4
Knebworth Rd 8
N16 . . . . 16 A4
Kneller Ho SW8 . . 171 C2
Kneller Rd SE4 . . . 66 A3
Knighten St E1 . . . 32 A1
Knighthead Point 28
E14 . . . . 41 C4
Knights Ho SE17 . 152 A3
Knightleas Ct NW2 . 9 B2
Knightrider Ct
EC4 . . . . 122 C4
Knightrider St
EC4 . . . . 122 B4
Knights Arc SW1 . 130 C3
Knight's Ave W5 . . 36 A4
KNIGHTSBRIDGE . 130 A2
Knightsbridge
SW7 . . . . 130 C3
Knightsbridge
SW1 . . . . 131 A3
Knightsbridge Gn
SW1 . . . . 130 C3

Knightsbridge Under
Sch SW7 . . . . **143** A3
Knights CI E9 . . . . . **17** B3
Knights Ho
Bermondsey SE1 . . **138** C4
South Lambeth
SW8 . . . . **162** B1
West Kensington
SW5 . . . . **140** C2
Knight's Ho SW10 **156** C2
Knights Rd E16 . . . . . **43** C4
Knight's Wlk
SE11 . . . . **150** A3
Knightswood Ct N6 . **4** C4
Knivet Rd SW6 . . . **155** B3
Knobs Hill Rd E15 . . **76** A1
Knoll Ho NW8 . . . . . **78** C2
Knoll SW18 . . . . **59** B2
Knolly's CI SW27,
SW16 . . . . **74** C1
Knolly's Rd SE27,
SW16 . . . . **74** C1
Knot Ho SE1 . . . . . **124** C1
Knottisford St E2 . . **25** B2
Knowlden Ho
E1 . . . . **32** B2
Knowle CI SW9 . . . . **62** C4
Knowledge Point Sch
N7 . . . . **14** B2
Knowles Hill Cres
SE13 . . . . **67** C2
Knowles Ho
Wandsworth
SW18 . . . . **59** A1
Willesden Green
NW10 . . . . **21** C4
Knowles Wlk SW4 . **61** B4
Knowlton Ho
SW9 . . . . **173** C4
Knowsley Rd
SW11 . . . . **168** C1
Knox Ct SW4 . . . . . **172** B2
Knox Ho SW15 . . . . . **47** B1
Knox St W1 . . . . . . **102** C4
Knoyle Ho W14 . . . **126** B2
Knoyle St SE14 . . . . **51** A4
Kobi Nazrul Prim Sch
E1 . . . . **111** C2
Kossuth St SE10 . . . **43** A1
Kotree Way SE1 . . **153** C4
Kramer Mews
SW5 . . . . **142** A1
Kreedman Wlk **8**
E8 . . . . **16** C3
Kreisel Wlk TW9 . . **44** B4
Kylemore Ct **4**
W12 . . . . **38** B4
Kylemore Rd NW6 . **10** C1
Kylestrome Ho
SW1 . . . . **145** C3
Kynance Mews
SW7 . . . . **128** B1
Kynance Pl SW7 . . **128** C1
Kynaston Ho **7**
SW2 . . . . **74** B3
Kynaston Rd N16 . . . **7** A1
Kyrle Rd SW11 . . . . **60** C1
Kyverdale Rd N16 . . . **7** B3

L

Laburnham Ct NW2 . **1** B2
Laburnum CI **5**
SE15 . . . . **50** B3
Laburnum Ct **26**
E2 . . . . **24** B4

Laburnum Ho
New Cross SE4 . . . . **51** B1
6 Stoke Newington
N16 . . . . **6** C2
Laburnum JMI Sch
E2 . . . . **24** B4
Lacey Ho **7** SE13 . . **52** B1
Lacine Ct SE16 . . . . **40** C4
Lackington St
EC2 . . . . **109** C4
Lackland Ho SE1 . . **153** A2
Lacland Ho SW10 . **157** B2
Lacon Rd SE22 . . . . **64** C3
Lacy Rd SW15 . . . . . **57** C3
Ladbroke Cres
W11 . . . . **31** A3
Ladbroke Gdns
W11 . . . . **31** B2 **112** C4
Ladbroke Gr
Kensal Town W10 . . **31** A4
Notting Hill
W11 . . . . . **31** B2 **112** C4
Ladbroke Grove Ho
W11 . . . . **112** C4
Ladbroke Grove Sta
W10 . . . . **31** A4
Ladbroke Ho E1 . . **111** A3
Ladbroke Mews
W11 . . . . **31** A1 **112** B1
Ladbroke Rd
W11 . . . . **112** C3
Ladbroke Sq
W11 . . . . . **31** B2 **113** A3
Ladbroke Terr
W11 . . . . **113** A4
Ladbroke Wlk
W11 . . . . **31** B1 **113** A3
Ladybower Ct **6**
E5 . . . . **17** C4
Ladycroft Rd SE13 . **67** A4
Lady Elizabeth Ho
SW14 . . . . **55** B4
Ladyfern Ho **16** E3 . . **26** C1
Lady Florence Ctyd **16**
SE8 . . . . **51** C3
Lady Margaret Rd
NW5 . . . . **13** B3
Lady Margaret Sch
SW6 . . . . **165** B3
Lady Somerset Rd
NW5 . . . . **13** A4
LADYWELL **66** C1
Ladywell CI SE4 . . . . **66** C3
Ladywell Hts SE4 . . . **66** B1
Ladywell Rd SE13 . . **67** A2
Ladywell Sta SE13 . **67** A2
Ladywell Water Twr
SE4 . . . . **66** C2
Lafitte Ho **27** N19 . . . **4** C4
Lafone Ho **11** SW2 . . **74** A4
Lafone St SE1 . . . . **138** C4
Lagado Mews
SE16 . . . . **32** C1
Lagonda Ho **11** E3 . . **26** C1
Lagonier Ho EC1 . . . **97** A3
Laindon Ho **6** N16 . . . **7** B3
Laing Ho SE5 . . . . . **48** B3
Lainson St SW18 . . . **70** C4
Lairdale CI SE21 . . . **75** B4
Laird Ho SE5 . . . . . **48** B3
Lairs Ct N7 . . . . **14** A2
Laitwood Rd
SW12 . . . . **73** A3
Lakanal SE5 . . . . . . **49** A2
Lake Ho SE1 . . . . . **136** C3

Laker Ct SW4 . . . . . **172** B2
Laker Pl SW15 . . . . . **58** A1
Lakeside Ct N4 . . . . . **6** B3
Lakeside Rd W14 . . . **39** C3
Lakeview **23** E3 . . **25** C3
Lake View Ct
SW1 . . . . **132** B2
Lakis CI NW3 . . . . . . **11** B4
Laleham Ho
E2 . . . . **24** B1 **98** C2
Lalor St SW6 . . . . . **164** B2
Lambard Ho **4**
SE10 . . . . **52** B3
Lamb Ct **18** E14 . . **33** A2
Lamberhurst Ho **14**
SE15 . . . . **50** B4
Lambert Ave TW9 . . **55** A4
Lambert Ho
Brixton SW9 . . . . . **173** B1
13 Crouch End N19 . . **4** C4
Lambert Rd SW2 . . . **62** B2
Lambert St N1 . . . . . **14** C1
LAMBETH **134** C3
Lambeth Acad
SW4 . . . . **61** B2
Lambeth Coll (Brixton
Ctr) SW2 . . . . **62** B2
Lambeth Coll
(Clapham Ctr)
SW4 . . . . **61** B2
Lambeth Coll (Tower
Bridge Ctr) SE1 . **124** B1
Lambeth Coll
(Vauxhall Ctr)
SW8 . . . . **171** B4
Lambeth Ct **8**
SW18 . . . . **58** C2
Lambeth High St
SE1 . . . . **148** A4
Lambeth Hill EC4 . **122** C4
Lambeth Hospl
SW9 . . . . **62** B4
Lambeth North Sta
SE1 . . . . **135** B2
Lambeth Pal* **134** C2
Lambeth Palace Rd
SE1 . . . . **134** B1
Lambeth Pier
SE1 . . . . **134** B1
Lambeth Rd SE1 . . **135** C1
SE27 . . . . **75** B2
Lambeth Twrs
SE11 . . . . **135** B1
Lambeth Wlk
SE11 . . . . **149** A4
Lambfold Ho **7** N7 . . **14** A2
Lamb Ho
28 Camberwell
SE5 . . . . **48** B3
11 Camberwell SE5 . **48** C2
Greenwich SE10 . . . **52** B4
Lamb La E8 . . . . **17** A1
Lamble St NW5 . . . . **12** C4
Lambolle Pl NW3 . . . **12** A2
Lambolle Rd NW3 . . **12** A2
Lambourn CI **9**
NW5 . . . . **13** B4
Lambourne Ho
NW8 . . . . **101** C4
Lambourn Rd
SW4 . . . . **61** A4
Lambrook Ho **13**
SE15 . . . . **49** C2
Lambrook Terr
SW6 . . . . **164** A4

Lamb's Bldgs EC1 . . **97** B1
Lamb's Conduit Pas
WC1 . . . . **106** C4
Lamb's Conduit St
WC1 . . . . **94** C1
Lamb's Mews N1 . . . **86** A3
Lamb's Pas EC1 . . . **97** B1
Lamb St E1 . . . . . . **110** C4
Lambton Ct **2** N19 . . **5** A3
Lambton Mews **4**
N19 . . . . **5** A3
Lambton Pl
W11 . . . . . . **31** B2 **113** A4
Lambton Rd N19 . . . . **5** A3
Lamb Wlk SE1 . . . . **138** A3
Lamerton Lo **10**
TW9 . . . . **44** B2
Lamerton St **8**
SE8 . . . . **51** C4
Lamington St **1**
W6 . . . . **39** A2
Lamlash St SE11 . . **150** A4
Lamley Ho SE10 . . . **52** A3
Lammas Rd E9 . . . . **17** C1
Lammermoor Rd
SW12 . . . . **73** A4
Lamont Rd SW10 . **157** B3
Lamont Rd Pas
SW10 . . . . **157** B3
Lampard Gr N16 . . . . **7** B3
Lampern Sq **19**
E2 . . . . **24** C2 **99** C4
Lampeter Sq W6 . . **154** A3
Lamplighter CI **34**
E1 . . . . **25** B1
Lampson Ho **6**
N19 . . . . **13** B4
Lanark Ho SE1 . . . **153** B1
Lanark Mans
Paddington W9 . . . . **89** A2
15 Shepherd's Bush
W12 . . . . **39** B4
Lanark Mews NW8 . **89** A3
Lanark Pl W9 . . . . . **89** A2
Lanark Rd W9 . . . . . **88** C3
Lanark Sq E14 . . . . . **42** A3
Lanbury Rd SE15 . . . **65** C3
Lancashire Ct
W1 . . . . **118** B4
Lancaster Ave SE21,
SE27 . . . . **75** B2
Lancaster CI
10 De Beauvoir Town
N1 . . . . **16** A1
Kensington W2 . . . **114** A3
Lancaster Cotts **3**
TW10 . . . . **54** A1
Lancaster Ct
Bayswater W2 . . . **115** A4
Parsons Green
SW6 . . . . **155** A1
West Norwood
SE27 . . . . **75** A1
Lancaster Dr
Canary Wharf E14 . . **34** B1
Maitland Pk NW3 . . **12** A2
Lancaster Gate
W2 . . . . **115** A4
Lancaster Gate Sta
W2 . . . . **115** B4
Lancaster Gr NW3 . **12** A2
Lancaster hall **14**
E16 . . . . **35** C1
Lancaster Ho
SW15 . . . . **47** B1
Lancaster Lo **2**
W11 . . . . **31** A3

Lancaster Ho
SW18 . . . . **71** A4
Lancaster Lo **2**
W11 . . . . **31** A3
Lancaster Mews
Bayswater W2 . . . **115** A4
2 Richmond TW10 . **54** A1
3 Wandsworth
SW18 . . . . **59** A2
Lancaster Pk
TW10 . . . . **54** A2
Lancaster Pl WC2 **120** C3
Dudden Hill NW10 . . **8** C3
Finsbury Pk N4 . . . . . **5** C4
Notting Hill W11 . . . **31** A3
Lancaster St SE1 . **136** B3
Lancaster Stables **2**
NW3 . . . . **12** A2
Lancaster Terr
W2 . . . . **115** B4
Lancaster Wlk
W2 . . . . **115** A2
Lancefield Ct
SE15 . . . . **65** A4
Lancefield St W10 . . **23** B2
Lancell St N16 . . . . . . **7** A2
Lancelot Pl SW7 . . **130** C3
Lancer Sq W8 . . . . **128** A4
Lanchester Ct
W2 . . . . **102** C1
Lanchester Way
SE14 . . . . **50** C2
Lancing St NW1 . . . . **93** B3
Lancresse Ct N1 . . . **24** A4
Landale Ho **4**
SE16 . . . . **40** B3
Landcroft Rd SE22 . **64** B1
Landells Rd SE22 . . **64** C1
Landford Rd SW15 . . **57** B4
Landin Ho **1** E14 . . . **33** C3
Landleys Field **21**
N7 . . . . **13** C3
Landmann Ho **18**
SE16 . . . . **40** A2
Landmann Way
SE14 . . . . **40** C1
Landmark Hts E5 . . **18** A4
Landon Pl SW1 . . . **130** C1
Landons CI E14 . . . . **34** B1
Landon Wlk **16**
E14 . . . . **34** A2
Landor Ct N16 . . . . . **16** A3
Landor Ho **7** SE5 . . **48** C3
Landor Rd SW9 . . . . **62** A4
Landor Wlk **11**
W12 . . . . **38** C4
Landrake NW1 . . . . . **83** A3
Landridge Rd
SW6 . . . . **164** C2
Landseer Ct **10** N19 . **5** A2
Landseer Ho
Battersea SW11 . . . **169** C3
Paddington NW8 . . . **89** C2
Westminster SW1 . **147** C3
Landseer Rd N19 . . . **5** A2
Landulph Ho
SE11 . . . . **149** C2
Landward Ct W1 . . **102** B2
Lane CI SW11 . . . . . . **72** B4
Lanercost CI SW2 . . **74** C2
Lanercost Rd SW2 . . **74** C2
Lane The NW8 . . . . . **78** C1
Laneway SW15 . . . . **57** A2

Laney Bldg EC1 . . . **107** B4
Lanfranc Rd E3 . . . . . **26** A3
Lanfrey Pl W14 . . **140** C1
Langbourne Ave
N6 . . . . **3** C2
Langbourne Ho **7**
SW2 . . . . **62** C2
Langbourne Mans
N6 . . . . **3** C2
Langbourne Pl
E14 . . . . **42** A1
Langbourne Prim Sch
SE21 . . . . **76** A1
Langdale N1 . . . **92** C4
Langdale Cl
Camberwell SE17 . . . **48** B4
Mortlake SW14 . . . . **55** A3
Langdale Ho SW1 **146** C1
Langdale Rd SE10 . . **52** B3
Langdale St **26** E1 . . **32** A3
Langdon Ct
Finsbury EC1 . . . . . . **86** B1
Harlesden NW10 . . . **21** A4
Langdon Ho **3**
E14 . . . . **34** B3
Langdon Park Rd
N6 . . . . **4** B4
Langdon Park Sec
Sch E14 . . . . **34** B3
Langdon Pl SW14 . . **55** B4
Langdon Way
SE1 . . . . **153** C3
Langford Cl
Shacklewell E8 . . . . **16** C3
St John's Wood
NW8 . . . . **79** A2
Langford Ct
SE8 . . . . **51** C4
Langford Ho **5**
SE8 . . . . **51** C4
Langford Pl NW8 . . **79** A2
Langford Prim Sch
SW6 . . . . **166** B2
Langford Rd SW6 . **166** B2
Langham Ct **4**
SW15 . . . . **57** C2
Langham Ho SW4 . . **61** B2
Langham Mans
SW5 . . . . **142** A1
Langham St
Chiswick W4 . . . . . . **46** A4
Fitzrovia W1 . . . . . **104** B3
Langham St W1 . . **104** B3
Lang Ho
South Lambeth
SW8 . . . . **162** A1
3 Tufnell Pk N19 . . . . **4** B1
Langholm Cl
SW12 . . . . **73** C4
Langhorne Ct **10**
NW8 . . . . **11** C1
Langhurst Ho
SW11 . . . . **169** B2
Langland Gdns
NW3 . . . . **11** A3
Langland Ho **10**
SE5 . . . . **48** C3
Langland Mans
NW3 . . . . **11** A3
Langler Rd NW10 . . **22** B3
Langley Ct
South Lambeth
SW8 . . . . **172** A4
Strand WC2 . . . . . **120** A4
Langley Dr W3 . . . . **37** A4

Langley Ho
11 Lower Clapton
E5 . . . . **17** A3
30 Paddington W2 . . **31** C4
Langley La SW8 . . **162** B4
Langley Mans
SW8 . . . . **162** B4
Langley St WC2 . . **106** A1
Langmead Ho **14**
E3 . . . . **27** A2
Langmore Ho E1 . **111** C1
Langport Ho **1**
SW9 . . . . **48** A1
Langridge **15** NW5 . . **12** C2
Langroyd Rd
SW17 . . . . **72** B2
Langside Ave
SW15 . . . . **56** C3
Lang St E1 . . . . **25** B1
Langston Hughes Cl
5 SE24 . . . . **63** A3
Langthorn Ct EC2 **109** C2
Langthorne Lo **30**
SW2 . . . . **74** C4
Langthorne St
SW6 . . . . **47** C3
Langton Cl WC1 . . . **95** A2
Langton Ct SW15 . . **58** B1
Langton Ho SE11 **149** A4
Langton Pl SW18 . . **70** C3
Langton Rd SW9 . . **48** A3
Langton St SW10 **157** A3
Langton Way SE3 . . **53** C3
Langtry Pl SW6 . . **155** C4
Langtry Rd NW8 . . **78** A3
Langtry Wlk NW8 . . **78** C4
Lanhill Rd W9 . . . . . **23** C1
Lanier Rd SE13 . . . . **67** C1
Lanner Ho **2**
SW11 . . . . **60** A4
Lannoy Point
SW6 . . . . **154** B2
Lanrick Rd E14 . . . . **35** A3
Lansbury Gdns **1**
E14 . . . . **34** C3
Lansbury Lawrence
Prim Sch E14 . . . . **34** A3
Lanscombe Wlk
SW8 . . . . **162** A1
Lansdell Ho **9**
SW2 . . . . **62** C1
Lansdowne Coll
W2 . . . . **114** A3
Lansdowne Cres
W11 . . . . . . **31** A2 **112** B3
Lansdowne Dr E8 . . **16** C1
Lansdowne Gdns
SW8 . . . . **172** A4
Lansdowne Gr
NW10 . . . . **8** A4
Lansdowne Hill
SE27 . . . . **75** A1
Lansdowne Ho
W11 . . . . . . **31** B1 **112** C2
Lansdowne Int Coll
Ltd SW7 . . . . **129** A1
Lansdowne Mews
W11 . . . . . . **31** B1 **112** C2
Lansdowne Pl
SE1 . . . . **137** C2
Lansdowne Rd
W11 . . . . . . **31** A2 **112** B3
Lansdowne Rise
W11 . . . . . . **31** A2 **112** B3
Lansdowne Row
W1 . . . . **118** B2

Lansdowne Sch
SW9 . . . . **62** B4
Lansdowne Terr
WC1 . . . . **94** B1
Lansdowne Way **1**
SW4,
SW8 . . . . **172** B3
Lansdowne Wlk
W11 . . . . **31** B1 **112** C2
Lansdowne Wood Cl
1 SE27 . . . . **75** A1
Lansdown Ho **28**
SE5 . . . . **48** B1
Lantern Cl SW15 . . **56** C3
Lantern Ho E14 . . . . **41** C4
Lanterns Ct E14 . . . . **41** C3
Lant Ho SE1 . . . . . **136** C3
Lantry Ct **1** SW13 . . **37** A3
Lant St SE1 . . . . . . **137** A3
Lanvanor Rd SE15 . . **50** B1
Lanyard Ho **4**
SE8 . . . . **41** B2
Lapford Cl W9 . . . . . **23** B1
Lapsang SE1 . . . . . **125** A1
Lapwing Twr **31**
SE8 . . . . **51** B4
Lapworth Ct W2 . . **100** B4
Lara Cl SE13 . . . . . . **67** B1
Larch Ave W3 . . . . . **29** A1
Larch Cl
Balham SW12 . . . . . **73** A2
12 Deptford SE8 . . . . . **51** B4
10 Upper Holloway
N19 . . . . **4** B1
Larch Ho **32** SE16 . . **40** B4
Larchmore Ct N19 . . **5** A2
Larch Rd NW2 . . . . . . **9** B4
Larcom St SE17 . . **151** A3
Larden Rd W3 . . . . . **38** A4
La Retraite RC Girls
Sch SW12 . . . . **73** B4
Larissa St SE17 . . **151** C3
Larix Ct NW10 . . . . . **21** C4
Larkfield Rd TW9 . . **54** A3
Larkhall La SW4 . . **171** C1
Larkhall Rise **4**
SW4 . . . . **171** B1
Lark Row E2 . . . . . . **25** B4
Larmenier & Sacred
Heart RC Prim Sch
W6 . . . . **39** C2
Larnaca Ho SE1 . . **138** C2
Larnach Rd W6 . . . . **47** C4
Larpent Ave SW15 . . **57** B2
La Saint Union RC Sec
Sch NW5 . . . . **3** C1
Lascelles Ho NW1 . . **90** B1
Lassell St SE10 . . . . **42** C1
Lasseter Pl SE3 . . . . **53** B4
Latchmere Rd
SW11 . . . . **168** C1
Latchmere St
SW11 . . . . **168** C2
Latham Ho E1 . . . . . **32** C3
Latimer SE17 . . . . . **152** A1
Latimer Ho
9 Homerton E9 . . . . **17** C2
11 Notting Hill
W11 . . . . . . **31** B2 **113** A3
Latimer Ind Est **1**
W10 . . . . **30** B3
Latimer Pl W10 . . . . **30** B3
Latimer Rd W10 . . . . **30** B3

Latimer Road Sta
W10 . . . . **30** C2
Latitude Ho NW1 . . **82** A3
Latona Rd SE15 . . . . **49** C4
Lattimer Pl W4 . . . . **46** A4
Latvia Ct SE17 . . . **151** A1
Latymer Ct W6 . . . . **39** C2
Latymer Upper Sch
W6 . . . . **38** C1
Lauderdale Mans
W9 . . . . **88** B3
Lauderdale Rd W9 . . **88** B3
Lauderdale Twr
EC2 . . . . **108** C4
Laud St SE11 . . . . . **148** C2
Laughton Ho **11**
SW2 . . . . **62** C1
Launcelot St SE1 . **135** B3
Launceston Pl
W8 . . . . **128** C1
Launch St E14 . . . . . **42** B3
Laundress La N16 . . . **7** C1
Laundry La **7** N1 . . . **15** B1
Laundry Rd W6 . . . **154** A3
Laura Pl E5 . . . . **17** B4
Laurel Bank Gdns
SW6 . . . . **165** A2
Laurel Cl **8** N19 . . . . **4** B2
Laurel Ct
Dalston E8 . . . . **16** B1
2 Putney SW15 . . . . **57** C2
9 Rotherhithe
SE16 . . . . **33** A1
Laurel Ho
9 Deptford SE8 . . . . **51** B4
5 Hamstead NW3 . . **11** A2
Laurel Rd SW13 . . . . **46** C1
Laurel St E8 . . . . **16** B2
Laurence Mews **2**
W12 . . . . **38** C4
Laurence Pountney
Hill EC4 . . . . **123** B4
Laurence Pountney La
EC4 . . . . **123** C4
Laurie Gr SE14 . . . . **51** A2
Laurie Ho
Newington SE1 . . . **136** B1
Notting Hill
W8 . . . . **31** C1 **113** B1
Laurier Rd NW5 . . . . **4** A1
Lauriston Ho **6**
E9 . . . . **17** C1
Lauriston Lo NW6 . . **10** B2
Lauriston Rd E9 . . . . **17** C1
Lauriston Sch E9 . . . **25** C4
Lausanne Rd SE15 . . **50** B2
Lavell St N16 . . . . . . **15** C4
Lavender Cl SW3 . . **157** C3
Lavender Ct **4** SW4 . **172** B3
Lavender Gdns
SW11 . . . . **60** B3
Lavender Gr E8 . . . . **16** C1
Lavender Hill
SW11 . . . . **60** C4
Lavender Ho
6 Richmond TW9 . . **45** A2
4 Rotherhithe
SE16 . . . . **32** C1
Lavender Rd
Battersea SW11 . . . . **59** C4
Rotherhithe SE16 . . . **33** A1
Lavender Sweep
SW11 . . . . **60** B3
Lavender Terr **2**
SW11 . . . . **60** A4
Lavender Wlk
SW11 . . . . **60** B3

Lavendon Ho NW8 . **90** B2
Lavengro Rd SE27 . . **75** B2
Lavenham Rd
SW18 . . . . **70** C3
Lavers Rd N16 . . . . . . **7** A1
Laverstoke Gdns
SW15 . . . . **68** C4
Laverton Mews
SW5 . . . . **142** B3
Laverton Pl SW5 . . **142** B3
Lavina Gr N1 . . . . . . **84** C2
Lavington Cl E9 . . . . **18** B2
Lavington St SE1 . . **122** B1
Lawdale Jun Sch
E2 . . . . **24** C2 **99** C4
Lawford Rd
Chiswick W4 . . . . . . **45** B3
De Beauvoir Town
N1 . . . . **16** A1
Kentish Town NW5 . . **13** B2
Lawfords Wharf **18**
NW1 . . . . **13** B1
Lawless Ho **5** E14 . . **34** B2
Lawless St **12** E14 . . **34** A2
Lawley St E5 . . . . . . **17** B4
Lawman Ct **2**
TW9 . . . . **44** B2
Lawn Cres TW9 . . . . **44** C1
Lawnfield Ct NW6 . . . **9** C1
Lawn House Cl
E14 . . . . **42** B4
Lawn La SW8 . . . . . **162** C4
Lawn Rd NW3 . . . . . **12** B3
Lawns The NW3 . . . . **11** B2
Lawrence Ave
NW10 . . . . **20** C4
Lawrence Bldgs **1**
N16 . . . . **7** B1
Lawrence Cl
Bow E3 . . . . **26** C3
6 Shepherd's Bush
W12 . . . . **30** A2
Lawrence Ct
1 South Acton
W3 . . . . **37** B3
Stoke Newington N16 . **7** B1
Lawrence Ho
20 Camden Town
NW1 . . . . **13** A1
Westminster SW1 . . **147** C3
Lawrence La EC2 . . **109** A2
Lawrence Mans
SW3 . . . . **158** A3
Lawrence Pl N1 . . . . **84** B4
Lawrence St
Canning Town E16 . . **35** B4
Chelsea SW3 . . . . . **158** A3
Lawrence Trad Est
SE10 . . . . **43** B2
Lawrence Univ
SW7 . . . . **143** A3
Lawson Cl SW19 . . . **69** C1
Lawson Ct **1** N4 . . . . **5** B3
Lawson Ho **7**
W12 . . . . **30** A2
Law St SE1 . . . . . . **137** C2
Lawton Rd E3 . . . . . **26** A2
Laxfield Ct E8 . . . . . **24** C4
Laxley Cl SE5 . . . . . **48** A3
Laxton Path **1**
SE4 . . . . **65** C3
Laxton Pl NW1 . . . . **92** B2
Layard Rd SE16 . . . . **40** A2
Layard Sq SE16 . . . . **40** A2
Laybourne Ho **18**
E14 . . . . **41** C4

Laycock Prim Sch N1 . . . 15 A2
Laycock St N1 . . . 14 C2
Layfield Ho SE10 . . . 43 C1
Laystall Ct EC1 . . . 95 B1
Laystall St EC1 . . . 95 B1
Layton Pl TW9 . . . 44 C2
Lazar Wlk N7 . . . 5 B2
Leabank Sq E9 . . . 18 C2
Leabourne Rd N16 . . . 7 C4
Leacroft Ave SW12 . . . 72 B4
Lea Ct W12 . . . 38 A4
Lea Int SE11 . . . 18 C3
Leake St
Lambeth SE1 . . . 135 B3
South Bank SE1 . . . 135 A4
Leamington Ct
Forest Hill SE26 . . . 76 C1
North Acton W3 . . . 28 C4
Leamington Ho W11 . . . 31 B4
Leamington Pk W3 . . . 28 C4
Leamington Rd Villas W11 . . . 31 B4
Leamore St W6 . . . 39 B2
Leamouth Rd E14 . . . 34 C3
Leander Ct
Hackney E9 . . . 17 B1
St Johns SE8 . . . 51 C2
Leander Rd SW2 . . . 62 C1
Leary Ho SE11 . . . 149 A1
Lea Sq E3 . . . 26 B4
Leatherdale St
Bethnal Green E1 . . . 25 B1
Globe Town E1 . . . 25 C2
Leatherhead Cl N16 . . . 7 B3
Leathermarket Ct SE1 . . . 138 A3
Leathermarket St SE1 . . . 138 A3
Leather Rd SE16 . . . 40 C2
Leathwaite Rd SW11 . . . 60 B2
Leathwell Rd SE8 . . . 52 A1
Lebanon Gdns SW18 . . . 58 C1
Lebanon Rd SW18 . . . 58 C2
Lebus Ho NW8 . . . 80 A1
Lechmere Rd NW2 . . . 9 A2
Leckford Rd SW18 . . . 71 B3
Leckhampton Pl SW2 . . . 74 C4
Lecky Ho NW2 . . . 9 A4
Lecky St SW7 . . . 143 B2
L'Ecole des Petits Sch SW6 . . . 166 A2
Leconfield Ave SW13 . . . 56 B4
Leconfield Ho SE5 . . . 64 A4
Leconfield Rd N5 . . . 15 C4

Lector Ct EC1 . . . 95 C1
Leda Ct SW9 . . . 163 B1
Ledam Bldg EC1 . . . 107 B4
Ledbury Ho SE22 . . . 64 A4
Ledbury Mews N W11 . . . 31 C3
Ledbury Mews W W11 . . . 31 C2 113 B4
Ledbury Rd W11 . . . 31 C3
Ledbury St SE15 . . . 49 C3
Ledo Ho N16 . . . 15 C4
Lee Conservancy Rd E9 . . . 18 B3
Lee Ct SE13 . . . 67 C3
Leeds Ct EC1 . . . 96 A2
Lee Ho N19 . . . 13 C3
Leeke St WC1 . . . 94 C4
Leeland Way NW10 . . . 8 B4
Leerdam Dr E14 . . . 42 B3
Lees Ct W1 . . . 117 B4
Lees Ho SE17 . . . 151 C1
Leeson Rd SE24 . . . 62 C3
Lees Pl W1 . . . 117 B4
Lee St E8 . . . 24 B4
Lee Valley Sp Ctr E10 . . . 19 A4
Leeve Ho W9 . . . 23 B2
Leeward Ct E1 . . . 125 C2
Leeway SE8 . . . 41 B1
Lefevre Wlk E3 . . . 26 C4
Leffern Rd W12 . . . 38 C4
Leff Ho NW6 . . . 10 A1
Lefroy Ho SE1 . . . 136 C3
Lefroy Rd W12 . . . 38 B4
Legard Rd N5 . . . 6 A1
Leggatt Rd E15 . . . 27 B3
Legge St SE13 . . . 67 B2
Leghorn Rd NW10 . . . 21 C3
Legion Cl N1 . . . 14 C1
Legion Terr E3 . . . 26 C4
Leicester Ct
Paddington W2 . . . 31 C4
St James WC2 . . . 119 C4
Leicester Ho
Brixton SW9 . . . 63 A4
Putney SW15 . . . 69 B4
Leicester Pl WC2 . . . 119 C4
Leicester Sq* WC2 . . . 119 C4
Leicester Square Sta WC2 . . . 119 C4
Leicester St WC2 . . . 119 C4
Leigham Ave SW16 . . . 74 A1
Leigham Hall SW16 . . . 74 A1
Leigham Hall Par SW16 . . . 74 A1
Leigham Vale SE27, SW16, SW2 . . . 74 C2
Leigh Ct SW2 . . . 62 C1
Leighfield Ho N4 . . . 6 B4
Leigh Gdns NW10 . . . 22 B3
Leigh Ho SW15 . . . 56 C2
Leigh Orchard Cl SW16 . . . 74 B1
Leigh Pl EC1 . . . 107 B4
Leigh Rd N5 . . . 15 A4
Leigh St WC1 . . . 94 A3
Leighton Cres NW5 . . . 13 B3
Leighton Gdns NW10 . . . 22 B3

Leighton Gr NW5 . . . 13 B3
Leighton House (Art Gall & Mus)* W14 . . . 127 A2
Leighton Pl NW5 . . . 13 B3
Leighton Rd NW5 . . . 13 B3
Leinster Ave SW14 . . . 55 B3
Leinster Gdns W2 . . . 114 C4
Leinster Mews W2 . . . 114 C4
Leinster Pl W2 . . . 100 C1
Leinster Sq W2 . . . 100 A1
Leinster Terr W2 . . . 114 C4
Leithcote Path SW16 . . . 74 B1
Leith Ho
Kentish Town N7 . . . 13 C3
Streatham SW2 . . . 74 B4
Leith Mans W9 . . . 88 A3
Leith Yd NW6 . . . 23 C4
Lelitia Cl E8 . . . 24 C4
Leman St E1 . . . 111 B1
Lemmon Rd SE10 . . . 53 A4
Le Moal Ho E1 . . . 32 B4
Lemsford Ct N4 . . . 6 B2
Lena Gardens Prim Sch W6 . . . 39 B3
Lena Gdns W6 . . . 39 B3
Lendal Terr SW4 . . . 61 C4
Len Freeman Pl SW6 . . . 154 C3
Lenham NW5 . . . 12 C2
Lenham Ho SE1 . . . 137 C3
Lennon Rd NW2 . . . 9 B2
Lennox Gdns
Knightsbridge SW1 . . . 130 C1
Willesden NW10 . . . 8 B4
Lennox Gdns Mews SW1 . . . 144 C4
Lennox Ho E9 . . . 17 B2
Lennox Rd N4, N7 . . . 5 C2
Lenthall Ho SW1 . . . 147 A1
Lenthall Rd E8 . . . 16 C1
Lenthorp Rd SE10 . . . 43 B2
Lenton Rise TW9 . . . 54 A4
Len Williams Ct NW6 . . . 23 C3
Leonard Ct
Bloomsbury WC1 . . . 94 A2
Kensington W8 . . . 127 B2
Leonard Day Ho NW5 . . . 13 A2
Leonard Pl N16 . . . 16 A4
Leonard St EC2 . . . 97 C2
Leonora Ho W9 . . . 88 C2
Leontine Cl SE15 . . . 49 C3
Leopards Ct EC1 . . . 107 B4
Leopold Bldgs E2 . . . 24 B2 98 C4
Leopold Mews E9 . . . 25 B4
Leopold Prim Sch NW10 . . . 8 B1
Leopold St E3 . . . 33 B4
Leopold Wlk SE11 . . . 148 C1
Leo St SE15 . . . 50 A3
Leo Yd EC1 . . . 96 B1
Leppoc Rd SW4 . . . 61 C2
Leroy St SE1 . . . 152 A4
Lerry Cl W14 . . . 155 A4

Lerwick Ho SW18 . . . 59 B3
Lesley Ct SW1 . . . 133 B1
Leslie Prince Ct SE5 . . . 48 C3
Leslie Rd E11 . . . 19 C4
Lessar Ave SW4 . . . 61 B1
Lessar Ct SW4 . . . 61 B1
Lester E3 . . . 27 A2
Leswin Pl N16 . . . 7 B1
Leswin Rd N16 . . . 7 B1
Letchford Gdns NW10 . . . 21 C2
Letchford Mews NW10 . . . 21 C2
Letchmore Ho W10 . . . 22 B1
Lethaby Ho SW4 . . . 62 A3
Lethbridge Cl SE13 . . . 52 B1
Letterstone Rd SW6 . . . 154 C1
Lettice St SW6 . . . 165 A3
Lett Rd E15 . . . 19 C1
Lettsom St SE5 . . . 49 A1
Levana Cl SW19 . . . 70 A3
Levant Ho E1 . . . 25 C1
Levehurst Way SW4, SW9 . . . 172 B2
Leven Rd E14 . . . 34 C3
Levendale Rd SE23 . . . 65 C1
Leverett St SW3 . . . 144 B4
Leverington Pl N1 . . . 97 C3
Lever St EC1 . . . 96 C3
Leverstock Ho SW3 . . . 144 B2
Leverton Pl NW5 . . . 13 B3
Leverton St NW5 . . . 13 B3
Levison Way N19 . . . 4 C3
Levita Ho NW1 . . . 93 C4
Levyne Ct EC1 . . . 95 B2
Lewesdon Cl SW19 . . . 69 C3
Lewes Ho
Bermondsey SE1 . . . 138 B4
Peckham SE15 . . . 49 C4
Leweston Pl N16 . . . 7 B4
Lewey Ho E3 . . . 26 B1
Lewin Rd SW14 . . . 55 C4
Lewis Ct SE16 . . . 40 A1
Lewis Gr SE13 . . . 67 B4
LEWISHAM . . . 67 B3
Lewisham Bridge Prim Sch SE13 . . . 67 A4
Lewisham Bsns Ctr SE14 . . . 50 C4
Lewisham Coll SE13 . . . 51 C1
Lewisham Ctr SE13 . . . 67 B4
Lewisham High St SE13 . . . 67 B3
Lewisham Hill SE13 . . . 52 B1
Lewisham Hospl SE13 . . . 67 A1
Lewisham Pk SE13 . . . 67 B1
Lewisham Rd SE13 . . . 52 B1
Lewisham Sta SE13 . . . 67 B3
Lewisham Way SE4, SE14 . . . 51 B2

Lewis Pl E8 . . . 16 C3
Lewis Silkin Ho SE15 . . . 50 B4
Lewis St NW1 . . . 13 A2
Lexden Rd W3 . . . 28 A1
Lexfield Ho N5 . . . 15 C4
Lexham Gardens Mews W8 . . . 128 B1
Lexham Gdns W8 . . . 142 A4
Lexham Mews W8 . . . 141 C4
Lexham Wlk W8 . . . 128 B1
Lexington St W1 . . . 119 A4
Lexton Gdns SW12 . . . 73 C3
Leyborne Pk TW9 . . . 44 C2
Leybourne Ho SE15 . . . 50 B4
Leybourne Rd NW1 . . . 13 A1
Leybourne St NW1 . . . 13 A1
Leyden Mans N19 . . . 5 A4
Leyden St E1 . . . 110 C3
Leydon Cl SE16 . . . 32 C1
Ley Ho SE1 . . . 137 A3
Leyland Ho E14 . . . 34 A2
Leylands SW18 . . . 58 B1
Leylang Rd SE14 . . . 50 C3
Leys Ct SW9 . . . 173 B1
Leysdown NW5 . . . 12 C2
Leysdown Ho SE17 . . . 152 B2
Leysfield Rd W12 . . . 38 C3
Leythe Rd W3 . . . 37 B4
LEYTON . . . 19 C4
Leyton Mills E10 . . . 19 B4
Leyton Rd E15 . . . 19 C2
Liardet St SE14 . . . 51 A4
Liberia Rd N5 . . . 15 A2
Liberty Mews SW12 . . . 61 A1
Liberty St SW9 . . . 173 A4
Libra Rd E3 . . . 26 B3
Library Mans W12 . . . 39 B4
Library Par NW10 . . . 21 A4
Library Pl E1 . . . 32 A2
Library St SE1 . . . 136 B3
Lichfield Ct TW9 . . . 54 A3
Lichfield Gdns TW10, TW9 . . . 54 A2
Lichfield Ho SE5 . . . 48 B1
Lichfield Rd
Mile End E3 . . . 26 A2
Richmond TW9 . . . 44 B2
West Hampstead NW2 . . . 10 A4
Lichfield Terr TW9 . . . 54 A2
Lichport Ct N4 . . . 6 A3
Lickey Ho W14 . . . 155 A4
Lidcote Gdns SW9 . . . 173 A1
Liddell Gdns NW10 . . . 22 B3
Liddell Rd NW6 . . . 10 C2
Lidfield Rd N16 . . . 15 C4
Lidgate Rd SE15 . . . 49 B3
Lidiard Rd SW18 . . . 71 B2
Lidlington Pl NW1 . . . 83 A1
Lidyard Rd N19 . . . 4 B3

Liffey Ct NW10 . . . . .8 C1
Liffords Pl SW13 . . . .46 B1
Lifford St SW15 . . . . .57 C3
Lighter Cl 16 SE16 . .41 A2
Lighterman Mews 13
E1 . . . . .32 C3
Lighterman's Rd
E14 . . . . .42 A4
Lighterman's Wlk
SW18 . . . . .58 C3
Light Horse Ct
SW1 . . . . .145 B1
Ligonier St
E2 . . . . .24 B1 98 C2
Lilac Ho SE4 . . . . .66 B4
Lilac Pl SE11 . . . . . .148 C3
Lilac St W12 . . . . .29 C2
Lilestone Est NW8 . .89 C1
Lilestone Ho NW8 . .89 C2
Lilestone St NW8 . . .90 A2
Lilford Ho 21 SE5 . . .48 B1
Lilford Rd SE5 . . . . . .48 A1
Lilian Baylis Ho
N1 . . . . .15 B2
Lilian Baylis Tech Sch
SE11 . . . . .149 A1
Lilley Cl E1 . . . . .125 C1
Lillian Ave W3 . . . . . .36 C4
Lillian Cl 16 N16 . . . .7 A1
Lillian Rd SW13 . . . . .47 A4
Lillie Ho N5 . . . . .14 C3
Lillie Rd SW6 . . . . .154 C3
Lillie Road Mans
SW6 . . . . .154 B3
Lilleshall Rd SW4 . . .61 B4
Lillie Yd SW6 . . . . . .155 B4
Lillingston Ho N7 . . .14 C4
Lily Cl W14 . . . . .39 C2
Lily Pl EC1 . . . . .107 C4
Lilyville Rd SW6 . . .164 C4
Limborough Ho 5
E14 . . . . .33 C4
Limburg Rd SW11 . . .60 A3
Limeburner La
EC4 . . . . .108 A2
Lime Cl E1 . . . . .125 C2
Lime Ct SW15 . . . . . .57 A4
Lime Gr W12 . . . . . . .39 B4
Limeharbour E14 . . .42 A4
Lime Ho 7 TW9 . . . . .45 A2
LIMEHOUSE 33 A2
Limehouse Cswy
E14 . . . . .33 B2
Limehouse Ct 5
E14 . . . . .33 C3
Lime House Ct 3
E14 . . . . .33 B3
Limehouse Cut 4
E14 . . . . .34 A4
Limehouse Fields Est
14 E14 . . . . .33 A4
Limehouse Link
(Tunnel) E14 . . . . . .33 B2
Limehouse Sta
E14 . . . . .33 A3
Limekiln Wharf 21
E14 . . . . .33 B2
Limerick Cl SW12 . . .73 B4
Limerick Ct 1
SW12 . . . . .73 B4
Limerston St
SW10 . . . . .157 A3
Lime St Pas EC3 . . .124 A4
Limes Ave
Barnes SW13 . . . . . . .46 B1

Limes Ave continued
Golders Green NW11 . .1 A4
Limes Ct NW6 . . . . . . .9 C1
Limes Field Rd
SW14 . . . . .56 A4
Limesford Rd
SE15 . . . . .65 C3
Limes Gdns SW18 . . .58 C1
Limes Gr SE13 . . . . . .67 B3
Limes St EC3 . . . . . .110 A1
Limes The
Camberwell SE5 . . . . .64 A4
Kensington
W2 . . . . .31 C3 113 C3
Limes Wlk SE15 . . . . .65 B3
Limetree Cl SW2 . . . .74 B3
Lime Tree Ct 8
E3 . . . . .33 C4
Limpsfield Ave
SW19 . . . . .69 C2
Limscott Ho 13 E3 . . .27 A2
Linacre Cl SE15 . . . . .65 A4
Linacre Ct W6 . . . . . .39 C1
Linacre Rd NW2 . . . . .9 A2
Linale Ho N1 . . . . . . .87 B1
Linberry Wlk 3
SE8 . . . . .41 B2
Lincoln Ave SW19 . . .69 C1
Lincoln Cl 16 . . . . . . .6 C4
Lincoln Ho
Bloomsbury WC1 . . .107 A3
9 Dartmouth Pk
NW5 . . . . .4 B1
2 Islington N1 . . . . . .15 B1
Knightsbridge SW1 130 C3
10 Putney SW15 . . . .58 A2
Lincoln Mews
NW6 . . . . .23 B4
Lincoln's Inn★
WC2 . . . . .107 A2
Lincoln's Inn Fields
WC2 . . . . .107 A2
Lincoln St SW3 . . .144 C3
Lindale SW19 . . . . . . .70 A2
Lindal Rd SE4 . . . . . .66 B2
Linden Ave NW10 . . .22 C3
Linden Ct
3 Battersea
SW11 . . . . .59 C3
8 Shepherd's Bush
W12 . . . . .30 B1
Linden Gdns
Chiswick W4 . . . . .37 C1
Notting Hill
W2 . . . . .31 C2 113 C3
Linden Gr SE15 . . . . .65 B4
Linden Ho 10 SE8 . . .51 B4
Linden Lodge Sch
SW19 . . . . .70 A3
Linden Mews
Kensington
W2 . . . . .31 C2 113 C3
Stoke Newington
N1 . . . . .15 C3
Lindens The W4 . . . . .45 B2
Lindfield Gdns
NW3 . . . . .11 B3
Lindfield Hts NW3 . . .11 B3
Lindfield St E14 . . . . .33 C3
Lindford Christie
Stadium The
W12 . . . . .30 A4
Lindisfarne Way
E9 . . . . .18 A4

Lindley Ho
13 Peckham SE15 . . .49 C3
9 Stepney E1 . . . . . . .32 B4
Lindley Pl TW9 . . . . .44 C2
Lindley St E1 . . . . . . .32 B4
Lindop Ho 5 E1 . . . . .26 A1
Lindore Rd SW11 . . . .60 B3
Lindo St SE15 . . . . . . .50 B1
Lindrop St SW6 . . . .166 C2
Lindsay Ct SW11 . . .167 C3
Lindsay Sq SW1 . . . .147 C2
Lindsell St 6
SE10 . . . . .52 B2
Lindsey Ho★
SW10 . . . . .157 C2
Lindsey Mews 18
N1 . . . . .15 B1
Lindsey St EC1 . . . .108 B4
Lind St SE8 . . . . .52 A1
Linfield WC1 . . . . .94 C3
Linford Ho 17 E2 . . . .24 C4
Linford St SW8 . . . .170 C3
Linford Street Bsns
Est SW8 . . . . .170 C4
Lingard Ho 11 E14 . .42 B3
Lingards Rd SE13 . . .67 B3
Lingfield Ho
18 Acton Green
W4 . . . . .37 B1
Lambeth SE1 . . . . . .136 B3
Lingham St SW9 . . .172 C1
Ling Rd E16 . . . . .35 C4
Ling's Coppice
SE21 . . . . .75 C2
Lingwell Rd SW17 . . .72 A1
Lingwood Rd E5 . . . . .7 C4
Linhope St NW1 . . . . .90 C1
Linkenholt Mans 3
W6 . . . . .38 B2
Link St E9 . . . . .17 B3
Links Yd
Spitalfields E1 . . . . . .111 A4
Spitalfields E1 . . . . . .111 A4
Link The W3 . . . . .28 A3
Linkway N4 . . . . .6 B4
Linkwood Wlk
NW1 . . . . .13 C1
Linnell Ho
Spitalfields E1 . . . . . .110 C4
St John's Wood
NW8 . . . . .78 C4
Linnell Rd SE5 . . . . . .49 A1
Linnet Mews
SW12 . . . . .72 C4
Linom Rd SW4 . . . . . .62 A3
Linscott Rd E5 . . . . . .17 B4
Linsey St
Bermondsey SE16 . . .153 B4
Bermondsey SE16 . . .139 C1
Linslade Ho
10 Hackney E2 . . . . . .24 C4
Marylebone NW8 . . . .90 B2
Linstead St 1
NW6 . . . . .10 C1
Linstead Way
SW18,SW19 . . . . .70 A4
Lintaine Cl W6 . . . . .154 B3
Linthorpe Rd N16 . . . .7 A4
Linton Ho
Lower Holloway
N7 . . . . .14 B4
2 Tower Hamlets
E3 . . . . .33 C4
Linton St N1 . . . . .87 A3
Linver Rd SW6 . . . .165 B2
Linwood Cl SE5 . . . . .49 B1
Lion Cl SE4 . . . . .66 C1

Lionel Ho 6 W10 . . . .31 A4
Lionel Mans 14
W14 . . . . .39 C3
Lionel Mews 13
W10 . . . . .31 A4
Lionel Road N
TW8 . . . . .36 A2
Lionel Road Prim Sch
TW8 . . . . .36 A2
Lionel Road S
TW8 . . . . .36 B1
Lion Gate Gdns
TW9 . . . . .54 B4
Lion Gate Mews
SW18 . . . . .70 C4
Lion House Sch
SW15 . . . . .57 C3
Lion Mills 30 E2 . . . . .24 C3
Lion Yd SW4 . . . . .61 C3
Lipton Rd 3 E1 . . . . . .32 C3
Lisburne Rd NW3 . . . .12 B4
Lisford St SE15 . . . . . .49 B2
Lisgar Terr W14 . . . .140 C4
Liskeard Gdns
SE3 . . . . .53 C2
Liskeard Ho SE11 . . .149 C2
Lisle Ct NW2 . . . . .1 A1
Lisle St WC2 . . . . . . .119 C4
Lismore Cir NW5 . . . .12 C3
Lismore Wlk 4
N1 . . . . .15 B2
Lissenden Gdns
NW5 . . . . .12 C4
Lissenden Mans
NW5 . . . . .12 C4
Lisson Cotts NW1 . . .102 B4
Lisson Gr NW1,NW8 . .90 A2
LISSON GROVE 90 B2
Lisson Ho NW1 . . . . .102 A4
Lisson St NW1 . . . . . .102 A4
Lister Cl W3 . . . . .28 C4
Lister Ct N16 . . . . .7 A2
Lister Ho
Greenwich SE3 . . . . . .53 A4
Marylebone W1 . . . .104 A2
Spitalfields E1 . . . . . .111 C4
Lister Hospl SW1 . . .146 A1
Lister Mews N7 . . . . .14 B4
Liston Rd SW4 . . . . . .61 B4
Listowel Cl SW9 . . . .163 C2
Listria La N16 . . . . .7 A2
Listria Pk N16 . . . . .7 A2
Litcham Ho 22 E1 . . . .25 C2
Litchfield Gdns
NW10 . . . . .8 C2
Litchfield St WC2 . . .119 C4
Lithos Rd NW3 . . . . . .11 B2
Little Albany St
NW1 . . . . .92 B2
Little Argyll St
W1 . . . . .104 C1
Little Boltons The
SW10 . . . . .142 B1
Little Britain EC1 . . .108 C3
Little Chelsea Ho
SW10 . . . . .157 A3
Little Chester St
SW1 . . . . .132 A2
Little Cloisters
SW1 . . . . .134 A2
Little College St
SW1 . . . . .134 A2
Little Combe Cl 1
SW15 . . . . .57 C1
Littlecote Cl SW19 . . .70 A4

Little Cottage Pl
SE10 . . . . .52 A3
Little Deans Yd
SW1 . . . . .134 A2
Little Dimocks
SW12 . . . . .73 A2
Little Dorrit Ct
SE1 . . . . .137 A4
Little Edward St
NW1 . . . . .92 B4
Little Essex St
WC2 . . . . .121 B4
Littlefield Cl N19 . . . .13 B4
Little George St
SW1 . . . . .134 A3
Little Green St
NW5 . . . . .13 A4
Little Marlborough St
W1 . . . . .104 C1
Little Newport St
WC2 . . . . .119 C4
Little New St EC4 . . .107 C2
Little Portland St
W1 . . . . .104 C2
Little Russell St
WC1 . . . . .106 A3
Little St James's St
SW1 . . . . .118 C1
Little St Leonards
SW14 . . . . .55 B4
Little Sanctuary
SW1 . . . . .134 A3
Little Smith St
SW1 . . . . .133 C2
Little Somerset St
E1 . . . . .110 C1
Little Titchfield St
W1 . . . . .104 C3
Littleton St SW18 . . .71 B2
Little Trinity La
EC4 . . . . .123 A4
Little Turnstile
WC1 . . . . .106 C3
LITTLE VENICE 101 A4
Little Venice★
W9 . . . . .100 C4
Littlewood SE13 . . . . .67 B1
Livermere Ct 3
E8 . . . . .24 B4
Livermere Rd E8 . . . .24 B4
Liverpool Gr SE17 . .151 B1
Liverpool Ho N7 . . . .14 C2
Liverpool Rd
Islington N1 . . . . .85 C3
Islington N1,N7 . . . . .14 C1
Newham E16 . . . . . . .35 A4
Liverpool St EC2 . . .110 A3
Liverpool Street Sta
EC2 . . . . .110 A3
Livesey Mus★
SE15 . . . . .50 B4
Livesey Pl SE15 . . . . .49 C4
Livingstone Ho 10
SE5 . . . . .48 B3
Livingstone Lo 18
W9 . . . . .31 C4
Livingstone Pl E14 . .42 B1
Livingstone Rd
5 Battersea
SW11 . . . . .59 C4
Mill Meads E15 . . . . . .27 B4
Livity Sch The
SW2 . . . . .62 A2
Livonia St W1 . . . . . .105 A1
Lizard St EC1 . . . . . . .97 A3
Llandovery Ho 7
E14 . . . . .42 B4

Llanelly Rd NW2 . . . . 1 B2
Llanvanor Rd NW2 . . 1 B2
Llewellyn Ho 10
  N19. . . . . 4 B1
Llewellyn Bldg SW1
  WC1 . . . . 95 B3
Lloyd Baker St
  WC1 . . . . 95 B3
Lloyd Ct
  Ladywell SE13 . . . . . 67 A2
  6 West Norwood
  SE27 . . . . 75 A1
Lloyd Ho N16 . . . . 6 C3
Lloyd's Ave EC3 . . 110 B1
Lloyd's Bldg*
  EC3 . . . . 110 A1
Lloyd's Pl SE3 . . . . . 53 A1
Lloyd Sq WC1 . . . . . 95 B4
Lloyd's Row EC1 . . . 96 A3
Lloyd St WC1 . . . . . 95 B4
Lloyd Villas SE4 . . . 51 C1
Loampit Hill SE13 . . 52 A1
Loampit Vale
  SE13 . . . . 67 B4
Loanda Cl SE8 . . . . . 41 B2
Loats Rd SW2 . . . . . 62 A1
Locarno Rd W3 . . . . 28 B1
Lochaline St W6 . . . 47 B4
Lochbie 4 N4 . . . . 5 A4
Lochinvar St
  SW12 . . . . 73 A4
Lochmore Ho
  SW1 . . . . 145 C3
Lochnagar St E14 . . 34 B4
Lockbridge Ct 8
  W9 . . . . 31 C4
Locke Ho
  Nine Elms SW8 . . 170 C4
  Stamford Hill N16 . . . 7 B3
Lockesfield Pl
  E14 . . . . 42 A1
Lockgate Cl E9 . . . . . 18 B3
Lockhart Cl N7 . . . . 14 B2
Lockhart St E3 . . . . . 26 B1
Lockhurst St E5 . . . 17 C4
Lockington Rd
  SW8 . . . . 170 B4
Lockmead Rd
  SE13 . . . . 67 B3
Lock Mews 9
  NW1 . . . . 13 C2
Lockside 17 E14 . . . 33 A2
Locksley St E14 . . . 33 B4
Lock View Ct 1
  E14 . . . . 33 A2
Lockwood Ho
  SE11 . . . . 163 B3
Lockwood Sq
  SE16 . . . . 40 A3
Lockyer Est SE1 . . 137 C3
Lockyer Ho
  7 Greenwich
  SE10 . . . . 43 B1
  Putney SW15 . . . . . 57 C4
  South Lambeth
  SW8 . . . . 162 A2
Lockyer St SE1 . . . 137 C3
Locton Gn 4 E3 . . . 26 B4
Loddiges Ho 5
  E9 . . . . 17 B1
Loddiges Rd E9 . . . . 17 B1
Loddon Ho NW8 . . . 89 C1
Loder St SE15 . . . . . 50 B3
Lodge Ave SW14 . . 56 A4
Lodge Rd NW8 . . . . 90 A3
Lodge The 3 W4 . . . 38 A3
Lodore St E14 . . . . . 34 B3

Lodsworth Ho
  SW11 . . . . 169 B3
Loftie St SE16 . . . . 139 C3
Lofting Ho 8 N1 . . . 14 C1
Lofting Rd N1 . . . . . 14 C1
Lofts on the Park 7
  E9 . . . . 17 C2
Loftus Rd W12 . . . . 30 A1
Loftus Rd (Queens
  Park Rangers FC)
  W12 . . . . 30 A1
Logan Mews 8 . . . 141 B4
Logan Pl W8 . . . . . 141 B4
Loggetts SE21 . . . . . 76 A2
Lohmann Ho 1
  SE11 . . . . 163 B4
Loleswoth Cl E1 . . 111 A3
Lollard St SE11 . . . 149 B3
Lollards Twr SE1 . . 134 C1
Loman St SE1 . . . . 136 B4
Lomas St E1 . . . . . 111 C4
Lombard Ct
  14 Acton W3 . . . . . 28 A1
  City of London EC3 123 C4
Lombard La EC4 . . 107 C1
Lombard Rd
  SW11 . . . . 167 B2
Lombard St EC3 . . 109 C1
Lombardy Pl W2 . . 114 B3
Lomley Ho 10
  SW2 . . . . 62 C1
Lomond Gr SE5 . . . 48 C3
Lomond Ho 10
  SE5 . . . . 48 C2
Loncroft Rd SE5 . . 49 A4
Londesborough Ho 1
  SE11 . . . . 16 A4
Londesborough Rd
  N16 . . . . 16 A4
London Acad of
  Computing &
  Electronics SW17 72 B1
London Aquarium*
  SE1 . . . . 134 C3
London Bridge SE1
  SE1 . . . . 123 C2
London Bridge City
  Pier SE1 . . . . 124 A2
London Bridge Hospl
  SE1 . . . . 123 C2
London Bridge Sta
  SE1 . . . . 123 C1
London Bridge Wlk
  SE1 . . . . 123 C2
London Britannia Coll
  N1 . . . . 97 B4
London Business Sch
  NW1 . . . . 90 C2
London Canal Mus*
  N1 . . . . 84 B2
London Central
  Mosque* NW8 . . . 90 B3
London Chest Hospl
  E2 . . . . 25 B3
London Clinic
  NW1 . . . . 91 C1
London Coll of
  Advanced Studies
  SE1 . . . . 123 B1
London Coll of Beauty
  Therapy W1 . . . . 105 A1
London Coll of Bsns &
  Computer Studies
  SE1 . . . . 61 C3

London Coll of
  Communication (Sch
  of Printing &
  Publishing)
  SE11 . . . . 136 B1
London Coll of
  Economics &
  Science NW10 . . 20 B1
London Coll of
  Fashion
  Broadgate
  EC2 . . . . 24 A1 98 B2
  Marylebone W1 . . 103 C1
  Marylebone W1 . . 104 A1
  Marylebone W1 . . 104 A1
  St Luke's EC1 . . . . 96 C1
London Coll of
  Fashion (Mare St)
  E8 . . . . 17 A1
London Coll of
  International
  Business Studies
  WC1 . . . . 106 B3
London Ct 3
  SW18 . . . . 58 C2
London Dungeon
  The* SE1 . . . . 123 C2
London Dungeon
London Electronics
  Coll SW5 . . . . . . 142 A3
London Eye
  (Millennium
  Wheel)* SE1 . . . 134 C4
London Fields East
  Side E8 . . . . 17 A1
London Fields Prim
  Sch E8 . . . . 25 A4
London Fields Sta
  E8 . . . . 17 A1
London Fields West
  Side E8 . . . . 16 C1
London Fire Brigade
  Mus* SE1 . . . . . . 136 C4
London Gas Mus
  The* E3,E16 . . . . 27 C1
London Ho 13 W6 . . 38 C2
London Ho TW9 . . . . 54 B4
London Ho NW8 . . . 80 B2
London Independent
  Hospl The E1 . . . 32 C4
London Int Coll N7 . 5 B1
London International
  Film Sch W1 . . . 106 A1
London La E8 . . . . . 17 A1
London Metropolitan
  Univ
  Islington N7 . . . . 14 C3
  Whitechapel E1 . . 110 C2
  Whitechapel E1 . . 110 C1
  Whitechapel E1 . . 124 C4
London Metropolitan
  Univ (Central Ho)
  E1 . . . . 111 B2
London Metropolitan
  Univ (Commercial
  Rd) E1 . . . . 111 C2
London Metropolitan
  Univ (Ladbroke Ho)
  N5 . . . . 15 A3
London Metropolitan
  Univ (Moorgate)
  EC2 . . . . 109 C3

London Metropolitan
  Univ (Spring Ho)
  N7 . . . . 14 C2
London Mews
  W2 . . . . 101 C2
London Nautical Sch
  The SE1 . . . . 121 C2
London Oratory Sch
  The SW6 . . . . . . 155 C2
London Pavilion
  SW1 . . . . 119 B3
London Peace
  Pagoda★
  SW3 . . . . 159 A2
London Rd SE1 . . 136 B2
London Sch of
  Economics &
  Political Science
  WC2 . . . . 107 A1
London St
  City of London
  EC3 . . . . 124 B4
  Paddington W2 . . 101 B1
London Stile 5
  W4 . . . . 36 C1
London Stock
  Exchange★ EC2 . 108 C2
London Terr 1
  E2 . . . . 24 C3
London Transport
  Mus★ WC2 . . . . . 120 B4
London Wall EC2 . 109 C3
London Wall Bldgs
  EC2 . . . . 109 C3
London Wetland Ctr★
  SW13 . . . . 47 A3
London Wetland
  Visitor Ctr★
  SW13 . . . . 47 A2
London Wharf 4
  E2 . . . . 25 A4
London Xtra Tuition
  Coll N4 . . . . 6 A2
London Zoo★
  NW1 . . . . 81 B2
Long Acre WC2 . . 106 B1
Longbeach Rd
  SW11 . . . . 60 B4
Longberrys NW2 . . 1 B1
Longbridge Way
  SE13 . . . . 67 B2
Longcliffe Ho
  SW18 . . . . 59 A2
Long Dr W3 . . . . . 29 A3
Longfellow Way
  SE1 . . . . 153 A3
Longfield Dr
  SW14 . . . . 55 A2
Longfield Est SE1 . 153 A3
Longfield St SW18 . 70 C4
Longford Ct
  1 Bedford Pk
  W12 . . . . 38 A4
  4 Clapton Pk E5 . 17 C4
Longford Ho
  E1 . . . . 32 B3
Longford St NW1 . 92 B2
Longford Wlk 9
  SW2 . . . . 74 C4
Longhope Cl SE15 . 49 B4
Longhurst Ho 8
  W9 . . . . 23 B2
Long La
  Bermondsey SE1 . 137 C3
  Holborn EC1 . . . . 108 B4
Longland Ct
  Bermondsey SE1 . 153 B2

Lla-Lor 237

Longland Ct continued
  Hackney E9 . . . . 18 A3
Longlands Ct
  W11 . . . . 31 B3 113 A4
Longleat Ho SW1 . . 147 B2
Longleigh Ho 8
  SE5 . . . . 49 A2
Longlents Ho 3
  NW10 . . . . 20 C4
Longley Ho 5
  N19 . . . . 13 B4
Longley St SE1 . . . 153 B4
Longman Ho
  6 Globe Town E2 . 25 C3
  10 Shoreditch E8 . 24 B4
Long Meadow 20
  N7 . . . . 13 C3
Longmoor Point 14
  SW15 . . . . 69 A3
Longmore St
  SW1 . . . . 146 C3
Longnor Rd E1 . . . . 25 C2
Long Pond Rd
  SE3 . . . . 53 A2
Long Rd SW4 . . . . . 61 B3
Longridge Ho
  SE1 . . . . 137 A1
Longridge Rd
  SW5 . . . . 141 C3
Longs Ct 2 TW9 . . 54 B3
Long's Ct W1 . . . . 119 C3
Longshore SE8 . . . . 41 B2
Long St E2 . . . 24 B2 98 C4
Longstaff Cres
  SW18 . . . . 70 C4
Longstaff Rd
  SW18 . . . . 58 C1
Longstone Ave
  NW10 . . . . 21 B4
Longthorne Ho 18
  E3 . . . . 26 B2
Longthorpe Ct 9
  W6 . . . . 38 C2
Longville Rd
  SE11 . . . . 150 B4
Long Wlk SE1 . . . . 138 B2
Longwood Dr
  SW15 . . . . 56 C1
Long Yd WC1 . . . . . 94 C1
Lonsdale Ho
  Fulham SW6 . . . . . 58 C4
  6 Stoke Newington
  N4 . . . . 6 B4
Lonsdale Mews
  Notting Hill W11 . . 31 B3
  4 Richmond TW9 . 44 C2
Lonsdale Pl N1 . . . 14 C1
Lonsdale Rd
  Barnes SW13 . . . . 46 B3
  Chiswick W4 . . . . 38 B2
  Kilburn NW6 . . . . 23 B4
  Notting Hill W11 . . 31 B3
Lonsdale Sq
  Islington N1 . . . . . 14 C1
  Islington N1 . . . . . 85 C4
Lopez Ho 9 SW9 . . 62 A4
Loraine Rd
  Chiswick W4 . . . . 45 A4
  Islington N7 . . . . . 14 B4
Lord David Pitt Ho 6
  SE24 . . . . 62 C3
Lorden Wlk
  E2 . . . . 24 C2 99 B3
Lord Hills Rd W2 . 100 B4

Lord Holland La
SW9 . . . . **173** C2
Lord Napier Pl
W6 . . . . .38 C1
Lord North St
SW1 . . . . **134** A1
Lord Roberts Mews
SW6 . . . . **156** A1
Lords Cl SE21 . . . . .75 B2
Lord's Cricket Mus*
NW8 . . . .**89** C3
Lordship Gr N16 . . . .6 C2
Lordship La N16 . . . .6 C2
Lordship La SE22 . . .64 B1
Lordship Park Mews
N16 . . . . .6 B2
Lordship Pk N16 . . . .6 C2
Lordship Pl SW3 . . **158** A3
Lordship Rd N16 . . . .6 C2
Lordship Terr N16 . . .6 C2
Lord's Indoor Cricket
Sch NW8 . . . .**90** A4
Lord's (MCC &
Middlesex Cty
Cricket Ground)*
NW8 . . . .**89** C4
Lord's View SW8 . . .**89** C3
Loreburn Ho **2**
N7 . . . . .14 B4
Lorenzo St N1,
WC1 . . . .**94** C4
Loris Rd W6 . . . . . .39 B3
Lorn Cl SW9 . . . . . **173** B2
Lorne Cl NW8 . . . . .**90** B3
Lorne Ct SW15 . . . .57 C1
Lorne Gdns **5**
W11 . . . . .39 C4
Lorne Ho
Hornsey N4 . . . . . . .5 B4
7 Tower Hamlets
E1 . . . . .33 A4
Lorne Rd
Finsbury Pk N4 . . . . .5 B3
3 Richmond TW10 . .54 B2
Lorn Rd SW9 . . . . . **173** B2
Lorraine Ct **10**
NW1 . . . . .13 A1
Lorrimore Rd
SE17 . . . . .48 A4
Lorrimore Sq
SE17 . . . . .48 A4
Lorton Ho **9** NW6 . .23 C4
Lostock Ho SW8 . . **171** B2
Lothair Rd S N4 . . . . .6 A4
Lothbury EC2 . . . . .**109** B2
Lothian Rd SW9 . . . .48 A2
Lothrop St W10 . . . .23 A2
Lots Rd SW10 . . . . **157** A1
Loudoun Rd NW8 . . .79 A3
Loughborough Ct **7**
SW9 . . . . .63 A4
Loughborough
Junction Sta
SW9 . . . . .63 A3
Loughborough Pk
SW9 . . . . .63 A3
Loughborough Prim
Sch SW9 . . . . .48 A1
Loughborough Rd SE5,
SW9 . . . . .48 A1
Loughborough St
SE11 . . . . **149** A1
Lough Rd N7 . . . . . .14 B2
Louisa Cl E9 . . . . . .25 C4
Louisa Gdns E1 . . . .25 C1

Louisa Ho SW15 . . .56 B3
Louisa St E1 . . . . . .25 C1
Louise Bennett Cl **9**
SE24 . . . . .63 A3
Louise De Marillac Ho
10 E1 . . . . .32 B4
Louise White Ho **1**
N19 . . . . .4 C3
Louisville Rd
SW17 . . . . .72 C1
Louvaine Rd
SW11 . . . . .59 C3
Lovat La EC3 . . . . . **124** A3
Lovatt Ct SW12 . . . .73 A3
Loveday Ho **2**
SW2 . . . . .74 C3
Lovegrove St SE1 . .49 C4
Lovegrove Wlk
E14 . . . . .34 B1
Love La EC2 . . . . . **109** A2
Lovelace Ho **12**
E8 . . . . .24 B4
Lovelace Rd SE21 . .75 B3
Lovelinch Cl SE15 . .50 B4
Lovell Ho E8 . . . . . .24 C4
Lovell Pl SE16 . . . . .41 A3
Loveridge Mews
NW6 . . . . .10 B2
Loveridge Rd
NW6 . . . . .10 B2
Lover's Wlk W1 . . . **117** B1
Lovette Rd E3 . . . . .26 C2
Lovetts Pl SW18 . . .59 A3
Love Wlk SE5 . . . . .48 C1
Lowden Rd SE24 . . .63 B3
Lowder Ho **6** E1 . . .32 A1
Lowe Ave E16 . . . . .35 C4
Lowell Ho **15** SE5 . .48 B3
Lowell St E14 . . . . .33 A3
Lower Addison Gdns
W14 . . . . **126** A3
Lower Belgrave St
SW1 . . . . **132** A1
LOWER CLAPTON . .17 B4
Lower Clapton Rd
E5 . . . . .17 B4
Lower Clarendon Wlk
9 W11 . . . . .31 A3
Lower Comm S
SW15 . . . . .57 A4
Lower Grosvenor Pl
SW1 . . . . **132** B2
Lower Grove Rd
TW10 . . . . .54 B2
LOWER HOLLOWAY .14 A3
Lower James St
W1 . . . . **119** A4
Lower John St
W1 . . . . **119** A4
Lower Lea Crossing
E14, E16 . . . . .35 A2
Lower Mall W6 . . . .39 A1
Lower Marsh SE1 . **135** B3
Lower Merton Rise
NW3 . . . . .12 A1
Lower Mortlake Rd
TW9 . . . . .54 B4
Lower Pk
Acton W3 . . . . .20 B1
6 Putney SW15 . . .57 C2
LOWER PLACE 20 B3
Lower Place Bsns Ctr
NW10 . . . . .20 B3
Lower Rd SE16 . . . .40 B4

Lower Richmond Rd
Mortlake SW14,
TW9 . . . . .55 A4
Putney SW15 . . . . .57 B4
Lower Robert St
WC2 . . . . **120** B3
Lower Sloane St
SW1 . . . . **145** B2
Lower Terr NW3 . . . .2 B1
Lower Thames St
EC3 . . . . **124** A3
Lowerwood Ct
W11 . . . . .31 A3
Loweswater Ho
E3 . . . . .26 B1
Lowfield Rd
Dagenham W3 . . . . .28 B3
Hampstead NW6 . . . .10 C1
Lowlands NW3 . . . . .12 A2
Lowman Rd N7 . . . .14 B4
Lowndes Cl SW1 . . **131** C1
Lowndes Ct
Knightsbridge
SW1 . . . . **131** A2
Marylebone W1 . . . **104** C1
Lowndes Lo SW1 . . **131** B1
Lowndes Pl SW1 . . **131** B1
Lowndes Sq SW1 . . **131** A3
Lowndes St SW1 . . **131** B2
Lowood Ho **11** E1 . .32 B2
Lowood St E1 . . . . .32 A2
Lowry Ct **3** SE16 . .40 A1
Lowther Ho
Pimlico SW1 . . . . . **147** A1
1 Shoreditch E8 . .24 B4
Lowther Prim Sch
SW13 . . . . .46 C4
Lowther Rd
Barnes SW13 . . . . .46 B2
Islington N7 . . . . . .14 C3
Lowth Rd SE5 . . . . .48 B1
Loxford Ho SW1 . . **145** C3
Loxham St WC1 . . . .94 B3
Loxley Rd SW18 . . .71 C3
LTC Coll London
W1 . . . . **104** C2
Lubavitch House Sch
(Jun Boys) E5 . . . . .7 B4
Lubbock Ho **21**
E14 . . . . .34 A2
Lubbock St SE14 . . .50 B3
Lucan Ho N1 . . . . . .87 C3
Lucan Pl SW3 . . . . **144** B3
Lucas Ct SW11 . . . **169** C3
Lucas Ho
Clapham SW8 . . . . **171** A2
Walham Green
SW10 . . . . **156** B2
Lucas St SE4, SE8 . .51 C2
Lucas Vale Prim Sch
SE8 . . . . .51 C2
Lucerne Mews
W8 . . . . **31** C1 **113** C2
Lucerne Rd N5 . . . .15 A4
Lucey Rd SE16 . . . **139** B1
Lucey Way SE16 . . **153** C4
Lucien Rd SW18 . . .71 A2
Lucraft Ho **12**
SW2 . . . . .74 A4
Lucy Ashe Ho
SE17 . . . . **150** B3
Lucy Brown Ho
SE1 . . . . **123** A1
Lucy Cres W3 . . . . .20 B1
Ludgate Broadway
EC4 . . . . **108** B1

Ludgate Cir EC4 . . **108** A1
Ludgate Hill EC4 . . **108** A1
Ludgate Ho EC4 . . **108** A1
Ludgate Sq EC4 . . **108** B1
Ludham NW5 . . . . .12 B3
Ludlow Ct W3 . . . . .37 B4
Ludlow St EC1 . . . . .96 C2
Ludovick Wlk
SW15 . . . . .56 A3
Ludwell Ho W14 . . **126** B2
Ludwick Mews
SE14 . . . . .51 A3
Lugard Ho **5** W12 . .30 A1
Lugard Rd SE15 . . . .50 A2
Luke Ho **2** E1 . . . . .32 A3
Luke St EC2 . . .24 A1 **98** A2
Lukin St E1 . . . . . . .32 B3
Lullingstone Ho **21**
SE15 . . . . .50 B4
Lullingstone La
SE13 . . . . .67 C1
Lulot Gdns N19 . . . .4 A2
Lulworth
Camden Town
NW1 . . . . .13 C1
Walworth SE17 . . . . .48 C4
Lulworth Ho SW8 . **162** C1
Lulworth Rd SE15 . .50 A1
Lumiere Ct **7**
SW17 . . . . .72 C2
Lumina Bldg **1**
E14 . . . . .34 B1
Lumley Ct WC2 . . . **120** B3
Lumley Flats
SW1 . . . . **145** B2
Lumley St W1 . . . . **103** C1
Lumsden Ho NW8 . .78 B3
Lunan Ho **4** E3 . . .26 B3
Lund Point E15 . . . .27 B4
Luntley Pl E1 . . . . . **111** B3
Lupin Cl SW2 . . . . .75 A2
Lupino Ct SE11 . . . **149** A4
Lupin Point SE1 . . **139** A3
Lupton St NW5 . . . .13 B4
Lupus St SW1 . . . . **147** A1
Luralda Gdns E14 . .42 C1
Lurgan Ave W6 . . . .47 C4
Lurline Gdns
SW11 . . . . **169** C4
Luscombe Ho
SW18 . . . . .58 B2
Luscombe Way
SW8 . . . . **162** A2
Lusher Ho SW15 . . .57 C1
Lushington Rd
NW10 . . . . .22 A3
Lushington Terr **11**
E8 . . . . .16 C3
Luton Pl SE10 . . . . .52 B3
Luton St NW8 . . . . .89 C1
Luttrell Ave SW15 . .57 A2
Lutyens Ho SW1 . . **146** C1
Luxborough Ho
W1 . . . . **103** B4
Luxborough St
W1 . . . . **103** B4
Luxborough Twr
W1 . . . . **103** B4
Luxemburg Gdns
W6 . . . . .39 C2
Luxford St SE16 . . . .40 C2
Luxmore St SE4 . . . .51 B2
Luxor St SE5 . . . . . .63 B4
Lyall Mews SW1 . . **131** B1
Lyall Mews W
SW1 . . . . **131** B1
Lyall St SW1 . . . . . **131** B1

Lyal Rd E3 . . . . . . .26 A3
Lyce e Francais
Charles de Gaulle
(French Univ Coll)
SW7 . . . . **143** B4
Lycee The SE11 . . **149** C1
Lycett Ho **10** SW2 . .74 A4
Lycett Pl **3** W12 . . .38 C4
Lydden Gr SW18 . . .71 A4
Lydden Rd SW18 . . .71 A4
Lydford NW1 . . . . . .83 A3
Lydford Cl **2** N16 . .16 A3
Lydford Rd
Brondesbury NW2 . . . .9 C2
Paddington W9 . . . . .23 B1
Lydgate Ho **8**
N16 . . . . .16 A3
Lydhurst Ave SW2 . .74 B2
Lydney Cl
Camberwell SE15 . . . .49 A3
Putney SW19 . . . . . .70 A2
Lydon Rd SW4 . . . .61 B4
Lydwell Ho SW8 . . **171** B1
Lyford Rd SW18 . . . .72 A3
Lygoe Ho **10** N6 . . . .4 C4
Lygon Ho
E2 . . . . .24 C2 **99** B4
Lygon Pl SW1 . . . . **132** A1
Lyham Cl SW2 . . . . .62 A1
Lyham Rd SW2 . . . .62 A1
Lyle Pk SW15 . . . . .57 C1
Lyly Ho SE1 . . . . . **137** C1
Lyme Gr **17** E9 . . . .17 B1
Lyme Grove Ho **2**
E9 . . . . .17 B1
Lyme St NW1 . . . . .82 C4
Lyminge Gdns SW17,
SW18 . . . . .72 A3
Lymington Mans
NW6 . . . . .11 A2
Lymington Rd
NW6 . . . . .11 A2
Lympstone Gdns
SE15 . . . . .49 C3
Lynbrook Gr SE15 . .49 A3
Lynch Wlk **2** SE8 . .51 B4
Lyncott Cres SW4 . .61 A3
Lyncourt SE3 . . . . .52 C1
Lyncroft Gdns
NW6 . . . . .1 C1
Lyncroft Mans **4**
NW6 . . . . .10 C3
Lyndale Ho **2** 1 B1
Lyndale Ave NW2 . . .1 B1
Lyndale Cl SE3 . . . .53 B4
Lynde Ho **2** SW4 . .61 C4
Lynden Gate
SW15 . . . . .69 A4
Lyndhurst Gdns
NW3 . . . . .11 C3
Lyndhurst Gr SE5,
SE15 . . . . .49 B1
Lyndhurst Ho **2**
SW15 . . . . .68 C4
Lyndhurst House Prep
Sch NW3 . . . . .11 C3
Lyndhurst Lo **3**
E14 . . . . .42 C2
Lyndhurst Rd
NW3 . . . . .11 C3
Lyndhurst Sq SE5 . .48 C3
Lyndhurst Sq SE15 .49 B2
Lyndhurst Terr
NW3 . . . . .11 C3
Lyndhurst Way
SE15 . . . . .49 B1

Lyneham Wlk E5 . . . .18 A3
Lynette Ave SW4 . . . .61 B1
Lynford French Ho
SE17 . . . . .150 C2
Lyngham Ct N4 . . .5 A4
Lynhurst Ct NW8 . . . . .79 B3
Lyn Mews 13 E3 . . . . .26 B2
Lynmouth Rd N16 . . .7 B3
Lynne Ct NW6 . . . . . .11 A1
Lynnett Ct E9 . . . . . . .18 A2
Lynn Ho SE15 . . . . . . .49 C4
Lynn Rd SW12 . . . . . .73 A4
Lynton Cl NW10 . . . . . .8 B3
Lynton Est SE1 . . . . .153 B3
Lynton Est SE1 . . . . .153 B3
Lynton Ho W2 . . . . . .100 B1
Lynton Lo N5 . . . . . . .15 A3
Lynton Mans SE1 . . .135 B2
Lynton Rd
  Acton W3 . . . . .28 A1
  Bermondsey SE1 . . .153 A3
  Paddington NW6 . . . .23 B3
Lynton Terr 4
  W3 . . . . .28 B3
Lynx Terr SW19 . . . . .70 C1
Lyon Ho NW8 . . . . . . .90 A1
Lyons Pl NW8 . . . . . . .89 B1
Lyon St N1 . . . . .14 B1
Lyons Wlk W14 . . . . .140 A4
Lyric Rd SW13 . . . . . .46 B2
Lysander Gr N19 . . . . .4 C3
Lysander Ho 10
  E2 . . . . .25 A3
Lysia Ct SW6 . . . . . . .47 C3
Lysias Rd SW12 . . . . .61 A1
Lysia St SW6 . . . . . . .47 C3
Lysons Wlk SW15 . . . .56 C2
Lytcott Gr SE22 . . . . .64 B2
Lytham St SE17 . . . .151 B1
Lyttelton Cl NW3 . . . .12 A1
Lytten Ct 6 W12 . . . . .38 C4
Lyttelton Ho 10 E9 . . . .17 B1
Lytton Ct WC1 . . . . . .106 B3
Lytton Gr SW15 . . . . .58 A1

M

Mabel Thornton Ho 12
  N16 . . . . .15 C4
Mableden Pl NW1,
  WC1 . . . . .93 C3
Mablethorpe Rd
  SW6 . . . . .154 A1
Mabley St E9 . . . . . . .18 A3
MacArthur Ho 4
  SW2 . . . . .74 A4
Macartney Ho
  SE10 . . . . .52 C3
Macaulay CE Prim
  Sch SW4 . . . . .61 A3
MacAulay Ct SW4 . . . .61 A4
MacAulay Ho
  2 Kensal Town
  W10 . . . . .31 A4
  10 Stoke Newington
  N16 . . . . .7 B2
MacAulay Rd SW4 . . . .61 A4
MacAulay Sq SW4 . . . .61 A3
McAuley Ct SE1 . . . .135 B2
McAuley Mews
  SE13 . . . . .52 B1
McAusland Ho 5
  E3 . . . . .26 B3
Macbeth Ho 4
  N1 . . . . .24 A3
Macbeth St W6 . . . . . .39 A1

McBride Ho 6 E3 . . . .26 B3
McCall Cl SW4 . . . . .172 A2
McCall Ho N7 . . . . . . .14 A4
McCarthy Ct
  SW11 . . . . .168 B3
Macclesfield Rd
  EC1 . . . . .96 C4
Macclesfield St
  W1 . . . . .119 C4
McCoid Way SE1 . . . .136 C3
McConnell Ho
  SW8 . . . . .171 B3
McCormick Ho 3
  SW2 . . . . .74 C3
McCrone Mews 3
  NW3 . . . . .11 C2
McCullum Rd E3 . . . . .26 B4
McDermott Cl
  SW11 . . . . .60 A4
McDermott Rd
  SE15 . . . . .64 C4
MacDonald Ho 4
  SW11 . . . . .169 B2
MacDonald Rd N19 . . .4 B2
McDougall Ct
  TW9 . . . . .44 C1
McDougall Ho
  E2 . . . . .25 A2
McDowall Cl E16 . . . . .35 B4
McDowall Rd SE5 . . . .48 B2
Macduff Rd SW11 . . .169 C4
Mace Cl E1 . . . . .32 A1
Mace St E2 . . . . .25 C3
McEwan Way E15 . . . .27 C4
Macey Ho
  Battersea SW11 . . . .168 A3
  10 Greenwich SE10 . .52 B4
Macfarlane Rd
  W12 . . . . .30 B1
McFarren Pl
  NW1 . . . . .91 C1
McGlashon Ho
  E1 . . . . .24 C1 99 B1
McGregor Ct
  N1 . . . . .24 A2 98 B4
McGregor Ho 2
  SW12 . . . . .73 C3
McGregor Rd W11 . . . .31 B4
Machell Rd SE15 . . . . .65 B4
McIntosh Ho 14
  SE16 . . . . .40 B2
McIntyre Ct 4 SW4 . .172 B2
Mackay Ho 33
  W12 . . . . .30 A2
Mackay Rd SW4 . . . . .61 A4
McKenna Ho 3
  E3 . . . . .26 B3
Mackennal St
  NW8 . . . . .80 B2
Mackenzie Cl 7
  W12 . . . . .30 A2
Mackenzie Rd N7 . . . .14 B2
Mackenzie Wlk
  E14 . . . . .33 C1
McKerrell Rd
  SE15 . . . . .49 C2
Mackeson Rd
  NW3 . . . . .12 B4
Mackie Ho 3
  SW2 . . . . .74 C4
Mackie Rd SW2 . . . . .74 C4
McKiernan Ct
  SW11 . . . . .168 A2

McKinnon Wood Ho
  E2 . . . . .24 C2 99 B3
Mackintosh La E9 . . . .17 C3
Macklin St WC2 . . . .106 B2
Mackonochie Ho
  EC1 . . . . .107 B4
Mackrow Wlk 1
  E14 . . . . .34 B2
Macks Rd SE16 . . . . .153 C4
Mackworth Ho
  NW1 . . . . .92 C4
Mackworth St
  NW1 . . . . .92 C4
Mac Laren Mews
  SW15 . . . . .57 B3
Maclean Rd SE23 . . . .66 A1
McLeod Ct SE21 . . . . .76 C3
McLeod's Mews
  SW7 . . . . .142 B4
MacLeod St SE17 . . .151 A1
Maclise Rd W14 . . . .126 A1
McManus Ho 7
  SW11 . . . . .59 C4
McMillan Ho SE4 . . . .66 A4
Macmillan Ho
  Cricklewood NW8 . . . .9 B4
  Lisson Gr NW8 . . . . .90 B3
McMillan St SE8 . . . . .51 C4
Mcmorran Ho 4
  N7 . . . . .14 A4
Macnamara Ho
  SW10 . . . . .157 B2
McNeil Rd SE5 . . . . . .49 A1
McNicol Dr NW10 . . . .20 B3
Maconochies Rd 2
  E14 . . . . .42 A1
Macquarie Way
  E14 . . . . .42 A2
Macready Ho W1 . . .102 B3
Macready Pl 2
  N7 . . . . .14 A4
Macroom Ho W9 . . . . .23 B2
Macroom Rd W9 . . . . .23 B2
Mac's Pl EC4 . . . . . .107 C2
Madame Tussaud's*
  NW1 . . . . .91 B1
Maddams St E3 . . . . . .27 A1
Maddocks Ho 3
  E1 . . . . .32 A2
Maddock Way
  SE17 . . . . .48 A4
Maddox St W1 . . . . .118 B4
Madinah Rd E8 . . . . . .16 C3
Madison Ho E3 . . . . . .27 B2
Madras Pl N7 . . . . . . .14 C2
Madrid St SW13 . . . . .46 C3
Madron St SE17 . . . .152 B2
Mafeking Ave
  TW8 . . . . .44 A4
Magdala Ave N19 . . . . .4 B2
Magdalene Cl 7
  SE15 . . . . .50 A1
Magdalen Pas E1 . . . .125 A4
Magdalen Rd
  SW18 . . . . .71 C3
Magdalen St SE1 . . .124 A1
Magee St SE11 . . . . .163 B4
Magellan Ho 18
  E1 . . . . .25 C1
Magellan Pl 28
  E14 . . . . .41 C2
Magnin Cl 8 E8 . . . . .24 C4
Magnolia Ho 2
  Richmond TW9 . . . . .45 A2
  Wandsworth SW11 . .60 B1

Magnolia Ho 13
  SE8 . . . . .51 B4
Magnolia Pl SW4 . . . .62 A2
Magnolia Rd W4 . . . . .45 A4
Magnolia Wharf
  W4 . . . . .45 A4
Magpie Ho 3 E3 . . . . .26 B4
Magpie Pl SE14 . . . . .51 A4
Magri Wlk 28 E1 . . . . .32 B4
Maguire St SE1 . . . .139 A4
Mahatma Gandhi Ind
  Est 3 SE24 . . . . . . .63 A3
Mahogany Cl
  SE16 . . . . .33 A1
Mahoney Ho SE14 . . . .51 B2
Maida Ave W2 . . . . . .89 A1
MAIDA VALE 88 A3
Maida Vale W9 . . . . . .88 B4
Maida Vale Sta
  W9 . . . . .88 B4
Maiden La
  Borough The SE1 . . .123 A2
  Camden Town NW1 . .13 C1
  Strand WC2 . . . . . .120 B4
Maidenstone Hill
  SE10 . . . . .52 B2
Maidstone Bldgs
  SE1 . . . . .123 B1
Maidstone Ho 4
  E14 . . . . .34 A3
Mail Coach Yd
  E2 . . . . .24 A2 98 B4
Main Yd E9 . . . . .18 C2
Maismore St SE15 . . . .49 C4
Maitland Cl 3
  SE10 . . . . .52 A3
Maitland Ct W2 . . . .115 B4
Maitland Ho
  Chelsea SW1 . . . . . .160 C4
  15 South Hackney
  E2 . . . . .25 B3
MAITLAND PARK 12 B2
Maitland Park Rd
  NW3 . . . . .12 B2
Maitland Park Villas
  NW3 . . . . .12 B2
Maitland Pl E5 . . . . . .17 B4
Majestic Ct N4 . . . . . . .6 A3
Major Cl SW9 . . . . . . .63 A4
Majorie Mews
  E1 . . . . .32 C3
Major Rd E15 . . . . . . .19 C3
Makepeace Ave N6 . . . .3 C2
Makepeace Mans
  N6 . . . . .3 C2
Makins St SW3 . . . . .144 B3
Malabar Ct 20
  W12 . . . . .30 A2
Malabar St E14 . . . . . .41 C4
Malam Ct SE11 . . . . .149 B3
Malam Gdns 3
  E14 . . . . .34 A2
Malay Ho 2 E1 . . . . . .32 B1
Malcolm Ho 13
  N1 . . . . .24 A3
Malcolm Pl E2 . . . . . .25 B1
Malcolm Rd E1 . . . . . .25 B1
Malcolmson Ho
  SW1 . . . . .147 C1
Malden Cres NW1 . . . .12 C2
Malden Pl NW5 . . . . . .12 C3
Malden Rd NW5 . . . . .12 C2
Maldon Cl
  Camberwell SE5 . . . .64 A4
  Shoreditch N1 . . . . . .87 A4

Maldon Cl continued
  Stratford New Town
  E15 . . . . .19 C3
Maldon Rd W3 . . . . . .28 B2
Malet Pl WC1 . . . . . .93 B1
Malet St WC1 . . . . . .105 C4
Maley Ave SE27 . . . . .75 A2
Malfort Rd SE5 . . . . . .64 A4
Malins Ct SW12 . . . . .60 C1
Mallams Mews 1
  SW9 . . . . .63 A4
Mallard Cl
  1 Hackney E9 . . . . . .18 B2
  Kilburn NW6 . . . . . . .23 C4
Mallard Ho
  2 Camberwell
  SE15 . . . . .49 B2
  St John's Wood
  NW8 . . . . .80 A1
Mallard Point 6
  E3 . . . . .26 C2
Mallet Ho 11
  SW15 . . . . .56 C2
Mallet Rd SE13 . . . . . .67 C1
Malling SE13 . . . . . . .67 A2
Mallinson Rd
  SW11 . . . . .60 B2
Mallon Gdns E1 . . . .111 A3
Mallord St SW3 . . . .157 C4
Mallory Bldgs EC1 . . .96 A1
Mallory Cl SE4 . . . . . .66 A3
Mallory St NW8 . . . . . .90 B2
Mallow Ct SE13 . . . . .52 B1
Mallow St EC1 . . . . . .97 B2
Mall Rd W6 . . . . .39 A1
Mall Studios 9
  NW3 . . . . .12 B3
Mall The
  Mortlake SW14 . . . . .55 B2
  St James SW1 . . . . .119 B1
Malmesbury 30 E2 . . .25 B3
Malmesbury Prim Sch
  E3 . . . . .26 B3
Malmesbury Rd
  Bow E3 . . . . .26 B3
  Newham E16 . . . . . . .35 A4
Malmesbury Terr
  E16 . . . . .35 B4
Malmsey Ho SE11 . . .149 A2
Malmsmead Ho
  E9 . . . . .18 A3
Malorees Jun & Inf
  Schs NW6 . . . . .9 C1
Malpas Rd
  Hackney E8 . . . . .17 A2
  New Cross SE4 . . . . .51 B1
Malta St EC1 . . . . . . .96 B2
Maltby St SE1 . . . . . .138 C2
Malthouse Dr W4 . . . .46 B4
Malthouse Pas
  SW13 . . . . .46 A1
Malting Ho E14 . . . . . .33 B2
Maltings W4 . . . . .36 C1
Maltings Cl SW13 . . . .46 A1
Maltings Lo W4 . . . . . .46 A3
Maltings Pl
  Bermondsey SE1 . . .138 B4
  Parsons Green
  SW6 . . . . .166 B3
Malt Mill SE1 . . . . . .124 C1
Malton Mews 4
  W10 . . . . .31 A3
Malton Rd W10 . . . . . .31 A3
Maltravers St
  WC2 . . . . .121 B4

Malt St SE1 .....49 C4
Malva Cl SW18 ....59 A2
Malvern Cl W10 ...31 B4
Malvern Ct
15 Shepherd's Bush
W12 ....38 C4
South Kensington
SW7 ....143 C4
Malvern Gdns NW2..1 C2
Malvern Ho
London N16 ......7 B3
SE17 ....151 A1
Malvern Mews
NW6 ....23 C2
Malvern Pl NW6...23 B2
Malvern Rd
Dalston E8 ......16 C1
Maida Vale NW6 ..23 C2
Upper Holloway N19 . 4 C3
Malvern Terr N1...85 B4
Malwood Rd
SW12 ....61 A1
Malyons Rd SE13..67 A2
Malyons Terr
SE13 ....67 A2
Managers St **8**
E14 ....34 B1
Manaton Cl SE15..65 A4
Manbre Rd W6....47 B4
Manchester Dr
W10 ....23 A1
Manchester Gr
E14 ....42 B1
Manchester Ho
SE17 ....151 A2
Manchester Mans
N19 ....4 C4
Manchester Mews
W1 ....103 B3
Manchester Rd
E14 ....42 B1
Manchester Sq
W1 ....103 C2
Manchester St
W1 ....103 B3
Manchuria Rd
SW11 ....60 C1
Manciple St SE1..137 C2
Mandalay Ho **6**
N16 ....15 C4
Mandalay Rd SW4..61 B2
Mandarin Ct **8**
SE8 ....51 C4
Mandela Cl **38**
W12 ....30 A2
Mandela Ho
E2 ......24 B2 98 C4
Mandela Rd E16...35 C3
Mandela St
Camden Town
NW1 ....83 A4
Kennington SW9..163 B1
Mandela Way
SE1 ....152 B4
Mandeville Ho
SE1 ....153 A2
Mandeville Cl **5**
SE3 ....53 B3
Mandeville Ctyd
SW11 ....169 B3
Mandeville Ho **8**
SW4 ....61 B2

Mandeville Pl W1 **103** C2
Mandrake Rd
SW17 ....72 B1
Mandrell Rd SW2..62 A2
Manette St W1...105 C1
Manfred **7**
Manfred Ct
SW15 ....58 B2
Manfred Rd SW15.58 B2
Manger Rd N7....14 A2
Manilla St E14....41 C4
Manitoba Ct **20**
SE16 ....40 B4
Manley Ct N16....7 B1
Manley Ho SE11..149 B2
Manley St NW1...81 B4
Manneby Prior N1 85 A1
Mannering Ho **18**
SW2 ....62 B2
Manningford Cl
EC1 ....96 A4
Manning Ho **3**
W11 ....31 A3
Manning Pl TW10 .54 B1
Manningtree Cl
SW19 ....70 A3
Manningtree St
E1 ....111 B2
Manny Shinwell Ho
SW6 ....155 A3
Manor Ave SE4...51 B1
Manor Circus
TW9 ....54 C4
Manor Ct
7 Brixton SW2 ...62 B2
Camberwell SE15 .49 B2
Gunnersbury W3 ..36 C2
Parsons Green
SW6 ....166 B3
Streatham SW16..74 A1
Manorfield Cl **3**
N19 ....13 B4
Manorfield Prim Sch
E14 ....34 A4
Manor Gdns
8 Chiswick W4...38 A1
Clapham SW4...171 A1
Gunnersbury W3 ..36 C2
Richmond TW10,
TW9 ....54 B3
Upper Holloway N7 . 5 A1
Manor Gr
Deptford SE8....51 B4
Richmond TW9...54 C4
Manor Gt SW15...58 A2
Manor Ho NW1...102 B4
Manor House Dr
NW6 ....9 C1
Manor House Sta
N4 ....6 A3
Manor Lo NW2...9 C2
Manor Mans
7 Hampstead
NW3 ....12 A2
Tufnell Pk N7....5 A1
Manor Mews
New Cross SE14..51 B1
Paddington NW6 ..23 C3
Manor Oak Mans
SE22 ....65 A1
Manor Par N16...7 B2
Manor Park Par
SE13 ....67 C3
Manor Park Rd
NW10 ....21 B4
Manor Pk TW9...54 B3

Manor Pl SE17 ...**150** C2
Manor Rd
Richmond TW10,
TW9 ....54 B3
Stamford Hill N16..7 A4
Manor Sch NW10..22 B4
Manor Street Est
SW3 ....158 B4
Manor The E11...118 A3
Manor Way W3...36 C2
Manresa Rd SW3..144 A1
Mansel Ct SW11..168 B3
Mansell Ho SW8..171 A4
Mansell Rd W3...37 C4
Mansell St E1....111 A1
Mansfield Ct **17**
E2 ....24 B4
Mansfield Ho
SW15 ....57 C1
Mansfield Mews
W1 ....104 A3
Mansfield Pl **28**
NW3 ....11 B4
Mansfield Rd
Acton W3 ......20 A1
Maitland Pk NW3 .12 B4
Mansfield St W1..104 A3
Mansford St E2...24 C3
Mansion Gdns NW3 . 2 A1
Mansion Ho*
EC4 ....109 B1
Mansion House **7**
EC4 ....109 B1
Mansion House St
EC2 ....109 B1
Mansion House Sta
EC4 ....123 A4
Mansions The
NW6 ....10 B2
Manson Mews
SW7 ....143 B3
Manson Pl SW7...143 B3
Manstone Rd
NW2 ....10 A3
Manston Ho W14.126 B1
Mantell Ho SW4..61 B2
Mantle Rd SE4...66 A4
Manton Ho N16...6 C1
Mantua St **23**
SW11 ....59 C4
Mantus Cl
Bethnal Green E1..25 B1
10 Stepney E1...25 B1
Mantus Rd E1....25 B1
Manville Gdns
SW17 ....73 A1
Manville Rd SW17.73 A1
Manwood Rd SE4 .66 B1
Many Gates SW12.73 A2
Mapesbury Ct
NW2 ....10 A3
Mapesbury Rd
NW2 ....10 A3
Mapeshill Pl NW2 . 9 B2
Mapes Ho **7** NW6.10 A1
Mape St E2 .....25 A1
Maple Ave W3...29 A1
Maple Cl SW4...61 C1
Maple Ct **3** NW2.. 9 C4
Mapledene Est SE16 C1
Mapledene Rd E8.16 C1
Maple Ho
5 Maitland Pk
NW3 ....12 B2

Maple Ho continued
5 New Cross SE8..51 B3
4 Richmond TW9..45 A2
Maple Leaf Sq **27**
SE16 ....40 C4
Maple Lo SW15...58 A1
Maple Mews NW6.78 A2
Maple Pl W1.....93 A1
Maples Pl **11** E1..32 A4
Maple St
5 Bethnal Green
E2 ....25 A3
Fitzrovia W1.....93 A1
Maplestead Rd
SW2 ....74 B4
Mapleton Cres
SW18 ....59 A1
Mapleton Rd
SW18 ....59 A1
Maple Wlk W10...22 C1
Maplin St E3.....26 B2
Marada Ho NW6..10 A1
Marais W4 ......45 B3
Marban Rd W9...23 B2
Marble Arch*
W1 ....117 A4
Marble Arch Sta
W1 ....103 A1
Marble Cl W3....28 A1
Marbleford Ct **4**
N6 ....4 C4
Marble Ho W9 ...23 B1
Marcella Rd SW9.173 B1
Marchant Ho **8**
SW2 ....62 B2
Marchant St SE14.51 A4
Marchbank Rd
W14 ....155 A4
March Ct SW15...57 A3
Marchmont Ho
TW10 ....54 B2
Marchmont St
WC1 ....94 A2
Marchwood Cl **8**
SE5 ....49 A3
Marcia Rd SE1...152 B3
Marcilly Rd SW18.59 C2
Marcol Ho W1...104 B2
Marcon Ct **20** E8.17 A3
Marcon Pl E8....17 A3
Marco Rd W6....39 B3
Marcus Ct TW8...44 A3
Marcus Garvey Mews
SE22 ....65 A2
Marcus Garvey Way
9 SE24 ....62 C3
Marcus Ho **14**
SE15 ....49 B2
Marcus St SW18..59 A1
Marcus Terr
SW18 ....59 A1
Marden Ho **8** E8..17 A3
Marden Sq SE16..40 A3
Mardyke Ho SE17 151 C4
Maresfield Gdns
NW3 ....11 B2
Mare St E8 ......17 A1
Margaret Bondfield
Ho
5 Bow E3 ......26 A3
22 Kentish Town
Margaret Ct W1..104 C2
Margaret Herbison Ho
SW6 ....155 A3
Margaret Ho **18**
W6 ....39 B1

Margaret Ingram Cl
SW6 ....154 C3
Margaret McMillan
Ho **80** N19 ......4 C4
Margaret Rd N16..7 B3
Margaret St W1..104 C2
Margaretta Terr
SW3 ....158 B4
Margaret White Ho
NW1 ....93 B4
Margate Rd SW2..62 B2
Margery Fry Ct N7..5 A1
Margery St WC1..95 B3
Margravine Gdns
Hammersmith W6..39 C1
West Kensington
W14 ....140 A2
Margravine Rd
W6 ....154 A4
Marham Gdns SW17,
SW18 ....72 A3
Maria Cl **5** SE1..153 C4
Maria Fidelis Convent
Sch (Lower) NW1 93 A3
Maria Fidelis Convent
Sch (Upper) NW1 93 B4
Marian Ct E9.....17 B3
Marian Pl E2.....25 A3
Marian Sq E2....25 A3
Marian St **2** E2...25 A3
Marian Way NW10..8 B1
Maria Terr E1....25 C1
Marie Curie SE5..49 A2
Marie Lloyd Ct **13**
SW9 ....62 B3
Marie Lloyd Gdns **1**
N19 ....5 A4
Marie Lloyd Ho
N1 ....87 B1
Marie Stopes Ct **3**
N19 ....5 A4
Marigold St SE16..40 A4
Marina Ct **12** E3..26 C2
Marina Point **1**
E14 ....42 A3
Marinefield Rd
SW6 ....166 B2
Marinel Ho **25** SE5.48 B3
Mariners Mews
E14 ....42 C2
Marine St **16** SE16.139 B2
Marine Twr **20**
SE8 ....51 B4
Marion Richardson
Prim Sch E1.....32 C3
Marischal Rd
SE13 ....67 C4
Maritime Ho **5**
SW4 ....61 B4
Maritime Quay **5**
E14 ....41 C1
Maritime St E3...26 B1
Marius Mans **3**
SW17 ....72 C2
Marius Rd SW17..72 C2
Marjorie Gr SW11.60 B3
Market Ct W1....104 C2
Market La W12...39 B4
Market Mews W1 118 A1
Market Pl
3 Acton W3 .....28 B1
5 Bermondsey
SE16 ....40 A2
Marylebone W1 ..104 C2
Market Rd
Barnsbury N7....14 A2

Market Rd continued
Richmond TW9 . . . . .54 C4
Market Sq E14 . . . . .34 A3
Market St E1 . . . . .110 C4
Market Studios 🕮
W12 . . . . .39 B4
Market Way E14 . . . . . . .34 A3
Market Yd Mews
SE11 . . . . .138 A2
Markham Pl SW3 . . . .144 C2
Markham Sq SW3 . . . .144 C2
Markham St SW3 . . . .144 B2
Mark La EC3 . . . . .124 B4
Markland Ho W10 . . . . .30 C2
Marksbury Ave
TW9 . . . . .54 C4
Mark Sq
EC2 . . . . .24 A1 98 A2
Mark St EC2 . . .24 A1 98 A2
Markstone Ho
SE1 . . . . .136 A3
Markyate Ho 🔟
W10 . . . . .22 B1
Marland Ho SW1 . . .131 A2
Marlborough
🕮 Putney SW19 . . . . . .69 C3
St John's Wood W9 . . . . .88 C4
Marlborough Ave 🕄
E8 . . . . .24 C4
Marlborough Cl
SE17 . . . . .150 B3
Marlborough Cres
W4 . . . . .38 A3
Marlborough Ct
Kensington W8 . . . . . . .127 A1
Marylebone W1 . . . . . .104 C1
Marlborough Day
Hospl NW8 . . . . .78 C2
Marlborough Flats
SW3 . . . . .144 B4
Marlborough Gr
SE1 . . . . .153 B1
Marlborough Hill
NW8 . . . . .79 A3
Marlborough Ho
Marylebone NW1 . . . . . .92 C2
Richmond TW10 . . . . . . .54 C2
Stoke Newington N4 . . . . .6 B3
Marlborough Ho
SW1 . . . . .119 A1
Marlborough Ho
SW19 . . . . .69 C1
Marlborough Lo
🕱 Stepney E1 . . . . . .25 B1
St John's Wood
NW8 . . . . .78 C1
Marlborough Mans 🕠
NW6 . . . . .10 C3
Marlborough Mews
🕮 SW2 . . . . .62 B3
Marlborough Pl
NW8 . . . . .79 A2
Marlborough Prim
Sch SW3 . . . . .144 B3
Marlborough Rd
Acton Green W4 . . . . . . .37 B1
Richmond TW10 . . . . . . .54 B1
St James SW1 . . . . . . .119 A1
Upper Holloway N19 . . . . .5 A2
Marlborough Rd
SW3 . . . . .144 B3
Marlborough Trad Est
TW9 . . . . .45 A2
Marlborough Yd
N19 . . . . .4 C2

Marlbury NW8 . . . . .78 B3
Marley Ho 🔟 W11 . .30 C2
Marley Wlk NW2 . . . . .9 B3
Marlin Ho SW15 . . . . .58 A2
Marloes Rd W8 . . . .128 A1
Marlow Ct NW6 . . . . . .9 C1
Marlow Bsns Ctr 🕄
SE14 . . . . .51 A3
Marlowe Ct SW3 . . .144 B3
Marlowe Ho 🕦
N16 . . . . .16 A4
Marlowes The NW8 . .79 B4
Marlow Ho
Bermondsey SE1 . . . . .138 C2
Kensington W2 . . . . . .100 B1
Spitalfields
E2 . . . . .24 B2 98 C3
Marlow Studio
Workshops
E2 . . . . .24 B2 98 C3
Marlow Way SE16 . . .40 C4
Marlstone Ho 🕦
W10 . . . . .23 A2
Marmara Apts 🕄
E16 . . . . .35 C2
Marmion Ho 🕦
SE22 . . . . .73 A4
Marmion Mews 🕄
SW11 . . . . .60 C4
Marmion Rd
SW11 . . . . .60 C3
Marmont Rd SE15 . . .49 C3
Marmora Ho E1 . . . . . .33 A4
Marmora Rd SE22 . . .65 B1
Marner Prim Sch
E3 . . . . .27 A1
Marne St W10 . . . . . .23 A2
Marney Rd SW11 . . . .60 C3
Marnfield Cres
SW2 . . . . .74 B3
Marnham Ave
NW2 . . . . .10 A4
Marnock Ho SE17 . . .151 B2
Marnock Rd SE4 . . . . .66 B2
Maroon St E14 . . . . . .33 A4
Marquess Rd N1 . . . .15 C2
Marquess Rd N
N1 . . . . .5 B3
Marquess Rd S 🕦
N1 . . . . .15 B2
Marquis Ct N4 . . . . . . .5 B3
Marquis Rd
Finsbury Pk N4 . . . . .5 C3
Kentish Town NW1 . . . . .13 C2
Marrick Cl SW15 . . . . .56 C3
Marrick Ho NW6 . . . . .78 B3
Marriott Rd N4 . . . . . . .5 B3
Marryat Ct 🕄 W6 . . .39 A2
Marryat Ho SW1 . . . .146 C1
Marryat Sq SW6 . . . . .54 A4
Marsala Rd SE13 . . . . .67 A3
Marsalis Ho 🕄 E3 . . .26 C2
Marsden Rd SE15 . . . .64 B4
Marsden St NW5 . . . .12 C2
Marshall Cl SW18 . . . .59 B1
Marshall Ct SW4 . . . .172 B3
Marshall Ho
Paddington NW6 . . . . . .23 B3
Shoreditch N1 . . . . .87 C2
Walworth SE17 . . . . . . .151 B2
Marshall St E10 . . . . .19 A4
Marshall's Pl
SE16 . . . . .139 A1
Marshall St W1 . . . . .105 A1

Marshalsea Rd
SE1 . . . . .137 A4
Marsham Ct
🕦 Putney SW19 . . . . .69 C3
Westminster SW1 . . . . .147 C4
Marsham St SW1 . . . .147 C4
Marsh Ct E8 . . . . .16 C2
Marsh Ho
SW1 . . . . .147 C1
Marsh Hill E9 . . . . . . .18 A3
Marsh La E10 . . . . . . .19 A1
Marsh St E14 . . . . . . .42 A2
Marsh Wall E14 . . . . . .42 A4
Marshwood Ho 🔟
NW6 . . . . .23 C4
Marsland Cl SE17 . . .150 B1
Marsom Ho N1 . . . . . .87 B1
Marston SE17 . . . . . .151 A4
Marston Cl NW6 . . . . .11 B1
Marston Ho SW9 . . . .173 C1
Marsworth Ho 🕄
E2 . . . . .24 C4
Martaban Rd N16 . . . . .7 B2
Martello St E8 . . . . . . .17 A1
Martello Terr E8 . . . . .17 A1
Martell Rd SE21 . . . . .75 C1
Martel Pl E8 . . . . .16 B2
Martha's Bldgs
EC1 . . . . .97 B2
Martha St E1 . . . . . . .32 B3
Martin Ct E14 . . . . . . .42 B4
Martindale SW14 . . . .55 B2
Martindale Ave 🕄
E16 . . . . .35 C2
Martindale Ho 🕥
E14 . . . . .34 A2
Martindale Rd
SW12 . . . . .73 A4
Martineau Ho
SW1 . . . . .146 C1
Martineau Mews
N5 . . . . .15 A4
Martineau Rd N5 . . . .15 A4
Martin Ho
Newington SE1 . . . . . .137 A1
South Lambeth
SW8 . . . . .162 A2
Martin La EC4 . . . . . .123 C4
Martlett Ct WC2 . . . .106 B1
Martlett Lo SW19 . . . .69 C3
Martley Ho SW8 . . . .171 A4
Martock Ct 🔟
SE15 . . . . .50 A2
Marton Rd 🕄 N16 . . . .7 A1
Marvel Ho 🕠 SE5 . . .48 C3
Marville Rd SW6 . . . .154 C1
Marvin St 🕄 E8 . . . . .17 A2
Marwell Ct SE3 . . . . . .52 C1
Mary Adelaide Cl
SW15 . . . . .68 B1
Mary Adelaide Ho
W2 . . . . .101 C4
Mary Ann Bldgs
SE8 . . . . .51 C4
Mary Datchelor Cl
SE5 . . . . .48 C2
Mary Dine Ct
SW8 . . . . .163 A1
Mary Gn NW8 . . . . . . .78 B4

Mary Ho
🕄 Hammersmith
W6 . . . . .39 B1
Stockwell SW9 . . . . . . .172 C1
Mary James Ho 🕯
E2 . . . . .24 C3
Mary Jones Ho 🕥
E14 . . . . .33 C2
Maryland Rd
Paddington W9 . . . . . . .23 C1
Stratford New Town
E15 . . . . .19 C3
Marylands Rd W9 . . . .88 A1
Maryland Wlk N1 . . . .86 C4
Mary Lawrenson Pl 🕕
SE3 . . . . .53 C3
MARYLEBONE 104 B2
Marylebone Flyover
NW1 . . . . .102 A3
Marylebone High St
W1 . . . . .103 C4
Marylebone La
W1 . . . . .103 C2
Marylebone Mews
W1 . . . . .104 A3
Marylebone Pas
W1 . . . . .105 A2
Marylebone Rd
NW1 . . . . .103 A4
Marylebone St
W1 . . . . .103 C3
Marylebone Sta
NW1 . . . . .90 C1
Mary Way SW19 . . . .147 A3
Mary McArthur Ho 🕮
N19 . . . . .4 C4
Mary Macarthur Ho
🕦 Globe Town E2 . . . .25 C2
W6 . . . . .154 A4
Maryon Mews
SE3 . . . . .53 C3
Mary Pl
W11 . . . . . .31 A2 112 A3
Mary's Ct NW8 . . . . . .90 B2
Mary Secole Cl 🕕
E8 . . . . .24 B4
Mary Smith Ct
SW5 . . . . .141 C3
Mary St
🕄 Canning Town
E16 . . . . .35 B4
Shoreditch N1 . . . . .87 A3
Mary Terr NW1 . . . . . .82 C3
Mary Wharne Ho 🕕
NW3 . . . . .12 B1
Masbro' Rd W14 . . . . .39 C3
Mascotte Rd 🕄
SW15 . . . . .57 C3
Masefield Ct SW15 . . .15 C3
Masefield Ho 🕕
NW6 . . . . .23 C2
Mashie Rd W3 . . . . . . .29 A3
Maskall Cl SW2 . . . . . .74 C3
Maskell Rd SW17 . . . .71 B1
Maskelyne Cl
SW11 . . . . .168 B4
Mason Cl
Bermondsey SE16 . . . .153 C2
Newham E16 . . . . .35 C2
Mason Ho
Bermondsey SE1 . . . . .153 C3
🕦 Hackney E9 . . . . . . .17 B1
Mason St W1 . . . . .118 B4
Mason's Ave EC2 . . . .109 B2
Mason's Pl EC1 . . . . . .96 C4

Mason St SE17 . . . . .151 C4
Mason's Yd
Finsbury EC1 . . . . .96 B4
St James SW1 . . . . . . .119 A2
Massie Rd E8 . . . . .16 C2
Massinger St SE1,
SE17 . . . . .152 A3
Massingham St
E1 . . . . .25 C1
Mast 🕦 SE16 . . . . . . .48 C1
Masterman Ho 🕄
SE5 . . . . .48 C3
Masters Dr SE16 . . . . .40 A1
Masters Lo 🕅 E1 . . . .32 B3
Master's St 🕦 E1 . . . .32 C4
Mast House Terr
E14 . . . . .41 C2
Mastin Ho SW18 . . . . .70 C3
Mastmaker Rd
E14 . . . . .41 C4
Matara Mews
SE17 . . . . .150 C1
Matching Ct 🕄 E3 . . .26 C2
Matham Gr SE22 . . . . .64 B3
Matheson Lang Ho
SE1 . . . . .135 B3
Matheson Rd
W14 . . . . .140 C3
Mathews Yd WC2 . . .106 A1
Mathieson Ct SE1 . . .136 B3
Mathison Ho
SW10 . . . . .156 C2
Matilda Ho E1 . . . . . .125 B2
Matilda St N1 . . . . . . .85 A4
Matlock Cl SE24 . . . . .63 B3
Matlock Ct
🕖 Herne Hill SE5 . . . . .63 C3
St John's Wood
NW8 . . . . .78 C2
Matlock St E14 . . . . . .33 A3
Maton Ho SW6 . . . . .154 C2
Matson Ho
🕪 Bermondsey
SE16 . . . . .40 A3
🕦 Homerton E9 . . . . . .17 C2
Matthew Cl W10 . . . . .22 C1
Matthew Parker St
SW1 . . . . .133 C3
Matthews Ho 🕠
E14 . . . . .33 C4
Matthews St
SW11 . . . . .168 C2
Matthias Ct 🕦
TW10 . . . . .54 A1
Matthias Ho 🕄
N16 . . . . .16 A3
Matthias Rd N16 . . . . .16 A3
Mattingly Way 🕄
SE15 . . . . .49 B3
Maude Ho 🕄 E2 . . . . .24 C3
Maude Rd SE5 . . . . . . .49 A2
Maudlins Gn E1 . . . . .125 B2
Maudsley Ho TW8 . . . .36 A1
Maudsley Hospl The
SE5 . . . . .48 C1
Maud St E16 . . . . .35 B4
Maud Wilkes Cl 🔟
NW5 . . . . .13 B3
Maugham Ct 🕄
W3 . . . . .37 B3
Mauleverer Rd
SW2 . . . . .62 A2
Maundeby Wlk
NW10 . . . . .8 A2

Maunsel St SW1... **147** B4
Maurer Ct 2 SE10.. **43** B3
Mauretania Bldg 11
 E1................. **32** C2
Maurice Ct 6 E1... **26** A2
Maurice Ho SW9.. **172** C2
Maurice St W12.... **30** A3
Mauritius Rd SE10.. **43** A2
Maury Rd N16....... **7** C1
Maverton Rd E3.... **26** C4
Mavor Ho N1...... **85** A3
Mawbey Ho N1..... **153** A1
Mawbey Pl SE1..... **153** A1
Mawbey Rd SE1.... **153** A1
Mawbey St SW8.... **162** A1
Mawdley Ho SE1.. **135** C3
Mawson Ct N1...... **87** C3
Mawson Ho EC1... **107** B4
Mawson La W4..... **46** B4
Maxden Ct SE15.... **64** C4
Maxted Rd SE15.... **64** B4
Maxwell Ct SE21... **76** C3
Maxwell Rd SW6.. **156** B1
Maya Cl SE15....... **50** A1
Mayall Rd SE24..... **63** A2
Maybury Ct W1.... **103** C3
Maybury Gdns
 NW10............. **9** A2
Maybury Mews N6... **8** A4
Maydew Ho SE16... **40** B2
Maydwell Ho 5
 E14............... **33** C4
MAYFAIR.......... **118** A3
Mayfair Pl W1.... **118** B2
Mayfield Ave W4.. **38** A2
Mayfield Cl
 Clapham Pk SW4... **61** C2
 Dalston E8......... **16** B2
Mayfield Ho 7
 Bethnal Green
 E2................. **25** A3
 Stamford Hill N16.... **7** A4
Mayfield Mans
 SW15............. **58** B2
Mayfield Rd
 Acton W3.......... **28** A2
 Bedford Pk W12... **38** A4
 Dalston E8......... **16** B1
Mayflower Cl
 SE16............. **40** C2
Mayflower Prim Sch
 E14............... **34** A3
Mayflower Rd
 SW9............. **62** A4
Mayflower St 1
 SE16............. **40** B4
Mayford NW1..... **83** A2
Mayford Rd SW12.. **72** B4
Maygood Ho N1... **85** B2
Maygood St N1.... **85** B2
Maygrove Rd NW6.. **10** B2
Mayhew Ct 2 SE5.. **63** C3
Maylands Ho
 SW3............. **144** B3
Maylie Ho 4 SE16.. **40** A4
Maynard Cl SW6.. **156** B1
Maynard Ho E1.... **26** A2
Maynards Quay
 E1................. **32** B2
Mayne Ct E8....... **16** C4
Mayo Ho 10 E1.... **32** B4
Mayola Rd E5...... **17** B4
Mayo Rd NW10.... **8** A2

May's Buildings Mews
 SE10............. **52** C3
Mays Ct WC2..... **120** A3
May's Ct SE10..... **52** C3
Maysoule Rd
 SW11............ **59** C3
May St W14........ **141** A1
Mayston Mews 3
 SE10............. **43** C1
Maythorne Cotts
 SE13............. **67** C1
Mayton St N7....... **5** B1
May Tree Ho SE4.. **66** B4
Maytree Wlk SW2.. **74** C2
Mayward Ho 7
 SE5............... **49** A2
Maze Hill SE10,
 SE3............... **53** A4
Maze Hill Lodge 7
 SE10............. **52** C1
Maze Hill Sta
 SE10............. **53** A4
Mazenod Ave
 NW6............. **10** C1
Maze Rd TW9..... **44** C3
Mead Cl 3 NW1... **12** C1
Meadcroft Rd
 SE17............. **48** A4
Meade Cl W4...... **44** C4
Meader Ct SE14... **50** C3
Mead Ho
 W11........ **31** B1 **112** C2
Mead Lo W4....... **37** C4
Meadowbank
 NW3............. **12** B1
Meadow Bank 8
 SW13............. **56** B2
Meadowbank Cl
 SW6............. **47** B3
Meadow Cl 9 E18.. **18** B3
Meadowcroft 1
 W4................ **36** C1
Meadowgate Sch
 SE4............... **66** A4
Meadow Mews
 SW8............. **162** C3
Meadow Pl
 Chiswick W4...... **46** A3
 South Lambeth
 SW8............. **162** B2
Meadow Rd SW8.. **162** C2
Meadow Row
 SE1............... **136** C1
Mead Pl E9........ **17** B2
Mead Row SE1... **135** B2
Meadway The 5
 SE28............. **52** C1
Meakin Est SE1... **138** A2
Meakin Ho N7..... **14** B3
Meard St W1...... **105** B1
Meath Ho SE24.... **63** A1
Meath St SW11... **170** A4
Mecklenburgh Pl
 WC1.............. **94** C2
Mecklenburgh Sq
 WC1.............. **94** C2
Mecklenburgh St
 WC1.............. **94** C2
Medburn St NW1.. **83** B2
Medcroft Gdns
 SW14............. **55** B3
Medfield St SW15.. **69** A4
Medhurst Cl 10
 E3................. **26** A3
Median Rd E5..... **17** B3
Medina Ct N7....... **5** C1
Medina Gr N7...... **5** C1
Medina Ho SE15.. **65** B3

Medina Rd N7...... **5** C1
Medlar St SE5..... **48** B2
Medley Rd NW6... **10** C2
Medora Rd SW2... **74** B4
Medresco Ho
 NW1.............. **11** C3
Medusa Rd SE6,
 SE13............. **67** A1
Medway Bldgs 23.. **26** A3
Medway Ct WC1... **94** A3
Medway Ho
 Bermondsey SE1.. **137** C3
 Paddington NW8.. **102** A4
 Stoke Newington
 N16............... **15** C4
Medway Mews 26
 E3................. **26** A3
Medway Rd E3.... **26** A3
Medway St SW1.. **133** C1
Medwin St SW4... **62** B3
Meecham Ct
 SW11............ **168** A2
Meeson St E5...... **18** A4
Meeting House Alley
 E1................ **32** A1
Meeting House La
 SE15............. **50** A3
Mehetabel Rd E9.. **17** B3
Melba Way SE13... **52** A2
Melbourne Ct
 Hackney E5....... **18** A4
 Paddington W9.... **89** A2
Melbourne Gr
 SE22............. **64** B3
Melbourne Ho
 W8....... **31** C1 **113** B1
Melbourne Mews
 SW9............. **173** B3
Melbourne Pl
 WC2............. **107** A1
Melbourne Sq
 SW9............. **173** B3
Melbray Mews
 SW6............. **164** C1
Melbreak Ho 11
 SE22............. **76** C3
Melbury Ct W8... **127** A2
Melbury Dr SE5... **49** A3
Melbury Ho 9
 SW8............. **162** C2
Melbury Rd W14.. **127** A2
Melchester 5
 W11............... **31** B3
Melchester Ho 1
 N19................ **4** C1
Melcombe Ct
 NW1............. **102** C4
Melcombe Ho
 SW8............. **162** C1
Melcombe Pl
 NW1............. **102** C4
Melcombe Prim Sch
 W6................ **47** C4
Melcombe St NW1 **91** A1
Meldon Cl SW6... **166** B4
Melford Ct
 Bermondsey SE1.. **138** B2
 Dulwich SE22..... **76** C4
Melford Rd SE21,
 SE22............. **76** C4
Melgund Rd N5... **14** C3
Melina Ct
 Putney SW15....... **57** A4
 St John's Wood
 NW8.............. **89** B3
Melina Pl NW8.... **89** B3
Melina Rd W12.... **39** A4
Melior Pl SE1..... **138** A4

Melior St SE1..... **138** A4
Melisa Ct N6....... **4** C4
Mellington Ct 2
 N16................ **7** C2
Mellis Ave TW9.... **45** A2
Mellish Ho 8 E1... **32** A3
Mellish St E14...... **41** C3
Mellish St W12... **239** B3
Mell St 6 SE10.... **43** A1
Melody La N5...... **15** B3
Melody Rd SW18.. **59** B2
Melon Pl W8...... **127** C4
Melon Rd SE15.... **49** C2
Melrose Ave
 Cricklewood NW2.. **9** B3
 Wimbledon SW19.. **70** C1
Melrose Ct SW18.. **58** B1
Melrose Gdns W6.. **39** B3
Melrose Ho
 Maida Vale NW6.. **23** C2
 Pimlico SW1..... **146** B2
Melrose Rd
 Barnes SW13...... **46** B1
 Wandsworth SW18.. **58** B1
Melrose Terr W6... **39** B3
Melton Ct 7 SW7.. **143** C3
Melton Ho E5....... **7** C2
Melton St NW1.... **93** B3
Melville Court Flats
 8 W12............ **39** A4
Melville Ho
 Brentford W4...... **36** C1
 Rotherhithe SE8... **41** A2
Melville Pl 4 N1... **15** B1
Melville Rd SW13.. **46** C2
Melville Villas Rd
 W3................ **28** C1
Melvin Ct 11 TW9 **44** C2
Melwood Ho 28
 E1................. **32** A3
Melyn Cl N7........ **13** C3
Memel Ct EC1..... **96** C1
Memel St EC1..... **96** C1
Menai Pl 2 E3..... **26** C3
Menard Ct EC1.... **97** A3
Mendham Ho
 SE1............... **138** A2
Mendip Ct
 12 Battersea
 SW11............. **59** B4
 Deptford SE14.... **50** B4
Mendip Dr NW2,
 NW2.............. **1** A2
Mendip Ho 2 N4.. **6** C4
Mendip Hos 12 E2.. **25** B2
Mendip Rd SW11.. **59** B4
Mendora Rd SW6.. **154** C2
Menelik Rd NW2... **10** B4
Menorah Prim Sch
 NW11............. **1** A4
Menotti St E2..... **24** C1 **99** C2
Menteath Ho 9
 E14................ **33** C3
Mentmore Terr
 E8................. **17** A1
Mentone Ct SW8.. **172** B4
Meon Rd W3....... **37** B4
Mepham St SE1... **121** B1
Merbury Ct SE13.. **67** C2
Mercator Pl 4
 E14................ **41** C1
Mercator Rd SE13.. **67** C3
Merceron Ho 3
 E2................. **25** B2
Merceron St E1.... **25** A1

Mercers Cl SE10... **43** B2
Mercer's Cotts 8
 E3................. **33** A3
Mercers Mews N7.. **13** C4
Mercers Pl W6.... **39** C2
Mercers Rd N19.... **4** C1
Mercer St WC2... **106** A1
Merchant Ct E1.... **32** B1
Merchants Ho
 SE10............. **42** C1
Merchant St E3.... **26** B2
Merchant Taylors
 Hall* EC3........ **109** C1
Merchon Ho N7... **13** B4
Mercia Gr SE13... **67** B3
Mercia Ho 2 SE5.. **48** B1
Mercie Ct SE22... **76** C3
Mercier Rd SW15.. **58** A2
Mercury Ct
 Brixton SW9..... **173** B4
 10 Millwall E14... **41** C2
Mercury Ho 6 E3.. **26** C4
Mercury Way
 SE14............. **50** C4
Mercy Terr SE13... **67** A2
Mere Cl SW15,
 SW19............. **69** C4
Meredith Ave NW2.. **9** B3
Meredith Ho 17
 N16............... **16** A3
Meredith Mews
 SE4............... **66** B3
Meredith St EC1... **96** A3
Meredith Twr W3.. **37** A3
Meredyth Rd
 SW13............. **46** C1
Meretone Cl SE4.. **66** A3
Mereton Mans 6
 SE8............... **51** C2
Mereworth Ho 5
 SE15............. **50** B4
Merganser Ct 17
 SE8............... **51** B4
Meridan Ct SE13... **67** C3
Meriden Ct SW3.. **144** A1
Meriden Ho 25 N1.. **24** A4
Meridian Building*
 SE10............. **52** C3
Meridian Ho SE10.. **43** A2
Meridian Pl E14... **42** B4
Meridian Prim Sch
 SE10............. **52** C4
Meridian Sq E15... **19** C1
Merivale Rd SW15.. **58** A3
Merlin Ho
 7 Chiswick W4.... **37** C1
 West Hampstead
 NW3.............. **11** A4
Merlin Sch SW15.. **58** A2
Merlin St WC1..... **95** B3
Merlin St EC1..... **95** B3
Mermaid Ct
 Bermondsey SE1.. **137** B4
 Rotherhithe SE16.. **33** B1
Mermaid Ho 8
 E14................ **34** B2
Mermaid Twr 2
 SE8............... **51** B4
Meroe Ct N16...... **7** A2
Merredene St
 SW2.............. **62** B1
Merrick Ho 2
 E9................. **18** B2
Merricks Ct 5
 SW14............. **55** A3
Merrick Sq SE1... **137** B2

Merrington Rd SW6 . . . . . 155 C4
Merritt Rd SE4 . . . . 66 B2
Merrivale NW1 . . . 83 A3
Merrow St SE17 . . 151 B1
Merrow Wlk SE17 151 C2
Merryfield SE3 . . . 53 B1
Merryweather Ct 5 N19 . . . . 4 C1
Mersey Ho 10 N7 . . 14 C3
Merstone Ho SW18 . . . 59 A1
Merthyr Terr SW13 . . . 47 B4
Merton Ave W4 . . . 38 B2
Merton Ho SW18 . . 70 C3
Merton La N6 . . . 3 C2
Merton Rd SE18 . . . 70 C4
Merton Rise NW3 . . 12 A1
Merton Road Ind Est SW18 . . . 70 C4
Merttins Rd SE15 . . 65 C2
Meru Cl NW5 . . . . 12 C3
Mervan Rd SW2 . . . 62 C3
Messaline Ave W4 . 38 B3
Messina Ave NW6 . . 10 C1
Messiter Ho N1 . . . 85 A3
Metcalfe Ho SW8. 171 B2
Meteor St SW11 . . . 60 C3
Methley Ho 8 N7 . . 5 B2
Methley St SE11 . . 149 C1
Methodist Central Hall* SW1 . . . . 133 C3
Methwold Rd W10 . 30 C4
Metropolis Apartments 5 SW1 . . . . 73 A3
Metropolitan Benefit Societies Almshouses 3 N1 . . . . 16 A2
Metropolitan Bsns Ctr 9 N1 . . . . 16 A1
Metropolitan Cl 2 E14 . . . . 33 C4
Mews St E1 . . . . 125 B2
Mews The
 Shoreditch N1 . . . 87 A4
 5 Upper Holloway N19 . . . . 5 A2
Mexborough N1 . . 82 C3
Mexfield Rd SW15 . 58 B2
Meyer Ho 1 SW12 . . . 73 A4
Meymott St SE1 . . 122 A1
Meynell Cres E9 . . 17 C1
Meynell Gdns E9 . . 17 C1
Meynell Rd E9 . . . 17 C1
Meyrick Ho 8 E14 . . . . 33 C4
Meyrick Rd
 Battersea SW11 . . . 60 A4
 Willesden NW10 . . . 9 A2
Miah Terr E1 . . . 125 C1
Micawber Ct N1 . . 97 A4
Micawber Ho SE16 . . . 139 C3
Micawber St N1 . . 97 A4
Michael Cliffe Ho EC1 . . . . 95 C3
Michael Faraday Ho SE17 . . . . 151 C1
Michael Faraday Sch SE17 . . . . 151 C1
Michael Rd SW6 . 166 B4
Michael Tippett Sch SE27 . . . . 75 B2

Michael Tippett Sch The SE11 . . . 149 C3
Michelangelo Ct 11 SE16 . . . . 40 A1
Michelle Ct W3 . . . 28 C2
Michels Almshouses 11 TW10 . . . . 54 A2
Michelsdale Dr 3 TW9 . . . . 54 A3
Michelson Ho SE11 . . . . 149 A3
Michel's Row 2 TW9 . . . . 54 A3
Michigan Ho E14 . . 41 C3
Mickledore E1 . . . 83 A1
Micklethwaite Rd SW6 . . . . 155 C3
Mickleton Ho 30 W2 . . . . 31 C4
Middlefield NW8 . . 79 B4
Middle Row W10 . . 23 A1
Middle Row Prim Sch W10 . . . . 23 A1
Middlesex Ct 5 W4 . . . . 38 B2
Middlesex Ho 1 W1 105 A4
Middlesex Pas EC1 . . . . 108 B3
Middlesex Pl 13 E9 . . . . 17 B2
Middlesex St E1 . . 110 C2
Middle St EC1 . . . 108 C4
Middle Temple* EC4 . . . . 121 B4
Middle Temple La EC4 . . . . 121 B4
Middleton Dr SE16 . . . . 40 C4
Middleton Gr N7 . . 14 A3
Middleton Ho
 Dalston E8 . . . . 16 B1
 Newington SE1 . . . 137 B1
Middleton Mews N7 . . . . 14 A3
Middleton Pl W1 . 104 C3
Middleton Rd
 Dalston E8 . . . . 16 B1
 Golders Green NW11 . 1 C4
Middleton St E2 . . 25 A2
Middleton Way SE13 . . . . 67 C3
Midford Pl W1 . . . 93 A1
Midhope Ho 6 WC1 . . . . 94 B3
Midhope St WC1 . . 94 B3
Midhurst Ct N8 . . . 5 A4
Midhurst Ho 6 E14 . . . . 33 B3
Midhurst Way E5 . . 16 C4
Midland Mainline Terminal NW1 . . . 83 C1
Midland Pl E14 . . . 42 B1
Midland Rd NW1 . . 83 C2
Midland Terr NW10 . . . . 21 A1
Midlothian Ho NW2 . 9 A4
Midlothian Rd E3 . . 26 B1
Midmoor Rd SW12 . . . . 73 B3
Midship Cl SE16 . . 32 C1
Midship Point E14 . 41 C4
Midstrath Rd NW10 . 8 A4
Midway Ho EC1 . . . 96 B4
Milborne Gr SW10 . . . . 143 A1
Milborne Ho 11 E9 . . . . 17 B2
Milborne St E9 . . . 17 B2

Milbrook Ct NW3 . . . 2 B3
Milcote St SE1 . . . 136 B3
Mildmay Ave N1 . . 15 C2
Mildmay Gr N N1 . . 15 C3
Mildmay Gr S N1 . . 15 C3
Mildmay Ho 6 SW15 . . . . 57 B2
Mildmay Mission Hospl E2 . . 24 B2 98 C3
Mildmay Pk N1 . . . 15 C3
Mildmay Rd N1 . . . 15 C3
Mildmay St N1 . . . 15 C2
MILE END 26 A1
Mile End Pl E1 . . . 25 C1
Mile End Rd E1, E3 . . . . 25 C1
Mile End Sta E3 . . 26 B2
Miles Bldgs NW1 . 102 A4
Miles Coverdale Prim Sch W12 . . . . 39 B4
Miles Ct E1 . . . . 32 A3
Miles Ho 5 SE10 . . 43 A1
Miles Lo E15 . . . . 19 C3
Miles Pl NW1 . . . 101 C4
Miles St SW8 . . . 162 B3
Milestone Green SW14 . . . . 55 C3
Milfoil St W12 . . . 29 C2
Milford Ct 5 N1 . . 7 A3
Milford La WC2 . . 121 B4
Milford Mews SW16 . . . . 74 B1
Milk St EC2 . . . . 109 A2
Milkwell Yd 7 SE5 . . . . 48 B2
Milkwood Rd SE24 . . . . 63 A3
Milk Yd E1 . . . . . 32 B2
Millais Rd E11 . . . 19 C4
Milland Ho 11 SW15 . . . . 68 C3
Millard Cl 21 N16 . . 16 A3
Millbank SW1 . . . 148 A3
Millbank Prim Sch SW1 . . . . 147 C3
Millbrooke Ct 7 SW15 . . . . 58 A2
Millbrook Ho 4 SE15 . . . . 49 C4
Millbrook Pl NW1 . 82 C2
Millbrook Rd SW9 . 63 A4
Millender Wlk SE16 . . . . 40 B2
Millennium Bridge* SE1, EC4 . . . . 122 C3
Millennium City Acad W1 . . . . 104 B3
Millennium Dr E14 . . . . 42 C2
Millennium Harbour E14 . . . . 41 C4
Millennium Pl 27 E2 . . . . 25 A3
Millennium Prim Sch SE10 . . . . 43 B3
Millennium Sq SE1 . . . . 139 A4
Millennium Way SE10 . . . . 43 A3
Miller Ho 9 SW2 . . 74 A4
Miller's Ave E8, N16 . . . . 16 B3
Miller's Ct 1 W4 . . 38 B1
Miller St NW1 . . . 82 C2

Miller's Terr 1 E8 . . 16 B3
Miller's Way W6 . . 39 B4
Millers Wharf Ho E1 . . . . 125 B1
Miller Wlk SE1 . . . 121 C1
Millfield N4 . . . . . 5 C2
Millfield La N6 . . . 3 B2
Millfield Pl N6 . . . 3 C2
Millfields Com Sch E5 . . . . 17 B4
Millgrove St SW11 . . . . 169 B2
Millharbour E14 . . . 42 A4
Mill Hill SW13 . . . 56 C4
Mill Hill Gr 11 W3 . 28 A1
Mill Hill Rd
 Barnes SW13 . . . . 46 C1
 South Acton W3 . . . 37 A4
Mill Hill Terr 9 W3 . . . . 28 A1
Milli Ho 4 SE13 . . . 67 B4
Milligan St E14 . . . 33 B2
Milliners Ho 58 SW18 . . . . 58 C3
Millington Ho N16 . . 6 C1
Mill La NW6 . . . . 10 B3
Millman Ct WC1 . . 94 C1
Millman Mews WC1 . . . . 94 C1
Millman Pl WC1 . . 95 A1
Millman St WC1 . . 94 C1
Millmark Gr SE14 . 51 A1
MILL MEADS 27 C3
Millner Ct SE4 . . . 51 B1
Mill Pl E14 . . . . . 33 A3
Mill Pond Cl SW8 . 161 C1
Millpond Est SE16 . 40 A4
Mill Row N1 . . . . 24 A4
Mills Ct EC2 . . 24 A2 98 A3
Mills Gr 1 E14 . . . 34 B4
Mills Ho SW8 . . . 171 A4
Millshott Cl SW6 . . 47 B2
Mills Row 1 W4 . . 37 C2
Mill St
 Bermondsey SE1 . . 139 A4
 Mayfair W1 . . . . 118 C4
Millstream Ho 14 SE16 . . . . 40 A4
Millstream Rd SE1 . . . . 138 C3
Mill Trad Est The NW10 . . . . 20 B2
MILLWALL 41 C3
Millwall Dock Rd E14 . . . . 41 C3
Millwood St 10 W10 . . . . 31 A4
Mill Yd E1 . . . . . 125 B4
Milman Rd NW6 . . 23 A3
Milman's Ho SW10 . . . . 157 B3
Milman's St SW10 157 B3
Milner Bldg N16 . . . 6 C1
Milner Ho 2 SW11 . . . . 59 C4
Milner Pl N1 . . . . 85 C4
Milner Sq N1 . . . . 15 A1
Milner St SW3 . . . 144 C4
Milnthorpe Rd W4 . . . . 45 C4
Milo Rd SE22 . . . . 64 B1
Milrood Ho 5 E1 . . 32 C4
Milroy Wlk SE1 . . 122 A2
Milson Rd W14 . . . 126 A2
Milsted Ho 2 E5 . . 17 A3
Milton Ave
 Becontree NW10 . . . 20 C4
 Crouch End N6 . . . 4 B4

Milton Cl SE1 . . . 152 C3
Milton Court Rd SE14 . . . . 51 A4
Milton Ct
 Fulham SW6 . . . . 58 A4
 St Luke's EC2 . . . 109 B4
 9 Wandsworth SW18 . . . . 58 C2
Milton Gr N16 . . . 16 A4
Milton Ho
 18 Bethnal Green E2 . . . . 25 B2
 2 Camberwell SE5 . . 48 C3
Milton House Mans E8 . . . . 16 B4
Milton Pk N6 . . . . 4 B4
Milton Pl 3 N7 . . . 14 C3
Milton Rd
 Acton W3 . . . . . 28 C1
 Crouch End N6 . . . 4 B4
 Mortlake SW14 . . . 55 C4
 Tulse Hill SE24 . . . 63 A2
Milton St EC1, EC2 109 B4
Milverton NW5 . . . 12 C3
Milverton Rd NW6 . . 9 B1
Milverton St SE11 . 149 C1
Milward St E1 . . . 32 A4
Mimosa St SW6 . . 165 A3
Mina Rd SE17 . . . 152 B2
Minchin Ho 10 E14 . . . . 33 C3
Mincing La EC3 . . 124 A4
Minera Mews SW1 . . . . 145 C4
Minerva Cl SW9 . . 163 C2
Minerva Rd NW10 . 20 C2
Minerva St E2 . . . 25 A3
Minerva Wlk EC1 . 108 B2
Minet Ave NW10 . . 21 A3
Minet Gdns NW10 . 21 A3
Minet Rd SW5, SW9 48 A1
Minford Gdns W14 . . . . 39 C4
Mingard Wlk N7 . . . 5 B1
Ming St E14 . . . . 33 C2
Minnow Wlk SE17 . . . . 152 B3
Minories EC3 . . . 124 C4
Minshull St SW8 . . 171 B3
Minson Rd E9 . . . 25 C4
Minstead Gdns SW15 . . . . 68 B4
Minster Ct EC3 . . 124 B4
Minster Rd NW2 . . 10 A3
Mint Bsns Pk 12 E16 . . . . 35 C4
Minton Ho SE11 . . 149 B4
Minton Mews 3 NW6 . . . . 11 A2
Mint St SE1 . . . . 137 A4
Mirabel Rd SW6 . . 155 A2
Miranda Cl 11 E1 . . 32 B4
Miranda Ho 10 N1 . 24 A3
Miranda Rd N19 . . 4 B3
Missenden SE17 . . 151 C1
Missenden Ho NW8 . . . . 90 A2
Mission Pl SE15 . . 49 C2
Mission Sq 13 TW8 . . . . 44 A4

Mission The
15 Bermondsey
SE16 . . . . 40 A4
14 Poplar E14 . . . . . . 33 B3

Misterton Ct
SW11 . . . . 167 C4

Mistral SE5 . . . . 49 A2
Mitali Pas E1 . . . . . . 111 B1
Mitcham Ho 9
SE5 . . . . 48 B2

Mitchell Brook Prim
Sch NW10 . . . . 8 A2
Mitchell Ct SW14 . . 56 A3
Mitchell Ho
Gunnersbury W4 . . . . 37 A1
6 Islington N1 . . . . 14 C1
57 Shepherd's Bush
W12 . . . . 30 A2
Mitchell's Pl SE21 . . 76 A4
Mitchell St EC1 . . . . 97 A2
Mitchison Rd N1 . . . 15 C2
Mitford Rd N19 . . . . . 5 A2
Mitre Bridge Ind Pk
W10 . . . . 22 A1
Mitre Rd SE1 . . . . . 135 C4
Mitre Sq EC3 . . . . . 110 B1
Mitre St EC3 . . . . . 110 B1
Mitre The 9 E14 . . . 33 B2
Mitre Way W10 . . . . 30 A4
Mizzen Ct E14 . . . . . 41 C4
Moatfield NW6 . . . . . 10 A1
Moat Pl Acton W3 . . 28 A3
Stockwell SW9 . . . . . 62 B4
Moat Sch The
SW6 . . . . 164 A2
Moberly Rd SW4 . . . 73 C4
Mobey Ct SW4 . . . . 172 A3
Mocatta Ho 9 E1 . . 25 A1
Modbury Gdns
NW5 . . . . 12 C2
Modder Pl SW15 . . . 57 C3
Model Cotts SW14 . . 55 B4
Modling Ho 8 E2 . . 25 C3
Moelwyn Hughes Ct
N7 . . . . 13 C3
Moffat Ho 24 SE5 . . 48 B3
Mohawk Ho 33 E3 . . 26 A3
Moira Ct SW17 . . . . 72 C2
Moira Ho SW9 . . . . 173 B4
Molasses Ho 1
SW11 . . . . 59 B4
Molasses Row 2
SW11 . . . . 59 B4
Mole Ct 2 W12 . . . 38 A4
Mole Ho NW8 . . . . . 89 C1
Molesey Ho
E2 . . . . 24 B1 98 C2
Molesford Rd
SW6 . . . . 165 B3
Molesworth Ho 9
SE17 . . . . 48 A4
Molesworth St
SE13 . . . . 67 B4
Molly Huggins Cl
SW12 . . . . 73 B4
Molton Ho N1 . . . . . 85 A3
Molyneux Ho N1 . . 102 B2
Molyneux St W1 . . 102 B3
Mona Rd SE15 . . . . . 50 B1
Mona St E16 . . . . . . 35 B4
Monck's Row
SW18 . . . . 58 B1
Monck St SW1 . . . . 133 C1
Monckton Ct
W14 . . . . 126 C2

Monclar Rd SE5 . . . . 63 C3
Moncorvo Cl
SW7 . . . . 130 A3
Moncrieff St SE15 . . 49 C1
Mondragon Ho
SW8 . . . . 172 B4
Monet Ct 18 SE16 . . 40 A1
Moneyer Ho N1 . . . . 97 B4
Monica Shaw Ct
NW1 . . . . 83 C1
Monier Rd E3 . . . . . . 18 C1
Monkbretton Ho
E2 . . . . 24 C2 99 B3
Monk Ct W12 . . . . . . 29 C1
Monk Dr E16 . . . . . . 35 C2
Monkridge 3 N8 . . . . 4 C4
Monksfield N4 . . . . . . 5 C2
Monkswell Ho
E2 . . . . 24 C2 99 B3
Monkton Ho
5 Bermondsey
SE16 . . . . 40 C4
22 Hackney E5 . . . . . 17 A3
Monkton St SE11 . . 149 C4
Monkwell Sq EC2 . . 109 A3
Monmouth Cl W4 . . . 37 C3
Monmouth Gr
TW8 . . . . 36 A2
Monmouth Ho
1 Camden Town
NW5 . . . . 13 A2
Wandsworth SW18 . . 58 C1
Monmouth Pl W2 . . 100 A1
Monmouth Rd W2 . . 31 C3
Monmouth St
WC2 . . . . 106 A1
Monnery Rd N19 . . . . 4 B1
Monnow Rd SE1 . . . 153 B3
Monroe Dr SW14 . . . 55 A2
Monroe Ho
10 Crouch End N19 . . . 4 C4
Lisson Gr NW8 . . . . . 90 B3
Monro Ho
18 Hampstead
NW3 . . . . 11 B4
Putney SW15 . . . . . . 57 A2
Monro Way E5 . . . . . 16 C4
Monsal Ct E5 . . . . . . 18 A4
Monsell Ct 4 N4 . . . . 6 A1
Monsell Rd N4, N5, . . 6 A1
Monson Prim Sch
SE14 . . . . 50 C3
Monson Rd
Deptford SE14 . . . . . 50 C3
Willesden Green
NW10 . . . . 22 A3
Montague Ave
SE4 . . . . 66 C3
Montague Cl SE1 . . 123 B2
Montague Pl
WC1 . . . . 105 C4
Montague Rd
Richmond TW10 . . . . 54 A1
Shacklewell E8 . . . . . 16 C3
Montague St
SE15 . . . . 50 B3
Montague St
Bloomsbury WC1 . . . 106 A4
City of London EC1 . . 108 C3
Montagu Mans
W1 . . . . 103 A4
Montagu Mews N
W1 . . . . 103 A2
Montagu Mews S
W1 . . . . 103 A2

Montagu Mews W
W1 . . . . 103 A2
Montagu Pl W1 . . . 103 A3
Montagu Row
W1 . . . . 103 A3
Montagu Sq W1 . . . 103 A3
Montagu St W1 . . . 103 A2
Montaigne Cl
SW1 . . . . 147 C3
Montana Bldg 4
SE13 . . . . 52 A2
Montana Rd SW17 . . 72 C1
Montcalm Ho E14 . . 41 C3
Montclare St
E2 . . . . 24 B1 98 C2
Monteagle Ct 27
N1 . . . . 24 A3
Monteagle Way
Nunhead SE15 . . . . . 65 A4
Shacklewell E5 . . . . . 7 C1
Montefiore Ct 2
N16 . . . . 7 B3
Montefiore St
SW8 . . . . 170 B1
Montego Cl 6
SW2 . . . . 62 C2
Montem Prim Sch
N7 . . . . 5 B1
Montem St N4 . . . . . 5 B3
Monteray Studios
W9 . . . . 23 A3
Montesquieu Terr 3
E16 . . . . 35 B3
Montford Pl SE11 . . 149 B1
Montfort Ho
4 Bethnal Green
E2 . . . . 25 B2
Cubitt Town E14 . . . . 42 B3
Montfort Pl SW19 . . 69 C3
Montgomery Ct
W4 . . . . 45 B4
Montgomery Ho 5
SW14 . . . . 55 C4
Montgomery Lo 38
E1 . . . . 25 B1
Montgomery Rd
W4 . . . . 37 B2
Montholme Rd
SW11 . . . . 60 B1
Monthope Rd E1 . . . 111 B3
Montolieu Gdns
SW15 . . . . 57 A2
Montpelier Gr
NW5 . . . . 13 B3
Montpelier Mews
SW7 . . . . 130 B2
Montpelier Pl
Knightsbridge
SW7 . . . . 130 B2
31 Stepney E1 . . . . 32 B3
Montpelier Rise
NW11 . . . . 1 A4
Montpelier Row
SE3 . . . . 53 B1
Montpelier Sq
SW7 . . . . 130 B3
Montpelier St
SW7 . . . . 130 B2
Montpelier Terr
SW7 . . . . 130 B3
Montpelier Vale
SE3 . . . . 53 B1
Montpelier Way
NW11 . . . . 1 A4

Montpelier Wlk
SW7 . . . . 130 B2
Montreal Pl WC2 . . 120 C4
Montrel Sq SW2 . . . 74 A3
Montrose Ave
NW6 . . . . 23 A3
Montrose Ct SW7 . . 129 C3
Montrose Ho
Belgravia SW1 . . . . 131 C3
Millwall E14 . . . . 41 C3
Montrose Pl SW1 . . 131 C3
Montrose Villas 5
W6 . . . . 38 C1
Montserrat Rd
SE15 . . . . 58 A3
Montserrat Rd
SW15 . . . . 58 A3
Monument Gdns
SE13 . . . . 67 B2
Monument St
EC3 . . . . 123 C4
Monument Sta
EC3 . . . . 123 C4
Monument The *
EC3 . . . . 123 C4
Monza Bldg The
E1 . . . . 32 B2
Monza St E1 . . . . . . 32 B2
Moodkee St SE16 . . 40 B3
Moody Rd SE15 . . . . 49 B2
Moody St E1 . . . . . . 25 C2
Moon St N1 . . . . 86 A4
Moorcroft Rd
SW16 . . . . 74 A1
Moore Ct SW14 . . . . 55 B4
Moore Ct N1 . . . . . . 86 A3
Moore Ho
18 Bethnal Green
E2 . . . . 25 B2
Greenwich SE10 . . . . 43 B1
7 Shadwell E1 . . . . 32 B2
Wandsworth SW17 . . 71 C1
Moore Park Ct
SW6 . . . . 156 B2
Moore Park Rd
SW6 . . . . 156 A1
Moore St SW3 . . . . 144 C4
Moorfields EC2 . . . . 109 B3
Moorfields Eye Hospl
EC1 . . . . 97 B3
Moorfields Highwalk
EC2 . . . . 109 B3
Moorgate EC2 . . . . 109 B3
Moorgate EC2 . . . . 109 B3
Moorgate Sta
EC2 . . . . 109 B3
Moorgreen Ho
EC1 . . . . 96 A4
Moorhouse Rd
W2 . . . . 31 C3
Moor La EC2 . . . . . 109 B3
Moorland Rd SW9 . . 63 A3
Moor Pl EC2 . . . . . 109 B3
Moor St W1 . . . . . . 105 C1
Morant St E14 . . . . . 33 C2
Mora Prim Sch
NW2 . . . . 9 B4
Mora Rd NW2 . . . . . . 9 B4
Mora St EC1 . . . . . . 97 A3
Moravian Cl SW3 . . 157 C3
Moravian Pl
SW10 . . . . 157 C3
Moravian St 10 E2 . . 25 B2
Moray Ho 9 E1 . . . . 26 A1
Moray Mews N4, N7 . 5 B2
Moray Rd N4, N7 . . . 5 B2

Mordaunt Ho
4 Becontree
NW10 . . . . 20 C4
Clapham SW8 . . . . . 171 B1
Mordaunt Rd
NW10 . . . . 20 C4
Mordaunt St SW9 . . 62 B4
Morden Ho 1
SW2 . . . . 62 C2
Morden La SE13 . . . . 52 B2
Morden Mount Prim
Sch SE13 . . . . 52 A1
Morden Rd SE3 . . . . 53 C1
Morden Road Mews
SE3 . . . . 53 C1
Morden St SE13 . . . . 52 A2
Morden Wharf Rd
SE10 . . . . 43 A3
Mordern Ho NW1 . . 90 B1
Morecambe Cl 3
E1 . . . . 32 C4
Morecambe St
SE17 . . . . 151 A2
More Cl
Canning Town E16 . . 35 B3
West Kensington
W14 . . . . 140 A3
Moredown Ho 3
E8 . . . . 16 C3
Moreland Ct 3
NW2 . . . . 1 C1
Moreland Prim Sch
EC1 . . . . 96 B3
Moreland St EC1 . . . 96 B4
Morella Rd SW11,
SW12 . . . . 72 B4
Moresby Wlk
SW8 . . . . 170 B1
More's Gdn SW3 . . 157 C3
Moreton Ho SE16 . . 40 A3
Moreton Pl SW1 . . . 147 A2
Moreton Rd SW1 . . 147 B2
Moreton Terr
SW1 . . . . 147 A2
Moreton Terr Mews N
SW1 . . . . 147 A2
Moreton Terr Mews S
SW1 . . . . 147 A2
Moreton Twr 3
W3 . . . . 28 A1
Morgan Ct SW11 . . 167 C2
Morgan Ho
Nine Elms SW8 . . . . 171 A4
Pimlico SW1 . . . . . . 147 A3
Morgan Rd
Islington N7 . . . . 14 C3
Notting Hill W10 . . . . 31 B4
Morgan St
Canning Town E16 . . 35 B4
Globe Town E3 . . . . 25 C2
Morgan's Wlk
SW11 . . . . 158 A1
Moriarty Cl N7 . . . . 14 A4
Morie St SW18 . . . . 59 A2
Morkyns Wlk
SE21 . . . . 76 A1
Morland Cl NW11 . . . 2 A3
Morland Est SE8 . . . 16 C1
Morland Ho
Kilburn NW6 . . . . . . 23 C4
Notting Hill W11 . . . . 31 A3
Somers Town NW1 . . 83 A1

Morland Ho continued
Westminster SW1 . **148** A4
Morland Mews
N1 . . . . **14** C1
Morley Coll SE1 . . **135** C2
Morley Ct SE13 . . . . **67** B3
Morley Ho
Stoke Newington
N16 . . . . **7** C2
Streatham SW2 . . . . **74** A4
W1 . . . . **104** B2
Morley Rd SE13 . . **67** B3
Morley St SE1 . . . **135** C3
Morna Rd SE5 . . . . **48** B1
Morning La E9 . . . . **17** B2
Morningside Prim Sch
E9 . . . . **17** B2
Mornington Ave
W14 . . . . **140** C3
Mornington Avenue
Mans W14 . . . . . **140** C3
Mornington Cres
NW1 . . . . **82** C2
Mornington Crescent
Sta NW1 . . . . **82** C2
Mornington Ct
NW1 . . . . **82** C2
Mornington Gr E3 . **26** C2
Mornington Mews 2
SE5 . . . . **48** B2
Mornington Pl
1 New Cross SE8 . **51** B3
Regent's Pk NW1 . **82** C2
Mornington Rd SE14,
SE8 . . . . **51** B3
Mornington St
NW1 . . . . **82** B2
Mornington Terr
NW1 . . . . **82** B2
Morocco St SE1 . **138** A3
Morpeth Gr E9 . . . . **25** C4
Morpeth Rd E9 . . . **25** C4
Morpeth Sec Sch
E2 . . . . **25** B2
Morpeth St E2 . . . . **25** C2
Morpeth Terr
SW1 . . . . **146** C4
Morrel Ct 11 E2 . . **24** C3
Morris Blitz Ct 2
N16 . . . . **16** B4
Morris Ct 3 SE5 . . **63** C3
Morris Gdns
SW18 . . . . **70** C4
Morris Ho
17 Bethnal Green
E2 . . . . **25** B2
Lisson Gr NW8 . . . **90** A1
1 Stockwell SW4 . **62** A3
10 Tufnell Pk N19 . **13** B4
Morrish Rd SW2 . . **74** A4
Morrison Bldgs
1 . . . . **111** B2
Morrison Ho SW2 . **74** C3
Morrison St SW11 . **60** C4
Morris Pl N4 . . . . . . **5** C2
Morris Rd E14 . . . . **34** A4
Morriss Ho 9
SE16 . . . . **40** A4
Morris St E1 . . . . . **32** A3
Morshead Mans
W9 . . . . **23** C2
Morshead Rd W9 . **23** C2
Mortain Ho 9
SE16 . . . . **40** A2
Morten Cl SW4 . . . **61** C1
Mortimer Cl
1 Child's Hill NW2 . **1** B1

Mortimer Cl continued
Streatham SW16 . . **73** C2
Mortimer Cres
NW6 . . . . **78** B3
Mortimer Ct NW8 . **79** A1
Mortimer Est NW6 . **78** A3
Mortimer Ho
6 Shepherd's Bush
W11 . . . . **30** C1
West Kensington
W14 . . . . **140** B3
Mortimer Lo 11
SW19 . . . . **70** A3
Mortimer Market
WC1 . . . . **93** A1
Mortimer PI NW6 . **78** A3
Mortimer Rd
De Beauvoir Town
N1 . . . . **16** A1
Kensal Green NW10 . **22** B2
Mortimer Sq W11 . **30** C2
Mortimer St W1 . . **105** A3
Mortimer Terr
NW5 . . . . **13** A4
MORTLAKE **55** B4
Mortlake High St
SW14 . . . . **55** C4
Mortlake Ho 7
W4 . . . . **37** B2
Mortlake Rd SW14,
TW9 . . . . **44** C2
Mortlake Sta
SW14 . . . . **55** B4
Mortlake Terr
TW9 . . . . **44** C3
Mortlock Cl SE15 . **50** A2
Morton Cl E1 . . . . . **32** B3
Morton Ho N1 . . . . **15** B1
Morton Mews
SW5 . . . . **142** A3
Morton Pl SE1 . . . **135** B1
Morton Rd N1 . . . . **15** B1
Morval Rd SW2 . . . **62** C2
Morven Rd SW17 . **72** B1
Morville Ho SW18 . **59** C1
Morville St E3 . . . . **26** C3
Morwell St WC1 . . **105** C3
Moscow Pl W2 . . . **114** A4
Moscow Rd W2 . . . **114** A4
Mosedale NW1 . . . **92** B3
Moseley Row
SE10 . . . . **43** B2
Mosque Tower
E1 . . . . **111** C3
Mossbourne Com
Acad 8 . . . . **16** C3
Mossbury Rd
SW11 . . . . **60** A4
Moss Cl E1 . . . . . . **111** C4
Mossford St E3 . . . **26** B1
Mossington Gdns
SE16 . . . . **40** B2
Mossop St SW3 . . **144** B4
Mostyn Gdns
NW10 . . . . **22** C3
Mostyn Gr E3 . . . . **26** C3
Mostyn Lo N5 . . . . **15** B4
Mostyn Rd SW9 . . **173** C3
Motcomb St SW1 . **131** B2
Mothers Sq The 15
E5 . . . . **17** A4
Motley Ave
EC2 . . . . **24** A1 **98** A2
Motley St SW8 . . . **170** C2
Moules Ct SE5 . . . **48** B3
Moulins Rd E9 . . . . **17** B1

Moulsford Ho
1 Lower Holloway
N7 . . . . **14** A3
8 Paddington W2 . **31** C4
Mounsey Ho 18
W10 . . . . **23** A2
Mount Adon Pk SE21,
SE22 . . . . **76** C4
Mountague PI 2
E14 . . . . **34** B2
Mountain Ho
SE11 . . . . **148** C2
Mount Angelus Rd
SW15 . . . . **68** B4
Mount Ararat Rd
TW10 . . . . **54** A2
Mountbatten Ho
N6 . . . . **3** C4
Mountbatten Mews
SW18 . . . . **71** B3
Mount Carmel
N7 . . . . **14** B3
Mount Carmel RC
Tech Coll for Girls
N19 . . . . **4** C3
Mountearl Gdns SW16,
SW2 . . . . **74** B1
Mount Ephraim La
SW16 . . . . **73** C1
Mount Ephraim Rd
SW16 . . . . **73** C1
Mountfield NW2 . . . **1** B2
Mountfield Ct
SE13 . . . . **67** C1
Mount Ford St
E1 . . . . **111** B2
Mountfort Cres
N1 . . . . **14** C1
Mountfort Terr 1
N1 . . . . **14** C1
Mountgrove Rd N5 . **6** B1
Mountjoy Ho EC2 . **108** C3
Mount Lodge SW4 . **61** C3
Mount Mills EC1 . . **96** B3
Mount Nod Rd SW16,
SW2 . . . . **74** B1
Mount PI 7 W3 . . . **28** A1
Mount Pleasant
WC1 . . . . **95** B1
Mount Pleasant Cres
N4 . . . . **5** B4
Mount Pleasant Rd
Lewisham SE13 . . . **67** B1
Willesden NW10 . . **22** B4
Mount Pleasant Villas
N4 . . . . **5** B4
Mount Rd SW18,
SW19 . . . . **71** A2
Mount Row W1 . . . **118** A3
Mounts Pond Rd SE3,
SE13 . . . . **52** C1
Mount Sq The 6
NW3 . . . . **2** B1
Mount St W1 . . . . **117** C3
Mount St W1 . . . . . **32** A4
Mount The
Hampstead NW3 . . **2** B1
Kensington
W8 . . . . **31** C1 **113** B1
Mount Vernon
NW3 . . . . **11** B4
Mountview 5
SW16 . . . . **74** B1
Mountview Cl
NW11 . . . . **2** B3
Mount Villas SE27 . **75** A1

Mourne Ho NW3 . . **11** B2
Mowatt Cl N19 . . . . **4** C3
Mowbray Rd NW6 . **10** A1
Mowlem Ho
E2 . . . . **25** B3
Mowlem St E2 . . . . **25** A3
Mowll St SW9 . . . **163** B1
Moxon St W1 . . . . **103** B3
Moye Cl 10 E2 . . . . **24** C3
Moylan Rd W6 . . . **154** B3
Moyle Ho SW1 . . . **161** A4
Moyne Ho 10 SW9 . **63** A3
Mozart St W10 . . . **23** B2
Mudchute Sta E14 . **42** A2
Mudie Ho 8 SW2 . **74** A4
Mudlarks Blvd 2
SE10 . . . . **43** B3
Muirdown Ave
SW14 . . . . **55** C3
Muir Dr SW18 . . . . **60** A1
Muirfield W3 . . . . . **29** A3
Muirfield Cl 22
SE16 . . . . **40** A1
Muirfield Cres
E14 . . . . **42** A3
Muir Rd E5 . . . . **7** C1
Mulberry Bsns Ctr
SE16 . . . . **40** C4
Mulberry Cl
Chelsea SW3 . . . **157** C3
East Dulwich SE22 . **64** C1
Hampstead NW3 . . **11** C4
Mulberry Ct
Finsbury EC1 . . . . **96** B3
Islington N5 . . . . . **15** A3
1 Leyton E11 . . . . **19** C4
10 Paddington W9 . **23** B2
Mulberry Ho
3 Bethnal Green
E2 . . . . **25** B2
6 Deptford SE8 . . **51** B4
Mulberry House Sch
The NW2 . . . . **10** A3
Mulberry Mews
SE14 . . . . **51** B2
Mulberry PI W6 . . **38** C1
Mulberry Rd E8 . . . **16** B1
Mulberry Sch for
Girls
Stepney E1 . . . . . . **32** A3
St George in t East
E1 . . . . **32** A2
Mulberry St E1 . . . **111** B2
Mulberry Wlk
SW3 . . . . **157** C3
Mulgrave Rd
West Kensington
W14 . . . . **154** C4
Willesden NW10 . . **8** B4
Mulkern Rd N19 . . . **4** C3
Muller Rd SW4 . . . **61** C1
Mullins Ho W1 . . . **105** B4
Mullens Ho 7
SW15 . . . . **57** B2
Mullet Gdns
E2 . . . . **24** C2 **99** C4
Mulletsfield WC1 . . **94** B3
Mullins Path
SW14 . . . . **55** C4
Mulready St NW8 . **90** A1
Multi Way W3 . . . . **38** A4
Multon Ho E9 . . . . **17** B1
Multon Rd SW18 . . **71** C4
Mulvaney Way
SE1 . . . . **137** C3

Mumford Rd SE24 . **63** A2
Muncaster Rd
SW11 . . . . **60** C2
Mundania Ct SE22 . **65** A1
Mundania Rd
SE22 . . . . **65** B1
Munday Ho SE1 . . **137** B1
Munday Rd E16 . . . **35** C2
Munden Ho 5 E3 . . **27** A2
Munden St W14 . . **140** A4
Mund St W14 . . . . **141** A1
Mundy Ho 6 W10 . **23** A2
Mundy St
N1 . . . . **24** A2 **98** B4
Munro Ho
Bermondsey SE1 . **137** C3
Lambeth SE1 . . . . **135** B3
Munro Mews W10 . **31** A4
Munster Ct SW6 . . **164** C2
Munster Rd SW6 . **154** B2
Munster Residences
SW6 . . . . **164** B4
Munster Sq NW1 . . **92** B2
Munton Rd SE1,
SE17 . . . . **151** A4
Murchison Ho 11
W10 . . . . **31** A4
Murdoch Ho 4
SE16 . . . . **40** B3
Murdock Cl E16 . . **35** B3
Murdock St SE15 . **50** A4
Muriel St N1 . . . . . **85** A4
Murphy Ho SE1 . . **136** B2
Murphy St SE1 . . . **135** B3
Murray Gr N1 . . . . **87** B1
Murray Mews
NW1 . . . . **13** C1
Murray St NW1 . . . **13** C1
Murray Terr NW3 . **11** C4
Musbury St E1 . . . . **32** B3
Muscal W6 . . . . . . **154** A4
Muscatel PI SE5 . . **49** A2
Muschamp Rd
SE15 . . . . **64** B4
Muscott Ho 18 E2 . **24** C4
Muscovy St EC3 . . **124** B4
Museum Ho 7 E2 . **25** B2
Museum in
Docklands ★
E14 . . . . **33** C2
Museum Mans
WC1 . . . . **106** A3
Museum of Brands ★
W11 . . . . **31** B3
Museum St WC1 . . **106** A2
Musgrave Cres
SW6 . . . . **165** C4
Musgrave Ct
SW11 . . . . **168** A4
Musgrove Ho 11
E9 . . . . **17** C2
Musgrove Rd
SE14 . . . . **51** A2
Musical Mus The ★
TW8 . . . . **44** A4
Musjid Rd SW11 . . **167** C1
Mus of Childhood
(V&A) ★ E2 . . . . . **25** B2
Mus of Culinary
History &
Alimentation ★
NW1 . . . . **83** A2

Mus of Garden
History★ SE1.... **134** C1
Mus of London★
EC2................. **108** C3
Mus of the Order of
St John★ EC1 ... **96** A1
Mustow PI NW6 .. **165** A2
Mutrix Rd NW6 ....**23** C4
Mutton PI NW1 ....**12** C2
Myatt Garden Prim
Sch SE4.............**51** B1
Myatt Ho SE5........**48** A1
Myatt Rd SW4 ......**48** A2
Myatts Field Ct
SE5...................**48** B2
Mycenae Rd SE3 ...**53** C4
Myddelton Pas
EC1...................**95** C4
Myddelton Sq EC1. **95** C4
Myddelton St EC1 . **95** C3
Myddelton Ave N4 ..**6** B2
Myers Ho **5** SW8 ...**162** A2
Myers La SE14 .....**50** C4
Mylius CI SE14 .....**50** B2
Mylne CI W6........**38** C1
Mylne St EC1........**85** B1
Mynterne Ct **16**
SW19.................**69** C3
Myrdle Ct E1........**111** C2
Myrdle St E1.........**111** C2
Myron PI SE13 .....**67** B4
Myrtle Ho SE14 ....**50** B2
Myrtle Rd W3........**28** B1
Myrtle Wlk **20** N1...**24** A3
Mysore Rd SW11 ...**60** B3
Myton Rd SE21 .....**75** C1
Mytton Ho SW8 ....**162** C1

N

N1 Shopping Ctr
N1......................**85** C2
Nags Head N7 ......**14** B4
Nags Head CI N7.. **14** C4
Nags Head Sh Ctr The
N7......................**14** B4
Naima Jewish Prep
Sch NW6.............**78** A2
Nainby Ho SE11 ...**149** B3
Nairne Gr SE5,
SE24..................**63** C3
Nairn St E14 ....**34** B4
Naish Ct N1..........**84** B4
Naldera Gdns SE3. **53** C4
Nalton Ho **4** NW6. **11** B1
Nankin St E14 .....**33** C3
Nansen Rd SW11 ..**60** C4
Nant Ct NW2.........**1** B2
Nantes CI SW18 ....**59** B3
Nant Rd NW2 ....**1** B2
Nant St E2 ....**25** A2
Naoroji St WC1.....**95** B3
Napier Ave
Deptford E14 ....**41** C1
Fulham SW6 ....**58** B4
Napier CI
New Cross SE14,
SE8 ....**51** B3
West Kensington
W14 ....**126** C2
Napier Ct
Fulham SW6 ....**58** B4
Shoreditch N1 ....**87** B2
Napier Gr N1........**87** A2
Napier Ho SE17 ....**48** A4
Napier PI W14 .....**126** C1
Napier Rd
College Pk NW10...**22** A2
Kensington W14...**126** C1
Napier Terr N1 .....**15** A1
Narbonne Ave
SW4..................**61** B2
Narborough St
SW6..................**166** A1
Narcissus Rd NW6. **10** C3
Narford Rd E5........**7** C2
Narrow St
6 Acton W3 ....**28** A1
Limehouse E14 ....**33** A2
Nascot St W12 .....**30** B3
Naseby Rd NW6 ....**11** B1
Nashe Ho SE1 .....**137** B1
Nash Ho
6 Millwall E14 .....**41** C3
Pimlico SW1........**146** B1
Nash Rd SE4 ......**66** A2
Nash St NW1........**92** B4
Nasmyth St W6 ....**39** A3
Nassau Rd SW13 ...**46** B2
Nassau St W1 .....**104** C3
Nassington Rd
NW3 ....**12** B4
Nathan Ho SE11...**149** C3
Nathaniel CI E1 ...**111** A3
National Army Mus★
SW3 ....**159** A4
National Fan Mus★
SE10 ....**52** B3
National Film
Theatre★
SE1 ....**121** A2
National Gallery★
W1 ....**119** C3
National Hospl The
WC1 ....**94** B1
National Maritime
Mus★ SE10 ....**52** C4
National Portrait
Gallery★ W1......**119** C3
National Portrait
Gallery (Annexe)★
SW1 ....**119** C2
National Theatre★
SE1 ....**121** A2
Natural History Mus★
SW7 ....**129** B1
Nat West Twr★
EC2 ....**109** C2
Nautilus Bldg The
EC1 ....**95** C4
Naval Row E14 ....**34** B2
Navarino Gr E8.....**16** C2
Navarino Mans E8..**16** C2
Navarino Rd E8 ...**16** C2
Navarre St
E2 ....**24** B1 **98** C2
Navenby Wlk **13**
E3 ....**26** C1
Navy St SW4 ....**61** C4
Naxos Bldg **3**
E14 ....**41** C4
Naylor Bldg W E1 .**111** B2
Naylor Ho
Clapham SW8......**171** B1
Walworth SE17.....**151** C2
5 West Kilburn
W10 ....**23** B2
Naylor Rd SE15.....**50** A3
Nayor Bldg E E1 ...**111** C2
Nazareth CI SE15...**50** A1
Nazrul St E2 .**24** B2 **98** C4
Nealden St SW9....**62** B4
Neal St WC2 ....**106** A1
Neal's Yd WC2 ....**106** A1
Neasden CI NW10 ...**8** A3
Neasden Junc
NW10...................**8** A4
Neasden La NW10 ...**8** A3
Neasden Sta NW10..**8** A3
Neate St SE5 ......**49** B4
Neathouse PI
SW1 ....**146** C4
Nebraska Bldg **11**
SE13 ....**52** A2
Nebraska St SE1 ..**137** B3
Neckinger SE16 ...**139** A2
Neckinger Est
SE16 ....**139** A2
Neckinger St SE1 .**139** A2
Nectarine Way
SE13 ....**52** A1
Nedahall Ct **4**
NW11...................**1** B4
Needham Ho
SE11 ....**149** B3
Needham Rd W11..**31** C3
Needleman St
SE16 ....**40** C4
Needwood Ho N4 ..**6** B3
Neilson-Terry Ct **9**
SW9 ....**62** B3
Neil Wates Cres **17**
SW2 ....**74** C3
Nella Rd W6 ....**47** C4
Nelldale Rd SE16..**40** B2
Nell Gwynn Ho
SW3 ....**144** B3
Nelson CI **2** NW6 ..**23** C2
Nelson Ct SE16....**33** B1
Nelson Dock Pier
SE16 ....**33** B1
Nelson Gdns
E2 ....**24** C2 **99** C4
Nelson Pas EC1 ...**97** A4
Nelson PI N1........**86** B1
Nelson Rd SE10 ...**52** B4
Nelson's Monument★
WC2 ....**120** A2
Nelson Sq SE1 ...**136** A4
Nelsons Row SW4..**61** C3
Nelson St
Canning Town E16 ..**35** B2
Stepney E1..........**32** A3
Nelsons Yd NW1...**82** C2
Nelson Terr N1 ....**86** B1
Nemoure Rd W3 ...**28** B2
Nepaul Rd **17**
SW11..................**60** A4
Nepean St SW15 ..**68** C4
Neptune Ct **13**
E14 ....**41** C2
Neptune Ho
2 Rotherhithe
SE16 ....**40** B3
14 Stoke Newington
N16....................**16** A3
Neptune St SE16 ..**40** B3
Nesham Ho **14** N1..**24** A4
Nesham St E1 .....**125** B2
Ness St SE16 ......**139** B2
Nestor Ho **13** E2...**25** A3
Netheravon Rd
W4 ....**38** B1
Netheravon Rd S
W4 ....**38** B1
Netherby Ho SW8 .**171** B1
Nethercombe Ho **1**
SE3 ....**53** C4
Nethercott Ho **27**
E3 ....**27**
Netherfield Rd
SW17 ....**72** C1
Netherford Rd
SW4 ....**171** A1
Netherhall Gdns
NW3 ....**11** B3
Netherhall Way
NW3 ....**11** B3
Netherleigh CI N6...**4** A3
Netherton Gr
SW10 ....**157** A3
Netherwood Rd
W14 ....**39** C4
Netherwood St
NW6 ....**10** C2
Netley **13** SE5 .....**49** A2
Netley Prim Sch
SW1 ....**92** C3
Netley Rd TW8 .....**44** A4
Netley St NW1 .....**92** C3
Nettlecombe NW1..**13** C1
Nettleden Ho
SW3 ....**144** B3
Nettlefold PI SE27..**75** A1
Nettleton Rd SE14..**50** C2
Nevada St SE10 ...**52** B4
Nevena Ct **3** SW2..**62** C2
Nevern Mans
SW5 ....**141** B2
Nevern PI SW5 ....**141** C3
Nevern Rd SW5 ...**141** B3
Nevern Sq SW5 ...**141** C3
Nevil Ho **7** SW9 ...**48** A1
Nevill Ct SW10 ....**156** C2
Neville CI
Acton W3 ....**37** B4
Paddington NW6 ...**23** B3
Peckham SE15 .....**49** C2
Somers Town NW1..**83** C1
Neville Ct **10**
SW12 ....**73** B4
Neville Gill CI
SW18 ....**59** A1
Neville Rd NW6 ....**23** B3
Neville St SW7 ....**143** B2
Neville Terr SW7 ..**143** B2
Nevill Rd N16 ......**7** A1
Nevinson CI SW18..**59** C1
Nevis Rd SW17 ....**72** C2
Nevitt Ho N1 ....**87** C1
New Atlas Wharf
E14 ....**41** C3
New Bentham Ct **10**
N1.....................**15** B1
Newbery Ho N1 ...**15** B1
Newbold Cotts **4**
E1 ....**32** B3
Newbolt Ho SE17 .**151** B2
New Bond St W1 ..**118** B4
New Bridge St
EC4 ....**108** A1
New Broad St
EC2 ....**110** A3
New Bsns Ctr The
NW10 ....**21** B2
Newburgh Rd W3 .**28** B1
Newburgh St W1 ..**105** A1
New Burlington Mews
W1 ....**118** C4
New Burlington PI
W1 ....**118** C4
New Burlington St
W1 ....**118** C4
Newburn Ho
SE11 ....**149** A2
Newburn St SE11 .**149** A2
Newbury Ct E5.....**18** A3
Newbury Ho
Brixton SW9 ....**48** A1
Kensington W2.....**100** B1
Newbury Mews
NW5 ....**12** C2
Newby CI **11** SW1 .**108** C4
New Butt La SE8 ..**51** C3
Newby NW1 ....**92** C4
Newby PI E14 .....**34** B2
Newby St SW8 ....**61** A4
New Caledonian
Wharf SE16 ....**41** B3
New Campden Ct **1**
NW3 ....**11** B4
Newcastle CI EC4 .**108** A2
Newcastle Ct EC4 .**123** A4
Newcastle Ho
NW1 ....**103** B4
Newcastle PI W2 ..**101** C4
Newcastle Row
EC1 ....**95** C1
New Cavendish St
W1 ....**104** A3
New Change EC4 .**108** C1
New Charles St
EC1 ....**96** B4
New Church Rd
SE5 Camberwell
.........................**48** B3
Camberwell SE5....**48** B3
New College Ct **6**
NW3 ....**11** B2
New College Mews **7**
N1.....................**14** C1
New Cottage Par **1**
NW1 ....**11** C1
Newcombe Ho N5..**15** B3
Newcombe St
W8 ....**31** C1 **113** C2
Newcomen Ho **5**
NW5 ....**13** A4
Newcomen Rd
SW11 ....**59** C4
Newcomen St
SE1 ....**137** B4
New Compton St
WC2 ....**106** A1
New Concordia Wharf
SE1 ....**139** A4
Newcourt Ho **26**
E2 ....**25** A2
Newcourt St NW8 .**80** A1
New Covent Garden
Flower Market
SW8 ....**162** A3
New Covent Garden
Fruit & Vegetable
Mkt SW8 ....**161** B3
New Crane PI E1 ..**32** B1
New Crescent Yd **1**
NW10 ....**21** B3
NEW CROSS
SE14 ....**51** B2
New Cross SE14....**51** B3
NEW CROSS GATE
SE14 ....**50** C2
New Cross Gate
SE14 ....**50** C2
New Cross Gate Sta
SE14 ....**51** A3

New Cross Hospl SE14 .... 50 B3
New Cross Rd SE14 .... 51 A2
New Cross Sta SE14 .... 51 B3
New Ct
  City of London EC4 .... 107 B1
  26 Hampstead NW3 .. 11 B4
  Stoke Newington N16 . 6 C3
New Den (Millwall FC) The SE16 .... 40 B1
Newdigate Ho 5 E14 .... 33 B3
Newell St E14 .... 33 B3
New End NW3 .... 2 C1
New End Prim Sch NW3 .... 11 B4
New End Sq NW3 .. 11 C4
Newent Cl SE15 .... 49 A3
New Fetter La EC4 .... 107 C2
Newfield Prim Sch NW10 .... 8 B1
New Globe Wlk SE1 .... 122 C2
New Goulston St E1 .... 110 C2
Newham Sch of Nursing E13 .... 27 C1
Newham Sixth Form Coll (Stratford Ctr) E15 .... 19 C1
Newham's Row SE1 .... 138 B3
Newhaven La 3 E16 .... 35 C4
NEWINGTON 150 B4
Newington Barrow Way N7 .... 5 B1
Newington Butts SE1, SE11 .... 150 B3
Newington Cswy SE1 .... 136 C2
Newington Gn N16 .... 15 C3
Newington Green Mans N16 .... 15 C3
Newington Green Prim Sch N16 .... 15 C3
Newington Green Rd N1 .... 15 C2
Newington Ind Est SE17 .... 150 B3
New Inn Broadway EC2 .... 24 A1 98 B2
New Inn Sq EC2 .... 24 A1 98 B2
New Inn St EC2 .... 24 A1 98 B2
New Inn Yd EC2 .... 24 A1 98 B2
New James Ct SE15 .... 65 A4
New Kent Rd SE1 .... 151 A4
New King's Prim Sch SW6 .... 165 C2
New King's Rd SW6 .... 165 C3
New King St SE8 .. 51 C4
Newland Ct EC1 .... 97 B2
Newland Ho E17 .... 50 C4
Newlands NW1 .... 92 C4

Newlands Quay E1 .... 32 B2
New London St EC3 .... 124 B4
Newlyn NW1 6 .... 83 A3
Newman Pas W1 .... 105 A3
Newman's Ct EC3 .... 109 C1
Newman's Row WC2 .... 107 A3
Newman St W1 .... 105 A3
Newmill Ho E3 .... 27 B1
Newmount St 9 E15 .... 19 C1
Newnes Path SW15 .... 57 A3
Newnham Ho 9 SW15 .... 57 C1
Newnham Terr SE1 .... 135 B2
New North Com Sch The N1 .... 15 C1
New North Pl EC2 .... 24 A1 98 A2
New North Rd N1 .. 87 B3
New North Road Bridge N1 .. 87 B3
New North St WC1 .... 106 C4
Newnton Cl N4 .... 6 C4
New Oxford St WC1 .... 106 A2
New Palace Yd SW1 .... 134 A3
New Park Ct 26 SW2 .... 74 A4
New Park Par 14 SW2 .... 74 A4
New Park Rd SW2 .. 74 A4
New Place Sq SE16 .... 40 A3
Newport Ave E14 .. 34 C2
Newport Ct WC2 .. 119 C4
Newport Ho 3 E3 .. 26 A2
Newport Pl WC2 .. 119 C4
Newport St SE11 .. 149 A4
New Priory Ct 3 NW6 .... 10 C1
New Providence Wharf E14 .... 34 C1
Newquay Ho SE11 .... 149 B2
New Quebec St W1 .... 103 A1
New Rd E1 .... 32 A4
New River Ct N5 .. 15 C4
New River Way N4 . 6 C4
New Row WC2 .... 120 A4
New St Sq EC4 .... 107 C2
New Scotland Yard* SW1 .... 133 B2
New Shepherd's Bush Mkt* W12 .... 39 B4
New Spring Gdns Wlk SE11 .... 148 B1
New Sq WC2 .... 107 A2
New Square Pas WC2 .... 107 B2
New St EC2 .... 110 B3
Newstead Ho N1 .. 85 C2
Newton Ave W3 .. 37 B4
Newton Gr W4 .... 38 A2
Newton Ho
  Clapham SW8 .. 171 B2
  Paddington NW8 .. 78 B4
  1 Stepney E1 .... 32 A3

Newton Pl E14 .... 41 C2
Newton Point 1 E16 .... 35 B3
Newton Prep Sch SW8 .... 170 B4
Newton Rd
  Acton W3 .... 37 B4
  Kensington W2 .. 100 A1
  Stratford New Town E15 .... 19 C3
Newton St WC2 .. 106 B2
Newton's Yd 14 SW18 .... 58 C2
New Tower Bldgs 21 E1 .... 32 A1
New Union Cl E14 .. 42 B3
New Union St EC2 .... 109 B3
Nicholas Ct
  Chiswick W4 .... 46 A3
  Golders Green NW11 .. 1 C4
Nicholas Ho 2 SW15 .... 56 C2
Nicholas La EC2, EC4 .... 123 C4
Nicholas Pas EC3 .... 123 C4
Nicholas Rd E1 .... 25 B1
Nicholay Rd N19 .. 4 C3
Nicholl Ho N4 .... 6 B3
Nicholl St E2 .... 24 C4
Nichols Cl N4 .... 5 C3
Nichols Ct E2 .... 24 B3
Nicholson Ho SE17 .... 151 B2
Nicholson St SE1 .... 122 A1
Nickleby Ho
  Bermondsey SE1 .. 139 B3
  7 Shepherd's Bush W11 .... 30 C1
Nickols Wlk SW18 .. 59 A3
Nicoll Ct NW10 .... 21 A4
Nicoll Rd NW10 .... 21 A4
Nicosia Rd SW18 .. 72 A4
Nigel Bldg EC1 .... 107 B4
Nigel Playfair Ave W6 .... 39 A1
Nigel Rd
  Peckham SE15 .. 65 A4
Nightingale Cl W4 .. 45 B4
Nightingale Ct
  4 Cubitt Town E14 .... 42 B3
  Finsbury Pk N4 .. 5 B2
Nightingale Gr SE13 .... 67 C2
Nightingale Ho
  31 Hoxton E1 .... 24 A4
  4 North Kensington W12 .... 30 B3
  St George in t East E1 .... 125 B2
Nightingale La SW11, SW12 .... 60 C1
Nightingale Lo 5 W9 .... 31 C4
Nightingale Mans 4 SW12 .... 60 C1
Nightingale Mews
  1 Bow E3 .... 26 A3
  Newington SE11 .. 150 A4

Nightingale Pl SW10 .... 157 A4
Nightingale Prim Sch E5 .... 16 C4
Nightingale Rd NW10 .... 21 B3
Nightingale Sch SW17 .... 72 A2
Nightingale Sq SW12 .... 72 C4
Nightingale Wlk SW18, SW4 .... 61 A1
Nile Cl N16 .... 7 B1
Nile Ho N1 .... 97 B4
Nile St N1 .... 97 B4
Nile Terr SE1, SE15 .... 153 A1
Nimegen Way 9 SE22 .... 64 A2
Nimrod Pas 4 N1 .. 16 A2
NINE ELMS 160 C2
Nine Elms La SW8 .... 161 B3
Nisbet Ho E9 .... 17 C3
Niton Rd TW9 .... 54 C4
Niton St SW6 .... 47 C3
No 2 Willow Rd* NW3 .... 12 A4
Nobel Ho 8 SE5 .. 48 B1
Noble Ct E1 .... 32 A2
Noble St EC2 .... 108 C2
Noel Coward Ho SW1 .... 147 A3
Noel Ho 3 NW3 .... 11 C1
Noel Rd Acton W3 .. 28 A3
  Islington N1 .... 86 B2
Noel St W1 .... 105 A1
Noko NW10 .... 22 C2
Nolan Way E5 .... 16 C4
Noll Ho N7 .... 5 B2
Norbiton Rd E14 .. 33 B3
Norbrooke St W12 .. 29 B2
Norburn St W10 .. 31 A4
Norcombe Ho 8 N19 .... 4 C1
Norcott Rd N16 .. 7 C1
Norcroft Gdns SE22 .... 76 C4
Norden Ho 25 E2 .. 25 A2
Nore Ct NW10 .... 8 C1
Norfolk Cres W2 .. 102 B2
Norfolk Ho
  City of London EC4 .... 122 C4
  Greenwich SE3 .... 53 A4
  4 Putney SW15 .. 69 B4
  Richmond TW10 .. 54 C2
  Shacklewell E8 .... 16 B4
  St Johns SE8 .... 51 C2
  Westminster SW1 . 147 C4
Norfolk House Rd SW16 .... 74 A1
Norfolk Mans
  Battersea SW11 .. 169 A3
  10 Wandsworth SW18 .... 58 C2
Norfolk Mews 4 W10 .... 31 A4
Norfolk Pl W2 .... 101 C2
Norfolk Rd
  St John's Wood NW8 .... 79 C3
  Willesden NW10 .. 8 A1
Norfolk Row SE1, SE11 .... 148 C4
Norfolk Sq W2 .... 101 C2

Norfolk Sq Mews W2 .... 101 C1
Norgrove St SW12 .. 72 C4
Norland Ho 13 W11 .... 30 C1
Norland Pl W11 .... 31 A1 112 B1
Norland Place Sch W11 .... 31 A1 112 B1
Norland Rd 18 W11 .... 30 C1
Norland Sq W11 .... 31 A1 112 B1
Norley Vale SW15 .. 68 C3
Norman Butler Ho 10 W10 .... 23 A1
Normanby Cl SW15 .... 58 B2
Normanby Rd NW10 .... 8 B4
Norman Ct
  Dulwich SE22 .... 76 C4
  Finsbury Pk N4 .. 5 C4
  Willesden NW10 .. 8 C1
Normand Croft Com Sch W14 .... 155 A4
Normand Mews W14 .... 154 B4
Normand Rd W14 .... 154 C4
Normandy Ho 6 E14 .... 42 B4
Normandy Rd SW9 .... 173 B3
Norman Gr E3 .... 26 A3
Norman Ho SW8 .... 162 A2
Normanhurst Rd SW2 .... 74 B2
Norman Rd SE10 .. 52 A3
Norman St EC1 .... 97 A3
Normanton Ave SW19 .... 70 C2
Normanton Ho 4 SW4 .... 61 B1
Norman Way W3 .. 28 A3
Norris Ho
  12 Hoxton N1 .... 24 A4
  9 South Hackney E9 .... 25 B4
Norris St SW1 .... 119 B3
Norroy Rd SW15 .. 57 C3
Norse Ho 25 SE5 .. 48 B1
Norstead Pl SW15 .. 68 C2
NORTH ACTON 20 C2
North Acton Rd NW10 .... 20 C2
North Acton Sta W3 .... 28 C4
Northampton Gr N1 .... 15 C3
Northampton Pk N1 .... 15 C2
Northampton Rd EC1 .... 95 C2
Northampton Sq EC1 .... 96 A3
Northampton St N1 .... 15 B1
North Audley St W1 .... 117 B4
North Ave 8 TW9 .. 44 C2
Northaw Ho 7 W10 .... 22 B1
North Bank NW8 .. 90 A3
North Block 19 E1 .. 32 B2

Northbourne Ho 21
E5 . . . . **17** A3
Northbourne Rd
SW4 . . . . .61 C2
North Bridge House
Sch NW3 . . . . .11 B2
North Bridge House
Senior Sch NW1 . . **82** A3
Northburgh St
EC1 . . . . **96** B2
North Carriage Dr
W2 . . . . **116** B4
Northchurch
SE17 . . . . **151** C2
Northchurch Ho 19
E2 . . . . .24 C4
Northchurch Rd
N1 . . . . .15 C1
Northchurch Terr
N1 . . . . .16 A1
North Circular Rd NW2,
NW10 . . . . 8 A3
North Colonnade The
E14 . . . . .34 A1
Northcote Lodge Sch
SW11 . . . . .60 B1
Northcote Rd
Wandsworth
SW11 . . . . .60 B2
Willesden NW10 . . . . . 8 A1
Northcourt W1 . . . **105** A4
North Cres
Marylebone WC1 . . **105** B4
Newham E16 . . . . . . .27 C1
Northcroft Ct 8
W12 . . . . .38 C4
North Cross Rd
SE22 . . . . .64 C2
North Ct SW1 . . . . **134** A1
Northdown St N1 . . **84** C1
North Dulwich Sta
SE21 . . . . .63 C2
NORTH END 2 B2
North End Ave NW3 . . 2 B2
North End Cres
W14 . . . . **140** C3
North End Ho
W14 . . . . **140** B3
North End Par
W14 . . . . **140** B3
North End Rd
Golders Green
NW11 . . . . 2 A3
West Kensington
W14 . . . . **141** A1
North End Way NW3 . . 2 B2
Northern Hts N8 . . . . 4 C4
Noreshk Ho 3
E1 . . . . .25 A1
North Eyot Gdns 3
W6 . . . . .38 B1
Northey St E14 . . . . .33 A2
Northfield Hall N6 . . . 3 C4
Northfield Ho 3
SE15 . . . . .49 C4
Northfield Rd N16 . . . 7 A4
Northfields SW18 . . . .58 C3
Northfields Prospect
SW18 . . . . .58 C3
Northfields Rd
W3 . . . . .28 B4
Northfleet Ho
SE1 . . . . **137** B4

North Flower Wlk
W2 . . . . **115** B3
North Gate NW8 . . . **80** A1
Northgate Ct 12
SW9 . . . . .62 C4
North Gower St
NW1 . . . . **93** A3
North Gr N6 . . . . 3 C4
North Greenwich Sta
SE10 . . . . .43 A4
North Hill Ct N6 . . . . . 3 C4
North Ho 3 SE8 . . . . .41 B1
Northiam WC1 . . . . . **94** B3
Northiam St E9 . . . . .25 A4
Northington St
WC1 . . . . **95** A1

North Lo 11 A4
Northmoor Ho 4 N4 . . 6 B4
North Worple Way
SW14 . . . . .55 C4
Norton Folgate
E1 . . . . **110** B4

Norton Ho
Globe Town E2 . . . .25 C3
Stepney E1 . . . . . . .32 A3
Stockwell SW9 . . . **173** A1
Norval Gn 9 SE5 . . . .48 B1
Norvic Ho 5 SE5 . . . .48 B1
Norway Gate SE16 . . .41 A3
Norway Pl E14 . . . . . .33 B3
Norway St SE10 . . . . .52 A4
Norwich Ho 5
E14 . . . . .34 A3
Norwich St EC4 . . **107** B2
Norwood Cl NW2 . . . . 1 A1
Norwood Ho 25
E14 . . . . .34 A2
Norwood Rd SE24,
SE27 . . . . .75 A3
Notley St SE5 . . . . . .48 C3
Notre Dame RC Girls
Sch SE1 . . . . **136** B1
Notting Barn Rd
W10 . . . . .22 C1
Nottingdale Sq
W11 . . . . . .31 A1 **112** A2
Nottingham Ct
WC2 . . . . **106** A1
Nottingham Ho
23 Camberwell

SE5 . . . . .48 B1
Stoke Newington N4 . . 6 B3
Nottingham Pl
W1 . . . . **103** B4
Nottingham Rd
SW17 . . . . .72 B3
Nottingham St
W1 . . . . **103** B4
Nottingham Terr
NW1 . . . . **91** B1
NOTTING HILL . . . **112** C3
Notting Hill Gate
W11 . . . . . .31 C1 **113** B2
Notting Hill Gate Sta
W11 . . . . . .31 C1 **113** B2
Nottingwood Ho
W11 . . . . . .31 A2 **112** A4
Nova Bldg 1 E14 . . .41 C2
Nova Ct E 3 E14 . . . .34 B1
Nova Ct W 4 E14 . . . .34 B1
Novello St SW6 . . . **165** B4
Nowell Rd SW13 . . . .46 C4
Noyna Rd SW17 . . . . .72 B1
Nucleus NW10 . . . . . .20 B2
Nuding Cl SE13 . . . . .66 C4
Nuffield Lo 14 W9 . . .31 C4
Nugent Ct 5 N19 . . . . 5 A3

Northways Par 2
NW3 . . . . .11 C1
Northwest Pl N1 . . . **85** C2
North Wharf Rd
W2 . . . . **101** B3
Northwick Cl NW8 . . **89** B2
Northwick Ho
NW8 . . . . **89** A2
Northwick Terr
NW8 . . . . **89** B2
North Wlk W2 . . . . **114** C3
Northwold Prim Sch
E5 . . . . 7 C2
Northwold Rd E5,
N16 . . . . 7 C2
North Wood Lo
NW11 . . . . 1 A4
Northwood Rd N6 . . . 4 A4
North Worple Way

Northwick Cl . . . .

Nugent Rd N19 . . . . . 5 A3
Nugent Terr NW8 . . **79** A1
Nun Ct EC2 . . . . . . **109** B2
NUNHEAD 65 B3
Nunhead Cres
SE15 . . . . .65 A4
Nunhead Gr SE15 . . .65 A4
Nunhead Gr SE15 . . .65 A4
Nunhead La SE15 . . .65 A4
Nunhead Sta SE15 . . .50 B1
Nursery Cl
New Cross SE4 . . . . .51 B1
Putney SW15 . . . . . .57 C3
Nursery La
North Kensington
W10 . . . . .22 B1
Shoreditch E2 . . . . . .24 B4
Nursery Rd
Hackney E9 . . . . .17 B2
Stockwell SW9 . . . . .62 B3
Nursery Row
SE17 . . . . **151** B3

Nutbourne St
W10 . . . . .23 A2
Nutbrook St SE15 . . .64 C4
Nutcroft Rd SE15 . . . .50 A3
Nutfield Rd
East Dulwich SE22 . . .64 B3
Leyton E15 . . . . .19 B4
Nutford Pl W1 . . . . **102** C2
Nuthurst Ave SW2 . . .74 B2
Nutley Terr NW3 . . . .11 C2
Nutmeg La E14 . . . . .34 C3
Nuttall St N1 . . . . . . .24 A3
Nutt St SE15 . . . . . . .49 B3
NW London Jewish
Day Sch NW6 . . . . .10 A1
Nye Bevan Ho

SW6 . . . . **154** C2
Nye's Wharf SE1,
SE15 . . . . .49 C4
Nylands Ave TW9 . . . .44 C1
Nynehead St SE14 . . .51 A3
Nyton Cl N19 . . . . 5 A3

O

O2 Millennium Dome
The* NW5 . . . . .35 A1
Oak Bank SE24 . . . . .63 B3
Oakbury Rd SW6 . . **166** B2
Oakcourt 15 SE15 . . .49 B3
Oak Cres E16 . . . . . . .35 A4
Oakcroft Ct SE13 . . . .53 C2
Oakcroft Rd SE13 . . . .52 C1
Oakdale Ct N19 . . . . . 5 A2
Oakdale Rd SE15 . . . .65 B4
Oakdene 3 SE15 . . . .50 A2
Oakdene Ho 11

N16 . . . . 7 A3
Oakden St SE11 . . . **149** C4
Oake Ct SW15 . . . . . .58 A2
Oakeford Ho
W14 . . . . **126** B1
Oakend Ho 10 N4 . . . 6 C4
Oakeshott Ave N6 . . . 3 C2
Oakey La SE1 . . . . **135** B2
Oakfield Ct
Clapham Pk SW4 . . . .62 A1
Finsbury Pk N8 . . . . . 5 A4
Oakfield Prep Sch
SE21 . . . . .75 C3
Oakfield Rd
Finsbury Pk N4 . . . . . . 5 C4
Wimbledon SW19 . . . .69 C1
Oakfield St SW10 . . **156** C4

Oakford Rd NW5 . . . .13 B4
Oak Gr NW2 . . . . .10 A4
Oakham Ho 5
W10 . . . . .22 B1
Oakhill Ave NW3 . . . .11 A4
Oakhill Ct
Honor Oak SE23 . . . . .65 B1
Putney SW15 . . . . . . .58 B2
Oak Hill Lo NW3 . . . .11 A4
Oak Hill Park Mews
NW3 . . . . .11 A4
Oak Hill Pk NW3 . . . .11 A4
Oakhill Pl SW15 . . . . .58 C2
Oakhill Rd SW15 . . . .58 B2
Oak Hill Way NW3 . . .11 A4
Oak Ho
13 Cubitt Town
E14 . . . . .42 B4
8 Maitland Pk
NW3 . . . . .12 B2
2 Richmond TW9 . . . .45 A2
9 Stoke Newington
N16 . . . . 6 C2
Oakhurst Gr SE22 . . .64 C3
Oakington Rd W9 . . . .23 C1
Oakington Way N8 . . . 5 A4
Oak La E14 . . . . .33 B2
Oaklands Ct
Dagenham NW10 . . . .21 A4
5 Shepherd's Bush
W12 . . . . .30 A1
Oaklands Gr W12 . . . .29 C1
Oaklands Ho SE4 . . . .66 B4
Oaklands Mews 1
NW2 . . . . 9 C4
Oaklands Pas 8 NW2 . . 9 C4
Oaklands Pl 8
SW4 . . . . .61 C3
Oaklands Rd
Cricklewood NW2 . . . . 9 C4
Mortlake SW14 . . . . . .55 C4
Oaklands Sec Sch
E2 . . . . .25 A2
Oakley Cres EC1 . . . **86** B1
Oakley Dr SE13 . . . . .67 C1
Oakley Gdns 3 SW3 **158** B4
Oakley Ho SW1 . . . **145** A4
Oakley Pl SE1 . . . . **152** C1
Oakley Rd N1 . . . . . . .15 C1
Oakley Sq NW1 . . . **83** A2
Oakley St SW3 . . . . **158** A4
Oak Lodge 14 SE13 . . . .47 C4
Oak Lodge
SE21 . . . . .75 C2
Oak Lodge Sch
SW12 . . . . .72 C4
Oakman Ho 20
SW19 . . . . .69 C3
Oakmead Rd
SW12 . . . . .73 A3
Oak Park Gdns
SW19 . . . . .69 C3
Oak Park Mews
N16 . . . . 7 B1
Oakshaw Rd
SW18 . . . . .71 A4
Oaks Sh Ctr The
W3 . . . . .28 B1
Oaks The
Brondesbury Pk
NW6 . . . . 9 C1
Willesden NW10 . . . . . 9 A1
Oak Tree Ct
Acton W3 . . . . .28 A2
8 Clapham Pk
SW4 . . . . .62 A2

Oak Tree Ho W9..... **88** A2
Oak Tree Rd NW8..... **90** A3
Oakview Lo NW11..... 1 B4
Oak Village NW5..... 12 C4
Oak Way W3..... 29 A1
Oakwell Ho SW8..... **171** B1
Oakwood Cl SE13..... 67 C1
Oakwood Ct W14..... **126** C2
Oakwood La W14..... **126** C2
Oakworth Rd W10..... 30 C4
Oast Ct 8 E14..... 33 B2
Oast Lo W4..... 46 A3
Oat La EC2..... **109** A2
Oatlands Ct 3
SW19..... 69 C3
Oatwell Ho SW3..... **144** B3
Oban Ho E14..... 34 C3
Oban St E14..... 34 C3
Oberon Ho 5 N1..... 24 A3
Oberstein Rd 18
SW11..... 59 C3
Oborne Cl SE24..... 63 A2
O'Brian Ho 10 E1..... 25 C2

Observatory Gdns
W8..... **127** C4
Observatory Mews
E14..... 42 C2
Observatory Rd
SW14..... 55 B3

Occupation Rd
SE17..... **150** C2
Ocean St E1..... 32 C4
Ockbrook 3 E1..... 32 B4
Ockendon Rd N1..... 15 C2
Ockley Rd SW16..... 74 A1
Octagon Arc EC2..... **110** A3
Octagon The W11..... **112** C4
Octavia Ho W10..... 23 A1
Octavia Mews 9
W9..... 23 B1
Octavia St SW11..... **168** B3
Octavius St SE8..... 51 C3
Odell Wlk 1 SE13..... 67 B4

Odeon Ct
Dagenham NW10..... 21 A4
1 Newham E16..... 35 C4
Odessa Rd NW10..... 21 C3
Odessa St SE16..... 41 B3
Odette Duval Ho 23
E1..... 32 B4
Odger St SW11..... **169** A2
Odhams Wlk
WC2..... **106** B1
Odin Ho 6 SE5..... 48 B1
O'Donnell Ct WC1..... 94 B2
O'Driscoll Ho 4
W12..... 30 A3
Offa's Mead E9..... 18 A4
Offenbach Ho 12
E2..... 25 C3
Offerton Rd SW4..... 61 B4
Offham Ho SE17..... **152** A3
Offley Ho 10 E9..... 17 C2
Offley Rd SW9..... **163** B2
Offord Rd N1..... 14 B1
Offord St N1..... 14 B1
Ogilvie Ho 12 E1..... 32 C3
Oglander Rd SE15..... 64 B4
Ogle St 4 W1..... **104** C4
O'Gorman Ho
SW10..... **157** A2
Ohio Rd 13 SE13..... 52 A2
Oil Mill La W6..... 38 C1
Okehampton Rd
NW10..... 22 C4

Okeover Manor
SW4..... 61 A3
Olaf St W11..... 30 C2
Old Bailey EC4..... **108** B1
Old Barrack Yd
SW1..... **131** B3
Old Bellgate Wharf
E14..... 41 C3
Old Bethnal Green Rd
E2..... 25 A2
Old Billingsgate Wlk
EC3..... **124** A3
Old Bldgs WC2..... **107** B2
Old Bond St W1..... **118** C3
Old Brewery Mews
NW3..... 11 C4
Old Broad St EC2..... **109** C2
Old Brompton Rd SW5,
SW7..... **143** A3
Old Burlington St
W1..... **118** C3
Oldbury Ct E9..... 18 A3
Oldbury Pl W1..... **103** C4
Old Castle St E1..... **111** A2
Old Cavendish St
W1..... **104** A1
Old Change Ct
EC4..... **108** C1
Old Chiswick Yd
W4..... 46 A4
Old Church Rd E1..... 32 C3
Old Church St
SW3..... **143** C1
Old Compton St
W1..... **105** B1
Old Court Ho W8..... **128** A3
Old Court Pl W8..... **128** A3
Old Covent Gdn*
WC2..... **120** B4
Old Dairy Mews
5 Balham SW12..... 72 C3
4 Camden Town
NW5..... 13 A2
Old Deer Park Gdns
TW9..... 54 A4
Old Devonshire Rd
SW12..... 73 A4
Old Dock Cl TW9..... 44 C4
Oldfield Gr SE16..... 40 C2
Oldfield Ho 14 W4..... 38 A1
Oldfield Mews N6..... 4 B4
Oldfield Rd
Bedford Pk W3,
W12..... 38 A4
Stoke Newington N16..... 7 A1
Willesden NW10..... 8 B1
Old Fish St Hill
EC4..... **122** C4
Old Fleet La EC4..... **108** A2
OLD FORD..... 26 B4
Old Ford Prim Sch
E3..... 26 B3
Old Ford Rd E2,E3..... 25 C3
Old Ford Trad Est 13
E3..... 26 C4
Old Forge Mews
W12..... 39 A4
Old Forge Rd N19..... 4 C2
Old Gloucester St
WC1..... **106** B4
Oldham Terr W3..... 28 B1
Oldhill St N16..... 7 C3
Old Hospital Cl SW12,
SW17..... 72 B3
Olding Ho 6
SW12..... 73 B4

Old Jamaica Bsns Est
SE16..... **139** B1
Old Jamaica Rd
SE16..... **139** B2
Old James St
SE15..... 65 A4
Old Jewry EC2..... **109** B1
Old Kent Rd
Deptford SE1,
SE15..... 50 A4
Walworth SE1,
SE15..... **152** B2
Old Laundry The 14
SW18..... 59 C3
Old Manor Ct NW8..... 79 A2
Old Manor Yd
SW5..... **142** A3
Old Market Sq
E2..... 24 B2 99 A4
Old Marylebone Rd
NW1..... **102** B3
Old Mitre Ct EC4..... **107** C1
Old Montague St
E1..... **111** B3
Old Nichol St
E2..... 24 B1 99 A2
Old North St WC1..... **106** C4
OLD OAK COMMON
..... 21 B1
Old Oak Common La
NW10..... 21 A1
Old Oak La NW10..... 21 B2
Old Oak Rd W3..... 29 B2
Old Orch The
NW3..... 12 B4
Old Palace Prim Sch
E3..... 27 A2
Old Paradise St
SE11..... **148** C4
Old Park Ave
SW12..... 60 C1
Old Park La W1..... **118** A1
Old Pye St SW1..... **133** B2
Old Pye Street Est
SW1..... **133** B1
Old Quebec St
W1..... **103** A1
Old Queen St
SW1..... **133** C3
Oldridge Rd SW12..... 73 A4
Old Royal Free Pl
N1..... **85** C3
Old Royal Free Sq
N1..... **85** C3
Old School Cl 12
SW19..... 69 B4
Old School Sq 12
E14..... 33 C3
Old School The
WC1..... **107** A4
Old Seacoal La
EC4..... **108** A1
Old South Lambeth
Rd SW8..... **162** B2
Old Spitalfields Mkt
E1..... **111** A4
Old Sq WC2..... **107** B2
Old St EC1..... **97** C2
Old Stable Mews
N5..... 6 B1
Old Street Sta EC1..... **97** C2
Old Sun Wharf
E14..... 33 A2
Old Swan Wharf
SW11..... **167** C4
Old Theatre Ct
SE1..... **123** A2
Old Town SW4..... 61 B4

Old Vicarage Sch
TW10..... 54 A1
Old Woolwich Rd
SE10..... 42 C1
Old York Rd SW18..... 59 A2
O'Leary Sq E1..... 32 B4
Olga Ho SE15..... 49 A3
Olga Prim Sch E3..... 26 A3
Olga St 20 E3..... 26 A3
Oliphant St W10..... 23 A2
Olive Blythe Ho 14
W10..... 23 A1
Oliver Bsns Pk
NW10..... 20 B3
Oliver Cl W4..... 45 A4
Olive Rd NW2..... 9 B4
Oliver Goldsmith Prim
Sch SE5..... 49 A2
Oliver Ho
Bermondsey SE16..... **139** B3
Notting Hill
W11..... 31 A2 **112** A3
Oliver House Prep
Sch SW4..... 61 A1
Oliver Mews SE15..... 49 C1
Oliver's Yd EC1..... **97** C2
Olive Tree Ho 7
SE15..... 50 B4
Olive Tree Sch The
SE13..... 67 A1
Olivette St 1
SW15..... 57 C4
Olive Waite Ho
NW6..... 11 A1
Ollerton Gn E3..... 26 B4
Ollgar Cl W12..... 29 B1
Olliffe St E14..... 42 B3
Olmar St SE1..... 49 C4
Olney Ho NW8..... **90** B2
Olney Rd SE17..... 48 B4
Olympia Ex Ctr*
W14..... **126** B1
Olympian Ct 3
E14..... 41 C2
Olympia Way
W14..... **126** B1
Olympia Yd W2..... **114** B3
Olympic Ho 10
W10..... 30 B3
Olympus Sq E5..... 7 C1
Oman Ave NW2..... 9 B4
Oman Ct W4..... 9 A4
Ombersley Ho N4..... 6 B4
Omeara St SE1..... **123** A1
Omega Cl E14..... 42 A3
Omega Ho SW10..... **157** A2
Omega Pl N1..... **84** B1
Omega St SE14..... 51 C2
Omega Works E3..... 18 C1
Ommaney Rd
SE14..... 51 A2
Omnibus Bsns Ctr
N7..... 14 A3
Ondine Rd SE15..... 64 B3
Onedin Point E1..... **125** C3
Onega Gate SE16..... 41 A3
O'Neill Ho NW8..... **79** C1
Ongar Ho 10 N1..... 15 C2
Ongar Rd SW6..... **155** C4
Onslow Ave TW10..... 54 A2
Onslow Avenue Mans
10 TW10..... 54 A2
Onslow Cl W9..... 54 A2
One Tree Cl SE23..... 65 B1
Onslow Ct SW10..... **143** A1

Onslow Gdns
SW7..... **143** B2
Onslow Lo 28
SW2..... 74 C4
Onslow Mews E
SW7..... **143** B3
Onslow Mews W
SW7..... **143** B3
Onslow Rd TW10..... 54 A1
Onslow Sq SW7..... **143** C3
Onslow St EC1..... **95** C1
Ontario St SE1..... **136** B2
Ontario Way E14..... 33 C2
Opal St SE11..... **150** A2
Open Air Theatre,
Regent's Pk*
NW1..... **91** B3
Openview SW17..... 71 C2
Operating Theatre
Mus & Herb Garret*
SE1..... **123** C1
Ophelia Gdns NW2..... 1 A1
Ophir Terr SE15..... 49 C2
Opie Ho NW8..... **80** B2
Oppenheim Rd
SE13..... 52 B1
Oppidan Apartments
NW6..... 11 C1
Oppidans Rd NW3..... 12 B1
Orange Pl SE16..... 40 B3
Orangery Gallery
The* W8..... **126** C3
Orange St WC2..... **119** C3
Orange Yd WC2..... **105** C1
Oransay Rd 28 N1..... 15 B2
Oratory La SW3..... **143** C2
Oratory RC Prim Sch
SW3..... **144** A2
Oratory The*
SW7..... **130** A1
Orbain Rd SW6..... **154** B1
Orbel St SW11..... **168** A3
Orb St SE17..... **151** B3
Orchard Cl
Honor Oak SE23..... 65 B1
Islington N1..... 15 B1
Kensal Town W10..... 31 A4
Orchard Ct
Barnes SW13..... 56 B4
Marylebone W1..... **103** B2
Orchard Dr SE3..... 53 A1
Orchard Ho
Camberwell SE5..... 48 B2
1 Rotherhithe
SE16..... 40 B3
Shepherd's Bush
W12..... 29 C1
Orchard Mead Ho
NW11..... 1 C2
Orchard Mews N1..... 15 C1
Orchard Pl E14..... 35 A2
Orchard Prim Sch
E9..... 17 B1
Orchard Rd
Highgate N6..... 4 A4
Richmond TW9..... 54 C4
Orchard Rise
TW10..... 55 A3
Richardson Ho
NW8..... **89** C1
Orchardson St
NW8..... **89** C1

Orchard Sq W14 . . . .140 C1
Orchard St W1 . . . .103 C2
Orchard The
Acton Green W4 . . . .37 C2
Lewisham SE3 . . . .52 C1
Orchid St W12 . . . .29 C2
Orde Hall St WC1 . . .106 C4
Orde Ho 10 N16 . . . .22 C4
Ordell Ct 25 E3 . . . .26 B3
Ordell Rd E3 . . . .26 B3
Ordnance Cres
SE10 . . . .43 A4
Ordnance Hill
NW8 . . . .79 C3
Ordnance Mews
NW8 . . . .79 C2
Ordnance Rd E16 . . .35 B4
Oregano Dr E14 . . . .34 C3
Oregon Bldg 3
SE13 . . . .52 A2
Orestes Mews 1
NW6 . . . .10 C3
Orford Ct SE27 . . . .75 A2
Oriana Ho 3 E14 . . .33 B2
Oriel Ct NW3 . . . .11 B4
Oriel Dr SW13 . . . .47 B4
Oriel Ho
Hackney E9 . . . .18 A2
Homerton E9 . . . .17 C2
Orient St SE11 . . . .150 A4
Orion Bsns Ctr
SE14 . . . .40 C1
Orion Ho 20 E1 . . . .25 A1
Orion Point 5
E14 . . . .41 C2
Orkney Ho N1 . . . .84 C4
Orkney St SW11 . . .169 B2
Orlando Rd SW4 . . .61 B4
Orleston Mews
N7 . . . .14 C2
Orleston Rd N7 . . . .14 C2
Orlop St SE10 . . . .43 A1
Orme Ct W2 . . . .114 A3
Orme Ct Mews
W2 . . . .114 B3
Orme Ho 8 E8 . . . .24 B4
Orme La W2 . . . .114 A3
Ormeley Rd SW12 . .73 A3
Ormerod Ho 3
SW9 . . . .62 A4
Orme Sq W2 . . . .114 A3
Ormiston Gr W12 . . .30 A1
Ormiston Rd SE10 . .43 C1
Ormond Cl WC1 . . .106 B4
Ormonde Ct SW15 . .57 B3
Ormonde Gate
SW3 . . . .145 A1
Ormonde Mans
WC1 . . . .106 B4
Ormonde Pl SW1 . . .145 C3
Ormonde Rd
SW14 . . . .55 B4
Ormonde Terr
NW8 . . . .80 C3
Ormond Ho 7 N16 . .6 C2
Ormond Mans
WC1 . . . .94 C1
Ormond Mews
WC1 . . . .94 B1
Ormond Rd N4,N19 . .5 A3
Ormond Yd SW1 . . .119 A2
Ormrod Ct W11 . . . .31 B3
Ormsby Lo 7 W4 . . .38 A3
Ormsby Pl N16 . . . .7 B1
Ormsby St E2 . . . .24 B3

Ormside St SE15 . . . .50 B4
Ornan Rd NW3 . . . .12 A3
Orpen Ho SW5 . . . .141 C3
Orpen Wlk N16 . . . .7 A1
Orpheus Ho 26 N19 . .4 C4
Orpheus St SE5 . . . .48 C2
Orsett Mews W2 . . .100 C2
Orsett St SE11 . . . .149 A2
Orsett Terr W2 . . . .100 C2
Orsman Rd N1 . . . .24 A4
Orton St E1 . . . .125 B1
Orville Rd SW11 . . .167 C2
Orwell Ct
Hackney E8 . . . .24 C4
Highbury N5 . . . .15 B4
Orwell Ho W12 . . . .29 C2
Osbaldeston Rd
N16 . . . .7 C3
Osbert St SW1 . . . .147 B3
Osborn Cl E8 . . . .24 C4
Osborne Rd
Finsbury Pk N4 . . .5 C3
Hackney E9 . . . .18 B2
South Acton W3 . . .37 A4
Willesden NW2 . . . .9 A2
Osborn St E1 . . . .111 A4
Osbourne Ho
TW10 . . . .54 C2
Oscar Faber Pl 3
N1 . . . .16 A1
Oscar St SE8 . . . .51 C1
Oseney Cres NW5 . .13 C2
Osier Ct E1 . . . .25 C1
Osier La SE10 . . . .43 B3
Osier Mews W4 . . . .46 B4
Osiers Rd SW18 . . .58 C3
Osier St E1 . . . .25 B1
Oslo Ct NW8 . . . .80 A1
Oslo Ho 2 SE5 . . . .48 B1
Oslo Sq SE16 . . . .41 A3
Osman Prim Sch
E1 . . . .111 C4
Osman Rd W6 . . . .39 B3
Osmington Ho
SW8 . . . .163 A1
Osmund St W12 . . . .29 B4
Osnaburgh St
NW1 . . . .92 B2
Osnaburgh Terr
NW1 . . . .92 B2
Osprey Ct NW3 . . . .11 A3
Osprey Ho
Camberwell SE15 . .49 B2
3 Limehouse E14 . .33 A2
Ospringe Ho SE1 . .121 C1
Ospringe Rd NW5 . .13 B4
Osram Ct W6 . . . .39 B3
Osric Path 5 N1 . . .24 A3
Ostade Rd SW2 . . . .74 B4
Osten Mews SW7 . .128 B1
Osterley Ho 5
E14 . . . .34 A3
Osterley Rd N16 . . .16 A4
Oswald Bldg SW8 . .160 A3
Oswald's Mead E9 . .18 A4
Osward Rd SW12,
SW17 . . . .72 B2
Oswell Ho 5 E1 . . . .32 A1

Oswin St SE11 . . . .150 A4
Oswyth Rd SE5 . . . .49 A1
Otford Cres SE4 . . . .66 B1
Otford Ho
Bermondsey SE1 . .137 C3
6 Deptford SE15 . . .50 B4
Otha Ho W6 . . . .172 B2
Othello Cl SE11 . . . .150 A2
Otis St E3 . . . .27 B2
Otley Ho N5 . . . .6 A1
Ottaway Ct E5 . . . .7 C1
Ottaway St E5 . . . .7 C1
Otterburn Ho 12
SE5 . . . .48 B3
Otter Cl E15 . . . .27 B4
Otto St SE17 . . . .48 A4
Our Lady of Dolours
RC Prim Sch W2 . .100 A4
Our Lady of Lourdes
RC Prim Sch
SE13 . . . .67 C4
Our Lady of Lourdes
RC Sch NW10 . . . .20 B4
Our Lady of Victories
RC Prim Sch
Putney SW15 . . . .57 C3
South Kensington
SW7 . . . .143 A3
Our Lady Queen of
Heaven RC Sch
SW19 . . . .69 C4
Our Lady RC Prim
Sch
Camden Town
NW1 . . . .83 A4
Poplar E14 . . . .33 B3
Our Lady & St Joseph
RC Prim Sch N1 . . .16 A2
Our Lady's Convent
RC High Sch N15 . .7 A4
Ouseley Rd SW12 . .72 B3
Outer Circ NW8 . . . .81 A1
Outgate Rd NW10 . .8 B1
Outram Pl N1 . . . .84 B4
Outwich St EC3 . . .110 B2
Outwood Ho 3
SW2 . . . .74 B4
Oval Mans SE11 . . .163 A4
Oval Pl SW8 . . . .163 A2
Oval Rd NW1 . . . .82 A4
Oval Sta SE11 . . . .163 B3
Oval The E2 . . . .25 A3
Oval The (Surrey Cnty
Crkt Gd) SE11 . . . .163 A4
Oval Way SE11 . . . .149 A1
Overbury Ho 5
E5 . . . .17 C4
Overbury St E5 . . . .17 C4
Overcliff Rd SE13 . .66 C4
Overhill Rd
SE22 . . . .76 C4
Overlea Rd E5 . . . .7 C4
Oversley Ho 17
W2 . . . .31 C4
Overstone Ho 18
E14 . . . .33 C3
Overstone Rd W6 . .39 B2
Overstrand Mans
SW11 . . . .169 B3
Overton Ho SW15 . .68 B4
Overton Rd SW9 . .173 C1
Overy Ho SE1 . . . .136 A3
Ovex Cl E14 . . . .42 B4
Ovington Ct SW3 . .130 B1
Ovington Gdns
SW3 . . . .130 B1

Ovington Mews
SW3 . . . .130 B1
Ovington Sq SW3 . .130 B1
Ovington St SW3 . .144 B4
Owen Ho 11 N19 . . .13 B4
Owen's Ct EC1 . . . .96 A4
Owen's Row EC1 . . .96 A4
Owen St EC1 . . . .86 A1
Owgan Cl SE5 . . . .48 C3
Oxberry Ave SW6 . .164 B2
Oxbridge Ct 4
W4 . . . .37 A1
Oxenden St SW1 . .119 B3
Oxenford St SE15 . .64 B4
Oxenham Ho 13
SE8 . . . .51 C4
Oxenholme
NW1 . . . .83 A1
Oxestalls Rd SE8 . .41 A1
Oxford & Cambridge
Mans NW1 . . . .102 B3
Oxford Cir W1 . . . .104 C1
Oxford Circus Ave
W1 . . . .104 C1
Oxford Circus Sta
W1 . . . .104 C1
Oxford Ct
City of London
EC4 . . . .123 B4
Gunnersbury W4 . . .37 A1
5 Paddington W2 . .31 C4
Oxford Dr SE1 . . . .124 A1
Oxford Gardens Prim
Sch W10 . . . .30 C3
Oxford Gate W6 . . .39 C2
Oxford Gdns
Brentford W4 . . . .44 C4
North Kensington
W10 . . . .30 C3
Oxford Ho N4 . . . .5 C3
Oxford Rd
Finsbury Pk N4 . . .5 C3
Paddington NW6 . . .23 C3
Putney SW15 . . . .58 A3
Oxford Rd N W4 . . .37 A1
Oxford Rd S W4 . . .37 A1
Oxford Sq W2 . . . .102 B1
Oxford St W1 . . . .104 B1
Oxley Cl SE1 . . . .153 A2
Oxonian St SE22 . . .64 B3
Oxo Tower Wharf
SE1 . . . .121 C3
Oxo Tw* SE1 . . . .121 C3
Oxted Ct N16 . . . .7 A3
Oyster Row E1 . . . .32 B3
Ozolins Way E16 . . .35 C3

P

Pablo Neruda Cl 4
SE24 . . . .63 A3
Pace Pl E1 . . . .32 A3
Pacific Ho 15 E1 . . .25 C1
Pacific Rd E16 . . . .35 C3
Pacific Wharf
SE16 . . . .32 C1
Packenham Ho
26 Crouch End N19 . .4 C4
Spitalfields
E2 . . . .24 B2 99 A4
Packington Sq N1 . .86 C4
Packington St N1 . .86 B3
Padbury SE17 . . . .152 B1
Padbury Ct
E2 . . . .24 B2 99 A3

Padbury Ho NW8 . . .90 B2
Paddenswick Ct 2
W6 . . . .39 A3
Paddenswick Rd
W6 . . . .38 C3
PADDINGTON 100 C3
Paddington Acad
W2 . . . .101 B3
Paddington Wy
W2 . . . .23 C1
Paddington Com
Hospl 9 W2 . . . .31 C4
Paddington Gn
W2 . . . .101 B4
Paddington Green
Prim Sch NW8 . . .89 B1
Paddington St
W1 . . . .103 B4
Paddington Sta
W2 . . . .101 B2
Paddock Cl SE3 . . .53 C1
Paddock Sch
SW15 . . . .56 B3
Paddock Way 11
SW15 . . . .69 B4
Padfield Rd SE5 . . .63 B4
Padstone Ho 50
E3 . . . .27 A2
Padstow Ho 12
E14 . . . .33 B2
Pagden St SW8 . . .170 B4
Pageant Cres
SE16 . . . .33 B1
Pageantmaster Ct
EC4 . . . .108 A1
Page Ho SE10 . . . .52 B4
Page St SW1 . . . .147 C4
Page's Wlk SE1 . . .138 B1
Paget Ho 16 E2 . . .25 B3
Paget Rd N16 . . . .6 C3
Paget St EC1 . . . .96 A4
Pagham Ho 3
W10 . . . .22 B1
Pagnell St SE14 . . .51 B3
Pagoda Ave TW9 . .54 B4
Pagoda Gdns SE3 . .52 C1
Pagoda Gr SE27 . . .75 B2
Paine Ct SE3 . . . .53 B4
Painsthorpe Rd
N16 . . . .7 A1
Painswick Ct 5
SE15 . . . .49 B3
Painters Mews
SE16 . . . .153 C4
Pakeman Ho 1 SE1 .136 B4
Pakeman Prim Sch
N7 . . . .5 B1
Pakeman St N7 . . . .5 B1
Pakenham Cl
SW12 . . . .72 C3
Pakenham St WC1 . .95 A2
Palace Ave W8 . . .128 B4
Palace Ct
Hampstead NW3 . . .11 A3
Kensington W2 . . .114 A3
Streatham SW2 . . .74 C2
Palace Garden Mews
W8 . . . .31 C1 113 C2
Palace Gate W8 . . .128 C3
Palace Gdns Mews
W8 . . . .114 B1
Palace Gn W8 . . . .114 A1
Palace Mans
W14 . . . .140 C4
Palace Mews
Belgravia SW1 . . .145 C3
Fulham SW6 . . . .155 A2

Palace Pl SW1 .... **132** C2
Palace Rd SE27, SW16,
SW2 .... **74** C2
Palace St SW1 .... **132** C2
Palatine Ave N16 .. **16** A4
Palatine Rd N16 ... **16** A4
Palazzo Apartments
⓫ N1 .... **11** C1
Palemead Cl SW6 .. **47** C2
Palermo Rd N10 ... **.21** C3
Palewell Common Dr
SW14 .... **55** C3
Palewell Pk SW14 .. **55** C3
Palfrey Pl SW8 ... **163** A2
Palgrave Gdns
NW1 .... **90** B2
Palgrave Ho
7 Camberwell
SE5 .... **48** B3
⓳ Maitland Pk
NW3 .... **12** B3
Palgrave Rd W12 .. **38** B3
Palissy St
E2 .... **24** B2 **98** C3
Pallant Ho SE1 ... **137** C1
Pallester Ct NW11.. **.1** A4
Palliser Ct W14 ... **140** A1
Palliser Ho
3 Greenwich
SE10 .... **43** B1
⓴ Stepney E1 ..... **25** C1
Palliser Rd W14 .. **140** A1
Pallister Terr
SW15 .... **68** B2
Pall Mall SW1 ... **119** B1
Pall Mall E SW1 .. **119** C2
Pall Mall Pl SW1 . **119** A1
Palm Ct
⓲ Camberwell
SE15 .... **49** B3
Stoke Newington N16 . **6** C2
Palmer Ho
6 Deptford SE14 .. **50** C3
5 Kentish Town
NW5 .... **12** C2
7 Tufnell Pk N19 .. **4** B1
Palmer Pl N7 ..... **14** C3
Palmers Rd
Globe Town E2 .... **25** C3
Mortlake SW14 .... **55** B4
Palmer St SW1 ... **133** B2
Palmerston Ct ⓴
E3 .... **25** C3
Palmerston Ho
Battersea SW11 ... **169** C3
Kensington
W8 ...... **31** C1 **113** B1
Palmerston Rd
Acton Green W3 ... **37** B3
Brondesbury NW6 .. **10** B1
Hampstead NW6 ... **10** C1
Mortlake SW14 .... **55** B3
Palmerston Way
SW8 .... **160** B1
Palm Gr W5 .... **36** A3
Palm Tree Ho **2**
SE14 .... **50** C3
Pamela Ct N1 ..... **87** B3
Pamela Ho ⓮ E8 .. **24** B4
Pamlion Ct N4 .... **5** A4
Panama Ho **6** E1 .. **32** C4
Pancras La EC2 ... **109** B1
Pancras Rd N1 .. **83** C2
Pandian Way **4**
NW5 .... **13** C2
Pandora Rd NW6 .. **10** C2
Pangbourne NW1 . **92** C3

Pangbourne Ave
W10 .... **30** B4
Pangbourne Ho **4**
N7 .... **14** A3
Pankhurst Cl **7**
SE14 .... **50** C3
Pankhurst Ho **2**
NW10 .... **30** B3
Panmure Cl N5 ... **15** A4
Pansy Gdns W12 .. **29** C2
Panton St SW1 ... **119** B3
Panyer Alley EC2 **108** C2
Paper Mill Wharf
E14 .... **33** A2
Papworth Gdns
N7 .... **14** B3
Papworth Way
SW9 .... **74** C4
Parade Mans ⓳
SE5 .... **48** B1
Parade Mews SE27,
SW2 .... **.75** A2
Parade The SW11 . **159** A2
Paradise Pas N7 .. **14** C3
Paradise Rd
Richmond TW10 ... **54** A2
South Lambeth
SW4 .... **172** A2
Paradise Row **2** .. **25** A2
Paradise St SE16 .. **40** A4
Paradise Wlk
SW3 .... **159** B4
Paragon Cl E16 ... **35** C3
Paragon Ho SE3 ... **53** B1
Paragon Mews
SE1 .... **151** C4
Paragon Pl SE3 ... **53** B1
Paragon Rd E9 ... **17** B2
Paragon The
Kidbrooke SE3 .... **53** C1
Walworth SE17 .. **151** C4
Paramount Bldg
EC1 .... **96** A2
Paramount Ct
WC1 .... **93** A1
Parbury Rd SE23 .. **66** A1
Pardoner St SE1 . **137** C2
Pardon St EC1 .... **96** B2
Parfett St E1 .... **111** C2
Parfitt Cl NW11 ... **1** A3
Parfrey St W6 ..... **47** B4
Paris Gdn SE1 ... **122** A2
Paris Ho ⓲ E2 .. **25** A3
Park Ave
Golders Green
NW11 .... **.2** A3
Mortlake SW14 .... **55** C3
Willesden NW2 .... **9** B2
Park Ave N NW10.. **.9** A3
Park Cl
Kensington W14 . **127** A2
Knightsbridge SW1 **130** C3
⓳ South Hackney
E9 .... **25** B4
Park Cres W1 .... **92** A1
Park Crescent Mews
E W1 .... **92** B1
Park Crescent Mews
W W1 .... **92** A1
Park Ct
Battersea SW11 .. **170** A4
Clapham Pk SW4 .. **61** C2
Dulwich SE21 ..... **75** C1
⓲ Hammersmith
W6 .... **38** C2
Upper Tooting
SW12 .... **72** C3

Park Dr Acton W3 ..**36** C3
Golders Green NW11.. **2** A3
Mortlake SW14 .... **55** C3
Park Dwellings **7**
NW3 .... **12** B3
Park End NW3 .... **12** A4
Parker Ct
Shoreditch N1 .... **87** A4
⓵ South Lambeth
SW4 .... **172** A3
Parke Rd SW13 ... **46** C2
Parker Mews
WC2 .... **106** B2
Parkers Row
SE16 .... **139** B3
Parker's Row SE1 **139** A3
Parker St WC2 ... **106** B2
Parkfield Ave
SW14 .... **56** A3
Parkfield Ct SE14 .. **51** B2
Parkfield Ind Est
SW11 .... **169** C2
Parkfield Rd
New Cross SE14 .. **51** B2
Willesden NW10 ... **.9** A1
Parkfields SW15 .. **57** B3
Parkfield St N1 .. **85** C2
Parkgate Gdns
SW14 .... **55** C2
Parkgate House Sch
SW11 .... **60** B3
Parkgate Mews N6 .. **4** B4
Parkgate Rd
SW11 .... **158** B1
Park Hall SE10 ... **52** C3
Park Hall Rd SE21 **75** C1
Park Hall Trad
Est SE21 .... **.75** C1
Parkham St
SW11 .... **168** A3
Park Heights Ct ⓶
E14 .... **33** B3
Park Hill
Clapham Pk SW4 .. **61** C2
Richmond TW10 ... **54** B1
Park Hill Ct SW17 **72** B1
Parkhill Rd NW3 .. **12** B3
Park Hill Wlk ⓾
NW3 .... **12** B3
Park Ho
8 Camberwell
SE5 .... **48** C2
Finsbury Pk N4 .... **6** A2
53 Hackney E9 ... **17** B1
Parkholme Rd E8 .. **16** C2
Parkhouse St SE5 . **48** C3
Parkhurst Ct N7 .. **14** A4
Parkhurst Rd N7 .. **14** A4
Parkinson Ct
Finsbury N1 ...... **97** B3
Shoreditch EC1 .. **97** C4
Parkinson Ho ⓭
E9 .... **17** B1
Park La
Mayfair W1 ..... **117** B3
Mill Meads E15 ... **27** C4
Parkland Ct W14 **126** A4
Parkland Gdns ⓲
SW19 .... **69** C3
Parklands
East Dulwich SE22 **65** A3
Highgate N6 ...... **.4** A4
Parklands Cl
SW14 .... **55** B2
Park Lea Ct N16 .. **7** A4

Park Lo
11 South Hampstead
NW8 .... **11** C1
⓾ Wapping E1... **32** A1
Willesden NW10 ... **9** B4
Park Lofts **9** SW4 **62** A3
Park Lorne NW8 .. **90** B3
Park Mans
Battersea SW11 .. **168** C3
Bedford Pk W6 ... **38** B3
Fulham SW6 ..... **164** B3
Knightsbridge SW1 **130** C3
St John's Wood
NW8 .... **80** A1
Vauxhall SW8 ... **162** B4
Parkmead SW15 ... **57** A1
Park Mews
Greenwich SE10 ... **43** B1
Kensal Rise W10 .. **23** A3
5 Park Par Acton W3 .. **36** C3
Dagenham NW10 .. **21** B3
Park Pl
Canary Wharf E14 . **33** C1
Gunnersbury W3 .. **36** C2
Shoreditch N1 ... **87** C4
St James SW1 ... **118** C2
Park Place Dr W3 . **36** C2
Park Place Ho **8**
SE10 .... **52** C4
Park Place Villas
W2 .... **101** A4
Park Rd
Chiswick W4 ..... **45** C4
Dagenham NW10 .. **21** A4
Lisson Gr NW1,
NW8 .... **90** B2
Richmond TW10 ... **54** B1
Park Rd E W3 ..... **37** B4
Park Rd N
Chiswick W4 ...... **37** C1
South Acton W3 ... **37** A4
Park Road E **11**
W3 .... **37** A4
Park Row SE10 ... **52** C4
PARK ROYAL **20** A2
Park Royal NW10 . **20** A4
Park Royal Bsns Ctr
NW10 .... **20** A1
Park Royal Metro Ctr
NW10 .... **20** A1
Park Royal Rd NW10,
W3 .... **20** B1
Park S SW11 .... **169** B3
Park St James
NW8 .... **80** C3
Park Sheen **3**
SW14 .... **55** A3
Parkshot TW9 .... **54** A3
Park Side NW2 .... **9** A4
Parkside
East Acton W3 .... **29** A1
Greenwich SE3 ... **53** B3
Park Side NW2 .... **9** A4
Parkside Bsns Est
SE8 .... **51** A4
Parkside Cres N7 .. **5** C1
Parkside Est E9 .. **25** C4
Parkside
(private)
Hospl SW19 ...... **69** C1
Parkside St SW11 **169** B3
Park Sq E NW1 ... **92** B2

Parkstead Rd
SW15 .... **57** A2
Parkstone Rd **5**
SE15 .... **49** C1
Park Stps W1 ... **116** B4
Park The NW11 ... **2** A3
Parkthorne Rd
SW12 .... **73** C4
Park Twrs W1 ... **118** A1
Park View
Dagenham W3 .... **28** B4
Highbury N5 ..... **15** B4
Willesden NW2 .... **9** B4
Parkview Ct SW6 **164** B1
Park View Ct
SW18 .... **58** C1
Park View Ho
SE24 .... **63** A1
Park View Mans
N4 .... **.6** A4
Park View Mews
SW9 .... **172** C2
Park View Rd
NW10 .... **.8** B4
Park Village E
NW1 .... **82** B1
Park Village W
NW1 .... **82** A1
Parkville Rd SW6 **154** C1
Park Vista SE10 .. **52** C4
Park Walk Prim Sch
SW10 .... **157** B3
Parkway NW1 .... **82** A3
Park Way W3 ..... **36** C2
Parkway Ho SW14 **55** C3
Park West W2 ... **102** B1
Park West Pl W1,
W2 .... **102** B2
Park Wlk
Chelsea SW10 ... **157** B4
Highgate N6 ...... **3** C4
Parkwood NW8 ... **80** C3
Parkwood Prim Sch
N4 .... **.6** A2
Parliament Ct
NW3 .... **12** A4
Parliament Hill
NW3 .... **12** A4
Parliament Hill Mans
NW5 .... **12** C4
Parliament Hill Sch
NW5 .... **12** C4
Parliament Mews
SW14 .... **45** B1
Parliament Sq*
SW1 .... **134** A3
Parliament St
SW1 .... **134** A4
Parliament View
Apartments
SE11 .... **148** C4
Parma Cres SW11 **60** B3
Parminter Ind Est ⓴
E2 .... **25** A3
Parmiter St E2 ... **25** A3
Parmoor Ct EC1 .. **96** C2
Parnell Cl W12 ... **39** A3
Parnell Ho WC1 . **105** C2
Parnell Rd E3 .... **26** B4
Parnham St E14 .. **33** A3
Parolles Rd N19 ... **4** B3
Parr Ct N1 .... **87** B2
Parrington Ho **1**
SW4 .... **61** C1
Parr Pl W4 .... **38** B2

Parr St N1 . . . . **87** B2
Parry Ho 52 E1 . . . . . . **32** A1
Parry Rd W10 . . . . . . **23** A2
Parry St SW8 . . . . **162** B4
Parsifal Coll NW3 . . 10 C4
Parsifal Ho NW3 . . . . 10 C4
Parsifal Rd NW6 . . . . 10 C3
Parsonage St E14 . . **42** B2
Parsons Gn SW6 . . **165** B3
PARSONS GREEN
. . . . **165** A4
Parsons Green La
SW6 . . . . **165** B4
Parsons Green Sta
SW6 . . . . **165** B3
Parsons Ho
Paddington W2 . . . . . **89** B1
2 Streatham
SW12 . . . . **74** A4
Parsons Lo NW6 . . . . 11 A1
Parthenia Rd
SW6 . . . . **165** C3
Partington Cl N19 . . . 4 C3
Parton Lo 14 E8 . . . . 16 B2
Partridge Cl EC1 . . . **96** A2
Partridge Ho 22
E3 . . . . 26 B3
Pascall Ho SE17 . . . . 48 B4
Pascal St SW8 . . . . **161** C2
Pascoe Rd SE13 . . . . **67** C2
Pasley Cl SE17 . . . . **150** C1
Passfield Dr E14 . . . 34 A4
Passfields W14 . . . . **140** C1
Passing Alley EC1 . . **96** B1
Passmore St SW1 **145** B2
Pastor St SE1,
SE11 . . . . **150** B4
Patcham Terr
SW8 . . . . **170** B4
Patent Ho E14 . . . . . 34 A4
Paternoster La
EC4 . . . . **108** B2
Paternoster Row EC2,
EC4 . . . . **108** B2
Paternoster Sq
EC4 . . . . **108** B2
Pater St W8 . . . . . . **127** B1
Patience Rd
SW11 . . . . **168** A1
Patience Villas
SE13 . . . . 67 C4
Patio Cl SW4 . . . . 61 C1
Patmore Ho 9
N16 . . . . 16 A3
Patmore St SW8 . . **171** A4
Patmos Rd SW9 . . . . 48 A2
Paton Cl E3 . . . . 26 C2
Paton Ho SW9 . . . . **172** C2
Paton St EC1 . . . . . . **96** C3
Patrick Coman Ho
EC1 . . . . **96** A3
Patrick Connolly Gdns
41 E3 . . . . 27 A2
Patriot Sq E2 . . . . . . 25 A3
Patrol Pl SE6 . . . . 67 A1
Pat Shaw Ho 2
E1 . . . . 25 C1
Patshull Pl NW5 . . . . 13 B2
Patshull Rd NW5 . . . 13 B2
Patten Ho N4 . . . . 6 B3
Patten Rd SW18 . . . . 72 A4
Patterdale NW1 . . . **92** B3
Patterdale Rd
SE15 . . . . 50 B3
Pattina Wlk SE16 . . 33 A1

Pattison Point 10
E16 . . . . 35 C4
Pattison Ho
Borough The SE1 . . **137** A4
1 Stepney E1 . . . . **32** C3
Pattison Rd NW2 . . . 1 C1
Pat Williams Ho
SE27 . . . . 75 B1
Paul Daisley Ct 2
NW6 . . . . 10 A1
Paulet Rd SE5 . . . . . 48 A2
Paul Ho 15 W10 . . . . 23 A1
Pauline Ho 1
E1 . . . . **111** C4
Paul Julius Cl E14 . 34 C2
Paul St EC2 . . 24 A1 **98** A2
Paultons Ho SW3 **157** C4
Paultons Sq SW3 **157** C4
Paultons St SW3 **157** C4
Pauntley Ho 6 N19 . 4 B3
Pauntley St 4 N19 . . 4 B3
Pavan Ct 20 E2 . . . . . **25** B2
Paveley Dr SW11 **158** A1
Paveley Ho N1 . . . . **84** C1
Paveley St NW8 . . . **90** B2
Pavement The
2 Hampstead
NW3 . . . . 11 B4
Hampstead NW3 . . . 11 C3
3 Paddington NW6 . 23 C2
Pavilion Mans 10
SW9 . . . . 62 B3
Pavilion Rd SW1 **131** A1
Pavilion Sq SW17 . . 72 B1
Pavilion St SW1 . . **131** A1
Pavilion Terr 8
W12 . . . . 30 B3
Pavillion Ct SW1 **160** A4
Pavitt Ct NW10 . . . . . 8 C1
Paxton Ho SE17 . . **151** A2
Paxton Rd W4 . . . . . 46 A4
Paxton Terr SW1 **160** B4
Paymal Ho 23 E1 . . 32 B4
Payne Ho N1 . . . . . . **85** A3
Payne Rd E3 . . . . 27 A3
Paynesfield Ave
SW14 . . . . 55 C4
Payne St SE8 . . . . . . 51 B4
Paynes Wlk W6 . . **154** A3
Peabody Ave
SW1 . . . . **146** B1
Peabody Bldgs
1 Camberwell
SE5 . . . . 48 C2
Walworth SE17 . . . **151** B3
Peabody Cl SW1 **160** B4
Peabody Ct
9 Camberwell
SE5 . . . . 48 C2
St Luke's EC1 . . . . . **97** A1
Peabody Est
18 Bethnal Green
E2 . . . . 25 A3
Borough The SE1 **122** C1
Fulham SW6 . . . . . **155** A4
17 Hammersmith
W6 . . . . 39 B1
Holborn EC1 . . . . . **95** C1
Lambeth SE1 . . . **121** C1
North Kensington
W10 . . . . 30 B4
4 Ratcliff E1 . . . . . **32** C2
St George in t East
E1 . . . . **125** B4

Peabody Est continued
St Luke's EC1 . . . . . **97** A1
Strand WC2 . . . . . **106** C1
Streatham SE24 . . . 75 B4
Westminster SW1 . **147** A4
Peabody Hill SE21 . 75 A3
Peabody Sq SE1 . **136** A3
Peabody Twr EC1 . . **96** C1
Peabody Yd N1 . . . . **86** C4
Peach Rd W10 . . . . 23 A2
Peacham Rd SE3 . . 53 B4
Peach Walk Mews 24
E3 . . . . 25 C3
Peacock St SE17 . . **150** B3
Peacock Yd SE17 . **150** B3
Peak Ho N4 . . . . 6 B3
Pearce Ho
Camden Town N19 . . 4 B1
7 Streatham SW2 . . 74 A4
Westminster SW1 . **147** C3
Pear Cl SE14 . . . . . . 51 A3
Pear Ct 21 SE15 . . . 49 B3
Peardon St SW8 . . **170** B1
Pearfield Ho 1
N5 . . . . 15 B3
Pearl St E1 . . . . 32 A1
Pearman St SE1 . **135** C3
Pear Pl SE1 . . . . . . **135** B4
Pearscroft Ct
SW6 . . . . **166** B3
Pearscroft Rd
SW6 . . . . **166** B3
Pearse St 3 SE15 . . 49 A4
Pearson Cl 4 SE5 . . 48 B2
Pearson Ho SW15 . . 47 B1
Pearson's Ave
SE14 . . . . 51 C2
Pearson St E2 . . . . . 24 B3
Peartree Ave
SW17 . . . . 71 B1
Pear Tree Cl 23
E2 . . . . 24 B4
Pear Tree Ct
Holborn EC1 . . . . . . **95** C1
Putney SW15 . . . . . 57 A3
Pear Tree Ho SE4 . . 66 B3
Peartree La E1 . . . . 32 B2
Peartree St EC1 . . . **96** C2
Pear Tree Way
SE10 . . . . 43 C2
Peary Pl E2 . . . . 25 B2
Peckarmans Wood
SE21, SE26 . . . . 76 C1
Peckett Sq 3 N5 . . . 15 A4
Peckford Pl SW9 **173** C1
PECKHAM 49 C2
Peckham Gr SE15 . . 49 A3
Peckham High St
SE15 . . . . 49 C2
Peckham Hill St
SE15 . . . . 49 C3
Peckham Park Prim
Sch SE15 . . . . 49 C3
Peckham Park Rd
SE15 . . . . 49 C3
Peckham Rd SE5 . . 49 A2
Peckham Rye
East Dulwich SE22 . 64 C3
Peckham SE15,
SE22 . . . . 65 A3
Peckham Rye Sta
SE15 . . . . 49 C1
Peckwater Ho 2
NW5 . . . . 13 C2

Peckwater St
NW5 . . . . 13 B3
Pedlars Wlk N7 . . . 14 A3
Pedley St
E1 . . . . 24 B1 **99** A1
Pedro St E5 . . . . 17 C4
Pedworth Gdns 4
SW18 . . . . 71 A4
Peel Gr E2 . . . . 25 B3
Peel Pass W8 . . . . **113** B1
Peel Prec NW6 . . . . 23 C3
Peel St W8 . . 31 C1 **113** B1
Peerless St EC1 . . . . **97** B3
Pegasus Cl N16 . . . 15 C4
Pegasus Ct
11 Acton W3 . . . . . 28 B3
Brentford TW8 . . . . 36 B1
College Pk NW10 . . 22 A2
Pegasus Ho 6 E1 . . 25 C1
Pegwell Ho 5 E5 . . 17 A3
Pekin St E14 . . . . . . 33 C3
Pekoe SE1 . . . . **125** A1
Peldon Ct TW10 . . . 54 B2
Pelham Cl SE5 . . . . 64 A4
Pelham Cres
SW7 . . . . **144** A3
Pelham Ho W14 . . . **140** C3
Pelham Pl SW7 . . . **144** A3
Pelham St SW7 . . . **143** C4
Pelican Ho 8 SE8 . . 41 B2
Pelican Pas 3 E1 . . 25 B1
Pelier St SE17 . . . . . 48 B4
Pella Ho W11 . . . . **149** A2
Pellant Rd SW6 . . **154** B2
Pellatt Rd SE22 . . . 64 B2
Pellerin Rd N16 . . . 16 A3
Pellew Ho 18 E1 . . . 25 A1
Pelling St E14 . . . . . 33 C3
Pelter St E2 . . 24 B2 **98** C4
Pember Rd NW10 . . 22 C2
Pemberton Ct 18
E1 . . . . 25 C2
Pemberton Gdns
N19 . . . . 4 B1
Pemberton Pl 2
E8 . . . . 17 A1
Pemberton Row
EC4 . . . . **107** C2
Pemberton Terr
N19 . . . . 4 B1
Pembridge Cres
W11 . . . . . 31 C2 **113** B4
Pembridge Gdns
W2 . . . . . . 31 C2 **113** C3
Pembridge Hall Sch
W2 . . . . . . 31 C2 **113** C3
Pembridge Mews
W11 . . . . . 31 C2 **113** B4
Pembridge Pl
Notting Hill
W2 . . . . . . 31 C2 **113** C4
3 Wandsworth
SW15 . . . . 58 C2
Pembridge Rd
W11 . . . . . 31 C2 **113** C3
Pembridge Sq
W2 . . . . . . 31 C2 **113** C3
Pembridge Villas
W11 . . . . . 31 C2 **113** B4
Pembroke W14 . . . **141** A3
Pembroke Ave N1 . . 84 B4
Pembroke Bldgs
NW10 . . . . 21 C2

Pembroke Cl
SW1 . . . . **131** C3
Pembroke Gdns
W8 . . . . **141** A4
Pembroke Gdns Cl
W8 . . . . **127** B1
Pembroke Ho
Acton W3 . . . . 37 B4
2 Chelsea SW1 . . . **131** B1
3 Clapham Pk
SW2 . . . . 62 A2
Kensington W2 . . . **100** B1
Putney SW15 . . . . . 56 C2
Pembroke Lo 2
SW16 . . . . 74 B1
Pembroke Mews
1 Bow E3 . . . . 26 A2
Kensington W8 . . . **127** B1
Pembroke Pl W8 . . **127** B1
Pembroke Rd W8 **141** B4
Pembroke Sq W8 **127** B1
Pembroke St N1 . . . 84 B4
Pembroke Studios
W8 . . . . **127** A1
Pembroke Terr
NW8 . . . . **79** B3
Pembroke Villas
W8 . . . . **141** B4
Pembroke Wlk
W8 . . . . **141** B4
Pembury Cl E5 . . . . . 17 A3
Pembury Ho SE5 . . 49 A1
Pembury Pl 15 E5,
E8 . . . . 17 A3
Pembury Rd E5 . . . . 17 A3
Pemell Cl 30 E1 . . . 25 B1
Pemell Ho 31 E1 . . . 25 B1
Penally Pl N1 . . . . . **87** C4
Penang St E1 . . . . . 32 A1
Penarth Ctr The
SE15 . . . . 50 B4
Penarth St SE15 . . . 50 B4
Pencombe Mews
W11 . . . 31 B2 **113** A4
Pencraig Way
SE15 . . . . 50 A4
Penda's Mead E9 . . 18 A4
Pendennis Ho 16
SE8 . . . . 41 A2
Penderyn Way N7 . 13 C4
Pendle Ho 15
SE26 . . . . 76 C1
Pendley Ho 16 E2 . 24 C4
Pendrell Ho WC2 **105** C1
Pendrell Rd SE4 . . . 51 A1
Penelope Ho
SW9 . . . . **173** B3
Penfield Lo 7 W9 . 31 C4
Penfields Ho N7 . . . 14 A2
Penfold Pl NW1 . . **102** A3
Penfold St NW8 . . . **89** C1
Penford St SE5 . . . 48 A1
Penhurst Mans
SW6 . . . . **164** C4
Peninsula Ct E14 . . 42 A3
Peninsular Park Rd
SE7 . . . . 43 C2
Penmayne Ho
SE11 . . . . **149** C2
Penmon Rd SE2 . . . 77 A1
Pennack Rd SE15 . 49 B4
Pennant Mews
W8 . . . . **142** A4
Pennard Mans 5
W12 . . . . 39 B4
Pennard Rd W12 . . 39 B4

Pennefather Ho
N1 . . . . **15** C2
Penner Cl SW19 . . . . **70** A2
Pennethorne Cl
E9 . . . . **25** B4
Pennethorne Ho
SW11 . . . . **59** C4
Pennethorne Rd
SE15 . . . . **50** A3
Penn Ho NW8 . . . . . **90** A1
Pennine La NW2 . . . 1 A2
Pennine Mans NW2 . 1 A2
Pennine Par NW2 . . . 1 A2
Pennington Ct
4 Rotherhithe
SE16 . . . . **33** A1
St George in t East
E1 . . . . **125** C3
Pennington St E1 . . **32** A2
Penn Rd N7 . . . . **14** A4
Penn St N1 . . . . **87** C3
Penny Ct SW10 . . . **157** A4
Pennyfields E14 . . . **33** C2
Pennyford Ct NW8 **89** B2
Penny Mews
SW12 . . . . **73** A4
Pennymore Wlk
W9 . . . . **23** B1
Penny Rd NW10 . . . **20** A2
Penpoll Rd E8 . . . . . **17** A2
Penrhyn Cres
SW14 . . . . **55** B3
Penrith Cl SW15 . . . **58** A2
Penrith Pl SE27 . . . **75** A2
Penrose Ho SE17 **150** C1
Penrose Ho SE17 **150** C1
Penrose St SE17 . . **150** C1
Penryn Ho SE11 . . **150** A2
Penryn St NW1 . . . **83** B2
Penry St SE1 . . . . . **152** B3
Pensbury Pl SW8 **171** A2
Pensbury St SW8 **171** A2
Pensford Ave
TW9 . . . . **44** C1
Penshurst **2** NW5 . **12** C2
Penshurst Ho **1**
SE15 . . . . **50** B4
Penshurst Rd E9 . . **17** C1
Pentland Cl NW11 . . 1 A2
Pentland Gdns
SW18 . . . . **59** B1
Pentland Ho
17 Camden Town
NW5 . . . . **12** C2
7 Stamford Hill N16 . **7** B3
Pentland Rd **1**
NW6 . . . . **23** C2
Pentland St SW18 . **59** B1
Pentlow St SW15 . . **57** B4
Pentney Rd SW12 . . **73** B3
Penton Gr N1 . . . . . **85** B1
Penton Ho N1 . . . . . **85** B1
Penton Pl SE17 . . **150** B2
Penton Rise WC1 . . **95** A4
Penton St N1 . . . . . **85** A1
PENTONVILLE **85** A1
Pentonville Rd N1 **84** C1
Pentridge St SE15 . **49** B3
Penwith Rd SW18 . **71** A2
Penwood Ho
SW15 . . . . **56** B1
Penywern Rd
SW5 . . . . **141** C2
Penzance Ho
SE11 . . . . **149** C2
Penzance Pl
W11 . . . . . **31** A1 **112** B2

Penzance St
W11 . . . . . **31** A1 **112** A2
Peony Gdns W12 . . **29** C2
Peperfield WC1 . . . **94** C3
Pepler Ho **17** W10 . **23** A1
Pepler Mews SE1 **152** C1
Peploe Rd NW6 . . . **22** C3
Peppermead Sq
SE13 . . . . **66** C2
Pepper St
Borough The SE1 . **136** C4
Millwall E14 . . . . . **42** A3
Peppie Cl N16 . . . . . . **7** A2
Pepsi Trocadero★
W1 . . . . **119** B3
Pepys Cres **2** E16 . **35** C1
Pepys Ent Ctr **18**
SE8 . . . . **41** B2
Pepys Ho
2 Bethnal Green
E2 . . . . **25** B2
Clapham Pk SW4 . . **61** C2
Pepys Rd SE14 . . . **50** C1
Pepys St EC3 . . . . **124** B4
Perceval Ave NW3 . **12** A3
Percheron Ct **3**
SW9 . . . . **62** B4
Perch St E8 . . . . . . **16** B4
Percival Rd SW14 . **55** B3
Percival St EC1 . . . **96** B3
Percy Cir WC1 . . . . **95** A4
Percy Laurie Ho **6**
SW15 . . . . **57** C3
Percy Mews W1 . . **105** B3
Percy Pas W1 . . . . **105** B3
Percy Rd
Newham E16 . . . . . **35** A4
Shepherd's Bush
W12 . . . . **38** C4
Percy St W1 . . . . . **105** B3
Peregrine Ho
6 Battersea
SW11 . . . . **60** A4
Finsbury EC1 . . . . . **96** B4
Perham Rd W14 . **140** B1
Perifield SE21 . . . . **75** B3
Perkins Ho **15** E14 . **33** B4
Perkins Rents
SW1 . . . . **133** B1
Perkins Sq SE1 . . **123** A2
Perley Ho **5** E3 . . . **33** B4
Perotti Ho SW6 . . . **59** A4
Perran Rd SE24,
SW2 . . . . **75** A2
Perren St NW5 . . . . **13** A2
Perrers Rd W6 . . . . **39** A2
Perring Est E3 . . . . **33** C4
Perrin's Ct **20**
NW3 . . . . **11** B4
Perrin's La NW3 . . . **11** B4
Perrin's Wlk NW3 . **11** B4
Perronet Ho SE1 **136** B1
Perry Ave W3 . . . . . **28** C3
Perry Ct **6** E14 . . . **41** C1
Perry Ho **24** SW2 . **74** A4
Perrymead St
SW6 . . . . **166** A3
Perryn Ho W3 . . . . **29** A2
Perryn Rd
Acton W3 . . . . **28** C2
3 Bermondsey
SE16 . . . . **40** A3
Perry's Pl W1 . . . . **105** B2
Perrywood Ho **17**
E5 . . . . **17** A3
Perseverance Works
E2 . . . . . . **24** A2 **98** A4

Perth Ct **5** SE5 . . . **63** C3
Perth Ho N1 . . . . . . **14** B1
Perth Rd N4 . . . . 5 C3
Petchey Acad The
E8 . . . . **16** B3
Peter Ave NW10 . . . . 9 A1
Peter Best Ho **1**
E1 . . . . **32** A3
Peterboat Cl SE10 . **43** A2
Peterborough Ct
EC4 . . . . **107** C1
Peterborough Mews
SW6 . . . . **165** B2
Peterborough Prim
Sch SW6 . . . . **165** C1
Peterborough Rd
SW6 . . . . **58** C4
Peterborough Villas
SW6 . . . . **166** A4
Peter Butler Ho
SE1 . . . . **139** B3
Peterchurch Ho
SE15 . . . . **50** A4
Petergate SW11 . . . **59** B3
Peter Heathfield Ho
4 E15 . . . . **27** C4
Peter Hills Ho
SE16 . . . . **153** B4
Peter Hills with St
Mary's & St Paul's CE
Prim Sch SE16 . . . **32** C1
Peter Ho SW8 . . . **162** A2
Peter James Ent Ctr
NW10 . . . . **20** B2
Peterley Bsns Ctr **21**
E2 . . . . **25** A3
Peters Ct W2 . . . . **100** B2
Peter's Ct SW4 . . . **62** A1
Petersfield Rd W3 . **37** B4
Petersfield Rise
SW15 . . . . **69** A3
Petersham Ho
SW7 . . . . **143** B4
Petersham La
SW7 . . . . **128** C2
Petersham Mews
SW7 . . . . **129** A1
Petersham Pl
SW7 . . . . **129** A2
Peter's La EC1 . . . **108** B4
Peter's St SW3 . . . **144** A2
Peterstow Cl
SW19 . . . . **70** A2
Petherton Ct
NW10 . . . . **22** C3
Petherton Ho N4 . . . 6 B3
Petherton Rd N5 . . **15** B3
Petiver Cl **28** E9 . . **17** B1
Petley Rd W6 . . . . . **47** C3
Peto Pl NW1 . . . . . . **92** B2
Peto St N E16 . . . . . **35** B3
Petrel Ct **8** SE21 . **75** C2
Petros Gdns **2**
NW3 . . . . **11** B2
Petticoat Lane Mkt★
E1 . . . . **110** C2
Petticoat Sq E1 . . **110** C2
Petticoat Twr E1 . **110** C2
Pettiward Cl
SW15 . . . . **57** B3
Petty France
SW1 . . . . **133** B2

Petty Wales EC3 . . **124** B3
Petworth Ho **16**
SE22 . . . . **64** A4
Petworth St
SW11 . . . . **168** B4
Petyt Pl SW3 . . . . **158** A3
Petyward SW3 . . . **144** B3
Pevensey Ct
4 South Acton
W3 . . . . **37** A4
West Norwood
SW16 . . . . **74** C1
Pevensey Ho **5**
E1 . . . . **33** A4
Peveril Ho SE1 . . . **137** C1
Pewsham Ho N4 . . . 6 B3
Peyton Pl SE10 . . . **52** B3
Pharamond NW2 . . . 9 C2
Phelp St SE17 . . . . **48** C4
Phelps Ho SW15 . . **57** C4
Phene St SW3 . . . **158** B4
Philadelphia Ct
SW10 . . . . **157** A1
Philbeach Gdns
SW5 . . . . **141** B2
Phil Brown Pl **3**
SW8 . . . . **61** A4
Philchurch Pl E1 . **111** C1
Philia Ho **4** NW1 . . **13** B1
Philip Blairman Ho
E1 . . . . **24** B1 **98** C1
Philip Ct W2 . . . . **101** B4
Philip Ho **8** NW6 . . **78** A3
Philip Turner Est **20**
E9 . . . . **17** B1
Philip Wlk SE15 . . . **64** C4
Phillimore Ct W8 **127** C3
Phillimore Gdns **1**
W8 . . . . **127** B3
Phillimore Gdns
Kensington W8 . . . **127** B3
Willesden NW10 . . . **22** B4
Phillimore Pl W8 **127** B3
Phillimore Terr
W8 . . . . **127** C2
Phillimore Wlk
W8 . . . . **127** C2
Phillip Ho E1 . . . . **111** A3
Phillipp St N1 . . . . **24** A4
Philpot La EC3 . . . **124** A4
Philpot Sq SW6 . . . **59** A4
Philpot St E1 . . . . . **32** A3
Philson Mans **1**
E1 . . . . **32** A3
Phipps Ho **10** W12 . **30** A2
Phipp St
EC2 . . . . . . **24** A1 **98** A2
Phoebeth Rd SE4 . . **66** C2
Phoenix Bsns Ctr **21**
E3 . . . . **33** C4
Phoenix Cl **18** E8 . **24** B4
Phoenix Ct
4 Brentford TW8 . . **36** A1
2 Deptford SE14 . **51** A4
Millwall E14 . . . . . **41** C2
Phoenix High Sch
W12 . . . . **29** C2
Phoenix Ho SW1 . **145** B4
Phoenix Lodge Mans
1 W6 . . . . **39** B2
Phoenix Pl WC1 . . . **95** A2
Phoenix Rd NW1 . . **93** B4
Phoenix Sch E3 . . . **26** B2
Phoenix Sch The
NW3 . . . . **11** B2
Phoenix St WC2 . . **105** C1

Pen–Pil 253

Phoenix Wharf Rd
SE1 . . . . **139** A3
Phyllis Hodges Ho
NW1 . . . . **83** B1
Physic Pl SW3 . . . **158** C4
Piccadilly W1 . . . . **118** C2
Piccadilly Arc
SW1 . . . . **118** C2
Piccadilly Circ★
W1 . . . . **119** B3
Piccadilly Circus Sta
SW1 . . . . **119** B3
Piccadilly Ct **5**
N7 . . . . **14** B2
Piccadilly Pl W1 . **119** A3
Pickard St EC1 . . . **96** B4
Pickering Cl **17**
E9 . . . . **17** C1
Pickering Ho
Kensington W2 . . . **100** B1
Stoke Newington N4 . 6 C4
Pickering Mews
W2 . . . . **100** B2
Pickering Pl SW1 **119** A1
Pickering St N1 . . . **86** B4
Pickets St SW12 . . **73** A4
Pickfords Wharf
N1 . . . . **86** C1
Pickwick Ho
Bermondsey SE16 . **139** B3
3 Shepherd's Bush
W11 . . . . **30** C1
Pickwick Rd SE21 . **76** A4
Pickwick St SE1 . . **136** C3
Pickworth Cl
SW8 . . . . **162** B1
Picton Ho **1** SW4 . **74** A4
Picton Pl W1 . . . . **103** C1
Picton St SE5 . . . . . **48** C3
Picture Ho **6**
SW16 . . . . **74** A2
Pied Bull Ct WC1 . **106** B3
Pied Bull Yd WC1 . **106** B3
Pier Head E1 . . . . . **32** A1
Pierhead Wharf **17**
E1 . . . . **32** A1
Pier Ho SW3 . . . . . **158** B3
Piermont Rd SE22 . **65** A2
Pierpoint Bldg **4**
E14 . . . . **41** C4
Pierrepoint Rd
W3 . . . . **28** A2
Pierrepoint Row
N1 . . . . **86** A2
Pier St E14 . . . . **42** B2
Pier Terr SW18 . . . . **59** B3
Piggott Ho **2** E2 . **25** C3
Pigott St E14 . . . . . **33** C3
Pilgrimage St
SE1 . . . . **137** B3
Pilgrim Ho SE1 . . **137** C1
Pilgrims Cloisters **5**
SE5 . . . . **49** A3
Pilgrims Ct SE3 . . . **53** C2
Pilgrim's La NW3 . **11** C4
Pilgrims Mews **12**
E14 . . . . **34** C2
Pilgrim's Pl **6**
NW3 . . . . **11** C4
Pilgrim St EC4 . . . **108** A1
Pilgrims Way NW1 . 4 C3
Pilgrims Way Prim
Sch SE15 . . . . **50** B4
Pilkington Rd **4**
SE15 . . . . **50** A1

Pilot Ind Ctr
NW10 . . . . 21 A1
Pilsden Cl SW19 . . . . 69 C3
Pilton Pl SE17 . . . . . 151 A2
Pimlico Rd SW1 . . . 147 B2
PIMLICO 146 C1
Pimlico Rd SW1 . . . 145 C2
Pimlico Sch SW1 . . 147 A1
Pimlico Wlk
N1 . . . . 24 A2 98 A4
Pinchin St E1 . . . . . 125 C4
Pincombe Ho
SE17 . . . . 151 B2
Pincott Pl SE4 . . . . . . 65 C4
Pindar St EC2 . . . . . 110 A4
Pine Apple Ct
SW1 . . . . 132 C2
Pine Ave E15 . . . . 19 C3
Pine Cl 11 N19 . . . . . . 4 B2
Pinedene 2 SE15 . . . 50 A2
Pinefield Cl E14 . . . . 33 C2
Pine Gr N4, N19 . . . . . 5 B2
Pine Ho Bow E3 . . . . 26 A4
21 Rotherhithe
SE16 . . . . 40 B4
Pinehurst Ct 6
W11 . . . . 31 B3
Pinelands 7
SE3 . . . . 53 B3
Pine Lo SW15 . . . . . . 58 A1
Pine Rd NW2 . . . . 9 C4
Pines Ct SW19 . . . . . 69 C3
Pine St EC1 . . . . 95 B2
Pine Tree Ho
SE14 . . . . 50 C3
Pinewood Ct SW4 . . 61 C1
Pinkham Mans
W4 . . . . 36 C1
Pinnace Ho E14 . . . . 42 B3
Pinnacle Ho EC3 . . 124 A3
Pinnacle The 7
N1 . . . . 87 A4
Pinner Ct NW8 . . . . . 89 B2
Pinner Ho 30 SE5 . . . 48 B1
Pintail Ct 80 SE8 . . . 51 B4
Pinter Ho SW9 . . . . 172 B1
Pioneer Cl W12 . . . . 30 A3
Pioneer St SE15 . . . . 49 C2
Pioneer Way W12 . . . 30 B3
Piper Cl N7 . . . . 14 B3
Pipers Ho SE10 . . . . 42 C1
Pippin Ho 17 W10 . . 30 C2
Pirbright Rd
SW18 . . . . 70 C3
Pitcairn Ho 1 E9 . . . 17 B2
Pitfield Ho N5 . . . . . . 15 B3
Pitfield St N1 . . . . . . 24 A3
Pitman Ho 4 SE8 . . . 51 C2
Pitman St SE5 . . . . . 48 B3
Pitmaston Ho 2
SE13 . . . . 52 B1
Pitsea Pl E1 . . . . 32 C3
Pitsea St E1 . . . . 32 C3
Pitt Ho 4 SW11 . . . . 59 C3
Pitt's Head Mews
W1 . . . . 117 C1
Pitt St W8 . . . . 127 C4
Pixley St E14 . . . . . . 33 B3
Planetree Ct W6 . . . . 39 C2
Plane Tree Ho
SE8 . . . . 51 A4
Plantain Pl SE1 . . . 137 B4
Plantation La EC3 . . 124 A4

Plantation The
SE3 . . . . 53 C1
Platehouse The 3
E14 . . . . 42 A1
Platina St EC2 . . . . . 97 C2
Plato Pl SW6 . . . . . 165 A2
Plato Rd SW2 . . . . . . 62 A3
Platt's La NW3 . . . . . . 1 C1
Platt St NW1 . . . . . . 83 B2
Plaxdale Ho SE17 . . 152 A3
Playfair St W6 . . . . . 39 B1
Playfield Cres
SE22 . . . . 64 B2
Playford Rd
Finsbury Pk N4 . . . . . . 5 B2
Finsbury Pk N4 . . . . . . 5 C2
Playhouse Yd
EC4 . . . . 108 A1
Plaza Sth Circ W1 . . 105 A2
Pleasance Rd
SW15 . . . . 57 A2
Pleasance The
SW15 . . . . 57 A3
Pleasant Pl N1 . . . . . 15 A1
Pleasant Row
NW1 . . . . 82 B3
Plender Ct NW1 . . . . 83 A3
Plender St NW1 . . . . 83 A3
Plevna St E14 . . . . . . 42 B3
Pleydell Ave W6 . . . . 38 B2
Pleydell Ct EC4 . . . 107 C1
Pleydell St EC4 . . . 107 C1
Plimsoll Cl E14 . . . . 34 A3
Plimsoll Rd N4 . . . . . . 6 A1
Plough Ct EC3 . . . . 123 C4
Plough La SE22 . . . . 64 B1
Ploughmans Cl
NW1 . . . . 83 B4
Plough Mews 19
SW11 . . . . 59 C3
Plough Pl EC4 . . . . 107 C2
Plough Rd SW11 . . . 59 C3
Plough St E1 . . . . . 111 B2
Plough Terr SW11 . . 59 C3
Plough Way SE16 . . . 41 A2
Plough Yd
EC2 . . . . 24 A1 98 B1
Plover Ho SW9 . . . . 163 B2
Plover Way SE16 . . . 41 A3
Plowman Ho
SW19 . . . . 69 C2
Plumbers Row
E1 . . . . 111 C2
Plumbridge St 7
SE10 . . . . 52 B2
Plume Ho SE10 . . . . 52 A4
Plummer Ct SE13 . . . 67 A1
Plummer Rd SW4 . . . 73 C4
Plumtree Ct EC4 . . 108 A2
Plymouth Ho 20
SE10 . . . . 52 A2
Plymouth Rd E16 . . . 35 C4
Plymouth Wharf
E14 . . . . 42 C2
Plympton Ave
NW6 . . . . 10 B1
Plympton Pl NW1 . . . 90 A1
Plympton Rd NW6 . . 10 B1
Plympton St NW1 . . . 90 A1
Pocklington Ct
SW15 . . . . 68 C3
Pocklington Lo 6
W12 . . . . 38 C3
Pocock St SE1 . . . . 136 B4
Podmore Rd
SW18 . . . . 59 B3

Poets Cnr★ SW1 . . 134 A2
Poet's Rd N5 . . . . . . 15 C3
Point Cl SE10 . . . . . . 52 B2
Pointer Sch The
SE3 . . . . 53 C3
Pointers Cl E14 . . . . 42 A1
Point Hill SE10 . . . . . 52 B2
Point Ho SE10 . . . . . 52 B2
Point Pleasant
SW18 . . . . 58 C3
Point Wharf La
TW8 . . . . 44 A3
Poland Ho 3 E15 . . . 27 C4
Poland St W1 . . . . . 105 A1
Polesworth Ho 16
W2 . . . . 31 C4
Polish Inst & Sikorski
Mus★ SW7 . . . . . 129 C3
Polish Univ Abroad
W6 . . . . 38 C2
Pollard Cl
Islington N7 . . . . 14 B4
Newham E16 . . . . . . 35 C2
Pollard Ho N1 . . . . . 84 C1
Pollard Row
E2 . . . . 24 C2 99 C4
Pollard St
E2 . . . . 24 C2 99 C4
Pollen St W1 . . . . . 104 B1
Pollitt Dr NW8 . . . . . 89 C2
Pollock Ho W10 . . . . 23 A1
Polperro Mans 3
NW6 . . . . 10 C3
Polperro Mews
SE11 . . . . 150 A4
Polygon Rd NW1 . . . 83 B1
Polygon The 4
St John's Wood
NW8 . . . . 79 C4
Pomell Way E1 . . . 111 A2
Pomeroy Ho W11 . . . 31 A3
Pomeroy Ho 5
E2 . . . . 25 C3
Pomeroy St SE14 . . . 50 B2
Pomfret Rd SE5 . . . . 63 A4
Pomoja La N19 . . . . . . 5 A2
Pomona Ho 10
SE8 . . . . 41 A2
Pond Cl SE3 . . . . 53 C1
Pond Cotts SE21 . . . 76 A3
Ponder St 8 N7 . . . . 14 B1
Pondfield Ho 4
N5 . . . . 15 B3
Pond Ho SW3 . . . . 144 A3
Pond Mead SE21 . . . 63 C1
Pond Pl SW3 . . . . . 144 A3
Pond Rd SE3 . . . . . . 53 B1
Pond Sq N6 . . . . 3 C3
Pond St NW3 . . . . . . 12 A3
Ponler St E1 . . . . . . 32 A3
Ponsard Rd NW10 . . 22 A2
Ponsford St E9 . . . . . 17 B2
Ponsonby Ho 13
E2 . . . . 25 B3
Ponsonby Pl SW1 . 147 C2
Ponsonby Rd
SW15 . . . . 69 A4
Ponsonby Terr
SW1 . . . . 147 C2
Ponton Ho SW2 . . . . 74 C3
Ponton Rd SW8 . . . 161 C3
Pont St Mews
SW1 . . . . 130 C1
Pont St SW1 . . . . . . 131 A1
Pontypool Pl SE1 . . 136 A4
Poole Cl SW15 . . . . . 16 A1

Poole Ho SE11 . . . . 135 A1
Poole Rd E9 . . . . 17 C2
Pooles Bldgs EC1 . . . 95 B1
Pooles La SW10 . . . 156 C1
Pooles Park Prim Sch
N4 . . . . 5 B2
Pooles Pk N4 . . . . 5 C2
Poole St N1 . . . . 87 B3
Pooley Ho E1 . . . . . . 25 C2
Pool Ho NW8 . . . . . 101 C4
Poolmans St SE16 . . 40 C4
Poonah St E1 . . . . . . 32 B3
Pope Ho
7 Bermondsey
SE16 . . . . 40 A2
8 Camberwell SE5 . . 48 C3
Pope John RC Prim
Sch W12 . . . . 30 A2
Pope's Head Alley
EC3 . . . . 109 C1
Pope's Rd SW9 . . . . 62 C4
Pope St SE1 . . . . . . 138 B3
Popham Ct N16 . . . . . 7 A1
Popham Gdns
TW9 . . . . 55 A4
Popham Rd N1 . . . . . 86 C4
Popham St
Islington N1 . . . . 86 B4
Shoreditch N1 . . . . . 86 C4
POPLAR 33 C3
Poplar Bath St 11
E14 . . . . 34 A2
Poplar Bsns Pk
E14 . . . . 34 B3
Poplar Cl E9 . . . . 18 B3
Poplar Ct 4 SW16 . . 74 B1
Poplar Gr W6 . . . . . . 39 B4
Poplar High St
E14 . . . . 34 A2
Poplar Ho
Brockley SE4 . . . . . . 66 B3
19 Rotherhithe
SE16 . . . . 40 C4
Poplar Mews 4
W12 . . . . 30 B1
Poplar Pl W2 . . . . . 114 B4
Poplar Rd SE24 . . . . 63 B3
Poplar Sta E14 . . . . . 34 A2
Poplars The NW5 . . . 13 B3
Poplar Wlk SE24 . . . 63 B3
Poppins Ct EC4 . . . 108 A1
Porchester Ct
W2 . . . . 100 B1
Porchester Gate
W2 . . . . 114 C3
Porchester Gdn Mews
W2 . . . . 100 B1
Porchester Gdns
W2 . . . . 114 B4
Porchester Ho 3
E1 . . . . 32 A3
Porchester Mews
W2 . . . . 100 B2
Porchester Pl
W2 . . . . 102 B1
Porchester Rd
W2 . . . . 100 B2
Porchester Sq
W2 . . . . 100 B2
Porchester Terr
W2 . . . . 114 C4
Porchester Terr N
W2 . . . . 100 B2
Porden Rd SW2 . . . . 62 B3
Porland Ct SE1 . . . 137 B2

Porlock Ho 5
SE26 . . . . 76 C1
Porlock St SE1 . . . . 137 C4
Porson Ct SE13 . . . . 67 A4
Portal Cl SE27 . . . . . 74 C1
Portal Way W3 . . . . . 28 C4
Portbury Cl 17
SE15 . . . . 49 C2
Portchester Cl
SE24 . . . . 63 C3
Portelet Ct 1 N1 . . . 24 A4
Portelet Rd E1 . . . . . 25 C2
Porten Ho SW14 . . 126 A1
Porten Rd W14 . . . 126 A1
Porter Sq N19 . . . . . . 5 A3
Porter St
Borough The SE1 . . 123 A2
Marylebone W1 . . . 103 A4
Porteus Rd W2 . . . 101 A4
Portfleet Pl 21 N1 . . 24 A4
Portgate Cl W9 . . . . 23 B1
Port Ho 6 SW11 . . . 59 B4
Port House The 8
E14 . . . . 42 A1
Portia Way E3 . . . . . 26 B1
Porticos The
SW3 . . . . 157 B3
Portinscale Rd
SW15 . . . . 58 B2
Portishead Ho 20
W2 . . . . 31 C4
Portland Ave N16 . . . . 7 B4
Portland Ct
7 De Beauvoir Town
N1 . . . . 16 A1
1 Deptford SE14 . . . 51 A4
Portland Gr SW8 . . 172 C4
Portland Ho 16
SW2 . . . . 74 C2
Portland Hospl for
Women & Children
The W1 . . . . 92 B1
Portland Mews
W1 . . . . 105 A1
Portland Pl W1 . . . 104 B3
Portland Place Sch
W1 . . . . 104 B3
Portland Place Sch
W1 . . . . 104 B4
Portland Rd
Notting Hill
W11 . . . . 31 A1 112 B2
Notting Hill
W11 . . . . 31 A2 112 A3
Portland Rise N4 . . . . 6 B3
Portland Sq 1 E1 . . . 32 A1
Portland St SE17 . . 151 B1
Portland Village
W6 . . . . 39 B3
Portman Ave
SW14 . . . . 55 C4
Portman Cl W1 . . . 103 B2
Portman Gate
NW1 . . . . 90 B1
Portman Hts 1
NW3 . . . . 1 C1
Portman Mews S
W1 . . . . 103 B1
Portman Pl E2 . . . . . 25 B2
Portman Sq W1 . . . 103 B2
Portman St W1 . . . 103 B1
Portman The NW11 . . 1 C4
Portman Twrs
W1 . . . . 103 A1
Portnall Rd W9 . . . . 23 B2
Portobello Ct Est
W11 . . . . 31 B3

Portobello Mews
W11 . . . . . . 31 C2 113 B3
Portobello Rd
W11 . . . . . . 31 B2 113 A4
Portobello Road
Mkt* W10 . . . . 31 A4
Portpool La E1 . . . . . . 94 C1
Portree St E14 . . . . . . 34 C3
Port Royal Pl 3
N16 . . . . 16 A3
Portsea Hall W2 . . 102 B1
Portsea Ho 3
SW15 . . . . 69 A3
Portsea Mews
W2 . . . . 102 B1
Portsea Pl W2 . . . . . 102 B1
Portslade Rd
SW8 . . . . 170 C2
Portsmouth Rd
SW15 . . . . 69 B4
Portsmouth St
WC2 . . . . 107 A1
Portsoken St E1,
EC3 . . . . 124 C4
Portswood Pl
SW15 . . . . 56 B1
Portugal St WC2 . . 107 A1
Poseidon Ct 9
E14 . . . . 41 C2
Postern The EC2 . . 109 A3
Post Office Way
SW8 . . . . 161 B2
Potier St SE1 . . . . . 137 C1
Potterne Cl 5
SW19 . . . . 69 C4
Potters Cl 5 SE15 . . 49 A3
Potters Fields
SE1 . . . . 124 B1
Potters Lo E14 . . . . . . 42 B2
Potters Rd SW6 . . . 166 C1
Pottery La
W11 . . . . . . 31 A1 112 B2
Pottery Rd TW8 . . . . . 44 A4
Pottery St SE16 . . . . . 40 A4
Pott St E2 . . . . 25 A2
Poullett Ho SW2 . . . . 75 A3
Poulton Cl E8 . . . . . . 17 A2
Poultry EC2 . . . . . . 109 B1
Pound La NW10 . . . . . . 8 C2
Pountney Rd
SW11 . . . . 60 C4
Povey Ho
Tulse Hill SW2 . . . . . 62 C1
Walworth SE17 . . . . 152 A3
Powell's Wlk W4 . . . . 46 B4
Powergate Bsns Pk
NW10 . . . . 20 C2
Power Ho 13 TW9 . . . . 44 C2
Power Ho The W4 . . . 38 B2
Power Rd W4 . . . . 36 C2
Powerscroft Rd
E5 . . . . 17 B4
Powis Gdns
Golders Green
NW11 . . . . 1 B4
Notting Hill W11 . . . . 31 B3
Powis Mews W11 . . 31 B3
Powis Pl WC1 . . . . . 94 B1
Powis Rd E3 . . . . 27 A2
Powis Sq W11 . . . . . 31 B3
Powis Terr W11 . . . . 31 B3
Powlesland Ct 21
E14 . . . . 33 A3
Powlett Ho NW1 . . . 13 A2
Powlett Pl NW1 . . . . 13 A1
Pownall Rd E8 . . . . . 24 C4

Powrie Ho SW11 . . 167 C2
Poynder Ct 3 N7 . . 14 A3
Poynders Ct 9
SW4 . . . . 61 B1
Poynders Gdns
SW12 . . . . 73 B4
Poynders Rd SW12,
SW4 . . . . 73 C4
Poynings Rd N19 . . . . 4 B1
Poynter Ho
Paddington NW8 . . . . 89 B2
10 Shepherd's Bush
W11 . . . . 30 C1
Poyntz Rd SW11 . . 168 C1
Poyser St E2 . . . . 25 A3
Praed Mews W2 . . 101 C2
Praed St W2 . . . . . 101 C2
Prague Pl SW2 . . . . 62 A2
Prah Rd N4 . . . . 5 C2
Prairie St SW8 . . . . 170 A1
Pratt Mews NW1 . . 82 C3
Pratt St NW1 . . . . . 82 C4
Pratt Wlk SE1,
SE11 . . . . 149 A4
Preachers Ct EC1 . . 96 B1
Prebend Gdns W4,
W6 . . . . 38 B2
Prebend Mans 4
W4 . . . . 38 B2
Prebend St N1 . . . . 86 C4
Precinct The
Islington N1 . . . . . . 86 C3
Islington N5 . . . . . . 15 A3
Premier Corner
NW6 . . . . 23 B3
Premier Ho 22 N1 . . 15 A1
Premier League Hall
of Fame* SE1 . . . 134 C4
Premier Park Rd
NW10 . . . . 20 A3
Premier Pk NW10 . . 20 A3
Premier Pl 17 E14 . . 33 C2
Prendergast Ho 7
SW4 . . . . 73 C4
Prendergast Sch
SE4 . . . . 66 C3
Prescot St E1 . . . . . 125 A4
Prescott Ho 18
SE17 . . . . 48 A4
Prescott Pl SW4 . . . 61 C3
Presentation Mews
SW2 . . . . 74 B3
President Dr E1 . . . . 32 A1
President Ho EC1 . . 96 B3
President St EC1 . . . 96 C4
Prestage Way 18
E14 . . . . 34 B2
Prested Rd SW11 . . 60 A3
Preston Cl SE1 . . . . 152 A4
Preston Gdns
NW10 . . . . 8 A2
Preston Ho
Bermondsey SE1 . . 138 C2
Walworth SE1 . . . . 152 A4
Preston Pl
Richmond TW10 . . . 54 A2
Willesden NW2 . . . . 8 C2
Preston's Rd E14 . . 34 B1
Prestwich Terr
SW4 . . . . 61 C2
Prestwood Ho 5
SE16 . . . . 40 A3
Prestwood St N1 . . 87 A1
Price Cl SW17 . . . . . 72 B1
Price Ho N1 . . . . . . 86 C3
Prices Ct SW11 . . . . 59 C4

Price's St SE1 . . . . . 122 B2
Price's Yd N1 . . . . . 85 A3
Prichard Ho
Battersea SW11 . . . 167 C3
Islington N1 . . . . . . 14 B1
Prideaux Ho 1 WC1 95 A4
Prideaux Pl
Acton W3 . . . . 28 C2
St Pancras WC1 . . . 95 A4
Prideaux Rd SW9 . . 62 A4
Pride Ct N1 . . . . 85 C2
Priestley Cl 1 N16 . . 7 B4
Priestley Ho
2 Camden Town
NW5 . . . . 13 A2
St Luke's EC1 . . . . . 97 A2
Priestman Point 23
E3 . . . . 27 A2
Priests Bridge
SW14 . . . . 56 A4
Priest's Ct EC2 . . . 108 C2
Prima Rd SW9 . . . . 163 B2
Primrose Cl 6 E3 . . 26 C3
Primrose Ct
2 Child's Hill NW2 . . 1 B1
Primrose Hill NW8 . . 80 C3
11 Streatham
SW12 . . . . 73 C4
Primrose Gdns
NW3 . . . . 12 B1
PRIMROSE HILL . . 12 B1
Primrose Hill EC4 . 107 C1
Primrose Hill Ct
NW3 . . . . 12 B1
Primrose Hill Rd
Primrose Hill NW1,
NW3 . . . . 12 B1
Primrose Hill NW3,
NW3 . . . . 80 C4
Primrose Hill Sch
NW1 . . . . 81 C4
Primrose Hill Studios
NW1 . . . . 81 B4
Primrose Ho
7 Peckham SE15 . . 49 C2
8 Richmond TW9 . . 44 B2
Primrose Mans
SW11 . . . . 169 B4
Primrose Mews 9
NW1 . . . . 12 B1
Primrose Sq E9 . . . . 25 B4
Primrose St EC2 . . 110 B4
Primrose Wlk 6
SE14 . . . . 51 A3
Primula St W12 . . . . 29 C3
Prince Albert Ct
NW8 . . . . 80 C3
Prince Albert Rd
NW8 . . . . 80 C3
Prince Arthur Ct 18
NW3 . . . . 11 B4
Prince Arthur Mews
17 NW3 . . . . 11 B4
Prince Arthur Rd
NW3 . . . . 11 B3
Prince Charles Rd
SE3 . . . . 53 B2
Prince Consort Ho
SE1 . . . . 148 B2
Prince Consort Rd
SW7 . . . . 129 B2
Princedale Rd
W11 . . . . . . 31 A1 112 B2
Prince Edward Mans
W2 . . . . . . 31 C3 113 C4

Prince Edward Rd
E9 . . . . 18 B2
Prince George Rd
N16 . . . . 16 A4
Princelet St E1 . . . . 111 A4
Prince of Orange La
3 SE10 . . . . 52 B3
Prince of Wales Dr
SW11 . . . . 169 B4
Prince of Wales
Mans
Battersea SW11 . . . 169 C4
Clapham SW4 . . . . . 61 A2
Prince of Wales Pas
NW1 . . . . 92 C3
Prince of Wales Rd
Blackheath Vale
SE3 . . . . 53 B2
Camden Town NW5 . 12 C2
Prince of Wales
Terr
Chiswick W4 . . . . . . 38 A1
Kensington W8 . . . 128 B3
Prince Regent Ct 2
SE16 . . . . 33 A1
Prince Regent Mews
NW1 . . . . 92 C3
Princes Arc SW1 . . 119 A2
Princes Ave W3 . . . . 36 C3
Princes Cir WC2 . . 106 A2
Princes Cl N4 . . . . . . 6 A3
Princes Coll WC1 . . 106 A2
Princes Court Bsns
Ctr 14 E1 . . . . 32 A2
Princes Ct
Brondesbury NW2 . . 10 A3
Hampstead NW3 . . . 11 C4
Stepney E1 . . . . 32 A2
Prince's Ct SE16 . . . 41 B3
Princes Gate
SW7 . . . . 129 C3
Prince's Gate
SW7 . . . . 130 A3
Princes Gate Ct
SW7 . . . . 129 C3
Princes Gate Mews
SW7 . . . . 129 C2
Princes Gdns
SW7 . . . . 129 C2
Princes Ho
W11 . . . . . . 31 C2 113 B3
Prince's Mews
6 Hammersmith
W6 . . . . 39 A1
Kensington W2 . . . 114 A4
Princes Rd
Kew TW10 . . . . 44 B2
Richmond TW10 . . . 54 B2
Prince's Rd SW14 . . 55 C4
Princes Rise SE13 . . 52 B1
Princes Riverside Rd
7 SE16 . . . . 32 C1
Princess Alexandra
School of Nursing
The E1 . . . . 32 A4
Princess Alice Ho 1
W10 . . . . 22 B1
Princess Beatrice Ho
SW10 . . . . 142 A1
Princess Cres N4 . . . 6 A2
Princess Cres N4,
N5 . . . . 6 A2
Princess Ct
Hampstead NW6 . . . 11 A1
Kensington W2 . . . 114 B4

Princess Ct continued
Marylebone W1 . . . 102 C3
Princess Frederica CE
Prim Sch NW10 . . 22 B3
Princess Grace Hospl
The W1 . . . . 91 B1
Princess Louise Cl 1
W2 . . . . 101 C4
Princess Louise Hospl
W10 . . . . 30 B4
Princess Mary Ho
SW1 . . . . 147 C3
Princess May Prim
Sch N16 . . . . 16 B4
Princess May Rd
N16 . . . . 16 A4
Princess Mews
NW3 . . . . 11 C2
Prince's Sq W2 . . . 114 A4
Princess Rd
Camden Town
NW1 . . . . 81 C4
Paddington NW6 . . . 23 C3
Princess St 1 SE1 . . 136 B1
Princes St N1 . . . . . 104 B1
Prince's St
City of London
EC2 . . . . 109 B1
Richmond TW10,
TW9 . . . . 54 A2
Princes St SE8 . . . . 51 B4
Princes Way
Acton W3 . . . . 36 C3
Putney SW19,
SW19 . . . . 70 A3
Princes Yd
W11 . . . . . . 31 A1 112 B1
Princethorpe Ho
W2 . . . . 100 A4
Princeton Ct
SW15 . . . . 57 C4
Princeton Mans
WC1 . . . . 106 C3
Principal Sq 9 E9 . . 17 C3
Printers Mews 13
E3 . . . . 26 A4
Printer St EC4 . . . . 107 C2
Printing House Yd
E2 . . . . 24 A2 98 B3
Printon Ho 8 E3 . . . 33 B4
Print Village Ind Est
SE15 . . . . 49 B1
Prior Bolton St
N1 . . . . 15 A2
Prioress Ho 2 E3 . . 27 A2
Prioress Rd SE27 . . 75 A1
Prioress St SE1 . . . . 137 C1
Priors Lo 4 TW10 . . 54 A1
Prior St SE10 . . . . . 52 B3
Prior Weston Prim
Sch
Broadgate EC1 . . . . 97 B2
St Luke's EC1 . . . . . 97 A1
Priory Ave W4 . . . . 38 A3
Priory Ct
City of London
EC4 . . . . 108 B1
Homerton E9 . . . . . . 17 C3
Nunhead SE15 . . . . . 65 B3
Roehampton SW15 . 56 B3
South Lambeth
SW8 . . . . 171 C2
Priory Gdns
Barnes SW13 . . . . . 56 B4
6 Chiswick W4 . . . . 38 A2

Priory Gn N1...... 84 C2
Priory Gr SW8.... 172 A3
Priory Ho
Clerkenwell EC1..... 96 A2
Pimlico SW1....... 147 B2
Spitalfields E1 .... 110 C4
Priory Hospl The
SW15............. 56 B3
Priory La SW15.... 56 B2
Priory Lo **7** W4....36 C1
Priory Mans
17 Maitland Pk
NW3.............. 12 B2
South Kensington
SW10............ 143 A1
Priory Park Rd
NW6.............. 23 B4
Priory Rd
Bedford Pk W4.....37 C3
Hampstead NW6 ... 11 A1
Richmond TW9.....44 C3
Priory St **10** E3.....27 A2
Priory Terr NW6....78 A4
Priory The SE1....136 A3
Priory Wlk SW10 ..143 A1
Pritchard Ho **20**
E2.............. 24 C3
Pritchard's Rd E2 ..24 C3
Priter Rd SE16 ...139 C1
Priter Road Hostel
SE16............ 139 C1
Probert Rd SW2....62 C2
Probyn Ho **1** SW1..147 C4
Probyn Rd SW2 ....75 A2
Procter Ho **12** SE5..48 C3
Procter St WC1 ...106 C3
Proctor Ho **1** SE1..153 B1
Prome Ho **3** N16 ..15 C4
Promenade Approach
Rd W4............46 A3
Promenade The
W4.............. 46 A2
Prospect Cotts
SW18............ 58 C3
Prospect Ho
1 Dalston E8 ....16 B2
Islington N1....... 85 B1
Newington SE1 ...136 B1
14 North Kensington
W10..............30 C3
Prospect House Sch
SW15............ 69 C4
Prospect Pl
2 Child's Hill NW2 ..1 B1
3 Chiswick W4......37 C1
6 Deptford SE8 .....51 B4
12 Hampstead NW3 ..2 C1
7 Lower Holloway
N7............... 14 A4
Wapping E1........32 B1
Prospect Quay
SW18............ 58 C3
Prospect Rd NW2 ..1 C1
Prospect St SE16 ..40 A4
Prospect Wharf
E1.............. 32 B2
Prospero Rd N19....4 C3
Prothero Rd SW6 ..154 C2
Proud Ho **10** E1 ....32 A3
Prout Gr NW10.....8 B4
Provence St N1 ....86 C2
Providence Ct E9 ..25 C4
Providence
Islington N1....... 86 A3

Providence Ct
continued
Mayfair W1........ 117 C4
Providence Pl N1 ..86 A3
Providence Row
N1.............. 84 C1
Providence Row Cl **50**
E2.............. 25 A2
Providence Sq
SE1.............. 139 B4
Providence Yd
E2......... 24 C2 99 B4
Provost Ct NW3....12 B2
Provost Rd NW3 ...12 B1
Provost St N1......97 B4
Prowse Pl NW1 ....13 B1
Prudent Pas EC2 ..109 A1
Prusom's Island **8**
E1.............. 32 A1
Prusom St E1......32 A1
Pryors Ho **1**.......2 C1
Public Record Office
TW9..............45 A3
Pudding La EC3 ...123 C4
Pudding Mill La
E15.............. 27 A4
Pudding Mill Lane Sta
E15.............. 27 A4
Puddle Dock EC4 ..122 B4
Pugin Ct N1........14 C1
Pulborough Rd
SW18............ 70 B4
Pulham Ho SW8...162 C1
Pullman Ct SW2....74 B3
Pullman Gdns
SW15............ 57 B1
Pulross Rd SW9....62 B4
Pulteney Cl **20** E3 ..26 B4
Pulteney Terr N1 ..85 A4
Pulton Ho SE4.....66 A3
Pulton Pl SW6 ....155 B1
Puma Ct E1........110 C4
Pump Ct EC4......107 B1
Pump House Cl
SE16.............40 B4
Pumphouse
Educational Mus
The* SE16........33 A1
Pumping Ho **8**
E14.............. 34 C2
Pumping Station Rd
W4..............46 A4
Pump La SE14.....50 B3
Punderson's Gdns
E2......... 25 A2
Purbeck Ho SW8 ..162 C1
Purbeck Est SE1 ..138 B3
Purbrook Ho **2**
SW15............ 69 A3
Purbrook St SE1 ..138 B2
Purcell Cres SW6 ..154 A2
Purcell Ho SW10 ..157 B3
Purcell Mews **2**
NW10............ 8 A1
Purcell St N1......24 A3
Purchese St NW1 ..83 C1
Purday Ho **4** W10..23 B2
Purdon Ho **11**
SE15............. 49 C2
Purdy St E3.......27 A1
Purley Ave NW2 ....1 A2
Purley Pl N1........15 A1
Purser Ho **3** SW2..62 C1
Pursers Cross Rd
SW6............. 165 A4
Purves Rd NW10 ..22 B3
Pusey Ho **20** E14 ..33 C3

Puteaux Ho **6** E2 ..25 C3
PUTNEY............57 B2
Putney Bridge App
SW6..............58 A4
Putney Bridge Rd
SW15............ 58 B3
Putney Bridge Sta
SW6..............58 B4
Putney Comm
SW15............ 57 B4
Putney Exchange
Shopping Ctr
SW15............ 57 C3
PUTNEY HEATH 57 B1
Putney Heath
SW15............ 57 B1
Putney Heath La
SW15............ 57 C1
Putney High Sch
SW15............ 57 C2
Putney High St
SW15............ 58 A3
Putney Hill SW15 ..57 C1
Putney Park Ave
SW15............ 56 C3
Putney Park La
SW15............ 57 A2
Putney Park Sch
SW15............ 57 A2
Putney Pier SW15 ..58 A4
Putney School of Art
& Design SW15....58 A3
Putney Sta SW15 ..58 A3
PUTNEY VALE 68 C1
Putney Wharf Twr
SW15............ 58 B4
Pyekwell Lo **13** E8..16 C3
Pylon Trad Est
E16.............. 34 C4
Pymers Mead
SE21............. 75 B3
Pynfolds SE16......40 A4
Pynnersmead
SE24............. 63 B2
Pyrford Ho **10**
SW9..............63 A3
Pyrland Rd
Richmond TW10 ...54 B1
Stoke Newington
N5.............. 15 C3
Pyrmont Gr SE27 ..75 A1
Pyrmont Rd W4....44 C4
Pytchley Rd SE22 ..64 A4

Q

Quadrangle Cl
SE1.............. 152 A4
Quadrangle The
Chelsea SW10 ....167 A4
Fulham SW6......154 A1
Herne Hill SE24 ....63 B2
3 North Kensington
W12..............30 B3
Paddington W2 ...102 A2
Quadrant Arc W1 ..119 A3
Quadrant Bsns Ctr
NW6..............23 A4
Quadrant Gr NW5..12 B3
Quadrant The
4 Kensal Green
W10..............22 C2
Richmond TW9....54 A3
Quaker Ct EC1 ....97 A2
Quaker St
E1...... 24 B1 98 C1

Quality Ct WC2.... 107 B2
Quantock Ho N16..7 B3
Quantock Mews **4**
SE15............. 49 C1
Quarrendon St
SW6............. 165 C2
Quarry Rd SW18 ...59 B1
Quarterdeck The
E14.............. 41 C4
Quartermile La E10,
E15.............. 19 A4
Quayside Ct **6**
SE16.............32 C1
Quebec & Crown
Wharves E14....33 B3
Quebec Ind Est
E16.............. 41 A3
Quebec Mews
W1.............. 103 A1
Quebec Way SE16 ..41 A4
Quebec Wharf **22**
E8.............. 24 A4
Quedgeley Ct **3**
SE15............. 49 B4
Queen Alexandra
Mans* WC1......94 A3
Queen Anne Mews
W1.............. 104 B3
Queen Anne Rd
E9.............. 17 C2
Queen Anne's Gate
SW1............. 133 B3
Queen Anne's Gdns
Bedford Pk W4....38 A3
Ealing W5..........36 A4
Queen Anne's Gr
Bedford Pk W4....38 A3
Ealing W5..........36 A4
Queen Anne St
W1.............. 104 A3
Queen Anne Terr **9**
E1.............. 32 A2
Queen Caroline St
W6.............. 39 B1
Queen Charlottes &
Chelsea Hospl
W12..............29 C3
Queen Ct WC1 ....94 B1
Queen Elizabeth **5**
SE5.............. 49 A3
Queen Elizabeth Hall
& Purcell Room*
SE1.............. 121 A2
Queen Elizabeth Ho
SW12............ 72 C4
Queen Elizabeth II
Con Ctr SW1 ....133 C3
Queen Elizabeth II
Jubilee Sch W9 ...23 B1
Queen Elizabeth II
Pier SE10..........35 B1
Queen Elizabeth's Cl
N16.............. 6 C2
Queen Elizabeth's Coll
15 SE10..........52 B3
Queen Elizabeth St
SE1.............. 138 C4
Queen Elizabeth's Wlk
N16.............. 6 C2
Queen Elizabeth Wlk
SW13............ 47 A2
Queenhithe EC4 ..123 A4
Queen Margaret Flats
22 E2...........25 A2
Queen Margarets Ct
N1.............. 16 A3

Queen Margaret's Gr
N1.............. 16 A3
Queen Mary's Gdns★
NW1.............. 91 B3
Queen Mary's Hospl
NW3.............. 2 B1
Queen Mary's Univ
Hospl SW15......56 C1
Queen Mary, Univ of
London E1........26 A1
Queen of Denmark Ct
SE16.............41 B3
Queen St Pl EC4 ..123 A4
Queensberry Mews W
SW7............. 143 B4
Queensberry Pl
SW7............. 143 B4
Queensberry Way
SW7............. 143 B4
Queensborough Mews
W2.............. 114 C4
Queensborough Terr
W2.............. 114 C4
Queensbridge Ct **1**
E2.............. 24 B3
Queensbridge Inf Sch
E8.............. 16 B1
Queensbridge Rd
Dalston E8, E2 ....16 B1
Shoreditch E2, E8...24 B4
Queensbury St N1..15 B1
Queen's CE Prim Sch
The TW9..........44 C3
Queen's Cir SW11 160 A1
Queen's Club Gdns
W14............. 154 B4
Queen's Club The
W14............. 140 B1
Queen's Coll W1 ..104 A3
Queens Cres
TW10............ 54 B2
5 Queen's Cres NW5 12 C2
Queens Ct
Battersea SW11 ...170 A4
Camberwell SE5 ...49 A1
4 Limehouse E14 ..33 B2
Queen's Ct
Barnes SW13 .....56 C4
Kensington W2 ...114 B3
8 Richmond TW10 ..54 B1
St John's Wood
NW8.............. 79 B2
Queensdale W11 ...30 C1
Queensdale Cres
W11.............. 30 C1
Queensdale Pl
W11...... 31 A1 112 A1
Queensdale Rd
Notting Hill W11 ...30 C1
Notting Hill
W11...... 31 A1 112 A1
Queensdale Wlk
W11...... 31 A1 112 A1
Queensdown Rd
E5.............. 17 A4
Queen's Dr N4 .....6 A2
Queen's Elm Par
SW3.............. 143 C2
Queen's Elm Sq
SW3.............. 143 C1
Queen's Gallery★
SW1............. 132 B3
Queen's Gate
SW7............. 129 A1

Queensgate Gdns
SW15 . . . . 57 A3
Queen's Gate Gdns
SW7 . . . . 129 A1
Queensgate Ho 34
E3 . . . . 26 B3
Queen's Gate Mews
SW7 . . . . 129 A2
Queensgate Pl 16
NW6 . . . . 10 C1
Queen's Gate Pl
SW7 . . . . 129 A2
Queen's Gate Pl Mews
SW7 . . . . 129 A2
Queen's Gate Sch
SW7 . . . . 143 B4
Queen's Gate Terr
SW7 . . . . 129 A2
Queen's Gate Villas
E9 . . . . 18 A1
Queen's Gdns W2 114 C4
Queen's Gdr W NW8 . 79 C3
Queen's Head Pas
EC2 . . . . 108 C2
Queen's Head St
N1 . . . . 86 B3
Queen's Head Yd
SE1 . . . . 123 B1
Queens Ho 1
SE17 . . . . .48 C4
Queen's House The*
SE10 . . . . 52 C4
Queensland Rd
N7 . . . . 14 C4
Queens Manor Sch
SW6 . . . . .47 C3
Queens Mans
NW6 . . . . 11 A3
Queen's Mans W6 . 39 C2
Queensmead NW8 . 79 C4
Queensmere Cl
SW19 . . . . .69 C2
Queensmere Ct
SW13 . . . . .46 C4
Queensmere Rd
SW19 . . . . .69 C2
Queen's Mews
W2 . . . . 114 A4
Queensmill Rd
SW6 . . . . .47 C3
Queensmill Sch
SW6 . . . . 165 C1
Queens Par 3 NW2 . 9 B2
Queens Park Com Sch
NW6 . . . . .22 C4
Queen's Park Ct 5
W10 . . . . .22 C2
Queen's Park Prim
Sch W10 . . . . .23 A1
Queen's Park Sta
NW6 . . . . .23 B3
Queen Sq WC1 . . . 106 B4
Queen's Quay
EC4 . . . . 123 A4
Queen's Rd
Mortlake SW14 . . . . . .55 C4
New Cross Gate SE14,
SE15 . . . . .50 B2
Richmond TW10 . . . .54 B1
Queen's Ride
SW13 . . . . .57 A4
Queen's Rise
TW10 . . . . .54 B1
Queen's Road Sta
SE15 . . . . .50 B2
Queen's Row SE17 .48 C4

R

Rabbit Row
W8 . . . . . . 31 C1 113 C2
Raby St E14 . . . . .33 A3
Racine 15 SE5 . . . . . .49 A2
Racton Rd SW6 . . . 155 B3
Radbourne Cl E5 . . .17 C4
Radbourne Ho
SW12 . . . . .73 C3
Radcliff Bldg EC1 . 107 B4

Queen St
City of London
EC4 . . . . 123 A4
Mayfair W1 . . . . 118 A2
Queens Terr NW8 . . 79 B2
Queenstown Mews
SW8 . . . . 170 A3
Queenstown Rd
SW8 . . . . 160 A2
Queenstown Road Sta
SW8 . . . . 170 B4
Queensville Rd SW12,
SW4 . . . . .73 C4
Queensway W2 . . . 114 A4
Queensway Sta
W2 . . . . 114 B3
Queenswood Ct 7
SW4 . . . . .62 A2
Queens Yd E9 . . . . . .18 C2
Queen's Yd W1 . . . . .93 A1
Queen Victoria
Meml* SW1 . . . . . 132 C4
Queen Victoria St
EC4 . . . . 122 C4
Queen Victoria Terr
12 E1 . . . . .32 A2
Quelch Ho 2 N19 . .13 C3
Quemerford Rd
N7 . . . . 14 B3
Quendon Ho 9
W10 . . . . .22 B1
Quenington Ct 5
SE15 . . . . .49 B4
Quenington Mans
SW6 . . . . 164 C4
Quennel Ho 7
SW12 . . . . .73 B4
Querrin St SW6 . . . 166 C1
Quested Ct 27 E8 . .17 A3
Quex Mews NW6 . . .23 C4
Quex Rd NW6 . . . . . .23 C4
Quick Rd W4 . . . . . . .38 A1
Quick St N1 . . . . .86 B1
Quick Street Mews
N1 . . . . 86 A1
Quickswood 3 NW3 .12 A1
Quill La SW15 . . . . . . .57 C3
Quill St N4 . . . . .5 C1
Quilp St SE1 . . . . . . 136 C4
Quilter St
E2 . . . . 24 C2 99 B4
Quilting Ct 23
SE16 . . . . .40 C4
Quince Rd SE13 . . . .52 A1
Quintin Ct W4 . . . . . .45 B3
Quintin Kynaston Sch
NW8 . . . . .79 B3
Quintock Ho 2
TW9 . . . . .44 C2
Quinton Ho SW8 . . 162 A2
Quinton St SW18 . . .71 B2
Quixley St 1 E14 . . .34 C2
Quorn Rd SE22 . . . . .64 A4

Radcliffe Ave
NW10 . . . . .21 C3
Radcliffe Coll
Marylebone W1 . . . . 104 C1
Soho W1 . . . . 105 B2
Radcliffe Ho 10
SE16 . . . . .40 A2
Radcliffe Path
SW8 . . . . 170 B1
Radcliffe Rd SE1 . . 138 B2
Radcliffe Sq SW15 . .57 C1
Radcot St SE11 . . . . 149 C1
Raddington Rd
W10 . . . . .31 A4
Radford Ho
7 Bow Comm E14 . . .34 A4
Islington N7 . . . . .14 B3
Radford Rd SE13 . . .67 B1
Radipole Rd SW6 . 164 C4
Radland Rd E16 . . . . .35 C3
Radlett Pl 12 SE16 . .40 C4
Radley Ct 18 SE16 . .40 C4
Radley Ho NW1 . . . . .90 C2
Radley La 30
SW19 . . . . .69 C3
Radley Mews W8 . . 127 C1
Radley Terr 1
E16 . . . . .35 B4
Radnor Lo 1 SW2 . 101 C1
Radnor Mews W2 . . 101 C1
Radnor Pl W2 . . . . . 102 A1
Radnor Rd
Kensal Rise NW6 . . . .23 A4
Peckham SE15 . . . . . .49 C3
Radnor St EC1 . . . . . .97 A3
Radnor Terr W14 . . 140 C4
Radnor Way
NW10 . . . . .20 A1
Radnor Wlk
Chelsea SW3 . . . . . . 144 C1
21 Millwall E14 . . . . . .41 C2
Radstock St
SW11 . . . . 158 A1
Radway Ho 38 W2 . .31 C4
Radwell Ho SW2 . . . .62 C2
Raeburn Ct 6
SW19 . . . . .69 C3
Raeburn St SW2 . . . .62 A3
Ragged School Mus
The* E3 . . . . .33 A4
Raglan Ct SW9 . . . . .62 C4
Raglan St NW5 . . . . . .13 A2
Ragley Cl W3 . . . . . . .37 B4
Rahere Ho EC1 . . . . . .96 C4
Railey Mews NW5 . . .13 B3
Railton Rd SE24 . . . . .63 A2
Railway App SE1 . . 123 C2
Railway Ave SE16 . . .40 B4
Railway Cotts W6 . . .39 B4
Railway Gr SE14 . . . .51 B3
Railway Rise SE22 . .64 A3
Railway Side
SW13 . . . . .56 A4
Railway St N1 . . . . . . .84 B1
Railway Terr SE13 . . .67 A2
Rainbow Ave E14 . . . .42 A1
Rainbow Ct 3
SE14 . . . . .51 A4
Rainbow Quay
SE16 . . . . .41 A3
Rainbow Sch The
SW17 . . . . .71 B2
Rainbow St SE5 . . . . .49 A3
Raines Ct N16 . . . . . . .7 B2
Raine's Foundation
Lower Sch E2 . . . . . . .25 A3

Raine's Foundation
Sch E2 . . . . .25 B3
Raine St E1 . . . . .32 A1
Rainford Ho 9 N7 . . 5 B2
Rainham Cl SW11 . . .60 A2
Rainham Ho NW1 . . . .83 A3
Rainham Rd NW10 . .22 B2
Rainhill Way 2 E3 . .26 C2
Rainsborough Ave
SE8 . . . . .41 A2
Rainsford Ct
NW10 . . . . .20 A3
Rainsford Ho 14
SW2 . . . . .62 B2
Rainsford Rd
NW10 . . . . .20 A3
Rainsford St W2 . . . 102 A2
Rainton Rd SE7 . . . . .43 C1
Rainville Rd W6 . . . . .47 B4
Raleigh Ct
7 Hammersmith
W12 . . . . .39 A4
2 Rotherhithe
SE16 . . . . .32 C1
Raleigh Gdns SW2, .62 B1
Raleigh Ho
Clapham SW8 . . . . . 171 B2
Isle of Dogs E14 . . . . .42 A4
Raleigh Mews N1 . . . .86 B3
Raleigh Rd TW9 . . . . .54 B4
Raleigh St N1 . . . . . . .86 B3
Ralph Ct W2 . . . . . . 100 B2
Ralston St SW3 . . . . 144 C1
Ramar Ho E1 . . . . . . 111 B4
Ramillies Cl SW2 . . . .62 A1
Ramillies Ho W1 . . . 105 A1
Ramillies Pl W1 . . . 104 C1
Ramillies Rd W4 . . . . .37 C3
Ramillies St W1 . . . 104 C1
Rampart St E1 . . . . . .32 A3
Rampayne St
SW1 . . . . 147 B2
Ramsay Ho NW8 . . . .80 A2
Ramsay Rd W3 . . . . . .37 B4
Ramsden Ho 1
SW12 . . . . .72 C4
Ramsey Ct
Putney SW15 . . . . . . .57 B1
6 Upper Holloway
N19 . . . . 4 C2
Ramsey Ho
5 Battersea
SW11 . . . . .59 C3
Kennington SW9 . . . 163 C1
Ramsey St
E2 . . . . 24 C1 99 C2
Ramsfort Ho 4
SE16 . . . . .40 A2
Ramsgate St 3 E8 . .16 B2
Ram St SW18 . . . . . . .59 A2
Randal Cremer JMI
Sch E2 . . . . .24 B3
Randall Cl SW11 . . . 168 A4
Randall Pl SE10 . . . . .52 B3
Randall Rd SE11 . . . 148 C3
Randall Row
SE11 . . . . 148 C3
Randell's Rd N1 . . . . .84 B4
Randolf Ct
Paddington NW6 . . . . 78 A1
St John's Wood
NW8 . . . . .78 C2
Randolph Ave W9 . . .88 C3
Randolph Cres W9 . .88 C2

Que–Rat 257

Randolph Gdns
NW6 . . . . .78 A1
Randolph Mews
W9 . . . . .89 A1
Randolph Rd W9 . . . .89 A1
Randolph St NW1 . . .13 B1
Ranelagh Ave
Barnes SW13 . . . . . . .46 C1
Fulham SW6 . . . . .58 B4
Ranelagh Gardens
Mans SW6 . . . . .58 A4
Ranelagh Gardens
(site of Chelsea
Flower Show)*
SW1 . . . . 145 C1
Ranelagh Gdns
5 Bedford Pk W6 . . . .38 B3
Chiswick W4 . . . . .45 B3
Fulham SW6 . . . . .58 B4
Ranelagh Gr SW1 145 C2
Ranelagh Ho
SW3 . . . . 144 C2
Ranelagh Mans
SW6 . . . . 165 A2
Ranelagh Rd
Dagenham NW10 . . . .21 B3
Pimlico SW1 . . . . 147 A1
Rangdon St EC3 . . . 110 C1
Ranger's House (The
Wernher
Collection)*
SE10 . . . . .52 C2
Rangers Sq SE10 . . .52 C2
Rangoon Ho 5
N16 . . . . .15 C4
Rankine Ho SE1 . . . 136 C1
Ranmere St SW12 . . .73 A3
Rann Ho 1 SW14 . . .55 C4
Rannoch Rd W6 . . . . .47 C4
Ransomes Dock Bsns
Ctr SW11 . . . . 158 B1
Ransomes Mews
SW11 . . . . 158 B2
Ranston St NW1 . . . 102 A4
Ranulf Rd NW2 . . . . . .10 B4
Ranwell Cl 20 E3 . . .26 B4
Ranwell Ho 20 E3 . .26 B4
Raphael Ct 9
SE16 . . . . .40 A1
Raphael St SW7 . . . 130 C3
Rapley Ho
E2 . . . . 24 C2 99 B3
Rashleigh Ct 3
SW8 . . . . .61 A4
Rashleigh Ho WC1 . .94 A3
Rastell Ave SW12 . . .73 C3
RATCLIFF 32 C2
Ratcliffe Cross St
E1 . . . . .32 C3
Ratcliffe Ho 10
E14 . . . . .33 A3
Ratcliffe La 18
E14 . . . . .33 A3
Ratcliffe Orch 9
E1 . . . . .32 C2
Rathbone Ho
5 Canning Town
E16 . . . . .35 B3
Kilburn NW6 . . . . .23 C4
Rathbone Mkt 3
E16 . . . . .35 B4
Rathbone Pl W1 . . . 105 B2
Rathbone St
Canning Town E16 . . .35 B3
Fitzrovia W1 . . . . 105 A3

Rathgar Rd SW9 . . . . . **63** A4
Rathmell Dr SW4 . . . **61** C1
Rattray Rd SW2 . . . . . **62** C2
Raul Rd SE15 . . . . **49** C2
Raveley St NW5 . . . . **13** B4
Ravenet Ct
Battersea SW11 . . . . **170** A3
Clapham SW4 . . . . . . **61** A2
Ravenet St SW11 . . **170** A3
Ravenfield Rd
SW17 . . . . **72** B1
Raven Ho **10** SE16 . . **40** C2
Ravenna Rd SW15 . . **57** C2
Raven Row E1 . . . . . **32** A4
Ravensbourne Ho
NW8 . . . . **102** A4
Ravensbourne Mans
8 SE8 . . . . **51** C4
Ravensbourne Pl
SE13 . . . . **52** A1
Ravensbury Rd
SW18 . . . . **71** A2
Ravensbury Terr
SW18 . . . . **71** A2
Ravenscar NW1 . . . . **82** C3
Ravenscourt **1**
N16 . . . . **7** C1
Ravenscourt Ave
W6 . . . . **38** C2
Ravenscourt Gdns
W6 . . . . **38** C2
Ravenscourt Ho **13**
W6 . . . . **39** A2
Ravenscourt Park
Mans **1** W6 . . . . . . **39** A3
Ravenscourt Park
Prep Sch W6 . . . . . **38** C2
Ravenscourt Park Sta
W6 . . . . **38** C2
Ravenscourt Pk
W6 . . . . **39** A2
Ravenscourt Pl
W6 . . . . **39** A2
Ravenscourt Rd
W6 . . . . **39** A2
Ravenscourt Sq
W6 . . . . **38** C3
Ravenscourt Theatre
Sch W6 . . . . **39** A2
Ravenscroft Ave
NW11 . . . . **1** B4
Ravenscroft Cl **4**
E16 . . . . **35** C4
Ravenscroft Ct
NW11 . . . . **1** B4
Ravenscroft Point **20**
E9 . . . . **17** C2
Ravenscroft Rd
Acton W4 . . . . **37** B2
Newham E16 . . . . . . **35** C4
Ravenscroft St
E2 . . . . **24** B2 **99** A4
Ravensdon St
SE11 . . . . **149** C1
Ravenshaw St
NW6 . . . . **10** B3
Ravenslea Rd SW11,
SW12 . . . . **72** B4
Ravensmede Way
W4 . . . . **38** B2
Ravenstone SE17 . **152** B1
Ravenstone Prim Sch
SW12 . . . . **72** C3
Ravenstone St
SW12 . . . . **72** C3

Ravenswood Rd
SW12 . . . . **73** A4
Ravensworth Ct
SW6 . . . . **155** B1
Ravensworth Rd
NW10 . . . . **22** A2
Raven Wharf SE1 . **138** C4
Ravey St
EC2 . . . . **24** A1 **98** A2
Rav Pinter Cl N16 . . . **7** A4
Rawlings St SW3 . . **144** C4
Rawlinson Ho
SE13 . . . . **67** C3
Rawlinson Point **8**
E16 . . . . **35** B4
Rawreth Wlk N1 . . . **87** A4
Rawson Ct SW11 . . **169** C3
Rawson St SW11 . . **170** A3
Rawstorne Pl EC1 . . **96** A4
Rawstorne St EC1 . **96** A4
Rayburne Ct W14 . . **126** A2
Raydon St N19 . . . . . **4** A2
Ray Ho
7 North Kensington
W10 . . . . **30** C3
Shoreditch N1 . . . . . **87** C3
Raymede Twr
W10 . . . . **30** C4
Raymond Bldgs
WC1 . . . . **107** A4
Raymouth Rd
SE16 . . . . **40** A2
Raynald Ho **3**
SW16 . . . . **74** A1
Rayne Ct SE1 . . . . . **138** C4
Rayne Ho
1 Balham SW12 . . **60** C1
Paddington W9 . . . . **88** A2
Rayner Ct **10** W12 . . **39** B4
Rayner's Rd SW15 . . **58** A2
Raynes Ct NW2 . . . . **10** A4
Raynham W2 . . . . . **102** A2
Raynham Ho **1**
E1 . . . . **25** C1
Raynham Rd W6 . . . **39** A2
Raynor Pl N1 . . . . . . **87** A4
Ray St EC1 . . . . **95** C1
Ray Wlk N7 . . . . **5** B2
Reachview Cl **17**
NW1 . . . . **13** B1
Reade Ct **6** W3 . . . **37** B3
Reade Wlk **5**
NW10 . . . . **8** A1
Read Ho SE11 . . . . . **163** B4
Reading Ho
Paddington W2 . . . **100** C1
Peckham SE15 . . . . . **49** C4
Reading La E8 . . . . . **17** A2
Reapers Cl NW1 . . . **83** B4
Reardon Ho **5** E1 . . **32** A1
Reardon Path **31**
E1 . . . . **32** A1
Reardon St E1 . . . . . **32** A1
Reaston St SE14 . . . **50** C3
Reay Prim Sch
SW9 . . . . **163** A1
Reckitt Rd W4 . . . . . **38** A1
Record St SE16 . . . . **50** B4
Rector St N1 . . . . . . **86** C3
Rectory Gdns **8**
SW4 . . . . **61** B4
Rectory Gr SW4 . . . **61** B4
Rectory Rd
Barnes SW13 . . . . . **46** C1
1 London W3 . . . . **28** B1
Shacklewell N16 . . . . **7** B1

Rectory Road Sta
N16 . . . . **7** B1
Rectory Sq E1 . . . . . **32** C4
Reculver Ho **2**
SE15 . . . . **50** B4
Reculver Rd SE16 . . **40** C1
Red Anchor Cl
SW3 . . . . **158** A3
Redan Pl W2 . . . . . **100** A1
Redan St W14 . . . . . **39** C3
Redan Terr SE5 . . . . **48** A1
Redbourne Ho **7**
E14 . . . . **33** B3
Redbourn Ho **10**
W10 . . . . **22** B1
Redbridge Gdns
SE5 . . . . **49** A3
Redburn St SW3 . . **158** C4
Redcar St SE5 . . . . . **48** B3
Redcastle Cl E1 . . . . **32** B2
Redchurch St
E2 . . . . **24** B1 **98** C2
Redcliffe Cl SW5 . . **142** A1
Redcliffe Gdns
Chiswick W4 . . . . . . **45** A3
Fulham SW10 . . . . **156** B4
Redcliffe Mews
SW10 . . . . **142** B1
Redcliffe Pl
SW10 . . . . **156** C3
Redcliffe Rd
SW10 . . . . **157** A4
Redcliffe Sch
SW10 . . . . **156** C4
Redcliffe Sq
SW10 . . . . **142** B1
Redcliffe St
SW10 . . . . **156** B4
Redclyf Ho **13** E1 . . **25** B1
Redcroft **5** NW6 . . **10** C2
Red Cross Cotts
SE1 . . . . **137** A4
Redcross Way
SE1 . . . . **123** A1
Reddins Rd SE15 . . . **49** C4
Rede Pl
W2 . . . . . . **31** C2 **113** C4
Redesdale St
SW3 . . . . **158** C4
Redfern Rd NW10 . . . **8** A1
Redfield La SW5 . . **142** A4
Redfield Mews
SW5 . . . . **141** C4
Redfiff Est SE16 . . . **41** B3
Redford Wlk N1 . . . . **86** C4
Redgate Terr
SW15 . . . . **57** C1
Redgrave Rd
SW15 . . . . **57** C4
Redhill Ct SW2 . . . . **74** C2
Redhill St NW1 . . . . **92** B4
Red House Sq **20**
N1 . . . . **15** B1
Redington Gdns
NW3 . . . . **11** A4
Redington Ho N1 . . . **85** A2
Redington Rd
NW3 . . . . **11** A4
Redlands Prim Sch
E1 . . . . **32** B4
Redlands Way
SW2 . . . . **74** B4
Red Lion Cl **9**
SE17 . . . . **48** C4
Red Lion Ct EC4 . . **107** C1
Red Lion Row
SE17 . . . . **48** B4

Red Lion Sq WC1 . **106** C3
Red Lion St WC1 . . **106** C3
Red Lion Yd W1 . . . **117** C2
Redlynch Ct W14 . . **126** B3
Redlynch Ho SW9 . **173** C4
Redman Bldg
EC1 . . . . **107** B4
Redman Ho SE1 . . . **137** A3
Redman's Rd E1 . . . **32** B4
Redmayne Ho
SW9 . . . . **173** A2
Redmead La E1 . . . **125** B1
Redmill Ho **52** E1 . . **25** A1
Redmond Ho N1 . . . **85** A3
Redmore Rd W6 . . . **39** A2
Red Pl W1 . . . . **117** C4
Red Post Hill SE21,
SE24 . . . . **63** C2
Redriff Prim Sch
SE16 . . . . **41** A4
Redriff Rd SE16 . . . . **41** A3
Red Rover SW13 . . . **56** C4
Redrup Ho **31**
SE14 . . . . **50** C4
Redruth Rd E9 . . . . . **25** B4
Red Sq The N16 . . . . **6** C1
Redstart Cl SE14 . . . **51** A3
Redvers St
E2 . . . . **24** A2 **98** B4
Redwald Rd E5 . . . . **17** C4
Redwood Cl
4 Bow E3 . . . . . . **26** C3
Rotherhithe SE16 . . . **33** A1
Redwood Ct
Brondesbury NW6 . . **10** A1
Crouch End N19 . . . . **4** C4
Redwood Mews **2**
SW4 . . . . **61** A4
Redwoods SW15 . . . **68** C3
Reece Mews SW7 . **143** B4
Reed Cl E16 . . . . **35** C4
Reedham St SE15 . . **64** C4
Reed Ho SW15 . . . . **56** C1
Reedholm Villas
N16 . . . . **15** C4
Reed Pl SW4 . . . . . . **61** C3
Reed's Pl NW1 . . . . **13** B1
Reedworth St
SE11 . . . . **149** C3
Reef Ho E14 . . . . **42** B3
Rees St N1 . . . . **87** A3
Reeves Ho
Lambeth SE1 . . . . . **135** B3
Mayfair W1 . . . . . . **117** B3
Reeves Mews W1 . **117** C3
Reeves Rd E3 . . . . . **27** A1
Reflection Ho
E2 . . . . **24** C1 **99** B2
Reform St SW11 . . **169** A2
Regal Cl E1 . . . . **111** C4
Regal La NW1 . . . . . **81** C3
Regal Pl
6 Tower Hamlets
E3 . . . . **26** B2
Walham Green
SW6 . . . . **156** B1
Regan Way N1 . . . . . **24** A3
Regatta Point
TW8 . . . . **44** B4
Regency Ct
3 Bow E3 . . . . . . **26** B3
14 South Hackney
E9 . . . . **25** B4
Regency Ho NW1 . . **92** B2
Regency La NW1 . . . **11** C1
Regency Mews
Camberwell SW9 . . . **48** A3

Regency Mews
continued
1 Willesden NW10 . . **8** C2
Regency Pl SW1 . . **147** C4
Regency St SW1 . . **147** C3
Regency Terr
SW7 . . . . **143** B2
Regency Wlk **8**
TW10 . . . . **54** A2
Regeneration Rd
SE16 . . . . **40** C1
Regent Cl
Lisson Gr NW8 . . . . **90** A3
1 Stamford Hill N16 . . **7** B4
Regent Ho W14 . . . **140** A4
Regent Pl W1 . . . . . **119** A4
Regent St SE24 . . . . **63** A2
Regents Bridge Gdns
SW8 . . . . **162** B2
Regents Canal Ho
10 E14 . . . . **33** A3
Regent's Coll NW1 **91** B2
Regents Ct E8 . . . . . **24** C4
Regents Gate Ho **20**
E14 . . . . **33** A2
Regents Lo **9**
SW2 . . . . **74** B3
Regents Mews
NW8 . . . . **79** A2
REGENT'S PARK★ . **92** A4
Regent's Park★
NW1 . . . . **81** B1
Regent's Park
Barracks NW1 . . . **82** B1
Regent's Park Rd
Camden Town
NW1 . . . . **81** B4
Primrose Hill NW3 . . **12** C1
Regent's Park Sta
NW1 . . . . **92** A1
Regent's Park Terr
NW1 . . . . **82** A4
Regent's Pl SE3 . . . . **53** C1
Regents Plaza
NW6 . . . . **78** A2
Regent Sq
23 Bromley E3 . . . **27** A2
St Pancras WC1 . . . **94** B3
Regent's Row E8 . . **24** C4
Regent St
Brentford W4 . . . . . **36** C1
7 Kensal Green
W10 . . . . **22** C2
Mayfair W1 . . . . . . **118** C4
Regents Wharf
2 Hackney E2 . . . **25** A4
Islington N1 . . . . . . **84** C2
Reginald Pl **6**
SE8 . . . . **51** C3
Reginald Rd SE8 . . . **51** C3
Reginald Sq SE8 . . . **51** C3
Regina Point SE16 . . **40** B3
Regina Rd N4 . . . . . . **5** B3
Regis Ct NW1 . . . . . **102** C4
Regis Pl **17** SW2 . . . **62** B3
Regis Rd NW5 . . . . . **13** A3
Regnart Bldgs
NW1 . . . . **93** A3
Reid Ct SW14 . . . . . **45** B1
Reighton Rd E5 . . . . **7** C2
Reizel Cl N16 . . . . . . **7** B3
Relay Rd W12 . . . . . **30** B1
Relf Rd SE15 . . . . . . **64** C4
Reliance Sq
E2 . . . . **24** A1 **98** B2
Relton Ct W3 . . . . . . **36** C4

Relton Mews
SW7 . . . . 130 B2
Rembrandt Cl E14 . . 42 C3
Rembrandt Ct 10
SE16 . . . . 40 A1
Rembrant Cl SW1 145 B3
Remington St N1 . . 86 B1
Remnant St WC2 . 106 C2
Remsted Ho NW6 . 78 A3
Remus Rd E3 . . . . . . 18 C1
Renaissance Wlk 4
SE10 . . . . 43 B3
Renbold Ho 8
SE10 . . . . 52 B3
Rendlesham Ho 3 E5,
N16 . . . . 7 C1
Rendlesham Rd E5 . 7 C1
Renforth St SE16 . . 40 B4
Renfrew Ho NW6 . . 78 A1
Renfrew Rd SE11 . 150 A3
Rennell Ho 13 E9 . 17 C2
Rennell St SE13 . . . 67 B4
Rennie Cotts 28
E1 . . . . 25 B1
Rennie Ct SE1 . . . . 122 A2
Rennie Ho 4 SE1 . 136 C1
Rennie St SE1 . . . . 122 A2
Renoir Ct 7 SE16 . . 40 A1
Renton Cl SW2 . . . . 62 B1
Rephidim St SE1 . 138 A1
Replingham Rd
SW18 . . . . 70 C3
Reporton Rd SW6 154 B1
Repton Ho NW1 . . 147 A3
Repton St E14 . . . . 33 A3
Reservoir Rd SE4 . . 51 A1
Reservoir Studios 14
E1 . . . . 32 C3
Resolution Way 4
SE8 . . . . 51 C3
Restell Cl SE3 . . . . 53 A4
Reston Pl SW7 . . . 128 C3
Restoration Sq
SW11 . . . . 167 C3
Retcar Pl N19 . . . . . . 4 A2
Retford St 24 A3
Retreat Ho 5 E9 . . 17 B2
Retreat Pl E9 . . . . . 17 B2
Retreat The SW14 . . 56 A4
Reunion Row E1 . . 32 A2
Reveley Sq SE16 . . 41 A4
Revelon Rd SE4 . . . 66 A4
Revelstoke Rd SW18,
SW19 . . . . 70 C2
Reverdy Rd SE1 . . 153 B3
Rewell St SW6 . . . 156 C1
Rex Pl W1 . . . . 117 C2
Reynard Cl SE4 . . . 66 B4
Reynard Pl SE14 . . 51 A4
Reynolds Cl SW19 . . 30 B2
Reynolds Ho
Finsbury Pk N4 . . . . 5 A3
18 South Hackney
E2 . . . . 25 B3
St John's Wood
NW8 . . . . 79 C1
Westminster SW1 . 147 C3
Reynolds Pl 12
TW10 . . . . 54 B1
Reynolds Rd
Acton Green W4 . . 37 B3
Nunhead SE15 . . . . 65 B3
Rheidol Mews 1 . . 86 C2
Rheidol Terr N1 . . . 86 C3
Rhoda St E2 . 24 B1 99 A2

Rhodes Ho
Shepherd's Bush
W12 . . . . 30 A2
Shoreditch N1 . . . . 97 B4
Rhodesia Rd SW9 172 B1
Rhodes St N7 . . . . . 14 B3
Rhodeswell Rd
E14 . . . . 33 B3
Rhondda Gr E3 . . . 26 B2
Rhyl Prim Sch
NW5 . . . . 12 C2
Rhyl St NW5 . . . . . . 12 C2
Ribbleside Ho 11 . . 23 C4
Ribbon Dance Mews
SE5 . . . . 48 C2
Ribstone Ho 12
E9 . . . . 17 C2
Ricardo St E14 . . . . 34 A3
Riceyman Ho WC1 . 95 B3
Richard Anderson Ct
7 . . . . 50 C1
Richard Atkins Prim
Sch SW2 . . . . 74 A4
Richard Burbidge
Mans SW13 . . . . . . 47 B4
Richard Cloudesley
Sch EC1 . . . . 96 C1
Richard Cobden Prim
Sch NW1 . . . . 83 A3
Richard Fox Ho N4 . 6 B1
Richard Ho 15
SE16 . . . . 40 B2
Richard Knight Ho
SW6 . . . . 165 C4
Richard Neale Ho 2
E1 . . . . 32 A2
Richardson Cl 10
E8 . . . . 24 B4
Richardson Ct
SW4 . . . . 172 B2
Richardson Ho 10
E14 . . . . 33 C4
Richardson's Mews
W1 . . . . 92 C1
Richard's Pl SW3 . 144 B4
Richard St 20 E1 . . 32 A3
Richbell WC1 . . . . 106 B4
Richbell Pl WC1 . . 106 C4
Richborne Terr
SW8 . . . . 163 A2
Richborough Ho
10 Deptford SE15 . 50 B4
14 Hackney E5 . . . . 17 A4
Richborough Rd
NW2 . . . . 10 A4
Richbourne Ct
W1 . . . . 102 B2
Richford Gate W6 . 39 B3
Richford St W6 . . . 39 B3
Rich La SW5 . . . . . 142 A2
Richland Ho 4
SE15 . . . . 49 C2
Richman Ho 10
SE8 . . . . 41 B1
RICHMOND 54 B3
Richmond Ave
Islington N1 . . . . . . 85 A4
Willesden NW10 . . . . 9 B2
Richmond Bldgs
W1 . . . . 105 B1
Richmond Circus
TW9 . . . . 54 A3
Richmond Coll
W8 . . . . 128 B2
Richmond Cres
N1 . . . . 85 B4

Richmond Ct
SW1 . . . . 131 A3
Richmond Gr N1 . . 15 A1
Richmond Healthcare
Hamlet Hospl
TW9 . . . . 54 A4
RICHMOND HILL . . 54 A1
Richmond Hill
TW10 . . . . 54 A1
Richmond Hill Ct 5
TW10 . . . . 54 A1
Richmond Ho
12 Forest Hill
SE26 . . . . 76 C1
Regent's Pk NW1 . 82 B1
Walworth SE17 . . . 151 B2
Richmond
International
Ctr 9 TW9 . . . . 54 B3
Richmond Mans
Earl's Ct SW5 . . . . 142 A2
Putney SW15 . . . . . 58 A4
Richmond Mews
W1 . . . . 105 B1
Richmond Park Rd
SW14 . . . . 55 C3
Richmond Rd
Dalston E8 . . . . 16 C1
Ealing W5 . . . . 36 A4
Richmond Sta
TW9 . . . . 54 A3
Richmond Terr
SW1 . . . . 134 A4
Richmond Way W12,
W14 . . . . 39 C4
Rich St E14 . . . . 33 B2
Rickard Cl SW2 . . . 74 C3
Rickett St SW6 . . . 155 C4
Rickman Ho 22 E2 . 25 B1
Rickman St 24 E1 . 25 B1
Rick Roberts Way
E15 . . . . 27 C3
Rickthorne Rd 7
N19 . . . . 5 A2
Riddell Ct SE1 . . . . 152 C2
Ridgdale St E3 . . . . 27 A3
Ridge Hill NW11 . . . 1 A3
Ridge Rd NW2 . . . . . 1 B1
Ridgeway 11
TW10 . . . . 54 A1
Ridgeway Dr W3 . . 36 C3
Ridgeway Gdns N6 . 4 B4
Ridgeway The
Acton W3 . . . . 36 C3
Golders Green NW11 . 1 A4
Ridgewell St E1 . . . 87 A4
Ridgmount Gdns
WC1 . . . . 105 B4
Ridgmount Pl
WC1 . . . . 105 B4
Ridgmount Rd
SW18 . . . . 59 A2
Ridgmount St
WC1 . . . . 105 B4
Ridgway Rd SW9 . . 63 A4
Riding House St
W1 . . . . 104 C3
Ridings Cl N6 . . . . . . 4 B4
Ridley Ho 14
SW11 . . . . 60 A4
Ridley Rd
Dalston E8 . . . . 16 B3
Willesden Green
NW10 . . . . 21 C3
Ridley Road Mkt
E8 . . . . 16 B3

Riffel Rd NW2 . . . . . . 9 B3
Rifle Ct SE11 . . . . . 163 C4
Rifle Pl W11 . . . . . . 30 C1
Rifle St E14 . . . . 34 A4
Riga Ho 12 E1 . . . . . 32 C4
Rigault Rd SW6 . . 164 B1
Rigden St E14 . . . . . 34 A3
Rigeley Rd NW10 . . 21 C2
Rigge Pl SW4 . . . . . 61 C3
Rigg Ho 2 SW4 . . . 74 A4
Rignold Ho 6 SE5 . 49 A1
Riley Ho
8 Bow E3 . . . . 26 C1
Chelsea SW10 . . . . 157 A2
1 Streatham SW4 . 73 C4
Riley Rd SE1 . . . . . 138 C2
Riley St SW10 . . . . 157 B2
Rill Ho 18 SE5 . . . . 49 A3
Rimini Ct SW12 . . . 72 B3
Rinaldo Rd SW12 . . 73 A4
Ringcroft St N7 . . . 14 C3
Ringford Ho SW18 . 58 B2
Ringford Rd SW18 . 58 C1
Ring Ho 18 E1 . . . . . 32 B2
Ringmer Ave
SW6 . . . . 164 B3
Ringmer Gdns 3
N19 . . . . 5 A2
Ringmer Ho 15
SE22 . . . . 64 A4
Ring Rd W12 . . . . . . 30 B1
Ringsfield Ho
SE17 . . . . 151 A1
Ringwood Gdns
17 Millwall E14 . . . 41 C2
Roehampton SW15 . 68 C3
Ripley Gdns SW14 . 55 C4
Ripley Ho
Mortlake SW14 . . . 56 A4
Nine Elms SW11 . . 160 C4
Riplington Ct
SW15 . . . . 69 A4
Ripplevale Gr N1 . 14 B1
Risborough SE17 . 150 C4
Risborough Ho
NW8 . . . . 90 B2
Risborough St
SE1 . . . . 136 B4
Risdon Ho 7 SE16 . 40 B4
Risdon St 17 SE16 . 40 B4
Riseholme Ct E9 . . 18 B2
Riseholme Ho 14
SE22 . . . . 64 A4
Riseldine Rd SE23 . 66 A1
Rising Hill St 5 N1 . 85 B2
Rising Sun Ct
EC1 . . . . 108 B3
Risley Ho 7 E9 . . . . 17 C2
Rita Rd SW8 . . . . . 162 C2
Ritchie Ho
Crouch End N19 . . . 4 C4
2 Rotherhithe
SE16 . . . . 40 B3
12 South Bromley
E14 . . . . 34 C3
Ritchie St N1 . . . . . . 85 C2
Ritherdon Rd
SW17 . . . . 73 A2
Ritson Ho N1 . . . . . 84 C3
Ritson Rd E8 . . . . . . 16 C2
Rivaz Pl E9 . . . . 17 B2
Riven Ct W2 . . . . . 100 B1
Riverains The
SW11 . . . . 167 B3
River Barge Cl
E14 . . . . 42 B4
Rivercourt Rd W6 . 39 A1

River Ct SE1 . . . . . 122 A3
Riverdale Dr
SW18 . . . . 71 A3
Riverfleet WC1 . . . . 94 B4
Riverford Ho 20
W2 . . . . 31 C4
River Ho SW13 . . . . 46 A1
Rivermead Ct
SW6 . . . . 58 B4
Rivermead Ho E9 . 18 A3
River Pl N1 . . . . 15 B1
River Plate Ho
EC2 . . . . 109 C3
Riversdale Prim Sch
SW18 . . . . 70 C3
Riversdale Rd N5 . . . 6 B1
Riversdene N5 . . . . . 6 B1
Rivers Ho 11 TW8 . 36 C1
Riverside
Battersea SW11 . . 158 B2
1 Rotherhithe
SE16 . . . . 40 B4
St Pancras WC1 . . 94 B4
Riverside Bsns Ctr
SW18 . . . . 71 A3
Riverside Ct SW8 161 C4
Riverside Dr W4 . . 46 A2
Riverside Gdns
W6 . . . . 39 A1
Riverside Ho 14
N1 . . . . 15 B1
Riverside Mans 21
E1 . . . . 32 B1
Riverside Prim Sch
SE16 . . . . 139 C3
Riverside Rd
Mill Meads E15 . . . 27 B3
Wandsworth SW17,
SW19 . . . . 71 B1
Riverside Workshops
SE1 . . . . 123 A2
River St EC1 . . . . . . 95 B4
River Terr W6 . . . . . 39 B1
Riverton Cl W9 . . . 23 B2
Riverview Gdns
SW13 . . . . 47 A4
Riverview Gr W4 . . 45 A4
Riverview Rd W4 . . 45 A4
River Way SE10 . . . 43 B3
Rivet Ho SE1 . . . . . 153 A2
Rivington Ct
NW10 . . . . 21 C4
Rivington Pl
EC2 . . . . 24 A2 98 B3
Rivington St
EC2 . . . . 24 A2 98 A3
Rivington Wlk 4
E8 . . . . 24 C4
Rixon St N7 . . . . 5 C1
Roach Rd E3 . . . . . . 18 C1
Roads Pl N19 . . . . . . 5 A2
Roan St SE10 . . . . . 52 B4
Robert Adam St
W1 . . . . 103 B2
Roberta St
E2 . . . . 24 C2 99 C3
Robert Bell Ho
3 SE16 . . . . 153 B4
Robert Blair Prim Sch
N7 . . . . 14 A2
Robert Browning
Prim Sch SE17 . . . 151 B2
Robert Cl W9 . . . . . 89 A1
Robert Dashwood
Way SE17 . . . . 150 C3

Robert Gentry Ho
W14 .... **140** B1
Robert Jones Ho
SE16 .... **153** B4
Robert Keen Cl 18
SE15 .... 49 C2
Robert Lowe Cl
SE14 .... 50 C3
Robert Owen Ho
Fulham SW6 ....47 C2
Spitalfields
E2 .... 24 B2 99 A4
Robert Owen Lo 4
E5 .... 17 A4
Roberts Ct
Islington N1 .... 86 B3
Willesden NW10 ...... 8 A2
Roberts Ho 5
SE27 .... 75 A1
Roberts Mews
SW1 .... 131 B1
Robertson Ho 11
SE10 .... 52 B2
Robertson Rd E15 ..27 B4
Robertson St
SW8 .... 170 B1
Robert's Pl EC1 .... 95 C2
Robert St
Regent's Pk NW1 .... 92 B3
Strand WC2 .... 120 B3
Robert Sutton Ho 20
E1 .... 32 B3
Robson Rd 7 E3 ....33 B4
Robin Ct E8 E14 ....42 B3
Robin Gr N6 .... 3 C2
Robin Ho NW8 ......80 A2
Robin Hood SW15 ..68 A1
Robin Hood Gdns 12
E14 .... 34 B2
Robin Hood La
E14 .... 34 B2
Robinscroft Mews 18
SE10 .... 52 A2
Robins Ct TW10 ....54 A1
Robin's Ct SW4 ....62 A1
Robinsfield Inf Sch
NW8 .... 80 A2
Robinson Ct
Islington N1 .... 86 B4
4 Richmond TW9 ....54 B3
Robinson Ho
6 North Kensington
W10 .... 30 C3
12 Tower Hamlets
E14 .... 33 C4
Robinson Rd E2 ....25 B3
Robinson St SW3 158 C4
Robsart St SW9 .. 173 B2
Robson Ave NW10 ..8 C1
Robson Ho SE21,
SE27 .... 75 B1
Roby Ho EC1 .... 96 C2
Rochdale Way 4
SE8 .... 51 C3
Roche Ho 15 E14 ..33 B2
Rochelle Cl SW11 ..59 C3
Rochelle Ct 11 E1 ..32 C4
Rochelle St
E2 .... 24 B2 98 C3
Rochemont Wlk 2
E8 .... 24 C4
Roche Sch The
SW18 .... 58 C2

Rochester Ct
1 Bethnal Green
E2 .... 25 A1
2 Camden Town
NW1 .... 13 B1
Rochester Ho
Bermondsey SE1 .. 137 C3
6 Deptford SE15 ....50 B4
Rochester Mews
NW1 .... 13 B1
Rochester Pl NW1 ..13 B1
Rochester Rd
NW1 .... 13 B2
Rochester Row
SW1 .... 147 A4
Rochester Sq
NW1 .... 13 B1
Rochester St
SW1 .... 133 B1
Rochester Terr
NW1 .... 13 B2
Rochester Wlk
SE1 .... 123 B2
Rochford Wlk 3
E8 .... 16 C1
Rochfort Ho 4
SE8 .... 41 B1
Rock Ave 13 SW14 ..55 C4
Rockell's Pl SE22 ..65 A1
Rockfield Ho SE10 ..52 B4
Rock Grove Way
SE16 .... 153 C4
Rockhall Rd NW2 ....9 C4
Rockingham Cl
SW15 .... 56 B3
Rockingham St
SE1 .... 136 C1
Rockland Rd
SW15 .... 58 A3
Rockley Ct 9
W14 .... 39 C4
Rockley Rd W14 ....39 C4
Rocks La SW13 ......56 C4
Rock St N4 .... 5 C2
Rockstraw Ho 5
NW3 .... 12 B1
Rockwood Ct N16 ..7 C4
Rocliffe St N1 ......86 B1
Rocque Ho SW6 .. 154 C2
Rodborough Rd
NW11 .... 1 C3
Rodenhurst Ct
SW4 .... 61 C2
Rodenhurst Rd
SW4 .... 61 C1
Roden St N7 .... 5 B1
Roderick Ho 3
SE16 .... 40 B2
Roderick Rd NW3 ..12 B4
Rodgers Ho 6
SW4 .... 73 C4
Rodin Ct N1 ....86 A3
Roding Ct 6 W12 ..38 A4
Roding Ho N1 ......85 B3
Roding Mews E1 125 C2
Roding Rd E5 ......18 A3
Rodmarton St
W1 .... 103 A3
Rodmell NW1 .... 94 B3
Rodmere St SE10 ..43 A1
Rodmill La SW2 ....74 A4
Rodney Ct NW8 ....89 A2
Rodney Ho
4 Cubitt Town
E14 .... 42 A2
Islington N1 .... 85 A1

Rodney Ho continued
Notting Hill
W11 .... 31 C2 113 B4
Rodney Pl SE17 .. 151 A4
Rodney Rd SE17 .. 151 B3
Rodney St N1 ......85 A1
Rodway Rd SW15 ..68 C4
Rodwell Rd SE22 ..64 B1
Roedean Cres
SW15 .... 56 A2
ROEHAMPTON 56 B2
Roehampton CE Prim
Sch SW15 .... 69 A4
Roehampton Cl
SW15 .... 56 B3
Roehampton Ct
SW13 .... 56 C4
Roehampton Gate
SW15 .... 56 A1
Roehampton High St
SW15 .... 68 C4
Roehampton La
Putney SW15 .... 56 C1
Roehampton SW15 ..69 A3
Roehampton Univ
(Digby Stuart Coll)
SW15 .... 56 B2
Roehampton Univ
(Froebel Coll)
SW15 .... 56 B1
Roehampton Univ
(Southlands Coll)
SW15 .... 56 C2
Roehampton Univ
(Whitelands Coll)
SW15 .... 68 C4
Roehampton Vale
SW15 .... 68 B2
Roffey St E14 ......42 B4
Rogate Ho 5 ......17 C2
Roger Dowley Ct 8
E2 .... 25 B3
Roger's Almshouses
2 SW9 .... 62 B3
Rogers Ct 14 E14 ..33 C2
Rogers Est 28 E2 ..25 B2
Rogers Ho 1
SW1 .... 147 C4
Rogers Rd E16 ......35 B3
Roger St WC1 ......95 A1
Rokeby Ho
8 Balham SW12 ......73 A4
Bloomsbury WC1 .... 94 C1
Rokeby Rd SE4 ......51 B1
Rokeby Sch E15 ..19 C1
Rokeland Ho SE4 ..66 A3
Roland Gdns
SW7 .... 143 A2
Roland Ho SW7 .. 143 A2
Roland Mews 1
E1 .... 32 C4
Roland Way
South Kensington
SW7 .... 143 A2
Walworth SE17 .... 151 C1
Rollins St SE15 ....50 B4
Rollit Ho N7 ....14 C3
Rollit St N7 ....14 C3
Rollo St SW11 .... 170 A3
Rollscourt Ave
SE24 .... 63 B2
Rolls Pas EC4 .... 107 B2
Rolls Rd SE1 ...... 153 A2
Rolt St SE8 .... 51 A4
Roman Cl 3 W3 ....37 A4
Roman Ct 4 N7 ....14 B2

Romanfield Rd
SW2 .... 74 B4
Roman Rd
Chiswick W4 .... 38 B2
Globe Town E2 E3 ..25 B3
25 Old Ford E3 ......26 B4
Roman Square Mkt 1
E3 .... 26 B3
Roman Way
Barnsbury N7 ....14 B2
4 Deptford SE15 ....50 B3
Roma Read Cl
SW15 .... 69 A4
Romayne Ho SW4 ..61 C4
Romberg Rd
SW17 .... 72 C1
Romborough Gdns
SE13 .... 67 B2
Romborough Way
SE13 .... 67 B2
Romer Ho 3 SW2 ..62 B2
Romero Cl SW9 ....62 B4
Romeyn Rd SW16 ..74 B1
Romford Ho 17
N1 .... 15 C2
Romford St E1 ......32 A4
Romilly Rd N4 .... 6 A2
Romilly St W1 .... 119 C4
Rommany Rd
SW27 .... 75 C1
Romney Cl
7 Deptford SE14 ....50 B3
North End NW11 .... 2 B3
Romney Ct
9 Hammersmith
W12 .... 39 B4
9 Hampstead
NW3 .... 12 A2
Romney Ho 2
E14 .... 34 C2
Romney Mews
W1 .... 103 B4
Romney Rd SE10 ..52 C4
Romney St SW1 .. 134 A1
Romola Rd SE24,
SW2 .... 75 A3
Ronald Ross Prim Sch
SW19 .... 70 A4
Ronald St E1 ....32 B3
Ronalds Rd N5 ......14 C3
Ronald Shaw N4 .... 5 C3
Rona Rd NW3 ......12 C4
Rona Wlk 20 N1 ....15 C2
Rondu Rd NW2 ......10 A3
Rood La EC3 ...... 124 A4
Rookery Rd SW4 ..61 B3
Rooke Way SE10 ..43 B1
Rookwood Rd N16 ..7 C4
Roosevelt Ct 12
SW19 .... 70 A3
Rootes Dr W10 ......30 C4
Ropemaker Rd
SE16 .... 41 A3
Ropemaker's Fields 7
E14 .... 33 B2
Ropemaker St
EC2 .... 109 B4
Roper La SE1 ...... 138 B3
Roper's Orch
SW3 .... 158 A3
Ropers Wlk 18
SE24 .... 74 C4
Ropery St E3 ....26 B1
Rope St SE16 ....41 A3
Ropewalk Gdns
E1 .... 111 C2
Ropley St 6 E2 ....24 C3

Rosa Alba Mews
N5 .... 15 B4
Rosalind Ho 25
N1 .... 24 A3
Rosaline Rd SW6 154 B1
Rosaline Terr
SW6 .... 154 B1
Rosa Parks Ho
SW9 .... 172 C1
Rosary Ct 17 E1 ....32 C4
Rosary Gdns SW7 143 A3
Rosary RC Prim Sch
NW3 .... 12 A3
Rosaville Rd SW6 154 C1
Rosbury SW15 ......58 A1
Roscastle Rd SE4 ..66 A2
Roscoe St EC1 ...... 97 A1
Roscommon Ho 2
NW3 .... 11 C3
Rose Alley
Borough The SE1 .. 123 A2
Broadgate EC2 .... 110 B3
Rosebank
2 Dagenham W3 ....28 C3
Fulham SW6 .... 47 B3
Rosebank Gdns
Bow E3 .... 26 B3
1 Dagenham W3 ....28 C3
Rosebank Way
W3 .... 28 C3
Rosebank Wlk
NW1 .... 13 C1
Rosebay Ho 20 E3 ..33 C4
Roseberry Pl E8 ....16 B2
Roseberry St SE16 ..40 A2
Rosebery Ave EC1 ..95 C3
Rosebery Ct
Holborn EC1 .... 95 B2
Mayfair W1 .... 118 A2
Rosebery Ho 4
E2 .... 25 B3
Rosebery Rd SW2 ..62 A1
Rosebery Sq EC1 ..95 B1
Rosebury Rd
SW6 .... 166 B1
Rose Bush Ct
NW3 .... 12 B3
Rosecroft Ave NW3 ..1 C1
Rose & Crown Ct
EC2 .... 108 C2
Rose & Crown Yard
SW1 .... 119 A1
Rose Ct
7 Dalston E8 .... 16 B1
Islington N1 .... 86 A3
Spitalfields E1 ...... 111 A3
Rosedale Ct N5 ....15 A4
Rosedale Ho N16 ....6 C3
Rosedale Rd TW9 ..54 A3
Rosedale Terr W6 ..39 A3
Rosedene NW6 ......22 C4
Rosedene Ave
SW16 .... 74 B1
Rosedew Rd W6 ....47 C4
Rosefield Gdns
E14 .... 33 C2
Roseford Ct 16
W12 .... 39 C4
Rosegate Ho 22
E3 .... 26 B3
Rosehart Mews 8
W11 .... 31 C3
Rosehill Rd SW18 ..59 B2
Roseland Ho SW6 ..58 A4
Roseleigh Ave N5 ..15 A4
Rosemary Branch
Bridge N1 .... 87 C4

Rosemary Ct **35**
SE8 . . . . 51 B4
Rosemary Dr **16**
E14 . . . . 34 C3
Rosemary Gdns
SW14 . . . . 55 B4
Rosemary Ho
Shoreditch N1 . . . . . 87 C3
Willesden NW10 . . 22 A4
Rosemary La
SW14 . . . . 55 B4
Rosemary Rd
Camberwell SE15 . . 49 B3
Wandsworth SW17 . . 71 B1
Rosemary St N1 . . . 87 C3
Rosemary Works Sch
N1 . . . . 87 C3
Rosemead Prep Sch
SE27 . . . . 75 B2
Rosemont Mans **11**
NW3 . . . . 11 A2
Rosemont Rd
Acton W3 . . . . 28 A2
Richmond TW10 . . . 54 A1
South Hampstead
NW3 . . . . 11 A2
Rosemont St
SW3 . . . . 144 C3
Rosemount Ct **2**
W3 . . . . 28 A1
Rosemount Lo
W3 . . . . 28 A2
Rosenau Cres
SW11 . . . . 168 C3
Rosenau Rd
SW11 . . . . 168 C3
Rosendale Prim Sch
SE21 . . . . 75 B2
Rosendale Rd SE21,
SE24 . . . . 75 B3
Roseneath Rd
SW11 . . . . 60 C1
Rosenthal Ho SE6 . . 67 A1
Rosenthal Rd SE6 . . 67 B1
Rosenthorpe Rd
SE15 . . . . 65 C2
Roserton St E14 . . . 42 B4
Rose Sq SW7 . . . . . 143 C2
Rose St
Holborn EC4 . . . . . . 108 B2
Strand WC2 . . . . . . 120 A4
Rosethorn Cl
SW12 . . . . 73 C4
Rosetta Cl SW8 . . . 162 B1
Rosetti Ct WC1 . . . . 105 B4
Roseway SE21 . . . . 63 C1
Rosewood Ct **2**
E11 . . . . 19 C4
Rosewood Gdns
SE13 . . . . 52 B1
Rosewood Ho **9**
NW3 . . . . 11 A2
Rosewood Sq
W12 . . . . 29 C3
Rosher Cl E15 . . . . . 19 C1
Rosina St E9 . . . . . . 17 C2
Roskell Rd SW15 . . . 57 C4
Roslin Ho **2** E1 . . . 32 C2
Roslin Rd W3 . . . . . 37 A3
Rosmead Rd
W11 . . . . . . 31 A2 112 B4
Rosoman Pl EC1 . . . 95 C2
Rosoman St EC1 . . . 95 C3
Ross Ct
1 Hackney E5 . . . . 17 A4
2 Putney SW15 . . . 69 C4
Rossdale Rd SW15 . . 57 B3
Rosse Gdns SE13 . . . 67 C1

Rossendale Way
NW1 . . . . 83 A4
Rossendale St E5 . . . 17 A4
Rossetti Gdns Mans
SW3 . . . . 158 C4
Rossetti Ho WC1 . . . 105 B4
Rossetti Mews
NW8 . . . . 79 C3
Rossetti Rd SE16 . . . 40 A1
Rossetti Studios
SW3 . . . . 158 B4
Ross Ho **8** E1 . . . . 32 A1
Rossington St E5 . . . 7 C2
Rossiter Rd SW12 . . 73 A3
Rosslyn Ave SW13 . . 56 B4
Rosslyn Ct NW3 . . . 12 A3
Rosslyn Hill NW3 . . 11 C3
Rosslyn Ho **8**
TW9 . . . . 44 B2
Rosslyn Mans
7 Hampstead
NW3 . . . . 11 B2
South Hampstead
NW6 . . . . 11 B2
Rosslyn Mews **7**
NW3 . . . . 11 C4
Rosslyn Park Mews
NW3 . . . . 11 C3
Rossmore Ct NW1 . . 90 C2
Rossmore Rd NW1 . . 90 B2
Rostrevor Mans
SW6 . . . . 164 C4
Rostrevor Mews
SW6 . . . . 164 C4
Rostrevor Rd
SW6 . . . . 164 C4
Rotary Lo **12** SE27 . 75 A1
Rotary St SE1 . . . . . 136 B2
Rothay NW1 . . . . . . 92 B4
Rothbury Rd E9 . . . . 18 C1
Rotheley Ho **59** E9 . 17 B1
Rotherfield Ct
De Beauvoir Town
N1 . . . . 15 C1
Shoreditch N1 . . . . 87 A4
Rotherfield Prim Sch
N1 . . . . 87 A4
Rotherfield St
Islington N1 . . . . . . 15 B1
Shoreditch N1 . . . . 87 A4
Rotherham Wlk
SE1 . . . . 122 A1
ROTHERHITHE 40 C3
Rotherhithe Bsns Est
SE16 . . . . 40 B2
Rotherhithe New Rd
SE16 . . . . 40 A1
Rotherhithe Old Rd
SE16 . . . . 40 C2
Rotherhithe Prim Sch
SE16 . . . . 40 C2
Rotherhithe St
SE16 . . . . 40 B4
Rotherhithe Sta
SE16 . . . . 40 B4
Rotherhithe Tunnel
SE16 . . . . 32 C1
Rother Ho SE15 . . . 65 A3
Rotherwick Rd
NW11 . . . . 1 C4
Rotherwood Rd
SW15 . . . . 57 C4
Rothery St N1 . . . . . 86 B4
Rothesay Ave SW14,
TW10 . . . . 55 A3
Rothesay Ct SE11 . . 163 B3
Rothley Ct NW8 . . . 89 B2

Rothsay St SE1 . . . . 138 A1
Rothsay Wlk **19**
E14 . . . . 41 C2
Rothschild Rd W4 . . 37 B3
Rothwell St
10 Hampstead
NW1 . . . . 12 B1
Primrose Hill NW1 . . 81 A4
Roth Wlk N7 . . . . . . 5 B2
Rotten Row SW1 . . 130 C4
Rotterdam Dr E14 . . 42 B3
Rouel Rd
Bermondsey SE16 . . 153 B4
Bermondsey SE16 . . 139 C2
Roundacre SW19 . . . 69 C2
Roundel Cl SE4 . . . . 66 B3
Roundwood Rd
NW10 . . . . 8 B2
Rounton Rd E3 . . . . 26 C1
Roupell Rd SW2 . . . 74 B3
Roupell St SE1 . . . . 121 C1
Rousden St NW1 . . . 13 B1
Rover Ho **6** N1 . . . 24 A4
Rowallan Rd SW6 . . 154 A1
Rowan Cl W5 . . . . . 36 A4
Rowan Ct
19 Camberwell
SE15 . . . . 49 B3
Wandsworth SW11 . . 60 B1
Rowan Ho
11 Bow E3 . . . . . 26 B4
Dagenham NW10 . . . 21 A1
3 Maitland Pk
NW3 . . . . 12 B2
Rowan Rd W6 . . . . . 39 C2
Rowan Terr W6 . . . . 39 C2
Rowan Wlk
7 Dartmouth Pk
N19 . . . . 4 B2
Kensal Town W10 . . 23 A1
Rowberry Cl SW6 . . 47 B3
Rowcross St SE1 . . . 153 A2
Rowditch La
SW11 . . . . 169 B2
Rowdon Ave NW10 . . 9 A1
Rowe Ho E9 . . . . . . 17 B2
Rowe La E9 . . . . . . 17 B3
Rowena Cres
SW11 . . . . 168 B1
Rowfant Rd SW12,
SW17 . . . . 72 C2
Rowhill Mans **11**
E5 . . . . 17 A4
Rowhill Rd E5 . . . . . 17 A4
Rowington Cl W2 . . 100 A4
Rowland Hill Ho
SE1 . . . . 136 A4
Rowland Hill St
NW3 . . . . 12 A3
Rowley Gdns N4 . . . 6 B4
Rowley Ho SE8 . . . . 51 C4
Rowley Ind Pk W3 . . 37 A3
Rowley Way NW8 . . 78 C4
Rowntree Cl NW6 . . 10 C2
Rowse Cl E15 . . . . . 27 B4
Rowstock **3** NW5 . . 13 C2
Rowstock Gdns
N7 . . . . 13 C3
Roxby Pl SW6 . . . . . 155 C4
Roxford Ho **2** E3 . . 27 A1
Roxley Rd SE13 . . . . 67 A1
Roxwell **10** NW1 . . . 13 A2
Roxwell Rd W12 . . . 38 C4

Royal Acad of Arts*
W1 . . . . 118 C3
Royal Acad of Dance
SW11 . . . . 167 C3
Royal Acad of Music
NW1 . . . . 91 C1
Royal Albert Hall*
SW7 . . . . 129 B3
Royal Arc W1 . . . . . 118 C3
Royal Armouries
The* E1 . . . . 124 C3
Royal Ave SW3 . . . . 144 C2
Royal Avenue Ho
SW3 . . . . 144 C2
Royal Ballet Sch The
Hammersmith
W14 . . . . 39 C1
St Giles WC2 . . . . . 106 B1
Royal Brompton
Hospl
Chelsea SW3 . . . . . 143 B2
Chelsea SW3 . . . . . 144 A2
Royal Cir SE27 . . . . 75 A1
Royal College of
Physicians Liby
NW1 . . . . 92 B2
Royal College St
NW1 . . . . 83 A4
Royal Coll of
Anaesthetists
NW1 . . . . 106 C3
Royal Coll of Art
SW7 . . . . 129 B3
Royal Coll of Art
Sculpture Sch
SW11 . . . . 158 A1
Royal Coll of
Midwives w1 . . . . 104 A3
Royal Coll of Music
SW7 . . . . 129 B2
Royal Coll of
Obstetricians &
Gynaecologists
NW1 . . . . 90 C2
Royal Coll of
Ophthalmologists
NW1 . . . . 91 B1
Royal Coll of
Paediatrics & Child
Health w1 . . . . . . 104 B4
Royal Coll of
Pathologists
SW1 . . . . 119 B1
Royal Coll of
Physicians NW1 . . 92 B2
Royal Coll of
Radiologists w1 . . 104 B4
Royal Coll of Science
SW7 . . . . 129 B2
Royal Coll of Speech
Language Therapists
SE1 . . . . 123 B1
Royal Coll of
Surgeons WC2 . . . 107 A2
Royal Courts of
Justice WC2 . . . . . 107 B1
Royal Cres
W11 . . . . . 31 A1 112 A1
Royal Crescent Mews
W11 . . . . 30 C1

Royal Ct
City of London
EC3 . . . . 109 C1
Royal Duchess Mews
SW12 . . . . 73 A4
Royal Exchange*
EC3 . . . . 109 C1
Royal Exchange Bldgs
EC3 . . . . 109 C1
Royal Festival Hall*
SE1 . . . . 121 A1
Royal Free Hospl
NW3 . . . . 12 A3
Royal Fusiliers Mus*
E1 . . . . 124 C3
Royal Geographical
Society SW7 . . . . 129 C3
Royal Hill SE10 . . . . 52 B3
Royal Hill Ct **2**
SE10 . . . . 52 B3
Royal Horticultural
Society (Lawrence
Hall & Conf Ctr)
SW1 . . . . 133 B1
Royal Horticultural
Society (Lindley
Hall) SW1 . . . . . . 147 B4
Royal Hospital (Army
Pensioners)*
SW1 . . . . 145 B1
Royal Hospital Rd
SW3 . . . . 145 A1
Royal Hospl and
Home SW15 . . . . . 58 A1
Royal Langford
Apartments NW6 . 78 A2
Royal London Est The
NW10 . . . . 20 C3
Royal London
Homeopathic Hospl
The WC1 . . . . 106 B4
Royal London Hospl
Archives & Mus*
E1 . . . . 32 A4
Royal London Hospl
(Mile End) The
E1 . . . . 25 C2
Royal London Hospl
(St Clements) The
E3 . . . . 26 B2
Royal London Hospl
(Whitechapel) The
E1 . . . . 32 A4
Royal Marsden Hospl
SW3 . . . . 143 C2
Royal Mews The*
SW1 . . . . 132 B2
Royal Mint Pl E1 . . . 125 B4
Royal Mint St E1 . . . 125 A4
Royal National
Orthopaedic Hospl
W1 . . . . 92 B1
Royal National TNE
Hospl The WC1 . . . 94 C4
Royal Naval Pl
SE14 . . . . 51 B3
Royal Oak Ct
N1 . . . . 24 A2 98 A4
Royal Oak Pl SE22 . . 65 A1
Royal Oak Rd **5**
E8 . . . . 17 A2
Royal Oak Sta
W2 . . . . 100 B3
Royal Oak Yd SE1 . . 138 A3

Royal Obsy The ★
SE10 .... 52 C3
Royal Opera Arc
SW1 .... 119 B2
Royal Orchard Cl
SW18 .... 70 A4
Royal Par
Blackheath Vale
SE3 .... 53 B1
Fulham SW6 .... 154 A2
🔟 Richmond TW9 .. 44 C2
Royal Pl 🔟 SE10 .. 52 B3
Royal Rd SE17 ...... 48 A4
Royal Sch Hampstead
The NW3 .... 11 C4
Royal St SE1 .... 135 A2
Royalty Ho W1 .... 105 B1
Royalty Mews
W1 .... 105 B1
Royalty Studios
W11 .... 31 A3
Royal United Services
Mus★ SW1 .... 120 A1
Royal Veterinary Coll
NW1 .... 83 B3
Royal Victoria Sta
E16 .... 35 C2
Royal Victor Pl E3 .. 25 C3
Roycroft Cl SW2 .... 74 C3
Roydon Cl SW11 .. 168 C2
Roy Ridley Ho
SW4 .... 61 C4
Roy Sq E14 .... 33 A2
Royston Cl
New Cross SE4 ...... 51 B1
🔟 Richmond TW9 .. 44 B2
Royston Ho 🔟
SE15 .... 49 C4
Royston St 🖸 E2 .. 25 B3
Rozel Cl 🖸 N1 ...... 24 A4
Rozel Rd SW4 .... 61 B4
Ruby St SE15 .... 50 A4
Ruby Triangle
SE15 .... 50 A4
Rucklidge Ave
NW10 .... 21 C3
Rudall Cres NW3 .. 11 C4
Rudbeck Ho 🔟
SE15 .... 49 C3
Ruddington Cl E5 .. 18 A4
Rudge Ho SE16 .. 139 C2
Rudgwick Terr
NW8 .... 80 B3
Rudhall Ho 🖪
SW2 .... 62 C1
Rudloe Rd SW12 .. 73 B4
Rudolf Pl SW8 .... 162 B3
Rudolph Rd NW6 .. 23 C3
Rudstone Ho 🔟
E3 .... 27 A2
Rudyard Ct SE1 .. 137 C3
Rufford St N1 ...... 84 B4
Rufford Street Mews
N1 .... 14 A1
Rufford Twr 🖪
W3 .... 28 A1
Rufus Bsns Ctr
SW18 .... 71 A2
Rufus Ho SE1 ...... 139 A2
Rufus St N1 .. 24 A2 98 A3
Rugby Mans W14 .. 140 A4
Rugby Rd W4 .... 38 A4
Rugby St WC1 ...... 94 C1
Rugg St E14 .... 33 C2

Rugless Ho 🖪 E14 .42 B4
Rugmere 🖪 NW1 .. 12 C1
Rumball Ho 🔟
SE5 .... 49 A3
Rumbold Rd SW6 156 B1
Rum Cl E1 .... 32 B2
Rumford Ho SE1 .. 136 C1
Rumsey Rd SW9 .... 62 B4
Runacres Ct SE17 150 C1
Runcorn Pl
W11 .... 31 A2 112 A4
Rundell Twr SW8 .. 172 C4
Running Horse Yd 🔟
TW8 .... 44 A4
Runnymede Ct
SW15 .... 68 C3
Runnymede Ho
Hackney E9 .... 18 A4
Richmond TW10 .... 54 C2
Rupack St 🖪 SE16 . 40 B4
Rupert Ct W1 ...... 119 B4
Rupert Gdns SW9 .. 48 A1
Rupert Ho SE11 .. 149 C3
🖸 Upper Holloway
N19 .... 4 C1
Rupert Rd
Bedford Pk W4 ...... 38 A3
Paddington NW6 .... 23 B3
Upper Holloway N19 .. 4 C2
Rupert St W1 ...... 119 B4
Rusbridge Cl E8 .. 16 C3
Ruscoe Rd E16 ...... 35 B3
Rushbrook Ho 🔟
SW8 .... 171 B2
Rushby Ct SW4 .... 172 A3
Rush Common Mews
🔟 SW2 .... 74 B4
Rushcroft Rd SW2,
SW9 .... 62 C3
Rushcutters Ct 🔟
SE16 .... 41 A2
Rushey Mead SE4 .. 66 C2
Rushford Rd SE4 .. 66 B1
Rush Hill Mews 🖪
SW11 .... 60 C4
Rush Hill Rd
SW11 .... 60 C4
Rushlake Ho
SW11 .... 169 B2
Rushmead 🖪 E2 .. 25 A2
Rushmere Ho 🖸
SW15 .... 68 C3
Rushmore Cres 🖸
E5 .... 17 C4
Rushmore Ho
🖸 Kentish Town
N7 .... 13 C3
W14 .... 126 B1
Rushmore Prim Sch
E5 .... 17 C4
Rushmore Rd
Clapton Pk E5 .... 17 C4
Hackney E5 .... 18 A4
Rusholme Rd
SW15 .... 58 A1
Rushton Ho SW8 171 B1
Rushton St N1 .... 87 C2
Rushworth St
SE1 .... 136 B3
Ruskin Ave TW9 .. 44 C3
Ruskin Ct SE5 ...... 63 C4
Ruskin Ho SW1 .. 147 C3
Ruskin Park Ho
SE5 .... 63 C4
Ruskin Wlk SE24 .. 63 B2
Rusper Ct SW9 .. 172 B1

Russell Cl W4 .... 46 B4
Russell Ct
Battersea SW11 .. 169 C3
Bloomsbury WC1 .... 94 A1
🖪 Peckham SE15 .. 50 A1
St James SW1 ...... 119 A1
Russell Gdns
W14 .... 126 A2
Russell Gdns Mews
W14 .... 126 A2
Russell Gr SW9 .. 173 C4
Russell Ho
🖪 Poplar E14 .... 33 C3
🖸 SW1 .... 146 C2
Russell Kerr Cl
W4 .... 45 B3
Russell Lo SE1 .. 137 B2
Russell Mans
WC1 .... 106 B4
Russell Pickering Ho
🖸 SW4 .... 62 A4
Russell Pl
Hampstead NW3 .... 12 A3
Rotherhithe SE16 .. 41 A3
Russell Rd W14 .. 126 B1
Russell Sq WC1 .... 94 A1
Russell Square Ho
WC1 .... 94 A1
Russell Square Sta
WC1 .... 94 A1
Russell St WC2 .. 120 B4
Russell's Wharf 🖪
W9 .... 23 B1
Russell Wlk 🖪
TW10 .... 54 B1
Russet Cres N7 ...... 14 B3
Russett Way SE13 .. 52 A1
Russia Dock Rd
SE16 .... 33 A1
Russia La E2 .... 25 B3
Russia Row EC2 .. 109 A1
Rusthall Ave W4 .... 37 C3
Rusthall Mans 🖪
W4 .... 37 C2
Ruston Mews
W11 .... 31 A3
Ruston St E3 .... 26 B4
Rust Sq SE5 .... 48 C3
Ruth Ct 🔟 E3 .... 26 A3
Ruth Ho W10 .... 23 A1
Ruthin Rd SE3 ...... 53 C4
Ruthven St E9 .... 25 C4
Rutland Cl SW14 .. 55 B4
Rutland Ct
Herne Hill SE5 ...... 63 C3
🖪 SW7 .... 130 B3
Rutland Gate
🖪 SW7 .... 130 B3
Rutland Gate Mews
SW7 .... 130 A3
Rutland Gdns
Barnes SW13 .... 46 C3
Knightsbr SW7 .. 130 B3
🖪 N4 .... 6 B4
Rutland Gdns Mews
SW7 .... 130 B3
Rutland Gr 🖸 W6 .. 39 A1
Rutland Ho
🔟 Putney SW15 ... 69 B4
W8 .... 128 A1
Rutland Mews E
SW7 .... 130 B2

Rutland Mews S
SW7 .... 130 A2
Rutland Mews W
SW7 .... 130 A2
Rutland Park Gdns 🖪
NW2 .... 9 B2
Rutland Park Mans 🖪
NW2 .... 9 B2
Rutland Pk NW2 .... 9 B2
Rutland Pl EC1 .... 108 B4
Rutland Rd E9 ...... 25 C4
Rutland St SW7 .. 130 B2
Rutland Studios
NW10 .... 21 C2
Rutley Cl SE11 ...... 48 A4
Rutt's Terr SE14 .... 50 C2
Ruvigny Gdns
SW15 .... 57 C4
Ruvigny Mans
SW15 .... 57 C4
Rycott Path SE22 .. 76 C4
Rycutf Sq SE3 ...... 53 B1
Rydal Ho 🖪 SW8 . 171 B1
Rydal Water NW1 .. 92 C3
Ryde Ho 🔟 NW6 .. 23 C4
Ryde Ct SW1 ...... 119 A2
Ryder Dr SE16 ...... 40 A1
Ryder Ho 🔟 E1 .... 25 B1
Ryder St SW1 .... 119 A2
Ryder's Terr NW8 .. 78 C2
Ryder Yd SW1 .... 119 A2
Ryde Vale Rd
SW12 .... 73 B2
Rydon St N1 .... 87 A4
Rydston Cl 🖸 N7 .. 14 B1
Ryecotes Mead
SE21 .... 76 A3
Ryecroft Rd SE13 .. 67 B2
Ryecroft St SW6 .. 166 A3
Ryedale SE22 ...... 65 A1
Ryefield Path 🖪
SW15 .... 68 C3
Ryegates 🖪 SE15 .. 50 A1
Rye Hill Pk SE15 .. 65 B3
Rye Ho 🔟 SE16 .... 40 B4
Rye La SE15 .... 49 C1
Rye Lane Mkt
SE15 .... 49 C1
Rye Oak Sch SE15 .. 65 A4
Rye Rd SE15 .... 65 C3
Rye Wlk SW15 ...... 57 C2
Ryfold Rd SW19 .... 70 C1
Ryland Rd NW5 .... 13 A2
Rylett Cres W12 .... 38 B3
Rylett Rd W12 .... 38 B3
Rylston Rd SW6 .. 154 C3
Rymer St SE24 ...... 63 A1
Rysbrack St SW1 130 C2

S

Saatchi Gallery Duke
of York's HQ ★
SW3 .... 145 A2
Sabbarton St 🖸
E16 .... 35 B3
Sabella Ct E3 .... 26 B3
Sabine Rd SW11 .... 60 C4
Sable St N1 .... 15 A1
Sacketts Ho SW9 173 C4
Sackville Ho 🔟
SW16 .... 74 A1
Sackville St W1 .. 119 A3
Sacred Heart High
Sch W6 .... 39 B2

Sacred Heart Jun Sch
W6 .... 39 C2
Sacred Heart Prim
Sch, Battersea
SW11 .... 168 A3
Sacred Heart RC
Prim Sch
Islington N7 .... 14 B3
Putney SW15 .... 56 C2
Sacred Heart RC Sec
Sch SE5 .... 48 B2
Saddlers Mews
SW8 .... 172 B4
Sadler Ho
🖸 Bromley E3 ...... 27 A2
EC1 .... 96 A4
Saffron Ave E14 .... 34 C2
Saffron Ct 🔟 N1 .. 15 C2
Saffron Hill EC1 .. 107 C4
Saffron Ho 🖸
SW1 .... 45 A2
Saffron St EC1 .... 107 C4
Saffron Wharf
SE1 .... 139 A4
Sage Mews SE22 .. 64 B2
Sage St E1 .... 32 B2
Sage Way WC1 .... 94 C3
Sailacre Ho 🔟
SE10 .... 43 B1
Sail Ct 🔟 E14 ...... 34 C2
Sailmakers Ct
SW6 .... 59 B4
Sail St SE11 .... 149 A4
Sainfoin Rd SW17 .. 72 C2
St Agnes Cl E9 ...... 25 B4
St Agnes Pl SE11 .. 48 A4
St Agnes RC Prim Sch
E3 .... 27 A2
St Agnes Sch
NW2 .... 1 A1
St Aidan's Prim Sch
N4 .... 5 C4
St Aidan's Rd
SE22 .... 65 A2
St Albans CE Prim
Sch EC1 .... 107 B4
St Alban's Gr W11 .. 1 C3
St Alban's Gr W8 .. 128 B2
St Alban's La NW11 .. 1 C3
St Albans Mans
W8 .... 128 B2
St Alban's Pl N1 .. 86 A3
St Alban's Rd
Dagenham NW10 .. 21 A4
Dartmouth Pk NW5 .. 4 A1
St Alban's St SW1 119 B3
St Albans Terr
W6 .... 154 A4
St Alban's Villas
NW5 .... 3 C1
St Alfege Pas
SE10 .... 52 B4
St Alfege with St
Peter's CE Prim Sch
SE10 .... 52 B4
St Aloysius RC Coll
N19 .... 4 B3
St Aloysius RC Inf Sch
NW1 .... 93 B4
St Aloysius RC Jun
Sch NW1 .... 83 B1
St Alphage Gdn
EC2 .... 109 A3

St Alphage Highwalk EC2.....109 A3
St Alphonsus Rd SW4.....61 C3
St Andrew & St Francis CE Prim Sch NW2.....8 C2
St Andrew's (Barnsbury) CE Prim Sch N1.....85 A4
St Andrew's CE Prim Sch SW9.....172 B1
St Andrews Chambers W1.....105 A2
St Andrews Cl 25 SE16.....40 A1
St Andrews Ct 44.....45 B2
St Andrew's Ct 2 SW18.....71 B2
St Andrew's Gr N16.....6 C2
St Andrew's Greek Sch NW1.....13 B2
St Andrew's Hill EC4.....108 B1
St Andrews Ho 11 SE16.....40 A3
St Andrew's Hospl E3.....27 A1
St Andrews Mans W1.....103 B3
St Andrews Mews Greenwich SE3.....53 C3
4 Streatham SW12.....73 C3
St Andrew's Mews N16.....7 A3
St Andrew's Pl NW1.....92 B2
St Andrew's Rd Dagenham W3.....29 A3
W14.....154 B4
Willesden NW2.....9 A2
St Andrew's Sq W11.....31 A3
St Andrew St EC4.....107 C3
St Andrews Way E3.....27 A1
St Andrew's Wharf SE1.....139 A4
St Anne RC Prim Sch E1.....24 C1 99 B1
St Anne's CE Prim Sch SW18.....59 A2
St Anne's Cl N6.....3 C1
St Anne's Ct Kensal Rise NW6.....23 A4
W1.....105 B1
St Anne's Flats NW1.....93 B4
St Anne's Pas E14.....33 B3
St Anne's RC Prim Sch SE11.....162 C4
St Anne's Row E14.....33 B3
St Anne St E14.....33 B3
St Anne's Trad Est 25 E14.....33 B3
St Ann's Cres SW18.....59 B1
St Ann's Gdns NW5.....12 C2
St Ann's Hill SW18.....59 B1
St Ann's Ho WC1.....95 B3
St Ann's La SW1.....133 C1

St Ann's Park Rd SW18.....59 B1
St Anns Rd SW13.....46 B2
St Ann's Rd W11.....30 C2
St Ann's St SW1.....133 C2
St Ann's Terr NW8.....79 C2
St Ann's Villas W11.....31 A1 112 A1
St Anselm's Pl W1.....118 A4
St Anselm's RC Prim Sch SW17.....72 C1
St Anthonys Cl SW17.....72 A2
St Anthony's Cl E1.....125 B2
St Anthony's Ct 2 Balham SW12.....60 C1
Upper Tooting SW17.....72 C2
St Anthony's Flats NW1.....83 B1
St Anthony's RC Prim Sch SE22.....64 C1
St Asaph Ct SE4.....65 C4
St Asaph Rd SE4.....65 C4
St Aubins Ct N1.....87 C4
St Augustine's CE High Sch NW6.....23 C3
St Augustine's CE Prim Sch NW6.....78 A2
St Augustine's Ho NW1.....93 B4
St Augustine's RC Prim Sch W6.....154 B3
St Augustine's Rd NW1.....13 C1
St Austell Rd SE13.....52 C1
St Barnabas Cl 11 SE22.....64 A2
St Barnabas & St Philip's CE Prim Sch W8.....127 B1
St Barnabas St SW1.....145 C2
St Barnabas Terr E9.....17 C3
St Barnabas Villas SW8.....172 B1
St Bartholomew's Hospl EC1.....108 B3
St Bede's RC Inf Sch SW12.....73 C3
St Benets Cl SW17.....72 C2
St Benet's Pl EC3.....123 C4
St Bernadette RC Jun Sch SW12.....73 B4
St Bernard Ho 6 E14.....42 B3
St Botolph St E1, EC3.....110 C2
St Brelades Ct N1.....87 C4
St Bride's Ave EC4.....108 A1
St Bride's Pas EC4.....108 A1
St Bride St EC4.....108 A2
St Catherines Cl SW17.....72 A2
St Catherine's Ct 8 W4.....38 A3
St Catherine's Dr SE14.....50 C1
St Catherines Mews SW3.....144 C4

St Cecilia's CE Sch SW18.....70 B3
St Chad's Pl WC1.....94 C4
St Chad's St WC1.....94 B4
St Charles' Hospl W10.....30 C4
St Charles RC Prim Sch W10.....30 C4
St Charles RC Sixth Form Coll W10.....30 C4
St Charles Sq W10.....30 C4
St Christina's Sch NW8.....80 B3
St Christophers Ct 18 N19.....4 C1
St Christopher's Ho NW1.....83 B1
St Christopher's Pl W1.....103 C2
St Christopher's Sch NW3.....11 C3
St Clair Ho 17 E3.....26 B2
St Clare St EC3.....110 C1
St Clement Danes CE Prim Sch WC2.....106 C1
St Clement & St James CE Prim Sch W11.....31 A1 112 A2
St Clement's Ct Barnsbury N7.....14 B2
7 SE14.....50 C4
8 Shepherd's Bush W11.....30 C2
St Clement's Ct EC3.....123 C4
St Clements Ho E1.....110 C3
St Clement's La WC2.....107 A1
St Clements Mans SW6.....47 C4
St Clements St N7.....14 C1
St Columb's Ho 10 W10.....31 A4
St Crispins Cl NW3.....12 A4
St Cross St EC1.....107 C4
St Cuthbert's Rd NW2.....10 B2
St Cuthbert with St Matthias Prim Sch SW5.....142 A2
St Davids Cl 27 SE16.....40 A1
St David's Sq E14.....42 A1
St Dionis Sch NW6.....165 A2
St Dominic RC Prim Sch NW5.....12 B3
St Dominics RC Prim Sch E9.....18 A2
St Donatt's Rd SE14.....51 B2
St Dunstan's Alley EC3.....124 A3
St Dunstan's Ave W3.....28 C2
St Dunstan's Ct EC4.....107 C1
St Dunstan's Gdns W3.....28 C2
St Dunstan's Hill EC3.....124 A3
St Dunstan's La EC3.....124 A3

St Dunstan's Rd W6.....39 C1
St Edmund RC Sch E14.....41 C2
St Edmund's Cl SW17.....72 A2
St Edmund's Cl NW8.....80 C3
St Edmund's Ct NW8.....80 C3
St Edmund's Sq SW13.....47 B4
St Edmund's Terr NW8.....80 C3
St Edward's RC Prim Sch NW1.....90 B1
St Elizabeth RC Prim Sch E2.....25 B3
St Elizabeth's RC Prim Sch TW10.....54 B1
St Elmo Rd W12.....38 B4
St Elmos Rd SE16.....41 A4
St Ermin's Hill SW1.....133 B2
St Ervan's Rd W10.....31 B4
St Eugene de Mazenod RC Prim Sch NW6.....10 C1
St Faith's CE Prim Sch SW18.....59 B2
St Faith's Rd SE24.....75 A3
St Francesca Cabrini Prim Sch SE23.....65 B1
St Francis' Ho NW1.....83 B1
St Francis of Assisi RC Prim Sch W11.....30 C2
St Francis Pl SW12.....61 A1
St Francis Rd SE22.....64 A3
St Francis Xavier Sixth Form Coll SW12.....61 A1
St Fridewides Mews 5 E14.....34 B3
St Gabriel's CE Prim Sch SW1.....146 C1
St Gabriels Cl 2 E14.....34 A4
St Gabriel's Rd NW2.....9 C3
St Gabriel Ho SW11.....169 C3
ST GEORGE IN THE EAST.....32 A2
St George's Ave N7.....13 C4
St George's Battersea CE Prim Sch SW8.....161 A1
St George's Bldgs SE11.....95 C2
St George's Cath NW1.....92 B4
St George's Cath RC Jun & Inf Sch SE1.....136 A2
St George's CE Prim Sch SE5.....49 A3
St George's Circ SE1.....136 A2
St Georges Cl SW8.....171 A4

St Georges Coll N7.....5 C1
St George's Ct SW15.....58 B3
St George's Ct Brompton SW3.....144 A4
Kensington SW7.....128 C1
Newington SE1.....136 A1
St George's Dr SW1.....146 C2
St George's Field W2.....102 B3
St George's Gr SW17.....71 C1
St Georges Hanover Sq Sch W1.....117 C3
St George's Ho NW1.....83 A1
St George's La EC3.....124 A4
St Georges Mews 11 NW1.....12 B1
St George's Mews 8 Rotherhithe SE8.....41 B2
SE1.....135 B3
St Georges Pl N7.....13 C4
St George's RC Cath SE1.....135 C2
St George's RC Sec Sch W9.....78 B1
St Georges Rd W4.....37 C4
St George's Rd Newington SE1.....136 A1
Richmond TW9.....54 B4
St George's Residences 4 SW2.....62 C2
St George's Rd EC4.....108 A2
St George's Sq E14.....33 A2
St George's Sq 1 SE8.....41 B2
SW1.....147 B1
St George's Square Mews SW1.....147 B1
St George St W1.....118 B4
St Georges Terr Hampstead NW1.....12 B1
NW1.....81 A4
St George's Way SE15.....49 A4
St George the Martyr CE Prim Sch WC1.....95 A1
St George Wharf SW8.....162 A4
St Gerards Cl SW4.....61 B2
St German's Pl SE3.....53 C2
St Gilda's RC Jun Sch N8.....5 A4
ST GILES.....106 A2
St Giles Cir WC1.....105 C2
St Giles Cl WC1.....106 A4
St Giles Ct WC2.....106 A2
St Giles High St WC2.....105 C2
St Giles Ho SW16.....71 A4
St Giles Hospl SE5.....49 A2
St Giles Pas WC2.....105 C1
St Giles Rd SE5.....49 A2
St Giles Twr 3 SE5.....49 A2
St Giles Ho 18 E2.....25 C3

St Helena Ho WC1. **95** B3
St Helena Rd SE16. **40** C2
St Helena St WC1 . **95** B3
St Helen's Gdns
  W10 . . . . **30** C3
St Helen's Pl EC3 **110** A2
St Helen's RC Sch
  SW9 . . . . **62** C4
St Helier Ct 4 N1 . **24** A4
St Hildas Cl SW17 . **72** A2
St Hilda's Cl NW6 . . **9** C1
St Hilda's Rd
  SW13 . . . . **47** A4
St Hildas Wharf
  E1 . . . . **32** B1
St Hubert's Ho 2
  E14 . . . . **41** C3
St Hughes Cl
  SW17 . . . . **72** A2
St Ives Ct NW2 . . . **10** A2
ST JAMES **119** B2
St James Ct
  Bethnal Green
  E2 . . . . **24** C2 **99** C3
  10 Brentford W4 . . **36** C1
St James's Ct
  Bedford Pk W4 . . . **37** C3
  SW1 . . . . **133** A2
St James Ho N5 . . . **14** C3
St James Independent
  Schs W14 . . . . . . **39** A3
St James Ind Mews
  SE1 . . . . **153** C1
St James's Mans
  NW6 . . . . **10** C1
St James Mews
  E14 . . . . **42** B3
St James's SE14. . **51** A2
St James's App
  EC2 . . . . . . **24** A1 **98** A1
St James's Ave 2 . **25** B3
St James School Flats
  6 N7 . . . . **14** C3
St James's Cl NW8 **80** C3
  Upper Tooting
  SW17 . . . . **72** B2
St James's Cloisters
  2 SE22 . . . . **64** B3
St James's Cres
  SW9 . . . . **62** C4
St James's Dr
  Balham SW12,
  SW17 . . . . **72** B4
  Upper Tooting
  SW17 . . . . **72** B3
St James's Gdns
  W11 . . . . . . **31** A1 **112** A2
St James's Gr
  SW11 . . . . **169** A2
St James's Hatcham
  CE Prim Sch
  SE14 . . . . **51** A2
St James's Market
  SW1 . . . . **119** B3
St James's Pal* . . . **119** A1
St James's Park Sta
  SW1 . . . . **133** B2
St James's Pas
  EC3 . . . . **110** B1
St James's Pk*
  SW1 . . . . **133** B4
St James's Sq
  SW1 . . . . **119** B2

St James's Rd
  Bermondsey SE1,
  SE16 . . . . **153** C4
  Peckham SE1 . . . . **49** C4
St James's & St
  Michael's CE Prim
  Sch W2 . . . . **115** A4
St James's Sq
  SW1 . . . . **119** A2
St James's St
  SW1 . . . . **118** C2
St James St W6 . . . **39** B1
St James's Terr
  NW8 . . . . **80** C4
  2 Upper Tooting
  SW12 . . . . **72** C3
St James's Terrace
  Mews 4 NW8 . . . . **80** C3
St James The Great
  RC Prim Sch
  SE15 . . . . **49** B2
St Joan of Arc RC
  Prim Sch N5 . . . . **15** B4
St John Evangelist RC
  Prim Sch N1 . . . . **86** A2
St John of Jerusalem
  CE Prim Sch E9 . . **17** B1
ST JOHN'S **51** C1
St John & St James
  CE Prim Sch E9 . . **17** B3
St John's Angell Town
  CE Prim Sch
  SW9 . . . . **173** B1
St John's Ave
  Dagenham NW10 . . **21** B4
  Putney SW15 . . . . **57** C2
St John's CE Prim
  Sch
  Fulham SW6 . . . . **164** B4
  SE17 . . . . **151** A3
  South Hackney E2 . **25** B3
St John's Church Rd
  E9 . . . . **17** B3
St John's Cl SW6 . **155** B2
St Johns Concert
  Hall* SW1 . . . . . . **134** A1
St John's Cres
  SW9 . . . . **62** C4
St Johns Ct 39 E1 . **32** A1
St John's Ct
  Finsbury Pk N4 . . . . **6** A2
  Hammersmith W6 . . **39** A2
  Lewisham SE13 . . . **52** B1
  5 South Hampstead
  NW3 . . . . **11** B2
Saint John's Ct
  N5 . . . . **15** A3
St John's Dr SW18 . **71** A3
St John's Est SE1 . **138** C3
St John's Gdns
  W11 . . . . . . **31** B2 **112** C3
St John's Gr
  2 Barnes SW13 . . **46** B1
  1 Richmond TW9 . **54** A3
  Upper Holloway N19 . . **4** B2
St John's Highbury
  Vale CE Prim Sch
  N5 . . . . **6** A1
St John's Hill
  SW11 . . . . **59** C3
St John's Hill Gr
  SW11 . . . . **59** C3
St Johns Ho 5
  SE17 . . . . **48** C4

St John's Ho 1
  E14 . . . . **42** B2
St John's La EC1 . **108** B4
St John's Lodge 3
  SE8 . . . . **51** C2
St John's Mans E5 . **17** B3
St John's Park Mans
  N19 . . . . **4** B1
St John's Path N1 . **96** A1
St John's Pk SE3 . . **53** C3
St John's Pl EC1 . . **96** A1
St John's RC Prim Sch
  SE16 . . . . **41** A4
St John's Rd
  Battersea SW11 . . **60** A3
  Canning Town E16 . **35** C3
  Richmond TW9 . . . **54** A3
St John's & St
  Clements CE Prim
  Sch SE15 . . . . **64** C4
St John's Sq EC1 . . **96** A1
St Johns Sta SE8 . . **51** C1
St John's St EC1 . . **96** A2
St John's Terr
  W10 . . . . **22** C1
St John's Upper
  Holloway CE Prim
  Sch N19 . . . . **4** C2
St John's Vale
  SE8 . . . . **51** C1
St John's Villas
  Upper Holloway N19 . . **4** C2
  W8 . . . . **128** B1
St John's Way N19 . **4** C3
ST JOHN'S WOOD
  . . . . **79** B1
St John's Wood Ct
  NW8 . . . . **89** C3
St John's Wood High
  St NW8 . . . . **80** A1
St John's Wood Park
  NW8 . . . . **79** B4
St John's Wood Pre-
  Prep Sch NW8 . . . **90** A4
St John's Wood Rd
  NW8 . . . . **89** C3
St John's Wood Sta
  NW8 . . . . **79** B2
St John's Wood Terr
  NW8 . . . . **80** A2
St John the Baptist
  CE Prim Sch N1 . . **87** C1
St John the Divine CE
  Jun & Inf Sch
  SE5 . . . . **48** A3
St Joseph's Cl
  W10 . . . . **31** A4
St Josephs Ct 3
  NW10 . . . . **21** B3
St Joseph's Flats
  NW1 . . . . **93** B4
St Joseph's Ho
  W6 . . . . **39** C2
St Joseph's Hospice
  E9, E8 . . . . **25** A4
St Joseph's RC Inf &
  Jun Schs SE5 . . . **48** B3
St Joseph's RC Prim
  Sch
  Chelsea SW3 . . . . **144** C3
  Deptford SE8 . . . . **51** C3
  Greenwich SE10 . . **43** A1
  Paddington W9 . . . **88** C3
  Rotherhithe SE16 . **40** B3
  St Giles WC2 . . . . **106** B2
  Upper Holloway N19 . **4** A3
  Wandsworth SW18 . **58** C2

St Joseph's RC Prim
  Sch continued
  Willesden NW10 . . . **8** A1
St Joseph's Sr
  SW8 . . . . **170** B4
St Joseph's Vale
  SE3 . . . . **67** C4
St Jude & St Paul's CE
  Prim Sch N1 . . . . **16** A2
St Jude's CE Prim Sch
  SE24 . . . . **63** A2
St Judes Ho 6
  W10 . . . . **23** B2
St Jude's Prim Sch
  SE1 . . . . **136** A1
St Jude's Rd E2 . . . **25** A3
St Jude St N16 . . . **16** A3
St Julian's Rd
  NW6 . . . . **23** C4
St Katharine's Ho
  N1 . . . . **85** B2
St Katharine's Prec
  NW1 . . . . **82** A2
St Katharine's Way
  E1 . . . . **125** A2
St Katherine's Row
  EC3 . . . . **110** B1
St Katherine's Wlk 1
  W11 . . . . **30** C1
St Kilda's Rd N16 . . **7** A3
St Laurence's
  CE Prim Sch
  NW6 . . . . **22** C4
St Lawrence Ct N1 **87** C4
St Lawrence Ho
  SE1 . . . . **138** B2
St Lawrence St
  E14 . . . . **34** B1
St Lawrence Terr
  W10 . . . . **31** A4
St Lawrence Way
  SW9 . . . . **173** C2
St Leonards
  SW14 . . . . **55** B4
St Leonard's Ct N1 **97** C4
St Leonard's Hospl
  N1 . . . . **24** A3
St Leonards Rd
  SW14 . . . . **55** B4
St Leonard's Rd
  Becontree NW10 . . **20** C1
  South Bromley E14 . **34** B4
St Leonard's Sq
  NW5 . . . . **12** C2
St Leonard's St E3 **27** A2
St Leonard's Terr
  SW3 . . . . **145** A1
St Loo Ave SW3 . . **158** B4
St Loo Ct SW3 . . . **158** C4
St Luke Prim Sch
  E16 . . . . **35** B3
ST LUKE'S **97** A2
St Luke's Ave SW4 . **61** C3
St Luke's CE Prim
  Sch
  Cubitt Town E14 . . . **42** C2
  Paddington W9 . . . **23** B2
  Shoreditch EC1 . . . **97** A3
St Luke's Cl EC1 . . **97** A2
St Luke's Ct 11 W11 . **31** B3
St Luke's Hospl
  W1 . . . . **92** C1
St Luke's Mews
  W11 . . . . **31** B3
St Luke's Rd W11 . **31** B4
St Luke's Sq E16 . . **35** B3
St Luke's St SW3 . **144** B2

St Margaret's Cres
  SW15 . . . . **57** A2
St Margaret's Ct
  Putney SW15 . . . . **57** A3
  SE1 . . . . **123** B1
St Margaret's La
  W8 . . . . **128** A1
St Margarets Rd
  W3 . . . . **37** A4
St Margaret's Rd
  Brockley SE4 . . . . **66** B3
  Kensal Green NW10 . **22** B2
St Margaret's Sch
  NW3 . . . . **11** A4
St Margaret St
  SW1 . . . . **134** A3
St Mark's CE Prim Sch
  SE11 . . . . **163** A4
St Marks Cl 5
  SE10 . . . . **52** B3
St Mark's Cres
  NW1 . . . . **81** C4
St Marks Gate 6 . . **18** B1
St Mark's Gr
  SW10 . . . . **156** B2
St Marks Ho 6
  SE17 . . . . **48** C4
St Mark's Hospl
  EC1 . . . . **96** B4
St Mark's Mans 14
  N4 . . . . **5** B2
St Mark's Pl W11 . . **31** A3
St Mark's Prim Sch
  N19 . . . . **5** A2
St Marks Rd 15
  NW10 . . . . **30** C3
North Kensington
  W10 . . . . **30** C4
  Notting Hill W11 . . . **31** A3
St Mark's Rise E8 . . **16** B3
St Mark St E1 . . . . **111** A1
St Martin-in-the-
  Fields High Sch for
  Girls SW2 . . . . . . **74** C3
St Martin's
  Almshouses NW1 . **82** C4
St Martin's Cl NW1 **82** C4
St Martins Ct N1 . . **24** A4
St Martin's Ct
  WC2 . . . . **120** A4
  West Norwood
  SE27 . . . . **75** A2
St Martin's La
  WC2 . . . . **120** A3
St Martin's Le Grand
  EC1 . . . . **108** C2
St Martin's Rd
  SW9 . . . . **172** C2
St Martin's St
  WC2 . . . . **119** C3
St Martin's Way
  SW17 . . . . **71** B1
St Mary Abbots CE
  Prim Sch W8 . . . . **128** A3
St Mary Abbot's Pl
  W8 . . . . **127** A1
St Mary Abbots Terr
  W14 . . . . **127** A1
St Mary at Hill
  EC3 . . . . **124** A3
St Mary Axe EC3 . **110** B2

St Marychurch St
SE16 . . . . 40 B4
St Mary Graces Ct
E1 . . . . 125 A3
St Marylebone CE Sch
The W1 . . . . 103 C4
St Mary le Bow
Church* EC2 . . . . 109 A1
St Mary- le-Park Ct
SW11 . . . . 158 B1
St Mary Magdalene
CE Prim Sch
Islington N7 . . . . 14 C2
Paddington W2 . . . 100 A4
Peckham SE15 . . . . . . 50 A1
St Mary Magdalen's
RC Prim Sch
Brockley SE4 . . . . . . 66 A3
Mortlake SW14 . . . . . 55 C4
St Mary Magdalen's
RC Jun Sch NW2 . . . 9 A2
St Mary Newington Cl
SE17 . . . . 152 B2
St Mary of the Angels
RC Prim Sch W2 . . 31 C3
St Mary RC Prim Sch
W10 . . . . 23 A1
St Mary & St Michael
Prim Sch E1 . . . . . . 32 B3
St Mary & St Pancras
CE Prim Sch
NW1 . . . . 83 B1
St Mary's Bryanston
Square CE Sch
W1 . . . . 102 C4
St Mary's CE Prim
Sch
Islington N1 . . . . 86 B4
Putney SW15 . . . . . . 57 C4
Willesden NW10 . . . . 8 A2
St Mary's CE Sch
NW10 . . . . 8 B3
St Mary's Est **2**
SE16 . . . . 40 B4
St Mary's Flats
NW1 . . . . 93 B4
St Mary's Gate
W8 . . . . 128 A1
St Mary's Gdns
SE11 . . . . 149 C4
St Mary's Gr
Barnes SW13 . . . . . . 57 A4
Chiswick W4 . . . . 45 A4
Islington N1 . . . . 15 A2
Richmond TW10,
TW9 . . . . 54 B3
St Mary's Ho N1 . . . 86 B4
St Mary's Hospl
W2 . . . . 101 C2
St Mary's Hospl
Medical Sch W2 101 C2
St Mary's Kilburn CE
Prim Sch NW6 . . . 23 C4
St Mary's Lewisham
CE Prim Sch
SE13 . . . . 67 A2
St Mary's Mans
Dagenham NW10 . . . 21 A4
Paddington W2 . . . 101 B4
St Mary's Mews
NW6 . . . . 11 C1
St Mary's Path N1 . 86 B4
St Mary's Pl W8 . . 128 A1
St Mary's RC Prim
Sch
Chiswick W4 . . . . 46 A4

St Mary's RC Prim Sch
continued
Clapham Pk SW4 . . . . 61 B2
Clapham SW8 . . . . . 170 B4
Hammersmith W14 . . 39 C3
Paddington NW6 . . . 23 C3
St Mary's Rd
Dagenham NW10 . . . 21 A4
Golders Green NW11 . 1 A4
Nunhead SE15 . . . . . 50 B1
St Mary's Sch
Hampstead NW3 . . 11 C3
St Mary's Sq W2 . 101 B4
St Mary's Stoke
Newington CE Prim
Sch N16 . . . . 7 A2
St Mary's Terr
W2 . . . . 101 B4
St Mary's Twr EC1 . 97 A1
St Mary's Wlk
SE11 . . . . 149 C4
St Matthews Ct
SE1 . . . . 136 C1
St Matthew's Ho **1**
SE17 . . . . 48 C4
St Matthew's Lo
NW1 . . . . 83 A2
St Matthew's Rd
SW2 . . . . 62 B2
St Matthew's Row
E2 . . . . 24 C1 99 B2
St Matthew's Sch
Westminster
SW1 . . . . 133 C2
St Matthew St
SW1 . . . . 133 B1
St Matthias CE Prim
Sch E2 . . . . . 24 B1 99 A2
St Matthias's CE Prim
Sch N16 . . . . 16 A4
St Mauritius Ho
SE13 . . . . 67 B2
St Maur Rd SW6 . . 165 A3
St Michael's Alley
EC3 . . . . 109 C1
St Michael's CE Prim
Sch
Camden Town
NW1 . . . . 82 C4
Highgate N6 . . . . 3 C4
Wandsworth SW18 . . 70 B4
St Michaels Ct **2**
E14 . . . . 34 B4
St Michael's Ct
NW1 . . . . 1 B4
St Michael's Flats
NW1 . . . . 83 B1
St Michael's Gdns
W10 . . . . 31 A4
St Michael's Rd
Cricklewood NW2 . . . 9 B4
Stockwell SW9 . . . 172 C2
St Michael's St
W2 . . . . 102 A2
St Michael Steiner
Sch The SW18 . . . . 58 C2
St Mildred's Ct
EC2 . . . . 109 B1
St Monica's RC Prim
Sch N1 . . . . 24 A2 98 A4
St Nicholas' Flats
NW1 . . . . 83 B1
St Nicholas Ho
SE8 . . . . 51 C4
St Nicholas Mans
SW17 . . . . 72 B2

St Nicholas St
SE8 . . . . 51 C2
St Norbert Gn SE4 . . 66 A3
St Norbert Rd SE4 . . 66 A3
St Olaf's Rd SW6 . 154 B1
St Olaves Ct W2 . . 114 A3
St Olave's Ct EC2 . 109 B1
St Olave's Est SE1 138 B4
St Olave's Gdns
SE11 . . . . 149 B4
St Olave's Mans
SE11 . . . . 149 B4
St Olav's Sq **2**
SE16 . . . . 40 B4
St Osmund's RC Prim
Sch SW13 . . . . 46 B2
St Oswald's Pl
SE11 . . . . 148 C1
St Oswulf St SW1 . 147 C3
St Owen Ho SE1 . . 138 B2
ST PANCRAS 94 B4
St Pancras
Almshouses **13**
NW5 . . . . 12 B3
St Pancras
Commercial Ctr
NW1 . . . . 83 A4
St Pancras Hospl
NW1 . . . . 83 B3
St Pancras
International Sta
WC1 . . . . 94 A4
St Pancras Way
NW1 . . . . 83 B4
St Patrick's Coll
W1 . . . . 105 B2
St Patrick's RC Prim
Sch NW5 . . . . . 13 A3
St Paul's Ave
Rotherhithe SE16 . . . 32 C1
Willesden NW2 . . . . . 9 B2
St Paul's Cath* . . . . . .
EC4 . . . . 108 C1
St Paul's Cath Sch
EC4 . . . . 108 C1
St Paul's CE Prim
Sch
Hammersmith W6 . . 39 B1
Hampstead NW3 . . 12 B1
SE17 . . . . 150 C2
St Paul's Church Yd
EC4 . . . . 108 C1
St Pauls Cres
NW1 . . . . 13 C1
St Paul's Ct
Clapham SW4 . . . . . . 61 C3
6 Upper Holloway
N19 . . . . 5 A2
St Paul's Dr E15 . . . 19 C3
St Paul's Girls' Sch
W6 . . . . 39 C2
St Pauls Mews
NW1 . . . . 13 C1
St Paul's Pl N1 . . . . 15 C2
St Pauls Rd TW9 . . 54 B4
St Paul's Rd N1 . . . 15 B2
St Paul's Sch
SW13 . . . . 39 C1
St Paul's Sta EC2 . 108 C2
St Paul St N1 . . . . . 87 A3
St Paul's Terr
SE17 . . . . 48 A4
St Pauls View
WC1 . . . . 95 B3
St Paul's Way E3 . . 33 C4

St Paul's Way Com
Sch E3 . . . . 33 C4
St Paul's with St
Michael's Prim Sch
E8 . . . . 24 C4
St Paul with St Luke
CE Prim Sch E3 . . 33 B4
St Peter & St Paul RC
Prim Sch EC1 . . . . 96 B2
St Peter's Alley
EC3 . . . . 109 C1
St Peter's Ave **37**
E2 . . . . 24 C3
St Petersburgh Mews
W2 . . . . 114 A3
St Petersburgh Pl
W2 . . . . 114 A3
St Peter's CE Prim
Sch
Chiswick W6 . . . . 38 C1
Paddington W9 . . . . . 23 C1
SE17 . . . . 151 B1
St Peter's Church Ct
N1 . . . . 86 B3
St Peters CE SI SW17 . 72 A2
St Peter's Cl **2** Stepney E1 . . 25 B1
St Peters Ct
New Cross SE4 . . . . . 51 B1
2B Stepney E1 . . . . 25 B1
St Peter's Eaton
Square Prim Sch
SW1 . . . . 132 B1
St Peter's Gdns
SE27 . . . . 74 C1
St Peter's Gr W6 . . 38 C2
St Peters Ho WC1 . 94 B3
St Peter's Ho
4 SE17 . . . . 48 C4
Stamford Hill N16 . . . 7 A4
St Peter's London
Docks CE Prim Sch
E1 . . . . 32 B1
St Peter's Pl W9 . . 88 A1
St Peter's Rd W6 . . 38 C1
St Peter's Sq
Chiswick W6 . . . . 38 B1
Hackney E2 . . . . 24 C3
St Peter's St N1 . . . 86 B3
St Peter's Street
Mews N1 . . . . 86 B2
St Peter's Terr
SW6 . . . . 154 B1
St Peter's Villas **3**
W6 . . . . 38 C2
St Peter's Way N1 . 16 A1
St Peter's Wharf **8**
W6 . . . . 38 C1
St Philip Ho WC1 . . 95 B3
St Philip Sq SW8 . 170 A1
St Philip's Rd E8 . . 16 C2
St Philip's Sch
SW7 . . . . 143 A3
St Philip St SW8 . . 170 A1
St Philip's Way N1 87 A3
St Quentin Ho
SW18 . . . . 59 C1
St Quintin Ave
W10 . . . . 30 C4
St Quintin Gdns **21**
W10 . . . . 30 B4
St Regis Hts NW3 . . 2 A1
St Richard's Ho
NW1 . . . . 93 B4
St Rule St SW8 . . . 170 C1
St Saviours SW4 . . . 61 A3

St Saviour's CE Prim
Sch
Bow Comm E14 . . . . 34 A4
Camberwell SE24 . . . 63 B4
Paddington W9 . . . . . 88 B1
St Saviours Ho
SE1 . . . . 139 B3
St Saviour's RC Prim
Sch SE13 . . . . 67 B3
St Saviour's Rd
SW2 . . . . 62 B2
St Saviours & St
Olaves CE Sch
SE1 . . . . 137 C1
St Saviour's Wharf
SE1 . . . . 139 A4
St Scholastica's RC
Prim Sch E5 . . . . . 7 C1
St Silas Pl NW5 . . . 12 C2
St Simon's Ave
SW15 . . . . 57 B2
St Stephen's Ave
W12 . . . . 39 A4
St Stephen's CE Prim
Sch
Paddington W2 . . . . . 31 C4
Shepherd's Bush
W12 . . . . 39 B4
St Johns SE8 . . . . . 51 C1
SW8 . . . . 162 C2
St Stephen's Cl
Maitland Pk NW5 . . 12 B3
NW8 . . . . 80 B3
St Stephen's Cres
W2 . . . . 31 C3
St Stephen's Gdns
Notting Hill W2 . . . . . 31 C3
4 Putney SW15 . . 58 B4
St Stephen's Gr
SE13 . . . . 67 B4
St Stephens Ho **7**
SE17 . . . . 48 C4
St Stephen's Mews **2**
W2 . . . . 31 C4
St Stephen's Rd
E3 . . . . 26 B3
St Stephen's Row
EC4 . . . . 109 B1
St Stephen's Terr
SW8 . . . . 162 C1
St Stephen's Wlk
SW7 . . . . 142 C3
St Swithin's La
EC4 . . . . 123 B4
St Swithun's Rd
SE13 . . . . 67 C1
St Thomas' CE Prim
Sch W10 . . . . 23 A1
St Thomas Ct **4**
NW1 . . . . 13 B1
St Thomas Ho **2**
E1 . . . . 32 C3
St Thomas More
Language Coll
SW3 . . . . 144 C3
St Thomas of
Canterbury RC Prim
Sch SW6 . . . . 154 C2
St Thomas Rd E16 . . 35 C3
St Thomas' Rd W4 . . 45 B4
St Thomas's Gdns
NW5 . . . . 12 C2

St Thomas's Hospl
SE1 . . . . **134** C2
**St Thomas's Hospl
Medical Sch** SE1 **134** C1
St Thomas's Pl 20
E9 . . . . 17 B1
St Thomas's Rd
Dagenham NW10 . . 21 A4
Highbury N4, N5 . . . . 5 C1
St Thomas's Sq E9 . . 17 B1
St Thomas St SE1 **123** C1
St Thomas's Way
SW6 . . . . **155** A2
**St Thomas the
Apostle Coll The**
SE15 . . . . 50 B2
**St Ursula's Convent
Sch** SE10 . . . . 52 C3
St Vincent De Paul Ho
24 E1 . . . . 32 B4
**St Vincent De Paul RC
Prim Sch** SW1 . . **133** A2
St Vincent Ho
SE1 . . . . **138** C2
**St Vincent's RC Prim
Sch**
Acton W3 . . . . 28 A2
Marylebone W1 . . **103** C3
St Vincent St W1 . **103** C3
Salamanca Pl
SE1 . . . . **148** C3
Salamanca St SE1,
SE11 . . . . **148** C3
Salcombe Gdns
SW4 . . . . 61 A3
Salcombe Lo NW5 . .12 C4
Salcombe Rd 23
N16 . . . . 16 A3
Salcombe Villas 13
TW10 . . . . 54 A2
Salcot N4 . . . . 5 B2
Salcott Rd SW11 . . 60 B2
Salehurst Rd SE4 . . 66 B1
Salem Ho 13 E9 . . . .17 C2
Salem Rd W2 . . . . **114** B4
Sale Pl W2 . . . . **102** A2
Salesian Coll
SW11 . . . . **168** A3
Sale St E2 . . . . 24 C1 **99** C2
Salford Ho 5 E14 . .42 B2
Salford Rd SW12,
SW2 . . . . 73 C3
Salisbury Cl SE17 . **151** B4
Salisbury Ct
Bermondsey SE16 . . **139** C1
Chiswick W4 . . . . 38 A2
EC4 . . . . **108** A1
Hackney E9 . . . . .18 A3
Salisbury Ho
2 Islington N1 . . . . . .15 A2
Islington N1 . . . . 86 A4
8 Poplar E14 . . . . . . 34 A3
Westminster SW1 . . **147** C2
Wimbledon SW19 . . 69 C1
Salisbury Mews
SW6 . . . . **154** C1
Salisbury Pl
Camberwell SW9 . . . .48 A3
Marylebone W1 . . . **102** C4
Salisbury Rd TW9 . .54 A3
Salisbury Sq EC4 . **107** C1
Salisbury St
10 Acton W3 . . . . . . 37 B4
NW8 . . . . **90** A1

Salisbury Terr
SE15 . . . . 65 B4
Salisbury Wlk N19 . . 4 B2
Salmon La E14 . . . . 33 A3
Salmon St 13 E14 . . 33 B3
Saltcoats Rd W4 . . . 38 A4
Saltdene N4 . . . . 5 B3
Salter Rd SE16 . . . . 33 A1
Salters' Hall Ct
EC4 . . . . **123** B4
Salter St
College Pk NW10 . . . .21 C2
1 Poplar E14 . . . . . 33 C2
Salterton Rd N7 . . . . .5 B1
Saltoun Rd SW2,
SW9 . . . . 62 C3
Saltram Cres W9 . . .23 C2
Saltwell St E14 . . . . 33 C2
Saltwood Gr SE17 **151** B1
Saltwood Ho 13
SE15 . . . . 50 B4
Salusbury Prim Sch
NW6 . . . . .23 B4
Salusbury Rd
NW6 . . . . .23 A4
Salutation Rd
SE10 . . . . .43 A2
Salvin Rd SW15 . . . .57 C4
Salway Rd E15 . . . . 19 C2
Salween Ho 2
N16 . . . . 15 C4
**Samaritan Hospl for
Women** NW1 . . **102** C4
Sambrook Ho 25
E1 . . . . 32 B4
Samels Ct W6 . . . . 38 C1
Samford Ho N1 . . . 85 B3
Samford St NW8 . . 90 A1
Sam Manners Ho 7
SE10 . . . . 43 A1
Sam March Ho 5
E14 . . . . 34 C3
Sampson St E1 . . **125** C1
Samuel Cl SE14 . . 50 C4
Shoreditch E8 . . . . . .24 B4
Samuel Ct
N1 . . . . .24 A2 **98** A3
Samuel Ho E8 . . . . .24 B4
Samuel Jones Ind Est
7 SE15 . . . . 49 A3
Samuel Lewis Bldgs
N1 . . . . .14 C2
**Samuel Lewis Trust
Dwellings**
6 Camberwell
SE5 . . . . .48 B2
Chelsea SW3 . . . . **144** A3
Walham Green
SW6 . . . . **155** C2
West Kensington
W14 . . . . **140** B4
Samuel Rhodes Sch
N1 . . . . 85 B4
**Samuel Richardson
Ho** W14 . . . . . . **140** C3
Samuel's Cl 2 W6 .39 B2
Samuel St SE15 . . 49 B3
Sancroft Ct SW11 **168** B4
Sancroft Ho SE11 **149** A2
Sancroft St SE11 **149** A2
Sanctuary Mews 18
E8 . . . . .16 B2
Sanctuary St SE1 **137** A4
Sanctuary The

Sanctuary The
continued
Westminster SW1 . . **133** C2
Sandale Cl N16 . . . . . 6 C1
Sandall Ho 7 E3 . . 26 A3
Sandall Rd NW5 . . 13 B2
Sandalwood Cl 1
E1 . . . . 26 A1
Sandalwood Ho 5
NW3 . . . . 11 A2
Sandbourne
4 Kensington
W11 . . . . 31 C3
Paddington NW8 . . . 78 B4
Sandbourne Rd
SE4 . . . . 51 A1
Sandbrook Rd N16 . .7 A1
Sandby Ho
6 Camberwell
SE5 . . . . 49 A2
6 Kilburn NW6 . . . .23 C4
Sandell St SE1 . . **135** B4
Sanderling Ct 20
SE8 . . . . 51 B4
Sanders Ho WC1 . .95 B4
Sanderson Ho 7
SE8 . . . . 41 B1
Sanderstead Ave
NW2 . . . . 1 A2
Sanderstead Cl
SW12 . . . . 73 B4
Sanders Way 3
N19 . . . . 4 C3
Sandfield WC1 . . . . 94 B3
Sandford Ct N16 . . . .7 A3
Sandford Row
SE17 . . . . **151** C2
Sandford St SW6 **156** B1
Sandgate Ho 15
E5 . . . . .17 A4
Sandgate La SW17,
SW18 . . . . 72 A3
Sandgate St SE15 . .50 A4
Sandgate Trad Est
SE15 . . . . 50 A4
Sandham Ct SW4 . **172** B3
Sandhills The
SW10 . . . . **157** A4
Sandhurst Ct SW2 . .62 A3
Sandhurst Ho 16
E1 . . . . 32 B4
Sandilands Rd
SW6 . . . . **166** A3
Sandison St SE15 . .64 C4
Sandland St WC1 **107** A3
Sandlings The SE15 50 A1
Sandmere Rd
SW4 . . . . 62 A3
Sandon Ho 5
SW2 . . . . 74 A4
Sandown Ho 2
W4 . . . . 37 B1
Sandpiper Cl SE16 . .41 B4
Sandpiper Ct
18 Cubitt Town
E14 . . . . 42 B3
1 SE8 . . . . 51 C3
Sandridge St 8
N19 . . . . 4 B2
Sandringham Cl
SW19 . . . . 69 C3
Sandringham Ct
Marylebone W1 . . **105** A1
Putney SW15 . . . . . . 57 C1

Sandringham Ct
continued
18 Rotherhithe
SE16 . . . . 32 C1
St John's Wood W9 . .89 A3
Sandringham Flats
WC2 . . . . **119** C4
Sandringham Ho
Richmond TW10 . . **54** C2
W14 . . . . **140** A4
Sandringham Rd
Dalston E8 . . . . 16 B3
Golders Green NW11 . .1 A4
Willesden NW2 . . . . . .9 A2
Sandrock Rd SE13 . .66 C4
SANDS END TW9 . . **89** A3
Sands End La
SW6 . . . . **166** B4
Sandstone TW9 . . . .44 C3
Sandstone Pl N19 . . .4 A2
Sandways 3 TW9 . . 44 C2
Sandwell Cres 2
NW6 . . . . 10 C2
Sandwell Mans 3
NW6 . . . . 10 C2
Sandwich Ho
18 Rotherhithe
SE16 . . . . 40 B4
WC1 . . . . **94** A3
Sandwich St WC1 . **94** A3
Sandycombe Rd
TW9 . . . . .54 C4
Sandy Lo N6 . . . . 4 B4
Sandy Rd NW3 . . . . . 2 A2
Sandy's Row E1 . . **110** B3
Sanford La 3 N16 . .7 B2
Sanford St SE14,
SE8 . . . . 51 A4
Sanford Terr N16 . . . 7 B1
Sanford Wlk SE14 . .51 A4
1 Stoke Newington
N16 . . . . .7 B2
Sangora Rd 17
SW11 . . . . 59 C3
Sankey Ho 29 E2 . .25 B3
Sansom Rd E11 . . . 19 C4
Sansom St
Camberwell SE5 . . . 48 C2
SE5 . . . . 48 C3
Sans Wlk EC1 . . . . 96 A2
Santley Ho SE1 . . **135** C3
Santley St SW4 . . . 62 B3
Santos Rd SW18 . . 58 C2
Sapcote Trad Ctr
NW10 . . . . 8 B2
Saperton Wlk
SE11 . . . . **149** A4
Sapperton Ct EC1 . .96 C2
Sapphire Ct E1 . . **125** B4
Sapphire Rd SE8 . .41 A2
Saracen St E14 . . . .33 C3
Sarah Ho
Roehampton SW15 . . 56 B3
8 Stepney E1 . . . . . 32 A3
Sarah Swift Ho
SE1 . . . . **137** C4
Sara Lane Ct 11
N1 . . . . .24 A3
Saratoga Rd E5 . . . 17 B4
Sardinia Ho WC2 **106** C1
Sardinia St WC2 . **106** C2
Sarjant Path
SW19 . . . . 69 C2
Sark Ho 5 N1 . . . . 15 B2

Sarnersfield Ho
SE15 . . . . 50 A4
Sarratt Ho 6 W10 . .30 B4
Sarre Rd NW2 . . . . . .10 B3
Sarsden Bldgs
W1 . . . . **103** C1
Sarsfeld Rd SW12,
SW17 . . . . .72 B3
Sartor Rd SE15 . . . 65 C3
Sarum Hall Sch
NW3 . . . . 12 A1
Sarum Ho
W11 . . . . 31 B2 **113** A3
Sassoon Ho SE15 . .50 B1
Satchwell Rd
E2 . . . . .24 C2 **99** B3
Saturn Ho 4 E3 . . .26 C4
Saul Ct 4 SE15 . . . .49 B4
Saunders Cl 13
E14 . . . . 33 B2
Saunders Ho 11
SW2 . . . . .74 C3
Saunders Ness Rd
E14 . . . . 42 C2
Saunders St SE11 **149** B4
Savage Gdns EC3 **124** B4
Savana N16 . . . . 7 A2
Savannah Cl 9
SE15 . . . . 49 B3
Savernake Ho N4 . . . . 6 C4
Savernake Rd
NW3 . . . . 12 B4
Saville Rd W4 . . . . . .37 C3
Saville Row W1 . . **118** C4
Savill Ho 2 SW4 . . .61 C1
Savona St SW8 . . **160** C1
Savoy Circus W3 . . .29 B2
Savoy Ct
Earl's Ct SW5 . . . . **141** C4
Strand WC2 . . . . . . **120** B3
Savoy Hill WC2 . . **120** C3
Savoy Mews SW9 . .62 A4
Savoy Pier WC2 . . **120** C3
Savoy Pl WC2 . . . **120** C3
Savoy Row WC2 . . **120** C4
Savoy St WC2 . . . **120** C3
Savoy Stps WC2 . . **120** C3
Savoy Way WC2 . . **120** C3
Sawkins Cl SW19 . .70 A2
Sawley Rd W12 . . . .29 C1
Sawmill Yd E3 . . . . 26 A4
Sawyer St SE1 . . . **136** C4
Saxby Rd SW2 . . . . 74 A4
Saxonbury Ct
5 Kentish Town
N7 . . . . .13 C3
2 Lower Holloway
N7 . . . . .14 A3
Saxoncroft Ho
SW16 . . . . 73 C1
Saxon Dr W3 . . . . . 28 A4
Saxonfield Cl SW2 . .74 B4
Saxon Hall W2 . . **114** A3
Saxon Ho 6 SW4 . .61 C3
Saxon Rd E3 . . . . . .26 B3
Saxton Cl SE13 . . . .67 C4
Sayer Ho SE4 . . . . 66 A3
Sayes Court St
SE8 . . . . 51 B4
Sayes Ct SE8 . . . . . 51 B4
Scafell NW1 . . . . . . **92** C4
Scala St W1 . . . . . **105** A4
Scampston Mews 5
W10 . . . . .30 C3
Scandrett St 38
E1 . . . . 32 A1
Scarba Wlk N1 . . . .15 C2

Scarborough Rd
N4 . . . . .5 C3
Scarborough St
E1 . . . . .111 A1
Scarlette Manor Wlk
10 SE24 . . . . .74 C4
Scarsbrook Ho 2
SW2 . . . . .62 C1
Scarsdale Pl W8 . 128 A2
Scarsdale Villas
W8 . . . . .127 C1
Scarth Rd SW13 . . .56 B4
Scawen Rd SE8 . . . .41 A1
Scawfell St E2 . . . . .24 B3
Sceptre Ho 10 E1 . .25 B1
Sceptre Rd E2 . . . . .25 B2
Schiller International
Univ SE1 . . . . . . .121 B1
Schofield Wlk SE3 . .53 C3
Sch of Pharmacy
WC1 . . . . .94 B2
Scholars Ct 5 N19 . .4 C3
Scholars Rd SW12 . .73 B3
Scholefield Rd N19 . .4 C2
Scholey Ho SW11 . . .60 A4
Schomberg Ho
SW1 . . . . .147 C4
Schonfeld Sq N16 . . .6 C3
School App
E2 . . . . .24 A2 98 B4
Schoolbank Rd
SE10 . . . . .43 B2
School Bell Cloisters
17 E3 . . . . .26 A3
Schoolbell Mews 18
E3 . . . . .26 A3
School Flats SW8 172 A3
School Ho SE1 . . . .152 A4
Schoolhouse La
E1 . . . . .32 C2
School Rd NW10 . . .20 C1
School Sq SE10 . . . .43 B3
Schooner Cl
Cubitt Town E14 . . . .42 C3
7 Rotherhithe
SE16 . . . . .40 C4
Schubert Rd
SW15 . . . . .58 B2
Science Mus ★
SW7 . . . . .129 B1
Sclater St
E1 . . . . . . .24 B1 99 A2
Scoles Cres SW2 . . .74 C3
Scoresby St SE1 . .122 A1
Scorton Ho 2 N1 . . .24 A3
Scotch Ho SW1 . .130 C3
Scoter Ct 28 SE8 . . .51 B4
Scotia Bldg 10 E1 . .32 C2
Scotia Ct 3 SE16 . .40 B3
Scotia Rd 2 SW2 . . .74 C4
Scotland Pl SW1 . .120 A1
Scotney Ho E9 . . . . .17 B2
Scotson Ho SE11 . .149 B3
Scotswood St SE1 . .95 C2
Scott Ct Albion ★
Clapham SW11 . . . .170 B1
17 Stoke Newington
N16 . . . . .7 A1
Scott Ellis Gdns
NW8 . . . . .89 B3
Scott Ho
2 Barnsbury N7 . . . .14 B2
Islington N1 . . . . . .87 B4
Lisson Gr NW8 . . . . .90 A1
17 Millwall E14 . . . .41 C4

Scotts Ct 6 W12 . . .39 A4
Scott's Rd W12 . . . .39 A4
Scott's Sufferance
Wharf SE1 . . . . .139 A3
Scott St E1 . . . . . . .25 A1
Scott Sq 17 EC4 . . . .23 B1
Scoulding Ho 12
E14 . . . . .41 C3
Scoulding Rd E16 . .35 C3
Scouler St E14 . . . . .34 C2
Scout App N5 . . . . . .8 A4
Scout La SW4 . . . . .61 B4
Scovell Cres SE1 . .136 C3
Scovell Rd SE1 . . .136 C3
Scriven Ct 2 E8 . . .24 B4
Scriven St E8 . . . . . .24 B4
Scrooby St SE6 . . . .67 A1
Scrope Bldg EC1 . .107 B4
Scrubs La NW10, W10,
W12 . . . . .22 A1
Scrutton Cl SW12 . .73 C4
Scrutton St
EC2 . . . . . . .24 A1 98 A1
Scutari Rd SE22 . . . .65 B2
Scylla Rd SE15 . . . .65 A4
Seabright St 27
E2 . . . . .25 A2
Seacole Cl W3 . . . . .28 C4
Seacon Twr 8
E14 . . . . .41 C4
Seaford Ho 10
SE16 . . . . .40 B4
Seaforth Cres N5 . . . .15 B3
Seaforth Lo 2
SW13 . . . . .46 B1
Seaforth Pl SW1 . .133 A2
Seagrave Lo SW6 . .155 C4
Seagrave Rd SW6 .155 C4
Seagrove Cl E1 . . . . .32 C4
Seagull La E16 . . . . .35 C2
Seal Ho SE1 . . . . .137 C2
Seal St E8 . . . . .16 B4
Searle Pl N4 . . . . . . .5 B3
Searles Cl SW11 . .158 B1
Searles Rd SE1 . . .151 C4
Searson Ho SE17 . .150 B3
Sears St SE5 . . . . . .48 C3
Seasalter Ho
SW9 . . . . .173 B4
Seaton Cl SW15 . . . .69 A4
Seaton Point E5 . . . .16 C4
Seavington Ho 2
SE5 . . . . .64 A4
Sebastian Ho 22
N1 . . . . .24 A3
Sebastian St EC1 . . .96 B3
Sebbon St N1 . . . . . .15 A1
Sebright Ho 22 E2 . .24 C3
Sebright Pas 26
E2 . . . . .24 C3
Secker Ho SW9 . . . . .48 A1
Secker St SE1 . . . .121 B1
Second Ave
East Acton W3 . . . . .29 B1
Kensal Town W10 . . .23 A1
Mortlake SW14 . . . . .56 A4
Sedan Way SE17 . .152 A2
Sedding St SW1 . . .145 B4
Seddon Ho EC2 . . . .108 C4
Seddon St WC1 . . . .95 A3
Sedgeford Rd
W12 . . . . .29 B1
Sedgewick Ho
SW19 . . . . .69 C2
Sedgley Ho N4 . . . . . .5 B2

Sedgmoor Pl SE5 . .49 A3
Sedgwick St E9 . . . . .17 C3
Sedleigh Rd SW18 . .58 B1
Sedlescombe Rd
SW6 . . . . .155 B4
Sedley Ho SE11 . . .149 A2
Sedley Pl W1 . . . . .104 A1
Seething La EC3 . . .124 B4
Sefton St SW15 . . . .57 B4
Sekforde St EC1 . . . .96 A2
Selbie Ho NW6 . . . . .10 C3
Selborne 3 NW11 . . .1 C4
Selborne Ho SE1 . . .137 B3
Selborne Rd 4
SE5 . . . . .48 C1
Selby Ho 10 SW4 . . .61 B1
Selby Sq 4 W10 . . . .23 A2
Selby St 3 E1 . .24 C1 99 C1
Selden Ho 2
SE15 . . . . .50 B1
Selden Rd SE15 . . . .50 B1
Selden Wlk N7 . . . . . .5 B2
Selden Ho
Nine Elms SW8 . . . .160 C1
Pimlico SW1 . . . . .146 C1
Selhurst Cl SW19 . . .69 C3
Selina Ho NW8 . . . . .89 C2
Selkirk Ho N1 . . . . . .84 C4
4 Stoke Newington
N16 . . . . .7 A1
Sellons Ave NW10 . .21 B4
Selma Ho 2 W12 . . .30 A3
Selman Ho 2 E9 . . . .18 A2
Selsdon Way E14 . . .42 A3
Selsea Pl N16 . . . . . .16 A3
Selsey St E14 . . . . . .33 C4
Selway Ho 5 SW8 . .172 B4
Selwood Ho 4 N4 . . .6 C4
Selwood Pl SW7 . . .143 B2
Selwood Terr
SW7 . . . . .143 B2
Selworthy Ho
SW11 . . . . .167 C4
Selwyn Ave TW9 . . .54 B4
Selwyn Ct 8
TW10 . . . . .54 B2
Selwyn Ho 8
SW15 . . . . .57 C1
Selwyn Rd Bow 8
E3 . . . . .26 B3
Willesden NW10 . . . .8 A1
Semley Gate E9 . . . .18 B2
Semley Ho SW1 . . .146 A3
Semley Pl SW1 . . . .146 A3
Senate St SE15 . . . .50 B1
Senators Lo 81 E3 . .26 A3
Sendall Ct 13
SW11 . . . . .59 C4
Senior St W2 . . . . .100 A4
Senrab St E1 . . . . . . .32 C3
Seraph Ct EC1 . . . . .96 C4
Serenaders Rd
SW9 . . . . .173 B1
Sergeant Ind Est The
SW18 . . . . .59 A1
Serica Ct 14 SE10 . .52 B3
Serjeants' Inn
EC4 . . . . .107 C1
Serlby Ct W14 . . . .126 C2
Serle St WC2 . . . . .107 A2
Sermon La EC4 . . .108 C1
Serpentine Ct 16
SE16 . . . . .40 C4
Serpentine Gallery ★
W2 . . . . .129 C4
Serpentine Rd
W2 . . . . .116 C1

Serpentine The ★
W2 . . . . .116 B1
Service Route No 1
E15 . . . . .19 C1
Service Route No 2 18
E15 . . . . .19 C1
Service Route No 3
E15 . . . . .19 C1
Servite Ho SE13 . . . .52 A2
Servite RC Prim Sch
SW10 . . . . .156 C4
Setchell Rd SE1 . . .152 C4
Setchell Way SE1 . .152 C4
Seth St 2 SE16 . . . .40 B4
Settlers Ct 11 E14 . .34 C2
Settles St 1 . . . . .111 C2
Settrington Rd
SW6 . . . . .166 A1
Seven Dials WC2 . .106 A1
Seven Mills Prim Sch
E14 . . . . .41 C4
Sevenoaks Rd SE4 . .66 B1
Seven Sisters Rd
Finsbury Pk N4 . . . . .5 C2
Stoke Newington N4, N7,
N15 . . . . .6 A4
Seven Stars Cnr
W12 . . . . .38 C3
Seven Stars Yd
E1 . . . . .111 A4
Severnake Cl E14 . . .41 C2
Severn Ave 2
W10 . . . . .23 A2
Severn Way NW10 . . .8 B3
Severus Rd SW11 . . .60 A3
Seville Ho E1 . . . . .125 C1
Seville Mews N1 . . .16 A1
Seville St SW1 . . . .131 A3
Sevington St W9 . . . .88 A1
Seward St EC1 . . . . .96 C3
Sewardstone Rd
E2 . . . . .25 B3
Sewell Ho 16 N16 . .16 A3
Sextant Ave E14 . . . .42 C2
Sexton Ct 7 E14 . . . .34 C2
Sexton's Ho 5
SE13 . . . . .52 B4
Seymour Ct
Putney SW15 . . . . . .57 A3
Upper Clapton N16 . . .7 C3
Seymour Gdns
SE4 . . . . .66 A4
Seymour Ho
Bloomsbury WC1 . . . .94 A2
Clapham SW8 . . . . .171 A2
Somers Town NW1 . . .93 C3
Seymour Mews
W1 . . . . .103 B2
Seymour Pl W1 . . .102 C2
Seymour Rd
Acton W4 . . . . .37 B2
Wandsworth SW18 . . .58 B1
Wimbledon SW19 . . .69 C1
Seymour St W1 . . .103 A1
Seymour Wlk
SW10 . . . . .156 C4
Seyssel St E14 . . . . .42 B2
Shaa Rd W3 . . . . . . .28 C2
Shabana Ct 3
W12 . . . . .30 A1
Shacklenton Ct 2
2 Dulwich SE21 . . . .75 C2
2 Isle of Dogs E14 . .41 C2
4 Shepherd's Bush
W12 . . . . .39 A4
Shackleton Ho 5
E1 . . . . .32 B1

SHACKLEWELL 16 B4
Shacklewell Ho 3
E8 . . . . .16 B4
Shacklewell La E8 . .16 B3
Shacklewell Prim Sch
E8 . . . . .16 B4
Shacklewell Rd
N16 . . . . .16 B4
Shacklewell Row
E8 . . . . .16 B4
Shacklewell St
E2 . . . . .24 B2 99 A3
Shad Thames
SE1 . . . . .139 A4
SHADWELL 32 B2
Shadwell Gdns E1 . .32 B2
Shadwell Pierhead
E1 . . . . .32 B2
Shadwell Pl 1 E1 . .32 B2
Shadwell Sta E1 . . .32 A2
Shaftesbury Ave
W1 . . . . .119 C4
Shaftesbury Ct
Borough The SE1 . . .137 B2
1 Herne Hill SE5 . . .63 C3
Shoreditch N1 . . . . .87 B1
Streatham SW16 . . . .73 C1
Shaftesbury Ctr
NW10 . . . . .22 C1
Shaftesbury Gdns
NW10 . . . . .21 A1
Shaftesbury Ho
Canning Town
E16 . . . . .35 B3
2 Stoke Newington
N16 . . . . .7 A1
W2 . . . . .114 B4
Shaftesbury Lo 9
E14 . . . . .34 A3
Shaftesbury Mews
3 Clapham Pk
SW4 . . . . .61 B2
W8 . . . . .127 C1
Shaftesbury Park
Chambers 1
SW11 . . . . .60 C4
Shaftesbury Rd
Finsbury Pk N4, N19 . .5 A3
Richmond TW9 . . . . .54 A4
Shaftesbury St N1 . .87 B1
Shaftesworth Ct
SW17 . . . . .72 B1
Shafto Mews
SW1 . . . . .131 A1
Shafton Rd E9 . . . . .25 C4
Shaftsbury Park Prim
Sch SW11 . . . . . . .169 B1
Shafts Ct EC3 . . . .110 A1
Shahjalal Ho 18
E2 . . . . .24 C3
Shakespeare Ave ★
NW10 . . . . .20 C4
Shakespeare Ho 3
E9 . . . . .17 B1
Shakespeare Rd
Acton W3 . . . . .28 B1
Brixton SE24 . . . . . .63 A3
Shakespeare's Globe
Theatre (site of) ★
SE1 . . . . .123 A2
Shakespeare Twr
EC2 . . . . .109 A4
Shakspeare Mews 7
N16 . . . . .16 A4

Shakspeare Wlk
N16 . . . . 16 A4
Shalbourne Sq E9 . .18 B2
Shalcomb St
SW10 . . . . 157 A3
Shalden Ho SW15 . .56 B1
Shalfleet Dr W10 . .30 C2
Shalford W10 . . . . . .21 C4
Shalford Ct N1 . . . . .86 A2
Shalford Ho SE1 . .137 C2
Shalimar Gdns
W3 . . . . .28 B2
Shalimar Lo W3 . . . .28 B2
Shalimar Rd W3 . . . .28 B2
Shalstone Rd SW14,
TW9 . . . . .55 A4
Shamrock St SW4 . .61 C4
Shandon Ct SE4 . . . .51 A1
Shandon Rd SW4 . . .61 B1
Shand St SE1 . . . . .138 B4
Shandy St E1 . . . . . .25 C1
Shan Ho WC1 . . . . . .94 C1
Shannon Ct █
Peckham SE15 . . . . .49 B3
Stoke Newington N16 . .7 A1
Willesden NW10 . . . . . .8 C2
Shannon Gr SW9 . . .62 B3
Shannon Pl NW8 . . .80 B2
Shanti Ct SW18 . . . .70 C3
Shapla Prim Sch
E1 . . . . .125 C3
Shardcroft Ave
SE24 . . . . .63 A2
Shardeloes Rd
SE14 . . . . .51 B1
Shard's Sq SE15 . . .49 C4
Shareburne Ho
SW2 . . . . .62 C2
Sharman Ho █
E14 . . . . .34 B3
Sharnbrook Ho
W6 . . . . .155 B4
Sharon Gdns E9 . . . .25 B4
Sharon Rd W4 . . . . . .37 C1
Sharp Ho SW8 . . . . .61 A4
Sharples Hall St █
NW1 . . . . .12 B1
Sharpness Ct █
SE15 . . . . .49 B3
Sharratt St SE15 . . .50 B4
Sharsted St SE17 . . .150 A1
Sharwood WC1 . . . . .85 A1
Shaver's Pl SW1 . . .119 B3
Shawbury Ct SE22 . .64 B2
Shawbury Rd
SE22 . . . . .64 B2
Shaw Cres █ E14 . . .33 A3
Shaw Ct
█ Acton Green
W3 . . . . .37 B3
█ Battersea SW11 . .59 C4
Upper Holloway N19 . . .5 A2
Shawfield St SW3 .144 B1
Shawford Ct █
SW15 . . . . .68 C4
Shaw Rd SE22 . . . . .64 A3
Shearling Way N7 . .14 A2
Shearsmith Ho
E1 . . . . .125 C4
Shearwater Ct ██
SE8 . . . . .51 B4
Sheba Pl E1 . . . . . . .24 B1
Sheba Pl E1 . . . .24 B1 99 A1
Sheen Common Dr
SW14, TW10 . . . . . .54 C2

Sheen Court Rd
TW10 . . . . .54 C3
Sheen Ct TW10 . . . .54 C3
Sheendale Rd
TW9 . . . . .54 B3
Sheen Gate Gdns
SW14 . . . . .55 B3
Sheengate Mans
SW14 . . . . .55 B3
Sheen Gr N1 . . . . . .85 B4
Sheen La SW14 . . . .55 B3
Sheen Mount Prim
Sch SW14 . . . . . . .55 A2
Sheen Pk TW10,
TW9 . . . . .54 A3
Sheen Rd TW10,
TW9 . . . . .54 B3
Sheen Wood
SW14 . . . . .55 B3
Sheepcote La
SW11 . . . . .169 A1
Sheep La E8 . . . . . . .25 A4
Sheffield Ho █
SE15 . . . . .49 B2
Sheffield Sq █ E3 . .26 B2
Sheffield St WC2 . .106 C1
Sheffield Terr
W8 . . . . .31 C1 113 C1
Shelbourne Ho █
N19 . . . . .4 C4
Shelbourne Rd
N17 . . . . .57 C2
Shelburne Rd N7 . . .14 B4
Shelbury Rd SE22 . .65 A2
Sheldon Ct SW8 . . .162 A1
Sheldon Ho █ E9 . . .17 C2
Sheldon Pl E2 . . . . .25 A3
Sheldon Rd NW2 . . . .9 C4
Sheldon Sq W2 . . . .101 A3
Sheldrake Ho █
SE16 . . . . .40 C2
Sheldrake Pl W8 . .127 B4
Shelduck Ct █
SE8 . . . . .51 B4
Shelford Pl N16 . . . . .6 C1
Shelgate Rd SW11 .60 B2
Shell Ctr SE1 . . . . .121 A1
Shelley Cl SE15 . . . .50 A1
Shelley Ct
Finsbury Pk N4 . . . . . .5 B3
█ SW3 . . . . .159 A4
Shelley Ho
██ Bethnal Green
E2 . . . . .25 B2
█ Chelsea SW1 . . . .160 C4
█ Stoke Newington
N16 . . . . .16 A4
Walworth SE17 . . . . .151 A2
Shelley Rd NW10 . . .20 C4
Shellgrove Rd
N16 . . . . .16 A3
Shellness Rd E5 . . . .17 A3
Shell Rd SE13 . . . . .67 A4
Shellwood Rd
SW11 . . . . .168 C1
Shelmerdine Cl
E3 . . . . .33 C4
Shelton St WC2 . . .106 A1
Shene Bldg EC1 . . .107 B4
Shene Sch SW14 . . .56 A3
Shenfield St N1 . . . .24 A3
Shenley Rd SE5 . . . .49 A2
Shepard Ho █
SW11 . . . . .59 C4
Sheperdess Pl N1 . .97 A4
Shepherd Cl W1 . . .117 B4

Shepherdess Wlk
N1 . . . . .87 A1
Shepherd Ho
Barnsbury N7 . . . . . . .14 A2
██ Poplar E14 . . . . .34 A3
Shepherd Mkt
W1 . . . . .118 A1
SHEPHERD'S BUSH
. . . . .30 A1
Shepherd's Bush
(Central Line) Sta
W12 . . . . .39 C4
Shepherd's Bush Gn
W12 . . . . .39 B4
Shepherd's Bush
(Hamm & City) Sta
W12 . . . . .30 B1
Shepherd's Bush
Market W12 . . . . . .39 B4
Shepherd's Bush Pl
W12 . . . . .39 C4
Shepherd's Bush Rd
W6 . . . . .39 B3
Shepherds Ct █
W12 . . . . .39 C4
Shepherd's La E9 . .17 C2
Shepherds Pl W1 . .117 B3
Shepherd St W1 . . .118 A1
Shepherd's Wlk
NW3 . . . . .11 C4
Sheppard Dr SE16 . .40 A1
Sheppard Ho
██ Hackney E2 . . . . .24 C3
█ Streatham SW2 . . .74 C3
Shepperton Rd N1 . .87 B4
Sheppey Ho SE11 . .149 C3
Shepton Ct SW11 . .167 C4
Shepton Hos █
E2 . . . . .25 B2
Sherard Ct N19 . . . . .5 A1
Sherard Ho ██ E9 . .17 B1
Sheraton Ho SW1 . .160 B4
Sheraton St W1 . . .105 B1
Sherborne Ho
Pimlico SW1 . . . . . . .146 B2
South Lambeth
SW8 . . . . .162 C1
Sherborne La
EC4 . . . . .123 C4
Sherborne St N1 . . .87 B4
Sherbourne Ct
SW5 . . . . .142 A4
Sherbrooke Ho █
E2 . . . . .25 B3
Sherbrooke Rd
SW6 . . . . .154 B1
Sherbrooke Terr
SW6 . . . . .154 B1
Shere Ho SE1 . . . . .137 B2
Sherfield Gdns
SW15 . . . . .56 B1
Sheridan Bldgs
WC2 . . . . .106 B1
Sheridan Ct
Earl's Ct SW5 . . . . . .142 A3
South Hampstead
NW6 . . . . .11 B1
South Lambeth
SW9 . . . . .173 A3
Sheridan Ho
SE11 . . . . .149 C3
█ Stoke Newington
N16 . . . . .7 A1
Sheridan Pl SW13 . .56 B4
Sheridan St ██ E1 . .32 A3
Sheringdale Prim Sch
SW18 . . . . .70 B3

Sheringham NW8 . .79 C4
Sheringham Ho
NW1 . . . . .102 B4
Sheringham Mews █
SW18 . . . . .71 B2
Sheringham Rd
N7 . . . . .14 C2
Sherlock Ct NW8 . . .79 B4
Sherlock Holmes
Mus ██ NW1 . . . . .91 A1
Sherlock Mews
W1 . . . . .103 C4
Sherren Ho ██ E1 . .25 B1
Sherrick Green Rd
NW10 . . . . .9 A3
Sherriff Ct NW6 . . . .10 C2
Sherriff Rd NW6 . . .10 C2
Sherrin Rd E10 . . . . .19 A4
Sherston Ct
Finsbury WC1 . . . . . . .95 B3
Newington SE1 . . . . .150 B4
Sherwin Ho SE11 . .163 B4
Sherwin Rd SE14 . . .50 C2
Sherwood NW6 . . . . .10 A1
Sherwood Cl
SW13 . . . . .57 A4
Sherwood Ct
█ Battersea
SW11 . . . . .59 B4
St Johns SE13 . . . . . .52 A1
█ W1 . . . . .102 C3
Sherwood Gdns
Bermondsey SE16 . . . .40 A1
Millwall E14 . . . . .41 C2
Sherwood Ho N4 . . . .6 B4
Sherwood St W1 . . .119 A4
Shetland Rd E3 . . . . .26 B3
Shillaker Ct W3 . . . .29 B1
Shillibeer Pl W1 . . .102 B3
Shillingford St █
N1 . . . . .15 A1
Shillingstone Ho
W14 . . . . .126 B1
Shinfield St W12 . . .30 B3
Shipka Rd SW12 . . .73 A3
Ship La SW14 . . . . . .45 B1
Shiplake Ho
E2 . . . . .24 B2 98 C3
Shipley Ho SW8 . . .171 B1
Ship & Mermaid Row
SE1 . . . . .138 A4
Ship St SE8 . . . . . . .51 C2
Ship Tavern Pas
EC3 . . . . .124 A4
Shipton Ho
█ Camden Town
NW1 . . . . .12 C2
██ Haggerston E2 . . .24 B3
Shipton St
E2 . . . . .24 B2 99 A4
Shipwright Rd
SE16 . . . . .41 A4
Shipwright Yd
SE1 . . . . .124 A1
Shirbutt St E14 . . . .34 A2
Shire Pl SW18 . . . . .71 B4
Shirland Mews
W9 . . . . .23 B2
Shirland Rd W9 . . . .23 C1
Shirley Gr SW11 . . . .60 C4
Shirley Ho █ SE5 . .48 C3
Shirley Rd W4 . . . . .37 C4
Shirley St E16 . . . . .35 B3
Shirlock Rd NW3 . . .12 B4
Shoe La EC4 . . . . . .107 C2

Shooters Hill Rd SE3,
SE10 . . . . .53 C4
Shoot-Up Hill
NW2 . . . . .10 A2
Shopstop SW11 . . . .60 A3
Shore Bsns Ctr ██
E9 . . . . .17 B1
SHOREDITCH 87 C1
Shoreditch Ct █
E8 . . . . .16 B1
Shoreditch High St
E2 . . . . .24 A1 98 B2
Shoreditch Ho N1 . .97 C3
Shoreham Cl
SW18 . . . . .59 A2
Shore Ho SW8 . . . . .61 A4
Shore Mews ██
E9 . . . . .17 B1
Shore Pl E9 . . . . . . .17 B1
Shore Rd E9 . . . . . . .17 B1
Shorncliffe Rd
SE1 . . . . .152 C2
Shorrolds Rd
SW6 . . . . .155 A2
Shortcroft Mead Ct
NW10 . . . . .8 C3
Shorter St EC3 . . . .125 A4
Shortlands W6 . . . . .39 C2
Short Rd W4 . . . . . . .46 A4
Shorts Gdns WC2 . .106 A1
Short St SE1 . . . . . .135 C4
Shottendale Rd
SW6 . . . . .165 B4
Shottfield Ave
SW14 . . . . .56 A3
Shottsford █
W11 . . . . .31 C3
Shoulder of Mutton
Alley ██ E14 . . . . .33 A2
Shouldham St
W1 . . . . .102 B3
Shreveport Ho ██
N19 . . . . .4 C4
Shrewsbury Ave
SW14 . . . . .55 C3
Shrewsbury Ho
Chelsea SW3 . . . . . . .158 A3
Kennington SE11 . . . .163 A3
Shrewsbury Mews █
W2 . . . . .31 C3
Shrewsbury Rd
W2 . . . . .31 C3
Shrewsbury St
W10 . . . . .22 B1
Shropshire Ho
WC1 . . . . .93 A1
Shroton St NW1 . . .102 B4
Shrubbery Cl N1 . . .87 A3
Shrubland Rd E8 . . .24 C4
Shrubs Ho SW1 . . . .147 C3
Shurland Gdns
SE15 . . . . .49 B3
Shuters Sq W14 . . .140 C1
Shuttle St
E1 . . . . .24 C1 99 B1
Shuttleworth Rd
SW11 . . . . .168 A2
Sibella Rd SW4 . . . .171 C1
Sicilian Ave WC1 . .106 B3
Sidbury St SW6 . . .164 A4
Siddons Ct WC2 . . .106 C1
Siddons Ho █
NW3 . . . . .12 B3
Siddons La NW1 . . . .91 A1
Sidford Ho SE1 . . . .135 A1
Sidford Pl SE1 . . . .135 A1
Sidgwick Ho SW9 . .172 B1

Sidings Mews N7 . . 14 C4
Sidlaw Ho N16 . . . . . . 7 B3
Sidmouth Ho
🔟 Camberwell
SE15 . . . . 49 C3
Marylebone W1 . . 102 B2
🔟 Streatham SW2 . . 74 C4
Sidmouth Mews
WC1 . . . . 94 C3
Sidmouth Par NW2 . . 9 B1
Sidmouth Rd NW2 . . . 9 B1
Sidmouth St WC1 . . 94 C3
Sidney Boyd Ct
NW6 . . . . 10 C1
Sidney Godley (VC)
Ho 🔟 E2 . . . . 25 B2
Sidney Gr EC1 . . . . 86 A1
Sidney Ho 4 E2 . . . 25 C3
Sidney Miller Ct 🔟
W3 . . . . 28 A1
Sidney Rd SW9 . . . 173 A1
Sidney Sq E1 . . . . . 32 B4
Sidney St E1 . . . . . . 32 B4
Sidworth St 6 E8 . . 17 A1
Siebert Rd SE3 . . . . 53 C4
Siege Ho 14 E1 . . . . 32 A3
Sigdon Rd E8 . . . . . 16 C3
Signal Ho
9 London E8 . . . . . 17 A1
SE1 . . . . 136 C3
Signmakers Yd
NW1 . . . . 82 B3
Silbury Ho 🔟
SE26 . . . . 76 C1
Silbury St N1 . . . . . . 97 B4
Silchester Rd
W10 . . . . 30 C3
Silesia Bldgs E8 . . . 17 A1
Silex St SE1 . . . . . . 136 B3
Silk Mills Path
SE13 . . . . 67 B4
Silk Mills Sq 10 . . . . 18 B2
Silk St EC2 . . . . . . 109 A4
Sillitoe Ho N1 . . . . . 87 C3
Silsoe Ho NW1 . . . . . 82 B1
Silverbirch Wlk 1
NW3 . . . . 12 C2
Silverburn Ho 4
SW9 . . . . 48 A2
Silver Cl SE14 . . . . . 51 A3
Silver Cres W4 . . . . 37 A2
Silver Ct N19 . . . . . . 4 B1
Silverdale NW1 . . . . 92 C4
Silverdale Ct EC1 . . 96 B2
Silvermere Rd
SE6 . . . . 67 A1
Silver Pl W1 . . . . . 119 A4
Silver Rd
Shepherd's Bush
W12 . . . . 30 C2
St Johns SE13 . . . . 67 A4
Silverthorn NW6 . . . 78 B3
Silverthorne Rd
SW8 . . . . 170 B1
Silverton Rd W6 . . . 47 C4
Silvertown Way
E16 . . . . 95 C1
Silver Wlk SE16 . . . 33 B1
Silvester Ho
27 Bethnal Green
E2 . . . . 25 B2
1 Notting Hill W11 . . 31 B3
6 Stepney E1 . . . . . 32 A3
Silvester Rd SE22 . . 64 B2
Silvester St SE1 . . . 137 B3
Silwex Ho
E1 . . . . 24 B1 98 C1

Silwood St SE16 . . . 40 B1
Sim La EC1 . . . . . . 137 C3
Simmonds Ct
SW5 . . . . 142 A3
Simmons Ho
Bethnal Green
E2 . . . . 24 C2 99 B3
Finsbury Pk N7 . . . . 5 B2
Simms Ct SW6 . . . 58 A4
Simms Rd SE1 . . . . 153 C3
Simon Cl
W11 . . . . 31 B2 113 A4
Simon Ct W9 . . . . . 23 C2
Simon Lo 1
SW19 . . . . 69 C3
Simon Marks Jewish
Prim Sch N16 . . . . 7 B2
Simonds Ho E15 . . . 19 C1
Simpson Dr W3 . . . 28 C3
Simpson Ho
Lisson Gr NW8 . . . 90 A3
Vauxhall SE11 . . . 148 C1
Simpson's Rd E14 . . 34 A2
Simpson St SW11 . . 168 A1
Sinclair Ct N5 . . . . . 15 B2
Sinclair Gdns
W14 . . . . 39 C4
Sinclair Ho 🔟
SW12 . . . . 73 A4
Sinclair Mans 13
W12 . . . . 39 C4
Sinclair Pl SE4 . . . . 66 C1
Sinclair Rd W14 . . . 126 A2
Sinclairs Ho 13 E3 . . 26 B3
Singer St EC2 . . . . . 97 C3
Sion Ho SE13 . . . . . 67 B3
Sion-Manning RC
Sch for Girls
Kensal Town W10 . . 31 A4
North Kensington
W10 . . . . 30 C4
Sir Abraham Dawes
Cotts SW15 . . . . . 58 A3
Sir Alexander Cl
W3 . . . . 29 B1
Sir Alexander Rd
W3 . . . . 29 B1
Sirdar Rd
W11 . . . . 31 A2 112 A3
Sir Francis Drake
Prim Sch SE8 . . . 41 A1
Sirinham Point
SW8 . . . . 163 A3
Sirius Bldg 18 E1 . . 125 C2
Sir James Barrie Prim
Sch SW8 . . . . 171 A3
Sir John Cass
Foundation &
Redcoat CE Sec Sch
E1 . . . . 32 C4
Sir John Cass's
Foundation Prim Sch
EC3 . . . . 110 B1
Sir John Kirk Cl 33
SE5 . . . . 48 B3
Sir John Lillie Prim
Sch SW6 . . . . 154 B3
Sir Oswald Stoll
Foundation The
SW6 . . . . 156 A2
Sir Thomas Abney
Sch N16 . . . . 6 C3
Sir Thomas More Est
SW3 . . . . 157 C3
Sir William Burrough
Prim Sch E14 . . . 33 A3

Sir William Powell's
Almshos SW6 . . . . 58 A4
Sise La EC4 . . . . . 109 B1
Siskin Ho 10 SE16 . . 40 C2
Sispara Gdns
SW18 . . . . 58 B1
Sissinghurst Ho 17
SE15 . . . . 50 B4
Sister Mabel's Way 15
SE15 . . . . 49 C3
Sisters Ave SW11 . . 60 B3
Sistova Rd SW12 . . 73 A3
Sistulu Pl SW9 . . . . 62 C4
Sitarey Ct 3 W12 . . 30 A1
Site of Changing of
the Guard*
SW1 . . . . 132 C3
Sivill Ho E2 . . . . . . 24 B2 99 A4
Siward Rd SW17 . . . 71 B1
Six Bridges Ind Est
SE1 . . . . 153 C1
Sixth Ave W10 . . . . 23 A2
Skardu Rd NW2 . . . 10 A3
Skeena Hill SW18,
SW19 . . . . 70 A3
Skeggs Ho 5 E14 . . 42 B3
Skegness Ho 3
N7 . . . . 14 B1
Skelbrook St
SW18 . . . . 71 B2
Skelgill Rd SW15 . . 58 B3
Skelton Cl 7 E8 . . . 16 B2
Skelton Ho N16 . . . 16 A3
Skelwith Rd W6 . . . 47 B4
Skenfrith Ho SE15 . . 50 A4
Sketchley Gdns
SE16 . . . . 40 C1
Skiffington Cl
SW2 . . . . 74 C3
Skinner Pl SW1 . . . 145 B3
Skinners Company
Sch (Upper) N16 . . 7 B4
Skinners La EC4 . . 123 A4
Skinner St EC1 . . . 95 C2
Skipsea Ho SW18 . . 59 C1
Skipton Ho SE4 . . . 66 A3
Skipwith Bldg
EC1 . . . . 107 B4
Skipworth Rd E9 . . 25 B4
Skua Ct 22 SE8 . . . 51 B4
Skyline Ct SE1 . . . 138 C1
Skyline Plaza Bldg
E1 . . . . 111 C2
Skylines E14 . . . . . 42 B4
Slade Ct NW2 . . . . 10 A3
Sladen Pl 12 E5 . . . 17 A4
Slagrove Pl SE13 . . 67 A2
Slaidburn St
SW10 . . . . 157 A3
Slaithwaite Rd
SE13 . . . . 67 B3
Slaney Pl 7 N7 . . . . 14 C3
Slaney Rd N7 . . . . . 14 C3
Sleaford Ho 3 E3 . . 26 C1
Sleaford Ind Est
SW8 . . . . 161 A1
Sleaford St SW8 . . 161 A1
Sleat Ho 11 E3 . . . . 26 B3
Slievemore Cl 8
SW4 . . . . 61 C4
Sligo Ho 6 E1 . . . . 25 C1
Slingsby Pl WC2 . . 120 A4
Slippers Pl SE16 . . . 40 A3
Slipway Ho 1 E14 . . 42 A1
Sloane Ave SW3 . . 144 B3
Sloane Avenue Mans
SW3 . . . . 144 C3

Sloane Ct E SW3 . . 145 B2
Sloane Ct W SW3 . . 145 B2
Sloane Gate Mans
SW1 . . . . 145 B4
Sloane Gdns SW1 . . 145 B3
Sloane Ho 7 E9 . . . 17 B1
Sloane Sq SW1 . . . 145 A3
Sloane Square Sta
SW1 . . . . 145 B3
Sloane St SW1 . . . 131 A1
Sloane Terr SW1 . . 145 B4
Sloane Terr Mans
SW1 . . . . 145 B4
Sly St 17 E1 . . . . . . 32 A3
Smallbrook Mews
W2 . . . . 101 B1
Smalley Cl N16 . . . . 7 B1
Smart's Pl WC1,
WC2 . . . . 106 B2
Smart St E2 . . . . . . 25 C2
Smeaton Ct SE1 . . 136 C1
Smeaton Rd SW18 . . 70 C4
Smeaton St E1 . . . . 32 A1
Smedley St SW4,
SW8 . . . . 171 C2
Smeed Rd E3 . . . . . 18 C1
Smiles Pl SE13 . . . . 52 B1
Smith Cl SE16 . . . . 32 C1
Smithfield Mkt
EC1 . . . . 108 B3
Smithfield St EC1 . . 108 A3
Smithies Ct E15 . . . 19 B3
Smith's Ct W1 . . . . 119 B4
Smith Sq SW1 . . . 134 A1
Smith St SW3 . . . . 144 C1
Smith's Yd SW18 . . 71 B2
Smith Terr SW3 . . . 144 C1
Smithwood Cl
SW19 . . . . 70 A2
Smithy St E1 . . . . . 32 B4
Smithy Street Sch
E1 . . . . 32 B4
Smugglers Way
SW18 . . . . 59 B3
Smyrk's Rd SE17 . . 152 B1
Smyrna Mans 8
NW6 . . . . 10 C1
Smyrna Rd NW6 . . . 10 C1
Smythe St E14 . . . . 34 A2
Snarsgate St W10 . . 30 B4
Sneath Ave NW11 . . 1 B4
Sneyd Rd NW2 . . . . 9 B4
Snowberry Cl E11 . . 19 C4
Snowbury Rd
SW6 . . . . 166 B1
Snowden St
EC2 . . . . 24 A1 98 A1
Snowe Ho SE27 . . . 75 A1
Snow Hill EC1 . . . . 108 A3
Snowman Ho NW6 . . 78 B4
Snowsfields SE1 . . 137 C4
Snowsfields Prim Sch
SE1 . . . . 138 A4
Soames St SE15 . . . 64 B4
Soane Ct 11 NW1 . . 13 B1
Soane Ho SE17 . . . 151 C1
Soane Mus The*
WC2 . . . . 106 C2
Soaphouse La
TW8 . . . . 44 A3
SOHO 105 B1
Soho* N1 . . . . 105 A1
Soho Parish CE Prim
Sch W1 . . . . 119 B4
Soho Sq W1 . . . . . 105 B2
Soho St W1 . . . . . . 105 B2
Sojourner-Truth Cl 11
E8 . . . . 17 A2

Solander Gdns
13 Shadwell E1 . . . 32 B2
Stepney E1 . . . . . . 32 A2
Soldene Ct N7 . . . . 14 B2
Solebay St E1 . . . . 26 A1
Solent Ho 6 E1 . . . 33 A4
Solent Rd NW6 . . . 10 C2
Soley Mews WC1 . . 95 B4
Solidarity Ho 5
NW10 . . . . 9 B2
Solna Ave SW15 . . 57 B2
Solomon's Pas
SE15 . . . . 65 A3
Solon New Rd
SW4 . . . . 62 A3
Solon Rd SW2 . . . . 62 A3
Solway Ho 12 E1 . . 25 C1
Solway Rd SE22 . . . 64 C3
Somali Rd NW2 . . . 10 B3
Somborne Ho
SW15 . . . . 68 C4
Sombrook Ho
SE11 . . . . 149 B3
Somer Ct SW6 . . . 155 B3
Somerfield Rd N4 . . 6 A2
Somerfield St
SE16 . . . . 40 C1
Somerford Gr N16 . . 16 B4
Somerford Grove Est
N16 . . . . 16 B4
Somerford St E1 . . . 25 A1
Somerford Way
SE16 . . . . 41 A4
Somerleyton Rd
SW9 . . . . 62 C3
Somers Cl NW1 . . . 83 B2
Somers Cres W2 . . 102 A1
Somerset Gdns
Highgate N6 . . . . . 3 C4
St Johns SE13 . . . . 52 A1
Somerset Ho
W2 . . . . 121 A4
Somerset Ho
SW19 . . . . 70 A1
Somerset Lo
SW15 . . . . 57 A3
Somerset Rd
Bedford Pk W4 . . . 37 C3
Wimbledon SW19 . . 70 A1
Somerset Sq
W14 . . . . 126 C3
Somers Pl SW2 . . . 74 B4
Somers Rd SW2 . . . 62 B1
SOMERS TOWN . . . 93 C4
Somers Town Est
NW1 . . . . 83 A1
Somerton Ave
TW9 . . . . 55 A4
Somerton Rd
Cricklewood NW2 . . 1 A1
Nunhead SE15 . . . . 65 A3
Somerville Ave
SW13 . . . . 47 B4
Somerville Ho 10
SW15 . . . . 57 C1
Somerville Point
SE16 . . . . 41 B4
Sonderburg Rd 13
N7 . . . . 5 B2
Sondes St SE17 . . . 48 C4
Sonia Gdns NW10 . . 8 B4
Sonning Ho
E2 . . . . 24 B2 98 C3
Sophia Cl N7 . . . . . 14 B2
Sophia Ho 10 W6 . . 39 B1

Sophia Sq **14** SE16 . . 33 A2
Sopwith Way
. . . . **160** A2
Sorrel La **17** E14 . . . . 34 C3
Sorrell Cl
Brixton SW2 . . . . . **173** C4
SE14 . . . . 51 A4
Soseki Mus★ SW4 . . 61 A4
Sotheby Rd N5 . . . . . 15 B4
Sotheran Cl **8** 24 C4
Sotheron Pl SW6 . . **156** B1
Soudan Rd SW11 . . **168** C3
Souldern Rd **10**
. . . . 39 C3
SOUTH ACTON . . . 37 A3
South Acton Sta W3,
W4 . . . . 37 B3
South Africa Rd
W12 . . . . 30 A2
Southall Pl SE1 . . **137** B3
Southam Ho **9**
. . . . 23 A1
Southampton Bldgs
WC2 . . . . **107** B3
Southampton Pl
WC1 . . . . **106** B3
Southampton Rd
NW5 . . . . 12 B3
Southampton Row
WC1 . . . . **106** B4
Southampton St
WC2 . . . . **120** B4
Southampton Way
SE5 . . . . 49 A3
Southam St W10 . . 23 A1
South Audley St
W1 . . . . **117** C2
South Ave TW9 . . . . 44 C1
SOUTH BANK 120 C1
South Bank Bsns Ctr
SW8 . . . . **161** C3
Southbank
International Sch
NW3 . . . . 11 B2
Southbank
International Sch
(Westminster
Campus) W1 . . . . **104** A4
Southbank Int Sch
W11 . . . 31 C2 **113** B3
South Bank Univ
London SW8 . . . . **171** C4
SE1 . . . . **136** B2
South Bermondsey
Sta SE16 . . . . 40 B1
South Black Lion La
7 W6 . . . . 38 C1
South Bldg SW1 . . **133** A2
South Block **20** E1 . . 32 B2
South Bolton Gdns
SW10 . . . . **142** B2
Southborough Ho
SE17 . . . . **152** B2
Southborough Rd
E9 . . . . 25 C4
SOUTH BROMLEY
. . . . 34 C4
South Building★
SE10 . . . . 52 C3
Southbury Ho **8**
SW9 . . . . **79** A4
South Camden Com
Sch NW1 . . . . **83** B2
South Carriage Dr
SW1, SW7 . . . . . . **130** C4

South Chelsea Coll
SW9 . . . . 62 B3
South Colonnade The
E14 . . . . 34 A1
Southcombe St
W14 . . . . **140** A4
Southcote Rd N19 . . 13 B4
Southcott Ho
31 Bromley E3 . . . . 27 A2
W9 . . . . **89** A1
South Cres
Newham E16 . . . . . 27 C1
WC1 . . . . **105** B3
South Ct **5** SW5 . . 57 C1
Southdean Gdns
SW19 . . . . 70 B2
Southdown N7 . . . . 14 A2
South Eastern Univ
N7 . . . . 5 B1
South Eaton Pl
SW1 . . . . **145** C4
South Edwardes Sq
W8 . . . . **127** B1
South End W8 . . . . **128** B2
South End Cl NW3 . . 12 A4
South End Gn
NW3 . . . . 12 A4
South End Rd
NW3 . . . . 12 A4
South End Row
W8 . . . . **128** B2
Southerngate Way
SE14 . . . . 51 A3
Southern Gr E3 . . . . 26 B1
Southern Row
W10 . . . . 23 A1
Southern St N1 . . . . **84** C2
Southern Way
SE10 . . . . 43 B3
Southerton Rd
W6 . . . . 39 B2
Southey Ho SE17 **151** A2
Southfield Lo W4 . . 37 C4
Southfield Prim Sch
W4 . . . . 38 A4
Southfield Rd W4 . . 37 C4
SOUTHFIELDS 71 A3
Southfields Com Coll
SW18 . . . . 70 C2
Southfields Rd
SW18 . . . . 58 C1
Southfields Sta
SW18 . . . . 70 B3
Southgate Ct N1 . . 15 C1
Southgate Gr N1 . . 15 C1
Southgate Rd N1 . . **87** C4
South Gr N6 . . . . . . 3 C3
South Grove Ho N6 . . 3 C3
SOUTH HACKNEY
. . . . 25 B4
SOUTH HAMPSTEAD
. . . . 11 B1
South Hampstead
High Sch NW3 . . 11 C2
South Hampstead
High Sch Jun Dept
NW3 . . . . 11 B2
South Hampstead Sta
NW8 . . . . 11 B1
South Hill Pk
NW3 . . . . 12 A4
South Hill Pk Gdns
NW3 . . . . 12 A4
Southill St E14 . . . . 34 A3

South Island Pl
SW9 . . . . **163** B1
SOUTH KENSINGTON
. . . . 143 A3
South Kensington Sta
SW7 . . . . **143** C4
South Kensington
Station Arc SW7 **143** C4
SOUTH LAMBETH
. . . . **172** B3
South Lambeth Pl
SW8 . . . . **162** B4
South Lambeth Rd
SW8 . . . . **162** B2
Southlands Dr
SW19 . . . . 69 C2
South Lo NW8 . . . . . **89** B4
South London
Montessori Sch
SW11 . . . . **168** A3
Southmead Prim Sch
SW19 . . . . 70 A3
Southmead Rd
SW19 . . . . 70 A3
South Molton La
W1 . . . . **104** A1
South Molton Rd
E16 . . . . 35 C3
South Molton St
W1 . . . . **104** A1
Southmoor Way
E9 . . . . 18 B3
Southolm St
SW11 . . . . **170** B3
South Par W4 . . . . . 37 C2
South Parade
SW3 . . . . **143** C2
South Park Mews
SW6 . . . . 59 A4
South Pl EC2 . . . . . **109** C3
South Pl Mews
EC2 . . . . **109** C3
South Quay Plaza
E14 . . . . 42 A4
South Quay Sta
E14 . . . . 42 A4
South Row SE3 . . . . 53 B1
South Sea St SE16 . . 41 B3
Southside N7 . . . . . 13 C4
South Side W6 . . . . 38 B3
Southside Ind Est
SW8 . . . . **170** C4
Southside Quarter
SW11 . . . . **168** C3
Southside Sh Ctr
SW18 . . . . 59 A1
South Sq WC1 . . . **107** B3
South St W1 . . . . . **117** C2
South Tenter St
E1 . . . . **111** A1
South Terr SW7 . . **144** A4
South Thames Coll
(Battersea Ctr)
SW11 . . . . **169** A3
South Thames Coll
(Putney Ctr)
SW15 . . . . 57 C2
South Thames Coll
(Roehampton Ctr)
SW15 . . . . 56 C1
South Thames Coll
(Wandsworth Ctr)
SW18 . . . . 59 A2
Southvale Rd SE3 . . 53 A1
Southview Ave
NW10 . . . . 8 B3

South Villas NW1 . . 13 C2
Southville SW8 . . **171** C3
SOUTHWARK 40 B2
Southwark Bridge SE1,
EC4 . . . . **123** A3
Southwark Bridge Rd
SE1 . . . . **123** A2
Southwark Cath★
SE1 . . . . **123** B2
Southwark Coll
SE1 . . . . **136** A4
Southwark Coll
(Blackfriars Ctr)
SE1 . . . . **122** A1
Southwark Coll
(Camberwell Ctr)
SE5 . . . . 49 A3
Southwark Coll
(Grange Ctr)
SE1 . . . . **138** B1
Southwark Coll
(Surrey Docks Ctr)
SE16 . . . . 40 C3
Southwark Park Est
11 SE16 . . . . 40 B3
Southwark Park Prim
Sch SE16 . . . . 40 A3
Southwark Park Rd
SE16 . . . . **153** B4
Southwark St
SE1 . . . . **122** C1
Southwater Cl **8**
E14 . . . . 33 B3
Southway Cl **9**
W12 . . . . 39 A4
Southwell Gdns
SW7 . . . . **142** C3
Southwell Ho
8 Bermondsey
SE16 . . . . 40 A2
13 Stoke Newington
N16 . . . . 16 A3
Southwell Rd SE5 . . 63 B4
South Wharf Rd
W2 . . . . **101** C2
Southwick Mews
W2 . . . . **101** C2
Southwick Pl W2 **102** A1
Southwick St W2 **102** A2
Southwick Yd
W2 . . . . **102** A1
Southwold Mans
W9 . . . . 23 C2
Southwood Ave N6 . . 4 A4
Southwood Ct EC1 **96** A3
Southwood Ho
W11 . . . 31 A2 **112** A4
Southwood Hospl
(Geriatric) N6 . . . . 3 C4
Southwood Hts N6 . . 4 A4
Southwood La N6 . . 3 C4
Southwood Lawn Rd
N6 . . . . 4 A4
Southwood Park
N6 . . . . 3 C4
Southwood Smith Ho
4 E2 . . . . 25 A2
Southwood Smith St
N1 . . . . **86** A3
South Worple Ave
SW14 . . . . 56 A4
Southwyck Ho
SW9 . . . . 62 C3
South Yd EC1 . . . . **109** B4
Sovereign Cl E1 . . 32 A2
Sovereign Cres
SE16 . . . . 33 A2

Sovereign Ct
3 Richmond TW9 . . 54 B3
10 Stepney E1 . . . . 32 A2
Sovereign Ho **23**
E1 . . . . 25 A1
Sovereign Mews **6**
E2 . . . . 24 B3
Sovereign Ho
NW10 . . . . 20 A2
Space Bsns Pk
NW10 . . . . 20 A2
Spa Ct SE16 . . . . **139** B3
Spafield St EC1 . . . . **95** B2
Spalding Ho SE4 . . 66 A2
Spanby Rd E3 . . . . 26 C1
Spaniards Cl NW11 . . 2 C3
Spaniards End
NW3 . . . . 2 C3
Spaniards Rd NW3 . . 2 B2
Spanish Pl W1 . . . **103** C2
Spanish Rd SW18 . . 59 B2
Spa Rd SE16 . . . . **139** A1
Sparke Terr **2**
E16 . . . . 35 B3
Sparkford Ho
SW11 . . . . **167** C4
Sparks Cl W3 . . . . 28 C3
Sparsholt Rd N19 . . 5 B3
Sparta St SE10 . . . 52 B2
Spa Sch SE1 . . . . **153** B4
Spa View **6** SW16 . . 74 B1
Speakers' Corner★
W1 . . . . **117** A4
Speakman Ho **4** . . 66 A4
Spear Mews SW5 **141** C3
Spears Rd N19 . . . . 5 A3
Spectrum Ho
NW5 . . . . 12 C4
Spedan Cl NW3 . . . . 2 B1
Speechly Mews
E8 . . . . 16 B3
Speed Ho EC2 . . . **109** B4
Speedwell St **8**
SE8 . . . . 51 C3
Speedy Pl WC1 . . . **94** A3
Speldhurst Rd
Bedford Pk W4 . . . 37 C3
Homerton E9 . . . . . 17 C1
Spellbrook Wlk
N1 . . . . **87** A4
Spelman Ho E1 . . **111** B3
Spelman St E1 . . . **111** B4
Spence Cl SE16 . . 41 B4
Spencer Gdns
SW14 . . . . 55 B2
Spencer Ho
Clapham SW8 . . . **171** B1
24 Putney SW19 . . 69 C3
Vale of Health NW3 . . 2 C1
Wimbledon SW19 . . 69 C1
Spencer House Mews★
SW1 . . . . **118** C2
Spencer Mews
Fulham W6 . . . . . **154** A4
South Lambeth
SW9 . . . . **172** B3
Spencer Park Ct
SW18 . . . . 59 C2
Spencer Pk SW18 . . 59 C2
Spencer Pl
10 Islington N1 . . 15 A1
SW1 . . . . **133** A2
Spencer Rd
Acton W3 . . . . 28 B1
Chiswick W4 . . . . . 45 B3
Wandsworth SW18 . . 59 C2
Spencer Rise NW5 . . 4 A1

Spencer St EC1 .... **96** A3
Spencer Wlk
26 Hampstead
NW3 ....11 B4
Putney SW15 .....57 C3
Spencer Yd SE3 ...53 B1
Spenlow Ho SE16 **139** C2
Spenser Gr N16 ...16 A4
Spenser Mews
SE21 ....75 C3
Spenser Rd SE24 ..63 A2
Spenser St SW1 ..**133** A2
Spens Ho WC1 .....**94** C1
Spensley Wlk N16...6 C1
Spert St E14 ....33 A2
Spey St E14 ....34 B4
Spezia Rd NW10 ...21 C3
Spice Ct
10 Battersea
SW11 ....59 B4
St George in the East
E1 ....**125** C2
Spice Quay Htss
SE1 ....**125** A1
Spicer Cl SE5, SW9..48 A1
Spicer Ho
E2 ....24 C2 **99** B3
Spindrift Ave E14...42 A2
Spinnaker Ho **21**
E14 ....41 C4
Spinney The
Barnes SW13 .....47 A4
Streatham SW16 ...73 C1
Spire Ct **18** TW10...54 A1
Spire Ho W2 ....**115** A4
Spirit Quay E1 ....32 A1
SPITALFIELDS 111 A4
Spital Sq E1 ......**110** B4
Spital St E1 ....**110** B4
Spital Yd E1 ......**110** B4
Splendid Wlk
SE16 ....40 B1
Spode Ho SE11 ..**135** B1
Spode Wlk NW3 ...11 A3
Sporle Ct **6** SW11..59 C4
Sprewell SW11 ....58 A1
Spriggs Ho **4** N1 ..15 A1
Sprimont Pl SW3 **144** C2
Springall St **9**
SE15 ....50 A3
Springalls Wharf
SE16 ....**139** B4
Springbank Wlk
NW1 ....13 C1
Spring Cott **10**
W12 ....38 C2
Spring Ct NW2 ....10 B2
Springdale Rd
N16 ....15 C4
Springett Ho **18**
SW2 ....62 B2
Springfield Ct
7 Dagenham W3 ...28 B3
Hampstead NW3 ...11 A2
Springfield Ho
Acton W3 ....28 B1
11 Camberwell SE5..49 A1
15 Dalston E8 .....16 A1
Springfield Hostel
SW17 ....72 A1
Springfield La
NW6 ....78 A3
Springfield Rd
NW8 ....79 A3
Springfield Wlk
NW6 ....78 A3

Spring Gdns
Islington N5 ....15 B3
SW1 ....**120** A2
Spring Gr W4 ......44 C4
Spring Grove Rd
TW10 ....54 B2
Spring Hill E5 ....7 C4
Springhill Cl SE5 ..64 A4
Spring Ho WC1.....**95** B3
Spring Mews W1 .**103** A4
Springpark Dr N4 ...6 B3
Spring Pl NW5 ....13 A3
Springrice Rd
SE13 ....67 C1
Spring Terr W2 ..**101** B1
Spring Terr TW10...54 A2
Springtide Cl **10**
SE15 ....49 C2
Springvale Ave
TW8 ....36 A1
Springvale Terr **5**
W14 ....39 C3
Springwater WC1 **106** C4
Springwell Ave
NW10 ....21 B4
Spring Wlk E1 ...**111** C4
Springwood Cl **8**
E3 ....26 C3
Spruce Ct W5 .....36 A3
Spruce Ho **18**
SE16 ....40 C4
Sprules Rd SE4....51 A1
Spurgeon St SE1 **137** B2
Spurling Rd SE22...64 B3
Spur Rd SE1 .....**135** B4
Spurstowe Rd E8...17 A2
Spurstowe Terr
E8 ....17 A3
Square Rigger Row **7**
SW11 ....59 B4
Square The
Hammersmith W6 ..39 B1
SW6 ....**165** B3
Squarey St SW17 ..71 B1
Squire Gdns NW8 ..89 C3
Squires Ct **3**
SW4 ....**172** B3
Squire's Mount
NW3 ....2 C1
Squirrels The
SE13 ....67 C3
Squirries St
E2 ....24 C2 **99** C3
Stable Ho **3** SE16..40 B4
Stables Way SE11 **149** B2
Stable Way W10....30 B3
Stable Yd Rd
SW1 ....**133** A4
Stacey St
Highbury N7 ....5 C1
Soho WC2 ....**105** C1
Stack Ho SW1 ...**145** C3
Stackhouse St
SW1 ....**130** C2
Stacy Path **15** SE5..49 A3
Stadium St SW10 ..**157** A1
Stafford Cl NW6...**23** C2
Stafford Cripps Ho
E2 ....25 B2
SW6 ....**155** A3
Stafford Ct
Kensington W8....**127** C2
South Lambeth
SW8 ....**172** B3
Stafford Ho SE1 ..**153** A2

Stafford Mans
18 Hammersmith
W14 ....39 C3
17 Stockwell SW4...62 A3
SW11 ....**158** C1
Stafford Pl SW1 ..**132** C2
Stafford Rd
Bow E3 ....26 B3
Maida Vale NW6 ...23 C2
Staffordshire St
Peckham SE15 ....49 C2
Peckham SE15 ....50 A2
Stafford St W1 ...**118** C2
Stafford Terr W8 .**127** B2
Stag La SW15 ....**68** A2
Stagshaw Ho **17**
SE22 ....64 A4
Stainer St SE1 ...**123** C1
Staining La EC2 .**109** A2
Stainsbury St **28**
E2 ....25 B3
Stainsby Rd E14...33 C3
Stalbridge Flats
W1 ....**103** C1
Stalbridge Ho
NW1 ....**82** C1
Stalbridge St
NW1 ....**102** B4
Stalham St SE16 ..40 A3
Stambourne Ho
SW8 ....**172** B4
Stamford Bridge
Stadium (Chelsea
FC) SW6 ....**156** A2
Stamford Brook Ave
W6 ....38 B3
Stamford Brook Gdns
1 W6 ....38 B3
Stamford Brook Mans
2 W6 ....38 B2
Stamford Brook Rd
W6 ....38 B2
Stamford Cl **2**
NW3 ....2 B1
Stamford Cotts
SW10 ....**156** B2
Stamford Ct W6...38 C2
Stamford Gr E **1**
N16 ....7 C3
Stamford Gr W **4**
N16 ....7 C3
STAMFORD HILL 7 A3
Stamford Hill N16...7 A3
Stamford Hill Mans **1**
N16 ....7 A4
Stamford Hill Sta
N16 ....7 A4
Stamford Hospl
W6 ....38 C2
Stamford Lo **2**
N16 ....7 B3
Stamford Mans **2**
N16 ....7 C3
Stamford Rd N1...16 A2
Stamford St SE1 .**121** C2
Stamp Pl E2 .24 B2 **99** A4
Stanard Cl N16 .....7 A4
Stanborough Ho **4**
E3 ....27 A1
Stanborough Pas
E8 ....16 B2
Stanbridge Mans
SW15 ....57 B4
Stanbridge Rd
SW15 ....57 B4

Stanbrook Ct W1 .**118** C2
Stanbury Ct **18**
NW3 ....12 B2
Stanbury Rd
Nunhead SE15 ....50 A1
Peckham SE15 ....50 A1
Standard Pl
EC2 ....24 A2 **98** B3
Standard Rd
NW10 ....20 C1
Standen Rd SW18 .70 C4
Standish Ho **6**
W6 ....38 C2
Standish Rd W6 ...38 C2
Stanesgate Ho **20**
SE15 ....49 C3
Stanfield Ho NW8 .**89** C2
Stanfield Rd **14**
E3 ....26 A3
Stanford Ct
Kensington W8....**128** B1
Walham Green
SW6 ....**166** B3
Stanford Pl SE1 ..**152** A3
Stanford Rd W8 ..**128** B2
Stanford St SW1 .**147** B3
Stangate SE1 ....**135** A2
Stanhope Cl **23**
SE16 ....40 C4
Stanhope Gate
W1 ....**117** C2
Stanhope Gdns
SW7 ....**143** A4
Stanhope Ho
4 Putney SW15 ...57 B2
SE8 ....51 B3
Stanhope Mews E
SW7 ....**143** A3
Stanhope Mews S
SW7 ....**143** A3
Stanhope Mews W
SW7 ....**143** A3
Stanhope Par
NW1 ....**92** C4
Stanhope Pl W2 .**102** C1
Stanhope Rd N6 ...4 B4
Stanhope Row
W1 ....**118** A1
Stanhope St NW1 .**92** C3
Stanhope Terr
W2 ....**115** C4
Stanier Cl SW5 ..**141** A1
Stanlake Mews **7**
W12 ....30 B1
Stanlake Rd W12...30 B1
Stanlake Villas **8**
W12 ....30 B1
Stanley Bldgs
NW1 ....**84** A1
Stanley Cl SW8 .**162** C3
Stanley Cohen Ho
EC1 ....**96** C1
Stanley Cres
W11 ....31 B2 **112** C4
Stanley Gdns
Bedford Pk W3 ....38 A4
Cricklewood NW2 ...9 B3
W11 ....31 B2 **112** C4
Stanley Gr SW11 .**169** C1
Stanley Ho **1**
Clapham SW8.....**171** B1
22 Poplar E14 ....33 C3
Stanley Holloway Ct
E16 ....35 C3
Stanley Mans
SW10 ....**157** A4

Stanley Mans continued
Upper Tooting
SW17 ....72 B2
Stanley Rd
Acton Green W3...37 B3
Mill Meads E15 ....27 C4
Mortlake SW14 ....55 A3
Stanley St SE14,
SE8 ....51 B3
Stanley Studios
SW10 ....**157** A4
Stanley Terr **8**
N19 ....5 A2
Stanliff Ho **8** E14 .41 C3
Stanmer St SW11 .**168** B2
Stanmore Gdns
TW9 ....54 B4
Stanmore Ho
SW8 ....**171** C2
Stanmore Pl NW1 .**82** B4
Stanmore Rd TW9 .54 B4
Stanmore St N1 .....84 C4
Stannard Cotts **27**
E1 ....25 B1
Stannard Mews
E8 ....16 C2
Stannard Rd E8 ...16 C2
Stannary Pl SE11 **149** C1
Stannary St SE11 **149** C1
Stansbury Sq **3**
W10 ....23 A2
Stansfeld Ho SE1 **153** A3
Stansfield Rd SW9 .62 B4
Stanstead Ho E3 ..27 B1
Stansted Express
Terminal EC2.....**110** A4
Stanswood Gdns
SE5 ....49 A3
Stanton Ct N16....15 C3
Stanton Ho **9**
SE10 ....52 B4
Stanton Rd SW13 .46 B1
Stanway Ct **22** N1 ..24 A3
Stanway St N1 ....24 A3
Stanwick Rd W14 **140** C3
Stanworth St SE1 **139** A3
Staplefield Cl **3**
SW2 ....74 A3
Stapleford Cl
SW19 ....70 A4
Staplehurst Ct
SW11 ....60 B1
Staplehurst Ho **18**
E5 ....17 C3
Staple Inn WC1 ..**107** B3
Staple Inn Bldgs
WC2 ....**107** B3
Staples Cl SE16 ...33 A1
Staple St SE1 ....**137** C3
Stapleton Hall N4 ...5 B4
Stapleton Hall Rd
N4 ....5 B4
Stapleton Ho **19**
E2 ....25 A2
Stapleton Rd
SW17 ....72 C1
Star Alley EC3 ...**124** B4
Starboard Way
E14 ....41 C3
Starcross St NW1 .93 A3
Stardome* NW1 ....91 B1
Starfield Rd W12 ..38 C4
Star & Garter Mans
SW15 ....57 C4
Starliner Ct N7....14 C2

Starling Ho NW8 . . **80** A2
Star PI E1 . . . . **125** C3
Star Rd W14 . . . . . . **140** C1
Star St W2 . . . . **102** A2
Star Works NW10 . . . . 21 C2
Star Yd WC2 . . . . . . **107** B2
Statham Ct N7 . . . . . 5 A1
Statham Gr N16 . . . . 6 C1
Statham Ho SW8 **170** C4
Station App
  Dagenham NW10 . . . . 21 B2
  Fulham SW6 . . . . 58 A4
  Richmond TW9 . . . . . 44 C2
Station Approach Rd
  W4 . . . . 45 B3
Station Ave
  5 Brixton SW9 . . . . 63 A4
  14 Richmond TW9 . . 44 C2
Station Cres SE3 . . . 43 C1
Station Ct 5 SE15 . . 50 B1
Stationers Hall Ct
  EC4 . . . . **108** B1
Station Gdns W4 . . . 45 B3
Station Mews Terr 4
  SE3 . . . . 43 C1
Station Par
  Cricklewood NW2 . . 9 B2
  Richmond TW9 . . . . 44 C2
  1 Upper Tooting
  SW12 . . . . 72 C3
Station Pas SE15 . . 50 B2
Station PI N4 . . . . . . 5 C2
Station Rd
  Barnes SW13 . . . . . . 46 B1
  Camden Town N19 . . 4 B1
  Harlesden NW10 . . . 21 B3
  Lewisham SE13 . . . . 67 B4
Station Rise SE27 . . 75 A2
Station St E15 . . . . . 19 C1
Station Terr
  Camberwell SE5 . . . 48 B2
  Kensal Rise NW10 . . 22 C3
Staunton Ho
  SE17 . . . . **152** A3
Staunton St SE8 . . . 51 B4
Staveley NW1 . . . . . **92** C4
Staveley Cl
  Hackney E9 . . . . 17 B3
  Lower Holloway N7 . 14 A4
  New Cross Gate
  SE15 . . . . 50 B2
  5 Peckham SE15 . . 50 A2
Staveley Gdns W4 . . 45 C2
Staveley Ho SE4 . . . 66 A2
Staveley Rd W4 . . . . 45 C3
Stavers Ho 8 E3 . . . 26 B2
Staverton Rd NW2 . . 9 B1
Stave Yard Rd
  SE16 . . . . 33 A1
Stavordale Lo
  W14 . . . . **127** A2
Stavordale Rd N5 . . 15 A4
Stayner's Rd E1 . . . 25 C1
Steadman Ct EC1 . . **97** A2
Stead St SE17 . . . . **151** B3
Stean St E8 . . . . 24 B4
Stebbing Ho 8
  W11 . . . . 30 C1
Stebondale St E14 . . 42 B2
Stebon Prim Sch
  E14 . . . . 33 C4
Stedham PI WC1 . . **106** A2
Stedman Ho
  SE17 . . . . **150** C3

Steele Rd
  Acton Green W4 . . . . 37 B3
  Becontree NW10 . . . 20 B3
Steele's Mews N
  NW3 . . . . 12 B2
Steele's Mews S
  NW3 . . . . 12 B2
Steel's La 23 E1 . . . 32 B3
Steen Way 7
  SE22 . . . . 64 A2
Steep Hill SW16 . . . 73 C1
Steeple Cl SW6 . . . **164** B1
Steeple Ct 1 E1 . . . 25 A1
Steeple Wlk N1 . . . **87** A4
Steerforth St
  SW18 . . . . 71 B2
Steers Way SE16 . . . 41 A4
Stelfax Ho W14 . . . **95** A4
Stephan Cl E8 . . . . . 24 C4
Stephen Cl 18
  SW19 . . . . 69 C3
Stephendale Rd
  SW6 . . . . **166** C2
Stephen Fox Ho 7
  W4 . . . . 38 A1
Stephen Hawking Sch
  E14 . . . . 33 A3
Stephen Mews
  W1 . . . . **105** B3
Stephen PI SW4 . . . 61 B4
Stephen Saunders Ct
  SW11 . . . . 60 A2
Stephens Ct 5 SE4 . . 66 A4
Stephenson Ho
  2 Gospel Oak
  NW5 . . . . 13 A4
  5 Maitland Pk
  NW3 . . . . 12 B3
  Newington SE1 . . . . **136** C2
Stephenson St
  Dagenham NW10 . . . 21 B2
  Newham E16 . . . . . . 35 A4
Stephenson Way
  NW1 . . . . **93** A3
Stephen St W1 . . . **105** B3
STEPNEY 32 C4
Stepney City E1 . . . 32 B4
Stepney Cswy E1 . . 32 C3
Stepney Gn E1 . . . . 32 C4
Stepney Greencoat CE
  Prim Sch The
  E14 . . . . 33 B3
Stepney Green Ct 4
  E1 . . . . 32 C4
Stepney Green Sch
  E1 . . . . 32 C4
Stepney Green Sta
  E1 . . . . 25 C1
Stepney High St
  E1 . . . . 32 C4
Stepney Way E1 . . . 32 B4
Sterling Cl NW10 . . . 8 C1
Sterling Gdns
  SE14 . . . . 51 A4
Sterling PI W5 . . . . . 36 A2
Sterling St SW7 . . **130** B2
Sterndale Rd W14 . . 39 C3
Sterne St W12 . . . . . 39 C4
Sternhall La SE15 . . 64 C4
Sternhold Ave SW12,
  SW2 . . . . 73 C2
Sterry St SE1 . . . . **137** B3
Steve Biko Ct
  W10 . . . . 22 C1
Steve Biko Rd N7 . . 5 C1

Stevedore St 8
  E1 . . . . 32 A1
Stevenage Rd
  SW6 . . . . 47 C2
Stevens Ave E9 . . . . 17 B2
Stevenson Cres
  SE16 . . . . 40 A1
Stevenson Ho
  Battersea SW11 . . **168** C1
  6 Clapham Pk
  SW2 . . . . 62 A2
  NW8 . . . . **78** C4
Stevens St SE1 . . . **138** B2
Steventon Rd W12 . . 29 B2
Stewart Headlam
  Prim Sch E1 . . . . . **25** A1
Stewart Ho SE1 . . **138** A1
Stewart Rd E15 . . . 19 C4
Stewart's Gr SW3 . **144** A2
Stewart's Rd SW8 **170** C4
Stewart St E14 . . . . 42 B4
Stew La EC4 . . . . . **122** C4
Steyne Ho
  Acton W3 . . . . 28 A1
  11 Acton W3 . . . . . . 28 B1
Steyne Rd W3 . . . . . 28 A1
Stifford Ho E1 . . . . . 32 B4
Stile Hall Gdns
  W4 . . . . 36 C1
Stile Hall Par 6
  W4 . . . . 36 C1
Stileman Ho 4 E3 . . 33 B4
Stillingfleet Rd
  SW13 . . . . 46 C4
Stillington St
  SW1 . . . . **147** A4
Stillness Jun & Inf
  Schs SE23 . . . . 66 A1
Stillness Rd SE23 . . 66 A1
Stirling Ct
  Clerkenwell EC1 . . . **96** A2
  Strand WC2 . . . . . **106** C1
Stirling Mans
  NW6 . . . . 11 B2
Stirling Rd
  South Acton W3 . . . 37 A3
  Stockwell SW9 . . . **172** B1
Stoatley Ho 10
  SW15 . . . . 68 C3
Stockbeck NW1 . . . **83** A1
Stockfield Rd
  SW16 . . . . 74 B1
Stockholm Ho E1 . **125** C4
Stockholm Rd
  SE16 . . . . 40 B1
Stockholm Way
  E1 . . . . **125** B2
Stockhurst Cl
  SW15 . . . . 47 C1
Stock Orchard Cres
  N7 . . . . 14 B3
Stock Orchard St
  N7 . . . . 14 B3
Stocks Ct 5 E1 . . . 25 C1
Stocks PI 16 E14 . . 33 B2
Stockton Ho 8
  E2 . . . . 25 A2
STOCKWELL 62 A4
Stockwell Ave
  SW9 . . . . 62 B4
Stockwell Gdns
  SW9 . . . . **172** C2
Stockwell Gn
  SW9 . . . . **172** C1

Stockwell La
  SW9 . . . . **172** C1
Stockwell Park Cres
  SW9 . . . . **173** A2
Stockwell Park Rd
  SW9 . . . . **173** A3
Stockwell Park Sch
  SW9 . . . . **172** C3
Stockwell Park Wlk
  SW9 . . . . 62 C4
Stockwell Prim Sch
  SW9 . . . . 62 B4
Stockwell St SE10 . . 52 B4
Stockwell Sta
  SW4 . . . . **172** B2
Stockwell Terr
  SW9 . . . . **172** C3
Stoddart Ho SW8 **163** A3
Stodmarsh Ho
  SW9 . . . . **173** C4
Stofford Cl SW19 . . . 70 A4
Stokenchurch St
  SW6 . . . . **166** A3
STOKE NEWINGTON
  . . . . 7 A2
Stoke Newington
  Church St N16 . . . . 7 A2
Stoke Newington
  Comm N16 . . . . . . 7 B2
Stoke Newington
  High St N16 . . . . . . 7 B1
Stoke Newington Rd
  N16 . . . . 16 B4
Stoke Newington Sch
  N16 . . . . 6 C1
Stoke Newington Sta
  N16 . . . . 7 B2
Stoke PI NW10 . . . . 21 B2
Stokesley St W12 . . 29 B3
Stondon Pk SE23 . . 66 A1
Stone Bldgs WC2 **107** A3
Stonebridge Ctr 8
  NW10 . . . . 20 C4
Stonebridge Sch The
  NW10 . . . . 20 C4
Stone Cl SW4 . . . **171** A1
Stonecutter St
  EC4 . . . . **108** A2
Stonefield N4 . . . . . . 5 B2
Stonefield Mans
  N1 . . . . **85** B3
Stonefield St N1 . . . **85** B4
Stonegate 8
  NW5 . . . . 12 C2
Stonehill Cl SW14 . . 55 C2
Stonehill Rd
  Brentford W4 . . . . . 36 C1
  Mortlake SW14 . . . . 55 C2
Stonehills Ct SE21 . 76 A1
Stonehill's Mans 3
  SW16 . . . . 74 A2
Stonehouse NW1 . . **83** A3
Stonehouse Ct
  EC2 . . . . **110** B2
Stonehouse Ho 2
  W2 . . . . 31 C4
Stoneleigh Lo 13
  TW9 . . . . 44 B2
Stoneleigh Mews 13
  E3 . . . . 26 A3
Stoneleigh PI
  W11 . . . . 30 C2
Stoneleigh St
  W11 . . . . 30 C2
Stoneleigh Terr
  N19 . . . . 4 A2

Stonell's Rd SW11 . . 60 B2
Stonenest St N4 . . . . 5 B3
Stones End St
  SE1 . . . . **136** C3
Stoneyard La E14 . . 34 A2
Stoney La E1 . . . . **110** B2
Stoney St SE1 . . . **123** B2
Stonhouse St
  SW4 . . . . 61 C3
Stonor Rd W14 . . . **140** C3
Stopes St SE15 . . . . 49 B3
Stopford Rd SE17 . **150** B1
Stopher Ho SE1 . . **136** B3
Storace Ho 6
  SW4 . . . . 62 A3
Storers Quay E14 . . 42 C2
Store St
  Bloomsbury WC1 . . **105** B4
  Stratford New Town
  E15 . . . . 19 C3
Storey Ct NW8 . . . **89** B3
Storey Ho 3 E14 . . 34 A2
Storey's Gate
  SW1 . . . . **133** C2
Stories Rd SE5 . . . . 64 A4
Storks Rd SE16 . . . **139** C2
Stormont House Sch
  E5 . . . . 17 A4
Stormont Rd
  Clapham SW11 . . . . 60 C3
  Highgate N6 . . . . . . 3 B4
Storrington WC1 . . **94** B3
Story St N1 . . . . 14 B1
Stothard Ho 25 E1 . . 25 B1
Stothard PI E1 . . . **110** B4
Stothard St 12 E1 . . 25 B1
Stott Cl SW18 . . . . . 59 C1
Stoughton Cl
  Roehampton SW15 . . 68 C3
  SE11 . . . . **149** A3
Stourcliffe Cl W1 . **102** C2
Stourcliffe St W1 . **102** C1
Stourhead Cl 6
  SW19 . . . . 69 C4
Stour Rd E3 . . . . . . 18 C1
Stowage SE8 . . . . . . 52 A4
Stowe Ho 11 N16 . . 7 A1
Stowe Rd W12 . . . . 39 A4
Stracey Rd NW10 . . 20 C4
Stradbroke Rd N5 . . 15 B4
Stradella Rd SE24 . . 63 B1
Straffan Lo 8
  NW3 . . . . 12 A2
Strafford Ho 9
  SE8 . . . . 41 B1
Strafford Rd W3 . . . 37 B4
Strafford St E14 . . . 41 C4
Strahan Rd E3 . . . . 26 A2
Straightsmouth
  SE10 . . . . 52 B3
Straker's Rd SE15 . . 65 A3
Strale Ho 17 N1 . . . 24 A4
STRAND **120** C4
Strand
  Strand WC2 . . . . . **120** C4
  Strand WC2 . . . . . **107** A1
Strand Dr TW9 . . . . 45 A3
Strand La WC2 . . . **121** B4
STRAND ON THE
  GREEN 44 C4
Strand-on-the-Green
  W4 . . . . 44 C4
Strand-on-the-Green
  Schs W4 . . . . 44 C4
Strang Ho N1 . . . . . **86** C3
Strangways Terr
  W14 . . . . **126** C1

Stranraer Way N1 . . . 14 A1
Strasburg Rd
SW11 . . . . 170 A3
STRATFORD 19 B2
Stratford Bus Sta
E15 . . . . 19 C1
Stratford Cir
(Newham 6th Form
Coll) E15 . . . . 19 C2
Stratford Gr SW15 . . 57 C2
Stratford
International Sta
(under constr)
E15 . . . . 19 B2
STRATFORD MARSH
. . . . 27 A4
STRATFORD NEW
TOWN 19 B3
Stratford Pl W1 . . . 104 A1
Stratford Rd W8 . . . 127 C1
Stratford Sh Ctr
E15 . . . . 19 C1
Stratford Sta E15 . . 19 C1
Stratford Studios
W8 . . . . 128 A1
Stratford Villas
NW1 . . . . 13 C1
Stratford Workshops
E15 . . . . 27 C4
Strathan Cl SE14 . . . 58 A1
Strathblaine Rd
SW11 . . . . 59 C3
Strathdon Dr
SW17 . . . . 71 C1
Strathearn Ho
W2 . . . . 116 A4
Strathearn Pl W2 . . 116 A4
Stratheden Par
SE3 . . . . 53 C3
Stratheden Rd
SE3 . . . . 53 C3
Strathleven Rd
SW2 . . . . 62 A2
Strathmore Ct
NW8 . . . . 90 A4
Strathmore Gdns
W8 . . . . . . 31 C1 113 C2
Strathmore Rd
SW19 . . . . 70 C1
Strathnairn St
SE1 . . . . 153 C3
Strathray Gdns
NW3 . . . . 12 A2
Strath Terr SW11 . . 60 A3
Strathville Rd
SW18 . . . . 71 A2
Stratton Ct 4 N16 . . 16 A1
Strattondale St
E14 . . . . 42 B3
Stratton St W1 . . . 118 B2
Strauss Rd W4 . . . . 37 C4
Streamline Mews
SE22 . . . . 76 C3
Streatham Cl
SW16 . . . . 74 A2
Streatham & Clapham
High Sch SW16 . . 73 C1
Streatham Ct
SW16 . . . . 74 A1
STREATHAM HILL
. . . . 74 A3
Streatham Hill
SW2 . . . . 74 A3
Streatham Hill &
Clapham High Sch
SW2 . . . . 74 B3

Streatham Hill Sta
SW2 . . . . 74 A2
Streatham PI SW2 . . 74 A4
Streatham St
WC1 . . . . 106 A2
Streathbourne Rd
SW17 . . . . 72 C1
Streatham Wells Prim
Sch SW2 . . . . 74 C2
Streatleigh Par 4
SW16 . . . . 74 A1
Streatley PI 17
Hampstead
NW3 . . . . 11 B4
Hampstead NW3 . . 11 C4
Streatley Rd NW6 . . 10 B1
Streimer Rd E15 . . . 27 B3
Strelley Way W3 . . . 29 A2
Stretton Mans 18
SE8 . . . . 51 C4
Strickland Ct
SE15 . . . . 64 C4
Strickland Ho
E2 . . . . 24 B2 99 A3
Strickland Row
SW18 . . . . 71 C4
Strickland St SE8 . . 51 C2
Stringer Hos 19
N1 . . . . 24 A4
Strode Ho 8 SW2 . . 74 C3
Strode Rd NW6 . . . 154 A2
Willesden NW10 . . . 8 C2
Strome Ho NW6 . . . 78 A1
Stronsa Rd W12 . . . 38 B4
Strood Ho SE1 . . . 137 C3
Stroud Cres SW15 . . 68 C1
Stroud Green Prim
Sch N4 . . . . 5 C3
Stroud Green Rd
N4 . . . . 5 C3
Stroudley Ho
SW8 . . . . 171 A4
Stroudley Wlk E3 . . 27 A2
Stroud Rd SW19 . . . 70 C1
Strout's PI
E2 . . . . 24 B2 98 C4
Strudwick Ct
SW4 . . . . 172 B3
Strutton Ground
SW1 . . . . 133 B1
Strype St E1 . . . . . 110 C3
Stuart Av W5 . . . . . 36 B4
Stuart Ho
Hammersmith W6 . . 39 B3
1 Homerton E9 . . . . 17 C1
5 Stockwell SW4 . . . 62 A3
W14 . . . . 140 A4
Stuart Mill Ho N1 . . 84 C1
Stuart Rd
Acton W3 . . . . 28 B1
Maida Vale NW6 . . . 23 C2
Nunhead SE15 . . . . 65 B3
Wimbledon SW19 . . 70 C1
Stubbs Dr SE16 . . . 40 A1
Stubbs Ho
Finsbury Pk N4 . . . . 5 B3
1 Globe Town E2 . . 25 C2
Stucley PI 11 NW1 . . 13 A1
Studdridge St
SW6 . . . . 165 C2
Studd St N1 . . . . . . 86 A4
Studholme Ct
NW3 . . . . 10 C4
Studholme St
SE15 . . . . 50 A3
Studio Pl SW1 . . . . 131 A3
Studios NW8 . . . . . 78 C2

Studios The
4 Clapham SW4 . . . 61 B3
SW8 . . . . 170 C4
Studland SE17 . . . 151 B2
Studland Ho E14 . . 33 A3
Studland St W6 . . . 39 A2
Studley Cl E5 . . . . . 18 A3
Studley Ct 13 E14 . . 34 C2
Studley Dr IG4 . . . . 24 C1
Studley Rd SW4 . . 172 B2
Stukeley St WC2 . . 106 B2
Stunell Ho 20
SE14 . . . . 50 C4
Sturdee Ho 2 E2 . . 24 C3
Sturdy Ho 22 E3 . . . 26 A3
Sturdy Rd SE15 . . . 50 A1
Sturgeon Rd
SE17 . . . . 150 C1
Sturge St SE1 . . . . 136 C4
Sturmer Way N7 . . . 14 B3
Sturminster Ho
SW8 . . . . 163 A1
Sturry St E14 . . . . . 34 A3
Sturt St N1 . . . . 87 A1
Stutfield St E1 . . . 111 C1
Stuttle Ho
E1 . . . . 24 C1 99 B1
Styles Gdns SW9 . . 63 A4
Styles Ho SE1 . . . . 122 A1
Stylus Apartments 23
E1 . . . . 111 B2
Sudbourne Prim Sch
SW2 . . . . 62 B2
Sudbourne Rd
SW2 . . . . 62 B2
Sudbrooke Rd
SW12 . . . . 60 C1
Sudbury Ct SW8 . . 171 C4
Sudbury Ho SW18 . . 59 A2
Sudeley St N1 . . . . . 86 B1
Sudlow Rd SW18 . . 58 C2
Sudrey St SE1 . . . . 136 C3
Suffield Ho SE17 . . 150 B2
Suffolk Ho 8 NW5 . . 4 B1
Suffolk La EC4 . . . 123 B4
Suffolk Pl SW1 . . . 119 C2
Suffolk Rd
Barnes SW13 . . . . . 46 C3
Willesden NW10 . . . 8 A1
Suffolk St SW1 . . . 119 C2
Sugar House La
E15 . . . . 27 B3
Sugar Loaf Wlk 8
E2 . . . . 25 B2
Sugden Rd SW11 . . 60 C3
Sulby Ho SE4 . . . . . 66 A3
Sulgrave Gdns 11
W6 . . . . 39 B4
Sulgrave Rd W6 . . . 39 B3
Sulina Rd SW2 . . . . 74 A4
Sulivan Ct SW6 . . . 165 B1
Sulivan Ent Ctr
SW6 . . . . 58 C4
Sulivan Prim Sch
SW6 . . . . 165 B1
Sulivan Rd SW6 . . 165 B1
Sulkin Ho 11 E2 . . . 25 C2
Sullivan Cl SW11 . . 60 A4
Sullivan Ct
Stamford Hill N16 . . 7 B3
SW5 . . . . 141 C4
Sullivan Ho
Chelsea SW1 . . . . 160 B4
Vauxhall SE11 . . . 149 A3
Sullivan Rd SE11 . . 149 C4
Sultan St SE5 . . . . 48 B3
Sumatra Rd NW6 . . 10 C2

Sumburgh Rd
SW12 . . . . 60 C1
Summercourt Rd
E1 . . . . 32 B3
Summerfield Ave
NW6 . . . . 23 A3
Summerhouse Rd
SE13 . . . . 67 C3
Summerhouse Rd
N16 . . . . 7 A2
Summerlands Ave
W3 . . . . 28 B2
Summerley St
SW18 . . . . 71 A2
Summers St EC1 . . . 95 B1
SUMMERSTOWN . . 71 B1
Summit Ct NW2 . . . 10 A3
Summit Est N16 . . . . 7 C4
Sumner Ave SE15 . . 49 B2
Sumner Bldgs
SE1 . . . . 122 C2
Sumner Ct SW8 . . 172 A4
Sumner Ho 1 E3 . . 34 A4
Sumner Pl SW7 . . 143 C3
Sumner Place Mews
SW7 . . . . 143 C3
Sumner Rd SE15 . . 49 B3
Sumner St SE1 . . . 122 C2
Sumpter Cl NW3 . . 11 B2
Sun Alley 6 W6 . . . 39 A2
Sunbeam Cres
W10 . . . . 22 B1
Sunbeam Rd
NW10 . . . . 20 C1
Sunbury Ave
SW14 . . . . 55 C3
Sunbury Ct 3
SE14 . . . . 50 C4
Sunbury Ho
E2 . . . . 24 B2 98 C3
Sunbury La SW11 . 167 C4
Sunbury Workshops
E2 . . . . 24 B2 98 C3
Sun Ct EC3 . . . . . . 109 C1
Sunderland Ct
SE22 . . . . 76 C4
Sunderland Ho 26
W2 . . . . 31 C4
Sunderland Terr
W2 . . . . 100 A2
Sundew Ave W12 . . 29 C2
Sundra Wlk 20 E1 . . 25 C1
Sundridge Ho 4
E9 . . . . 17 C1
Sunley Ho E1 . . . . 111 A3
Sunlight Sq 2 E2 . . 25 A2
Sunningdale Ave
W3 . . . . 29 A2
Sunningdale Cl 22
SE16 . . . . 40 A1
Sunningdale Gdns
W8 . . . . 127 C1
Sunninghill Ct 9
W3 . . . . 37 B4
Sunninghill Rd
SE13 . . . . 52 A1
Sunnyhill Cl E5 . . . 18 A4
Sunmead Rd
SW15 . . . . 57 A2
Sunnyside 4 NW2 . . 1 B1
Sunnyside Ho 3
NW2 . . . . 1 B1
Sunnyside Rd N19 . . 4 C4
Sun Pas SE16 . . . . 139 B2
Sunray Ave SE5,
SE24 . . . . 63 C3

Sun Rd W14 . . . . . 140 C1
Sun St Pas EC2 . . . 110 A3
Sunset Rd SE5 . . . . 63 C3
Sun St EC2 . . . . . . 109 C4
Sunwell Cl SE15 . . . 50 A2
Surcot Ho W4 . . . . 171 C1
Surma Cl E1 . . 24 C1 99 C1
Surrendale Pl W9 . . 23 C1
Surrey Canal Rd SE14,
SE16, SE8 . . . . . . 50 C4
Surrey Cres 11
W4 . . . . 36 C1
Surrey Gr SE17 . . . 152 A1
Surrey Ho 8 SE16 . . 32 C1
Surrey La SW11 . . . 168 B3
Surrey Quays Rd
SE16 . . . . 40 C4
Surrey Quays Sh Ctr
SE16 . . . . 40 C3
Surrey Quays Sta
SE16 . . . . 65 C4
Surrey Row SE1 . . 136 B4
Surrey Sq SE17 . . . 152 B2
Surrey Square Inf Sch
SE17 . . . . 152 A2
Surrey Square Jun
Sch SE17 . . . . . . 152 A2
Surrey St WC2 . . . 121 A4
Surrey Terr SE17 . . 152 B2
Surrey Water Rd
SE16 . . . . 32 C1
Surridge Ct SW9 . . 172 B2
Surr St N7 . . . . 14 A3
Susan Constant Ct 11
E14 . . . . 34 C2
Susan Rd SE3 . . . . 53 C1
Sussex Cl N19 . . . . . 5 A2
Sussex Ct
4 Barnes SW13 . . . 46 B1
Greenwich SE10 . . . 52 B4
Paddington W2 . . . 101 B1
Sussex Gdns W2 . . 101 C1
Sussex Ho
Hampstead NW3 . . 12 A2
Richmond TW9 . . . 44 B1
Sussex House Sch
SW1 . . . . 144 C4
Sussex Lo W2 . . . . 101 C1
Sussex Mans
South Kensington
SW7 . . . . 143 B3
Strand WC2 . . . . . 120 B4
Sussex Mews E
W2 . . . . 101 C1
Sussex Mews W
W2 . . . . 115 C4
Sussex Pl
23 Hammersmith
W6 . . . . 39 B1
Lisson Gr NW1 . . . . 90 C2
Paddington W2 . . . 101 C1
Sussex Sq W2 . . . 115 C4
Sussex St SW1 . . . 146 B2
Sussex Way
Upper Holloway N7 . . 5 A1
Upper Holloway N7,
N19 . . . . 5 A2
Upper Holloway N19 . 4 C3
Sutherland Ave
W9 . . . . 88 C2
Sutherland Ct
3 Paddington W9 . . 23 C1
Stoke Newington N16 . 6 C1

Sutherland Gdns
SW14 . . . . .56 A4
Sutherland Gr SW18,
SW19 . . . . .70 B4
Sutherland Ho
Kensington W8 . . . .**128** A1
7 Putney SW15 . . .69 B4
9 South Hampstead
NW6 . . . . .11 B2
Sutherland Pl W2 . .31 C3
Sutherland Rd
W4 . . . . .46 A4
Sutherland Row
SW1 . . . .**146** B2
Sutherland Sq
SE17 . . . .**150** C1
Sutherland St
SW1 . . . .**146** B2
Sutherland Wlk
SE17 . . . .**151** A1
Sutterton St N7 . . .14 B2
Sutton Court Mans
W4 . . . . .45 B4
Sutton Court Rd
W4 . . . . .45 B4
Sutton Ct
Chiswick W4 . . . . .45 B4
8 Hackney E5 . . .17 A4
Sutton Est SW3 . . .**144** B2
Sutton Est The **8**
W10 . . . . .30 B4
Sutton House*
E9 . . . . .17 B3
Sutton La EC1 . . . .**96** B1
Sutton La N W4 . . .37 B1
Sutton La S W4 . . .45 B4
Sutton Pl E9 . . . . .17 B3
Sutton Row W1 . . .**105** C2
Sutton Sq E9 . . . . .17 B3
Sutton St E1 . . . . .32 B3
Suttons Way EC1 . .**97** A1
Sutton Way W10 . . .30 B4
Swaby Rd SW17,
SW18 . . . . .71 B2
Swaffield Prim Sch
SW18 . . . . .71 B4
Swaffield Rd
SW18 . . . . .71 B4
Swain's La N6 . . . . .4 A2
Swainson Rd W7 . . .14 C4
Swainson Rd W3 . . .38 B4
Swain St NW8 . . . .**90** A2
Swallow Cl SE14 . . .50 C2
Swallow Ct **4** W9 . .31 C4
Swallowfield W1 . . .**92** B3
Swallow Ho NW8 . . .**80** A2
Swallow Pl
24 Poplar E14 . . . . .33 B3
W1 . . . .**104** B1
Swallow St W1 . . . .**119** A3
Swanage E5 . . . . .16 A1
Swanage Ho SW8 **162** C1
Swanage Rd SW18 .59 B1
Swanbourne
SE17 . . . .**150** C3
Swanbourne Ho
NW8 . . . .**90** A2
Swan Bsns Ctr **8**
W4 . . . . .37 C2
Swan Ct
Chelsea SW3 . . . .**144** B1
Parsons Green
SW6 . . . .**155** B1
Poplar E14 . . . . . . .33 B3

Swan Ctr SW17 . . . .71 B1
Swandon Way
SW18 . . . . .59 A3
Swanfield St
E2 . . . . . .24 B2 **99** A3
Swan Ho N1 . . . . . .15 C1
Swan La EC4 . . . . .**123** C3
Swan Lane Pier
E1 . . . .**123** A1
Swanlea Sec Sch
E1 . . . . .25 A1
Swanley Ho SE17 . .**152** B2
Swan Mead SE1 . . .**138** A1
Swan Mews
Stockwell SW9 . . .**172** C2
SW6 . . . .**165** B4
Swanmore Ct
SW18 . . . . .59 B1
Swann Ho **12**
SE10 . . . . .52 B3
Swan Pas E1 . . . . .**125** B3
Swan Pl SW13 . . . .46 B1
Swan Rd SE16 . . . .40 B4
Swanscombe Ho **11**
W11 . . . . .30 C1
Swanscombe Point **7**
E16 . . . . .35 B4
Swanscombe Rd
5 Chiswick W4 . . .38 A1
Shepherd's Bush
W11 . . . . .30 C1
Swan St SE1 . . . . .**137** A3
Swanton Gdns
SW19 . . . . .69 C3
Swanwick Cl
SW15 . . . . .68 B4
Swan Wlk SW3 . . . .**158** C4
Swan Yd N1 . . . . . .15 A2
Swaton Rd E3 . . . .26 C1
Swaythling Ho
SW15 . . . . .56 B1
Swedenborg Gdns
E1 . . . . .32 A2
Sweden Gate
SE16 . . . . .41 A2
Swedish Quays
SE16 . . . . .41 A3
Swedish Sch The
SW13 . . . . .46 C4
Sweeney Cres
SE1 . . . .**139** A3
Sweyn Pl SE3 . . . . .53 C1
Swift Ho
10 Stepney E1 . . . . .32 B3
15 Stoke Newington
N16 . . . . .7 A1
SW9 . . . .**163** C2
Swift St SW6 . . . . .**164** C4
Swinbrook Rd
W10 . . . . .31 A4
Swinburne Ct **4**
SE5 . . . . .63 C3
Swinburne Ho **15**
E2 . . . . .25 B2
Swinburne Rd
SW15 . . . . .56 C3
Swindon St W12 . . .30 B1
Swinford Gdns
SW9 . . . . .63 A4
Swingfield Ho **4**
E9 . . . . .25 B4
Swinley Ho NW1 . . .92 B4
Swinnerton St E9 . .18 A3
Swinton Ho
E2 . . . . . . .24 C2 **99** B3
Swinton Pl WC1 . . .**94** C4
Swinton St WC1 . . .**94** C4

Swiss Cottage
NW3 . . . . .11 C1
Swiss Cottage Sch
South Hampstead
NW3 . . . . .11 C1
St John's Wood
NW8 . . . .**79** C4
Swiss Cottage Sta
NW3 . . . . .11 C1
Swiss Re Building*
EC2 . . . .**110** A2
Swiss Terr **7**
NW3 . . . . .11 C1
Switch Ho **4** E14 .34 C2
Sybil Phoenix Cl
SE8 . . . . .40 C1
Sybil Thorndike
Casson Ho SW5 .**141** C1
Sybil Thorndike Ho **12**
N1 . . . .**15** B1
Sycamore Ave E3 . .26 B4
Sycamore Cl W3 . . .29 A1
Sycamore Ct
Kilburn NW6 . . . . .23 C4
Tufnell Pk N19 . . . . .4 C1
Sycamore Gdns W6,
W12 . . . . .39 A3
Sycamore Gr SE6 . .67 B1
Sycamore Ho
16 Maitland Pk
NW3 . . . . .12 B2
1 Rotherhithe
SE16 . . . . .40 C4
3 Shepherd's Bush
W6 . . . . .39 A4
2 Stoke Newington
N16 . . . . .6 C2
Sycamore Lo
SW15 . . . . .57 A4
Sycamore Mews **4**
SW4 . . . . .61 B4
Sycamore St EC1 . .**96** C1
Sycamore Wlk **1**
W10 . . . . .23 A1
Sydcote SE21 . . . . .75 B3
Sydenham Hill SE21,
SE22, SE23, SE26,
SE19 . . . . .76 C1
Sydenham Hill Sta
SE21 . . . . .76 B1
Sydner Mews N16 . .16 B4
Sydner Rd N16 . . . .16 B4
Sydney Cl SW3 . . .**143** C3
Sydney Ho **4** W4 . .38 A2
Sydney Mews
SW3 . . . .**143** C3
Sydney Pl SW7 . . .**144** A3
Sydney Rd TW10, ...54 A3
Sydney St SW3 . . .**144** A2
Sylva Cotts **3** SE8 .51 C2
Sylva Ct **3** SW15 . .69 C4
Sylvan Ct NW6 . . . .**78** A4
Sylvan Gr
Hampstead NW2 . . .9 C4
SE15 . . . . .50 A4
Sylvester Ho **7**
E8 . . . . .17 A2
Sylvester Path **8**
E8 . . . . .17 A2
Sylvester Rd E8 . . .17 A2
Sylvia Pankhurst Ho
14 E2 . . . . .25 C2
Sylvia Young Theatre
Sch NW1 . . . .**90** B1

Symes Mews NW1. .**82** C2
Symington Ho
SE1 . . . .**137** B1
Symington Mews
E9 . . . . .17 C3
Symister Mews
N1 . . . . . .24 A2 **98** A3
Symons St SW3 . . .**145** A3
Symphony Mews **15**
W10 . . . . .23 A2
Syringa Ho SE4 . . . .66 B4

T

Tabard Ct **6** E14 . . .34 B3
Tabard Ho SE1 . . . .**137** C2
Tabard St SE1 . . . .**137** B2
Tabernacle St EC2 . .**97** C2
Tableer Ave SW4 . . .61 C2
Tabley Rd N7 . . . . .14 A4
Tabor Rd W6 . . . . .39 A3
Tachbrook Est
SW1 . . . .**147** C1
Tachbrook Mews
SW1 . . . .**146** C4
Tachbrook St
SW1 . . . .**147** A3
Tack Mews SE4. . . .66 C4
Tadema Ho NW8 . . .**89** C1
Tadema Rd SW10 .**157** A1
Tadmor St W12 . . . .30 C1
Tadworth Ho SE1 . .**136** A3
Taeping St E14 . . . .42 A2
Taffrail Ho **2** E14 . .42 A1
Taft Way **44** E3 . . .27 A2
Tailworth St E1 . . .**111** B3
Tait Ct
10 Old Ford E3 . . . .26 B4
SW8 . . . .**171** C4
Tait Ho SE1 . . . . .**121** C1
Takhar Mews
SW11 . . . .**168** B1
Talacre Rd NW5 . . .12 C2
Talbot Ct EC3 . . . .**123** C4
Talbot Grove Ho **10**
W11 . . . . .31 A3
Talbot Ho
Highbury N7 . . . . . .5 C1
Poplar E14 . . . . . . .34 A3
Talbot Pl SE3 . . . . .53 A1
Talbot Rd
Camberwell SE22 . .64 A3
Notting Hill W2 . . . .31 C3
Notting Hill W11 . . .31 B3
Talbot Sq W2 . . . .**101** B1
Talbot Wlk
Notting Hill W11 . . .31 A3
Willesden NW10 . . . .8 A2
Talbot Yd SE1 . . . .**123** B1
Talcott Path **12**
SW2 . . . . .74 C3
Talfourd Pl SE15 . . .49 B2
Talfourd Rd SE15 . .49 B2
Talgarth Rd
Hammersmith W6 . .39 B1
W14 . . . .**140** B2
Talia Ho E14 . . . . .42 B4
Talina Ctr SW6 . . .**166** C3
Talleyrand Ho SE5 .48 B1
Tallis St EC4. . . . .**121** C4
Talma Rd SW2 . . . .62 C3
Talmud Torah Chaim
Meirim Sch N16. . . .7 B3

Talmud Torah
Machzikei Hadass
Sch E5 . . . . .7 C4
Talmud-Torah Yetev-
Lev N16 . . . . .7 C4
Talwin St E3 . . . . .27 A2
Tamar Cl **24** E3 . . .26 B4
Tamar Ho
10 Cubitt Town
E14 . . . . .42 B4
SE11 . . . .**149** C2
Tamarind Ct **8**
W3 . . . . .28 B3
Tamarind Ho **4**
SE15 . . . . .49 C3
Tamarind Yd E1 . . .**125** C2
Tamarisk Sq W12 . .29 B2
Tamworth N7 . . . . .14 A2
Tamworth St
SW6 . . . .**155** B3
Tangier Rd TW10 . . .55 A4
Tangley Gr SW15 . .68 B4
Tangmere WC1 . . . .**94** C3
Tanhurst Ho **27**
SW2 . . . . .74 B4
Tankerton St WC1 . .**94** B3
Tanner Ho SE1 . . .**138** B3
Tanner's Hill SE8 . .51 C2
Tanners Mews
SE8 . . . . .51 A2
Tanner St SE1 . . . .**138** B3
Tanners Yd **83** E2. .25 A3
Tannery Ho E1 . . . .**111** B4
Tannington Terr
N5 . . . . .5 C1
Tansley Cl N7 . . . . .13 C3
Tanswell St SE1 . . .**135** B3
Tantallon Rd
SW12 . . . . .72 C3
Tant Ave E16 . . . . .35 B3
Tanza Rd NW3 . . . .12 B4
Tapley Ho SE1 . . . .**139** B3
Taplow NW3 . . . . . .11 C1
Taplow Ho
E2 . . . . . .24 B2 **98** C3
Taplow St N1 . . . . .**87** A1
Tappesfield Rd
SE15 . . . . .65 B4
Tapp St E1 . . . . . .25 A1
Taranto Ho **14** E1 . .32 C4
Tarbert Rd SE22 . . .64 A2
Tarbert Wlk E1 . . . .32 B2
Tarling Rd E16 . . . .35 B3
Tarling St E1 . . . . .32 B3
Tarnbrook Ct
SW1 . . . .**145** B3
Tarn St SE1 . . . . .**136** C1
Tarns The NW1 . . . .**92** C4
Tarplett Ho **22**
SE14 . . . . .50 C4
Tarragon Cl SE14 . .51 A3
Tarranbrae NW6 . . .10 A1
Tarrant Ho E2 . . . .25 B2
Tarrant Pl W1 . . . .**102** C3
Tarrantt Ho W14 . .**126** A2
Tarriff Cres SE8 . . .41 B2
Tarrington Cl
SW16 . . . . .73 C1
Tartan Ho **15** E14 . .34 B3
Tarver Rd SE17 . . .**150** B2
Tarves Way SE10 . . .52 A3
Tasker Ho **7** E14 . . .33 B4
Tasker Lo W8 . . . .**127** B4
Tasker Rd NW3 . . . .12 B3
Tasman Ct **3** E14 . .42 A2
Tasman Ho **17** E1. .32 A1
Tasman Rd SW9 . . .62 A4

Tasso Rd W6 . . . . **154** A4
Tasso Yd W6 . . . . **154** A3
Tatchbury Ho
SW15 . . . . 56 B1
Tate Britain★
SW1 . . . . **148** A3
Tate Ho **13** E2 . . . . 25 C3
Tate Modern★
EC4 . . . . **122** B2
Tatham Pl NW8 . . . . . . **79** C2
Tatnell Rd SE23 . . . . . . 66 A1
Tatton Cres E5, N16 . . 7 A4
Tatum St SE17 . . . . . . **151** C3
Tauheed Cl N4 . . . . 6 B2
Taunton Ho W2 . . . . . **100** C1
Taunton Mews
NW1 . . . . **90** C2
Taunton Pl NW1 . . . . . **90** C2
Tavern Cl SE1 . . . . **137** A1
Taverner Ho N16 . . . . . 6 C1
Taverners Cl
W11 . . . . . 31 A1 **112** A4
Taverner Sq **4**
N5 . . . . 15 B4
Tavern La SW9 . . . . . **173** C2
Tavistock Cl N16 . . . . 16 A3
Tavistock Cres
W11 . . . . 31 B4
Tavistock Ct WC1 . . . . **93** C2
Tavistock Ho **3**
W11 . . . . 31 B4
Tavistock Mews **3**
W11 . . . . 31 B3
Tavistock Pl WC1 . . . . **94** A3
Tavistock Rd
Dagenham NW10 . . . . 21 B3
Notting Hill W11 . . . . . 31 B4
Tavistock Rd WC1 . . . . **93** C2
Tavistock St WC2 . . . **120** B4
Tavistock Terr N19 . . 4 C1
Tavistock Twr
SE16 . . . . 41 A3
Taviton St WC1 . . . . . . **93** B2
Tavy Cl SE11 . . . . **149** C2
Tawny Way SE16 . . . . 40 C2
Taybridge Rd
SW11 . . . . 60 C3
Tayburn Cl E14 . . . . . . 34 B3
Tay Ho **10** E3 . . . . 26 B3
Tayler Ct NW8 . . . . **79** B4
Taylor Ave TW9 . . . . . . 45 A1
Taylor Cl SE8 . . . . 51 B4
Taylor Ct E15 . . . . 19 B3
Taylor Ho **10** SW2 . . 74 C3
Taylor's Gn W3 . . . . . . 29 A3
Taylor's La NW10 . . . . 8 A1
Tayport Cl N1 . . . . 14 A1
Tayside Ct **6** SE5 . . . 63 C3
Teak Cl SE16 . . . . 33 A1
Tealby Ct N7 . . . . 14 B2
Teal Ct **30** SE8 . . . . . 51 B4
Teale St E2 . . . . 24 C3
Teal St **1** SE10 . . . . . 43 B3
Teather St **1** SE5 . . 49 A3
Tebbs Ho **1** SW2 . . . . 74 C4
Tedman Ct SE13 . . . . . 67 B3
Ted Roberts Ho **25**
E2 . . . . 25 A3
Tedworth Gdns
SW3 . . . . **144** C1
Tedworth Sq
SW3 . . . . **144** C1
Teesdale Cl E2 . . . . . . 25 A3
Teesdale St E2 . . . . . . 25 A3
Teesdale Yd **34**
E2 . . . . 25 A3
Tee The W3 . . . . 29 A3

Teignmouth Cl **6**
SW4 . . . . 61 C3
Teignmouth Rd
NW2 . . . . 9 C2
Telegraph Hill NW3 . . 2 A1
Telegraph Pl E14 . . . . 42 A2
Telegraph Rd
SW15 . . . . 69 B4
Telegraph St EC2 . . . **109** B2
Telephone Pl
SW6 . . . . **155** A4
Telfer Cl **4** W3 . . . . . 37 B4
Telfer Ho EC1 . . . . **96** B3
Telferscot Prim Sch
SW12 . . . . 73 C3
Telferscot Rd
SW12 . . . . 73 C3
Telford Ave SW12 . . . .
SW2 . . . . 74 A3
Telford Avenue Mans
7 SW2 . . . . 74 A3
Telford Ho
8 Kensal Town
W10 . . . . 31 A4
Telford Parade Mans
1 SW2 . . . . 74 A3
Telford Rd W10 . . . . . 31 A4
Telford Terr SW1 . . . **160** C4
Telford Way W3 . . . . . 29 A4
Tell Gr SE22 . . . . 64 B3
Telscombe Ho
SW11 . . . . **169** B3
Temair Ho **1**
SE10 . . . . 52 B3
Temeraire Pl TW8 . . . 36 B1
Temeraire St SE16 . . 40 B4
Temperley Rd
SW12 . . . . 72 C4
Templar Ho NW2 . . . . 10 B2
Templars Ho E15 . . . . 19 A3
Templar St SE5 . . . . . 48 A1
Temple Ave EC4 . . . . **121** C4
Templecombe Rd
E9 . . . . 25 B4
Temple Cl
Stepney E1 . . . . 32 C4
SW8 . . . . **172** B4
Temple Dwellings **7**
E2 . . . . 25 A3
Temple Ho
13 Battersea
SW11 . . . . 60 A4
4 Tufnell Pk N7 . . . . 4 B1
Temple La EC4 . . . . . **107** C1
Templemead Cl
W3 . . . . 29 A3
Templemead Ho
E9 . . . . 18 A4
Temple Mill La E10,
E15 . . . . 19 B4
Temple Mills Rd
E15 . . . . 19 A3
TEMPLE MILLS 19 A3
Temple Mills Rd
E15 . . . . 19 B4
Temple Pl WC2 . . . . **121** A4
Temple Rd
Acton Green W4 . . . . 37 B3
Richmond TW9 . . . . . 54 B4
Temple Sheen
SW14 . . . . 55 B2
Temple Sheen Rd
SW14 . . . . 55 B3
Temple St E2 . . . . 25 A3
Temple Sta WC2 . . . **121** B4
Templeton Cl **5**
N16 . . . . 16 A3

Templeton Pl
SW5 . . . . **141** C3
Temple West Mews
SE11 . . . . **136** A1
Templewood Ave
NW3 . . . . 2 A1
Templewood Gdns
NW3 . . . . 2 A1
Templewood Point
NW2 . . . . 1 B2
Tenbury Ct SW12 . . . 73 C3
Tenby Ho
Islington N7 . . . . 14 C4
W2 . . . . **100** C1
Tench St E1 . . . . 32 A1
Tenda Rd SE16 . . . . . 40 A2
Tendring Ho SW2 . . . 62 C1
Tenham Ave SW2 . . . 73 C2
Tenison Ct W1 . . . . . **118** C4
Tenison Way SE1 . . . **121** B1
Tenniel Cl W2 . . . . . . **114** B4
Tennis St SE1 . . . . . . **137** B4
Tennyson Ho
SE17 . . . . **151** A2
Tennyson Rd NW6 . . 23 B4
Tennyson St SW8 . . **170** A1
Tensing Ho N1 . . . . . . 15 A2
Tenterden Ho
SE17 . . . . **152** B2
Tenterden St W1 . . . **104** B1
Tenter Ground
E1 . . . . **110** C3
Tent St E1 . . . . 25 A1
Tequila Wharf
E14 . . . . 33 A3
Terborch Way **6**
SE22 . . . . 64 A2
Tercelet Terr
NW3 . . . . 11 B4
Teredo St SE16 . . . . . 40 C3
Terling Ho **9**
W10 . . . . 30 B4
Terling St SW11 . . . **86** C4
Terminus Pl SW1 . . **132** B1
Terrace Gdns
SW13 . . . . 46 B1
Terrace La TW10 . . . . 54 A1
Terrace Rd E9 . . . . . . 17 B1
Terrace The
Barnes SW13,
SW14 . . . . 46 A1
EC4 . . . . **107** C1
Kilburn NW6 . . . . 23 C4
10 Rotherhithe SE8 . 41 B2
Terrano Ho **1**
TW9 . . . . 45 A2
Terrapin Ct SW17 . . 73 A1
Terrapin Rd SW17 . . 73 A1
Terrick St W12 . . . . . 30 A3
Territorial
SE11 . . . . **149** C3
Terry Ho SW2 . . . . . . 74 C3
Tersha St TW9 . . . . . . 54 B3
Tessa Sanderson Pl
6 SW8 . . . . 61 A4
Testerton Wlk **3**
W11 . . . . 30 C2
Tetcott Rd SW10 . . . **156** C1
Teversham La
SW8 . . . . **172** B4
Teviot St E14 . . . . 34 B4
Teyham Ct SW11 . . . 60 B1
Thackeray Ct
Chelsea SW3 . . . . . . **144** C2
West Kensington
W14 . . . . **126** A1

Thackeray Ho
College Pk NW10 . . . 21 C2
WC1 . . . . **94** A2
Thackeray Mews
E8 . . . . 16 C2
Thackeray Rd
SW8 . . . . **170** B1
Thackeray's
Almshouses SE6 . . 67 A1
Thackeray St W8 . . **128** B2
Thalia Cl SE10 . . . . . 52 C4
Thame Rd SE16 . . . . 40 C4
Thames Ave
SW10 . . . . **167** A4
Thames Bank
SW14 . . . . 45 B1
Thames Christian Coll
SW11 . . . . 59 C4
Thames Circ E14 . . . 41 C2
Thames Cres W4 . . . 46 A3
Thames Ct **10**
SE15 . . . . 49 B3
Thames Hts SE1 . . . **138** C4
Thameside Ctr
TW8 . . . . 44 B4
Thames Link Ho **7**
TW9 . . . . 54 A3
Thames Pl SW15 . . . 57 C4
Thames Quay
Millwall E14 . . . . 42 A4
SW10 . . . . **167** A3
Thames Rd W4 . . . . . 44 C4
Thames Reach
W6 . . . . 47 B4
Thames Row TW9 . . 44 B4
Thames St SE10 . . . . 52 A4
Thames Village
W4 . . . . 45 B2
Thames Wlk
SW11 . . . . **158** A2
Thane Mans N7 . . . . . 5 B1
Thanet Ho
1 West Norwood
SE27 . . . . 75 A1
Thanet Ho WC1 . . . . . **94** A3
Thanet Lo NW2 . . . . . 10 A2
Thanet St WC1 . . . . . **94** A3
Thane Villas N7 . . . . . 5 B1
Thane Works N7 . . . . 5 B1
Thavies Inn EC4 . . . **107** C2
Thaxted Ct N1 . . . . . **87** C1
Thaxted Ho SE16 . . . 40 B2
Thaxton Rd W14 . . . **155** A4
Thayer St W1 . . . . . . **103** C2
Theatre Mus★ . . . . .
WC2 . . . . **120** B4
Theatre Sq E15 . . . . . 19 C2
Theatre St SW11 . . . 60 B4
Theberton St N1 . . . **86** A4
Theed St SE1 . . . . . . **121** C1
Thelbridge Ho **28**
E3 . . . . 27 A2
Theobalds Ct N4 . . . . 6 B2
Theobald's Rd
WC1 . . . . **106** C4
Theobald St SE1 . . . **137** B1
Theodore Ct SE13 . . 67 C1
Theodore Ho **1**
SW15 . . . . 56 C2
Theodore Rd SE13 . . 67 C1
Therapia Rd SE22 . . . 65 B1
Theresa Rd W6 . . . . . 38 C2
Therfield Ct N4 . . . . . 6 B2
Thermopylae Gate
E14 . . . . 42 A2
Theseus Ho **2**
E14 . . . . 34 C3

Theseus Ho continued
2 E14 . . . . 34 C3
Theseus Wlk N1 . . . . **86** B1
Thessaly Ho SW8 . . **160** C1
Thessaly Rd SW8 . . **171** A4
Thetford Ho SE1 . . . **138** C2
Thetis Terr TW9 . . . . . 44 C4
Third Ave
East Acton W3 . . . . . 29 B1
West Kilburn W10 . . . 23 A2
Thirleby Rd SW1 . . . **133** A1
Thirlmere NW1 . . . . . **92** B4
Thirlmere Ho **19**
N16 . . . . 15 C4
Thirsk Rd SW11 . . . . 60 C3
Thistle Gr SW7 . . . . **143** A1
Thistle Ho **10** E14 . . 34 B3
Thistlewood Cl **3**
N7 . . . . 5 B2
Thistly Ct SE8 . . . . . . 52 A4
Thomas Baines Rd
SW11 . . . . 59 C4
Thomas Burt Ho **8**
E2 . . . . 25 A2
Thomas Buxton Jun &
Inf Sch E1 . . . . 24 C1 **99** C1
Thomas Crowell Ct **29**
N1 . . . . 16 A3
Thomas Doyle St
SE1 . . . . **136** B2
Thomas Fairchild
Com Sch N1 . . . . **87** A2
Thomas Ho
3 Hackney E9 . . . . 17 B2
4 Stockwell SW4 . . 62 A3
Thomas Hollywood
Ho **3** E2 . . . . 25 B3
Thomas Jones Prim
Sch W11 . . . . 31 A3
Thomas Milner Ho **8**
SE15 . . . . 49 C3
Thomas More Ho
EC2 . . . . **108** C3
Thomas More Sq
E1 . . . . **125** B3
Thomas More St
E1 . . . . **125** B3
Thomas North Terr **4**
E16 . . . . 35 B4
Thomas Pl W8 . . . . **128** A1
Thomas Rd E14 . . . . 33 C4
Thomas Road Ind Est
4 E14 . . . . 33 C3
Thomas's London Day
Schs SW11 . . . . **167** C3
Thomas's Prep Sch
Clapham SW11 . . . . 60 B2
Thompson Ave
Richmond TW9 . . . . . 54 C4
6 SE5 . . . . 48 B3
Thompson Ho
1 Kensal Town
W10 . . . . 23 A1
SE14 . . . . 50 C4
Thompson Rd
SE22 . . . . 64 B2
Thomson Ct **4** E8 . . 16 C2
Thomson Ho
Pimlico SW1 . . . . . **147** C1
Walworth SE17 . . . **152** A3
Thorburn Ho
SW1 . . . . **131** B3
Thorburn Sq SE1 . . **153** B3
Thoresby Ho N16 . . . . 6 C1
Thoresby St N1 . . . . . **97** A4

Thornaby Ho **15**
Thornbill Ho **1**
E2 ....25 A2
SE15 ....49 C3
Thornbury Cl N16 ...16 A4
Thornbury St
W11 ....31 C2 113 A4
Thornbury Ho N6 ...4 B3
Thornbury Rd
SW2 ....62 A1
Thornbury Sq N6 ...4 B3
Thorncliffe Ct
SW2 ....62 A1
Thorncliffe Rd
SW2 ....62 A1
Thorncombe Rd
SE22 ....64 A2
Thorncroft St
SW8 ....162 A1
Thorndale Ho **16**
N16 ....7 A3
Thorndean St
SW18 ....71 B2
Thorndike Cl
SW10 ....156 C2
Thorndike Ho
SW1 ....147 B2
Thorndike Rd **21**
N1 ....15 C2
Thorndike St
SW1 ....147 B3
Thorne Cl E16 .....35 C3
Thorne Ho
34 Bethnal Green
E2 ....25 B2
4 Cubitt Town E14 ..42 B3
Thorne Pas **7**
SW13 ....46 B1
Thorne Rd SW8 ...162 B1
Thorness St SW18 ..59 B1
Thorne St SW13,
SW14 ....56 A4
Thornewill Ho **8**
E1 ....32 B2
Thorney Cres
SW11 ....157 C1
Thorneycroft Ho **11**
W4 ....38 A1
Thorney Ct W8 ...128 C3
Thorney Hedge Rd
W4 ....37 A2
Thorney St SW1 ...148 A4
Thornfield Ho
E14 ....33 C2
Thornfield Rd
W12 ....39 A4
Thornford Rd
SE13 ....67 B2
Thorngate Rd W9 ...23 C1
Thornham Gr E15 ..19 C3
Thorn Ham Ho
SE1 ....137 C2
Thornham St SE10 ..52 A4
Thornhaugh St
WC1 ....93 C1
Thornhill Bridge
Wharf N1 ....84 C3
Thornhill Cres N1 ...14 B1
Thornhill Gr N1 ...14 C1
Thornhill Ho
15 Chiswick W4 ......38 A1
Islington N1 ....14 C1
Thornhill Mews
SW15 ....58 B3
Thornhill Prim Sch
N1 ....14 C1
Thornhill Rd N1 ....85 B4
Thornhill Sq N1 ....14 B1
Thornicroft Ho
SW9 ....173 A1
Thornley Pl **2**
SE10 ....43 A1
Thornsett Rd
SW18 ....71 A3
Thornton Ave
Chiswick W4 ....38 A2
Streatham SW2 ....73 C3
Thornton Ct N1 .....14 A3
Thornton Gdns
SW12 ....73 C3
Thornton Ho
SE17 ....152 A3
Thornton Pl W1 ...103 A4
Thornton Rd
Mortlake SW14 ....55 C4
Streatham SW12,
SW2 ....73 C3
Thornton St SW9 .173 B2
Thornville St SE8 ...51 C2
Thornwood Gdns
W8 ....127 B4
Thornwood Lo
W8 ....127 B4
Thornycroft Ct
TW9 ....44 B1
Thorold Ho SE1 ...136 C4
6 Streatham SW2 ...74 A4
Thorparch Rd
SW8 ....161 C1
Thorpebank Rd
W12 ....29 C1
Thorpe Cl W10 .....31 A3
Thorpedale Rd N4...5 B3
Thorpe Ho N1 ....85 A3
Thorverton Rd
NW2 ....1 A1
Thoydon Rd E3 .....26 A3
Thrale St SE1 ......123 A1
Thrasher Cl **20** E8 ...24 B4
Thrawl St E1 ....111 A3
Thrayle Ho **2**
SW9 ....62 B4
Threadgold Ho **8**
N1 ....15 C2
Threadneedle St
EC2,
EC3 ....109 C1
Three Colts La E2 ..25 A1
Three Colts St E14 ..33 B2
Three Cups Yd
WC1 ....107 A3
Three Kings Yd
W1 ....118 A4
Three Mill La E3 ...27 B2
Three Mills Studios
E14 ....27 B2
Three Nun Ct EC2 ..109 A2
Three Oak La SE1 ..138 C4
Threshers Pl
W11 ....31 A2 112 A4
Thring Ho SW9 ....172 C2
Throgmorton Ave
EC2 ....109 C2
Throgmorton St
EC2 ....109 C2
Thrush St SE17 ...150 C2
Thurland Ho **3**
SE16 ....40 A2
Thurland Rd SE16 ..139 B2
Thurleigh Ave
SW12 ....60 C1
Thurleigh Ct
SW12 ....60 C1
Thurleigh Rd
SW12 ....60 C1
Thurloe Cl SW7 ...144 A3
Thurloe Ct SW3 ...144 A3
Thurloe Pl SW7 ...143 C4
Thurloe Place Mews
SW7 ....143 C4
Thurloe Sq SW7 ...144 A4
Thurloe St SW7 ...143 C4
Thurlow Hill SE21 ..75 B2
Thurlow Ho **17**
SW16 ....74 A1
Thurlow Park Rd
SE21,
SE24 ....75 B2
Thurlow Rd NW3 ..11 C3
Thurlow St SE17 ...152 A1
Thurlow Terr
NW5 ....12 C3
Thurlow Twrs
SE27 ....74 C1
Thurlow Wlk
SE17 ....152 A1
Thurnscoe NW1 ....82 C3
Thursley Gdns
SW19 ....69 C2
Thursley Ho **10**
SW2 ....74 B4
Thurso Ho NW6 ....78 A1
Thurston Ind Est
SE13 ....67 A1
Thurston Rd SE8,
SE13 ....52 A1
Thurtle Rd E2 ....24 B3
Thurtle Rd E2 ....27 A1
Tibberton Sq N1 ...86 C4
Tibbets Cl SW19 ..69 C3
Tibbet's Corner
SW19 ....69 C4
Tibbet's Ride
SW19 ....69 C4
Tiber Cl **10** E3 ......26 C4
Tiber Gdns N1 ....84 B3
Tickford Ho NW8 ...90 A3
Tidal Basin Rd
E16 ....35 B2
Tidbury Ct SW8 ...160 C1
Tidemill Prim Sch
SE8 ....51 C3
Tideswell **10** NW5 ..13 A4
Tideswell Rd
SW15 ....57 B3
Tideway Ct **3**
SE16 ....32 C1
Tideway Ho E14 ....41 C4
Tideway Ind Est
SW8 ....161 A3
Tideway Wharf
SW13 ....46 A1
Tideway Yd SW13 ..46 A1
Tidey St E3 ....33 C4
Tidworth Ho **13**
SE22 ....64 A4
Tidworth Rd E3 ....26 C1
Tierney Rd SW2 ....74 A3
Tierney Terr SW2 ..74 A3
Tiger Ho WC1 ....93 C3
Tiger Way E5 ....17 A4
Tignel Ct W3 ....36 C4
Tilbury Cl **14** SE15 ..49 B3
Tilbury Ho **4**
SE14 ....50 C4
Tildesley Rd SW15 .57 B1
Tilehurst NW1 ....92 B3
Tilehurst Rd SW17,
SW18 ....71 C3
Tile Kiln La N6 ......4 B3
Tileyard Rd N7 .....14 A1
Tilford Gdns
SW19 ....69 C3
Tilford Ho **8** SW2 ..74 B4
Tilia Rd E5 ....17 A4
Tilia Wlk **2** SW9 ..63 A3
Tiller Ho **24** N1 .....24 A4
Tiller Rd E14 ....41 C3
Tillet Sq SE16 ....41 A4
Tillet Way
E2 ....24 C2 99 B4
Tilling Ho **1** SE15 ..65 A4
Tillman Ho **8**
SW2 ....74 B3
Tillman St E1 ....32 A3
Tilloch St **1** N1 ....14 B1
Tillotson Ct SW8 ..161 C1
Tilney Ct EC1 ....97 A2
Tilney Gdns **1** N1 ..15 C2
Tilney St W1 ....117 C2
Tilson Cl **2** SE15 ...49 A3
Tilson Gdns SW2,
SW4 ....74 A4
Tilson Ho SW2 ......74 A4
Tilson Rd SW6 ......54 A4
Tilton St SW6 ......154 B3
Tiltwood The W3 ..28 B2
Timberland Cl **11**
SE15 ....49 C3
Timber Mill Way
SW4 ....61 C4
Timber Pond Rd
SE16 ....40 C4
Timber St EC1 ....96 C2
Time Sq E8 ....16 B3
Timothy Cl **1**
SW4 ....61 B2
Timsbury Wlk **5**
SW15 ....68 C3
Tina Ct SW16 ....74 C1
Tindal St SW9 ....48 A2
Tinniswood Cl N5 ..14 C3
Tinsley Rd E1 ....32 B4
Tintagel Cres
SE22 ....64 B3
Tintagel Ct EC1 .....96 A2
Tintern Cl SW15 ...58 A2
Tintern Ho
Belgravia SW1 .....146 A3
Regent's Pk NW1 ...82 B1
Tintern St SW4 .....62 A3
Tinworth St SE11 ..148 B2
Tipthorpe Rd
SW11 ....60 C4
Tiptree **1** NW1 ....13 A1
Tisbury Ct W1 ......119 B4
Tisdall Pl SE17 ....151 C3
Tissington Ct **4**
SE16 ....40 C2
Titan Bsns Est **3**
SE8 ....51 C3
Titan Ct TW8 ....36 B1
Titchborne Row
W2 ....102 B1
Titchfield Rd NW8 ..80 C4
Titchwell Rd
SW18 ....71 C3
Tite St SW3 ....158 C4
Titmuss St W12 ....39 B4
Tiverton Rd NW6,
NW10 ....22 C4
Tiverton St SE1 ...136 C2
Tivoli Ct SE16 ....33 B1
Tobago St **12** E14 ..41 C4
Tobin Cl NW3 ....12 A1
Toby La E1 ....26 A1
Todber Ho W14 ...126 A2
Todds Wlk N7 ....5 B2
Tokenhouse Yd
EC2 ....109 B2
Toland Sq SW15 ...56 C2
Tolchurch **2** W11 ..31 C3
Toldos Yakov Yosef
sch N16 ....6 C2
Tolhurst Dr **4**
W10 ....23 A2
Tollbridge Cl W10 ..23 A1
Tollet St E1 ....25 C1
Tollgate Dr SE21 ..76 A2
Tollgate Ho NW6 ...78 A2
Tollhouse Way N19 ..4 B2
Tollington Ct N4 .....5 B2
Tollington Ho
N19 ....5 A1
Tollington Pk N4 ....5 B2
Tollington Pl N4 .....5 B2
Tollington Rd N7 ...14 B4
Tollington Way N7 ..5 A1
Tolmers Sq NW1 ...93 A2
Tolpaide Ho SE11 .149 B3
Tolpuddle St N1 ....85 B2
Tolsford Rd E5 ......17 A3
Tom Groves Cl
E15 ....19 C3
Tom Hood Cl E15...19 C3
Tom Jenkinson Rd **5**
E16 ....35 C1
Tomkyns Ho SE11 .149 B3
Tomline Ho SE1 ..122 C1
Tomlin's Gr E3 ......26 C2
Tomlinson Cl
5 Gunnersbury
W4 ....37 A1
Spitalfields
E2 ....24 B2 99 A3
Tomlin's Terr E14 ..33 A3
Tomlins Wlk **4** N7 ..5 B2
Tompion Ho **4** 96 B2
Tompion St EC1 ....96 B3
Tom Smith Cl
SE10 ....53 A4
Tomson Ho SE1 ...138 C2
Tom Williams Ho
SW6 ....154 C3
Tonbridge Hos
WC1 ....94 A3
Tonbridge St WC1 ..94 A3
Toneborough
NW8 ....78 B3
Tonsley Hill SW18 ..59 A2
Tonsley Pl SW18 ...59 A2
Tonsley Rd SW18 ..59 A2
Tonsley St SW18 ..59 A2
Took's Ct EC4 .....107 B2
Tooley St SE1 ......124 A1
Tooting Bec Sta
SW17 ....72 C1
Topham Ho **8**
SE10 ....52 B3
Topham St EC1 .....95 B2
Topiary Sq **1** TW9 ..54 B4
Topmast Point **28**
E14 ....41 C4
Torbay Ct **18** NW1 ..13 A1
Torbay Mans NW6 ..23 B4
Torbay Rd NW6 ....10 B1
Torbay St **1** NW1 ..13 A1
Tor Ct W8 ....127 C4
Tor Gdns W8 ....127 B4
Tornay Ho
Hackney E9 ....17 B1
N1 ....84 C2
Torquay St W2 .....100 A3

Torrence Ho 6
N19 . . . . 4 B2
Torrens Ct SE5 . . . . . 63 C4
Torrens Rd SW2 . . . . 62 B2
Torrens St EC1 . . . . . 86 A1
Torres Sq E14 . . . . . 41 C1
Torriano Ave NW5 . 13 C3
Torriano Cotts
NW5 . . . . 13 B3
Torriano Jun & Inf
Schs NW5 . . . . 13 C3
Torriano Mews
NW5 . . . . 13 B3
Torridge Gdns
SE15 . . . . 65 B3
Torridon Ho No 4 . . 78 A1
Torrington Pl
Bloomsbury WC1 . . 105 B4
St George in East
E1 . . . . 125 C2
Torrington Sq
WC1 . . . . 93 C1
Tortington Ho 1
SE15 . . . . 50 A3
Torwood Rd SW15 . 56 C2
Tothill Ho SW1 . . . . 147 C4
Tothill St SW1 . . . . 133 C3
Totland Ho SW18 . . 59 A1
Tottan Terr E1 . . . . . 32 C3
Tottenhall 5
NW1 . . . . 12 C1
Tottenham Court Rd
W1 . . . . 105 A4
Tottenham Court
Road Sta W1 . . . . 105 C2
Tottenham Mews
W1 . . . . 105 B4
Tottenham Rd N1 . 16 A2
Tottenham St W1 . . 105 A4
Totteridge Ho
SW11 . . . . 167 C2
Touchard Ho N1 . . . 97 C3
Toulmin St SE1 . . . . 136 C3
Toulon St SE5 . . . . . 48 B3
Toulouse Ct 2
SE16 . . . . 40 A1
Tounson Ct SW1 . . . 147 C3
Tournay Rd SW6 . . . 155 A2
Toussaint Wlk
SE16 . . . . 139 C2
Tovy Ho S1 . . . . 153 B1
Towcester Rd E3 . . . 27 B1
Tower 42 * EC2 . . . 110 A2
Tower Br App E1,
EC3 . . . . 32 A1
Tower Bridge * E1, EC3,
SE1 . . . . 124 C2
Tower Bridge Bsns
Complex SE16 . . . 40 A3
Tower Bridge Bsns Sq
SE1 . . . . 138 C4
Tower Bridge Piazza
SE1 . . . . 124 C1
Tower Bridge Prim
Sch SE1 . . . . 138 C4
Tower Bridge Rd
SE1 . . . . 138 A3
Tower Bridge Sq
SE1 . . . . 138 C4
Tower Cl NW3 . . . . 11 C3
Tower Ct
Brockley SE4 . . . . 66 A3
Stamford Hill E5 . . . 7 B4
St Giles WC2 . . . . . 106 A1

Tower Ct continued
St John's Wood
NW8 . . . . 80 B2
Towergate SE1 . . . . 152 A4
Towergate Ho 56
E3 . . . . 26 B3
Tower Gateway Sta
EC3 . . . . 124 C4
TOWER HAMLETS
. . . . 33 B4
Tower Hamlets Coll
Poplar E14 . . . . . . 34 A2
Poplar E14 . . . . . . 34 A3
Stepney E1 . . . . . . 32 C3
Tower Hill EC3 . . . . 124 C4
Tower Hill Sta
EC3 . . . . 124 C4
Tower Mans SE1 . . 138 C1
Tower Mews E5 . . . 18 A3
Tower Millennium
Pier EC3 . . . . 124 C3
Tower Mill Rd 7
SE15 . . . . 49 A3
Tower Pl E EC3 . . . 124 B3
Tower Pl W EC3 . . . 124 B3
Tower Rd NW10 . . . 8 C1
Tower Rise TW9 . . . 54 A4
Tower Royal EC4 . . 123 B4
Towers Pl TW10 . . . 54 A2
Tower St WC2 . . . . 106 A1
Towers The
Dartmouth Pk NW5 . 4 A1
R Richmond TW9 . . 54 B3
Tower Terr SE4 . . . . 66 A3
Tower The* EC3 . . . 124 C3
Towerview SE13 . . . 66 C2
Tower Wharf SE1 . . 138 C4
Tower Wlk SE1 . . . . 152 A4
Towncourt Path N4 . 6 B3
Townhall Ave 3
W4 . . . . 37 C1
Town Hall Rd
SW11 . . . . 60 B4
Town Hos EC1 . . . . 96 B1
Townley Rd SE22 . . 64 A2
Townley St SE17 . . 151 B2
Townmead Bsns Ctr
SW6 . . . . 59 B4
Townmead Rd
Richmond TW9 . . . 45 A1
Sands End SW6 . . . 166 C1
Townsend Ho
SE1 . . . . 153 C3
Townsend Mews 3
SW18 . . . . 71 B1
Townsend Prim Sch
SE17 . . . . 152 A3
Townsend St SE1,
SE17 . . . . 152 A4
Townsend Yd N6 . . 4 A3
Townshend Ct
NW8 . . . . 80 B2
Townshend Est
NW8 . . . . 80 A2
Townshend Rd
Primrose Hill NW8 . 80 A3
Richmond TW9 . . . 54 B3
Townshend Terr
TW9 . . . . 54 B3
Towns Ho 4 SW4 . . 61 C4
Towpath Wlk E9 . . 18 B3
Toynton St SE27 . . 75 B2
Toxteth Ho N4 . . . . 6 B4
Toynbee St E1 . . . . 110 C3
Tracey Ave NW2 . . 9 B3

Tracy Ho 15 E3 . . . . 26 B2
Tradescant Ho 15
E9 . . . . 17 B1
Tradescant Rd
SW8 . . . . 162 B1
Trade Twr 8
E1 . . . . 59 B4
Trade Winds Ct
E1 . . . . 125 C2
Trading Estate Rd
NW10 . . . . 20 B1
Traemore Ct
SW16 . . . . 74 C1
Trafalgar Ave
SE15 . . . . 49 B4
Trafalgar Cl 1
SE16 . . . . 41 A2
Trafalgar Gdns
Stepney E1 . . . . . . 32 C4
W8 . . . . 128 B2
Trafalgar Gr SE10 . . 52 C4
Trafalgar Ho
SE17 . . . . 151 A2
Trafalgar Mews
E9 . . . . 18 B2
Trafalgar Point 2
N1 . . . . 15 C1
Trafalgar Rd SE10 . . 43 A1
Trafalgar Sq*
SW1 . . . . 119 C2
Trafalgar St SE17 . . 151 C2
Trafalgar Way E14 . . 34 B1
Trafford Cl E15 . . . . 19 A3
Trafford Ho N1 . . . . 87 C2
Tragail SW15 . . . . . 58 A2
Trahorn Cl E1 . . . . . 25 A1
Traitors Gate* 124 C2
Tralee Ct 51 SE16 . . 40 A1
Tramway Ave E15 . . 19 C1
Trance Way W3 . . . 36 C3
Tranmere Ho 7
N7 . . . . 14 C3
Tranmere Rd SW17,
SW18 . . . . 71 B2
Tranquil Pas SE3 . . 53 B1
Tranquil Vale SE3 . . 53 A1
Transept St NW1 . . 102 B3
Transom Cl SE16 . . 41 A2
Transom Sq E14 . . . 42 A1
Tranton Rd SE16 . . 40 A3
Trappes Ho 2
SE16 . . . . 40 A2
Travers Ho 6
SE10 . . . . 43 B1
Travers Rd N7 . . . . 5 C1
Travis Ho SE10 . . . 52 B2
Treadgold Ho 7
W11 . . . . 30 C2
Treadgold St W11 . 30 C2
Treadway St E2 . . . 25 A3
Treasury Bldgs
SW1 . . . . 134 A4
Treaty St N1 . . . . . 84 C3
Trebeck St W1 . . . . 118 A1
Treborough Ho
W1 . . . . 103 B4
Trebovir Rd SW5 . . 141 C3
Treby St E3 . . . . . . 26 B1
Trecastle Way 7
N7 . . . . 13 C4
Tredegar Mews 10
E3 . . . . 26 B2
Tredegar Rd E3 . . . 26 B3
Tredegar Sq E3 . . . 26 B2
Tredegar Terr E3 . . 26 B2
Trederwen Rd E8 . . 24 C4

Treen Ave SW13 . . 56 B1
Trees The N16 . . . . 6 C2
Trefil Wlk N7 . . . . . 14 A4
Trefoil Rd SW18 . . 59 B2
Tregarvon Rd
SW11 . . . . 60 C3
Trego Rd E9 . . . . . 18 C1
Tregothnan Rd
SW9 . . . . 62 A4
Tregunter Rd
SW10 . . . . 142 C1
Treherne Ct SW9 . . 48 A2
Trehern Rd 12
SW14 . . . . 55 C4
Trehurst St E9 . . . . 18 A3
Trelawney Est E9 . . 17 B2
Trelawney Ho
SE1 . . . . 136 C4
Trelawn Rd SW2 . . 62 C2
Trellis Sq 1 E3 . . . . 26 B2
Tremadoc Rd
SW4 . . . . 61 C3
Tremaine Cl SE4 . . 51 C1
Trematon Ho
SE11 . . . . 149 C2
Tremlett Gr N19 . . . 4 B1
Tremlett Mews N19 . 4 B1
Trenchard St
SE10 . . . . 42 C1
Trenchold St
SW8 . . . . 162 A3
Trendell Ho 8
E14 . . . . 33 C3
Trenmar Gdns
NW10 . . . . 22 A2
Trentham St SW18 . 70 C3
Trent Ho SE15 . . . . 65 B3
Trent Rd SW2 . . . . 62 B2
Treport St SW18 . . 71 A4
Tresco Ho SE11 . . 149 B2
Tresco Rd SE15 . . . 65 A3
Tresham Cres
NW8 . . . . 90 A2
Tresham Wlk E9 . . . 17 B3
Tressider Ho 10
SW4 . . . . 73 C4
Tressel Cl 20 N1 . . 15 A1
Tressillian Cres
SE4 . . . . 66 C4
Tressillian Rd SE4 . 66 C4
Trevanion Rd
W14 . . . . 140 B2
Trevelyan Gdns
NW10 . . . . 22 B4
Trevelyan Ho
6 Globe Town E2 . . 25 C2
SE5 . . . . 48 A3
Treveris St SE1 . . . 122 B1
Treverton St W10 . 22 C1
Treverton Twr
W10 . . . . 30 C4
Treves Ho
E1 . . . . 24 C1 99 C1
Treville St SW15 . . 69 A4
Trevithick Ho
13 Bermondsey
SE16 . . . . 40 A2
3 Gospel Oak
NW5 . . . . 13 A4
Trevithick St SE8 . . 51 C4
Trevor Pl SW7 . . . . 130 B3
Trevor Roberts
Tutorial Coll
NW8 . . . . 11 C1

Trevor Sq SW7 . . . 130 B3
Trevor St SW7 . . . . 130 B3
Trevose Ho SE11 . . 149 A2
Trewint St SW18 . . 71 B2
Triangle Ct SE1 . . . 123 A1
Triangle Est The
SE11 . . . . 149 B1
Triangle Ho SE1 . . 138 C4
Triangle Pl SW4 . . . 61 C3
Triangle Rd 7 E8 . . 25 A4
Triangle The
Crouch End N19 . . . 4 C4
EC1 . . . . 96 B2
Hackney E8 . . . . . 25 A4
Trident Ho 14 E14 . 34 B3
Trident St SE16 . . . 40 C2
Trieste Ct SW12 . . 72 B3
Trig La EC4 . . . . . . 122 C4
Trigon Rd SW8 . . . 163 A2
Trillington Ho
W12 . . . . 29 C1
Trimdon NW1 . . . . 83 A3
Trimmer Wlk 1
TW8 . . . . 44 A4
Trim St SE8 . . . . . . 51 B4
Trinder Gdns N19 . 5 A3
Trinder Rd N4, N19 . 5 A3
Trinidad Ho 17
E14 . . . . 33 B2
Trinidad St E14 . . . 33 B2
Trinity Church Rd
SW13 . . . . 47 A4
Trinity Church Sq
SE1 . . . . 137 A2
Trinity Cl
3 Clapham SW4 . . 61 B3
Lewisham SE13 . . . 67 C3
Trinity Cotts TW9 . . 54 B4
Trinity Cres SW17 . 72 C2
Trinity Ct
Finsbury EC1 . . . . . 94 C2
2 Hoxton N1 . . . . 24 A4
Rotherhithe SE16 . . 41 A4
Willesden NW2 . . . 9 B3
Trinity Gdns
Stockwell SW9,
SW9 . . . . 62 B3
Trinity Gn 1 E1 . . . 32 B4
Trinity Gr 8 SE10 . . 52 B2
Trinity Ho SE1 . . . . 137 A2
Trinity Homes 14
SW2 . . . . 62 B3
Trinity Mews
SW18 . . . . 70 C3
Trinity Pl EC3 . . . . 124 C3
Trinity Rd
Richmond TW9 . . . 54 B4
Wandsworth SW17,
SW18 . . . . 72 A4
Trinity Rise SE24,
SW2 . . . . 75 A4
Trinity St Mary's CE
Prim Sch SW12 . . 72 C3
Trinity Sq EC3 . . . . 124 B4
Trinity St
9 Newham E16 . . . 35 C4
SE1 . . . . 137 B2
Trinity Way W3 . . . 29 B2
Trio Pl SE1 . . . . . . 137 A3
Tristan Ct 34 SE8 . . 51 B4
Triton Ct EC2 . . . . 97 C1
Triton Ho 2 E14 . . 42 A2
Triton Sq NW1 . . . 92 C2
Tritton Rd SE21,
SE27 . . . . 75 C1

Trocette Mans
SE1. . . . . **138** B2
Trojan Ct NW6 . . . . . 10 A1
Trojan Ind Est
NW10 . . . . 8 B2
Troon Cl **34** SE16 . . . 40 A1
Troon Ho **6** E14 . . . . 33 A3
Troon St E1 . . . . 33 A3
Tropical Ct **2**
W10 . . . . 22 C2
Trossachs Rd
SE22 . . . . 64 A2
Trothy Rd SE1 . . . **153** C3
Trotman Ho **1**
SE14 . . . . 50 B2
Trott St SW11 . . . **168** A3
Trotwood Ho **3**
SE16 . . . . 40 A4
Troubridge Ct **12**
W4 . . . . 37 B1
Troutbeck NW1 . . . **92** B3
Troutbeck Rd
SE14 . . . . 51 A2
Trouville Rd SW4 . . 61 B1
Trowbridge Rd E9 . . 18 B2
Trower Ho **5** E9 . . . 18 A2
Troy Ct W8 . . . . . . **127** B2
Troyes Ho NW3 . . . . 12 B3
Troy Town SE15 . . . . 64 C4
Troy Town Flats
SE15 . . . . 64 C4
Truman's Rd **24**
N16 . . . . 16 A3
Trump St EC2 . . . . **109** A1
Trundle St SE1 . . . **136** C4
Trundleys Rd SE8 . . 51 A4
Trundley's Rd SE8 . . 40 C1
Trundley's Terr
SE8 . . . . 41 A2
Truro Ho **25** W2 . . . . 31 C4
Truro St NW5 . . . . . . 12 C2
Trussley Rd W6 . . . . 39 B3
Trust Wlk SE21 . . . . 75 A3
Tryon Cres E9 . . . . . 25 B4
Tryon St SW3 . . . . **144** C2
Tubbs Rd NW10 . . . . 21 B3
Tudor Cl
Crouch End N6 . . . . 4 B4
Hampstead NW3 . . . 12 A2
Tulse Hill SW2 . . . . 62 B1
Tudor Coll WC1 . . . **94** A3
Tudor Ct
Kingsland N1 . . . . . 16 A2
5 Rotherhithe
SE16 . . . . 32 C1
South Acton W5 . . . 36 C4
Tudor Est NW10 . . . 20 A3
Tudor Gdns SW14 . . 56 A4
Tudor Gr E9 . . . . . . 17 B1
Tudor Ho
Brook Green W14 . . 39 C2
34 Hackney E9 . . . 17 B1
Tudor Mews 2
NW10 . . . . 8 C2
Tudor Rd E9 . . . . . . 25 A4
Tudor St EC4 . . . . **121** C4
Tudor Way W3 . . . . 36 C4
Tufnell Ct **19** E3 . . 26 B4
Tufnell Mans **7**
N7 . . . . 13 C4
TUFNELL PARK 13 C4
Tufnell Park Mans **2**
N7 . . . . 5 A1
Tufnell Park Prim Sch
N7 . . . . 13 C4

Tufnell Park Rd N19,
N7 . . . . 13 C4
Tufnell Park Sta
N19 . . . . 13 B4
Tufton Ct SW1 . . . **134** A1
Tufton St SW1 . . . **134** A1
Tugela St SE6 . . . . . 50 A2
Tuitis Ho **28** E9 . . . 17 B1
TULSE HILL 75 A4
Tulse Hall
Tulse Hill SW2 . . . . 74 C4
Tulse Hill SW27 . . . 75 A2
Tulse Hill Sta
SE27 . . . . 75 A2
Tulse Ho SW2 . . . . . 62 C1
Tulsemere Rd SE21,
SE27 . . . . 75 B2
Tunbridge Ct **1**
SE26 . . . . 76 C1
Tunbridge Ho EC1 . . **96** A4
Tunis Rd W12 . . . . . 30 A1
Tunley Gn **12** E14 . . 33 B4
Tunley Rd
Dagenham NW10 . . 21 A4
Upper Tooting SW17,
SW17 . . . . 72 C2
Tunnel Avenue Trad
Est SE10 . . . . 42 C4
Tunnel Rd SE16 . . . . 40 B4
Tunstall Ct **14**
TW9 . . . . 44 B2
Tunstall Rd SW9 . . . 62 B3
Tunstall Wlk **10**
TW8 . . . . 44 A4
Tunworth Cres
SW15 . . . . 56 B1
Tun Yd SW8 . . . . . . 61 A4
Tupman Ho **10**
SE16 . . . . **139** B3
Turberville Ho **1**
SW9 . . . . 62 B4
Turenne Cl SW18 . . . 59 B3
Turin St E2 . . . . 24 C2 **99** B3
Turk's Head Yd
EC1 . . . . **108** A4
Turks Row SW3 . . **145** A2
Turle Rd N4 . . . . 5 B2
Turleway Cl N4 . . . . 5 B3
Turnagain La EC4 **108** A2
Turnberry Cl **24**
SE16 . . . . 40 A1
Turnberry Quay **1**
E14 . . . . 42 A3
Turnbull Ho N1. . . **86** B4
Turnchapel Mews **1**
SW4 . . . . 61 A4
Turner Cl **7** SW9 . . 48 A2
Turner Ct
9 Herne Hill SE24 . 63 B3
24 Rotherhithe
SE16 . . . . 40 B4
Turner Ho
Finsbury Pk N4 . . . . 5 B3
24 Millwall E14 . . 41 C4
St John's Wood
NW8 . . . . 80 A2
Strand WC2 . . . . . **120** B3
Westminster SW1 . **147** C3
Turner Lo **10**
SW19 . . . . 69 C3
Turner Pl SW11 . . . . 60 A2
Turner St E1 . . . . . **115** B3
Turner St E15 . . . . . 19 B4
Turner's Rd E3 . . . . 33 B4
Turner St
Canning Town E16 . . 35 B3
Stepney E1 . . . . . . 32 A4
Turneville Rd
W14 . . . . **154** C4

Turney Prim & Sec
Specl Sch SE21 . . . 75 B4
Turney Rd SE21 . . . . 75 C4
Turnham Green Sta
W4 . . . . 38 A2
Turnham Green Terr
W4 . . . . 38 A2
Turnham Ho SE4 . . . 66 A3
Turnham Prim Sch
SE4 . . . . 66 A3
Turnmill Ho **8**
SW2 . . . . 62 C2
Turnmill St EC1 . . **108** A4
Turnpike Cl SE8 . . . 51 B3
Turnpike Ho EC1 . . **96** B3
Turnpin La **3**
SE10 . . . . 52 B4
Turpentine La
SW1 . . . . **146** B1
Turpin Ho SW11 . . **170** A4
Turpin Way N19 . . . 4 C3
Turquand St SE17 . **151** A3
Turret Gr SW4 . . . . . 61 B4
Turville Ho NW8 . . . 90 A2
Turville Rd
E2 . . . . . . 24 B1 **98** C2
Tuscan Ho **38** E2 . . 25 B2
Tuskar St SE10 . . . . 43 A1
Tuttle Ho SW1 . . . **147** C1
Tweedale Ct E15 . . . 19 B3
Tweed Ho E14 . . . . . 27 B1
Tweezer's Alley
WC2 . . . . **121** B4
Twelvetrees Bsns Pk
E16 . . . . 27 C1
Twelvetrees Cres
E3 . . . . 27 B1
Twice Times
Montessori Sch
SW6 . . . . **165** C2
Twig Folly Cl **21**
E2 . . . . 25 C3
Twilley St SW18 . . . 71 A4
Twine Ct E1 . . . . . . 32 B2
Twisden Rd NW5 . . . 13 A4
Twyford CE High Sch
W3 . . . . 28 A1
Twyford Ho N5 . . . . 6 A1
Twyford St N1 . . . **84** C4
Twynholm Mans
SW6 . . . . **154** A2
Tyburn Tree (site
of)* W2 . . . . **116** C4
Tyburn Way W1 . . **117** A4
Tye St E2 . . . . 24 C3
Tyer's Est SE1 . . . **138** A4
Tyers Gate SE1 . . . **138** A3
Tyers St SE11 . . . . **148** C2
Tyers Terr SE11 . . **149** A1
Tyler Cl E2 . . . . . **24** B3
Tyler Ho SE3 . . . . . 52 C1
Tyler St
Greenwich SE10 . . . 43 A1
SE10 . . . . 53 A4
Tylney Ho **10** E1 . . . 32 A3
Tymperley Ct
SW19 . . . . 70 A3
Tyndale La N1 . . . . . 15 A1
Tyndale Mans N1 . . 15 A1
Tyndale Terr **18**
N1 . . . . 15 A1
Tyneham Cl **10**
SW11 . . . . 60 C4
Tyneham Rd
SW11 . . . . 60 C4

Tynemouth St
SW6 . . . . **166** C2
Tyne St E1 . . . . . . **111** A2
Tynsdale Rd NW10 . . 8 A2
Tynte Ct E9 . . . . 18 A3
Tynwald Ho **16**
SE26 . . . . 76 C1
Type St E2 . . . . 25 C3
Tyrawley Rd SW6 . **166** A4
Tyrells Ct **3** SE15 . . 65 A4
Tyrrell Ho SW1 . . . **161** A4
Tyrrell Rd SE22 . . . . 64 C3
Tyrwhitt Rd SE4 . . . 66 C4
Tyson Rd SE23 . . . . 65 B1
Tyson Rd SE1 . . . . **95** C3

U

Uamvar St E14 . . . . 34 A4
Udall St SW1 . . . . **147** A3
Udimore Ho **11**
W10 . . . . 30 B4
Uffington Rd
NW10 . . . . 22 A4
Ufford St SE1 . . . . **135** C4
Ufton Gr N1 . . . . . . 15 C1
Ufton Rd N1 . . . . . . 16 A1
Uhura Sq **2** N16 . . . 7 A1
Ujima Ct N19 . . . . . . 5 A3
Ullin St E14 . . . . . . 34 B4
Ullswater SW15 . . . 57 C1
Ullswater Ho SE15 . . 50 B4
Ullswater Rd
Barnes SW13 . . . . . 46 C3
West Norwood SE27,
SW16 . . . . 75 A2
Ulster Pl NW1 . . . . **92** A1
Ulster Terr NW1 . . **92** A2
Ulundi Rd SE3 . . . . 53 A4
Ulva Rd SW15 . . . . 57 C3
Ulverscroft Rd
SE22 . . . . 64 C2
Ulverstone Rd
SE27 . . . . 75 A2
Ulysses Rd NW6 . . . 10 B3
Umberston St E1 . . 32 A3
Umbria St SW15 . . . 56 C1
Una Ho **7** NW5 . . . . 13 A2
Undercliff SE10 . . . . 52 B2
Undercliff Rd
SE13 . . . . 67 A4
Underhill Ho **7**
E14 . . . . 33 C4
Underhill Pas
NW1 . . . . **82** B4
Underhill St NW1 . . **82** B3
Undershaft EC3 . . **110** A1
Underwood Ho
W6 . . . . 39 A3
Underwood Rd
E1 . . . . 24 C1 **99** C1
Underwood Row
N1 . . . . **97** A4
Underwood St N1 . **97** A4
Undine Rd E14 . . . . 42 A2
Unicorn Bldg **14**
E1 . . . . 32 C2
Unicorn Sch TW9 . . 44 B2

Union Cl E11 . . . . . . 19 C4
Union Ct
46 Paddington W2 . **31** C4
2 Richmond TW10 . . 54 A2
South Lambeth
SW4 . . . . **172** A1
Union Dr E1 . . . . . . 26 A1
Union Gr SW8 . . . **171** C2
Union Mews SW9 . **172** A1
Union Pk **11** SE10 . . 43 B1
Union Rd SW8 . . . **171** C1
Union Sq N1 . . . . . **87** A3
Union St
Mill Meads E15 . . . . 27 C4
SE1 . . . . **122** C1
Union Wharf N1 . . . **87** A2
Union Wlk
E2 . . . . 24 A2 **98** B4
Union Yd W1 . . . . **104** B1
Unity Cl NW10 . . . . . 8 C2
Unity Mews NW1 . . **83** B2
Univ Coll Jun Sch
NW3 . . . . 11 B4
Univ Coll London
Bloomsbury WC1 . . **93** B2
Bloomsbury WC1 . . **94** B3
Univ Coll London
(Windeyer Inst)
W1 . . . . **105** A4
Univ Coll London
(Wolfson Ho)
NW1 . . . . **93** A4
University Coll Hospl
WC1 . . . . **93** A2
University Coll Sch
NW3 . . . . 11 B3
University Mans
SW15 . . . . 57 C4
University St WC1 . . **93** A1
Univ of California
WC1 . . . . **105** C3
Univ of East London
(Duncan Ho) E15 . . 27 C4
Univ of Greenwich
SE10 . . . . **52** C4
Univ of Greenwich
Rachel McMillan
Campus SE8 . . . . **51** C4
Univ of London
WC1 . . . . **93** C1
Univ of London
(King's Coll Hall)
SE5 . . . . **63** C4
Univ of London
(Queen Mary &
Westfield Coll)
E1 . . . . 26 A1
Univ of Westminster
NW1 . . . . **92** C2
Univ of Westminster
(Cavendish Campus)
W1 . . . . **104** C3
Univ of Westminster
(Marylebone
Campus) W1. . . **103** B3
Univ of Westminster
(Regent Campus)
W1 . . . . **104** C3
Univ of Westminster
(Regent Campus,
Univ HQ) W1. . . **104** B2
Unwin Cl SE15 . . . . 49 C4
Unwin Rd SW7 . . **129** C2
Upbrook Mews
W2 . . . . **101** A1
Upcerne Rd
SW10 . . . . **157** A1

Upcott Ho
33 Bromley E3 . . . . .27 A2
4 Hackney E9 . . . . .17 B1
Upgrove Manor Way
12 SE24 . . . . . . .74 C4
Upham Park Rd
W4 . . . . .38 A2
Upland Rd SE22 . . . .64 C1
Uplands CI SW14 . . .55 A2
Upnall Ho 15 SE15 . .50 B4
Upnor Way SE17 . . .152 B2
Upper Addison Gdns
W14 . . . . .126 A4
Upper Bank St
E14 . . . . .34 A1
Upper Bardsey Wlk 7
N1 . . . . .15 B2
Upper Belgrave St
SW1 . . . . .131 C2
Upper Berkeley St
W1 . . . . .103 A1
Upper Brockley Rd
SE4 . . . . .51 B1
Upper Brook St
W1 . . . . .117 B4
Upper Caldy Wlk 8
N1 . . . . .15 B2
Upper Camelford Wlk
14 W10 . . . . .31 A3
Upper Cheyne Row
SW3 . . . . .158 A4
Upper Clarendon Wlk
12 W11 . . . . .31 A3
Upper Dengie Wlk
N1 . . . . .86 C4
Upper Grosvenor St
W1 . . . . .117 B3
Upper Ground
SE1 . . . . .121 B2
Upper Gulland Wlk 8
N1 . . . . .15 B2
Upper Hampstead
Wlk 20 NW3 . . . . .11 B4
Upper Handa Wlk 1
N1 . . . . .15 B2
Upper Harley St
NW1 . . . . .91 C1
Upper Hawkwell Wlk
N1 . . . . .87 A4
UPPER HOLLOWAY
. . . . .4 C2
Upper Holloway Sta
N19 . . . . .4 C2
Upper James St
W1 . . . . .119 A4
Upper John St
W1 . . . . .119 A4
Upper Lismore Wlk 8
N1 . . . . .15 B2
Upper Mall W6 . . . . .39 A1
Upper Marsh SE1 . .135 A2
Upper Montague St
W1 . . . . .102 C3
Upper North St E3,
E14 . . . . .33 C4
Upper Park Rd
NW3 . . . . .12 B3
Upper Phillimore
Gdns W8 . . . . . . .127 B3
Upper Ramsey Wlk 15
N1 . . . . .15 C2
Upper Rawreth Wlk
N1 . . . . .87 A4
Upper Richmond Rd
SW15 . . . . .57 B3

Upper Richmond Rd
W TW10, SW14,
SW15 . . . . .55 B3
Upper St Martin's La
WC2 . . . . .120 A4
Upper St N1 . . . . . .86 A3
Upper Tachbrook St
SW1 . . . . .147 A4
Upper Talbot Wlk 8
W10 . . . . .31 A3
Upper Terr NW3 . . . .2 B1
Upper Thames St
EC4 . . . . .123 A4
Upper Tollington Pk
N4 . . . . .5 C3
UPPER TOOTING . . .72 B1
Upper Tooting Park
Mans 1 SW17 . . . .72 C2
Upper Tooting Pk
SW17 . . . . .72 B2
Upper Tooting Rd
SW17 . . . . .72 B2
Upper Tulse Hill
SW2 . . . . .74 B3
Upper Wimpole St
W1 . . . . .103 C4
Upper Woburn Pl NW1,
WC1 . . . . .93 C3
Upstall St SE5 . . . . .48 A2
Upton CI NW2 . . . . . .1 A1
Urban Mews N4 . . . . .6 A4
Urlwin St SE5 . . . . .48 B4
Urlwin Wlk SW9 . . . .48 A2
Urmston Dr SW19 . . .70 A3
Urmston Ho 4
E14 . . . . .42 B2
Ursula Mews N4 . . . .6 B3
Ursula St SW11 . . . .168 A3
Urswick Rd E5, E9 . .17 B3
Usborne Mews
SW8 . . . . .163 A2
Usher Rd E3 . . . . . .26 B3
Usk Rd SW11 . . . . . .59 B3
Usk St E2 . . . . .25 C2
Utah Bldg 3 SE13 . .52 A2
Utopia Ho 3 NW2 . . .9 C2
Utopia Village
NW1 . . . . .81 B4
Uverdale Rd
SW10 . . . . .157 A1
Uxbridge Rd W12 . . .30 A1
Uxbridge St
W8 . . . . 31 C1 113 B2

V

Vadnie Bish Ho
NW5 . . . . .13 B2
Vaine Ho 4 E9 . . . . .18 A2
Vale CI W9 . . . . . . .88 C3
Vale Ct
East Acton W3 . . . .29 B1
St John's Wood W9 . .88 C3
Vale End SE22 . . . . .64 B3
Vale Est The W3 . . .29 A1
Vale Gr Acton W3 . . .28 C1
Stoke Newington N4 . .6 B4
Valens Ho 1 SW2 . . .74 C3
Valentia Pl SW9 . . . .62 C3
Valentine Ho
1 Clapham Pk
SW4 . . . . .61 B1
28 Old Ford E3 . . . .26 B4
Valentine Pl SE1 . . .136 A4
Valentine Row SE1 . .17 C2

Valentine Row
SE1 . . . . .136 A3
VALE OF HEALTH . . .2 C1
Vale of Health NW3 . .2 C1
Vale Rd N4 . . . . . . .6 B4
Vale Rise NW11 . . . .1 B3
Vale Row N5 . . . . . .6 A1
Vale Royal N7 . . . . .14 A1
Vale Sch The
SW7 . . . . .128 C1
Vale The
Cricklewood NW11 . .1 A4
East Acton W3 . . . .29 A1
SW3 . . . . .157 C4
Valetta Rd W3 . . . . .38 B4
Valette Ho E9 . . . . .17 B2
Valette St E8 . . . . . .17 A2
Valiant Ho
4 Cubitt Town
E14 . . . . .42 B4
SW11 . . . . .167 C3
Vallance Rd
E1 . . . . .24 C1 99 C1
Valliere Rd NW10 . . .21 C2
Val McKenzie Ave
N7 . . . . .5 C1
Valmar Rd SE5 . . . . .48 B2
Valmar Trad Est
SE5 . . . . .48 B2
Valois Ho 1 SE1 . . .138 C2
Valonia Gdns
SW18 . . . . .58 B1
Vanbern Ho NW5 . . .12 C2
Vanbrugh Ct
SE11 . . . . .149 C3
Vanbrugh Fields
SE3 . . . . .53 B3
Vanbrugh Hill SE10,
SE3 . . . . .53 B4
Vanbrugh Ho 8
E9 . . . . .17 B1
Vanbrugh Park Rd
SE3 . . . . .53 B3
Vanbrugh Park Rd W
SE3 . . . . .53 B3
Vanbrugh Pk SE3 . . .53 B3
Vanbrugh Rd W4 . . .37 C3
Vanbrugh Terr
SE3 . . . . .53 B2
Vanburgh Ho E1 . . .110 C4
Vancover Ho 33
E1 . . . . .32 A1
Vanderbilt Rd
SW18 . . . . .71 B3
Vanderbilt Villas 1
W12 . . . . .39 C4
Vandon Ct SW1 . . . .133 A2
Vandon Pas SW1 . . .133 A2
Vandon St SW1 . . . .133 A2
Vandyke CI SW15 . . .57 C1
Vandy St
EC2 . . . . .24 A1 98 A1
Vane CI NW3 . . . . . .11 C4
Vane St SW1 . . . . . .147 A4
Vange Ho 10 W10 . . .30 B4
Van Gogh Ct E14 . . .42 C3
Vanguard Bldg 6
E14 . . . . .41 C4
Vanguard Ho 11
E8 . . . . .17 A1
Vanguard St SE8 . . .51 C2
Vanguard Trad Ctr
E15 . . . . .27 B4
Vanneck Sq SW15 . .56 C2
Vanner Point 27
E9 . . . . .17 C2

Vansittart St 7
SE14 . . . . .51 A3
Vanston PI SW6 . . .155 C2
Vantage Mews 7
E14 . . . . .34 B1
Vantage PI W8 . . . .127 C1
Vantrey Ho SE11 . . .149 B3
Varcoe Rd SE16 . . . .40 B1
Vardens Rd SW11 . . .59 C3
Varden St E1 . . . . . .32 A3
Vardon CI W3 . . . . .28 C3
Vardon Ho SE10 . . . .52 B2
Varey Ho E1 . . . . . .26 A2
Varley Ho 5 NW6 . . .23 C4
Varma Ct SE3 . . . . .53 C2
Varna Rd SW6 . . . .154 C1
Varndell St NW1 . . . .92 C4
Varsity Row SW14 . .45 B1
Vascroft Est
NW10 . . . . .20 A1
Vassall Ho 3 E3 . . . .26 A2
Vassall Rd SW9 . . . .163 C1
Vat Ho SW8 . . . . . .162 B2
Vauban Est SE16 . . .139 A1
Vauban St SE16 . . . .139 A1
Vaudeville Ct N4 . . . .5 C2
Vaughan Ave W6 . . .38 B2
Vaughan Est
E2 . . . . .24 B2 98 C4
Vaughan Ho SE1 . . .136 A4
Vaughan Rd SE5 . . . .63 B4
Vaughan St SE16 . . .41 B4
Vaughan Way E1 . . .125 C2
Vaughan Williams CI
SE8 . . . . .51 C3
VAUXHALL 148 B1
Vauxhall Bridge Rd
SW1 . . . . .147 A3
Vauxhall Cross SE1,
SW8 . . . . .148 B1
Vauxhall Gr SE8 . . .162 C4
Vauxhall Prim Sch
SE11 . . . . .149 A2
Vauxhall St SE11 . . .149 A2
Vauxhall Sta
SW8 . . . . .148 B1
Vauxhall Wlk
SE11 . . . . .148 C2
Vawdrey CI E1 . . . . .25 B1
Vaynor Ho N7 . . . . .14 A4
Vectis Ct SW18 . . . . .59 A1
Veda Rd SE13 . . . . .66 C3
Velde Way 1
SE22 . . . . .64 A2
Vellacott Ho 3
W12 . . . . .30 A3
Velletri Ho 17 E2 . . .25 C3
Venables St NW8 . . .101 C4
Vencourt PI W6 . . . .38 C1
Venetian Rd SE5 . . . .48 B1
Venice Ct 14 SE5 . . .48 B3
Venn Ho N1 . . . . . . .85 A3
Venn St SW4 . . . . . .61 B3
Ventnor Rd SE14 . . . .50 C3
Ventura Ho 2
SW2 . . . . .62 A3
Venue St E14 . . . . . .34 B4
Venus Ho
7 Millwall E14 . . . .41 C2
8 Old Ford E3 . . . .26 C4
Vera Ct W2 . . . . . . .100 A2
Vera Rd SW6 . . . . . .164 B4
Verbena Gdns
W6 . . . . .38 C1
Verdi Cres W10 . . . . .23 A3
Verdun Rd SW13 . . . .46 C3
Vere Bank SW19 . . . .70 B3

Vereker Rd W14 . . . .140 B1
Vere St W1 . . . . . . .104 A1
Verity CI W11 . . . . . .31 A3
Verity Ho 20 E3 . . . .26 B2
Vermeer Ct E14 . . . .42 C3
Vermont Rd SW18 . . .59 A1
Verne Ct 9 W3 . . . . .37 B3
Verneer Gdns
SE15 . . . . .65 B3
Verney Ho
Lisson Gr NW8 . . . . .90 A2
South Kensington
SW10 . . . . .156 C4
Verney Rd SE16 . . . .40 A1
Verney Way SE16 . . .40 A1
Vernon Ct NW2 . . . . .1 B1
Vernon Ho SE11 . . . .149 A1
Vernon Mews
W14 . . . . .140 B3
Vernon PI WC1 . . . .106 B3
Vernon Rd Bow E3 . .26 B3
Mortlake SW14 . . . . .55 C4
Vernon Rise WC1 . . .95 A4
Vernon Sq WC1 . . . .95 A4
Vernon St W14 . . . .140 B3
Vernon Yd
W11 . . . . . . .31 B2 112 C4
Verona Ct
Chiswick W4 . . . . . .38 A1
10 SE14 . . . . .50 C4
Veronica Ho
Brockley SE4 . . . . . .66 B4
8 Bromley E3 . . . . .27 A2
Veronica Rd SW17 . .73 A2
Verran Rd SW12 . . . .73 A4
Verulam Bldgs
WC1 . . . . .107 A4
Verulam Ho
W6 . . . . .39 B4
Verulam St EC1 . . . .107 B4
Vervain Ho 2
SE15 . . . . .49 C3
Verwood Ho SW8 . . .163 A1
Verwood Lo 1
E14 . . . . .42 C2
Vesage Ct EC1 . . . .107 C3
Vesey Path 15 E14 . .34 A3
Vespan Rd W12 . . . .38 C4
Vesta Ct SE1 . . . . . .138 A3
Vesta Ho 9 E3 . . . . .26 C4
Vesta Rd SE4, SE14 . .51 A1
Vestry Mews 12
SE5 . . . . .49 A2
Vestry Rd SE5 . . . . .49 A1
Vestry St N1 . . . . . . .97 B4
Viaduct PI 23 E2 . . . .25 A2
Viaduct St E2 . . . . . .25 A2
Vian St SE13 . . . . . .67 A4
Vibart Gdns SW2 . . .74 B4
Vibart Wlk N1 . . . . . .84 B4
Vicarage Ave SE3 . . .53 C3
Vicarage Cres
SW11 . . . . .167 B3
Putney SW15 . . . . . .68 C4
W8 . . . . .128 A4
Vicarage Dr SW14 . . .55 C2
Vicarage Gate
W8 . . . . .114 A1
Vicarage Gdns
Mortlake SW14 . . . . .55 C2
W8 . . . . .31 C1 113 C1
Vicarage Gr SE5 . . . .48 C2
Vicarage Rd SW14 . .55 C2

280 Vic–Wal

Vicarage Wlk
SW11 .... 167 C4
Vicar's Cl E9 ..... 25 B4
Vicars Hill SE13 ...67 A3
Vicar's Rd NW5 ...12 C3
Viceroy Ct NW8 ...80 B2
Viceroy Rd SW8 ..172 A4
Vic Johnson Ho 5
E3 ....26 B4
Vickery Ct EC1 ....97 A2
Vickery Ho 13
SW4 ....61 C3
Vickery's Wharf 3
E14 ....33 C3
Victor Cazalet Ho
N1 ....86 A4
Victoria & Albert
*Mus*** SW7 .....129 C1
Victoria Ave EC2 .110 B3
Victoria Bldgs 13
E8 ....25 A4
Victoria Chambers
EC2 ....24 A1 98 A2
Victoria Coach Sta
SW1 ....146 A3
Victoria Coll SE17 107 B2
Victoria Cotts
7 Richmond TW9 ..44 C2
Spitalfields E1 ....111 B4
Victoria Ct
5 Clapham Pk
SW4 ....61 C1
South Acton W3 ...37 B4
St George in East
E1 ....125 B3
Victoria Dr SW19 .69 C3
Victoria Emb
WC2 ....121 B3
Victoria Gdns
W11 .....31 C1 113 B2
Victoria Gr W8 ...128 C2
Victoria Gr Mews
W2 ....114 A3
Victoria Hall 18
E16 ....35 C1
Victoria Ho
6 Clapham Pk
SW4 ....61 C1
2 Shepherd's Bush
W12 ....38 C4
SW1 ....146 A2
Victoria Ind Est
W3 ....29 A4
Victoria Mans
8 Islington N7 ....14 C3
Willesden NW10 ...9 A1
Victoria Mews
Kilburn NW6 ....23 C3
Wandsworth SW18 .71 B3
Victoria Mills 1
E15 ....27 C4
Victorian Gr N16 ...7 A1
Victorian Rd N16 ...7 B1
Victoria Park Ct 11
E9 ....17 B1
Victoria Park Ind Ctr
E9 ....18 B1
Victoria Park Lofts
E9 ....25 C4
Victoria Park Rd
E9 ....17 C1
Victoria Park Sq
E2 ....25 B2
Victoria Pas NW8 .89 B2

Victoria Place Sh Ctr
SW1 ....146 B4
Victoria Rd
Finsbury Pk N4 ....5 B3
Kensington W8 ...128 C2
Kilburn NW6 ....23 B4
Mortlake SW14 ....55 C4
North Acton NW10 .21 A1
Victoria Rise SW4 ..61 A4
Victoria Sq SW1 ..132 B2
Victoria St SW1 ..133 A1
Victoria Sta SW1 .146 B4
Victoria Terr
Dagenham NW10 ...21 A1
Finsbury Pk N4 ....5 C3
Victoria
(Underground)
SW1 ....132 B1
Victoria Villas
TW9 ....54 B3
Victoria Wharf
E14 ....33 A2
Victoria Yd 11
E1 ....111 C1
Victor Rd NW10 ...22 A2
Victory Pl
6 Limehouse E14 ..33 A2
SE17 ....151 B4
Victory Sch SE17 ..151 A4
Victory Way SE16 ..41 A4
Victory Wlk SE8 ...51 C2
Video Ct N4 ....5 A4
Vienna Ct N6 .....3 B4
Viewfield Rd
SW18 ....58 B1
Viewpoint 3 N5 ...15 A3
Vigo St W1 ....118 C3
Viking Cl 13 E3 ...26 A3
Viking Ho 6 SE5 ..48 B1
Village Cl NW3 ....11 C3
Village Mount 19
NW3 ....11 B4
Village Sch The
NW3 ....12 B2
Village The SW11 .60 B4
Villa Rd SW9 .....62 C4
Villas On The Heath
NW3 ....2 B1
Villa St SE17 .....151 C1
Villiers Ct SW11 .168 B4
Villiers Rd NW2 ...8 C2
Villiers St WC2 ...120 B2
Vince Ct N1 ....97 C3
Vincent Ct
Finsbury Pk N4 ....5 A3
Marylebone W1 ...102 C2
South Lambeth
SW9 ....173 A3
Vincent Mews 1
E3 ....26 C3
Vincent Rd W3 ....37 B3
Vincents Cl SE16 ..41 A4
Vincent Sq SW1 ..147 B4
Vincent St
Canning Town E16 ..35 B4
Westminster SW1 .147 C4
Vincent Terr N1 ...86 B2
Vince St EC1 ....97 C3
Vine Ct E1 ....111 C3
Vinegar St E1 .....32 A1
Vinegar Yd SE1 ...138 A4
Vine La SE1 ....124 B1
Vine Rd SW13 .....56 B4
Vine St Bridge
EC1 ....95 C1
Vine Sq W14 ......141 A1

Vines Sch The
SW11 ....60 C3
Vine St W1 ....119 A3
Whitechapel EC3 ...110 C1
Vineyard Path
SW14 ....55 C4
Vineyard Sch The
TW10 ....54 A1
Vineyard The
TW10 ....54 A1
Vineyard Wlk EC1 ..95 B2
Viney Ct 9 SW4 ...61 C1
Vine Yd SE1 ......137 A4
Viney Rd SE13 ....67 A4
Vining St SW2,
SW9 ....62 C3
Vinson Ho 10 N1 ..87 C1
Vintners Ct EC4 ..123 A4
Viola Sq W12 .....29 B2
Violet Cl 32 SE8 ..51 B4
Violet Hill NW8 ...78 C1
Violet Hill Ho NW8 78 C1
Violet Rd E3 ......27 A1
Violet St E2 ......25 A1
Virgil Pl W1 ......102 C3
Virgil St SE1 .....135 A2
Virginia Ct 7
SE16 ....40 C4
Virginia Ho 3 E14 .34 B2
Virginia Prim Sch
E2 ....24 B2 98 C3
Virginia Rd
E2 ....24 B2 98 C3
Virginia St E1 .....125 C3
Virginia Wlk SW2 .62 B1
Viscount Ct 9
W11 ....31 C3
Viscount St EC1 ..108 C4
Vista Bldgs 18 E3 .26 B2
Vitae Apartments 7
W6 ....38 C3
Vittoria Ho N1 ....85 A3
Vittoria Prim Sch
N1 ....85 B2
Vivian Comma Cl 3
N4 ....6 A1
Vivian Ct NW6 ....78 A2
Vivian Ho N4 .....6 C4
Vivian Rd E3 ......26 A3
Vogans Mill SE1 ..139 A4
Vogler Ho 4 E1 ...32 B2
Vollasky Ho 1 E1 .111 B4
Voltaire
2 Camberwell
SE5 ....49 B2
15 Richmond TW9 .44 B2
Voltaire Ct SW11 .169 C2
Voltaire Rd SW4 ..61 C4
Volt Ave NW10 ....21 A2
Vorley Rd N19 .....4 B2
Voss St E2 ....24 C2 99 C3
Voyager Bsns Est
SE16 ....139 B2
Vulcan Rd SE4 ....51 B1
Vulcan Sq E14 ....41 C2
Vulcan Terr SE4 ..51 B1
Vulcan Way N7 ...14 B2
Vyner Ct E5 ....7 C2
Vyner Rd W3 ......28 C2
Vyner St E2 ....25 A4

W

Wadcroft Ct SE4 ..66 B4
Wadding St SE17 .151 B3
Waddington Rd
E15 ....19 C2
Waddington St
E15 ....19 C2
Wade Ho SE1 .....139 B3
Wadeson St E2 ...25 A3
Wade's Pl E14 ....34 A2
Wadham Gdns
NW3 ....80 A4
Wadham Rd SW15 .58 A3
Wadhurst Rd W4 ..37 C3
Wager St E3 ....26 B1
Waghorn St SE15 ..64 C4
Wagner St SE15 ....50 B3
Wainford Cl SW19 .69 C3
Wainwright Ho 3
E1 ....32 B1
Waite St SE15 ....49 B4
Waithman St EC4 108 A1
Wakefield Ho 6
SE15 ....49 C2
Wakefield Mews
WC1 ....94 B3
Wakefield St WC1 .94 B3
Wakeford Cl SW4 .61 B2
Wakeham St 9
N1 ....15 C2
Wakehurst Rd
SW11 ....60 B2
Wakeling Ho 8
SE27 ....75 A1
Wakeling St 11
E14 ....33 A3
Wakelin Ho 10 N1 .15 B2
Wakeman Rd
NW10 ....22 C2
Wakley St EC1 ....96 A4
Walberswick St
SW8 ....162 B1
Walbrook EC4 ....123 B4
Walbrook Ct N1 ...24 A3
Walbrook Wharf
EC4 ....123 B4
Walburgh St E1 ...32 A3
Walcorde Ave
SE17 ....151 A3
Walcot Gdns
SE11 ....149 B4
Walcot Ho 9
SE22 ....64 A4
Walcot Sq SE11 ..149 C4
Walcott St SW1 ..147 A4
Waldeck Gr SE27 ..75 A1
Waldeck Rd
Brentford W4 .....44 C4
Mortlake SW14 ...55 B4
Waldeck Terr
SW14 ....55 B4
Waldegrave Ho 5
SW15 ....57 B2
Waldemar Ave
SW6 ....164 B2
Waldemar Avenue
Mans SW6 ....164 B4
Walden Ct SW8 ..171 C4
Walden Ho
Clapham SW11 ...169 B2
SW1 ....145 C3
Walden St E1 .....32 A3
Waldo Cl SW4 ....61 B2
Waldo Rd NW10 ..22 A2

Waldron Ho 17
SW2 ....62 B2
Waldron Mews
SW3 ....157 C4
Waldron Rd SW18 .71 B1
Walerand Rd SE13 52 B1
Waleran Flats
SE1 ....152 A4
Wales Cl SE15 ....50 A4
Wales Farm Rd
W3 ....28 C4
Waley St 1 E1 ....33 A4
Walford Ho 28 E1 .32 A3
Walford Rd N16 ...16 A4
Walham Ct 15
NW3 ....12 B2
Walham Gn Mews,
SW6 ....155 B2
WALHAM GREEN
SW6 ....156 A1
Walham Green Arc
SW6 ....155 C2
Walham Yd SW6 .155 C2
Walham Ho NW1 ..83 B1
Walker Mews 7
SW2 ....62 C2
Walkerscroft Mead
SE21 ....75 B3
Walker's Ct W1 ..119 B4
Walkers Lo 18 E14 .42 B4
Walker's Pl SW15 .58 A3
Walkinshaw Ct 9
N1 ....15 B1
Walkynscroft 1
SE15 ....50 A1
*Wallace Collection**
W1 ....103 B2
Wallace Ct NW1 ..102 B3
Wallace Ho N7 ...14 B2
Wallace Lo N4 .....5 C3
Wallace Rd N1, N5 .15 B2
Wallbutton Rd
SE4 ....51 A1
Wall Ct N4 ....5 B3
Waller Rd SE14 ...50 C1
Wallett Ct 11 NW1 .13 B1
Wallflower St
W12 ....29 B2
Wallgrave Rd
SW5 ....142 A3
Wallingford Ave
W10 ....30 C3
Wallis Alley SE1 ..137 A4
Wallis Cl SW11 ...59 C4
Wallis Ho 1 SE14 .51 A2
Wallis Rd E9 ......18 C2
Wallorton Gdns
SW14 ....55 C3
Wall St N1 ....15 C2
Wallwood St E14 ..33 B4
Walmer Ho 8
W10 ....30 C3
Walmer Pl W1 ....102 C4
Walmer Rd
North Kensington
W10 ....30 B4
W11 .....31 A2 112 A3
Walm La NW2 .....9 B2
Walney Wlk 6 N1 ..15 B2
Walnut Cl SE8 ....51 B4
Walnut Ho 11 E3 ..26 B4
Walnut Tree Cl
SW13 ....46 B2
Walnut Tree Ho
SW10 ....156 B3
Walnut Tree Rd
Brentford TW8 ....44 B4

Walnut Tree Rd
continued
Greenwich SE10 . . . . . . 43 A1
Walnut Tree Walk
Prim Sch SE11 . . **149** B4
Walnut Tree Wlk
SE11 . . . . **149** B4
Walpole Ave TW9 . . 44 B1
Walpole Ct
7 Hammersmith
W14 . . . . 39 C3
South Hampstead
NW6 . . . . 11 B1
Walpole Gdns W4 . . 37 B1
Walpole Mews
NW8 . . . . 79 B3
Walpole St SW3 . . **145** A2
Walsham Cl N16 . . . . . 7 C3
Walsham Ho
New Cross Gate
SE14 . . . . 50 C1
SE17 . . . . **151** B2
Walsham Rd SE14 . . 50 C1
Walsingham NW8 . . **79** C4
Walsingham Lo
SW13 . . . . 46 C2
Walsingham Mans
SW6 . . . . **156** B2
Walsingham Pl SW4,
SW11 . . . . 60 C1
Walsingham Rd E5 . . 7 C1
Walter Besant Ho 20
E1 . . . . 25 C2
Walter Ct 3 W3 . . 28 B3
Walter Green Ho
SE15 . . . . 50 B2
Walter Ho SW10 . . **157** B2
Walter Northcott Ho
2 NW6 . . . . 10 C3
Walters Cl SE17 . . **151** A3
Walters Ho
3 Camberwell
SE5 . . . . 49 A1
Islington N1 . . . . . . **86** B4
SE17 . . . . 48 A4
Walter Sickert Hall
N1 . . . . **86** C1
Walter St E2 . . . . . . 25 C2
Walters Way SE23 . 65 C1
Walter Taylor Ct
SE4 . . . . 66 B3
Walter Terr E1 . . . . 32 C3
Walterton Rd W9 . . 23 C1
Waltham Green Ct
SW6 . . . . **156** A1
Waltham Ho NW8 . . 78 C4
Stockwell SW9 . . . . **173** A1
Walton Cl SW8 . . . **162** B2
Walton Gdns W3 . . 28 A4
Walton Ho
E2 . . . . 24 B1 **99** A2
Upper Holloway N7 . . 5 B1
Wandsworth SW18 . 58 C1
Walton Pl SW3 . . **130** C2
Walton St SW3 . . **130** B1
Walton Way W3 . . 28 A4
Walt Whitman Cl 6
SE24 . . . . 63 A3
WALWORTH **152** A3
Walworth Pl SE17 **151** A1
Walworth Rd
SE17 . . . . **151** A2
Walworth Sch
SE17 . . . . **152** B1
Wanborough Dr
SW15 . . . . 69 A3

Wandle Ct 4 W12 . 38 A4
Wandle Ho NW8 . . **102** A4
Wandsworth SW18 . 71 A4
Wandle Rd SW17 . . 72 A2
Wandle Way
SW18 . . . . 71 A3
Wandon Rd SW6 . . **156** B1
WANDSWORTH . . . **58** C1
Wandsworth Bridge
Rd SW6 . . . . **166** A3
Wandsworth Common
Sta SW12 . . . . 72 C4
Wandsworth Common
West Side SW11 . . 60 B1
Wandsworth Gyratory
SW18 . . . . 59 A2
Wandsworth High St
SW18 . . . . 59 A2
Wandsworth Mus* . .
SW18 . . . . 59 A2
Wandsworth Plain
SW18 . . . . 59 A2
Wandsworth Rd
SW8 . . . . **162** A1
Wandsworth Road Sta
SW4 . . . . **171** A1
Wandsworth Town
Sta SW18 . . . . 59 A3
Wangford Ho 13
SW9 . . . . 63 A3
Wanless Rd SE24 . 63 B4
Wanley Rd SE5 . . . . 63 C3
Wansbeck Rd E3,
E9 . . . . 18 B1
Wansdown Pl
SW6 . . . . **156** A2
Wansey St SE17 . . **151** A3
WAPPING 32 A1
Wapping Dock St 19
E1 . . . . 32 A1
Wapping High St
E1 . . . . 32 A1
Wapping La E1 . . . . 32 A1
Wapping Sta E1 . . 32 B1
Wapping Wall E1 . . 32 B1
Warbeck Rd W12 . . 39 A4
Warburg Ho
E2 . . . . 24 C2 **99** B3
Warburton Cl 6
N1 . . . . 16 A2
Warburton Ct
SE15 . . . . 64 C4
Warburton Ho 5
E8 . . . . 25 A4
Warburton Rd 8
E8 . . . . 25 A4
Warburton St 6
E8 . . . . 25 A4
Wardalls Ho 12
SE8 . . . . 51 B4
Wardell Ho 7
SE10 . . . . 52 B4
Warden Rd NW5 . . 12 C2
Wardens Gr SE1 . . **122** C2
Wardle St E9 . . . . . 17 C3
Wardley St SW18 . 71 A4
Wardlow 8 NW5 . . 13 A4
Wardo Ave SW6 . **164** A4
Wardour Mews
W1 . . . . **105** A1
Wardour St W1 . . **105** B1
Ward Point SE11 . **149** B3
Wardrobe Pl EC4 . **108** B1

Wardrobe Terr
EC4 . . . . **122** B4
Wareham Ct 2
N1 . . . . 16 A1
Wareham Ho
SW8 . . . . **162** C2
Warfield Rd NW10 . 22 C2
Warfield Yd 2
NW10 . . . . 22 C2
Wargrave Ho
E2 . . . . 24 B2 **98** C3
Warham St SE5 . . **48** A3
Waring Ho
E2 . . . . 24 C2 **99** C3
Warley Ho N1 . . . . . 15 C2
Warley St E2 . . . . . 25 C2
Warlock Rd W9 . . . 23 C1
Warlters Cl N7 . . . . 14 A4
Warlters Rd N7 . . . 14 A4
Warltersville Mans
N19 . . . . 5 A4
Warltersville Rd N4, N8,
N19 . . . . 5 A4
War Meml Homes
W4 . . . . 45 C3
Warmington Rd
SE24 . . . . 63 B1
Warmsworth NW1 . 82 C3
Warndon St SE16 . 40 B2
Warneford St E9 . . 25 A4
Warner Ho
4 Homerton E9 . . . 17 C2
Lewisham SE13 . . . . 52 A1
SE1 . . . . **136** A3
Warner Pl
E2 . . . . 24 C2 **99** C4
Warner Rd SE5 . . . 48 B2
Warner St EC1 . . . . 95 B1
Warner Yd EC1 . . . . 95 B1
Warnford Ho
SW15 . . . . 56 A1
Warnham WC1 . . . . 94 C3
Warnham Ho 6
SW2 . . . . 74 B4
Warple Mews W3 . 38 A4
Warple Way W3,
W12 . . . . 38 A4
Warren Ave SW14,
TW10 . . . . 55 A3
Warren Cl SE21 . . . 75 B4
Warren Ct N1 . . . . **85** B2
Warrender Rd
N19 . . . . 13 B4
Warren Gdns E15 . 19 C3
Warren Ho 8 E3 . . 27 A2
Warren Mews W1 . **92** C1
Warren St W1 . . . **92** C1
Warren Street Sta
NW1 . . . . **93** A2
Warriner Gdns
SW11 . . . . **169** B3
Warrington Cres
W9 . . . . **88** C2
Warrington Gdns
W9 . . . . **88** C2
Warspite Ho 3
E14 . . . . 42 A2
Warton Rd E15 . . . 27 B4
Warwick W14 . . . . **141** A3
Warwick Ave W9 . **88** C1
Warwick Bldg
SW8 . . . . **160** A3
Warwick Chambers
W8 . . . . **127** B2

Warwick Cres
W2 . . . . **100** C4
Warwick Ct WC1 . **107** A3
Warwick Dr SW15 . 57 A4
Warwick Gdns
W14 . . . . **141** A4
Warwick Ho
Brixton SW9 . . . . . **173** B1
6 Putney SW15 . . . 69 B4
Stoke Newington N4 . 6 B3
Warwick House St
SW1 . . . . **119** C2
Warwick La EC4 . . **108** B1
Warwick Lo NW2 . . 10 A3
Warwick Mans
SW5 . . . . **141** B4
Warwick Pas EC4 . **108** B2
Warwick Pl W9 . . **100** C4
Warwick Pl N
SW1 . . . . **146** C3
Warwick Rd SW5 . **141** A4
Warwick Row
SW1 . . . . **132** B2
Warwickshire Path
SE8 . . . . 51 B3
Warwick Sq
Holborn EC4 . . . . . **108** B2
Pimlico SW1 . . . . . **146** C2
Warwick Sq Mews
SW1 . . . . **146** C3
Warwick St W1 . . **119** A4
Warwick Way
SW1 . . . . **146** B4
Warwick Yd EC1 . . **97** A1
Wasdale NW1 . . . . **92** B3
Washbrook Ho
SW2 . . . . 62 C1
Washington Bldg 1
SE13 . . . . 52 A2
Washington Cl 5
E3 . . . . 27 A2
Washington Ho
SW1 . . . . **130** C3
Washington Rd
SW13 . . . . 46 C3
Watchfield Ct 2
W4 . . . . 37 B1
Watcombe Cotts
TW9 . . . . 44 C4
Watercress Pl N1 . 16 A1
Waterden Cres E9 . 18 C3
Waterden Rd E15 . 18 C2
Waterford Rd
SW6 . . . . **156** A1
Waterford Way
NW10 . . . . 8 C3
Water Gardens The
W2 . . . . **102** B2
Watergate EC4 . . . **122** A4
Watergate St SE8 . **51** C4
Watergate Wlk
WC2 . . . . **120** B2
Waterhead NW1 . . **92** C4
Waterhouse Cl
Hammersmith W6 . 39 C1
Hampstead NW3 . . 11 C3
Waterlegate Cl E14 . 41 C3
Water La
16 Camden Town
NW1 . . . . 13 A1
SE14 . . . . 50 B3
Waterloo Bridge SE1,
WC2 . . . . **121** A3
Waterloo Cl E9 . . . **17** B3
Waterloo East Sta
SE1 . . . . **121** C1

Waterloo Gdns
26 Islington N1 . . . . 15 A1
South Hackney E2 . . **25** B3
Waterloo Int Sta
SE1 . . . . **135** A4
Waterloo Pier
SE1 . . . . **134** C4
Waterloo Pl
Kew TW9 . . . . 44 C4
9 Richmond TW9 . . 54 A3
SW1 . . . . **119** B2
Waterloo Sta SE1 . **135** B4
Waterloo Terr N1 . 15 A1
Waterlow Ct NW11 . 2 A4
Waterlow Rd N19 . . 4 B3
Waterman Bldg 2
E14 . . . . 41 C4
Watermans Ct 2
TW8 . . . . 44 A4
Waterman St
SW15 . . . . 57 C4
Waterman Way
E1 . . . . 32 A1
Watermead Ho E9 . 18 B3
Watermeadow La
SW6 . . . . **166** C1
Water Mews SE15 . 65 B3
Watermill Ct SE13 . 67 A4
Watermint Quay
N16 . . . . 7 C4
Water's Edge SW6 . 47 B2
Waterside N1 . . . . **86** C1
Waterside Cl
Bermondsey SE16 . **139** C3
Old Ford E3 . . . . . . 26 B4
Waterside Ct SE13 . 67 C3
Waterside Pl NW1 . 81 C4
Waterside Point
SW11 . . . . **158** B2
Waterson St
E2 . . . . 24 B2 **98** C4
Waters Pl SW15 . . 47 B1
Waters St WC2 . . . **121** B4
Waterview Ho 18
E14 . . . . 33 A4
Waterworks Rd
SW2 . . . . 62 B1
Watford Cl SW11 . **168** B3
Watford Rd E16 . . 35 C4
Watkins Ho 11
E14 . . . . 42 B4
Watkinson Rd N7 . 14 B2
Watling Ct EC4 . . **109** A1
Watling Gdns
NW2 . . . . 10 A2
Watling St 5
6 Camberwell
SE15 . . . . 49 A4
City of London EC4 . **109** A1
Watney Cotts
SW14 . . . . 55 B4
Watney Mkt* E1 . . 32 A3
Watney Rd SW14 . 55 B4
Watney St E1 . . . . 32 A3
Watson Ho 15 . . . . 32 C3
Watson Ho 3
SW2 . . . . 74 A4
Watsons Mews
W1 . . . . **102** B3
Watson's St SE8 . . 51 C3
Watts Gr E3 . . . . . 34 A4
Watts Ho 6 W10 . . 31 A4
Watts St SE15 . . . . 49 B2
Wapping E1 . . . . . . 32 A1

Wat Tyler Rd SE10 ..52 C2
Wavel Ct
 7 Streatham
 SW16 ....74 A1
 7 Wapping E1......32 B1
Wavel Mews NW6 ..11 A1
Wavendon Ave
 W4 ....37 C1
Waveney Ave
 SE15 ....65 A3
Waveney Cl E1 ..125 C2
Waveney Ho SE15 ..65 A3
Waverley Ct
 5 Brondesbury
 NW6 ....10 A1
 W1 ....103 C4
Waverley Pl
 Finsbury Pk N4 ....6 A3
 St John's Wood
 NW8 ....79 B2
Waverley Rd N8 .....5 A4
Waverly Ct NW3 ..12 B2
Waxham NW5 .....12 B3
Waxlow Rd NW10 ..20 C3
Wayford St SW11 168 B1
Wayland Ave E8 ..16 C3
Wayland Ho SW9 173 B2
Waylett Ho SE11 ..149 B1
Waylett Pl SE27 ..75 A1
Wayman Ct E8 ....17 A2
Waynflete Sq
 10 North Kensington
 W10 ....30 C3
 10 Shepherd's Bush
 W10 ....30 C2
Waynflete St
 SW18 ....71 B2
Wayside
 Golders Green
 NW11 ....1 A3
 Mortlake SW14 ..55 B2
Weald Cl 10 SE16...40 A1
Weardale Ho N4 ....6 A4
Weardale Rd SE13 ..67 C3
Wearmouth Ho 1
 E3 ....33 B4
Wear Pl 12 E2.....25 A2
Wearside Rd SE13 ..67 A3
Weatherbury 6
 W2 ....31 C3
Weatherbury Ho 3
 N19 ....4 C1
Weatherley Cl E3 ..33 B4
Weaver Ct 2 E2 ..25 A1
Weaver Ho
 E1 .....24 C1 99 B1
Weaver's La SE1 ..124 B1
Weaver St
 E1 .....24 C1 99 B1
Weavers Way
 6 Camden Town
 NW1 ....13 C1
 NW1 ....83 B4
Webb Cl NW10 ..22 B1
Webb Ct W3 .....37 A4
Webber Row SE1 ..136 A3

Webber St SE1 ....136 A3
Webb Est E5 ....7 C4
Webb Ho SW8....161 C1
Webb Pl NW10 ....21 B2
Webb Rd SE3......53 B4
Webb's Rd SW11 ..60 B2
Webb St SE1 .....138 A1
Webheath 1 NW6...10 B1
Webster Ho 10
 N16 ....16 A3
Webster Rd SE16 139 C1
Weddell Ho 21 E1 ..25 C1
Wedderburn Rd
 NW3 ....11 C3
Wedgewood Ho
 SW1 ....146 C1
Wedgewood Mews
 W1 ....105 C1
Wedgewood Wlk
 NW3 ....11 A3
Wedgwood Ho
 17 Globe Town E2 ..25 C2
 SE11 ....235 B1
Wedlake St W10 ..23 A1
Wedmore Gdns
 N19 ....4 C2
Wedmore St N19...4 C1
Weech Rd NW6 ...10 C4
Weedington Rd
 NW5 ....12 C3
Weedon Ho W12 ..29 C3
Weekley Sq SW11 ..59 C4
Weighhouse St
 W1 ....103 C1
Weimar St SW15 ..58 A4
Weir Ho 8 SW12..73 B4
Weir Rd
 Streatham SW12 ..73 B4
 Wimbledon SW18,
 SW19 ....71 A1
Weir's Pas NW1 ..93 C4
Weiss Rd SW15 ..57 C4
Welbeck Ct E14 ..140 C4
Welbeck Mans 10
 NW6 ....10 C3
Welbeck St W1 ..104 A2
Welbeck Way W1 ..104 A2
Welby Ct SE5 ....48 A2
Welby St SE5 .....48 A2
Weldon Ct SE8 ..51 C1
Welford Ct
 1 Camden Town
 NW1 ....13 A1
 Clapham SW8....170 C1
Welland Ho SE15 ..65 B3
Welland Mews
 E1 ....125 C2
Welland St SE10..52 B4
Wellclose Sq E1 ..125 C3
Wellclose St 1
 E1 ....125 C3
Wellday Ho 2 E9 ..18 A2
Weldon Ct 1
 SE21 ....75 C2
Weller Ho SE16..139 B3
Weller St SE1 ....136 C4
Welles Ct 1 E14 ..33 C2
Wellesley Ave W6 ..39 A3
Wellesley Ct W9 ..88 C4
Wellesley Ho NW1..93 B3
Wellesley Pl
 Camden Town
 NW5 ....12 C3
 NW1 ....93 B3
Wellesley Rd
 Gospel Oak NW5 ..12 C3

Wellesley Rd continued
 Gunnersbury W4 ..37 A1
Wellesley St E1 ..32 C4
Wellesley Terr N1 ..97 A4
Wellfit St 8 SE24 ..63 A4
Wellgarth Rd NW11..2 A3
Wellington Arch★
 ....131 C4
Wellington Bldgs
 19 Bow E3 ....26 C2
 SW1 ....145 C1
Wellington Cl
 Kensington W11....31 C3
 New Cross Gate
 SE14 ....50 C2
Wellington Ct
 Knightsbridge
 SW1 ....130 C3
 St John's Wood
 NW8 ....79 C1
 Strand WC2 ....120 A4
 Wandsworth SW18..60 A2
Wellington Gr
 SE10 ....52 C3
Wellington Ho 18
 NW3 ....12 B1
Wellington Hospl The
 NW8 ....79 C1
Wellington Mans
 N16 ....16 B4
Wellington Mews
 East Dulwich SE22 ..64 C3
 1 Islington N7 ....14 B2
 Streatham SW16 ..73 C1
Wellington Mus
 (Apsley Ho)★
 SW1 ....131 C4
Wellington Pl
 NW8 ....89 C4
Wellington Prim Sch
 E3 ....26 C2
Wellington Rd
 Kensal Green
 NW10 ....22 C2
 St John's Wood
 NW8 ....79 C1
 Wimbledon SW19..70 C2
Wellington Row
 E2 ....24 C2 99 B4
Wellington Sq
 SW3 ....144 C2
Wellington St
 WC2 ....120 C4
Wellington Terr 2
 E1 ....32 A1
Wellington Way
 E3 ....26 C2
Well La SW14 ....55 B2
Well Rd NW3 ......2 C1
Wells Ct
 21 Hampstead
 NW3 ....11 B4
 1 Paddington NW6..23 C3
 Stoke Newington
 N16 ....16 A3
Wells Ho
 Finsbury EC1 ....96 A4
 12 Kensal Town
 W10 ....23 A1
 New Cross Gate
 SE4 ....51 A1
 9 Rotherhithe
 SE16 ....40 B3
Wells Ho The 2
 W11 ....31 C4
Wells House Rd
 NW10 ....29 A4

Wellside Gdns
 SW14 ....55 B2
Wells Mews W1 ..105 A2
Wells Pl SW18 ....71 B4
Wells Rd W12 ....39 B4
Wells Rise NW8 ..80 C3
Wells Sq WC1 ....95 A3
Wells St W1 .....105 A2
Wells Terr N4 .....5 C2
Well St E9 ....17 B1
Wells Way
 Brompton SW7 ..129 B2
 Camberwell SE5 ..49 A4
Well Walk NW3 ...2 C1
Wellwood Ct
 SW15 ....57 B3
Welmar Works
 SW4 ....61 C3
Welsford St SE1 ..153 B3
Welsh Ho 14 E1 ..32 A1
Welshpool Ho 22
 E8 ....24 C4
Welshpool St 1
 E8 ....25 A4
Welstead Ho 26
 E1 ....32 A3
Welstead Way W4..38 B2
Weltje Rd W6 ....38 C1
Welton Ct SE5 ....49 A2
Welton Ho E1 ....32 C4
Welwyn St E2 ....25 B2
Wembury Mews N6..4 B4
Wembury Rd N6....4 A3
Wemyss Rd SE3...53 B1
Wendell Park Prim
 Sch W12 ....38 B4
Wendell Rd W12 ..38 B4
Wendling NW5 ....12 B3
Wendon St E3 ....26 B4
Wendover SE17 ..152 A1
Wendover Ct
 Acton W3 ....20 A1
 Becontree W3 ....20 B1
 4 Child's Hill NW2 ..1 C1
 W1 ....103 B3
Wendover Ho W1 ..103 B3
Wendover Rd
 NW10 ....21 B3
Wengham Ho
 W12 ....29 C2
Wenham Ho SW8 160 C1
Wenlake Ho EC1...96 C2
Wenlock Ct N1 ...87 C1
Wenlock Rd N1 ...87 A1
Wenlock St N1 ...87 B1
Wennington Rd
 E3 ....26 C3
Wensdale Ho E5 ..7 C2
Wensleydale Ho 8
 N4 ....6 B4
Wentworth Cres
 SE15 ....49 C3
Wentworth Ct
 W6 ....154 A3
 Wandsworth SW18 ..59 A1
Wentworth Dwellings
 E1 ....110 C2
Wentworth Ho 4
 SE3 ....53 C3
Wentworth Mews
 E3 ....26 B2
Wentworth St E1 111 A3
Werrington St NW1..83 A1
Werter Rd SW15 ..58 A3
Wesleyan Pl NW5 ..13 A4

Wesley Ave NW10 ..20 C2
Wesley Cl
 Finsbury Pk N7 .....5 B2
 SE17 ....150 B3
Wesley Ct W1 ....103 C1
Wesley Ho SE24 ..63 C1
Wesley Rd NW10 ..20 B4
Wesley Sq W11 ...31 A3
Wesley St W1 ....103 C3
Wessex Ct SW15...57 C2
Wessex Gardens Prim
 Sch NW11 ......1 A3
Wessex Gdns NW11..1 A3
Wessex St 1 E2 ...153 A1
Wessex St E2 .....25 B2
Wessex Way NW11..1 A3
West 12 SW12.....39 C4
Westacott Cl N19...4 C3
West Acton Prim Sch
 W3 ....28 A3
West Arbour St
 E1 ....32 C3
West Bank N16.....7 A4
Westbere Rd NW2 ..10 A3
West Block 18 E1...32 B2
Westbourne Ave
 W3 ....28 C3
Westbourne Cres
 W2 ....115 B4
Westbourne Ct
 W2 ....100 C2
Westbourne Gdns
 W2 ....100 A2
Westbourne Gr
 Notting Hill W2,
 W11 ....31 C3
 W11 ......31 B2 113 A4
WESTBOURNE GREEN
 ....88 A2
Westbourne Gr Mews
 7 W11 ....31 C3
Westbourne Gr Terr
 W2 ....100 A1
Westbourne Ho
 SW1 ....146 A2
Westbourne Park Rd
 Notting Hill W2 ...31 C3
 Notting Hill W11 ..31 B3
Westbourne Park Sta
 W11 ....31 B4
Westbourne Park
 Villas W2 ......100 A3
Westbourne Rd
 N7 ....14 B2
Westbourne St
 W2 ....115 B4
Westbourne Terr
 W2 ....101 A2
Westbourne Terrace
 Mews W2 ......100 C2
Westbourne Terrace
 Rd W2 ....100 C3
Westbridge Cl
 W12 ....29 C2
Westbridge Prim Sch
 SW11 ....168 A3
Westbridge Rd
 SW11 ....168 A4
WEST BROMPTON
 ....156 A4
West Brompton Sta
 SW5 ....141 C1
Westbrook Ho
 5 Bethnal Green
 E2 ....25 B2

Westbrook Ho
continued
5 Clapham Pk
SW4 . . . . .61 B2
Westbury Ct SW4. .61 A1
Westbury Ho 6
NW10 . . . . .8 A1
Westbush Ct 1
W12 . . . . .39 A4
West Carriage Dr
W2 . . . .**116** A2
West Central St
WC1 . . . .**106** A2
Westchester Ho
W2 . . . .**102** C1
Westcliff Ho 13
N1 . . . . .15 C2
Westcombe Ct 1
SE3 . . . . .53 B3
Westcombe Hill SE3,
SE10 . . . . .53 C4
Westcombe Park Rd
SE3 . . . . .53 B3
Westcombe Park Sta
SE3 . . . . .43 C1
Westcott Ho 1
E14 . . . . .34 A2
Westcott Rd SE17 . .48 A4
West Cotts NW6 . . .10 C3
Westcroft Cl NW2 . .10 A4
Westcroft Sq W6 . .38 C2
Westcroft Way
NW2 . . . . .10 A4
West Cromwell Rd
W14 . . . .**141** A2
West Cross Route W10,
W11 . . . . .30 C2
Westdean Cl
SW18 . . . . .59 A1
Westdown Rd E15 . .19 B4
WEST DULWICH . . .75 B2
West Dulwich Sta
SE21 . . . . .75 C3
West Eaton Pl
SW1 . . . .**145** B4
West Eaton Pl Mews
SW1 . . . .**145** B4
West Ella Rd NW10 . .8 A1
West End Ct NW6 . .11 A1
West End La NW6 . .11 A2
Westerdale Ct N5 . .15 A4
Westerdale Rd 2
SE10 . . . . .43 C1
Westerham NW1 . . .**82** C3
Westerham Ho
SE1 . . . .**138** A2
Western Ave W3 . . .28 C3
Western Avenue Bsns
Pk W3 . . . . .20 A1
Western Beach Apts
E16 . . . . .35 C1
Western Ct 4
7 Dagenham W3 . .28 C3
5 Kilburn W9 . . . . .23 B3
Western Eye Hospl
NW1 . . . .**102** C4
Western Gateway
E16 . . . . .35 C2
Western Ho 3
W9 . . . . .23 B1
Western La SW12. . .72 C4
Western Mews
W9 . . . . .23 B1
Western Pl 10
SE16 . . . . .40 B4

Western Rd
Becontree NW10 . . . .20 B1
Brixton SW9 . . . . . . .62 C4
Western Terr 3
W6 . . . . .38 C1
Western Wharf 2
SE15 . . . . .49 C4
Westferry Cir E14 . .33 C1
Westferry Rd E14 . .42 B3
Westferry Sta E14 . .33 C2
Westfield NW3 . . . .10 C4
Westfield Cl
SW10 . . . .**156** C1
Westfield Ct 1
W10 . . . . .22 C2
Westfield Ho 6
SE16 . . . . .40 C2
Westfields SW13 . . .56 B4
Westfields Ave
SW13 . . . . .56 A4
Westfields Rd W3 . .28 A4
Westfield Way E1 . .26 A1
West Garden Pl
W2 . . . .**102** B1
Westgate Bsns Ctr
2 Kensal Town
W10 . . . . .23 A1
North Kensington
W10 . . . . .22 C1
Westgate Ct 3
SW9 . . . . .62 C4
Westgate St E8 . . . .25 A4
Westgate Terr
SW10 . . . .**156** B4
West Gdns E1 . . . . .32 A2
West Gr SE10 . . . . .52 C2
Westgrove La
SE10 . . . . .52 B2
West Halkin St
SW1 . . . .**131** B2
West Hall Rd TW9 . .45 A2
WEST HAMPSTEAD
. . . . .10 C4
West Hampstead
Mews NW6 . . . . . .11 A2
West Hampstead Sta
NW6 . . . . .10 C2
West Hampstead
Thameslink Sta
NW6 . . . . .10 C2
West Harding St
EC4 . . . .**107** C2
Westhay Gdns
SW14 . . . . .55 A2
West Heath Ave
NW11 . . . . .1 C3
West Heath Cl NW3 . .1 C1
West Heath Ct
NW11 . . . . .1 C3
West Heath Dr
NW11 . . . . .1 C3
West Heath Gdns
NW3 . . . . .1 C1
West Heath Rd
NW3 . . . . .2 A1
WEST HILL 58 B1
West Hill
Highgate N6 . . . . .3 C3
Putney SW15 . . . . . .58 A1
Westhill Ct
W11 . . . . . .31 B2 **113** A4
West Hill Ct N6 . . . . .3 C1
Westhill Pk
Dartmouth Pk N6 . . . .3 C2
Highgate N6 . . . . .3 B2
West Hill Prim Sch
SW18 . . . . .58 C1

West Hill Rd SW18. .58 B1
West Ho 9 SW12. . . .73 B4
Westhope Ho
E2 . . . . .24 C2 **99** C3
Westhorpe Rd
SW15 . . . . .57 B4
West House Cl
SW19 . . . . .70 A3
West India Ave
E14 . . . . .33 C1
West India Dock Rd
E14 . . . . .33 C2
West India Ho 1
E14 . . . . .33 C2
West India Quay Sta
E14 . . . . .33 C2
WEST KENSINGTON
. . . .**140** B3
West Kensington Ct
W14 . . . .**140** C3
West Kensington
Mans W14 . . . . . .**140** C2
West Kensington Sta
W14 . . . .**140** C2
WEST KILBURN 23 A2
West La SE16. . . . . .40 A4
Westlake 3 SE16 . . .40 B2
Westland Pl N1 . . . .**97** B4
Westlands Terr 2
SW12 . . . . .61 B1
Westleigh Ave
SW15 . . . . .57 B2
West London Stad
The W12. . . . . .9 C2
Westly Ct NW2 . . . . .9 C2
Westmacott Ho
NW8 . . . .**89** C1
West Mall
W11 . . . . .31 C1 **113** C2
Westmark Point 13
SW15 . . . . .69 A3
West Mersea Cl
E16 . . . . .35 C1
West Mews SW1 . .**146** C2
Westmill Ct N4 . . . . .6 B2
WESTMINSTER . . .**133** A1
Westminster Abbey*
SW1 . . . .**134** A2
Westminster Abbey
Choir Sch SW1 . . .**133** C2
Westminster Acad
NW1 . . . .**102** A4
Westminster Acad
(Sch of English)
W1 . . . .**105** A2
Westminster Boating
Base SW1 . . . .**161** B4
Westminster Bridge
SE1, SW1 . . . .**134** B3
Westminster Bridge
Rd SE1 . . . .**134** C3
Westminster Cath
. . . .**132** C1
Westminster Cath
Choir Sch SW1 . . .**147** A4
Westminster Cath RC
Prim Sch SW1 . . . .**147** C2
Westminster City Hall
SW1 . . . .**133** A2
Westminster City Sch
SW1 . . . .**133** A2

Westminster
Kingsway Coll
Battersea SW11 . . . .**169** C4
St Pancras WC1 . . . .**94** C3
Westminster
Kingsway Coll
(Regent's Park Ctr)
NW1 . . . .**92** C2
Westminster Pier
SW1 . . . .**134** B4
Westminster Sch
SW1 . . . .**134** A2
Westminster Sta
SW1 . . . .**134** B3
Westminster Under
Sch SW1 . . . .**147** B3
Westmore Ct
SW15 . . . . .58 A2
Westmoreland Ho
NW10 . . . . .21 C2
Westmoreland Pl
SW1 . . . .**146** B1
Westmoreland Rd
Barnes SW13 . . . . . .46 C2
Camberwell SE17 . . .48 C4
Westmoreland St
W1 . . . .**103** C3
Westmoreland Terr
SW1 . . . .**146** B1
WEST NORWOOD
. . . . .75 B1
West Norwood Sta
SE27 . . . . .75 A1
Westonbirt Ct 6
SE15 . . . . .49 B4
Weston Ct N4 . . . . . .6 B1
Weston Ed Ctr The
SE5 . . . . .48 B1
West One Ho W1 . .**104** C3
West One Sh Ctr
W1 . . . .**104** A1
Weston Ho
4 Brondesbury
NW6 . . . . .10 A1
8 South Hackney
E9 . . . . .17 B1
Weston Rise N1,
WC1 . . . .**95** A4
Weston St SE1 . . . .**137** C4
Weston Wlk 3 E8,
E9 . . . . .17 A1
Westover Hill NW3 . .1 C2
Westover Rd
SW18 . . . . .59 B1
West Park Ave
TW9 . . . . .45 A2
West Park Rd
TW9 . . . . .44 C2
West Parkside
Greenwich SE10 . . . .43 B3
Greenwich SE10 . . . .43 C2
West Plaza E14 . . . .34 A1
Westpoint SW15 . . .57 C1
West Point 3 SE1 . .**153** B2
Westpoint Trad Est
W3 . . . . .28 A4
Westport St E1 . . . .32 C3
West Poultry Ave
EC1 . . . .**108** A3
West Quarters
W12 . . . . .29 C3
West Rd
Chelsea SW3 . . . . .**159** A4
Clapham Pk SW4 . . . .61 C2
Westrow SW15 . . . .57 B1

Wes–Wey **283**

West Row W10 . . . . .23 A1
West Sheen Vale
TW9 . . . . .54 B3
Westside 11 W6 . . .38 C2
Westside Ct 7
W9 . . . . .23 C1
West Silvertown Sta
E16 . . . . .35 C1
West Smithfield
EC1 . . . .**108** B3
West Sq SE11 . . . . .**136** A1
West St
30 Bethnal Green
E2 . . . . .25 A3
Soho WC2 . . . .**105** C1
West Temple Sheen
SW14 . . . . .55 A3
West Tenter St
E1 . . . .**111** A1
Westvale Mews
W3 . . . . .38 A4
Westview Cl
North Kensington
W10 . . . . .30 B3
Willesden NW10 . . . . .8 B3
Westville Rd W12 . .38 C4
West Warwick Pl
SW1 . . . .**146** C3
Westway W10,
W12 . . . . .29 C2
Westway (Elevated
Rd) W10 . . . . .31 B4
Westway Lo 55
W2 . . . . .31 C4
Westwell 4 NW5 . . .12 C2
Westwick Gdns
W14 . . . . .39 C4
Westwood Bsns Ctr
NW10 . . . . .21 A1
Westwood Gdns
SW13 . . . . .56 B4
Westwood Ho
6 Shepherd's Bush
W12 . . . . .30 B1
5 Stoke Newington
N4 . . . . .6 C4
Westwood Park Trad
Est W3 . . . . .20 A1
Westwood Rd
SW13 . . . . .56 B4
Wetherby Gdns
SW5 . . . .**142** C3
Wetherby Mans
SW5 . . . .**142** A3
Wetherby Mews
SW5 . . . .**142** A2
Wetherby Pl SW7 . .**143** A3
Wetherell Rd E9 . . .25 C4
Wevco Wharf
SE15 . . . . .50 A4
Wexford Ho 11 E1 . .32 A4
Wexford Rd SW12 . .72 B4
Weybourne St
SW18 . . . . .71 B2
Weybridge Ct 19
SE16 . . . . .40 A1
Weybridge Ho N4 . . .6 B4
Weybridge Point
SW11 . . . .**169** A2
Weydown Cl
SW19 . . . . .70 A3
Weyhill Ho 26 SE5 . .48 B1
Weyhill Rd E1 . . . .**111** C2
Wey Ho NW8 . . . . . .**89** C1

Weymouth Ct
5 Haggerston E2 . . . . 24 B3
10 Streatham SW2 . . 74 B4
Weymouth Ho
Fitzrovia W1 . . . . . **104** B4
South Lambeth
SW8 . . . . **162** C1
Weymouth Mews
W1 . . . . **104** A4
Weymouth St W1 . . **104** A4
Weymouth Terr
E2 . . . . 24 B3
Whadcoat St N4 . . . . 5 C2
Whaddon Ho
11 Camberwell
SE5 . . . . 64 A4
SW1 . . . . **131** A3
Wharfdale Ho N1 . . **84** B2
Wharfdale Ct **5**
E5 . . . . 17 C4
Wharfdale Rd
SW10 . . . . **142** A1
Wharf La **12** E14 . . . 33 B3
Wharf Pl E2 . . . . 25 A4
Wharf Rd
King's Cross NW1 . . **83** C3
Shoreditch N1 . . . . **86** C1
Wharf Road NW1 . . **84** A2
Wharfside Rd E16 . . 35 A4
Wharf St E16 . . . . . . 35 A4
Wharf View Ct **13**
E14 . . . . 34 B3
Wharncliffe Ho **8**
SW15 . . . . 57 B2
Wharton St N1 CW10 . . 3 A2
Wharton Ho SE1 . . **138** C2
Wharton St WC1 . . . **95** A3
Whateley Rd SE22 . . 64 B2
Whatman Ho **10**
E14 . . . . 33 B3
Wheatland Ho **7**
SE22 . . . . 64 A4
Wheatlands Rd
SW17 . . . . 72 C1
Wheatley Ho
Gospel Oak NW5 . . . 13 A4
3 Putney SW15 . . . . 68 C4
Wheatley St W1 . . . **103** C3
Wheat Sheaf Cl
E14 . . . . 42 A2
Wheatsheaf La
Fulham SW6 . . . . . . 47 B3
SW8 . . . . **162** B2
Wheatsheaf Terr
SW6 . . . . **155** A1
Wheatstone Ho **7**
W10 . . . . 31 A4
Wheatstone Rd
W10 . . . . 31 A4
Wheeler Ct **5**
SW11 . . . . 59 C4
Wheeler Gdns N1 . . **84** B4
Wheeler La E1 . . . . **110** C4
Wheelhouse The **4**
E14 . . . . 42 A1
Wheelwright St
N7 . . . . 14 B1
Wheldon Ct SE1 . . **138** C4
Wheler Ho
E1 . . . . 24 B1 **98** C1
Wheler St
E1 . . . . **98** C1
Whellock Rd W4 . . . 38 A3
Whetstone Park
WC2 . . . . **106** C2

Whewell Rd N19 . . . . 5 A2
Whichcote St
SE1 . . . . **121** B1
Whidborne Bldgs
WC1 . . . . **94** A3
Whidborne Cl SE8 . . 51 C1
Whidborne St
WC1 . . . . **94** B3
Whippingham Ho **22**
E3 . . . . 26 B2
Whiskin St EC1 . . . . **96** A3
Whistler Mews **23**
SE15 . . . . 49 B3
Whistlers Ave
SW11 . . . . **157** C1
Whistler St N5 . . . . . 15 A3
Whistler Twr
SW10 . . . . **156** C1
Whistler Wlk
SW10 . . . . **157** A2
Whiston Ho **18** N1 . . 15 A1
Whiston Rd E2 . . . . . 24 C4
Whitbread Ctr EC1 . . **97** B1
Whitbread Rd SE4 . . 66 B3
Whitby Ave NW10 . . 20 A2
Whitby Ct **6** N7 . . . . 14 A4
Whitby Ho NW8 . . . **78** C3
Whitby St
E1 . . . . 24 B1 **98** C2
Whitcher Cl SE14 . . . 51 A4
Whitcher Pl NW1 . . . 13 B2
Whitchurch Ho **16**
W10 . . . . 30 C3
Whitchurch Rd
W11 . . . . 30 C2
Whitcomb Ct W1 . . **119** C3
Whitcomb St
WC2 . . . . **119** C3
Whitcome Mews
TW9 . . . . 45 A2
Whiteacre Mews
SE11 . . . . **149** C1
Whitebeam Ave
E14 . . . . 42 C1
Whitear Wlk E15 . . . 19 C2
Whitebeam Cl
SW9 . . . . **163** A1
Whitebeam Ho **3**
NW3 . . . . 12 B2
White Bear Pl **1**
NW3 . . . . 11 C4
White Bear Yd
EC1 . . . . **95** B1
WHITECHAPEL . . . **110** C1
Whitechapel High St
E1 . . . . **111** A2
Whitechapel Mkt
E1 . . . . **111** C3
Whitechapel Rd
E1 . . . . **111** C2
Whitechapel Sta
E1 . . . . **111** A4
Whitechurch La
E1 . . . . **111** B2
Whitechurch Pas
E1 . . . . **111** B2
White City W10 . . . . 30 B3
White City Cl W12 . . 30 B2
White City Est
W12 . . . . 30 A2
White City Rd
W12 . . . . 30 B2
White City Sta
W12 . . . . 30 B2
Whitecliff Ho
SW18 . . . . 59 A1

White Conduit St
N1 . . . . **85** C2
Whitecross Pl
EC2 . . . . **109** C4
Whitecross St EC1 . . **97** A1
White Cube The, Art
Gallery **9**
N1 . . . . . . 24 A2 **98** A3
Whitefield Cl
SW15 . . . . 58 A1
Whitefriars St
EC4 . . . . **107** C1
Whitehall SW1 . . . . **120** B1
Whitehall Ct SW1 . **120** B1
Whitehall Gdns
Chiswick W4 . . . . . 45 A4
SW1 . . . . **120** A1
Whitehall Mans **8**
N19 . . . . 4 B3
Whitehall Park Rd
W4 . . . . 45 A4
Whitehall Pk N19 . . . 4 B3
Whitehall Pl WC2,
SW1 . . . . **120** A1
White Hart La
Mortlake SW13 . . . . 56 A4
Willesden NW10 . . . 8 B2
White Hart St
Holborn EC4 . . . . . **108** B2
Kennington SE11 . . **149** C2
White Hart Yd
SE1 . . . . **123** B1
Whitehaven St
NW8 . . . . **90** A1
Whitehead Cl
SW18 . . . . 71 B4
Whitehead Ho **8**
SW15 . . . . 57 C2
Whitehead's Gr
SW3 . . . . **144** B3
White Ho
Battersea SW11 . . **167** C2
2 Streatham SW4 . . 73 C4
White Horse La
E1 . . . . 32 B1
Whitehorse Mews
SE1 . . . . **136** A2
Whitehorse Rd E1 . . 33 A4
White Horse Rd
E1 . . . . 33 A3
White Horse St
W1 . . . . **118** B1
White Horse Yd
EC2 . . . . **109** B2
White Ho The
NW1 . . . . **92** B2
White Kennett St
E1 . . . . **110** B2
Whitelands Cres
SW18 . . . . 70 A4
Whitelands Ho
SW3 . . . . **145** A2
Whiteley Ho **5**
SW4 . . . . 73 C4
Whiteleys Ctr W2 . **100** B1
White Lion Ct
EC3 . . . . **110** A1
White Lion Hill
EC4 . . . . **122** B4
White Lion St N1 . . . **85** C1
White Lion Yd W1 . **118** A4
Whitelock Ho **21**
E9 . . . . 17 C2
White Lyon Ct
EC2 . . . . **108** C4

Whiteness Ho
SW9 . . . . **173** B4
White Post La E9 . . . 18 C2
White Post St SE14,
SE15 . . . . 50 B3
White's Grounds
SE1 . . . . **138** B4
White's Grounds Est
SE1 . . . . **138** B4
White's Row E1 . . . **110** C3
White's Sq SW4 . . . . 61 C3
Whitestone La NW3 . 2 B1
Whitestone Wlk
NW3 . . . . 2 B1
Whitethorn St E3 . . . 33 C4
Whitfield Ct SW4 . . **172** A3
Whitfield Gdns
W1 . . . . **105** A4
Whitfield Ho NW8 . . **90** A1
Whitfield Pl W1 . . . . **93** A1
Whitfield St W1 . . . **105** A4
Whitgift Ho
Battersea SW11 . . **168** A4
Lambeth SE11 . . . **148** C4
Whitgift St SE11 . . **148** C4
Whittington Ave
EC3 . . . . **110** A1
Whitley Ho SW1 . . **161** A4
Whitlock Dr SW19 . . 70 A3
Whitman Ho **20**
E2 . . . . 25 B2
Whitman Rd E3 . . . . 26 A1
Whitmore Gdns
NW10 . . . . 22 B3
Whitmore Ho **20**
E1 . . . . 24 A4
Whitmore Prim Sch
N1 . . . . **87** C3
Whitmore Rd N1 . . . 24 A4
Whitnell Ct **7**
SW15 . . . . 57 C2
Whitnell Way
SW15 . . . . 57 C2
Whitney Ho **6**
SE22 . . . . 64 A4
Whitstable Ho **11**
W10 . . . . 30 C3
Whitsters Ho SE1 . **138** C4
Whittaker Ct
SW4 . . . . **172** B3
Whittaker St SW1 . **145** B3
Whittaker Way
SE1 . . . . **153** C4
Whittingham Ct
W4 . . . . 46 A3
Whittingstall Mans
SW6 . . . . **165** A3
Whittingstall Rd
SW6 . . . . **165** A3
Whittington Hospl
The N19 . . . . 4 B2
Whittlebury Ho N4 . . 6 B4
Whitton NW3 . . . . . 12 B1
Whitton Wlk **3** E3 . . 26 C2
Whitworth Ho
SE1 . . . . **137** A1
Whitworth St
SE10 . . . . 43 A1
Whorlton Rd SE15 . . 65 A4
Whytlaw Ho **10** E3 . . 33 B4
Wicker St **32** E1 . . . 32 A3
Wickfield Ho
SE16 . . . . **139** C3
Wickford Ho **5**
E1 . . . . 25 B1
Wickford St E1 . . . . 25 B1

Wickham Cl E1, ... 32 B4
Wickham Gdns
SE4 . . . . 66 B4
Wickham Ho
SW15 . . . . 57 C1
Wickham Mews
SE4 . . . . 51 B1
Wickham Rd SE4 . . . 66 B4
Wickham St SE11 . **148** C2
Wick La
Hackney E3 . . . . . . 18 B1
Stratford Marsh E3 . 26 C4
Wicklow Ho N16 . . . . 7 B3
Wicklow St WC1 . . . **94** C4
Wick Rd
Hackney E9 . . . . . . 17 C2
Hackney E9 . . . . . . 18 A2
Wickstead Ho
TW8 . . . . 36 B1
Wicksteed Ho
SE1 . . . . **137** A1
Wickway Ct **7**
SE15 . . . . 49 B4
Wickwood St SE5 . . 48 A1
Widdenham Rd
N7 . . . . 14 B4
Widecombe Ho **32**
SE5 . . . . 48 B1
Widegate St E1 . . . **110** B3
Widford **8** NW1 . . . 13 A2
Widford Ho N1 . . . **86** A1
Widley Rd W9 . . . . . 23 C1
Widnes Ho **6** N7 . . 14 C3
Wigmore Hall*
W1 . . . . **104** A2
Wigmore Pl W1 . . . **104** A2
Wigmore St W1 . . . **103** C2
Wigram Ct SW11 . . **168** A4
Wigram Ho **7**
E14 . . . . 34 A2
Wigton Pl SE11 . . . **149** C1
Wilberforce Ho **3**
SW11 . . . . 59 C4
Wilberforce Mews **3**
SW4 . . . . 61 C3
Wilberforce Prim Sch
W10 . . . . 23 A2
Wilberforce Rd
Finsbury Pk N4 . . . . 6 A2
Highbury N4, N5 . . . 6 B1
Wilbraham Ho
SW8 . . . . **162** A1
Wilbraham Pl
SW1 . . . . **145** B4
Wilby Mews
W11 . . . . 31 B1 **113** A2
Wilcox Cl SW8 . . . **162** B2
Wilcox Ho **3** E3 . . . 33 B4
Wilcox Pl SW1 . . . **133** A1
Wilcox Rd SW8 . . . **162** A2
Wildcroft Manor
SW15 . . . . 69 B4
Wildcroft Rd
SW15 . . . . 69 B4
Wild Ct WC2 . . . . . **106** C2
Wilde Cl E8 . . . . 24 C4
Wilde Pl SW18 . . . . 71 C4
Wilderness Mews
SW4 . . . . 61 A3
Wilderton Rd N16 . . . 7 A4
Wild Goose Dr
SE14 . . . . 50 B2
Wilding Ho **17** E9 . . 17 C2
Wild's Rents SE1 . . **138** A2
Wild St WC2 . . . . . **106** C1
Wildwood Gr NW3 . . 2 B3
Wildwood Rd NW11 . 2 B4

Wildwood Rise
NW11 . . . . 2 B3
Wildwood Terr
NW3 . . . . 2 B3
Wilfred Fienburgh Ho
N7 . . . . 13 C4
Wilfred St SW1 . . . . . 132 C2
Wilfrid Gdns W3 . . . . 28 B4
Wilkes Rd 3 TW8 . . . 44 A4
Wilkes St E1 . . . . . . 111 A4
Wilkie Ho SW1 . . . . . 147 C2
Wilkins Ho SW1 . . . . 160 C4
Wilkinson Ho N1 . . . . 87 C1
Wilkinson St SW8 . . 162 C1
Wilkinson Way
W4 . . . . 37 C4
Wilkin St NW5 . . . . . 13 A2
Wilks Pl N1 . . . . 24 A3
Willan Wall E16 . . . . 35 B2
Willard St SW8 . . . . . 61 A4
Willbury Ho 4 N7 . . 13 C3
Willcott Rd W3 . . . . . 28 A1
Willenfield Rd
NW10 . . . . 20 B3
WILLESDEN 8 B1
**Willesden Community
Hospl The** NW10 . . . 8 C1
WILLESDEN GREEN
. . . . 22 A4
Willesden Green Sta
NW2 . . . . 9 B2
**Willesden Junction
Sta** NW10 . . . . 21 B2
Willesden La NW2,
NW6 . . . . 9 C2
Willes Rd NW5 . . . . . 13 A2
Willett Ho SW9 . . . . . 62 A4
William Banfield Ho
SW6 . . . . 164 C2
William Blake Ho 2
SE15 . . . . 49 C1
William Bonney Est 10
SW4 . . . . 61 C3
**William Booth Meml
Training Coll** SE5 . 48 C1
William Brown Ct
SE27 . . . . 75 A2
William Caslon Ho 28
E2 . . . . 25 A3
William Channing Ho
6 E2 . . . . 25 A2
William Cl SE13 . . . . 67 B4
**William Davis Prim
Sch** E2 . . . . 24 C1 99 B2
William Dromey Ct
NW6 . . . . 10 B1
William Dunbar Ho
NW6 . . . . 23 B3
William Ellis Sch
NW5 . . . . 3 C4
William Ellis Way
SE16 . . . . 139 C1
William Evans Ho 9
SE8 . . . . 40 C2
William Gdns
SW15 . . . . 57 A2
William Guy Gdns 47
E3 . . . . 27 A2
William Harvey Ho 1
SW19 . . . . 70 A3
**William Hogarth Prim
Sch The** W4 . . . . . 38 A1
William Hunt Mans
SW13 . . . . 47 B4
William IV St
WC2 . . . . 120 A3

William Margrie Cl 1
SE15 . . . . 49 C1
William Mews
SW1 . . . . 131 A3
William Morris Acad
W6 . . . . 39 C1
William Morris Ho
W6 . . . . 47 C4
William Morris Way
SW6 . . . . 166 C1
**William Patten Prim
Sch** N16 . . . . 7 B2
William Pl 87 E3 . . 26 B3
William Rathbone Ho
3 E2 . . . . 25 A2
William Rd NW1 . . . . 92 C3
**William Rushbrooke
Ho** SE16 . . . . 153 B4
William Saville Ho 2
NW6 . . . . 23 B3
William's Bldgs 1
E2 . . . . 25 B1
Williams Cl SW6 . . 154 B2
Williams Coll EC1 . 107 C3
Williams Ho
10 Bow E3 . . . . 26 C2
3 Hackney E9 . . . . 25 A4
4 Streatham SW2 . 74 C3
Williams La SW14 . 45 B1
Williamson Cl
SE10 . . . . 43 B1
Williamson Ct
SE17 . . . . 150 C1
Williamson St N7 . 14 A4
William Sq 15
SE16 . . . . 33 A2
William St SW1 . . . 131 A3
**William Tyndale Prim
Sch** N1 . . . . 15 A1
William Winter St 29
SW2 . . . . 74 C4
Willingham Cl 4
NW5 . . . . 13 B3
Willingham Terr
NW5 . . . . 13 B3
Willington Rd
SW9 . . . . 62 A4
Willis Ho 8 E14 . . . 34 A2
Willis St E14 . . . . . . 34 A3
Willoughby Ho
EC2 . . . . 109 B3
34 Wapping E1 . . . 32 A1
Willoughby Rd
NW3 . . . . 11 C4
Willoughby St
WC1 . . . . 106 A3
Willoughbys The
SW14 . . . . 56 A3
Willow Ave SW13 . 46 B1
Willowbank SW6 . . 58 A4
Willowbank Rd
SE15 . . . . 49 B4
Willow Bridge Rd
N1 . . . . 15 B2
Willow Cotts TW9 . 44 C4
Willow Ct
Brixton SW9 . . . . . . 173 B3
Chiswick W4 . . . . . . 46 A3
EC2 . . . . 24 A1 98 A2
Islington N7 . . . . . . 14 B3
40 Paddington W2 . 31 C4
3 Streatham SW16 74 B1
Willowdene
Highgate N6 . . . . . . 3 B4
3 Peckham SE15 . 50 A2
5 SE15 . . . . 50 A3

Willow Farm La
SW15 . . . . 57 A4
Willow Hall NW3 . . 11 C4
Willow Ho
1 Maitland Pk
NW3 . . . . 12 B2
North Kensington
W10 . . . . 22 C1
Willow Lo
Fulham SW6 . . . . . . 47 C2
Putney SW15 . . . . . 57 A4
Willow Lodge 10
SW8 . . . . 61 A4
Willowmere SE13 . 67 A2
Willow Pl SW1 . . . 147 A4
Willow Rd
Ealing W5 . . . . 36 A4
Hampstead NW3 . . 12 A4
Willow St
EC2 . . . . 24 A1 98 A2
Willows Terr
NW10 . . . . 21 B3
Willow Tree Cl
14 Old Ford E3 . . . 26 B4
Wandsworth SW18 71 A3
Willow Vale W12 . . 29 C1
Willow Way 9
W11 . . . . 30 C2
Willow Wlk SE1 . . 152 C4
Willsbridge Ct 1
SE15 . . . . 49 B4
Wilman Gr E8 . . . . 16 C1
Wilmcote Ho W2 . . 100 A4
Wilmer Gdns 22
N1 . . . . 24 A4
Wilmer Ho 6 E3 . . 26 A3
Wilmer Lea Cl
E15 . . . . 19 C1
Wilmer Pl N16 . . . . 7 B2
Wilmers Ct 5
NW10 . . . . 20 C4
Wilmington Ave
W4 . . . . 45 C3
Wilmington Sq
WC1 . . . . 95 B3
Wilmington St
WC1 . . . . 95 B3
Wilmot Cl SE15 . . . 49 C3
Wilmot Pl NW1 . . . 13 B1
Wilmot St E2 . . . . . 25 A1
Wilna Rd SW18 . . . 71 B4
Wilsham St
W11 . . . . 31 A1 112 A2
Wilshaw Ho 10
SE8 . . . . 51 C3
Wilshaw St SE14 . 51 C2
Wilson Gr SE16 . . . 40 A4
Wilson Ho
Clapham SW8 . . . . . 171 B1
South Hampstead
NW6 . . . . 11 B1
Wilson's Pl E14 . . . 33 B3
Wilson's Rd W6 . . . 39 C1
Wilson St EC2 . . . . 109 C4
Wiltern Ct NW2 . . . 10 A2
Wilton Ave W4 . . . . 38 A1
Wilton Cres SW1 . . 131 B3
Wilton Ct
1 Richmond
TW10 . . . . 54 A2
1 Stepney E1 . . . . 32 A3
Wilton Est E8 . . . . 16 C2
Wilton Ho 3 SE22 . 64 A4
Wilton Mews
SW1 . . . . 131 C2
Wilton Pl SW1 . . . . 131 B3

Wilton Rd SW1 . . . 146 C4
Wilton Row SW1 . . 131 B3
Wilton Sq N1 . . . . . 87 B4
Wilton St SW1 . . . . 132 A2
Wilton Terr SW1 . . 131 B2
Wilton Villas N1 . . . 87 B3
Wilton Way E8 . . . . 16 C2
Wiltshire Cl SW3 . . 144 C3
Wiltshire Ct 2 N4 . 5 B3
Wiltshire Rd SW9 . 62 C4
Wiltshire Row N1 . 87 C3
Wimbart Rd SW2 . . 74 B4
**Wimbledon Lawn
Tennis Mus** *
SW19 . . . . 70 A1
Wimbledon Park Ct
SW19 . . . . 70 B3
**Wimbledon Park
Montessori Sch**
SW18 . . . . 70 C4
**Wimbledon Park Prim
Sch** SW19 . . . . 71 A2
Wimbledon Park Rd
SW18, SW19 . . . . . . 70 B3
Wimbledon Park Side
SW19 . . . . 69 C3
Wimbledon Park Sta
SW19 . . . . 70 C1
**Wimbledon Stadium
Bsns Ctr** SW17 . . 71 A1
**Wimbledon Windmill
Mus** * SW19 . . . . . 69 C1
Wimbolt St
E2 . . . . 24 C2 99 B4
Wimborne Ho
Canning Town E16 . 35 B2
Marylebone NW1 . . 90 B1
South Lambeth
SW8 . . . . 163 A1
Upper Tooting
SW12 . . . . 73 B1
Wimbourne Ct N1 . 87 B2
Wimbourne St N1 . 87 B2
Wimpole Mews
W1 . . . . 104 A3
Wimpole St W1 . . . 104 A2
Winans Wlk SW9 . 173 B1
Winant Ho 19 E14 . 34 A2
Wincanton Rd
SW18 . . . . 70 B4
Winchelsea Cl
SW15 . . . . 57 C2
Winchelsea Ho 16
SE16 . . . . 40 B4
Winchelsea Rd
NW10 . . . . 20 C4
Winchendon Rd
SW6 . . . . 165 A4
Winchester Ave
NW6 . . . . 10 A1
Winchester Cl
SE17 . . . . 150 B3
Winchester Ct
Richmond TW9 . . . . 54 B4
8 W8 . . . . 128 A4
Winchester Ho
Bayswater W2 . . . . 100 C1
Chelsea SW3 . . . . . 157 C3
24 Tower Hamlets
E3 . . . . 26 B2
Winchester Pal *
SE1 . . . . 123 B2
Winchester Pl
8 Dalston E8 . . . . 16 B3
Highgate N6 . . . . . . 4 A3
Winchester Rd
Highgate N6 . . . . . . 4 A3

Winchester Rd
continued
South Hampstead
NW3 . . . . 11 C1
Winchester Sq
SE1 . . . . 123 B2
Winchester St
Acton W3 . . . . 37 B4
SW1 . . . . 146 B2
Winchester Wlk
SE1 . . . . 123 B2
Winchfield Ho
SW15 . . . . 56 B1
Winch Ho
Isle of Dogs E14 . . 42 A3
SW10 . . . . 157 A2
Winchilsea Ho
NW8 . . . . 89 C3
Wincott St SE11 . . 149 C3
Windermere NW1 . 92 B4
12 Putney SW15 . 57 C1
Windermere Ave
NW6 . . . . 23 A4
Windermere Ct
SW13 . . . . 46 B4
Windermere Ho
E3 . . . . 26 B1
Windermere Point 3
SE15 . . . . 50 B3
Windermere Rd
N19 . . . . 4 B2
Winders Rd SW11 . 168 A2
Windham Rd TW9 . 54 B4
Windlass Pl SE8 . . 41 A2
Windlesham Gr
SW19 . . . . 69 C3
Windmill NW6 . . . . 106 C3
Windmill Alley 7
W4 . . . . 38 A2
Windmill Cl
Bermondsey SE1 . . 153 C4
4 Lewisham SE13 . 52 B1
Windmill Ct NW2 . . 10 A2
Windmill Dr
Clapham SW4 . . . . . 61 A2
Cricklewood NW2 . . 1 A1
Windmill Gdns
SW2 . . . . 62 B1
Windmill Hill
Hampstead NW3 . . 2 B1
1 Hampstead NW3 . 11 B4
Windmill Ho
E14 . . . . 41 C2
SW1 . . . . 121 C1
Windmill La E15 . . 19 C2
Windmill Pas 10
W4 . . . . 38 A2
Windmill Rd
Chiswick W4 . . . . . . 38 A2
Roehampton SW19 . 69 A1
Wandsworth SW18 . 59 C1
Windmill Row
SE11 . . . . 149 B1
Windmill St W1 . . . 105 B3
Windmill Wlk
SE1 . . . . 135 C4
Windrose Cl SE16 . 40 C4
Windrush Cl
Battersea SW11 . . . 59 C3
Chiswick W4 . . . . . . 45 B3
Windrush Ho
NW8 . . . . 101 C4
Windrush Rd
NW10 . . . . 20 C4

Windsock Cl 1
SE16 . . . . 41 B2

Windsor Ct
Battersea SW11 . . 167 C2
Bayswater W2 . . . . 114 A4
Chelsea SW3 . . . . . . 144 B2
2 Clapham SW4 . . . . 61 B3
Fulham SW6 . . . . . . 58 A4
20 Rotherhithe
SE16 . . . . 32 C1
4 Wandsworth
SW18 . . . . 58 C2
West Hampstead
NW3 . . . . 10 C4

Windsor Gdns W9 . .23 C1

Windsor Ho
4 Acton Green
W4 . . . . 37 B1
Brondesbury NW2 . 10 A2
4 Globe Town E2 . . 25 C2
Regent's Pk NW1 . . 92 B4
Shoreditch N1 . . . . 87 A2
Stoke Newington N4 . .6 B4

Windsor Pl SW1 . . 147 A4

Windsor Rd
Richmond TW9 . . . . 44 B1
Upper Holloway N7 . . .5 A1
Willesden NW2 . . . . . 9 A2

Windsor St N1 . . . . 86 B4
Windsor Terr N1 . . 97 A4

Windsor Way
W14 . . . . 140 A4
Windsor Wharf E9 . 18 B3
Windsor Wlk SE5 . . 48 C1

Windspoint Dr
SE15 . . . . 50 A4
Windus Rd N16 . . . . 7 B3
Windus Wlk N16 . . . 7 B3
Wine Cl E1 . . . . 32 B2

Wine Office Ct
EC4 . . . . 107 C2

Winfield Ho
SW11 . . . . 167 C2

Winford Ct 16
SE15 . . . . 49 C2
Winford Ho E3 . . . . 18 B1
Winforton St SE10 . 52 B2
Winfrith Rd SW18 . 71 B3

Wingate Ho
28 Bromley E3 . . . . . 27 A2
8 Stoke Newington
N16 . . . . 15 C4
Wingate Rd W6 . . . 39 A3
Wingfield Ct 5
E14 . . . . 34 C2

Wingfield Ho
Paddington NW6 . . 78 A2
Spitalfields
E2 . . . . 24 B2 98 C3

Wingfield Mews
SE15 . . . . 64 C4
Wingfield St SE15 . 64 C4
Wingford Rd SW2 . 62 A1
Wingham **3** NW5 . . 12 C2

Wingmore Rd
SE24 . . . . 63 B4
Wingrad Ho **18** E1 . . 32 B4
Wingrave SE17 . . . 151 B3
Wingrave Rd W6 . . 47 B4
Wingreen NW8 . . . . 78 B4
Winicotte Ho W2 . 101 C4
Winifrede Paul Ho **7**
NW5 . . . . 13 A4
Winkley St **6** E2 . . 25 A3

Winkworth Cotts 14
E1 . . . . 25 B1
Winnett St W1 . . . . 119 B4

Winnington Ho
16 Kensal Town
W10 . . . . 23 A1
8 SE5 . . . . 48 B3
Winscombe St N19 . .4 A2

Winsham Gr
SW11 . . . . 60 C2
Winsham Ho NW1 . 93 C4
Winslade Rd SW2 . 62 A2

Winsland Mews
W2 . . . . 101 B2
Winsland St W2 . . 101 B2
Winsley St W1 . . . . 105 A2
Winslow SE17 . . . . 152 A1
Winslow Rd W6 . . . 47 B4

Winstanley Rd
SW11 . . . . 59 C4
Winston Ho N1 . . . . 93 C2
Winston Rd N16 . . . 15 C4
Winston Wlk **2**
W4 . . . . 37 C2

Winterbourne Ho
W11 . . . . . . 31 A2 112 A3
Winter Box Wlk
TW10 . . . . 54 B2

Winterbrook Rd
SE24 . . . . 63 B1
Winterfold Cl
SW19 . . . . 70 A2

Winterleys 7
NW6 . . . . 23 B3
Winter Lo SE16 . . . 153 C1
Winterslow Ho **20**
SE5 . . . . 48 B1
Winterton Ho **18**
E1 . . . . 32 B3

Winterton Pl
SW10 . . . . 157 A4

Winterwell Rd
SW2 . . . . 62 A2
Winthorpe Rd
SW15 . . . . 58 A3

Winthrop Ho 10
W12 . . . . 30 A2
Winthrop St E1 . . . . 32 A4
Winton Prim Sch
N1 . . . . 84 C1

Wirrall Ho 18
SE26 . . . . 76 C1
Wisbech **5** N4 . . . . . 5 B3
Wisden Ho SW8 . . 163 A3
Wise Rd E15 . . . . . . 27 C4
Wiseton Rd SW17 . 72 B3
Wisley Ho SW1 . . . 147 B2
Wisley Rd SW11 . . . 60 C2
Wisteria Ho SE4 . . 66 A4
Wisteria Rd SE13 . . 67 C3
Wistow Ho **14** E2 . . 24 C4
Witanhurst La N6 . . .3 C3
Witan St E2 . . . . 25 A2
Witchwood Ho **10**
SW9 . . . . 62 C4
Witcombe Point **14**
SE15 . . . . 49 C2
Witham Ct SW17 . . 72 B1
Witham Ho **54** SE5 . 48 B1
Witherington Rd
N5 . . . . 14 C3
Withers Pl EC1 . . . . 97 A2
Withycombe Rd
SW19 . . . . 69 C4
Withy Ho **4** E1 . . . . 25 C1
Witley Ho **2** SW2 . 74 B4

Witley Point 8
SW15 . . . . 69 A3
Witley Rd N19 . . . . . 4 B2
Wittering Ho
SW11 . . . . 169 A2
Wivenhoe Cl SE15 . 65 A4
Wix Prim Sch
SW4 . . . . 61 A3
Wix's La SW4 . . . . . 61 A3

Woburn Ct
22 Bermondsey
SE16 . . . . 40 A1
Richmond TW9 . . . . 54 B4
Woburn Pl WC1 . . . 94 A1
Woburn Sq WC1 . . . 93 C1
Woburn Wlk WC1 . . 93 C3
Wodeham Gdns **1**
E1 . . . . 32 A4
Wodehouse Ave
SE5 . . . . 49 B2
Wodehouse Ho **10**
W3 . . . . 37 B3
Woking Cl SW15 . . . 56 B3
Wolcot Ho NW1 . . . 83 A1
Wolfe Cres **34**
SE16 . . . . 40 C4
Wolfe Ho **16** W12 . . 30 A2
Wolfson Ct
Golders Green
NW11 . . . . 1 A4
SE1 . . . . 139 A4
Wolftencroft Cl
SW11 . . . . 59 C4
Wollaston Cl SE1 . 150 C4
Wollotan Ho N1 . . . 85 C2
Wolseley Ave SW18,
SW19 . . . . 70 C2
Wolseley Gdns
W4 . . . . 45 A4
Wolseley Rd W4 . . . 37 B2
Wolseley St SE1 . . 139 A3
Wolsey Cl NW5 . . . . 11 B1
Wolsey Ho **3**
NW5 . . . . 13 C2

Wolsey Mews
NW5 . . . . 13 B2
Wolsey Rd N1 . . . . . 15 C3
Wolsey St E1 . . . . . . 32 B4
Woverley Se10 . . . . 52 A2
Wolverton SE17 . . 152 A2
Wolverton Gdns
W6 . . . . 39 C2
Wontner Cl **6** N1 . . 15 B1
Wontner Rd SW12,
SW17 . . . . 72 B2
Woodall Ct **18** E14 . 34 A2
Woodberry Down
Com Prim Sch N4 . . 6 B4
Woodberry Gr N4 . . 6 B4
Woodbine Terr E9 . 17 B2
Woodborough Rd
SW15 . . . . 57 A3
Woodbourne Ave
SW16 . . . . 73 C1
Woodbourne Cl
SW16 . . . . 74 A1
Woodbridge Cl **10**
N7 . . . . 5 B2
Woodbridge Ho
N16 . . . . 6 C1
Woodbridge St
EC1 . . . . 96 A2
Woodchester Sq
W2 . . . . 100 A4

Woodchurch Ho
SW9 . . . . 173 B4
Woodchurch Rd
NW6 . . . . 11 A1
Wood Cl E2 . . 24 C1 99 B2
Woodcock Ho **4**
E14 . . . . 33 C4
Woodcote Ho **4**
SE8 . . . . 51 B4
Woodcott Ho **1**
SW15 . . . . 68 C4
Woodcroft Mews
SE8 . . . . 41 A2
Wood Dene **6**
SE15 . . . . 50 A2
Woodfall Rd N4 . . . . 5 C2
Woodfall St SW3 . 144 C1
Woodfarrs SE5 . . . . 63 C3
Wood Field NW3 . . 12 B3
Woodfield Ave
SW16 . . . . 73 C1
Woodfield Ct
SW16 . . . . 73 C1
Woodfield Gr
SW16 . . . . 73 C1
Woodfield Pl W9 . . 23 B1
Woodfield Rd W9 . . 31 B4
Woodford Ct **15**
W12 . . . . 39 C4
Woodger Rd W12 . . 39 B4
Woodhall NW1 . . . . 92 C3
Woodhall Ave
SE21 . . . . 76 B1
Woodhall Dr SE21 . 76 B1
Woodhall Ho
SW18 . . . . 59 C1
Woodheyes Rd
NW10 . . . . 8 A3
Wood Ho
Clapham SW4 . . . 171 C2
6 Paddington NW6 . 23 B3
Woodhurst Rd W3 . 28 B2
Woodison St E3 . . . 26 A1
Wood La W12 . . . . . 30 B2
Woodland Cres
18 Rotherhithe
SE16 . . . . 40 C4
SE10 . . . . 53 A4
Woodland Gr
SE10 . . . . 43 A1
Woodland Hts
SE3 . . . . 53 A4
Woodland Mews
SW16 . . . . 74 A1
Woodlands **3** SW4 . 61 A3
Woodlands Ave
W3 . . . . 28 A1
Woodlands Ct
NW10 . . . . 22 C4
Woodlands Gt
SW15 . . . . 58 B2
Woodlands Park Rd
SE10 . . . . 53 A4
Woodlands Rd
SW13 . . . . 56 B4
E8 . . . . 16 B2
Woodlands The
Highbury N5 . . . . . . 15 B4
12 Hornsey N8 . . . . . 5 A4
Woodlands Way
SW15 . . . . 58 B2
Woodland Wlk
9 Greenwich
SE10 . . . . 43 A1
Hampstead NW3 . . 12 A3

Wood Lane High Sch
W12 . . . . 30 A3
Woodlawn Cl
SW15 . . . . 58 B2
Woodlawn Rd
SW6 . . . . 47 C2
Woodlea Rd N16 . . . 7 A1
Woodleigh Gdns
SW16 . . . . 74 A1
Woodman Mews
TW9 . . . . 45 A2
Woodmans Gr
NW10 . . . . 8 B3
Woodmans Mews
W12 . . . . 30 A4
Woodmere Cl **11**
SW11 . . . . 60 C4
Woodpecker Mews
SE13 . . . . 67 C3
Woodpecker Rd **6**
SE14 . . . . 51 A4
Wood Point **8**
E16 . . . . 35 C4
Woodquest Ave
SE24 . . . . 63 B2
Woodruff Ho **12**
SW2 . . . . 62 C1
Woodrush Cl
SE14 . . . . 51 A3
Woodseer St E1 . . 111 B4
Woodsford SE17 . . 151 B1
Woodsford Sq
W14 . . . . 126 B4
Woods Ho SW8 . . . 170 C4
Wood's Mews W1 . 117 B4
Woodsome Rd
NW5 . . . . 4 A1
Wood's Pl SE1 . . . 138 B1
Woodspring Rd
SW19 . . . . 70 A2
Wood's Rd SE15 . . . 50 A2
Wood St
Chiswick W4 . . . . . . 38 A1
City of London EC2 . 109 A2
Woodstar Ho **3**
SE15 . . . . 49 C3
Woodstock Ave
NW11 . . . . 1 A4
Woodstock Ct
SE11 . . . . 149 A2
Woodstock Gr
W12 . . . . 39 C4
Woodstock Ho **2**
N5 . . . . 15 B4
Woodstock Mews
W1 . . . . 103 C3
Woodstock Rd
Bedford Pk W4 . . . . 38 A3
Finsbury Pk N4 . . . . . 5 C3
Golders Green NW11 . .1 B3
Woodstock St
W1 . . . . 104 A1
Woodstock Studios **17**
W12 . . . . 39 C4
Woodstock Terr
E14 . . . . 34 A2
Woodthorpe Rd
SW15 . . . . 57 A3
Woodview Cl N4 . . . . 6 A4
Woodville Ct **3**
SE10 . . . . 52 B2
Woodville Ho SE1 . 138 C2
Woodville Rd
Golders Green
NW11 . . . . 1 A4
Paddington NW6 . . 23 B3

Woodville Rd continued
Stoke Newington
N16 . . . . 16 A3
Woodwarde Rd
SE22 . . . . 64 A1
Woodwell St
SW18 . . . . 59 B2
Wood Wharf SE10 . . 52 B4
Woodyard Cl NW5 . . 12 C3
Woodyard La
SE21 . . . . 76 A4
Woolcombes Ct 4
SE16 . . . . 32 C1
Wooler St SE17 . . 151 C2
Woolf Ct 7 W3 . . . . 37 B3
Woolf Mews WC1 . . 94 A2
Woolley Ho SW9 . . 63 A4
Woollon Ho 1 E1 . . 32 B3
Woolmore Prim Sch
E14 . . . . 34 B2
Woolmore St E14 . . 34 B2
Woolneigh St
SW6 . . . . 166 A1
Woolpack Ho 1
E9 . . . . 17 B2
Woolridge Way
E9 . . . . 17 B1
Woolstaplers Way
SE16 . . . . 153 B4
Woolstone Ho 7
E2 . . . . 24 C4
Woolven Ho SE3 . . 53 B4
Wooster Gdns
E14 . . . . 34 C3
Wooster Pl SE1 . . 151 C4
Wootton St SE1 . . 121 C1
Worcester Ct 44
W2 . . . . 31 C4
Worcester Dr W4 . . 38 A4
Worcester Gdns
SW11 . . . . 60 B2
Worcester Ho
Bayswater W2 . . . . 100 C1
3 Islington SE11 . . 15 B1
Lambeth SE11 . . . 135 B1
9 Putney SW15 . . 69 B4
Worcester Mews 2
NW6 . . . . 11 A2
Wordsworth Ho
NW6 . . . . 23 C2
Wordsworth Pl 11
NW5 . . . . 12 B3
Wordsworth Rd
Bermondsey SE1 . . 153 A3
Stoke Newington
N16 . . . . 16 A4
Worfield St SW11 . 158 B1
Worgan St
Rotherhithe SE16 . . 40 C2
SE11 . . . . 148 C2
Working Men's Coll
The NW1 . . . . 83 A2
World's End Pas
SW10 . . . . 157 B2
World's End Pl
SW10 . . . . 157 A2
World Trade Ctr
London E14 . . . . . . 42 A4
Worlidge St W6 . . 39 B1
Worlingham Rd
SE22 . . . . 64 B3
Wormholt Park Prim
Sch W12 . . . . 29 C2

Wormholt Rd
W12 . . . . 29 C1
Wormwood St
EC2 . . . . 110 A2
Wornington Rd
W10 . . . . 31 A4
Woronzow Rd
NW8 . . . . 80 A3
Worple St SW14 . . 55 C4
Worple Way TW10 . . 54 A3
Worship St
EC2 . . . . 24 A1 98 A1
Worsley Gr E5 . . . . 16 C4
Worsopp Dr SW4 . . 61 B2
Worth Gr SE17 . . . 151 B1
Worthington Ho
EC1 . . . . 95 C4
10 Streatham SW2 . . 74 C4
Wotton Cl E14 . . . . 34 C2
Wotton Rd 18 SE8 . . 51 B4
Wouldham Rd E16 . . 35 B3
Wrayburn Ho
SE16 . . . . 139 C3
Wray Cres N4 . . . . . 5 B2
Wray Ct N4 . . . . 5 B2
Wray St WC1 . . . . . 95 A1
Wren Ave NW2 . . . . 9 B4
Wren Cl E16 . . . . . . 35 B3
Wren Ho
20 Bow E3 . . . . 26 A3
SW1 . . . . 147 B1
Wren Landing E14 . 33 C1
Wrenn Ho SW13 . . 47 B4
Wren Rd SE5 . . . . . 48 C2
Wren St WC1 . . . . 95 A2
Wrentham Ave
NW10 . . . . 22 C3
Wren View N6 . . . . 4 B3
Wrestlers Ct EC3 . 110 A2
Wrexham Rd E3 . . 26 C3
Wrigglesworth St
SE14 . . . . 50 C3
Wright Cl SE13 . . . 67 C3
Wright Ho SW15 . . 57 A2
Wright's Gn SW4 . . 61 C3
Wright's La W8 . . 128 A2
Wright's Rd E3 . . . 26 B3
Wrights Wlk
SW14 . . . . 55 C4
Wrotham Ho SE1 . 137 C2
Wrotham Rd 13
NW1 . . . . 13 B1
Wrottesley Rd
NW10 . . . . 21 C3
Wroughton Rd
SW11 . . . . 60 B1
Wroxton Rd SE15 . . 50 B1
Wr Twr Pl N1 . . . . . 86 A2
Wulfstan St W12 . . 29 B3
Wyatt Cl SE16 . . . . 41 B4
Wyatt Dr SW13 . . . 47 A3
Wyatt Ho
Blackheath Vale
SE3 . . . . 53 B1
NW8 . . . . 89 C1
Wyatt Park Mans 1
SW2 . . . . 74 A2
Wyatt Park Rd
SW2 . . . . 74 B2
Wyatt Rd N5 . . . . . . 6 B1
Wybert St NW1 . . . 92 C2
Wycherley Cl SE3 . 53 B3
Wychwood End N6 . 4 B4

Wychwood Ho N4 . . 6 B4
Wyclif Ct EC1 . . . . 96 A3
Wycliffe Rd
SW11 . . . . 169 C2
Wyclif St EC1 . . . . 96 A3
Wycombe Gdns
NW11 . . . . 1 C2
Wycombe Ho NW8 . 90 A2
Wycombe Pl
SW18 . . . . 59 B1
Wycombe Sq
W8 . . . . 31 C1 113 B1
Wyersdale Ho N4 . . 6 B4
Wye St SW11 . . . . 167 C1
Wyfold Rd SW6 . . 154 A1
Wyke Rd E3 . . . . . . 18 C1
Wyldes Cl NW11 . . . 2 B3
Wyllen Cl E1 . . . . . 25 B1
Wymering Mans 9
W9 . . . . 23 C2
Wymering Rd W9 . 23 C2
Wymondham Ct
NW8 . . . . 79 C4
Wymond St SW15 . 57 B4
Wynan Rd E14 . . . . 42 A1
Wyndham Cres N19 . 4 B1
Wyndham Deedes Ho
50 E2 . . . . 24 C3
Wyndham Ho
SW1 . . . . 145 B3
Wyndham Mews
W1 . . . . 102 C3
Wyndham Pl W1 . 102 C3
Wyndham Rd SE5 . 48 B3
Wyndhams Ct 4
E8 . . . . 16 B1
Wyndham St W1 . . 102 C4
Wyndham Yd W1 . 102 C3
Wyneham Rd
SE24 . . . . 63 C2
Wynford Rd N1 . . . 85 A2
Wynne Ho SE14 . . 50 C2
Wynne Rd SW9 . . . 173 B1
Wynnstay Gdns
W8 . . . . 127 C2
Wynter Ho SW9 . . 173 A1
Wynter St SW11 . . 59 B3
Wynton Pl W3 . . . . 28 A3
Wynyard Ho SE11 . 149 A2
Wynyard Terr
SE11 . . . . 149 A2
Wynyatt Ho EC1 . . 96 A4
Wynyatt St EC1 . . 96 A4
Wytham Ho NW8 . . 89 C1
Wythburn Ct W1 . 102 C2
Wythburn Pl W1 . 102 C2
Wyvil Prim Sch
SW8 . . . . 162 B2
Wyvil Rd SW8 . . . 162 A2
Wyvis St E14 . . . . . 34 A4

Y

Yabsley St E14 . . . . 34 B1
Yaldam Ho SE1 . . 152 A3
Yalding Ho 20 E5 . . 17 A3
Yalding Rd SE16 . . 153 B4
Yale Ct NW6 . . . . . 11 A3
Yardley St WC1 . . . 95 B3
Yard The N1 . . . . . . 84 B1
Yarmouth Pl W1 . . 118 A1

Yarnfield Sq 15
SE15 . . . . 49 C2
Yarrow Ho
12 Cubitt Town
E14 . . . . 42 B3
16 North Kensington
W10 . . . . 30 B4
Yatesbury Ct E5 . . 18 A3
Yates Ct NW2 . . . . . 9 C2
Yates Ho E2 . . 24 C2 99 C4
Yatton Ho 13 W10 . 30 B4
Yeadon Ho 17
W10 . . . . 30 B4
Yearby Ho W10 . . . 22 B1
Yeate St N1 . . . . . . 15 C1
Yeats Cl NW10 . . . . 8 A2
Yeldham Ho W6 . . 39 C1
Yeldham Rd W6 . . 39 C1
Yelverton Rd
SW11 . . . . 167 C1
Yeoman Cl SE27 . . 75 A1
Yeoman's Row
SW3 . . . . 130 B1
Yeoman St SE8 . . . 41 A2
Yeoman's Yd E1 . . 125 A4
Yeo St E3 . . . . 34 A4
Yeovil Ho
Finsbury Pk N7 . . . . 5 B2
North Kensington
W10 . . . . 22 B1
Yerbury Prim Sch
N19 . . . . 4 C1
Yerbury Rd N19 . . . 4 C1
Yeshivo Horomo
Tadmudical Coll
N16 . . . . 7 B3
Yesodey Hatorah Sch
N16 . . . . 7 B4
Yet Lev Ct E5 . . . . 7 C3
Yewfield Rd NW10 . 8 B2
Yew Gr NW2 . . . . . . 9 C4
Yew Ho SE14 . . . . . 51 B1
Yew Tree Cl 3
SE13 . . . . 67 B4
Yew Tree Cl 8
N16 . . . . 6 C2
Yew Tree Rd W12 . 29 B2
Yoakley Rd N16 . . . 7 A2
Yoke Cl N7 . . . . 14 A2
Yonge Pk N4, N7 . . 5 C1
York Ave
Mortlake SW14 . . . . 55 B2
Walworth SE17 . . . 151 A2
York Bldgs WC2 . . 120 B3
York Bridge NW1 . . 91 B2
York Cl 11 SE5 . . . 48 B1
York Gate NW1 . . . 91 C1
York Gr SE15 . . . . . 50 B2
York Hill SE27,
SW16 . . . . 75 A1
York House Pl
W8 . . . . 128 A4

Yorkley Ho 3
W10 . . . . 22 B1
York Mans
Battersea SW11 . . 169 C4
Marylebone W1 . . . 103 B4
Walworth SE17 . . . 151 A2
York Mews NW5 . . 13 A3
York Pl
Battersea SW11 . . . 59 C4
WC2 . . . . 120 B3
York Place Mans
NW1 . . . . 103 A4
York Rd
Battersea SW11,
SW18 . . . . 59 C4
Dagenham W3 . . . . 28 C3
4 Richmond TW10 . 54 B2
SE1 . . . . 135 A4
York Rise NW5 . . . . 4 A1
York Road Bsns Ctr
SW11 . . . . 167 B1
York St Chambers
W1 . . . . 102 C4
Yorkshire Cl N16 . . 7 A1
Yorkshire Grey Pl 13
NW3 . . . . 11 B4
Yorkshire Grey Yd
WC1 . . . . 106 C3
Yorkshire Rd E14 . . 33 A3
York Sq 12 E14 . . . . 33 A3
York St W1 . . . . . . 103 A4
York Terr E NW1 . . 91 C1
York Terr W NW1 . . 91 B1
Yorkton St E2 . . . . 24 C3
York Way
Barnsbury N1, N7,
NW1 . . . . 14 A1
N1 . . . . 84 B3
York Way Ct
Islington N1 . . . . . . 84 C3
Islington N1 . . . . . . 84 B3
Young's Bldgs EC1 . 97 A2
Youngs Brewery
Visitor Ctr★
SW18 . . . . 59 A2
Youngs Ct SW11 . 169 C3
Young St W8 . . . . 128 A3
Yoxall Ho 2 W10 . . 22 B1
Yukon Rd SW12 . . 73 A4

Z

Zampa Rd SE16 . . . 40 B1
Zander Ct
E2 . . . . 24 C2 99 C4
Zangwill Ho NW6 . 23 B3
Zealand Ho 11
SE5 . . . . 48 B1
Zealand Rd E3 . . . . 26 A3
Zennor Rd SW12 . . 73 B3
Zenoria St SE22 . . 64 B3
Zetland Ho W8 . . 128 A2
Zetland St E14 . . . 34 B4
Zeus Ho N1 . . . . . . 97 B3
Zion Ho 6 E1 . . . . . 32 B3
Zoar St SE1 . . . . . 122 C2
Zodiac Ho 3 E3 . . . 26 C1
Zoffany St N19 . . . . 4 C2

List of numbered locations

This atlas shows thousands more place names than any other London street atlas. In some busy areas it is impossible to fit the name of every place.

Where not all names will fit, some smaller places are shown by a number. If you wish to find out the name associated with a number, use this listing.

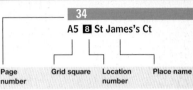

34

A5 8 St James's Ct

Page number | Grid square | Location number | Place name

1
- B1 **1** Mortimer Cl
- **2** Primrose Ct
- **3** Sunnyside Ho
- **4** Sunnyside
- **5** Prospect Pl
- B4 **1** Berkeley Ct
- **2** Exchange Mans
- **3** Beechcroft Ct
- **4** Nedahall Ct
- C1 **1** Portman Hts
- **2** Hermitage Ct
- **3** Moreland Ct
- **4** Wendover Ct

2
- B1 **1** Hampstead Sq
- **2** Stamford Ct
- **3** Mount Sq The

4
- B1 **1** Hunter Ho
- **2** Fisher Ho
- **3** Lang Ho
- **4** Temple Ho
- **5** Palmer Ho
- **6** Carlisle Ho
- **7** Durham Ho
- **8** Suffolk Ho
- **9** Lincoln Ho
- **10** Llewellyn Ho
- **11** Fell Ho
- **12** Aveling Ho
- **13** Merryweather Ct
- **14** Brennands Ct
- **15** St Christophers Ct
- **16** Francis Terrace Mews
- B2 **1** Flowers Mews
- **2** Archway Cl
- **3** Sandridge St
- **4** Bovingdon Cl
- **5** Cawell Ct
- **6** Torrence Ho
- **7** Rowan Wlk
- **8** Laurel Cl
- **9** Forest Way
- **10** Larch Cl
- **11** Pine Cl
- **12** Alder Mews
- **13** Aspen Cl
- B3 **1** Calvert Ct

- **2** Academy The
- **3** Whitehall Mans
- **4** Pauntley St
- **5** Archway Hts
- **6** Pauntley Ho
- C1 **1** Melchester Ho
- **2** Norcombe Ho
- **3** Weatherbury Ho
- **4** Wessex Ho
- **5** Archway Bsns Ctr
- **6** Harford Mews
- **7** Opera Ct
- **8** Rupert Ho
- **9** All Saints Church
- C2 **1** Bowerman Ct
- **2** Gresham Pl
- **3** Hargrave Mans
- **4** Church Garth
- **5** John King Ct
- **6** Ramsey Ct
- C3 **1** Louise White Ho
- **2** Levison Way
- **3** Sanders Way
- **4** Birbeck Ho
- **5** Scholars Ct
- C4 **1** Eleanor Rathbone Ho
- **2** Christopher Lo
- **3** Monkridge
- **4** Marbleford Ct
- **5** High London
- **6** Garton Ho
- **7** Hilltop Ho
- **8** Caroline Martyn Ho
- **9** Arthur Henderson Ho
- **10** Margaret Mcmillan Ho
- **11** Enid Stacy Ho
- **12** Mary McArthur Ho
- **13** Bruce Glasier Ho
- **14** John Wheatley Ho
- **15** Keir Hardie Ho
- **16** Monroe Ho
- **17** Iberia Ho
- **18** Lygoe Ho
- **19** Lambert Ho
- **20** Shelbourne Ho
- **21** Arkansas Ho
- **22** Lafitte Ho
- **23** Shreveport Ho
- **24** Packenham Ho

- **25** Orpheus Ho
- **26** Fayetville Ho
- **27** Bayon Ho

5
- A1 **1** Northview
- **2** Tufnell Park Mans
- **3** Fulford Mans
- **4** Tollington Ho
- A2 **1** Bracey Mews
- **2** Christie Ct
- **3** Ringmer Gdns
- **4** Kingsdown Rd
- **5** Cottenham Ho
- **6** St Paul's Ct
- **7** Rickthorne Rd
- **8** Stanley Terr
- **9** Arundel Lo
- **10** Landseer Ct
- A3 **1** Beeches The
- **2** Lambton Ct
- **3** Nugent Ct
- **4** Lambton Mews
- **5** Mews The
- A4 **1** Marie Lloyd Gdns
- **2** Edith Cavell Cl
- **3** Marie Stopes Ct
- **4** Jessie Blythe La
- **5** Barbara Rudolph Ct
- **6** Hetty Rees Ct
- **7** Leyden Mans
- **8** Brambledown
- **9** Lochbie
- **10** Lyngham Ct
- **11** High Mount
- **12** Woodlands The
- B2 **1** Berkeley Wlk
- **2** Lazar Wlk
- **3** Thistlewood Cl
- **4** Tomlins Wlk
- **5** Andover Rd
- **6** Barmouth Ho
- **7** Chard Ho
- **8** Methley Ho
- **9** Rainford Ho
- **10** Woodbridge Ct
- **11** Allerton Wlk
- **12** Falconer Wlk
- **13** Sonderburg Rd
- **14** St Mark's Mans
- **15** Athol Ct
- B3 **1** Lawson Ct

- **2** Wiltshire Ct
- **3** Fenstanton
- **4** Hutton Ct
- **5** Wisbech
- C2 **1** Brookfield
- **2** Churnfield

6
- A1 **1** Hurlock Ho
- **2** Blackstock Ho
- **3** Vivian Comma Cl
- **4** Monsell Ct
- B4 **1** Finsen Ho
- **2** Keynsham Ho
- **3** Kilpeck Ho
- **4** Knaresborough Ho
- **5** Leighfield Ho
- **6** Lonsdale Ho
- **7** Groveley Ho
- **8** Wensleydale Ho
- **9** Badminton Ct
- C2 **1** Chestnut Cl
- **2** Sycamore Ho
- **3** Lordship Ho
- **4** Clissold Ho
- **5** Beech Ho
- **6** Laburnum Ho
- **7** Ormond Ho
- **8** Yew Tree Ct
- **9** Oak Ho
- C4 **1** Selwood Ho
- **2** Menlip Ho
- **3** Ennerdale Ho
- **4** Delamere Ho
- **5** Westwood Ho
- **6** Bernwood Ho
- **7** Allerdale Ho
- **8** Chattenden Ho
- **9** Farningham Ho
- **10** Oakend Ho

7
- A1 **1** Gujarat Ho
- **2** Marton Rd
- **3** Painsthorpe Rd
- **4** Selkirk Ho
- **5** Defoe Ho
- **6** Edward Friend Ho
- **7** Sheridan Ho
- **8** Barrie Ho
- **9** Arnold Ho
- **10** MacAulay Ho

- **11** Stowe Ho
- **12** Carlyle Ho
- **13** Shaftesbury Ho
- **14** Lillian Cl
- **15** Swift Ho
- **16** Dryden Ho
- **17** Scott Ct
- **18** Kingsfield Ho
- **19** Uhura Sq
- **20** Hartopp Ct
- A3 **1** Godstone Ct
- **2** Farnham Ct
- **3** Milford Ct
- **4** Cranleigh Ct
- **5** Haslemere Ct
- **6** Belmont Ct
- **7** Hockworth Ho
- **8** Garratt Ho
- **9** Fairburn Ho
- **10** Thorndale Ho
- **11** Oakdene Ho
- **12** Briardale Ho
- B1 **1** Lawrence Bldgs
- **2** Cottage Wlk
- **3** Batley Pl
- B2 **1** Garnham St
- **2** Garnham Ho
- **3** Sanford La
- **4** Sanford Wlk
- **5** Abney Gdns
- **6** Fleet Wood
- B3 **1** Stamford Hill Mans
- **2** Montefiore Ct
- **3** Berwyn Ho
- **4** Clent Ho
- **5** Chiltern Ho
- **6** Laindon Ho
- **7** Pentland Ho
- B4 **1** Regent Ct
- **2** Stamford Lo
- **3** Holmwood Ct
- C1 **1** Ravenscourt
- **2** Mellington Ct
- **3** Rendlesham Ho
- **4** Carroll Ct
- C2 **1** Cazenove Mans
- **2** Chedworth Ho
- **3** Aldergrove Ho
- **4** Abbotstone Ho
- **5** Briggeford Cl
- **6** Inglethorpe Ho
- **7** Ashdown Ho

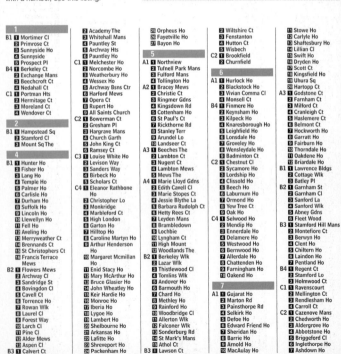

8 Epping Ho
9 Cypress Cl
C3 1 Stamford Gr E
2 Stamford Mans
3 Grove Mans
4 Stamford Gr W

8

A1 1 Beveridge Rd
2 Purcell Mews
3 George Lansbury Ho
4 Charles Hobson Ho
5 Reade Wlk
6 Westbury Ho
7 Bridge Ct
A4 1 Grange Ct
2 Green Ct
C2 1 Regency Mews
2 Tudor Mews
3 Utopia Ho
4 Bell Flats
5 Angel Ct

9

B2 1 Rutland Park Gdns
2 Rutland Park Mans
3 Queens Par
4 Harcourt Ho
5 Solidarity Ho
6 Electra Ct
7 Cassandra Ct
8 Carlton Ct
C4 1 Oaklands Mews
2 Acer Ct
3 Maple Ct
4 Argyle Mans

10

A1 1 Christ Church Ct
2 Paul Daisley Ct
3 Fountain Ho
4 Kingston Ho
5 Waverley Ct
6 Weston Ho
7 Mapes Ho
8 Athelstan Gdns
9 Leff Ho
B1 1 Alma Birk Ho
2 Brooklands Ct
3 Brooklands Court Apartments
4 Cleveland Mans
5 Buckley Ct
6 Webheath
C1 1 Linstead St
2 Embassy Ho
3 Acol Ct
4 Kings Wood Ct
5 Douglas Ct
6 King's Gdns
7 Carlton Mans
8 Smyrna Mews
9 New Priory Ct
10 Queensgate Pl
11 Brondesbury Mews
C2 1 Dene Mans
2 Sandwell Cres
3 Sandwell Mans
4 Hampstead West
5 Redcroft
C3 1 Orestes Mews
2 Walter Northcott Ho
3 Polperro Mans
4 Lyncroft Mans
5 Marlborough Mans

6 Alexandra Mans
7 Cumberland Mans
8 Cavendish Mans
9 Ambassador Ct
10 Welbeck Mans
11 Inglewood Mans
12 Dennington Park Mansions

11

A2 1 Beswick Mews
2 Worcester Mews
3 Minton Mews
4 Doulton Mews
5 Laurel Ho
6 Sandalwood Ho
7 Iroko Ho
8 Banyan Ho
9 Rosewood Ho
10 Ebony Ho
11 Rosemont Mans
12 Exeter Mews
B1 1 Harrold Ho
2 Glover Ho
3 Byron Ct
4 Nalton Ho
B2 1 Petros Gdns
2 Heath Ct
3 Imperial Twrs
4 Fairhurst
5 St John's Ct
6 New College Ct
7 Chalford
8 Rosslyn Mans
9 Sutherland Ho
B4 1 Windmill Hill
2 Highgrove Point
3 Gainsborough Ho
4 Holly Bush Hill
5 Heath Mans
6 Holly Bush Steps
7 Pavilion Ct
8 Holly Berry La
9 New Campden Ct
10 Holly Bush Vale
11 Benham's Pl
12 Prospect Pl
13 Yorkshire Grey Pl
14 Gardnor Mans
15 Ellerdale Cl
16 Monro Ho
17 Prince Arthur Mews
18 Prince Arthur Ct
19 Village Mount
20 Perrin's Ct
21 Wells Ct
22 Bakers Pas
23 Spencer Wlk
24 Bird In Hand Yd
25 Kings Well
26 New Ct
27 Streatley Pl
28 Mansfield Pl
29 Upper Hampstead Wlk
C1 1 New College Par
2 Northways Par
3 Noel Ho
4 Campden Ho
5 Centre Hts
6 Hickes Ho
7 Swiss Terr
8 Leitch Ho
9 Jevons Ho
10 Langhorne Ct
11 Park Lo

12 Avenue Lo
C2 1 Belsize Park Mews
2 Baynes Mews
3 McCrone Mews
C3 1 Belsize Court Garages
2 Roscommon Ho
3 Akenside Ct
C4 1 White Bear Pl
2 Wells Ho The
3 Boades Mews
4 Flask Cotts
5 Coach House Yd
6 Pilgrim's Pl
7 Rosslyn Mews

12

A2 1 Banfi Ho
2 Glenloch Ct
3 Havercourt
4 Holmefield Ct
5 Gilling Ct
6 Howitt Cl
7 Manor Mans
8 Straffan Lo
9 Romney Ct
10 Lancaster Stables
11 Eton Garages
B1 1 Hancock Nunn Ho
2 Higginson Ho
3 Duncan Ho
4 Mary Wharrie Ho
5 Rockstraw Ho
6 Cleaver Ho
7 Chamberlain St
8 Sharples Hall St
9 Primrose Mews
10 Rothwell St
11 St Georges Mews
B2 1 Alder Ho
2 Hornbeam Ho
3 Whitebeam Ho
4 Aspen Ho
5 Rowan Ho
6 Beech Ho
7 Chestnut Ho
8 Oak Ho
9 Willow Ho
10 Sycamore Ho
11 Maple Ho
12 Hazel Ho
13 Elaine Ct
14 Faircourt
15 Walham Ct
16 Stanbury Ct
17 Priory Mans
18 Wellington St
19 Grange The
B3 1 Cayford Ho
2 Du Maurier Ho
3 Isokon Flats
4 Palgrave Ho
5 Garnett Ho
6 Stephenson Ho
7 Park Dwellings
8 Siddons Ho
9 Mall Studios
10 Park Hill Wlk
11 Wordsworth Ho
12 Fraser Regnart Ct
13 St Pancras Almshouses
C1 1 Bridge Ho
2 Hardington
3 Mead Cl
4 Rugmere
5 Tottenhall

6 Beauvale
7 Broomfield
C2 1 Silverbirch Wlk
2 Penshurst
3 Wingham
4 Westwell
5 Chislet
6 Burmarsh
7 Shipton Ho
8 Stonegate
9 Leysdown
10 Headcorn
11 Lenham
12 Halstow
13 Fordcombe
14 Cannington
15 Langridge
16 Athlone Ho
17 Pentland Ho
18 Beckington
19 Hawkridge
20 Edington

13

A1 1 Ferdinand Ho
2 Harmood Ho
3 Hawley Rd
4 Hawley Mews
5 Leybourne St
6 Barling
7 Tiptree
8 Havering
9 Candida Ct
10 Lorraine Ct
11 Donnington Ct
12 Welford Ct
13 Torbay Ct
14 Bradfield Ct
15 Torbay St
16 Water La
17 Leybourne Rd
18 Haven St
19 Stucley Pl
20 Lawrence Ho
A2 1 Ashington
2 Priestley Ho
3 Leonard Day Ho
4 Old Dairy Mews
5 Monmouth Ho
6 Alpha Ct
7 Una Ho
8 Widford
9 Heybridge
10 Roxwell
11 Hamstead Gates
A4 1 Denyer Ho
2 Stephenson Ho
3 Trevithick Ho
4 Brunel Ho
5 Newcomen Ho
6 Faraday Ho
7 Winifrede Paul Ho
8 Wardlow
9 Fletcher Ct
10 Tideswell
11 Grangemill
12 Hambrook Ct
13 Calver
B1 1 Cherry Tree Ct
2 Chichester Ct
3 Durdans Ho
4 Philia Ho
5 Bernard Shaw Ct
6 Foster Ct
7 Bessemer Ct
8 Hogarth Ct
9 Rochester Ct

10 Soane Ct
11 Wallett Ct
12 Inwood Ct
13 Wrotham Rd
14 St Thomas Ct
15 Caulfield Ct
16 Bruges Pl
17 Reachview Ct
18 Lawfords Wharf
B3 1 Eleanor Ho
2 Falkland Pl
3 Kensington Ho
4 Willingham Cl
5 Kenbrook Ho
6 Aborfield
7 Great Field
8 Appleford
9 Forties The
10 Maud Wilkes Cl
11 Dunne Mews
12 Dowdeny Cl
B4 1 Benson Ct
2 Tait Ho
3 Manorfield Cl
4 Greatfield Cl
5 Longley Ho
6 Lampson Ho
7 Davidson Ho
8 Palmer Ho
9 Lambourn Cl
10 Morris Ho
11 Owen Ho
C1 1 Hillier Ho
2 Gairloch Ho
3 Cobham Mews
4 Bergholt Mews
5 Blakeney Cl
6 Weavers Way
7 Allensbury Pl
C2 1 Rowstock
2 Peckwater Ho
3 Wolsey Ho
4 Pandian Way
5 Busby Mews
6 Caledonian Sq
7 Canal Bvd
8 Northpoint Sq
9 Lock Mews
10 Carters Cl
11 York Ho
12 Hungerford Rd
13 Cliff Road Studios
14 Cliff Ct
15 Camelot Ho
16 Church Studios
17 Camden Terr
C3 1 Blake Ho
2 Quelch Ho
3 Lee Ho
4 Willbury Ho
5 Howell Ho
6 Holmsbury Ho
7 Leith Ho
8 Betchworth Ho
9 Rushmore Ho
10 Dugdale Ho
11 Horsendon Ho
12 Colley Ho
13 Coombe Ho
14 Ivinghoe Ho
15 Buckhurst Ho
16 Saxonbury Ct
17 Charlton Ct
18 Apollo Studios

4 Sidney Ho
5 Pomeroy Ho
6 Puteaux Ho
7 Doric Ho
8 Modling Ho
9 Longman Ho
10 Ames Ho
11 Alzette Ho
12 Offenbach Ho
13 Tate Ho
14 Norton Ho
15 St Gilles Ho
16 Harold Ho
17 Velletri Ho
18 Bridge Wharf
19 Gathorne St
20 Bow Brook The
21 Twig Folly Cl
22 Palmerston St
23 Lakeview
24 Peach Walk Mews
25 Caesar Ct

26

A1 1 Formosa Ho
2 Galveston Ho
3 Arabian Ho
4 Greenland Ho
5 Coral Ho
6 Anson Ho
7 Cambay Ho
8 Lindop Ho
9 Moray Ho
10 Azov Ho
11 Sandalwood Cl
12 Broadford Ho
A2 1 Imperial Ho
2 Newport Ho
3 Vassall Ho
4 Maurice Ct
5 Creed Ct
6 Christopher France Ho
7 Beaumont Ct
8 Pembroke Mews
A3 1 Nightingale Mews
2 Bunsen Ho
3 Bunsen St
4 Beatrice Webb Ho
5 Margaret Bondfield Ho
6 Wilmer Ho
7 Sandall Ho
8 Butley Ct
9 Josseline Ct
10 Dalton Ho
11 Brine Ho
12 Ford Cl
13 Viking Cl
14 Stanfield Rd
15 Stoneleigh Mews
16 Ruth Ct
17 School Bell Cloisters
18 Schoolbell Mews
19 Medhurst Cl
20 Olga St
21 Conyer St
22 Diamond Ho
23 Daring Ho
24 Crane Ho
25 Exmoor Ho
26 Grenville Ho
27 Hyperion Ho
28 Sturdy Ho
29 Wren Ho
30 Ardent Ho

31 Senators Lo
32 Hooke Ho
33 Mohawk Ho
34 Ivanhoe Ho
35 Medway Mews
B2 1 Trellis Sq
2 Sheffield Sq
3 Howcroft Ho
4 Astra Ho
5 Frye Ct
6 Byas Ho
7 George Lansbury Ho
8 Regal Pl
9 Coborn Mews
10 Tredegar Mews
11 Cavendish Terr
12 Lyn Mews
13 Buttermere Ho
14 Coniston Ho
15 Tracy Ho
16 Hanover Pl
17 St Clair Ho
18 Longthorne Ho
19 Vista Bldgs
20 Verity Ho
21 Icarus Ho
22 Whippingham Ho
23 Hamilton Ho
24 Winchester Ho
B3 1 Roman Square Mkt
2 John Bond Ho
3 McKenna Ho
4 Dennis Ho
5 McAusland Ho
6 McBride Ho
7 Libra Rd
8 Dave Adams Ho
9 Regency Ct
10 Tay Ho
11 Sleat Ho
12 Brodick Ho
13 Lunan Ho
14 Cruden Ho
15 Anglo Rd
16 Mull Ho
17 Sinclairs Ho
18 Driffway Ho
19 Clayhall Ct
20 Berebinder Ho
21 Barford Ho
22 Partridge Ho
23 Gosford Ho
24 Dornoch Ho
25 Dunnet Ho
26 Enard Ho
27 Fraserburgh Ho
28 Forth Ho
29 Stavers Ho
30 Rosegate Ho
31 Crowngate Ho
32 Queensgate Ho
33 Towergate Ho
34 Ordell Ct
35 William Pl
B4 1 Hampstead Wlk
2 Waverton Ho
3 Elton Ho
4 Locton Gn
5 Birtwhistle Ho
6 Clare Ho
7 Magpie Ho
8 Hornbeam Sq
9 Rowan Ho
10 Barge La

11 Walnut Ho
12 Birdsfield La
13 Atkins Ct
14 Willow Tree Cl
15 Jasmine Sq
16 Tait Ct
17 Ranwell Ho
18 Ranwell Cl
19 Tufnell Ct
20 Pulteney Ct
21 Vic Johnson Ho
22 Lea Sq
23 Iceni Ct
24 Tamar Cl
25 Roman Rd
26 Valentine Ho
C1 1 Fairmont Ho
2 Healy Ho
3 Zodiac Ho
4 Buick Ho
5 Consul Ho
6 Bentley Ho
7 Cresta Ho
8 Daimler Ho
9 Riley Ho
10 Jensen Ho
11 Lagonda Ho
12 Ireton St
13 Navenby Wlk
14 Burwell Wlk
15 Leadenham Ct
16 Sleaford Ho
17 Bow Triangle Bsns Ctr
C2 1 Bow Ho
2 Denmark Pl
3 Marsalis Ho
4 Lovette Ho
5 Drapers Almshouses
6 Mallard Point
7 Creswick Wlk
8 Bevin Ho
9 Huggins Ho
10 Williams Ho
11 Harris Ho
12 Marina Ct
13 Electric Ho
14 Matching Ct
15 Wellington Bldgs
16 Grafton Ho
17 Berkeley Ho
18 Columbia Ho
C3 1 Vincent Mews
2 Menai Pl
3 Heathfield Ct
4 Redwood Cl
5 Acorn Ct
6 Primrose Cl
7 Briar Ct
8 Springwood Cl
C4 1 Ironworks
2 Juno Ho
3 Chariot Cl
4 Saturn Ho
5 Hadrian Ct
6 Mercury Ho
7 Forum Cl
8 Venus Ho
9 Vesta Ho
10 Tiber Ct
11 Gemini Ho
12 Crown Close Bsns Ctr
13 Old Ford Trad Ctr

27

A1 1 Broxbourne Ho

2 Roxford Ho
3 Biscott Ho
4 Stanborough Ho
5 Hillstone Ct
A2 1 Bradley Ho
2 Prioress Ho
3 Alton Ho
4 Foxley Ho
5 Munden Ho
6 Canterbury Ho
7 Corbin Ho
8 Barton Ho
9 Jolles Ho
10 Rudstone Ho
11 Baxter Ho
12 Baker Ho
13 Insley Ho
14 Hardwicke Ho
15 Glebe Ct
16 Priory St
17 Sadler Ho
18 Ballinger Point
19 Henshall Point
20 Dorrington Point
21 Warren Ho
22 Fairlie Ct
23 Regent Sq
24 Hackworth Point
25 Priestman Point
26 Wingate Ho
27 Nethercott Ho
28 Thelbridge Ho
29 Bowden Ho
30 Kerscott Ho
31 Southcott Ho
32 Birchdown Ho
33 Upcott Ho
34 Langmead Ho
35 Limscott Ho
36 Northleigh Ho
37 Huntshaw Ho
38 Chagford Ho
39 Ashcombe Ho
40 Shillingford Ho
41 Patrick Connolly Gdns
42 Lester Ct
43 Franklin St
44 Taft Way
45 Washington Cl
46 Veronica Ho
47 William Guy Gdns
48 Denbury Ho
49 Holsworthy Ho
50 Padstone Ho
B2 1 Miller's House Visitor Ctr
C1 1 Crescent Court Bsns Ctr
2 Ashmead Bsns Ctr
3 Forward Bsns Ctr The
C4 1 Victoria Mills
2 Hallings Wharf Studios
3 Poland Ho
4 Peter Heathfield Ho
5 Burford Rd

28

A1 1 Lantry Ct
2 Rosemount Ct
3 Moreton Twr
4 Acton Central Ind Est
5 Rufford Twr
6 Narrow St

1 Mount Pl
2 Sidney Miller Ct
3 Mill Hill Terr
4 Cheltenham Pl
5 Mill Hill Gr
6 Benjamin Ho
7 Arlington Ct
8 Lombard Ct
9 Steyne Ho
B1 1 Rectory Rd
2 Derwentwater Mans
3 Market Pl
4 Hooper's Mews
5 Cromwell Ct
6 Locarno Rd
7 Edgecote Ct
8 Harleyford Manor
9 Coopers Ct
10 Avingdor Ct
11 Steyne Ho
B3 1 Avon Ct
2 Bromley Lo
3 Walter Ct
4 Lynton Terr
5 Acton Ho
6 Fells Haugh
7 Springfield Ct
8 Tamarind Ct
9 Lynton Ct
10 Aspen Ct
11 Pegasus Ct
12 Friary Park Ct
C3 1 Rosebank Gdns
2 Rosebank
3 Edinburgh Ho
4 Western Ct
5 Kilronan

30

A1 1 Arlington Ho
2 Lugard Ho
3 Shabana Ct
4 Sitarey Ct
5 Oaklands Ct
6 Davenport Mews
A2 1 Abercrombie Ho
2 Bathurst Ho
3 Brisbane Ho
4 Bentinck Ho
5 Ellenborough Ho
6 Lawrence Ct
7 Mackenzie Ct
8 Carteret Ho
9 Calvert Ho
10 Winthrop Ho
11 Auckland Ho
12 Blaxland Ho
13 Havelock Cl
14 Hargraves Ho
15 Hudson Ho
16 Phipps Ho
17 Lawson Ho
18 Hastings Ho
19 Wolfe Ho
20 Malabar Ct
21 Commonwealth Ave
22 Charnock Ho
23 Canning Ho
24 Cornwallis Ct
25 Commonwealth Ave
26 Champlain Ho

27 Grey Ho
28 Durban Ho
29 Baird Ho
30 Campbell Ho
31 Mitchell Ho
32 Denham Ho
33 Mackay Ho
34 Evans Ho
35 Davis Ho
36 Mandela Cl
A3 1 Holborn Ho
2 Clement Danes Ho
3 Vellacott Ho
4 O'Driscoll Ho
5 King Ho
6 Daley Ho
7 Selma Ho
8 Garrett Ho
B1 1 Linden Ct
2 Frithville Ct
3 Blomfield Mans
4 Poplar Mews
5 Hopgood St
6 Westwood Ho
7 Stanlake Mews
8 Stanlake Villas
9 Alexandra Mans
B3 1 Latimer Ind Est
2 Pankhurst Ho
3 Quadrangle The
4 Nightingale Ho
5 Gordon Ct
6 Ducane Cl
7 Browning Ho
8 Pavilion Terr
9 Ivebury Ct
10 Olympic Ho
B4 1 Galleywood Ho
2 Edgcott Ho
3 Cuffley Ho
4 Addlestone Ho
5 Hockliffe Ho
6 Sarratt Ho
7 Firle Ho
8 Sutton Est The
9 Terling Ho
10 Danes Ho
11 Udimore Ho
12 Vange Ho
13 Binbrook Ho
14 Yeadon Ho
15 Yatton Ho
16 Yarrow Ho
17 Clement Ho
18 Danebury
19 Coronation Ct
20 Calderon Pl
21 St Quintin Gdns
C1 1 St Katherine's Wlk
2 Dorrit Ho
3 Pickwick Ho
4 Dombey Ho
5 Caranday Villas
6 Mortimer Ho
7 Nickleby Ho
8 Stebbing Ho
9 Boxmoor Ho
10 Poynter Ho
11 Swanscombe Ho
12 Darnley Terr
13 Norland Ho
14 Hume Ho
15 Boundary Ho
16 Norland Rd

17 Helix Ct
C2 1 Frinstead Ho
2 Hurstway Wlk
3 Testerton Wlk
4 Grenfell Wlk
5 Grenfell Twr
6 Barandon Wlk
7 Treadgold Ho
8 St Clements Ct
9 Willow Way
10 Florence Ho
11 Dora Ho
12 Carton Ho
13 Agnes Ho
14 Marley Ho
15 Estella Ho
16 Waynflete Sq
17 Pippin Ho
18 Baseline Business Studios
C3 1 Kelfield Ct
2 Downing Ho
3 Crosfield Ct
4 Robinson Ho
5 Scampston Mews
6 Girton Villas
7 Ray Ho
8 Walmer Ho
9 Goodrich Ct
10 Arthur Ct
11 Whitstable Ho
12 Kingsnorth Ho
13 Bridge Ct
14 Prospect Ho
15 St Marks Rd
16 Whitchurch Ho
17 Blechynden Ho
18 Waynflete Sq
19 Bramley Ho
20 Dixon Ho

31

A3 1 Malton Mews
2 Lancaster Lo
3 Manning Ho
4 Galsworthy Ho
5 Hudson Ho
6 Cambourne Mews
7 Upper Talbot Wlk
8 Kingsdown Cl
9 Lower Clarendon Wlk
10 Talbot Grove Ho
11 Clarendon Wlk
12 Upper Clarendon Wlk
13 Camelford Wlk
14 Upper Camelford Wlk
15 Camelford Ct
A4 1 Murchison Ho
2 MacAulay Ho
3 Chesterton Ho
4 Chiltern Ho
5 Lionel Ho
6 Watts Ho
7 Wheatstone Ho
8 Telford Ho
9 Golborne Mews
10 Millwood St
11 St Columb's Ho
12 Norfolk Mews
13 Lionel Mews
B3 1 Silvester Ho
2 Golden Cross Mews
3 Tavistock Mews
4 Clydesdale Ho

5 Melchester
6 Pinehurst Ct
7 Denbigh Ho
B4 1 Blagrove Rd
2 All Saints Ho
3 Tavistock Ho
4 Leamington Ho
C3 1 Shottsford
2 Tolchurch
3 Casterbridge
4 Sandbourne
5 Anglebury
6 Weatherbury
7 Westbourne Gr Mews
8 Rosehart Mews
9 Viscount Ct
10 Hereford Mans
11 Hereford Mews
C4 1 Ascot Ho
2 Ashgrove Ct
3 Lockbridge Ct
4 Swallow Ct
5 Nightingale Lo
6 Hammond Lo
7 Penfield Lo
8 Harvey Lo
9 Hunter Lo
10 Barnard Lo
11 Falcon Lo
12 Johnson Lo
13 Livingstone Lo
14 Nuffield Lo
15 Finch Lo
16 Polesworth Ho
17 Oversley Ho
18 Derrycombe Ho
19 Buckshead Ho
20 Combe Ho
21 Culham Ho
22 Dainton Ho
23 Devonport Ho
24 Honwell Ho
25 Truro Ho
26 Sunderland Ho
27 Stonehouse Ho
28 Riverford Ho
29 Portishead Ho
30 Mickleton Ho
31 Keyham Ho
32 Moulsford Ho
33 Shrewsbury Mews
34 St Stephen's Mews
35 Westway Lo
36 Langley Ho
37 Brindley Ho
38 Radway Ho
39 Astley Ho
40 Willow Ct
41 Larch Ct
42 Elm Ct
43 Beech Ct
44 Worcester Ct
45 Union Ct
46 Leicester Ct
47 Kennet Ct
48 Oxford Ct
49 Fazerley Ct

32

A1 1 China Ct
2 Wellington Terr
3 Stevedore St
4 Portland Sq
5 Reardon Ho
6 Lowder Ho

7 Meeting House Alley
8 Farthing Fields
9 Oswell Ho
10 Park Lo
11 Doughty Ct
12 Inglefield Sq
13 Chopin's Ct
14 Welsh Ho
15 Hilliard Ho
16 Clegg St
17 Tasman Ho
18 Ross Ho
19 Wapping Dock St
20 Bridewell Pl
21 New Tower Bldgs
22 Tower Bldgs
23 Chimney Ct
24 Jackman Ho
25 Fenner Ho
26 Franklin Ho
27 Frobisher Ho
28 Flinders Ho
29 Chancellor Ho
30 Beechey Ho
31 Reardon Path
32 Parry Ho
33 Vancover Ho
34 Willoughby Ho
35 Sanctuary The
36 Dundee Ct
37 Pierhead Wharf
38 Scandrett St
39 St Johns Ct
A2 1 Newton Ho
2 Richard Neale Ho
3 Maddocks Ho
4 Cornwall St
5 Brockmer Ho
6 Dellow Ho
7 Bewley Ho
8 Artichoke Hill
9 Queen Anne Terr
10 King Henry Terr
11 King Charles Terr
12 Queen Victoria Terr
13 Sovereign Ct
14 Princes Court Bsns Ctr
15 Kingsley Mews
A3 1 Peter Best Ho
2 Mellish Ho
3 Porchester Ho
4 Dickson Ho
5 Joscoyne Ho
6 Silvester Ho
7 Wilton Ct
8 Sarah Ho
9 Bridgen Ho
10 Tylney Ho
11 Greenwich Ct
12 Damien Ct
13 Philson Mans
14 Siege Ho
15 Jacob Mans
16 Proud Ho
17 Sly St
18 Barnett St
19 Kinder St
20 Richard St
21 Hungerford St
22 Colstead Ho
23 Melwood Ho
24 Wicker St
25 Langdale St
26 Chapman St
27 Burwell Cl

28 Walford Ho
29 Welstead Ho
30 Norton Ho
31 Turnour Ho
32 Luke Ho
33 Dunch St
34 Sheridan St
A4 1 Wodeham Gdns
2 Castlemaine St
3 Court St
B1 1 John Rennie Wlk
2 Malay Ho
3 Wainwright Ho
4 Riverside Mans
5 Shackleton Ho
6 Whitehorn Ho
7 Wavel Ct
8 Prusom's Island
B2 1 Shadwell Pl
2 Gosling Ho
3 Vogler Ho
4 Donovan Ho
5 Knowlden Ho
6 Chamberlain Ho
7 Moore Ho
8 Thornewill Ho
9 Fisher Ho
10 All Saints Ct
11 Coburg Dwellings
12 Lowood Ho
13 Solander Gdns
14 Chancery Bldgs
15 Ring Ho
16 Juniper St
17 Gordon Ho
18 West Block
19 North Block
20 South Block
21 Ikon Ho
B3 1 Woollon Ho
2 Dundalk Ho
3 Anne Goodman Ho
4 Newbold Cotts
5 Kerry Ho
6 Zion Ho
7 Longford Ho
8 Bromehead St
9 Athlone Ho
10 Jubilee Mans
11 Harriott Ho
12 Brayford Sq
13 Clearbrook Way
14 Rochelle Ct
15 Winterton Ho
16 Swift Ho
17 Brinsley Ho
18 Dean Ho
19 Foley Ho
20 Robert Sutton Ho
21 Montpelier Pl
22 Glastonbury Pl
23 Steel's La
24 Masters Lo
25 Stylus Apartments
26 Arta Ho
B4 1 Fulneck
2 Gracehill
3 Ockbrook
4 Fairfield
5 Dunstan Hos
6 Cressy Ct
7 Cressy Hos
8 Callahan Cotts
9 Lindley Ho
10 Mayo Ho
11 Wexford Ho

12 Sandhurst Ho
13 Addis Ho
14 Colverson Ho
15 Beckett Ho
16 Jarman Ho
17 Armsby Ho
18 Wingrad Ho
19 Miranda Cl
20 Drake Ho
21 Ashfield Yd
22 Magri Wlk
23 Jean Pardies Ho
24 St Vincent De Paul Ho
25 Sambrook Ho
26 Louise De Marillac Ho
27 Dagobert Ho
28 Le Moal Ho
29 Odette Duval Ho
30 Charles Auffray Ho
31 Boisseau Ho
32 Clichy Ho
33 Paymal Ho

C1
1 Clarence Mews
2 Raleigh Ct
3 Katherine Cl
4 Woolcombes Ct
5 Tudor Ct
6 Quayside Ct
7 Princes Riverside Rd
8 Surrey Ho
9 Tideway Ct
10 Edinburgh Ct
11 Falkirk Ct
12 Byelands Cl
13 Gwent Ct
14 Lavender Ho
15 Abbotshade Rd
16 Bellamy's Ct
17 Blenheim Ct
18 Sandringham Ct
19 Hampton Ct
20 Windsor Ct
21 Balmoral Ct
22 Westminster Ct
23 Beaton Wlk

C2
1 Barnardo Gdns
2 Roslin Ho
3 Glamis Est
4 Peabody Est
5 East Block
6 Highway Trad Ctr The
7 Highway Bsns Pk The
8 Cranford Cotts
9 Ratcliffe Orch
10 Scotia Bldg
11 Mauretania Bldg
12 Compania Bldg
13 Sirius Bldg
14 Unicorn Bldg
15 Keeper Wharf

C3
1 Pattison Ho
2 St Thomas Ho
3 Arbour Ho
4 Bladen Ho
5 Antill Terr
6 Majorie Mews
7 Billing Ho
8 Dowson Ho
9 Lipton Rd
10 Chalkwell Ho
11 Corringham Ho
12 Ogilvie Ho

13 Edward Mann Cl
14 Reservoir Studios
15 Lighterman Mews

C4
1 Roland Mews
2 Beatrice Ho
3 Morecambe Cl
4 Stepney Green Cl
5 Milrood Ho
6 Panama Ho
7 Galway Ho
8 Jacqueline Ho
9 Crown Mews
10 Caspian Ho
11 Darien Ho
12 Riga Ho
13 Flores Ho
14 Taranto Ho
15 Aden Ho
16 Master's St
17 Rosary Ct

33

A1
1 Edward Sq
2 Prince Regent Ct
3 Codrington Ct
4 Pennington Ct
5 Cherry Ct
6 Ash Ct
7 Beech Ct
8 Hazel Ct
9 Laurel Ct

A2
1 St Georges Sq
2 Drake Ho
3 Osprey Ho
4 Fleet Ho
5 Gainsborough Ho
6 Victory Pl
7 Challenger Ho
8 Conrad Ho
9 Lock View Ct
10 Shoulder of Mutton Alley
11 Frederick Sq
12 Helena Sq
13 Elizabeth Sq
14 Sophia Sq
15 William Sq
16 Lamb Ct
17 Lockside
18 Adriatic Bldg
19 Ionian Bldg
20 Regents Gate Ho

A3
1 Hearnshaw St
2 Berry Cotts
3 Causton Cotts
4 Elizabeth Blount Ct
5 Carr St
6 Shaw Cres
7 Darnley Ho
8 Mercer's Cotts
9 Troon Ho
10 Ratcliffe Ho
11 Wakeling St
12 York Sq
13 Anglia Ho
14 Cambria Ho
15 Caledonia Ho
16 Ratcliffe La
17 Bekesbourne St
18 John Scurr Ho
19 Regents Canal Ho
20 Basin App
21 Powlesland Ct

A4
1 Waley St
2 Edith Ramsay Ho
3 Andaman Ho
4 Atlantic Ho

5 Pevensey Ho
6 Solent Ho
7 Lorne Ho
8 Cromarty Ho
9 Dakin Pl
10 Greaves Cotts
11 Donaghue Cotts
12 Ames Cotts
13 Waterview Ho
14 Limehouse Fields Est

B2
1 Hamilton Ho
2 Imperial Ho
3 Oriana Ho
4 Queens Ct
5 Brightlingsea Pl
6 Faraday Ho
7 Ropemaker's Fields
8 Oast Ct
9 Mitre The
10 Bate St
11 Joseph Irwin Ho
12 Padstow Ho
13 Bethlehem Ho
14 Saunders Ct
15 Roche Ho
16 Stocks Pl
17 Trinidad Ho
18 Grenada Ho
19 Kings Ho
20 Dunbar Wharf
21 Limekiln Wharf
22 Belgrave Ct
23 Eaton Ho

B3
1 Dora Ho
2 Flansham Ho
3 Gatwick Ho
4 Ashpark Ho
5 Newgate Ho
6 Midhurst Ho
7 Redbourne Ho
8 Southwater Cl
9 Andersens Wharf
10 Whatman Ho
11 Butler Ho
12 Fitzroy Ho
13 Salmon St
14 Mission The
15 Arithan Ho
16 Britley Ho
17 Cheadle Ho
18 Elland Ho
19 Wharf La
20 Docklands
21 Park Heights Ct
22 Grosvenor Ct
23 Lime House Ct
24 Swallow Pl
25 St Anne's Trad Est

B4
1 Wearmouth Ho
2 Elmslie Point
3 Grindley Ho
4 Stileman Ho
5 Wilcox Ho
6 Huddart St
7 Robeson St
8 Couzens Ho
9 Perley Ho
10 Whytlaw Ho
11 Booker Cl
12 Tunley Grn
13 Callingham Cl
14 Bowry Ho
15 Perkins Ho
16 Printon Ho
17 Tasker Ho

C2
1 West India Ho

2 Berber Pl
3 Birchfield Ho
4 Elderfield Ho
5 Thornfield Ho
6 Gorsefield Ho
7 Arborfield Ho
8 Colborne Ho
9 East India Bldgs
10 Compass Point
11 Salter St
12 Garland Ct
13 Bogart Ct
14 Fonda Ct
15 Welles Ct
16 Rogers Ct
17 Premier Pl
18 Kelly Ct
19 Flynn Ct
20 Mary Jones Ho
21 Cannon Dr
22 Horizon Bldg

C3
1 Landin Ho
2 Thomas Road Ind Est
3 Vickery's Wharf
4 Abbotts Wharf
5 Limehouse Ct
6 Charlesworth Ho
7 Gurdon Ho
8 Trendell Ho
9 Menteath Ho
10 Minchin Ho
11 Donne Ho
12 Old School Sq
13 Anglesey Ho
14 Gough Wlk
15 Baring Ho
16 Gladstone Ho
17 Hopkins Ho
18 Granville Ho
19 Overstone Ho
20 Pusey Ho
21 Russell Ho
22 Stanley Ho

C4
1 Bredel Ho
2 Linton Ho
3 Matthews Ho
4 Woodcock Ho
5 Limborough Ho
6 Maydwell Ho
7 Underhill Ho
8 Meyrick Ho
9 Ambrose Ho
10 Richardson Ho
11 Carpenter Ho
12 Robinson Ho
13 Bellmaker Ct
14 Lime Tree Ct
15 Bracken Ho
16 Bramble Ho
17 Berberis Ho
18 Bilberry Ho
19 Ladyfern Ho
20 Rosebay Ho
21 Invicta Cl
22 Phoenix Bsns Ctr
23 Metropolitan Cl
24 Busbridge Ho

34

A2
1 Westcott Ho
2 Corry Ho
3 Malam Gdns
4 Blomfield Ho
5 Devitt Ho
6 Leyland Ho
7 Wigram Ho

8 Willis Ho
9 Balsam Ho
10 Finch's Ct
11 Poplar Bath St
12 Lawless St
13 Storey Ho
14 Abbot Ho
15 Woodall Cl
16 Landon Wlk
17 Goodhope Ho
18 Goodfaith Ho
19 Winant Ho
20 Goodspeed Ho
21 Lubbock Ho
22 Goodwill Ho
23 Martindale Ho
24 Holmsdale Ho
25 Norwood Ho
26 Constant Ho

A3
1 Colebrook Ho
2 Essex Ho
3 Salisbury Ho
4 Maidstone Ho
5 Osterley Ho
6 Norwich Ho
7 Clarissa Ho
8 Elgin Ho
9 Shaftesbury Lo
10 Shepherd Ho
11 Jeremiah St
12 Elizabeth Cl
13 Chilcot Cl
14 Fitzgerald Ho
15 Vesey Path
16 Ennis Ho
17 Kilmore Ho
18 Cygnet House N
19 Cygnet House S

A4
1 Sumner Ho
2 David Hewitt Ho
3 St Gabriels Cl
4 Limehouse Cut
5 Colmans Wharf
6 Foundary Ho
7 Radford Ho

B1
1 Lumina Bldg
2 Nova Ct W
3 Nova Ct E
4 Aurora Bldg
5 Arran Ho
6 Kintyre Ho
7 Vantage Mews
8 Managers St
9 Horatio Pl
10 Concordia Wharf

B2
1 Discovery Ho
2 Mountague Pl
3 Virginia Ho
4 Collins Ho
5 Lawless Ho
6 Carmichael Ho
7 Commodore Ho
8 Mermaid Ho
9 Bullivant St
10 Anderson Ho
11 Mackrow Wlk
12 Robin Hood Gdns
13 Prestage Way

B3
1 Glenkerry Ho
2 Carradale Ho
3 Langdon Ho
4 Balfron Twr
5 St Frideswides Mews

6 Tabard Ct
7 Delta Bldg
8 Findhorn St
9 Kilbrennan Ho
10 Thistle Ho
11 Heather Ho
12 Tartan Ho
13 Sharman Ho
14 Trident Ho
15 Wharf View Ct

B4 1 Mills Gr
2 St Michaels Ct
3 Duncan Ct

C2 1 Quixley St
2 Romney Ho
3 Pumping Ho
4 Switch Ho
5 Wingfield Ct
6 Explorers Ct
7 Sexton Ct
8 Keel Ct
9 Bridge Ct
10 Sail Ct
11 Settlers Ct
12 Pilgrims Mews
13 Studley Ct
14 Wotton Ct
15 Cape Henry Ct
16 Bartholomew Ct
17 Adventurers Ct
18 Susan Constant Ct
19 Atlantic Ct

C3 1 Lansbury Gdns
2 Theseus Ho
3 Adams Ho
4 Jones Ho
5 Sam March Ho
6 Arapiles Ho
7 Athenia Ho
8 Julius Ho
9 Jervis Bay Ho
10 Helen Mackay Ho
11 Gaze Ho
12 Ritchie Ho
13 Blairgowrie Ct
14 Circle Ho
15 Dunkeld Ho
16 Rosemary Dr
17 Sorrel La
18 East India Dock Road Tunnel

35

B3 1 Newton Point
2 Sparke Terr
3 Montesquieu Terr
4 Crawford Point
5 Rathbone Ho
6 George St
7 Emily St
8 Fendt Ct
9 Sabbarton St
10 Briary Ct
11 Shaftesbury Ho

B4 1 Radley Terr
2 Bernard Cassidy St
3 Rathbone Mkt
4 Thomas North Terr
5 Mary St
6 Hughes Terr
7 Swanscombe Point
8 Rawlinson Point
9 Kennedy Cox Ho
10 Cooper St

C1 1 Capulet Mews
2 Pepys Cres
3 De Quincey Mews
4 Hardy Ave
5 Tom Jenkinson Rd
6 Kennacraig Cl
7 Charles Flemwell Mews
8 Gatcombe Rd
9 Badminton Mews
10 Holyrood Mews
11 Britannia Gate
12 Dalemain Mews
13 Bowes-Lyon Hall
14 Lancaster hall
15 Victoria Hall

C2 1 Clements Ave
2 Martindale Ave
3 Balearic Apts
4 Marmara Apts
5 Baltic Apts
6 Coral Apts
7 Aegean Apts
8 Capital East Apts

C4 1 Odeon Ct
2 Edward Ct
3 Newhaven La
4 Ravenscroft Cl
5 Douglas Rd
6 Ferrier Point
7 Harvey Point
8 Wood Point
9 Trinity St
10 Pattinson Point
11 Clinch Ct
12 Mint Bsns Pk

36

A1 1 Burford Ho
2 Hope Cl
3 Centaur Ct
4 Phoenix Ct

C1 1 Surrey Cres
2 Forbes Ho
3 Haining Cl
4 Melville Ct
5 London Stile
6 Stile Hall Par
7 Priory Lo
8 Kew Bridge Ct
9 Meadowcroft
10 St James Ct
11 Rivers Ho

37

A1 1 Churchdale Ct
2 Cromwell Ct
3 Cambridge Rd S
4 Oxbridge Ct
5 Tomlinson Cl
6 Gunnersbury Mews
7 Grange The
8 Gunnersbury Cl
9 Bellgrave Lo

A4 1 Cheltenham Pl
2 Beaumaris Twr
3 Arundel Ho
4 Pevensey Ct
5 Jerome Twr
6 Anstey Ct
7 Bennett Ct
8 Gunnersbury Ct
9 Barrington Ct
10 Hope Gdns
11 Park Road E

B1 1 Arlington Park Mans
2 Sandown Ho
3 Goodwood Ho
4 Windsor Ho
5 Lingfield Ho
6 Ascot Ho
7 Watchfield Ct
8 Belgrave Ct
9 Beverley Ct
10 Beaumont Ct
11 Harvard Rd
12 Troubridge Ct
13 Branden Lo
14 Fromow's Cnr

B2 1 Chiswick Green Studios
2 Bell Ind Est
3 Fairlawn Ct
4 Dukes Gate
5 Dewsbury Ct
6 Chiswick Terr
7 Mortlake Ho

B3 1 Blackmore Twr
2 Bollo Ct
3 Kipling Twr
4 Lawrence Ct
5 Maugham Ct
6 Reade Ct
7 Woolf Ct
8 Shaw Ct
9 Verne Ct
10 Wodehouse St
11 Greenock Rd
12 Garden Ct
13 Barons Gate
14 Cleveland Rd
15 Carver Ct
16 Chapter Ct
17 Beauchamp Ct
18 Holmes Ct
19 Copper Mews

B4 1 Belgrave Ct
2 Buckland Wlk
3 Frampton Ct
4 Telfer Ct
5 Harlech Twr
6 Corfe Twr
7 Barwick Ho
8 Charles Hocking Ho
9 Sunninghill Ct
10 Salisbury St
11 Jameson Pl
12 Castle Cl

C1 1 Chatsworth Lo
2 Prospect Pl
3 Townhall Ave
4 Devonhurst Pl
5 Heathfield Ct
6 Horticultural Pl
7 Merlin Ho
8 Garth Rd
9 Autumn Rise

C2 1 Disraeli Cl
2 Winston Wlk
3 Rusthall Mans
4 Bedford Park Mans
5 Essex Place Sq
6 Holly Rd
7 Homecross Ho
8 Swan Bsns Ctr
9 Jessop Ho

38

A1 1 Glebe Ct
2 Devonshire Mews
3 Binns Terr
4 Ingress St
5 Swanscombe Rd
6 Brackley Terr
7 Stephen Fox Ho
8 Manor Gdns
9 Coram Ho
10 Flaxman Ho
11 Thorneycroft Ho
12 Thornhill Ho
13 Kent Ho
14 Oldfield Ho

A2 1 Chestnut Ho
2 Bedford Ho
3 Bedford Cnr
4 Sydney Ho
5 Bedford Park Cnr
6 Priory Gdns
7 Windmill Alley
8 Castle Pl
9 Jonathan Ct
10 Windmill Pas
11 Chardin Rd
12 Gable Ho

A3 1 Fleet Ct
2 Ember Ct
3 Emlyn Gdns
4 Clone Ct
5 Brent Ct
6 Abbey Ct
7 Ormsby Lo
8 St Catherine's Ct
9 Lodge The

A4 1 Longford Ct
2 Mole Ct
3 Lea Ct
4 Wandle Ct
5 Beverley Ct
6 Roding Ct
7 Crane Ct

B1 1 Miller's Ct
2 British Grove Pas
3 British Grove S
4 Berestede Rd
5 North Eyot Gdns

B2 1 Flanders Mans
2 Stamford Brook Mans
3 Linkenholt Mans
4 Prebend Mans
5 Middlesex Ct

B3 1 Stamford Brook Gdns
2 Hauteville Court Gdns
3 Ranelagh Gdns

C1 1 Chiswick Common Gdns
2 North Verbena Gdns
3 Western Terr
4 Verbena Gdns
5 Montrose Villas
6 Hammersmith Terr
7 South Black Lion La
8 St Peter's Wharf

C2 1 Hamlet Ct
2 Derwent St
3 Westcroft Ct
4 Black Lion Mews
5 St Peter's Villas
6 Standish Ho
7 Chambon Pl
8 Court Mans
9 Longthorpe Ct
10 Charlotte Ct
11 Westside
12 Park Ct
13 London Ho

C3 1 Elizabeth Finn Ho
2 Ashchurch Ct
3 King's Par
4 Inver Ct
5 Ariel Ct
6 Pocklington Lo
7 Vitae Apartments

C4 1 Becklow Gdns
2 Victoria Ho
3 Lycett Pl
4 Kylemore Ct
5 Alexandra Ct
6 Lytten Ct
7 Becklow Mews
8 Northcroft Ct
9 Bailey Ct
10 Spring Cott
11 Landor Wlk
12 Laurence Mews
13 Hadyn Park Ct
14 Askew Mans
15 Malvern Ct

39

A1 1 Prince's Mews
2 Aspen Gdns
3 Hampshire Hog La
4 Blades Ct

A2 1 Albion Gdns
2 Flora Gdns
3 Lamington St
4 Felgate Mews
5 Galena Ho
6 Albion Mews
7 Albion Ct
8 King Street Cloisters
9 Dimes Pl
10 Clarence Ct
11 Hampshire Hog La
12 Marryat Ct
13 Ravenscourt Ho

A3 1 Ravenscourt Park Mans
2 Paddenswick Ct
3 Ashbridge Ct

A4 1 Westbush Ct
2 Goldhawk Mews
3 Sycamore Ho
4 Shackleton Ct
5 Drake Ct
6 Scotts Ct
7 Raleigh Ct
8 Melville Court Flats
9 Southway Cl

B1 1 Bridge Avenue Mans
2 Bridgeview
3 College Ct
4 Beatrice Ho
5 Amelia Ho
6 Edith Ho
7 Joanna Ho
8 Mary Ho
9 Adela Ho
10 Sophia Ho
11 Henrietta Ho
12 Charlotte Ho
13 Alexandra Ho
14 Bath Pl
15 Elizabeth Ho
16 Margaret Ho
17 Peabody Est
18 Eleanor Ho
19 Isabella Ho
20 Caroline Ho
21 Chancellors Wharf
22 Sussex Pl

B2
1 Phoenix Lodge Mans
2 Samuel's Cl
3 Broadway Arc
4 Brook Ho
5 Hammersmith Broadway
6 Broadway Ctr The
7 Cambridge Ct
8 Ashcroft Sq
B4 1 Verulam Ho
2 Grove Mans
3 Frobisher Ct
4 Library Mans
5 Pennard Mans
6 New Shepherd's Bush Mkt
7 Kerrington Ct
8 Granville Mans
9 Romney Ct
10 Rayner Ct
11 Sulgrave Gdns
12 Bamborough Gdns
13 Hillary Ct
14 Market Studios
15 Lanark Mans
C3 1 Grosvenor Residences
2 Blythe Mews
3 Burnand Ho
4 Bradford Ho
5 Springvale Terr
6 Ceylon Rd
7 Walpole Ct
8 Bronte Ct
9 Boswell Ct
10 Souldern Rd
11 Brook Green Flats
12 Haarlem Rd
13 Stafford Mans
14 Lionel Mans
15 Barradell Ho
C4 1 Vanderbilt Villas
2 Bodington Ct
3 Kingham Cl
4 Clearwater Terr
5 Lorne Gdns
6 Cameret Ct
7 Bush Ct
8 Shepherds Ct
9 Rockley Ct
10 Grampians The
11 Charcroft Ct
12 Addison Park Mans
13 Sinclair Mans
14 Fountain Ct
15 Woodford Ct
16 Roseford Ct
17 Woodstock Studios

40
A1 1 Hockney Ct
2 Toulouse Ct
3 Lowry Ct
4 Barry Ho
5 Lewis Ct
6 Gainsborough Ct
7 Renoir Ct
8 Blake Ct
9 Raphael Ct
10 Rembrandt Ct
11 Constable Ct
12 Da Vinci Ct
13 Gaugin Ct
14 Michelangelo Ct
15 Monet Ct
16 Weald Cl

17 Jasmin Lo
18 Birchmere Lo
19 Weybridge Ct
20 Florence Ho
21 Gleneagles Cl
22 Sunningdale Cl
23 Muirfield Cl
24 Turnberry Cl
25 St Andrews Cl
26 Kingsdown Cl
27 St Davids Cl
28 Galway Cl
29 Edenbridge Cl
30 Birkdale Cl
31 Tralee Ct
32 Woburn Ct
33 Belfry Ct
34 Troon Cl
35 Holywell Cl
A2 1 Market Pl
2 Trappes Ho
3 Thurland Ho
4 Ramsfort Ho
5 Hambley Ho
6 Holford Ho
7 Pope Ho
8 Southwell Ho
9 Mortain Ho
10 Radcliffe Ho
11 Southwark Park Est
12 Galleywall Road Trad Est
13 Trevithick Ho
14 Barlow Ho
15 Donkin Ho
16 Landmann Ho
17 Fitzmaurice Ho
18 Dodd Ho
A3 1 Perryn Rd
2 Chalfont Ho
3 Prestwood Ho
4 Farmer Ho
5 Gataker Ho
6 Gataker St
7 Cornick Ho
8 Glebe Ho
9 Matson Ho
10 Hickling Ho
11 St Andrews Ho
A4 1 Butterfield Cl
2 Janeway Pl
3 Trotwood Ho
4 Maylie Ho
5 Cranbourn Pas
6 Cranbourn Ho
7 Cherry Garden Ho
8 Burton Ho
9 Morriss Ho
10 Dixon's Alley
11 King Edward The Third Mews
12 Cathay St
13 Mission The
14 Millstream Ho
B2 1 Damory Ho
2 Antony Ho
3 Roderick Ho
4 Pedworth Gdns
5 Banner Ct
6 Rotherhithe Bsns Est
7 Beamish Ho
8 Corbetts Pas
9 Gillam Ho
10 Richard Ho
11 George Walter Ho
12 Westlake

13 Adron Ho
14 McIntosh Ho
B3 1 Blick Ho
2 Neptune Ho
3 Scotia Ct
4 Murdoch Ho
5 Edmonton Ct
6 Niagara Ct
7 Columbia Point
8 Ritchie Ho
9 Wells Ho
10 Helen Peele Cotts
11 Orchard Ho
12 Dock Offices
13 Landale Ho
14 Courthope Ho
15 Hithe Gr
16 China Hall Mews
B4 1 Mayflower St
2 St Mary's Est
3 Rupack St
4 Frank Whymark Ho
5 Adams Gardens Est
6 Hatteraick St
7 East India Ct
8 Bombay Ct
9 Stable Ho
10 Grannary The
11 Riverside
12 Cumberland Wharf
13 Seaford Ho
14 Hythe Ho
15 Sandwich Ho
16 Winchelsea Ho
17 Rye Ho
18 Kenning St
19 Western Pl
20 Ainsty St
21 Pine Ho
22 Beech Ho
23 Larch Ho
24 Turner Ct
25 Seth St
26 Risdon Ho
27 Risdon St
28 Aylton Est
29 Manitoba Ct
30 Calgary Ct
31 Irwell Est
32 St Olav's Sq
33 City Bsns Ctr
C2 1 John Kennedy Ho
2 Brydale Ho
3 Balman Ho
4 Tissington Ct
5 Harbord Ho
6 Westfield Ho
7 Albert Starr Ho
8 John Brent Ho
9 William Evans Ho
10 Raven Ho
11 Egret Ho
12 Fulmar Ho
13 Dunlin Ho
14 Siskin Ho
15 Sheldrake Ho
16 Buchanan Ct
17 Burrage Ct
18 Biddenham Ho
19 Ayston Ho
20 Empingham Ho
21 Deanshanger Ho
22 Codicote Ho
23 Buryfield Ct
C4 1 Schooner Ct
2 Dolphin Ct
3 Clipper Cl

4 Deauville Ct
5 Colette Ct
6 Coniston Ct
7 Virginia Ct
8 Derwent Ct
9 Grantham Ct
10 Serpentine Ct
11 Career Ct
12 Lacine Ct
13 Fairway Ct
14 Harold Ct
15 Spruce Ho
16 Cedar Ho
17 Sycamore Ho
18 Woodland Cres
19 Poplar Ho
20 Adelphi Ct
21 Basque Ct
22 Quilting Ct
23 Chargrove Ct
24 Radley Ct
25 Greenacre Sq
26 Maple Leaf Sq
27 Stanhope Ct
28 Hawke Pl
29 Drake Ct
30 Brass Talley Alley
31 Monkton Ho
32 James Ho
33 Wolfe Cres

41
A2 1 Trafalgar Ct
2 Hornblower Cl
3 Cunard Wlk
4 Caronia Ct
5 Carinthia Ct
6 Freswick Ho
7 Graveley Ho
8 Husbourne Ho
9 Crofters Ct
10 Pomona Ho
11 Hazelwood Ho
12 Cannon Wharf Bsns Ctr
13 Bence Ho
14 Clement Ho
15 Pendennis Ho
16 Lighter Cl
17 Mast Ct
18 Rushcutters Ct
19 Boat Lifter Way
B1 1 Gransden Ho
2 Daubeney Twr
3 North Ho
4 Rochfort Ho
5 Keppel Ho
6 Camden Ho
7 Sanderson Ho
8 Berkeley Ho
9 Strafford Ho
10 Richman Ho
11 Hurleston Ho
12 Grafton Ho
13 Fulcher Ho
14 Citrus Ho
B2 1 Windsock Cl
2 St George's Mews
3 Linberry Wlk
4 Lanyard Ho
5 Golden Hind Pl
6 James Lind Ho
7 Pelican Ho
8 Bembridge Ho
9 Terrace The

23 Topmast Point
24 Turner Ho
25 Constable Ho
26 Knighthead Point

42
A1 **1** Slipway Ho
2 Taffrail Ho
3 Platehouse The
4 Wheelhouse The
5 Chart House The
6 Port House The
7 Beacon Ho
8 Blasker Wlk
9 Maconochies Rd
A2 **1** Brassey Ho
2 Triton Ho
3 Warsprite Ho
4 Rodney Ho
5 Conway Ho
6 Exmouth Ho
7 Akbar Ho
8 Arethusa Ho
9 Tasman Ct
10 Cutty Sark Ho
A3 **1** Turnberry Quay
2 Balmoral Ho
3 Aegon Ho
4 Marina Point
B2 **1** St John's Ho
2 Betty May Gray Ho
3 Castleton Ho
4 Urmston Ho
5 Salford Ho
6 Capstan Ho
7 Frigate Ho
8 Galleon Ho
9 Barons Lo
B3 **1** Cardale St
2 Hickin St
3 John McDonald Ho
4 Thorne Ho
5 Skeggs Ho
6 St Bernard Ho
7 Kimberley Ho
8 Kingdon Ho
9 Killoran Ho
10 Alastor Ho
11 Lingard Ho
12 Yarrow Ho
13 Sandpiper Ct
14 Nightingale Ct
15 Robin Ct
16 Heron Ct
17 Ferndown Lo
18 Crosby Ho
B4 **1** Llandovery Ho
2 Rugless Ho
3 Ash Ho
4 Elm Ho
5 Cedar Ho
6 Castalia Sq
7 Aspect Ho
8 Normandy Ho
9 Valiant Ho
10 Tamar Ho
11 Watkins Ho
12 Alice Shepherd Ho
13 Oak Ho
14 Ballin Ct
15 Martin Ct
16 Grebe Ct
17 Kingfisher Ct
18 Walkers Lo

10 Antilles Bay
C2 **1** Verwood Lo
2 Fawley Lo
3 Lyndhurst Lo
4 Blyth Cl
5 Farnworth Ho
6 Francis Cl

43
A1 **1** Bellot Gdns
2 Thornley Pl
3 King William La
4 Bolton Ho
5 Miles Ho
6 Mell St
7 Sam Manners Ho
8 Hatcliffe Alm-
shouses
9 Woodland Wlk
10 Earlswood Cl
B1 **1** Baldrey Ho
2 Christie Ho
3 Dyson Ho
4 Cliffe Ho
5 Moore Ho
6 Collins Ho
7 Lockyer Ho
8 Halley Ho
9 Kepler Ho
10 Sailacre Ho
11 Union Pk
B3 **1** Teal St
2 Maurer Ct
3 Mudlarks Blvd
4 Renaissance Wlk
5 Alamaro Lo
C1 **1** Layfield Ho
2 Westerdale Rd
3 Mayston Mews
4 Station Mews Terr

44
A4 **1** Ferry Sq
2 Watermans Ct
3 Wilkes Rd
4 Charlton Ho
5 Albany Par
6 Albany Ho
7 Alma Ho
8 Griffin Ct
9 Cressage Ho
10 Tunstall Wlk
11 Trimmer Wlk
12 Running Horse Yd
13 Mission Sq
14 Distillery Wlk
B2 **1** Primrose Ho
2 Lawman Ct
3 Royston Ct
4 Garden Ct
5 Capel Lo
6 Devonshire Ct
7 Celia Ct
8 Rosslyn Ho
9 Branstone Ct
10 Lamerton Lo
11 Kew Lo
12 Dunraven Ho
13 Stoneleigh Lo
14 Tunstall Ct
15 Voltaire
C2 **1** Clarendon Ct
2 Quintock Ho
3 Broome Ct
4 Lonsdale Mews
5 Elizabeth Cotts
6 Sandways

7 Victoria Cotts
8 North Ave
9 Grovewood
10 Hamilton Ho
11 Melvin Ct
12 Royal Par
13 Power Ho
14 Station Ave
15 Blake Mews

45
A2 **1** Terrano Ho
2 Oak Ho
3 Aura Ho
4 Maple Ho
5 Cedar Ho
6 Saffron Ho
7 Lime Ho
8 Lavender Ho
9 Juniper Ho

46
B1 **1** Melrose Rd
2 Seaforth Lo
3 St John's Gr
4 Sussex Ct
5 Carmichael Ct
6 Hampshire Ct
7 Thorne Pas
8 Brunel Ct
9 Beverley Path

47
C4 **1** Cobb's Hall
2 Dorset Mans
3 St Clements Mans
4 Bothwell St
5 Hawksmoor St

48
A1 **1** Langport Ho
2 Iveagh Ho
3 Newark Ho
4 Edgehill Ho
5 Hopton Ho
6 Ashby Ho
7 Nevil Ho
A2 **1** Fairbairn Gn
2 Hammelton Ho
3 Foxley Sq
4 Silverburn Ho
5 Butler Ho
6 Dalkeith Ho
7 Turner Cl
8 Bathgate Ho
9 Black Roof Ho
A4 **1** Faunce Ho
2 Garbett Ho
3 Harvard Ho
4 Doddington Pl
5 Kean Ho
6 Jephson Ho
7 Cornish Ho
8 Bateman Ho
9 Molesworth Ho
10 Walters Ho
11 Cruden Ho
12 Brawne Ho
13 Prescott Ho
14 Chalmer's Wlk
15 Copley Cl
16 King Charles Ct
B1 **1** Bergen Ho
2 Oslo Ho
3 Viking Ho
4 Jutland Ho
5 Norvic Ho

6 Odin Ho
7 Baltic Ho
8 Nobel Ho
9 Mercia Ho
10 Kenbury Gdns
11 Zealand Ho
12 Elsinore Ho
13 Norse Ho
14 Denmark Mans
15 Dane Ho
16 Canterbury Cl
17 York Cl
18 Kenbury Mans
19 Parade Mans
20 Winterslow Ho
21 Lilford Ho
22 Bartholomew Ho
23 Guildford Ho
24 Boston Ho
25 Hereford Ho
26 Weyhill Ho
27 Lichfield Ho
28 Lansdown Ho
29 Honiton Ho
30 Pinner Ho
31 Baldock Ho
32 Widecombe Ho
33 Nottingham Ho
34 Witham Ho
35 Barnet Ho
36 Empress Mews
B2 **1** Bertha Neubergh
Ho
2 Mornington Mans
3 Badsworth Rd
4 Pearson Ct
5 Elm Tree Ct
6 Samuel Lewis Trust
Dwellings
7 Milkwell Yd
8 Keswick Ho
9 Mitcham Ho
B3 **1** Boundary Ho
2 Day Ho
3 Burgess Ho
4 Carlyle Ho
5 Myers Ho
6 Thompson Ave
7 Palgrave Ho
8 Winnington Ho
9 Brantwood Ho
10 Lowell Ho
11 Jessie Duffett Ho
12 Otterburn Ho
13 Crossmount Ho
14 Venice Ct
15 Bowyer St
16 Livingstone Ho
17 Gothic Ct
18 Coniston Ho
19 Harlynwood
20 Carey Ct
21 Finley Ct
22 Grainger Ct
23 Hayes Ct
24 Moffat Ho
25 Marinel Ho
26 Hodister Cl
27 Arnot Ho
28 Lamb Ho
29 Kipling Ho
30 Keats Ho
31 Kenyon Ho
32 New Church Rd
33 Sir John Kirk Cl
C1 **1** Selborne Rd
2 Hascombe Terr

C2 **1** Joiners Arms Yd
2 Butterfly Wlk
3 Cuthill Wlk
4 Colonades The
5 Artichoke Mews
6 Peabody Bldgs
7 Brighton Ho
8 Park Ho
9 Peabody Ct
10 Lomond Ho
11 Lamb Ho
12 Kimpton Ct
13 Belham Wlk
14 Datchelor Pl
15 Harvey Rd
C3 **1** Masterman Ho
2 Milton Ho
3 Pope Ho
4 Chester Ct
5 Marvel Ho
6 Flecker Ho
7 Landor Ho
8 Leslie Prince Ct
9 Evelina Mans
10 Langland Ho
11 Drinkwater Ho
12 Procter Ho
13 Shirley Ho
14 Drayton Ho
15 Bridges Ho
16 Cunningham Ho
17 Hood Ho
18 Herrick Ho
19 Dekker Ho
20 Houseman Way
21 Coleby Path
C4 **1** Queens Ho
2 Arnside Ho
3 Horsley St
4 St Peter's Ho
5 St Johns Ho
6 St Marks Ho
7 St Stephens Ho
8 St Matthew's Ho
9 Red Lion Cl
10 Boyson Rd
11 Bradenham

49
A1 **1** Springfield Ho
2 Craston Ho
3 Walters Ho
4 Edgecombe Ho
5 Fowler Ho
6 Rignold Ho
7 Chatham Ho
A2 **1** Barnwell Ho
2 Brunswick Villas
3 St Giles Twr
4 Bentley Ho
5 Dawson Ho
6 Dryden Ho
7 Mayward Ho
8 Longleigh Ho
9 Fairwall Ho
10 Bodeney Ho
11 Sandby Ho
12 Vestry Mews
13 Netley
14 Lakanal
15 Racine
A3 **1** Tower Mill Rd
2 Tilson Cl
3 Granville Sq
4 Edgar Wallace Cl
5 Potters Cl
6 Dorton Cl

7 Samuel Jones Ind Est
8 Dibden Ho
9 Marchwood Cl
10 Pilgrims Cloisters
11 Beacon Ho
12 Teather St
13 Stacy Path
14 Rumball Ho
15 Ballow Cl
16 Rill Ho
A4 1 Downend Ct
2 Andoversford Ct
3 Pearse St
4 Watling St
5 Gandolfi St
B2 1 Colbert
2 Voltaire
3 Finch Mews
4 Charles Coveney Rd
5 Bamber Rd
6 Crane St
7 Curlew Ho
8 Mallard Ho
9 Tern Ho
10 Crane Ho
11 Falcon Ho
12 Bryanston Ho
13 Basing Ct
14 Marcus Ho
15 Sheffield Ho
B3 1 Painswick Ct
2 Sharpness Ct
3 Mattingly Way
4 Hordle Prom N
5 Burcher Gale Gr
6 Calypso Cres
7 Hordle Prom S
8 Cinnamon Cl
9 Savannah Cl
10 Thames Ct
11 Shannon Ct
12 Amstel Ct
13 Danube Ct
14 Tilbury Ct
15 Hordle Prom E
16 Indus Ct
17 Oakcourt
18 Palm Ct
19 Rowan Ct
20 Blackthorn Ct
21 Pear Ct
22 Lidgate Rd
23 Whistler Mews
24 Boathouse Wlk
B4 1 Willsbridge Ct
2 Cam Ct
3 Quedgeley Ct
4 Saul Ct
5 Quenington Ct
6 Westonbirt Ct
7 Wickway Ct
C1 1 William Margrie Cl
2 William Blake Ho
3 Quantock Mews
4 Choumert Sq
5 Parkstone Rd
6 Atwell Rd
C2 1 Canal Head Public Sq
2 Angelina Ho
3 Jarvis Ho
4 Richland Ho
5 Honeywood Ho
6 Wakefield Ho
7 Primrose Ho
8 Hardcastle Ho

9 Dunstall Ho
10 Springtide Cl
11 Purdon Ho
12 Flamborough Ho
13 Lambrook Ho
14 Witcombe Point
15 Yarnfield Sq
16 Winford Ct
17 Portbury Cl
18 Robert Keen Cl
C3 1 Thornbill Ho
2 Vervain Ho
3 Woodstar Ho
4 Tamarind Ho
5 Hereford Retreat
6 Haymerle Ho
7 Furley Ho
8 Thomas Milner Ho
9 Applegarth Ho
10 Freda Corbett Cl
11 Rudbeck Ho
12 Henslow Ho
13 Lindley Ho
14 Collinson Ho
15 Sister Mabel's Way
16 Timberland Cl
17 Hastings Cl
18 Sidmouth Ho
19 Budleigh Ho
20 Stanesgate Ho
21 Breamore Ho
22 Ely Ho
23 Gisburn Ho
C4 1 Bowles Rd
2 Western Wharf
3 Northfield Ho
4 Millbrook Ho
5 Denstone Ho
6 Deerhurst Ho
7 Caversham Ho
8 Battle Ho
9 Cardiff Ho
10 Bridgnorth Ho
11 Exeter Ho
12 Grantham Ho
13 Aylesbury Ho
14 Royston Ho

50

A1 1 Walkynscroft
2 Ryegates
3 Hathorne Cl
4 Pilkington Rd
5 Russell Ct
6 Heaton Ho
7 Magdalene Cl
8 Iris Ct
A2 1 Willowdene
2 Pinedene
3 Oakdene
4 Beechdene
5 Hollydene
6 Wood Dene
7 Staveley Cl
8 Carnicot Ho
9 Martock Ct
10 Cherry Tree Ct
11 Kendrick Ct
A3 1 Tortington Ho
2 Credenhill Ho
3 Bromyard Ho
4 Hoyland Ct
5 Willowdene
6 Ashdene
7 Acorn Par
8 Havelock Ct
9 Springall St

10 Harry Lambourn Ho
11 Grenier Apartments
B1 1 Honiton Gdns
2 Selden Ho
3 Hathway Ho
4 Hathway St
5 Station Ct
B2 1 Trotman Ho
2 Boddington Ho
3 Heydon Ho
4 Boulter Ho
B3 1 Ambleside Point
2 Grasmere Point
3 Windermere Point
4 Roman Way
5 Laburnum Ct
6 Juniper Ho
7 Romney Ct
8 Hammersley Ho
9 Hutchinson Ho
10 Hammond Ho
11 Fir Tree Ho
12 Glastonbury Ct
13 Highbridge Ct
14 Filton Ct
15 Chiltern Ct
16 Cheviot St
B4 1 Penshurst Ho
2 Reculver Ho
3 Mereworth Ho
4 Camber Ho
5 Chiham Ho
6 Otford Ho
7 Olive Tree Ho
8 Aspen Ho
9 Lewis Silkin Ho
10 Richborough Ho
11 Dover Ho
12 Eynsford Ho
13 Horton Ho
14 Lamberhurst Ho
15 Canterbury Ind Pk
16 Upnall Ho
17 Sissinghurst Ho
18 Rochester Ho
19 Saltwood Ho
20 Leybourne Ho
21 Lullingstone Ho
C3 1 Richard Anderson Ct
2 Palm Tree Ho
3 Edward Robinson Ho
4 Antony Ho
5 Gerrard Ho
6 Palmer Ho
7 Pankhurst Cl
C4 1 Harrisons Ct
2 Grantley Ho
3 Sunbury Ct
4 Tilbury Ct
5 Graham Ct
6 Connell Ct
7 St Clements Ct
8 Henderson Ct
9 Jennotts Ct
10 Verona Ct
11 Heywood Ho
12 Francis Ct
13 Hind Ho
14 Donne Ho
15 Carew Ct
16 Burbage Ho
17 Newland Ho
18 Dobson Ho
19 Dalton Ho

20 Greene Ct
21 Redrup Ho
22 Tarplett Ho
23 Stunell Ho
24 Gasson Ho
25 Bryce Ho
26 Barnes Ho
27 Barkwith Ho
28 Bannister Ho
29 Apollo Ind Bsns Ctr

51

A2 1 Archer Ho
2 Browning Ho
3 Hardcastle Ho
4 Brooke Ho
5 Wallis Ho
A3 1 Batavia Ho
2 Marlowe Bsns Ctr
3 Batavia Mews
4 Woodrush Cl
5 Alexandra St
6 Primrose Wlk
7 Vansittart St
8 Granville Ct
9 Cottesbrook St
10 Ewen Henderson Ct
11 Fordham Ho
A4 1 Portland Ct
2 Phoenix Ct
3 Rainbow Ct
4 Hawke Twr
5 Chubworthy St
6 Woodpecker Rd
7 Hercules St
B3 1 Austin Ho
2 Exeter Way
3 Crossleigh Ct
4 Mornington Pl
5 Maple Ho
B4 1 Chester Ho
2 Lynch Wlk
3 Arlington Ho
4 Woodcote Ho
5 Cornbury Ho
6 Prospect Pl
7 Akintaro Ho
8 Mulberry Ho
9 Laurel Ho
10 Linden Ho
11 Ashford Ho
12 Wardalls Ho
13 Magnolia Ho
14 Howard Ho
15 Larch Cl
16 Ibis Ct
17 Merganser Ct
18 Wotton Rd
19 Kingfisher Sq
20 Sanderling Ct
21 Dolphin Twr
22 Mermaid Twr
23 Scoter Ct
24 Shearwater Ct
25 Brambling Ct
26 Kittiwake Ct
27 Diana Cl
28 Guillemot Ct
29 Marine Twr
30 Teal Ct
31 Lapwing Twr
32 Violet Cl
33 Skua Ct
34 Tristan Ct
35 Rosemary Ct
36 Cormorant Ct
37 Shelduck Ct

38 Eider Ct
39 Pintail Ct
C2 1 Admiralty Ct
2 Harton Lodge
3 Sylva Cotts
4 Pitman Ho
5 Heston Ho
6 Mereton Mans
7 Indiana Bldg
8 St John's Lodge
C3 1 Sandpiper Ct
2 Flamingo Ct
3 Titan Bsns Est
4 Rochdale Way
5 Speedwell St
6 Reginald Pl
7 Fletcher Path
8 Frankham Ho
9 Cremer Ho
10 Wilshaw Ho
11 Castell Ho
12 Holden Ho
13 Browne Ho
14 Resolution Way
15 Lady Florence Ctyd
16 Covell Ct
17 Bittern Ho
18 Albion Ho
C4 1 Dryfield Wlk
2 Blake Ho
3 Hawkins Ho
4 Grenville Ho
5 Langford Ho
6 Mandarin Ct
7 Bittern Ct
8 Lamerton St
9 Ravensbourne Mans
10 Armada St
11 Armada Ct
12 Benbow Ho
13 Oxenham Ho
14 Caravel Mews
15 Hughes Ho
16 Stretton Mans

52

A2 1 Washington Bldg
2 California Bldg
3 Utah Bldg
4 Montana Bldg
5 Oregon Bldg
6 Dakota bldg
7 Idaho Bldg
8 Atlanta Bldg
9 Colorado Bldg
10 Arizona Bldg
11 Nebraska Bldg
12 Alaska Bldg
13 Ohio Bldg
14 Charter Bldgs
15 Flamsteed Ct
16 Friendly Pl
17 Dover Ct
18 Robinscroft Mews
19 Doleman Ho
20 Plymouth Ho
A3 1 Finch Ho
2 Jubilee The
3 Maitland Cl
4 Ashburnham Retreat
B1 1 Ellison Ho
2 Pitmaston Ho
3 Aster Ho

4 Windmill Cl
6 Hermitage The
6 Burnett Ho
7 Lacey Ho
8 Darwin Ho
9 Pearmain Ho
B2 1 Penn Almshouses
2 Jervis Ct
3 Woodville Ct
4 Darnall Ho
5 Renbold Ho
6 Lindsell St
7 Plumbridge St
8 Trinity Gr
9 Hollymount Cl
10 Cade Tyler Ho
11 Robertson Ho
B3 1 Temair Ho
2 Royal Hill Ct
3 Prince of Orange La
4 Lambard Ho
5 St Marks Cl
6 Ada Kennedy Ct
7 Arlington Pl
8 Topham Ho
9 Darnell Ho
10 Hawks Mews
11 Royal Pl
12 Swanne Ho
13 Maribor
14 Serica Ct
15 Queen Elizabeth's Coll
B4 1 Crescent Arc
2 Greenwich Mkt
3 Turnpin La
4 Durnford St
5 Sexton's Ho
6 Bardsley Ho
7 Wardell Ho
8 Clavell St
9 Stanton Ho
10 Macey Ho
11 Boreman Ho
12 Clipper Appts
C4 1 Frobisher Ct
2 Hardy Cotts
3 Palliser Ho
4 Bernard Angell Ho
5 Corvette Sq
6 Travers Ho
7 Maze Hill Lodge
8 Park Place Ho

53
B3 1 Westcombe Ct
2 Kleffens Ct
3 Ferndale Ct
4 Combe Mews
5 Mandeville Cl
6 Pinelands Cl
C3 1 Mary Lawrenson Pl
2 Bradbury Ct
3 Dunstable Ct
4 Wentworth Ho
C4 1 Nethercombe Ho
2 Holywell Cl

54
A1 1 Lancaster Cotts
2 Lancaster Mews
3 Bromwich Ho
4 Priors Lo

6 Richmond Hill Ct
6 Glenmore Ho
7 Hillbrow
8 Heathshott
9 Friars Stile Pl
10 Spire Ct
11 Ridgeway
12 Matthias St
A2 1 Lichfield Terr
2 Union Ct
3 Carrington Lo
4 Wilton Ct
5 Egerton Ct
6 Beverley Lo
7 Bishop Duppa's Almshouses
8 Regency Wlk
9 Clear Water Ho
10 Onslow Avenue Mans
11 Michels Almshouses
12 Albany Pas
13 Salcombe Villas
A3 1 St John's Gr
2 Michel's Row
3 Michelsdale Dr
4 Blue Anchor Alley
5 Clarence St
6 Sun Alley
7 Thames Link Ho
8 Benns Wlk
9 Waterloo Pl
10 Northumbria Ct
B1 1 Chester Ct
2 Evesham Ct
3 Queen's Ct
4 Russell Wlk
5 Charlotte Sq
6 Jones Wlk
7 Hilditch Ho
8 Isabella Ct
9 Damer Ho
10 Eliot Ho
11 Fitzherbert Ho
12 Reynolds Pl
13 Chisholm Rd
B2 1 Alberta Ct
2 Beatrice Rd
3 Lorne Rd
4 York Rd
5 Connaught Rd
6 Albany Terr
7 Kingswood Ct
8 Selwyn Ct
9 Broadhurst Ct
B3 1 Towers The
2 Longs Ct
3 Sovereign Ct
4 Robinson Ct
5 Calvert Ct
6 Bedford Ct
7 Hickey's Almshouses
8 Church Estate Almshouses
9 Richmond International Bsns Ctr
10 Abercorn Mews

55
A3 1 Hershell Ct
2 Deanhill Ct
3 Park Sheen
4 Furness Lo
5 Merricks Ct
C4 1 Rann Ho

2 Craven Ct
3 John Dee Ho
4 Kindell Ho
5 Montgomery Ho
6 Avondale Ho
7 Addington Ct
8 Dovecote Gdns
9 Firmston Ho
10 Glendower Gdns
11 Chestnut Ave
12 Trehern Rd
13 Rock Ave

56
C2 1 Theodore Ho
2 Nicholas Ho
3 Bonner Ho
4 Downing Ho
5 Jansen Ho
6 Fairfax Ho
7 Devereux Ho
8 David Ho
9 Leigh Ho
10 Clipstone Ho
11 Mallet Ho
12 Arton Wilson Ho

57
B2 1 Inglis Ho
2 Ducie Ho
3 Wharncliffe Ho
4 Stanhope Ho
5 Waldegrave Ho
6 Mullens Ho
C1 1 Balmoral Ho
2 Glenalmond Ho
3 Selwyn Ho
4 Keble Ho
5 Bede Ho
6 Gonville Ho
7 Magdalene Ho
8 Armstrong Ho
9 Newnham Ho
10 Somerville Ho
11 Balliol Ho
12 Windermere
13 Little Combe Cl
14 Classinghall Ho
15 Chalford Ct
16 Garden Royal
17 South Ct
18 Anne Kerr Ct
19 Ewhurst
C2 1 Geneva Ct
2 Laurel Ct
3 Cambalt Ho
4 Langham Ct
5 Lower Pk
6 King's Keep
7 Whitnell Ct
8 Whitehead Ho
9 Halford Ho
10 Humphry Ho
11 Jellicoe Ho
C3 1 Olivette St
2 Mascotte Rd
3 Glegg Pl
4 Crown Ct
5 Charlwood Terr
6 Percy Laurie Ho

58
A2 1 Claremont
2 Downside
3 Cavendish Cl
4 Ashcombe Ct

5 Carltons The
6 Espirit Ho
7 Millbrooke Ct
8 Coysh Ct
9 Keswick Hts
10 Lincoln Ho
11 Avon Ct
B2 1 Keswick Broadway
2 Burlington Mews
3 Cambria Lo
4 St Stephen's Gdns
5 Atlantic Ho
6 Burton Lo
7 Manfred Ct
8 Meadow Bank
9 Hooper Ho
10 Aspire Bld
C2 1 Pembridge Pl
2 Adelaide Rd
3 London Ct
4 Windsor Ct
5 Westminster Ct
6 Fullers Ho
7 Bridge Pk
8 Lambeth Ct
9 Milton Ct
10 Norfolk Mans
11 Francis Snary Lo
12 Bush Cotts
13 Downbury Mews
14 Newton's Yd

59
A2 1 Fairfield Ct
2 Blackmore Ho
3 Lancaster Mews
4 Cricketers Mews
5 College Mews
6 Arndale Wlk
B4 1 Molasses Ho
2 Molasses Row
3 Cinnamon Row
4 Calico Ho
5 Calico Row
6 Port Ho
7 Square Rigger Row
8 Trade Twr
9 Ivory Ho
10 Spice Ct
11 Sherwood Ct
12 Mendip Ct
13 Chalmers Ho
14 Coral Row
15 Ivory Sq
16 Kingfisher Ho
C3 1 Burke Ho
2 Fox Ho
3 Buxton Ho
4 Pitt Ho
5 Ramsey Ho
6 Beverley Cl
7 Florence Ho
8 Linden Ct
9 Dorcas Ct
10 Johnson Ct
11 Agnes Ct
12 Hilltop Ct
13 Courtyard The
14 Old Laundry The
15 Oberstein Rd
16 Fineran Ct
17 Sangora Rd
18 Harvard Mans
19 Plough Mews
C4 1 Benham Cl
2 Milner Ho
3 McManus Ho

4 Wilberforce Ho
5 Wheeler Ct
6 Sporle Ct
7 Holliday Sq
8 John Parker Sq
9 Carmichael Cl
10 Fenner Sq
11 Clark Lawrence Ct
12 Shaw Ct
13 Sendall Ct
14 Livingstone Rd
15 Farrant Ho
16 Jackson Ho
17 Darien Ho
18 Shepard Ho
19 Ganley Ct
20 Arthur Newton Ho
21 Chesterton Ho
22 John Kirk Ho
23 Mantua St
24 Heaver Rd
25 Candlemakers

60
A4 1 Kiloh Ct
2 Lanner Ho
3 Griffon Ho
4 Kestrel Ho
5 Kite Ho
6 Peregrine Ho
7 Hawk Ho
8 Inkster Ho
9 Harrier Ho
10 Eagle Hts
11 Kingfisher Ct
12 Lavender Terr
13 Temple Ho
14 Ridley Ho
15 Eden Ho
16 Hertford Ct
17 Nepaul Rd
C1 1 Rayne Ho
2 St Anthony's Ct
3 Earlsthorpe Mews
4 Nightingale Mans
C4 1 Shaftesbury Park Chambers
2 Selborne
3 Rush Hill Mews
4 Marmion Mews
5 Crosland Pl
6 Craven Mews
7 Garfield Mews
8 Audley Cl
9 Basnett Rd
10 Tyneham Cl
11 Woodmere Cl

61
A4 1 Turnchapel Mews
2 Redwood Mews
3 Phil Brown Pl
4 Bev Callender Cl
5 Keith Connor Cl
6 Tessa Sanderson Pl
7 Daley Thompson Way
8 Rashleigh Ct
9 Abberley Mews
10 Willow Lodge
11 Beaufoy Rd
B1 1 Joseph Powell Cl
2 Cavendish Mans
3 Westlands Terr
4 Cubitt Ho
5 Hawkesworth Ho
6 Normanton Ho

7 Eastman Ho
8 Couchman Ho
9 Poynders Ct
10 Selby Ho
11 Valentine Ho
12 Gorham Ho
13 Deauville Mans
14 Deauville Ct
B2 1 Timothy Cl
2 Shaftesbury Mews
3 Brook Ho
4 Grover Ho
5 Westbrook Ho
6 Hewer Ho
7 Batten Ho
8 Mandeville Ho
9 George Beare Lo
B3 1 Polygon The
2 Windsor Ct
3 Trinity Cl
4 Studios The
5 Bourne Ho
B4 1 Clapham Manor Ct
2 Clarke Ho
3 Gables The
4 Sycamore Mews
5 Maritime Ho
6 Rectory Gdns
7 Floris Pl
C1 1 Parrington Ho
2 Savill Ho
3 Blackwell Ho
4 Bruce Ho
5 Victoria Ct
6 Victoria Ho
7 Belvedere Ct
8 Ingram Lo
9 Viney Ct
10 Bloomsbury Ho
11 Belgravia Ho
12 Barnsbury Ho
C3 1 Kendoa Rd
2 Felmersham Ct
3 Abbeville Mews
4 Saxon Ho
5 Gifford Ho
6 Teignmouth Cl
7 Holwood Pl
8 Oaklands Pl
9 Wilberforce Mews
10 William Bonney Est
C4 1 Chelsham Ho
2 Lynde Ho
3 Greener Ho
4 Towns Ho
5 Hugh Morgan Ho
6 Roy Ridley Ho
7 Lendal Terr
8 Slievemore Cl
9 Cadmus Cl
10 Clapham North Bsns Ctr

62
A2 1 King's Mews
2 Clapham Court Terr
3 Clapham Ct
4 Clapham Park Terr
5 Pembroke Ho
6 Stevenson Ho
7 Queenswood Ct
8 Oak Tree Ct
9 Park Lofts
10 Ashby Mews
A3 1 Morris Ho
2 Gye Ho
3 Clowes Ho

4 Thomas Ho
5 Stuart Ho
6 Storace Ho
7 Bedford Ho
8 Ascot Ct
9 Ascot Par
10 Ashmere Ho
11 Ashmere Gr
12 Ventura Ho
13 Vickery Ho
14 Stafford Mans
15 Beresford Ho
A4 1 Callingham Ho
2 Russell Pickering Ho
3 Ormerod Ho
4 Lopez Ho
5 Coachmaker Mews
B2 1 Beatrice Ho
2 Florence Ho
3 Evelyn Ho
4 Diana Ho
5 Brixton Hill Ct
6 Austin Ho
7 Manor Ct
8 Camsey Ho
9 Romer Ho
10 Gale Ho
11 Byrne Ho
12 Farnfield Ho
13 Marchant Ho
14 Rainsford Ho
15 Springett Ho
16 Mannering Ho
17 Waldron Ho
B3 1 Freemens Hos
2 Roger's Almshouses
3 Gresham Almshouses
4 Exbury Ho
5 Glasbury Ho
6 Dalbury Ho
7 Fosbury Ho
8 Chalbury Ho
9 Neilson-Terry Ct
10 Pavilion Mans
11 Daisy Dormer Ct
12 George Lashwood Ct
13 Marie Lloyd Ct
14 Trinity Homes
15 Lethaby Ho
16 Edmundsbury Ct Est
17 Regis Pl
18 Marlborough Mews
19 Alpha Ho
20 Beta Pl
21 Cedars Ho
B4 1 Turberville Ho
2 Thrayle Ho
3 Percheron Ct
4 Draymans Ct
C1 1 Eccleston Ho
2 Scarsbrook Ho
3 Purser Ho
4 Rudhall Ho
5 Hardham Ho
6 Heywood Ho
7 Haworth Ho
8 Birch Ho
9 Lansdell Ho
10 Lomley Ho
11 Laughton Ho
12 Woodruff Ho
13 Bascome St

14 Dudley Mews
15 Herbert Mews
16 Blades Lo
17 Dick Shepherd Ct
18 Charman Ho
19 Morden Ho
20 Bishop Ct
21 Blackburn Ct
22 Leigh Ct
23 John Conwey Ho
24 Bristowe Cl
C2 1 Crownstone Ct
2 Brockwell Ct
3 Nevena Ct
4 St George's Residences
5 Hanover Mans
6 Fleet Ho
7 Langbourne Ho
8 Turnmill Ho
9 Walker Mews
10 Cossar Mews
11 Carter Ho
12 Electric Mans
13 Electric La
14 Connaught Mans
15 Clifton Mans
16 Hereford Ho
17 Chaplin Ho
18 Brixton Oval
19 Lord David Pitt Ho
20 Marcus Garvey Way
21 Montego Cl
22 Bob Marley Way
23 Leeson Rd
C4 1 Buckmaster Cl
2 Albemarle Ho
3 Goodwood Mans
4 Angell Park Gdns
5 Fyfield Rd
6 Howard Ho
7 Harris Ho
8 Broadoak Ct
9 Burgate Ct
10 Witchwood Ho
11 Blacktree Mews
12 Chartham Ct
13 Chilham Ct
14 Northgate Ct
15 Westgate Ct
16 Dover Mans

63
A3 1 Mahatma Gandhi Ind Est
2 Dylan Rd
3 Bessemer Park Ind Est
4 Pablo Neruda Cl
5 Langston Hughes Cl
6 Walt Whitman Cl
7 James Joyce Wlk
8 Alice Walker Cl
9 Louise Bennett Cl
10 Chadacre Ho
11 Burwood Ho
12 Pyrford Ho
13 Wangford Ho
14 Ashford Ho
15 Kenwood Ho
16 Moyne Ho
17 Elveden Ho
18 Carrara Cl
19 Broughton Dr
20 Angela Davis Ind Est

21 Tilia Wlk
22 County Ho
A4 1 Mallams Mews
2 Amberley Ct
3 Harper Ho
4 Leicester Ho
5 Station Ave
6 Wellfit St
7 Loughborough Ct
8 Belinda Rd
9 Higgs Ind Est
C3 1 Shaftesbury Ct
2 Mayhew Ct
3 Morris Ct
4 Swinburne Ct
5 Perth Ct
6 Tayside Ct
7 Matlock Ct
8 Hunter Ct
9 Turner Ct

64
A2 1 Velde Way
2 Delft Way
3 Arnhem Way
4 Isel Way
5 Kempis Way
6 Terborch Way
7 Steen Way
8 Deventer Cres
9 Nimegen Way
10 Hilversum Cres
11 St Barnabas Ct
A4 1 Harfield Gdns
2 Karen Ct
3 Seavington Ho
4 Appleshaw Ho
5 Birdsall Ho
6 Whitney Ho
7 Wheatland Ho
8 Wilton Ho
9 Walcot Ho
10 Whaddon Ho
11 Melbreak Ho
12 Ledbury Ho
13 Tidworth Ho
14 Riseholme Ho
15 Ringmer Ho
16 Petworth Ho
17 Stagshaw Ho
18 Ivybridge Ho
19 Inwood Ho
20 Gatcombe Ho
21 Felbridge Ho
22 Cowdray Ho
B3 1 Dulwich Mews
2 St James's Cloisters
C2 1 Dorothy Charrington Ho
2 Keswick Ct
3 Kendall Ct
4 Halliwell Ct

65
A4 1 Tilling Ho
2 Goodwin Ho
3 Tyrells Ct
4 Citron Terr
5 Basswood Ct
6 Cheam St
C3 1 Laxton Path
2 Barlings Ho
3 Bayfield Ho
4 Coston Wlk
5 Coverham Ho
6 Gateley Ho

7 Dereham Ho
8 Greenwood Ho
9 Hilton Ho
10 Goodall Ho
11 Horsley Ho
12 Jordan Ho

67
B4 1 Bankside Ave
2 Elder Wlk
3 Yew Tree Cl
4 Mill Ho

68
C3 1 Farnborough Ho
2 Rushmere Ho
3 Horndean Cl
4 Highcross Way
5 Timsbury Wlk
6 Foxcombe Rd
7 Ryefield Path
8 Greatham Wlk
9 Gosport Ho
10 Stoatley Ho
11 Milland Ho
12 Clanfield Ho
13 Fareham Ho
14 Grayswood Point
C4 1 Woodcott Ho
2 Lyndhurst Ho
3 Wheatley Ho
4 Allbrook Ho
5 Bordon Wlk
6 Chilcombe Ho
7 Vicarage Ct
8 Shawford Ct
9 Eastleigh Wlk
10 Kings Ct
11 Somborne Ho

69
A3 1 Ramsdean Ho
2 Purbrook Ho
3 Portsea Ho
4 Blendworth Point
5 Eashing Point
6 Hindhead Point
7 Hilsea Point
8 Witley Point
9 Buriton Ho
10 Grateley Ho
11 Hascombe Ho
12 Dunhill Point
13 Westmark Point
14 Longmoor Point
15 Cadnam Point
B4 1 Cumberland Ho
2 Devonshire Ho
3 Cornwall Ho
4 Norfolk Ho
5 Leicester Ho
6 Warwick Ho
7 Sutherland Ho
8 Carmarthen Ho
9 Worcester Ho
10 Rutland Ho
11 Paddock Way
C3 1 Sandringham Cl
2 Eastwick Ct
3 Oatlands Ct
4 Banning Ho
5 Grantley Ho
6 Caryl Ho
7 Duncombe Ho

6 Chilworth Ct
9 Kent Lo
10 Turner Lo
11 Marlborough
12 Parkland Gdns
13 Lewesdon Cl
14 Pines Ct
16 Ashtead Ct
16 Mynterne Ct
17 Arden
18 Stephen Ct
19 Marsham Ct
20 Doradus Ct
21 Acorns The
22 Heritage Ho
23 Conifer Ct
24 Spencer Ho
25 Chartwell
26 Blenheim
27 Chivelston
28 Greenfield Ho
29 Oakman Ho
30 Radley Lo
31 Simon Lo
32 Admirals Ct
C4 1 Brett Ho
2 Brett House Cl
3 Sylva Ct
4 Ross Ct
5 Potterne Cl
6 Stourhead Cl
7 Fleur Gates
8 Greenwood

70
A3 1 William Harvey Ho
2 Highview Ct
3 Cameron Ct
4 Galgate Cl
5 Green Ho The
6 King Charles Wlk
7 Florys Ct
8 Augustus Ct
9 Albert Ct
10 Hertford Lo
11 Mortimer Lo
12 Allenswood
13 Ambleside
14 Hansler Ct
15 Roosevelt Ct

71
B2 1 Beemans Row
2 St Andrew's Ct
3 Townsend Mews
4 Sheringham Mews

72
C2 1 Upper Tooting Park Mans
2 Cecil Mans
3 Marius Mans
4 Boulevard The
5 Elmfield Mans

6 Holdernesse Rd
7 Lumiere Ct
C3 1 Heslop Ct
2 St James's Terr
3 Boundaries Mans
4 Station Par
5 Old Dairy Mews
C4 1 Hollies Way
2 Endlesham Ct

73
A3 1 Holbeach Mews
2 Hildreth Street Mews
3 Coalbrook Mans
4 Hub Buildings The
5 Metropolis Apartments
A4 1 Meyer Ho
2 Faraday Ho
3 Hales Ho
4 Frankland Ho
5 Graham Ho
6 Gibbs Ho
7 Dalton Ho
8 Ainslie Wlk
9 Rokeby Ho
10 Caistor Ho
11 Ivanhoe Ho
12 Catherine Baird Ct
13 Marmion Ho
14 Devonshire Ct
15 Blueprint Apartments
B4 1 Limerick Ct
2 Homewoods
3 Jewell Ho
4 Glanville Ho
5 Dan Bryant Ho
6 Olding Ho
7 Quennel Ho
8 Weir Ho
9 West Ho
10 Neville Ct
11 Friday Grove Mews
C3 1 Sinclair Ho
2 MacGregor Ho
3 Ingle Ho
4 St Andrews Mews
C4 1 Riley Ho
2 Bennett Ho
3 White Ho
4 Rodgers Ho
5 Dumphreys Ho
6 Homan Ho
7 Prendergast Ho
8 Hutchins Ho
9 Whiteley Ho
10 Tresidder Ho
11 Primrose Ct
12 Angus Ho
13 Currie Ho

74
A1 1 De Montfort Ct
2 Leigham Hall Par
3 Leigham Hall

4 Endsleigh Mans
5 John Kirk Ho
6 Raebarn Ct
7 Wavel Ct
8 Homeleigh Ct
9 Howland Ho
10 Beauclerk Ho
11 Bertrand Ho
12 Drew Ho
13 Dowes Ho
14 Dunton Ho
15 Raynald Ho
16 Sackville Ho
17 Thurlow Ho
18 Astoria Mans
A2 1 Wyatt Park Mans
2 Broadlands Mans
3 Stonehill's Mans
4 Streatleigh Par
5 Dorchester Ct
6 Picture Ho
A3 1 Beaumont Ho
2 Christchurch Ho
3 Staplefield Cl
4 Chipstead Ho
5 Coulsdon Ho
6 Conway Ho
7 Telford Avenue Mans
8 Telford Parade Mans
9 Wavertree Ct
10 Hartswood Ho
11 Wray Ho
A4 1 Picton Ho
2 Rigg Ho
3 Watson Ho
4 MacArthur Ho
5 Sandon Ho
6 Thorold Ho
7 Pearce Ho
8 Mudie Ho
9 Miller Ho
10 Lycett Ho
11 Lafone Ho
12 Lucraft Ho
13 Freeman Ho
14 New Park Par
15 Argyll Ct
16 Dumbarton Ct
17 Kintyre Ct
18 Cotton Ho
19 Crossman Hos
20 Cameford Ct
21 Parsons Ho
22 Brindley Ho
23 Arkwright Ho
24 Perry Ho
25 New Park Ct
26 Tanhurst Ho
27 Hawkshaw Ct
B1 1 Carisbrooke Ct
2 Pembroke Lo
3 Willow Ct
4 Poplar Ct
5 Mountview

6 Spa View
B3 1 Charlwood Ho
2 Earlswood Ho
3 Balcombe Ho
4 Claremont Cl
5 Holbrook Ho
6 Gwynne Ho
7 Kynaston Ho
8 Tillman Ho
9 Regents Lo
10 Hazelmere Ct
11 Dykes Ct
B4 1 Archbishop's Pl
2 Witley Ho
3 Outwood Ho
4 Dunsfold Ho
5 Deepdene Lo
6 Warnham Ho
7 Albury Lo
8 Tilford Ho
9 Elstead Ho
10 Thursley Ho
11 Brockham Ho
12 Capel Lo
13 Leith Ho
14 Fairview Ho
15 Weymouth Ct
16 Ascalon Ct
17 China Mews
18 Rush Common Mews
C3 1 Valens Ho
2 Loveday Ho
3 Strode Ho
4 Ethelworth Ct
5 Harbin Ho
6 Brooks Ho
7 Godolphin Ho
8 Sheppard Ho
9 McCormick Ho
10 Taylor Ho
11 Saunders Ho
12 Talcott Path
13 Derrick Ho
14 Williams Ho
15 Baldwin Ho
16 Churston Cl
17 Neil Wates Cres
18 Burnell Ho
19 Portland Ho
C4 1 Ellacombe Ho
2 Booth Ho
3 Hathersley Ho
4 Brereton Ho
5 Holdsworth Ho
6 Dearmer Ho
7 Cherry Cl
8 Greenleaf Cl
9 Longford Wlk
10 Scarlette Manor Wlk
11 Chandlers Way
12 Upgrove Manor Way
13 Ropers Wlk
14 Tebbs Ho
15 Bell Ho

16 Worthington Ho
17 Courier Ho
18 Mackie Ho
19 Hamers Ho
20 Kelyway Ho
21 Harriet Tubman Cl
22 Estoria Cl
23 Leckhampton Pl
24 Scotia Rd
25 Charles Haller St
26 Sidmouth Ho
27 Hunter Ct
28 Onslow Lo
29 William Winter Ct
30 Langthorne Lo

75
A1 1 Thanet Ho
2 Chapman Ho
3 Beaufoy Ho
4 Easton Ho
5 Roberts Ho
6 Lloyd Ct
7 Kershaw Ho
8 Wakeling Ho
9 Edridge Ho
10 Jeston Ho
11 Lansdowne Wood Cl
12 Rotary Lo
C2 1 Welldon Ct
2 Coppedhall
3 Shackleton Ct
4 Bullfinch Ct
5 Gannet Ct
6 Fulmar Ct
7 Heron Ct
8 Petrel Ct
9 Falcon Ct
10 Eagle Ct
11 Dunnock Ct
12 Dunlin Ct
13 Cormorant Ct
14 Oak Lodge
15 Corfe Lodge

76
C1 1 Tunbridge Ct
2 Harrogate Ct
3 Bath Ct
4 Leamington Ct
5 Porlock Ho
6 Cissbury Ho
7 Eddisbury Ho
8 Dundry Ho
9 Silbury Ho
10 Homildon Ho
11 Highgate Ho
12 Richmond Ho
13 Pendle Ho
14 Tynwald Ho
15 Wirrall Ho
16 Greyfriars

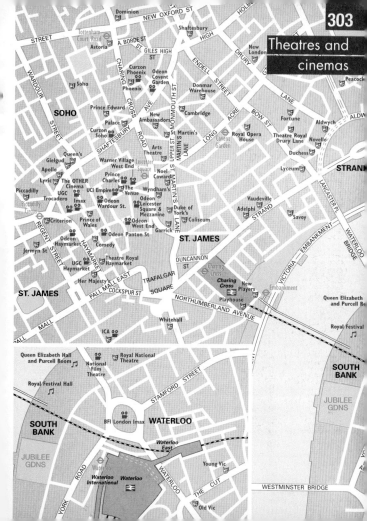

Dominion
NEW OXFORD ST
HOLB
Tottenham
Court Road
STREET
Shaftesbury
A. BORDE ST
GILES HIGH
ST
Astoria
HIGH
CHARING
Curzon
Phoenix
Odeon
Covent
Garden
Donmar
Warehouse
New London
DRURY
LANE
Peacock
WARDOUR
Soho
Phoenix
ENDELL
STREET
ACRE
BOW ST
Prince Edward
SOHO
New
Ambassadors
Cambridge
Royal Opera
House
Fortune
Aldwych
ALDW
Palace
Curzon
Soho
St Martin's
LONG
Theatre Royal
Drury Lane
Novello
Covent
Garden
Duchess
Gielgud
Queen's
SHAFTESBURY
ROAD
Arts
Theatre
Leicester
Square
Noel
Coward
Lyceum
STRAND
STREET
Apollo
Warner Village
West End
Prince
Charles
UPPER ST MARTIN'S LANE
MONMOUTH ST
Lyric
The OTHER
Cinema
UCI Empire
The
Venue
Wyndham's
Vaudeville
LANCASTER PL
Piccadilly
UGC
Trocadero
Imax
Odeon
Wardour St.
Odeon
Leicester
Square &
Mezzanine
Duke of
York's
Adelphi
STRAND
Savoy
WATERLOO
Piccadilly
Circus
Criterion
Prince of
Wales
Odeon Panton St
Odeon
West End
Coliseum
STRAND
BRIDGE
Jermyn St
REGENT STREET
Odeon
Haymarket
Comedy
Garrick
ST. JAMES
VICTORIA
EMBANKMENT
UGC
Haymarket
Theatre Royal
Haymarket
DUNCANNON
ST
Charing
Cross
New
Players
Embankment
Queen Elizabeth
and Purcell Re
ST. JAMES
Her Majesty's
PALL MALL EAST
COCKSPUR ST
TRAFALGAR
SQUARE
Playhouse
NORTHUMBERLAND AVENUE
Royal/Festival
ALL
MALL
ICA
Whitehall
Queen Elizabeth Hall
and Purcell Room
National
Film
Theatre
Royal National
Theatre
SOUTH
BANK
JUBILEE
GDNS
Royal/Festival Hall
STAMFORD
STREET
WATERLOO
SOUTH
BANK
JUBILEE
GDNS
BFI London Imax
Waterloo
East
YORK
ROAD
Waterloo
Waterloo
International
Waterloo
WATERLOO
Young Vic
THE CUT
Old Vic
WESTMINSTER BRIDGE

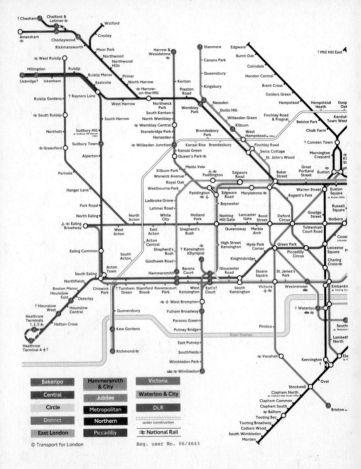

MAYOR OF LONDON

24 hour travel information
020 7222 1234

Website
tfl.gov.uk

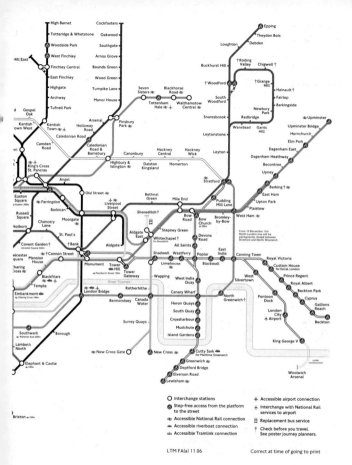

Interchange stations
Step-free access from the platform to the street
Accessible National Rail connection
Accessible riverboat connection
Accessible Tramlink connection

Accessible airport connection
Interchange with National Rail services to airport
Replacement bus service
Check before you travel. See poster journey planners.

LTM FA(a) 11.06

Correct at time of going to print

Textphone
020 7918 3015

Transport for London

UNDERGROUND

First published 2001 by

Philip's, a division of
Octopus Publishing Group Ltd
2–4 Heron Quays
London E14 4JP

Third edition 2007
First impression 2007

LONBC

© Philip's 2007

Spiral-bound
ISBN-10 0-540-09044-1 (spiral-bound)
ISBN-13 978-0-540-09044-0 (spiral-bound)

Perfect-bound
ISBN-10 0-540-09045-X (perfect-bound)
ISBN-13 978-0-540-09045-7 (perfect-bound)

Hardback (navy)
ISBN-10 0-540-09107-3
ISBN-13 978-0-540-09107-2

Hardback (pink)
ISBN-10 0-540-09108-1
ISBN-13 978-0-540-09108-9

Hardback (red)
ISBN-10 0-540-09110-3
ISBN-13 978-0-540-09110-2

Hardback (grey)
ISBN-10 0-540 09111-1
ISBN-13 978-0-540 09111-9

Hardback (green)
ISBN-10 0-540-09113-8
ISBN-13 978-0-540-09113-3

Hardback (brown)
ISBN-10 0-540-09115-4
ISBN-13 978-0-540-09115-7

Printed and bound in Spain
by Cayfosa-Quebecor.

NOTES